SOTHEBY'S
INTERNATIONAL PRICE GUIDE

1986-87 EDITION

(including 1985 prices)

General Editor: John L. Marion

THE VENDOME PRESS
NEW YORK   PARIS

Produced and designed by Philip Wilson Publishers Ltd
Russell Chambers, Covent Garden, London WC2E 8AA

Designer: Christopher Matthews

House editor: Vanessa Brett
Administrator: Pauline Somerville
Assistant house editor (New York): Elizabeth White

First published in Great Britain by Penguin Books Ltd
Harmondsworth, Middlesex

First published in the United States of America by
The Vendome Press, 515 Madison Avenue, N.Y., N.Y. 10022
Distributed in the United States of America by
Rizzoli International Publications, 597 Fifth Avenue, N.Y., 10017
Distributed in Canada by Methuen Publications

Library of Congress Cataloging-in-Publication Data
Main entry under title:
Sotheby's international price guide.
1. Sotheby's (Firm)—Prices. 2. Antiques—
Prices. I. Marion, John. II. Sotheby's (Firm)
NK1133.S68 1985 707'.5 8515730

Printed and bound in France
by Maury-Imp. S.A. (Malesherbes) and A.G.M. (Forges-les-Eaux)
Paper : Calypso, Arjomari-Prioux

ISBN 0-86565-065-9
ISBN 0-86565-066-7 (pbk.)

Contents

Bold headings indicate main sections; inset headings indicate articles within these sections.

Preface

The first edition of *Sotheby's International Price Guide* was published last Fall and rapidly established itself as the most reliable guide on the market. It quickly sold out, and its success has brought us two new European publishers. This 1986-87 guide, therefore, will be published simultaneously in English, German, French and Italian, which we feel is a tribute to the book's accuracy and utility to all who work to develop the "eye" that is the mark of the true collector.

Because of the larger edition, there are now 16 more color pages and 32 more in black and white, making a total of 736 pages. A completely new selection of 8,000 objects is included with sale dates and the prices they fetched at auction worldwide. Although there are a few items included which fetched very large sums of money (of a sort that most of us can only dream about owning), the majority of objects come from the middle and lower price range of items, ranging from about $100 upwards.

This year more emphasis is placed on the specialist articles written by Sotheby's experts. Each of the twenty-three articles discusses a particular area of collecting and gives information about the current market. There is something of interest to everyone: topics of a popular nature, such as "altered and restored furniture"; subjects for collectors of relatively modest means, such as "Silhouettes", "Electroplate" or "Tunbridgeware", are balanced by articles relating to more expensive items, such as a study of American chairs. Readers may also be tempted by some articles to break new ground and learn about areas which may be new to them—ivories, Japanese prints, or Italian maiolica, for example. For the first time this edition has much reference information in the form of a glossary of terms, biographical details of artists and craftsmen, makers' marks and charts, including dates of monarchs and dynasties.

All this material has been chosen with the aim of building up over future editions a substantial body of useful information for the collector, which will compliment the basic aim of the guide—to illustrate the widest possible cross-section of objects and the prices they realized in the international art market.

JOHN L. MARION
Chairman and President
Sotheby's North America

Sotheby's Principal Auction Locations

United Kingdom

34-35 Bond Street,
London W1A 2AA.
Telephone (01) 493 8080.

Booth Mansion,
28 Watergate Street,
Chester, CH1 2NA.
Telephone (0244) 315531.

Summers Place,
Billingshurst,
Sussex RH14 9AD.
Telephone (040 381) 3933.

United States

1334 York Avenue,
New York,
N.Y. 10021.
Telephone (212) 606 7000.

Holland

102 Rokin,
1012 KZ Amsterdam.
Telephone (20) 27 56 56.

Hong Kong

901-5 Lane Crawford House,
70 Queen's Road Central,
Hong Kong.
Telephone (5) 248 121.

Italy

Palazzo Capponi,
Via Gino Capponi 26,
50121 Florence.
Telephone (55) 2479021.

Monaco

Sporting d'Hiver,
B.P.45, Place du Casino,
MC 98001 Monaco Cedex.
Telephone (93) 30 88 80.

South Africa

13 Biermann Avenue,
Rosebank, Johannesburg 2196.
Telephone (11) 880 3125.

Spain

Plaza de la Independencia 8,
28001 Madrid.
Telephone (1) 232 6488 & 6572.

Switzerland

24 Rue de la Cité,
CH 1204 Geneva.
Telephone (22) 21 3377.

20 Bleicherweg, CH-8022,
Zurich.
Telephone (1) 202 0011.

Opportunites for Collectors

The art market is livelier than ever, and both 1985 and 1986 were exciting years at Sotheby's. Too often the publicity surrounding the most dramatic events in the art world gives the impression that collecting is an area reserved for the wealthy and sophisticated. In reality, the art market offers many opportunities to all who are willing to explore, and the current strength of the market can be largely attributed to the participation of new private buyers, many of whom are laying the foundations for the important collections of the future.

Like many other markets, the art market is ruled by supply and demand, which are in turn influenced by new scholarship, museum exhibitions, the constant shifting of wealth around the world, life styles, and those ineffable and fickle elements of taste and fashion. With so many parts to the equation, trends are difficult to identify and predictions impossible. Nevertheless, works of art can add immeasurably to your life, enriching your mind and enhancing your home.

Last spring we interviewed a number of the knowledgeable experts at Sotheby's to find out where the opportunities are today to acquire works of art that epitomize the style and taste of their own time and are now for various reasons relatively undervalued. Interestingly, such possibilities exist in virtually every collecting area from antiquity to the eighteenth and nineteenth centuries and even to the 1950s, just now coming into vogue. Allow us therefore to take you on a buying tour of history.

Let's start in ancient Egypt. Good small bronzes, miracles of casting for their time, can be purchased for under $3,000 while scarabs carved in decorative stones are available in the $300 to $500 range. There is plentiful material in both areas, and it is relatively easy, with good advice, to build up a defined collection that should increase in value as it grows. As for classical Greece, both Athenian and South Italian black-figure, red-figure, and polychrome pottery are increasing in popularity. Exceptional pieces reach mid-five figures but lovely examples can be found from $200 to $3,000.

Works of art of the middle ages and the Renaissance can be an even more fertile area to investigate. Medieval art, particularly sculpture, is very good value and Gothic wood carvings seem to be attracting growing interest. Tapestries can be great buys, providing they are in good condition. Once they sold for as much as old master paintings, but as people moved from castles to condominiums, tapestries lost their position in the household. Their artistic value is unique and the scenes they depict perfectly convey the spirit of the middle ages and the Renaissance.

Mementos of the glories of the Renaissance are still accessible today. Renaissance jewels, exquisite examples of courtly life, can cost as little as $2,000, although a splendid gold, enamel, and jeweled design would be about ten times as much. The profusion of nineteenth century imitations has kept prices low, but a careful buyer can find real treasures.

The bronzes and painted enamels of the sixteenth century have a specialized audience and are currently undervalued. Bronze plaquettes—complete expressions of the Renaissance ideal—range from $150 upwards to about $3,000. Limoges enamels, with their lustrous finish and delicately painted scenes in grisaille, blue and white, and rainbow colors, are a delight to the eye and should be back in fashion soon.

The very mention 'blue and white' brings to mind the Chinese and Japanese export wave of the seventeenth and eighteenth centuries. This porcelain is quite plentiful and nice examples can be found for between $500 and $750. At the moment, there are unusual opportunities to buy early ceramics from the Han, Tang, and Song dynasties, in particular unglazed Tang pottery figures and Song bowls and dishes, because so much has recently come on the market. Chinese snuff bottles are still very inexpensive with simple porcelain bottles selling for $75 and more intricate designs for $450 to $600. Jade carvings are a good area for collectors, choice examples fetching between $500 and $750.

Returning to Europe, the cabinetwork of eighteenth century France certainly represents one of the great moments in the history of decorative arts. While the finest marquetry and lacquer furniture makes exceptional prices, there are excellent buys in gilded bronze clocks and andirons ($4,000 to $10,000), which are the perfect expression of the rococo spirit. Among the furniture, pieces from the Louis XIV era, particularly ungilded carved wood consoles, show a unique flair for design and are currently less expensive than those of the later periods.

For the most part, eighteenth century American furniture is now out of reach, and collectors are turning to the handsome designs of the Federal period. Similarly, there is strong interest in the English regency style.

The eighteenth century does offer many possibilities in silver and ceramics. There are good buys in mid-century Georgian silver sauce boats, coffee and tea pots, salvers and tea kettles on lampstands. The workmanship is elaborate, the silver content is high, and the prices are in the $2,000 to $3,000 range—just as they were twenty years ago. In the same field, there is enormous demand and very high prices for the work of Paul de Lamerie, Nicholas Sprimont, and other major Huguenot makers.

Ceramics of this period are an extraordinary bargain in France and England, often costing less than similar pieces made today. Twelve Sevrès plates can go for as little as $50 per piece and bring with them a sense of history. In Great Britain, look to the small factories such as New Hall, Liverpool, and Lowestoft as well as the Welsh factories of Swansea and Nantgarw.

We have arrived at the nineteenth century, with its profusion of styles and abundant material. Starting with an esoteric field, near Eastern weapons are better and more luxuriously made than contemporary European examples and far less expensive. A totally silver-encrusted sword with an ivory handle can be had for between $800 and $900. Also from this part of the world come Oriental rugs and carpets, which are currently enjoying a revival of interest. Rugs rose greatly in value after OPEC and then fell when the Shah was deposed. Now there is particular interest in Caucasian, Turkman, and Eastern Turkestan tribal pieces, and small Southwest Persian pieces are a true find at prices between $2,000 and $2,500.

Returning to silver, American pewter and silver of the late eighteenth and early nineteenth century is on the rise but still reasonable: a good quality porringer can cost between $2,000 and $2,500. Since scholarship in this period is just beginning, the decorative arts are awaiting discovery and a concomitant increase in value.

Mid to late nineteenth century porcelain offers some excellent buys. English wares such as pâte-sur-pâte by Minton and the earthenware pieces by Deck and Longwy, the French equivalent of the aesthetic movement in England, are already moving up in price in anticipation of the major exhibition at the Metropolitan Museum next year.

Moving back to unusual places in the same period, there is plenty of good tribal African sculpture that has such an interesting relationship to modern taste; think of Picasso and of last year's 'Primitivism in 20th Century Art' at the Museum of Modern Art. A hundred years is a long time in tribal art, and value comes from ritual use as well as age. The range of pieces below $5,000 should tempt collectors. Look at Dan masks from Liberia, sculpture from Baule of the Ivory Coast or Dogon sculpture from Mali, all of which are relatively inexpensive. And while considering the primitive art of this period, you should perhaps turn your attention to transitional Navajo textiles and Southwest pottery, which are in the same price range.

Back in Europe, let's look at jewelry, particularly nineteenth century cameos and engraved stones. Mostly made in Italy in a variety of materials—coral, agates, shell, moonstones—these are gems of the carver's art and seem to be coming back into fashion.

Like the oceans, there are small and large waves in the history of taste, and the smart collector spots them before they get too close to shore. Without question, the wave breaking this fall is the aesthetic of the Wiener Werkstatte, that dazzling moment in the Vienna of Freud and the Mayerling scandal when Josef Hoffmann, Otto Wagner, Koloman Moser, Josef Maria Olbrich and so many others produced a myriad of objects from silver and jewelry to posters and books in a style that mingled severity and decadence. Klimt and Schiele—nearly unsaleable twenty years ago—are practically priceless today and everything in the decorative arts is likely to follow as the immense Vienna exhibition arrives at the Museum of Modern Art after showing to capacity audiences in Vienna and Paris.

We are in the twentieth century and could start projecting good values for the twenty-first. There is already interest in the jewelry of the 40's—wristwatches by Patek Philippe and Rolex, bracelets and necklaces by Mauboussin, Van Cleef & Arpels, and others—and even the objects of the 1950's, familiar icons of our own youth, are finding a place in the market. Like everything else we have mentioned, these perfectly reflect their time and place. If you seek objects that do the same, you cannot go very wrong.

ALEXIS GREGORY
The Vendome Press

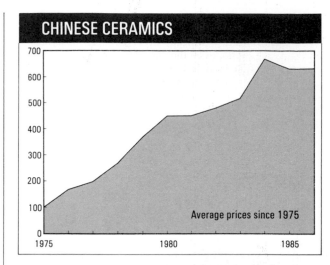

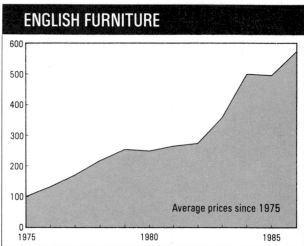

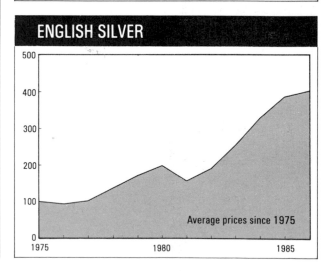

An Economic Review of the Art Market

During the twelve month period to mid-summer 1986 strong outside forces had a significant impact on the art market, both on prices achieved and on the nature of participation. The art market as a whole is subject to the influence of underlying economic factors, however individual areas of the market are affected by other factors specifically related to that field. This always makes it difficult to draw any wider conclusions. While there has not been substantial growth over the past year, the market remains strong and healthy.

Through the second half of 1985 the market underwent a period of consolidation at the high levels established after a number of years of sustained growth; activity was not as frenetic as that seen during the corresponding period the previous year. Buyers and sellers adjusted their expectations towards rather more realistic price levels. During this period demand remained firm for the finest quality works which were also fresh to the market. An interesting and encouraging development, however, was the resurgence of interest in items in the middle range of the market which traditionally are somewhat more price sensitive. The current strength of the art market can also partly be attributed to the emergence of large numbers of new private buyers. In the long term, new collectors will undoubtedly stimulate the entire market, benefiting all concerned.

The first few months of 1986 were quiet. However, from April there was a significant increase in activity. This was a particular achievement given that it was accomplished without the strong US dollar and consequent American participation which had provided so much of the impetus behind earlier growth patterns. From the spring of 1986 the strength of the Yen was a feature which led to a significant revival of Japanese participation.

One of the main beneficiaries of this increased Japanese presence has been the Impressionist and Modern paintings sectors. There has long been a strong Japanese influence in this area; it was their withdrawal from it in 1974 during the first oil shock, which precipitated a decline at that time. The weakness of the dollar has also added a fillip to participation by British and other European buyers. Traditionally sectors such as Impressionist and Modern art and jewellery are used as a barometer to gauge the climate of the overall market .

One of the features of the period under consideration was the appearance at auction of large quantities of material in one collecting field at one time, which has not adversely affected price levels. In London, thirty-eight Flemish Old Master paintings were offered for sale at Sotheby's from a single collection, including eighteen by Pieter Breughel the younger. Many of them had only been acquired at auction within the last decade (regarded as a short time for resale), which added to the risk of offering so many works by one artist at the same time. However, the popularity of the artist, the sound history of the works and their easily identifiable, attractive and cheerful nature, all contributed to a highly successful sale. A second example was the disposal at Christie's in Amsterdam of some 150,000 pieces of Chinese porcelain destined for the export market, recovered from the China Sea. The circumstances of the find resulted in exceptional prices, illustrating the extra value that can be added even to modest quality works with important or romantic historical connections. Because of these special features, it was not anticipated that the high prices would have a long-term impact on the market for Chinese ceramics and this has proved to be the case.

Chinese ceramics is one of the three sectors chosen for closer examination (see figs on facing page). It has been one of the most volatile areas of the art market over the past decade. Part of the rapid growth immediately following 1975 is accounted for by the fact that there had been a major fall in prices just prior to that date. More recently, growth has been inhibited by the economic uncertainties concerning the future of Hong Kong, home of many of the major participants in this field; and erratic supply has also been a problem.

English furniture has been one of the success stories of recent years. While the dollar was strong, an active American interest kept prices moving on a firm upward trend. Over the last few months, the weakness of the dollar has deterred American interest but their place has been taken by greater interest from British and other European collectors.

Another sector which has shown strength over the past ten years is English silver. In the early 1980s dealers from the United Kingdom were deterred neither by American interest nor by the strength of the dollar. Competition for pieces of the very best quality helped to ensure a steady increase in prices over a long term.

The objects in this edition were sold in 1985

The condition of an object is crucial to its value. Although condition is mentioned in some sections of this guide, the description may not be detailed. Many entries give no indication of condition, but in the majority of cases it can be assumed that the entry is in reasonably good condition, bearing in mind the date of the piece and the nature of its material. Readers are asked to remember this when comparing similar pieces and to take into consideration fluctuations in the market.

English Monarchs

1558 Elizabeth I
1603 James I
1625 Charles I
1653 (Commonwealth)
1660 Charles II
1685 James II
1689 William and Mary
1694 William III
1702 Anne
1714 George I
1727 George II
1759 George III
1811 (Prince of Wales Regent)
1820 George IV
1830 William IV
1837 Victoria
1901 Edward VII
1910 George V
1937 Edward VIII
1937 George VI
1952 Elizabeth II

French Monarchs and Periods

1589 Henri IV
1610 Louis XIII
1643 Louis XIV
1715 Louis XV
1774 Louis XVI
1792 The Republic ⎫
1795 Directory ⎬ Directoire
1799 Consulate ⎭
1804 Empire
1814 Louis XVIII ⎫
1824 Charles X ⎬ Restauration
1830 Louis Phillipe ⎭
1848 Second Republic
1852 Napoleon III
1870 Third Republic

American furniture periods

1620-90   Jacobean or 'Pilgrim century'
1690-1725 William and Mary
1725-60   Queen Anne
1750-80   Chippendale
1780-1810 Federal

Abbreviations used in the captions of sale locations

A	Amsterdam	Glen	Gleneagles	J	Jerusalem	NP	Nostell Priory
Belg	Belgravia	H	Houston	JHB	Johannesburg	NY	New York
C	Chester	HH	Hopetoun House	L	London	S	Sussex
Ct	Capetown	HK	Hong Kong	LA	Los Angeles	St.M	St. Moritz
F	Florence	HS	House Sale	M	Monaco		
G	Geneva	HU	Honolulu	MA	Manchester		

Furniture and Decorations

1
A Regency stencilled and painted small bookcase, *c.*1815, 82.5cm (32½in) high, *NY 8 Oct,* $2,090 (£1,412)

2
A George III set of mahogany wall shelves, *c.*1765, altered, 104cm (41in) high, *C 3 Oct,* £682 ($955)

3
A George III mahogany and pine book cabinet, *c.*1800, 135cm (53in) high, *S 22 Jan,* £1,100 ($1,304)

4
A George IV mahogany bookcase, *c.*1825, 229cm (7ft 6in) high, *S 15 Oct,* £1,155 ($1,709)

5
A George III brass-mounted mahogany revolving bookstand, *c.*1800, 164cm (6ft 4½in) high, *NY 26 Jan,* $13,750 (£12,387)

6
An Edwardian mahogany revolving bookcase, 50cm (19½in) wide, *S 5 Feb,* £429 ($506)

7
A Louis XV/XVI ormolu-mounted kingwood and tulipwood parquetry bookcase, third quarter 18th century, with 'rouge royale' marble top, 98cm (38½in) high, *NY 5 Oct,* $2,090 (£1,482)

8
A Louis XVI mahogany and tulipwood bookcase, last quarter 18th century, 149cm (58¾in) high, *NY 5 Oct,* $2,860 (£2,028)

1

2

3

4

5

6

7

8

1

An Empire mahogany bookcase, 265cm (8ft 8½in), M 24 June, FF 188,700 (£15,205; $20,375)

2

A Russian birchwood bookcase, c.1830, 237.5cm (7ft 9½in) high, L 31 May, £1,210 ($1,621)

3

An early George III breakfront library secretaire bookcase, c.1760, 265cm (8ft 8½in), L 8 Mar, £18,700 ($20,944)

4

An early George III mahogany breakfront bookcase, c.1745, 281cm (9ft 2½in) high, L 15 Nov, £9,900 ($13,860)

5

A George III inlaid satinwood and mahogany breakfront secretary bookcase, late 18th century, 248cm (8ft 1½in) high, NY 26 Jan, $13,750 (£12,387)

6

A George III breakfront secretary cabinet, early 19th century, 268cm (8ft 9½in) high, NY 13 Apr, $6,600 (£5,280)

7

A George III mahogany breakfront library bookcase, c.1770, 293cm (9ft 7½in) wide, NY 26 Jan, $13,200 (£11,891)

8

A late George III mahogany breakfront bookcase, c.1810, 298cm (9ft 9½in) wide, L 15 Nov, £8,580 ($12,012)

9

A George III mahogany breakfront bookcase, c.1780, 245cm (8ft ½in) high, L 8 Mar, £9,350 ($10,472)

10

A George III mahogany breakfront bookcase, c.1790, on later plinth, 305cm (10ft), L 26 July, £4,510 ($6,629)

11

A George IV mahogany breakfront bookcase, c.1825, 232cm (7ft 7½in) high, S 15 Oct, £3,080 ($4,558)

1

2

3

4

5

6

7

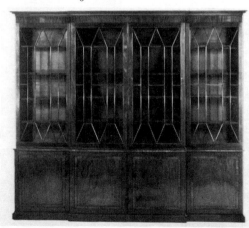

8

9

10

11

1
A George IV mahogany
bookcase, *c.*1830, 237cm
(93in) high, *C 17 Jan,*
£2,310 ($2,772)

2
A Victorian mahogany
breakfront bookcase,
*c.*1850, 244cm (8ft) wide,
S 11 June,
£2,640 ($3,472)

3
A Victorian walnut
bookcase, *c.*1860, 213cm
(7ft) high, *L 22 Feb,*
£2,145 ($2,445)

4
A Victorian flame
mahogany breakfront
secretaire bookcase, *c.*1850,
340cm (134in) wide,
C 7 Jan,
£4,180 ($5,016)

5
A George III style
mahogany bookcase,
*c.*1910, 221cm (7ft 3in)
high, *C 3 Oct,*
£1,870 ($2,618)

6
A Victorian mahogany
bookcase, *c.*1850, 223cm
(7ft 4in) high, *C 5 Sept,*
£1,012 ($1,487)

7
A George III style faded
mahogany and satinwood
breakfront bookcase, 19th
century, 190cm (6ft 2½in)
high, *NY 26 Jan,*
$6,050 (£5,450)

8
A Renaissance Revival
carved oak library book-
case, 19th century, 209cm
(82in), *S 8 Jan,*
£484 ($581)

1   2   3

4   5   6

7   8

1
A William and Mary walnut secretaire, late 17th century, altered, 165cm (5ft 5in) wide, *L 22 Nov,* £3,190 ($4,466)

2
A William and Mary marquetry secretaire chest, *c.*1680, inlaid with flowers and ebony panels within oyster and plain walnut veneer, 159cm (5ft 2½in) wide, *L 8 Mar,* £13,200 ($14,784)

3
A Queen Anne walnut-veneered double-domed bureau bookcase, *c.*1700, 199cm (6ft 6in) high, *L 26 July,* £6,050 ($8,893)

4
A Queen Anne burr-elm double-domed bureau cabinet, *c.*1710, 196cm (6ft 5in) high, *L 26 Apr,* £14,300 ($18,161)

5
A late George II mahogany bureau cabinet, *c.*1750, 242cm (7ft 11½in) high, *L 14 June,* £5,720 ($7,607)

6
A George II mahogany bureau cabinet, mid 18th century, in three parts, 215cm (7ft 11in) high, *L 12 Apr,* £2,860 ($3,661)

7
A George III mahogany secretaire chest on chest, *c.*1760, 193cm (6ft 4in) high, *C 18 Apr,* £2,200 ($2,860)

8
A painted satinwood secretaire cabinet, 19th century, the upper part fitted with adjustable bookshelves, 193cm (6ft 4in) high, *C 17 Jan,* £6,820 ($8,184)

1

2

4

5

7

8

3

6

1

An early George III mahogany secretaire bookcase, *c.*1770, 222cm (7ft 3½in) high, *L 14 June,* £5,280 ($7,022)

2

A George III inlaid mahogany slant-front bureau cabinet, late 18th century, the upper part reconstructed, 220cm (7ft 4in) high, *NY 13 Apr,* $6,600 (£5,280)

3

A George III mahogany secretaire bookcase, *c.*1780, 221cm (7ft 3in) high, *L 26 July,* £2,750 ($4,042)

4

A George III mahogany secretaire bookcase, *c.*1790, 222cm (7ft 3½in) high, *S 22 Jan,* £7,700 ($9,125)

5

A late Georgian mahogany secretaire bookcase, early 19th century, 238cm (7ft 10in) high, *C 28 Feb,* £935 ($1,047)

6

A late George III mahogany secretaire bookcase, *c.*1820, with associated upper part, 226cm (7ft 5in) high, *C 3 Oct,* £1,155 ($1,617)

7

A George IV mahogany secretaire bookcase, *c.*1820, the writing drawer revealing satinwood-veneered small drawers and pigeonholes, 221cm (7ft 3in) high, *S 11 June,* £2,200 ($2,893)

8

An Edwardian mahogany and marquetry bureau bookcase, *c.*1900, 229cm (7ft 6in) high, *C 3 Oct,* £748 ($1,047)

9

A Victorian mahogany secretaire bookcase, *c.*1860, 224cm (7ft 4in) high, *C 2 May,* £1,265 ($1,657)

1

2

3

4

5

6

7

8

9

1
A Queen Anne walnut-veneered kneehole desk, *c.1710*, stamped from W Williamson & Sons, Guildford, with recessed sliding cupboard, *L 14 June*, £5,500 ($7,315)

2
A George I walnut-veneered bureau, *c.1720*, 106cm (42in) high, *L 7 June*, £3,520 ($4,681)

3
A George II inlaid walnut kneehole desk, second quarter 18th century, 80cm (31½in) wide, *NY 13 Apr*, $3,575 (£2,860)

4
An early 18th century oak bureau, 84cm (33in) high, *L 27 Sept*, £2,640 ($3,907)

5
A George III mahogany bureau, *c.1760*, 109cm (43in) wide, *S 11 June*, £2,035 ($2,676)

6
A George III mahogany bureau, *c.1770*, 109cm (43in) wide, *S 19 Feb*, £825 ($949)

7
A George III mahogany bureau, *c.1775*, 102cm (40in) high, *C 3 Oct*, £1,705 ($2,387)

8
A George III mahogany bureau, late 18th century, the fall front enclosing a plain fitted interior, 104cm (41in) high, *C 18 Apr*, £1,595 ($2,073)

9
A George III satinwood bureau, *c.1790*, with later inlay, 111cm (43½in) high, *S 22 Jan*, £935 ($1,108)

10
A George III oak bureau, *c.1790*, 115.5cm (45½in), *C 28 Feb*, £748 ($838)

11
A George III satinwood-veneered cylinder bureau, *c.1790*, crossbanded in rosewood, 151cm (59½in) high, *L 8 Mar*, £9,900 ($11,088)

12
A Regency inlaid mahogany cylinder top bureau cabinet, *c.1810*, 174cm (5ft 8½in) high, *NY 26 Jan*, $1,760 (£1,585)

13
A George III mahogany tambour writing desk, *c.1780*, 96.5cm (38in) wide, *L 27 Sept*, £2,640 ($3,907)

14
A George III inlaid mahogany and purple-heart tambour writing table, *c.1790*, 81cm (32in) high, *NY 8 June*, $2,530 (£2,008)

15
A George III painted satinwood reading or writing table, *c.1790*, painted with trailing flowers, 90.5cm (35½in) wide, *L 7 June*, £792 ($1,053)

1 2 3
4 5 6
7 8 9
10 11 12
13 14 15

1
A George III mahogany
pedestal desk, c.1790,
later feet, 104cm (41in)
wide, S 15 Oct,
£1,540 ($2,279)

2
A late George III
mahogany writing table,
c.1800, 151cm (59½in)
wide, L 15 Nov,
£3,300 ($4,620)

3
A Victorian figured
walnut pedestal desk,
with leather inset top,
123cm (48½in) wide,
S 8 Jan,
£1,430 ($1,716)

4
A George III mahogany
pedestal partner's desk,
early 19th century, 152cm
(5ft) wide, NY 26 Jan,
$8,250 (£7,432)

5
A Victorian gilt-brass
mounted burr-walnut
pedestal desk, 19th
century, 137cm (54in)
wide, NY 1 Nov,
$4,400 (£3,055)

6
A satinwood pedestal
writing desk, c.1880,
129.5cm (51in) wide,
L 19 July,
£1,650 ($2,310)

7
A Regency mahogany
Carlton House writing
desk, c.1810, 162.5cm (5ft
4in) wide, L 14 June,
£17,600 ($23,408)

8
A George III style
mahogany 'Carlton
House' writing table,
c.1920, 120cm (47in)
wide, S 23 July,
£1,485 ($2,198)

9
A mahogany roll top
desk, c.1900, 152.5cm
(60in) wide, C 17 Oct,
£660 ($977)

10
A Wooton & Co standard
grade walnut patent desk,
c.1875, 167cm (5ft 6in)
high, L 19 July,
£3,300 ($4,620)

1

2

3

4

5

7

6

8

9

10

1
A William IV rosewood
Davenport, 56cm (22in)
wide, *S 5 Feb,*
£660 ($779)

2
A William IV rosewood
Davenport, *c.*1825, 93cm
(36½in) high,
NY 13 Apr,
$3,410 (£2,728)

3
A Victorian walnut
Davenport, *c.*1870, 86cm
(34in) high, *C 3 Oct,*
£1,265 ($1,771)

4
A Victorian walnut secre-
taire Wellington chest,
*c.*1850, 122cm (48in) high,
S 12 Nov,
£968 ($1,355)

5
A Victorian mahogany
Davenport, *c.*1860, with
ebonised mouldings and
crossbanding, 107cm
(42in) high, *S 11 June,*
£1,155 ($1,519)

6
An Edwardian satinwood
cylinder bureau, *c.*1910,
108cm (42½in) high,
S 16 Apr,
£616 ($801)

7
A Victorian walnut and
kingwood crossbanded
bonheur du jour, *c.*1870,
with gilt-metal mounts,
142cm (56in) high,
S 12 Nov,
£1,045 ($1,463)

8
A satinwood bonheur du
jour, *c.*1890, 109cm (43in)
high, *L 22 Feb,*
£858 ($978)

9
An Edwardian mahogany
bureau bookcase, 102cm
(40in) wide, *S 30 Apr,*
£748 ($965)

10
An Edwardian mahogany
lady's writing desk, *c.*1900,
74cm (29in) wide,
C 28 Feb,
£396 ($444)

11
An Edwardian mahogany
bureau de dame, *c.*1900,
crossbanded in satin-
wood, stamped Gregory
& Co, 212 and 214 Regent
St, *C 3 Oct,*
£1,705 ($2,387)

12
A George III style break-
front mahogany pedestal
desk, *c.*1920, 152.5cm (5ft)
wide, *C 14 Mar,*
£990 ($1,128)

13
A Louis XV style boulle
bureau plat, English,
*c.*1840, 142cm (56in) long,
L 8 Nov,
£2,530 ($3,795)

1
**A Chippendale carved
maple slant-front desk,**
New England, *c.*1785,
111cm (43½in) high,
NY 26 Oct,
$8,525 (£6,003)

2
**A Federal mahogany
slant-front desk,** *c.*1800,
117cm (46in) wide,
NY 2 Feb,
$2,310 (£1,957)

3
**A Chippendale carved
mahogany slant-front
desk,** Eastern Massachu-
setts, *c.*1780, 111cm
(43¾in) high, *NY 26 Oct,*
$6,875 (£4,841)

4
**A Queen Anne carved
walnut secretary-bookcase,**
Philadelphia, *c.*1740, in
two parts, 205cm (6ft
8½in) high, *NY 2 Feb,*
$19,800 (£18,000)

5
**A Federal mahogany
lady's secretary,** New
York, *c.*1810, in two parts,
136cm (53½in) high,
NY 1 Feb,
$3,575 (£3,250)

6
**A Federal carved
mahogany secretary-
bookcase,** attributed to
Duncan Phyfe, New
York, *c.*1810, in two parts,
244cm (8ft) high,
NY 1 Feb,
$42,900 (£39,000)

7
**A Queen Anne carved
cherrywood slant-front
desk on frame,** Connec-
ticut, *c.*1760, 102cm (40in)
high, *NY 26 Oct,*
$13,750 (£9,683)

8
**A Chippendale caved
walnut kneehole desk,**
Middle Atlantic States,
*c.*1780, 92cm (36in) wide,
NY 2 Feb,
$5,500 (£4,661)

9
**A Chippendale carved
walnut slant-front desk,**
Lancaster, Pennsylvania,
*c.*1780, 109cm (43in) high,
NY 26 Oct,
$6,600 (£4,647)

10
**A Federal inlaid
mahogany writing desk,**
Middle Atlantic States,
*c.*1790, 87cm (34in) high,
NY 2 Feb,
$1,210 (£1,025)

1

2

3

4

5

6

7

8

9

10

1
A Dutch walnut bureau cabinet, c.1725, later mirrored doors, 243cm (8ft) high, *L 31 May,* **£3,960 ($5,306)**

2
A South German ivory-inlaid walnut-veneered bureau cabinet, c.1740, the upper part with an ivory panel of Venus and Cupid, the lower part with a small ivory landscape cartouche, 218cm (7ft 2in) high, *L 29 Nov,* **£13,200 ($18,480)**

3
A South German walnut bureau cabinet, mid 18th century, the upper cupboard door inlaid with a rustic scene, three long drawers outlined in mahogany, 193cm (7ft 4in), *L 24 May,* **£7,480 ($9,948)**

4
An Italian inlaid walnut bureau, c.1730, in crossbanded wood, inlaid throughout with scrollwork, flowers, cherubs and grotesques, 114cm (45in) wide, *L 24 May,* **£6,600 ($8,778)**

5
A North Italian rosewood bureau, c.1730, quarter-veneered and crossbanded with tulipwood and boxwood stringing. 132cm (52in) wide, *L 24 May,* **£3,080 ($4,096)**

6
A North Italian walnut-veneered bureau, mid 18th century, the serpentine flap enclosing a fitted interior with a well, 122cm (48in) wide, *L 18 Dec,* **£2,200 ($3,080)**

7
An Italian walnut-veneered writing desk, Lombardy, mid 18th century, 112cm (44in) high, *F 26 Mar,* **L 15,000,000 (£6,012; $7,635)**

8
An Italian walnut-veneered bureau, Rome, c.1760, 140cm (55in) wide, *F 26 Mar,* **L 10,000,000 (£4,008; $5,090)**

9
A Central Italian inlaid walnut-veneered bureau, second half 18th century, 127cm (50in) wide, *F 26 Mar,* **L 6,000,000 (£2,405; $3,054)**

1   2   3
4   5
6   7
8   9

1
A Venetian walnut-veneered bureau cabinet, mid 18th century, *F 26 Mar,* **L 28,000,000 (£11,222; $14,253)**

2
An Austrian walnut bureau cabinet, *c.*1770 200cm (6ft 7in) high, *L 31 May,* £2,530 ($3,390)

3
An Austrian neoclassical ormolu-mounted mahogany drop front secretaire, *c.*1810, in two parts, the upper with ebony ovals bearing ormolu plaques, 197cm (6ft 5½in), *NY 24 May,* $4,675 (£3,710)

4
An Italian walnut-veneered bureau, Emilia, late 18th century, 139cm (54¾in) high, *F 26 Mar,* **L 3,500,000 (£1,403; $1,782)**

5
A German brass-mounted burr-walnut slant front desk, third quarter 18th century, 108cm (42½in) high, *NY 24 May,* $4,510 (£3,579)

6
An Italian walnut and fruitwood parquetry writing table, second quarter 19th century, 78cm (30½in) high, *NY 23 Mar,* $1,045 (£893)

7
A Venetian walnut-veneered writing desk, mid 18th century, 106cm (41¾in) wide, *F 26 Mar,* **L 30,000,000 (£12,024; $15,271)**

8
A Dutch satinwood bon-heur du jour, late 18th century, crossbanded in tulipwood, 116cm (46in) high, *L 31 May,* £3,300 ($4,422)

9
A Dutch walnut and marquetry bureau de dame, mid 19th century, 104cm (41in) high, *L 21 June,* £1,540 ($2,002)

10
A Dutch secretaire à abattant, *c.*1790, quarter-veneered in kingwood with mahogany and tulipwood, with late 19th century floral marquetry, 154cm (5ft ½in) high, *L 31 May,* £3,630 ($4,864)

11
A Dutch mahogany reading/writing cabinet, 19th century, 100cm (39in) high, *A 26 Feb,* **Dfl 1,392 (£341; $382)**

12
A Viennese Vernis Martin bureau de dame, by A Forster of Vienna, *c.*1860, gilt-metal mounts, 98cm (38½in) high, *L 22 Mar,* £1,705 ($2,046)

1   2   3

4   5   6

7

8

9

10   11   12

1
A Louis XIV bureau
Mazarin, *c.*1700, inlaid
with Berainesque designs
in brass on an ebony
ground, altered, 82cm
(32½in) wide, *L 24 May,*
£3,960 ($5,267)

2
A Régence ormolu-
mounted ebonised
bureau plat, *c.*1720, 132cm
(52in) wide, *NY 24 May,*
$8,250 (£6,547)

3
A Louis XV ormolu-
mounted tulipwood and
kingwood marquetry
table à écrire, mid 18th
century, 72cm (28¼in)
high, *NY 24 May,*
$4,180 (£3,317)

4
A Louis XV ormolu-
mounted tulipwood and
kingwood parquetry table
à écrire, alterations, 93cm
(36¾in) wide, *NY 24 May,*
$1,980 (£1,571)

5
A Louis XV rosewood
marquetry table à écrire,
81.5cm (32in) wide,
M 24 June,
FF 55,500
(£4,472; $5,993)

6
A Louis XV ormolu-
mounted kingwood and
parquetry bureau en
pente, mid 18th century,
105cm (41½in) high,
NY 23 Mar,
$4,950 (£4,231)

7
A Louis XV veneered
bureau plat, stamped P.
Roussel, gilt-bronze
mounts, 119cm (47in)
wide, *M 23 June,*
FF 111,000
(£8,944; $11,985)

8
A Louis XVI ormolu-
mounted tulipwood and
fruitwood parquetry table
à écrire, *c.*1780, 72cm
(28¼in) high, *NY 24 May,*
$5,775 (£4,583)

9
A Louis XV/XVI ormolu-
mounted mahogany table
à écrire, signed S Oeben,
later trestle supports,
109cm (42¾in) wide,
NY 12 Oct,
$6,050 (£4,291)

10
A Louis XV bureau plat,
mid 18th century, 162cm
(5ft 4in) wide, *L 5 July,*
£19,800 ($27,324)

11
A Louis XV/XVI
ormolu-mounted tulip-
wood parquetry table à
écrire, *c.*1775, attributed
to Dusautoy, with oval
veined white marble top,
75cm (29½in) high,
NY 4 May,
$16,500 (£13,750)

12
A late Louis XVI
mahogany dressing and
writing table, *c.*1790, the
hinged mirror-lined top
with recessed marble
panel, 89cm (35in) wide,
L 5 July,
£1,210 ($1,670)

13
A Louis XVI mahogany
table à écrire, Riesener,
from the Petit Trianon,
M 23 June,
FF 377,400
(£30,411; $40,751)

1
A Louis XVI satinwood
veneered oval table à
écrire, stamped N. Petit,
white marble top, gilt-
bronze decoration, 75cm
(29½in) high, *M 23 June,*
FF 111,000
(£8,944; $11,985)

2
A Louis XVI secretaire à
abattant, stamped
J Stumpff, with rosewood,
amaranth and bois satiné
marquetry, marble top,
140cm (55in) high,
M 23 June,
FF 38,850
(£3,131; $4,195)

3
A Louis XVI marquetry
table à écrire, stamped
Jeanne, *M 24 June,*
FF 11,100 (£894; $1,199)

4
A Louis XVI ormolu-
mounted mahogany
bureau à cylindre, late
18th century, with liver
and white mottled mar-
ble galleried top, 107cm
(42in) high, *NY 23 Mar,*
$4,675 (£3,996)

5
A Louis XVI satinwood
and mahogany bonheur
du jour, *c.*1790, the upper
part with Carrara marble
top, gilt-brass mouldings,
L 5 July,
£1,870 ($2,581)

6
A Louis XVI mahogany-
veneered bureau à
cylindre, 130.5cm (51¼in)
wide, *M 24 June,*
FF 88,800
(£7,156; $9,588)

7
An Empire mahogany
cylinder bureau cabinet,
*c.*1810, with gilt brass
mounts, one signed
Andrieu, 185.5cm (6ft
1in) high, *C 17 Jan,*
£1,485 ($1,782)

8
An Empire secretaire à
abattant, early 19th cen-
tury, mahogany-
veneered, with gilt-
bronze mounts, 142cm
(4ft 8in) high, *M 24 June,*
FF 24,420
(£2,035; $2,747)

9
An Empire mahogany
secretaire à abbatant,
early 19th century,
ormolu-mounted, with
verde antico top, 140cm
(4ft 7in) high, *NY 24 May,*
$4,400 (£3,492)

10
A Directoire mahogany
secretaire à abbatant,
*c.*1795, with grey marble
top, 145cm (57in) high,
C 18 Apr,
£1,485 ($1,931)

11
An Empire mahogany
bureau plat, *c.*1815, with
leather-lined top, 114cm
(3ft 9in) wide, *L 18 Dec,*
£3,410 ($4,774)

12
A Directoire mahogany
bureau plat, late 18th
century, with ormolu
mounts, the sides now
with leather-lined slide,
127cm (50in) wide,
NY 23 May,
$3,410 (£2,915)

13
A Directoire mahogany
bureau plat, *c.*1800, fitted
with pull-out slides,
130cm (51in) wide, *C 3 Oct,*
£1,870 ($2,618)

14
A Louis Philippe
ebonized and gilt-bronze
Davenport, *c.*1830, 89cm
(35in) wide, *C 3 Oct,*
£550 ($770)

15
A Napoleon III bureau
en pente, with gilt-bronze
mounts, inlaid with
mother-of-pearl, 99cm
(39in) high, *NY 22 June,*
$825 (£644)

1

2

3

4

5

6

7

8

9

10

11

12

13

14

15

1

A brass-inlaid ebonised writing table, c.1850, the top lined in green leather, 124cm (49in) wide, *L 22 Feb,* £1,540 ($1,756)

2

A marquetry bureau de dame, c.1870, with tulipwood crossbanding, 68cm (27in) wide, *L 8 Nov,* £792 ($1,188)

3

A French tulipwood secretaire à abattant, c.1860, in the form of a semainier, with gilt-metal mounts, rouge royale marble top, 140cm (55in) high, *S 11 June,* £1,430 ($1,880)

4

An inlaid walnut bureau de dame, c.1870, 140cm (55in) high, *L 19 July,* £902 ($1,263)

5

An ivory-inlaid ebonised bonheur-du-jour, c.1880, 111cm (43½in) high, *L 21 June,* £550 ($715)

6

A French tulipwood-veneered secretaire à abattant, c.1910, the lock stamped Krieger Paris, with mottled green marble top and Wedgwood type oval plaque, 151cm (59½in) high, *L 21 June,* £1,485 ($1,931)

7

A tulipwood veneered bonheur-du-jour, c.1890, stamed Krieger, gilt-brass mouldings, 75cm (29½in) wide, *L 21 June,* £1,925 ($2,502)

8

A Louis XV-style kingwood parquetry bonheur-du-jour, c.1890, incorporating a clock with enamel dial, by Janvier, 104cm (51in) high, *S 14 May,* £682 ($907)

9

A 'plum pudding' mahogany bureau à cylindre, late 19th century, signed P Sormani & Fils, Paris, 91.5cm (36in) wide, *L 8 Nov,* £2,200 ($3,300)

10

A Vernis Martin bureau à cylindre, c.1900, with mirror back, 152.5cm (5ft) high, *L 22 Mar,* £968 ($1,162)

11

A Louis XV style bureau plat, with leather-lined top, 147.5cm (58in) wide, *C 14 Feb,* £1,265 ($1,480)

12

A Louis XV style gilt-bronze mounted tulipwood bureau plat, late 19th century, 163cm (5ft 4in) wide, *NY 22 June,* $3,630 (£2,835)

1
A Regency inlaid partridge wood writing table, early 19th century, 76cm (30in) high, *NY 11 Oct,* $3,740 (£2,652)

2
A George III mahogany writing table, last quarter 18th century, 105cm (41½in) wide, *NY 1 Nov,* $3,575 (£2,482)

3
A late George III mahogany library writing table, *c.*1805, 91cm (36in) wide, *L 15 Nov,* £3,300 ($4,620)

4
A George III mahogany library or writing table, *c.*1780, 139cm (54¾in) wide, *L 1 Feb,* £6,160 ($7,022)

5
A George III carved and inlaid mahogany writing table, last quarter 18th century, 160cm (5ft 3in) wide, *NY 13 Apr,* $11,000 (£8,800)

6
A William IV double-sided mahogany library table, *c.*1830, 122cm (48in) wide, *L 26 July,* £1,870 ($2,748)

7
A George III mahogany library table, *c.*1805, 119cm (3ft 11in) wide, *L 27 Sept,* £2,860 ($4,233)

8
A late George III brass-mounted inlaid and carved satinwood writing table, 19th century, 117cm (46in) wide, *NY 1 Nov,* $14,850 (£10,312)

9
An early Victorian rosewood library table, 121cm (47½in) wide, *S 5 Feb,* £330 ($389)

10
A Victorian maple writing table, *c.*1870, 122cm (48in) wide, *C 28 Feb,* £550 ($616)

1   2   3

4

5

6

7   8

9   10

1
A late 16th century-style oak draw-leaf table, 266cm (8ft 8in) fully extended, *S 29 Oct*, £704 ($1,049)

2
A James I style oak side table, 295cm (9ft 8in) long, *L 26 Apr*, £1,320 ($1,676)

3
A Charles II oak gateleg table, late 17th century, 150cm (59in) wide, *L 22 Nov*, £1,760 ($2,464)

4
A William and Mary elmwood drop-leaf table, 76cm (30in) wide, *L 17 July*, £4,620 ($6,699)

5
A Charles I semi-circular oak folding table, *c.*1630, 76cm (30in) wide, *L 26 Apr*, £1,705 ($2,165)

6
A Victorian burr walnut Sutherland table, 86cm (34in) wide, *S 7 May*, £308 ($394)

7
A Queen Anne oak and elm gateleg table, early 18th century, 181cm (5ft 11in) wide, *C 11 July*, £2,970 ($4,128)

8
A mid Georgian red walnut gateleg table, *c.*1750, 72cm (28½in) high, *C 11 July*, £825 ($1,147)

9
A George II mahogany drop-leaf table, 123cm (48½in) wide, *S 9 July*, £319 ($427)

10
A George III mahogany spider gateleg table, late 18th century, length open 91cm (36in), *NY 11 Oct*, $3,080 (£2,184)

1

2

3

4

5

6

7

8

9

10

1
A George III mahogany circular dining table, c.1800, in two parts, 130cm (51in) wide, *C 18 Apr,* £880 ($1,144)

2
A George III mahogany 'D'-end extending dining table, c.1770, with a later drop-leaf central section, 245cm(8ft ½in) wide fully extended, *S 19 Mar,* £2,530 ($3,112)

3
A George III mahogany twin-pedestal table, c1800, extending with two leaves and usable as a single pedestal table, 282cm (9ft 3in) fully extended, *S 15 Oct,* £7,920 ($11,721)

4
A Regency mahogany extending dining table, c.1810, with telescopic action and three leaf insertions, 287cm (9ft 5in) fully extended, *S 12 Nov,* £3,300 ($4,620)

5
A George IV Regency mahogany extending dining table, c.1825, with four extra leaves, 336cm (11ft) extended, *L 8 Mar,* £4,620 ($5,174)

6
A William IV mahogany dining table, c.1835, attributed to Johnson & Jupe, mid 19th century, the expandable top with segmental leaves, 173cm (5ft 8in) diam closed, *L 15 Nov,* £41,800 ($58,520)

7
A Victorian oak 'D'-end extending dining table, 301cm (9ft 10¾in) fully extended, together with a leaf stand, *S 2 Apr,* £550 ($698)

8
A Regency mahogany twin-pedestal dining table, with two spare leaves, 265cm (8ft 8½in), *S 30 Apr,* £1,485 ($1,916)

9
An Edwardian mahogany 'D'-end dining table, c.1900, 213cm (7ft), *C 6 June,* £1,320 ($1,782)

1

4

6

8

2

3

5

7

9

1
A mahogany drum library table, early 19th century, with inset leather panels, 104cm (41in) diam, *C 17 Jan*, £1,705 ($2,046)

2
A George III mahogany breakfast table, *c.*1800, 140cm (55in) wide, *C 17 Jan*, £1,650 ($1,980)

3
A late George III mahogany drum-top library table, early 19th century, 99cm (3ft 3in) diam, *L 22 Nov*, £6,050 ($8,470)

4
A late George III mahogany breakfast or dining table, *c.*1800, 115cm (45½in) wide, *L 8 Mar*, £6,600 ($7,392)

5
A Regency centre table, *c.*1815, in pale mahogany with coromandel-wood crossbanding, 114cm (45in) wide, *L 10 May*, £3,190 ($4,115)

6
A George IV rosewood-veneered table, *c.*1820, 121cm (47½in) diam, *L 15 Nov*, £5,500 ($7,700)

7
A Victorian burr-walnut marquetry library table, *c.*1850, 140cm (55in) diam, *L 22 Feb*, £2,365 ($2,696)

8
An early Victorian rose-wood table, second quarter 19th century, 132cm (52in) diam, *NY 13 Apr*, $1,925 (£1,540)

9
A George III style satin-wood breakfast table, *c.*1900, 122cm (48in) wide, *C 17 Jan*, £3,190 ($3,828)

10
A Victorian walnut and marquetry pedestal table, *c.*1850, 145cm (57in) diam, *S 11 June*, £3,960 ($5,207)

1

2

3

4

5

6

7

8

9

10

1
A George III mahogany tilt-top occasional table, *c.*1770, 76cm, (30in) diam, *S 17 Sept,* £396 ($594)

2
A William and Mary walnut tripod candlestand, early 18th century, 70cm (27½in) high, *NY 1 Nov,* $1,980 (£1,375)

3
A George II walnut tripod table, second quarter 18th century, 69cm (27in) high, *NY 1 Nov,* $1,430 (£993)

4
A George II mahogany tripod table, *c.*1750, the stem carved with Gothic tracery and leaves, 70cm (27½in) high, *L 14 June,* £6,600 ($8,778)

5
A nest of three Regency rosewood tables, *c.*1810, 51cm (20in) wide, *S 12 Nov,* £935 ($1,309)

6
A nest of four Regency mahogany tables, first quarter 19th century, each on 'bamboo' trestle supports, 70cm (27½in) high, *NY 11 Oct,* $2,090 (£1,482)

7
A set of Regency rosewood quartetto tables, *c.*1810, 72cm (28¼in) high, *L 12 Apr,* £2,310 ($2,957)

8
A George III satinwood occasional table, the oval top segmentally veneered, 69cm (27in) high, *L 14 June,* £4,400 ($5,852)

9
A late George III maplewood occasional table, *c.*1810, 76cm (30in) high, *L 14 June,* £3,410 ($4,535)

10
A George III mahogany centre table, last quarter 18th century, 59cm (23¼in) wide, *NY 11 Oct,* $1,045 (£741)

11
A George III mahogany occasional table, *c.*1790, with oval top, 76cm (30in) high, *C 12 July,* £825 ($1,147)

12
An occasional table, Edwards & Roberts, with rosewood and flower marquetry, 56cm (22in) wide, *S 8 Jan,* £407 ($488)

13
A serpentine walnut and marquetry table, *c.*1850, the frieze inlaid with Jacobean Revival marquetry strapwork, 115cm (45½in) wide, *L 19 July,* £1,100 ($1,540)

14
A Victorian coromandel ivory inlaid centre table, *c.*1870, 115cm (45¼in) wide, *L 8 Nov,* £2,750 ($4,125)

1
A late George III
rosewood-crossbanded
mahogany sofa table,
*c.*1810, 94cm (37in) closed,
L 14 June,
£3,300 ($4,389)

2
A Regency rosewood sofa
table, *c.*1810, 94cm (37in)
closed, *S 22 Jan,*
£2,200 ($2,607)

3
A Regency rosewood-
veneered sofa table,
*c.*1810, with 'D'-shaped
flaps, 145cm (57in) open,
L 8 Mar,
£9,900 ($11,088)

4
A Regency mahogany
sofa table, *c.*1810, 89cm
(35in) wide closed,
S 19 Feb,
£990 ($1,138)

5
An early George III
mahogany Pembroke
table, *c.*1765, 99cm (27in)
wide, *L 14 June,*
£1,760 ($2,340)

6
A George III satinwood
Pembroke table, *c.*1785,
98cm (38½in) wide,
L 22 Nov,
£3,520 ($4,928)

7
A George III inlaid
mahogany marquetry
Pembroke table, late 18th
century, marquetry later,
72cm (28¼in) high,
NY 8 June,
$1,430 (£1,135)

8
A George III mahogany
Pembroke table, *c.*1790,
79cm (31in) wide,
S 15 Oct,
£385 ($570)

9
A George III Pembroke
table, *c.*1790, mahogany
and rosewood cross-
banded, inlaid with
satinwood stringing,
76cm (30in) wide,
S 19 Feb,
£770 ($885)

10
A late George III Pem-
broke work table,
mahogany and rosewood
crossbanded, 53cm (21in)
wide, *S 5 Mar,*
£506 ($567)

11
A George III mahogany
drawing room reading or
writing table, *c.*1800, with
ratchet adjustable top,
74cm (29in) high,
C 17 Jan,
£2,970 ($3,564)

12
A mid Georgian walnut
reading table, *c.*1750, with
two candle slides, 74cm
(29in) high, *C 17 Jan,*
£528 ($634)

13
A George III mahogany
architect's table, late 18th
century, 90cm (35½in)
wide, *NY 8 Oct,*
$3,575 (£2,416)

1

2

3

4

5

6

7

8

9

10

11

12

13

1
A Charles II oak side table, *c.*1675, 84cm (33in) wide, *L 27 Sept*, £1,430 ($2,116)

2
A William and Mary walnut-veneered side table, *c.*1700, 78cm (30½in) wide, *L 27 Sept*, £2,640 ($3,907)

3
A William and Mary oak side table, *c.*1700, 84cm (33in) wide, *S 22 Jan*, £418 ($495)

4
A George I gilt-gesso side table, first quarter 18th century, with later marble top, *NY 26 Jan*, $17,050 (£15,360)

5
A George II mahogany side table, *c.*1750, in the style of Thomas Chippendale, the frieze now with a drawer, 135cm (53in) wide, *L 14 June*, £6,820 ($9,070)

6
A George III mahogany side table, *c.*1820, 87cm (34in) high, *C 18 Apr*, £352 ($458)

7
A George III serpentine-fronted mahogany side table, *c.*1780, 179cm (5ft 10½in) wide, *L 10 May*, £2,860 ($3,689)

8
A William IV mahogany side table, *c.*1830, 197cm (6ft 6in) wide, *L 10 May*, £880 ($1,135)

9
A George III inlaid mahogany serpentine serving table, late 18th century, 127cm (50in) wide, *NY 8 June*, £2,750 (£2,183)

10
A George III style mahogany side or serving table, late 19th century, 170cm (67in) wide, *C 18 Apr*, £1,595 ($2,074)

11
A pair of George III painted and inlaid satinwood demi-lune side tables, last quarter 18th century, 106cm (41¾in) wide, *NY 26 Jan*, $9,900 (£8,918)

12
A Regency mahogany side table, *c.*1810, in the manner of Gillow, 94cm (37in) wide, *S 15 Oct*, £1,650 ($2,442)

13
A Regency brass-inlaid rosewood-veneered side table, *c.*1810, with bow-fronted *St Anne* marble top and mirrored back panel, 97cm (38in) wide, *L 22 Nov*, £1,870 ($2,618)

14
A Victorian parcel-gilt rosewood console table, *c.*1840, with marble top, the base with mirror back, 135cm (53in), *L 22 Feb*, £935 ($1,066)

1
A Regency inlaid faded burr yew-wood work table, first quarter 19th century, the divided top opening to form an inset leather surface, 70cm (27½in) high, *NY 26 Jan,* $1,760 (£1,585)

2
A William IV inlaid rosewood work and games table, second quarter 19th century, the top enclosing a backgammon well, 74cm (29¼in) high, *NY 8 June,* $1,870 (£1,484)

3
A Victorian mahogany combined games and work table, c.1860, with revolving fold-over top above a frieze drawer and sliding work bag, 76cm (30in) high, *C 11 July,* £308 ($428)

4
A Victorian walnut combined games and work table, c.1870, flanked by pull-out chessboard, fitted with a frieze drawer and walnut wool bag, 72cm (28½in) square, *C 18 Apr,* £572 ($744)

5
A late George III rosewood chess table, c.1820, with boxwood and harewood chessboard, 71cm (28in) high, *L 10 May,* £550 ($710)

6
A George IV rosewood drop-leaf games table, c.1825, with ebony and ivory chessboard top, 48cm (19in) wide closed, *S 16 Apr,* £936 ($1,217)

7
An early George II walnut triple-top games table, c.1735, 76cm (30in) wide, *L 12 Apr,* £3,300 ($4,224)

8
A late George II walnut games table, c.1750, inset with a baize playing surface, 89cm (35in) wide, *C 17 Jan,* £1,320 ($1,584)

9
An early George III mahogany serpentine card table, c.1770, 89cm (35in) wide, *L 14 June,* £5,940 ($7,900)

10
A George III rosewood games table, c.1800, 91.5cm (36in) wide, *C 17 Jan,* £704 ($845)

11
A pair of George III satinwood and rosewood inlaid card tables, last quarter 18th century, each with baize-lined gaming surface, 97cm (38in) wide, *NY 13 Apr,* $7,975 (£6,380)

12
A George III mahogany tea table, c.1780, inlaid with single strings, 84cm (33in) wide, *C 11 July,* £1,265 ($1,758)

13
A George III mahogany and kingwood cross-banded semi-circular card table, c.1790, the fold-over top revealing a green baize lining, 91.5cm (36in) wide, *S 17 Sept,* £495 ($743)

14
A George III satinwood-veneered card table, c.1790, of 'D'-shape, 91cm (36in) wide, *L 14 June,* £2,530 ($3,364)

1   2   3

4   5   6

7   8

9   10   11

12   13   14

1
**A George IV rosewood
card table,** *c.*1825, with
green baize lining, brass
claw feet, 91.5cm (36in)
wide, *S 23 July,*
£715 ($1,058)

2
**A William IV mahogany
card table,** *c.*1830, the
fold-over top revealing a
baize lining, 86cm (34in)
wide, *S 17 Sept,*
£275 ($413)

3
**A Regency brass inlaid
mahogany games table,**
first quarter 19th cen-
tury, 91cm (36in) wide,
NY 8 June,
$1,265 (£1,004)

4
**A Victorian rosewood
card table,** 91cm (35¾in)
wide, *S 9 July,*
£418 ($560)

5
**A tulipwood and walnut
serpentine marquetry
card table,** *c.*1850, with
swivelling top, gilt-metal
rococo mounts, 87cm
(34in) wide, *L 19 July,*
£968 ($1,355)

6
**A pair of ebonised and
amboyna card tables,**
*c.*1860, each with
moulded swivelling top,
90cm (35½in) wide,
L 19 July,
£2,035 ($2,849)

7
**A Victorian rosewood
envelope card table,**
*c.*1900, the fold-over top
with claret baize lining,
52cm (20½in) wide,
S 17 Sept,
£440 ($660)

8
**A George III-style
mahogany and satinwood
crossbanded card table,**
*c.*1910, 91.5cm (36in)
wide, *S 22 Jan,*
£715 ($847)

9
**A George IV maplewood
pedestal table,** *c.*1825,
bearing the remains of a
label by Seddon, 75cm
(29½in) high, *L 26 July,*
£660 ($970)

10
A Victorian slate table,
*c.*1850, probably Ashbur-
ton, the top inlaid with
floral festoons in hard-
stones, including
malachite, 43.5cm (17in)
diam, *S 11 June,*
£682 ($897)

11
**A George III mahogany
tripod table,** *c.*1800, the
top lined with later green
and gilt-tooled leather,
84.5cm (33¼in) diam,
L 1 Feb,
£1,045 ($1,191)

12
**A George IV pollard elm
pedestal table,** *c.*1830, fitted with one dummy and
one real drawer, 97cm
(38in) open, *C 3 Oct,*
£1,925 ($2,695)

1
A painted and turned pine and maple tavern table, New England, c.1750, 112cm (44in) wide, *NY 2 Feb,* $7,425 (£6,292)

2
A carved and stained maple shoe-foot hutch table, American, 1740-60, 117cm (46in) diam, *NY 26 Oct,* $9,350 (£6,584)

3
A Queen Anne carved curly maple lowboy, New England, 1760-80, 99cm (39in) wide, *NY 26 Oct,* $9,350 (£6,584)

4
A Queen Anne carved mahogany dressing table, Philadelphia, c.1765, 84cm (33in), *NY 2 Feb,* $18,700 (£15,847)

5
A Chippendale mahogany kneehole dresssing table, Middle Atlantic States, c.1780, 84cm (33in) wide, *NY 2 Feb,* $2,310 (£1,957)

6
A Federal curly maple-inlaid mahogany corner basin stand, Eastern New England, c.1810, 98cm (38½in) high, *NY 26 Oct,* $2,750 (£1,936)

7
A Classical carved mahogany dressing table, school of Duncan Phyfe, New York, c.1815, 97cm (38in) wide, *NY 2 Feb,* $2,970 (£2,516)

8
A Chippendale carved mahogany card table, Philadelphia, c.1770, 86cm (34in) wide, *NY 2 Feb,* $28,600 (£24,237)

9
A Federal inlaid walnut card table, Southern, c.1800, 95cm (37½in) wide, *NY 2 Feb,* $3,575 (£3,029)

10
A Federal inlaid mahogany card table, New England, c.1810, 89cm (35in) wide, *NY 2 Feb,* $3,300 (£2,796)

1

2

3

4

5

6

7

8

9

10

1
A Federal curly maple card table, New England, *c.*1810, 89cm (35in), *NY 2 Feb*, $1,100 (£932)

2
A Federal carved and crossbanded mahogany card table, New York, *c.*1815, 92cm (36in) wide, *NY 1 Feb*, $16,500 (£15,000)

3
A Federal inlaid mahogany Pembroke table, Annapolis or Baltimore, *c.*1795, 103cm (40¾in), *NY 26 Oct*, $8,250 (£5,809)

4
A Federal carved mahogany Pembroke table, New York, *c.*1815, 104cm (41in), *NY 1 Feb*, $3,850 (£3,500)

5
A Federal curly maple Pembroke table, New York State, *c.*1815, width extended 94cm (37in), *NY 2 Feb*, $4,400 (£3,728)

6
A Queen Anne carved cherrywood drop-leaf dining table, Pennsylvania, *c.*1765, 129cm (51in), *NY 26 Oct*, $4,950 (£3,485)

7
A Chippendale carved walnut drop-leaf dining table, Pennsylvania, *c.*1780, width extended 160cm (5ft 3in), *NY 2 Feb*, $2,970 (£2,516)

8
A Queen Anne carved maple tavern table, New England, 1740-70, 89cm (35¼in) wide, *NY 26 Oct*, $6,600 (£4,647)

9
A Federal carved mahogany library table, attributed to Duncan Phyfe, New York, *c.*1815, width extended 117cm (46in), *NY 2 Feb*, $11,000 (£9,322)

10
A Federal carved mahogany and giltwood brass-mounted side table, New York, *c.*1810, 84cm (33in) high, *NY 1 Feb*, $8,250 (£7,500)

1   2

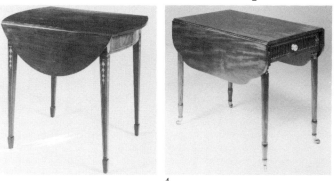

3   4   5

6   7   8

9   10

1
A Chippendale carved
mahogany tilt-top tea
table, Pennsylvania,
c.1780, 85cm (33½in)
diam, *NY 26 Oct*,
$9,350 (£6,584)

2
A Federal satinwood-
inlaid mahogany oval
tilt-top candlestand,
probably New York,
c.1795, 70cm (27½in) high,
NY 26 Oct,
$4,125 (£2,904)

3
A Federal carved maple
tilt-top candlestand, New
England, c.1810, 70cm
(27½in) high, *NY 2 Feb*,
$1,540 (£1,305)

4
A Federal inlaid
mahogany work table,
labelled Andrew Ander-
son, New York, c.1795,
NY 2 Feb,
$4,950 (£4,194)

5
A Federal mahogany
work table, c.1810, 74cm
(29in) high, *NY 2 Feb*,
$2,530 (£2,144)

6
A Federal carved
mahogany three-part
dining table, New York,
c.1810, extended length
267cm (8ft 9in),
NY 26 Oct,
$15,400 (£10,845)

7
A carved pine tripod-
base side table, Eastern
Shore, Maryland, first
quarter 19th century,
75cm (29½in) high,
NY 2 Feb,
$1,100 (£1,000)

8
An American Renais-
sance marquetry walnut
and rosewood centre
table, c.1860, 117cm (46in)
wide, *NY 30 Mar*,
$660 (£532)

9
An American Rustic
'Adirondack' hickory
table, c.1890, the oval top
composed of half
branches, 160cm (5ft 3in)
diam, *NY 30 Mar*,
$990 (£798)

1
A Tuscan walnut table,
*c.*1550, 371cm (12ft 2in)
long, *L 24 May,*
£17,050 ($22,677)

2
An Italian walnut table,
late 16th century, 346cm
(13ft 4in) long,
NY 11 May,
$1,870 (£1,520)

3
**A Flemish oak draw-leaf
table,** mid 17th century,
L 31 May,
£1,430 ($1,916)

4
**A Flemish oak draw-leaf
table,** mid 17th century,
top and leaves replaced,
142cm (56in) closed,
L 18 Dec,
£1,980 ($2,772)

5
**A Venetian giltwood con-
sole,** late 17th/early 18th
century, with onyx top,
135cm (51in) wide,
NY 8 Nov,
$19,800 (£13,944)

6
**A Flemish walnut side
table,** *c.*1690, 110cm (44in)
wide, *L 24 May,*
£3,300 ($4,389)

7
**A German giltwood side
table,** mid 18th century,
with marble top, 158cm
(5ft 2in) long, *NY 5 Oct,*
$7,700 (£5,460)

8
**A German maplewood
backgammon table,** late
17th/early 18th century,
with divided top open-
ing to reveal a well with
carved circular game
pieces, 102cm (40in) wide
closed, *L 24 May,*
£5,500 ($7,315)

1

2

3

4

5

6

7

8

1

A pair of North Italian painted and giltwood console tables, *c*.1700, with faux marble tops and plinths, 119cm (46½in) wide, *L 29 Nov*, £5,500 ($7,700)

2

A Venetian carved pinewood side table, mid 18th century, with serpentine mottled green and cream marble top, 142cm (56in) wide, *L 24 May*, £6,600 ($8,778)

3

A Cape yellowwood and hardwood table, *c*.1700, 183cm (6ft) long, *JHB 18 June*, **R** 15,500 (£6,055; $8,174)

4

A Dutch marquetry card table, mid 18th century, later marquetry decoration, 73.5cm (29in) high, *L 18 Dec*, £1,100 ($1,540)

5

An Italian walnut parquetry card table, *c*.1740, 85cm (33½in) wide, *L 31 May*, £660 ($884)

6

A Lombard marquetry dressing table, late 18th century, 78cm (30½in) high, *L 18 Dec*, £1,012 ($1,417)

7

An Italian giltwood centre table, late 18th century, with white marble top, 88cm (34½in) diam, *NY 5 Oct*, $2,310 (£1,638)

8

An Italian painted console table, late 18th century, the top veneered in liver, beige and ochre mottled marble, 92cm (36in) high, *NY 23 Mar*, $2,530 (£2,162)

9

A Dutch mahogany and marquetry table, 18th century, 85cm (33½in) wide, *A 26 Feb*, **Dfl** 4,640 (£1,137; $1,274)

10

A pair of North Italian white painted and parcel gilt consoles, last quarter 18th century, 146cm (57½in) wide, *NY 4 May*, $33,000 (£27,500)

1

2

3

4

5

6

7

8

9

10

1
A Cape teak side table, *c.*1790, 81cm (32in) wide, *CT 13 May,* **R 1,000 (£417; $538)**

2
A Cape stinkwood and yellowwood side table, *c.*1800, 90cm (35½in) wide, *CT 13 May,* **R 2,600 (£1,083; $1,397)**

3
An Austrian fruitwood and burr-walnut work table, early 19th century, 78cm (30in), *NY 5 Oct,* **$2,750 (£1,950)**

4
A Dutch mahogany and marquetry side table, early 19th century, 73.5cm (29in), *C 17 Jan,* **£1,320 ($1,584)**

5
An Italian mahogany painted and parcel-gilt gueridon, early 19th century, with *verde antico* marble top, 81cm (32in) diam, *NY 9 Nov,* **$5,500 (£3,873)**

6
An Italian console table, early 19th century, 83cm (32¾in) wide, *M 25 June,* **FF 6,660 (£555; $749)**

7
An Italian marble-topped giltwood centre table, *c.*1840, the black marble top inlaid with three white doves, 71cm (28in) diam, *L 21 June,* **£1,540 ($2,002)**

8
An Italian tilt-top table, *c.*1860, inlaid with various woods, 98cm (38½in) diam, *NY 22 June,* **$1,320 (£1,031)**

9
A Scandinavian mahogany centre table, Sweden or Norway, *c.*1850, 130cm (51in) wide, *L 22 Mar,* **£1,375 ($1,650)**

10
A Florentine wood and pietra dura table, early 19th century, stamped E Miccinesi Firenze, 163cm (64in) wide, *M 24 June,* **FF 199,800 (£16,650; $22,478)**

11
An Italian ebonised and gilt-wood and pietra dura gueridon, *c.*1860, 80cm (31½in) high, *NY 22 June,* **$3,575 (£2,792)**

12
An Italian bone-walnut and brass-inlaid ebony and ebonised centre table, *c.*1870, probably Milan, *L 22 Mar,* **£1,705 ($2,046)**

13
An Italian walnut centre table, *c.*1880, with rectangular top, 93cm (36½in) wide, *L 8 Nov,* **£1,815 ($2,723)**

1
A Louis XIV giltwood side table or cabinet stand, c.1700, with later mottled green and white marble top, 142cm (56in) long, *L 5 July,* £3,080 ($4,250)

2
A Louis XIV giltwood centre table, late 17th century, with veined white and grey marble top, 165cm (5ft 5in) long, *NY 4 May,* $19,800 (£16,500)

3
A Régence giltwood centre table, c.1720, with *fleur de peche* marble top, 100cm (35½in) long, *NY 4 May,* $6,600 (£5,500)

4
A Louis XV giltwood centre table, with *rouge royale* marble top, now fitted with one drawer, 94cm (37in) long, *NY 23 Mar,* $4,400 (£3,761)

5
A Louis XVI mahogany three-tier gueridon, last quarter 18th century, 74cm (29in) high, *NY 24 May,* $990 (£785)

6
An Empire ormolu-mounted mahogany gueridon, first quarter 19th century, signed Chapuis, with circular veined black and white marble top, 83cm (32¾in) diam, *NY 9 Nov,* $9,900 (£6,972)

7
An Empire carved gilt-wood centre table, early 19th century, possibly Italian, the circular 'scagliola' top decorated in the Etruscan style, 85cm (33½in) diam, *L 5 July,* £12.100 ($16,698)

8
An Empire ormolu-mounted centre table, early 19th century, with brown and grey marble top, 90cm (35½in) diam, *NY 23 Mar,* $3,575 (£3,056)

9
A Charles X Kyrolean birch centre table, c.1825, 132cm (52in) diam, *NY 5 Oct,* $4,400 (£3,120)

10
A Napoleon III painted and nacre-inlaid black lacquer and parcel-gilt centre table, third quarter 19th century, with oval top, 142cm (48in) long, *NY 22 June,* $1,320 (£1,031)

11
A Charles X gilt-bronze centre table, c.1820, with later *verde antico* marble top, 81cm (32in) high, *L 29 Nov,* £12,650 ($17,710)

12
A gilt-bronze centre table, in Louis XVI style, c.1860, after the model by Weisweiler, with *verde antico* marble top, 71cm (28in) wide, *L 21 June,* £4,950 ($6,435)

1

2

3

4

5

6

7

8

9

10

11

12

1
A gilt-bronze mounted
mahogany centre table,
*c.*1890, 87cm (34in) wide,
L 22 Mar,
£880 ($1,056)

2
A tulipwood centre table,
with gilt-bronze mounts,
*c.*1880, 81cm (32in) diam,
L 22 Mar,
£1,100 ($1,320)

3
A Louis XV style
mahogany centre table,
*c.*1900, with marble top
and gilt bronze mounts,
77cm (30½in) wide,
C 11 July,
£440 ($612)

4
An Empire style gilt-
metal mounted mahog-
any centre table, early
20th century, with oval
white marble top, 86cm
(34in) wide, *NY 30 Mar,*
$1,650 (£1,331)

5
A Louis XVI style
ormolu-mounted lacquer
gueridon, 19th century,
the circular top decor-
ated with river landscape
in iron red and gilt on a
black ground, 61cm (21in)
diam, *NY 5 Oct,*
$5,500 (£3,900)

6
A mahogany and lacquer
table, *c.*1880, stamped
Henry Dasson, with
griotte marble top, 60cm
(35½in) wide, *L 21 June,*
£3,960 ($5,148)

7
A Louis XV kingwood
parquetry table, *c.*1760,
with serpentine top, 73cm
(28½in) wide, *L 5 July,*
£1,430 ($1,973)

8
A Louis XV fruitwood
side table, mid 18th cen-
tury, 74cm (29¼in) long,
NY 23 Mar,
$4,070 (£3,479)

9
A Louis XV oak console
table, mid 18th century,
with serpentine mottled
brown and white marble
top, 86cm (33¾in) high,
NY 8 Nov,
$4,125 (£2,905)

10
An early Louis XV pain-
ted console, second quar-
ter 18th century, with
liver mottled marble top,
155cm (5ft 1in) long,
NY 23 Mar,
$7,150 (£6,111)

11
A Louis XVI mahogany-
veneered console, stam-
ped Avril, *c.*1775, white
marble top, 144cm
(56½in) wide, *M 24 June,*
FF 66,600
(£5,367; $7,191)

12
A pair of Louis XVI
brass-mounted mahogany
small consoles, *c.*1775,
with white and grey mot-
tled marble tops, 94cm
(33in) high, *NY 23 Mar,*
$4,510 (£3,855)

13
A Louis XVI mahogany-
veneered console, stam-
ped L Moreau, gilt-
bronze mounts, 80cm
(31½in) high, *M 23 June,*
FF 99,900
(£8,050; $10,787)

14
A mahogany table, early
19th century, 75cm
(29½in) wide, *M 24 June,*
FF 6,105 (£509; $687)

1   2   3

4   5   6

7   8   9

10   11

12   13   14

1
An Empire ormolu-mounted walnut console, early 19th century, with brown and grey mottled marble top, 131cm (51½in) long, *NY 23 Mar,* $1,100 (£940)

2
A Régence walnut games table, c.1720, the top now covered with suede, 80cm (31½in) wide, *NY 8 Nov,* $7,700 (£5,423)

3
An early Louis XV kingwood and walnut tric-trac table, c.1730, the top reversing to reveal a chess-board and with interior inlaid for backgammon, gilt-bronze mounts, *L 5 July,* £13,200 ($18,216)

4
A Louis XV ormolu-mounted fruitwood and kingwood parquetry tric-trac table, mid 18th century, the top reversing to reveal a well for backgammon, 98cm (38½in) long, *NY 5 Oct,* $3,850 (£2,730)

5
A Napoleon III gilt-bronze mounted boulle marquetry card table, c.1860, the top opening to reveal a felt-lined playing surface, 90cm (35in) wide, *NY 30 Mar,* $1,980 (£1,597)

6
An ebonised and boulle card table, c.1860, with fold-over top, 89cm (35in) wide, *C 17 Jan,* £935 ($1,122)

7
An ormolu-mounted kingwood serpentine display table, c.1900, the top with a panel of glass enclosing a velvet-lined interior, 70cm (27½in) wide, *L 8 Nov,* £1,430 ($2,145)

8
A late Louis XVI fruitwood dining table, late 18th century, with four leaves of later date, 152cm (5ft 2in) diam, *NY 9 Nov,* $11,000 (£7,746)

9
A Louis XVI brass-mounted fruitwood drop-leaf dining table, last quarter 18th century, 137cm (54in) long, *NY 24 May,* $2,200 (£1,746)

10
A Louis XVI mahogany bouillotte table, c.1785, with grey and white marble top, 72.5cm (28½in) high, *L 5 July,* £2,640 ($3,643)

11
Two similar satinwood tricoteuse tables, c.1830, both 71cm (28in) high, *L 22 Mar,* £3,630 ($4,356)

12
A rosewood and marquetry table à rognon, c.1890, signed J. Werner, 76cm (30in) high, *L 22 Mar,* £1,155 ($1,386)

13
A serpentine parquetry table, mid 19th century, in Louis XV style, galleries replaced, gilt-bronze mounts, 72cm (28½in) high, *L 22 Mar,* £1,045 ($1,254)

14
A marquetry table, c.1900, with serpentine top, gilt-brass mounts, 51cm (20in) wide, *L 21 June,* £638 ($829)

1   2   3

4   5

6   7   8

9   10   11

12   13   14

1
A Louis XV ormolu-mounted tulipwood and marquetry table de toilette, mid 18th century, 79cm (35in) wide, *NY 23 Mar,* $3,025 (£2,585)

2
A late Louis XV tulipwood and marquetry poudreuse, *c.*1770, with serpentine top, 75cm (29½in) wide, *L 18 Dec,* £2,200 ($3,080)

3
A Louis XV ormolu-mounted tulipwood, purplewood and fruitwood marquetry table de toilette, mid 18th century, stamped Jme, the top with lifting mechanism to form a bookstand reversing to a leather-lined writing surface, 79cm (31¼in) wide, *NY 12 Oct,* $44,000 (£31,206)

4
A Louis XVI tulipwood-veneered coiffeuse, *c.*1780, 81cm (32in) wide, *L 31 May,* £1,320 ($1,769)

5
A Louis XV rosewood marquetry table 'en chiffonnière', brèche d'Alep marble top, bronze mounts, 82cm (32¼in) high, *M 23 June,* FF 149,850 (£12,075; $16,180)

6
A Louis XV marquetry serpentine table en chiffonnière, *c.*1750, 41cm (16in) wide, *L 5 July,* £2,860 ($3,947)

7
A Louis XV ormolu-mounted parquetry fruitwood table en chiffonniére, mid 18th century, 68cm (26in) high, *NY 23 Mar,* $2,200 (£1,880)

8
A Louis XV/XVI ormolu-mounted kingwood and fruitwood marquetry table en chiffonnière, *c.*1775, signed Boudin, the circular top veneered to represent an oriental boating scene, 73cm (28½in) high, *NY 23 Mar,* $3,575 (£3,056)

9
A kingwood parquetry and gilt-metal mounted table en chiffonnière, *c.*1800, 73cm (29in) high, *S 15 Oct,* £1,485 ($2,198)

10
A Louis XVI ormolu-mounted kingwood and tulipwood parquetry table de toilette, *c.*1775, 93cm (36½in) wide, *NY 24 May,* $6,050 (£4,801)

11
An Empire ormolu-mounted dressing table, early 19th century, 140cm (55¼in) high, *NY 24 May,* $2,200 (£1,746)

12
A tulipwood and mahogany table en chiffonnière, in Louis XVI style, *c.*1900, with green and white mottled marble top, 78cm (30½in) high, *L 21 June,* £858 ($1,115)

13
A Louis XV style gilt-bronze mounted tulipwood dressing table, early 20th century, F Linke, of kidney shape, 125cm (49in) wide, *NY 30 Mar,* $8,800 (£7,097)

1
A Queen Anne walnut side table, *c.*1710, 78cm (30½in) wide, *L 8 Mar,* £3,190 ($3,573)

2
A George I Suffolk walnut lowboy, *c.*1725, signed W N Marsh, Woodbridge, 71cm (28in) wide, *L 1 Feb,* £2,090 ($2,383)

3
A Queen Anne inlaid walnut dressing table, 79cm (31in) wide, *NY 11 Oct,* $4,675 (£3,316)

4
A Queen Anne oak lowboy, *c.*1710, 70cm (27½in) high, *C 17 Jan,* £660 ($792)

5
A George II mahogany kneehole dressing table, *c.*1750, on later feet, 81cm (32in), *S 15 Oct,* £1,045 ($1,547)

6
A George III dressing table, *c.*1770, in the manner of John Cobb and in the French style, 69cm (2ft 3½in) wide, *L 12 Apr,* £3,300 ($4,224)

7
A Victorian mahogany side or dressing table, *c.*1845, with a rectangular moulded top, wheels on castors, 79 x 114cm (31 x 45in), *C 6 June,* £374 ($505)

8
A George III mahogany dressing table, *c.*1800, *S 22 Jan,* £825 ($978)

9
A mahogany dressing table, *c.*1810, 83cm (33in), *S 15 Oct,* £495 ($733)

10
A George IV mahogany kneehole dressing table, *c.*1825, 114cm (45in) wide, *S 16 Apr,* £1,342 ($1,745)

11
A George IV mahogany dressing table, *c.*1825, formerly with gallery, 122cm (48in) wide, *S 16 Apr,* £748 ($972)

12
A walnut pedestal dressing table, *c.*1870, 188cm (74in), *S 16 Apr,* £506 ($642)

13
A Lamb of Manchester mahogany dressing table, *c.*1860, 176cm (5ft 9in) high, *L 22 Feb,* £605 ($690)

14
A Victorian gilt-bronze-mounted walnut dressing table, *c.*1870, with white marble top, 191cm (6ft 3in) high, *L 22 Feb,* £1,265 ($1,442)

1
A Federal maple four poster bedstead, American, *c.*1810, 206cm (6ft 8in) long, *NY 1 Feb,* $2,640 (£2,400)

2
A George III style mahogany four poster bed, late 19th century, the posts 210cm (90½in) high, *C 11 May,* £1,265 ($1,758)

3
A lacquered brass double bed, mid 19th century, 140cm (55in) wide, *C 2 May,* £440 ($576)

4
An Italian marquetry bedroom suite, *c.*1870, comprising six pieces, all decorated in 17th century style, wardrobe 209cm (5ft 10in) wide, *L 8 Nov,* £8,800 (£13,200)

5
A George III mahogany cradle, early 19th century, 102cm (40in), *C 16 May,* £330 ($439)

6
A Queen Anne oak cradle, *c.*1700, 100cm (39in), *S 16 Apr,* £440 ($527)

7
A George III mahogany bedside commode, *c.*1800, 71cm (28in) high, *C 17 Jan,* £968 ($1,162)

8
A George III mahogany tray-top bedside commode, *c.*1790, 53cm (21in) wide, *S 23 July,* £770 ($1,140)

9
A George III walnut bedside commode, *c.*1760, 74cm (29in) high, *C 3 Oct,* £605 ($847)

10
An Edwardian mahogany and marquetry bedroom suite, *c.*1900, comprising a wardrobe, dressing table and bedside cupboard, *C 18 Apr,* £935 ($1,216)

11
An Edwardian satinwood bedside cupboard, floral painted, 38cm (15in) wide, *S 9 July,* £418 ($560)

12
A Louis XV rosewood-veneered bedside table, stamped Schmitz JME, 82cm (32¼in) high, *M 23 June,* FF 38,850 (£3,131; $4,195)

13
A Louis XV ormolu-mounted tulipwood and purplewood parquetry bedside cupboard, third quarter 18th century, with two grey marble shelves, 85cm (33½in) high, *NY 8 Nov,* $16,500 (£11,620)

1

An Italian pietra dura and wood casket, 17th century, with plaques inlaid with various coloured stones, casket rebuilt, 38cm (15in) wide, *NY 11 May,* $4,290 (£3,489)

2

A North Italian walnut casket, late 17th century, the sliding cover concealing a separate compartment, 31cm, (12¼in) wide, *NY 22 Nov,* $1,320 (£904)

3

A Dutch marquetry chest, 17th/18th century, 68cm (26¾in) wide, *A 26 Feb,* **Dfl 4,872** (£1,194; $1,337)

4

An Italian silver and tortoiseshell veneered box, first half 18th century, the inside veneered in coloured wood with Chinese figures, 32.5cm (12¾in) wide, *NY 11 May,* $5,500 (£4,472)

5

A Spanish walnut casket, 17th century, 65cm (25½in) wide, *NY 11 May,* $2,310 (£1,878)

6

A Spanish walnut vargueno, on later stand, *c.*1650, 107cm (3ft 4in) wide, *L 18 Dec,* £1,815 ($2,541)

7

A Dutch wunderkammer casket, late 17th century, veneered in exotic woods, ivory and mother-of-pearl, 62cm (24½in) wide, *NY 11 May,* $3,575 (£2,907)

8

A German marquetry box, mid 17th century, in pale wood, inlaid with hunting scenes, 47cm (16½in) wide, *L 31 May,* £1,265 ($1,695)

9

A George III inlaid mahogany collector's cabinet, early 19th century, with two tiers of drawers in contrasting specimen woods, 102cm (44in) high, *NY 13 Apr,* $6,600 (£5,280)

10

A late George III mahogany croft or filing cabinet, with drawers numbered 1-39, 125cm (49in) wide, *S 8 Jan,* £484 ($528)

11

An oak chest on stand, late 19th century, inlaid with roundels, flanked by ebony panels with ivory and box inlay, 115cm (45¼in) high, *C 17 Jan,* £418 ($502)

12

A North Italian walnut inlaid casket, 16th century, three sides mounted with Gothic tracery panels and inlaid with multicoloured wood strips, 57cm (22½in) wide, *NY 22 Nov,* $3,080 (£2,110)

13

A Charles I oak food hutch, *c.*1640, 90cm (35½in) wide, *HS 4 June,* £2,090 ($2,822)

14

A Charles II oak food safe, dated 1671, 93cm (37in) wide, *L 26 Apr,* £1,210 ($,1,536)

15

A William and Mary oak spice cupboard, *c.*1690, 48.5cm (19in) wide, *S 23 July,* £385 ($570)

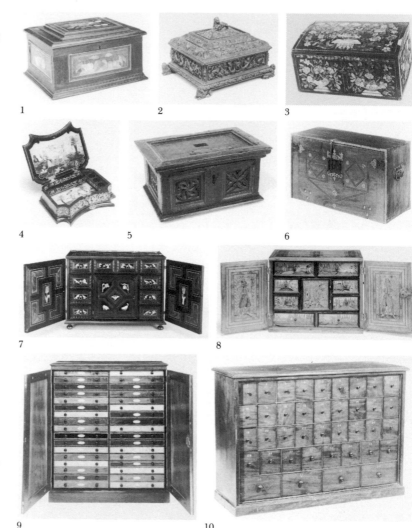

1   2   3

4   5   6

7   8

9   10

11   12

13   14   15

1
A French oak Gothic linen fold chest, first half 16th century, carved with 'fleur de lis' Gothic tracing, 104cm (41in) wide, *NY 11 May,* $3,300 (£2,683)

2
A James I oak chest, early 17th century, 109.5cm (43¼in) wide, *L 26 Apr,* £1,210 ($1,536)

3
A Charles I oak chest, c.1630, 132cm (52in) wide, *L 26 Apr,* £715 ($908)

4
An oak coffer, third quarter 17th century, 136cm (53½in) wide, *C 11 July,* £418 ($581)

5
An oak and elm coffer, c.1690, 114cm (45in) wide, *C 16 May,* £495 ($658)

6
A Queen Anne walnut and feather-banded blanket chest, c.1710, later hide-lined interior and tray, later feet, 113cm (44¼in) wide, *S 16 Apr,* £1,155 ($1,502)

7
A George I oak mule chest, c.1720, now with fixed top, altered, 140cm (55in) wide, *S 23 July,* £352 ($521)

8
An English tulipwood and porcelain-mounted jewellery cabinet, c.1860, stamped Edwards & Roberts, with gilt-bronze mounts and five Sevres-style porcelain plaques, 99cm (39in) high, *L 22 Mar,* £2,530 ($3,036)

9
A japanned cabinet on giltwood stand, late 17th century, 151cm (59½in) high, *L 26 July,* £4,510 ($6,629)

10
A William and Mary oyster-veneered rosewood cabinet on stand, late 17th century, 172cm (5ft 8in), *L 15 Nov,* £4,620 ($6,468)

11
A Flemish marquetry cabinet, in two parts, mid 17th century, inlaid with green-stained and natural ivory, ebony, and walnut, on later bracket feet, altered, 190cm (6ft 3in) high, *L 24 May,* £15,400 ($20,482)

12
An inlaid rosewood cabinet, 1880s, by Gillows, inlaid in ivory, mother-of-pearl and light wood with Mannerist Revival motifs, 179cm (5ft 10½in), *L 19 July,* £4,290 ($6,006)

13
An Italian bone inlaid walnut side cabinet, c.1880, in two parts, 254cm (8ft 4in), *NY 22 June,* $4,510 (£3,523)

1 2 3 4 5 6 7 8 9 10 11 12 13

1
A Charles II oak cupboard, c.1680, 127cm (50in) high, S 15 Oct, £770 ($847)

2
A Charles II oak cupboard, c.1680, 104cm (39in) high, C 17 Jan, £660 ($792)

3
An oak court cupboard, early 18th century, later cornice, 148cm (58¼in) high, C 3 Oct, £858 ($1,201)

4
A South German burr-walnut, beech and fruit-wood parquetry cupboard on chest, second half 18th century, 211cm (6ft 11in) high, NY 24 May, $6,325 (£5,019)

5
A Tyrolean armoire, dated 1722, painted with flower panels on a green ground, 188cm (6ft 2in) high, L 18 Dec, £1,925 ($2,695)

6
A Swiss walnut armoire, mid 18th century, with rectangular yew-wood panels, 173cm (5ft 8in) high, HS 2 July, £1,650 ($2,277)

7
A Flemish carved oak cupboard, mid 17th century, in two parts, 198cm (6ft 6in) high, L 31 May, £3,410 ($4,569)

8
A Cologne marquetry cupboard, mid 17th century, 216cm (7ft 11in) high, L 29 Nov, £3,300 ($4,620)

1   2   3

4   5   6

7   8

1

**A Queen Anne carved
walnut kasten,** Pennsyl-
vania, 1750-80, 234cm (7ft
10in) wide, *NY 2 Feb,*
$11,000 (£9,322)

2

A German oak schrank,
late 17th century, 203cm
(6ft 8½in), *NY 22 Nov,*
$3,960 (£2,712)

3

**A Dutch walnut and
marquetry secretaire
press cupboard,** *c.*1770,
inlaid with satinwood
and mother-of-pearl,
260cm (8ft 6in) high,
S 15 Oct,
£6,600 ($9,768)

4

**A Dutch mahogany
cabinet,** late 18th century,
217cm (7ft 2in) high,
A 29 Oct,
Dfl 2,760 (£657; $979)

5

A Dutch walnut cabinet,
231cm (7ft 7in), *A 4 June,*
Dfl 18,560
(£4,199; $5,669)

6

**A George III style satin-
wood and kingwood
crossbanded gentleman's
wardrobe,** circa 1870,
bearing stencil and trade
plate of S & H Jewell,
Holborn, 200cm (6ft 7in)
high, *S 23 July,*
£1,045 ($1,547)

7

**A Louis XIV rosewood
veneered cupboard,**
182cm (5ft 11½in) high,
M 23 June,
FF 61,050
(£4,919; $6,592)

8

**A painted satinwood
wardrobe,** late 19th century, 190cm (75in) high,
C 18 Apr,
£2,640 ($3,432)

1
A George IV mahogany breakfront wardrobe, 227cm (7ft 5¼in) wide, *S 13 Aug,*
£935 ($1,393)

2
A George II mahogany press, *c.*1800, inlaid with satinwood bands, 224cm (7ft 4in) high, *C 18 Apr,*
£1,980 ($2,574)

3
A George III mahogany press, *c.*1800, with alterations, 198cm (6ft 6in), *C 20 June,*
£858 ($1,158)

4
A George III oak linen press, late 18th century, with two dummy and two real drawers, *C 25 July,*
£748 ($1,100)

5
A George III oak press, *c.*1760, 191cm (6ft 3in) high, *S 19 Mar,*
£990 ($1,218)

6
An oak linen press, mid 18th century, 194cm (76½in) high, *C 11 July,*
£1,100 ($1,529)

7
A George III mahogany wardrobe, *c.*1770, 204cm (6ft 8½in) high, *L 8 Mar,*
£11,000 ($12,320)

8
A George III mahogany press, *c.*1800, 205cm (6ft 9in), *C 17 Oct,*
£572 ($847)

9
A George III inlaid bird's eye maple linen press, last quarter 18th century, 208cm (6ft 10in), *NY 13 Apr,*
$4,400 (£3,520)

10
A William and Mary walnut-veneered cabinet on chest, *c.*1690 with 'cushion' frieze drawer above a pair of doors, 163cm (5ft 4½in), *L 7 June,*
£2,750 ($3,657)

11
A George II oak clothes press, 217.5cm (7ft 2in) high, *HS 4 June,*
£1,430 ($1,931)

1

2

3

4

5

6

7

8

9

10

11

1
A Charles II oak chest, *c.*1660, 102cm (40in) wide, *L 26 Apr,* £825 ($1,047)

2
A Charles II oak chest, *c.*1660, in two parts, 102cm (40in) wide, *L 26 Apr,* £2,860 ($3,632)

3
A William and Mary walnut marquetry chest of drawers, late 17th century, 95cm (37½in) wide, *NY 1 Nov,* $11,550 (£8,020)

4
A William and Mary chest on stand, *c.*1700, 174cm (5ft 8½in) high, *L 26 Apr,* £1,980 ($2,514)

5
A William and Mary walnut chest on stand, late 17th century, altered stand, 120cm (47in) high, *L 22 Nov,* £3,300 ($4,620)

6
A William and Mary walnut chest on stand, *c.*1700, 173cm (5ft 8in) high, *NY 11 Oct,* $5,500 (£3,907)

7
A William and Mary walnut and marquetry chest, *c.*1690, later feet, faults, 97cm (38in) wide, *S 15 Oct,* £2,090 ($3,093)

8
A Queen Anne walnut yewtree veneered chest, *c.*1710, 100cm (39¼in) wide, *C 11 July,* £1,870 ($2,599)

9
A George I walnut tall-boy, *c.*1725, 186cm (6ft 1½in) high, *L 22 Nov,* £6,600 ($9,240)

10
A George I yew-wood and walnut chest on chest, *c.*1720, 166cm (5ft 5in) high, *S 15 Oct,* £5,280 ($7,814)

1

2

3

4

5

6

7

8

9

10

1
A George III style oak chest on chest, late 19th century, 157.5cm (62in) wide, *C 17 Oct,* £550 ($814)

2
A George III mahogany chest on chest, Irish, last quarter 18th century, 183cm (6ft) high, *NY 26 Jan,* $6,600 (£5,945)

3
An early George III mahogany tallboy, *c.*1770, 212cm (6ft 11½in) high, *L 12 Apr,* £2,750 ($3,520)

4
A George III mahogany tallboy, *c.*1760, 190cm (6ft 3in) high, *L 12 Apr,* £2,310 ($2,957)

5
A George I small walnut chest, *c.*1720, 76cm (30in) wide, *S 15 Oct,* £9,900 ($10,890)

6
A George III mahogany chest, *c.*1750, 80cm (31½in) wide, *S 12 Nov,* £1,430 ($2,002)

7
A George III mahogany serpentine chest, *c.*1780, 115cm (45½in) wide, *C 3 Oct,* £1,155 ($1,617)

8
A George III faded mahogany serpentine chest of drawers, third quarter 18th century, 102cm (40in) wide, *NY 13 Apr,* $4,400 (£3,520)

9
A George III mahogany and pine chest on chest, 103cm (40½in) wide, *S 9 July,* £660 ($884)

10
A George III mahogany serpentine dressing chest, *c.*1765, 116cm (45½in) wide, *L 27 Sept,* £3,410 ($4,774)

11
A George III mahogany serpentine chest of drawers, last quarter 18th century, 107cm (42in) wide, *NY 11 Oct,* $14,300 (£10,142)

12
A George III mahogany chest on chest, *c.*1760, 184cm (6ft ½in) high, *S 19 Feb,* £1,210 ($1,391)

13
A George III mahogany serpentine chest of drawers, *c.*1775, 113cm (44½in) wide, *NY 11 Oct,* $6,875 (£4,876)

14
A George III satinwood-veneered bowfront chest, *c.*1790, 102cm (40in) wide, *L 8 Mar,* £7,700 ($8,624)

1
A George III mahogany commode, c.1810, 118cm (46½in) wide, C 17 Jan, £2,750 ($3,300)

2
A harewood and marquetry serpentine commode, in the manner of Moore of Dublin, c.1900, 104cm (41in), C 3 Oct, £2,420 ($3,388)

3
A George III mahogany serpentine chest, c.1770, 102cm (40in), S 16 Apr, £4,510 ($5,863)

4
A George III serpentine mahogany commode, in the French style, c.1770, 120cm (47in) wide, L 14 June, £11,550 ($15,361)

5
A George III inlaid mahogany serpentine-fronted chest of drawers, 109cm (43in) wide, NY 8 Oct, $1,760 (£1,189)

6
A teak and brass-bound secretaire military chest, in two parts, early 19th century, 92cm (36in), S 5 Feb, £935 ($1,103)

7
A George III mahogany bowfront chest, early 19th century, 82.5cm (32½in) wide, C 2 May, £440 ($576)

8
A Victorian mahogany Wellington chest, c.1850, 122cm (48in) high, S 23 July, £902 ($1,335)

(page 54) **1**
A Chippendale maple chest-on-chest, New England, c.1790, 193cm (6ft 4in), NY 26 Oct, $8,250 (£5,809)

(page 54) **2**
A Chippendale cherrywood chest of drawers, Connecticut, 1790-1810, 109cm (43in) wide, NY 2 Feb, $5,225 (£4,427)

(page 54) **3**
A Chippendale mahogany reverse-serpentine chest of drawers, Massachusetts, c.1780, 100cm (31½in) wide, NY 2 Feb, $11,000 (£9,322)

1

2

3

4

5

6

7

8

Captions to figs 1, 2 & 3
are on page 53.

4
A Chippendale mahogany serpentine-front chest of drawers, New England, c.1775, 117cm (42in) wide, *NY 26 Oct,* $9,900 (£6,971)

5
A Chippendale birch-wood chest of drawers, New England, 1780-1800, 108cm (42½in) wide, *NY 26 Oct,* $3,630 (£2,556)

6
A Queen Anne cherry-wood bonnet-top chest-on-chest, Connecticut, c.1780, in three sections, 224cm (7ft 4in) high, *NY 26 Oct,* $27,500 (£19,366)

7
A Federal inlaid curly maple bow-front chest of drawers, New England, c.1800, 109cm (42½in) wide, *NY 2 Feb,* $1,980 (£1,677)

8
A Federal inlaid mahogany bow-front chest of drawers, New England, c.1810, 104cm (41in) wide, *NY 26 Oct,* $2,200 (£1,549)

9
A Queen Anne cherry-wood bonnet-top high-boy, possibly by Issac Tryon, Glastonbury, Connecticut, c.1760, in two parts, 211cm (6ft 11in) high, *NY 2 Feb,* $39,600 (£33,550)

10
A Classical mahogany gilt-metal mounted marble-top chest of drawers, stamped Charles Honore Lannuier, New York, c.1815, 124cm (49in) wide, *NY 26 Oct,* $11,550 (£8,133)

11
A Federal mahogany chest of drawers, New York, c.1815, 123cm (48½in) wide, *NY 1 Feb,* $4,125 (£3,750)

1

2

3

6

4

5

7

8

9

10

11

1
A Louis XIV kingwood parquetry commode, *c.*1710, with bowfronted top and gilt-bronze mounts, 119cm (3ft 11in) wide, *L 5 July,* £15,400 ($21,252)

2
A Louis XIV commode, gilt-bronze mounts, 126cm (49½in) wide, **M 24 June,** FF 26,640 (£2,220; $2,997)

3
A Louis XIV walnut commode, early 18th century, brass mouldings, possibly re-veneered, 123cm (48½in) wide, *L 29 Nov,* £6,600 ($9,240)

4
A Régence ormolu-mounted kingwood parquetry commode, first quarter 18th century, 134cm (52¾in) wide, *NY 9 Nov,* $14,300 (£10,070)

5
A Louis XV tulipwood bombé commode, *c.*1750, with grey and beige marble top, 129cm (51in) wide, *L 5 July,* £5,500 ($7,590)

6
A Louis XV kingwood and tulipwood bombé commode, *c.*1740, marble top, gilt-bronze mounts, *L 5 July,* £4,620 ($6,376)

7
A Louis XV satinwood marquetry commode, *c.*1750 stamped M Criaerd, 92cm (36¼in) high, *M 24 June,* FF 66,600 (£5,367; $7,191)

8
A Louis XV small parquetry bombé commode, *c.*1750, stamped M Criaerd, with white-mottled rust marble top, gilt-bronze mounts, 82cm (32½in) high, *L 29 Nov,* £12,650 ($17,710)

9
A Louis XV tulipwood small commode, *c.*1745, the serpentine top with later leather inset, gilt-bronze mounts, 75cm (29½in) high, *L 5 July,* £5,500 ($7,590)

1

2

3

4

5

6

7

8

9

1
A Louis XV ormolu-mounted kingwood and tulipwood parquetry commode, mid 18th century, with liver and white mottled marble top, 143cm (45in) wide, *NY 23 Mar,* $8,250 (£7,051)

2
An early Louis XV kingwood parquetry serpentine commode, *c.*1725, with mottled peach and grey marble top, 126cm (49½in) wide, *L 5 July,* £5,280 ($7,286)

3
A Louis XV rosewood marquetry commode, stamped A M Criaerd, gilt-bronze mounts, *M 23 June,* FF 222,000 (£17,889; $23,971)

4
A Louis XV/XVI transitional ormolu-mounted tulipwood, purplewood and fruitwood parquetry commode, *c.*1775, with grey 'Ste. Anne' marble top, ormolu mounts, 85cm (33½in) high, *NY 8 Nov,* $5,500 (£3,873)

5
A Louis XVI mahogany demi-lune commode, *c.*1775, with white and violette marble top, gilt-bronze mounts, 98cm (38½in) wide, *L 29 Nov,* £3,850 ($5,390)

6
A Louis XV/XVI transitional breakfront commode, *c.*1775, with mottled grey marble top, 128cm (50½in) wide, *L 31 May,* £1,485 ($1,990)

7
A Louis XV/XVI transitional parquetry breakfront commode, *c.*1775, stamped L Boudin, with mottled grey and white marble top, gilt-bronze mounts, 130cm (51in) wide, *L 5 July,* £6,380 ($8,804)

8
A Louis XVI parquetry walnut commode, late 18th century, 122cm (48in) wide, *NY 5 Oct,* $1,870 (£1,326)

9
A Louis XVI ormolu-mounted painted commode, with grey mottled marble top, *faux bois* and pale blue painted decoration, 113cm (44½in) wide, *NY 5 Oct,* $4,620 (£3,276)

10
A Louis XVI mahogany commode, *c.*1785, with mottled grey marble top, 128cm (50½in), *L 5 July,* £3,520 ($4,858)

11
A Louis XV/XVI ormolu-mounted kingwood and tulipwood parquetry commode, *c.*1775, with grey mottled marble breakfront top, 127cm (50in), *NY 24 May,* $4,125 (£3,273)

1

2

3

4

5

6

7

8

9

10

11

1
An Empire ormolu-mounted mahogany commode, early 19th century, with black mottled marble top, 102cm (48in) wide, *NY 23 Mar,* $2,200 (£1,880)

2
An Empire ormolu-mounted mahogany commode, early 19th century, with black mottled marble top, 132cm (52in) wide, *NY 24 May,* $2,310 (£1,833)

3
A pair of kingwood and tulipwood petite commodes, *c.*1890, gilt-bronze mounts, 76cm (30in) high, *L 22 Mar,* £2,860 ($3,432)

4
A gilt-bronze mounted rosewood commode, in Louis XV style, *c.*1880, the carcass partly 18th century, with serpentine russe marble top and gilt-bronze mounts, *L 8 Nov,* £1,100 ($1,650)

5
A rosewood and marquetry petite commode, *c.*1900, with serpentine brown marble top, gilt-bronze mounts, 87cm (34¼in) high, *L 21 June,* £715 ($930)

6
A rosewood, parquetry and marquetry break-front commode, *c.*1900, by Paul Sormani, with brèche violette marble top, gilt-brass mounts, 128cm (50¼in) wide, *C 3 Oct,* £4,400 ($6,424)

7
A Louis XV kingwood-veneered marble-topped serpentine commode, mid 19th century, 157cm (5ft 2in) wide, *L 21 June,* £4,400 ($5,720)

8
A Louis XV style tulip-wood and rosewood commode, 20th century, with serpentine grey mottled marble top and gilt-metal mounts, 135cm (53in) wide, *L 22 Mar,* £2,860 ($3,432)

9
A Louis XV style gilt-bronze mounted tulip-wood parquetry commode, *c.*1890, stamped F Durand Fils, with rouge marble top, 132cm (52in) wide, *NY 22 June,* $5,500 (£4,296)

10
A Louis XV style king-wood, tulipwood and parquetry petite commode, 20th century, with brèche d'alep marble top and gilt-bronze mounts and sabots, 87cm (33in) high, *C 18 Apr,* £748 ($972)

11
A marble top parquetry commode, *c.*1900, stamped Vve P Sormani & Fils, with mottled purple and grey marble top, 138cm (50½in) wide, *L 21 June,* £5,280 ($6,864)

12
A Louis XVI style rose-wood and marquetry petite commode, *c.*1890, with marble top and gilt-brass mounts, 83cm (32½in), *C 3 Oct,* £440 ($616)

13
A French satinwood and brass-mounted semainier, *c.*1880, 146cm (57½in) high, *S 15 Oct,* £2,200 ($3,256)

14
A Louis XV/XVI style gilt-bronze mounted tulipwood chest of drawers, late 19th century, stamped Kreiger, Paris, with white marble top and two faux and five real drawers, 152cm (5ft) high, *NY 22 June,* $2,970 (£2,320)

1　　2　　3

4　　5　　6

7　　8

9　　10　　11

12　　13　　14

1
A Flemish stained wood
chest, early 18th century,
95cm (37in), *L 31 May,*
£1,210 ($1,621)

2
A Swedish elmwood
parquetry commode,
mid 18th century, 114cm
(45in) wide, *L 29 Nov,*
£3,300 ($4,620)

3
A German inlaid walnut
chest of drawers, mid
18th century, 104cm
(41in) wide, *NY 5 Oct,*
$2,750 (£1,950)

4
A German walnut
commode, with
serpentine-fronted
drawers, 123cm (48½in)
wide, *HS 16 July,*
£3,960 ($5,742)

5
A German marquetry
commode, mid 18th cen-
tury, with grey and cream
marble top, 132cm (52in)
wide, *L 24 May,*
£6,600 ($8,778)

6
A South German
miniature fruitwood
commode, mid 18th cen-
tury, the top inlaid with
eight pointed star in
ebony, maple and fruit-
wood, 30.5cm (12in)
wide, *NY 11 May,*
$1,430 (£1,163)

7
A Dutch walnut
commode, 18th century,
82cm (32¼in) high,
A 2 July,
Dfl 9,048 (£2,006; $2,769)

8
A South German ormolu-
mounted walnut and
burr-walnut marquetry
chest of drawers, mid
18th century, 121cm
(47in) wide, *NY 23 Mar,*
$5,610 (£4,795)

9
A walnut parquetry
commode, *c.*1760, North
Italian or South German,
102cm (40in) wide,
L 24 May,
£8,800 ($11,704)

10
An Italian walnut-
veneered and ivory inlaid
chest of drawers, Pied-
mont, *c.*1760, 121cm
(47½in), *F 26 Mar,*
L 9,500,000
(£3,808; $4,836)

11
An Italian kingwood
commode, mid 18th cen-
tury, with later grey
marble top, 130cm (51in)
wide, *L 24 May,*
£3,520 ($4,682)

1
A pair of Italian pickled burr-walnut chests of drawers, mid 18th century, 126cm (49in), *NY 5 Oct*, $2,475 (£1,755)

2
An Italian provincial ormolu-mounted chest of drawers, mid 18th century, 123cm (48½in) wide, *NY 23 Mar*, $4,400 (£3,761)

3
A South German walnut commode, *c.*1790, with broad crossbanding and quarter-veneered top, 114cm (45in) wide, *S 19 Feb*, £2,860 ($3,289)

4
An Austrian chest of drawers, second half 18th century, veneered and inlaid in walnut, mahogany, and other woods, *F 26 Mar*, L 2,800,000 (£1,122; $1,425)

5
A pair of Lombard commodes, mid 18th century, each inset with panels of burrwood within walnut bandings, 131cm (51½in) wide, *L 29 Nov*, £3,520 ($4,928)

6
An Italian ormolu-mounted burr-walnut and parquetry chest of drawers, third quarter 18th century, 113cm (44¼in) wide, *NY 5 Oct*, $1,540 (£1,092)

7
An Italian neoclassical ormolu-mounted fruit-wood and parquetry chest of drawers, late 18th century, 114cm (44¾in) wide, *NY 23 Mar*, $4,675 (£3,996)

8
An Italian chest of drawers, Lombardy, late 18th century, veneered in walnut and various woods, 124cm (48¾in) wide, *F 26 Mar*, L 6,000,000 (£2,405; $3,054)

9
A Lombardy marquetry small chest, *c.*1800, 86cm (34in) high, *L 18 Dec*, £902 ($1,263)

10
A Dutch mahogany and marquetry commode, early 19th century, 94 x 97cm (37 x 38¼in), *C 11 July*, £1,265 ($1,758)

11
A Danish marquetry D-shaped commode, early 19th century, 107cm (42in) wide, *L 21 June*, £1,375 ($1,788)

1

2

3

4

5

6

7

8

9

10

11

1
A Louis XV rosewood
encoignure, *c.*1750, 80cm
(31½in) high, *S 11 June,*
£825 ($1,085)

2
A Louis XV ormolu-
mounted lacquer
encoignure, mid 18th
century, decorated in
brown, green, red and
gilt on a yellow lacquer
ground, 92cm (36in),
NY 5 Oct,
$2,200 (£1,560)

3
An ormolu-mounted
mahogany corner cup-
board, in Louis XVI
style, *c.*1880, stamped
Wright & Mansfield, 104
New Bond Street, with
grey and white marble
top, 69cm (27¼in) wide,
L 19 July,
£1,210 ($1,694)

4
A pair of French tulip-
wood and marquetry
encoignures, *c.*1910, each
with a red serpentine
marble top and gilt-
bronze mounts, 90cm
(35½in) high, *L 21 June,*
£1,650 ($2,145)

5
A Dutch painted wood
corner cupboard, 18th
century, 130cm (51in)
high, *A 26 Feb,*
Dfl 3,712 (£910; $1,019)

6
A Queen Anne walnut
hanging corner cupboard,
*c.*1710, 88cm (34in) high,
C 12 July,
£2,310 ($3,211)

7
A George II chinoiserie
hanging corner cup-
board, *c.*1740, black
japanned and gilt, 108cm
(42½in) high, *S 19 Mar,*
£385 ($474)

8
A George III mahogany
bow front hanging wall
cupboard, *c.*1780, 109cm
(43in) high, *C 11 May,*
£440 ($612)

9
A George III oak standing
corner cupboard, *c.*1780,
208cm (6ft 10in) high,
C 3 Oct,
£935 ($1,309)

10
A George III mahogany
corner cupboard, *c.*1800,
117.5cm (46in) high,
C 17 Jan,
£825 ($990)

11
A late George III
mahogany hanging
corner cupboard, *c.*1800,
119.5cm (47in) high,
C 28 Nov,
£396 ($554)

12
A George III mahogany
bow front standing corner
cupboard, *c.*1790, 234cm
(7ft 6in) high, *C 11 July,*
£2,310 ($3,211)

13
A Dutch mahogany
corner cabinet, late 18th
century, 219cm (7ft 2in)
high, *A 26 Feb,*
Dfl 9,280
(£2,275; $2,547)

1

2

3

4

5

6

7

8

9

10

11

12

13

1
A Dutch marquetry and walnut display cabinet-on-chest, *c.*1760, 188cm (6ft 2in) high, *S 11 June,* £2,200 ($2,893)

2
A Regency display cabinet, in two parts, *c.*1805, 207cm (6ft 9½in) high, *L 8 Mar,* £4,950 ($5,544)

3
A George III mahogany cabinet, *c.*1800, 224cm (7ft 4in) high, *S 15 Oct,* £2,310 ($3,419)

4
An early George III mahogany display cabinet, *c.*1770, 221cm 7ft 3in) high, *L 4 June,* £9,900 ($13,167)

5
A pair of Dutch walnut and marquetry corner display cabinets, late 18th/early19th century, 182cm (6ft 11in) high, *C 11 July,* £4,400 ($6,116)

6
A Dutch walnut and marquetry display cabinet, 19th century, 203cm (6ft 8in), *L 31 May,* £1,980 ($2,653)

7
A pair of Louis XVI style gilt-bronze and porcelain mounted ebonised-wood side cabinets, English, *c.*1860, 183cm (6ft), *NY 22 June,* $1,430 (£1,117)

8
A Victorian thuyawood and ebonised Bonheur-du-Jour, *c.*1870, with gilt-metal mounts and 'Sevres'-style porcelain plaques, the raised back with mirror-lined recess, 138cm (54½in), *S 23 July,* £990 ($1,465)

9
A Victorian display cabinet, *c.*1860, walnut and thuyawood crossbanded, with gilt-metal mounts, 150cm (59in) high, *S 19 Mar,* £990 ($1,218)

10
A Victorian bow-fronted painted satinwood display cabinet, *c.*1880, 198cm (6ft 6in) high, *L 22 Feb,* £2,750 ($3,101)

11
A Victorian marquetry and rosewood side cabinet, *c.*1860, cross-banded in tulipwood, 193cm (6ft 4in) high, *L 22 Feb,* £3,080 ($3,511)

12
A French gilt-bronze mounted kingwood-veneered display cabinet, *c.*1890, with mottled apricot marble top, 170cm (5ft 7in) high, *L 8 Nov,* £1,870 ($2,805)

13
A Louis XVI style gilt-bronze mounted tulip-wood display cabinet, *c.*1900, two mounts inscribed J P Legastelois, 188cm (6ft 2in), *NY 30 Mar,* $1,760 (£1,419)

1
A Napoleaon III boulle
marquetry display
cabinet, second half 19th
century, inlaid in brass,
127cm (50in), *NY 30 Nov,*
$1,870 (£1,255)

2
A French gilt-bronze
mounted kingwood-
veneered display cabinet,
*c.*1900, 192cm (6ft 3½in),
L 8 Nov,
£5,280 ($7,920)

3
A mahogany display
cabinet, late 19th century,
with gilt-bronze mounts
and Vernis Martin
panels, 171.5cm (55½in)
high, *L 8 Nov,*
£660 ($990)

4
A French kingwood and
Vernis Martin vitrine,
*c.*1880, painted and with
gilt-brass mounts, 196cm
(6ft 5in) high, *C 17 Jan,*
£1,925 ($2,310)

5
A Louis XV style gilt-
bronze mounted king-
wood marquetry display
cabinet, *c.*1890, 173cm
(5ft 8in), *NY 22 June,*
$3,850 (£3,007)

6
A George III style inlaid
mahogany vitrine
étagère, *c.*1870, Edwards
and Roberts, 94cm (37in)
high, *NY 30 Mar,*
$825 (£665)

7
A satinwood and
marquetry side cabinet,
*c.*1900, in the manner of
Edwards & Roberts,
201cm (6ft 7in) high,
C 18 Apr,
£6,380 ($8,294)

8
An Edwardian rosewood
and inlaid side cabinet,
138cm (54¼in) wide,
S 7 May,
£506 ($648)

9
An Edwardian mahog-
any display cabinet,
satinwood-banded, 87cm
(34¼in), *S 9 July,*
£352 ($472)

10
An Edwardian mahog-
any display cabinet,
*c.*1910, inlaid with satinwood stringing, 135cm
(53in) high, *S 19 Feb,*
£616 ($708)

11
An Edwardian mahog-
any centre display
cabinet, *c.*1900, 129.5cm
(51in) high, *C 6 June,*
£352 ($475)

12
A Victorian oak standing
corner cupboard, *c.*1860,
207cm (6ft 9½in) high,
S 16 Apr,
£715 ($929)

13
A pair of Edwardian
satinwood corner display
cabinets, *c.*1900, 188cm
(6ft 2in) high, *C 17 Jan,*
£2,750 ($3,300)

1
An English ormolu and 'Sevres' porcelain mounted kingwood and tulipwood side cabinet, *c.*1845, 188cm (6ft 2in) wide, *L 22 Mar,*
£15,950 ($19,140)

2
A Victorian figured walnut display cabinet, *c.*1860, with gilt-metal mouldings, 138cm (54½in) wide, *L 22 Feb,*
£1,705 ($1,944)

3
A Victorian ebony-veneered and ivory inlaid side cabinet, *c.*1865-75, the inlay inspired by Dr Christopher Dresser, and with the manufacturer's label of Hewettson & Milner, 205cm (6ft 9in) wide, *L 19 July,*
£1,705 ($2,387)

4
A Victorian walnut credenza, *c.*1870, with painted porcelain panels and gilt brass mounts, 184cm (6ft ½in) wide, *C 17 Jan,*
£748 ($898)

5
A Victorian gilt-bronze and porcelain mounted walnut and ebonised side cabinet, *c.*1860, 190cm (6ft 3in), *NY 30 Mar,*
$2,860 (£2,306)

6
A burr-walnut side cabinet, *c.*1860, with tulipwood crossbandings, gilt-metal mouldings, 181cm (5ft 11in) wide, *L 22 Feb,*
£2,200 ($2,508)

7
A Victorian walnut credenza, *c.*1860, with gilt-brass bandings and caryatid figures, originally with a mirrored back, 157cm (5ft 9in) wide, *C 17 Jan,*
£1,595 ($1,914)

8
A boulle side cabinet, *c.*1860, inlaid with a cut-brass foliage on a red tortoiseshell ground, 210cm (6ft 10in) wide, *L 19 July,*
£880 ($1,232)

9
A pair of Louis XVI style gilt-bronze mounted mahogany side cabinets, late 19th century, with marble tops, 105cm (41½in) high, *NY 30 Mar,*
$3,300 (£2,661)

10
An ebonised boulle display cabinet, *c.*1860, 182cm (5ft 11½in) wide, *L 21 June,*
£1,100 ($1,430)

11
An American Renaissance carved walnut side cabinet, *c.*1865, J & J W Meeks, New York, 208cm (7ft 10in) high, *NY 30 Nov,*
$6,600 (£4,429)

12
A Napoleon III brass inlaid and ebonised side cabinet, *c.*1850, with white marble top and parcel-gilt electrotype panels, 142cm (4ft 8in) wide, *L 8 Nov,*
£1,210 ($1,815)

13
A Napoleon III white and gilt side cupboard, by Guéret Frères, *c.*1865, the pair of glazed doors flanked by figures of Pan and Flora, 191cm (6ft 3½in) wide, *L 8 Nov,*
£990 ($1,485)

14
A pair of porcelain-mounted tulipwood-veneered pedestal cabinets, *c.*1860, each with white marble top and Sevres-type plaque, *L 22 Mar,*
£4,400 ($5,280)

1
An Italian walnut side
cabinet, early 17th cen-
tury, 153cm (5ft) wide,
L 31 May,
£1,705 ($2,285)

2
A George III inlaid
satinwood bow-fronted
cabinet, late 18th century,
89cm (35in) wide,
NY 26 Jan,
$8,250 (£7,432)

3
An early George III
serpentine mahogany side
cabinet, *c.*1765, 118cm
(46½in) wide, *L 15 Nov,*
£5,720 ($8,008)

4
A pair of Italian neo-
classical kingwood and
fruitwood parquetry cab-
inets, late 18th century,
74cm (29in), *NY 24 May,*
$2,750 (£2,182)

5
A Dutch marquetry and
mahogany side cabinet,
*c.*1810, 91.5cm (36in)
high, *S 16 Apr,*
£605 ($787)

6
A Regency mahogany
side cabinet, early 19th
century, the top with two
mirror-backed shelves,
150cm (59in) wide,
NY 8 June,
$3,300 (£2,619)

7
A Louis XVI mahogany
buffet, grey marble top,
145cm (57in) wide,
M 24 June,
FF 22,200
(£1,789; $2,397)

8
A George III mahogany
bowfront side cabinet,
*c.*1810, with a pair of
silk-lined panelled cup-
boards, 81.5cm (32in)
high, *L 8 Mar,*
£2,750 ($3,080)

9
A Regency rosewood
dwarf side cabinet, *c.*1810,
the doors with pleated
silk panels, 89cm (35in)
high, *S 17 Sept,*
£770 ($1,155)

10
A Regency amboyna side
cabinet, first quarter 19th
century, after a design by
George Smith, 168cm (5ft
6in), *NY 1 Nov,*
$4,950 (£3,437)

11
A Victorian mahogany
serpentine-fronted
cabinet, *c.*1850, with
arched mirror back,
152cm (5ft) high,
S 17 Sept,
£715 ($1,073)

12
A pair of Regency inlaid
mahogany side cabinets,
first quarter 19th cen-
tury, 123cm (48¼in) wide,
NY 13 Apr,
$8,800 (£7,040)

13
A South African Cape
stinkwood and yellow-
wood cupboard, early
19th century, 120cm
(47in) wide, *JHB 8 July,*
R 6,000 (£2,230; $3,099)

1

A William and Mary oak dresser base, *c.*1690, 191cm (75in) wide, *C 17 Jan,* £4,620 ($5,544)

2

A George I oak dresser, *c.*1720, 150cm (59in) wide, *S 14 May,* £704 ($936)

3

A George II oak dresser base, *c.*1750, with cross-banded moulded top, 171cm (5ft 7¼in) long, *L 26 Apr,* £2,750 ($3,492)

4

A George III oak dresser, *c.*1800, 193cm (76in) long, *C 31 Jan,* £1,760 ($2,077)

5

A William and Mary oak dresser, 186cm (6ft 1in) high, *S 12 Nov,* £2,530 ($3,542)

6

A George II oak dresser, *c.*1750, 149cm (58½in) wide, *S 19 Mar,* £3,410 ($4,194)

7

A George III oak dresser, *c.*1790, 154cm (5ft ½in) wide, *S 11 June,* £2,200 ($2,893)

8

A George III oak dresser, *c.*1780, with pine super-structure, 193cm (76in) high, *C 17 Jan,* £3,850 ($4,620)

9

An oak dresser, late 18th century, 185cm (6ft 1in) high, *C 17 Jan,* £1,485 ($1,782)

10

A George III oak and elm dresser, *c.*1760, 298cm (9ft 9½in) high, *L 26 Apr,* £2,200 ($2,794)

1
A George IV mahogany
sideboard, c.1820, 152.5cm
(5ft), L 27 Sept,
£2,750 ($4,070)

2
A George III style
mahogany sideboard,
with a brass rail above
a drawer and two cup-
boards, 20th century,
152.5cm (5ft) wide,
C 28 Feb,
£770 ($862)

3
A Federal carved
mahogany serving table,
the top with reeded edge,
tapering legs on brass
ball feet, New York,
c.1805, 92cm (36in),
NY 26 Oct,
$4,400 (£3,098)

4
A Federal mahogany
serving table, New York,
c.1815, 91cm (36in) wide,
NY 1 Feb,
$3,300 (£3,000)

5
A George IV mahogany
chiffonier, the raised
open tierback with
pierced brass gallery, the
panel doors flanked by
pilasters, c.1825, 120cm
(47in) high, S 19 Feb,
£605 ($696)

6
A William IV rosewood
chiffonier, c.1830, 145cm
(57in) high, C 11 May,
£638 ($887)

7
A George IV ormolu-
mounted rosewood side
cabinet, c.1825, 111cm
(43½in) wide, L 15 Nov,
£2,860 ($4,004)

8
A George III-style
mahogany serving table,
the legs carved with
flowers and paterae,
c.1900, 122cm (48in)
wide, S 14 May,
£407 ($541)

9
An early Victorian
mahogany sideboard, the
doors flanked by open
shelves, 220cm (7ft 3in)
wide, S 5 Feb,
£572 ($675)

10
A Victorian mahogany
sideboard, c.1850, the
breakfront top above two
panelled doors flanking a
door and a recess, 213cm
(7ft) wide, C 17 Jan,
£880 ($1,056)

1
A George III mahogany sideboard, *c.*1800, 161cm (5ft 3½in) wide, *C 17 Jan,* £968 ($1,162)

2
A George III mahogany sideboard, *c.*1775, with five drawers panelled as six, with associated ivory handles, 200cm (6ft 6¾in) wide, *L 12 Apr,* £5,280 ($6,758)

3
A George III inlaid mahogany serpentine-fronted sideboard, last quarter 18th century, the drawer flanked by a cellaret drawer at one side and a cupboard door the other, 137cm (54in) wide, *NY 26 Jan,* $3,960 (£3,567)

4
A George III inlaid mahogany serpentine-fronted sideboard, *c.*1800, the drawer flanked by a deep cellaret drawer at each side, 161cm (5ft 3½in) wide, *NY 8 June,* $2,750 (£2,183)

5
A George III mahogany serpentine-fronted sideboard, *c.*1790, on reduced legs, 203cm (6ft 8in) wide, *S 16 Apr,* £3,740 ($4,682)

6
A George III mahogany sideboard, *c.*1800, with ebony banded top, 180cm (5ft 11in) wide, *C 11 July,* £2,365 ($3,287)

7
A Federal inlaid mahogany sideboard, New England, *c.*1805, 185.5cm (6ft 1in) wide, *NY 26 Oct,* $4,675 (£3,292)

8
A late George III mahogany breakfront sideboard, *c.*1820, the superstructure fitted with tambour cupboards, 166.5cm (65½in) wide, *C 14 Mar,* £1,012 ($1,153)

9
A Regency mahogany sideboard, *c.*1815, inlaid with ebonised stringing, 183cm (6ft) wide, *S 17 Sept,* £1,540 ($2,310)

10
A Regency breakfront sideboard, *c.*1810, mahogany and satinwood crossbanded, 185cm (6ft 1in) wide, *S 11 June,* £1,485 ($1,953)

1

2

3

4

5

6

7

8

9

10

1
A Queen Anne oak box-seat settle, *c.*1710, 142cm (56in) wide, *S 16 Apr,* £605 ($787)

2
An oak hall seat, *c.*1750, 140cm (55in) wide, *C 16 May,* £1,155 ($1,536)

3
A George II walnut double-chairback sofa, *c.*1740, 125cm (49in) wide, *L 8 Mar,* £14,300 ($16,016)

4
A Victorian walnut nine piece drawing room suite, *c.*1860, comprising a chaise longue, a gentleman's and lady's chair and six side chairs, *C 17 Jan,* £2,640 ($3,168)

5
A giltwood conversation chair, *c.*1880, 140cm (55in) wide, *C 3 Oct,* £902 ($1,263)

6
A Victorian chaise longue, 183cm (6ft) overall, *C 14 Nov,* £308 ($431)

7
A George III-style settee, *c.*1870, satinwood and upholstered, 191cm (6ft 3in) wide, *S 19 Feb,* £770 ($885)

8
A George III tapestry-covered mahogany settee, late 18th century, 247cm (8ft 1in) long, *NY 1 Nov,* $17,050 (£11,840)

9
A reproduction Victorian faded red leather Chesterfield, 20th century, 181cm (5ft 11in) wide, *C 3 Oct,* £990 ($1,386)

10
A Regency mahogany settee, *c.*1820, *C 17 Jan,* £858 ($1,030)

11
A late George III mahogany hall bench, *c.*1800, 147cm (58in) long, *L 14 June,* £4,180 ($5,559)

12
A Victorian walnut chaise longue, *c.*1860, 185cm (6ft 1in) long, *C 17 Jan,* £352 ($422)

13
A Victorian walnut settee, *c.*1870, *C 18 Apr,* £528 ($686)

14
A pair of William IV rosewood settees, *c.*1830 213cm (7ft) long, *L 7 June,* £1,100 ($1,463)

1

A pair of George III white painted and parcel-gilt serpentine-fronted window seats, last quarter 18th century, *NY 8 June,* $7,700 (£6,111)

2

A George IV mahogany 'X' framed stool, *c.*1825, 71cm (28in) wide, *S 15 Oct,* £462 ($684)

3

An early Victorian rosewood foot stool, *c.*1850, 41cm (16in) wide, *C 2 May,* £297 ($389)

4

A pair of stained beech foot stools, 20th century, *C 14 Nov,* £352 ($493)

5

A pair of Flemish walnut stools, *c.*1660, the tops covered in flame-stitch woolwork, 56cm (22in) wide, *L 24 May,* £3,300 ($4,389)

6

A pair of Régence stools, *M 23 June,* FF 28,860 (£2,326; $3,116)

7

A Louis XIV walnut long stool, *c.*1690, the top woven with flowers in blue, green and brown, 82cm (32½in) wide, *L 29 Nov,* £2,860 ($4,004)

8

A pair of Louis XV beechwood benches, mid 18th century, signed P Remy, 69cm (27in), *NY 4 May,* $7,700 (£6,417)

9

A pair of Louis XV giltwood stools, *M 24 June,* FF 42,180 (£3,515; $4,745)

10

An early Louis XV giltwood foot-stool, second quarter 18th century, 56cm (22in) wide, *NY 12 Oct,* $4,400 (£3,121)

11

A pair of Louis XV giltwood tabourets, mid 18th century, signed Delanois, 46cm (18in) wide, *NY 9 Nov,* $6,325 (£4,454)

12

An Italian painted and parcel-gilt bench, first half 18th century, *NY 23 Mar,* $1,430 (£1,222)

13

A Louis XV oak banquette, mid 18th century, 89cm (35in) wide, *NY 9 Nov,* $6,600 (£4,648)

14

A Napoleon III giltwood 'rope' stool, 1860-70, in the manner of Fournier, 55cm (21½in) wide, *L 22 Mar,* £3,410 ($4,092)

15

A Louis XV walnut banquette, mid 18th century, 123cm (48½in) wide, *NY 8 Nov,* $2,750 (£1,937)

16

A Louis XVI giltwood tabouret, last quarter 18th century, 49cm (19¼in) diam, *NY 12 Oct,* $4,400 (£3,121)

1 2 3

4 5 6

7 8

9 10 11

12 13 14

15 16

1
A Charles II walnut stool,
c.1685, 54cm (21in) wide,
L 14 June,
£2,310 ($3,072)

2
A George I walnut stool,
c.1720, 51cm (20in) wide,
S 22 Jan,
£704 ($834)

3
A George I walnut stool,
c.1740, the slip seat covered with an Oriental
rug fragment, 51cm (20in)
wide, NY 2 Feb,
$4,675 (£3,961)

4
A pair of George II
needlework-covered wal-
nut stools, c.1730, the
drop-in seats covered in
red and blue flowers on a
buff ground, 52cm
(20½in) wide, L 14 June,
£12,650 ($16,824)

5
A George III cross-
banded mahogany
curule-form stool, last
quarter 18th century,
NY 8 Oct,
$2,200 (£1,486)

6
A George III carved
mahogany stool, 72cm
(28¼in) wide, NY 26 Jan,
$9,900 (£8,918)

7
A George III mahogany
stool, c.1785, 58.5cm
(23in) wide, L 8 Mar,
£2,640 ($2,957)

8
A George III satinwood
window seat, c.1790, 85cm
(33½in) wide, C 12 July,
£2,970 ($4,128)

9
A George III mahogany
window seat, c.1760, in
the French taste, 94cm
(37in) wide, C 12 July,
£6,820 ($9,480)

10
A Charles II oak stool,
c.1680, 37cm (14½in)
high, HS 4 June,
£1,100 ($1,485)

11
A Charles II oak joint
stool, c.1680, with later
moulded top, 46cm (18in)
wide, HS 4 June,
£440 ($594)

12
A pair of George II
mahogany stools, c.1740,
S 12 Nov,
£1,155 ($1,617)

13
A James I oak armchair,
c.1605, L 15 Nov,
£2,750 ($3,850)

14
A Charles II oak panel-
back armchair, c.1660,
L 26 Apr,
£1,078 ($1,369)

15
A Charles II turkeywork-
covered walnut armchair,
c.1650, L 26 Apr,
£1,815 ($2,305)

16
A Commonwealth oak
wainscot armchair,
c.1650, C 17 Jan,
£1,595 ($1,914)

17
An elm turner's armchair,
c.1660, L 26 Apr,
£330 ($419)

18
A Charles II oak box-seat
settle, c.1680, 180cm (5ft
11in) wide, S 23 June,
£528 ($781)

19
A set of four William and
Mary oak and elm side
chairs, c.1690, C 18 Apr,
£2,530 ($3,289)

1
A composed set of eight
yew and elm Windsor
armchairs, *C 31 Oct,*
£3,190 ($4,785)

2
A Victorian Windsor
yew-wood armchair,
*c.*1840, *S 11 June,*
£462 ($608)

3
A matched set of five
George III ladder-back
chairs, *c.*1800, ash and
elm, *S 11 June,*
£605 ($796)

4
A stained oak Windsor
chair, early 18th century,
107cm (46in), *L 17 July,*
£935 ($1,356)

5
A composed set of five
ash ladder-back chairs,
early 19th century,
C 20 June,
£1,540 ($2,079)

6
A set of six George III
oak chairs, *c.*1770,
S 17 Sept,
£825 ($1,238)

7
A harlequin set of six
George III ash chairs,
*c.*1800, spindle-back, with
rush-seats, *S 19 Mar,*
£1,100 ($1,353)

8
A set of six George IV
ladder-back chairs,
*c.*1825, ash and elm,
including two armchairs,
S 14 May,
£902 ($1,200)

9
A set of four elm and yew
Windsor armchairs,
*c.*1800, *L 26 Apr,*
£4,620 ($5,867)

10
A pair of Queen Anne
walnut side chairs, first
quarter 18th century,
NY 26 Jan,
$1,540 (£1,387)

11
A set of six George I
walnut chairs, *c.*1720,
L 8 Mar,
£23,100 ($25,872)

12
A George I walnut chair,
*c.*1720, with needlework-
covered seat, *L 14 June,*
£2,860 ($3,803)

13
A set of eight George II
red walnut dining chairs,
*c.*1740, possibly Irish, the
drop-in seats covered in
19th century floral tapestry, *L 14 June,*
£34,100 ($45,353)

14
A set of six walnut chairs,
mid 18th century,
L 22 Nov,
£2,970 ($4,158)

15
A George II mahogany
armchair, *c.*1755,
L 26 July,
£1,045 ($1,536)

16
A George II carved
mahogany armchair,
*c.*1755, *L 14 June,*
£3,190 ($4,242)

17
A set of twelve mahogany
dining chairs, including
a pair of armchairs, six
*c.*1770, six 19th century,
C 3 Oct,
£5,720 ($8,008)

18
A set of six early George
III mahogany dining
chairs, *c.*1765, in the style
of Robert Manwaring,
L 15 Nov,
£5,060 ($7,084)

19
A set of six George III
mahogany dining chairs,
*c.*1780, *C 3 Oct,*
£1,760 ($2,464)

1 2 3 4

5 6 7 8

9 10 11 12

13 14 15 16

17 18 19

1
An early George III
mahogany 'cock-pen'
armchair, c.1770,
L 14 June,
£2,970 ($3,950)

2
A set of eleven early
George III mahogany
dining chairs, c.1770,
including three arm-
chairs, *L 8 Mar,*
£7,700 ($8,624)

3
A set of eight George III
mahogany dining chairs,
c.1775, including two
armchairs, *C 3 Oct,*
£2,860 ($4,004)

4
A set of seven George III
mahogany dining chairs,
c.1790, including an
armchair, *L 7 June,*
£3,520 ($4,681)

5
A set of eight George III
mahogany dining chairs,
c.1790, *C 17 Jan,*
£1,540 ($1,848)

6
A George III mahogany
wheel back armchair,
c.1780, *C 18 Apr,*
£880 ($1,144)

7
A set of six late George
III mahogany chairs,
c.1800, *L 1 Feb,*
£748 ($853)

8
A set of eight George III
mahogany dining chairs,
c.1800, including a pair
of armchairs, *S 11 June,*
£4,400 ($5,786)

9
A set of eight George III
mahogany chairs, c.1800,
including a pair of arm-
chairs, *L 15 Nov,*
£3,850 ($5,390)

10
A set of sixteen late
George III mahogany
dining chairs, c.1805,
including a pair of arm-
chairs, *L 8 Mar,*
£9,460 ($10,595)

11
A set of four Regency
'bamboo' armchairs,
c.1820, *L 7 June,*
£2,970 ($3,950)

12
A pair of Regency
grained beechwood
'bamboo' armchairs, first
quarter 19th century,
decoration restored,
NY 26 Jan,
$19,800 (£17,837)

13
A George III mahogany
elbow chair, c.1810,
C 6 June,
£220 ($297)

14
A set of six Regency
mahogany dining chairs,
c.1810, including a pair
of armchairs, *L 26 July,*
£2,200 ($3,234)

15
A set of six Regency
mahogany dining chairs,
c.1820, *L 10 May,*
£1,155 ($1,490)

16
A set of six Regency
beech rail-back chairs
c.1810, stained to simu-
late rosewood and with
cut-brass inlay, *S 17 Sept,*
£1,595 ($2,393)

17
A set of six George IV
rosewood dining chairs,
c.1825, *C 3 Oct,*
£792 ($1,109)

18
A set of six George IV
provincial mahogany
chairs, c.1825, including
two armchairs, *S 14 May,*
£990 ($1,317)

19
A set of six Regency
elmwood dining chairs,
c.1810, *L 26 Apr,*
£660 ($838)

1 2 3
4 5 6 7
8 9 10 11
12 13 14 15
16 17 18 19

1
A set of eight **Regency mahogany dining chairs**, first quarter 19th century, comprising two armchairs and six side chairs, *NY 1 Nov*, $8,250 (£5,729)

2
A set of four **Regency gilt-bronze inlaid mahogany side chairs**, first quarter 19th century, *NY 1 Nov*, $2,200 (£1,527)

3
A set of eight **George III mahogany dining chairs**, *c.1800, C 11 July*, £2,750 ($3,823)

4
A set of eight **Regency mahogany rail-back chairs**, *c.1810*, including two armchairs, *S 11 June*, £4,400 ($5,786)

5
A set of seven **William IV mahogany dining chairs**, *c.1830*, including a pair of armchairs, *L 7 June*, £1,210 ($1,609)

6
A set of twelve **William IV mahogany dining chairs**, *c.1835, L 14 June*, £6,050 ($8,046)

7
A set of six **William IV mahogany library chairs**, *c.1830, C 11 July*, £858 ($1,193)

8
A set of twenty-four late **Victorian mahogany side chairs**, *c.1870, C 7 June*, £1,430 ($1,931)

9
A set of six **Victorian mahogany balloon-back dining chairs**, *S 29 Oct*, £792 ($1,180)

10
A set of thirteen **Victorian mahogany dining chairs**, *c.1865*, including an armchair, *C 3 Oct*, £3,740 ($5,236)

11
A set of eight **Charles II style walnut dining chairs**, 20th century, including two armchairs, *C 3 Oct*, £990 ($1,386)

12
A set of eight **George III style mahogany dining chairs**, including a pair of armchairs, *c.1900, C 17 Jan*, £968 ($1,162)

13
A set of eight **mahogany dining chairs**, of Chippendale inspiration, *c.1900*, including a pair of armchairs, *L 22 Feb*, £4,840 ($5,518)

14
A set of twelve **Scottish mahogany dining chairs**, in late George II style and including a pair of armchairs, *L 14 June*, £11,000 ($14,630)

15
A set of six **George III style mahogany dining chairs**, late 19th century, including a pair of armchairs, *C 11 July*, £3,960 ($5,504)

16
A set of four **Edwardian salon chairs**, rosewood and inlaid, *S 5 Feb*, £275 ($325)

17
A set of eight **George III style black painted and cane armchairs**, modern, *S 22 Jan*, £1,650 ($1,955)

18
A set of six **George III style mahogany dining chairs**, *c.1900, C 18 Apr*, £1,045 ($1,359)

19
A set of ten **George II style mahogany dining chairs**, *c.1920, C 11 July*, £1,870 ($2,599)

1   2   3
4   5   6   7
8   9   10   11
12   13   14   15
16   17   18   19

1
A George I walnut
'Shepard's Crook' arm-
chair, c.1720, *NY 11 Oct*,
$2,530 (£1,794)

2
A George II mahogany
armchair, c.1755,
L 22 Nov,
£2,420 ($3,388)

3
A George II needlepoint
upholstered walnut wing
armchair, second quar-
ter 18th century,
NY 1 Nov,
$16,500 (£11,458)

4
A George II mahogany
armchair, c.1755, *L 8 Mar*,
£5,500 ($6,160)

5
A George III mahogany
library armchair, c.1760,
L 14 June,
£3,410 ($4,535)

6
A pair of George III solid
satinwood armchairs,
c.1790, *L 14 June*,
£9,350 ($12,435)

7
A pair of George III
carved mahogany arm-
chairs, last quarter 18th
century, *NY 13 Apr*,
$20,900 (£16,720)

8
A pair of George III
giltwood armchairs, in
the French style, *L 8 Mar*,
£7,700 ($8,624)

9
A set of three George III
painted armchairs, c.1780,
now painted white,
L 14 June,
£3,850 ($5,120)

10
A George III painted
satinwood armchair,
c.1790, in the manner of
George Seddon, *L 8 Mar*,
£2,530 ($2,834)

11
A George III japanned
armchair, c.1785,
S 19 Mar,
£1,980 ($2,435)

12
An early Victorian
carved rosewood armchair,
second quarter 19th cen-
turym, *NY 26 Jan*,
$5,500 (£4,954)

13
A Victorian rosewood
salon armchair, c.1850,
C 3 Oct,
£341 ($477)

14
A pair of Victorian wal-
nut salon chairs, c.1860,
C 8 Aug,
£286 ($426)

15
A walnut salon suite, mid
19th century, comprising
an armchair, a low chair,
and a sofa, *L 19 July*,
£1,430 ($2,002)

16
Two Victorian walnut
and mahogany framed
balloon-back chairs,
S 3 Dec,
£572 ($801)

17
A George III style
mahogany wing armchair,
20th century, *C 6 June*,
£550 ($743)

18
A set of seven painted
satinwood chairs, c.1900,
in the style of Seddon,
including an armchair,
L 22 Feb,
£3,080 ($3,511)

19
A bergère suite, with
dual-caning, comprising
a pair of armchairs and a
triple chair-back settee,
183cm (6ft) wide, *S 19 Feb*,
£1,210 ($1,391)

1

2

3

4

5

6

7

8

9

10

11

12

13

14

15

16

17

18

19

1
A Regency mahogany bergère, *c*.1810, *C 18 Apr*, £1,188 ($1,544)

2
A late Georgian mahogany library bergère, *c*.1820, *C 18 Apr*, £550 ($715)

3
A set of Regency metamorphic library steps, *c*.1820, in the manner of Morgan and Saunders, the beechwood frame closing to form an armchair, *L 14 June*, £2,860 ($3,803)

4
A George IV mahogany Daw's Patent armchair, *c*.1825, covered in nailed hide, *S 19 Mar*, £1,650 ($2,030)

5
A Regency mahogany curule armchair, after a design by Thomas Hope, first quarter 19th century, *NY 1 Nov*, $9,350 (£6,493)

6
A Regency carved mahogany caned armchair, first quarter 19th century, *NY 13 Apr*, $8,250 (£6,600)

7
A Regency mahogany hall porter's chair, *c*.1810, covered in rexine, 169cm (5ft 6½in) high, *L 10 May*, £2,090 ($2,696)

8
A George IV mahogany and cane bergère, *c*.1825, *S 19 Mar*, £660 ($812)

9
A George III mahogany library armchair, *c*.1800, *C 3 Oct*, £1,078 ($1,509)

10
A set of four George IV mahogany hall chairs, *c*.1820, *L 14 June*, £1,265 ($1,682)

11
A pair of George III mahogany hall chairs, *c*.1790, *S 11 June*, £572 ($752)

12
A George II elmwood corner armchair, mid 18th century, possibly of colonial origin, *NY 26 Jan*, $2,310 (£2,081)

13
A George III mahogany corner armchair, *NY 13 Apr*, $1,540 (£1,232)

14
A Georgian mahogany corner armchair, *c*.1760, *C 11 July*, £484 ($673)

15
An early Victorian mahogany patent armchair, second quarter 19th century, *NY 8 June*, $6,050 (£4,802)

16
A mahogany and upholstered bath chair, *c*.1840, 104cm (41in) high, *S 17 Oct*, £330 ($488)

17
A George IV mahogany patent adjustable armchair, *c*.1825, *S 19 Feb*, £1,265 ($1,455)

1
A French late Gothic walnut chair, *c.*1500, with hinged box seat, 164cm (5ft 4½in) high, *L 24 May,* £3,520 ($4,682)

2
A French Renaissance inlaid highback seat, mid 16th century, inlaid with leaves highlighted in black and red wax, 229cm (7ft 6½in) high, *NY 11 May,* $3,575 (£2,907)

3
A Louis XIV walnut armchair, late 17th century, *NY 11 May,* $1,980 (£1,610)

4
A pair of Louis XVI walnut armchairs, last quarter 17th century, with contemporary upholstery, *NY 11 May,* $5,225 (£4,248)

5
A pair of Régence caned walnut chaises à la reine, *c.*1720, *NY 8 Nov,* $1,650 (£1,162)

6
A pair of Régence fauteuils, *M 23 June,* FF 77,700 (£6,261; $8,390)

7
A set of four Régence fauteuils, *M 24 June,* FF 88,800 (£7,156; $9,588)

8
A pair of Régence beechwood caned fauteuils à la reine, *c.*1720, *NY 24 May,* $2,860 (£2,269)

9
A Louis XV giltwood child's bergère, mid 18th century, *NY 12 Oct,* $1,980 (£1,404)

10
A Louis XV bergère, lacquered in cream, *M 24 June,* FF 16,650 (£1,342; $1,798)

11
A Louis XV caned beechwood fauteuil de bureau, mid 18th century, *NY 12 Oct,* $4,400 (£3,121)

12
A set of four Louis XV giltwood chaises à la reine, mid 18th century, *NY 24 May,* $2,200 (£1,746)

13
A Louis XV beechwood fauteuil, *c.*1750, stamped IB, LeLarge, *L 5 July,* £1,100 ($1,518)

14
A set of three early Louis XV walnut chairs, *c.*1730, *L 5 July,* £1,375 ($1,898)

1

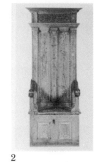

2

3

4

5

6

7

8

9

10

11

12

13

14

1
A set of four Louis XV
beechwood fauteuils à la
reine, mid 18th century,
NY 23 Mar,
$31,900 (£27,265)

2
A pair of Louis XV caned
natural wood fauteuils,
one stamped Ch. Nor-
mand, *M 24 June,*
FF 11,100 (£894; $1,199)

3
A set of four Louis XV
fauteuils, stamped
H Amand, *M 24 June,*
FF 27,750
(£2,236; $2,996)

4
A set of four Louis XV
chairs, attributed to
Nogaret, *M 24 June,*
FF 79,920
(£6,440; $8,630)

5
A pair of Louis XV
giltwood fauteuils à la
reine, mid 18th century,
signed Tilliard,
NY 12 Oct,
$66,000 (£46,809)

6
A Louis XV walnut ber-
gère à oreilles, mid 18th
century, *NY 9 Nov,*
$7,150 (£5,035)

7
A Louis XV/XVI tran-
sitional giltwood suite,
stamped F Geny, *c.*1775,
comprising five arm-
chairs and a sofa, *L 5 July,*
£7,700 ($10,626)

8
A pair of Louis XV
beechwood bergères à la
reine, mid 18th century,
signed I. DeLanois,
NY 12 Oct,
$14,300 (£10,142)

9
A pair of Louis XVI
walnut chaises en cab-
riolet, *c.*1775, *NY 23 Mar,*
$2,860 (£2,444)

10
A set of Louis XVI oak
chairs en cabriolet, *c.*1775,
NY 24 May,
$3,575 (£2,837)

11
A Louis XVI painted side
chair, last quarter 18th
century, *NY 23 Mar,*
$935 (£799)

French cabinet-makers
m.=made Master

Henri Amand, m.1749

Etienne Avril, m.1774

Léonard Boudin,
m.1761

A. M. Criaerd, m.1747

Mathieu Criaerd,
m.1738

Louis Delanois, m.1761

Adrien Delorme,
m.1748

Jean-Pierre Dusautoy,
m.1779

Adrien-Delorme
Faizelot, m.1748

Georges Jacob, m.1765

Guillaume Kemp,
m.1764

Claude Leclerc, m.1785

Jean-Baptiste Lelarge,
m.1738

Louis Moreau, m.1764

Charles-Francois
Normand, m.1745

Simon Oeben, m.1764

François Igance Papst,
m.1785

Nicolas Petit, m.1761

Pierre Remy, m.1750

Jean-Henri Riesener,
m.1768

Pierre Roussel, m.1745

Joseph Schmitz, m.1761

Claude II Sené, m.1769

Jean-Chrysostome
Stumpff, m.1766

Nicolas Tilliard,
m.1736

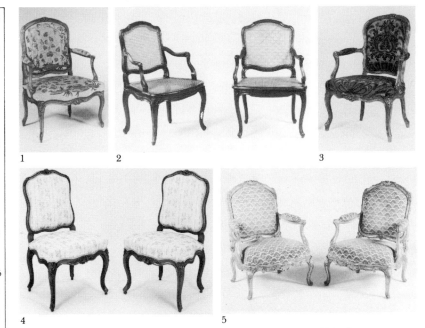

1 2 3

4 5

6 7

8 9 10 11

1
A Louis XVI caned mahogany fauteuil de cabinet, last quarter 18th century, attributed to Georges Jacob, with circular revolving seat, *NY 9 Nov*, $9,900 (£6,972)

2
A pair of Louis XVI mahogany side chairs, late 18th century, signed G Iacob, made for the Duc De Penthièvre (grandson of Louis XIV and Mame de Montespan), for the Chateau de Chanteloup, Amboise, *NY 9 Nov*, $9,900 (£6,972)

3
A Louis XVI mahogany bergère, last quarter 18th century, signed C Leclerc, *NY 9 Nov*, $6,875 (£4,842)

4
A pair of Louis XVI grey-painted marquises, last quarter 18th century, signed C Sené, 81.5cm (32in) wide, *NY 4 May*, $30,800 (£25,667)

5
A Louis XVI bergère, last quarter 18th century, *M 24 June*, FF 7,215 (£601; $812)

6
A set of six Louis XVI grey-painted side chairs, last quarter 18th century, one signed G Iacob, *NY 4 May*, $19,800 (£16,500)

7
A suite of Louis XVI giltwood seat furniture, last quarter 18th century, signed G Iacob, comprising four fauteuils à la reine and a canapé (length reduced). *NY 4 May*, $14,300 (£11,917)

8
A Louis XVI painted canapé, last quarter 18th century, signed C Sené, 164cm (5ft 4½in) long, *NY 4 May*, $4,950 (£4,125)

9
A set of eight Empire mahogany dining chairs, first quarter 19th century, *NY 23 Mar*, $7,700 (£6,581)

10
A Second Empire mahogany salon suite, late 19th century, comprising a pair of fauteuils and five side chairs, inlaid with gilt-bronze foliage, *L 8 Nov*, £2,090 ($3,135)

11
A pair of Empire mahogany armchairs, *c.1810, C 18 Apr*, £1,210 ($1,573)

12
An Empire mahogany and parcel-gilt bergère, early 19th century, later ormolu mounts, *NY 23 Mar*, $1,650 (£1,410)

13
A pair of Charles X mahogany fauteuils à la reine, *c.1825, NY 5 Oct*, $3,850 (£2,730)

1

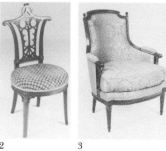
2

3

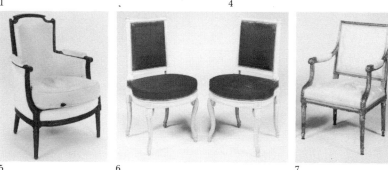
4

5

6

7

8

9

10   11   12   13

1
A Charles X fauteuil prie-Dieu, c.1825, M 25 June,
FF 7,770 (£648; $874)

2
A pair of Empire mahogany fauteils à la reine, first quarter 19th century, NY 9 Nov,
$6,325 (£4,454)

3
A gilt-bronze-mounted mahogany three-piece salon suite, c.1890, comprising a pair of bergères and a sofa, sofa 141cm (55½in) wide, L 22 Mar,
£1,925 ($2,310)

4
A painted and parcel-gilt suite, in Louis XVI style, c.1870, comprising a pair of fauteuils and a set of four chairs, L 22 Mar,
£2,860 ($3,432)

5
A brass-mounted tulipwood-veneered salon suite, c.1850, comprising three chairs, a scoopback chair and a sofa, sofa 195cm (6ft 5in) wide, L 8 Nov,
£3,850 ($5,775)

6
A set of four French giltwood chairs, in Louis XVI style, c.1870, L 21 June,
£858 ($1,115)

7
A set of three Louis XIV-style armchairs, carved giltwood, upholstered in Genoa velvet, S 9 July,
£418 ($560)

8
A Louis XVI style walnut duchesse, c.1900, 188cm (6ft 2in) long, C 18 Apr,
£1,100 ($1,430)

9
A pair of Louis XVI style giltwood armchairs, late 19th century, NY 22 June,
$990 (£773)

10
A Louis XV style giltwood small bergère, c.1900, C 18 Apr,
£462 ($601)

11
A Louis XV style giltwood bergère, c.1900, C 18 Apr,
£495 ($644)

12
A Louis XVI style giltwood suite, c.1900, comprising a canapé and six armchairs, upholstered in Aubusson tapestry, NY 22 June,
$9,625 (£7,519)

1
A set of six Tuscan walnut armchairs, 16th century, *F 26 Mar,*
L 8,000,000
(£3,206; $4,072)

2
A Flemish walnut armchair, late 17th century, *L 18 Dec,*
£1,100 ($1,540)

3
A Venetian walnut chair, early 18th century, *HS 2 July,*
£418 ($577)

4
A pair of Genoese walnut armchairs, *c.1740,* *L 29 Nov,*
£5,280 ($7,392)

5
A pair of Venetian walnut armchairs, *c.1750,* *F 26 Mar,*
L 6,000,000
(£2,405; $3,054)

6
A pair of Genoese walnut armchairs, mid 18th century, *F 26 Mar,*
L 3,700,000
(£1,483; $1,883)

7
A Dutch walnut armchair, mid 18th century, *A 26 Feb,*
Dfl 4,640 (£1,137; $1,274)

8
A pair of Venetian lacquered wood cabriolet armchairs, 18th century, *M 25 June,*
FF 13,320
(£1,110; $1,499)

9
A set of twelve Northern Italian dining chairs, mid 18th century, now painted and gilded, together with six matching copies of later date, *NY 8 Nov,*
$7,975 (£5,616)

10
A pair of Italian painted and parcel-gilt armchairs, mid 18th century, *NY 5 Oct,*
$1,870 (£1,326)

11
A Venetian giltwood settee, mid 18th century, 186cm (6ft 1in), *NY 23 Mar,*
$2,200 (£1,880)

12
A pair of Italian rococo painted and parcel gilt armchairs, mid 18th century, painted and highlighted with gilding, *NY 23 Mar,*
$1,540 (£1,316)

13
A pair of Italian painted and parcel-gilt armchairs, mid 18th century, *NY 5 Oct,*
$1,540 (£1,092)

14
A pair of North Italian painted and parcel-gilt armchairs, *c.1785,* *L 24 May,*
£2,310 ($3,072)

15
Five Dutch chairs and one armchair, by A Struys, green painted, late 18th century, *A 26 Feb,*
Dfl 6,960 (£1,706; $1,911)

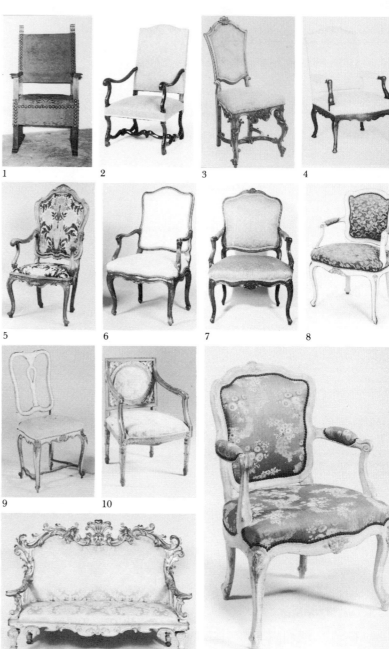

1
Twelve Italian walnut dining chairs, late 18th century, composed of a set of ten and a pair very similar, stamped with labels for the Palazzo Reali de Modena and the Palazzo Moncalieri, *L 24 May,*
£8,800 ($12,584)

2
A set of six Dutch elm dining chairs, *c.*1785, *L 18 Dec,*
£1,650 ($2,310)

3
A set of four Dutch painted chairs, late 18th century, *L 31 May,*
£638 ($855)

4
A pair of Italian armchairs, late 18th century, traces of original grey paint, now highlighted with gilding, *NY 24 May,*
$1,430 (£1,134)

5
A set of six Viennese mahogany dining chairs, *c.*1790, the backs inlaid with brass lozenges, *L 24 May,*
£3,740 ($4,974)

6
A set of four Italian beechwood armchairs, *c.*1820, *NY 24 May,*
$9,900 (£7,857)

7
A set of four Italian fruitwood marquetry side chairs, early 19th century, the top rail inlaid with dolphins, *NY 23 Mar,*
$1,540 (£1,316)

8
A set of six brass-inlaid mahogany chairs, early 19th century, German or Austrian, *L 24 May,*
£1,760 ($2,341)

9
A pair of South German walnut and parcel-gilt armchairs, *c.*1820, *L 18 Dec,*
£3,190 ($4,466)

10
A set of six Portuguese rosewood chairs, *c.*1840, the backs with 'Chippendale' Gothic splats, *L 22 Mar,*
£1,760 ($2,112)

11
A pair of marquetry armchairs, South German/North Italian in 17th century style, the back inlaid with village scenes heightened in ivory, *L 8 Nov,*
£3,850 ($5,775)

12
A set of six bentwood dining chairs, *c.*1880, including two armchairs, by Jacob & Joseph Kohn, Austria, *C 28 Nov,*
£572 ($808)

13
A pair of Italian ivory-inlaid walnut Savonarola chairs, *c.*1880, each cross-bar inlaid with a pewter and ivory figure, *L 22 Mar,*
£1,320 ($1,584)

14
A South African Cape fruitwood tolletjies side chair, early 18th century, *JHB 29 Apr,*
R 3,300 (£1,375; $1,801)

15
A pair of South African Cape stinkwood tub chairs, *c.*1790, *CT 13 May,*
R 650 (£271; $350)

16
A South African Cape teak transitional tulbagh side chair, 18th century, *JHB 8 July,*
R 580 (£216; $300)

17
A South African Cape teak tolletjies armchair, early 18th century, *JHB 29 Apr,*
R 6,200 (£2,583; $3,384)

Regional Characteristics in 18th century American Chairs

As centres of cabinet- and chair-making became established in the early decades of the 18th century, various regions in the colonies developed individual preferences in design and construction techniques. While there are exceptions to these characteristics, it is often possible to attribute American furniture to a region or school of cabinet-makers or even to an individual craftsman on the basis of specific types of carving, proportion, and construction.

The chairs illustrated here each represent one of the major centres — Philadelphia, Newport, New York, Massachusetts — and illustrate the elements of either the Queen Anne or the Chippendale styles.

The Queen Anne chairs are all similar in form, with tall, slender proportions, a vase-form splat, and cabriole legs. Made of walnut, often used as the primary wood during the early 18th century, these chairs have the elegant lines and restrained decoration associated with the Queen Anne style.

Frequently, the attribution of a piece to a specific cabinet-making centre is based on a combination of features rather than on a single characteristic. The balloon-shaped seat on the chairs in fig.3 is often seen on Philadelphia chairs but it is also found on Queen Anne chairs from Newport (fig.1) and Massachusetts (fig.2). However, the trifid feet and the distinctive shell-carving on the knees make it possible to ascribe these chairs to the Philadelphia area.

The design of the chairs illustrated in fig.1 incorporates a number of elements associated with Boston cabinet-makers: a baluster-shaped splat, chamfered back legs, block-and-ring-turned side stretchers, and a swelled medial stretcher. Although several of these characteristics are shared by the chairs in fig.2, the distinctive volute-and-shell carved crest and central reel-turned stretcher between the legs suggest a Newport origin.

—1—

A pair of Queen Anne walnut side chairs, Newport, Rhode Island, 1740-60, *NY 26 Oct,* $23,100 (£16,267)

—2—

Two similar Queen Anne carved walnut balloon seat side chairs, Massachusetts 1740-60, *NY 1 Feb 1986,* $17,600 (£13,750)

—3—

A Queen Anne carved walnut chair, Philadelphia, c.1735, *NY 1 Feb,* $13,750 (£10,742)

—4—

A set of three Chippendale mahogany side chairs, New York, c.1780, *NY 2 Feb,* $7,150 (£6,059)

—5—

A Chippendale carved mahogany side chair, attributed to Benjamin Randolph, Philadelphia, c.1770, *NY 1 Feb,* $24,200 (£18,906)

—1—

—2—

—3—

—4—

—5—

During the second half of the 18th century, a new rococo spirit brought a much freer approach to furniture design. There was a fresh interest in brilliantly carved and figured surfaces, and mahogany became the preferred wood. A new enthusiasm for surface ornamentation can be seen in the backs, or 'splats,' of side chairs during the period. In contrast to the solid splat typical of the Queen Anne period, these splats were pierced and often carved with delicate foliate decoration. Claw-and-ball feet on chairs (as on the legs of case pieces) were characteristic of this period. Among the other new design elements were the Marlborough leg, hairy-paw foot and scrolled toe, and also the Gothic lancet-arch and trefoil in chair backs.

Philadelphia emerged as a major cabinet-making centre, and a mahogany side chair (fig.5) attributed to Benjamin Randolph, one of the city's finest cabinet-makers, exhibits the crisp carving typical of this school.

The New York interpretation of the Chippendale style is illustrated by a pair of chairs (fig.7) made about the same time as the Randolph chair. As is customary in New York seating furniture, the overall proportions of the seat and back are lower and wider than in pieces made in other centres. The cupid's bow crest and pierced diamond and scrolled splat are characteristic of New York cabinet-work.

Perhaps the most familiar element of the Chippendale style is the claw-and-ball foot, which is found on case pieces as well as on seat furniture. Craftsmen in Newport, New York and Philadelphia used this form, and their interpretations clearly illustrate regional distinctions. Frequently on Newport pieces, three-dimensional talons grasp a slightly oblong ball. On New York pieces, the talons and ball are combined and somewhat squared, while on Philadelphia pieces the ball is round but slightly flattened. The most extravagant version, developed in Philadelphia, is the 'hairy-paw' foot, which is found on only a few pieces. Among them is the elaborately carved Chippendale side chair (fig.6) attributed to Thomas Affleck, another eminent Philadelphia cabinet-maker, which realised $275,000 (£197,840) in 1982, the highest price ever paid for a chair at auction.

● LESLIE KENO ●

Further reading
Morrison H. Heckscher, *American Furniture in the Metropolitan Museum of Art*, 1985
Brock Jobe and Myrna Kaye, *New England Furniture: The Colonial Era*, 1984.
Michael Moses, *Mastercraftsmen of Newport*, 1984

—6—
A Chippendale carved mahogany hairy paw foot side chair, Thomas Affleck, Philadelphia, *c.*1770, *NY 23 Oct, 1982*
$275,000 (£197,840)

—7—
A pair of Chippendale carved mahogany side chairs, New York, *c.*1770, *NY 2 Feb,*
$11,000 (£7,857)

—8—
A pair of Chippendale mahogany side chairs, Reading, Pennsylvania, *c.*1785, *NY 2 Feb,*
$3,300 (£3,000)

—9—
top left **detail of hairy paw Fig. 6 (Philadelphia)**

top right **detail of Fig. 5 (Philadelphia)**

bottom left (**Newport**)

bottom right **detail of Fig. 4 (New York)**

—6—

—7—

—8—

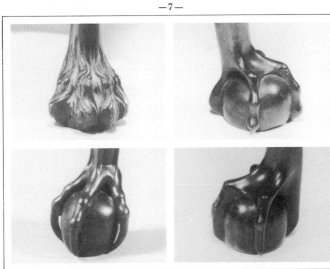

—9—

1

A Classical mahogany
side chair, attributed to
Duncan Phyfe, New
York, c.1805, the legs
painted gold and black,
NY 26 Oct,
$3,575 (£2,517)

2

A set of eight Federal
mahogany side chairs,
New York, c.1820,
NY 2 Feb,
$4,400 (£3,728)

3

A set of ten Federal curly
maple rush seat side
chairs, New York State,
c.1825, *NY 1 Feb,*
$19,800 (£18,000)

4

A Shaker painted maple
rocking armchair, Union
Village, Ohio, mid 19th
century, painted black
over the old red,
NY 2 Feb,
$1,320 (£1,118)

5

A Shaker maple rocking
armchair, Mt Lebanon,
New York, c.1910,
NY 2 Feb,
$715 (£605)

6

A Windsor comb-back
armchair, Philadelphia,
c.1775, *NY 2 Feb,*
$4,675 (£3,961)

7

A Windsor bow-back
armchair, branded
S Jacques, late 18th cen-
tury, *NY 2 Feb,*
$1,540 (£1,400)

8

A painted Windsor con-
tinuous armchair, c.1795,
NY 2 Feb,
$2,750 (£2,330)

9

A bow-back Windsor side
chair, c.1815, the chair
painted black, the seat
painted tan, *NY 1 Feb,*
$550 (£500)

10

A pair of American lami-
nated rosewood pierced
back side chairs, c.1885,
John Henry Belter, New
York, *NY 30 Nov,*
$5,500 (£3,691)

11

A set of six painted and
decorated rust seat side
chairs, New England,
c.1835, painted and sten-
cilled in green and gold
on a black ground,
NY 1 Feb,
$1,430 (£1,300)

12

An American laminated
rosewood suite, John
Henry Belter, New York,
c.1855, comprising a set-
tee and a pair of side
chairs, *NY 30 Mar,*
$5,225 (£4,214)

13

An American rosewood
upholstered settee, c.1860,
230cm (7ft 6in), *NY 30 Nov,*
$3,575 (£2,399)

14

A poplar settee, Pennsyl-
vania, c.1840, 183cm (6ft)
long, *NY 2 Feb,*
$660 (£600)

15

A Classical mahogany
sofa, attributed to
Samuel Field McIntire,
Salem Massachusetts,
c.1825, 208cm (6ft 10in)
long, *NY 2 Feb,*
$6,600 (£5,593)

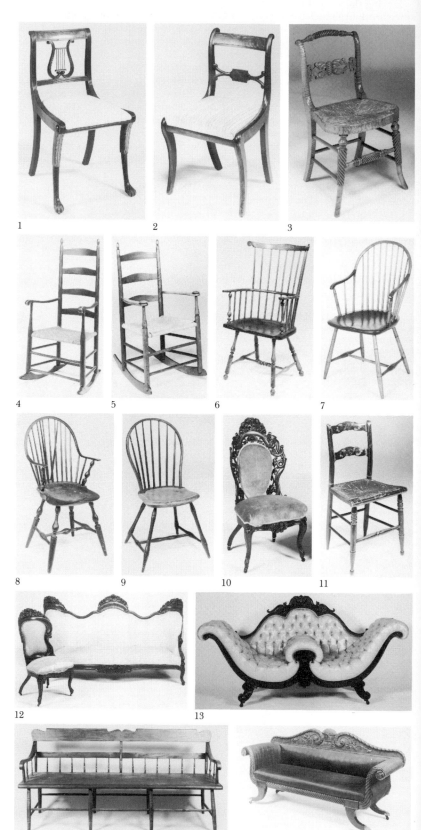

1 2 3
4 5 6 7
8 9 10 11
12 13
14 15

1
A Louis XV provincial ormolu-mounted fruit-wood bureau, mid 18th century, 107cm (42in) wide, *NY 23 Mar*, $2,860 (£2,600)

2
A Louis XV provincial walnut bureau, mid 18th century, *L 31 May*, £1,925 ($2,580)

3
An Empire provincial mahogany writing table, early 19th century, with leather inset writing surface, *NY 23 May*, $1,100 (£940)

4
A composite set of ten Liegeois chairs, *c.*1740, including three armchairs, *L 24 May*, £6,380 ($8,485)

5
A Louis XV provincial beechwood suite, *c.*1750, comprising five armchairs and a settee, settee 169cm (5ft 6½in) wide, *L 18 Dec*, £2,860 ($4,004)

6
A Louis XV provincial walnut armchair, mid 18th century, *NY 23 Mar*, $1,650 (£1,410)

7
An early Louis XV provincial painted side table, *c.*1730, with mottled apricot and cream marble top, later serpentine base, 156cm (5ft 1½in) wide, *L 24 May*, £26,400 ($35,112)

8
A Louis XV provincial oak side table, mid 18th century, probably Southern France, with liver and grey mottled marble top, 211cm (6ft 11in) wide, *NY 12 Oct*, $33,000 (£23,404)

9
A Louis XV provincial beechwood window seat, mid 18th century, 224cm (7ft 4in) long, *NY 24 May*, $2,970 (£2,357)

10
A Louis XVI provincial walnut settee, last quarter 18th century, *NY 23 Mar*, $1,100 (£940)

1
A Louis XV/XVI provincial steel-mounted bibliotheque, third quarter 18th century, with brown and grey mottled marble top, 145cm (47in) wide, *NY 23 Mar,*
$1,870 (£1,598)

2
A Régence oak provincial commode, *c.*1730, with grey and white marble top, 147cm (58in) wide, *L 18 Dec,*
£3,190 ($4,466)

3
An early Louis XV provincial walnut serpentine commode, *c.*1730, 130cm (51in) wide, *L 18 Dec,*
£3,300 ($4,620)

4
A Louis XV provincial chestnutwood commode, *c.*1740, with brass lock-plates, 125cm (49in) wide, *HS 2 July,*
£3,520 ($4,858)

5
A Louis XV provinicial brass-mounted fruitwood commode, mid 18th century, 155cm (53in) wide, *NY 24 May,*
$5,225 (£4,146)

6
A Louis XV provincial walnut commode, *c.*1745, 94cm (37in) wide, *S 14 May,*
£616 ($819)

7
A Louis XVI provincial ormolu-mounted fruitwood commode, last quarter 18th century, 108cm (42½in) wide, *NY 23 Mar,*
$2,970 (£2,538)

8
A Louis XV provincial oak commode, *c.*1765, 127cm (55in) wide, *L 31 May,*
£1,870 ($2,506)

9
A Restauration provincial cherrywood chiffonier, *c.*1825, 159cm (5ft 2½in) high, *HS 2 July,*
£770 ($1,063)

10
A Louis XV provincial oak display cabinet, *c.*1740, 253cm (8ft 3½in) high, *L 18 Dec,*
£2,420 ($3,388)

11
A pair of Louis XV provincial chestnutwood food cupboards, mid 18th century, 147.5cm (58in) high, *L 18 Dec,*
£1,540 ($2,156)

1

2

3

4

5

6

7

8

9

10

11

1
A Louis XV provincial oak armoire, mid 18th century, reduced in height, later cornice, 202cm (6ft 7½in), *NY 23 Mar,* $1,760 (£1,504)

2
A Louis XV provincial oak armoire, *c.*1770, 219cm (7ft 2in) high, *L 18 Dec,* £990 ($1,386)

3
A Louis XV oak armoire, mid 18th century, 242cm (8ft) high, *C 17 Jan,* £1,705 ($2,046)

4
A Louis XV oak cupboard, mid 18th century, 221cm (7ft 3in) high, *C 17 Jan,* £1,100 ($1,320)

5
A Louis XV carved oak cupboard, *c.*1770, 224cm (7ft 4in) high, *S 11 June,* £2,970 ($3,901)

6
A Louis XV walnut buffet à deux corps, mid 18th century, 236cm (7ft 9in) high, *NY 24 May,* $4,620 (£3,666)

7
A Louis XVI provincial walnut armoire, late 18th century, 234cm (7ft 8in), *NY 23 Mar,* $4,950 (£4,231)

8
A Louis XVI provincial oak armoire, last quarter 18th century, 244cm (8ft) high, *NY 23 Mar,* $3,190 (£2,726)

1

2

3

4

5

6

7

8

1
A Biedermeier satin-birch centre table, *c.*1820, with oval top, 126cm (49½in) wide, *L 18 Dec,* £1,980 ($2,772)

2
A Biedermeier ebonised and bois-clair sofa table, early 19th century, 199cm (46½in) open, *L 31 May,* £1,320 ($1,769)

3
A Biedermeier mahogany demi-lune chest of drawers, first quarter 19th century, 92cm (36½in) wide, *NY 5 Oct,* $3,300 (£2,340)

4
A Biedermeier fruitwood commode, *c.*1820, in oyster-cut wood with ebony mouldings, 124cm (49in) wide, *L 18 Dec,* £1,815 ($2,541)

5
A Biedermeier mahogany duet music stand, first half 19th century, with one static and one folding desk, and adjustable stem, *L 3 Apr,* £770 ($993)

6
A Biedermeier mahogany and marquetry games table, *c.*1825, 95cm (37½in) wide, *L 24 May,* £7,700 ($10,241)

7
A set of four Biedermeier walnut side chairs, *c.*1820, *NY 24 May,* $2,750 (£2,182)

8
A Biedermeier fruitwood settee, first quarter 19th century, 232cm (7ft 8in) long, *NY 23 Mar,* $2,750 (£2,350)

1

2

3

4

5

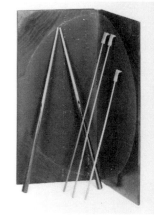

6

7

8

1
A Biedermeier satin-birch bookcase or vitrine, *c.*1820, 193cm (6ft 4in) high, *L 18 Dec*, £2,420 ($3,388)

2
A Biedermeier ash secretaire, *c*1820, the upper part with bow-fronted cupboard faced with ebonised pillars, 152cm (5ft) high, *L 18 Dec*, £3,960 ($5,544)

3
A Bidermeier mahogany pier cabinet, *c.*1830, 173cm (5ft 8in) high, *S 14 May*, £1,078 ($1,434)

4
A pair of Beidermeier fruitwood and ebonised display cabinets, *c.*1830, 184cm (6ft 1in) high, *L 18 Dec*, £2,420 ($3,388)

5
A Biedermeier ash cylinder bureau cabinet, *c.*1830, 214cm (7ft) high, *L 24 May*, £3,300 ($4,389)

6
A Biedermeier birch fall front secretaire, early 19th century, with ebonised interior, 138cm (54½in) high, *NY 23 Mar*, $3,575 (£3,056)

7
A Biedermeier oak and birch side board, first half 19th century, 204cm (88in) wide, *NY 5 Oct*, $2,475 (£1,755)

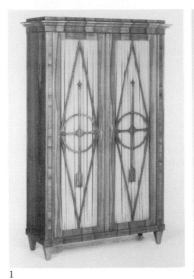

1

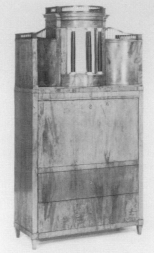

2

3

4

5

6

7

Altered and Restored Furniture

When one writes a catalogue description of an item of furniture it is customary to start from the top and to continue down to the base. Conversely, when one is ascertaining the amount of alteration to which a piece of furniture has been subjected, it is better to work from the base upward. For it is at floor-level that most furniture will suffer the most wear; during moving the feet are particularly prone to suffer damage in handling. Frequently the bracket feet on 18th century items have been replaced, or the height may have been reduced where the feet have worn (fig.1).

It is common for the rarer early 18th century items to have suffered deterioration. Such pieces were veneered onto a carcase of pine or deal, which are softwoods and are liable to woodworm. The pieces might have stood on a flagstone floor, and the washing-down of the floor would have caused the supports to absorb water, with the result that the timber would rot in due course. Consequently much furniture of this period has been restored by the replacement of legs and feet. (fig.3). This structural factor should always be taken into account when inspecting furniture for old repairs. A mahogany

—1—
A George III small mahogany chest, *c.*1760, with associated top, on reduced bracket feet, restored, 81cm (32in), *S 17 Sept,*
£682 ($1,023)

—2—
A George I solid walnut chest, *c.*1720, now on turned feet, 76cm (30in) wide, *C 11 July,*
£1,320 ($1,835)

—3—
A Dutch walnut and marquetry centre table, *c.*1690, later turned beech supports, now on castors, restored, 112cm (44in) wide, *S 11 June,*
£1,210 ($1,591)

—4—
A George II style gilt-wood and gesso pier table, incorporating some early 18th century pieces, 155cm (61in) wide, *C 18 Apr,*
£2,530 ($3,289)

—5—
A William and Mary oak chest on stand, *c.*1700, in two parts, the legs reduced in height and altered, 165cm (5ft 5in) high, *L 26 July,*
£550 ($808)

—1—

—2—

—3—

—4—

—5—

sideboard has a large, heavy carcase, and if the piece is moved carelessly the legs can break, necessitating repair or replacement. Sofa tables similarly suffer damage to their feet.

Oak furniture of the 16th and 17th centuries is likely to have undergone alteration, as it has been in use for hundreds of years, despite the fact that it is in the solid form and not veneered. Feet are often cut down, and consequently the stretcher rails are now at floor level. Often the original stem feet or bun feet have been replaced by the subsequently fashionable bracket feet (fig.9).

—6—
A George II mahogany side table, c.1740, on later acanthus carved cabriole legs, 75cm (29½in) wide, S 11 June, £1,210 ($1,591)

—7—
A mahogany low boy, reconstructed, 76cm (30in) high, C 8 Aug, £836 ($1,246)

—8—
A Charles II oak cupboard, c.1680, restored and with later top and plinth, 98cm (38½in) wide, C 17 Jan, £330 ($396)

—9—
A James II elm and fruitwood chest, c.1680, in two parts, on later bracket feet, 99cm (39in) square, C 17 Jan, £1,155 ($1,386)

—10—
A North Italian walnut and pine side table, c.1700, the associated rectangular top with a marble inset and inlaid surround, 100cm (39½in) wide, S 14 May, £902 ($1,200)

—11—
A William and Mary marquetry chest on stand, late 17th century, the stand re-constructed, 117cm (46½in) high, L 26 July, £5,060 ($7,438)

—6—

—7—

—8—

—9—

—10—

—11—

Larger items may have become so weak in the structural frame that they have to be reconstructed. This would involve replacing worn or damaged sections and rebuilding the piece with original parts. There is also the type of item which is referred to as *made-up*. To produce this, the cabinet-maker takes components from items of furniture from various periods, and makes a piece from these. For example, part of a 17th century coffer and table might be used to make a court cupboard or buffet, (figs.12 and 13). Pieces such as these are numerous, as the fashion for oak in the late Victorian period and during the early part of this century created a demand that was often met by the construction of these so-called antiques. It was easier and more profitable for a retailer to set a cabinet-maker to work on such an item, than to send out a buyer in quest of an original piece. Furthermore, the made-up pieces could be designed to a specific size, to satisfy fashion and a client's demands.

The whims of changing fashion also led to the improvement of items from their original form. The Victorians carved bold foliate scrolls onto plain 17th century oak furniture. Late 18th century satinwood has often been more elaborately painted in the 19th century than was originally conceived (fig.15).

To reveneer furniture to increase its value and appeal is not uncommon (fig.16). Oak bureaux and chests-of-drawers would normally be reveneered in walnut. Original examples, as has been stated, would normally have been veneered on pine or deal, so that a solid oak carcase may well indicate that subsequent reveneering has occurred.

A major alteration is the combining of two items into a single piece. There are various reasons for this: the original piece might well have been in two sections, which became separated over the years; an owner might have been unable to house a piece in its original form, or part might have been damaged or destroyed. Items that lend themselves to remaining as two

—12—
An Elizabeth I-style carved oak buffet, made-up, 170cm (5ft 7in) high, *S 19 Mar,* £825 ($1,015)

—13—
An Elizabethan-style carved oak court cupboard, made-up, 122cm (48in) wide, *S 11 June,* £440 ($579)

—14—
An oak joined back wainscot armchair, partly mid 17th century, the top rail inscribed John Cort, *C 17 Jan,* £418 ($502)

—15—
A George III oval satinwood-veneered Pembroke table, *c.*1780, with mid-19th century painted floral decoration, *L 12 Apr,* £4,180 ($5,350)

—12—

—13—

—14—

—15—

—16—

A George III painted satinwood bureau, late 18th century, re-veneered and painted, *c.*1900, 89cm (35in) wide, *L 22 Feb,* £3,190 ($3,637)

—17—

A George II walnut bureau, largely early 18th century, re-veneered and with restorations, 107cm (42in) high, *C 18 Apr,* £1,870 ($2,431)

—18—

A George II walnut oak bureau, *c.*1730, inlaid with featherbanding, formerly with a bookcase surmount, 84cm (31in) wide, *S 11 June,* £2,200 ($2,893)

—19—

A George III mahogany bureau, *c.*1750, with later Kingwood crossbanding and satinwood inlay, 94cm (37in) wide, *S 19 Feb,* £1,155 ($1,328)

—20—

A George III serpentine mahogany sideboard, *c.*1780, inlay on legs, *c.*1900, 206cm (6ft 9in) wide, *L 8 Mar,* £7,700 ($8,624)

—16—

—17—

—18—

—19—

—20—

pieces are chests-on-chests, sometimes referred to as tall-boys, which are easily modified into two chests-of-drawers. The bringing together of two items has often been referred to as a *marriage* — a term, however, which is not a guide to the age of both sections. If one takes a bureau bookcase as an example, the upper section, if considered to be the same age as the bureau, could be described as *associated* (fig.21): should the bookcase be later than the bureau, then it could be referred to as a *later* bookcase. Oak coffers may well have later tops, as the originals broke from their hinges, became damaged or were lost. Dressers are often found with unrelated shelf-backs.

Chairs can be subjected to considerable wear and as a consequence their legs and backs may well have been repaired. Single chairs might have been converted into armchairs at a later stage; such conversions can often be identified by a poor colour match and an unbalanced design. Chairs might be copied to match an existing set, and often the differing weight will betray these later examples. Again, a set of original chairs might be dismantled and the components combined with modern parts to produce a large *made-up* set. A table may be found to have a top or base different from that with which it started life — an alteration which, as so often, might have been prompted by damage to part of the original piece (fig.23).

—21—
A George III mahogany bureau bookcase, *c.*1760, with associated upper section, 223cm (7ft 6in) high, *S 22 Jan,* $2,090 (£2,477)

—22—
A mahogany break-front secretaire bookcase, partly early 19th century, with alterations and additions, 234cm (7ft 10in), *C 3 Oct,* £1,815 ($2,541)

—23—
A Regency mahogany three-pedestal dining table, *c.*1810, the top and bottom associated, 422cm (13ft 10in) long, *L 14 June,* £7,700 ($10,241)

—21—

—22—

—23—

Obviously the extent of restoration will be reflected in the value of an item of furniture. Some repairs are to be expected and will have little effect on the auction price, but some of the more severe restorations and changes can reduce a piece's financial worth. However, the scarcity of certain rare pieces can make even these considerations relatively insignificant.

Further reading

Herbert Cescinsky, *English Furniture of the 18th century*

Ralph Edwards, *The Dictionary of English Furniture*, 1954

● ANTHONY ROGERS ●

—24—
A George III mahogany bureau bookcase, *c.*1780, with associated upper part, later handles and feet, 225cm (7ft 4½in) high, *C 11 July,* £1,870 ($2,599)

—25—
A George III-style oak dresser, made-up, 150cm (59in) wide, *S 19 Feb,* £2,530 ($2,909)

—26—
A mahogany bureau bookcase, partly 18th century, but probably remodelled later, 221cm (7ft 3in) high, *C 18 Apr,* £1,980 ($2,574)

—27—
A George III mahogany cylinder bureau, *c.*1800, the top possibly associated, 130cm (38½in) high, *C 18 Apr,* £2,530 ($3,289)

—28—
A George III mahogany tripod table, *c.*1770, the top and base contemporary but associated, 69cm (27in), *C 12 July,* £550 ($764)

—24—

—25—

—26—

—27—

—28—

1
A Shaker birch wall shelf,
Canterbury, New Hampshire, *c.*1840, 122cm
(48in), *NY 2 Feb,*
$825 (£699)

2
A Shaker drying rack,
*c.*1830, painted grey,
106cm (42in) wide,
NY 2 Feb,
$192 (£162)

3
A Shaker maple and pine oval carrier, Mt Lebanon,
New York, *c.*1930, 37cm
(14½in), *NY 2 Feb,*
$330 (£279)

4
A Shaker poplar utility box, Mt Lebanon, New
York, *c.*1860, 34cm
(13½in) wide, *NY 2 Feb,*
$330 (£279)

5
A Monarch inlaid walnut and cast-iron snooker table, third quarter 19th
century, B A Stevens,
Toledo, Ohio, with
various accessories,
280cm (9ft 2in) long,
NY 30 Nov,
$7,979 (£5,352)

6
A Victorian cast-iron paraffin oil heater, *c.*1860,
with Gothic pierced
sides, 84cm (33in),
C 20 June,
£82 ($111)

7
A painted cast-iron umbrella stand, *c.*1850,
possibly Coalbrookdale,
84cm (33in), *C 20 June,*
£308 ($415)

8
A late Victorian mahogany three-quarter size snooker table, by Herbert Holt, 265cm (8ft
8½in) by 130cm (51in),
S 2 Apr,
£1,265 ($1,606)

9
A carved walnut umbrella stand, *c.*1880, 88.5cm
(34¾in) high, *NY 30 Mar,*
$1,870 (£1,508)

10
A Victorian mahogany hall stand, *c.*1870, 230.5cm
(7ft 7in) high, *C 6 June*
£1,375 ($1,856)

11
A George III oak linen press, *c.*1800, 173cm (68in)
high, *C 28 Mar,*
£935 ($1,187)

12
A Swiss carved bear umbrella stand, *c.*1900,
112cm (44in) high,
S 11 June,
£792 ($1,041)

1
**A George III rosewood
canterbury,** *c.*1800, 50cm
(19½in) high, *S 19 Mar,*
£550 ($677)

2
**A Regency rosewood
canterbury,** *c.*1810, 56cm
(22in) high, *S 11 June,*
£990 ($1,302)

3
**A George III mahogany
four-division canterbury,**
*c.*1800, 50cm (19½in)
wide, *S 15 Oct,*
£1,320 ($1,954)

4
**A George IV mahogany
canterbury,** *c.*1825, 84cm
(33in) high, *L 10 May,*
£1,100 ($1,419)

5
**A Victorian walnut can-
terbury,** *c.*1860, *C 28 Feb,*
£374 ($419)

6
**A Regency brass-
mounted rosewood can-
terbury,** *c.*1810, 80cm
(31½in) high, *NY 13 Apr,*
$8,525 (£6,820)

7
**A Victorian walnut can-
terbury,** *c.*1860, 88cm
(26½in) high, *L 22 Feb,*
£858 ($978)

8
**A Victorian rosewood
whatnot,** *c.*1880, 109cm
(42¾in) high, *C 11 July,*
£495 ($688)

9
**A George III mahogany
whatnot,** *c.*1800, 107cm
(42in) high, *C 18 Apr,*
£935 ($1,216)

10
**A Victorian rosewood
whatnot,** *c.*1850, 103cm
(40½in) high, *C 18 Apr,*
£605 ($787)

11
A mahogany whatnot,
*c.*1820, 160cm (63in) high,
C 18 Apr,
£1,045 ($1,359)

12
**A George III mahogany
whatnot,** *c.*1800, 137cm
(54in) high, *S 12 Nov,*
£715 ($1,001)

13
**A Victorian rosewood
whatnot,** *c.*1850, 117cm
(46in) high, *S 16 Apr,*
£704 ($915)

14
**A Dutch mahogany
hanging corner étagère,**
*c.*1770, with bow front
tambour cupboard,
102cm (40in) high,
C 12 July,
£1,595 ($2,217)

15
**A set of late George III
rosewood hanging
shelves,** *c.*1785, crossbanded in tulipwood,
127cm (50in) high,
L 14 June,
£5,720 ($7,607)

1
A George II dumb
waiter, *c*.1755, 83cm
(32½in) high, *L 7 June*,
£1,595 ($2,121)

2
A George II walnut
dumb waiter, *c*.1750,
110cm (43½in) high,
L 1 Feb,
£1,155 ($1,316)

3
A George III mahogany
dumb waiter, *c*.1790,
109cm (43in) high,
C 17 Jan,
£605 ($726)

4
A George III mahogany
wine cistern on stand,
c.1775, 64cm (25¼in)
wide, *NY 11 Oct*,
$4,400 (£3,121)

5
A George III mahogany
cellarette, *c*.1780, 53cm
(21in) high, *NY 1 Nov*,
$3,575 (£2,482)

6
A George III brass
mounted mahogany wine
cooler, *c*.1800, lead liner,
56cm (22in) high,
NY 13 Apr,
$1,760 (£1,400)

7
A George III brass bound
mahogany wine cooler,
c.1770, on a contempor-
ary fluted stand, 75cm
(29½in) high, *C 11 May*,
£2,310 ($3,211)

8
A George III mahogany
cellarette, *c*.1800, 64cm
(25in) high, *C 3 Oct*,
£1,045 ($1,463)

9
A George III mahogany
wine cooler, *c*.1805,
restored, 66cm (26in)
wide, *C 31 Oct*,
£286 ($429)

10
A Regency mahogany
wine cooler, *c*.1820, in
the manner of Gillows,
69cm (27½in) wide,
L 14 June,
£5,720 ($7,607)

11
A William IV carved
mahogany wine cooler,
c.1835, of sarcophagus
form, 97cm (38in) wide,
S 15 Oct,
£2,310 ($3,419)

12
A George III satinwood
cutlery box, *c*.1790,
original fitted interior,
38cm (15in) high, *C 17 Jan*,
£528 ($634)

13
A George III satinwood
and marquetry cutlery
box, *c*.1770, 41cm (16in)
high, *L 22 Nov*,
£770 ($1,078)

14
A pair of Federal inlaid
mahogany knife boxes,
American, *c*.1790, silver
mounts, 37cm (14½in)
high, *NY 2 Feb*,
$2,970 (£2,700)

1
A Cape teak brass-bound
water vat, 19th century,
95cm (37½in) high,
JHB 29 Aug,
R 1,700 (£533; $784)

2
An English revolving
wine cistern in lignum
vitae, late 17th century,
with brass tap, 58cm
(22¾in) high, *L 20 Mar,*
£3,800 ($4,674)

3
A pair of George III
brass-mounted mahogany
plate buckets, *c.*1770,
41cm (16¼in), *NY 1 Nov,*
$8,250 (£5,729)

4
A mahogany plate and
cutlery stand, early 19th
century, 76cm (30in)
high, *C 18 Apr,*
£2,860 ($3,718)

5
A Regency mahogany
plate and cutlery stand,
*c.*1820, 79cm (31in) high,
L 8 Mar,
£3,850 ($4,312)

6
An early George III
mahogany tray, *c.*1760,
with brass-inlaid mould-
ing, 71cm (28in),
L 8 Mar,
£2,420 ($2,710)

7
A George III mahogany
cheese coaster, *c.*1800, on
brass castors, 40.5cm
(16in) wide, *HS 4 June,*
£682 ($921)

8
A walnut cheese coaster,
*c.*1810, 43cm (17in) wide,
C 17 Jan,
£220 ($264)

9
A mahogany and brass-
bound plate bucket,
*c.*1810, 56cm (22in) high,
C 17 Jan,
£792 ($950)

10
A George III coopered
mahogany bread dish,
*c.*1790, the sides bound in
brass, 37cm (14½in) wide,
C 17 Jan,
£616 ($739)

11
A French rosewood
liqueur case, *c.*1890, 32cm
(13½in) wide, *S 19 Mar,*
£451 ($555)

12
A Napoleon III gilt-
bronze mounted boulle
marquetry decanter set,
*c.*1860, with four decanters and fourteen liqueur
glasses, 28cm (11in) high,
NY 30 Mar,
$1,430 (£1,153)

13
An early George III
mahogany dining room
pedestal and urn, *c.*1775,
the urn with detachable
lid, 165cm (5ft 5in),
L 8 Mar,
£3,080 ($3,450)

1
A Victorian walnut music cabinet, *c.*1860, 105cm (41½in) high, *S 19 Mar,* £770 ($947)

2
A walnut music canterbury, Lamb of Manchester, 1870, 87cm (34in) high, *C 18 Apr,* £1,265 ($1,645)

3
An early 19th century mahogany music stand, *c.*1810, 96cm (38in) high, *L 1 Feb,* £1,870 ($2,132)

4
An ebony and marquetry music cabinet, *c.*1880, 121cm (47½in) high, *C 7 June,* £352 ($475)

5
An Empire style gilt-bronze mounted mahogany music stand, *c.*1880, 102cm (40in) high, *NY 22 June,* $715 (£558)

6
An Empire gilt-metal and painted wood music stand, first quarter 19th century, 130cm (51in) high, *NY 5 Oct,* $1,210 (£858)

7
A Victorian walnut adjustable duet piano stool, *c.*1880, 107cm (42in) wide, *S 14 May,* £528 ($702)

8
A walnut and gilt piano stool, mid 19th century, with adjustable seat, *C 3 Oct,* £484 ($678)

9
An English rosewood duet music stand, *c.*1835, adjustable desks and stem, *L 3 Apr,* £770 ($993)

10
A William IV mahogany and parcel-gilt duet stand, *c.*1830, adjustable stem, 89cm (35in) wide, *C 16 May,* £286 ($380)

11
A patent iron and brass music stool, C H Hare & Son, *c.*1890, 47cm (18½in) wide, *C 7 June,* £187 ($252)

12
A Sheraton revival mahogany and marquetry music stand, *c.*1900, 135cm (53in) high, *C 17 Jan,* £484 ($581)

1
A set of mahogany library steps, c.1840, 71cm (28in), *C 14 Nov,*
£495 ($693)

2
A Victorian oak folio stand, c.1870, 94cm (37in), *S 16 Apr,*
£990 ($1,287)

3
A Regency mahogany book carrier, c.1800, 43cm (17in) wide, *HS 16 July,*
£880 ($1,276)

4
A George IV rosewood book carrier, c.1825, 66cm (26in) wide, *L 14 June,*
£770 ($1,024)

5
A Regency burr walnut book trough, c.1810, 42cm (16½in), *S 22 Jan,*
£506 ($600)

6
A malachite and gilt-bronze inkstand, c.1870, 27cm (10½in) wide, *L 21 June,*
£990 ($1,287)

7
A Restauration bronze and gilt-bronze inkstand, c.1820, in the form of a neo-classical barge, with twined snake handles, 37cm (14½in) wide, *L 5 July,*
£1,265 ($1,746)

8
A Louis XIV boulle ink-stand, early 18th century, with brass scrolling foliage on a tortoiseshell ground, 35.5cm (14in), *L 5 July,*
£1,210 ($1,670)

9
A Regency boulle ink-stand, c.1820, in ebonised wood and cut brass, the base with a drawer, 31cm (16in) wide, *L 8 Mar,*
£638 ($715)

10
A Charles X ormolu-mounted maple jar-dinière, c.1830, 109cm (43in) wide, *NY 5 Oct,*
$1,760 (£1,248)

11
A Regency rosewood pen tray, c.1810, on gilt ball feet, 23cm (6in) wide, *C 17 Jan,*
£484 ($581)

12
A Victorian writing box, c.1870, walnut and brass mounted, 35cm (13¾in) wide, *S 19 Mar,*
£352 ($433)

13
A pair of ormolu-mounted marquetry jar-dinières, c.1870, with lidded tops, 94cm (37in), *L 22 Mar,*
£660 ($792)

14
A mahogany jardinière, 19th century, 52cm (20½in), *A 22 May,*
Dfl 899 (£209; $277)

15
A Victorian combined stationery and writing box, c.1900, rosewood, with brass carrying handles, 37cm (14½in) wide, *S 11 June,*
£308 ($405)

1
A set of four lead garden figures of the Seasons, 18th century, probably English, 48.5cm (19in), *L 4 July*, £3,740 ($5,161)

2
A sandstone figure of a lion couchant, 46cm (18in) wide, *C 28 Nov*, £374 ($524)

3
An English pine and wire birdcage, late 19th century, 38cm (15in) high, *NY 8 Oct*, $1,100 (£743)

4
A rustic cast-iron garden seat, *c*.1870, with wooden seat, 156cm (61in), *S 17 Sept*, £550 ($825)

5
A lead cistern, English, dated 1779, 90cm (35½in) wide, *S 19 Mar*, £704 ($866)

6
A white-lacquered cast-iron garden suite, end 19th century, comprising eight pieces, garden seat 126cm (49½in) wide, *M 25 June*, FF 33,300 (£2,775; $3,746)

7
A wrought iron demi lune seat, English, early 19th century, 279.4cm (9ft 2in) wide, *C 11 July*, £968 ($1,346)

8
A pair of Gothic style cast-iron benches, English, late 19th century, with slat seats, *NY 30 Nov*, $3,300 (£2,215)

9
A Coalbrookdale bronze fern garden seat, 1870s, known as the 'Osmunda Regalis' seat, 175cm (5ft 9in) wide, *L 19 July*, £8,020 ($12,628)

10
A pair of cast-iron garden benches, American, 19th century, stamped Peter Tinmes & Son, Bkyn, NY, *NY 22 June*, $5,500 (£4,296)

11
A pair of cast-iron garden urns, 19th century, 76cm (30in) high, *C 5 Sept*, £506 ($743)

12
A pair of cast-iron garden urns, *c*.1840, 76cm (30in) high, *L 26 July*, £1,100 ($1,617)

13
A pair of cast-iron garden urns, *c*.1830, 61cm (24in) high, *L 8 Mar*, £2,420 ($2,710)

1   2   3

4   5

6

7   8

9   10

11   12   13

An ormulu, marble and bluejohn urn, mid 19th century, 17cm (6½in) high, *S 19 Feb,* £968 ($1,113)

A bluejohn vase, 19th century, 13cm (5¼in) high, *C 18 Apr,* £308 ($400)

A pair of French brass azze, *c.*1850, stamped VP, each supported by three cherub terms, 21.5cm (8½in) high, *L 22 Mar,* £572 ($686)

4
A pair of Louis XVI gilt-bronze and white marble vases, *c.*1780, of classical form, 26cm (10½in), *L 5 July,* £1,540 ($2,125)

5
A pair of Louis XVI ormolu and marble cassolettes, *c.*1775, 30cm (11¾in) high, *NY 4 May,* $8,800 (£7,333)

6
A set of four gilt-metal curtain tie backs, American, *c.*1835, 15cm (6in) diam, *NY 2 Feb,* $1,210 (£1,025)

7
A pair of French gilt-bronze mounted 'verde antico' marble urns, *c.*1880, 64cm (25in) high, *L 8 Nov,* £3,080 ($4,620)

8
A George II mahogany pole screen, *c.*1750, the banner worked in 'gros' and 'petit' point, 170cm (5ft 7in) high, *L 8 Mar,* £2,310 ($2,587)

9
A Chippendale pole screen, Massachusetts, probably Salem, *c.*1780, with adjustable floral needlework panel, 149cm (58½in) high, *NY 2 Feb,* $2,750 (£2,500)

10
A pair of George III mahogany pole screens, *c.*1775, with oval upholstered screens, 147cm (58in) high, *NY 8 June,* $2,200 (£1,746)

11
A pair of late George III painted satinwood pole screens, early 19th century, the panel interiors painted with landscape scenes, 145cm (57in), *L 8 Mar,* £1,815 ($2,033)

12
A pair of Victorian rosewood pole screens, *c.*1840, 141cm (53½in) high, *S 11 June,* £572 ($752)

13
A pair of fire screens, *c.*1850, lacquered in gold and polychrome, with adjustable rectangular screen, 146cm (57½in) high, *C 17 Jan,* £572 ($686)

1   2   3
4   5   6
7   8   9
10   11   12   13

1
A set of rosewood and
brass mechanical bellows,
c.1820, 63.5cm (25in),
C 17 Jan,
£374 ($449)

2
A set of mechanical bel-
lows, c.1830, with beech
body and brass mounted
funnel, lacking wheel,
68.5cm (27in), *C 17 Jan,*
£33 ($40)

3
A Louis XV walnut bel-
lows, mid 18th century,
with ormolu tip, 71.5cm
(28¼in) high, *NY 9 Nov,*
$5,500 (£3,873)

4
A pair of Victorian cast-
iron and steel fenders,
c.1860, each with 'Gothic'
arches, 142 and 131cm
(56 and 51½in), *C 11 July,*
£550 ($765)

5
A pair of American brass
and wrought-iron and-
irons, 18th century, 50cm
(19½in) high, *NY 2 Feb,*
$495 (£419)

6
A George III mahogany
and brass-bound peat
bucket, c.1760, 36cm
(14in) wide, *S 15 Oct,*
£1,155 ($1,709)

7
A George III mahogany
and brass-bound oval
peat bucket, c.1770, with
brass liner, 33cm (13in)
wide, *S 22 Jan,*
£495 ($587)

8
A pair of Egyptian
Revival bronze andirons,
c.1890, 94.5cm (37¼in)
high, *NY 22 June,*
$2,310 (£1,805)

9
A japanned and glazed
coal scuttle, c.1850, of
'Gothic' outline, the
cover with mother-of-
pearl panels, 61cm (24in)
wide, *C 12 Dec,*
£187 ($262)

10
A George III mahogany
navette-form brass-bound
peat bucket, late 18th
century, 30cm (11¾in)
high, *NY 8 June,*
$1,430 (£1,135)

11
A pair of American brass
and wrought-iron eagle-
engraved andirons,
Philadelphia, c.1795,
46cm (18in) high,
NY 2 Feb,
$7,150 (£6,500)

12
A pair of Louis XVI
gilt-bronze chenets, 43cm
(17in) high, *M 24 June,*
FF 49,950
(£4,025; $5,393)

13
A pair of Louis XV style
gilt-bronze chenets, late
19th century, sold with a
fender, 44cm (17½in)
high, *NY 30 Mar,*
$880 (£710)

14
A pair of Louis XV
gilt-bronze chenets,
c.1740, 35cm (14½in)
high, *L 5 July,*
£2,640 ($3,643)

1
A George III carved
gesso and pine mantel-
piece, late 18th century,
NY 1 Nov,
$4,950 (£3,437)

2
A George III carved pine
mantelpiece, mid 18th
century, 201cm (6ft 7in)
wide, NY 26 Jan,
$9,350 (£8,423)

3
A Victorian fire screen,
c.1870, carved and gilt-
gesso framed, 107cm
(42in) high, S 19 Feb,
£374 ($430)

4
A George III carved
white marble chimney-
piece, c.1700, in the style
of Robert Adam, with
steel basket grate and
engraved steel surround.
117cm (46in) wide,
L 15 Nov,
£13,200 ($18,480)

5
A Victorian rosewood fire
screen, c.1870, with
needlework panel, 121cm
(47½in) high, C 14 Mar,
£187 ($213)

6
A pair of Flemish walnut
and parcel-gilt torchères,
mid 18th century, 111cm
(43½in), L 24 May,
£2,750 ($3,658)

7
A pair of George III
carved giltwood and gesso
torchères, c.1780, the tops
with Vitruvian scrolls
and flowerheads,
L 15 Nov,
£3,300 ($4,620)

8
An Italian carved pine
torchère, c.1800, 112cm
(44in) high, L 8 Nov,
£792 ($1,188)

9
An Italian polychrome
blackamoor figure, hold-
ing a torchère, c.1800,
230cm (7ft 6½in) high,
L 8 Nov,
£1,870 ($2,805)

10
A pair of parcel-gilt
bronze torchères, by
Barbedienne of Paris,
1875, signed, 218cm (7ft
2in), L 22 Mar,
£14,850 ($17,820)

11
A set of four Louis XVI
style giltwood torchères,
c.1900, 160cm (5ft 3in)
high, NY 30 Mar,
$2,475 (£1,996)

1

2

3

4

5

6

7

8

9

10

11

1
A pair of late Louis XIV gilt-bronze wall-lights, early 18th century, 18cm (7in), *L 5 July*, £1,100 ($1,518)

2
A set of four Louis XV ormolu two-light wall-lights, mid 18th century, 53.5cm (21in), *NY 8 Nov*, $14,300 (£10,070)

3
A pair of Louis XV ormolu two-light wall-lights, mid 18th century, 32cm (16½in), *NY 5 Oct*, $2,200 (£1,560)

4
A pair of Louis XV gilt-bronze wall-lights, *c.*1765, in the form of entwined lily branches, 49cm (19in), *L 5 July*, £10,450 ($14,421)

5
A pair of George III gilt-brass and cut-glass five-light wall-lights, late 18th century, *NY 1 Nov*, $5,225 (£3,628)

6
A pair of Louis XVI ormolu three-light wall-lights, last quarter 18th century, 56cm (22in), *NY 4 May*, $11,000 (£9,167)

7
A pair of Empire gilt-bronze wall-lights, *c.*1800, 43cm (17in), *L 29 Nov*, £5,500 ($7,700)

8
A set of four Louis XVI style gilt-bronze sconces, 71cm (28in), *NY 22 June*, $3,025 (£2,363)

9
A pair of Empire style parcel-gilt-bronze two-light sconces, 19th century, each in the form of a winged female figure, 58cm (23in), *NY 30 Mar*, $715 (£577)

10
A William and Mary brass table candlestand, 20.5cm (8in), *L 26 Apr*, £1,265 ($1,606)

11
A pair of Louix XIV ormolu candlesticks, late 17th century, the bases with addorsed dolphins, 19cm (7½in), *NY 24 May*, $1,980 (£1,571)

12
A pair of Régence candlesticks, *c.*1720, 18cm (7in), *NY 9 Nov*, $9,900 (£6,972)

13
A pair of Louis XV ormolu candlesticks, mid 18th century, each with asymmetrical nozzle, 24cm (9½in), *NY 8 Nov*, $4,125 (£2,905)

14
A pair of early George III gilt-bronze candlesticks, *c.*1760, detachable nozzles, 26cm (10½in), *L 14 June*, £1,100 ($1,463)

15
A pair of George III mahogany and brass candlesticks, *c.*1780, 34cm (13½in), *L 22 Nov*, £715 ($1,001)

16
A pair of Louis XVI ormolu candlesticks, last quarter 18th century, 29cm (11½in), *NY 5 Oct*, $1,870 (£1,326)

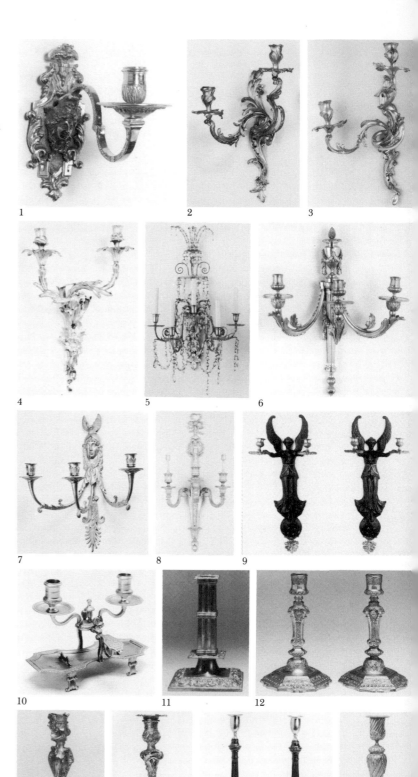

1   2   3
4   5   6
7   8   9
10   11   12
13   14   15   16

1
A pair of Louis XVI
ormolu three-light
candelabra, last quarter
18th century, the bases
with white marble panels
and Jasperware medal-
lions, 47cm (18½in),
NY 9 Nov,
$51,700 (£36,408)

2
A pair of Louis XVI
patinated and gilt-bronze
candelabra, 56cm (22in),
M 23 June,
FF 49,950
(£4,025; $5,393)

3
A pair of late Louis XVI
ormolu and patinated
bronze four-light candel-
abra, late 18th century,
41cm (16in), *NY 4 May,*
$3,300 (£2,750)

4
A pair of Regency gilt-
bronze gas lamps, *c.*1815,
58cm (33in), *L 8 Mar,*
£2,090 ($2,341)

5
A pair of Empire parcel-
gilt bronze five-light
candelabra, 19th century,
80cm (32½in), *NY 30 Mar,*
$1,870 (£1,508)

6
A pair of George IV
yew-wood candlesticks,
*c.*1825, 20.5cm (8in),
L 26 July,
£396 ($542)

7
A pair of George IV gilt
and patinated bronze
candlesticks, *c.*1820, now
fitted for electricity, 42cm
(16½in) high, *C 18 Apr,*
£1,012 ($1,316)

8
A pair of Charles X
ormolu candlesticks,
*c.*1825, 30cm (11¾in),
NY 23 Mar,
$2,310 (£1,974)

9
A pair of Charles X
ormolu six-light candel-
abra, *c.*1825, 61.5cm
(24¼in), *NY 9 Nov,*
$6,325 (£4,454)

10
A pair of gilt-bronze
table candelabra, *c.*1840,
52cm (20½in), *L 22 Feb,*
£660 ($752)

11
A pair of gilt-bronze and
porcelain candlesticks,
*c.*1860, 31cm (12in),
L 22 Mar,
£1,210 ($1,452)

12
A pair of French bronze
and gilt-bronze candel-
abra, *c.*1880, 73cm
(28¾in) high, *A 26 Feb,*
Dfl 2,204 (£540; $605)

13
A pair of bronze and
gilt-bronze table candel-
abra, *c.*1880, on 'griotte'
marble bases, 46cm
(18in), *L 21 June,*
£1,100 ($1,430)

14
A pair of Louis XVI style
gilt-bronze candelabra,
late 19th century, each
with stems formed from
three addorsed female
figures, *L 8 Nov,*
£1,320 ($1,980)

15
A pair of Régence style
gilt-bronze candlesticks,
*c.*1880, 26cm (10¼in)
high, *C 18 Apr,*
£495 ($634)

1
A gilt and patinated bronze student's lamp, 1830, with green tôle shades, 50cm (19½in) high, *C 18 Apr,*
£1,760 ($2,288)

2
A pair of Empire ormolu bouillotte lamps, first quarter 19th century, with adjustable green 'tôle peinte' shades, 64cm (25in), *NY 9 Nov,*
$10,450 (£7,359)

3
A Louis XVI style ormolu bouillotte lamp, first half 19th century, with later green tôle shade, *NY 24 May,*
$1,760 (£1,396)

4
A pair of parcel-gilt cast-iron and glass Argand lamps, second half 19th century, 53.5cm (21in), *NY 30 Nov,*
$1,100 (£738)

5
A pair of Regency parcel-gilt bronze Argand lamps, c.1820, with label of Johnston Brookes & Co./ Manufacturers/London, 36cm (14¼in), *NY 8 Oct,*
$935 (£632)

6
A pair of gilt metal and etched glass Argand lamps, American, c.1830, 43cm (17in), *NY 1 Feb,*
$3,850 (£3,500)

7
A painted and gilt tin and glass Kerosene lamp, probably Continental, early 19th century, 53cm (21in), *NY 1 Feb,*
$770 (£700)

8
A ruby glass and gilt bronze oil lamp, c.1860, 62cm (24½in), *C 6 June,*
£396 ($535)

9
A gilt-bronze and cut-glass oil lamp, late 19th century, 58.5cm (23in), *C 6 June,*
£187 ($252)

10
A blown amethyst glass and cast-metal hurricane lamp, American, early 19th century, lower section 35cm (14in), *NY 2 Feb,*
$3,575 (£3,029)

11
A Regency brass lantern, c.1825, of hexagonal shape, 79cm (31in), *L 12 Apr,*
£2,200 ($2,816)

12
A George IV gilt-metal lantern, of hexagonal shape, 91cm (36in), *L 8 Mar,*
£2,200 ($2,464)

13
A pair of Empire bronze and gilt-bronze lamps, by Carcel, early 19th century, 97cm (38in), *L 5 July,*
£15,400 ($21,252)

14
A pair of Venetian bronze lanterns, 19th century, adapted for electricity, 52cm (20½in), *F 26 Mar,*
L 2,600,000 (£1,042; $1,323)

15
A Victorian copper and white metal station lamp, c.1840, 115.5cm (45½in) high, *C 5 Sept,*
£440 ($646)

1   2   3   4   5   6   7   8   9   10   11   12   13   14   15

1
An early Georgian brass six-light chandelier, first quarter 18th century, 48cm (19in), *NY 1 Nov,* $2,475 (£1,718)

2
A Baltic gilt-bronze and glass chandelier, *c.*1795, 100cm (39½in), *L 24 May,* £6,600 ($8,778)

3
A gilt-bronze and rock crystal chandelier, late 18th century, 90cm (35½in), *M 24 June,* FF 55,500 (£4,472; $5,993)

4
An Empire ormolu and patinated bronze four-light chandelier, early 19th century, 83cm (32½in), *NY 24 May,* $2,750 (£2,182)

5
A brass chandelier, English or Dutch, 19th century, *NY 2 Feb,* $5,775 (£4,894)

6
A Louis XV style gilt-metal and glass twelve-light chandelier, of cage form, 112cm (44in), *NY 22 June,* $2,310 (£1,805)

7
A Regency style gilt-bronze and glass nine-light chandelier, modern, 97cm (38in), *NY 30 Mar,* $1,980 (£1,597)

8
An Empire style silvered metal and glass six-light chandelier, 87cm (34in), *NY 30 Mar,* $1,430 (£1,153)

9
A gilt-bronze twelve-light chandelier, third quarter 19th century, 94cm (37in), *L 22 Mar,* £660 ($792)

1
A William and Mary walnut wall mirror, *c.*1690, the replaced bevelled plate contained by cyma mouldings, 71cm (28in) high, *C 17 Jan,*
£605 ($726)

2
A William and Mary oyster and marquetry mirror, *c.*1700, formerly with a cresting, 110cm (43½in) high, *NY 26 Jan,*
$4,400 (£3,963)

3
A George I giltwood reverse etched and blue glass overmantel mirror, *c.*1725, 155cm (5ft 1in) wide, *NY 13 Apr,*
$3,850 (£3,080)

4
An Irish Regency cut-glass mirror, *c.*1815, 66cm (26in) high, *NY 26 Jan,*
$3,850 (£3,468)

5
A Dutch carved-wood overmantel, late 17th century, with a baroque strapwork surround, now with polychrome paint, 160cm (5ft 3in), *L 18 Dec,*
£1,100 ($1,540)

6
An Italian giltwood mirror, early 18th century, 184cm (6ft ½in), *NY 24 May,*
$2,970 (£2,357)

7
An Italian giltwood and verre eglomisé mirror, late 17th century, the border with silver scroll-work on a red ground, 157cm (5ft 2in) high, *L 24 May,*
£11,000 ($14,630)

8
A late Louis XIV gilt-wood and gesso girandole mirror, *c.*1710, 55cm (21½in) high, *L 5 July,*
£715 ($987)

9
A Régence giltwood mirror, *c.*1715, the cresting flanked by hoho birds, 173cm (5ft 8in) high, *NY 4 May,*
$10,450 (£8,708)

10
A Louis XV giltwood mirror, mid 18th century, 150cm (59in) high, *NY 23 Mar,*
$4,400 (£3,761)

11
A Régence style giltwood mirror, 19th century, 191cm (6ft 3in), *NY 22 June,*
$4,400 (£3,437)

12
A pair of Venetian rococo giltwood mirrors, mid 18th century, surmounted by an architectural cresting, 161cm (5ft 3½in), *NY 8 Nov,*
$5,775 (£4,067)

13
A pair of North Italian giltwood mirrors, mid 18th century, the crestings with chinoiserie parasols, 191cm (6ft 3in), *L 29 Nov,*
£7,700 ($10,780)

14
A George II gilt-gesso mirror, *c.*1735, 118cm (46½in) high, *L 1 Feb,*
£2,860 ($3,260)

15
A George II giltwood pier glass, *c.*1735, cartouche and mirror replaced, 187cm (6ft 1½in) high, *L 8 Mar,*
£2,640 ($2,957)

16
An early George III gilt-wood wall mirror, *c.*1760, 137cm (54in), *L 26 July,*
£2,640 ($3,880)

17
A George III giltwood mirror, *c.*1765, with a chinoiserie structure at the cresting, 155cm (5ft 1in), *NY 1 Nov,*
$14,850 (£10,312)

18
An early George III gilt-wood wall mirror, *c.*1760, the cresting surmounted by an exotic bird, 183cm (6ft) high, *L 8 Mar,*
£4,180 ($4,682)

1   2   3

4   5   6

7   8   9   10

11   12   13   14

15   16   17   18

1
An Italian neoclassical giltwood pier mirror, last quarter 18th century, surmounted by hoho birds, 175cm (5ft 9in), *NY 23 Mar,*
$6,875 (£5,876)

2
A pair of George III giltwood pier glasses, *c.*1795, 211cm (6ft 11in) high, *L 8 Mar,*
£23,100 ($25,872)

3
A George III giltwood overmantel glass, late 18th century, cresting lacking, 159cm (5ft 2½in) wide, *L 15 Nov,*
£2,640 ($3,696)

4
An Italian mirror, carved and gilt, *c.*1850, 220cm (7ft 2½in) high, *S 19 Mar,*
£5,060 ($6,224)

5
A George II style walnut wall mirror, 20th century, 104cm (41in) high, *C 16 May,*
£275 ($366)

6
A George III mahogany wall mirror, *c.*1770, 108cm (42½in) high, *C 3 Oct,*
£2,530 ($3,542)

7
A Chippendale parcel-gilt and walnut mirror, American, *c.*1770, with removable candle-holders, 152cm (59¾in), *NY 2 Feb,*
$12,100 (£11,000)

8
A pair of mid Georgian style mahogany wall mirrors, *c.*1910, 104cm (41in), *C 17 Jan,*
£462 ($554)

9
A pair of giltwood pier glasses, mid 19th century, 184cm (6ft ½in), *L 12 Apr,*
£3,300 ($4,224)

10
An American giltwood wall mirror, *c.*1825, 94cm (37in) high, *NY 1 Feb,*
$17,600 (£16,000)

11
A gilt composition overmantel mirror, *c.*1780, 188cm (74in) wide, *C 12 Dec,*
£462 ($647)

1
A Regency giltwood and ebonised convex mirror, c.1815, 94cm (37in) high, NY 13 Apr, $4,675 (£3,740)

2
A Regency gilt gesso girandole, c.1815, 58.5cm (23in) high, C 18 Apr, £1,045 ($1,359)

3
A Regency gilt gesso convex wall mirror, c.1815, 124.5cm (49in) high, C 17 Jan, £770 ($924)

4
A Queen Anne walnut toilet mirror, c.1710, restored, 96cm (38in) high, S 11 June, £550 ($723)

5
A late Georgian rosewood toilet mirror, c.1810, 62cm (24½in) high, C 6 June, £220 ($297)

6
A George III mahogany toilet mirror, c.1790, 61cm (24in) high, C 12 July, £275 ($382)

7
A Regency brass-inlaid toilet mirror, c.1820, 68cm (24½in) high, L 14 June, £1,056 ($1,404)

8
A Federal carved mahogany cheval glass, New York, c.1810, 165cm (5ft 5in), NY 1 Feb, $3,630 (£3,300)

9
A Federal inlaid mahogany and ivory shaving mirror, c.1810, 48cm (19in) high, NY 1 Feb, $1,100 (£1,000)

10
A Federal inlaid mahogany dressing mirror, American, c.1810, 69cm (27in) high, NY 2 Feb, $715 (£605)

11
A George IV mahogany spiral-reeded cheval dressing mirror, c.1825, S 16 Apr, £638 ($829)

12
An early Victorian mahogany cheval mirror, 95cm (37½in) wide, S 13 Aug, £132 ($197)

13
A Victorian mahogany cheval mirror, c.1850, 198cm (78in) high, C 17 Oct, £660 ($977)

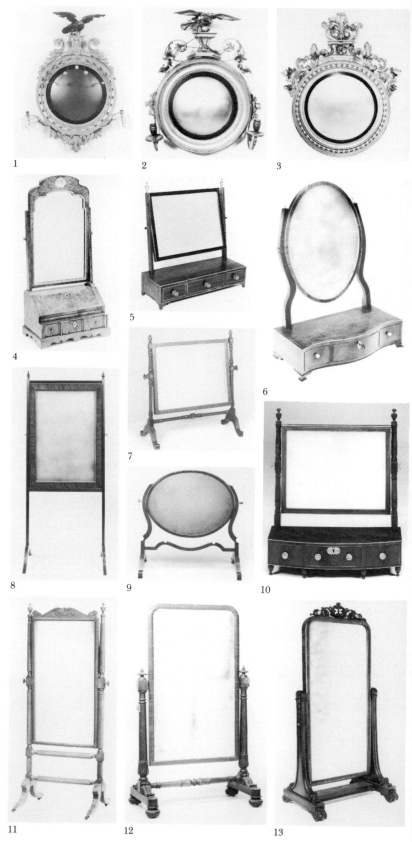

1
A painted and stencilled tin basket, 19th century, painted red, 30cm (12in) wide, *NY 1 Feb,*
$770 (£700)

2
A pair of Empire tôle peinte verrières, 19th century, with polychrome reserves depicting fowl and game, on a green ground, 32.5cm (12¾in) wide, *NY 23 Mar,*
$2,530 (£2,162)

3
A pair of painted and decorated tin vases, Continental, early 19th century, with faux marble bases, 24cm (9½in), *NY 1 Feb,*
$1,210 (£1,100)

4
A tôle jardiniere, *c.*1800, japanned and gilt with figures on a red ground, 41cm (16in) wide, *C 3 Oct,*
£770 ($1,078)

5
A pair of tôle chestnut urns, late 18th century, painted and gilt with flowers on a black ground, *C 12 July,*
£1,375 ($1,911)

6
An American tin plate warming stand, 19th century, painted black and gold and stencilled with leaves, 73cm (28½in), *NY 1 Feb,*
$1,210 (£1,100)

7
A William IV pair of tôle urns and covers, *c.*1825, with gilt flowers on black, 32cm (12½in), *L 7 June,*
£1,980 ($2,633)

8
A Regency papier-mâché jardiniere on stand, *c.*1820, the body decorated in imitation of Chinese lacquer, 73cm (28¾in), *L 27 Sept,*
£1,430 ($2,116)

9
A Pontypool japanned tin tray, early 19th century, 78cm (31in) wide, *S 14 May,*
£330 ($439)

10
A George IV papier-mâché tray, *c.*1825, with burgundy ground, 80cm (31½in) wide, *S 22 Jan,*
£880 ($1,043)

11
A pair of Regency papier-mâché fans, *c.*1820, transfer decorated within a gilt border, ebony handle, 46cm (18in) long, *C 18 Apr,*
£308 ($400)

12
A Regency tôle peinte tray, *c.*1815, the reserve depicting a classically draped woman and a lion, 76cm (30in), *NY 8 Oct,*
$1,540 (£1,041)

13
A Victorian japanned and tinned coal bin, *c.*1860s, with painted flowers on a black ground, 56cm (22in) wide, *S 17 Sept,*
£440 ($660)

14
A Victorian papier-mâché work table, *c.*1860, decorated with gilt and inlaid with mother-of-pearl, the cover revealing a green silk-lined interior with compartments, 47cm (18½in) diam, *S 16 Apr,*
£462 ($601)

15
A Regency gilt-decorated scarlet japanned papier-mâché tray, *c.*1810, on later stand, 67cm (26½in) high, *NY 1 Nov,*
$6,875 (£4,774)

Tunbridgeware

Buying souvenirs has long been popular as a way of remembering visits and holidays. Tunbridgeware is the name given to souvenirs from Tunbridge Wells in Kent. The wares were made in a variety of woods using different decorative techniques, the most commonly found today being the inlaid pieces dating from the 19th century. However, unlike many other souvenirs from resorts developed in the 19th century, Tunbridgeware is known from the 17th century, its popularity starting with the visit of King Charles II in 1663 to the Wells.

The range of mementoes available during the early years of Tunbridge Wells' popularity largely consisted of tea caddies, dressing boxes, snuff boxes, punch ladles and numerous similar items. In addition to these, various drinking vessels, including wassail bowls and standing cups, were also produced. Many of these pieces would have been turned from Lignum Vitae (tree of life) which was imported from the West Indies for the medicinal properties it was believed to possess. However, the limited information available suggests that local timbers such as yew, cherry and holly, provided most of the basic raw materials.

—1—
A selection of Tunbridgeware, *S 11 Dec, 1983,*
£650 ($968)

—2—
A Tunbridgeware rosewood tea caddy, *c.*1840, the interior with two smaller tea caddies and glass mixing bowl, 34.5cm (13½in) long, *Belg 5 Aug, 1981,*
£370 ($765)

—3—
A Tunbridgeware rosewood work box, *c.*1840, complete with various accessories, 27cm (10½in) wide, *Belg 5 Aug, 1981,*
£410 ($848)

—1—

—2—

—3—

It is difficult to build up an image of early Tunbridgeware as no 17th or 18th century manufacturers labelled their work, unlike their 19th century counterparts. Although Sir Ambrose Heal's *London Furniture Makers 1660-1840* lists several stockists, it is unlikely that any of these actually ran workshops. The earlier wares would almost certainly have followed the prevailing decorative trends in cabinet making, such as floral marquetry in Charles II's reign, and lacquer in the early 18th century. To supplement this trade, plain white-wood boxes were produced for customers to demonstrate their own decorative talents. Towards the end of the 18th century painted souvenirs became more prevalent. The wide assortment of trifles made included cribbage boards, sewing accessories, various games and spice boxes. Many of these gifts would have been labelled 'A present from Tunbridge Wells'. These messages were also adapted for Brighton and Margate, with transfers depicting views of the respective towns.

The style of Tunbridgeware then changed to the renowned geometric form favoured throughout the 19th century. This can be seen as a natural development of the fashion for contrasting veneers in cabinet making. Early forms of parquetry in Tunbridgeware were dominated by the cube pattern and 'Vandyke' border, which resembled a series of interlocking triangular segments. Traditional means of selecting veneers were costly and laborious so the Tunbridgeware industry responded by pioneering a cheaper and more efficient method of production in order to take full advantage of public demand. The technique for producing decorative veneers on a large scale has been attributed to James Burrows, who was in partnership with his brother George between 1820 and about 1842.

—4—
A Tunbridgeware rosewood work table, *c.*1840, the top enclosing an adjustable writing surface, above a needlework bag, 80cm (31½in) high, *Belg 5 Aug, 1981,* £550 ($1,138)

—5—
A Tunbridgeware coromandel cigar box, by Edmund Nye, mid 19th century, inlaid with cube pattern within a geometric border, 20cm (8in) high, *Belg 5 Aug, 1981* £225 ($465)

—6—
A Victorian walnut tilt-top Tunbridgeware pedestal table, *c.*1850, 107cm (42in) wide, *S 22 Jan,* £902 ($1,069)

—7—
A Tunbridgeware cube pattern parquetry box, *c.*1830, 20cm (8in) wide, *S 11 Dec, 1983,* £55 ($81)

—8—
A mahogany Tunbridgeware tea caddy, *c.*1825, 23cm (11in) wide, *S 19 Mar,* £154 ($189)

—9—
A Tunbridgeware rosewood pen box, by William Upton, Brighton, mid 19th century, 25cm (9¾in) long, *Belg 5 Aug, 1981,* £200 ($414)

—4—

—6—

—5—

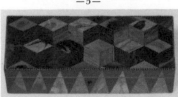

—7—

—8—

—9—

The new 'mosaic' method entailed the assembly of different coloured wooden sticks into a cylindrical or rectangular block. The pattern for these mosaic blocks was prepared on a graph chart, each square representing the cross-section of one of the coloured wooden sticks. After the bundle of sticks has been glued and dried, transverse sections of veneer were sawn thus creating uniform repetitions of the surface design. An indication of just how fine the mosaic patterns can be is given by the number of tesserae (individual pieces) found in some Tunbridgeware designs. It has been calculated, for example, that a stamp box bearing Queen Victoria's profile is formed of as many as one thousand tesserae. A variation on the principle of mosaic veneer was achieved by turning the blocks on a lathe, which revealed different coloured sticks according to the depth the blade reached at any given point. The sticks were built around a solid core of wood to enable the piece to be hollowed out without wasting the carefully assembled sticks. Naturally enough, this type of decoration is described as 'stickware'.

These techniques were also used in conjunction with contrasting veneers. Rosewood, holly, sycamore and walnut were amongst those most commonly used. Floral pattern borders based on 'Berlin woodwork' became almost universal amongst the decorative repertoire used in mosaic ware from the 1840s onwards. These borders were later augmented by bird and animal mosaics, including butterflies, which are now particularly sought after. In the 1850s and 1860s pictorial designs became even more ambitious with local architecture becoming the focus of attention. The more popular subjects include Eridge, Dover and Tonbridge Castle, in addition to ruined abbeys such as Muckrose.

Tunbridgeware was represented at the Great Exhibition of 1851 by three eminent manufacturers: Robert Russell, Edmund Nye and Henry Hollamby. Nye, whose company was famous for being chosen to make a birthday present for Princess Victoria in 1826, included amongst his exhibits a table depicting a galleon in full sail, which was acclaimed for its 'perfect imitation of nature'. Towards the end of Victoria's reign the industry declined and by 1902 the only surviving firm was Boyce Brown and Kemp. Although the company was liquidated in 1927, Thomas Green bought up the veneer stock and attempted to revive the trade in Rye during the 1930s. Unfortunately this last vestige of the industry came to an abrupt end when Thomas Green's premises were destroyed during the Second World War.

—10—
A Tunbridgeware coromandel box, by Thomas Barton, c.1870, the top inlaid with a view of Battle Abbey, 23cm (9½in), *Belg 5 Aug, 1981,* £250 ($517)

—11—
A Tunbridgeware pollarded satinwood collector's cabinet, c.1840, the front enclosing four drawers, 24cm (9½in) wide, *S 11 Dec, 1983,* £520 ($722)

—12—
A Tunbridgeware rosewood bezique marker, c.1850, by T Barton, 13cm (5in) wide, *S 11 Dec, 1983* £75 ($104)

—13—
A selection of Tunbridgeware, *S 11 Dec, 1983* £143 ($198)

—10—

—11—

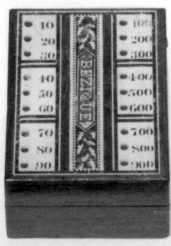

—12—

—13—

Tunbridgeware has wide popular appeal and the market for it has developed over a long period. However, it appears at auction relatively infrequently and, as a result, price records are nearly always set when a group is seen in the salerooms. Potential collectors would benefit from a visit to the Municipal Museum at Tunbridge Wells, which has a large collection illustrating the development of Tunbridgeware over more than two hundred years and exhibits demonstrating construction techniques in a typical workshop setting.

Further reading

Edward H. & Eva R. Pinto, *Tunbridgeware and Scottish Souvenir Woodware*, 1970

● FERGUS LYONS ●

—14—
A Tunbridgeware jewellery box, *c.*1825, 25cm (10in) wide, *S 11 June,* £330 ($434)

—15—
A Tunbridgeware and holly sewing casket, *c.*1830, the cover depicting Erith Castle, the interior with tray and Tunbridgeware-mounted accessories, 23cm (9¼in), *S 23 July,* £462 ($684)

—16—
A Tunbridgeware rosewood and ebony banded jewellery box, *c.*1850, the lid with a panel depicting Herstmonceux Castle, 24cm (9½in) wide, *S 11 Dec, 1983,* £140 ($194)

—17—
A Tunbridgeware inkstand, *c.*1840, 28.5cm (11in) wide, *C 18 Apr,* £341 ($443)

—18—
A Tunbridgeware and rosewood writing slope, *c.*1850, the dual hinged top inlaid with cube parquetry and a view of Battle Abbey, 31cm (12in), *C 18 Apr,* £352 ($458)

—19—
A Tunbridgeware coromandel letter case, *c.*1860, by T Barton, late Nye, with central sycamore panel, 24cm (9½in) wide, *S 11 Dec, 1983,* £80 ($111)

—20—
A Tunbridgeware rosewood writing slope, *c.*1870, inlaid with a view of Hever Castle, 30.5cm (12in) wide, *Belg, 5 Aug, 1981,* £270 ($558)

—14—

—15—

—16—

—17—

—18—

—19—

—20—

1
**A Scottish burr birch
snuff box,** 19th century,
lined with tortoiseshell,
11cm (4¼in) wide,
S 19 Mar,
£49 ($61)

2
**A Victorian shoe snuff
box,** *c.*1880, mahogany
and ebonised, with brass
detail, 9cm (3½in) long,
S 19 Mar,
£187 ($230)

3
**An English painted
satinwood lady's box,** late
19th century, the top
with a pastoral scene
(flaked), 27.5cm (10½in)
diam, *NY 1 Feb,*
$467 (£396)

4
**A Victorian mahogany
snuff box walking stick,**
*c.*1883, dated 1883, 90cm
(35½in) long, *S 19 Mar,*
£374 ($412)

5
**An Anglo-Indian ivory,
ebony and porcupine-
quill work box,** *c.*1830,
the hinged lid enclosing
a removable tray, 25.5cm
(10in), *L 8 Mar,*
£880 ($986)

6
**A painted and decorated
pine work box,** New Eng-
land, *c.*1825, the lid with
a landscape and ruins,
29cm (11½in), *NY 2 Feb,*
$1,100 (£932)

7
**A William IV rosewood
and brass-bound work
box,** *c.*1830, with
countersunk handles, the
base with writing drawer,
30.5cm (12in) wide,
S 15 Oct,
£176 ($260)

8
**A Victorian coromandel
needlework box,** *c.*1840,
with mother-of-pearl
floral sprays, velvet-lined
interior with compart-
ments, 30cm (12in) wide,
S 15 Oct,
£209 ($309)

9
**A turned sycamore
tobacco jar,** 18th cen-
tury, lead lined, 32cm
(12½in) high, *C 18 Apr,*
£319 ($415)

10
**A late George III solid
burr-maple wool box,**
*c.*1810, detached cover,
C 3 Oct,
£132 ($185)

11
A burr apple tea caddy,
English, early 19th cen-
tury, 20cm (8in) high,
NY 1 Feb,
$550 (£500)

12
**An early George III
mahogany waste-paper
basket,** *c.*1770, with oval
frame and brass handle,
48 x 37cm (19 x 14½in),
C 12 July,
£1,925 ($2,676)

13
A Victorian eggcup stand,
*c.*1880, with alternating
bands of rosewood and
sycamore mounted with
ivory, 55cm (21¾in) high,
S 19 Mar,
£1,540 ($1,894)

14
**A carved and inlaid
mahogany hanging
candlebox,** probably
Maryland, first quarter
19th century, 53cm (21in)
high, *NY 2 Feb,*
$660 (£600)

15
**A George II mahogany
birdcage,** second quarter
18th century, 43cm
(17in), *NY 1 Nov,*
$3,025 (£2,100)

1
A George III yew-wood
tea caddy, c.1790, 16.5cm
(6½in) wide, S 19 Mar,
£385 ($430)

2
A George III tea caddy,
c.1790, 15cm (6in) wide,
S 19 Mar,
£374 ($460)

3
A George III tea caddy,
c.1800, tortoiseshell and
mother-of-pearl inlaid,
S 19 Mar,
£396 ($487)

4
A pear-wood gourd-shaped
tea caddy, early 19th
century, 13cm (5in)
high, L 8 Mar,
£1,320 ($1,478)

5
A George III mahogany
and rosewood banded tea
caddy, c.1800, 18cm (7in)
wide, S 22 Jan,
£99 ($117)

6
A Regency rosewood tea
caddy, c.1810, 22cm
(8½in) wide, S 15 Oct,
£286 ($423)

7
A George III satinwood
tea caddy, c.1780, 12cm
(4¾in) high, C 18 April,
£99 ($129)

8
A George III satinwood
tea caddy, c.1790, 19cm
(7½in) wide, C 17 Jan,
£484 ($581)

9
A Regency inlaid tor-
toiseshell tea caddy, early
19th century, 12cm
(4¾in) high, NY 13 Apr,
$495 (£396)

10
A Regency penwork tea
caddy, c.1815, decorated
in black and white with
chinoiserie boating
scene and flowers, 37cm
(14½in) wide, L 8 Mar,
£1,100 ($1,232)

11
A George III oval tea
caddy, c.1790, cross-
banded in tulipwood
with mahogany body,
28cm (11in) wide,
L 15 Nov,
£748 ($1,047)

12
A George III oval rolled
paperwork tea caddy,
c.1790, 20cm (8in)
wide, L 14 June,
£792 ($1,053)

13
A George IV rosewood
teapoy, c.1825, the
hinged cover revealing a
pair of lidded canisters,
43cm (17in) wide,
S 12 Nov,
£495 ($693)

14
A harewood urn-shaped
tea caddy, 19th century,
26.5cm (10in), L 8 Mar,
£1,760 ($1,971)

15
A George III oval tea
caddy, c.1795, the body
with a cameo on both
sides, green ground,
13cm (5in) high, L 8 Mar,
£2,860 ($3,203)

Textiles

1
A Commonwealth needle-work picture, *c.*1650, worked in petit point and showing Queen Esther inviting the King and Maman to the Banquet, 39 x 51cm (15½ x 20in), *L 17 July,* £4,840 ($7,018)

2
A Charles I stumpwork picture, mid-17th century, 30 x 44cm (11¾ x 17½in), *L 8 Mar,* £2,860 ($3,203)

3
An English needlework panel, 17th century, depicting the sacrifice of Isaac, 34.5 x 45.5cm (13½ x 18in), *NY 11 May,* $1,210 (£984)

4
A Charles II embroidered picture, *c.*1670, depicting King Solomon and the Queen of Sheba, 26 x 36.5cm (10½ x 14¼in), *S 17 Sept,* £990 ($1,485)

5
A Charles II embroidered miniature, *c.*1650, 11.5cm (4½in) diam, *L 26 Sept,* £550 ($825)

6
A Flemish silk embroid-ered guild panel, dated 1652, applied with fish and lobster, the light blue coloured silk ground replaced, 43cm (17in) high, *NY 22 Nov,* $1,320 (£904)

7
A George I embroidered satin picture, *c.*1720, the ivory ground embroid-ered with brilliant silks, 21 x 23cm (8¼ x 9in), *L 17 July,* £2,200 ($3,190)

8
A silk embroidered panel, dated 1698, depicting two Apostles, 40cm (15¾in) diam., *NY 11 May,* $275 (£224)

9
A pair of English petit point embroidered pictures, mid-17th cen-tury, with gilt and black moulded frames, 15 x 23cm (6 x 9in), *C 14 Feb,* £660 ($759)

1

2

3

4

5

6

7

8

9

1
Two Italian silk-embroidered panels, 18th century, 64 x 42cm (25 x 16½in) and 20 x 42cm (8 x 16½in), *NY 11 May*, $660 (£537)

2
A pair of Italian silk-embroidered panels, late 17th century, 334 x 64cm (10ft 11½in x 2ft 1½in), *L 24 May*, £2,090 ($2,780)

3
A pair of Flemish or Sheldon tapestry cushion covers, c.1600, from a series of six, 46cm (18in) square, *HS 20 Nov*, £13,200 ($18,744)

4
A Victorian woolwork picture, worked in gros point heightened with cut steel and glass beads, 57 x 78cm (22½ x 30½in), *S 9 July*, £715 ($958)

5
A pair of French Chinoiserie embroidered wall-hangings, c.1730, 221 x 175cm (7ft 3in x 5ft 9in), *L 24 May*, £3,300 ($4,389)

6
An embroidered firescreen panel, early 18th century, with yellow grospoint ground and petit point centre, *L 9 May*, £1,100 ($1,419)

7
A tapestry cushion cover, early 17th century, English or North German, 56 x 110cm (22 x 43in), *L 24 May*, £3,960 ($5,267)

8
A length of French needlepoint lace, mid-18th century, worked in buttonhole stitch, 40 x 308cm (15¼ x 121in), *L 9 May*, £660 ($851)

9
A lace table cover, probably Burano, c.1880, 308 x 117cm (10ft 1½in x 3ft 10in), *NY 22 Nov*, $3,960 (£2,712)

10
A length of French point de France needlepoint lace, c.1710, *L 9 May*, £2,420 ($3,122)

1

2

3

4

5

6

7

8

9

10

1
A pair of needlework pictures: The Shepherd and Shepherdess, probably English, c.1800, painted and embroidered on silk, 30.5 x 24cm (12 x 9½in), *NY 1 Feb,* $990 (£839)

2
A pair of embroidered silk pictures, South African, 1836, 1837, one with splits in the ground, 44 x 30cm (14¼ x 11¾in) and 46 x 32cm (18 x 12½in), *L 17 July,* £1,265 ($1,834)

3
A pair of English caricature collage pictures, c.1770, one of 'Capn Shandy and Corporal Trim', the other of a fashionable lady, 20.5 x 29cm (8¼ x 11½in) and 22 x 28.5cm (8½ x 11¼in), *L 8 Mar,* £1,540 ($1,724)

4
A silk-embroidered mourning picture, Sacred to the Memory of Mrs Catharine Patten, Portland, Maine, dated 1816, some repairs, 53 x 62cm (21 x 24½in), *NY 1 Feb,* $3,080 (£2,610)

5
A silk-embroidered mourning picture, In Memory of Mrs Mary F. Train, possibly Miss Rowson School, Boston, dated 1810, 55 x 40.5cm (21¾ x 16in), *NY 1 Feb,* $330 (£280)

6
A Charles II border band sampler, c.1650, worked with Adam and Eve and animals and insects in coloured silks, 33 x 16cm (13 x 6¼in), *L 8 Mar,* £660 ($739)

7
An embroidered satin still life of flowers, in pastel silks on an ivory ground, 63cm (21in) diam, *HS 16 July,* £352 ($510)

8
A pair of English silkwork pictures, c.1800, of young gentlemen, 20.5cm (8in) and two pictures of young ladies, 21 and 18.5cm (8¼ and 7½in), *S 14 May,* £935 ($1,244)

9
A Charles I border band sampler, dated 1647, worked in brilliant silks, signed, 79 x 18cm (31 x 7in), *L 26 Sept,* £1,320 ($1,980)

1

2

3

4

5

6

7

8

9

1
A needlework sampler,
1842, probably
American, entitled 'Pity
and Protect the Slave',
S 19 Mar,
£902 ($1,109)

2
A needlework sampler,
Pennsylvania, 1810,
NY 1 Feb,
$3,850 (£3,263)

3
A needlework sampler,
Ohio, 1824, *NY 26 Oct,*
$6,325 (£4,454)

4
**An English needlework
sampler,** 1829, *S 9 July,*
£550 ($737)

5
**An English needlework
sampler,** Hannah
Richardson Ag'd 11,
1773, *S 14 May,*
£1,078 ($1,434)

6
A needlework sampler,
Pennsylvania, December
6, 1823, *NY 28 June,*
$1,980 (£1,523)

7
A needlework sampler,
probably Lebanon,
Pennsylvania, 1817,
NY 1 Feb,
$770 (£653)

8
An English sampler,
1784, *L 17 July,*
£825 ($1,196)

9
**An English linen worked
sampler,** Elizabeth
Lovell, aged 11 years,
C 17 Jan,
£308 ($370)

10
An English sampler,
1801, *L 17 July,*
£715 ($1,037)

11
An English sampler,
1833, *L 17 July,*
£308 ($447)

12
A needlework sampler,
probably English,
mid-19th century,
NY 1 Feb,
$440 (£373)

1

2

3

4

5

6

7

8

9

10

11

12

1
A pieced and appliqued quilt, probably Pennsylvania, 19th century, composed of red, pink, green, and yellow fabric in a Blossom and Bud pattern, minor staining, 224 x 173cm (7ft 4in x 5ft 8in), *NY 28 June,* $660 (£507)

2
A cotton Amish crib quilt, American, 20th century, in a Star of the East pattern, 102 x 127cm (40 x 50in), *NY 1 Feb,* $770 (£653)

3
A pieced cotton Mennonite quilt, Lancaster, Pennsylvania, *c.*1900, composed of green, purple, blue, brown, red, orange and yellow fabric in the Joseph's Coat pattern, 210cm (6ft 9in) square, *NY 28 June,* $1,210 (£930)

4
A patchwork quilt, late 19th century, in individual squares of Honeycomb, Log Cabin, Tumbling Black, Crazy Quilt and other designs, 161cm (5ft 3½in) square, *C 29 Nov,* £308 ($431)

5
A patchwork coverlet, late 19th century, with tumbling block centre and log cabin design border, 60 x 152cm (87 x 60in), *L 17 July,* £264 ($383)

6
A patchwork coverlet, of late 18th and early 19th century printed and polished cottons, with log cabin design centre, 229 x 264cm (104 x 90in), *L 17 July,* £495 ($717)

1

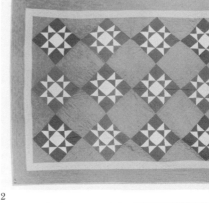
2

3

4

5

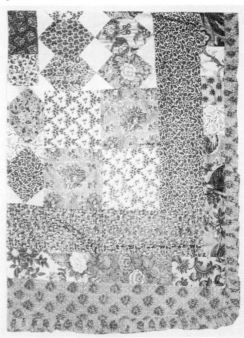
6

1
A pieced and appliqued calico star Friendship quilt, New Jersey, dated 1841, 285cm (9ft 4in) sq *NY 1 Feb,* $715 ($606)

2
A pieced and appliqued calico quilt, probably Pennsylvania, 19th century, Sunflower, and Leaf pattern, 254cm (8ft 4in) square, *NY 28 June,* $1,210 (£930)

3
A pieced all-silk Star of Bethlehem quilt, probably Pennsylvania, 19th century, 203cm (6ft 8in) square, *NY 28 June,* $1,320 (£1,015)

4
A pieced and appliqued cotton quilt, American, mid-19th century, President's Wreath pattern, 254cm (8ft 4in) sq, *NY 26 Oct,* $1,100 (£775)

5
A pieced wool and cotton Amish quilt, Pennsylvania, *c.*1890, Sunshine and Shadow pattern, 183cm (6ft) sq, *NY 28 June,* $1,100 (£846)

6
A red, white and blue pieced cotton quilt, American, 19th century, President's Wreath pattern, 193 x 203cm (6ft 4in x 6ft 8in), *NY 28 June,* $550 (£423)

7
A pieced red and green calico quilt, probably Pennsylvania, 19th century, 254cm (8ft 4in) square, sold with a rug, 19th century, *NY 28 June,* $192 (£147)

8
A pieced cotton President's Wreath quilt, probably Pennsylvania, 19th century, 193cm (76in) square, *NY 1 Feb,* $1,760 (£1,492)

9
An American pictorial hooked rug, 19th century, 81 x 252cm (2ft 8in x 5ft), *NY 28 June,* $715 (£550)

10
An American pictorial hooked rug, 19th century, 75 x 125cm (2ft 5½in x 4ft 1½in), *NY 28 June,* $1,430 (£1,100)

1

2

3

4

5

6

7

8

9

10

Costume

Have you ever discovered an old trunk or wardrobe filled with costume? What was your reaction? Admittedly costume found this way can at first appear dull, lifeless and unappealing, but did you see something more in the folded dresses and limp dusty garments? Pause before you throw them on the bonfire or give them away—take a closer look.

Costume can bring us as close as it is possible to get to the living presence of a past age. It reflects the forms and fashions dictated by past times on the human figure—from 18th century pannier dresses with huge side extensions to each hip, to the sharp-pointed winkle picker shoes worn by teenagers in the 1960s.

Costume also reflects social trends. It is particularly interesting to note the change of shape and style in women's clothes in the 19th and early 20th century: from constricting boning and lacing of Victorian times to the relative ease of the post-1914 period. Changed social and political conditions induced by World War I meant that women had for the first time to take a major role outside the home, which necessitated clothes that would allow freer movement and general comfort.

Long floor-length skirts no longer impeded the impatient strides of women eager for emancipation. The freedom and excesses so much associated with post-war Europe in the mad 1920s were also reflected in dress of the time. For women the skirts went up, the neckline down. A similar phenomenon was witnessed after 1945, when after the privations of rationing and clothing coupons, Dior's 'New Look' caused a revolution in women's dress, with minute 'wasp' waists and voluminous yards of material in the full skirts.

Not only does costume reveal the style of a particular period, but also the status and personality of the original wearer. It can be very amusing to discover, for example, an evening dress of gargantuan proportions in the most dreadful colour combinations, trimmed with silk flowers, ribbons and everything else that could be crammed on, and to wonder what the wearer looked like and the sort of comments the dress inspired! There can be no doubt, however, that the dramatic and elegant black-and-white striped gown illustrated (fig. 2) was owned and worn by an extremely fashionable young woman in the London of the 1890s.

—1—
An open robe of turquoise damask satin, *c.*1740, later altered, together with a sky-blue quilted silk petticoat, *L 26 Sept,* £1,870 ($2,805)

—2—
A late Victorian gown, English, 1890s, of black and white striped silk, *L 26 Sept,* £506 ($759)

—1—

—2—

Today private collectors and museums throughout the world eagerly seek good costume specimens. They are looking for rare, early examples of men's and women's costume in good condition, or fine examples of more recent couturier gowns. Sotheby's sells costume dating up to the 1960s providing it is by a famous designer, a fine example of a particular style, and in good condition. Condition is extremely important. Stains, tears and alterations drastically reduce the value of a piece.

It must be stressed that not all costume sold at auction goes to museums. There is an increasing number of private collectors who buy old costume to wear. Sturdy late 19th and early 20th century underwear in particular is often bought for summer wear. Beaded dresses and stylish evening gowns of the 1930s in good condition are eagerly sought by women looking for high quality, unique evening wear. For example a black sequinned and beaded 1920s gown, in good condition but by an unknown maker, recently made £880 ($1,320) (fig. 4). Dresses of similar period but by famous designers, such as Chanel, can reach four figures. It is interesting that some modern fashion phases affect the prices of antique pieces. During the 'New Romantic' phase of early 1985, lace, waistcoats, and frilly cotton underwear became more saleable.

Another area which sold strongly was printed cotton garments. Many collectors are trying to acquire early examples of block-printed gowns. In past years emphasis had been placed on rich silks and more expensive fabrics. For decades the more humble cotton dress was overlooked in favour of brocaded silks. Now this imbalance is being corrected and the humble chintz is taking its rightful place in many major museum exhibitions. This trend was reflected in the price of £2,860 ($4,290) paid for a block-printed drop-front gown of *c*.1800 (fig. 6).

—3—
Three Victorian corsets, probably English, late 1890s, one black cotton, one ribbed white cotton and one of pale green cotton, *L 26 Sept,* **£187 ($281)**

—4—
A black sequinned and eau-de-nil beaded tunic, *c*.1928, *L 26 Sept,* **£880 ($1,320)**

—5—
A lady's pink damask satin shoe, *c*.1720, with woven bands of silver fabric, *L 9 May,* **£275 ($355)**

—6—
A block-printed cotton lady's dress, *c*.1800, with multi-coloured floral design, *L 26 Sept,* **£2,860 ($4,290)**

—3—

—5—

—4—

—6—

Collectors are particularly anxious to buy men's costume, which is more rare than women's fashions. Arguably the reason for this scarcity is because women generally take more care of their clothes, whereas men wear their clothes out completely or give them away when no longer wanted. Everyday suits, trousers, jackets and coats from the 19th and early 20th century are particularly difficult to find. Most costume of this date which has survived tends to be evening wear or ceremonial dress. This is the reason why in May 1985 £900 ($1,080) was paid for an 1840s suit comprising beige pants, navy blue Melton-cloth coat and pale blue and white waistcoat. 18th century menswear in particular has jumped in price. Whereas in 1980 a good suit of this period would fetch merely hundreds of pounds, similar pieces today can fetch thousands.

The record price of £13,750 ($17,738) was paid for another man's costume—the suit worn by William James as Black Rod of Ireland in 1751 (fig. 7). The cut brown and black velvet on an ivory silk ground was a striking and unusual fabric to use. The suit was found nailed onto its case, complete with gilt-metal topped ebony cane. The early date and historical importance, together with the attractiveness of the suit, combined to push its price way above the estimate. It is important to note that any costume sold with documentation or a strong provenance detailing the identity of the original owner, is far more desirable than anonymous specimens.

As costume is a rather large and difficult subject to display properly, many private collectors are turning to accessories— bags, gloves, hats and shoes, which take up less room. Shoes in particular have made a great jump in price. Even single shoes, if early enough and in good condition, can be saleable. Collectors of accessories are always keen to know any historical details of the original owner, which is reflected in the price. This can be seen by the interest shown in King Leopold of the Belgians' pink silk baby shoes (fig. 11).

—7—

A brown and cream cut velvet coat and breeches, as worn by William James, Black Rod of Northern Ireland, 1751, with silver brocade cuffs and silver and wire buttons, L 9 May, £13,750 ($17,738)

—8—

An Eton Montem tailcoat, scarlet, with 'Eton Hall' buttons bearing the school crest and dated 1844, L 26 Sept, £330 ($495)

—9—

A gold lamé and sequinned evening gown and matching coat, by Chiberta, Mayfair, worn by Lady Docker at the Paris Motor Show in 1956, L 26 Sept, £286 ($429)

—10—

A pair of 18th century pink satin baby shoes, embroidered in silver thread, 14cm (5½in) long, L 9 May, £462 ($596)

—11—

A pair of cerise pink silk infant's shoes, c.1835, reputed to have been King Leopold of the Belgians' first pair of shoes, L 9 May, £484 ($624)

—12—

A pair of lady's peach satin-damask shoes, c.1730, with stitched maroon morocco heels, L 26 Sept, £715 ($1,073)

—7—

—8—

—9—

—11—

—10—

—12—

Although prices have risen dramatically in five years, they have probably not risen far enough. Costume is still an expanding field—one in which there are sure to be interesting developments as new private collectors enter the market and museums improve and extend their displays. In England there is the recently opened and much celebrated costume collection at the Victoria and Albert Museum which has already attracted tens of thousands of devotees. In Paris, even more recently Yvonne Deslandres opened the highly acclaimed Musée des Arts de la Mode, a section of the Louvre museum. It is reassuring to know that in almost every major European country you will be able to find specialist museums devoted entirely to the conservation, investigation and exhibition of costume in all of its diverse forms.

So please, next time you open that wardrobe, chest or trunk, look a little more closely, and just consider, the contents may not be rags but potential riches!

● KERRY TAYLOR ●

Further reading

Georgina Howell, *In Vogue*, 1978

Victoria & Albert Museum, *Four Hundred Years of Fashion*, 1984

Cunnington & Beard, *A Dictionary of English Costume*, 1960

C. Willett Cunnington & Phillips Cunnington, *Handbook of English Costume in the Nineteenth Century*, 1970

—13—
A collection of Edwardian infants' coats, capes and dresses, *c.*1900, eleven pieces, *L 26 Sept*, £220 ($330)

—14—
An agricultural smock, English, *c.*1900, of coarse drabbet, embroidered in scarlet silks, *L 17 July*, £660 ($957)

—15—
A Victorian child's dress, *c.*1850, of striped pale green satin, slight staining, *C 14 Feb*, £176 ($202)

—16—
An 18th century open robe, *c.*1740, of beige silk brocade woven with brown and ivory flowers, later alterations, with gold and ivory brocade under-skirt, *L 26 Sept*, £404 ($606)

—17—
A lady's silk gown, late 1850s, in shot mauve and grey, *L 26 Sept*, £605 ($908)

—13—

—14—

—15—

—16—

—17—

Some museums with major collections of costume

Metropolitan Museum of Art
5th Avenue and
82nd Street
New York

The Victoria and Albert Museum
Cromwell Road
London

Munich City Museum
St Jakobs Platz 1
Munich

Costume Museum
11 avenue du
President-Wilson
Paris

Museum of Fashion and Costume
Palais Galliera
10 avenue Pierre
de Servie
Paris

Musée des Arts de la Mode
Pavillon de Marsan
Palais du Louvre
Paris

1
A Burgundian Renaissance tapestry, mid-16th century, 265 x 216cm (8ft 8in x 7ft 11in), *L 29 Nov,* £6,600 ($9,240)

2
A Felletin 'Nine Heroes' tapestry, second half 16th century, 285 x 265cm (9ft 4in x 8ft 8in), *NY 11 May,* $16,500 (£13,415)

3
A Flemish hunting tapestry, *c.*1600, 310 x 320cm (10ft 2in x 10ft 5in), *NY 11 May,* $11,000 (£8,943)

4
A Flemish tapestry panel, late 16th century, 130 x 290cm (4ft 4in x 9ft 6in), *NY 11 May,* $8,250 (£6,707)

5
A Gobelins Metamorphoses tapestry, of Acis and Galatea, *c.*1700, attributed to Jan Jans, 325 x 285cm (10ft 8in x 9ft 5in), *L 5 July,* £4,950 ($6,831)

6
A Flemish verdure tapestry, *c.*1630, 400 x 380cm (13ft 1in x 12ft 6in), *NY 11 May,* $4,840 (£3,935)

7
A pastoral tapestry, probably Oudenarde, mid-17th century, 330 x 300cm (10ft 10¼in x 9ft 10½in), *M 24 June,* FF 133,200 (£10,733; $14,382)

8
A Brussels tapestry, *c.*1660, by G. Van Leefdael, 370 x 340cm (12ft 1in x 11ft 1in), *NY 11 May,* $19,800 (£16,098)

9
A Beauvais pastoral tapestry, late 17th century, 292 x 351cm (9ft 7in x 11ft 6in). *NY 22 Nov,* $5,500 (£3,767)

10
A French hunting tapestry, late 17th century, 230 x 280cm (7ft 6in x 9ft 3in), *NY 11 May,* $7,150 (£5,813)

1

2

3

4

5

6

7

8

9

10

1
A Flemish verdure tapestry, late 17th century, probably Oudenarde, woven mainly in shades of blue, 290 x 335cm (9ft 6in x 11ft), *L 24 May*, £4,510 ($5,998)

2
A Flemish verdure tapestry panel, 18th century, 185 x 155cm (6ft 1in x 5ft 1in), *NY 22 Nov*, $1,760 (£1,205)

3
A Flemish verdure tapestry panel, early 18th century, 302 x 190cm (9ft 11in x 6ft 3in), *NY 22 Nov*, $5,225 (£3,579)

4
A Beauvais 'Ports de Mer' tapestry, *c.*1725, 292 x 192cm (9ft 7¼in x 6ft 3½in), *M 24 June*, **FF 144,300** (£11,628; $15,581)

5
An Aubusson medallion tapestry, *c.*1770, 236 x 139cm (7ft 9in x 4ft 7in), *L 29 Nov*, £6,820 ($12,068)

6
A Lille pastoral tapestry, 18th century, 210 x 260cm (7ft x 8ft 6in), *NY 11 May*, $2,750 (£2,236)

7
A Flemish Teniers tapestry, 19th century, 235 x 200cm (7ft 8in x 6ft 6in), *L 24 May*, £2,090 ($2,780)

1

2

3

4

5

6

7

1
A Florentine armorial tapestry portiere, c.1600, woven with the Medici arms supported by a prince represting the Grand Duke of Tuscany, 265 x 175cm (8ft 8in x 5ft 8in), *L 29 Nov,* **£9,900 ($13,860)**

2
A Brussels armorial tapestry, first half 17th century, 260 x 245cm (8ft 5in x 8ft 1in), *NY 11 May,* **$7,700 (£6,260)**

3
A Flemish armorial tapestry, 17th century, 365 x 285cm (12ft x 9ft 5in), *NY 11 May,* **$6,050 (£4,919)**

4
A Bessarabian carpet, mid-19th century, signed, 279 x 185cm (9ft 2in x 6ft 1in), *NY 13 Apr,* **$10,450 (£8,360)**

5
A Spanish rug, possibly Cuenca, late 17th century, with dark blue floral pattern on ochre ground, 325 x 160cm (10ft 8in x 5ft 3in), *NY 22 Nov,* **$7,150 (£4,897)**

6
A Bessarabian carpet, with walnut field, 362 x 213cm (11ft 10in x 7ft), *L 31 July,* **£770 ($1,147)**

7
A Bessarabian carpet, last quarter 19th century, 320 x 239cm (10ft 6in x 7ft 10in), *NY 23 Nov,* **$13,200 (£9,041)**

1

2

3

4

5

6

7

1
An Aubusson carpet,
*c.*1850, the ivory field
with aubergine medal-
lion, 410 x 340cm (13ft
6in x 11ft 2in), *M 25 June,*
FF 88,800
(£7,400; $9,990)

2
An Aubusson carpet, the
rose field with ivory
medallion and green
surround, 330 x 262cm
(10ft 10in x 8ft 7in),
S 29 Jan,
£1,650 ($1,955)

3
An Aubusson rug, *c.*1860,
with apple green
ground, and maroon
surround with buff and
red 'damask' panels,
148cm (4ft 10in) square,
L 5 July,
£4,400 ($6,072)

4
An Aubusson carpet, with
plum madder field and
ivory border, restored,
490 x 288cm (16ft 2in x
9ft 5in), *L 17 Apr,*
£3,960 ($5,148)

5
An Aubusson carpet,
third quarter 19th cen-
tury, with central ivory
reserve on two-tone
raspberry field, reduced
in size, 727 x 396cm
(23ft 10in x 13ft),
NY 8 June,
$3,850 (£3,056)

6
An Aubusson carpet, late
19th century, with pale
gold field and black
surround, 340 x 305cm
(11ft 2in x 10ft),
NY 26 Jan,
$4,675 (£4,212)

7
An Aubusson carpet, with
ivory field, 505 x 406cm
(16ft 7in x 13ft 4in),
L 16 Oct,
£3,960 ($5,861)

8
An Aubusson carpet, with
ivory field, 484 x 480cm
(15ft 10in x 15ft 9in),
L 31 July,
£11,550 ($17,210)

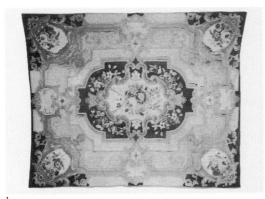
1

2

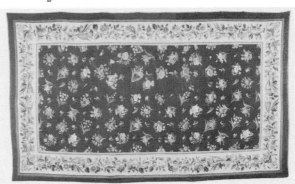
3

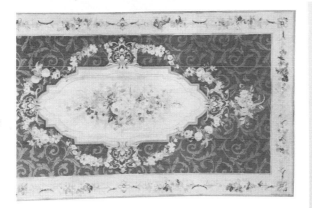
4

5

6

7

8

1
A Russian needlework rug, 295 x 182cm (9ft 8in x 6ft), *L 16 Oct,* £3,520 ($5,210)

2
A Russian needlework carpet, 341 x 255cm (11ft 2in x 7ft 5in), *L 6 Feb,* £4,400 ($4,972)

3
A European needlework rug, 290 x 158cm (9ft 6in x 5ft 2in), *L 31 July,* £3,850 ($5,737)

4
An English needlework carpet, third quarter 19th century, with ivory and black panels containing red, blue and green bouquets, 315 x 201cm (10ft 4in x 6ft 7in), *NY 13 Apr,* $9,350 (£7,480)

5
An English needlework rug, last quarter 19th century, with ivory field, and cornflower blue border, minor restoration, 292 x 163cm (9ft 7in x 5ft 4in), *NY 8 June,* $5,775 (£4,583)

6
A European needlework rug, probably English, last quarter 19th century, stains, 369 x 254cm (12ft 1in x 8ft 4in), *NY 26 Jan,* $15,950 (£14,369)

7
An English needlework carpet, last quarter 19th century, the field woven with ivory reserves, gold and straw banding, 427 x 323cm (14ft x 10ft 7in), *NY 18 May,* $22,000 (£17,460)

8
A French needlework carpet, 18th century, restored, 437 x 374cm (14ft 4in x 12ft 3in), *NY 26 Jan,* $16,500 (£14,865)

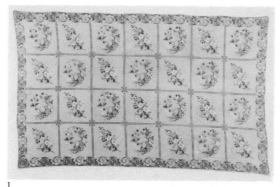

1

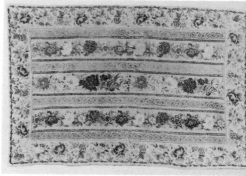

2

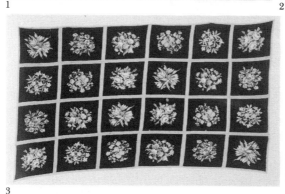

3

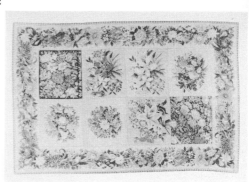

4

5

6

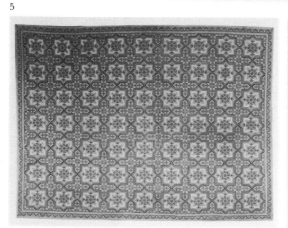

7

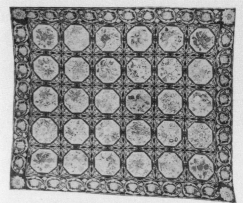

8

Clocks and Watches

Article ● Wristwatches *pp* 156-159

See also

● Colour illustrations *pp* 338-339 ● Jewellery *pp* 509-511

1
A George I brass-mounted walnut bracket clock, first quarter 18th century, Charles Molins, London, 34cm (13½in), *NY 26 Jan,* $7,700 (£6,936)

2
A George I ebony bracket clock, John Latham, London, early 18th century, *NY 26 Jan,* $5,500 (£4,954)

3
A George I ebonised bracket timepiece, the dial signed Jos. Williamson London, 28cm (11in), *L 5 Dec,* £1,980 ($2,772)

4
An ebony quarter-repeating bracket timepiece, in the manner of Joseph Knibb, the dial and backplate signed Jonathan Puller Londini fecit, 31cm (12¼in), *L 28 Feb,* £5,720 ($6,635)

5
An ebony-veneered quarter-repeating bracket clock, *c.*1685, the dial and backplate signed Joseph Knibb London, 30.5cm (12in), *L 25 Apr,* £14,300 ($18,447)

6
A Queen Anne ebony-veneered quarter-repeating bracket timepiece, the backplate signed Langley Bradley London, later anchor escapement, 35.5cm (14in), *L 25 July,* £2,310 ($3,396)

7
An ebonised quarter-repeating bracket timepiece, the dial signed Anth. Pluet London, 37cm (14½in), *L 25 Apr,* £2,200 ($2,838)

8
A George II ebonised chiming bracket clock, the dial signed Daniel Torin & Moses Fontaine no. 475, 61cm (24in), *L 8 Oct,* £3,190 ($4,721)

9
A George II walnut bracket clock, the dial and backplate signed John Ellicott London, 47cm (18½in), *L 5 Dec,* £8,250 ($11,550)

10
A late George II ebonised quarter-repeating bracket clock, the dial signed Stepn. Rimbault London, 49cm (19in), *L 25 Apr,* £1,540 ($1,987)

11
A George III ebonised alarum bracket timepiece, the dial signed John Wareham London, 30cm (12in), *L 8 Oct,* £1,540 ($2,279)

12
A George III mahogany bracket clock, the dial signed Willm. Jourdain, London, 51cm (20in), *L 5 Dec,* £1,650 ($2,310)

13
A burr-walnut quarter-repeating bracket clock, signed Wm. Webster Exchange Alley London, 47cm (18½in), *L 5 Dec,* £9,350 ($13,090)

14
A George III mahogany clock, *c.*1780, the dial signed Barton, Kendall, 51cm (20in), *C 17 Jan,* £1,045 ($1,254)

15
A George III burr-chestnut bracket clock, signed Fladgate & Willder, London, 31cm (12¼in), *L 6 June,* £4,620 ($6,145)

1   2   3   4
5   6   7   8
9   10   11   12
13   14   15

1
A George III mahogany chiming bracket clock, the dial signed Rich, Style London, 48cm (19in), *L 6 June,* £3,520 ($4,682)

2
A late George III mahogany musical bracket clock, the dial and backplate signed Evill & Son Bath, five tune selection dial, 58.5cm (23in), *L 5 Dec,* £1,980 ($2,772)

3
An ebonised repeating bracket clock, *c.*1760, the chapter ring signed Geor. Creswell, Brewood, 48cm (19in), *S 25 July,* £770 ($1,132)

4
A George III mahogany bracket clock, the dial signed John Meek London, 44.5cm (17½in), *L 6 June,* £1,540 ($2,048)

5
A George III ebony-veneered bracket clock, *c.*1820, the dial and backplate signed Carter, London, 79cm (29in), *S 25 July,* £968 ($1,423)

6
An early 19th century, mahogany mantel regulator, *c.*1806, the dial signed Reid & Auld Edinr., altered pendulum and suspension, 43cm (17in), *L 28 Feb,* £2,420 ($2,807)

7
A glass and gilt-bronze mantel clock, late 19th century, 33cm (13in), *S 21 Feb,* £792 ($911)

8
An English ormolu mantel timepiece, *c.*1830, the fusee and chain movement signed Payne, 163 New Bond Street, 36.5cm (14½in), *L 5 Dec,* £748 ($1,047)

9
An ebonised repeating bracket clock, *c.*1840, 25cm (10in), *S 13 June,* £990 ($1,317)

10
A mahogany balloon mantel clock, the dial and movement signed James McCabe Royal Exchange London 2461, 46cm (18in), *L 6 June,* £1,870 ($2,487)

11
A George IV mahogany bracket clock, *c.*1835, the movement signed Bennet, Wing & Co., London, no.850, 37cm (14½in), *C 17 Jan,* £495 ($594)

12
A mahogany bracket clock, *c.*1845, the dial signed J. Pennington & Co., Liverpool, 51cm (21in), *C 17 Jan,* £352 ($422)

1　　　　　2　　　　　3

4　　　　　5　　　　　6

7　　　　　8　　　　　9

Clock
In general (see WATCH), any timekeeper not designed to be carried in the pocket or worn; in particular (see TIMEPIECE), a clock that strikes the hours every hour.

Watch
A timekeeper with a balance, and designed to be carried in the pocket or worn.

Timepiece
A timekeeper that does NOT strike regularly, but may repeat.

Clockwatch
A watch that strikes the hours regularly.

Regulator
A clock (usually a timepiece) designed for precision timekeeping.

10　　　　　11　　　　　12

1

A George III mahogany bracket clock, *c.*1815, the dial and backplate signed Barraud's, Cornhill, London, bell missing, 42cm (16½in), *S 21 Feb,* £792 ($911)

2

A rosewood and cut brass bracket clock, *c.*1820, 34cm (13½in), *C 17 Jan,* £374 ($449)

3

A George III brass-inlaid ebonised bracket clock, the dial and movement signed Thos. Moss London 185, 38cm (15in), *L 25 July,* £715 ($1,051)

4

An early 19th century satinwood chiming bracket clock, the dial signed Payne, 163 New Bond Street, *L 5 Dec,* £1,210 ($1,694)

5

A George III mahogany bracket clock, *c.*1820, the dial and plates signed Desbois & Wheeler, Grays Inn Passage, the plates numbered 128, 53cm (21in), with matching wall bracket, *S 13 June,* £2,530 ($3,365)

6

A Victorian mahogany chiming bracket clock, *c.*1890, the dial and movement signed Barraud & Lunds, London, 59.5cm (23½in), *L 10 Jan,* £935 ($1,122)

7

A rosewood and mahogany quarter striking bracket clock, the dial signed G Cachard successor to Henry Favre London, the movement signed G Cachard London, 33cm (12½in), *L 6 June,* £2,090 ($2,780)

8

A rosewood bracket clock, *c.*1830, the dial and backplate signed Brockbank & Atkins, London, no 1987, 39cm (15½in), *C 18 Apr,* £1,045 ($1,359)

9

A mahogany mantel clock, the movement signed James McCabe Royal Exchange London, 24cm (9½in), *L 10 Jan,* £1,650 ($1,980)

10

A Victorian mahogany mantel timepiece, the dial and movement signed Chas. Frodsham & Co., Clockmakers to the Queen 84 Strand, London, no. 1942, 25cm (9¾in), *L 8 Oct,* £1,155 ($1,709)

11

A rosewood bracket clock, *c.*1840, the dial and backplate signed Bludnell, Clerkenwell, London, no. 5547, 41cm (16¼in), *C 18 Apr,* £330 ($429)

12

A Victorian mahogany chiming bracket clock, *c.*1890, 71cm (29in), *L 10 Jan,* £990 ($1,188)

13

An oak bracket clock, *c.*1880, 56cm (22in), *C 16 May,* £440 ($585)

14

A walnut and gilt bronze chiming bracket clock, *c.*1900, 69cm (27in), *C 17 Jan,* £825 ($990)

Lantern Clock
A particular early (circa 1600-1750) type of metal-cased weight-driven wall clock; also used of later spring-driven copies.

Cartel Clock
A type of decorative spring-driven wall clock, usually metal-cased and very often French; 18th century or later.

1
A gold and enamel desk
clock, c.1928, the dial
signed Cartier, on
onyx and gem-set base,
6cm (2½in), *L 28 Oct,*
£6,600 ($9,834)

2
A Viennese ormolu
Grande Sonnerie alarum
travelling clock, the
dial signed Charles Le
Roy, with later lever
platform, 16.5cm (6½in),
L 28 Feb,
£682 ($791)

3
A rosewood alarum dial
timepiece, c.1850, the
dial inscribed Delaselle
& Christie, Cannon
Street, London, 32cm
(12½in), *C 3 Oct,*
£528 ($777)

4
A Federal mahogany and
eglomisé shelf clock,
c.1820, signed Aaron
Willard, Boston, 87cm
(34½in), *NY 26 Oct,*
$9,350 (£6,584)

5
An early Victorian
mahogany wall clock,
c.1840, the dial signed
Alldridge, Birming-
ham, 109cm (43in),
C 18 Apr,
£352 ($458)

6
A mahogany Act of
Parliament timepiece,
the case signed John
Daviss Windsor, 150cm
(59in), *L 25 July,*
£1,980 ($2,911)

7
A black-japanned tavern
dial timepiece, c.1760,
the dial signed Ebenezer
Court, Bedford, *C 17 Jan,*
£2,420 ($2,904)

8
A mahogany wall time-
piece, c.1760, the dial
signed James Wood,
Dorchester, *S 25 July,*
£1,100 ($1,617)

9
A late George III
mahogany wall timepiece,
the dial signed Vulliamy
London, 69cm (27in),
L 8 Oct,
£1,430 ($2,116)

10
A Cape mahogany wall
clock, c.1820, the dial
signed L Twentyman,
Cape of Good Hope,
the movement signed
Hadley & Moore, 55cm
(21½in), *JHB 29 Apr,*
R 3,200 (£1,333; $1,746)

11
A mahogany tavern clock,
c.1780, the dial signed
Pinkney, London,
132cm (52in), *S 21 Feb,*
£715 ($822)

12
A black japanned tavern
timepiece, c.1750, the
dial signed Borrett,
Stowmarket, 150cm
(59in), *HS 16 July,*
£3,300 ($4,785)

13
An American walnut wall
clock, c.1850, with
Tunbridge inlay, 96.5cm
(38in), *C 16 May,*
£132 ($176)

Pendule D'Officier
A type of metal-cased French travelling clock,
usually late 18th or early 19th century.

Mystery, Mysterieuse
A timekeeper in which the means of maintaining
motion are not obvious. In one type there is no
visible connection between the hands and the
movement.

Automaton
A timekeeper with animated figures(s) actuated by
the movement.

Striking
In particular, sounding the hours regularly
(almost always on one bell or gong); more
generally, of a timekeeper with any type of
striking or chiming mechanism.

Quarter-striking
Sounding every quarter on up to three bells or
gongs.

1
A German walnut wall
clock, c.1880, 71cm
(28in), C 28 Feb,
£330 ($370)

2
A rosewood quarter
striking Vienna regulator,
1870, 115cm (45¼in),
A 26 Feb,
Dfl 5,800 (£1,422; $1,592)

3
A maple and mahogany
'Vienna' wall timepiece,
the movement support
stamped R Maurer,
Eisenbach, 73.5cm
(29in), L 8 Oct,
£462 ($684)

4
A walnut Grande Sonnerie
Vienna regulator, the
dial signed L Hoeber,
31 Duke Street, Gros-
venor Square, London,
187cm (6ft 1½in), L 5 Dec,
£3,300 ($4,620)

5
A 'stoelklok' Goslinck
Ruempol, 1746, 65cm
(25½in), A 25 Nov,
Dfl 8,740 (£2,080; $2,912)

6
A Black Forest wall clock,
c.1840, 39cm (15½in),
L 28 Feb,
£319 ($370)

7
A Black Forest wood
automaton travelling
clockmaker timepiece,
c.1880, American-type
metal movement, 38cm
(15in), G 12 Nov,
SF 3,300 (£1,078; $1,509)

8
A Black Forest quarter-
striking automaton wall
clock, c.1840, dial
cracked, one bell lack-
ing, L 8 Oct,
£2,090 ($3,093)

9
An ebonised cuckoo clock,
c.1880, 51cm
(20in), C 28 Nov,
£1,210 ($1,694)

10
An oak 'stoelschippertje',
19th century, 67cm
(26¼in), A 4 June,
Dfl 6,496 (£1,470; $1,984)

11
A Black Forest wall clock,
c.1850, pendulum and
side doors replaced,
12cm (4¾in), L 25 Apr,
£330 ($426)

12
A French clock picture,
19th century, 58 x 71cm
(22¾ x 28in), A 25 Nov,
Dfl 5,520 (£1,314; $1,840)

1   2   3   4

5   6   7

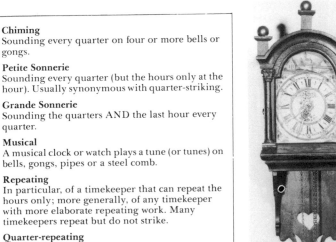

8   9

10   11   12

Chiming
Sounding every quarter on four or more bells or
gongs.

Petite Sonnerie
Sounding every quarter (but the hours only at the
hour). Usually synonymous with quarter-striking.

Grande Sonnerie
Sounding the quarters AND the last hour every
quarter.

Musical
A musical clock or watch plays a tune (or tunes) on
bells, gongs, pipes or a steel comb.

Repeating
In particular, of a timekeeper that can repeat the
hours only; more generally, of any timekeeper
with more elaborate repeating work. Many
timekeepers repeat but do not strike.

Quarter-repeating
Repeating the hours and quarters.

Minute-repeating
Repeating the hours, quarters and minutes (up to
14) within each quarter, usually on two bells or
gongs.

1
**A mahogany longcase
clock,** the dial signed
Tho Lumpkin London,
calendar ring lacking,
L 10 Jan,
£1,155 ($1,386)

2
**An early 18th century
burr-walnut chiming
longcase clock,** the dial
signed Mary-Anne
Viet London, 264cm
(8ft 4in), *L 8 Oct,*
£14,300 ($21,164)

3
**A marquetry longcase
clock,** the dial signed
Ben Hutchinson
London, inlaid on an
ebony ground and
veneered in walnut,
208cm (6ft 10in),
L 25 Apr,
£4,400 ($5,976)

4
**An early 18th century
Dutch walnut marquetry
quarter-striking alarum
longcase clock,** the dial
signed Johannes Dort-
mondt Amsterdam,
234cm (7ft 8in), *L 28 Feb,*
£4,840 ($5,614)

5
A walnut longcase clock,
early 18th century,
signed Jno Tantum, in
Loscoe, 231cm (7ft 7in),
restored, *C 11 July,*
£5,060 ($7,033)

6
**A mahogany longcase
clock,** late 18th century,
signed Wm Troop,
London, 243cm (7ft
11½in), *S 17 Oct,*
£1,650 ($2,442)

7
**An oak and mahogany
longcase clock,** *c.1780,*
the dial signed Fletcher,
Leeds, 225cm (7ft 4½in),
C 17 Jan,
£550 ($660)

8
**A George III mahogany
longcase clock,** *c.1790,*
the dial signed John
Howells, St Catherin's,
224cm (7ft 3in), *C 17 Jan,*
£1,870 ($2,244)

9
An oak longcase clock,
c.1780, signed Joseph
Atkinson, 208cm (7ft
2in), *C 6 June,*
£308 ($416)

10
An oak longcase clock,
mid 18th century, the
dial signed John Shaw,
on later plinth, *C 17 Jan,*
£330 ($396)

11
**A George III mahogany
longcase clock,** the dial
signed J Coates London,
213cm (7ft), *L 5 Dec,*
£2,640 ($3,696)

12
**An oak and mahogany
longcase clock,** *c.1760,*
signed Thomas Richard-
son, Weaverham, 208cm
(6ft 10in), *C 3 Oct,*
£924 ($1,349)

13
**A George III longcase
clock,** the movement
c.1780, the case
reconstructed, the dial
signed Jno Fisher
Preston, 226cm (7ft
5in), *C 17 Jan,*
£550 ($660)

14
**An inlaid mahogany
longcase clock,** the dial
signed William Allam
London, 242cm (7ft
11in), *L 6 June,*
£2,200 ($2,926)

15
**A George III oak longcase
clock,** last quarter 18th
century, signed Will
Ball, Bicester, 206cm
(6ft 9in), *NY 1 Nov,*
$2,310 (£1,604)

1   2   3   4   5

6   7   8   9   10

11   12   13   14   15

1
A George III mahogany longcase clock, last quarter 18th century, signed James and Jacob Butler, Boulton, 221cm (7ft 3in), *NY 13 Apr,* $2,530 (£2,024)

2
A George III mahogany longcase clock, the dial signed Justin Vulliamy London, 219cm (7ft 2in), *L 5 Dec,* £11,000 ($11,540)

3
A mahogany George III longcase clock, late 18th century, signed John Holmes, London, 220cm (7ft 2½in), *S 21 Feb,* £7,260 ($8,349)

4
A George III inlaid mahogany longcase clock, last quarter 18th century, signed George Cordell, London, 257cm (8ft 5in), *NY 13 Apr,* $4,950 (£3,960)

5
A George III mahogany longcase clock, the dial signed Willm. Tomkins, London, 234cm (7ft 8in), *C 18 Apr,* £1,705 ($2,217)

6
A George III walnut longcase clock, last quarter 18th century, Benson, West Haven, 218cm (7ft 2in), *NY 1 Nov,* $2,750 (£1,909)

7
A George III inlaid mahogany longcase clock, last quarter 18th century, William Barr & Son, Hamilton, painted with female figures representing England, Scotland, Wales and Ireland, 230cm (7ft 6½in), *NY 1 Nov,* $3,300 (£2,291)

8
An oak and mahogany longcase clock, *c.*1780, signed J N Holt, Rochdale, 217.5cm (7ft 2in), *C 14 Nov,* £440 ($616)

9
A mahogany longcase clock, *c.*1820, the dial inscribed Thos. Hargreaves, Burnley, 256cm (8ft 5in), *C 17 Jan,* £935 ($1,122)

10
A mahogany longcase clock, *c.*1810, the dial signed R Lawson, Hindley, 239cm (7ft 10in), *C 3 Oct,* £682 ($996)

11
A mahogany longcase clock, the dial signed Helm Ormskirk, 252cm (8ft 3in), *L 8 Oct,* £3,300 ($4,884)

12
A mahogany longcase clock, *c.*1810, the dial signed Henry Lymington, 240cm (7ft 10½in), *C 3 Oct,* £1,375 ($2,007)

13
A mahogany longcase clock, early 19th century, signed Rd. Gilkes, Whitchurch, 224cm (7ft 4in), *S 13 June,* £1,430 ($1,902)

14
A mahogany longcase clock, early 19th century, the dial signed Phil Thache, London, 201cm (6ft 7in), *S 18 Apr,* £770 ($1,001)

15
A William IV mahogany longcase clock, *c.*1830, 215cm (7ft ½in), *C 18 Apr,* £308 ($400)

1   2   3   4   5

6   7   8   9   10

11   12   13   14   15

1
A George III mahogany
longcase clock, c.1820,
signed G Booth,
Aberdeen, 238cm (7ft
9½in), S 21 Feb,
£2,750 ($3,162)

2
A mahogany longcase
clock, c.1860, the dial
signed Andw Millar,
Edinburgh, 198cm (6ft
6in), S 13 June,
£1,980 ($2,633)

3
A mahogany regulator,
c.1870, the dial signed
J J Stockall & Sons Ltd,
London EC, 193cm (6ft
4in), S 13 June,
£1,870 ($2,487)

4
A mahogany regulator,
c.1830, the dial signed
Richd Sayer, Annell,
replaced pediment,
190cm (6ft 3in), S 18 Apr,
£2,860 ($3,718)

5
A 19th century mahogany
regulator, the dial signed
Frank Slee, Holsworthy,
199cm (6ft 6in), L 25 July,
£1,540 ($2,264)

6
A mahogany grandmother
clock, 19th century,
174cm (5ft 8½in), C 3 Oct,
£935 ($1,365)

7
An oak longcase clock,
late 19th century, signed
John Watson, Black-
burn, 249cm (8ft 2in),
C 3 Oct,
£1,155 ($1,686)

8
An ebonised oak chiming
longcase clock, c.1890,
231cm (7ft 7in), C 17 Jan,
£550 ($660)

9
An Edwardian inlaid
rosewood chiming long-
case clock, the case inlaid
with finely etched bone,
238cm (7ft 10in), L 25 Apr,
£4,400 ($5,676)

10
A carved oak chiming
longcase clock, the dial
signed John Armour
Kilmares, 242cm (7ft
11in), L 6 June,
£1,320 ($1,756)

11
A mahogany longcase
clock, c.1913, the dial
signed Ollivant &
Botsford, Manchester,
236cm (7ft 9in), C 3 Oct,
£1,980 ($2,891)

12
An Edwardian mahogany
chiming longcase clock,
in Chippendale style
case, 280cm (9ft 2in),
L 25 July,
£3,740 ($5,498)

13
A Dutch striking mar-
quetry longcase clock,
the dial signed R Penny
London, 221cm (7ft 3in),
L 25 Apr,
£2,640 ($3,406)

14
A Dutch 18th century
walnut marquetry long-
case clock, the dial
signed Paulus Bramer
Amsterdam, 219cm (7ft
2in), L 25 July,
£2,420 ($3,557)

15
A Dutch inlaid walnut
and fruitwood floral
marquetry longcase
clock, early 18th century,
signed Johannes Logge,
Amsterdam, later bun
feet, 214cm (7ft),
NY 1 Nov,
$7,700 (£5,347)

1   2   3   4   5

6   7   8   9   10

11   12   13   14   15

1
A Louis V style king-wood veneered and ormolu longcase clock, *c.*1870, the dial signed Le Faucheur à Paris, 226cm (89in), *S 13 June,* £5,500 ($7,315)

2
A Louis XV gilt-bronze-mounted kingwood parquetry longcase clock, mid 18th century, the dial signed Tallon Fils à Paris 1769, 214cm (7ft), *L 5 July,* £12,100 ($16,698)

3
A Napoleon III style gilt-bronze mounted Boulle marquetry regulator, late 19th century, inlaid with scenes from the Commedia dell 'Arte, 234cm (7ft 8in), *NY 22 June,* $2,750 (£2,148)

4
A Chippendale carved walnut tall-case clock, *c.*1780, David Rittenhouse, Philadelphia, some restoration, 203cm (7ft 10in), *NY 2 Feb,* $10,450 (£8,855)

5
A Chippendale mahogany tall-case clock, *c.*1780, by Samuel Hill, Harrisburg, Pennsylvania, 263cm (8ft 7½in), *NY 2 Feb,* $14,300 (£13,000)

6
A Chippendale carved walnut tall-case clock, *c.*1780, by George Miller, Germantown, Pennsylvania, restoration and repairs, 244cm (8ft), *NY 26 Oct,* $6,050 (£4,260)

7
A Federal inlaid cherry-wood tall-case clock, Western Pennsylvania, *c.*1810, 234cm (7ft 10in), *NY 2 Feb,* $5,500 (£4,661)

1   2   3

4   5   6   7

1
A Louis XV gilt-bronze-mounted bracket clock, mid 18th century, the dial signed Jean-Lavoy à Paris, 56cm (22in), *L 5 July,* £3,300 ($4,554)

2
An early Louis XV Boulle bracket clock, *c.*1730, the dial signed Thullier Fils à Paris, later Brocot escapement, with ormolu mounts depicting Diana and her dog, 84cm (33in), *L 5 July,* £1,375 ($1,898)

3
An early Louis XV Boulle clock and bracket, the dial signed Gilbert à Paris, with a figure of Time as cresting and Diana below the dial, 92cm (36in), *G 12 Nov,* SF 12,100 (£3,954; $5,535)

4
A Louis XV gilt-bronze cartel clock, *c.*1765, the dial signed Lamy au Louvre, 79cm (31in), *L 5 July,* £4,400 ($6,072)

5
A Louis XV gilt-bronze cartel clock, signed Mesnil à Paris, 74cm (29in), *M 23 June,* FF 111,000 (£8,944; $11,985)

6
A Louis XVI gilt-bronze cartel clock, *c.*1780, the dial signed Imbert L'ainé à Paris, pendulum lacking, 81cm (32in), *L 5 July,* £1,100 ($1,518)

7
A Louis XVI ormolu and marble mantel clock, late 18th century, signed Maniere à Paris, surmounted by a figure of Athena, 64cm (25in), *S 17 Oct,* £1,595 ($2,361)

8
A Louis XVI gilt-bronze mantel clock, *c.*1785, signed Henri Voisin à Paris, the case with figures of Venus and Cupiad, 32cm (12½in), *L 5 July,* £2,200 ($3,036)

9
A Louis XVI gilt-bronze and marble mantel clock, signed Filon à Paris, decorated with figures after Boizot, 51cm (20in), *M 24 June,* FF 24,420 (£1,968; $2,637)

10
A Louis XVI ormolu and marble mantel clock, 32cm (12½in), *G 12 Nov,* SF 3,300 (£1,078; $1,509)

11
An Empire gilt bronze patinated mantel clock, surmounted by Cupid in a cradle, *A 26 Feb,* Dfl 3,712 (£910; $1,019)

12
A Restauration bronze and gilt-bronze mantel clock, *c.*1820, 43.5cm (17½in), *L 5 July,* £2,860 ($3,947)

1   2   3   4

5   6   7

8   9

10   11   12

1
**An Empire ormolu and
bronze patinated mantel
clock,** signed Thomire
Paris, 93cm (36½in),
A 4 June,
Dfl 31,210 (£7,086; $9,566)

2
**A Restauration ormolu
mantel clock,** in Louis
XV style, the cracked
dial signed S Devaulx
Palais Royal 124, 28cm
(11in), *L 28 Feb,*
£528 ($612)

3
A gilt-bronze cartel clock,
mid 19th century,
signed Bertoud à Paris,
the base with a cherub
veiling a female figure
of Night, 108cm (42½in),
L 21 June,
£3,410 ($4,569)

4
**An Empire gilt-bronze
mounted mahogany
mantel clock,** *c.*1820,
39.5cm (5½in), *L 5 July,*
£1,045 ($1,442)

5
**A large lacquered brass
Charles X mantel clock,**
*c.*1825, the dial signed
Angedin à Paris, 64cm
(25in), *C 17 Jan,*
£880 ($1,056)

6
**A French rosewood mantel
clock,** *c.*1840, 49cm
(19½in), *C 3 Oct,*
£352 ($514)

7
**A French rosewood
mantel regulator clock,**
the dial, signed Frappier
Breveté, 66cm (26in),
L 28 Feb,
£3,520 ($4,083)

8
**A Restauration bronze
and ormolu mantel clock,**
pendulum lacking,
flanked by a figure of a
young warrior, 56cm
(22in), *L 25 Apr,*
£550 ($710)

9
**An Empire gilt-bronze
mantel clock,** flanked by
figures of Ulysses and
Penelope, *A 26 Feb,*
Dfl 7,192 (£1,763; $1,974)

10
**A French mantel time-
piece,** *c.*1850, the dial
signed Chas. Frodsham,
Maker to the Queen, 84
Strand, 33cm (13in),
L 25 Apr,
£748 ($965)

11
An ormolu cartel clock,
*c.*1860, 74cm (29in),
S 13 June,
£638 ($849)

12
**An Empire ormolu pen-
dule d'officier,** the dial
signed Robert &
Courvoisier, 19cm
(7½in), *L 25 Apr,*
£2,530 ($3,264)

13
**A gilt-metal light
powered mantel time-
piece,** signed Patek
Philippe Geneve,
no 872578, 21.5cm
(8½in), *L 28 Feb,*
£1,760 ($2,042)

1　　　　2　　　　3

4　　　5　　　6　　　7

8　　　　9　　　　10

11　　　　12　　　　13

1
An 18th century Bohemian ebonised grande sonnerie bracket clock, the dial signed Jacob Koebel in Pest, 44cm (17¼in), *L 8 Oct*, £1,540 ($2,279)

2
A German neoclassical painted and parcel-gilt mantel clock, first quarter 19th century, inscribed Ge, Adam Follermann in Wurzburg, 48cm (19in), *NY 24 May*, $1,650 (£1,309)

3
A late 18th century Austrian fruitwood quarter-striking bracket clock, the cracked dial signed Jno. Michael Hofer in Wien, 46cm (18in), *G 12 Nov*, SF 3,080 (£4,312; $6,036)

4
A Viennese grand sonnerie mantel clock, *c.*1830, 68.5cm (27in), *L 10 Jan*, £396 ($475)

5
An ormolu and 'Sèvres' porcelain clock garniture, *c.*1860, signed Raingo Frères Paris, no. 339, the case surmounted by a porcelain vase with a bucolic scene reserved on *bleu-celeste* ground, 77.5cm (30½in), and a pair of vases 55cm (21¾in), *L 21 June*, £5,940 ($7,960)

6
A gilt-bronze, champlevé and jasper clock garniture, 38cm (15in), flanked by a pair of ovoid urns, 32cm (12½in), *c.*1890, *C 17 Jan*, £792 ($950)

7
An ormolu and porcelain clock garniture, *c.*1865, the dial painted with a pastoral scene within gilt borders on a *gros-bleu* ground, the movement no. 560 Japy Freres, 32.5cm (12¾in), with two conforming vases, 26cm (10¼in), *L 22 Mar*, £1,100 ($1,320)

8
An ormolu and 'Sèvres' porcelain composed clock garniture, *c.*1860, the movement stamped JBD, 50cm (19¾in), with a pair of ewers, 40.5cm (16in), *L 22 Mar*, £2,420 ($2,904)

9
A Louis XVI style gilt-bronze three-piece clock garniture, *c.*1860, the dial signed Raingo Fres/ Paris, clock 62cm (24½in), *NY 30 Mar*, $6,600 (£5,323)

10
A Louis XVI style gilt-bronze and marble three-piece clock garniture, *c.*1890, comprising a clock and two candelabra, assembled, the clock signed Leroy/ Paris, candelabra 49.5cm (19½in), *NY 22 June*, $1,045 (£816)

11
A Louis XV style gilt-bronze clock garniture, *c.*1900, clock 86cm (34in), *NY 30 Mar*, $4,675 (£3,770)

12
A gilt-bronze and porcelain clock garniture, *c.*1870, the clock with pink porcelain and 'jewelled' dial, with two candelabra, clock 46cm (18in), *NY 30 Nov*, $1,980 (£1,328)

1   2   3   4

5   6

7   8

9

10

11   12

1
**A gilt-brass rococo mantel
clock**, *c.*1870, the movement stamped S Marti,
56cm (22in), *L 8 Nov,*
£1,100 ($1,650)

2
An ormolu mantel clock,
*c.*1870, 46cm (18in),
S 13 June,
£418 ($556)

3
**A French glazed ormolu
mantel clock,** *c.*1850, the
dial indistinctly signed
Sevenier & G Gore...,
the movement stamped
Lefrand A Paris 409,
46cm (18in), *L 5 Dec,*
£715 ($1,001)

4
**A silvered and gilt-
bronze and onyx mantel
clock,** *c.*1865, the dial
signed Chles. Oudin,
Palais-Royal 52, the
movement with the
stamp of Japy Frères,
67cm (26½in), *L 8 Nov,*
£2,970 ($4,455)

5
**A Louis XVI style gilt-
bronze mantel clock,**
*c.*1900, signed Linke,
56cm (22in), *NY 30 Nov,*
$3,520 (£2,362)

6
**A figural bronze and
marble mantel clock,**
*c.*1880, signed
F Barbedienne, Fon-
deur, 52cm (30½in),
NY 22 June,
$770 (£602)

7
**A Louis XVI style gilt-
bronze and marble figural
mantel clock,** the dial
signed Charpentier/
Bronzier/A Paris/Rue
d'Orleans, 44cm (17½in),
NY 30 Mar,
$1,210 (£976)

8
**An ormolu, bronze and
marble mantel clock,**
*c.*1870, the cracked
dial signed Martinot A
Paris, the movement
stamped Japy Frères,
no. 463, on red marble
plinth, bell lacking
29.5cm (11½in), *L 22 Mar,*
£792 ($950)

9
**An ormolu and 'Sèvres'
porcelain mantel clock,**
*c.*1860, the movement
Japy Frères, the case
inset with twelve
'jewelled' porcelain
panels, 48.5cm (19in),
L 22 Mar,
£4,620 ($5,544)

10
**A tortoiseshell, ormolu
and porcelain mantel
clock,** *c.*1870, the dial
signed Glading, 38cm
(15in), *S 21 Feb,*
£319 ($367)

1

2

3

4

5

6

7

8

9

10

1
An ormolu and porcelain clock garniture, *c.*1860, the dial signed Raingo Frères à Paris, the case inset with painted porcelain panels, 28cm (11in), with two matching candlesticks, 28cm (11in), *L 10 Jan,* £990 ($1,188)

2
An ormolu and porcelain composed clock garniture, *c.*1860, with painted dial, 30cm (11¾in), and a pair of ormolu candelabra, 37cm (14½in), *L 21 June,* £1,650 ($2,211)

3
A gilt and bronzed spelter and marble clock garniture, *c.*1870, the movement with the stamp of Samuel Marti, 43cm (17in), and a pair of conforming candelabra, 47cm (18½in), *L 22 Mar,* £726 ($871)

4
An Empire style ormolu, bronze and marble clock garniture, the Japy Frères movement contained in a chariot case, the dial forming a wheel, 42.5cm (16¾in), and a pair of conforming candelabra, 56.5cm (22¼in), *L 21 June,* £2,310 ($3,095)

5
An Egyptian Revival gilt-bronze mounted basalt mantel clock, *c.*1900, 44cm (17in), *NY 30 Mar,* $770 (£621)

6
A French mystery clock, *c.*1880, the movement stamped Brevete GIT 1135, the female figure swivelling on a concealed pivot, 62cm (24½in), *L 28 Feb,* £2,200 ($2,552)

7
A French bronzed spelter mystery timepiece, *c.*1870, the movement stamped GLT Paris, the sphere rotating round a central post, driving link lacking, 71cm (28in), *L 25 Apr,* £2,860 ($3,689)

8
A spelter and brass mantel clock, *c.*1890, the movement with Brocot escapement, associated parts, 67cm (26½in), *C 17 Jan,* £330 ($396)

9
A French ormolu and enamel mantel clock, the dial signed Le Roy & Fils Palais Royal Paris, the case inlaid with polychrome enamel, 52cm (20½in), *L 10 Jan,* £660 ($792)

10
A patinated bronze mantel clock, *c.*1870, 56cm (22in), *C 17 Jan,* £396 ($475)

11
A Boulle mantel clock, *c.*1860, the movement stamped E J P Brevete, the case veneered with red shell inlaid with brass, 63.5cm (25in), *L 22 Mar,* £495 ($594)

12
A Boulle bracket clock, the dial signed Grottendieck Bruxelles, 104cm (41in), *L 28 Feb,* £2,420 ($2,807)

13
An ormolu and mahogany mantel clock, *c.*1880, in Régence style, with a Brocot escapement, 95cm (37½in), *L 22 Mar,* £1,980 ($2,376)

14
A white marble and ormolu lyre clock, *c.*1890, the movement stamped S Marti, 46.5cm (18¼in), *L 22 Mar,* £935 ($1,122)

15
An ormolu and white marble lyre clock, *c.*1870, the S Marti movement stamped J D, Brocot escapement, 54.5cm (21½in), *L 21 June,* £2,035 ($2,727)

16
An ormolu cartel clock, *c.*1865, the dial signed Costain, Galerie de la Madeleine à Paris, the movement by A D Mougin, 46cm (18in), *L 21 June,* £748 ($1,002)

1

An ormolu cathedral mantel clock, *c.*1840, the dial signed Bourdin Sr. de Souriau Hr. Du Roi, 24 Rue de la Paix, A Paris, Japy Frères movement, 63.5cm (25in), *L 5 Dec,* £715 ($1,001)

2

A Victorian skeleton timepiece, *c.*1860, 31cm (12¼in), *L 6 June,* £385 ($512)

3

A skeleton clock, the chapter ring signed T Morgan Manchester, 61cm (24in), *L 25 July,* £1,870 ($2,749)

4

An eight-day silvered metal and brass lighthouse clock, *c.*1880, probably French, 25.5cm (10in), *NY 30 Oct,* $1,760 (£1,231)

5

An alarum capucine, first quarter 19th century, the dial signed Guy Reffey A Lyon, 30cm (12in), *G 12 Nov,* **SF 5,500 (£1,797; $2,515)**

6

A French alarum lantern clock, *c.*1700, the dial signed Raoul Deunnepart A Paris, the front cresting piece engraved with a grotesque mask, 35.5cm (14in), *G 12 Nov,* **SF 3,520 (£1,150; $1,610)**

7

A lantern clock, 17th century the front cresting piece signed Thomas Loomes Londini, with converted anchor escapement, formerly with alarum, 39.5cm (15½in), *L 8 Oct,* £1,760 ($2,091)

8

An early 18th century striking table clock, signed Johan Anth. Kleinschmit im Wien, later silver chapter ring and central disk, restored, base 14cm (5½in) square, *L 28 Feb,* £3,300 ($3,828)

9

A Viennese silver-gilt and enamel standing clock, *c.*1880, with earlier circular movement, 19cm (7½in), *NY 17 June,* $1,650 (£1,299)

10

A gilt-metal desk timepiece, in the manner of Thomas Cole, 19cm (7½in), *L 28 Feb,* £1,100 ($1,276)

11

A French sedan timepiece, early 19th century, the movement signed Le Roy, with replaced lever escapement, 28cm (11in), *S 13 June,* £330 ($439)

12

A Watson-Webb rack gravity clock, *c.*1920, 26cm (10¼in), *L 6 June,* £220 ($293)

13

A Swiss silver-gilt and blue enamel minute repeating desk clock, *c.*1920, 9cm (3½in), *NY 14 Jan,* $3,080 (£2,775)

1
A gilt-brass repeating alarum carriage clock, Margaine movement, *C 17 Jan*, £506 ($607)

2
A repeating carriage clock, 19cm (7½in), *S 17 Oct*, £297 ($440)

3
An engraved brass repeating carriage clock, with alarm, *c.*1870, retailed by Bailey & Co., Philadelphia, 13.5cm (5½in), *NY 17 June*, $605 (£476)

4
A gilt-brass carriage clock, *c.*1880, by Drocourt, 16cm (6¼in), *C 18 Apr*, £550 ($715)

5
A brass alarum carriage clock, *c.*1860, by Drocourt, retailed by Payne & Co., later lever escapement, 16cm (6¼in), *C 3 Oct*, £396 ($578)

6
A repeating carriage clock, inscribed Dent, 61 Strand, London, the lever escapement with Soldano stamp and bell strike, 16cm (6½in), *S 13 June*, £990 ($1,317)

7
A gilt-metal quarter repeating grande sonnerie carriage clock with alarm, *c.*1900, L & E Fabre, Buenos Aires, 14.5cm (5¾in), *NY 14 Jan*, $1,210 (£1,090)

8
A gilt brass petite sonnerie repeating carriage clock, *c.*1900, 12.5cm (5in), *NY 14 Jan*, $715 (£644)

9
A French gilt-brass carriage clock, *c.*1890, 19cm (7½in), *C 18 Apr*, £418 ($543)

10
A gilt-metal repeating carriage clock with alarm, *c.*1900, by Bolviller, Paris, 16cm (6¼in), *NY 4 Apr*, $1,320 (£1,109)

11
An oval grande sonnerie carriage clock, the dial signed Robert Pleissner Dresden, minute wheel faulty, 15.5cm (6in), *L 28 Feb*, £3,300 ($3,828)

12
A French calendar carriage timepiece, later lever escapement, 13cm (5¼in), *L 8 Oct*, £396 ($586)

13
A gilt-metal and champlevé enamel repeating carriage clock with alarum, *c.*1900, with multicoloured enamel decoration, 16cm (6¼in), *NY 4 Apr*, $3,080 (£2,588)

14
An English bronze carriage clock, signed E I Dent London, and numbered 663, lacking repeat button, 22cm (8¾in), *L 28 Feb*, £3,960 ($4,594)

Chronograph or Stopwatch
A watch with a seconds hand that can be started, stopped and returned to zero at will.

Chronometer
A precision timekeeper (usually a watch) with a detent escapement. Now also used (especially on the Continent) of watches tested to a certain standard of precision.

Oignon
The popular name given to the large and rather bulbous French watches of the late 17th and early 18th centuries.

Pair Cased
Two cases for one watch. The inner case containing the movement, removed from the outer for winding. Almost universal in English watches from about 1650 to 1800, but less common on the Continent.

1
A porcelain-mounted carriage clock, the side panels signed Simonnet, the lever movement stamped GL 102, 17cm (6¾in), *L 25 Apr,* £1,320 ($1,703)

2
A repeating carriage clock, with alarm, base inscribed 'Gustave Badolett, Geneve', 14cm (5½in), *S 18 Apr,* £495 ($644)

3
A porcelain-mounted carriage timepiece, in the Japanese taste, the lever movement with the stamp of Richard et Cie, 8.5cm (3¼in), *L 5 Dec,* £1,320 ($1,848)

4
A porcelain-mounted carriage clock, in the Japanese taste, the lever movement with the stamp of Henri Jacot, numbered 5339, *L 25 July,* £2,090 ($3,072)

5
A gilt-metal oval grande sonnerie repeating carriage clock with alarm, *c.*1880, 14cm (5½in), *NY 17 June,* $1,650 (£1,299)

6
A miniature carriage timepiece, base numbered 6520, 7cm (2¾in), *L 25 Apr,* £748 ($965)

7
A miniature silver and pale blue enamel carriage timepiece, *c.*1900, with Swiss lever movement, 6.5cm (2½in), *L 6 June,* £418 ($556)

8
A miniature 9 carat gold carriage timepiece, hallmarked 1911, the dial signed Mappin & Webb, Paris, 45cm (1¾in), *L 8 Oct,* £528 ($781)

9
A miniature silver and blue enamel carriage timepiece, early 20th century, the dial signed Theo B Starr Inc, the lever movement by Concord Watch Co, 4cm (1½in), *C 18 Apr,* £297 ($386)

10
A miniature carriage timepiece, the dial signed Hawley & Co., the movement with later detached lever platform, 6.5cm (2½in), *L 28 Feb,* £286 ($332)

11
A silver pair-cased verge watch, early 18th century, no. 334 by Thomas Peirce of London, 5.5cm (2½in), *L 25 July,* £660 ($970)

12
A silver virgule watch, late 18th century, by Louis Duchene of Geneva, signed and numbered 47316, 8cm (3in), *L 25 July,* £1,320 ($1,940)

13
A silver repeating oignon watch, signed Dufour à Paris, *c.*1710, 6cm (2½in), *NY 17 June,* $825 (£650)

14
A repoussé gold pair cased verge watch, 1737, by True. Good of London, repousse with a mythological scene, 4.5cm (1¾in), *L 5 Dec,* £1,210 ($1,694)

15
A silver pair cased verge clockwatch, *c.*1690, by Michel Dehecq of Paris, later single hand, 6cm (2½in), *L 25 Apr,* £2,420 ($3,122)

16
A silver quarter repeating oignon with pendulum bob, *c.*1700, by Josue Panier of Paris, 5.5cm (2¼in), *NY 17 June,* $3,025 (£2,381)

17
A repoussé silver quarter striking verge calendar chaise watch with alarum, first half 18th century, signed Johann Daniel Delle in Fridberg, the back repoussé with a scene of Daniel in the Lions' Den 11.5cm (4½in), *L 28 Oct,* £15,400 ($22,946)

18
A silver pair cased verge coach watch, hallmarked 1863, no. 1, 7.5cm (3in), *L 25 Apr,* £605 ($780)

1
A gold fusee keyless lever watch, Charles Frodsham, hallmarked London 1920, 5.5cm (2in), *L 6 June,* £880 ($1,170)

2
A gold free sprung keyless lever watch, Charles Frodsham, hallmarked 1894, 5.5cm (2in), *L 25 July,* £1,210 ($1,779)

3
A gold keyless lever watch, 18 carat, signed William Rogers, Liverpool, hallmarked London 1889, 5.5cm (2in), *C 11 July,* £363 ($505)

4
A gold watch, *c.*1920, 18 carat, Patek Philippe & Co, Geneva, 4.5cm (1¾in), *NY 4 Apr,* $550 (£462)

5
A gold keywound lever watch, hallmarked London, 1878, 18 carat, 6cm (2½in), *C 11 July,* £286 ($398)

6
A gold watch, *c.*1915, Patek Philippe & Co, Geneva, 18 carat, 5cm (2in), *NY 14 Jan,* $1,650 (£1,486)

7
A yellow gold English plunge quarter repeating pocket watch, 1821, 18 carat, movement signed Green Ward & Co, London, *S 13 June,* £1,100 ($1,463)

8
A gold calender watch, Girard Perregaux, Chaux-de-Fonds, 18 carat, 5cm (2in), *NY 14 Jan,* $1,100 (£991)

9
A gold minute repeating watch, *c.*1910, 18 carat, Patek Philippe & Co, Geneva, 5cm (2in), *NY 14 Jan,* $4,400 (£3,964)

10
A gold centre seconds keyless lever watch, T Rushton, Leeds, hallmarked Birmingham 1890, 18 carat, 5.5cm (2¼in), *C 3 Oct,* £330 ($482)

11
A gold hunting case minute repeating calendar watch with carillon, moon phases and chronograph, *c.*1880, 18 carat, 5.5cm (2¼in), *NY 30 Oct,* $3,575 (£2,500)

12
A gold keyless lever chronograph, signed L Leroy & Co, Hgers à Paris, no. 27355, 5cm (2in), *G 12 Nov,* SF 2,860 (£935; $1,309)

13
A keyless lever chronograph, 14 carat, the dial inscribed Tiffany & Co, New York, 5cm (2in), *C 17 Jan,* £286 ($343)

14
A gold chronograph with pulsemeter, *c.*1900, 18 carat, Vacheron & Constantin, Geneva, 5cm (2in), *NY 17 June,* $1,210 (£953)

15
A German hunting case chronograph with register, *c.*1910, A Lange & Sohne, Glasshutte I/Sa. 18 carat, 5.5cm (2¼in), *NY 4 Apr,* $9,350 (£7,857)

Hunting Cased
A watch with front and back cover.

Half Hunter, Half Hunting Cased
The front cover with a small aperture showing the hands and dial centre beneath.

Open-faced
With a glass over the dial, but no further cover.

Bras-en-L'Air
A watch in which, when the pendant is depressed, the time is shown by a figure with two arms pointing to the hours and minutes.

1   2   3

4   5   6

7   8   9

10   11   12

13   14   15

1
A gold half hunting cased keyless lever watch, hallmarked Chester ? 1932, 18 carat, the movement by Thos. Russell & Son Liverpool, 5cm (2in), *C 11 July,* £385 ($535)

2
A gold hunting cased keyless lever watch, 18 carat, inscribed Thos. Russell & Sons, hallmarked Chester 1918, 5cm (2in), *C 3 Oct,* £363 ($530)

3
A gold hunting cased double dial calendar watch, *c.*1900, 5cm (2in), *NY 17 June,* $1,100 (£866)

4
A gold and turquoise-set quarter repeating lever watch, 1825, Viner & Co, London, with Lepine calibre movement, 5cm (2in), *L 6 June,* £1,870 ($2,487)

5
A gold minute repeating keyless lever watch, Patek Philippe, the dial inscribed Tiffany & Co, 5.5cm (2¼in), *L 25 July,* £2,970 ($4,366)

6
A silver pocket chronometer, 1806, signed Jno.R. Arnold London, 6.5cm (2½in), *L 5 Dec,* £4,620 ($6,468)

7
A gold centre seconds union chronometer, 1867, Edward White, from Dents, London, 5cm (2in), *L 25 Apr,* £715 ($922)

8
A gold open faced key wound pocket chronometer, 18 carat, Robt. Best, Royl. Exchange, London, hallmarked London 1817, 5cm (2in), *C 17 Jan,* £902 ($1,082)

9
A silver open faced double wheel duplex watch, Urban Jürgensen, Copenhagen, 5.5cm (2¼in), *G 12 Nov,* SF 4,510 (£1,474; $2,064)

10
An American gold chronograph with register, A W W.Co, Waltham, *c.*14 carat, 5cm (2in), *NY 14 Jan,* $1,210 (£1,090)

11
A gold minute repeating watch with perpetual calendar and moon phases, *c.*1900, Vacheron & Constantin, Geneva, 18 carat, 5cm (2in), *NY 17 June,* $11,000 (£8,661)

12
A gold multi-dialled watch with compass, *c.*1800, with subsidiary dials for the time in Paris, Cairo, Cayenne and Pondicheri, 6cm (2in), *L 28 Oct,* £5,500 ($8,195)

13
A gold double dialled watch-form perpetual calendar with moon phases, *c.*1790, stamped CFC, 5.5cm (2¼in), *NY 17 June,* $1,760 (£1,385)

14
A Swiss gold keyless lever calendar watch, signed Retouret, Feant Grand Quai 18, Geneva, 5cm (2in), *G 12 Nov,* SF 4,840 (£1,582; $2,215)

Verge Escapement
A recoil escapement, and the first escapement applied to mechanical timekeepers. In use continuously from 1300 to 1900.

Cylinder Escapement
An escapement invented by George Graham in 1726. A cylinder, with a segment cut away, forms part of the balance staff. Early examples had steel cylinders and brass escape wheels. From about 1760 some high-grade watches had ruby cylinders and steel escape wheels, to reduce wear.

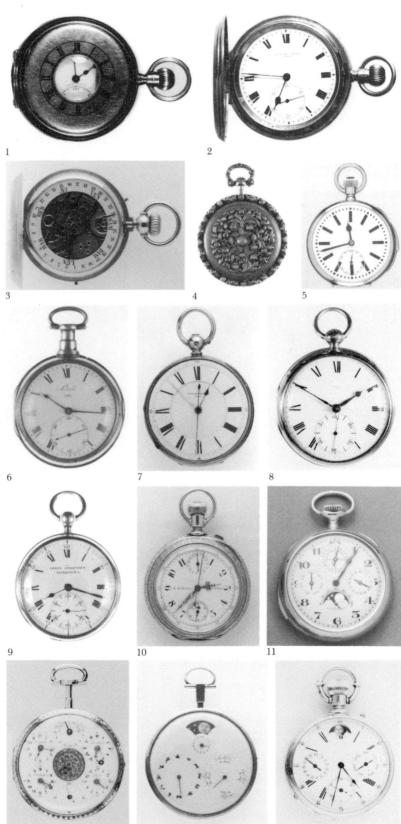

1
A silver pair case quarter-repeating coach watch with alarum, c.1740, signed Miroir, London, the case signed C F Winter, L, 12cm 4¾in), *NY 17 June,* $11,000 (£8,661)

2
An oval gilt-metal verge watch, c.1600, by Nicholas Vallin, signed, 5.5cm (2¼in) long, *L 28 Feb,* £2,970 ($3,445)

3
A gold minute repeating duplex watch, hall-marked 1819, 5.5cm (2¼in), *L 28 Oct,* £2,090 ($3,114)

4
A gold and champlevé enamel pair cased cylinder watch, c.1830, by Courvoisier & Compe, signed 4.5cm (1¾in), *G 12 Nov,* SF 3,520 (£1,150; $1,610)

5
A gold and champlevé enamel ring watch, c.1840, dial 2cm (¾in), with Breguet type male winding key, *L 28 Feb,* £1,760 ($2,042)

6
A lady's gold and diamond hunting case watch, c.1905, Patek Philippe & Co, Geneva, 18 carat, 3cm (1¼in), *NY 30 Oct,* $1,430 (£1,000)

7
A gold and enamel hunting case minute repeating automaton watch, c.1890, 18 carat, 5.5cm (2¼in), *NY 14 Jan,* $2,750 (£2,477)

8
A Swiss gold, red enamel and rose-diamond set keyless cylinder watch, late 19th century, 2cm (¾in), *L 28 Feb,* £484 ($561)

9
A silver calendar watch with regulator dial, c.1810, 5.5cm (2¼in), *NY 17 June,* $990 (£780)

10
A gold quarter-repeating automaton, c.1820, bearing the signature Breguet à Paris, 6cm (2½in), *G 12 Nov,* SF 22,000 (£7,190; $10,066)

11
A gold, pearl and rose-diamond set keyless lever watch and brooch, Vacheron & Constantin, 2.5cm (1in), *L 10 Jan,* £880 ($1,056)

12
A gilt metal pedometer, c.1800, Spencer & Perkins, London, 5.5cm (2¼in), *NY 17 June,* $440 (£346)

13
A gold and enamel watch, c.1930, Ulysse Nardin, Locle, 5cm (2in), *NY 4 Apr,* $825 (£693)

14
A gold and diamond skeleton pocket watch, Audemars Piguet, 18 carat, *G 15 May,* SF 12,100 (£3,538; $4,706)

15
A pigskin covered steel calendar watch, c.1935, signed Movado, closed 5cm (2in), *L 28 Feb,* £638 ($740)

16
A gold pistol form watch key, second quarter 19th century, 7.5cm (3in), *NY 4 Apr,* $770 (£647)

17
A gold Dunhill lighter watch, c.1940, 9 carat, 5.5cm (2in), *NY 30 Oct,* $1,540 (£1,077)

Lever Escapement
A type of precision escapement invented in the 18th century and employed in the great majority of marine and pocket chronometers.

Detent Escapement
A type of precision escapement invented in the 18th century and employed in the great majority of marine and pocket chronometers. At first the detent was pivoted, but the spring detent is now almost universal.

1
A gold Dunhill lighter watch, 1928, 5.5cm (2in) high, *L 28 Feb,* £748 ($968)

2
A gold coin watch in the form of a $20 piece, 1924, 3.5cm (1¼in), *L 28 Oct,* £1,650 ($2,459)

3
A gold hunting cased Grande Sonnerie clock-watch, *c.*1900, La Rochette, Chaux-de-Fonds, 14 carat, 5.5cm (2¼in), *NY 30 Oct,* $4,950 (£3,462)

4
A gold half hunting cased minute repeating watch, *c.*1889, retailed by Tiffany & Co, 18 carat, 5cm (2in), *NY 17 June,* $2,970 (£2,338)

5
A gold hunting cased pocket chronometer, Charles Frodsham, hallmarked London, 1874, 6cm (2½in), *S 18 Apr,* £3,740 ($4,862)

6
A gold hunting cased watch, *c.*1885, Patek Philippe & Co, Geneva, 5cm (2in), *NY 4 Apr,* $2,640 (£2,218)

7
A gold hunting cased pocket chronometer, 19th century, Robert Roskell of Liverpool, 5cm (2in), *L 6 June,* £638 ($849)

8
A gold keyless free-sprung half hunting cased lever chronograph, hall-marked London 1887, 18 carat, 5cm (2in), *C 3 Oct,* £748 ($1,093)

9
A gold hunting cased Swiss minute repeating keyless lever perpetual calendar chronograph, signed J E Dufour & Cie, E Wirth, Succr. Geneva, 5.5cm (2¼in), *G 12 Nov,* **SF 25,300** (£8,268; $11,575)

10
A gold thin hunting cased watch, *c.*1915, Patek Philippe & Co, Geneva, 18 carat, 5cm (2in), *NY 14 Jan,* $1,540 (£1,387)

11
A Swiss gold and enamel hunting-cased cylinder watch, *c.*1850, with polychrome enamel lakeside scene, 3cm (1¼in), *L 28 Feb,* £550 ($638)

12
A gold hunting cased keyless lever chronograph, Hall & Co, hallmarked London 1882, 18 carat, *C 17 Jan,* £440 ($528)

13
A gold half hunting cased minute repeating keyless lever watch, hallmarked 1894, 5.5cm (2¼in), *L 6 June,* £1,650 ($2,195)

14
A gold hunting cased minute repeating lever watch, J R Losada, London, hallmarked 1861, 4cm (1½in), *L 19 Jan,* £3,520 ($4,224)

15
A hunting cased keyless lever watch, A Lange & Sohne, Glashutte, Dresden, 5.5cm (2¼in), *S 21 Feb,* £1,155 ($1,328)

Duplex Escapement
The escapement in its widely used form was invented by Thomas Tyrer in 1782. It was popular during the first half of the 19th century.

Tourbillon
A type of revolving carriage carrying the escapement of a watch. As it turns through 360° the effects of errors are neutralised. Invented by A L Breguet and patented in 1801.

Karrusel
A type of revolving carriage patented in 1894 by Bahne Bonniksen, in which (unlike the tourbillon) the carriage and escape wheel are driven separately.
GLOSSARY CONTINUED ON P.160

Wristwatches

Wristwatches are a relatively new collecting area and one that has seen tremendous growth over the last six years. Although the wristwatch represents a significant aspect of horological history, collectors today are generally more interested in a watch's design and wearability than in its technical qualities.

The first group of wristwatches to be offered at auction appeared in the mid-1970s at Sotheby's New York. The highlight, a Patek Philippe perpetual calendar wristwatch, realized $3,000 (£2,000); the same watch has since fetched $11,550 (£7,700) in the saleroom. From then on, the appearance of wristwatches at auction was haphazard at best, and it was not until 1980 that a specialized section of wristwatches was offered. This venture was prompted by rumours that the Swiss were about to abandon the production of mechanical watches in favour of quartz Six years later, these rumours have proved only partially true, as there are still a number of watchmakers—Patek Philippe, Rolex, Vacheron and Constantin—which continue to produce mechanical watches.

—1—
An 18-carat gold wristwatch, retailed by Asprey, c.1915, 5cm (2in), *NY 14 Jan,* $660 (£595)

—2—
An 18-carat gold oval Curvex wristwatch, Bueche Girod, 5.5cm (2¼in), *NY 30 Oct,* $1,210 (£846)

—3—
An 18-carat striped white and yellow gold Rolex Prince wristwatch, 1928, 4cm (1½in), *L 28 Feb,* £3,740 ($4,338)

—4—
A stainless steel and gold duo dial Prince wristwatch, Rolex Prince Chronometer, c.1935, case, dial and movement signed, 4.5cm (1¾in), *NY 4 Apr,* $3,410 (£2,866)

—5—
A stainless steel and gold-filled octagonal water resistant wristwatch, Rolex Oyster, c.1927, case, dial and movement signed, 4cm (1½in), *NY 17 June,* $880 (£693)

—6—
An 18-carat gold day/date centre seconds oyster wristwatch, Rolex, with fitted President bracelet, 3.5cm (1¼in), *L 28 Feb,* £3,850 ($4,466)

—7—
An 18-carat gold wristwatch, with matching gold bracelet, Rolex, Cellini, King Midas, 3.5cm (1¼in), *NY 17 June,* $3,300 (£2,598)

—8—
An 18-carat gold GMT-Master oyster Perpetual, Rolex with gold bracelet, 4cm (1½in), *L 6 June,* £2,420 ($3,219)

—9—
An 18-carat two-colour gold digital Rolex Prince wristwatch, 1930, 4cm (1½in), *L 6 June,* £4,400 ($5,852)

—10—
A 9-carat two-colour gold wristwatch, Rolex, 1930, 4cm (1½in), *L 28 Feb,* £770 ($893)

—11—
A 9-carat gold Rolex oyster wristwatch, 1934, bezel 3cm (1¼in), *L 28 Feb,* £572 ($664)

—12—
A 9-carat gold Rolex Prince wristwatch, 1929, 4.5cm (1¾in), *L 28 Feb,* £1,650 ($1,914)

—1—

—2—

—3—

—4—

—5— —6— —7— —8—

—9— —10— —11— —12—

Multi-calibrated chronograph. One which combines more than one calibrated scale, such as telemeter, pulsemeter etc.

Perpetual Chronograph. A watch which has both perpetual calendar and chronograph work.

Reprinted dial. A restored or refinished dial—done for purposes of cleaning.

The results of the 1980 sale were mixed, but encouraging enough to warrant continuing the venture. By mid-1981, the market for pocket watches had reached a peak and then fallen, and attention began to shift more and more to the wristwatch. Since then, wristwatches have emerged as a separate collecting field that continues to grow and become more clearly defined.

The auction pattern has been similar in London; although the numbers and variety of wristwatches offered in London has not been as great as in New York, the price trends are parallel.

Last autumn saw the first sale of wristwatches in Geneva.

In this field, there are three main areas of interest: the design of the case, technical complication, and the design of the dial. The cases most sought after are those that have unusual shapes, such as the rectangular or square form, and round watches with unusual bezels or interesting lugs. Also influential is the colour of the case, whether yellow or pink gold, platinum or a combination of these tones. Lastly, a premium will also be paid if the case is water-resistant.

—13—
An 18-carat gold wristwatch, Patek Philippe & Co, Geneva, 1965, 3.5cm (1¼in), *NY 14 Jan*, $1,430 (£1,288)

—14—
An 18-carat pink gold wristwatch, Patek Philippe & Co, Geneva, c.1956, case, dial and movement signed, 3.5cm (1¼in), *G 12 Nov*, SF 2,200 (£719; $1,007)

—15—
A lady's white gold and diamond wristwatch, Patek Philippe & Co, Geneva, translucent blue enamel gold dial, the bezel set with 36 single-cut diamonds, with 18-carat white gold strap, 2.5cm (1in), *NY 14 Jan*, $3,740 (£3,369)

—16—
An 18-carat gold automatic wristwatch, modern, Patek Philippe & Co, Geneva, with gold bracelet, 3.5cm (1¼in), *L 28 Feb*, £1,980 ($2,297)

—17—
A stainless steel chronograph with register, Patek Philippe & Co, Geneva, c.1940, case, dial and movement signed, 3.5cm 1¼in), *NY 4 Apr*, $1,870 (£1,571)

—18—
An 18-carat gold wristwatch, Patek Philippe & Co, Geneva, c.1946, case, dial and movement signed, 3cm (1¼in), *NY 4 Apr*, $1,100 (£924)

—19—
An early transitional 18-carat gold wristwatch with enamel dial, Patek Philippe & Co, Geneva, case, dial, movement and cuvette signed, 4cm 1½in), *NY 30 Oct*, $3,300 (£2,308)

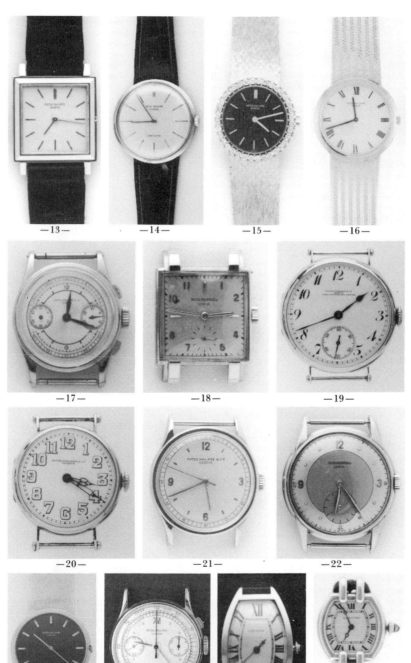

—13—   —14—   —15—   —16—

—17—   —18—   —19—

—20—   —21—   —22—

—23—   —24—   —25—   —26—

—20—
An 18-carat early gold wristwatch with enamel dial, Patek Philippe & Co, Geneva, c.1910, case, dial, cuvette and movement signed, 3cm (1¼in), *NY 30 Oct*, $1,650 (£1,154)

—21—
An 18-carat pink gold sweep seconds wristwatch, Patek Philippe & Co, Geneva, c.1935, case, dial and movement signed, 4cm (1½in), *NY 4 Apr*, $1,540 (£1,294)

—22—
An 18-carat gold wristwatch, Patek Philippe & Co, Geneva, c.1947, case, dial and movement signed, 3.5cm (1¼in), *NY 14 Jan*, $990 (£892)

—23—
An 18-carat white gold self-winding wristwatch, Patek Philippe & Co, Geneva, with integral gold bracelet, 3.5cm (1¼in), *NY 30 Oct*, $2,310 (£1,615)

—24—
An 18-carat pink gold chronograph wristwatch with tachometer and registers, Patek Philippe & Co, Geneva, 1946, case, dial and movement signed, 3cm (1¼in) diam, *G 12 Nov*, SF 11,000 (£3,595; $5,033)

—25—
An early platinum elongated tonneau form wristwatch, Cartier, c.1910, 4.5cm (1¾in), *NY 4 Apr*, $3,850 (£3,235)

—26—
An 18-carat gold lady's wristwatch, Cartier, the movement by the European Watch & Clock Company, 2.5cm (1in) long, *L 6 June*, £968 ($1,287)

Within the area of complications, there are several choices. Moon phases, based on the 29½-day moon cycle, will show whether the moon is full or in the quarter, in the half or new moon phase. The chronograph wristwatch has several varieties with calibrated scales for Tachometer, Pulsemeter or Telemeter. A combination of scales and the addition of registers will enhance the value of the watch. In addition, there are also chronographs that include phases of the moon, perpetual calendars and other models with simple calendar and moon phases. Perhaps the simplest complication a watch can have is a self-winding mechanism. This area was explored in great depth in the earlier part of the century, and there are many interesting examples of different ways of arriving at the most efficient self-winding mechanism.

Dial design is perhaps the last element to make its mark on wristwatch collecting. In the past, a reprinted dial was overlooked, but today the originality of the dial has become important in assessing the value of a watch. A refinished dial, particularly on a multi-calibrated chronograph, can have a serious effect on the desirability of a watch. Other factors that influence value include the type of numerals (whether Arabic, Roman or geometric applications) and whether they are printed or painted.

—27—
An 18-carat gold moon phase calendar wristwatch, Ulysse Nardin, Locle, *c.*1950, case, dial and movement signed, 3.5cm (1¼in) diam, *NY 30 Oct,*
$1,430 (£1,000)

—28—
An 18-carat gold early chronograph wristwatch with enamel dial, tachometer and registers, Ulysse Nardin, Locle & Geneva, *c.*1930, case, dial, movement and cuvette signed, 4cm (1½in), *NY 30 Oct,*
$1,980 (£1,385)

—29—
An 18-carat pink gold Curvex wristwatch, Ulysse Nardin, Locle, *c.*1920, case, dial and movement signed, 5cm (2in), *NY 14 Jan,*
$1,650 (£1,486)

—30—
An 18-carat pink gold chronograph wristwatch with tachometer and additional time dial, Universal Geneve, Aero Compax, *c.*1945, 4cm (1½in), *NY 14 Jan,*
$1,540 (£1,387)

—31—
An 18-carat gold chronograph wristwatch with moon phases, calendar and register, Universal Tri-Compax, Geneva, *c.*1945, 4cm (1½in), *NY 30 Oct,*
$1,540 (£1,077)

—32—
An 18-carat gold chronograph wristwatch with tachometer enamel dial, and register, Universal Watch, *c.*1920, 4cm (1½in), *NY 4 Apr,*
$935 (£786)

—33—
An aluminium German aviator's wristwatch, A Lange & Sohne, *c.*1945, 5.5cm (2¼in), *NY 17 June,*
$880 (£693)

—34—
A gold automatic skeleton wristwatch, Gerald Genta, retailed by Van Cleef & Arpels, 3.5cm (1¼in), sold with pair of matching cuff links, *L 6 June,*
£2,860 ($3,804)

—35—
An 18-carat gold wristwatch, by the International Watch Company of Schaffhausen, 3cm (1¼in), *L 6 June,*
£660 ($878)

—36—
An 18-carat gold chronograph wristwatch with tachometer and register, Longines, *c.*1945, 3.5cm (1¼in), *NY 17 June,*
$935 (£736)

—37—
An 18-carat gold lozenge form wristwatch, Jaeger Le Coultre, *c.*1945, 3.5cm (1¼in), *NY 4 Apr,*
$1,650 (£1,387)

—38—
An 18-carat gold wristwatch, 1926, Vacheron & Constantin, 3cm (1¼in), *L 6 June,*
£1,155 ($1,536)

—39—
An 18-carat gold tank wristwatch, Cartier, European Watch & Clock Co, Inc, *c.*1950, 2.5cm (1in), *NY 30 Oct,*
$1,650 (£1,154)

—40—
An 18-carat gold and enamel tank wristwatch, Cartier, Paris, 1935, movement signed Jaeger Le Coultre, 3.5cm (1¼in), *NY 14 Jan,*
$3,300 (£2,973)

As important as the appearance of a watch is the maker's name. The greatest share of the market of old wristwatches is held by Patek Philippe, probably because they manufactured models in every category and their designs are by far the most classically handsome. The next most eminent maker is Rolex; I refer specifically to their watches made before 1960, when the Modern Oyster Perpetual became their leading production model. Models by Cartier are also highly sought after, particularly those dating from the period before 1950. With a few exceptions, Cartier watches are collected for their case and dial designs, but occasionally a complicated Cartier does appear. Smaller makers (Vacheron and Constantin, Audemars Piguet, Le Coultre, Movado, Universal Genève, and Omega) are also collected, usually for watches that are more than a simple timepiece.

Further reading

Negretti and Nencini, *I Signori del Tempo*, 1986

Khalert, Mühe, Brunner, *Armbanduhren*, 1983

Zagoory and Can, *A Time to Watch*, 1984

Calibrated scale. A scale with graduated measurement found in chronograph such as telemeter or tachometer.

Tonneau. A case style usually looking, more or less, like a shaped rectangle.

Register. A subsidiary dial which records lapsed time.

Sweep seconds. The seconds hand is mounted to the centre wheel as opposed to a watch with subsidiary seconds.

● DARYN SCHNIPPER ●

—41—
A 14-carat white gold Mysterieuse wristwatch, Jaeger Le Coultre and Vacheron & Constantin, the black dial signed Le Coultre, 3.5cm (1¼in), L 6 June, £1,430 ($1,902)

—42—
An 18-carat gold self-winding wristwatch, Vacheron & Constantin, Geneva, case, dial and movement signed, 3cm (1¼in) long, NY 4 Apr, $880 (£739)

—43—
An 18-carat gold Curvex wristwatch, Vacheron & Constantin, Geneva, 1915, case, dial and movement signed, 4.5cm (1¾in), NY 14 Jan, $1,540 (£1,387)

—44—
A gold automatic wristwatch, 1963, Piaget, and retailed by Asprey, with gold bracelet, 3cm (1¼in), L 28 Feb, $990 ($1,148)

—45—
An 18-carat gold chronograph wristwatch, 1945, Vacheron & Constantin, 3.5cm (1¼in), G 12 Nov, SF 7,150 (£2,337; $3,272)

—46—
An 18-carat gold Omega Seamaster, the back stamped 'Apollo XI 1969, Moon', gold bracelet, 4cm (1½in), diam, L 28 Feb, $1,870 ($2,169)

—47—
An 18-carat gold wristwatch with calendar and moon phases, Omega c.1945, 3cm (1¼in) diam, NY 14 Jan, $990 (£892)

—48—
An 18-carat gold skeletonised wristwatch, Breguet, no. 591, dial and case signed, 3.5cm (1¼in), NY 4 Apr, $4,400 (£3,697)

—49—
A gold driver's wristwatch, Gruen Curvex, c.1939, 4cm (1½in), NY 30 Oct, $1,100 (£769)

—50—
A white gold and lapis lazuli square wristwatch, Piaget, with 18-carat Piaget white gold buckle, 2.5cm (1in), NY 17 June, $1,760 (£1,385)

—51—
An 18-carat lady's gold and lapis lazuli bracelet wristwatch, Piaget, retailed by Tiffany & Co, the bracelet with oval buckle form links, 3cm (1¼in), NY 4 Apr, $1,980 (£1,664)

—52—
An 18-carat gold self-winding skeletonised wristwatch, Audemars Piguet, c.1970, 3cm (1¼in), NY 17 June, $5,225 (£4,114)

—53—
An 18-carat gold and enamel wristwatch, Le Coultre Watch Co, 1970, with pink gold deployant buckle, 4cm (1½in), NY 30 Oct, $4,125 (£2,885)

—41—   —42—   —43—   —44—

—45—   —46—   —47—

—48—   —49—   —50—

—51—

—52—   —53—

1
A late George III
mahogany barometer-
cum-timepiece, the dial
signed Willm. Terry
London no 138, the
silvered plate signed
Lione & Somalvico
112cm (44in), *L 5 Dec,*
£990 ($1,386)

2
A mahogany wheel
barometer, *c.*1840, the
plate signed C W
Dixey, 3 New Bond
Street, London, 104cm
(41in), *C 17 Jan,*
£374 ($449)

3
A mahogany barometer,
early 19th century, the
level signed Fras.
Saltry & Co, Holbourn
Hill, London, no 94,
C 18 Apr,
£1,045 ($1,359)

4
A mahogany stick baro-
meter, with silvered
scales, inscribed
Troughton & Simms,
London, 99cm (39in),
S 21 Feb,
£1,760 ($2,024)

5
A George III mahogany
stick barometer, *c.*1800,
signed Torre & Co,
London, 95cm (37½in),
C 17 Jan,
£352 ($422)

6
An early 19th century
bow-fronted mahogany
stick barometer, signed
W & S Jones Holborn
London, 100cm (39½in),
L 5 Dec,
£2,420 ($3,388)

7
A George III mahogany
stick barometer, *c.*1770,
with later silvered
plate 92cm (36in),
C 3 Oct,
£275 ($402)

8
A Dutch mahogany baro-
meter, signed Reballio,
Rotterdam, 131cm
(51½in), *A 29 Oct,*
Dfl 5,060 (£1,205; $1,795)

9
A Dutch mahogany baro-
meter, by A Peia,
Amsterdam, 135cm
(53in), *C 3 Oct,*
£1,870 ($2,730)

10
An eight-day marine
chronometer, by Brock-
bank, Atkins & Moore,
no 2112, bezel 15.5cm
(6in) diam, *L 5 Dec,*
£2,640 ($3,696)

11
A two-day marine
chronometer, by Frod-
sham & Keen, Liverpool,
no 4007, 18.5cm (7¼in),
NY 4 Apr,
$880 (£739)

12
A two-day marine
chronometer, by James
Murray of London and
numbered 829, bezel
12.5cm (5in) diam,
L 25 July,
£1,210 ($1,779)

13
A small marine chrono-
meter, early 19th
century, by Louis
Berthoud, no 54, bezel
8cm (3in) diam, *L 25 Apr,*
£10,450 ($13,481)

14
A marine chronometer,
signed John Arnold &
Son, London, no 18,
11.5cm (4½in), *L 28 Feb,*
£10,450 ($12,122)

CONTINUED FROM P.155
Free-sprung
Of a watch which can only be regulated by
adjusting the screws on the balance, and lacking a
regulation pointer. Chronometers and many
high-grade watches are free-sprung.

Keyless
Of a watch that is wound from the crown and does
not have a separate key.

Jump Hour
An hour hand which does not advance steadily,
but jumps forward an hour at a time.

1   2   3   4   5

6   7   8   9

10

11

12   13   14

1
A Charles I carved and inlaid oak press cupboard, *c.*1625, 162cm (5ft 4in) wide, *L 26 Apr,*
£3,190 ($4,051)

2
A Charles II table armchair, *c.*1680, the solid seat above a guilloche-carved drawer, *L 26 Apr,*
£3,300 ($4,191)

3
A Dutch marquetry screen, *c.*1840, inlaid on one side with dense floral marquetry and on the other with lighter sprays, 219cm (7ft 2in) high, *L 29 Nov,*
£15,400 ($21,560)

1

2

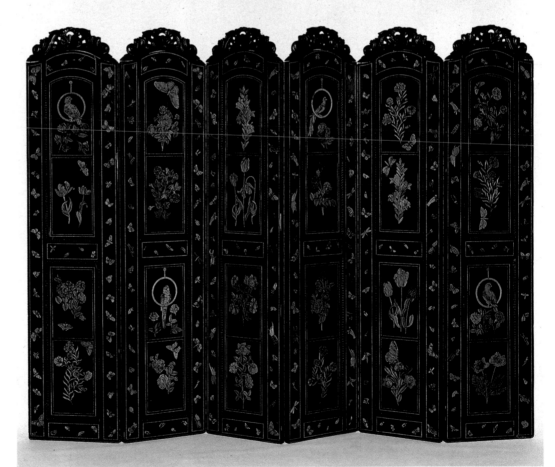

3

1
**A George I walnut con-
certina-action games
table,** first quarter 18th
century, the top enclos-
ing a baize-lined gaming
surface, 91cm (36in) wide,
NY 1 Nov,
$23,100 (£16,041)

2
**A pair of George III
satinwood card tables,**
*c.*1780, crossbanded in
purpleheart, 92cm (3ft)
wide, *L 8 Mar,*
£10,120 ($11,334)

1

2

A **Queen Anne walnut
side table,** c.1715, 76cm
(30in) wide, *L 8 Mar,*
£5,280 ($5,914)

A **George II giltwood
wall mirror,** c.1730, with
later rectangular plate,
165cm (5ft 5in) high,
L 8 Mar,
£4,400 ($4,928)

A **George I burr yew-
wood and walnut, inlaid
chest on chest,** c.1725,
185cm (6ft 1in) high,
NY 26 Jan,
$11,000 (£9,909)

A **George III inlaid burr
yew-wood and satinwood
Pembroke table,** last
quarter 18th century,
width open 88cm
(34½in), *NY 26 Jan,*
$14,300 (£12,882)

1

3

2

4

1
A set of fourteen mahogany dining chairs, ten
c.1835, *L 15 Nov*,
£17,600 ($24,640)

2
A set of twelve George
III mahogany dining
chairs, late 18th century,
together with two matching armchairs of later
date, *NY 8 June*,
$23,100 (£18,333)

3
A set of ten George III
style mahogany dining
chairs, including two
armchairs, *NY 1 Nov*,
$28,600 (£19,861)

4
A pair of Regency
mahogany bergères,
c.1810, with caned
back and now leather-
upholstered, *L 14 June*,
£17,050 ($22,676)

1

2

3

4

1
A George III mahogany library table, late 18th century, with inset leather writing surface, and alternate drawers and false drawer-fronts, 112cm (44in) wide, NY 13 Apr, $7,700 (£6,160)

2
A George III mahogany writing table c.1800, with leather-lined top, 122cm (48in) wide, L 8 Mar, £8,800 ($9,856)

3
A pair of George III inlaid mahogany secretaire cabinets, last quarter 18th century, 222cm (7ft 3½in), NY 1 Nov, $18,700 (£12,986)

4
A George III serpentine mahogany sideboard, c.1780, 185cm (6ft 1in) wide, L 14 June, £7,150 ($9,510)

1

2

3

4

1
A pair of Louis XV ormolu wall lights, mid-18th century, 56cm (22in) high, *NY 9 Nov,* $26,400 (£18,592)

2
A Russian Tula cut-steel candelabrum, late 18th century, one of a pair given in the late 18th century to the Duchess of Alba, later famous for having been painted by Goya, 47cm (18½in) high, in original case, *L 24 May,* £10,450 ($13,899)

3
A pair of Louis XV tôle-peinte wine coolers, *c.*1740, decorated in imitation of oriental lacquer, 21.5c (8½in), *L 5 July,* £8,250 ($11,385)

1

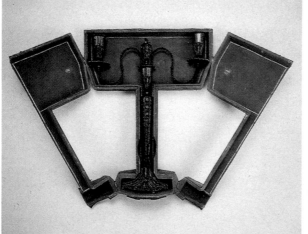

2

3

1
**A pair of Louis XV
ormolu chenets,** mid-18th
century, representing a
male musician and a
female figure, 31cm
(12¼in) high, *NY 8 Nov,*
$23,100 (£16,268)

2
**An early Louis XV king-
wood parquetry
commode,** *c.*1725, 126cm
(4ft 1½in) wide, *L 5 July,*
£5,280 ($7,286)

3
**A Louis XV ormolu-
mounted black lacquer
commode,** mid-18th cen-
tury, signed Delorme,
JME, with *verde antico*
marble top, decorated
with panels of chinois-
eries, 148cm (4ft 10in)
wide, *NY 4 May,*
$132,000 (£110,000)

4
**A Louis XV/XVI tran-
sitional marquetry
commode,** stamped
G Kemp JME, *c.*1775,
now with grey marble top,
gilt-bronze mounts,
115cm (45¼in) wide,
L 29 Nov,
£19,250 ($26,950)

5
**A Louis XV/XVI tran-
sitional bureau à cylindre,**
*c.*1770, the top and cylinder front inlaid with
musical trophies, 99cm
(39in) high, *L 29 Nov,*
£11,550 ($16,170)

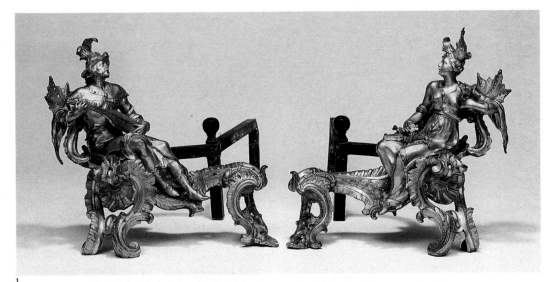

1

2

3

4

5

1
**A Régence gilded wood
mirror,** 196cm (6ft 5in)
high, *M 23 June,*
**FF 111,000
(£8,944; $11,985)**

2
**A Lombard marquetry
commode,** *c.*1790, the
quartered rosewood
ground with leaf border,
central roundel of
Classical figures, 121cm
(47½in) wide, *L 24 May,*
£6,600 ($8,778)

3
**A German marquetry
table,** attributed to David
Roentgen, *c.*1765, raised
on de-mountable cabriole
legs, 76cm (32in) high,
L 24 May,
£7,480 ($9,948)

4
**A Louis XVI sycamore
parquetry table à écrire,**
last quarter 18th century,
in the manner of
Craemer, the frieze
drawer fitted with a writing surface and inkwell
and powder box, 69cm
(27¼in) high, *NY 4 May,*
$9,900 (£8,250)

5
**A Genoese walnut-
veneered commode,** mid-
18th century, 120cm (3ft
11in) wide, *L 29 Nov,*
£5,280 ($7,392)

1
A South German parcel-
gilt walnut bureau-
cabinet, mid-18th cen-
tury, the doors each with
removable panel, 224cm
(7ft 4in) high, *L 29 Nov,*
£9,680 ($13,552)

2
A German walnut and
parquetry commode,
c.1750, 150cm (59in) wide,
L 29 Nov,
£7,150 ($10,010)

1

2

1
A pair of Italian painted torchères, last quarter 18th century, each with white marble top, 122cm (48in), *NY 12 Oct,* $23,100 (£16,383)

2
A German ormolu-mounted tulipwood and kingwood marquetry writing table, mid-18th century, 83cm (32¾in) wide, *NY 9 Nov,* $16,500 (£11,620)

1

2

1
A pair of Directoire mahogany guéridons, late 18th century, each with circular veined green marble top, 102cm (40¼in) high, *NY 9 Nov,* $27,500 (£19,366)

2
An Empire mahogany-veneered bronze-mounted dressing table, attributed to Jacob Frères, *M 24 June,* **FF 79,920** (£6,440; $8,630)

3
A Directoire mahogany commode, *c.*1795, with grey marble top, banded in gilt brass, 117cm (46in) wide, *C 18 Apr,* £3,960 ($5,148)

1

2

3

1
A gilt-metal-mounted
painted and kingwood-
veneered vitrine, *c.*1890,
the lower parts of each
door with a bombé Ver-
nis Martin panel, 196cm
(6ft 5in) high, *L 22 Mar,*
£3,190 ($3,828)

2
A Victorian inlaid satin-
wood Carlton House
writing table, *c.*1890,
122cm (48in) wide,
L 22 Feb,
£11,550 ($13,167)

3
A pair of boulle brass and
pewter side cabinets,
*c.*1860, with gilt-
metal masks and mount,
139cm (55in) high,
L 22 Mar,
£3,740 ($4,488)

4
A satinwood bonheur du
jour, by Henry Dasson,
1878, with rust and beige
marble top and a pair of
doors each with a
Japanese lacquer panel,
111cm (44in) high,
L 21 June,
£4,070 ($5,291)

5
A tulipwood and king-
wood marquetry centre
table, by Zwiener, *c.*1880,
74cm (29in) high,
L 22 Mar,
£5,500 ($6,600)

1

3

2

4

5

1
A Federal satinwood and rosewood inlaid mahogany card table, Massachusetts, *c*.1805, 89cm (35in) wide, *NY 1 Feb,* $12,650 (£11,500)

2
A Queen Anne cherry-wood slant-front desk on frame, Connecticut, *c*.1750, 107cm (42in) high, *NY 2 Feb,* $18,700 (£15,847)

3
A Chippendale walnut step-back cupboard, Pennsylvania, *c*.1775, in two sections, 218cm (7ft 1¾in) high, *NY 26 Oct,* $23,100 (£16,267)

4
A Chippendale walnut side chair, Philadelphia, 1760-80, *NY 2 Feb,* $11,550 (£10,500)

5
A Federal inlaid mahogany sideboard, probably Baltimore, Maryland, *c*.1800, 183cm (6ft) wide, *NY 2 Feb,* $28,600 (£26,000)

1

2

3

4

5

1
**An appliqued and
Trapunto chintz and
cotton quilt,** Cordelia
Young, Montgomery
County, Maryland,
*c.*1823, minor stain and
discolouration, 2.54 x
2.54m (100 x 100in)
NY 1 Feb,
$9,075 (£7,691)

2
**A Charles II silk-
embroidered and raised
work picture,** English,
*c.*1660, some restoration,
34 x 45cm (13½ x 17¾in),
L 17 July,
£1,870 ($2,712)

3
**A silk-embroidered
mourning picture,** Eliza
Durnford, Connecticut,
1800, 61 x 48cm (24 x
19in); together with a
watercolour hatchment
of the Durnford family
coat of arms, 52 x 46cm
(20½ x 18in),
NY 28 June,
$23,100 (£17,769)

1

2

3

**French tapestry-woven
carpet** of Bessarabian
design, last quarter 19th
century, 574 x 412cm
(18ft 8in x 13ft 6in),
NY 13 Apr,
$46,200 (£36,960)

**An English needlepoint
carpet,** first quarter
20th century, 406 x
198cm (13ft 4in x 6ft 6in),
NY 26 Jan,
$9,900 (£8,919)

1

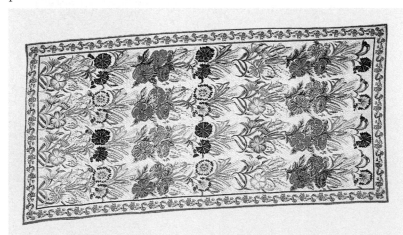

2

1
A prisoner-of-war bone model of H.M.S. 'Royal Sovereign', French, early 19th century, 52 x 64cm (20½ x 25¼in), *L 23 Oct,* **£11,000 ($16,500)**

2
An engraved and polychromed baby sperm whale jaw, American, 19th century, one side engraved with a whaling ship, the reverse with a wounded sperm whale, 47cm (18½in) long, *NY 28 June,* **$6,600 (£5,076)**

3
A punched tin coffee pot, marked W. Shade for Mary Shade, Pennsylvania, dated March 18, 1848, 28.5cm, (11¼in) high, *NY 26 Oct,* **$2,640 (£1,859)**

4
A wrigglesware tinware coffee pot, probably Pennsylvania, early 19th century, bearing the wrigglesware serpent maker's mark, 25.5cm (10¾in) high, *NY 26 Oct,* **$2,420 (£1,704)**

1

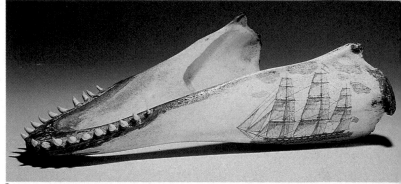

2

3   4

Folk Art

See also
● Colour illustrations *p 176* ● Textiles *pp 122-125*

1
A double-sided inn sign 'Queen Victoria', English, mid-19th century, painted on both faces with a portrait of the Queen, 140 x 114cm (55 x 45in), *L 17 July,* £770 ($1,117)

2
A carved and gilded pine butcher shop trade sign, 19th century, gesso cracked and flaking, 94cm (37in) high, *NY 28 June,* $4,675 (£3,596)

3
A carved and painted wood 'Yale Locks Locksmith' trade sign, American, late 19th/early 20th century, cut from a single plank of wood in the form of a large key, 105cm (41½in) long, *NY 28 June,* $1,760 (£1,353)

4
A carved and painted wood cigar store figure, attributed to Samuel Robb, New York, *c.*1880, some wear, 114cm (45in) high, *NY 1 Feb,* $6,600 (£5,593)

5
A moulded and painted tin advertising sign, American, early 20th century, in the form of a black child in red shirt and yellow straw hat, some dents, 132cm (52in) high, *NY 26 Oct,* $1,980 (£1,394)

6
An outsize teapot shop sign, English, early 20th century, in papier-mâché, 76cm (30in) high, *L 17 July,* £1,045 ($1,515)

7
A carved and painted wood cigar store Indian Princess, S. A. Robb, New York, late 19th century, some wear, 178cm (70in) high overall, *NY 28 June,* $6,050 (£4,653)

8
A carved and painted wood blacksmith trade sign, Maine, late 19th/early 20th century, carved in the form of a large horse-shoe, 69cm (27¼in) high, *NY 28 June,* $1,430 (£1,100)

9
A painted tinware hatter's trade sign, 19th century, some flaking, 20cm (8in), *NY 1 Feb,* $990 (£839)

1

2

3

5

6

7

8

9

1
A gilded and painted sheet-metal soldier weathervane, American 19th century, 49.5cm (19½in) high, *NY 28 June*, $2,860 (£2,200)

2
A moulded and gilded copper Massasoit Indian weathervane, Harris & Co., Boston, late 19th century, with much original gilding, 97cm (38in), *NY 28 June*, $34,100 (£26,230)

3
A cast-iron horse weathervane, New England, c.1860, 71cm (28in) high, *NY 26 Oct*, $9,350 (£6,585)

4
A cast-iron horse weathervane, New England, c.1860, bullet holes in rear leg, 70cm (27½in) high, *NY 1 Feb*, $9,900 (£8,390)

5
A moulded and gilded copper rooster weathervane, New England, mid-19th century, with traces of gilded and yellow polychroming, 74cm (29in) high, *NY 26 Oct*, $3,300 (£2,324)

6
A moulded and gilded copper game cock weathervane, probably Harris & Co., Boston, Massachusetts, third quarter 19th century, 51cm (20in), *NY 1 Feb*, $1,870 (£1,585)

7
A sheet-metal American flag lightning rod finial, c.1890, 38cm (15in) high, *NY 1 Feb*, $1,045 (£886)

8
A painted tin cow weathervane, Walter Crawford, New York State, c.1890, retaining much original polychrome, 83cm (32½in) high, *NY 28 June*, $2,750 (£2,115)

9
A moulded copper cow weathervane, L. W. Cushing & Son, Waltham, Massachusetts, third quarter 19th century, 61cm (24in) high, *NY 28 June*, $3,850 (£2,961)

10
A moulded copper 'Black Hawk' weathervane, Harris & Co., Boston, 19th century, with traces of original gilding and subsequent polychrome, some tiny holes, 60cm (23½in) high, *NY 28 June*, $1,980 (£1,523)

11
A moulded copper and zinc steer weathervane, probably Cushing & White, Co., Waltham, Massachusetts, third quarter 19th century, 71.5cm (28in) high, *NY 1 Feb*, $3,025 (£2,564)

1
A two-man hand-operated portable fire pump, late 19th century, slightly distressed, 127cm (50in) high, *S 2 Oct*, £506 ($744)

2
A lace pillow, bobbins and accessories, English, mainly 19th century, *L 17 July*, £495 ($718)

3
A Hemming clamp, East European, mid-19th century, with pin cushion mounted above 17th-century style dolphin, re-gilded, 21cm (8¼in), *L 26 Sept*, £352 ($528)

4
A Welsh love spoon, 19th century, of carved elm, the grip pierced and carved with a heart, *L 17 July*, £209 ($303)

5
Two love spoons probably Welsh, 19th century, one pierced and carved with leaves and sunflowers, the other pierced with cartwheel and star motifs, *L 17 July*, £528 ($766)

6
Three pastry crimpers, English, early 19th century, one with carved fruitwood handle, 18cm (7in), another with oak handle and double wheel, 16cm, (6¼in) and another with chip-carved handle, 17cm (6¾in), *L 17 July*, £242 ($351)

7
Two pastry crimpers, English, early 19th century, one with oak handle and ivory wheel, 18cm (7in), (the other of fruitwood carved with love tokens, 14cm (5½in), *L 17 July*, £165 ($239)

8
A copper standing horse weathervane, English, mid-19th century, 185cm (73in) high, *L 17 July*, £2,530 ($3,669)

9
A copper cockerel weathervane, mid-19th century, of hand-beaten construction, 56cm (22in) long, *L 17 July*, £495 ($718)

10
A painted and wrought-iron child's sled, American, late 19th century, the platform painted with a sailboat, and yellow tulips and blue scrolls on a red ground, 120cm (47in) long, *NY 28 June*, $770 (£592)

11
A decorated elm staff, English, dated 1817, the top carved in the form of a hot air balloon, 103cm (40½in), *L 17 July*, £1,430 ($2,074)

12
A pair of sailor's shell Valentines, Barbadian, late 19th century, the mahogany cases mounted with coloured shells, each 23cm (9in) wide, *L 5 June*, £880 ($1,170)

13
An engraved powder horn, American, probably Pennsylvania, early 19th century, engraved with various figures including an American eagle, 33cm (13in) long, *NY 28 June*, $1,540 (£1,184)

14
A painted cast-iron velocipede, New York, c.1870, the horse with cast-iron head and wood body painted red, 75cm (29½in) high, *NY 28 June*, $1,100 (£846)

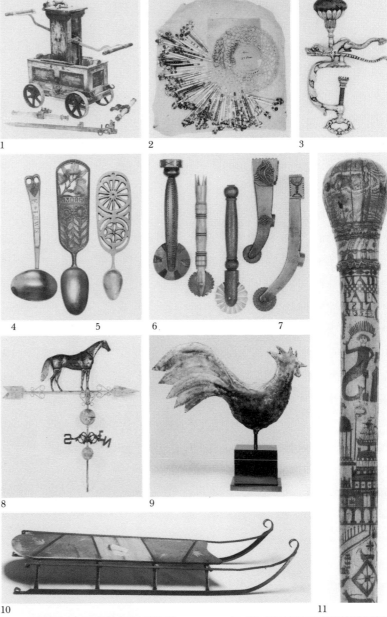

1

2

3

4

5

6

7

8

9

10

11

12

13

14

1
A carved and painted wood yarn winder, third quarter 19th century, 90cm (35½in) high, *NY 1 Feb,* $2,750 (£2,331)

2
A tinware coffee pot, Pennsylvania, 19th century, decorated on each side with red fruit and yellow foliage on black ground, some flaking, 28cm (11in), *NY 1 Feb,* $935 (£792)

3
A carved cherrywood watch hutch, probably Connecticut, early 19th century, 24cm (9½in) high, *NY 1 Feb,* $770 (£653)

4
A grain-painted pine miniature dome-trunk, probably New England, 19th century, with red-brown swirls and green sponge painting on an ochre ground, 70cm (17½in) wide, *NY 28 June,* $2,530 (£1,946)

5
A painted wood miniature dome-top trunk, probably Continental, early 19th century, painted with red and white designs on a black ground, 27cm (10¾in) high, *NY 28 June,* $935 (£719)

6
A painted and decorated toleware miniature document box, Stevens Plains, Maine, early 19th century, painted in red, white, yellow and green, on a black ground, 11 x 16cm (4½ x 6¼in), *NY 28 June,* $605 (£465)

7
A painted bentwood bride's box, Continental, 18th century, 19cm (7in) high, *NY 28 June,* $770 (£592)

8
A salt-glazed and cobalt blue decorated stoneware crock, M. Woodruff & Co., Cortland, New York, 19th century, 23.5 cm (9¼in), *NY 1 Feb,* $6,875 (£5,826)

9
A salt-glaze decorated stoneware crock, A.O. Whittemore, Havana, New York, 19th century, decorated in cobalt blue, 19cm (7½in), *NY 1 Feb,* $1,430 (£1,212)

10
A carved walnut mahogany cake board, signed J. Y. Watkins, New York, early 19th century, 28 x 28.5cm (11 x 11¼in), *NY 28 June,* $825 (£634)

11
A group of four glazed stoneware crocks, New England, 19th century, heights 19 to 32cm (7½ to 12½in), *NY 28 June,* $1,210 (£930)

12
A salt-glaze stoneware jug, New York, *c.*1810, decorated with cobalt-blue leaves, 39cm (15½in), *NY 1 Feb,* $522 (£442)

13
A salt-glaze stoneware pot, Cheesequake, New Jersey, *c.*1770, the sides impressed with stylised tulip motifs, 33cm (13in), *NY 1 Feb,* $467 (£396)

14
A salt-glaze stoneware pitcher, American, 1800-20, decorated with cobalt-blue bands and floral motif, 33cm (13in), *NY 1 Feb,* $605 (£513)

15
A salt-glaze stoneware pot, probably by Thomas Commeraw, New York, *c.*1800, the sides decorated with cobalt-blue leaves, 26cm (10in), *NY 1 Feb,* $302 (£256)

16
A salt-glaze stoneware pot, possibly by John Remmey, New York, *c.*1815, decorated in cobalt blue, 36cm (14in), *NY 1 Feb,* $550 (£466)

17
A salt-glaze stoneware pot, New York, *c.*1770, the sides decorated with cobalt blue motifs, cracked, 37cm (14½in), *NY 1 Feb,* $660 (£559)

1   2   3

4   5

6   7

8   9

10   11

12   13   14   15   16   17

1
A ship's figurehead,
English, mid-19th
century, arms missing,
130cm (52in) high,
L 5 June,
£990 ($1,317)

2
A ship's figurehead,
English, mid-19th
century, repainted,
142cm (56in) high,
L 5 June,
£2,420 ($3,219)

3
**A carved and polychromed
wood figure of Santa
Claus,** attributed to
North Tonowanda, New
York, *c.*1880, with dark
red and white costume,
and yellow pouch, 56cm
(22in), *NY 26 Oct,*
$20,900 (£14,718)

4
**A carved and painted
wood and tin sailor boy
whirligig,** *c.*1890, 52cm
(20½in), *NY 1 Feb,*
$715 (£606)

5
**A carved and painted
wood figure of a man
chopping wood,** 20th
century, 29cm (11½in)
high, *NY 1 Feb,*
$522 (£442)

6
**A carved and painted pine
head of a man,** North
Carolina, early 20th
century, painted white,
with fabric collar and
buttons, 46cm (18in)
high, *NY 28 June,*
$1,760 (£1,353)

7
**A sailor-made woolwork
picture,** English, late
19th century, with inset
photographic portrait,
45 x 51cm (17¾ x 20in),
L 5 June,
£374 ($497)

8
A sailor-work picture,
*c.*1850, 32 x 46cm (12½
x 18in), *S 19 Mar,*
£462 ($568)

9
**A carved and poly-
chromed side show head,**
*c.*1920, 51cm (20in) high,
NY 1 Feb,
$770 (£653)

10
A woolwork picture,
English, mid-19th
century, 33 x 49cm (13 x
19¼in), *L 5 June,*
£550 ($732)

11
A woolwork picture,
of the frigate 'Star of
Bengal', 49.5 x 37cm
(19½ x 14in), *C 29 Nov,*
£231 ($323)

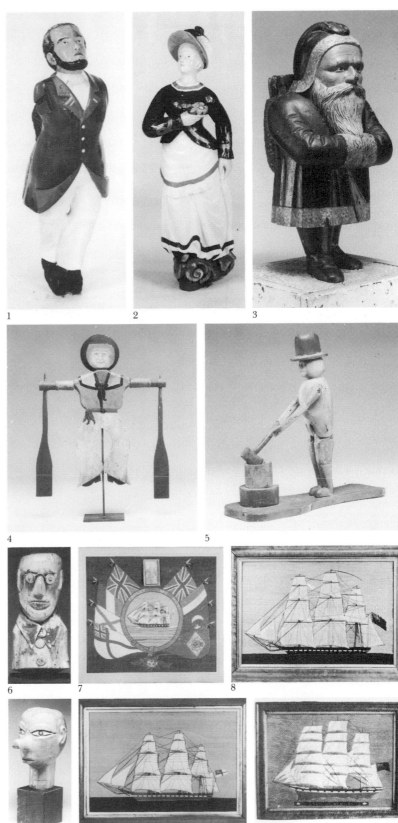

1

2

3

4

5

6

7

8

9

10

11

1

An early pair of scrim-shawed whale's teeth, Scottish, *c.*1830, decorated with husband and wife in traditional costume, both tips chipped, 18cm (7in) high, *L 5 June,* £660 ($878)

2

A pair of scrimshawed whale's teeth, engraved with a British whaler, chips, 14.5cm (5¾in) high, *A 7 Oct,* Dfl 1,552 (£366; $541)

3

An engraved sperm whale's tooth, American, mid-19th century, with a comport with tree and an American eagle on one side, and a Victorian lady on the reverse, 20cm (8in) high, *NY 1 Feb,* $660 (£559)

4

A scrimshawed whale's tooth from the American whaler 'Pactolus', American, dated 1837, with inscription and portrait of the whale below, 19cm (7½in) long, *L 5 June,* £5,500 ($7,315)

5

A scrimshawed pan bone, English, mid-19th century, depicting an admiral's barge approaching a warship off the Dover cliffs, 17.5 x 24.5cm (7 x 9½in), *L 5 June,* £1,540 ($2,048)

6

A scrimshawed busk, English, mid-19th century, depicting Stirling Castle, 34cm (13½in), *L 5 June,* £286 ($300)

7

A polychromed and scrimshawed busk, English, mid-19th century, with five different sailing ships on one face and a whaling scene on the reverse, 35cm (13¾in) long, *L 5 June,* £495 ($658)

8

A scrimshawed whalebone busk, English, early 19th century, 33cm (13in), *L 5 June,* £528 ($702)

9

A walking stick, of carved, painted and gilded whalebone and wood, American, dated 1826, with inscription, 97cm (38¼in), *NY 28 June,* $1,320 (£1,015)

10

A whale harpoon, early 19th century, 92cm (36in), *L 5 June,* £286 ($380)

11

A whalebone and whale ivory swift, American, mid-19th century, 43cm (17in) high, *L 5 June,* £2,200 ($2,926)

12

A prisoner-of-war model of a two decker, French, early 19th century, 76 x 107cm (30 x 42in), *NY 15 Feb,* $11,000 (£9,483)

13

A prisoner-of-war-work bone domino box, English *c.*1810, the inner lid pierced for cribbage with drawn and coloured naval scene, and containing a complete set of dominoes and four cribbage pegs, 17cm (6¾in), *L 5 June,* £1,760 ($2,341)

14

A prisoner-of-war bone games casket, early 19th century, the pine casket, applied with bone panels, containing a set of bone playing cards, dominoes, a pair of dice and a teetotum, 25.5cm (10in) long, *L 17 July,* £770 ($1,117)

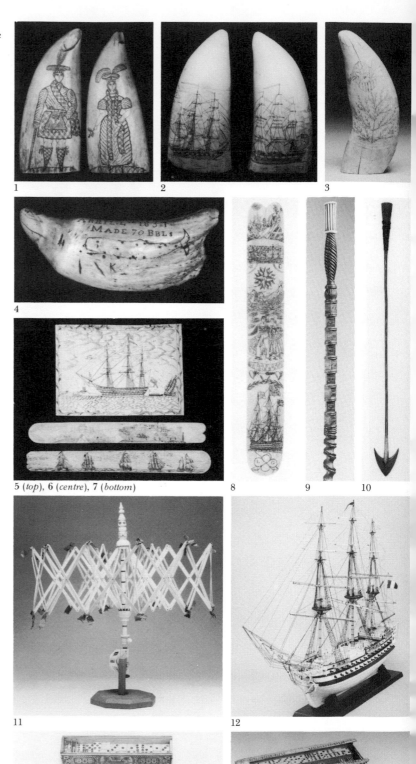

1

2

3

4

5 (*top*), 6 (*centre*), 7 (*bottom*)

8   9   10

11

12

13

14

1
A lithographed paper-on-wood sailing vessel 'Volunteer', *c.*1880, the orange and yellow hull with sailors fishing, 102cm (40in) long, *NY 13 Apr,* $1,210 (£968)

2
A prisoner-of-war bone model of an 80-gun ship-of-the-line, early 19th century, stated to be of the Spanish ship 'San Joseph' captured by Nelson at the Battle of St. Vincent, 38 x 42cm (15 x 16½in), *L 5 June,* £2,860 ($3,804)

3
A shipping diorama, English, mid-19th century, 99cm (39in) long, *L 5 June,* £825 ($1,097)

4
A diorama of an American clipper, English, *c.*1870, 53 x 76cm (21 x 30in), *L 5 June,* £462 ($614)

5
A prisoner-of-war bone model of a frigate, French, early 19th century, stern panel restored, some rigging missing, 42 x 71cm (16½ x 28in), *L 23 Oct,* £5,500 ($8,250)

6
A shipbuilder's model of the Amazon steam ships TSS Belam and Labrea, Scottish, *c.*1891, 135cm (53in) long, *L 5 June,* £2,200 ($2,926)

7
A lacquered wooden model of a ship, 134cm (52¾in) long, *A 7 Oct,* Dfl 2,760 (£652; $964)

8
A model of a merchant ship, mid-19th century, 64cm (25in) long, *L 5 June,* £605 ($805)

9
A carved ivory shipping diorama, continental, mid-19th century, with stern view of a frigate on gilt brass frame, 8.5 x 7.5cm (3½ x 3in), *L 23 Oct,* £1,045 ($1,568)

10
A waterline model of a clipper, English, 19th century, 50cm (19¾in) long, *L 5 June,* £418 ($556)

11
A sailor-made model of a brig, English, late 19th century, 34cm (13½in) long, *L 5 June,* £770 ($1,024)

12
A wooden model of the yacht 'Seahawk', 1960, 100cm (39¼in) long, *A 7 Oct,* Dfl 1,006 (£237; $350)

13
A prisoner-of-war bone model of a ship-of-the-line, French, early 19th century, lacking masts and rigging, 15cm (6in) long, *L 23 Oct,* £1,430 ($2,145)

Instruments of Science and Technology

See also ● Colour illustrations *p 337*

1
A Newton & Co Foucault's gyroscope, English, *c.*1880, with accessories, *L 23 Oct,* £550 ($825)

2
A Carpentier tangent galvanometer, French, *c.*1880, 30.5cm (12in) high, *L 23 Oct,* £275 ($413)

3
A Duboscq brass polarimeter, French, mid-19th century, 101cm (40in) long, *L 11 June,* £990 ($1,287)

4
A Duboscq brass saccharimeter, French, mid-19th century, 46cm (18in) long, with two polarising tubes, *L 11 June,* £220 ($286)

5
A travelling orrery, *c.*1800, in gilt brass and silvered brass, the major stars in wood and ivory, three missing, 12cm (4¾in), *NY 17 June,* $2,090 (£1,645)

6
A Dollond model fire pump, English, late 18th century, 46cm (18in) wide, *L 23 Oct,* £1,870 ($2,805)

7
A school-room orrery, *c.*1900, 54cm (21¼in) wide, *L 23 Oct,* £825 ($1,238)

8
A vacuum pump, English, late 18th century, 33cm (13in) high, *L 23 Oct,* £660 ($990)

9
A turner's sclerometer, English, *c.*1900, 48.5cm (19in), sold with four weights, *C 22 Oct,* £165 ($248)

1

2

4

3

5

7

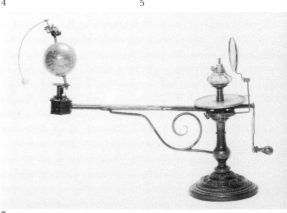

6

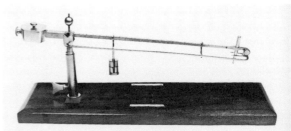

8

9

1
A Jacques Senecal ivory Bloud-type diptych dial, Dieppe, late 17th century, 6 x 7cm (2¼ x 2¾in) closed, *L 11 June,* £1,155 ($1,501)

2
A Mason brass pocket sundial, English, early 19th century, 7.5cm (3in) diam, *L 11 June,* £308 ($400)

3
A silver 'perpetual calendar', German, early 18th century, 4.5cm (1¾in) diam, *L 20 Feb,* £660 ($759)

4
A Jones brass universal equinoctial dial, *c.*1797, stamped T. Butler, 1797, 9.5cm (3¾in) wide, *S 13 June,* £396 ($527)

5
A small Roch Blondeau silver horizontal dial, French, late 17th century, with hinged gnomon, 5cm (2in) long, *L 20 Feb,* £682 ($784)

6
A gilt brass astronomical ring dial, Johannes Sommer, Augsburg, late 17th century, with maker's signature and names of cities and their latitudes, 8cm (3in) diam, *NY 17 June,* $1,650 (£1,299)

7
A brass ring dial, English, 18th century, 5.5cm (2in) diam, with contemporary magnifying glass, *C 26 June,* £352 ($475)

8
A brass analemmatic dial, English, *c.*1700, 16 x 10cm (6¼ x 4in) fully open, *L 23 Oct,* £3,080 ($4,620)

9
A brass universal equinoctial dial, South German, *c.*1780, 7cm (2¾in) long, *L 11 June,* £440 ($572)

10
A Macquart silver Butterfield-type dial, French, *c.*1770, 7cm (2¾in) long, *L 11 June,* £1,210 ($1,573)

11
A Lorenz Grassl brass universal equinoctial dial, Nuremberg, 18th century, crack to glass, *A 25 Feb,* **Dfl 1,218 (£299; $334)**

12
A John Bleuler brass universal equinoctial dial, English, *c.*1800, 11cm (4¼in) diam, *L 20 Feb,* £902 ($1,037)

13
A Claude Langlois brass universal equinoctial dial, French, mid-18th century, 7.5cm (3in) wide, *L 23 Oct,* £550 ($825)

14
A Baradelle silver horizontal dial, French, late 18th century, 7 x 8.5cm (2¾ x 3¼in), *L 20 Feb,* £2,200 ($2,530)

15
A Butterfield brass gunners level, French, early 18th century, signed 'Butterfield a Paris', 10cm (4in) high, *L 23 Oct,* £902 ($1,353)

16
A brass gunners' rule, English, mid-18th century, lacking iron tips, 17cm (6¾in) long, *L 11 June,* £495 ($643)

1
A pair of brass dividers, English, late 17th century, 30.5cm (12in), *L 20 Feb*, £1,320 ($1,518)

2
An iron and gilt-bronze compass, French, first half 17th century, 24cm (9½in) radius, *L 20 Feb*, £2,750 ($3,163)

3
A pair of brass and steel dividers, probably German, late 17th century, 16.5cm (6½in) radius, *L 20 Feb*, £308 ($354)

4
A compass, English, dated 1747, engraved 'Joseph Willson, June 1745', 15cm (6in) wide, *L 23 Oct*, £242 ($363)

5
A W. C. Cox brass plain theodolite, English, *c.*1800, 31cm (12¼in) high, *L 23 Oct*, £550 ($825)

6
A brass transit theodolite, English, *c.*1900, 37.5cm (14¾in) high, *L 11 June*, £495 ($643)

7
A Casartelli brass theodolite, English, late 19th century, tube 23cm (9in), *C 22 Oct*, £396 ($594)

8
A Benjamin Gray double waywiser, English, mid-19th century, with brass dial engraved with scales for miles, furlongs and poles, 31cm (12½in) diam, *L 20 Feb*, £990 ($1,139)

9
An early brass graphometer, Low Countries, late 17th century, 20cm (8in) wide, *L 20 Feb*, £2,090 ($2,404)

10
A J. Bennett mahogany waywiser, English, mid-18th century, 137cm (54in) wide, *L 23 Oct*, £440 ($660)

11
A boxwood nocturnal, English, early 18th century, 25.5cm (10in) long, *L 5 June*, £2,970 ($3,951)

12
A Troughton & Simms brass miner's dial, English, mid-19th century, 26cm (10¼in) wide, *L 23 Oct*, £308 ($462)

13
A G. Riva brass plane-table compass, Venetian, late 17th century, compass diam, 8cm (3in), *L 11 June*, £1,540 ($2,002)

14
A brass Holland circle, Dutch, second half 17th century, 28.5cm (11¼in) diam, *L 11 June*, £5,280 ($6,864)

1
A Kelvin White spherical binnacle compass, American, early 20th century, 33cm (13in) high, *L 5 June,* £352 ($468)

2
A Jesse Ramsden brass bridge-frame sextant, English, *c.*1790, 20cm (8in) radius, *L 20 Feb,* £2,640 ($3,036)

3
A J. Parkes & Sons brass sextant, English, late 19th century, 17cm (6¾in) radius, *L 23 Oct,* £638 ($957)

4
A John Berge brass sextant, English, 1800-1808, 12.5cm (5in) radius, *L 23 Oct,* £1,760 ($2,640)

5
An Abraham ebony octant, English, early 19th century, 24cm (9½in) radius, *L 5 June,* £330 ($439)

6
A mahogany Hadley's quadrant, English, mid-18th century, horizon glasses lacking filters, 46cm (18in) radius, *L 5 June,* £1,760 ($2,341)

7
A bronze ship's bell, dated 1774, 36cm (14in) diam, *L 23 Oct,* £440 ($660)

8
A Siebe Gorman & Co. brass and copper diver's helmet, English, early 20th century, 46cm (18in) high, *L 23 Oct,* £770 ($1,155)

9
A J. W. Ray & Co. brass ship's telegraph, English, early 20th century, 117cm (46in), *L 23 Oct,* £440 ($660)

10
A Kelvin & Hughes Ltd ship's binnacle compass, English, *c.*1940, 135cm (53in) high, *L 20 Feb,* £748 ($860)

11
A loadstone, probably English, late 17th century, with silver coloured mounts, 2.5cm (1in) high, *L 23 Oct,* £715 ($1,073)

12
A brass-bound loadstone, English, 17th century, lacking metal poles, 4.5cm (1¾in) high, *L 5 June,* £495 ($658)

13
A Royal Navy pine grog barrel, English, early 20th century, 72cm (28in) high, *L 5 June,* £242 ($322)

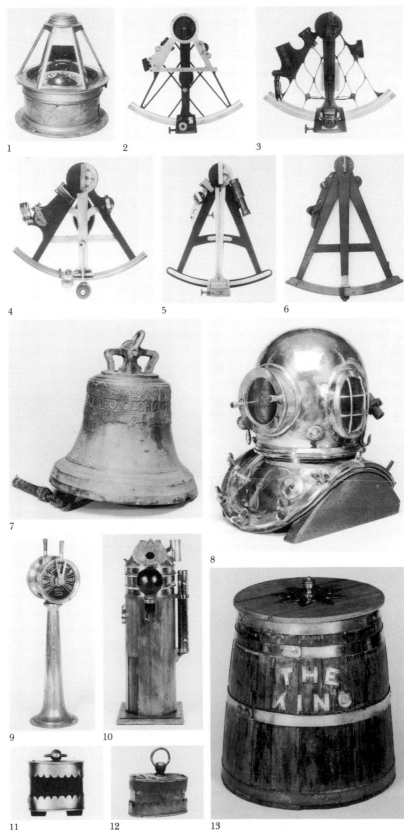

1
A 1-inch brass reflecting pocket telescope, late 18th century, length of tube 13cm (5¼in), *S 21 Feb,* £836 ($961)

2
A 1¼-inch pocket refracting telescope, Italian, 19th century, signed Giuseppe Moschino in Genoua, ivory mounts, extended length 10cm (4in), *L 23 Oct,* £165 ($248)

3
A ½-inch horn and leather refracting telescope, probably Italian, 18th century, extended length 84cm (33in), *L 23 Oct,* £330 ($495)

4
A W. Watkins 5¼-inch brass reflecting Gregorian telescope, English, *c.*1790, with various accessories, the tube 80.5cm (31¾in) long, *L 23 Oct,* £3,850 ($5,775)

5
A Dudley Adams 4-inch brass Gregorian reflecting telescope on stand, English, late 18th century, length of tube 65cm (25½in), *L 23 Oct,* £1,870 ($2,805)

6
A 1½-inch Horne & Thornthwaite brass refracting telescope, English, *c.*1850, with six draws, extended length 67.5cm (26½in), *L 5 June,* £121 ($161)

7
An Ebsworth 1½-inch refracting telescope, English, *c.*1825, with four silver-plated draws and mounts, extended length 71cm (28in), *L 5 June,* £440 ($585)

8
A Peter and John Dollond 2¾-inch refracting telescope, English, late 18th century, lacking steadying strut, length of tube 112cm (44in), *L 20 Feb,* £1,210 ($1,392)

9
A 3-inch refracting astronomical 'Alpha' telescope, English, 1912, 89cm (35¼in) long, *C 20 Mar,* £418 ($514)

10
A 2-inch Jesse Ramsden brass refracting telescope on stand, English, late 18th century, replacement eye-piece, length of tube 64cm (25in) long, *L 20 Feb,* £660 ($759)

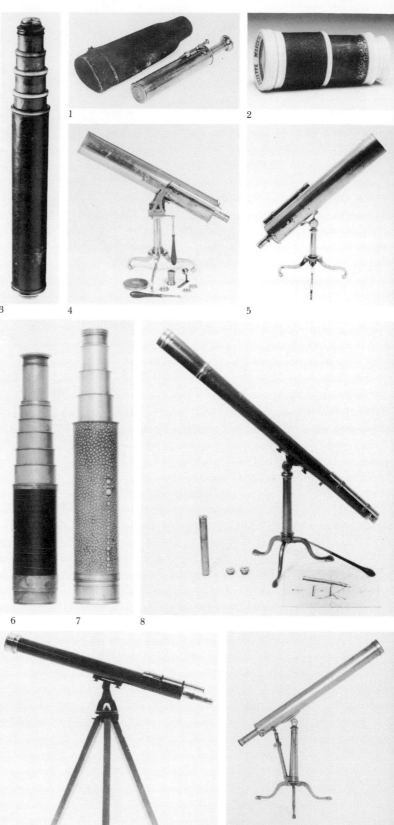

1

2

3   4   5

6   7   8

9   10

1
An Edward Scarlett brass screw-barrel microscope, English, *c.*1730, signed, on ivory handle, 6.5cm (2½in) long, *L 20 Feb,* £990 ($1,139)

2
A Bate brass solar microscope, English, *c.*1800, signed, 36cm (14in) long, with six bone slides, rack and pinion focusing defective, *L 11 June,* £550 ($715)

3
A William Cary brass monocular microscope, English, *c.*1830, signed, 23cm (9in) high, *L 11 June,* £418 ($543)

4
A Dollond brass cuff-type microscope, English, late 18th century, signed, with various accessories, *L 20 Feb,* £2,090 ($2,404)

5
A Cuff-type microscope, English, *c.*1770-80, 27cm (10½in) high, *L 11 June,* £1,650 ($2,145)

6
A Smith & Beck brass binocular microscope, English, *c.*1860, signed, 43cm (17in) high, with various accessories, *L 23 Oct,* £880 ($1,320)

7
A Henry Crouch brass binocular microscope, English, *c.*1870, No. 1785, with various accessories, 41cm (16in) high, *L 20 Feb,* £1,320 ($1,518)

8
An R. & J. Beck brass binocular microscope, English, *c.*1870, plano/concave mirror restored, 48cm (19in) high, *L 20 Feb,* £440 ($506)

9
An H. & W. Crouch brass binocular microscope, English, *c.*1880, signed, 36cm (14in) high, with various accessories, *L 23 Oct,* £715 ($1,073)

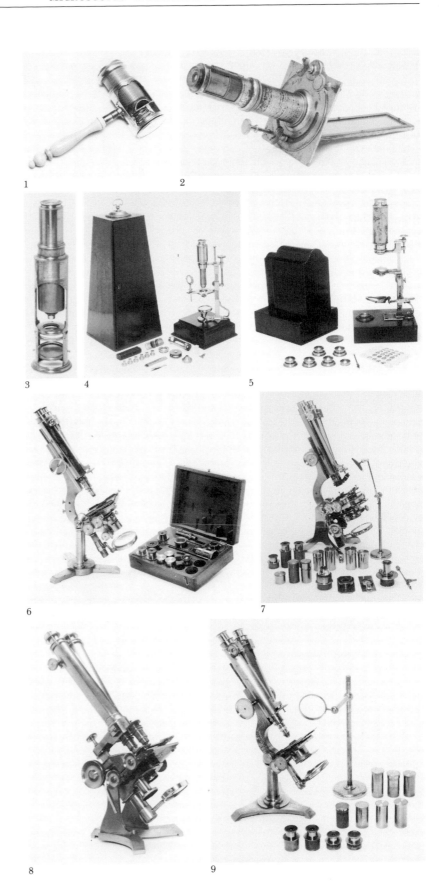

1
A rosewood hour glass,
English, c.1800, with
brass waist, 22cm (8½in),
L 5 June,
£770 ($1,024)

2
An hour-glass, probably
French, late 18th cen-
tury, mounted in cut-
brass stand, 30.5cm
(12in), L 11 June,
£1,100 ($1,430)

3
A 5½-inch Cary star globe,
English, early 20th
century, signed, patent
no. 21540, L 23 Oct,
£286 ($429)

4
A 2¾-inch pocket terres-
trial globe, English, late
18th century, some
damage, 8cm (3¼in)
diam, L 20 Feb,
£440 ($506)

5
A Dudley Adams 3-inch
pocket globe, English,
early 19th century,
8.5cm (3½in) diam,
L 23 Oct,
£935 ($1,403)

6
A pair of mahogany
celestial and terres-
trial library globes, by J W
Cary, the former dated
1800, the latter 1806,
122cm (48in) overall,
C 12 July,
£14,850 ($20,642)

7
A pair of Isaac Habrecht
8-inch terrestrial and
celestial globes, late 17th
century, published by
Johann Christoph
Weigel in Nuremberg,
33cm (13in) high,
L 23 Oct,
£14,300 ($21,450)

8
A pair of celestial and
terrestrial globes,
c.1820, by J W Cary,
103cm (40in), L 8 Mar,
£19,800 ($22,176)

9
A Malby's celestial globe,
Enlgish, mid-19th cen-
tury, with revision as to
1860, 109cm (43in)
high, L 23 Oct,
£1,430 ($2,145)

10
A Cary 15-inch terrestrial
library globe, English,
c.1840, printed with the
tracks of the principal
18th century navigators,
97cm (38in) high,
L 20 Feb,
£4,180 ($4,807)

11
A Bett's patent new port-
able terrestrial globe,
English, c.1890,
printed on polished
cotton, 74cm (29in),
C 26 June,
£220 ($297)

12
A Chadburn & Son
weather station, English,
late 19th century, 63cm
(25in) wide, L 11 June,
£660 ($858)

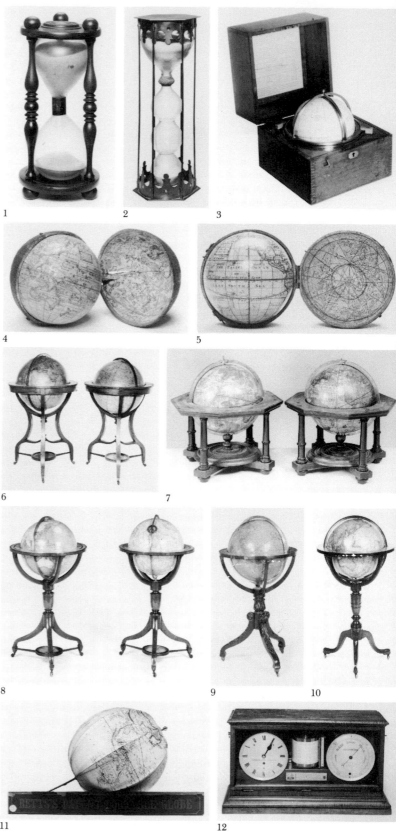

1
A cased set of Jacobus Listingh coin weights, Dutch, dated 1659, 16cm (6¼in) wide, *L 20 Feb,* £3,080 ($3,542)

2
An Avery shop-counter balance, English, late 19th century, 114cm (45in), *L 20 Feb,* £275 ($316)

3
A George III cast brass wool weight, late 18th century, 17cm (6¾in) long, *L 11 June,* £770 ($1,001)

4
A De Grave imperial brass half-bushel measure, *c.*1890, inscribed 'Orange River Colony', 53cm (20¾in) wide, *JHB 29 Aug,* R 3,700 (£1,160; $1,705)

5
A brass imperial gallon measure, 1896, inscribed 'Zuid Afrikaansche Republiek', 16.5cm (6½in) high, *JHB 29 Apr,* R 1,700 (£708; $927)

6
A set of brass cup weights, Danish, late 18th century, outer case 11.5cm (4½in), *L 11 June,* £440 ($572)

7
A set of eleven De Grave, Short & Fanner brass imperial measures, English, 1854, 1 bushel to ¼ gill, largest 50cm (19¾in) diam, *L 20 Feb,* £3,300 ($3,795)

8
A set of seven brass weights, dated 1883, from 56lb to 1lb, *C 18 Apr,* £484 ($629)

9
A set of five bronze weights, dated 1835, 31 to 14cm (12 to 5½in), *C 17 Jan,* £660 ($792)

10
Five De Grave, Short & Fanner imperial measures, English, *c.*1855, largest 51cm (20in) diam, *L 23 Oct,* £1,210 ($1,815)

11
A set of eight Bate imperial brass measures, English, *c.*1835, 1 gallon to ¼ gill, largest 19.5cm (7¾in) diam, *L 20 Feb,* £1,430 ($1,645)

12
A composite set of sixteen brass spherical imperial weights, English, *c.*1909, 56lb to ½ dram, weights 4oz and above, largest 24cm (9½in), *L 20 Feb,* £1,540 ($1,771)

13
A set of four De Grave & Co Ltd. brass imperial weights, English, *c.*1909, 50lb to 5lb, the largest 23cm (9in) wide, *L 20 Feb,* £660 ($759)

1
An S Maw Son & Thompson amputation set,
English, last quarter
19th century, comprising ten items, case 40cm
(15¾in) wide, *L 11 June,*
£528 ($686)

2
A set of surgical instruments, F Arnold,
Baltimore, Md., *c.*1890,
case 42cm (16½in) long,
NY 14 Jan,
$1,760 (£1,586)

3
A set of dental instruments, with coral,
mother-of-pearl or ivory
handles, *c.*1859, a
number of tools stamped
H G Kern, Philada., box
51cm (20in) long,
NY 4 Apr,
$7,700 ($6,471)

4
A Thomas Machell's
combination saw and forceps, English, *c.*1815,
15cm (6in), *L 11 June,*
£1,100 ($1,430)

5
A mechanical bone saw,
German, mid-19th century, 32cm (12½in),
L 11 June,
£1,320 ($1,716)

6
A pair of steel amputation
pincers, Continental,
17th century, 31cm
(12¼in), *L 11 June,*
£385 ($505)

7
An iron amputation fork,
probably English,
early 18th century,
L 11 June,
£308 ($400)

8
Four gynaecological
instruments, English,
*c.*1900, *L 20 Feb,*
£330 ($380)

9
A cupping and bleeding
set, English, mid-19th
century, case 25cm
(10in) wide, *L 11 June,*
£572 ($743)

10
A set of tracheotomy
instruments, probably
French, mid-19th century, case 15cm (6in)
wide, *L 20 Feb,*
£330 ($380)

11
A medicine chest, English, early 19th century,
with various accessories
including five concealed
poison bottles, 29cm
(11½in) wide, *L 20 Feb,*
£968 ($1,113)

12
A trepanning set, *c.*1865,
S 25 July,
£528 ($776)

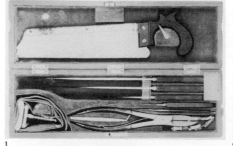

1

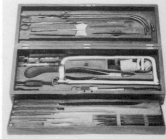

2

3

4

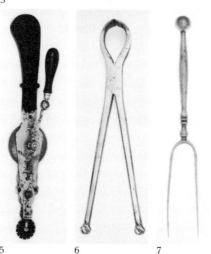

5

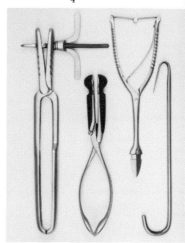

6

7

8

9

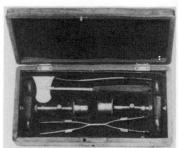

10

11

12

1
A medicine chest,
English, mid-18th
century, with six glass
bottles and pewter and
glass funnel, 23cm (9in)
wide, *L 11 June,*
£550 ($715)

2
**An Alfred Carter
gynaecological couch,**
*c.*1890, 152.5cm (60in)
long, *S 13 June,*
£209 ($278)

3
**A silver-plated hearing
aid,** English, late 19th
century, signed F C Rain
& Sons, 14cm (5½in),
NY 4 Apr,
$715 (£601)

4
**A pair of silver 'ana-
tomical' hearing aids,**
French, mid 19th
century, 5cm (2in) long,
L 20 Feb,
£550 ($633)

5
An early steel ear trumpet,
probably German,
early 19th century, 21cm
(8¼in), *L 20 Feb,*
£495 ($569)

6
**A brass telescopic ear
trumpet,** French, mid-
19th century, stamped
C.C.O. Paris, 34cm
(13½in) long, *L 20 Feb,*
£374 ($430)

7
**A copper and brass 'bell
resonator' ear trumpet,**
English, mid-19th
century, 15cm (6in)
long, *L 20 Feb,*
£198 ($278)

8
A silver medical etui,
mid-18th century, con-
taining four items,
incomplete, 14.5cm
(5¾in) high, *L 20 Feb,*
£286 ($329)

9
**A Mudge's patent pewter
inhaler,** English, *c.*1820,
30.5cm (12in) high,
L 11 June,
£264 ($343)

10
**An Adams patent pair of
silver spectacles,** London,
dated 1799, *L 23 Oct,*
£2,200 ($3,300)

11
A tooth key, probably
French, late 18th
century, 13cm (5in),
L 20 Feb,
£220 ($253)

12
A tooth key, English,
*c.*1730, 11cm (4¼in),
L 20 Feb,
£385 ($443)

13
A dental key, French,
early 18th century, 15cm
(5¾in), *L 20 Feb,*
£462 ($531)

14
A set of ivory false teeth,
mid-19th century, some
discolouration,
C 26 June,
£396 ($534)

15
A Pelican tooth extractor,
18th century, 15cm
(6in), *L 11 June,*
£572 ($743)

16
A mechanical irrigator,
French, late 19th
century, 24cm (9¾in),
L 23 Oct,
£286 ($429)

17
**A Lister-type antiseptic
spray,** French, late 19th
century, signed Mathieu
a Paris, 25.5cm (10in),
L 23 Oct,
£308 ($462)

18
**A wax dental display
model,** early 20th cen-
tury, 24cm (9½in) long,
sold with a case of wax
models of 'Diseases of
the Teeth' with twenty-
four exhibits, 31cm
(12in), *C 26 June,*
£440 ($594)

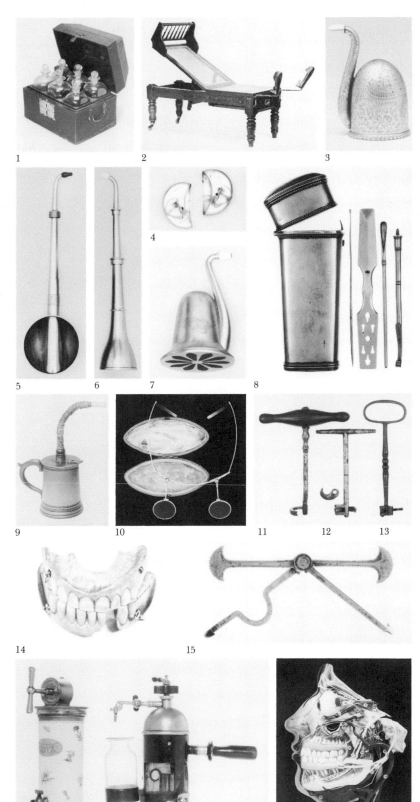

1
A Hall typewriter,
American, *c.*1880s, No.
1535, 39cm (15½in)
long, *C 20 Mar,*
£286 ($352)

2
A Williams No. 2 type-
writer, American, *c.*1895,
C 20 Mar,
£330 ($406)

3
A Hammond No. 1 type-
writer, American, *c.*1884,
L 20 Feb,
£605 ($696)

4
An 'Improved No. 2
Columbia typewriter',
American, *c.*1890,
25.5cm (10in) wide,
L 20 Feb,
£1,430 ($1,645)

5
A Lambert typewriter,
*c.*1900, made by Sidney
Herbert, 29cm (11½in)
wide, *L 23 Oct,*
£418 ($627)

6
A Salter Model Five type-
writer, No. 878, English,
*c.*1892, *L 23 Oct,*
£2,090 ($3,135)

7
A Merritt typewriter,
American, *c.*1890,
31cm (12¼in) long,
L 11 June,
£440 ($572)

8
A Hammond No. 1 type-
writer, American,
*c.*1884, *L 11 June,*
£715 ($929)

9
A Lambert typewriter,
American, *c.*1900,
No. 8703, *L 11 June,*
£330 ($429)

10
A black-lacquered metal
child's sewing machine,
A 28 June,
Dfl 603 (£136; $184)

1

2

3

4

5

6

7

8

9

10

Musical Instruments

See also
- Colour illustrations *pp* 340-341 ● Mechanical musical instruments and musical boxes *pp* 525-527
- Rock 'n roll *p* 533

1
A two-keyed stained pear-wood tenor oboe, (Vox Humana) by William Milhouse, Newark *c.*1775, 72.5cm (28½in), *L 3 Apr,* £1,980 ($2,554))

2
An American six-keyed boxwood flute, by A. & W. Geib, New York, *c.*1820, sounding length 59.5cm (23½in), *L 3 Apr,* £1,210 ($1,561)

3
An eight-keyed cocus-wood flute, by Rudall & Rose, London, *c.*1830, sounding length 58.5cm (23in), *L 3 Apr,* £2,310 ($2,980)

4
A ten-keyed boxwood oboe by Carl August Grenser, Dresden 1791, keywork with later adaptations, 57cm (22½in), *L 12 Dec,* £1,600 ($2,240)

5
An ivory descant (soprano) recorder, Continental, early 18th century, 35cm (13¾in), *L 3 Apr,* £3,960 ($5,108)

6
A one-keyed ivory flute, probably French, early 18th century, unstamped, one joint restored, sounding length 55cm (21½in), *L 12 Dec,* £1,300 ($1,820)

7
A one-keyed boxwood flute, by Astor, London, *c.*1800, sounding length 54cm (21¼in), *L 3 Apr,* £605 ($780)

8
A stained boxwood treble (alto) recorder, by Urquhart, early 18th century, 50cm (19½in), *L 3 Apr,* £3,520 ($4,541)

9
An eleven-keyed stained maple bassoon, by H. Grenser & Wiesner, Dresden, *c.*1825, 126cm (49¾in), *L 3 Apr,* £3,520 ($4,541)

10
A six-keyed tenoroon, English, *c.*1800, approx length 164cm (64½in), *L 3 Apr,* £1,045 ($1,348)

11
A German bassoon by Heckel, Biebrich-am-Rhein, late 19th century, 132cm (52in), *L 3 Apr,* £1,320 ($1,703)

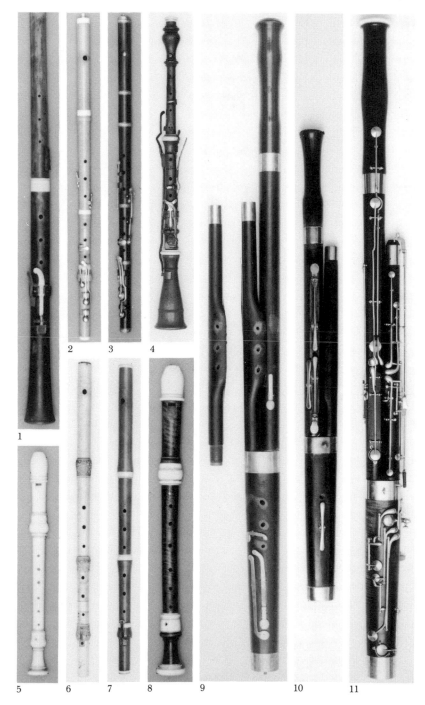

1 2 3 4 5 6 7 8 9 10 11

1
A double action pedal harp by Sebastian and Pierre Erard, London, mid-19th century, *L 12 Dec,* £1,500 ($2,100)

2
A 'Salzedo Model' harp by Lyon & Healy, Chicago, 1930, *NY 19 June,* $6,600 (£5,197)

3
A double action pedal harp by John Egan, Dublin, restorable for decorative purposes only, *L 12 Dec,* £400 ($560)

4
A pair of kettle drums, German or Austrian, first half 18th century, 48cm (19in) and 46cm (18¼in) diam., *L 3 Apr,* £2,200 ($2,838)

5
A French serpent, *c.*1825, with brass mounts and ivory mouthpiece (damaged), overall length 228.5cm (7ft 6in), *L 3 Apr,* £880 ($1,135)

6
An English glass-keyed glockenspiel by George Smart, London, *c.*1805, 43.5cm (17in) long, with two beaters, *L 3 Apr,* £880 ($1,135)

7
A set of Northumbrian small pipes by Robert Reid, North Shields, *c.*1840, *L 12 Dec,* £700 ($980)

8
A set of Scottish pastoral pipes, *c.*1830, chanter 52cm (20½in) long, *L 3 Apr,* £1,430 ($1,845)

9
A composite set of Irish Union pipes in B flat, *c.*1850, the chanter by Michael Egan and the drone stock by Colgan, 114.5cm (45in) long, *L 4 July,* £2,640 ($3,643)

10
An alto sarrusophone in E flat, by Gautrot-Marquet, Paris, late 19th century, 71.5cm (28¼in), *L 12 Dec,* £1,400 ($1,960)

1

4

2

5

3

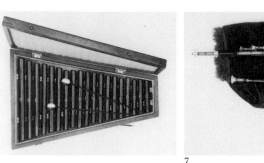

6   7

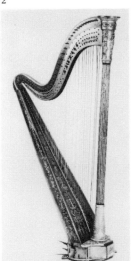

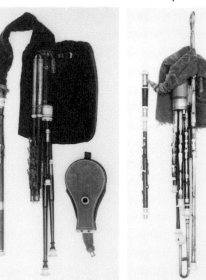

8   9   10

1
An English spinet, by Stephen Keene, London 1706, later stand, 170cm (5ft 6½in), *L 3 Apr,* £11,000 ($14,190)

2
An English grand piano by John Broadwood and Son, London 1798, on later stand, 228 x 107cm (7ft 5¾in x 3ft 6in), *L 12 Dec,* £3,800 ($5,320)

3
An English square piano by John Pohlman, London, *c.*1780, 172cm (5ft 7¾in), *L 4 July,* £1,540 ($2,125)

4
A Viennese or German grand pianoforte, school of Haschka, *c.*1825, 230.5 x 125cm (7ft 6¾in x 4ft 1¼in), *L 12 Dec,* £1,800 ($2,520)

5
An Italian grand pianoforte, by Carol Tremino, Rome, *c.*1780, in poor condition, 199.5cm (6ft 6½in) long, *L 3 Apr,* £3,080 ($3,973)

6
A French combined piano, sewing table and writing desk, second quarter 19th century, 85.5 x 52cm (35½ x 20½in), *L 12 Dec,* £1,400 ($1,960)

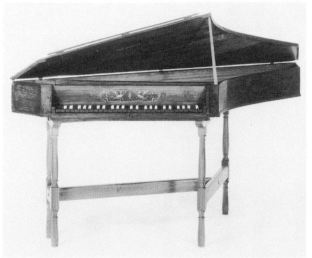

1

2

3

4

5

6

1
An Italian violin by Girolamo Amati (Hieronymus II), Cremona, 1693, *L 4 July,* £39,600 ($54,648)

2
An Italian violin by Bernardo Calcanius, Genoa, first half 18th century, *NY 19 June,* $13,200 (£10,394)

3
An Italian violin by Antonio Gragnani, Livorno, 1784, *L 14 Nov,* £17,600 ($24,640)

4
An Italian violin by Gioffredo Benedetto Rinaldi, Turin, 1873, *L 3 Apr,* £3,740 ($4,825)

5
An Italian violin by Giovanni Battista Ceruti, Cremona, 1813, 35.5cm *L 3 Apr,* £24,200 ($31,218)

6
An Italian violin by Giulio Degani, Venice, 1898, *L 3 Apr,* £3,410 ($4,399)

7
An Italian violin by Giovanni Schwarz, Venice, 1905, *L 14 Nov,* £3,960 ($5,544)

8
An Italian violin by Giovanni Gaida, Ivrea, 1906, *L 14 Nov,* £5,500 ($7,700)

9
An Italian violin by Vittorio Bellarosa, Naples, *c.*1920, *NY 19 June,* $4,400 (£3,464)

10
An Italian violin by Giuseppe Pedrazzini, Milan, 1923, *L 14 Nov,* £8,140 ($11,396)

11
An Italian violin by Nicolo Iginio Sderci, Florence, 1954, *NY 19 June,* $3,300 (£2,598)

12
An Italian violin by Ageo Castaldini, Bologna, *c.*1964, *NY 19 June,* $1,650 (£1,299)

1

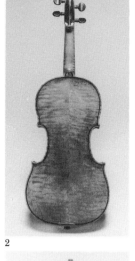
2

3

4

5

6

7

8

9

10

11

12

1
A violin by Jacob Stainer,
Absam 1677, *NY 19 June,*
$23,100 (£18,189)

2
A German violin by
Matthias Hornsteiner,
Mittenwald, *c.1790,*
L 3 Apr,
£1,650 ($2,129)

3
An English violin by
Thomas Urquhart,
London, *c.1680,*
L 14 Nov,
£3,080 ($4,312)

4
An English violin by
Emanuel Whitmarsh,
London, 1910, *L 3 Apr,*
£715 ($922)

5
An English violin by W. E.
Hill & Sons, London,
1911, *L 19 Sept,*
£3,630 ($5,082)

6
An English violin by
William Robinson,
London, 1947, *L 3 Apr,*
£660 ($851)

7
A gold and tortoiseshell-
mounted viola bow by
J. S. Finkel, 70 grams,
L 3 Apr,
£1,210 ($1,561)

8
A silver-mounted double
bass bow by Victor
Fétique, Paris, *L 19 Sept,*
£1,870 ($2,618)

9
An English silver-
mounted violin bow by
William Tubbs, London,
53 grams, *L 14 Nov,*
£1,045 ($1,463)

10
A silver-mounted violon-
cello bow by John Dodd,
London, 80 grams,
L 14 Nov,
£1,540 ($2,156)

11
An ivory-mounted violin
bow by John Dodd, last
quarter 19th century,
55 grams, *NY 19 June,*
£990 (£780)

1

2

3

4

5

6

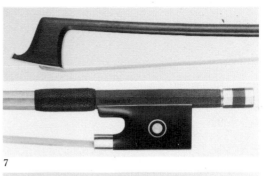

7

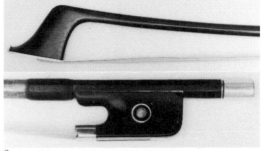

8

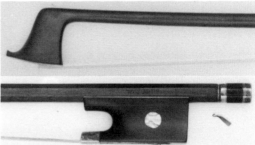

9

10

11

1
A French violin by
Jacques Boquay, Paris,
first half 18th century,
NY 19 June,
$4,400 (£3,464)

2
A French violin, Chap-
puy school, *c.*1780,
L 14 Nov,
£1,980 ($2,772)

3
A French violin by Justin
Maucotel, Mirecourt,
second quarter 19th
century, *L 4 July,*
£1,210 ($1,669)

4
A French violin by
Honore Derazey, Paris,
mid-19th century,
NY 19 June,
$4,125 (£3,248)

5
A French violin by Paul
Bailly, Paris, 1899,
L 19 Sept,
£2,530 ($3,542)

6
A French violin, by
Charles Jean-Baptiste
Collin-Mézin, Paris,
1899, *L 3 Apr,*
£1,100 ($1,419)

7
A French violin by
Charles Brugère, Paris,
1909, *L 14 Nov,*
£3,520 ($4,928)

8
A French violin, by
Charles Louis Buthod,
Mirecourt, *L 3 Apr,*
£858 ($1,107)

9
**A silver-mounted violon-
cello bow,** by André
Vigneron, Paris,
74 grams. *L 3 Apr,*
£1,760 ($2,270)

10
**A silver-mounted violin
bow,** by Eugene Sartory,
Paris, 65 grams,
NY 19 June,
$2,860 (£2,252)

11
**A silver-mounted violin
bow** by Alfred Lamy,
Paris, 58 grams, later
adjuster, *NY 19 June,*
$2,200 (£1,732)

1   2   3   4

5   6   7   8

9

10

11

1
A Swedish violoncello by
Johann Öhberg, Stock-
holm, third quarter 18th
century, labelled Aug.
Waidele, Musikinstru-
mentafar, Göteborg, Rep.
920, 75cm (29½in),
L 12 Dec,
£2,900 ($4,060)

2
An English violoncello by
William Forster Junior,
London, *c.*1810, 73cm
(28¾in), *L 3 Apr,*
£5,940 ($7,663)

3
An English violoncello
by Benjamin Banks,
Salisbury, 73cm (28¾in),
L 14 Nov,
£6,380 ($8,932)

4
An English viola by
Joseph Hill, London,
1758, 40.5cm (16in),
L 14 Nov,
£13,200 ($18,480)

5
A French viola by Charles
Jean-Baptiste Collin-
Mézin, Paris, 1899,
39.5cm (15½in), *L 14 Nov,*
£2,420 ($3,388)

6
A French viola by Hip-
polyte Chrétien Silvestre,
Lyon, 1881, 41cm (16in),
L 4 July,
£9,680 ($13,358)

7
A French viola by Gabriel
Magnière, Mirecourt,
1895, 40cm (15½in),
L 14 Nov,
£1,210 ($1,694)

8
An Italian viola by
Stefano Conia, Cremona,
1973, 42cm (16½in),
L 3 Apr,
£1,100 ($1,419)

9
An Italian viola by Giulio
Cesare Gigli, Rome,
mid-18th century, 38cm
(15in), *NY 19 June,*
$5,775 (£4,547)

10
An American violin, by
John Justice Hull,
Kingston, Pennsylvania,
*c.*1914, *NY 19 June,*
$1,100 (£866)

1 2 3

4 5 6

7 8 9 10

1
A double bass ascribed to a member of the Testore family, string stop 105.5cm (41½in), *L 14 Nov*, **£11,550 ($16,170)**

2
An English double bass by Thomas Kennedy, London, mid-19th century, string stop 104.5cm (41¼in), *L 3 Apr*, **£13,200 ($17,028)**

3
An English double bass, Forster School, late 18th century, string stop 108cm (42½in), *L 14 Nov*, **£7,700 ($10,780)**

4
A French guitar by René François Lacôte, Paris, 1830, 44cm (17¼in), *L 12 Dec*, **£950 ($1,330)**

5
An Italian guitar by Gennaro Fabricatore, Naples, *c.*1830, 45.5cm (18in), *NY 19 June*, **$2,200 (£1,732)**

6
A French guitar, mid 19th century, labelled C. Boullangier, from Vuillaume & Gand of Paris, London address, 44cm (17¼in), *L 12 Dec*, **£380 ($532)**

7
A Norwegian hardan-gerfele, by Ellef Johnsen, Stenkjedalen, Böv 1864, 34.5cm (14in), *L 12 Dec*, **£1,200 ($1,680)**

8
A German bass viola da gamba by Jacob Meinertzen, Berlin, *c.*1700, 63cm (24¾in), *L 12 Dec*, **£18,000 ($25,200)**

9
A Viola d'Amore, probably Viennese, late 18th century, the pegbox with carved female head, 39cm (15¼in), *L 4 July*, **£1,430 ($1,973)**

10
A Norwegian hardan-gerfele by Bjarne Øen, Bø, 1966, inlaid with bone and mother-of-pearl, 35.5cm (14in), *L 3 Apr*, **£1,100 ($1,419)**

1   2   3

4   5   6   7

8   9   10

Glass

See also
● Colour illustrations *pp* 342-343 ● Decorative arts from 1880 *pp* 284-291 ● Russian works of art *p* 430
● Antiquities *p* 577 ● Islamic works of art *p* 610 ● Chinese works of art *p* 674

1
A Dutch engraved goblet, c.1750, the bowl engraved with a church and inscribed T WELVAREN VAN LAND EN KERK, 21cm (8¼in), *L 1 July,* £286 ($395)

2
A Dutch engraved goblet, c.1750, inscribed HET WEL VAAREN VAN DEEZEN HÜYZE, 21.5cm (8½in), *L 1 July,* £242 ($334)

3
A Dutch engraved 'friendship' glass, c.1750, the funnel bowl decorated in wheel engraving and inscribed VRINTSHAP, 20cm (7¾in), *L 2 July,* £638 ($880)

4
A Dutch engraved light-baluster wine glass, c.1750, 18cm (7in), *L 2 July,* £550 ($759)

5
A Dutch engraved Royal armorial goblet, c.1745, decorated with the arms of William IV of Orange within the ribbon of the Garter, 19.5cm (7½in), *L 2 July,* £396 ($546)

6
A Dutch engraved armorial goblet, c.1745, the bowl engraved with the arms of the city of Amsterdam, 18.5cm (7½in), *L 2 July,* £396 ($546)

7
A Dutch engraved glass, G. V. Rossum, 1759, decorated with pheasants and inscribed 'VRIENDSCHAP' (Friendship), 19cm (7½in), *A 25 Feb,* Dfl 16,240 (£3,980; $4,458)

8
A Dutch engraved glass, mid-18th century, 22cm (8¾in), *A 25 Feb,* Dfl 8,120 (£1,990; $2,229)

9
A Dutch engraved glass, signed and dated Matthijs Sax, 15 September 1785, on metal foot, 20cm (8in), *A 3 June,* Dfl 928 (£210; $283)

10
A goblet with cover, 18th century, engraved with a cherub amongst flowers and leaves, 29.5cm (11½in), *A 3 June,* Dfl 1,392 (£315; $425)

11
A Dutch engraved glass, attributed to Jacob Sang, c.1760, 18cm (7in), *A 25 Feb,* Dfl 5,104 (£1,251; $1,401)

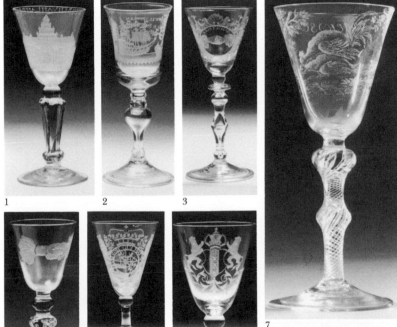

1   2   3

4   5   6

7

8   9   10   11

1
A light-baluster wine glass,
*c.*1745, 16.5cm (6½in),
L 2 July,
£143 ($197)

2
A wine glass, *c.*1740, 19cm
(7½in), *L 2 July,*
£242 ($334)

3
A wine glass, *c.*1720,
15.6cm (6in), *L 2 July,*
£242 ($334)

4
A wine glass, *c.*1730,
16.5cm (6½in), *L 2 July,*
£330 ($455)

5
A baluster goblet, *c.*1720,
21.5cm (8½in), *L 2 July,*
£176 ($243)

6
A large goblet, *c.*1730,
22.5cm (8¾in), *L 2 July,*
£82 ($113)

7
An engraved goblet,
*c.*1735, 18cm (7in),
L 2 July,
£572 ($789)

8
**A bobbin-knopped wine
glass,** *c.*1730-40, 20cm
(7¾in), *L 2 July,*
£1,650 ($2,277)

9
**An armorial engraved
goblet,** *c.*1750, the bowl
decorated with a coat of
arms inscribed below
'LIBERTATIS
PRIMITIAE', 19.6cm
(7¾in), *L 2 July,*
£286 ($395)

10
An incised twist wine glass,
mid-18th century,
14.3cm (5½in), *L 2 July,*
£176 ($243)

11
An incised-twist flute,
mid-18th century, 17cm
(6½in), *L 2 July,*
£176 ($243)

12
A mixed-twist glass,
*c.*1760, the stem with
corkscrew air gauze and
opaque thread, 17.5cm
(6¾in), *L 2 July,*
£209 ($288)

13
A colour-twist wine glass,
*c.*1760, the stem enclosing a central opaque
corkscrew entwined
with translucent red and
royal blue threads, 14cm
(5½in), *L 2 July,*
£858 ($1,184)

14
**An engraved opaque-twist
wine glass,** *c.*1760, 19cm
(7½in), *L 2 July,*
£209 ($288)

15
**A colour and mixed-twist
wine glass,** *c.*1760, the
stem enclosing a central
opaque-twist core
entwined with an air-
gauze corkscrew and
translucent mid-blue
thread, 14.5cm (5¾in),
L 2 July,
£1,210 ($1,670)

1
A mixed-twist flute, c.1760, the stem with opaque gauze core and outer corkscrew air threads, 18.6cm (7¼in), L 2 July, £176 ($243)

2
A wine glass, with multi-spiral opaque-twist stem, 17.5cm (6¾in), L 2 July, £77 ($106)

3
An opaque-twist goblet, c.1760, 16cm (6¼in), L 2 July, £176 ($243)

4
A colour-twist firing glass, c.1770, 10cm (4in), L 2 July, £1,540 ($2,125)

5
A colour-twist flute, c.1770, 20cm (7¾in), L 2 July, £935 ($1,290)

6
A colour-twist goblet, c.1770, with opaque-twist threads in red, peppermint green and royal blue, 18.5cm (7¼in), L 2 July, £1,320 ($1,822)

7
A colour-twist wine glass, c.1770, 14.5cm (5¾in), L 2 July, £1,870 ($2,581)

8
A colour-twist wine glass, c.1770, the bowl engraved with bird and fruiting vine, the stem enclosing an opaque-white corkscrew edged in translucent green entwined with a brown thread, 16cm (6¼in), L 1 July, £396 ($546)

9
A ratafia, c.1760, 18cm (7in), L 1 July, £330 ($455)

10
A pro-Hanoverian wine glass, c.1745, the bowl engraved with the white horse of Hanover below a ribbon inscribed 'LIBERTY', the heraldic rose of Westphalia on the reverse, 16cm (6¼in), L 1 July, £605 ($836)

11
A Jacobite wine glass, c.1745, 14cm (5½in), L 1 July, £352 ($486)

1   2   3

4   5   6   7

8   9   10   11

1
An engraved wine glass,
*c.*1760. 21.5cm (8½in),
L 2 July,
£176 ($243)

2
A tartan-twist wine glass,
*c.*1770, the stem
enclosing opaque-white,
translucent blue, red
and green spiral
threads, 14cm (5½in),
L 2 July,
£550 ($759)

3
An engraved goblet, the
bowl engraved with the
infant Bacchus seated on
a barrel, inscribed below
'TICIAE PATER', 19cm
(7½in), *L 2 July,*
£572 ($789)

4
An engraved wine glass,
15.5cm (6in), *L 2 July,*
£104 ($144)

5
A Williamite wine glass,
*c.*1800, engraved with an
equestrian portrait of
William III, inscribed
on the reverse 'BOYNE
1ST JULY 1690' and round
the rim 'THE GLORIOUS
AND IMMORTAL MEMORY OF
KING WILLIAM III', 14cm
(5½in), *L 2 July,*
£495 ($683)

6
**A Beilby enamelled wine
glass,** *c.*1770, 15cm (6in),
L 2 July,
£506 ($698)

7
**A Beilby enamelled wine
glass,** *c.*1770, the bowl
painted in white enamel
with a meander of
scrolls, 14.3cm (5½in),
L 2 July,
£440 ($607)

8
**A Beilby enamelled wine
glass,** 14cm (5½in) high,
L 1 July,
£990 ($1,366)

9
**A Beilby enamelled wine
glass,** *c.*1770, the bowl
decorated in white
enamel with a scene of
ruins set amongst trees
and shrubs, 14.5cm
(5¾in), *L 1 July,*
£1,980 ($2,732)

10
**A Beilby enamelled
colour-twist wine glass,**
1767, the bowl painted
in colours with a three-
masted sailing ship
inscribed above 'the
Providence', painted on
the reverse 'JO.N
ELLIOT 1767', chipped,
16.5cm (6½in), *L 2 July,*
£11,550 ($15,939)

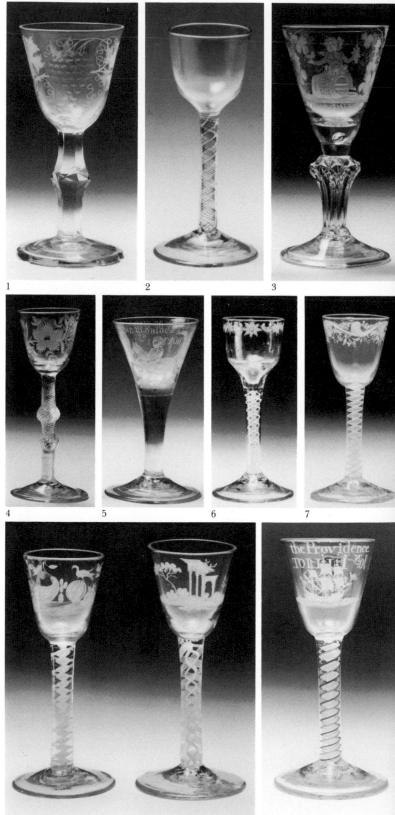

1 2 3

4 5 6 7

8 9 10

candlestick and sconce,
1760, 25.5cm (10in),
2 July,
715 ($987)

suite of drinking glasses,
1820, with gilt decor-
tion, comprising twenty-
even pieces, 14.5cm
¾in) to 21.5cm (8½in),
16 Jan,
550 ($660)

taperstick, *c.*1760,
5cm (6in), *L 2 July,*
495 ($683)

serving decanter jug
nd stopper, *c.*1720, 33cm
13in), *L 1 July,*
550 ($759)

pair of marked Cork
ecanters and stoppers,
1800, 26cm (10¼in),
HB 18 June,
1,600 (£625; $844)

commemorative Sun-
erland goblet, *c.*1821,
nscribed 'Presented by
Brother John Colling-
wood to the Caledonian
ociety, January 25th
821', 20.5cm (8in),
16 Jan,
341 ($409)

An Irish cut-glass pedestal
owl, early 19th century,
4cm (9½in), *C 10 July,*
253 ($352)

A pair of covered vases,
9th century, chips,
2cm (12½in), *A 28 Mar,*
Dfl 1,624 (£376; $477)

An Irish cut-glass pedestal
owl, early 19th century,
4cm (9½in), *C 10 July,*
363 ($505)

0
An Irish cut fruit bowl,
1800, 20.5cm (8in)
igh, *L 2 July,*
418 ($577)

1
A cut bowl, first half 19th
entury, 24.5cm (9½in),
17 May,
Dfl 1,102 (£256; $340)

12
An Irish cut fruit bowl,
*c.*1800, 21.5cm (8½in),
L 2 July,
£418 ($577)

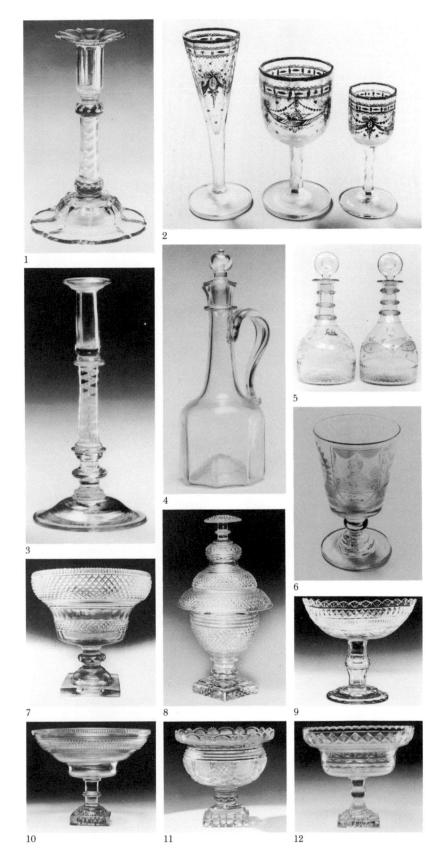

1

2

3

4

5

6

7

8

9

10

11

12

1
A glass-of-lead goblet, last quarter 17th century, of 'roemer' form, 29.5cm (11½in), *L 1 July*, £770 ($1,063)

2
A Saxon blued glass enamelled flask, dated 1613, in the shape of a wheel lock pistol, pewter nozzle, some repair, 34.5cm (13½in), *NY 15 Feb*, $1,760 (£1,517)

3
An Italian flask, 18th century, decorated with lion's head masks on the body and handle, 14cm (5½in), *F 26 Mar*, L 520,000 (£208; $265)

4
A set of six Venetian glass-mounted fruit knives, two dated 1847, another signed 'FC', with later silverplated blades, 21cm (8¼in), *NY 15 June*, $715 (£559)

5
A dated sealed wine bottle, 1797, *S 14 Nov*, £253 ($354)

6
An 'All Souls Common Room' sealed green glass wine bottle, early 19th century, 27cm (10¾in), *S 14 Nov*, £44 ($62)

7
A sealed green glass wine bottle, early 19th century, embossed with a crest, 29cm (11½in), *S 14 Nov*, £77 ($108)

8
A green-glazed bottle, 18th century, with polychrome decoration, 30cm (11¾in), *A 4 Sept*, Dfl 1,725 (£397; $583)

9
A German opaque-blue glass pewter-mounted tankard, 18th century, 25.5cm (10in), *L 1 July*, £1,045 ($1,442)

10
A Central European 'milchglas' enamelled tankard, mid-18th century, 15.5cm (6in), *L 1 July*, £352 ($486)

11
A Central European 'milchglas' enamelled flask, mid-18th century, 12.5cm (5in), *L 1 July*, £242 ($334)

12
A blue-tinted Central European enamelled flask, mid-18th century, 17cm (6½in), *L 1 July*, £572 ($789)

13
A Central European enamelled flask, mid-18th century, 18cm (7in), *L 1 July*, £330 ($455)

14
A Central European enamelled flask, mid-18th century, 13cm (5in), *L 1 July*, £286 ($395)

15
An enamelled 'milchglas' jug and cover, 18th century, probably German, some cracks, 22cm (8¾in), *A 25 Feb*, Dfl 1,044 (£256; $287)

16
A Bohemian 'milchglas' tankard, mid-18th century, 17.5cm (7in), *C 10 July*, £341 ($474)

1

2

3

4

5　6　7

8

9

10　11

12

13

14

15

16

Silesian 'zwischengold' portrait goblet and cover, 1790, by Johann gismund Menzel, armbrunn, 23.5cm in), *L 1 July*, 3,850 ($5,313)

pair of French white paline finger bowls, 1825, 7.5cm (3in) high, *25 June*, F 9,990 (£832; $1,124)

French white opaline ustard pot, *c.*1825, ecorated in blue and old, 14.5cm (5¾in), *25 June*, F 5,550 (£462; $624)

French white opaline lass, *c.*1825 decorated grey and gold, 15.5cm in), *M 25 June*, F 7,215 (£601; $812)

Bohemian transparent-namelled beaker, *c.*1830-0, painted in colours ith a hunting scene, ilt inscription and rim, 1cm (4¼in), *L 1 July*, 418 ($577)

Bohemian flashed and ngraved spa beaker, 1840, the amber bowl ith polished circlets, ome engraved with amed aspects of the pa, 14cm (5½in), *1 July*, 385 ($531)

Bohemian transparent-namelled portrait beaker, ate 19th century, ainted with a portrait of Goethe, rim chip, 12cm 4¾in), *L 1 July*, 550 ($759)

Viennese transparent-namelled topographical eaker, by Anton Koth-asser, *c.*1820, 10.5cm 4in), *L 1 July*, 1,650 ($2,277)

Viennese transparent-namelled beaker, by Anton Kothgasser, *c.*1820, initialled, 1cm (4¼in), some hips, *L 1 July*, 5,280 ($7,286)

10
A Bohemian enamelled goblet, 19th century, gilt borders, 17cm (6¾in), *A 3 June*, **Dfl 1,044 (£236; $319)**

11
A Bohemian 'red hyalith' spill vase, Bouquoy Glasshouse, *c.*1830, decorated in marbled red and a chinoiserie gilt vignette, 12cm (4¾in), *L 1 July*, £495 ($683)

12
A Bohemian 'lithyalin' scent bottle and stopper, Egermann or possibly Bouquoy, *c.*1830-40, the body with calcedony-style marbling overpainted with gilt flower sprays, 15.5cm (6in), *L 1 July*, £1,210 ($1,670)

13
A Bohemian gilt 'red hyalith' piggin, *c.*1830, gilt with chinoiserie insects and sprigs, interior gilt, small chips, 4.5cm (1¾in), *L 1 July*, £143 ($197)

1

2 3 4

5 6

7

8 9

10

11

12 13

1
A French black opaline glass, Napoleon III period, 39cm (15¼in), *M 25 June,* **FF 3,330 (£277; $375)**

2
A Bohemian silver-gilt-mounted and 'jewelled' amber overlay vase, mid-19th century, mounted with a Renaissance-style collar, 19cm (7½in), *NY 15 Feb,* **$550 (£474)**

3
A ruby flash dessert service, late 19th century, comprising seven pieces, slight damage, *C 10 July,* **£715 ($994)**

4
A pair of ruby-flashed cut glass urns, 28.5cm (11¼in), *L 20 June,* **£484 ($653)**

5
A pair of ruby glass decanters and stoppers, decorated with gilt foliage, 34cm (13¼in), *C 26 Mar,* **£1,595 ($2,026)**

6
A cameo glass scent bottle, *c.*1886, carved in white relief on a red glass ground, silver cover, stopper missing, 10cm (4in), *C 2 Oct,* **£275 ($401)**

7
A large Bohemian engraved ruby-flashed vase, *c.*1850, 57cm (22½in), *L 1 July,* **£550 ($1,006)**

8
A Bohemian gilt and enamelled glass overlay vase, mid-19th century, the green glass overlaid with white painted panels enamelled with roses, 34cm (13½in), *S 10 July,* **£374 ($501)**

9
A Bohemian ruby-flashed glass table service, *c.*1860, comprising 53 pieces, some chips, *L 7 Nov,* **£1,760 ($2,640)**

10
A pair of Bohemian overlay bottles and stoppers, the green glass overlayed in white, and painted with portrait medallions 25cm (9¾in), *C 12 Feb,* **£374 ($655)**

11
A Baccarat cut glass tumbler, with enamelled metal enclosure of pink rose and green leaves, some surface wear, 8.5cm (3¼in) diam, *NY 15 June,* **$935 (£730)**

12
A pair of overlay glass vases, 1860s, applied with a portrait medallion on a cranberry glass ground gilt with foliage, 30.5cm (12in), *C 10 July,* **£418 ($581)**

13
A pair of overlay vases, 1860s, applied with portraits of young girls on a cranberry and gilt foliate ground, 30cm (11¾in), *C 10 July,* **£528 ($734)**

pair of Stevens and
Villiams fancy glass
ases, 28cm (11in),
10 Dec,
154 ($216)

n overlay vase, late
9th century, probably
y Stevens and Wil-
ams, in cream
palescent glass over-
aid in flesh pink, 20cm
¾in), L 2 July,
1,210 ($1,670)

n 'Alexandrite' intaglio
nd cameo overlay vase,
y Stevens and Wil-
ams, c.1880, in
merald-green over
itron, 31.5cm (12½in),
2 July,
1,210 ($1,670)

A gilt cranberry glass
essert service, c.1880,
omprising eighteen
ieces, S 25 Mar,
1,155 ($1,467)

A silver-mounted cameo
lass biscuit barrel,
1885, the silver marked
ondon 1885, L 2 July,
935 ($1,290)

A pair of enamelled and
ilt mallet-form decanters,
toppers and stands,
econd half 19th cen-
ury, pale-green with
pink and blue roses
nd gilt line borders,
21cm (8¼in), S 25 Mar,
£528 ($671)

A cameo vase, probably
Webb, c.1880, in mid-
night blue translucent
glass overlaid in opaque
white, 23cm (9in),
L 2 July,
£935 ($1,290)

A pair of Thomas Webb
& Sons ivory cameo
glass vases, c.1900,
unsigned, with elephant
head handles, 22cm
(8¾in), NY 17 May,
$2,200 (£1,746)

9
A Thomas Webb & Sons
two-colour cameo glass
vase, c.1900, unsigned,
in strawberry red over-
laid in white, 20.5cm
(8in), NY 17 May,
$1,045 (£829)

10
A pair of Bohemian ruby
flash lustres, 35cm
(13¾in), C 3 Sept,
£308 ($453)

11
A pair of enamelled and
gilt Bohemian overlay
glass lustres, mid-19th
century, decorated with
gilt-ground classical
portrait medallions,
minor chips to prisms,
31.5cm (12½in), S 10 July,
£385 ($516)

12
A pair of overlay glass
lustres, 1870s, 27.5cm
(10¾in), C 10 July,
£462 ($642)

13
A pair of overlay glass
lustres, 1870s, with
panels painted with
portraits of young
girls, gilding rubbed,
27.5cm (10¾in), C 10 July,
£308 ($428)

1   2   3
4   5   6
7   8   9   8   10
11   12   13

1
A Clichy patterned-millefiori weight, 7.7cm (3in), *L 1 July*, £715 ($987)

2
A Clichy translucent blue-ground weight of patterned-millefiori type, 7.8cm (3in), *L 1 July*, £352 ($486)

3
A Clichy patterned-millefiori translucent red-ground weight, 8.1cm (3in), *L 1 July*, £880 ($1,214)

4
A Clichy signed scattered millefiori weight, signed 'C' 6.7cm (2¾in), *NY 15 June*, $825 (£645)

5
A Clichy barber's pole or chequer weight, 6.6cm (2½in), *L 1 July*, £880 ($1,214)

6
A Clichy garland weight, (small bruise), 7.9cm (3¼in), *NY 15 June*, £385 (£301)

7
A Clichy colour-ground weight, 8cm (3in), *L 1 July*, £495 ($683)

8
A Clichy red-ground weight, 6.7cm (2½in), *L 1 July*, £660 ($911)

9
A Clichy swirl weight, 6.7cm (2¾in), *NY 15 June*, $1,045 (£816)

10
A Clichy blue and white swirl weight, (slight surface wear), 5.3cm (2¼in), *NY 15 June*, $715 (£559)

11
A Clichy pansy weight, 7.5cm (3in), *L 1 July*, £6,050 ($8,349)

12
A Clichy faceted pink clematis weight, bruised 7cm (2¾in), *L 1 July*, £1,210 ($1,670)

13
A Clichy pedestal weight, 7.4cm (3in), *L 1 July*, £12,650 ($17,457)

14
A Clichy pedestal weight, 6.7cm (2½in), *L 1 July*, £1,045 ($1,442))

15
A Baccarat red primrose weight, 6.8cm (2½in), *L 1 July*, £528 ($730)

16
A Baccarat miniature primrose weight, 5.1cm (2in), *NY 15 June*, $935 (£730)

17
A Baccarat garlanded double clematis weight, 6.7cm (2¾in), *NY 15 June*, $1,210 (£945)

18
A Baccarat clematis bud weight, (minute surface wear), 7.6cm (3in), *NY 15 June*, $522 (£408)

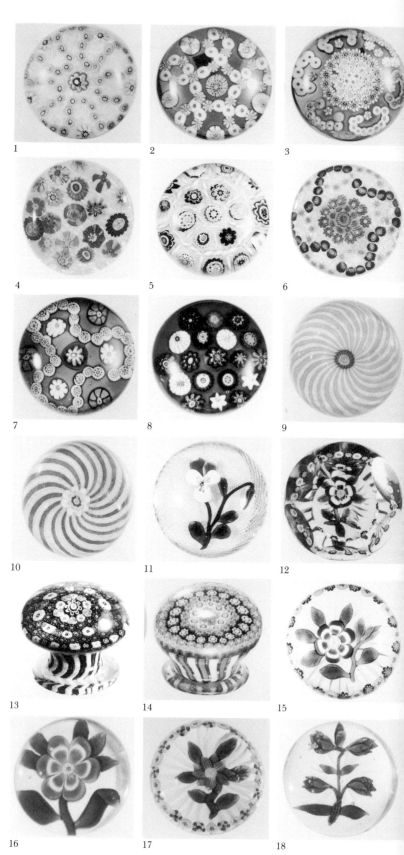

1 2 3
4 5 6
7 8 9
10 11 12
13 14 15
16 17 18

1
A Baccarat garlanded
butterfly weight, (minute
surface wear), 8.3cm
(3¼in), *NY 15 June,*
$900 (£703)

2
A Baccarat scattered-
millefiori weight, 7cm
(2¾in), *L 1 July,*
£440 ($607)

3
A Baccarat pom-pom and
garlanded paperweight,
6.5cm (2½in), *S 14 Nov,*
£1,100 ($1,540)

4
A Baccarat patterned
millefiori weight, (pitted
near base), 8.6cm
(3½in), *NY 15 June,*
$3,190 (£2,492)

5
A Baccarat garlanded
sulphide weight, 7.3cm
(2¾in), *NY 15 June,*
$605 (£472)

6
A Baccarat miniature
sulphide weight, 5.4cm
(2¼in), *NY 15 June,*
$165 (£129)

7
A Baccarat miniature
sulphide weight, 5.1cm
(2in), *NY 15 June,*
$247 (£193)

8
A Baccarat garlanded
clematis weight (minute
wear, one air bubble)
8.3cm (3¼in), *NY 15 June,*
$1,100 (£869)

9
A Baccarat double
clematis and garland
weight, 7.2cm (2¾in),
L 1 July,
£605 ($835)

10
A St Louis faceted upright
bouquet weight, 7.5cm
(3in), *L 1 July,*
£1,430 ($1,973)

11
A St Louis fuchsia weight,
7.3cm (2¾in), *NY 15 June,*
$2,310 (£1,805)

12
A St Louis strawberry
weight, 6cm (2¾in),
NY 15 June,
$1,870 (£1,461)

13
A St Louis purple dahlia
weight, 6.3cm (2½in),
L 1 July,
£1,210 ($1,670)

14
A St Louis fruit weight,
6.7cm (2¾in), *NY 15 June,*
$715 (£559)

15
A St Louis crown weight,
base damaged, 6.4cm
(2½in), *L 1 July,*
£297 ($410)

16
A St Louis concentric-
millefiori weight, 6.7cm
(2½in), *L 1 July,*
£1,870 ($2,581)

17
A St Louis faceted nosegay
mushroom weight, 8.4cm
(3¼in), *L 1 July,*
£990 ($1,366)

18
A St Louis concentric-
mushroom weight, signed
and dated SL 1848,
7.4cm (3in), *L 1 July,*
£1,760 ($2,429)

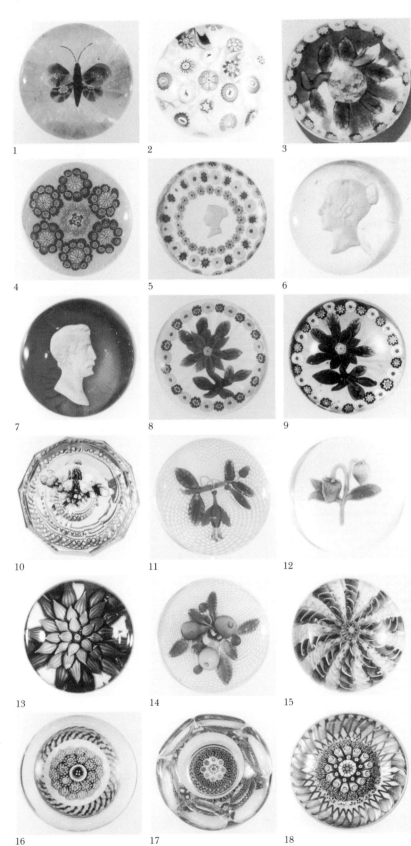

1   2   3
4   5   6
7   8   9
10   11   12
13   14   15
16   17   18

1
A St. Louis crown weight, (bubbles in glass), 7.6cm (3in), *NY 15 June,* $1,210 (£945)

2
A St. Louis concentric millefiori weight, 6.8cm (2½in), *L 1 July,* £1,540 ($2,125)

3
A St. Louis pom-pom weight, 6.5cm (2½in), *L 1 July,* £1,430 ($1,973)

4
A St. Louis concentric millefiori weight, signed SL 1848, 6.6cm (3in), *L 1 July,* £605 ($835)

5
A St. Louis paperweight small compote, 7.6cm (3in), *NY 15 Feb,* $715 (£616)

6
A St. Louis concentric sheaf weight, inscribed 248 in diamond point, 7.4cm (3in), *L 1 July,* £1,320 ($1,822)

7
Paul Ysart footed parrot weight, signed 'PY' on a single cane, 8.5cm (3¼in), *NY 15 Feb,* $770 (£664)

8
A Paul Ysart garlanded flat bouquet weight, signed 'PY' on a single cane, 7.3cm (2¾in), *NY 15 June,* $715 (£559)

9
A Paul Ysart fish weight, signed 'PY' on a single cane, 7.4cm (2¾in), *NY 15 June,* $660 (£516)

10
A Paul Stankard oriental floral design weight, signed and numbered, 7cm (2¾in), *NY 15 June,* $935 (£730)

11
A Charles Kaziun pedestal rose weight, signed 'K' underneath, 7cm (2¾in), *NY 15 June,* $605 (£473)

12
A Charles Kaziun pansy weight, signed with a gold foil 'K' underneath, 5.7cm (2¼in), *NY 15 June,* $1,045 (£816)

13
A Sandwich poinsettia weight, 7.3cm (2¾in), *NY 15 June,* $825 (£645)

14
A Sandwich magnum holly weight, (slight surface wear), 10.2cm (4in), *NY 15 June,* $825 (£645)

15
A New England apple weight, 8.3cm (3¼in), *NY 15 June,* $770 (£602)

16
A Paul Stankard botanical interpretation weight, signed and numbered, 6.4cm (2½in), *NY 15 June,* $660 (£516)

17
A Whitefriars paperweight doorstop, containing spirals of multi-coloured concentric millefiori canes, 5.2cm (6in), *NY 15 Feb,* $605 (£522)

18
A patterned-millefiori weight, of unknown origin, 7.6cm (3in), *L 1 July,* £770 ($1,063)

European Ceramics

Raeren stoneware
ug, dated 1600, brown
aze, minor chips,
2cm (8¾in), *L 5 Mar,*
550 ($616)

Raeren stoneware jug,
ated 1594, faulty
andle, 20cm (8in),
26 June,
fl 1,334 (£302; $407)

'Steinzeug' ewer,
6th century, 17.5cm
7in), *A 25 Feb,*
fl 6,148 (£1,507; $1,688)

Creussen tankard, dated
685, with moulded
rieze depicting a bear
unt, picked out in
oloured enamels,
inged pewter cover,
7cm (6¾in), *L 26 Nov,*
5,280 ($7,392)

Creussen stoneware
ankard, 1670-75,
pplied with moulded
igures of Christ and
he Apostles, later
nounts on handle, 15cm
6in), *L 25 June,*
2,420 ($3,267)

Creussen stoneware
ewter-covered tankard,
ate 17th century, with
frieze depicting a bear
unt, cover incised
693, minor chips, 16cm
6¼in), *NY 22 Nov,*
4,950 (£3,390)

A Westerwald stoneware
ug, 18th century,
oloured in blue and
grey, 25.5cm (10in),
C 12 Nov,
187 ($261)

A Westerwald stoneware
jug, c.1700, decorated
with floral motifs and a
portrait of Mary Stuart,
slight cracks, 14.5cm
5¾in), *A 3 June,*
Dfl 1,856 (£420; $567)

9
**A Waldenburg stoneware
humpen,** *c.*1580-90,
pewter-mounted,
applied with three
classical figures, 19cm
(7½in), *L 25 June,*
£3,410 ($4,604)

10
**A Mettlach pewter-
mounted stein,** late 19th
century, impressed
marks, 24cm (9½in),
S 14 Aug,
£308 ($459)

11
A Mettlach tankard,
decorated and signed by
Henri Schlitt, with
pewter mount, 18cm
(7in), *C 29 Jan,*
£363 ($428)

12
A Mettlach stein, early
20th century, pewter-
mounted, impressed
marks including pattern
number 1759, 23cm
(9in), *C 16 Jan,*
£253 ($304)

13
**A pair of Mettlach stone-
ware vases,** late 19th
century, with panels
of the seasons,
impressed marks
including shape num-
ber 1462, 34.3cm
(13½in), *C 10 July,*
£308 ($428)

1 2 3

4 5 6

7 8 9

10 11 12 13

1
An Ansbach faience tankard, *c.*1772, decorated in high temperature colours, later pewter mounts, hair cracks, AP/72 in blue, 23.5cm (9½in), *L 5 Mar,* £3,960 ($4,435)

2
A Bayreuth faience 'Enghalskrug', *c.*1730, decorated in shades of blue, later pewter cover, BK/H in blue, 28.5cm (11½in), *L 5 Mar,* £3,960 ($4,435)

3
A Bayreuth faience miniature Walzenkrug, 1745-7, painted in manganese and cobalt blue, pewter mounts, blue BFS/B mark of Frankel and Schreck, 10cm (4in), *L 26 Nov,* £990 ($1,386)

4
An Erfurt faience tankard, *c.*1760-70, painted in blue, green, manganese, iron-red, yellow and black, pewter cover dated 1770, 24cm (9½in), *L 26 Nov,* £550 ($770)

5
A Nuremburg faience tankard, first half 18th century, painted in blue with a king carrying a bunch of barley, pewter mounts, lid incised 'BM 1 38', cracks, 18cm (7in), *L 26 Nov,* £1,870 ($2,618)

6
A Thuringian faience tankard (Walzenkrug), pewter-mounted, probably third quarter 18th century, the lid dated 1786, *L 25 June,* £605 ($817)

7
A Frankfurt faience 'Birnkrug', early 18th century, painted in greyish cobalt blue, pewter lid inscribed 'GCE 1708', 26cm (10in), *L 5 Mar,* £495 ($554)

8
A South German faience 'Walzenkrug', 18th century, painted in blue, pewter mounts, 'H' mark in blue, 27cm (10½in), *L 26 Nov,* £1,100 ($1,540)

9
A German faience pewter-mounted tankard, second half 18th century, handle repaired, slight cracks, 28cm (11in), *C 10 July,* £418 ($581)

10
A North German faience goblet, 18th century, the exterior with fine manganese glaze, 11cm (4¼in), *L 5 Mar,* £440 ($493)

11
An Hispano-Moresque plate, Catalonia, late 15th century, painted in copper lustre, chipped, 32cm (12½in) diam., *L 25 June,* £275 ($371)

12
A Hanau faience dish, 1740-45, painted in turquoise, marked No. 3/P, 31cm (12¼in), *L 5 Mar,* £1,430 ($1,602)

13
An Hispano-Moresque plate, 16th century, broken and repaired, 46cm (18in), *NY 22 Nov,* $1,430 (£979)

14
An Hispano-Moresque charger, 17th century, the underside painted with stylised foliate scrolls, cracked, 39cm (15¼in), *S 10 July,* £264 ($354)

1   2   3   4

5   6   7   8

9   10   11

12

13   14

1
Dutch Delft candlestick, by Lambertus Cleffius, with chinoiserie decoration, *A 25 Feb*, fl 5,800 (£1,422; $1,592)

2
A set of three Dutch Delft drug jars, second half 18th century, mark IVH for Hendrick van Hoorn, minor chips, 18cm (7in), *L 26 Nov*, 990 ($1,386)

3
A Tuscan albarello, 15th century, painted in tones of blue and ochre, 20.2cm (8in), *L 5 Mar*, 2,860 ($3,203)

4
Two French faience Strasbourg-type blue and white platters, 1725-35, painter's marks 7X or XL on one and an encircled dot in blue on the other, 39.5 and 37.5cm (15½ and 14¾in), sold with a similar damaged dish, *NY 8 Nov*, 440 (£310)

5
Six Dutch tiles depicting William V of Orange, 18th century, each 37.5 x 24cm (14¾ x 9½in), *A 7 Feb*, Dfl 6,032 (£1,478; $1,730)

6
Six Dutch Delft tiles, 35.5 x 26cm (13¾ x 10¼in), *A 7 Feb*, Dfl 1,740 (£426; $499)

7
Six Dutch Delft tiles, inscribed Bakhuizen tot Rotterdam 1769, each 38 x 25.5cm (15 x 10in), *A 7 Feb*, Dfl 1,392 (£341; $399)

8
A Dutch Delft tile, Rotterdam, 17th century, flaking, *A 3 June*, Dfl 11,368 (£2,572; $3,472)

9
Three Dutch Delft tiles, first half 17th century, depicting a cow, a hare and an elephant, some flaking, *A 26 June*, Dfl 1,624 (£367; $412)

10
A Faenza plate, in the manner of Filippo Comerio, last quarter 18th century, 24.5cm (9¾in) diam., *F 26 Mar*, L 700,000 (£281; $356)

11
A French faïence vegetable dish and cover, Moustiers, 18th century, decorated in blue, 30cm (12in) wide, *M 25 June*, FF 8,880 (£740; $999)

12
A French faïence plate, Montpellier, 18th century, decoration on yellow ground, 34.5cm (13½in) diam., *M 25 June*, FF 9,990 (£833; $1,124)

13
A French faïence tureen and cover, third quarter 18th century, 22.5cm (8¾in), *L 5 Mar*, £682 ($764)

14
A Palissy-type lead-glazed dish, early 17th century, moulded in the centre with bacchanalian revellers, cracked, 24cm (9½in) diam., *L 25 June*, £308 ($416)

15
A Strasbourg faïence woodcock tureen and cover, Paul Hannong, 1750-54, modelled by Jean-Guillaume (Johann Wilhelm) Lanz, 30cm (12in), *NY 8 Nov*, $56,100 (£39,507)

1

A Dutch Delft blue and white deep dish, late 17th century, chip and hair crack, 38.5cm (15in), *NY 4 May,* $247 (£206)

2

A Dutch Delft blue and white Wan Li-style charger, 1690-1710, painted in shades of blue trekked in black, 39.5cm (15½in), *NY 4 May,* $990 (£825)

3

A Dutch Delft blue and white plate, early 18th century, illegible mark, 34.5cm (13½in), *NY 4 May,* $440 (£367)

4

A Dutch Delft polychrome deep dish, De Drye Clocken Factory, mid-18th century, painted in blue, green, orange and yellow, IVL monogram and numeral 3 mark, 34.5cm (13½in), *NY 4 May,* $687 (£573)

5

A Dutch Delft-doré dish, first quarter 18th century, painted in colours in Imari style, minor chips and wear, 35cm (13¾in), *L 5 Mar,* £2,310 ($2,587)

6

A Dutch Delft blue and white dish with crowned monogram, 18th century, 35cm (13¾in), *A 25 Feb,* Dfl 1,392 (£341; $382)

7

A Dutch Delft blue and white plate, dated 1656, *A 3 June,* Dfl 5,568 (£1,260; $1,701)

8

A Dutch Delft polychrome patriotic plate, dated 1748, commemorating the birth of William V of Orange, painted in iron-red, yellow and blue, numeral 2(?) mark in iron-red, 22.5cm (8¾in), *NY 4 May,* $330 (£275)

9

A pair of Dutch Delft blue and white plates, 18th century, *A 26 June,* Dfl 394 (£89; $120)

10

A Dutch Delft polychrome charger, late 18th century, painted in iron-red, blue, yellow, manganese, green and blue, 36cm (14in), *NY 4 May,* $330 (£275)

11

A pair of Dutch Delft tulip vases, 18th century, coloured in blue, green and red, marked in red Adriaen Kocks, some restoration, 21cm (8¼in) high, *M 25 June,* FF 7,215 (£601; $812)

12

A Dutch Delft blue and white tobacco box with cover, 18th century, 18cm (7in), *A 25 Feb,* Dfl 2,436 (£597; $669)

13

A pair of Dutch Delft marriage plates, dated 1785, *A 25 Feb,* Dfl 2,552 (£625; $700)

14

A Dutch Delft plaque, 18th century, with chinoiserie decoration, 34.5 x 33cm (13½ x 13in), *A 25 Feb,* Dfl 8,584 (£2,104; $2,356)

15

A pair of Dutch Delft shoes, painted in blue with flower sprays, 18th century, chips and hairline cracks, 11cm (4¼in), *C 16 Jan,* £1,265 ($1,518)

16

A Dutch Delft butter tub with cover, 18th century, 11.5cm (4½in), *A 25 Feb,* Dfl 4,640 (£1,137; $1,274)

17

A Dutch Delft polychrome jar and cover, 19th century, painted in blue, terracotta and green, chip, 67cm (26½in), *NY 8 Nov,* $1,760 (£1,239)

1 2 3

4 5 6

7 8 9

10 11 12

13 14

15 16 17

Italian Maiolica

Tin-glazed earthenware was first produced in Italy in the 11th or 12th century. The technique was originally developed in Mesopotamia, whence it was transmitted to North Africa, Spain and Italy. The term 'maiolica' is derived from the Tuscan name for the island of Majorca, through which Italian merchants shipped Valencian lustred pottery en route to Italy in the 15th century. Today 'maiolica' is used to describe all Italian and Sicilian earthenware with a tin-glaze.

Maiolica wares of the archaic period—that is, before the 15th century—were mostly painted in manganese brown and copper-green (fig.4)—the latter having a tendency to run is normally used as a wash, which is contained within the more readily controlled manganese outline. These early designs, often executed on a cross-hatched ground were mainly geometric or vegetal, and show Eastern influence. Such wares are frequently attributed to Orvieto or Viterbo in central Italy, both of which were important pottery manufacturing areas; recent excavations, however, suggest that comparable types were also made elsewhere in Italy.

The 15th century witnessed the change from the restricted green and manganese palette to a full range of primary colours. From the second quarter of the century the so-called 'severe' style appears; initially painted in green and brown, wares of this group are distinguished by the way in which the predominating Gothic decoration was tailored to the contours of the dish or vessel, the object not being subordinated to the design. Such designs were more complicated than those of the earlier wares, the main theme being enclosed within a frame or on a ground of dense scrolling foliage, much like contemporary illuminated manuscripts.

—1—
An Italian jar, Savona, late 17th century, painted in deep blue with Salvata Mundi, 43cm (17in), *F 28 May,* L 5,200,000 (£2,019; $1,666)

—2—
A Faenza albarello, early 16th century, painted in blue, cracked, 17cm (6¾in), *F 26 Mar,* L 1,300,000 (£521; $667)

—3—
A Faenza albarello, c.1540-50, with a portrait of a man inscribed 'VALERIO', footrim chipped, 33cm (13in), *L 25 June,* £3,080 ($4,158)

—4—
A Viterbo jug, 15th century, painted in green pigment and covered in grey glaze, 20.5cm (8in), *L 5 Mar,* £3,300 ($3,696)

—5—
A Calabrian maiolica albarello, 17th century, painted in cobalt, ochre, green, and yellow on a blue ground, 25.5cm (10¼in), *L 25 June,* £990 ($1,337)

—6—
An Urbino figure of a huntsman, early 17th century, probably Patanazzi workshop, some repairs, 24cm (9½in) high, *L 25 June,* £880 ($1,188)

—1—

—2—

—3—

—4—

—5—

—6—

Another group which appeared at about this time is painted in very deep cobalt oxide (*zaffara*), so thickly applied as to stand out in relief. These pieces are decorated in a Near Eastern style; oak leaves are frequently used as a ground pattern. The commonest form is the typically Tuscan high-shouldered oviform drug jar, with angular handles flanking the neck (fig.8).

In the second half of the 15th century the full chromatic range of primary colours is employed: in addition to manganese, green and cobalt, ochre, yellow and (rarely) a brownish red are used. Figurative subjects are treated in a more realistic or humanistic manner with profile portraits enclosed in contour panels on a ground of vibrant curling foliage between curving pointed and overlapping leaves or stylised peacock feathers.

Towards the end of the 15th century maiolica wares painted with narrative themes based on contemporary prints began to appear. These early figure subjects, however, were still encircled by borders of grotesques with ornamentation in the classical Roman style. Border decoration, although out of fashion during the second quarter of the 16th century, never entirely disappeared, in spite of the advance of the *istoriato* school. This school, of which Urbino and Venice were the protagonists, used maiolica only as a vehicle for the painted subject, the entire surface of the plate or vase being treated as a canvas or fresco. Themes were taken either from the Bible or from classical mythology, and the designs were often after engravings by Marcantonio Raimondi based in turn on Raphael. This group is part of a larger family of wares called *stile bella* ('beautiful style'), in which the vessel or dish was once more reduced to a subordinate role. At Faenza in the early 16th century maiolica painters used a distinctive blue ground known as *berettino*, mainly in conjunction with scrollwork and grotesque borders. This *berettino* type of decoration was later adopted in other areas—particularly in the north of Venice and Bassano.

—7—

A Venetian maiolica plaque, third quarter 16th century, painted with a bust of 'Pasqual Maripetra' (or Pasquale Malipiero, Doge of Venice 1437-62), 18 x 15cm (7⅛ x 6in), *L 25 June*, £3,520 ($4,752)

—8—

A pair of Tuscan double-handled albarelli, third quarter 16th century, perhaps Cafaggiolo, decorated in blue between ochre borders, flaked and chipped, 14cm (5½in), *L 26 Nov*, £990 ($1,386)

—9—

A Southern Italian jug, decorated in polychrome with a portrait of St Catherine of Alexandria, dated 1660, 20cm (8in), *F 25 Sept*, **L 600,000 (£220; $330)**

—10—

A Faenza maiolica crespina, mid 16th century, cracked, 28cm (11in), *L 5 Mar*, £1,100 ($1,232)

—11—

A signed Urbino plaque, c.1530-40, by Francesco Xanto Avelli da Rovigo, painted with Darius the Great marrying Attusa, cracked 30.3 x 28cm (12¼ x 11in), *L 9 Oct, 1984*, £11,000 ($14,300)

—7—

—8—

—9—

—10—

—11—

Another sub-family of the *stile bella* group consists of dishes painted with bust portraits of young maidens, often inscribed in a ribbon or scroll with the subject's name. The great exponent of this genre was Nicolo Pellipario, who worked at Castel Durante (fig.12). Pellipario, his son Guido Durantino (who established the famous factory at Fontana) and Francesco Xanto Avelli (fig.11) were arguably the finest *istoriato* painters during the second quarter of the 16th century (figs. 13-19).

In *c.*1500 the technique of lustring maiolica in the manner of Hispano-Moresque ware reached Italy, where it was most fully developed at Deruta (fig.20) and, a little later, in the workshop (or *bottega*) of Maestro Giorgio Andreoli at Gubbio; he added metallic lustres to wares painted at Castel Durante and elsewhere (fig.21).

—12—
Castel Durante saucer dish, *c.*1530-40, painted in the manner of Nicola Pellipario, restored, 23.2cm (9⅛in), 5 July, 1984, £2,750 ($3,822)

—13—
An Urbino trefoil cistern, 1600, probably by the Fontana workshop, painted after Raphael with a scene of Mount Helicon with Apollo and the nine Muses, minor restoration, 49cm (19¼in), 26 Nov, £9,020 ($12,628)

—14—
An Urbino istoriato dish, Fontana workshop, 1550-60, painted with Cloelia and her companions crossing the Tiber to escape from the Etruscans, extensive damage, 46cm (18in), L 25 June, £2,750 ($3,713)

—15—
An Urbino istoriato maiolica plate, mid 16th century, painted with the legend of Narcissus and Echo in tones of blue, yellow, ochre, white, green and blue, chips and crack, 22.5cm (8¾in), NY 22 Nov, £2,860 (£1,959)

—16—
An Urbino istoriato dish, 1540, painted in typical colours with a scene depicting Isaac blessing Jacob, some restoration, 26.5cm (10½in), L 5 Mar, £4,620 ($5,174)

—17—
An Urbino istoriato fragment, *c.*1530, probably painted by the Milan Marsyas painter, showing St Jerome, the fragment being the central portion of a dish, cracked, 20cm, (8in), L 25 June, £880 ($1,188)

—18—
An Italian istoriato maiolica plate, possibly Urbino and first half 16th century, depicting Alexander the Great before Diogenes, painted in blue, ochre, yellow, white and green, rim restored, originally a tazza, 26cm (10¼in), NY 10 May, $2,420 (£1,967)

—19—
A Venetian plate, late 16th century, decorated with Pan in a landscape, chip, 19.5cm (7¾in), L 26 Nov, £550 ($770)

—12—

—13—

—14—

—15—

—16—

—17—

—18—

—19—

Grotesque borders enjoyed a revival in the second half of the 16th century, the workshops of the Fontana and Patanazzi factories, in particular, re-interpreting them in an academic style, whereas those of Pesaro, Deruta (fig.22, 23) and Faenza adopted a freer approach.

Concurrently with this movement away from the narrative style an increasing emphasis was placed on form rather than on decoration. In consequence, dishes and vessels in contemporary silver or bronze forms were sparingly painted in ochre, yellow and cobalt only. This *compendiario* style, as it is known, was especially favoured at Faenza, where the rich white-glazed maiolica served as a brilliant counterpoint to the spare decoration (fig.24). This type of decoration proved fashionable not only in other Italian maiolica-producing areas, but also in France, Holland and England. The pictorial style

did not, however, disappear altogether but continued, albeit in a somewhat debased form, in Urbania (formerly Castel Durante), in Sienna and in the Abruzzi.

The 17th century saw the emergence into prominence of hitherto unimportant centres. At Montelupo in Tuscany maiolica painters produced a unique, vigorously executed ware which depicts strutting soldiers, painted in a bold palette and set against saffron skies (fig.25). Further south, the Grue family and other potters of Castelli used a subtle autumnal palette to paint idyllic landscapes with classical ruins, hunting subjects (fig.26) or, occasionally, religious themes—all taken from contemporary engravings (fig.29, 30, 31).

In the north-eastern region of Liguria huge quantities of blue and white maiolica wares were manufactured, mainly for pharmaceutical purposes. These were invariably loosely drawn

—20—
A Deruta plate, c.1520-30, decorated in gold-lustre and blue with a portrait of a young lady, rim restored, 22.5cm (8¾in), *L 26 Nov,*
£715 ($1,001)

—21—
A Gubbio maiolica nuptial dish, c.1530-40, 26cm (10in), *L 5 July 1984,*
£3,740 ($4,862)

—22—
An Italian Deruta dish, 17th century, with polychrome decoration, small cracks, 21.5cm (8½in), *M 25 June,*
FF 4,440 (£370; $500)

—23—
A Deruta charger, painted with St Francis receiving the stigmata, in cobalt blue, white and gold lustre, 41.5cm (17¼in), *L 12 June 1984,*
£14,850 ($19,305)

—24—
A Faenza Casa Pirota dish, 1520-30, 25.8cm (10¼in) diam, *L 5 July 1984,*
£11,000 ($14,300)

—25—
An Italian maiolica dish, Montelupo, early 17th century, cracks, 32.5cm (12¾in), *L 25 June,*
£308 ($416)

—20—

—21—

—22—

—23—

—24—

—25—

...ith disjointed vignettes of putti, trees and buildings in a ...ebased *compendiario* style (fig.22). Sicily was also a major ...roducer of utilitarian wares—again, mainly drug jars. In most ...ases, the designs and styles were copied from the more ...ophisticated mainland wares of Faenza and Venice (fig.27).

Maiolica has always been popular amongst European ...ollectors, and recently American buyers have been showing a ...reater interest in the subject. Damage appears to have a ...elatively more serious effect on prices realised for later ...aiolica than for the early wares. To a certain extent, buyers are ...repared to accept cracks and chips on 15th century wares ...ather than on 17th and 18th century pieces. It would also ...ppear that damage to a narrative dish has a greater effect on its ...alue than comparable damage to a dish with abstract floral or ...eometric design.

● GORDON LANG ●

Further reading

B. Rackham, *Guide to Italian Maiolica*, Victoria & Albert Museum, 1940

A. N. Kube, *Italian Maiolica XV-XVIII Centuries*, 1976

J. Giacometti, *Les Majoliques des Musées National*, 1974

G. Liverani, *La Maiolica Italiana*, 1960

J. Lessmann, *Italienische Majolika*, 1979

—26—
A Castelli armorial maiolica deep dish, mid ...7th century, painted with a hunting scene by a ...ollower of Antonio Lolli, ...ubdued polychrome ...alette, chips and glaze ...racks, 28cm (11in), *L 5 Mar*, £1,540 ($862)

—27—
An Italian albarello, Venice, late 16th century, 16cm (6¼in), *F 20 May*, L 2,800,000 (£1,087; $1,435)

—28—
A Sienna maiolica dish, c.1730-50, probably pain-ed by Ferdinando Mario Campani, in Flemish ...tyle, with shepherds and ...hepherdesses, 32.5cm (13¾in), *L 5 Mar*, £1,155 ($1,294)

—29—
A South-Italian plate, Castelli or Naples, late 17th century, painted in the style of Francesco Grue, some chips, 28cm (11in) diam, *F 28 May*, L 3,200,000 (£1,243; $1,640)

—30—
An Italian dish, probably from Naples, late 17th century, painted with a hunting scene, slight chips, 41.5cm (16¼in), *F 28 May*, L 2,600,000 (£1,009; $1,331)

—31—
A Castelli saucer, mid 18th century, painted by Carmine Gentili with a mythological subject, minor chips, 12.5cm (5in), *L 5 Mar*, £770 ($862)

—26—

—27—

—28—

—29—

—30—

—31—

1
A Liverpool Delftware bowl, *c.*1760, inscribed 'Trade and Navigation' and painted with coloured flowers, cracked, 23.5cm (9¼in), *S 25 Mar,* £187 ($237)

2
An English Delftware 'Adam and Eve' charger, *c.*1700, naively painted in blue, yellow, aubergine and green, cracked, 35cm (13¾in), *L 21 May,* £1,100 ($1,474)

3
A Bristol Delftware plate, *c.*1720-30, painted in yellow, rust-red, blue and manganese, minor rim chips, 22.5cm (8¾in), *L 23 July,* £858 ($1,270)

4
A Bristol Delftware polychrome 'Adam and Eve' charger, 1700-10, painted in turquoise, blue and yellow, 30cm (11¾in), *NY 12 Apr,* $1,430 (£1,144)

5
A London Delftware polychrome 'Oak Leaf' charger, *c.*1680, repaired, 34cm (13¼in), *NY 12 Apr,* $660 (£528)

6
A Bristol Delftware plate, the border in *bianco-sopra-bianco*, *c.*1765, 23cm (9in), *S 10 July,* £93 ($125)

7
An English manganese-decorated Delftware plate, second quarter 18th century, 22.5cm (8¾in), *S 10 July,* £60 ($81)

8
A blue and manganese Bristol Delftware plate, *c.*1770, 23cm (9in), *S 10 July,* £104 ($140)

9
A Delftware Royal Portrait 'Blue Dash' charger, *c.*1685-90, probably London, painted in blue, yellow and ochre with a portrait of William III, chips, 40cm (15¾in), *L 21 May,* £10,450 ($14,003)

10
A London polychrome Delftware 'Royal Portrait' plate, *c.*1690-95, riveted, 22cm (8¾in), *L 21 May,* £990 ($1,327)

11
A Bristol Delftware plate, *c.*1720-30, painted in yellow, rust-red, blue and manganese, 22.5cm (8¾in), *L 23 July,* £858 ($1,270)

12
A 'scratch blue' salt-glazed stoneware plate, mid-18th century, cracked 21.8cm (8⅝in), *S 25 Mar,* £3,080 ($3,912)

13
An English Delftware dish, late 17th century, painted in blue, chips and crazing, 28.5cm (11¼in), *L 23 July,* £550 ($814)

1
An English Delftware syrup jar, first half 18th century, 20.5cm (8in), *L 21 May*, £660 ($884)

2
An English Delftware drug jar, first half 18th century, chipped, 17.5cm (7in), *L 21 May*, £418 ($585)

3
A Liverpool Delftware blue and white bottle, mounted as a lamp, 1760-79, 22cm (8¾in), *NY 12 Apr*, $522 (£418)

4
A Bristol Delftware tea caddy, *c.*1750, painted in blue, slight glaze chipping, 12cm (4½in), *L 22 Oct*, £990 ($1,485)

5
A Liverpool Delftware tile, *c.*1765, printed by Sadler and Green, in greenish-brown, 12.5cm (5in), *S 10 July*, £104 ($140)

6
A Liverpool Delftware tile, *c.*1765, printed by Sadler and Green in black/sepia, 12.5cm (5in), *S 10 July*, £99 ($133)

7
Two London Delftware bin labels, 1750-60, 13.5cm (5¼in), *NY 12 Apr*, $220 (£176)

8
Two London Delftware bin labels, 1750-60, 13.5cm (5¼in), *NY 12 Apr*, £220 ($176)

9
Two London Delftware bin labels, 1750-60, 14cm (5½in), *NY 12 Apr*, $247 (£198)

10
A London Delftware bin label, 1750-60, glaze crackled, 13.5cm (5¼in), *NY 12 Apr*, $110 (£88)

11
A polychrome Delftware dish, *c.*1760, naively painted in orange, green, yellow and blue, minor rim chips, 33.5cm (13¼in), *L 22 Oct*, £308 ($462)

12
A Delftware salt, *c.*1730, probably Bristol, the body washed in manganese within iron-red and blue borders, some restoration, 5.5cm (2¼in), *L 26 Feb*, £715 ($801)

13
A pair of Delftware hexafoil salts, early 18th century, English or Dutch, each on three feet and painted in dark blue, glaze chips, 8cm (3¼in), *L 26 Feb*, £660 ($739)

14
An English Delftware charger, *c.*1700, painted in cobalt, manganese and green with a portrait of William III, chipped, 35cm (13¾in), *L 21 May*, £1,540 ($2,064)

15
A Lambeth Delftware ballooning plate, *c.*1780, painted in ochre and manganese, slight wear, 23cm (9in), *L 22 Oct*, £1,320 ($1,980)

7, 8, 9, 10 (*top to bottom*)

1
A medieval London pottery jug, 13th century, traces of yellow and ochre glaze, chips, 43cm (17in), *L 22 Oct*, £1,430 ($2,145)

2
An early Staffordshire slipware baking dish, *c.*1720-30, in light and brown slip against a cream ground, 42cm (16½in), *L 22 Oct*, £25,300 ($37,950)

3
A Staffordshire slipware baking dish, *c.*1720-30, press-moulded with a flower design, lead glaze, chips and cracks, 36cm (14¼in), *L 22 Oct*, £2,750 ($4,125)

4
A Staffordshire slipware baking dish, late 18th century, the red stoneware body decorated with brown slip trailed in cream, some wear and chips, 43cm (17in), *L 22 Oct*, £462 ($693)

5
A Staffordshire slipware strainer, late 18th century, repaired, 26.7cm (10½in), *C 16 Jan*, £660 ($792)

6
A documentary Nottingham stoneware 'carved jug', 1703, lustrous brown salt-glaze, repaired, 10cm (4in), *L 21 May*, £2,970 ($3,980)

7
A Whieldon-type teapot and cover, *c.*1760, with green flower sprays against tortoiseshell ground, damage to handle, chips, 14.5cm (5¾in), *S 14 Nov*, £638 ($893)

8
A slipware baking dish, dated 1852, slip-trailed in cream against a brown ground, chips, 33.5cm (13in), *L 17 July*, £385 ($558)

9
A Whieldon-type toy teapot, and cover, mid-18th century, in dark brown and cream tortoiseshell glaze, chipped and restored, 9cm (3½in), *S 25 Mar*, £638 ($810)

10
A Staffordshire agateware jug and cover, *c.*1740, veined in reddish-brown, buff and blue, bird knop, hair crack, 16cm (6¼in), *S 14 Nov*, £1,320 ($1,848)

11
An Andrew Abbott slipware baking dish, 1781-3, with slip trails combed into a feathered pattern, repaired, chips, 46cm (18in), *L 17 July*, £440 ($638)

12
A Whieldon-type 'Dolphin' sauce boat, *c.*1770-75, with green and brown glazes on the creamware body, chips and hair crack, 14.5cm (5¾in), *L 26 Feb*, £275 ($308)

13
A Staffordshire salt-glazed solid agate model of a cat, *c.*1745, with brown slip and cobalt blue markings on a cream ground, 10cm (4in), *C 29 Oct*, £858 ($1,278)

14
A Whieldon figure of a rabbit, *c.*1750-60, glazed in cream, grey and green, 11.5cm (4½in) long, *L 26 Feb*, £3,960 ($4,435)

15
An agateware cat, *c.*1740, chipped, 11.7cm (4½in), *S 10 July*, £1,320 ($1,769)

1

2

3

4

5

6

7

8

9

10

11

12

13

14

15

1
A Leeds creamware coffee pot and cover, 1770s, decorated in bright colours, 26cm (10¼in), *C 2 Oct,*
£440 ($642)

2
A set of five Neale & Co creamware salts, late 18th century, painted in sepia, patt. no. 181 in sepia, impressed 'WILSON', 7.7cm (3in) high, sold with a double ogee pot and cover 'en suite', 13.4cm (5¼in), *C 10 July,*
£418 ($581)

3
A creamware teapot and cover, *c.*1780, probably North Country, chipped, 12.5cm (5in), *S 10 July,*
£253 ($339)

4
A Staffordshire salt-glaze teapot and cover, *c.*1750-60, chipped, cracks, 9.5cm (3¾in), *L 21 May,*
£440 ($590)

5
A salt-glazed stoneware tea caddy, *c.*1750, probably Nottingham, toffee-brown glaze, 11cm (4¼in), *L 23 July,*
£660 ($977)

6
A pearlware cruet, *c.*1800, comprising seven pieces, the oil bottle with detachable cover, central handle missing, minor chips, stand 20cm (8in) diam, *L 26 Feb,*
£660 ($739)

7
Three Staffordshire salt-glazed coffee cups, and a salt-glazed plate, *C 4 June,*
£572 ($772)

8
A creamware coffee pot and a cover, *c.*1780, damaged, 28.6cm (11¼in), *C 17 Apr,*
£209 ($272)

9
A Melbourne creamware sauceboat, 1770s, restored, 19cm (7½in), another 'en suite', and a double-ogee salt 'en suite', *C 2 Oct,*
£132 ($192)

10
A lead-glazed earthenware cup, *c.*1760, the buff-coloured ware touched in green under a greenish clear glaze, 6cm (2½in), *S 14 Nov,*
£880 ($1,232)

11
A blue and white pearlware mug, dated 1788, 12cm (4¾in), sold with a Liverpool blue and white tankard, 12.5cm (5in), *C 15 Oct,*
£187 ($277)

12
A Leeds creamware dish with cover, 18th century, 26cm (10¼in) long, *A 3 June,*
Dfl 1,740 (£394; $531)

13
A Leeds creamware tea set, 18th century, eight pieces, slight damage, *A 3 June,*
Dfl 8,816 (£1,995; $2,693)

1

A garniture of ironstone vases, c.1830, 22cm (8¾in), *S 10 July,* £418 ($560)

2

A Mason's ironstone jug, c.1825, impressed mark, 14cm (5½in), *S 25 Mar,* £286 ($363)

3

Three Mason's ironstone jugs, decorated with an Imari pattern, green dragon handles, 24.1cm (9½in), 21.5cm (8½in) and 17.7cm (7in), *C 3 Sept,* £330 ($485)

4

A Bristol creamware jug, inscribed 'Betsey Draper 1834', painted in the manner of William Fifield, enamel flaked, 20cm (8in), *HS 4 June,* £165 ($223)

5

A Dillwyn, Swansea, earthenware plate, c.1825-30, naively painted, green border, 20cm (8in), *L 23 July,* £440 ($651)

6

A Mason's ironstone vase and cover, c.1820, cracked, 69.7cm (27½in), *C 16 Jan,* £330 ($396)

7

A Staffordshire earthenware jug, early 19th century, painted in red enamel and silver lustre, 11.5cm (4½in), *L 23 July,* £231 ($342)

8

A North Country tythe pig pottery jug, the base with an impressed inscription 'His Grease The Reverend shepherd of his Flock, the Lord Bishop of shearemclean', damaged, 23.5cm (9¼in), £176 ($211)

9

A Mason's ironstone vase and cover, the body painted with butterflies and birds amongst gilt flowers on a dark blue glazed ground, chipped, 52.5cm (20¾in), *C 17 Apr,* £880 ($1,144)

10

A David Wilson, Hanley, earthenware jug, c.1815, pale-brown reliefs against a 'mirror' silver lustre ground, hair crack, impressed, 14.5cm (5¾in), *L 23 July,* £176 ($260)

11

A Pratt-type jug, early 19th century, chipped, 15.3cm (6in), *S 25 Mar,* £506 ($643)

Bailey & Batkin silver-
lustre wig-stand, c.1815,
surmounted by a lion,
20cm (8in), *L 23 July,*
£220 ($326)

Staffordshire silver-
lustre bust of Nelson,
early 19th century, 20cm
(8in), *L 23 July,*
£275 ($407)

Doulton & Watts salt-
glazed spirit flask, early
19th century, 18.4cm
(7¼in), *C 4 June,*
£132 ($178)

silver-ground jug,
early 19th century,
decorated with panels
of inset wedged
coloured clays, 16.5cm
(6½in), *L 23 July,*
£220 ($326)

Staffordshire silver
lustre egg cruet, early
19th century, one cup
repaired, chips, 20cm
(8in) wide, *L 23 July,*
£132 ($195)

Derbyshire 'Bargeware'
teapot and cover, 1884,
29.5cm (11½in), *L 17 July,*
£220 ($319)

Wemyss (Plichta) pig,
1930s, ears and trotters
in pink, printed mark,
42cm (16½in), *L 22 Oct,*
£1,265 ($1,898)

A salt-glazed stoneware
money box, 1842,
impressed 'George
Goodwin, Decr. 9th, 1842',
damaged, 15cm (6in)
high, *S 10 July,*
£286 ($383)

A satirical creamware
plate, c.1815, entitled
'Symptoms of Walking
made Easy', 18.5cm
(7¼in), *S 16 Jan,*
£66 ($79)

0
A satirical pearlware
plate, c.1815, entitled
'Symptoms of Grave-
Digging', chip, 18.5cm
(7¼in), *S 16 Jan,*
£77 ($92)

11
A medium pot lid,
'Napirima, Trinidad',
(Ball 225), *C 29 Oct,*
£110 ($163)

12
A small pot lid, 'The
Trysting Place', (Ball
118), *C 29 Oct,*
£110 ($163)

13
A medium pot lid,
'Wellington', (Ball 160),
C 29 Oct,
£71 ($106)

14
A large pot lid, 'Queen
Victoria on Balcony',
(Ball 150), *C 29 Oct,*
£176 ($262)

1

2

3

4

5

6

7

8

9

10

11

12

13

14

1
A Staffordshire salt-glaze bear jug and cover, c.1740, detachable head, tail repaired, 26cm (10¼in), *L 21 May*, £1,980 ($2,653)

2
A Nottingham brown stoneware bear jug and cover, c.1760, replacement metal collar and link, 27.5cm (10¾in), *NY 15 Feb*, $880 (£759)

3
An Obadiah Sherratt mantelpiece ornament c.1835, the details brightly and naively coloured, minor damage, 28.5cm (11¼in), *L 22 Oct*, £880 ($1,320)

4
An Obadiah Sherratt group of 'The Death of Munrow', c.1830, a tiger gnawing the head of the lieutenant, repaired chips, 34.5cm (13½in), *NY 12 Apr*, $7,975 (£6,380)

5
An Obadiah Sherratt 'Bull Baiting' group, c.1835, some restoration, 37cm (14½in), *L 21 May*, £2,200 ($2,948)

6
A Dixon Austin & Co pink lustre watch stand, c.1825, damaged, impressed mark, 27cm (10½in), *L 23 July*, £682 ($1,009)

7
A 'Temple of Chronus' watch stand, c.1815-20, coloured to simulate yellow-grey marble, restored, 23.5cm (9¼in), *L 23 July*, £462 ($684)

8
A pair of North Country money boxes, early 19th century, damaged, 15cm (6in), *S 25 Mar*, £550 ($699)

9
A Pratt-type money box clock group, early 19th century, details picked out in ochre, blue, green, black and pink, restored, 22.2cm (8¾in), *S 25 Mar*, £715 ($908)

10
A Staffordshire spill vase, c.1820, on stepped base marbled in red and blue, damaged, 12.7cm (5in) wide, *S 25 Mar*, £286 ($363)

11
A Staffordshire pearlware spill holder castle, early 19th century, 13cm (5⅛in), *S 25 Mar*, £385 ($489)

12
A Pratt-style money box, c.1820 12.5cm (5in), *C 29 Oct*, £99 ($147)

13
An earthenware pastille burner, impressed date 1928, 21.5cm (8½in), *C 6 Aug*, £440 ($655)

14
A pottery spill vase, c.1800, possibly Scottish, in the form of a rock applied with a sheep and lamb, some restoration, 19cm (7½in), *L 21 May*, £352 ($472)

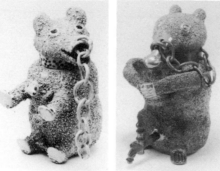

1 2 3

4 5

6 7 8 9

10 11

12 13 14

1
A pair of Staffordshire lions, *c.*1840, after Ralph Wood originals, glazed in translucent brown, damaged, 36.3cm (14¼in), *C 16 Jan,*
£1,100 ($1,320)

2
A pair of Staffordshire models of rabbits, second half 19th century, 25.4cm (10in), *C 12 Mar,*
£1,375 ($1,568)

3
A Staffordshire pearlware bull-baiting group, early 19th century, restored, 15.5cm (6in), *S 25 Mar,*
£825 ($1,048)

4
A polychrome pottery model of a lion, late 18th century, with bright yellow glaze, 9cm (3½in), *C 29 Oct,*
£550 ($819)

5
A cow creamer and cover, early 19th century, sponged in black and deep pink, 13.5cm (5¼in), *C 29 Oct,*
£187 ($278)

6
A pearlware pug, early 19th century, the rust coloured dog seated on a tasselled green cushion, restored, 9cm (3½in), *S 25 Mar,*
£286 ($363)

7
A pair of groups of poodles and their puppies, second half 19th century, 20.3cm (8in), *C 6 Aug,*
£154 ($229)

8
A Staffordshire figure of a greyhound, second half 19th century, 19cm (7½in), *C 6 Aug,*
£63 ($94)

9
A Pratt-type model of a deer, late 18th century, sponged in ochre, restored, 14cm (5½in), *S 10 July,*
£297 ($398)

10
A Staffordshire figure of the murderer William Palmer, *c.*1856, 28.5cm (11¼in), *L 22 Oct,*
£1,430 ($2,145)

11
A Staffordshire model of Palmer's House, *c.*1856, 19.5cm (7¾in), *L 22 Oct,*
£495 ($743)

12
A Staffordshire model of Palmer's house, *c.*1856, damaged, 23cm (9in), *S 16 Jan,*
£220 ($264)

13
A Staffordshire pearlware bull-baiting group, 1790-1810, after the Ralph Wood model, one horn restored, 34.5cm (13½in), *NY 12 Apr,*
$4,510 (£3,608)

14
A composite set of Dixon and Austin 'Seasons', *c.*1825, slight wear, two cracked, three with impressed mark, 23cm (9in), *L 23 July,*
£1,540 ($2,279)

1
A Ralph Wood figure of a ram, 1770s, green glazed, chipped, 15.5cm (6in), *C 2 Oct,* £440 ($642)

2
A pair of Staffordshire groups, mid-19th century, 22.8cm (9in), *C 6 Aug,* £132 ($197)

3
A Ralph Wood pearlware bust of Handel, *c.*1800, minor restoration, impressed Ra Wood and 80, 23cm (9in), *S 14 Nov,* £638 ($893)

4
A pair of Ralph Wood figures, *c.*1770-80, Neptune and a girl in 18th century dress playing a tambourine, glazed green, some repair and chips, 28.5 and 30cm (11¼ and 11¾in), *L 22 Oct,* £1,650 ($2,475)

5
A Staffordshire 'costume' group, *c.*1810, repaired, 19.7cm (7¾in), *C 16 Jan,* £1,320 ($1,584)

6
A Staffordshire group of two children, early 19th century, chips, 21cm (8¼in), sold with a Staffordshire figure of a sheep and lamb, *c.*1800, chips, 12cm (4¾in), *L 22 Oct,* £418 ($627)

7
A Staffordshire group, early 19th century, repaired, 20.3cm (8in), *C 16 Jan,* £1,650 ($1,980)

8
A 'Tythe Pig' group, early 19th century, 14cm (5½in), *C 29 Oct,* £242 ($360)

9
A figure of a sportsman's companion, *c.*1800, of Pratt type, 19cm (7½in), *L 26 Feb,* £385 ($431)

10
A Ralph Wood figure of a gardener, *c.*1770-80, restored, chips, 19.5cm (7¾in), *L 23 July,* £715 ($1,058)

11
A Ralph Wood figure of Chaucer, impressed mark on reverse of base, 'Ra Wood, Burslem, 155', *C 6 Aug,* £968 ($1,442)

12
A pearlware group of 'Charity', early 19th century, 18.5cm (7¼in), *S 25 Mar,* £77 ($98)

13
A pearlware figure of an actor, in 17th century dress, early 19th century, 24cm (9½in), *S 25 Mar,* £105 ($133)

14
A pearlware figure of a boy representing 'Winter', early 19th century, chipped, 19.3cm (7⅝in), *S 25 Mar,* £110 ($140)

15
A pearlware figure of an actor, probably Shylock, early 19th century, 12cm (4¾in), *S 25 Mar,* £110 ($140)

16
A Staffordshire pearlware figure of a girl representing 'Summer', early 19th century, impressed 'Summer', 19.5cm (7¾in), *S 25 Mar,* £302 ($384)

1

2

3

4

5

6

7

8

9

10

11

12

13

14

15

16

1
A Minton 'majolica' tureen and cover, 1873, in typical bright 'majolica' glazes, chip and crack, 26.5cm (10½in), *L 21 May,* £2,090 ($2,801)

2
A Minton 'majolica' game pie dish, cover and liner, 1860, impressed number 668, 31.5cm (12½in), *L 23 July,* £495 ($733)

3
A George Jones 'majolica' cheese dish and cover, *c.*1875, moulded with insects amongst water-lilies, chips and crack, impressed mark and PODR mark, base 28cm (11in), *L 22 Oct,* £572 ($858)

4
A George Jones 'majolica' centrepiece, *c.*1870, with lilac and pale blue bowl, impressed PODR mark and pattern no. 3205, 20cm (8in), *L 22 Oct,* £1,980 ($2,970)

5
A George Jones 'majolica' centrepiece, *c.*1870, impressed PODR mark, 20cm (8in), *L 21 May,* £3,850 ($5,159)

6
A 'majolica' game tureen and cover, *c.*1870, damaged, 35cm (13¾in), *S 15 May,* £880 ($1,170)

7
Two George Jones 'majolica' flower-holders, *c.*1870, one in the form of an ass, the other of a camel, camel repaired, chips, *L 21 May,* £4,400 ($5,896)

8
A George Jones 'majolica' salmon dish and cover, *c.*1880, impressed PODR mark, pattern no. 2464, 48.5cm (19in), *L 21 May,* £2,750 ($3,689)

9
A pair of 'majolica' goats, 1870s, damaged, 40.7cm (16in), *C 10 July,* £1,650 ($2,294)

10
A Holdcroft 'majolica' jardinière and stand, *c.*1870, impressed mark, restored, 23cm (9in), *S 15 May,* £88 ($117)

11
A J Holdcroft 'majolica' umbrella stand, *c.*1875, glazed in green, brown, blue and yellow, damaged, impressed mark and '8', 82cm (32¾in), *L 21 May,* £715 ($958)

12
A Minton 'majolica' jug, 1873, coloured in bright yellow, green, blues, aubergine and white, impressed mark '437' and date code, 25cm (9⅞in), *S 15 May,* £1,760 ($2,341)

13
A Minton 'majolica' heron and fish ewer, impressed mark, for 1869, after a model by H Protat, chip to crest, 54cm (21¼in), *S 23 Jan,* £1,925 ($2,281)

14
A pair of J Holdcroft 'majolica' vases, *c.*1875, some damage, 63.5 and 59.5cm (25 and 23½in), *L 23 July,* £1,430 ($2,116)

15
A Minton 'majolica' centrepiece, *c.*1863, impressed marks including an obscured date code possibly for 1863, damaged, 54.6cm (21½in), *C 17 April,* £2,640 ($3,432)

1   2   3

4   5   6

7   8

9

10   11   12

13   14   15

1
A Minton 'majolica' jardinière, 1871, impressed marks and date code, chipped, 36.8cm (14½in), *C 10 July*, £484 ($673)

2
An assembled set of twelve Minton 'majolica' oyster plates, dated 1873 and 1876, each with green and brown tortoiseshell glaze, ten with impressed Minton marks, and each numbered 1323, 30cm (9in), *NY 12 Apr*, $1,100 (£880)

3
A Minton 'majolica' jardinière, 1869, chip and flakes, impressed mark, shape no. 532, 60cm (23½in) wide, *L 23 July*, £330 ($488)

4
A Minton 'majolica' garden seat, dated 1896, covered in streaky turquoise glaze, impressed Minton mark, shape no. 588, 53cm (20¾in) high, *NY 12 Apr*, $550 (£440)

5
A pair of Minton 'majolica' lamps, dated 1868, minor repairs, impressed Minton marks, shape no. 476, 37cm (14½in) wide, *NY 12 Apr*, $2,200 (£1,760)

6
A Minton 'majolica' 'Aesthetic' garden seat, 1881, impressed marks and date code, 46cm (18in), *S 15 May*, £1,760 ($2,341)

7
A Minton 'majolica' teapot and cover, 1875, in the form of a monkey in a blue jerkin grasping a large fruit, spout restored, shape no. 1844, 14cm (5½in), *L 22 Oct*, £825 ($1,238)

8
A Minton 'majolica' sweetmeat dish, 1868, modelled as a blue tit on a branch bearing a large leaf, impressed mark, shape no. 1881, 20.5cm (8in), *L 22 Oct*, £440 ($660)

9
A Minton 'majolica' teapot and cover, 1872, in the form of a crouching cockerel, impressed mark, shape no. 1909, 20cm (8in), *L 26 Feb*, £2,420 ($2,710)

10
A Minton 'majolica' jug, 1869, with green leaves and white flowers beneath the lilac rim, impressed mark, shape no. 1228, 16.5cm (6½in), *L 22 Oct*, £396 ($594)

11
A Minton 'majolica' oyster stand, 1869, with revolving base, glazed in green, brown and white, chip, impressed mark, shape no. 636, 25.5cm (10in), *L 26 Feb*, £1,980 ($2,218)

12
A Minton 'majolica' 'Rhenish' jug, *c.1867*, impressed mark and date code for 1867, repaired, 27.5cm (10¾in), *S 15 May*, £60 ($80)

13
A pair of 'majolica'-glazed figures, *c.1870*, representing Summer and Autumn, chips, 38 and 37cm (15 and 14½in), *L 23 July*, £418 ($619)

14
A Minton 'majolica' figure of a grape harvester, 1866, impressed mark and date code, some damage, 41cm (16in), *S 23 Jan*, £495 ($587)

15
A Minton oval plaque, 1883, glazed in turquoise blue, impressed mark, 43cm (17in), *L 22 Oct*, £275 ($413)

English Commemorative Wares

Whether it is a keen interest in social history, an eye for shape and decoration or just a passing interest in one's fellow man, the commemorative collector will already have or will rapidly acquire these attributes. The term 'commemorative' need not be confined to the ubiquitous coronation mug; as the collector will quickly discover, the scope is very broad. Every conceivable celebration has been recorded, with ceramics as perhaps the most popular medium. Royal events are the most numerous but there are also many other topics such as military and political battles, the commissioning or launching of a ship to the opening of a railway, the celebration of a sporting achievement or simply a birth or marriage in a family. These invariably provide a fascinating insight and popular animated view of the event.

Up until the end of the 18th century, the tin glazed or so-called 'delft' centres tended to be the source of commemorative wares, with London, the West Country, Liverpool, Glasgow and Dublin the main areas of production. Here attribution can be difficult, even to decide whether a piece is English or Continental. Probably some of the earliest wares are the charming group of so-called 'blue dash' chargers which often bore the naively painted portrait of the reigning monarch, for instance a related plate painted with William and Mary, dated 1691 (fig.1). Other delft wares are illustrated on pp.224-5.

—1—
A London Delftware dated 'Royal Portrait' plate, 1691, some flaking, 21.5cm (8½in), L 22 Oct, £2,860 ($4,290)

—2—
A pearlware jug commemorating the marriage of Princess Charlotte and Prince Leopold, 1816, restored spout, 22cm (8¾in), S 25 Mar, £352 ($447)

—3—
A creamware commemorative jug, 1785, painted with red inscription and flower sprays in famille-rose enamels, 21.5cm (8½in), C 10 Dec, £176 ($246)

—4—
A yellow-ground Staffordshire jug, early 19th century, bat-printed with titled portraits of Col. Wardle and Miss Taylor, crack, 16.5cm (6½in), L 22 Oct, £264 ($396)

—5—
A Liverpool creamware jug, c.1800, printed with a picture of the Guillotine and a cartoon entitled 'French Liberty', restored, 18.5cm (7¼in); sold with another, printed with a scene entitled 'Susan's Farewell', damaged, C 2 Oct, £165 ($240)

—1—

—2—

—4—

—3—

—5—

The royal theme is perhaps the most popular amongst collectors and can be followed chronologically to the present day. Queen Victoria and Prince Albert certainly gave rise to more than their share of material in this respect: some examples sold in 1985 are illustrated as figs.9, 10, 11 & 12; another is a rare Davenport mug (fig.6) made for the town of Preston on the occasion of Victoria's coronation. Early Victoria commemoratives are certainly a lot scarcer than pieces made for the Queen's Diamond Jubilee in 1897; however the three Doulton jugs shown in fig.7 still made £418 ($560), probably because of the desirability of Doulton in its own right. Continuing the royal theme, fig.8 shows a Grindley porcelain Edward VIII coronation mug for 1937, which is unusual because, following his abdication, factories and suppliers were ordered to destroy all commemorative wares depicting the King actually wearing the crown. Many uncrowned portrait mugs exist, and the myth of rarity, and therefore high value, which surrounds these is sadly misplaced.

—6—
A Davenport commemorative mug, commemorating the coronation of Queen Victoria, and titled 'Success to the Town and Trade of Preston', transfer-printed in underglaze blue, restored, printed mark, 7.5cm (3in), L 22 Oct, £363 ($545)

—7—
A set of three Royal Doulton stoneware commemorative jugs, 1897, commemorating Queen Victoria's Diamond Jubilee, glazed in blue, green and brown, impressed mark, 15, 18.5 and 23cm (6, 7 and 9in), L 21 May, £418 ($560)

—8—
A Grindley porcelain 'Edward VIII Coronation' mug, 1937, printed mark, 7cm (2¾in), S 16 Jan, £83 ($99)

—9—
A commemorative jug, 1840, commemorating the marriage of Queen Victoria and Prince Albert, printed in puce with two portraits of the royal couple, yellow and copper lustre ground, 16cm (6¼in), L 23 July, £132 ($195)

—10—
A Victoria Coronation earthenware plate, c.1838, printed in black, 18cm (7in), S 16 Jan, £121 ($145)

—11—
A marriage of Victoria and Albert earthenware plate, c.1840, printed in black, slight restoration, 20.5cm (8in), S 16 Jan, £77 ($92)

—12—
A marriage of Victoria and Albert earthenware loving cup, c.1840, printed in blue, restored, 12cm (4¾in), S 16 Jan, £209 ($251)

—13—
An Admiral Rodney mask mug, 16.5cm (6½in), C 4 June, £462 ($624)

—6— —7— —8— —9— —10— —11— —12— —13—

The use of fine bodied potteries became popular from the late 18th century onwards and, following the development of the ceramics industry during the industrial revolution, the mass production of commemoratives in this medium became widespread. These were mainly creamwares, pearlwares and, from the early 19th century, ironstone. The centre for much of this production was Stoke-on-Trent, with many of the famous names in potting history working there. Perhaps the most renowned of these was Josiah Wedgwood, whose influence was profound and who brought the name of Wedgwood and English products to the rest of Europe, Asia and, of course, to North America, producing many commemorative pieces specially for the American market. Representative of the creamwares is the jug illustrated in fig. 14, which was decorated at the Robinson and Rhodes workshop. Saltglazed stoneware was also popular and figs.16, 17 & 19,

shows some amusing spirit flasks, another can be seen on p.229 fig. 3.

The toby jug has often been used as a popular form of caricature. Fig.15 shows a jug in the form of Winston Churchill, which was designed by Clarice Cliff (whose work can also be seen on page 295); these jugs usually bring between £500 and £800 ($750 and $1,200). The same firm produced a set of First World War generals designed by Sir F. Carruthers Gould (p.262 fig. 10) — the set of eleven can be worth in excess of £2,000 ($3,000). On the sporting theme, examples abound and figs.20 and 21 show two boxing jugs. Pugilistic commemoratives illustrate the great heroism of the early bare knuckle fighters. Often the printed or painted subjects can be traced to contemporary engraved sources, which introduces another interest to such a collection. Other sports, such as golf or cricket, are given equal attention (see also p.541) but many others can be

—14—
A creamware commemorative jug, 1781, painted perhaps at the Rhodes workshop, with black inscription and coloured flower sprays, restored, 17.5cm (7in), C 2 Oct, £198 ($289)

—15—
A Wilkinson toby jug of Churchill, 1940's, designed by Clarice Cliff, black printed marks including number 262 and facsimile signature, 30cm (11¾in), C 10 July, £550 ($765)

—16—
A commemorative stoneware spirit flask moulded with portraits of Queen Victoria and Prince Albert, 21cm (8¼in), C 4 June, £187 ($252)

—17—
A saltglazed stoneware gin flask, probably depicting Queen Caroline, impressed with the slogan 'My hope is in the people', 28cm (11in), C 10 Dec, £220 ($308)

—18—
A pearlware inscribed and dated jug, 1812, naively painted with a scene of a blacksmith at work, an inscription, and the blacksmith's arms, resist lustre rim, star crack, 19.5cm (7¾in), L 23 July, £440 ($651)

—14—

—17—

—15—

—18—

—16—

—19—
A Bourne saltglazed spirit flask moulded in the form of Daniel O'Connell, with the slogan 'Irish Reform Cordial', impressed marks for Denby and Codnor Park, 19.5cm (7¾in), C 4 June, £220 ($297)

—20—
A Staffordshire commemorative 'Boxing' jug, c.1810-15, with two panels depicting the boxers Molineux and Cribb, mid-blue ground, rim chip, 15cm (5¾in), L 23 July, £440 ($651)

—21—
A commemorative boxing jug, 1824, printed and naively painted with titled scenes of the boxers Spring and Langan, orange and copper lustre borders, rim chip restored, 11.5cm (4½in), L 23 July, £462 ($684)

Jack Langan, the Irish champion, was defeated by Tom Spring on the 8th June 1824 in a fight at Chichester. The fight lasted 77 rounds before Tom Spring won the championship belt of England.

—19—

—20—   —21—

much more rare.

A collector may choose to concentrate on the very broad theme of dated pieces. These can provide accurate dating of styles and materials, with often the early dated pieces of pottery being the only source of chronological information relating to a period of production. Thematic collecting need not, of course, be confined to ceramics alone, as many other commemorative items were produced, from pressed glass to match box tops, cigarette cards (see pp.531 & 541), biscuit and tobacco tins (figs.22 and 24).

Many collectors choose to buy modern commemorative wares, which are often produced as 'limited editions'. However if this type of collecting is being considered, a long term view must be borne in mind, as the market for such pieces today is very poor. Limited editions are often alluringly advertised as being infallible investments which, as auction results show, is totally misleading. They do 'complete the picture' of commemorative wares to the present day but the collector should be very selective and buy only good quality items from well-known manufacturers.

—22—

A glass rolling-pin, c.1900, with printed portraits of the British leaders in the Transvaal War, 40cm (15¾in) long, *JHB 7 Feb*, **R 230 (£150; $176)**

—23—

A creamware coronation mug, c.1820, printed with a portrait of George IV, restored, 7.5cm (3in); sold with a jug, printed with bust portraits of Queen Caroline, repaired, 12cm, (4¾in), *C 2 Oct*, **£440 ($642)**

—24—

A presentation chocolate tin, 1900, inscribed 'New Year Greetings from Her Majesty', presented to the British troops serving in South Africa, 15cm (6in), *JHB 7 Feb*, **R 110 (£51; $60)**

—25—

A Copeland Transvaal War Tyg, c.1900, printed and impressed marks, hair-cracks, restoration, 14cm (5½in), *S 16 Jan*, **£99 ($119)**

—26—

A George IV coronation mug, c.1829, probably Samuel Alcock, small hair-crack to handle, 8.5cm (3¼in), *S 16 Jan*, **£209 ($251)**

—27—

A commemorative creamware jug, 1821, bat-printed in sepia with two portraits of George IV, pink lustre borders, 12.5cm (5in), *L 26 Feb*, **£528 ($591)**

—22—

—23—

—24—

—25—

—26—

—27—

The market for commemorative wares is continuing to develop but unfortunately few dealers specialise in this area alone. Auction houses now give the theme to sections of sales wherever possible, which has helped to validate the subject. Both the auction houses and well-established trade are the best source of information, particularly when first starting to collect. High prices are usually only obtained for items in pristine condition and caution with marks is advisable as many can be spurious, or only indicate that the piece is in a particular style. As in any collecting field, the advice of a friendly dealer or auctioneer will prove invaluable.

Further reading:

John & Jennifer May *Commemorative Pottery, 1780-1900,* 1972

Exhibition catalogue *Royal Wedding Exhibition,*
produced by the Commemorative Collector's Society 1981

● PAUL MACK ●

—28—
A Royal Doulton earthenware memorial loving cup, depicting George V, 1936, printed mark, crack, 12cm (4¾in), *S 16 Jan,*
£27 ($33)

—29—
A Copeland Tyg, *c.*1900, marked Subscriber's Copy, T Goode & Co, South Audley St London, commemorating the British victory in the Second Anglo-Boer War, 14cm (5½in), *JHB 7 Feb,*
R 1,150 (£537; $628)

—30—
A Minton 'Edward VIII Coronation' beaker, 1937, printed mark no. 451/2000, 10.5cm (4¼in), *S 16 Jan,*
£104 ($125)

—31—
A Doulton Boer War commemorative stoneware jug, *c.*1900, 21cm (8¼in), impressed marks, *S 15 May,*
£132 ($176)

—32—
A Royal Doulton loving-cup, by Noke and Fenton, 1937, commemorating the coronation of George VI and Queen Elizabeth, 26.5cm (10½in), *JHB 23 May,*
R 420 (£175; $231)

—33—
A Coalport blue and white plate, *c.*1900, inscribed with the names of the battles and generals in the Boer War up to 1900, with central portrait of Lord Roberts, *JHB 7 Feb,*
R 300 (£140; $164)

—34—
A commemorative plate, 1900, marked W L, inscribed 'War declared in South Africa by President Kruger Oct 11th 1899 . . .' 24cm (9½in) diam, *JHB 7 Feb,*
R 250 (£117; $137)

—28—

—29—   —30—

—31—

—32—

—33—   —34—

1

A Meissen sugar box and cover, 1725-30, painted in iron-red, violet, green, brown and gilt, 14.5cm (5¾in), *L 26 Nov,* £2,750 ($3,850)

2

A pair of Meissen beakers, 1730-35, painted in Imari style with *indianische Blumen*, crossed swords and sign in underglaze blue, 8cm (3⅛in), *L 25 June,* £495 ($668)

3

A Meissen tea caddy, *c.*1740, minor wear and chip, crossed swords in blue, gilder's mark G, 9.5cm (3¾in), *L 5 Mar,* £935 ($1,047)

4

A Meissen sugar box and cover, 1723-4, the cover and sides with chinoiserie scenes, KPM and crossed swords in underglaze blue, 12cm (4¾in), *L 26 Nov,* £9,900 ($13,860)

5

A Meissen tea caddy and cover, *c.*1740, painted with 'Schwarzlot' merchant scenes, gilt scrollwork, crossed swords in blue, 11cm (4¼in), *L 5 Mar,* £3,740 ($4,189)

6

A Meissen beaker, *c.*1740, the upper part with hunting scenes after J E Riedinger, the lower part with purple *camaieu* panels, crossed swords in underglaze blue, 2 in gilt, 13.5cm (5¼in), *L 26 Nov,* £1,980 ($2,772)

7

A Meissen bowl, *c.*1740, after an Arita original, slightly rubbed, crossed swords and 'K' in underglaze blue, 22.5cm (9in), *L 26 Nov,* £1,430 ($2,002)

8

A Meissen kakiemon plate, *c.*1740, painted with the 'Schmetterling' pattern, rubbed, crossed swords in underglaze blue, 22.2cm (8¾in), *L 25 June,* £341 ($460)

9

A set of twelve Meissen plates, *c.*1740, 'Schmetterling', (butterfly) pattern each painted in kakiemon palette, two repaired, five with imperfections, crossed swords in underglaze blue, impressed numerals, 23.5 to 24cm (9¼ to 9½in), *NY 10 Oct,* $3,025 (£2,145)

10

An early Meissen 'Hausmaler' slop bowl, 1725-30, decorated in Augsburg in the Seuter workshop, gilding rubbed, 17cm (6¾in), *L 26 Nov,* £715 ($1,001)

11

A Meissen celadon ground coffee cup and saucer, *c.*1730, decorated in Kakiemon style, crossed swords in underglaze blue, impressed 55, 12.5cm (5in), *L 26 Nov,* £1,430 ($2,002)

12

A Meissen yellow-ground tea cup and saucer, *c.*1750, painted with *deutsche Blumen*, crossed swords in underglaze blue, *L 5 Mar,* £418 ($468)

13

A Meissen ecuelle, cover and a stand, *c.*1750, the stand painted by a different hand, crossed swords in underglaze blue, 17cm (6¾in), *L 5 Mar,* £825 ($924)

14

A Meissen gold-mounted snuff box, *c.*1765, with a coloured view of 'Schloss Pillnitz', 10.5cm (4¼in), *L 5 Mar,* £4,180 ($4,682)

15

A Meissen cylindrical tankard, *c.*1740, minor wear, faint crossed swords in underglaze blue, later silvered metal cover, 16.5cm (6½in), *NY 8 Nov,* $5,775 (£4,067)

16

A Meissen teapot and cover, *c.*1760, repair, crossed swords in underglaze blue, 11cm (4¼in), *NY 8 Nov,* $1,210 (£852)

pair of Meissen saucer
shes, third quarter 18th
ntury, painted with
utsche Blumen, crossed
ords in underglaze
ue, incised numerals,
.5cm (11¼in),
10 July,
40 ($612)

pair of Meissen vases,
750, painted with
utsche Blumen, repair,
ossed swords in
derglaze blue and
e with impressed 22,
cm (8in), NY 8 Nov,
760 (£1,239)

pair of Meissen peony
shes, c.1765, chips
d repair, crossed
ords and dot marks
underglaze blue, 25
d 24.5cm (9¾ and
in), NY 8 Nov,
640 (£1,859)

pair of Meissen ornith-
ogical dishes, late 18th
ntury, crossed swords
underglaze blue,
pressed 67, 38cm
5in), NY 10 Oct,
090 (£1,482)

Meissen part dinner
rvice, Marcolini
eriod, c.1790, compris-
g forty nine pieces,
ch painted with
utsche Blumen, chips
d hair cracks, crossed
ords and star marks,
rious incised and
pressed marks, plates
.5 to 24cm (8¾ to
in), NY 8 Nov,
870 (£1,317)

Meissen ornithological
sh, 1760-70, crossed
ords in underglaze
ue and impressed 54
d 4, 39cm (15½in),
Y 10 Oct,
80 (£624)

Meissen leaf-shaped
sh, Marcolini period,
1800, painted by
schentsch in under-
aze blue, crossed
ords with double hilts
d star, painter's mark
' and three dots in
nderglaze blue, 30.5cm
2in), L 26 June,
275 ($371)

8
A Meissen tray, Marcolini period, last quarter
18th century, 35cm
(13¾in), A 3 June,
Dfl 2,088 (£472; $638)

9
**A Meissen 'Indian
Flowers' assembled part-
dinner service,** the
majority 20th century,
comprising 144 pieces,
the majority with cros-
sed swords in under-
glaze blue, cake stand
40.5cm (16in),
NY 30 Mar,
$3,410 (£2,750)

10
**A Meissen dinner, tea and
dessert service,** late 18th
century, comprising 131
pieces, crossed swords
in underglaze blue,
C 26 Feb,
£1,265 ($1,417)

11
A Meissen deep basin,
late 18th century, cros-
sed swords mark and IX
in underglaze blue,
incised numeral, 44cm
(17¼in), C 10 July,
£902 ($1,254)

12
**A Meissen assembled
part dinner service,** the
majority 20th century,
comprising 156 pieces,
each painted in colour-
ful deutsche Blumen,
some chips and cracks,
crossed swords in
underglaze blue, tureen
stand 50cm (19¾in),
NY 30 Mar,
$2,200 (£1,774)

13
A Meissen coffee service,
19th century, compris-
ing 39 pieces, A 28 Mar,
Dfl 5,336 (£1,236; $1,567)

14
**A Meissen cabinet cup
and saucer,** third quarter
19th century, crossed
swords in underglaze
blue, saucer 12.5cm
(5in); sold with a gilt
ground Berlin trem-
bleuse cup, cover and
saucer, late 19th cen-
tury, damaged, sceptre
in underglaze blue,
saucer 14cm (5½in),
L 7 Nov,
£352 ($528)

1 2 3
4 5
6 7 8
9 10
11 12
13 14

1
A pair of Meissen 'Schneeballen' circular bowls and covers, c.1825, each encrusted with yellow-centred small white blossoms heightened in puce, gilded rims, crossed swords in underglaze blue, impressed 16 and 58, 20cm (8in), *NY 10 Oct,* $1,980 (£1,404)

2
An assembled set of twelve Meissen game plates, late 19th century, chip, crossed swords in underglaze blue, 21cm (8¼in), *NY 22 June,* $770 (£601)

3
A pair of Meissen 'named view' vases and covers, c.1860, painted with a view of Dresden or Pillnitz within gilt borders on a blue ground, some restoration, crossed swords in underglaze blue, Russian retailer's label, 63.5cm (25in), *L 20 June,* £1,760 ($2,376)

4
A Meissen centrebasket, late 19th century, crossed swords in underglaze blue, slight repairs, 32cm (12½in), *C 17 Apr,* £792 ($1,030)

5
A Meissen centrepiece, 1880, some damage, crossed swords in underglaze blue, inscribed 2772, 49.5cm (19½in), *L 20 June,* £990 ($1,337)

6
A Meissen 'armorial' mantel clock and stand, painted with the arms of Augustus the Strong of Saxony, losses and repairs, crossed swords in underglaze blue, incised model no. 452, 70.5cm (27¾in), *NY 22 June,* $1,650 (£1,289)

7
Six Meissen Capodimonte-style cabinet plates, late 19th century, each painted with two cupids, crossed swords in underglaze blue, 30cm (9in), *NY 30 Mar,* $715 (£577)

8
A Meissen clockcase, third quarter 19th century, centre finial of clockcase missing, crossed swords in underglaze blue, incised f 36, 28cm (11in), *L 7 Nov,* £682 ($1,023)

9
A pair of Meissen vases and covers, 19th century, decorated with *indianische Blumen,* chip, hair cracks and repair, AR marks in underglaze blue, 44cm (17¼in), *NY 8 Nov,* $4,125 (£2,905)

10
A Meissen 'Limoges Enamels' vase, c.1880, painted *en grisaille,* crossed swords in underglaze blue, 16.5cm (6½in), *L 20 June,* £495 ($668)

11
A pair of Meissen Capodimonte vases, late 19th century, crossed swords in underglaze blue, impressed 68, 28.5cm (11¼in), *NY 15 Feb,* $467 (£403)

12
A Meissen swan tureen, late 19th century, after a model by J. J. Kaendler, cancelled crossed swords in underglaze blue, incised no. E 98, 37cm (14½in), *NY 30 Mar,* $1,760 (£1,419)

13
A pair of Meissen vases and covers, late 19th century, chips, crossed swords in underglaze blue, 34cm (13½in), *L 7 Nov,* £825 ($1,238)

14
A Meissen wine jug in the form of a bear, mid-19th century, incised no. 1001, crossed swords in underglaze blue, 26.5cm (10½in), *S 10 July,* £638 ($855)

15
A Meissen vase and cover, mid-19th century, losses and repair, crossed swords in underglaze blue, 86.5cm (34in), *NY 30 Nov,* $2,420 (£1,624)

1 2 3 4 5 6 7 8 9 10 11 12 13 14 15

1 German porcelain needle case, 1760-65, probably Meissen, painted in polychrome, 11.5cm (4½in), *L 26 Nov,* £1,012 ($1,417)

2 Berlin chocolate cup, cover and saucer, c.1780, sceptre marks in underglaze blue, *L 5 Mar,* £2,200 ($2,464)

3 A pair of Berlin candlesticks, late 19th century, KPM marks, *A 8 Feb,* Dfl 858 (£210; $246)

4 Berlin 'named view' cabinet cup and saucer, c.1815, set on paw feet, sceptre in underglaze blue, saucer 15cm (6in), *S 20 June,* £385 ($520)

5 Berlin part tête-à-tête, mid-19th century, comprising eleven pieces, painted eagle medallion, and sceptre mark in underglaze blue, KPM and orb in red, *S 25 Mar,* £880 ($1,118)

6 A pair of Berlin vases and covers, c.1880, with panels of 18th century lovers within gilt borders on a blue ground, both knops and one handle repaired, sceptre in underglaze blue, 40.5cm (15¾in), *S 20 June,* £1,045 ($1,411)

7 A pair of Berlin vases, late 19th century, painted and signed by Madler *en grisaille,* as pairs, now mounted as table lamps, cancelled sceptre marks in underglaze blue, 41cm (16¼in), *NY 30 Mar,* £415 ($577)

8 A set of ten Berlin reticulated plates and a covered sucrier, 1790-1800, repairs and chips, sceptre marks in underglaze blue, various impressed or incised numerals, plates 25cm (9¾in), *NY 4 May,* £1,310 (£1,925)

9 A set of six Berlin dessert plates, c.1900, each with garden flowers, minor chips, sceptre in underglaze blue, printed orb and KPM, 22cm (8¼in), *L 7 Nov,* £495 ($743)

10 A Berlin soup tureen and cover, late 19th century, painted with drinking scenes, sceptre mark in underglaze blue, 35.5cm (14in), *C 2 Oct,* £385 ($562)

11 A set of twelve Berlin pierced plates, c.1900, each painted with garden flowers, sceptre in underglaze blue, printed orb and KPM in red, 22cm (8½in), *L 7 Nov,* £660 ($990)

12 A Boettger tea bowl and saucer, c.1730, saucer cracked, gilder's mark 85, *L 5 Mar,* £528 ($591)

13 A Boettger porcelain tea caddy, c.1715, chip, 10cm (4in), *L 26 Nov,* £770 ($1,078)

14 A pair of Dresden vases and covers, late 19th century, each painted with 18th century rustic figures and flowers, chips, KPM in underglaze blue, 52cm (20½in), *L 7 Nov,* £715 ($1,073)

1

A pair of Dresden pot-pourri vases and covers, *c.*1880, 42.5cm (16¾in), *C 12 Feb,* £374 ($655)

2

A pair of Dresden covered vases, *c.*1880 each with the arms of Augustus the Strong and hunting scenes, pseudo AR cipher in underglaze blue, 54.5cm (21½in), *NY 30 Mar,* $990 (£798)

3

A pair of vases and covers, Saxony, 19th century, marked in blue, damaged, 55cm (21½in), *M 25 June,* FF 11,000 (£925; $1,249)

4

A pair of German Schnee-ballen 'covered vases' late 19th century, losses and repairs, pseudo crossed swords and star marks in underglaze blue, 55cm (21¾in), *NY 30 Nov,* $1,980 (£1,329)

5

A Fürstenberg part tea and coffee service, *c.*1800, comprising eight pieces, each decorated with moulded figures, F in underglaze blue, covered wares 13.5 to 12.5cm (5¼ to 5in), *NY 4 May,* $715 (£596)

6

A Höchst solitaire, 1765-74, comprising eight pieces, decorated in gilt and enamels, chips, wheel marks and crown in underglaze blue, with various numerals, 30.5cm (12in), *L 26 Nov,* £5,720 ($8,008)

7

A pair of Höchst tea cups and saucers, 1765-70, one saucer possibly married, wheel marks in underglaze blue, various numerals, sold with a Vienna ogee-shaped tea cup and saucer, shield marks in underglaze blue, impresses 17 or 24, diam 7.5 and 12.5cm (3 and 5in), *NY 10 Oct,* $495 (£351)

8

A Fürstenberg tea cup and saucer, *c.*1765, decorated in purple *camaieu,* F in underglaze blue, *L 5 Mar,* £440 ($493)

9

A Kloster Veilsdorf coffee service, *c.*1770, comprising seventeen pieces, painted in iron-red with travellers in landscapes, 'CV' in underglaze blue, painter's mark T, 17.5cm (7in), *L 26 Nov,* £2,640 ($3,696)

10

A pair of Fürstenberg plates, *c.*1770, painted by C G Albert, chip, script F in underglaze blue, impressed numbers, 24.2cm (9½in), *L 25 June,* £825 ($1,114)

11

A Nymphenburg soup plate, 1760-65, painted with a landscape in green and purple, impressed shield mark and incised 46, 25cm (9⅞in), *L 25 June,* £550 ($743)

12

A pair of Ludwigsburg coffee cups, *c.*1770, crowned interlaced C's in underglaze blue, 6.5cm (2½in), *NY 4 May,* $247 (£206)

13

A Ludwigsburg teapot and cover, *c.*1765, painted in green, brown, blue and iron-red, crowned interlaced C's in underglaze blue, 9cm (3½in), *NY 4 May,* $1,100 (£917)

14

A Wallendorf part tea and coffee service, *c.*1780, W in underglaze slate blue, 27 pieces, *L 25 June,* £1,430 ($1,931)

1 2 3 4

5

6 7

8

9

10

11

12 13 14

Vienna part tête-à-
te, early to late 19th
ntury, comprising
ght pieces, all with
ield marks, various
pressed numerals,
ry 36cm (14in),
Y 4 May,
,100 (£917)

'Vienna'-decorated
rtrait vase, c.1900,
inted by Wagner (?),
gned indistinctly,
eptre mark in under-
aze blue, 26.5cm
0½in), NY 22 June,
,320 (£1,031)

'Vienna' covered vase
'Song', c.1900, the
nels on a green/
llow ground, finial
placed, 42cm (6½in),
Y 30 Mar,
75 (£222)

'Vienna' portrait vase,
910, painted and
gned by H Weigel,
ided brown ground,
eudo shield mark,
5cm (12in), NY 30 Mar,
70 (£621)

'Vienna' porcelain
vered vase on stand,
900, pseudo shield
ark in underglaze
ue, 52cm (20½in),
Y 30 Mar,
430 (£1,153)

'Vienna'-decorated
rl Magnus Hutschen-
ter cabinet plate, late
th century, painted
d signed by Melzer,
pressed shield mark
underglaze blue,
5cm (9½in), L 7 Nov,
05 ($908)

pair of 'Vienna' dishes,
e 19th century, each
inted with the Graces
d Cupid, shield
rks in underglaze
ue, 35.5cm (14¼in),
2 Oct,
68 ($1,413)

pair of 'Vienna' vases
d covers, late 19th
ntury, each painted
d signed by A Otto,
os bleu ground, shield
ark, 54.5cm (21½in),
2 Oct,
420 ($3,533)

9
A 'Vienna' Gilbert &
Sullivan subject plate,
late 19th century,
painted and signed by
Dittrich, with a portrait
of Yum Yum, shield in
underglaze blue, 24.5cm
(9¾in), S 28 June,
£233 ($317)

10
A German oval plaque,
c.1800, painted en
grisaille, 16.5cm (6½in),
L 5 Mar,
£352 ($394)

11
A German porcelain
snuff box, 1770-80, prob-
ably Berlin, gilt metal
mounts, some wear, 7cm
(2¾in), L 5 Mar,
£990 ($1,109)

12
An Ansbach porcelain
soup plate, c.1770,
decorated with the so-
called 'Berliner Muster',
green-ground border,
chip, A in underglaze
blue, 25.5cm (10in),
L 5 Mar,
£1,045 ($1,170)

1
A Mettlach wall plaque,
1897, decorated after
Stahl, inscribed, in
white relief against a
grey-green ground,
impressed mark, pattern
no. 2443, 46.5cm
(18¼in), *L 7 Nov,*
£286 ($429)

2
A Berlin plaque of Diana
at her bath, third
quarter 19th century,
painted after Boucher,
impressed sceptre and
KPM, 19 x 25.5cm
(7½ x 10in), *NY 30 Nov,*
$2,310 (£1,550)

3
A Meissen plaque, mid-
19th century, painted in
the style of Franz Xavier
Petter, crossed swords
in underglaze blue,
incised 'Brobe' (trial
piece), 37.5 x 28cm (14¾
x 11in), *L 7 Nov,*
£6,600 ($9,900)

4
A Berlin plaque, late 19th
century, painted and
signed by R Dittrich,
after Landelle, depict-
ing Ruth in a field of
corn, impressed sceptre
and KPM, 46.5 x 28cm
(18¼ x 11in), *L 20 June,*
£2,420 ($3,267)

5
A Berlin plaque, late 19th
century, painted with
'Ruth in the Cornfield',
after Landelle, unsigned,
impressed sceptre and
KPM, 24 x 16.5cm (9½
x 6½in), *L 7 Nov,*
£638 ($957)

6
A Dresden plaque, late
19th century, impressed
numerals, 32 x 22cm
(12½ x 8½in), *L 7 Nov,*
£2,090 ($3,135)

7
A Berlin plaque, third
quarter 19th century,
painted by Brodel with
an Eastern maiden,
signed, impressed
sceptre and KPM, 36.5
x 25.5cm (14¼in x 10in),
L 7 Nov,
£2,310 ($3,456)

8
A Berlin plaque of 'The
Finding of Moses', late
19th century, painted
after Paul Delaroche
by Fr Till, signed,
impressed sceptre and
KPM, 24 x 16cm (9½ x
6½in), *NY 30 Mar,*
$1,980 (£1,597)

9
A Berlin plaque, mid-19th
century, painted after
Muller, impressed
sceptre and KPM, 25.5
x 19cm (10 x 7½in),
L 7 Nov,
£2,200 ($3,300)

10
A Berlin plaque, late
19th century, painted
by Schunzel, after
C Kiessel, impressed
sceptre and KPM, 18.5
x 11.5cm (7¼ x 4½in),
L 20 June,
£1,045 ($1,411)

11
A Berlin plaque, late
19th century, of 'La
Belle Chocolatiere',
painted by E Ems after
Liotard, signed,
impressed sceptre and
KPM, 25 x 19cm (9¾ x
7½in), *L 7 Nov,*
£715 ($1,073)

1

2

3

4

5

6

7

8

9

10

11

Copenhagen covered
[v]ase, mid-19th century,
[p]ainted with two views
[o]f the Amalienborg
[P]alace, triple wave
[m]arks in underglaze
[bl]ue, 82cm (32¼in),
[N]Y 30 Nov,
[3],410 (£2,289)

[a]n Oude Loosdrecht cup
[an]d saucer, 18th century,
[M]OL mark in under-
[gl]aze blue, A 3 June,
[f]l 1,508 (£341; $461)

[A] Weesp tureen and cover,
[1]8th century, 28.5cm
[1]1¼in), A 25 Feb,
[f]l 9,512 (£2,331; $2,611)

[a]n Oude Loosdrecht blue
[an]d white part dinner
[se]rvice, c.1775, com-
[p]rising 41 pieces, MOL
[m]arks in underglaze
[bl]ue, square dish
[2]5.5cm (10in), NY 4 May,
[$]2,310 (£1,925)

[a]n Oude Loosdrecht oval
[so]up tureen, cover and
[st]and, c.1775, damage,
[al]l with incised MOL,
[3]2 and 39.5cm (12½ and
[1]5½in), NY 8 Nov,
[$]605 (£426)

[A] Capodimonte cup
[an]d saucer, c.1750,
[so]me chips and wear,
[bl]ue fleur-de-lys marks,
[A] 5 Mar,
[$]7,260 ($8,131)

[A] pair of Zurich saucers,
[c.]1770, 'Z' and dots
[in] underglaze blue,
[so]ld with two Nyon
[sa]ucers, c.1780, fish
[m]ark in underglaze
[bl]ue, 13.5cm (5¼in),
[A] 26 Nov,
[$]85 ($539)

[A] Du Paquier Vienna
[be]aker, c.1730, painted
[in] iron-red, purple,
[li]ght-blue, green, yellow
[an]d gilding, 8cm (3in),
[A] 25 June,
[$]770 ($1,040)

[A] Vienna cabbage leaf
[ju]g and cover, mid-18th
[ce]ntury, 13cm (5in),
[A] 16 July,
[$]08 ($447)

10
A Vienna chocolate cup,
cover and saucer, c.1798,
shield mark in under-
glaze blue, L 5 Mar,
£935 ($1,047)

11
A pair of Naples vases,
signed by Raffaele
Giovine, dated 1823,
with portraits of Francis
I of Bourbon and his
consort, gilding rubbed,
34.5cm (13½in), F 28 May,
L 11,500,000
(£4,466; $5,895)

12
A pair of Vienna ice-pails
and covers, 1804, decor-
ated in Etruscan style,
chip, shield mark in
underglaze blue, 39cm
(15¼in), L 26 Nov,
£3,740 ($5,236)

**Sèvres gilders, enamel-
lers and painters**

François Joseph
Alconcle, 1758-81,
painter
Baudouin (the elder),
1750-1800, gilder
François Boucher,
1703-70, painter
Etienne-François
Bouillat, late 18th cen-
tury, painter
Boulanger (the elder),
1754-84, gilder
Antoine Gabriel Boul-
lemier, 1802-42, gilder
Charles Buteux,
1756-82, painter
Carrié, 1752-7, painter
Antoine-Toussaint
Cornailles, 1755-1800,
painter
Etienne Evans, 1752-
1806, painter
Denis Leve, 1754-1805,
painter
Pierre-Antoine
Mereaud, 1754-91,
painter
Charles Morin, gilder
Nicquet, 1764-92,
painter
Guillaume Noel,
1755-1804, painter
Pajou, 1751-9, painter
Pierre-Joseph Rosset,
1753-95, painter
Vincent Taillandier,
1750-75, painter and
enameller
Charles Tandart,
1756-60, painter
Jean-Baptiste Tandart
(mid-18th century)
Claude Antoine Tardy,
1755-95, painter
Thevenet (the elder),
1741-77, painter

1

A Vincennes cup and saucer, *c.*1753, (*'goblet calabre'*), interlaced L's and central dot in blue enamel, cup incised 'f', chip restored, 7.5cm (3in), *L 26 Nov,* £2,640 ($3,696)

2

A Vincennes sucrier and cover, *c.*1750, interlaced L's in underglaze blue, small chip, 11cm (4¼in), *L 5 Mar,* £9,900 ($11,088)

3

A pair of Sèvres green-ground plates, 1758, decorated by Guillaume Noël, interlaced L's, incised CT, 26cm (10¼in), *L 5 Mar,* £825 ($924)

4

A Sèvres coffee cup and saucer, 1763, decorated by Thévenet père, interlaced L's, date letter and painter's mark, cup 7cm (3in), *NY 4 May,* $1,540 (£1,283)

5

A Sèvres apple-green teapot and cover, 1770-75, with later painting by Pajou, interlaced L's, painter's mark and gilder's mark for Boulanger père, knop repaired, 12.5cm (5in), *NY 4 May,* $495 (£413)

6

A Sèvres blue lapis ground cup and saucer, 1759, interlaced L's in underglaze blue, date letter G and painter's mark, minor chip, *L 5 Mar,* £990 ($1,109)

7

An assembled set of twelve Sèvres plates, dated 1763-76, interlaced L's, date letters and unidentified painters marks, rim chip, 23.5 and 24cm (9¼ and 9½in), *NY 4 May,* $1,540 (£1,283)

8

An assembled pair of Sèvres wine coolers, dated 1759 and 1763, painted by Méreaud and Denis Levé, interlaced L's, date letters and painters marks, 10.5cm (4¼in), *NY 4 May,* $2,200 (£1,833)

9

An assembled pair of Sèvres verrieres, *c.*1773, interlaced L's, painted by Nicquet, gilder's mark for Baudouin père, hair crack and chips, 29.5 and 30cm (11½ and 11¾in), *NY 10 Oct,* $1,980 (£1,404)

10

A Sèvres pomade box and cover, 18th century, interlaced L's, 9.5cm (3¾in), *F 28 May,* L 550,000 (£214; $282)

11

A Sèvres wine cooler, from the Madame du Barry service, 1771, interlaced L's, date letter and incised 3 cf (?) marks, 17cm (6¾in), *NY 8 Nov,* $6,600 (£4,648)

12

A pair of Sèvres jugs, one painted by Tardy, gilded details, interlaced L's, slight wear, 12cm (4¾in), *L 5 Mar,* £550 ($616)

13

Two Sèvres cups and saucers, last quarter 18th century, various marks, *L 5 Mar,* £605 ($678)

14

A Sèvres cup and saucer, 1775, (*gobelet litron*), enamelled by Nicquet, interlaced L's, date letter, gilder's mark for Baudouin père, slight wear, *L 5 Mar,* £1,650 ($1,848)

15

A pair of Sèvres 'Premiere Republique' cups and saucers, 1794, (*gobelet litron*), in *pâte tendre,* incised 40 and 46, painters marks, slight scratching, *L 5 Mar,* £517 ($579)

16

A Sèvres coffee can and saucer, 1789, probably painted by Huny, decorated in gilding, purple and blue, interlaced L's, date letters, painter's mark and incised 46 and 29, *L 5 Mar,* £748 ($838)

See p.247 for details of Sèvres gilders, enamellers and painters

A pair of St Cloud toilet
pots and covers, *c.*1740,
mounted in silver, 11
and 11.5cm (4¼ and
4½in), *NY 21 May,*
$2,530 (£2,024)

A pair of St Cloud cups
and trembleuse saucers,
second quarter 18th
century, sold with a
matching cup and
saucer, one handle
repaired, *C 10 July,*
£385 ($535)

A Mennecy bourdaloue,
18th century, marked
DVA, 23cm (9in),
M 25 June,
FF 8,325 (£694; $937)

A pair of French por-
celain coffee cans and
saucers, early 19th cen-
tury, one handle re-
stuck, incised B on
cups, *L 5 Mar,*
£660 ($739)

A Chantilly dish, 1735-45,
decorated after a kak-
emon original, 21.4cm
(8½in), sold with a sim-
ilar tea bowl and saucer,
NY 8 Nov,
$605 (£426)

A Chantilly cuspidor,
*c.*1735, painted after a
Kakiemon original,
13.4cm (5¼in),
NY 8 Nov,
$660 (£465)

A pair of Paris vases,
Restoration period,
32cm (12½in), *M 25 June,*
FF 22,200 (£1,850;
$2,498)

A Chantilly-style gold-
mounted snuffbox and
cover, modern gold
mounts, 8cm (3¼in),
NY 21 May,
$247 (£198)

A St Cloud-style cat-form
bonbonnière and cover,
probably Samson, late
19th century, silver
mount, *NY 21 May,*
$220 (£176)

10
A French biscuit vase,
19th century, with gilt
metal mounts, 50.5cm
(19¾in), *A 3 June,*
Dfl 14,060 (£919; $1,240)

11
A Vieux Paris yellow-
ground vase-form clock,
1820-30, chips, 33cm
(13in), *NY 4 May,*
$935 (£779)

12
A Paris part tea-service,
*c.*1800, comprising
18 pieces, chips and
cracks, *L 5 Mar,*
£528 ($591)

13
A Vieux Paris mytholog-
ical square tray, Duc
d'Angouleme Factory,
*c.*1800, iron-red
factory mark, 34cm
(13½in) wide, *NY 8 Nov,*
$440 (£310)

14
A Vieux Paris part tea
and coffee service, *c.*1820,
comprising 21 pieces,
some wear, pots 26 and
21cm (10¼ and 8¼in),
NY 8 Nov,
$605 (£426)

15
A Tressemannes & Vogt
Limoges plate, 1892-99,
made for President
Benjamin Harrison at
the White House, prin-
ted marks, 24cm (9½in),
NY 1 Feb,
$935 (£792)

16
A pair of Vieux Paris
lavender-ground vases,
mounted as lamps,
1815-25, one handle
repaired, 37.5cm
(14¾in), *NY 4 May,*
$3,025 (£2,521)

17
A Paris dessert service,
mid to late 19th century,
comprising 43 pieces,
with the arms of the
Royal House of Savoy,
one cover cracked,
plate 23cm (9in) diam,
L 21 Mar,
£1,980 ($2,396)

18
A Paris part coffee ser-
vice, Nast factory, *c.*1810,
comprising ten pieces,
painted factory mark,
some damage, coffee pot
22.5cm (8¾in), *L 26 Nov,*
£275 ($385)

1
A Samson ewer and
basin, c.1900, in late 18th
century Compagnie des
Indes style, painted seal
mark, ewer restored,
ewer 31cm (12in) high,
L 20 June,
£385 ($520)

2
A Jacob Petit clockcase,
c.1840, surmounted by a
portrait of a French
courtesan, signed, chips,
40cm (15¾in), *L 7 Nov,*
£638 ($957)

3
A Samson vase and cover,
in Chinese style, late
19th century, some
repair, 104cm (41in),
C 16 Jan,
£1,265 ($1,518)

4
A Paris clockcase, c.1830,
surmounted by a group
of lovers in richly decorated clothes, one hand
missing, chips, 51cm
(20in) *L 20 June,*
£385 ($520)

5
A Jacob petit clockcase,
c.1840 in the form of a
brightly coloured and
gilt cathedral, small
cracks, painted marks,
20.2cm (19¾in),
NY 15 Feb,
$1,210 (£1,043)

6
A Paris pâte-sur-pâte gilt-
metal-mounted oil lamp,
c.1880, decorated with
Bacchic children on a
celadon ground, 33.5cm
(13¼in), *L 7 Nov,*
£242 ($363)

7
A pair of Paris vases, mid
19th century, minor
chips, 34cm (13¼in),
L 21 Mar,
£990 ($1,198)

8
A pair of Paris vases and
covers, c.1870, with
panels on a *rose Pom-
padour* ground, replace-
ment knops, some
restoration, 43cm (14in),
L 20 June,
£572 ($772)

9
A pair of Paris vases,
c.1860, each with a scene
of 18th century lovers
on an *eau-de-nil* ground,
gilding rubbed, 58.5cm
(23in), *L 21 Mar,*
£495 ($599)

10
A pair of French biscuit
porcelain candlesticks,
late 19th century, chips,
30cm (11¾in), *S 14 Nov,*
£165 ($231)

11
A pair of French gilt-
bronze-mounted pearlware
vases, late 19th century,
each painted by F
Gardon, signed, illegible
mark, 47.5cm (18¾in),
NY 30 Mar,
$935 (£754)

12
A pair of French ice pails,
covers and liners, late
19th century, gilding
rubbed, 29cm (11½in),
L 21 Mar,
£1,210 ($1,464)

13
A pair of Paris jardinieres
and stands, mid 19th
century, each with por-
traits on a green ground,
small chips and cracks,
gilding rubbed, 33cm
(13in), *L 20 June,*
£1,210 ($1,634)

14
A French ewer with basin,
c.1850, with polychrome
decoration on a blue
ground, ewer 29.5cm
(11½in), *M 25 June,*
FF 11,655 (£971; $1,311)

1

2

3

4

5

6

7

8

9

10

11

12

13

14

1
A 'Sèvres' gilt-bronze-mounted and 'jewelled' jardiniere, mid 19th century, the porcelain indistinctly inscribed, 32.5cm (12¾in), L 20 June, £1,320 ($1,782)

2
A 'Sèvres' gilt-bronze-mounted vase, mid 19th century, the body painted with a continuous frieze, 37cm (14½in), L 21 Mar, £2,860 ($3,461)

3
A 'Sèvres' gilt-bronze-mounted vase, mid 19th century, with a frieze of cherubs on a *gros bleu* ground, 34cm (13in), L 7 Nov, £1,430 ($2,145)

4
A 'Sèvres' gilt-bronze-mounted vase, late 19th century, covered in *bleu-du-roi* glaze, 82cm (32¼in), NY 22 June, $4,125 (£3,222)

5
A pair of 'Sèvres' Napoleonic coverd vases, late 19th century, each painted by H Desprez with a battleground scene, signed, *bleu-du-roi* borders, M Imp le de Sèvres marks, 56cm (22in), NY 30 Mar, $3,300 (£2,661)

6
A 'Sèvres' gilt-bronze-mounted covered vase, c.1910, painted by Turpn with scenes reserved on pale blue ground, signed, printed Louis-Philippe marks, 54.5cm (21½in), NY 30 Mar, $550 (£444)

7
A pair of gilt-metal-mounted 'Sèvres' vases, late 19th century, interlaced L's, slight wear, 57cm (22½in), L 20 June, £770 ($1,040)

8
A pair of gilt-metal-mounted 'Sèvres' vases, c.1890, interlaced Ls, slight wear, 49cm (19¼in), L 20 June, £550 ($743)

9
A pair of 'Sèvres' gilt-bronze-mounted vases and covers, late 19th century, painted by Berre, signed, painted interlaced Ls, one cover cracked, 73cm (28¾in), L 21 Mar, £5,720 ($6,921)

10
A 'Sèvres' gilt-bronze-mounted vase and cover, late 19th century, painted by A Maglin signed, interlaced Ls, 107cm (42in), L 21 Mar, £6,380 ($7,720)

11
A 'Sèvres' gilt-bronze-mounted covered vase, late 19th century, painted by Collot on a *bleu-du-roi* ground, signed, flaking, interlaced L's, 76.5cm (30in), NY 22 June, $660 (£515)

12
A pair of gilt-bronze-mounted and 'jewelled' 'Sèvres' vases and covers, third quarter 19th century, each body painted in the style of Morin on a 'gros-bleu' ground, slight wear, 68cm (26¾in), L 20 June, £2,420 ($3,267)

13
A 'Sèvres' gilt-bronze-mounted vase, 19th century, painted by Quentin, 61.6cm (24¼in), NY 30 Mar, $1,430 (£1,153)

14
A 'Sèvres' gilt-bronze-mounted vase and cover, painted with lovers on a *bleu-du-roi* ground, 69.2cm (27¼in), NY 30 Mar, $550 (£444)

15
A pair of 'Sèvres' gilt-bronze-mounted vases and covers, painted by Poitevin, signed, painted and printed marks, 165cm (65in), NY 30 Mar, $12,100 (£9,758)

1
A Meissen figure of a miner as a 'Bergmusikant' c.1750, modelled by Johann Joachim Kaendler and Peter Reinicke, playing a triangle (mostly missing), crossed swords in underglaze blue, 20cm (8in), *NY 4 May,* $2,970 (£2,475)

2
A Meissen figure of a miner as a 'Bergmusikant' c.1750, modelled by Johann Joachim Kaendler and Peter Reinicke, chips, crossed swords in underglaze blue, 20cm (8in), *NY 4 May,* $3,080 (£2,567)

3
A Meissen figure of Harlequin playing the bagpipes, c.1750, modelled by J J Kaendler, chips, crossed swords in underglaze blue, 14cm (5½in), *NY 8 Nov,* $990 (£697)

4
A Meissen figure of a lutenist, mid-18th century, modelled by J J Kaendler or P Reinicke, some restoration, 12.5cm (5in), *L 25 June,* £440 ($594)

5
A pair of Meissen figures of musicians, mid-19th century, crossed swords in underglaze blue, incised 1337 and 1352, chips, 33cm (13in) and 32cm (12½in), *L 20 June,* £770 ($1,040)

6
A Meissen crinoline group of lovers on a settee, late 19th century, minor losses, crossed swords in underglaze blue, incised number W56, 15cm (6in), *NY 30 Mar,* $1,430 (£1,153)

7
A Meissen figure of a masquerader, c.1745-50, crossed swords in underglaze blue, incised 10, ribbon damaged, *L 25 June,* £1,760 ($2,376)

8
A Meissen figure of a fishwife, c.1745, modelled by J J Kaendler, crossed swords in underglaze blue, restorations, 19.5cm (7¾in), *L 25 June,* £550 ($743)

9
A Meissen figure of a pastry-seller, c.1755, from the Cris de Paris series, by P. Reinicke and J J Kaendler, underglaze blue crossed swords, restored, minor chips, 13.5cm (5¼in), *L 25 June,* £660 ($891)

10
A Meissen Commedia dell 'Arte figure of Coviello, c.1775, modelled by J J Kaendler, crossed swords and star in underglaze blue, incised D 43, some damage and restoration, 17cm (6¾in), *L 25 June,* £1,320 ($1,782)

11
A Meissen figure of a fish seller, c.1759, from the 'Cris de Paris' series, modelled by J J Kaendler and Reinicke, crossed swords in underglaze blue, repaired, 14.6cm (5¾in) high, *C 17 Apr,* £495 ($642)

12
A Meissen figure of a cook, c.1740-45, probably modelled by J J Kaendler, some damage, traces of a blue mark, 15cm (6in), *L 26 Nov,* £418 ($585)

1   2   3   4

5   6

7   8   9

10   11   12

1

A Meissen figure of a
blacksmith, mid-18th
century, crossed swords
in underglaze blue,
12cm (4¾in), *L 5 Mar,*
£330 ($370)

2

A Meissen figure of a
potter, *c.*1750, by J J
Kaendler, from the
series of craftsmen,
probably decorated in
Thuringia in the 18th
century, hair cracks,
crossed swords in
underglaze blue, 19cm
(7½in), *L 5 Mar,*
£1,100 ($1,232)

3

A Meissen figure of a
trinket-seller, *c.*1765, by
J J Kaendler and
P Reinicke, restoration,
crossed swords and dot
in underglaze blue, 'v'
in gilding, 16.5cm
(6½in), *L 5 Mar,*
£660 ($739)

4

A Meissen figure of a
bird-catcher, *c.*1755,
repairs, crossed swords
in underglaze blue,
14.5cm (5¾in), *NY 8 Nov,*
$550 (£387)

5

A Meissen figure of a
shepherdess, mid-18th
century, chips, crossed
swords in underglaze
blue, 15.5cm (6in),
L 5 Mar,
£660 ($739)

6

A Meissen group of a
shepherd and shepherdess,
late 19th century, minor
chips, crossed swords
in underglaze blue,
incised number A.41,
18cm (7in), *NY 30 Mar,*
$715 (£577)

7

A Meissen figure of 'La
Belle Chocolatière', mid-
19th century, inspired
by the painting by
Liotard, crossed swords
in underglaze blue,
incised V86, minor
chips, 37cm (14½in),
L 21 Mar,
£462 ($559)

8

A Meissen group of a
**beggar-woman and
children**, *c.*1745, by J J
Kaendler, restorations,
traces of crossed swords
in blue, 22.5cm (8¾in),
L 26 Nov,
£880 ($1,232)

9

A Meissen sweetmeat
figure of a Turk, mid-
18th century, modelled
by J F Eberlein, small
chips, crossed swords in
underglaze blue, 17.5cm
(7in), *L 26 Nov,*
£638 ($893)

10

A Meissen figure of a
girl with a bird, *c.*1745,
probably modelled by
J J Kaendler, bird's left
wing restored, crossed
swords in underglaze
blue, 12.5cm (5in),
NY 21 May,
$715 (£572)

11

A Meissen figure of an
**Indian chieftain with a
covered sweetmeat
basket**, *c.*1750 and
probably later decor-
ated, modelled by J J
Kaendler and J F Eber-
lein, crossed swords in
underglaze blue,
impressed numeral 50
twice, 19.5cm (7¾in),
NY 8 Nov,
$880 (£619)

12

A Meissen figure of a
blackamoor, *c.*1745, with
puce, iron-red and
yellow feathered head-
dress, some damage and
restoration, 15.5cm
(6in), *NY 8 Nov,*
$550 (£387)

13

A Meissen figure of a
nodding Chinese boy,
*c.*1750, probably
modelled by J J
Kaendler, restored, cros-
sed swords in underglaze
blue, 21.5cm (8½in),
L 26 Nov,
£792 ($1,109)

1   2   3   4

5   6   7

8   9   10

11   12   13

1
Two Meissen figures,
mid-19th century, chips,
crossed swords in
underglaze blue, incised
D66 and H58, 19.5 and
20cm (7¾ and 8in),
L 7 Nov,
£638 ($957)

2
**A Meissen figure of a lady
with two pugs,** c.1880,
after a model by J J
Kaendler, chips, crossed
swords in underglaze
blue, 28cm (11in),
L 7 Nov,
£825 ($1,238)

3
**A pair of Meissen figures
of 'Love' and 'Matrimony',**
crossed swords in under-
glaze blue, incised 'F73',
damaged, 18.8cm
(7¼in), *S 25 Mar,*
£825 ($1,048)

4
A pair of Meissen figures,
mid-19th century,
crossed swords in under-
glaze blue, incised 2868
and B65, some restor-
ation, 49cm (19¼in) and
50cm (19½in), *L 21 Mar,*
£1,320 ($1,597)

5
**A pair of Meissen figures
of a lady and gallant,**
crossed swords mark in
underglaze and over-
glaze blue, deleted,
incised numerals,
repaired, 47cm (18½in),
C 17 Apr,
£2,860 ($3,718)

6
**A Meissen figure of a
woman asleep,** late 19th
century, crossed swords
in underglaze blue,
chipped, 18.4cm (7¼in),
S 10 July,
£418 ($560)

7
**A Meissen group of Count
von Brühl's tailor,** late
19th century, minor
chipping, 42.5cm
(16¾in), *S 25 Mar,*
£1,650 ($2,096)

8
**A Meissen group repre-
senting War,** second half
19th century, modelled
as Vulcan, crossed
swords in blue, incised
'D80', impressed '51',
damaged, 25.5cm (10in),
S 10 July,
£506 ($678)

9
A pair of Meissen figures
of cherubs, late 19th
century, 19cm (7½in),
C 10 Dec,
£374 ($524)

10
**A pair of Meissen figures
of cherubs,** c.1880, minor
chips, crossed swords in
underglaze blue, incised
K116 and K117, 14cm
(5½in), *L 7 Nov,*
£352 ($528)

11
A Meissen group of Juno,
late 19th century,
small chips, crossed
swords in underglaze
blue, incised number
0.199, 22cm (8¾in),
NY 30 Mar,
$935 (£754)

1

2

3

4

5

6

7

8

9

10

11

1
A Meissen musical group, late 19th century, crossed swords in underglaze blue, incised R60, 25cm (9¾in), *L 21 Mar,*
£528 ($639)

2
A Meissen rustic celebration group, *c.*1880, crossed swords in underglaze blue, incised D96, 50cm (19¾in), *L 20 June,*
£1,210 ($1,634)

3
A pair of Meissen figures of muses, mid-19th century, crossed swords in underglaze blue, incised L65 and L66, 26.5cm (10½in), *L 21 Mar,*
£440 ($532)

4
A Meissen allegorical group of 'Asia', early 19th century, from a set of the 'Four Continents', crossed swords, star and II mark in underglaze blue, incised number 687, 32.5cm (12¾in), *NY 4 May,*
$1,100 (£917)

5
A Meissen figure of a monkey drum-carrier, 1753-65, repairs, 13.5cm (5¼in), *L 5 Mar,*
£1,100 ($1,232)

6
A Meissen figure of a monkey playing the French horn, crossed swords in underglaze blue, impressed number 12, 14.5cm (5¾in), *L 5 Mar,*
£528 ($591)

7
A Meissen figure of a monkey musician, 1753-65, damage, restoration, impressed numeral 1, 14cm (5½in), *L 5 Mar,*
£528 ($591)

8
A Meissen figure of a monkey bagpiper, 1753-65, crossed swords in underglaze blue, impressed numeral 1, 14cm (5½in), *L 5 Mar,*
£1,100 ($1,232)

9
A Meissen figure of a monkey playing the viola da gamba, 1753-65, crossed swords in underglaze blue, 12cm (4¾in), *L 5 Mar,*
£1,760 ($1,971)

10
A Meissen figure of a monkey playing the viola de gamba, crossed swords in underglaze blue, impressed number 19, 12.5cm (5in), *L 5 Mar,*
£528 ($591)

11
A Meissen figure of a pug, mid-18th century, crossed swords in underglaze blue, 11.5cm (4½in), *S 25 Mar,*
£605 ($768)

12
A Meissen figure of a husky dog, late 19th century, crossed swords in underglaze blue, incised model number K. 41/60, 23cm (9in), *NY 30 Mar,*
$550 (£444)

13
A Meissen figure of a Bolognese terrier, *c.*1748, modelled by Johann Joachim Kaendler, crossed swords in underglaze blue, 18.5cm (7¼in), *NY 8 Nov,*
$7,700 (£5,422)

14
A Meissen figure of a leopard, mid-18th century, crossed swords in underglaze blue, 13.5cm (5¼in), *L 26 Nov,*
£880 ($1,232)

15
A Meissen figure of a hoopoe, late 19th century, swords and dot mark in blue, 32.3cm (12¾in), *C 17 Apr,*
£572 ($744)

16
A pair of Meissen figures of canaries, mid-18th century, crossed swords in blue, chipped, 10.5cm (4¼in), *L 25 June,*
£880 ($1,188)

17
A pair of Meissen figures of swans, *c.*1774, crossed swords and dot marks in underglaze blue, 10.5 and 10cm (4¼ and 4in), *NY 8 Nov,*
$770 (£542)

18
A pair of Meissen game birds, late 19th century, crossed swords in underglaze blue, incised 2475, 20cm (8in) and 21.5cm (8½in), *L 21 Mar,*
£605 ($732)

1 2 3
4 5 6 7 8
9 10 11 12
13 14 15
16 17 18

1
A Berlin figure of a blackamoor with a covered sweetmeat basket, c.1770, adapted probably by Friedrich Elias Meyer from the Meissen original, repairs and chip, sceptre mark in underglaze blue, 19cm (7½in), *NY 8 Nov*, $1,870 (£1,317)

2
A Frankenthal figure of a harvester, c.1762-70, modelled by J W Lanz, damage, crown and CT, incised M mark, 13.4cm (5¼in), *L 26 Nov*, £902 ($1,263)

3
A Frankenthal figure of a girl holding a doll in swaddling clothes, c.1756, marked in blue with rampant lion, 'PH' monogram for Paul Hannong, slight chips, 10.5cm (4in), *C 16 Jan*, £1,012 ($1,214)

4
A Frankenthal figure of a boy flautist, c.1770, crowned CT monogram above AB monogram in underglaze blue, incised numerals, repaired, 14.3cm (5½in), *C 17 Apr*, £374 ($486)

5
A Fürstenberg figure of a woman, c.1774, modelled by J Ch Rombrich, restoration to right arm, F in blue, 15cm (6in), *L 26 Nov*, £715 ($1,001)

6
A Höchst group of lovers in autumn, c.1765, the rococo arbour entwined with grapes, some restoration, wheel mark in underglaze blue, incised triangle, Y, UC, 28cm (11in), *L 26 Nov*, £6,600 ($9,240)

7
An early Höchst figure of 'The Bowing Chinaman', 1750-53, modelled by the 'Master of the Turkish Emperors', slight repair, impressed letters I and IH, painter's monogram AL for Adam Ludwig, 9cm (3½in), *NY 21 May*, $1,320 (£1,056)

8
A Ludwigsburg figure of a sportsman, c.1770, repaired, 10.7cm (4¼in), *C 17 Apr*, £330 ($429)

9
A Höchst figure of a woman, c.1770, probably modelled by J P Melchior, wheel mark in underglaze blue, chipped, 16.5cm (6½in) high, *C 17 Apr*, £902 ($1,173)

10
A pair of Ludwigsburg figures of a shepherd and shepherdess, 1768-78, by Pierre Francois Lejeune, restorations, interlaced C's in underglaze blue, 12.5cm (5in), *L 26 Nov*, £2,200 ($3,080)

11
A Ludwigsburg figure of a peasant, 1768-78, by Pierre Francois Lejeune and probably painted by D Chr Sausenhofer, restored interlaced C's beneath crown in underglaze blue, 13cm (5in), *L 26 Nov*, £990 ($1,386)

12
A Ludwigsburg figure of a birdseller, 1768-78, by Pierre Francois Lejeune, repair, interlaced C's beneath crown in underglaze blue, 12.5cm (5in), *L 26 Nov*, £1,100 ($1,540)

13
A Wallendorf figure of a man reading from a scroll, 1790s, 15.3cm (6in), *C 10 July*, £330 ($459)

14
A Ludwigsburg figure of a woman playing a hurdy-gurdy, c.1765, slight damage, 12.1cm (4¾in), *C 10 July*, £253 ($352)

15
A Vienna figure of a blackamoor, 1744-49, with colourful feather skirt and yellow boots, chip and slight damage, incised shield mark, 14.5cm (5¾in), *NY 8 Nov*, $1,760 (£1,239)

1   2   3   4

5   6   7   8

9   10   11   12

13   14   15

1
A pair of Royal Dux figures of a goatherd and a shepherdess, c.1910, minor chips, impressed and applied pink triangle mark, and shape numbers, 63.5 and 62.5cm (25 and 24in), *L 21 Mar*, £792 ($958)

2
A pair of Royal Dux figures of fish sellers, 44.4cm (17½in), *C 4 June*, £275 ($371)

3
A Limbach allegorical figure of 'Autumn', 1775-80, holding grapes in both hands, triple slash mark, incised 17cm (6¾in), *NY 8 Nov*, $1,210 (£852)

4
A Mennecy figure of a seated lady, 1755-60, chip and hair crack, 23cm (9in), *NY 8 Nov*, $3,300 (£2,324)

5
A Cozzi figure of a Chinese boy with a pheasant, c.1770, in gilt-edged puce robe, firing crack, 11.5cm (4½in), *NY 21 May*, $715 (£572)

6
A pair of Copenhagen allegorical figures of 'Winter' and 'Spring', mid 19th century, triple wave marks in underglaze blue, 18.5 and 19cm (7¼ and 7½in), *NY 21 May*, $467 (£374)

7 & 8
A pair of Copenhagen figures of vegetable sellers, c.1783, repairs, triple wave marks in underglaze blue, 17.5 and 17cm (7 and 6¾in), *NY 21 May*, $770 (£616)

9
A Copenhagen figure of a poultry seller, late 18th century, carrying a basket of eggs (handle broken) and a chicken, triple wave mark in underglaze blue, 16cm (6¼in), *NY 21 May*, $330 (£264)

10
A Copenhagen group of harlequin and child, c.1790, wearing a black mask and pale puce and yellow costume, repair and chips, 19cm (7½in), *NY 21 May*, $770 (£616)

11
A pair of Gilles Jeune coloured biscuit figures, third quarter 19th century, cracks, applied blue tablet mark, and numerals, 61 and 59.5cm (24 and 23½in), *L 7 Nov*, £1,540 ($2,310)

12
A pair of French bisque figures of a lady and gallant, 43cm (17in), *C 12 Feb*, £396 ($693)

13
A Mennecy white porcelain group, mid 18th century, depicting two musicians, 17cm (6¾in) high, *M 25 June*, FF 5,550 (£463; $624)

14
A pair of French biscuit figures, depicting a man with a watering can and his companion with a basket of flowers, 60cm (23½in), *C 14 May*, £418 ($556)

15
A Dresden group of 'Valet de chiens au cor', late 19th century, modelled after Oudry, crossed swords in blue, chips and crack, 38cm (15in), *L 20 June*, £550 ($743)

16
A set of four Samson figures of 'The Elements', c.1900, chips, impressed numerals, 18.5 to 21.5cm (7¼ to 8½in), *L 7 Nov*, £220 ($330)

1

2

3

4

5

6

7

8

9

10

11

12

13

14

15

16

1
A Bow figure of a pedlar, 1755-6, in the white, hair crack, some restoration, 17cm (6¾in), *L 26 Feb*, £880 ($986)

2
A Bow figure of a Thames waterman, 1753-5, cap chipped, left hand restored, 20cm (8in), *S 10 July*, £3,960 ($5,306)

3
An early Bow figure of Kitty Clive, *c.*1750, the actress in her part in Garrick's farce 'Lethe', some wear, hair crack, 31cm (12¼in), *L 22 Oct*, £2,750 ($4,125)

4
A Bow figure of Cybele or Ceres, *c.*1762-5, some damage, 23cm (9in), *L 26 Feb*, £462 ($517)

5
A Bow lion, *c.*1750, ear chip, 10cm (4in), *L 22 Oct*, £2,750 ($4,125)

6
A Bow figure of a flautist, *c.*1755, in the white, flute missing, chips and repair to one foot, 9.5cm (3¾in), *L 21 May*, £396 ($531)

7
A pair of Bow figures of a shepherd and shepherdess, *c.*1755, damaged, 14.5cm (5¾in), *S 25 Mar*, £1,265 ($1,607)

8
A Bow figure of a nun, chipped, 15.8cm (6¼in), *C 17 Apr*, £209 ($272)

9
A pair of Bow figures of a shepherd and shepherdess, 1760-65, minor repair, 18cm (7in), *NY 10 Oct*, $825 (£585)

10
A pair of Bow figures representing Freedom and Matrimony, *c.*1755-60, each with hand missing, chips and some restoration, 18cm (7in), *L 26 Feb*, £792 ($887)

11
A Bow figure of a boy in Turkish attire, *c.*1765, representing Asia, chipped, iron-red dagger and anchor marks, 14cm (5½in), *S 14 Nov*, £297 ($416)

12
A pair of Bow figures of Fire and Water, *c.*1765, restored, chipped, 22.3cm (8¼in), *C 10 July*, £495 ($688)

13
A Bow candlestick group of Harlequin and Columbine, *c.*1765, some restoration, 27cm (10½in), *L 22 Oct*, £660 ($990)

14
A Bow group of 'Birds in Branches', *c.*1760, some chips and restoration, incised S, 17cm (6¾in), *L 22 Oct*, £935 ($1,403)

15
Four Bow figures representing the Seasons, *c.*1765, some damage and restoration, two with anchor, dagger and crescent marks, 17cm (7¾in), *L 26 Feb*, £1,870 ($2,094)

1
A pair of Derby bocage
figures of stags at lodge,
c.1770, restored, 18 and
18.5cm (7 and 7¼in),
NY 12 Apr,
$467 (£374)

2
A Derby figure of a pug
dog, c.1800, incised 3,
5.5cm (2¼in), L 23 July,
£396 ($586)

3
A Derby figure of a
pointer, late 18th cen-
tury, tail restored,
16cm (6¼in), L 22 Oct,
£319 ($479)

4
A Derby 'Pale Family'
figure of a seated girl,
c.1756-8, repaired,
12cm (4¾in), L 26 Feb,
£330 ($370)

5
A Derby figure of
'Summer', c.1758, wearing
a wheat-ear garland and
holding corn and corn-
flowers, 10.8cm (4¼in)
high, C 16 Jan,
£605 ($726)

6
A pair of Bloor Derby
figures of a milkmaid
and milkman, c.1830,
restored, yoke missing,
printed circular mark,
18 and 17cm (7 and
6¾in), L 23 July,
£572 ($847)

7
A Derby group of
musicians with a dancing
dog, 1765-70, after a
painting by Carle
Vanloo, chips, 26cm
(10¼in), NY 12 Apr,
$1,430 (£1,144)

8
A Derby sweetmeat figure
of a seated shepherd,
1760-65, some colour
possibly added later,
23.5cm (9¼in), NY 10 Oct,
$1,320 (£936)

9
A Derby figure of
Britannia, c.1765, chips,
32cm (12½in), L 21 May,
£198 ($265)

10
A Derby figure of Diana,
c.1770-80, restored, 26cm
(10in), L 21 May,
£286 ($383)

11
A Derby figure of George
IV, c.1830, some
restoration, 32cm
(11½in), L 22 Oct,
£330 ($495)

12
A Derby figure of
Shakespeare, c.1790,
after Scheemakers,
restored, 28.5cm (11¼in)
high, S 25 Mar,
£198 ($251)

13
A pair of Derby figures
of pastoral musicians,
c.1765, modelled as a
youth playing the bag-
pipes and a girl the
mandolin, some res-
toration, 23cm (9in),
L 23 July,
£770 ($1,140)

14
A pair of Derby figures
of 'The Dresden Shepherd
and Shepherdess', c.1820,
some chips and resto-
ration, incised no 55/2,
21cm (8¼in), L 23 July,
£462 ($684)

15
A set of four Derby
figures of 'The Seasons',
c.1825, repairs and
chips, painted crowned
crossed batons and D
in red, 22.5 to 24.5cm
(8¾ to 9½in), L 23 July,
£330 ($488)

1
A pair of Chelsea figures
symbolic of Freedom
and Matrimony, c.1760,
some restoration, gold
anchor marks, 19cm
(7½in), L 21 May,
£1,430 ($1,916)

2
A Chelsea figure of a
rabbit seller, 1756-69,
after a Meissen original,
small restorations,
firing fault, gold anchor
mark, 14cm (5½in),
L 23 July,
£1,870 ($2,768)

3
A Chelsea figure of a
cooper, c.1765, 13cm
(5in), L 22 Oct,
£825 ($1,238)

4
A Chelsea figure of 'The
Night Watchman', c.1760,
from the 'Cries of Paris'
series, gold anchor
mark, damaged, 15.2cm
(6in) high, S 25 Mar,
£1,045 ($1,327)

5
A Longton Hall group of
Hercules and the Nemean
Lion, c.1755-6, tail
restored, some cracks,
14cm (5½in), L 26 Feb,
£605 ($678)

6
A pair of Longton Hall
figures of a gardener and
companion, c.1755-60,
some repairs and chips,
12 and 11cm (4¾ and
4¼in), L 26 Feb,
£792 ($887)

7
A pair of Longton Hall
figures of an abbess and
a novice, c.1755-6, some
restoration, 12.5cm
(5in), L 26 Feb,
£748 ($838)

8
A pair of Royal Worcester
'Queen Anne Boy and
Girl Comports', 1884, in
Kate Greenaway style
clothes, printed and
impressed crowned
circle marks, 16cm
(6¼in), L 23 July,
£352 ($521)

9
A Staffordshire model of
a hound, c.1830, crack,
21cm (8¼in), L 23 July,
£297 ($440)

10
A Royal Doulton figure of
Columbine, wearing a
pink dress, HN 1297,
impressed date 3.3.29,
15.2cm (6in), C 6 Aug,
£495 ($738)

11
A pair of Royal Worcester
candlestick figures,
1899, purple printed
mark including a date
code, 50.8cm (20in),
C 16 Jan,
£792 ($950)

12
A Royal Doulton figure of
'Siesta', 1928, printed
mark, title and HN1305,
16.5cm (6½in), L 26 Feb,
£1,980 ($2,218)

13
A Royal Doulton figure of
'The Sentimental Pierrot',
c.1925, printed and
painted marks, title and
HN36, 14cm (5½in),
L 22 Oct,
£1,650 ($2,475)

14
A Royal Doulton figure of
'The Bather', 1930,
printed mark and
numbered HN687,
19.5cm (7¾in), L 26 Feb,
£352 ($394)

15
A Royal Doulton figure of
'Priscilla', HN1340,
impressed date 3.2.31,
19.6cm (7¾in), C 14 May,
£98 ($117)

16
A Royal Doulton figure of
'the young Miss Nightin-
gale', HN2010, 24.1cm
(9½in) high, C 12 Mar,
£385 ($439)

17
A Royal Doulton figure of
Mephistopheles and
Marguerite, c.1940, the
double-sided figure
modelled as a maiden
on one side and the devil
on the other, printed
and painted marks, title
and HN775, 19.5cm
(7¾in), L 21 May,
£660 ($884)

1   2   3   4

5   6   7

8   9   10

11   12   13

14   15   16   17

1
A Robinson & Leadbeater
Parian figure of Venus,
late 19th century,
minor chips, moulded
initials mark, 75.5cm
(29¾in), *L 21 May,*
£528 ($706)

2
A Copeland Parian figure
of 'Egeria', 1874, after an
original by J H Foley,
RA, impressed factory
marks and date code,
moulded artist's name,
71.8cm (28¼in), *S 15 May,*
£506 ($673)

3
A Parian figure of a
bather, *c.*1870, after a
drawing by Fragonard,
65cm (25½in), *S 15 May,*
£418 ($556)

4
A Goss coloured Parian
figure of a classical
maiden, *c.*1866, printed
mark in sepia, 43.7cm
(17¼in) high, *C 10 July,*
£220 ($306)

5
A Copeland Parian group
of a boy and girl, seated
on a rock, impressed
mark, 29cm (11½in)
high, *S 15 May,*
£396 ($527)

6
A Copeland Parian badger
hunting group, *c.*1880,
impressed mark, 31cm
(12¼in) high, *S 15 May,*
£242 ($322)

7
A Copeland Parian figure
of Sir Walter Scott,
modelled by J Steel,
33cm (13in) high,
C 14 May,
£165 ($219)

8
A Copeland Parian group
of 'The Sleep of Sorrow
and the Dream of Joy',
*c.*1875, after the original
sculpture by Raphael
Monti, chips, impressed
marks, 47cm (18½in),
L 21 May,
£902 ($1,209)

9
A Ridgway Bates & Co
Parian figure of Venus
and Cupid, by J Gibson,
1858, 47cm (18½in),
A 25 Feb,
Dfl 2,900 (£711; $796)

10
A Copeland Parian bust
of 'The Veiled Bride',
1861, after the original
sculpture by Raphael
Monti, printed mark,
37cm (14½in), *L 23 July,*
£1,210 ($1,791)

11
A Goss Parian bust of
Benjamin Disraeli,
Earl of Beaconsfield,
1881, impressed mark,
40cm (15¼in), *L 26 Feb,*
£935 ($1,047)

12
A Minton Parian group of
two naked girls, 30.4cm
(12in) high, *C 14 May,*
£286 ($380)

1
A Royal Doulton
character jug entitled
the 'Toothless Granny',
*c.*1935-45, 16.5cm (6½in),
C 29 Oct,
£616 ($917)

2
A Royal Doulton 'Punch
and Judy man' character
jug, *c.*1964-9, 19cm
(7½in), *C 6 Aug,*
£341 ($508)

3
A Royal Doulton
'Gondolier' character jug,
*c.*1964-9, 19cm (7½in),
C 14 May,
£374 ($497)

4
A Royal Doulton
character jug entitled
'Friar Tuck', *c.*1951-60,
16.5cm (6½in), *C 29 Oct,*
£198 ($295)

5
A Royal Doulton
character jug entitled
'Uncle Tom Cobbleigh',
*c.*1952-60, 16.5cm
(6½in), *C 29 Oct,*
£198 ($295)

6
A Royal Doulton clown
jug, *c.*1951-5, white-
haired version, 15.8cm
(6¼in), *C 29 Jan,*
£484 ($571)

7
A Royal Doulton 'Old
King Cole' character jug,
*c.*1939-60, 14.6cm (5¾in),
C 12 Mar,
£176 ($201)

8
A Royal Doulton 'Lord
Nelson' character jug,
*c.*1958-68, 19cm (7½in),
C 12 Mar
£187 ($213)

9
A Royal Doulton 'Sam
Johnson' character jug,
*c.*1950-60, 16.5cm
(6½in), *C 12 Mar,*
£198 ($226)

10
A set of eleven Wilkinson
Ltd. 'First World War'
Toby jugs, 1914-18, each
designed by Sir F
Carruthers Gould,
damages and repairs,
printed mark and fac-
simile signature, 26 to
30.5cm (10¼ to 12in),
L 26 Feb,
£1,870 ($2,094)

11
A pearlware 'hearty good
fellow' Toby jug, early
19th century, restored,
29.8cm (11¾in), *S 25 Mar,*
£108 ($137)

12
A Ralph Wood Toby jug,
*c.*1770-80, some resto-
ration, 25cm (9¾in),
L 23 July,
£605 ($895)

13
A Staffordshire Toby jug
and cover, late 18th cen-
tury, after a Ralph
Wood original, 24.5cm
(10in) high, *C 10 July,*
£682 ($948)

14
A prattware Toby jug,
*c.*1800, damage to rim,
24cm (9½in), *L 23 July,*
£374 ($554)

15
A Yorkshire Toby jug, late
18th century, holding a
bottle and glass, hat
restored, 20cm (8in),
L 21 May,
£242 ($324)

16
An unusual pearlware
Toby jug of the Squire,
*c.*1800, minor imperfec-
tions, 29cm (11½in),
NY 15 Feb,
$1,320 (£1,138)

Bristol sauceboat, 1775, with moulded flowers and scroll border picked out in pink, painted cross in blue, 18.5cm (7¼in), *L 21 May,* £880 ($1,179)

Bristol butter boat, 1775, with moulded fruits and puce scrolls, 11cm (4¼in), *L 26 Feb,* £550 ($616)

Richard Champion's Bristol cup and saucer, 1774, from the Sarah Smith service, with floral monogram in pink and gilding, some wear, blue enamel cross, *L 22 Oct,* £352 ($528)

Bristol christening mug, 1775, painted with pendant bands of pink roses, painted cross in blue, 7.5cm (3in), *L 21 May,* £440 ($590)

Bristol dessert basket, 1770-72, the exterior with blue floral motifs, handles restored, chips, 21.5cm (8½in), *L 21 May,* £484 ($649)

A pair of Bristol dessert dishes, *c.*1775, chip and some wear, painted cross in blue, 25.5cm (10in), *L 21 May,* £462 ($647)

An early Bow jug, *c.*1750, painted in famille-rose enamels, chips and scratching, 8.5cm (3¼in), *L 21 May,* £660 ($844)

A pair of Bow plates, *c.*1765-8, transfer-printed and enamelled, chips and rubbing, 23cm (9in), *L 21 May,* £308 ($413)

A Bow 'jumping boy' pattern plate, *c.*1760, painted in underglaze blue, chip, wear, 16.5cm (6½in), *L 26 Feb,* £229 ($246)

10
A Bow mug, *c.*1751, painted in vivid blue, chips, 12cm (4¾in), *S 14 Nov,* £1,375 ($1,925)

11
A Bow mug, *c.*1770, boldly enamelled, chip, 14.5cm (5¾in), *L 22 Oct,* £528 ($792)

12
A pair of Bow flower ornaments, *c.*1765, chipped and restored, 19cm (7½in), *S 10 July,* £605 ($811)

13
A pair of Bow baskets of flowers, *c.*1765, chips, 12 and 11cm (4¾ and 4¼in), *NY 12 Apr,* $770 (£616)

14
A Bow 'birds in branches' candlestick, *c.*1760, repairs, numeral 2 mark, 22cm (8¾in), *NY 12 Apr,* $302 (£242)

15
A blue printed cabbage leaf jug, *c.*1770, probably Caughley, chipped, 22.5cm (8¾in), *S 25 Mar,* £572 ($726)

16
A Bow saucer-dish, *c.*1758-60, painted in famille-verte style, slight wear, 17.5cm (7in), *L 26 Feb,* £495 ($554)

17
A Chelsea mug, 1752-6, painted red anchor, 14cm (5½in), *L 26 Feb,* £1,320 ($1,478)

1 2

3 4 5

6 7 8

9 10 11

12 13 14

15 16 17

1
A Chelsea lemon box and cover, late red/early gold anchor period, c.1758, repair and chips, 17.5cm (6¾in) long, NY 12 Apr, $247 (£198)

2
A pair of Chelsea 'May-blossom' bowls and covers, gold anchor period, c.1765, chips, restorations and hair crack, 18.5 and 17.5cm (7¼ and 7in) diam, NY 12 Apr, $330 (£264)

3
A pair of Chelsea pots of flowers, gold anchor period, 1760-65, chips, 20 and 19.5cm (8 and 7¾in), NY 12 Apr, $357 (£286)

4
A Chelsea 'birds in branches' candlestick group, c.1760, repair and cracks, candlestick missing, gold anchor mark, 18cm (7in), NY 12 Apr, $412 (£329)

5
A Chelsea 'Hans Sloane' plate, c.1756, chip, painted red anchor, 21cm (8¼in), L 23 July, £1,045 ($1,547)

6
A Chelsea mug, 1752-6, damaged, red anchor mark, 12.1cm (4¾in), C 10 July, £715 ($994)

7
A set of six Chelsea fruit plates, c.1757, chips, wear, two with red anchor mark, 21.5 to 21cm (8½ to 8¼in), NY 12 Apr, $495 (£396)

8
A pair of Chelsea leaf dishes, c.1758-60, each painted in 'Fable' style, restoration, cracks and flaking, red and gold anchor marks, 21.5cm (8½in), L 23 July, £660 ($977)

9
A Chelsea dessert plate, 1752-6, chip, painted red anchor, 15.5cm (6in), L 21 May, £264 ($354)

10
A Chelsea 'mazarine blue' oval dish, 1760-65, gold anchor, 31.5cm (12½in), NY 12 Apr, $770 (£616)

11
A pair of Chelsea silver-shaped dishes, c.1760-65, gold anchor marks, 24cm (9½in), L 21 May, £902 ($1,209)

12
A Chelsea leaf dish, c.1760, moulded in the form of a leaf laid on a basket, firing flaws, brown anchor, 27.5cm (10¾in), L 21 May, £385 ($516)

13
A pair of Chelsea sauce-boats, c.1754, red anchor marks, minor damage, 19.5cm (7¾in), S 25 Mar, £5,060 ($6,426)

14
A Chelsea fruit basket, c.1755, red anchor mark, 28cm (11in) wide, S 25 Mar, £1,540 ($1,956)

15
A Chelsea 'Fable' tea bowl and saucer, 1749-52, painted by Jefferyes Hamett o'Neale, the bowl with the fable of the Horse and the Loaded Ass, and the saucer with the Bear and the Man, crack and restoration, bowl with raised anchor, bowl 7cm (2¾in), L 22 Oct, £2,310 ($3,465)

16
A Chelsea leaf dish, c.1755, formed as seven overlapping leaves in shades of green and yellow, minor imperfections, red anchor, 16cm (6½in), NY 10 Oct, $2,090 (£1,482)

17
A Chelsea partridge tureen and cover, c.1755, the bird with brown, tan and grey plumage, chips, beak restored, red anchor and nos. 2 and 72, 13.5cm (5¼in), L 22 Oct, £770 ($1,155)

18
A Chaffer's Liverpool, blue and white mug, c.1760-65, 11.5cm (4½in), L 23 July, £715 ($1,058)

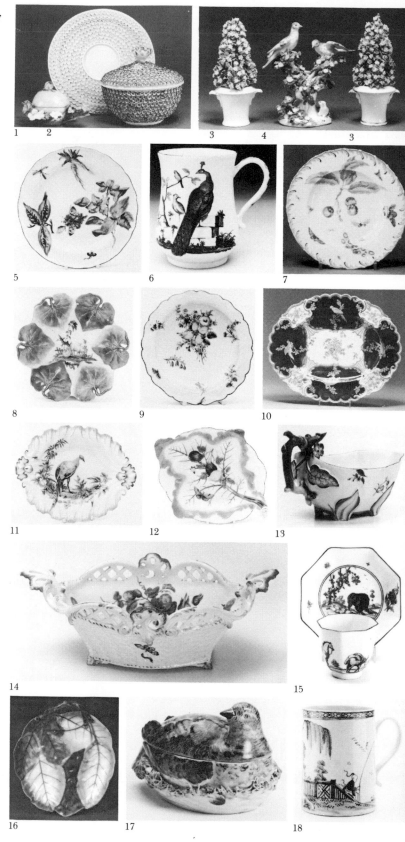

1
A Liverpool Japan pattern teapot and cover, *c.*1770, enamelled and gilt with *kiku mon*, slight wear, 12.5cm (5in), *L 21 May,* £605 ($811)

2
A Christian's Liverpool coffee pot and cover, painted in greens and pinks, 24cm (9½in), *C 15 Oct,* £231 ($342)

3
A Christian's Liverpool 'thirsty mask' cream jug, *c.*1770, the spout worked into a mask with protruding tongue, chips, 10cm (4in), *L 21 May,* £330 ($442)

4
A Pennington's Liverpool coffee pot and cover, *c.*1780, painted in a famille-rose palette, 25.3cm (10in), *C 10 July,* £363 ($505)

5
A Lowestoft blue and white ale beaker, *c.*1765-70, painted with John Barleycorn, cracks, painted workman's mark, 7cm (2¾in), *L 22 Oct,* £2,200 ($3,300)

6
A Lowestoft coffee pot and cover, *c.*1780, the body enamelled in famille-rose style with floral sprays, cracked, 26.5cm (10⅜in), *S 10 July,* £418 ($560)

7
A Lowestoft baluster vase and cover, *c.*1785-90, painted after a Chinese exportware original, 14cm (5½in), *L 21 May,* £1,650 ($2,211)

8
A Plymouth blue and white mug, *c.*1769, painted with an oriental-style landscape, rim restored, mark in underglaze blue, 16.5cm (6½in), *L 22 Oct,* £330 ($495)

9
A pair of Coalport double-handled bowls and covers, *c.*1830, on scroll feet, 12cm (4¾in), *HS 16 July,* £880 ($1,276)

10
A Coalport basket, *c.*1820-30, chipped, 20.5cm (8in), *HS 16 July,* £264 ($383)

11
A Coalport potpourri vase, cover and liner, *c.*1830, picked out in turquoise and gilding, slight chipping, 29cm (11½in), *HS 16 July,* £770 ($1,117)

12
A set of eleven dessert plates, *c.*1830, and another similar, all of Coalport type, slight wear, 22cm (8¾in), *L 26 Feb,* £770 ($862)

13
A pair of Coalport Sèvres-style serving plates, the porcelain *c.*1810, decorated at a later date, interlaced L's, 36 and 35.5cm (14¼ and 14in), *NY 21 May,* $467 (£374)

14
A pair of Coalport vases and covers, *c.*1900, painted and signed by E. O. Ball with a view of Loch Ness and Loch Earn, printed crown mark, 18.5cm (7¼in), *L 21 May,* £418 ($560)

15
A John Rose, Coalport, tea service, *c.*1810, comprising 31 pieces, each decorated with a 'Japan' pattern in underglaze blue, iron-red and green, some damage, *L 26 Feb,* £1,760 ($1,971)

16
A pair of Derby sauce-boats, *c.*1756-60, painted in rose, iron-red, yellow and green, one handle restored, chips, 19.5cm (7¾in), *L 22 Oct,* £352 ($528)

1   2   3
4   5   6   7
8   9   10
11   12   13
14   15   16

1
A Coalbrookdale miniature tea service, *c.*1830, sucrier restored, *S 3 Apr,* £176 ($227)

2
A Derby mug, *c.*1770, slight scratching, 14cm (5½in), sold with another smaller Derby mug painted with birds, 9.5cm (3¾in), *L 21 May,* £858 ($1,150)

3
A pair of Derby dessert plates, *c.*1810, perhaps painted by Thomas Tatlow, one with a perch and the other with a trout, crown, crossed batons and D in red, 22cm (8¾in), *L 21 May,* £880 ($1,179)

4
A Derby vase, early 19th century, damaged, 42cm (16½in), *C 16 Jan,* £660 ($792)

5
A pair of Derby potpourri vases and covers, *c.*1820, decorated in underglaze blue, iron-red and gilding with an 'Imari' pattern, repair, crowned crossed batons and D in red, 14cm (5½in), *L 21 May,* £352 ($472)

6
A Derby tea and coffee service, *c.*1810, comprising forty three pieces, decorated with a 'Japan' pattern in underglaze blue, iron-red and gilding, cracks and repairs, crowned batons and D, cake plate 21.5cm (8½in), *L 23 July,* £396 ($586)

7
A Derby tea and coffee service, *c.*1850-60, comprising 56 pieces, one tea cup cracked, *C 16 Jan,* £1,650 ($1,980)

8
A Royal Crown Derby cabinet plate, 1926, painted by A Gregory, signed, green-ground rim, printed crowned initials mark, 22.5cm (8¾in), *L 26 Feb,* £385 ($431)

9
A pair of Royal Crown Derby vases, 41.9cm (16½in), *C 28 Feb,* £682 ($764)

10
A Swansea plate, *c.*1820, painted by William Pollard, slight wear, printed Swansea mark, 21cm (8¼in), *L 26 Feb,* £550 ($616)

11
A Swansea cup and saucer, *c.*1820, with pink roses on turquoise and gilt ground, slight wear, printed mark sold with a Swansea vase, *c.*1820, chipped, Swansea and trident, 11cm (4¼in), *L 21 May,* £352 ($472)

12
A Nantgarw plate, 1813-22, impressed Nantgarw C W, 24cm (9½in), *L 26 Feb,* £605 ($678)

1
A Minton porcelain
tea service, c.1810, comprising eighteen pieces,
some staining and
wear, painted 'Sevres'
marks and number 670,
sold with two Spode
saucers, c.1810, with the
same pattern, L 22 Oct,
£770 ($1,155)

2
A Minton porcelain yellow
ground tea and coffee
service, c.1840, 56 pieces,
C 26 Mar,
£770 ($978)

3
A pair of Minton porcelain vases, c.1870,
impressed mark and
indistinct date cypher,
crazed, 19.5cm (7¾in),
L 15 May,
£99 ($132)

4
A Minton earthenware
dish, 1869, painted by
W S Coleman, signed,
impressed mark, 27.5cm
(10¾in), L 23 July,
£462 ($684)

5
A Mintons earthenware
wall plaque, 1873, painted
by E Broughton, signed,
after Reynolds,
impressed mark, 39cm
(15¼in), L 23 July,
£385 ($570)

6
A Minton pottery ewer,
c.1870, in Henri Deux
St Porchaire style,
modelled by Charles
Toft, repaired handle,
printed marks, 23cm
(9in), C 2 Oct,
£352 ($513)

7
A copper lustre pottery
jug, c.1830, repaired,
78cm (30¾in), C 14 Apr,
£825 ($1,073)

8
A Copeland earthenware
green-glazed hedgehog
crocus pot and stand,
mid-19th century, stand
impressed 'Copeland',
30.5cm (12in), S 10 July,
£352 ($472)

9
A Staffordshire silver
resist lustre earthenware
jug, c.1815, transfer-
printed in black and
enamelled in various
colours, all on a silver
lustre ground, 11cm
(4¼in), NY 12 Apr,
$385 (£308)

10
A Mintons pâte-sur-pâte
porcelain vase, 1901, the
cream body gilt in
relief, with brown panel
of white amorini,
probably by Alboine
Birks, some wear,
impressed marks, 35.5cm
(14in), L 21 May,
£748 ($1,002)

11
A Staffordshire silver
resist lustre earthenware
'Husbandman's' jug, c.1815,
21cm (8¼in), NY 12 Apr,
$412 (£329)

12
A Staffordshire earthen-
ware pink lustre jug,
dated 1817, the pale
buff ground transfer-
printed in black, 17cm
(6¾in), NY 1 Feb,
$550 (£466)

1

A pair of London dec-orated Nantgarw plates, *c.*1813-22, 22cm (8½in), L 26 Feb, £572 ($641)

2

A London-decorated Nantgarw plate, *c.*1820, blue and gilt borders, scratches, impressed mark, 23.5cm (9¼in), L 21 May, £440 ($590)

3

A New Hall tea and coffee service, late 18th century, comprising thirty five pieces, decorated with pink roses, slight wear, patt no. 83, C 2 Oct, £792 ($1,156)

4

A Rockingham tea and coffee service, *c.*1835, comprising thirty six pieces, each decorated with grey and gilt scrolls, cracks and wear, printed griffin mark, patt no. 1170, teapot 18cm (7in), L 22 Oct, £352 ($528)

5

A Rockingham inkwell, liner and cover, late 1820s, griffin mark and wording in red, 6.6cm (2⅝in) diam, S 25 Mar, £572 ($726)

6

A Rockingham miniature teapot and cover, *c.*1830, applied with blue and yellow blossom, puce mark CL2, chipped, 7cm (2¾in), HS 16 July, £330 ($479)

7

A garniture of three Spode spill vases, *c.*1825, each painted and gilt with a famille-rose pattern, one restored, one with pattern no. 868, 11 and 13.5cm (4¼ and 5¼in), L 21 May, £286 ($383)

8

A Spode 'beaded new shape jar', *c.*1810-20, painted with colourful flowers and foliage on a blue and gilt ground, painted mark and pattern no. 1166, 13cm (5in), L 21 May, £715 ($958)

9

A Spode garniture of three spill vases, *c.*1825, painted with famille-rose flowers, pattern no. 868 in red and gilding, one inscribed SPODE 11.7cm (4½in) and 15.8cm (6¼in), C 17 Apr, £902 ($1,173)

10

A set of six Spode 'Japan' pattern plates, *c.*1825, each decorated in underglaze blue, iron-red, green and gilding, painted mark and pattern no. 2251, 20cm (8in), L 21 May, £550 ($737)

11

A Belleek shell ornament, *c.*1880, printed and impressed marks, 12.5cm (5in), S 23 Oct, £825 ($1,238)

12

A Belleek 'naiads flower pot', late 19th century, 27cm (10½in), L 21 May, £858 ($1,150)

13

A Belleek covered ice bucket, 1863-91, repair, printed black mark, 46.5cm (18¼in), NY 30 Nov, $1,320 (£886)

1

2

3

4

5

6

7

8

9

10

11

12

13

Belleek basket, 1891-
926, with creamy
ustrous glaze, minor
hips, impressed mark,
2.5cm (8¾in), L 26 Feb,
2,310 ($2,587)

Belleek tinted basket
nd cover, 1891-1926,
mpressed mark, 20.5cm
in), L 26 Feb,
1,540 ($1,725)

Belleek basket and
over, 1863-91, repair,
hips, impressed mark,
9cm (11½in) wide,
22 Oct,
1,100 ($1,650)

Davenport Imari
attern cabaret set,
1880, comprising 15
ieces, printed mark,
3 Sept,
484 ($711)

A pair of Copeland vases,
1870, painted by C F
Hurten, signed, hair
racks, slight wear, 50cm
19¾in), L 21 May,
4,620 ($6,191)

A Copeland vase, c.1895,
ainted by C F Hurten,
igned, with pink, white
nd yellow roses on a
ale-green ground,
rinted mark, 63.5cm
25in), L 23 July,
1,265 ($1,872)

A pair of Copeland
cachepots, c.1870,
printed marks, 18.5cm
7¼in), S 23 Oct,
£550 ($825)

A Staffordshire pastille
burner and base, c.1830,
in the form of a church
applied with brightly
coloured flowers, chips,
13.5cm (5¼in), L 23 July,
£748 ($1,107)

A Goss model of the
Priest's House, Prestbury,
early 20th century,
printed goshawk mark
and title in black,
chimney repaired, 9cm
(3½in) high, C 16 Jan,
£268 ($343)

10
**A Staffordshire porcel-
laneous model of Trinity
College,** mid-19th cen-
tury, titled on the
base, 20.3cm (8in) high,
C 4 June,
£143 ($193)

11
**A Staffordshire porcelain
pastille burner,** c.1830,
15.2cm (6in) high,
C 4 June,
£209 ($282)

12
**A Goss model of Shake-
speare's house,** early 20th
century, 7.6cm (3in),
C 12 Feb,
£46 ($80)

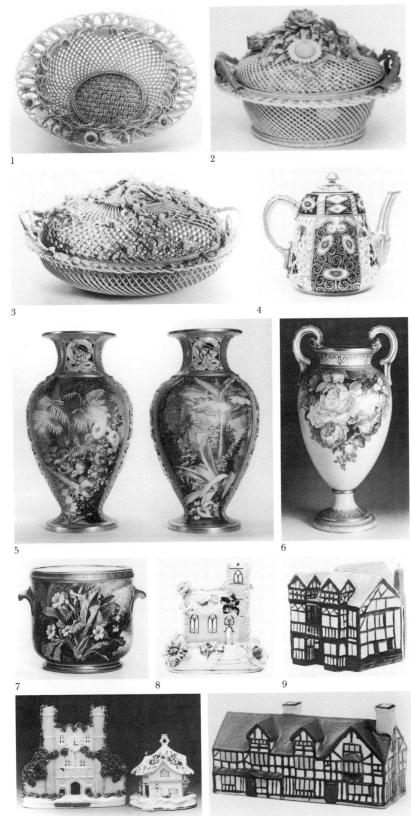

1

2

3

4

5

6

7

8

9

10

11

12

Early 19th Century English Dinner Services

Until 1710, when the first hard-paste porcelain to be made in Europe was produced at Meissen, near Dresden in Germany, virtually all porcelain in England and on the Continent was imported from China and Japan, and was considered a treasured luxury. In 1708, with the chartering of England's Honourable East India Company, trade with the Orient burgeoned, and within a quarter of a century the supply of 'chinaware' from the east began to meet the steadily rising demand in the west, providing every form of table and tea ware for almost every level of household. Simultaneously, small porcelain factories were springing up in the cultural centres of Germany, Austria, Italy and France. Finally, in the mid-1740s, England's own porcelain factories began production at Bow and

Chelsea in London, and slightly later at Longton Hall, Derby, Bristol, Worcester, Liverpool, Lowestoft, Plymouth and Caughley. Towards the end of the century the potteries of Staffordshire, with Wedgwood in the forefront, were in full production, supplying useful and ornamental wares at prices so internationally competitive that they ultimately forced the closing not only of the Dutch Delft potteries across the Channel in Holland, but also of the Honourable East India Company, whose elegant imports were to lose their edge to the new generation of early 19th century English porcelain products. Among the most prominent of these were the Worcester factories of Flight and Barr (1792-1804), Barr, Flight and Barr (1804-13), Flight, Barr and Barr (1813-40) and Chamberlain

—1—

A Wedgwood Queen's Ware dessert service, 1810-15, comprising twenty five pieces, each transfer-printed in sepia and heightened in coral and gilding with the 'Darwin Water Lily' pattern, some repair and cracks, impressed mark and potter's marks, plate 21cm (8¼in), *L 26 Feb,* **£2,200 ($2,464)**

—2—

A Wedgwood pearlware dessert service, early 19th century, comprising thirty-three pieces, enamelled and printed with oriental flowers in 'famille rose' style with trellised salmon borders, impressed marks, *S 10 July,* **£2,420 ($3,243)**

—1—

—2—

1788-1852); and the Staffordshire factories of New Hall 1781-1835), Minton (1793-   ), Coalport (1795-   ), Spode c.1784-1833), Ridgway (1814-30), Davenport (1793-1887) and Rockingham (1745-1842, producing porcelain from c.1826).

The proliferation and success of the Staffordshire pottery and porcelain factories were due to their proximity to suitable clays, their ready adaptation to the advances and technology of the Industrial Revolution and an excellent network of roads and waterways, combined with the rising demands of a newly affluent middle class. By the middle of the 19th century these factories had developed into the dominant pottery and porcelain-makers of the western world.

—3—
A Wedgwood Queen's Ware dessert service, late 18th century, comprising thirty pieces, patt. no. 1472 in gilding, some damage, C 16 Jan, £2,200 ($2,640)

—4—
A Wedgwood Queen's Ware dinner service, 1790-1810, comprising forty-five pieces, each painted in sepia and green, impressed marks, minor chips, tureen 47.5cm (18¾in), L 23 July, £1,155 ($1,709)

—5—
A Wedgwood blue and white part dinner service, 1810-15, comprising thirty pieces, each transfer-printed in underglaze blue with the 'Darwin Water Lily' pattern, some damage, largest serving dish 52cm (20½in), L 23 July, £1,265 ($1,872)

—6—
A Wedgwood Queen's Ware part dinner service, early 19th century, pattern no. 899, comprising fifty eight pieces, each with a border of blue daisies, some damage, largest serving dish 39cm (15¼in), L 23 July, £935 ($1,384)

—7—
A Wedgwood porcelain dessert service, c.1910, comprising eighteen pieces, each painted with flower panels between blue and gilt decoration, printed marks, painted numerals, plate 21.5cm (8½in), L 21 May, £572 ($766)

—8—
A Staffordshire porcelain dessert service, third quarter 19th century, comprising twenty three pieces, each painted with a landscape, seascape or riverscape, some wear and cracks, plate 22.5cm (8¾in), L 26 Feb, £528 ($591)

—9—
A Staffordshire earthenware dinner service, third quarter 19th century, comprising one hundred and fifty three pieces, patt. no. 4975, some damage and wear, venison dish 49.5cm (19½in), L 23 July, £1,485 ($2,198)

—10—
A Staffordshire ironstone 'Japan' pattern dinner service, probably Ridgway, Morley, Wear & Co., 1835-42, patt. no. 3/669, comprising fifty pieces, each transfer-printed in underglaze blue and painted in iron-red, salmon, rose, blue, brown, green and gold, marks printed in underglaze blue, tureens 19 and 21.5cm (7½ and 8½in), NY 12 Apr, $1,540 (£1,232)

—3—

—4—

—5—

—6—

—7—

—8—

—9—

—10—

Stylistically, England's earliest porcelain factories had taken their cues initially from the Meissen factory, producing wares and figures first in the oriental taste and then in the rococo, with a slight detour into botanical and naturalistic forms. In the 1760s and 1770s, they proceeded to the French taste, imitating the products of the Sèvres factory outside Paris, whose wares were being collected avidly by Queen Charlotte, wife of King George III, and members of her court; and finally, they turned toward the restraint of neoclassicism that pervaded most of the visual arts in the late 18th century. Interestingly, this sequence of styles repeated itself almost exactly in the first sixty years of the 19th century, becoming adapted to or modified by the difference in the vision of the Regency and early Victorian eye. It was also aided by the improved technology that now provided the factories with a greatly expanded palette of enamel colours, and, more importantly, a range of more durable clay bodies that permitted a wider variety of shapes and forms than had been attempted hitherto.

Nothing glittered more brightly than the Regency dining table fully arrayed for the dinner party that was as much a theatrical event as a social gathering. The table was virtually reset between courses, providing a stage for the display of the hostess's fashionable services (no minor factor in the prosperity of the English porcelain industry). It may be to that tradition that we can attribute the survival of a large quantity of early 19th century dinner and dessert services, and while many of these services have lost a substantial number of pieces through 150 years of wear and breakage, and others have been split into smaller groups and single pieces, a popular pattern that may have been in production for almost a century (fig.11) can still survive in sufficient quantity for a modern collector to reassemble a usable service from diverse pieces.

—11—
A Spode porcelain '967' pattern dinner service, *c.*1810, comprising one hundred and five pieces, each painted in iron-red, green, underglaze blue and gilding, some repairs and cracks, sold in seventeen lots, *NY 22 Apr,* $27,850 (£20,035)

—12—
A Spode ironstone part dinner service, early 19th century, comprising thirty-one pieces, each piece printed and painted with an Imari pattern, printed seal marks in blue, patt. no. 2054 in iron-red, *C 16 Jan,* £418 ($502)

—13—
A Mason's ironstone dinner service, *c.*1850, comprising ninety-eight pieces, each piece printed in sepia and picked out in an Imari palette with oriental boats and islands, printed marks in sepia, *C 16 Jan,* £2,860 ($3,432)

—11—

—12—

—13—

The revival of interest in early 19th century English table services parallels the revival of taste for Regency furniture; today's collector of the decorative arts has become a 'period purist'. But that is only one aspect of a multi-faceted market. It is perhaps just as significant that the buyer of such a dinner service may have looked at modern services and found them to be up to five times more expensive and considerably less appealing. In such cases an early 19th century service seems an irresistible bargain, particularly when it is borne in mind that it should increase in value over the years, unlike a modern service. It is, too, one of the great discoveries of the collector of modest means that an 18th or early 19th century breakfront cabinet filled with porcelain of the period furnishes a large expanse of wall attractively and far more economically than a painting of equivalent quality.

—14—
Staffordshire ironstone dinner service, *c.*1830, patt. no. 103, comprising forty eight pieces, each painted in underglaze blue, coloured enamels and gilding, painted crown in underglaze blue, dinner plate 26cm (10¼in), *L 26 Feb,* £1,760 ($1,971)

—15—
A pair of Mason's ironstone soup tureens, covers and stands, *c.*1825, painted with 'willow pattern' landscapes, one cover repaired and slight wear, printed pelmet mark, stand 33cm (13in), *L 26 Feb,* £748 ($838)

—16—
A Mason's ironstone dinner service, 1840-50, comprising one hundred and ten pieces, some damage, largest serving dish 54.5cm (21½in), *L 22 Oct,* £880 ($1,320)

—17—
A John Ridgway 'Imperial Stone China' dinner service, *c.*1835, comprising fifty-four pieces, each painted in underglaze blue, enamels and gilding, some damage and staining, printed coat-of-arms mark, dinner plate 25cm (9¾in), *L 26 Feb,* £825 ($924)

—18—
A Mason's 'Patent Ironstone China' part dinner service, *c.*1830, comprising thirty three pieces, each painted in ironred, underglaze blue and gilding, some chips and cracks, impressed mark, venison dish 52.5cm (20½in), *L 22 Oct,* £990 ($1,485)

—19—
A Coalport porcelain dinner service, 1805-10, comprising one hundred and eight pieces, each painted with colourful flowers, some damage and wear, largest serving dish 55.5cm (19¾in), *L 22 Oct,* £4,400 ($6,600)

—14—

—15—

—16—

—17—

—18—

—19—

While there are bargains to be found within the range of the early 19th century English pottery and porcelain services, there also are many examples that are almost shockingly expensive (fig.20). Generally, however, this is a market in which predictability in taste and price prevails and quality supersedes quantity. The highest prices tend to be fetched by services from the best known factories: in porcelain the Worcester factories (fig.26), Coalport (fig.24), Spode and Derby; and in ironstone (the durable type of pottery from which the largest surviving services were made) Mason's (fig.23). But beyond the maker, it is the decoration which plays the most important part in determining price. The most expensive are botanical services (fig.21) (particularly those inscribed with the floral identification on each piece), the various oriental patterns (figs.11 & 35) derived and anglicized from both Japanese Imari and Chinese famille-rose prototypes; armorial services (fig.26); and services painted with feathers, shells, identified topographical views or other specific subjects attributable to a known painter (figs.25 & 31). Many of the last type have been split over the years by dealers and collectors, and the rare appearance of one on the market intact is something of a *cause célèbre*.

—20—

An English pearlware botanical assembled part dinner service, 1800-10, comprising 15 items, plates 25 and 18.5cm (9¾ and 7¼in) diam, *NY 12 Apr,* $4,675 (£3,740)

—21—

An English pearlware botanical assembled part dessert service, 1790-1800, comprising twelve pieces, some with impressed marks, botanical inscriptions in red, plates 21.5 to 21cm (8½ to 8¼in), *NY 12 Apr,* $3,850 (£3,080)

—22—

A James Neale & Co pearlware botanical part dessert service, 1780-86, comprising 8 pieces, impressed crowned G marks, 20 to 27.5cm (8 to 10¾in), *NY 12 Apr,* $3,190 (£2,552)

—23—

A Mason's ironstone dinner service, c.1820, comprising 67 pieces, *S 25 Mar,* £2,530 ($3,213)

—24—

A Coalport porcelain dessert service, c.1830, comprising 18 pieces, *C 16 Jan,* £1,375 ($1,650)

—25—

A pair of Derby porcelain kidney-shaped dishes, c.1797, painted by John Brewer, entitled "The menagerie Hafod" and "West front of Hafod", crowned crossed batons & D mark, 25cm (10in) wide, *L 20 May, 1980,* £1,100 ($2,585)

—26—

A Chamberlain's Worcester crested part dinner service, c.1820, comprising 103 pieces, some pieces marked, tureen 12in (30.5cm) wide, *NY 12 Apr,* $5,225 (£4,180)

—20—

—21—

—22—

—23—

—24—

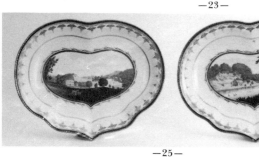

—25—

—26—

Earthenwares (creamware, pearlware and ironstone) are less expensive than their porcelain counterparts because they were more easily mass-produced and tend to be decorated partially or wholly by transfer-printing rather than hand-enamelling. The more desirable of these services are usually those decorated with the most enamelling (fig.2 & 29) and bearing the least obvious printing. It is the ironstone services that are bought most often for use rather than for display; their durability and cheerfulness make them particularly popular (fig.27).

—27—
Davenport stone china 'Japan' pattern part dinner service, 1815-20, comprising one hundred and thirteen pieces, pattern no. 135, marks and painter's marks, tureens 36 and 32.5cm (14¼ and 13in) long, *NY 12 Apr,* $10,450 (£8,360)

—28—
Davenport stone china 'famille rose' part dinner service, 1810-20, comprising seventy six pieces, each transfer-printed in underglaze blue and enamelled in rose, iron-red, purple, green and yellow, most pieces with anchor and table mark, some covers missing and cracks, largest platter 46.5cm (18¼in), *NY 12 Apr,* $3,575 (£2,860)

—29—
Spode creamware dessert service, early 19th century, comprising fifteen pieces, some rubbing and repair, pattern. no. 1557 in black, impressed factory mark, *C 2 Oct,* £440 ($642)

—30—
Davenport porcelain dessert service, *c.*1860, patt. no. 967, comprising eight plates and an oval dish, printed anchor and crown marks, plate 23cm (9in), *L 21 May,* £770 ($1,032)

—31—
A pair of Derby porcelain landscape plates, from the Hafod service, 1797, painted by John Brewer, crowned crossed batons, D marks and patt. no. 67, 23cm (9in), *L 20 May, 1980,* £1,050 ($2,467)

—32—
Sir James Duke & Sons stone china dessert service, comprising twelve plates and five shaped comports, *c.*1860, patt. no. 414367, impressed hand device, *L 3 Apr,* £638 ($823)

—27—

—28—

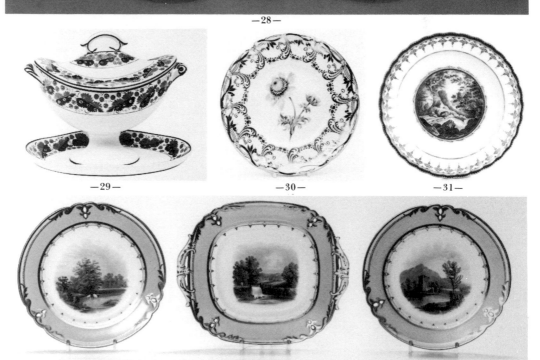

—29—   **—30—**   **—31—**

—32—

The best bargains are to be found in several categories which all fall into the 1820-40 period. First there are services decorated simply with floral bouquets (fig.36) or with bouquets within unfashionably coloured borders, such as cobalt-blue, olive-green or magenta (but not if they are bordered in the always popular apple-green, apricot (fig.33) or yellow); and especially services of this type that are unmarked and unattributable to a particular factory. (While generally unmarked, services of this period often can be attributed to a known factory when the shapes of the component pieces are identical to those of a marked service.) Second are the services decorated with un-named landscape views or unidentifiable crests; but here again, the border colour dictates the level of saleability. Third

are the heavily moulded services, precursors of Victorianism, which may be of high quality but are too ornate to suit the average modern taste (fig.34). Fourth are services decorated only with transfer-printing (fig. 5). And last are services of unwieldy size—a service of 200 pieces is rarely worth double its counterpart of 100 pieces, since modern dinner parties (like the storage cupboards) have developed into more intimate affairs, and few hostesses today entertain on the grand scale for which many early 19th century services were made.

The buyers of these services, like collectors of antiques in other fields, recognize that, in this age of stress and confusion, it is innate in human nature to cling to the past: to the tried and true, and to a taste that has proved itself over the years.

● LETITIA ROBERTS ●

—33—
A Coalport porcelain dinner service, c.1830, patt. no. 951, comprising 162 pieces, some damage and wear, 52.5cm (20¾in), L 21 May, **£2,420 ($3,243)**

—34—
A Davenport porcelain dessert service, 1840-45, comprising 32 pieces, pattern no. 8751, in red or gilding, S 25 Mar, **£1,320 ($1,676)**

—35—
A G L Ashworth & Bros. Ltd. ironstone dinner service, late 19th century, comprising 99 pieces, each decorated in early 19th century taste, repair, venison dish 53cm (21in), L 21 May, **£7,920 ($10,613)**

—36—
A Flight, Barr & Barr part dessert service, c.1830, comprising 8 pieces, small chips, slight wear, impressed mark, fruit stand 31.5cm (12½in) diam, L 22 Oct, **£440 ($660)**

—37—
A Mintons porcelain dessert service, 1880-81, patt. no. G3439, comprising twelve plates and three stands, slight wear, impressed mark and date code, plate 23cm (9in), L 21 May, **£605 ($811)**

—38—
A Mintons porcelain dessert service, c.1875, patt. no. G.2213, comprising two tazze and twelve plates, impressed marks and date codes, plates 23cm (9in), S 28 Nov, **£495 ($733)**

—33—

—36—

—34—

—37—

—35—

—38—

Further reading

Monographs on Specific Factories

Coalport

Godden, Geoffrey A., *Coalport and Coalbrookdale Porcelains*, 1981 (revised from the 1970 edition).

Daniel

Berthoud, Michael, *H. & R. Daniel, 1822-1846*, 1980.

Davenport

Lockett, T. A., *Davenport Pottery and Porcelain, 1794-1887*, 1972.

Derby

Twitchett, John, *Derby Porcelain*, 1980.

Mason's

Godden, Geoffrey A., *Godden's Guide to Mason's China and the Ironstone Wares*, 1980.

Minton

Godden, Geoffrey A., *Minton Pottery and Porcelain of the First Period, 1793-1850*, 1968.

New Hall

Holgate, David, *New Hall and Its Imitators*, 1971.

Ridgway

Godden, Geoffrey A., *Ridgway Porcelains*, 1985.

Rockingham

Cox, Alwyn and Angela, *Rockingham Pottery and Porcelain, 1745-1842*, 1983.

Spode

Whiter, Leonard, *Spode*, 1970.

Worcester

Godden, Geoffrey A., *Chamberlain-Worcester Porcelain, 1788-1852*, 1982.

Sandon, Henry, *Flight and Barr Worcester Porcelain, 1783-1840*, 1978.

General Reference

Godden, Geoffrey A., *British Porcelain, An Illustrated Guide*, 1974.

Godden, Geoffrey A., *Encyclopedia of British Pottery and Porcelain Marks*, 1964 (and subsequent revised editions).

Godden, Geoffrey A., *An Illustrated Encylopedia of British Pottery and Porcelain*, 1968.

Godden, Geoffrey, *Godden's Guide to English Porcelain*, 1978.

Godden, Geoffrey (Editor and Main Author), *Staffordshire Porcelain*, 1983.

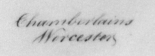

Chamberlain's Worcester, *c.*1800

Chamberlain & Co, Worcester, *c.*1840-45

G.L. Ashworth & Bros, Hanley, makers of Masons Patent Ironstone China, *c.*1862

Worcester, Flight, Barr & Barr, *c.*1813-40

Josiah Spode, Stoke-on-Trent, *c.*1820

Minton, Stoke-on-Trent, *c.*1875

Wedgwood, Etruria, 1st half 19th century

-39—
Hicks, Meigh and Johnson ironstone dinner service, 1825-35 comprising one hundred and four pieces, printed royal arms in underglaze blue, damaged, 16 Jan, 6,820 ($8,184)

1
An early blue and white Worcester cream boat, c.1753-5, painted in underglaze blue with 'The Cream Boat Warbler' pattern, workman's mark in underglaze blue, 13.5cm (5¼in), L 21 May, £2,090 ($2,801)

2
An early Worcester cream boat, c.1752-5, printed with two 'smoky primitives', one of a castle, the other of rustic dwellings, chips, 11cm (4½in), L 26 Feb, £1,870 ($2,094)

3
An early Worcester octagonal tea bowl, c.1753-5, painted in a famille verte palette with oriental style flowers and insects, 5.5cm (2¼in), L 21 May, £1,320 ($1,769)

4
A Worcester miniature tea bowl and saucer, c.1756-8, painter's marks, L 26 Feb, £880 ($986)

5
A Worcester tea bowl and saucer, c.1755, painted in underglaze blue, saucer chipped and cracked, painter's marks, L 21 May, £352 ($472)

6
A Worcester blue and white hors d'oeuvre dish, c.1760, painted in underglaze blue with 'the willow rock bird', open crescent mark in blue, chipped, 9cm (3¼in), S 25 Mar, £286 ($363)

7
A Worcester teapot and cover, c.1770, decorated with the 'Dragons in Compartments' pattern, knop and spout restored, seal mark in underglaze blue, 13cm (5in), L 21 May, £825 ($1,106)

8
A miniature Worcester teapot and cover, c.1756, painted with 'The Rock Warbler' pattern, chips, workman's mark, 8cm (3½in), S 25 Mar, £572 ($726)

9
A Worcester cauliflower tureen and cover, c.1760, 11cm (4¼in), L 23 July, £902 ($1,335)

10
A Worcester polychrome teapot and cover, 1760s, brightly enamelled with a Chinese scene, chipped spout, 16.5cm (6½in), S 14 Nov, £462 ($647)

11
An assembled pair of Worcester 'pine cone' pattern baskets, c.1775, transfer-printed in underglaze blue, hatched crescent marks in underglaze blue, 23 and 22.5cm (9 and 8¾in), NY 12 Apr, $990 (£792)

12
A Worcester basin, c.1765, painted in cobalt blue with a chinoiserie landscape, painted crescent mark, 28cm (11in), L 22 Oct, £682 ($1,023)

13
A Worcester 'Kakiemon' pattern dish, c.1765-70, painted in the atelier of James Giles, slight wear, 19.5cm (7¾in), L 21 May, £319 ($427)

14
A Worcester 'Japan' pattern fluted dish, c.1770, painted in an Imari palette, slight wear, seal mark, 18cm (7in), L 21 May, £275 ($369)

15
A Worcester 'Japan' pattern trio, c.1770, comprising tea bowl, coffee cup and saucer, each painted with orange gilt-diaper bands between demi-*kiku mon*, slight wear, L 21 May, £242 ($324)

16
A Worcester jug, c.1770, printed in black outline and coloured with chinoiserie figures, slight scratching, W mark, 9cm (3½in), L 21 May, £264 ($354)

A pair of 'brocade' pattern Worcester dishes, c.1770, each painted in polychrome enamels and gilding, some wear, gold crescent marks, 26.5cm (10½in), L 21 May, £770 ($1,032)

A Worcester 'Japan pattern Worcester dishes, c.1765-70, painted with iron-red *mon* and gilt leaves and flowers, chip, seal mark in underglaze blue, 14.5cm (5¾in), L 26 Feb, £418 ($468)

A pair of Worcester blue-scale dishes, first period, c.1770, painted in the atelier of James Giles, seal marks in underglaze blue, 24cm (9¾in), NY 1 Feb, £2,530 (£2,144)

A Worcester vase, c.1770, brilliantly enamelled with the phoenix pattern, powder blue ground, seal mark, 18.5cm (7¼in), L 21 May, £429 ($575)

A Worcester deep dish, c.1770, script W, slight wear, 32.5cm (12¾in), L 21 May, £1,100 ($1,474)

A pair of Worcester oval dishes, c.1770, with flower panels on blue-scale ground, slight wear, script W marks, 26.5cm (10½in), L 21 May, £1,045 ($1,400)

A Worcester milk jug and cover, c.1770, painted with kakiemon inspired flowers on the mottled scale ground, slight wear, chip, crescent mark, L 21 May, £605 ($811)

A Worcester apple-green-ground mug, c.1770, painted with brightly coloured exotic birds, firing imperfections, 12cm (4¾in), L 26 Feb, £880 ($986)

9
A Worcester tea canister and cover, c.1770, brilliantly enamelled with birds, blue-scale ground, chip, seal mark in underglaze blue, 17cm (6¾in), L 22 Oct, £1,210 ($1,815)

10
A pair of Barr, Flight & Barr plates, c.1807-13, each painted with the 'Lord Henry Thynne' pattern and named scenes, impressed crown and BFB, L 21 May, £880 ($1,179)

11
A Worcester teapot and cover, c.1770, painted in the manner of James Giles, 13.5cm (5¼in), L 26 Feb, £748 ($838)

12
A Worcester armorial mug, c.1770, painted with the arms of Thurlow, 12cm (4¾in), L 26 Feb, £1,045 ($1,170)

13
A Worcester trio, c.1770, comprising coffee cup, tea cup and saucer, 'wet blue' borders, some wear, crescent marks, L 21 May, £231 ($310)

14
A Worcester puce-scale milk jug, c.1770, painted in the atelier of James Giles, slight wear, crossed swords and 9 in underglaze blue, 11.5cm (4½in), L 22 Oct, £2,750 ($4,125)

1   2

3   4   5

6   7   8

9   10   11

12   13   14

1
A Worcester King of Prussia mug, c.1760, printed in black after Robert Hancock, firing fault and chip, 12cm (4¾in), *L 22 Oct,* £330 ($495)

2
A Worcester mug, c.1760-65, transfer-printed in black after Robert Hancock with 'The Whitton Anglers' and 'Milking Scene', *L 21 May,* £561 ($752)

3
A Flight and Barr Worcester porcelain tea service, c.1795, comprising twenty seven pieces, each painted and gilt with bands of brown scrolling foliage, *L 21 May,* £484 ($649)

4
A Worcester goblet, c.1810, probably Barr, Flight & Barr, painted with brightly coloured feathers, simulated grey veined marble, 12cm (4¾in), *L 26 Feb,* £2,530 ($2,834)

5
A Worcester teapot stand, c.1770, printed in puce with anglers in a river, some wear, 14.5cm (5¾in), *L 21 May,* £165 ($221)

6
A Barr, Flight & Barr part tea and coffee service, 1807-13, comprising twenty nine pieces, most pieces with impressed crowned BFB marks, *NY 10 Oct,* $2,860 (£2,028)

7
A Barr, Flight & Barr named view sugar bowl, c.1810, painted with two views of Fountains Abbey, Yorkshire, impressed BFB beneath a crown, 19cm (7½in), *C 2 Oct,* £297 ($433)

8
A pair of Barr, Flight & Barr dessert tureens and covers, c.1810, impressed and puce printed marks, 16cm (6¼in) high, *S 25 Mar,* £1,980 ($2,515)

9
A Barr, Flight & Barr tea cup and saucer, c.1807, gilding rubbed, saucer with painted mark, saucer 14cm (5½in), *L 21 May,* £1,760 ($2,358)

10
A Flight, Barr & Barr tea cup and saucer, c.1813-40, painted with a band of flower studies on a cream ground, some wear, impressed crown and FBB, *L 21 May,* £286 ($383)

11
A Flight, Barr & Barr candleholder, c.1815, painted with a panel illustrating Canto 5 of the 'Lady of the Lake', gilding rubbed, script marks, 17cm (6¾in), *L 22 Oct,* £770 ($1,155)

12
A Chamberlain & Co flower-encrusted basket, c.1840, chips, painted red Chamberlain and Co, Worcester, *L 21 May,* £660 ($884)

13
A Chamberlains Worcester dessert service, c.1800, comprising sixteen plates and a shell-shaped dish, some wear, chips, painted mark, plate 21cm (8¼in), *L 22 Oct,* £715 ($1,073)

14
A Flight, Barr & Barr plate, c.1815, painted with three vignettes of rustic figures, apple-green ground, impressed crown and FBB and printed mark, 22.5cm (8¾in), *L 21 May,* £385 ($516)

1
A Worcester chocolate cup and stand, c.1770, enamelled in blue with stripes alternating with gilt lines and ermine, slight wear, saucer 15cm (6in), *L 21 May*, £330 ($442)

2
A Worcester chestnut basket, cover and stand, c.1770, red anchor mark on basket and stand, one handle missing, 25cm (10in), *HS 16 July*, £858 ($1,244)

3
A Royal Worcester vase, 1920, pierced by George Owen, signed, printed crowned circle mark, 22.5cm (8¾in), *L 23 July*, £2,530 ($3,744)

4
A Worcester 'Dolphin' ewer, c.1765-70, hair crack, 8cm (3¼in), *L 22 Oct*, £638 ($957)

5
A Worcester 'Kempthorne' pattern teapot and cover, c.1770, 14.5cm (5¾in), and matching stand, restored, seal mark, 14.5cm (5¾in), *L 21 May*, £528 ($708)

6
A set of six Royal Worcester plates, post-1956, each painted by J. Cook, F Higgins, J Smith or Sibley Lewis, signed, printed crowned circle mark, 27cm (10½in), *L 23 July*, £550 ($814)

7
A Worcester sucrier and cover, c.1770, chip, crescent mark, 12cm (4¾in), *L 22 Oct*, £330 ($495)

8
A Worcester polychrome vase, c.1760, 11.7cm (4⅝in), *S 10 July*, £682 ($914)

9
A pair of Royal Worcester jars and covers, modern, painted by Freeman, signed, printed crowned circle mark and shape numbers, 18cm (7in), *L 21 May*, £770 ($1,032)

10
A Royal Worcester pot-pourri vase and cover, late 19th century, printed marks, 32cm (12½in), *C 12 Nov*, £330 ($462)

11
A pair of Worcester leaf-shaped dishes, c.1770, enamelled in the atelier of James Giles, crack, some wear, 26.5cm (10½in), *L 21 May*, £352 ($472)

12
A Royal Worcester tea service, 1925, painted by E Spilsbury, signed, comprising 38 pieces, purple printed marks with date codes, *C 17 Apr*, £275 ($358)

13
A pair of Grainger's Worcester vases, 1880s, printed marks, 34cm (13½in), *S 31 May*, £242 ($319)

14
A Royal Worcester vase, 1909, painted by John Stinton, signed, printed crowned circle mark, 33cm (15in), *L 26 Feb*, £1,870 ($2,094)

15
A Royal Worcester vase, 1929, painted by H Stinton, signed, printed crowned circle mark, 19.5cm (7¾in), *L 23 July*, £418 ($619)

16
A set of six Royal Worcester coffee cups and saucers, 1931, painted by H Stinton, or Stinton signed, printed crowned circle mark, sold with six silver-gilt coffee spoons, *L 21 May*, £1,540 ($2,064)

17
A Royal Worcester vase and cover, 1907, painted by Harry Davis, signed, printed mark in puce with date code, 29.2cm (11½in), *C 16 Jan*, £935 ($1,122)

18
A Royal Worcester ewer, c.1900, painted by C H Baldwyn, signed, printed crowned circle mark, 40cm (15¾in), *L 22 Oct*, £2,200 ($3,300)

1
A Wedgwood creamware
punch pot and cover,
1780s, printed in black,
probably by Sadler &
Green, minor chips,
impressed Wedgwood,
20cm (8in), *S 14 Nov,*
£1,540 ($2,156)

2
A Wedgwood creamware
transfer-printed and
enamelled jug, dated
1783, one side with a
black and yellow sailing
ship, the other printed
in black with Diana,
impressed Wedgwood,
22cm (8½in), *NY 12 Apr,*
$1,650 (£1,320)

3
A Wedgwood & Bentley
black basaltes portrait
medallion of Sir
William Hamilton,
*c.*1772, small crack,
16cm (6¼in), *L 21 May,*
£3,960 ($5,306)

4
A pair of Wedgwood black
basaltes vases, early
19th century, each in
the form of a Greek
'krater', one damaged,
chips, impressed mark,
20.5cm (8in), *L 23 July,*
£385 ($570)

5
A Wedgwood black
basaltes vase and cover,
early 19th century,
knop damaged, 35cm
(13¾in), *C 16 Jan,*
£462 ($554)

6
A Wedgwood black
basaltes vase and cover,
early 19th century,
impressed mark, 33.5cm
(13¼in), *C 16 Jan,*
£396 ($475)

7
A pair of Wedgwood &
Bentley 'porphyry' vases,
*c.*1770, decorated to
simulate mottled green
hardstone, with medal-
lions of the 'Three
Graces' and 'Sacrifice to
Aesculapius', damaged,
moulded circular mark,
24cm (9½in), *L 23 July,*
£1,375 ($2,035)

8
A pair of Wedgwood
black basaltes figures of
griffins, late 18th/early
19th century, each sup-
porting a candle nozzle,
some repairs, impressed
marks, 34cm (13½in),
NY 12 Apr,
$1,430 (£1,144)

9
A pair of Wedgwood blue-
jasper-dip potpourri
vases, covers and stands,
third quarter 19th cen-
tury, one vase cracked,
chips, impressed
mark, 65cm (25½in),
L 26 Feb,
£1,870 ($2,094)

10
A pair of Wedgwood blue
jasper-dip and gilt-metal
lustres, mid-19th cen-
tury, one glass drop
incomplete, impressed
mark, 18cm (7in),
L 26 Feb,
£528 ($591)

11
A matched pair of
Wedgwood blue and white
jasper bough pots and
covers, late 19th century,
one base repaired,
impressed mark, 18 and
18.5cm (7 and 7¼in),
NY 12 Apr,
$275 (£220)

12
A pair of Wedgwood three-
colour jasper mantle
ornaments, mounted in
gilt-metal, late 19th
century, impressed
mark, 30.5cm (12in),
NY 12 Apr,
$1,650 (£1,320)

13
A pair of Wedgwood three-
colour jasperware vases
and covers, 19th century,
one cover chipped,
36cm (14¼in), *S 25 Mar,*
£1,045 ($1,327)

14
A pair of Wedgwood
black basaltes triton
candlestick figures, 1862
or 1888, impressed
marks, repaired, 27.5cm
(10¾in), *S 25 Mar,*
£253 ($321)

15
A Wedgwood black-jasper-
dip Portland Vase, late
19th century, small
chip, impressed mark,
25.5cm (10in), *L 23 July,*
£990 ($1,465)

Three Wedgwood blue and white jasper portait medallions, late 19th century, depicting Sir William Hamilton, Earl St Vincent and Admiral Duncan, framed, impressed Wedgwood marks, 11.5cm (4½in) and 10cm (4in), *C 16 Jan,* 220 ($264)

A pair of Wedgwood black-jasper-dip cabinet plates, mid- to late 19th century, impressed mark, 22cm (8¾in), *23 July,* 968 ($1,433)

A Wedgwood earthenware vase, 1865, painted by Edouard Rischgitz, signed, minor chip, impressed mark, *22 Oct,* 660 ($990)

A Wedgwood Three-Colour jasper cup, cover and stand, early 19th century, impressed Wedgwood, *C 16 Jan,* 550 ($660)

A Wedgwood porcelain dessert service, *c.*1900, comprising eighteen pieces, slight wear, printed and impressed marks, 23cm (9in), *21 May,* 352 ($472)

A Wedgwood Fairyland Lustre 'Malfrey Pot and Cover', *c.*1925, decorated in the 'Coral and Bronze' palette with the 'Candlemass' design, printed urn mark, 24cm (9½in), *26 Feb,* 3,300 ($3,696)

A Wedgwood flame Fairyland Lustre vase, 1920s, decorated with the 'Torches' pattern, small chip, printed urn mark, incised shape number 2177, Z4968, 29cm (11½in), *L 21 May,* 990 ($1,327)

8
A Wedgwood flame Fairy-land Lustre 'Trumpet' vase, 1920s, decorated with the 'Butterfly Women' design, printed urn mark, Z5360, incised shape number 2810, 20cm (8in), *L 22 Oct,* £528 ($792)

9
A Wedgwood 'Lahore' lustre vase and cover, 1920-29, printed urn mark, incised shape number 2311, Z5266, 21cm (8¼in), *L 26 Feb,* £2,200 ($2,464)

10
A Wedgwood Fairyland Lustre bowl, 1920s, the interior decorated with the 'Woodland Elves' pattern, the exterior with 'Poplar Trees', slight wear, printed urn mark, Z4968, 27.5cm (10¾in), *L 21 May,* £440 ($590)

11
A Wedgwood Fairyland Lustre pedestal bowl, 1920s, decorated with a version of the 'Fairy Gondola' design, printed Portland vase mark, inscribed Z5340, 27cm (10½in), *C 2 Oct,* £638 ($931)

12
A Wedgwood Fairyland Lustre octagonal bowl, 1920s, Portland Vase mark in gilding, 21.5cm (8½in), *C 17 Apr,* £561 ($729)

13
A Wedgwood Fairyland Lustre octagonal bowl, 1920s, printed Portland Vase mark, 18cm (7in), *C 16 Jan,* £715 ($858)

Decorative Arts from 1880

1
A Tiffany Favrile glass and bronze bud vase, 1899-1920, inscribed, the amber glass vase decorated with green feathering and fitting into bronze support, 63.5cm (25in), *NY 18 May*, $1,430 (£1,135)

2
A Tiffany Favrile glass vase, 1899-1920, inscribed 'Louis C Tiffany', the opalescent sea-green sides decorated with pale green and mustard feathering, 56cm (22in), *NY 18 May*, $3,410 (£2,706)

3
A Tiffany Favrile glass Jack-in-the-Pulpit vase, *c*.1912, in amber iridescent glass tinged with magenta, aqua, salmon and gold, base cracked, 44.5cm (17½in). *NY 18 May*, $935 (£742)

4
A Tiffany Favrile glass Jack-in-the-Pulpit vase, *c*.1916, in blue iridescent glass tinged with amber and pink, 49cm (19¼in), *NY 18 May*, $14,850 (£11,786)

5
A Tiffany Favrile glass cabinet vase, *c*.1900, in deep-aubergine decorated with silver-blue feathering, 9.5cm (3¾in), *NY 18 May*, $1,320 (£1,048)

6
A Tiffany Favrile paper-weight glass finger bowl and under-plate, 1892-1928, the clear glass decorated with rose, amber and green lotus blossoms and foliage, plate 18.5cm (7¼in) diam, *NY 18 May*, $880 (£698)

7
A set of ten Tiffany Favrile intaglio-carved punch cups, 1899-1920, each amber iridescent cup carved with vine clusters and leaves, 9cm (3½in) high, *NY 6 Dec*, $1,650 (£1,115)

8
A Tiffany Favrile glass vase, *c*.1896, in greyish mint-green decorated in deep-green, 42.5cm (16¾in) high, *NY 18 May*, $3,520 (£2,794)

9
A Tiffany Favrile glass stoppered decanter and six liquer glasses, 1892-1928, in amber iridescent glass, decanter 25.5.cm (10in), *NY 18 May*, $1,430 (£1,135)

10
A Tiffany glass vase, *c*.1900, in iridescent opalescent glass streaked in gold, 32cm (12½in), *M 17 Mar*, FF 17,760 (£1,586; $1,951)

1

2

5

6

7

8

9   10

1
A Daum landscape lamp, c.1900, cameo mark, in yellow glass mottled in red and overlaid in green, 43cm (17in), M 17 Mar, FF 33,300 (£2,973; $3,657)

2
A Handel painted-glass and patinated-metal landscape lamp, early 20th century, the shade in tones of green, yellow, orange and brown, rim chip and missing finial, 56cm (22in), NY 23 Feb, $1,430 (£1,336)

3
A Rateau gilt-bronze lamp, c.1925, impressed mark, 37cm (14½in), NY 7 Dec, $2,530 (£1,709)

4
A Degue cameo glass and wrought-iron landscape lamp, c.1930, signed in cameo, the shade and base in yellow glass mottled with cherry-red and overlaid in chocolate, 38.5cm (15½in), NY 17 May, $1,760 (£1,397)

5
A Scheider 'Le Verre Francais' cameo glass and wrought-iron lamp, c.1930, embedded candy-cane mark, the shade in grey mottled with dusty rose and overlaid in pumpkin, 37cm (14½in) high, NY 17 May, $990 (£786)

6
An Edgar Brandt bronze lamp with Daum shades, c.1925, 49cm (19¼in), M 6 Oct, FF 23,310 (£2,027; $3,000)

7
A Tiffany Favrile glass and bronze turtle-back tile border lamp, 1900-1920, the shade with amber glass and turtle-back tiles, 51.5cm (20¼in), NY 18 May, $7,700 (£6,111)

8
A Tiffany Favrile glass and bronze four-branch candelabrum, the shades decorated in green and the candlecups set with green glass 'jewels', 42.5cm (17¾in), NY 18 May, $2,860 (£2,270)

9
A Tiffany Favrile glass and gilt-bronze seven-light lily lamp, 1899-1920, the shades in tones of iridescent amber, 51 cm (20¼in), NY 18 May, $4,675 (£3,710)

10
A Tiffany Favrile glass and bronze geometric lamp, 1899-1920, the shade in mint-green with yellow ivy-leaf band, 58.5cm (23in) high, NY 18 May, $3,740 (£2,968)

11
A Tiffany Favrile glass and bronze candlestick lamp, 1899-1920, the shade decorated in rust and yellow, 44cm (17¼in), NY 18 May, $1,430 (£1,135)

12
A Tiffany Studios leaded glass table lamp, c.1900, the shade with apple blossom design in blue, white, pink and dark green against an apple green ground, 67cm (26½in) high, L 2 May, £10,450 ($13,480)

13
A Tiffany Favrile glass poppy shade, 1899-1920, with brilliant red and green poppies against turquoise and blue ground, 41cm (16in) diam, together with an American patinated-metal base, NY 7 Dec, $11,000 (£7,432)

14
A Tiffany Favrile glass and bronze pomegranate lamp, 1899-1920, the shade with lemon-yellow tiles and band of green pomegranates, 42cm (16½in) high, NY 6 Dec, $2,420 (£1,635)

1
A Val Saint-Lambert vase,
c.1900, cameo mark,
in clear glass overlaid
in white, brown and
green, 60.5cm (23¾in),
M 6 Oct,
FF 38,850 (£3,379; $5,001)

2
**An F Marquis iridescent
glass vase,** c.1900,
engraved mark, in pale
green glass decorated
with peacock/green
lustre, 16.5cm (6½in),
L 4 Dec,
£176 ($246)

3
**A Muller Freres cameo
glass vase,** c.1900, signed,
decorated in shades of
green, the top cut with
artichoke leaves, 34.5cm
(13½in), NY 6 Dec,
$1,320 (£892)

4
**A Muller Freres cameo
glass landscape vase,**
c.1900, cameo mark, in
yellow glass overlaid in
orange and brown,
28.5cm (11¼in), L 4 Dec,
£825 ($1,155)

5
**A Daum cameo glass
vase,** c.1900, cameo mark
in mottled grey glass
tinged with amber/
green, overlaid in grey/
green and russet,
34.5cm (13½in), L 5 July,
£418 ($577)

6
A Daum cameo glass vase,
c.1900, cameo mark,
with mauve streaked
glass overlaid in green,
and red enamelled
berries, 70cm (27½in),
L 17 Oct,
£968 ($1,433)

7
A Daum glass vase, c.1900,
engraved mark, tinged
with orange, yellow and
blue, overlaid in green,
decorated with white
and mauve violets, 18cm
(7in), M 6 Oct,
FF 12,765 (£1,110; $1,643)

8
**A Daum etched and
carved cameo glass vase,**
c.1900, engraved mark,
in mottled yellow and
pink glass, overlaid in
red and green, 14.5cm
(5¾in), L 5 July
£1,210 ($1,670)

9
**A Daum glass bottle and
stopper,** c.1900, gilt
mark, in clear glass with
mauve interior, decor-
ated in red, white and
black enamelling, gilt
details, 8cm (7in),
M 6 Oct,
FF, 3,552 (£309; $458)

10
**A Daum etched and
enamelled glass vase,**
c.1900, gilt mark 'Daum
Nancy', decorated in
brown and green
enamels with gilt
details, 29cm (11¼in),
L 2 May,
£715 ($922)

11
**A Daum Nancy cameo
glass vase,** c.1910, signed
in intaglio, in acid-
etched creamy glass
overlaid in cherry red,
51cm (20in), NY 17 May,
$1,540 (£1,222)

12
**A Daum Nancy cameo
glass vase,** c.1910, cameo
mark, in mottled grey
and purple glass over-
laid in orange and
green, 52cm (20½in),
NY 23 Feb,
$1,760 (£1,645)

13
**A Daum Nancy cameo
glass vase,** c.1910, cameo
mark, in blue-grey glass
streaked in green,
overlaid in green and
brown, 66.5cm (26¼in),
NY 23 Feb,
$1,760 (£1,645)

1

2

3

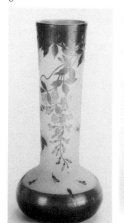

4

5

6

7

8

9

10

11

12

13

Daum acid-etched glass
ase, *c.*1925, engraved
mark, in dark green
lass, 26cm (10¼in),
M 17 Mar,
F 3,885 (£346; $425)

Daum etched green
lass vase, 1920s, marked
Daum Nancy France',
0cm (11¾in), *L 15 Feb,*
462 ($536)

Daum Nancy cameo
lass landscape vase,
1912, cameo mark,
he yellow, apricot,
almon and rose sides
verlaid in burgundy,
9.5cm (11½in),
Y 23 Feb,
4,070 (£3,804)

Daum etched glass
ase, 1920s, engraved
gnature, 20.5cm (8in),
5 July,
418 ($577)

Daum acid-etched pink
lass vase, 1920s, marked,
4cm (9½in), *L 5 July,*
418 ($577)

Daum acid-etched glass
owl, *c.*1930, inscribed
ark, with thick brown
lass walls on frosted
round, 36cm (14in),
Y 17 May,
2,970 (£2,357)

Daum glass vase with
ajorelle iron mounts,
1925, engraved mark
the form of a bucket,
e colourless glass with
ust decoration, 30cm
1¾in), *M 6 Oct,*
F 6,600 (£574; $850)

Loetz iridescent glass
ase, *c.*1900, in ruby
ed glass with peacock/
old lustre, 23cm (9in),
15 Feb,
935 ($1,085)

n iridescent glass vase,
1900, attributed to
oetz, in ruby red glass
ith feathered pink/
eacock lustre, 31cm
2¼in), *L 2 May,*
374 ($482)

10
A Loetz iridescent glass
vase, *c.*1900, in amber
glass overlaid in blue
and green, 14cm (5½in),
NY 23 Feb,
$495 (£463)

11
A Loetz iridescent glass
vase, *c.*1900, inscribed
'Loetz/Austria', in
shades of blue decorated
with silver-blue, 30cm
(11¾in), *NY 23 Feb,*
$1,100 (£1,028)

12
A Loetz iridescent glass
vase, *c.*1900, in deep
red decorated with
silver-blue, 20cm (8in),
NY 23 Feb,
$715 (£668)

13
A Loetz iridescent glass
vase, *c.*1900, inscribed
'Loetz/Austria', in
deep amber tinged with
silver-blue, 23cm (9in),
NY 23 Feb,
$550 (£514)

14
A Loetz iridescent glass
vase, *c.*1900, in yellow-
green glass streaked
with blue, green, violet
and light blue, 17cm
(6¾in), *NY 23 Feb,*
$2,090 (£1,953)

15
Two Loetz iridescent glass
vases, *c.*1900, both in
yellow-green glass
decorated with silver-
blue, 12.5cm (4¾in),
NY 23 Feb,
$660 (£617)

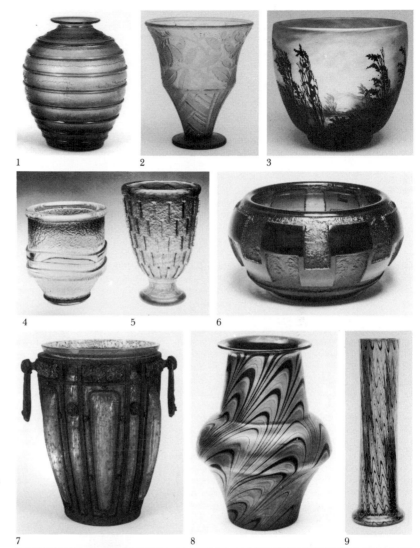

1
A Gallé cameo glass lamp,
*c.*1900, base and shade
with cameo mark, in
yellow tinted grey glass,
overlaid in deep red
blossom, 56.5cm
(22¼in), *L 4 Dec,*
£11,000 ($15,400)

2
A Gallé cameo glass lamp,
*c.*1900, cameo mark, in
grey glass tinted in
orange pink and
streaked throughout in
deep blue and green,
59cm (23¼in), *L 5 July,*
£7,150 ($9,867)

3
A Gallé glass lamp, *c.*1900,
cameo mark, in yellow
glass overlaid in blue
and mauve, 26cm (10¼in),
M 6 Oct,
FF 63,270
(£5,502; $8,232)

4
**A Gallé cameo glass table
lamp,** *c.*1900, shade and
base each with cameo
mark, in yellow glass
overlaid with pink and
dark red prunus blos-
som, 28.5cm (11¼in),
L 4 Dec,
£7,700 ($10,780)

5
A Gallé glass bowl, *c.*1900,
cameo mark, in opales-
cent glass shot with blue
and amber, overlaid in
red, 7.5cm (3in) wide,
M 6 Oct,
FF 7,215 (£628; $929)

6
A Gallé cameo glass vase,
*c.*1900, cameo mark, in
red/pink glass overlaid
in red, 15.5cm (6in),
M 6 Oct,
FF 7,770 (£676; $1,000)

7
A Gallé cameo glass vase,
*c.*1910, cameo mark, in
grey/blue glass overlaid
in rose and olive-green,
16.5cm (6½in), *M 6 Oct,*
FF 6,600 (£574; $850)

8
A Gallé cameo glass vase,
*c.*1910, cameo mark, in
grey glass overlaid in
mauve, 59cm (23¼in),
M 6 Oct,
FF 13,875
(£1,207; $1,787)

9
A Gallé cameo glass vase,
*c.*1900, cameo mark, in
pink glass tinted in blue,
overlaid in pink/mauve
and pale green, 46cm
(18in), *L 4 Dec,*
£2,090 ($2,926)

10
A Gallé cameo glass vase,
*c.*1900, cameo mark, in
grey glass overlaid in
mauve, 34.5cm (13½in),
M 6 Oct,
FF 4,995 (£434; $642)

11
A Gallé glass vase, *c.*1900,
cameo mark, in yellow
glass overlaid in red,
16.5cm (6½in), *M 6 Oct,*
FF 7,770 (£676; $1,000)

12
**A Gallé cameo landscape
glass vase,** *c.*1900, cameo
mark, in amber glass
overlaid in brown, 35cm
(13¾in), *M 6 Oct,*
FF 13,320
(£1,160; $1,717)

13
**A Gallé glass bonbon-
nière,** *c.*1900, cameo
mark, in opalescent grey
glass overlaid in brown,
14.5cm (5¾in) diam,
M 6 Oct,
FF 6,438 (£560; $829)

14
**A Gallé mould-blown
cameo glass clematis vase,**
*c.*1925, cameo mark, in
frosty-white overlaid in
apple green, 25.5cm
(10in), *NY 17 May,*
$2,750 (£2,183)

1 2 3 4 5 6 7 8 9 10 11 12 13 14

1

A Gallé enamelled glass bottle and stopper, c.1890, engraved mark, the clear glass decorated in blue, yellow and green enamelled flowers, outlined in gilding, 30cm (11¾in), L 2 May, £330 ($425)

2

A Gallé enamelled glass vase, c.1890, marked, decorated in blue, rust, black, white and mauve enamels, outlined in gilding, 27cm (10½in), M 6 Oct, FF 12,210 (£1,062; $1,572)

3

A Gallé cameo landscape glass vase, c.1910, cameo mark, in yellow glass overlaid in brown, 25.5cm (10in), M 6 Oct, FF 7,770 (£676; $1,000)

4

A Gallé cameo glass box and cover, c.1900, cameo mark, the body with apple-green tint, the cover in light pink overlaid in deep red, 13cm (5in) diam, L 17 Oct, £506 ($708)

5

A pair of Gallé cameo glass sconces, c.1900, cameo signature, in grey glass tinged with blue, 24cm (9½in), NY 7 Dec, $3,300 (£2,229)

6

A Gallé cameo glass vase, c.1900, cameo signature, the dusty-rose walls splashed in white and overlaid in lavender and green, 43cm (17in), NY 23 Feb, $3,850 (£3,598)

7

A Gallé cameo glass vase, c.1900, cameo mark, in pink glass overlaid in green and brown, 9cm (3½in), L 15 Feb, £286 ($332)

8

A Gallé cameo glass bowl, c.1900, cameo mark, in pink/grey glass overlaid with purple and grey/green, L 5 July, £506 ($698)

9

A Gallé cameo glass vase, c.1900, cameo mark, in grey glass overlaid in purple, 16.5cm (6½in), L 4 Dec, £462 ($647)

10

A Gallé cameo glass vase, c.1900, signed in cameo, 45cm (17¾in), NY 23 Feb, $1,210 (£1,131)

11

A Gallé cameo glass vase, c.1900, cameo signature, in citron-yellow glass overlaid in blue and violet, 32cm (12½in) high, NY 23 Feb, $1,980 (£1,850)

12

A Gallé cameo glass vase, c.1900, cameo signature, in lemon-yellow glass tinged with grey and cranberry, 35.5cm (14in), NY 23 Feb, $1,650 (£1,542)

13

A Gallé cameo glass vase, c.1900, cameo signature, in grey glass splashed with pink, overlaid in white, violet and green, 35.5cm (14in), NY 23 Feb, $770 (£720)

14

A Gallé cameo glass vase, c.1900, cameo signature, in misty white glass overlaid in violet and deep purple, 56cm (22in), NY 23 Feb, $2,640 (£2,467)

1
A Lalique glass scent bottle and stopper, c.1920, impressed mark, moulded with classical figures, with brown staining, 15.5cm (6in), *L 17 Oct*, £418 ($619)

2
A Lalique glass bottle and stopper, c.1925, inscribed 'R Lalique' and numbered 6, moulded with pairs of frolicking couples, 29cm (11½in), *NY 7 Dec*, $2,200 (£1,486)

3
Two Lalique glass scent bottles, c.1925, the first moulded 'R Lalique France', the latter, a display bottle, acid stamped 'R Lalique, Worth/Made in France'. both with enamelled blue decoration, 9 and 28cm (3½ and 11in), *NY 17 May*, $880 (£698)

4
A Lalique opalescent glass vase, 1920s, engraved 'R Lalique France', moulded with naked women pouring water from urns, 18cm (7in), *L 17 Oct*, £1,045 ($1,547)

5
A Lalique glass vase, 1930s, stencilled mark, with deep blue staining, 24cm (9½in), *L 2 May*, £572 ($737)

6
A Lalique glass liquer set, 1930s, stencilled marks, comprising decanter and stopper and six glasses, stems and decanter neck with blue staining, decanter 20cm (8in), *L 2 May*, £572 ($737)

7
Two Lalique glass scent bottles, 1930s, 22 and 18.5cm (8¾ and 7¼in), *L 2 May*, £418 ($539)

8
A Lalique glass clock vase, c.1930, moulded mark, the face by Ato, 15.5cm (6in), *L 2 May*, £682 ($879)

9
A Lalique scent bottle and stopper, 'Amphytrite', 1930s, incised 'R Lalique' and numbered 514, the glass with faint blue staining, 9.5cm (3½in), *S 23 Oct*, £396 ($594)

10
A Lalique glass bottle and stopper, stencilled mark, moulded with stars, deep blue staining, 26.5cm (10in), *L 5 July*, £605 ($835)

11
A Lalique glass flower-form candle-holder, c.1930, engraved mark 23cm (9in), *L 15 Feb*, £308 ($357)

12
A Lalique moulded amber glass figure, 'Suzanne', c.1932, moulded mark, 24cm (9½in), *NY 23 Feb*, $4,620 (£4,318)

13
A pair of Lalique glass scent bottles, 1930s, stencilled mark, moulded as sea urchins, black enamel details, 9.5cm (3¾in), *L 5 July*, £176 ($243)

14
A Lalique glass figure of a bird, c.1930, moulded mark 'R Lalique France', light amethyst tint, 14.5cm (5¾in), *L 17 Oct*, £308 ($456)

1
A Wiener Werkstätte glass goblet, designed by Otto Prutscher, c.1910, the colourless glass cased in red, 21cm (8¼in), *L 2 May*, £1,210 ($1,560)

2
A Wiener Werkstätte enamelled glass vase, 1920s, in deep blue glass enamelled in black and white, 15cm (6in), *L 4 Dec*, £660 ($924)

3
A Wiener Werkstätte green glass vase, c.1910/20, the design attributed to Josef Hoffmann, with 'WW' monogram, 14.5cm (5¾in), *L 2 May*, £770 ($993)

4
An Argy Rousseau 'pate de cristal' box and cover, 1920s, marked, the amber and grey body decorated in white, yellow and brown, 8cm (3in), *L 4 Dec*, £1,320 ($1,848)

5
A Walter 'pate de cristal' vase, designed by H Berge, moulded marks, the pink-grey glass mottled in mauve, ochre and green, 18cm (7in), *L 2 May*, £2,090 ($2,696)

6
A Schneider glass vase, c.1920, signed, with lime-green body decorated with blue, tangerine base and plum foot, 42cm (16½in), *NY 17 May*, $2,860 (£2,270)

7
A Goupy enamelled glass bottle and stopper, c.1925, marked, decorated with blue, white and black enamelled flowers, 20.5cm (8in), *M 6 Oct*, FF 2,775 (£242; $358)

8
A Libbey intaglio-carved glass vase, c.1925, acid stamped mark, the black glass carved to grey, with green highlights, 35cm (13¾in), *NY 23 Feb*, $1,100 (£1,028)

9
An Orrefors smoked glass coupe, c.1925, in deep smoked blue/grey glass, 15cm (6in), *L 4 Dec*, £352 ($493)

10
An Argy Rousseau 'pate de cristal' bowl, 1920s, 11cm (4¼in) diam, *L 4 Dec*, £4,290 ($6,006)

11
A Schneider glass vase, 1920s, signed, in blue mottled glass with yellow glass stringing, 26.5cm (10¼in), *C 2 Oct*, £231 ($337)

12
A vase decorated by Maurice Marinot, c.1930, signed, in colourless glass with acid-etched panels and green marbling, 15cm (6in), *M 6 Oct*, FF 44,400 (£3,861; $5,714)

13
A Francois Decorchement 'pate de cristal' vase, 1929-30, marked, the amber glass with burgundy marbling, *M 17 Mar*, FF 33,300 (£2,973; $3,656)

14
A Charles Boyton glass tazza, 1930s, signed, 27.5cm (10¾in), *L 4 Dec*, £165 ($231)

15
A Venetian glass vase, designed by Guido Balsamo Stella for Salir, c.1930, the pale blue glass engraved with mermaids and aquatic motifs, 37cm (14½in), *NY 7 Dec*, $1,430 (£966)

16
An Orrefors glass drinking set, designed by Vicke Lindstrand, 1940s, comprising decanter and twelve glasses, all engraved with circus figures, decanter 29.5cm (11½in), *L 5 July*, £660 ($911)

17
A Nuutajarvi Notsjo glass bottle, designed by Kaj Franck, 1960s, signed and numbered 65, the clear glass body with trails of black, 34cm (13¼in), *L 4 Dec*, £209 ($293)

1
A De Morgan 'Persian'
vase, early 1900s,
painted by Fred Pas-
senger, marked, 57cm
(22½in), *S 23 Oct,*
£12,100 ($18,150)

2
A De Morgan lustre vase,
decorated by Fred
Passenger, 1890s, pain-
ted 'W De Morgan
Fulham and artist's
initials, decorated in
mauve, pale-blue and
yellow, 32.5cm (12¾in),
L 3 May,
£880 ($1,126)

3
Two ruby lustre tiles,
*c.*1900, probably painted
by Charles Passenger,
Wedgwood's moulded
Portland vase mark,
15cm (6in), *S 15 May,*
£297 ($395)

4
A pair of ruby lustre
tiles, *c.*1900, probably
painted by Charles
Passenger, Wedgwood's
moulded Portland vase
mark, 15cm (6in),
S 15 May,
£297 ($395)

5
Two ruby lustre tiles,
*c.*1900, probably painted
by Charles Passenger,
Wedgwood's moulded
Portland vase mark,
15cm (6in), *S 15 May,*
£297 ($395)

6
Two ruby lustre tiles,
*c.*1900, probably decor-
ated by Charles Pas-
senger, Wedgwood's
moulded Portland vase
mark, 15cm (6in),
S 15 May,
£286 ($380)

7
A pair of ruby lustre tiles,
*c.*1900 probably painted
by Charles Passenger,
Wedgwood's moulded
Portland vase mark,
15cm (6in), *S 15 May,*
£66 ($88)

8
A De Morgan ruby lustre
vase, decorated by James
Hersey, 1888-97,
impressed Sand's End
mark, painted initials
and numbered 2227, rim
chips, 21cm (8¼in),
L 3 May,
£330 ($422)

9
A Moorcroft Macintyre
vase, with purple and
blue wisteria on a cream
ground, 26cm (10¼in),
C 29 Jan,
£462 ($545)

10
A Moorcroft ginger jar
and cover, 28.5cm
(11¼in), *C 14 May,*
£385 ($512)

11
A Moorcroft pottery
'Hazledene' vase, *c.*1920,
signed, decorated in
blue-grey, green and
blue, 42cm (16½in),
NY 23 Feb,
$1,045 (£977)

12
A Moorcroft Macintyre
tyg, *c.*1900, printed mark,
painted signature,
tube-lined with tulips
and cornflowers in
green, blue and red,
11cm (4¼in), *L 3 May,*
£264 ($337)

13
A Moorcroft Macintyre
'Florian Ware' vase,
*c.*1900, printed Florian
mark, painted signa-
ture, tube-lined with
poppies and leaves in
blue and green, 30.5cm
(12in), *L 5 July,*
£330 ($455)

14
A Moorcroft Macintyre
'Florian Ware' vase,
*c.*1900, printed marks,
painted signature, tube-
lined with poppies and
leaves in shades of blue,
30cm (11¾in), *L 3 May,*
£330 ($422)

15
A Moorcroft 'Hazeldene'
vase, 1912, printed
Liberty mark, painted
signature, tube-lined
with trees in green, blue
and yellow, 30cm
(11¾in), *L 3 May,*
£990 ($1,267)

16
A pair of Moorcroft
vases, *c.*1920, green
script signature,
impressed Burslem
mark, trailed in white
slip with dark coloured
glazes, 32cm (12½in),
C 16 Jan,
£1,100 ($1,320)

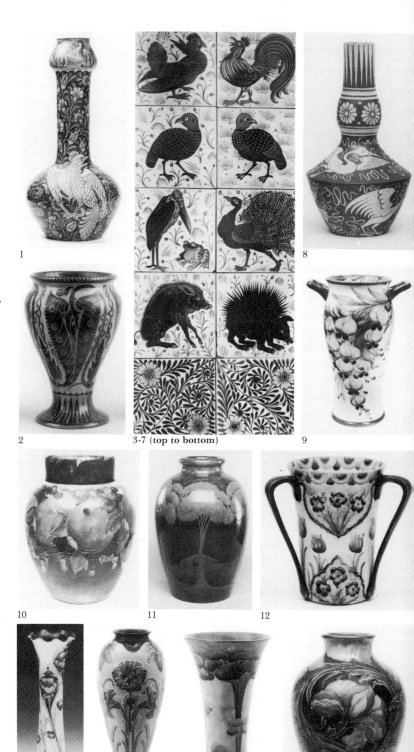

1

2

3-7 (top to bottom)

8

9

10

11

12

13

14

15

16

1
A pair of Florence Barlow vases, with Lucy A Barlow's monogram, each with four oval panels of robins, 20cm (8in) high, *C 6 Aug,* £638 ($951)

2
A pair of Royal Doulton vases, decorated by Florence Barlow, 1902, impressed marks, incised artist's monogram 349, painted in green and white slips against a mottled green glazed ground, 31.5cm (12½in), *L 5 July,* £638 ($880)

3
A pair of Royal Doulton vases, decorated by Hannah Barlow and Florence Roberts, 1903, impressed marks, incised artists' monograms and numerals, each neck and foot glazed in green, white and ochre, 41.5cm (16¼in), *L 3 May,* £495 ($633)

4
A Doulton jug, decorated by Florence Barlow, 1890s, impressed marks the body with a bird in brown and green against a buff ground, *L 3 May,* £1,100 ($1,408)

5
A pair of Royal Doulton vases, decorated by Hannah Barlow, 1906, impressed marks, incised artist's monogram, 20cm (8in), *L 3 May,* £352 ($450)

6
A Doulton vase, decorated by Hannah Barlow and Eliza Simmance, 1890s, impressed Lambeth marks, minor rim flake, 44cm (17¼in), *L 4 Dec,* £330 ($462)

7
A Doulton Lambeth vase, decorated by Hannah Barlow and Alice Budden, 1880s, impressed Lambeth mark, *L 5 July,* £198 ($273)

8
A pair of Doulton vases, decorated by Frank Butler, 1883, impressed Lambeth mark, assistant's monograms of Ernest Bishop, 36cm (14¼in), *L 3 May,* £220 ($281)

9
A pair of Doulton vases, decorated by Frank Butler, 1884, impressed Lambeth mark, incised with foliage glazed green and ochre against a buff ground, 31.5cm (12¼in), *L 4 Dec,* £264 ($370)

10
A Doulton stoneware vase, 1890s, decorated by Frank Butler, 43cm (17in), *S 15 May,* £748 ($995)

11
A pair of Doulton stoneware vases, decorated by Frank Butler, 1890s, coloured in pale-lilac, green, brown and white, 43.5cm (17¼in), *S 23 Jan,* £3,190 ($3,780)

12
A pair of Doulton stoneware vases, early 20th century, decorated by Eliza Simmance, minor restoration, 47cm (18½in), *S 15 May,* £1,430 ($1,902)

13
A pair of Doulton stoneware vases, designed by Frank Butler, incised monogram of Bessie Newbury on one, the floral design picked out in blue, brown and green, 28cm (11in), *C 29 Oct,* £572 ($852)

14
A pair of Doulton stoneware vases, designed by Mary Mitchell, signature of the assistant Mary Aitken, 28cm (11in), *C 29 Oct,* £594 ($885)

15
A Royal Doulton jardiniere and stand, c.1900, impressed marks, the body with flowers and leaves glazed in blue and green, some cracks, 94cm (37in), *L 3 May,* £418 ($535)

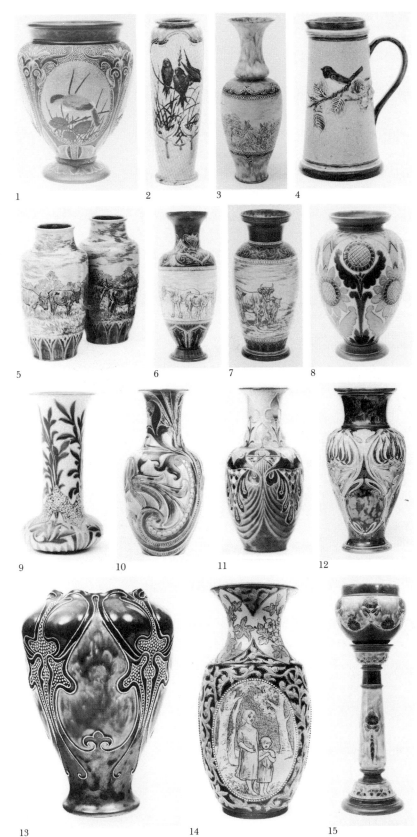

1
A **Burmantofts jardinière and stand,** c.1900, impressed marks 1943 and 1944, glazed in deep turquoise, 109cm (43in), *L 3 May,* £330 ($422)

2
An **Elton lustre vase,** c.1900, incised mark, glazed in veined and crackled gold and silver, 41.5cm (16¼in), *L 3 May,* £297 ($380)

3
An **Elton lustre jug,** c.1900, painted mark, glazed in crackled silver and gold veined in green, 38cm (15in), *L 3 May,* £506 ($648)

4
A **Maw & Co. Ltd 'Diver' vase,** designed by Walter Crane, 1890s, decorated in crimson with bands of maidens and stylised porpoises, 22.5cm (8¾in), *L 4 Dec,* £968 ($1,355)

5
A **Maw & Co. Ltd. 'Swans' vase,** designed by Walter Crane, 1890s, painted cipher, decorated in iridescent amber-yellow against a cream ground, 23cm (9in), *L 3 May,* £1,760 ($2,252)

6
A **Royal Doulton 'Chang' vase,** by F Allen and Harry Nixon, 1920s, marked, decorated in deep-blue on crimson ground, 23cm (9in), *L 3 May,* £770 ($985)

7
A **Royal Doulton 'Chang' vase,** by Noke and Harry Nixon, 1930s, marked and impressed 7814, the body thinly glazed in black with trails of ashen-white, 11.5cm (4½in), *L 3 May,* £418 ($535)

8
A **Royal Doulton 'Chinese Jade' vase,** by Harry Nixon, 1929, marked, the body glazed in white and green, with trails of ashen-white shaded in jade-green, 19cm (7½in), *L 3 May,* £1,320 ($1,689)

9
A **Ruskin high-fired vase,** 1906, impressed mark and date, glazed in turquoise, green and mauve, 19.5cm (7¾in), *L 3 May,* £209 ($267)

10
A **Wedgwood black basalt vase,** designed by Keith Murray, 1930s, designer's facsimile signature, 14cm (5½in), *L 5 July,* £286 ($395)

11
A **Carlton ware lustre-glazed 'Jazz Age' vase,** 1930s, printed mark, decorated in orange, red and green against royal blue ground, gilt details, 20cm (8in), *L 2 May,* £880 ($1,135)

12*
A **Martin Brothers 'John Barleycorn' jug,** 1910, incised mark and date, glazed honey-brown, minor flakes, 17.5cm (7in), *L 4 Dec,* £770 ($1,078)

13
A **Martin Brothers jug,** 1896, incised mark and date, decorated with buff heads against lustrous brown ground, 24cm (9½in), *L 3 May,* £352 ($450)

14
A **Martin Brothers stand,** 1886, incised marks and date, glazed in green, brown and blue against a buff ground, minor crack, 41cm (16in), *L 3 May,* £385 ($493)

15
A **pair of Martin Brothers 'Gourd' vases,** 1908, incised marks and date, with green grooves against a buff ground, chips, 26.5cm (10½in), *L 3 May,* £330 ($422)

16
A **Martin Brothers pottery bird,** c.1900, inscribed, glazed in pale blue, inky blue, beige and ochre, restorations, 33cm (13in), *NY 7 Dec,* $3,300 (£2,229)

A Clarice Cliff Newport
Pottery Bizarre biscuit
barrel and cover, 1930s,
printed marks, painted
in blue, green, purple,
orange and black,
15.5cm (6in), L 15 Feb,
£143 ($166)

A pair of Clarice Cliff
Newport Pottery vases,
1936, printed marks,
painted in pink, blue
and shades of green,
15cm (6in), C 29 Oct,
£231 ($344)

A Clarice Cliff Newport
Pottery Bizarre jug,
1930s, printed marks,
additional stencilled
Wilkinson Ltd marks,
painted in orange,
yellow and brown, 28cm
(11in), L 2 May,
£308 ($397)

A Clarice Cliff Newport
Pottery 'Fantasque'
Bizarre vase, 1930s,
printed marks, painted
in colourful palette
with stylised landscapes,
21cm (8¼in), L 2 May,
£418 ($539)

A Clarice Cliff Newport
Pottery Bizarre jug, 1930s,
printed marks, painted
in orange, yellow and
brown, 30cm (11¾in),
L 2 May,
£550 ($709)

A Clarice Cliff Newport
Pottery Bizarre jug, 1930s,
printed marks, painted
in yellow, purple, green
and brown, on cream
ground, 29cm (11½in),
C 4 Dec,
£385 ($539)

A Clarice Cliff Newport
Pottery Bizarre double-
handled vase, 1930s,
30cm (11¾in), C 10 July,
£550 ($765)

A Clarice Cliff Newport
Pottery Bizarre 'Fan-
tasque' wall plate, 1930s,
printed marks, painted
with a single red tulip,
with green leaves,
yellow, blue and black
details, 26cm (10¼in),
C 5 July,
£176 ($243)

9
A Clarice Cliff Wilkinson
Ltd dinner service, 1930s,
printed marks, com-
prising thirty pieces,
painted in brown,
orange and turquoise,
L 15 Feb,
£330 ($383)

10
A Clarice Cliff Newport
Pottery Bizarre 'Latona'
charger, 1930s, printed
marks, with red and
black design, L 2 May,
£220 ($283)

11
A Clarice Cliff Newport
Pottery Bizarre teaset,
1930s, printed marks,
comprising twenty-
three pieces, L 15 Feb,
£440 ($510)

12
A Clarice Cliff Newport
pottery vase, 1930s,
signed, decorated in
blue and lilac glaze
against a turquoise and
inky blue ground, 15cm
(6in), L 2 May,
£440 ($567)

13
A Clarice Cliff 'Early
Morning' tea service,
1930s, printed marks,
comprising nine pieces,
painted with blue and
black trees in a green
landscape, C 29 Oct,
£792 ($1,180)

14
A Clarice Cliff Newport
Pottery 'Archaic' Bizarre
vase, 1930s, printed
marks, impressed num-
ber 373, painted with
Isnic design in blue,
yellow, red and green,
18cm (7in), L 2 May,
£660 ($851)

1

2

3

4

5

6

7

8

9

10

11

12

13

14

1
An 'Amphora' eggshell
porcelain vase, *c.*1900,
marked 'Amphora Hol-
land SS W 651 M 244',
with polychrome decor-
ation on white ground,
29cm (11½in), *M 6 Oct,*
FF 15,540
(£1,352; $2,001)

2
A Gallé pottery cat,
*c.*1880, marked 'E. Gallé
Nancy', decorated in
polychrome with flowers
on a blue ground,
33.5cm (13¼in), *M 6 Oct,*
FF 18,870
(£1,641; $2,429)

3
A Sèvres pottery vase
with Austrian silver
mounts. *c.*1900, the body
with blue and violet
flambé glaze, 25.5cm
(10in), *NY 7 Dec,*
$2,090 (£1,412)

4
A Zsolnay lustre-glazed
earthenware vase, 1900,
moulded mark, decor-
rated in bronze, purple,
crimson and green,
26.5cm (10½in), *L 2 May,*
£550 ($709)

5
A Sèvres pottery vase,
decorated by Taxile
Doat, *c.*1901, the grey
and ochre body applied
with cream florets, 18cm
(7in), *NY 18 May,*
$1,430 (£1,135)

6
A Zsolnay Pecs iridescent
pottery bowl, early 20th
century, impressed
5100/1/453 1/2, painted
with dragonflies in
flight above foliage and
sunbeams in ochre,
deep burgundy and gilt
against purple irides-
cent ground, 10cm (4in),
NY 18 May,
$990 (£786)

7
A Reissner Stellmacher
and Kessel 'Amphora'
vase, *c.*1900, printed
factory mark, decorated
in rich pastel colouring
with gilt details, 15.5cm
(6in), *L 5 July,*
£484 ($668)

8
A Sèvres porcelain vase,
the porcelain 1899, the
decoration by Henri
Lasserre, 1900, painted
with salmon-coloured
blossoms and green
leafage, 49cm (18¼in),
NY 18 May,
$1,650 (£1,310)

9
A Rozenburg 'eggshell'
vase, decorated by J W
van Rossum, 1913,
A 3 June,
Dfl 4,872 (£1,102; $1,488)

10
A Rozenburg 'eggshell'
vase, with polychrome
decoration, 16.5cm
(6½in), *A 25 Feb,*
Dfl 12,552 (£625; $701)

11
A Longwy Atelier Prima-
vera crackle-glazed moon
flask, 1920s, stencilled
factory marks, detailed
in pale grey/blue
against beige/grey
crackled ground, 29.5cm
(11½in), *L 15 Feb,*
£187 ($217)

12
A Velsen pottery jug,
with polychrome decor-
ation, 16cm (6¼in),
A 26 June,
Dfl 394 (£89; $120)

13
A Wouter box with cover,
1980, grey glazed,
34.5cm (13½in) diam,
A 25 Feb,
Dfl 185 (£45; $51)

1

2

3

4

5

6

7

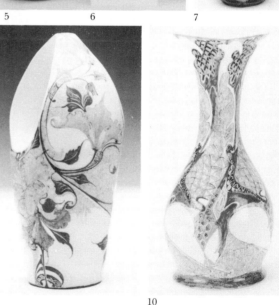

8

9

10

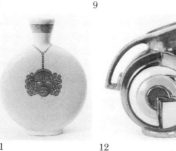

11

12

13

1
A Royal Dux porcelain figure of a bather, 1910, with triangle mark, impressed 1361, the young girl in a green and peach swimsuit, 55cm (21¾in), *NY 18 May,* $1,320 (£1,048)

2
A Royal Dux nude figure, 1930s, with triangle mark, 29cm (11½in), *L 5 July,* £198 ($273)

3
A Rosenthal porcelain figure of a dancer, *c.*1920, possibly representing Nijinsky, printed factory mark, impressed K/566 and inscribed Mettner, 41cm (16¼in), *NY 18 May,* $605 (£480)

4
A Royal Dux ceramic group of flamenco dancers, after a model by Weiss, 1930s, signed, with triangle mark, gilt and natural glaze to simulated bronze and ivory, 22.5cm (8¾in), *L 5 July,* £264 ($364)

5
A Lenci figure of a native woman, 1930s, marked, 55.5cm (21¾in), *L 15 Feb,* £440 ($510)

6
A Lenci figure of a young woman walking two dogs, 1930s, marked, wearing brown and red check costume, 40cm (15¾in), *L 17 Oct,* £330 ($488)

7
A Goldscheider earthenware figure of a woman sitting on a suitcase, 1930s, impressed factory marks, designer's facsimile signature (?) Da Ron', in blue costume with black hat, 25cm (9¾in), *L 2 May,* £880 ($1,135)

8
A Goldscheider earthenware wall mask, 1920s, printed factory mark, numbered 6288 12, the young woman with orange hair and holding a black mask, 36cm (14in), *L 17 Oct,* £462 ($684)

9
A Royal Doulton earthenware figure, entitled Folly, 1936, HN 1750, 24cm (9½in), *S 23 Oct,* £990 ($1,485)

10
A Goldschieder earthenware head of a young woman, 1920s, printed marks 'Goldscheider Wien Made in Austria', numbered 7546, with orange curls and turquoise dress, 19.5cm (7¾in), *L 5 July,* £220 ($304)

11
A Goldscheider earthenware head of a young woman, 1920s, printed factory marks, numbered 7586, 26.5cm (10½in), *L 15 Feb,* £308 ($357)

12
A Haviland Limoges porcelain teapot, designed by Edouard Marcel Sandoz, 1920s, printed factory marks, the bird with yellow beak and blue and white body, 16cm (6¼in), *L 2 May,* £143 ($184)

13
A Richard Ginori porcelain teapot, designed by Gio Ponti, 1930s, printed mark 'Decorazione Eseguita da Richard Ginori 30=10', each side with stencilled scene from boxing match, 13.5cm (5¼in), *L 2 May,* £484 ($624)

1 2 3

4 5 6

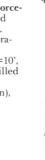

7 8 9 10

11 12 13

1
A Bernard Leach stone-
ware vase, 1960s,
impressed BL and St
Ives seals, with fluting
beneath a rich *tenmoku*
glaze, 25.8cm (10in),
L 4 Dec,
£715 ($1,001)

2
A Bernard Leach stone-
ware vase, 1950s,
impressed BL and St
Ives seals, brushed in
brown and glazed in
creamy mushroom,
14cm (5½in), *L 4 Dec,*
£220 ($308)

3
A Hamada Shoji stone-
ware dish, 1950s, brushed
in mottled brown
against a pale-green
ground, 19.5cm (7¾in),
L 4 Dec,
£330 ($462)

4
A Bernard Leach St Ives
slipware bowl, 1920s,
impressed BL and St
Ives seals, rim chip,
17.5cm (7in), *L 3 May,*
£165 ($211)

5
A Hamada Shoji St Ives
stoneware bowl, c.1922,
impressed sho and St
Ives seals, glazed in
ashen-white, hair crack,
22.5cm (8¾in), *L 4 Dec,*
£462 ($647)

6
A Hamada Shoji St Ives
stoneware vase, 1920-23,
impressed sho and St
Ives seals, glazed in
deep-rust, 22cm (8¾in),
L 3 May,
£825 ($1,056)

7
A David Leach St Ives
stoneware vase, c.1940,
impressed St Ives seal,
glazed in pale celadon,
rust and grey, 44.5cm
(17½in), *L 3 May,*
£264 ($337)

8
A Hans Coper black
stoneware vase, 1970s,
impressed HC seal,
15cm (6in), *L 3 May,*
£3,520 ($4,505)

9
A Hans Coper stoneware
vase, 1970s, impressed
HC seal, with patches
of 'sharkskin' texturing
stained brown beneath
an ashen-white glaze,
21cm (8¼in), *L 3 May,*
£1,980 ($2,534)

10
An Hans Coper stoneware
vase, 1950s, impressed
seal, with circles
beneath a mottled grey
and brown glaze, 15cm
(6in), *L 4 Dec,*
£605 ($847)

11
A Lucie Rie stoneware
bowl, 1950s, impressed
LR seal, glazed in
speckled ashen-white
and banded in brown,
12cm (4¾in), *L 4 Dec,*
£198 ($277)

12
A Lucie Rie stoneware
bowl, 1950s, impressed
LR seal, glazed in ashen-
white and banded in
brown, 15.5cm (6¼in)
wide, *L 4 Dec,*
£242 ($339)

13
A Lucie Rie porcelain
bowl, impressed LR
seal, with brown rings
against a cream ground,
6.5cm (2½in), *L 4 Dec,*
£209 ($293)

14
A Lucie Rie porcelain
vase, c.1960, impressed
LR seal, with *sgraffito*
lines through a
manganese-brown glaze,
13.5cm (5¼in), *L 4 Dec,*
£385 ($539)

15
A Lucie Rie porcelain
bowl, 1960s, impressed
LR seal, with *sgraffito*
band of cross-hatching
beneath a celadon
glaze, 10.5cm (4¼in),
L 4 Dec,
£330 ($462)

16
A Lucie Rie porcelain
vase, 1960s, impressed
LR seal, glazed in spirals
of green and ashen-
white, *L 3 May,*
£495 ($633)

1
A Lucie Rie porcelain bowl, 1970s, impressed LR seal, glazed in rich brown and bronze, 22cm (8¾in), *L 3 May,* £1,210 ($1,548)

2
A Michael Cardew Winchcombe Pottery slipware bowl, 1930s, impressed Winchcombe Pottery seal, 35cm (13¾in), *L 4 Dec,* £275 ($385)

3
A Michael Cardew Wenford Bridge stoneware bowl, 1960s, impressed MC and Wenford Bridge seals, 25.5cm (10in) diam, *L 3 May,* £165 ($211)

4
A Michael Cardew Winchcombe Pottery slipware tureen and cover, 1930s, impressed MC and Winchcombe Pottery seals, 13.5cm (5¼in), *L 4 Dec,* £154 ($216)

5
A Michael Cardew Wenford Bridge stoneware bread crock and cover,1970s, impressed MC and Wenford Bridge seals, rich brown glaze, 39cm (15¼in), *L 3 May,* £462 ($591)

6
A Michael Cardew Winchcombe Pottery slipware bowl, late 1930s, impressed MC and Winchcombe Pottery seals, 40cm (15¾in), *L 3 May,* £187 ($239)

7
A Michael Cardew Wenford Bridge stoneware bowl, 1970s, impressed WC and Wenford Bridge seals, with bands in mustard slip against a brown ground, 30cm (11¾in) diam, *L 3 May,* £352 ($450)

8
A Michael Cardew slipware jug, 1930s, impressed MC seal, 26cm (10¼in), *L 3 May,* £242 ($310)

9
A William Staite Murray stoneware bowl, 1930s, impressed pentagon seal, 22cm (8¾in), *L 4 Dec,* £209 ($293)

10
A Katharine Pleydell-Bouverie stoneware vase, 1940s, impressed KPB seal, with fluting beneath a crackled celadon glaze, 14cm (5½in), *L 4 Dec,* £242 ($339)

11
A Katharine Pleydell-Bouverie stoneware vase, 1940s, impressed KB seal, 23.5cm (9¼in), *L 4 Dec,* £330 ($462)

12
A Rookwood standard glaze pottery Indian portrait mug, 'Chief Tah-Boo-Cha-Ket', decorated by Frederick Sturgis Laurence, *c.*1900, 837, 13.5cm (5¼in), *NY 23 Feb,* $1,430 (£1,336)

13
A Natzler pottery bowl, 1965, signed and numbered N706, 24.5cm (9½in) diam, *NY 23 Feb,* $1,650 (£1,542)

14
A Natzler pottery vase, mid-20th century, signed, glazed in watery blue, 9.5cm (3¾in), *NY 23 Feb,* $605 (£565)

15
A Linda Gunn-Russell earthenware teapot, 1984, painted in cream and blue against a terracotta ground, 23cm (9in), *L 4 Dec,* £396 ($554)

16
A Robin Welch stoneware bowl, 1984, decorated in green and ashen-white slips, 44cm (17¼in) diam, *L 4 Dec,* £264 ($370)

17
An Eileen Nisbet porcelain sculpture, 'Flyer', 1984, incised and painted in blue, orange and yellow, 28cm (11in), *L 4 Dec,* £308 ($431)

1

A gold, rubellite, demantoid garnet and diamond pendant-locket, *c.*1900, the interior with two glazed locket compartments, *NY 15 Oct,* $2,310 (£1,638)

2

A René Foy gold, enamel and opal brooch, *c.*1900, reverse engraved 'Rene Foy', *L 4 Dec,* £1,760 ($2,464)

3

A pair of wrought iron hair combs, 1920s, attributed to Edgar Brandt, each surround with a pair of coiled serpents, 9.5cm (4in) wide, *L 17 Oct,* £352 ($521)

4

A gold, enamel and freshwater pearl necklace, *c.*1900, each panel with rose and green enamel floral spray, *NY 15 Oct,* $4,950 (£3,511)

5

A Ronson black enamelled chromium plated metal combined lighter and cigarette case, 1930s, marked 'Ronson YTA Case Tuxedo Made in USA...*, L 17 Oct,* £121 ($179)

6

An eighteen-carat gold, diamond and pearl pendant necklace, *c.*1900, *NY 12 June,* $3,410 (£2,706)

7

A Guy fils gold pendant, marked 'Guy fils 20 rue de la Paix, Paris', with small diamonds and red and blue cabochon stones, *M 6 Oct,* FF 44,400 (£3,861; $5,714)

8

A gold, enamel and diamond brooch, *c.*1900, applied with green and purple translucent enamel, *NY 12 June,* $1,045 (£829)

9

A gold, plique-à-jour, diamond and baroque pearl pendant, French, *c.*1910, one diamond missing, some repair, *NY 15 Oct,* $2,860 (£2,028)

10

A Marcus & Co. plique-à-jour enamel and conch pearl wisteria brooch, *c.*1900, some losses to enamel, *NY 22 Apr,* $7,700 (£6,160)

1

2

3

4

6

7

5

8

9

10

1 Gorham Co silver centrepiece, Providence, RI, 1899, the base engraved, 37cm (14½in), NY 18 May, £990 (£786)

2 Gorham Co silver three-piece coffee set, with matching tray, Providence RI, Martelé, 1897, chased with winged maidens amongst daisies and foliage, coffee pot 29.5cm (11½in), NY 18 May, £9,350 (£7,421)

3 Tiffany & Co silver bowl, New York, c.1880, 'Japanese Style', overlaid with copper and gold, 21.5cm (8½in), NY 18 May, £1,210 (£960)

4 Gorham Mfg. Co silver centrepiece bowl, Providence RI, 1905, 'Martelé' style, applied and chased with vines, 36cm (14¼in), NY 7 Dec, £935 (£631)

5 Whiting Mfg. Co silver and mixed metal jug, Providence, RI, c.1884, 'Japanese Style', applied on one side with a gilt dragonfly and the other with a gilt iris flower, 24.5cm (9½in), NY 7 Dec, £10,175 (£6,875)

6 Cardeilhac silver chocolate jug, Paris, c.1900, chased with tulips and curling fronds, 24.5cm (9½in), NY 23 Feb, £3,850 (£3,598)

7 Cardeilhac silver coffee pot, Paris, c.1900, 20cm (8in), M 6 Oct, F 6,600 (£579; $857)

8 René Lalique silver and opalised glass chalice, c.1900, stamped 'Lalique 5', 19cm (7½in), M 6 Oct, F 124,320 (£10,810; $15,999)

9 A Christofle 'Gallia' electroplated metal tea and coffee service, c.1900, comprising six pieces, each piece with clover and linear motifs, samovar 40cm (15¾in), L 5 July, £1,870 ($2,580)

10 A WMF electroplated frame, c.1900, 37cm (14½in), L 15 Feb, £572 ($664)

11 A pair of WMF electroplated candelabra, c.1900, 48cm (19in), L 2 May, £2,200 ($2,838)

12 An engraved decanter with electroplated mounts, c.1900, 38.5cm (15¼in), F 29 May, L 900,000 (£350; $462)

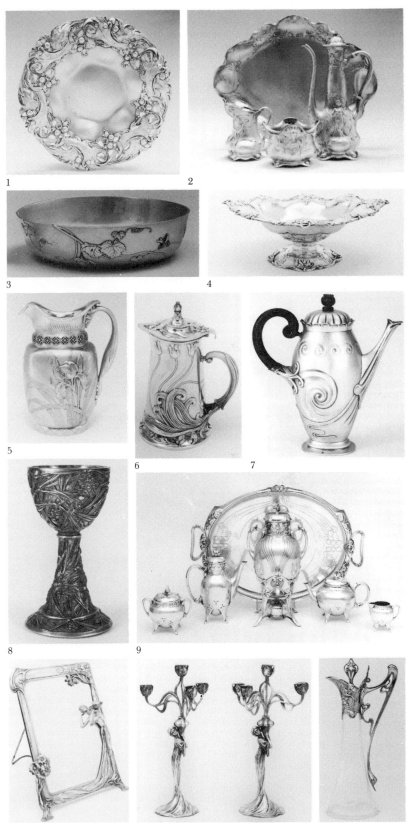

1
A James Dixon & Sons electroplated toast rack, designed by Christopher Dresser, 1880s, 13.5cm (5¼in), *L 4 Dec,* £4,180 ($5,852)

2
A Hukin & Heath electroplated condiment set, designed by Christopher Dresser, 1878, *L 4 Dec,* £3,960 ($5,544)

3
An electroplate-mounted glass claret jug, 1880s, after a design by Christopher Dresser, ebonised wood handle, 21.5cm (8½in), *L 5 July,* £176 ($243)

4
A Hukin & Heath electroplated sugar basket and spoon, designed by Christopher Dresser, 1880s, engraved, 16.5cm (6½in), with similar Walker & Hall sugar basket, 1880s, 15.5cm (6in), *L 2 May,* £220 ($283)

5
A W S Connell tea and coffee set, designed by Kate Harris, London, 1902, comprising teapot and Turkish coffee/chocolate pot, sugar basin and cream jug, coffee pot 16.5cm (6½in), *L 2 May,* £2,200 ($2,838)

6
A Hukin & Heath electroplated tea service, designed by Christopher Dresser, *c.*1880, comprising five pieces, each engraved in 'Aesthetic' taste, hot water jug 22.5cm (8¾in), *L 2 May,* £7,150 ($9,223)

7
A Hukin & Heath silver teapot, London, 1901, maker's mark of Heath & Middleton for Hukin & Heath, wicker-covered handle, 16cm (6¼in), *L 5 July,* £308 ($425)

8
A Guild of Handicraft Ltd. silver double loop handled dish, designed by C R Ashbee, London, 1907, 26cm (10¼in), *L 4 Dec,* £990 ($1,386)

9
A Guild of Handicraft Ltd. silver loop handled bowl, designed by C R Ashbee, London 1902, set with a green stone, 20cm (8in), *L 5 July,* £715 ($987)

10
An A & J Zimmermann silver frame, Birmingham, 1905, *L 17 Oct,* £99 ($147)

11
A silver-mounted shaped oblong photograph frame, Birmingham, 1904, maker's mark H & A, decorated in blue-green and yellow enamel, 17.5cm (7in) high, *C 7 Aug,* £396 ($590)

12
A James Dixon & Sons silver-mounted photograph frame, Chester, 1905, stamped with a maiden amongst flowers and scrolls, 32cm (12½in), *C 1 May,* £594 ($778)

13
A William Hutton & Sons Ltd. silver and enamel frame, London, 1903, with blue-green enamel ground, 20cm (8in), *L 17 Oct,* £770 ($1,140)

14
A Gilbert Marks silver cup and cover, London, 1900, set with a fire opal, 42cm (16½in), *L 4 Dec,* £990 ($1,386)

An A & J Zimmermann
Ltd. three-piece tea
set, Birmingham, 1907,
C 4 Sept,
£330 ($485)

A set of six Sybil Dunlop
silver coffee spoons with
matching sugar tongs,
London, 1927, 11cm
(4¼in), L 5 July,
£275 ($379)

A Liberty & Co 'Cymric'
silver spoon, Birming-
ham, 1923, C 13 Nov,
£231 ($323)

A set of six Liberty &
Co silver and enamel
cake forks and six
teaspoons, Birmingham,
1929, each finial with
blue and green
enamelled design, fork
12.5cm (5in), L 2 May,
£440 ($567)

A set of six Liberty & Co
'Cymric' silver coffee
spoons, Birmingham,
1902, 11cm (4¼in),
L 5 July,
£308 ($425)

A set of six Liberty & Co
'Cymric' silver and
enamel buttons, Bir-
mingham, 1903, detailed
in turquoise enamel, 2cm
(¾in), L 17 Oct,
£93 ($138)

An Artificers Guild silver
bowl, London, 1913,
23cm (9in), L 4 Dec,
£418 ($585)

A Liberty & Co silver
chalice, Birmingham,
1901, the design
attributed to Archibald
Knox or Rex Silver,
set with blue, amber and
green stones, 25cm
(9¾in), L 4 Dec,
£7,150 ($10,010)

A Liberty & Co silver
and enamel vase, Bir-
mingham, 1899, the
design attributed to
Archibald Knox,
detailed in orange-gold
enamel and set with a
row of pale green stones,
19cm (7½in), L 5 July,
£3,740 ($5,161)

10
A pair of A E Jones silver
and wood candlesticks,
Birmingham, 1922,
20cm (8in), L 4 Dec,
£154 ($216)

11
A Liberty & Co 'Cymric'
silver and shagreen
tobacco box and cover,
Birmingham, 1901, the
design attributed to
Archibald Knox, 19.5cm
(7¾in), L 4 Dec,
£5,720 ($8,008)

12
A John Paul Cooper silver-
mounted shagreen
covered box and cover,
c.1920, 12cm (4¾in),
L 4 Dec,
£748 ($1,047)

13
A pair of Omar Ramsden
silver wine coasters,
London, 1934, engraved
'Omar Ramsden me
Fecit', 14cm (5½in) diam,
L 2 May,
£3,520 ($4,540)

1

2   3   4   5

6   7

8   9   10

11   12   13

1
A pair of James Dixon and Sons silver candlesticks, Sheffield, 1908, 23.5cm (9¼in), *L 17 Oct,* £264 ($391)

2
A Dunstan Pruden silver-gilt chalice and paten, London 1945, chalice 19.5cm (7¾in), *L 15 Feb,* £286 ($332)

3
An electroplated three-piece coffee-set, *c.*1930, with green bakelite finials and handles, and four matching cups and saucers, *C 16 Oct,* £715 ($1,058)

4
A set of six Bernard Instone silver and enamel fruit knives, Birmingham, 1929, facsimile signature, the handles in pink, green and blue cloisonné enamels, 14cm (5½in), *L 17 Oct,* £220 ($326)

5
A Charles Boyton silver dish, London, 1938, lightly hammered, 30cm (12in) diam, *L 2 May,* £1,760 ($2,270)

6
A Cube Teapots Ltd. electroplated tea set, 1930s, teapot 11cm (4¼in) high, *L 17 Oct,* £165 ($244)

7
A silvered-metal five-piece tea and coffee service, Ravinet D'Enfant, *c.*1935, with lucite handles, coffee pot 26cm (10¼in) high, *NY 7 Dec,* $3,300 (£2,229)

8
A silver flask, 1930s, indistinct maker's name, stamped 'Sterling', 22.5cm (8¾in), *L 17 Oct,* £418 ($619)

9
A French silver three-piece tea and coffee service, BF & Cie, Paris, *c.*1925, coffee pot 15cm (6in), *NY 6 Dec,* $1,100 (£743)

10
A Cohr silver and ivory cocktail shaker, *c.*1930, 24cm (9½in), *M 6 Oct,* FF 7,770 (£676; $1,000)

11
A Puiforcat silver tea service, *c.*1930, each piece stamped 'Jean E Puiforcat Paris', maker's mark 'E.P.', max. height 17cm (6¾in), *M 6 Oct,* FF 31,080 (£2,703; $4,000)

Wiener Werkstätte
ilver six-piece tea and
offee service, designed
y Josef Hoffmann,
1925, the tray with
ooden base painted
lack, coffee pot 16.5cm
½in), *NY 18 May,*
15,400 (£12,222)

Wiener Werkstätte
ilver vase by Josef
Ioffmann, *c.*1905,
7.5cm (7in), *M 17 Mar,*
F 27,750
£2,477; $3,046)

ive pieces of Wiener
Verkstätte table silver
esigned by Josef
Ioffmann, 1904,
1 17 Mar,
F 111,000
£9,910; $12,189)

A Wiener Werkstätte
ilver eight-light candela-
rum designed by
osef Hoffmann, 21cm
8¼in), *NY 7 Dec,*
12,100 (£8,175)

A Wiener Werkstätte
ilver basket, probably
esigned by Josef Hoff-
nann, *c.*1905, 27.5cm
10¾in), *NY 7 Dec,*
2,530 (£1,709)

A pair of Argentor
ilvered-metal vases,
1920, after a design
y Josef Hoffmann,
ith glass liners, 17cm
6¾in), *L 15 Feb,*
374 ($434)

A Wiener Werkstätte
ea and coffee service,
esigned by Josef
Ioffmann, *c.*1920, the
offee pot made to match
1930, teapot 15cm
6in), *L 4 Dec,*
6,600 ($9,240)

A tureen and cover and
auce boat on stand,
1930 after a design by
osef Hoffmann, (see
10.7), tureen 25.5cm
10in) diam, *L 4 Dec,*
935 ($1,309)

9
A Wiener Werkstätte
silvered-metal vase,
designed by Josef Hoff-
mann, *c.*1910, hammered
surface, 28.5cm (11¼in),
M 6 Oct,
FF 14,430
(£1,255; $1,857)

10
A Wiener Werkstätte
silver and ivory tea ser-
vice, designed by Josef
Hoffmann, *c.*1920,
comprising teapot,
sugar basin, milk jug,
sugar tongs and tray,
with hammered finish,
tray 41cm (16in) wide,
M 6 Oct,
FF 88,800
(£7,722; $11,428)

11
A Nestler silver bowl,
*c.*1910, hammered
surface, 30cm (11¾in)
diam, *M 6 Oct,*
FF 19,980
(£1,737; $2,571)

1

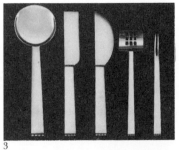

2

3

4

5

6

7

8

9

10

11

Georg Jensen Silver

Georg Jensen started his workshop in Copenhagen in 1904 after training as a silversmith and a sculptor. His objective was to be commercially successful with modern designs rather than reproductions of antique silver. During the first two years, the small workshop on Bredgade concentrated on the production of jewellery. By 1907, in collaboration with the designer Johan Rohde, Jensen was offering a variety of hollow-ware and flatware.

By attracting such talented designers as Johan Rohde, Gundorph Albertus, Harald Nielsen and Sigvard Bernadotte, and insisting on a high standard of design and workmanship, the silversmithy won acclaim in every major international exhibition of the applied arts before World War II. Henning Koppel and Tias Eckhoff were just two of the many others who joined the firm after Jensen's death and continued to produce popular and award-winning designs. Today, the workshop is owned by Royal Copenhagen Porcelain and has retail outlets all over the world. It continues to thrive with a small cadre of master craftsmen, still employing hand and hammer.

The variety of flatware services offered at auction in 1985 and illustrated here provides an interesting survey of the different styles of the silversmith's many designers. Georg Jensen's 'Blossom' (fig. 6) and 'Beaded' (fig. 7) and Johan Rohde's 'Acorn' (figs. 1 & 2) and 'Acanthus' illustrate the influence of nature on these two early collaborators. From Gundorph Albertus' 'Cactus' (fig. 8), Harald Nielsen's 'Pyramid' (fig. 4), Sigvard Bernadotte's 'Bernadotte' (fig. 5) to Tias Eckhoff's 'Cypress' (fig. 3), we see the firm's elegant progression toward modernism.

Most of the Jensen flatware services seen in the saleroom have been assembled over the years, with pieces bearing different Jensen trademarks. Generally, the more complete and comprehensive the set, the higher the price per piece will be. In December 1985 one set of 'Acorn' sold for $55 (£40) per piece; one lot later another sold for $135 (£96) per piece. Although both sets were for twelve, the second included, in addition to the basics, more unusual implements such as ice cream forks, grapefruit spoons and lobster picks, as well as many serving utensils. These sets are acquired primarily for use by private buyers.

—1—
A flatware service, Georg Jensen, Copenhagen, designed by Johan Rohde, comprising 342 pieces, in the 'Acorn' pattern, *NY 7 Dec,* **$60,500 (£40,878)**

—2—
A flatware service, Georg Jensen, Copenhagen, designed by Johan Rohde, comprising 276 pieces, in the 'Acorn' pattern, *NY 7 Dec,* **$25,300 (£17,094)**

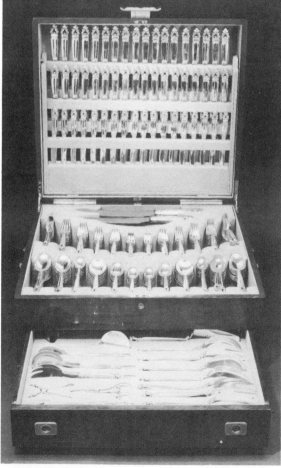

—1—

—2—

—3—
A **flatware service,** Georg Jensen, Copenhagen, designed by Tias Eckhoff, comprising 70 pieces, in the 'Cypress' pattern, *NY 7 Dec,* $3,575 (£2,415)

—4—
A **flatware service,** Georg Jensen, Copenhagen, designed by Harald Nielsen, comprising 240 pieces, in the 'Pyramid' pattern, *NY 7 Dec,* $22,000 (£14,864)

—5—
A **flatware service,** Georg Jensen, Copenhagen, designed by Sigvard Bernadotte, comprising 258 pieces, in the 'Bernadotte' pattern', *NY 7 Dec,* $17,600 (£11,891)

—6—
Nine serving pieces, Georg Jensen, Copenhagen, numbered 84 and 84A, designed by Georg Jensen, in the 'Blossom' pattern, *NY 7 Dec,* $1,980 (£1,337)

—7—
A **flatware service,** Georg Jensen, Copenhagen, designed by Georg Jensen, comprising 76 pieces, in the 'Beaded' pattern, *NY 7 Dec,* $4,400 (£2,972)

—8—
A **flatware service,** Georg Jensen, Copenhagen, designed by Gundorph Albertus, comprising 294 pieces, in the 'Cactus' pattern, *NY 7 Dec,* $12,100 (£8,175)

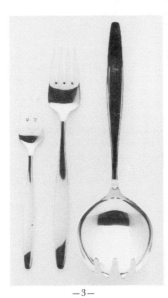
—3—

—4—

1904-8

1915-27

1925-32

Since 1945

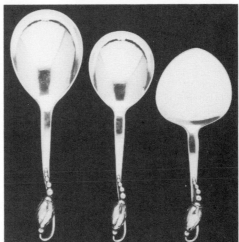
—5—

—7—

—8—

Gundorph Albertus
1887-1970

Sigvard Bernadotte
1907-

Tias Eckhoff
1926-

Georg Jensen
1866-1935

Jorgen Jensen
1895-1966

Henning Koppel
1918-1981

Harald Nielsen
1892-1977

Johan Rohde
1856-1935

In addition to different flatware designs, Jensen also produced a variety of hollow-ware, most commonly bowls, tazze, and tea and coffee services. During the silversmithy's first three decades, much of this silver was applied or chased with grape bunches or stylized berried foliage. Harald Nielsen, one of Georg Jensen's closest colleagues, bridged this early naturalism into modernism with his striking clean designs adorned with stylized fowl or fish, as in the cocktail shaker with the cock finial (fig. 10) and the fish platter and cover with the dolphin finial (fig. 12). Gradually, geometric shapes took over, typified by Sigvard Bernadotte's work. Henning Koppel's designs, such as the tea and coffee service illustrated (fig. 13) launched the silversmithy into futurism.

Several discontinued or specially commissioned designs were offered at Sotheby's in 1985. The rarity of the lamp in fig. 9 was reflected in the price of $3,575 (£2,416). This was made after 1945 but must have been designed at least as early as 1918, since an individual lamp appears in a photograph of that date of the Jensen shop at 21 Bredgade, Copenhagen. Jensen jewellery, still being produced today, seldom appears at auction. Usually composed only of silver and a few semi-precious stones, the jewellery attracts only modest prices. An exception is the platinum and diamond ring c.1910, which sold for $1,870 (£1,417) in November 1984 (fig. 11).

—9—
A lamp, Georg Jensen, Copenhagen, numbered 79, probably designed by Georg Jensen, 70cm (27½in), *NY 7 Dec,* $3,575 (£2,416)

—10—
A cocktail shaker, Georg Jensen, Copenhagen, numbered 774, designed by Harald Nielsen, the cover with rooster and grapevine finial, 28cm (11in), *NY 18 May,* $1,210 (£960)

—11—
A platinum and diamond ring, c.1910, Georg Jensen, Copenhagen, *NY 17 Nov,* $1,870 (£1,417)

—12—
A covered serving dish dish with mazarin, Georg Jensen, Copenhagen, numbered 600, designed by Harald Nielsen, the mazarin pierced with fish scales and tail, dolphin finial, 63cm (24¾in), *NY 23 Feb,* $10,175 (£9,509)

—13—
A five-piece tea and coffee service with matching tray, Georg Jensen, Copenhagen, numbered 1017, designed by Henning Koppel in 1963, coffee pot 16cm (6¼in), *NY 7 Dec,* $8,800 (£5,945)

—9—

—10—

—11—

—12—

—13—

Despite the relatively short span of the silversmithy's existence, the age of a piece does have an influence on auction prices. Auction prices for designs still being produced today are often substantially below the current retail levels. After 1945 the manufacturer's stamp ceased to vary. Dating of styles that have been in continuous production is therefore dependent on other clues such as dated inscriptions, country import marks or recollections of the owner, (which are not always reliable). Silver made before 1906 is extremely rare because of the early concentration on jewellery. The majority of the pieces that appear in the saleroom date from 1920 or later. The teapot, covered sugar bowl and footed bowl (figs. 16, 17 & 18) are all dated 1919 and brought more than post World War II examples would have done.

Most Jensen silver collectors feel that eighty-odd years of existence is no excuse for symptoms of old age and are sensitive about condition. This is reflected in price. Buyers will inspect for altered surfaces caused by buffing, lacquering or removal of monograms and inscriptions. Those who will accept another's monogram can sometimes find bargains.

The market for Jensen silver is strongest in New York, although it also sells well in London. The Danish silversmithy has a tradition of success in America, which began in 1915 when William Randolph Hearst bought most of their exhibit at the San Francisco World Fair. A showroom was established on Fifth Avenue in New York by 1920. The popularity of Jensen silver encouraged many American and Mexican silversmiths to make similar designs. During the late 1930s and early 1940s, many American manufacturers introduced flatware patterns based on Johan Rohde's best-selling 'Acorn' pattern, with names like 'Danish', 'Copenhagen', 'Oakleaf', 'King Christian' and 'Danish Baroque'. The most successful imitator was the International Silver Company of Meriden, Connecticut, which introduced their 'Royal Danish' pattern in 1939. Later, International employed a designer named Alphonse LaPaglia to start a line of 'Jensen style' silver hollow-ware. Some

—14—
salver, c.1905, Georg
Jensen, Copenhagen,
designed by Georg
Jensen, 38.5cm (15in)
wide, L 5 July,
£1,210 ($1,670)

—15—
**serving spoon and a
serving spoon and fork**,
1925/35, 19.5 and 15cm
(7¾ and 6in), L 5 July,
£165 ($228)

—16—
teapot, Georg Jensen,
Copenhagen, 1919,
numbered 182, designed
by Johan Rohde, 15cm
(6in), NY 7 Dec,
$660 (£445)

—17—
footed bowl, Georg
Jensen, Copenhagen,
1919, numbered 6,
designed by Johan
Rohde, 12.5cm (5in),
NY 7 Dec,
$715 (£483)

—18—
covered sugar bowl,
Georg Jensen, Copen-
hagen, 1919, numbered
93, designed by Johan
Rohde, 14cm (5½in),
NY 7 Dec,
$660 (£445)

—19—
vase, 1930s, Georg
Jensen, Copenhagen,
designed by Jorgen
Jensen, 16.5cm (6½in),
4 Dec,
$748 ($1,047)

—14—

—15—

—16—   —17—   —18—   —19—

renditions are misleadingly stamped USA Georg Jensen Inc. The Woodside Sterling Company of New York produced several coffee services remarkably similar to Georg Jensen's own 'Blossom' pattern. A Woodside set (fig. 27) offered in February 1985, brought less than half the price of an original set sold in December (fig. 25). Mexican silversmiths were particularly prolific in their output of 'Blossom' pattern serving pieces as well as hollow-ware with grape-bunch decoration (fig. 28). These copies appear from time to time at auction and always bring a fraction of the price of their genuine counterparts.

Several museums around the world have Jensen silver in their permanent collections. As early as 1914, the Louvre in

—20—
A pair of dishes, c.1935, Georg Jensen, Copenhagen, 10.5cm (4¼in), *L 15 Feb,* £462 ($536)

—21—
A pill box, 1950s, Georg Jensen, Copenhagen, designed by Henning Koppel, 5cm (2in), *L 4 Dec,* £264 ($370)

—22—
A five-piece tea and coffee service, Georg Jensen, Copenhagen, numbered 45C, designed by Johan Rohde, coffee pot 27.5cm (10¾in), *NY 23 Feb,* $4,400 (£4,112)

—23—
A jug and a footed bowl, Georg Jensen, Copenhagen, the jug c.1930, numbered 385B, the bowl c.1940, numbered 778, designed by Gundorph Albertus, 13.5 and 11cm (5¼ and 4¼in), *NY 7 Dec,* $880 (£594)

—24—
A footed bowl, c.1940, Georg Jensen, Copenhagen, numbered 19A, designed by Georg Jensen, 17cm (6¾in), *NY 7 Dec,* $1,320 (£891)

—20—

—21—

—22—

—23—   —24—   —23—

Paris chose a footed bowl like the one in fig. 24, designed in 1912, for their permanent collection. A few museums have sponsored retrospective exhibitions of Jensen silver, most notably the Renwick Gallery of Washington D.C. in 1980. The inclusion of pieces of identical design or of the piece itself in important exhibitions, museum collections and literature can influence prices. For example the work of Henning Koppel has increased dramatically in value following the memorial exhibition at the Kunstindustrimuseet in Copenhagen in 1982.

Fashion plays a part in every collecting field, but Jensen's continued insistence on originality of design and quality of production should protect buyers against the vicissitudes of changing taste.

● SARAH NEGREA ●

Further reading

Graham Hughes, *Modern Silver*, New York and London, 1967

Jorgen E. R. Moller, *Georg Jensen The Danish Silversmith*, Copenhagen, 1984

W. Schwartz, *Georg Jensen*, Copenhagen, 1958

Exhibition catalogue, *Georg Jensen Silversmithy*, Renwick Gallery of the National Collection of Fine Arts, Washington DC, 1980

Edgar Kaufman, Jr. *Fifty Years of Danish Silver in the Georg Jensen Tradition*, Museum of Modern Art, New York, 1984

—25—
A three-piece coffee service with matching tray, Georg Jensen, Copenhagen, numbered 2D and 2T, designed by Georg Jensen in the 'Blossom' pattern, coffee pot 21cm (8¼in), *NY 7 Dec,* $5,775 (£3,902)

—26—
A three-piece coffee service, Georg Jensen, Copenhagen, numbered 600A, designed by Harald Nielsen, coffee pot 18.5cm (7¼in), *NY 7 Dec,* $2,860 (£1,932)

—27—
An American 'Danish Style' three-piece coffee service with matching silver tray, Woodside Sterling Co, c.1925, in a modified 'Blossom' pattern, coffee pot 19.5cm (7¾in), *NY 23 Feb,* $2,090 (£1,953)

—28—
A pair of Mexican tazze, de Matteo, 16.5cm (6½in), *NY 11 May,* $550 (£387)

—29—
A Mexican punch bowl, Sanborns, c.1945, 35.5cm (14in) diam, *NY 11 May,* $1,100 (£774)

—25—

—26—

—27—

—28— —29—

1
A Hagenauer electroplated hand mirror, 1930s, stamped 'WHW made in Vienna Austria', 29cm (11½in), *L 4 Dec,* £198 ($277)

2
A Paul Kiss silver cup and cover, Vienna, 1927, chased with emblematic scenes of workers and set with coloured stones, some damaged 34cm (13¼in) high, *NY 6 Dec,* $1,045 (£706)

3
A Gorham & Co. copper and silver plated vase, c.1915, 42cm (16½in), *C 3 Oct,* £462 ($647)

4
An Austrian electroplated mirror, c.1900, cast with crouched nude figure above, 52cm (20½in), *L 2 May,* £660 ($851)

5
A David Anderson enamelled cream jug and sugar basin, 1903, with red enamel body, the necks with blue and green enamelled cornflowers, *L 4 Dec,* £418 ($585)

6
A Danish silver dish, designed by F Hingelberg, 1936, 45cm (17¾in) wide, *L 15 Feb,* £1,210 ($1,404)

7
A pair of Gallia silvered-metal salts, c.1930, 5 and 5.5cm (2 and 2¼in) high, *NY 6 Dec,* $550 (£372)

8
A German chromium-plated cocktail shaker and accessories, c.1930, stamped D.R.G.M. with factory mark, the wings fitted as removable flasks, the tail with shot glasses and a funnel, the nose with larger flask and fruit strainer, 32cm (12½in) high, *NY 6 Dec,* $1,430 (£966)

9
A set of twelve Philippe Wolfers silver spoons and twelve forks, Brussels, c.1925, *NY 18 May,* $990 (£786)

10
A Henry van de Velde silver and tortoiseshell caviar knife, maker's mark, 19cm (7½in), *M 6 Oct,* FF23,310(£2,027;$3,000)

11
A Tiffany copper teapot, c.1900, ivory handle, 23cm (9in), length overall, *NY 7 Dec,* $880 (£594)

12
A French bronze-mounted pottery vase, c.1900, impressed with monogram EO, with streaked blue-grey glaze shading to *sang de boeuf,* restored, 50cm (19½in), *NY 23 Feb,* $1,100 (£1,028)

13
A Henry Louis Levasseur bronze ewer, c.1900, impressed E.V.527, golden brown patina, 32cm (12½in), *NY 23 Feb,* $1,045 (£977)

14
A Jean Dunand patinated-metal vase and liner, c.1930, marked, patterned in silver on a brown ground, 39.5cm (15½in), *NY 18 May,* $1,760 (£1,397)

Raoul Larche 'Loïe
Fuller' gilt-bronze lamp,
1900, signed and
numbered 573, 45.5cm
(18in), M 17 Mar,
FF 111,000
(£9,911; $12,190)

WMF silvered-pewter
mirror, c.1900, the
mirror plate supported
by a maiden with robes
continuing into a foot,
55.5cm (19½in),
NY 28 May,
$1,320 (£1,048)

Marion Wilson pewter
mantel clock, c.1910,
monogrammed 'MHW',
repousse with a galleon
steered by a cherub,
40.5cm (16in), L 5 July,
£264 ($364)

Hagenauer chromed
and enamelled-metal
mirror, c.1930, marked
and numbered 1257,
56cm (22in), NY 23 Feb,
$5,500 (£5,140)

A pair of Kayserzinn
pewter candlesticks,
c.1900, stamped
'Kayserzinn 4427',
42.5cm (16¾in), L 5 July,
£1,540 ($2,125)

A polished chrome
mantel clock, designed
by Gilbert Rohde for
the Herman Miller
Company, c.1937, 28cm
(11in) long, NY 23 Feb,
$1,210 (£1,131)

A WMF pewter dish,
c.1900, cast with a young
woman reclining amidst
flowers, 34.5cm (13½in),
L 4 Dec,
£528 ($739)

A WMF electroplated
metal centrepiece,
c.1900, decorated with
maidens, scrollwork
and floral motifs, 46cm
(18in) wide, L 15 Feb,
£451 ($523)

A WMF electroplated
pewter liqueur set, c.1900,
one glass missing, 38cm
(15in), L 4 Dec,
£275 ($385)

10
A pair of Kayserzinn
pewter candelabra,
c.1900, cast factory
marks, each with three
cups supported by a bat
with extended wings,
30.5cm (12in), NY 7 Dec,
$3,025 (£2,043)

11
A pair of James Dixon &
Sons pewter candelabra,
c.1905, 23cm (9in),
L 1 Feb,
£550 ($638)

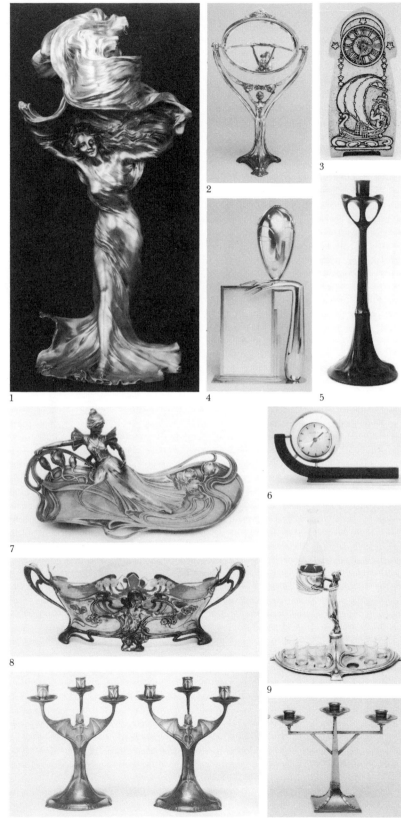

1

2

3

4

5

6

7

8

9

10

11

1
A bronze mirror, dated
1900, 63cm (24¾in),
L 17 Oct,
£935 ($1,384)

2
**A wrought iron part
staircase,** *c.*1900, with
forty uprights with
stylised stems, lacking
hand rail and steps,
L 17 Oct,
£990 ($1,465)

3
**A green enamelled cast
iron umbrella stand,**
*c.*1900, 60.5cm (23¾in),
L 17 Oct,
£220 ($326)

4
**A Coalbrookdale cast
iron umbrella stand,**
designed by Christopher
Dresser, *c.*1875, stamped
'Coalbrookdale', 82cm
(32¼in) high, *L 4 Dec,*
£352 ($493)

5
**A set of Russell Workshops
wrought iron fire irons,**
1930s, comprising
stand, poker, tongs and
shovel, 51.5cm (20¼in),
L 2 May,
£286 ($368)

6
**A wrought iron chande-
lier,** designed by
Edgar Brandt, *c.*1920,
impressed 'E Brandt',
minor losses, 79.5cm
(30¼in) high, *NY 23 Feb,*
$825 (£771)

7
**A pair of cast and
wrought-iron two-arm
candle sconces,** designed
by Ernest Gimson,
*c.*1905, 36cm (14¼in),
NY 18 May,
$825 (£655)

8
**A pair of wrought-iron
and gilt-bronze figural
andirons,** early 20th
century, each cast with a
hooded monk's head,
61cm (24in) high,
NY 23 Feb,
$715 (£668)

9
**A pair of Edgar Brandt
wrought iron bookends,**
1920s, stamped 'E
Brandt', each with a
kneeling gazelle, 17.5cm
(7in), *L 4 Dec,*
£990 ($1,386)

10
**A patinated-copper fire
fender,** possibly English,
*c.*1905, cast and pierced
with iris blossoms, 75cm
(29½in) high, *NY 18 May,*
$1,705 (£1,353)

1   2   3

4   5   6

7   8

9   10

1
A Gustav Stickley hammered copper and glass domed chandelier, 1910, 51.5cm (20¼in) high without chain, NY 23 Feb, $6,875 (£6,425)

2
A pair of metal and glass bedside lamps, attributed to Loetz, the bases in white metal, the adjustable shades in iridescent glass with amber spots and purple lines, 31cm (12¼in), M 17 Mar, FF12,210(£1,090;$1,340)

3
A Daum Nancy etched glass chandelier, c.1925, signed in intaglio, 58.5cm (23in) high, NY 18 May, 880 (£698)

4
A pair of Lalique opalescent glass ceiling shades, 1930s, shades 30.5cm (12in) diam, 4 Dec, 968 ($1,355)

5
A Perzel aluminium and glass ceiling light, c.1930, 66cm (26in) diam, 15 Feb, 935 ($1,085)

6
A pair of silvered-bronze and moulded glass two-arm sconces, designed by Genet et Michon, 1922, chips, 51cm (20in), NY 7 Dec, 1,100 (£743)

7
A Perzel copper and glass lampstand, 174cm (5ft ½in), M 17 Mar, FF 11,100 (£991; $1,218)

8
A Wiener Werkstatte electroplated copper lamp, designed by Josef Hoffmann, 1920s, with original green silk shade, 36cm (14in) high, 4 Dec, 1,430 ($2,002)

9
A nickel lamp, designed by René Prou for the Compagnie des Wagons-its, c.1930, 56.5cm (22¼in), M 17 Mar, F 6,660 (£595; $732)

10
A glass and chromium-plated metal 'Saturn' ceiling light, 1930s, 53cm (20¾in) diam, sold with a pair of chromium-plated metal wall lights, 1930s, L 2 May, £198 ($255)

11
A chromed-metal and red glass floor lamp, designed by J Kuyken, c.1930, minor chips, 175cm (5ft 9in), NY 7 Dec, $5,775 (£3,902)
(A similar lamp illustrated in last year's guide was wrongly captioned)

12
A chromed-metal and frosted glass table lamp, 1930s, the mushroom shade with five inset frosted glass flanges, 71.5cm (28¼in), L 2 May, £308 ($397)

13
A Perzel chrome metal and glass hanging lamp, 102cm (40¼in), M 17 Mar, FF11,100 (£991; $1,218)

1
A Gallé inlaid fruitwood
sewing table, *c.*1900,
signed, 76cm (30in)
high, *NY 7 Dec,*
$4,400 (£2,972)

2
A Gallé fruitwood
marquetry two-tier table,
*c.*1900, signed, 110cm
(43½in) high, *NY 7 Dec,*
$1,320 (£891)

3
A Gallé fruitwood table,
*c.*1900, 81cm (32in) wide,
M 6 Oct,
FF42,180(£3,668;$5,429)

4
A Gallé fruitwood
marquetry two-handled
tray, *c.*1900, signed,
inlaid with a view of a
ruin and vines, the
handles as soaring
birds, 67cm (26½in),
NY 23 Feb,
$1,650 (£1,542)

5
A Eugène Gaillard table,
*c.*1900, 80cm (31½in)
high, *M 17 Mar,*
FF68,820(£6,144;$7,557)

6
A Majorelle inlaid
mahogany table, *c.*1900,
inlaid signature, the top
inlaid with branches of
flowering orchid,
78.5cm (31in) high,
L 15 Feb,
£1,155 ($1,340)

7
Two armchairs and two
matching side chairs,
100.5 and 112cm (43½
and 44cm) high, *L 5 July,*
£572 ($789)

8
A Majorelle grandfather
clock, 227cm (8ft 5½in)
high, *M 17 Mar,*
FF 53,280 (£4,757; $5,851)

9
A Majorelle inlaid
sideboard, *c.*1900, the top
with travertine panel,
the uprights with
ormolu mounts, 144cm
(56¾in) high, *L 15 Feb,*
£1,430 ($1,659)

10
A Majorelle mahogany
and bronze table,
M 17 Mar,
FF 133,200
(£11,892; $14,627)

1

2

3

4

5

6

7

8

9

10

1
A pair of Mundus white-painted armchairs, designed by Josef Hoffmann, c.1905, *M 6 Oct*, **FF 45,510 (£3,957; $5,857)**

2
A pair of J & J Kohn armchairs, designed by Koloman Moser, c.1905, 86cm (34in), *M 6 Oct*, **FF 42,100 (£3,661; $5,418)**

3
An Emile Jacques Ruhlmann macassar armchair, c.1925, 87.5cm (34½in), *M 17 Mar*, **FF 25,530 (£2,279; $2,803)**

4
An ivory-inlaid macassar and shagreen dressing table and matching chair, designed by Emile-Jacques Ruhlmann, c.1925, table 122cm (48in) high, *NY 18 May*, **$22,000 (£17,460)**

5
A Jean Michel Franck vellum cabinet/bar, c.1935, 86cm (34in) high, *M 6 Oct*, **FF 77,700 (£6,757; $10,000)**

6
An Emile Jacques Ruhlmann macassar post tray, c.1925, 36cm (14in) long, *M 6 Oct*, **FF 17,760(£1,545; $2,286)**

7
A brass and mirrored peach glass screen, attributed to Jacques Adnet, c.1930, each panel 105 x 30cm (41½ x 12in), *NY 7 Dec*, **$1,100 (£743)**

8
A Dalbert bronze table mirror, c.1930, brown patina, 46.5cm (18¼in), *NY 7 Dec*, **$2,750 (£1,858)**

9
A mahogany and bird's-eye maple chest of drawers, designed by Gilbert Rohde for Herman Miller, c.1936, 93cm (36½in) high, *NY 23 Feb*, **$1,320 (£1,234)**

10
A Pierre Chareau desk, c.1930 128cm (50¼in) wide, *M 17 Mar*, **FF 555,000 (£49,553; $60,950)**

1
A Carlo Zen inlaid
mahogany mirror,
*c.*1905, 240cm (8ft ¼in)
high, *L 4 Dec,*
£2,750 ($3,580)

2
A Carlo Bugatti inlaid
wood, copper and suede
chair, *M 6 Oct,*
FF 11,100 (£966; $1,430)

3
A Carlo Bugatti lady's
writing desk and chair,
*c.*1900, desk 98cm
(38½in) high, *M 6 Oct,*
FF 47,730
(£4,151; $6,143)

4
A Carlo Bugatti inlaid
wood, copper and vellum
chair, *c.*1900, *M 17 Mar,*
FF 17,760
(£1,585; $1,949)

5
A Carlo Bugatti inlaid
wood, copper and vellum
desk, *c.*1900, 75.5cm
(29¾in), *M 17 Mar,*
FF 76,590
(£6,838; $8,410)

6
A Bugatti corner chair,
*c.*1900, *L 15 Feb,*
£1,650 ($1,914)

7
An Austrian copper and
patinated metal table,
*c.*1905, 57cm (22½in)
high, *M 17 Mar,*
FF 6,105 (£545; $670)

8
Two inlaid mahogany
chairs, *c.*1909,
L 4 Dec,
£352 ($493)

9
A wood and parcel gilt
suite, *c.*1900, comprising
sofa, pair of armchairs,
and a pair of chairs,
sofa 116cm (45½in) wide,
M 17 Mar,
FF 35,520
(£3,171; $3,900)

10
A quartered oak dressing
table, and chair *c.*1910,
148cm (58in) high,
NY 18 May,
$1,100 (£873)

11
A J & J Kohn wood and
copper stand, *c.*1900,
143.5cm (56½in),
M 6 Oct,
FF 61,050
(£5,309; $7,857)

1

2   3

4   5

6

7

8

9

10

11

1
An Austrian bentwood
hall stand, *c.*1900, after a
design by Josef Hoff-
mann, *L 15 Feb,*
£550 ($638)

2
A nest of four J & J
Kohn bentwood tables,
designed by Josef
Hoffmann, *c.*1910,
NY 23 Feb,
$6,050 (£5,654)

3
A bentwood rocking
chair, *c.*1915, *NY 7 Dec,*
$770 (£520)

4
A bentwood chaise longue,
*c.*1900, *NY 7 Dec,*
$4,125 (£2,787)

5
A J & J Kohn bentwood
settee, designed by
Gustav Siegel, *c.*1902,
NY 23 Feb,
$2,970 (£2,776)

6
A Thonet bentwood
dressing table, designed
by Josef Hoffmann,
*c.*1905, *M 17 Mar,*
FF 6,660 (£595; $731)

7
Two J & J Kohn wooden
armchairs, designed by
Josef Hoffmann, *c.*1905,
M 17 Mar,
FF 14,985 (£1,337; $1,644)

8
A J & J Kohn 'Fleder-
maus' chair, designed
by Josef Hoffmann,
*c.*1905, *L 2 May,*
£308 ($397)

9
A J & J Kohn armchair,
designed by Otto Wag-
ner, *c.*1900, *L 5 July,*
£682 ($941)

10
A J & J Kohn bentwood
mirror, designed by
Koloman Moser, *c.*1910,
NY 7 Dec,
$6,875 (£4,645)

11
A pair of J & J Kohn
wooden stools, designed
by Josef Hoffmann,
*c.*1905, *M 17 Mar,*
FF 15,540 (£1,387; $1,706)

12
An oval beech table,
manufactured by Fischel,
*c.*1910, *NY 23 Feb,*
$1,650 (£1,542)

1

A Morris & Co embroidered fire screen, c.1889, probably from the drawing-room of Bullerswood, mahogany frame, 111cm (43¾in) high, *L 4 Dec,* £1,100 ($1,540)

2

A Wylie & Lockhead white-painted writing bureau, probably designed by E A Taylor, c.1900, set with a pink and green glass panel, 168cm (5ft 6in) high, *L 2 May,* £935 ($1,206)

3

A Guild of Handicrafts Ltd cabinet, designed by C R Ashbee, c.1906, green stained oak case, the upper doors inlaid with ivory carnations and with stained and gilt interiors, 141cm (55½in) high, *L 2 May,* £25,800 ($33,282)

4

A Morris & Co mahogany washstand, 1890s, stamped and numbered 1409, 123cm (48½in) high, *L 17 Oct,* £308 ($456)

5

An oak dresser, designed by C F A Voysey, c.1900, with brass strapwork hingeplates, 150.5cm (59¼in) high, *L 4 Dec,* £31,900 ($44,600)

6

A set of six oak chairs, designed in the offices of Richard Norman Shaw, c.1880, comprising two armchairs and four side-chairs, 117 and 102cm (46 and 40in) high, *L 2 May,* £715 ($922)

7

A set of six J S Henry mahogany chairs, c.1900, comprising two armchairs and four side-chairs, 98.5 and 93cm (38¾ and 36½in) high, *L 2 May,* £1,760 ($2,270)

8

A Morris & Co 'Sussex' settee, 1880s, rush seat, 153cm (5ft ¼in) long, *L 2 May,* £264 ($340)

1

2

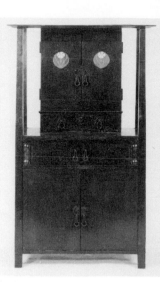

3

4

5

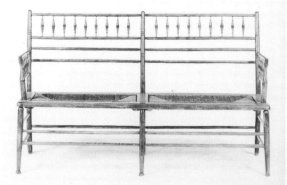

6   7   8

1
A Liberty & Co 'Thebes'
stool, c.1900, applied
label, 37cm (14½in),
, 4 Dec,
£484 ($678)

2
An inlaid oak sideboard,
1880s, 196.5cm (5ft
5½in), L 17 Oct,
£660 ($977)

3
An ebonised occasional
table, designed by E W
Godwin, c.1880, 69.5cm
(27¼in), L 5 July,
£187 ($258)

4
An Aesthetic Movement
firescreen, 1880s, with
stained glass panel,
105cm (41¼in), L 17 Oct,
£209 ($309)

5
An ebonised Aesthetic
Movement cabinet, 1880s,
a pair of doors set with
painted and gilt panels
of children, in the style
of W S Coleman, 142cm
(56in) high, L 15 Feb,
£715 ($829)

6
A Gothic bureau, 1880s,
163cm (5ft 3in) high,
L 4 Dec,
£385 ($539)

7
A Gothic table, 1880s,
64.5cm (25½in) high,
L 15 Feb,
£165 ($191)

8
A Liberty & Co 'Thebes'
stool, 1890s, 37cm
(14½in), L 15 Feb,
£605 ($702)

9
An inlaid oak chest of
drawers, 1880s, inlaid
with chevron bands,
129.5cm (50¾in) high,
L 4 Dec,
£495 ($693)

10
A Liberty & Co washstand,
c.1900, affixed label,
124cm (48¾in), L 15 Feb,
£638 ($740)

11
A Robson & Sons inlaid
mahogany music cabinet,
c.1905, with applied
label, the doors inlaid
in fruitwoods and
mother-of-pearl, 122cm
(48in) high, L 4 Dec,
£1,320 ($1,848)

1

2

3

4

5

6

7

8

9

10

11

1
A pewter-inlaid and marquetry stained-oak rocker, designed by Harvey Ellis for Gustav Stickley, c.1905, *NY 23 Feb,* $1,760 (£1,645)

2
A carved oak dining table, designed by Charles Rohlfs, 1907, 137cm (54¼in) wide without leaves, *NY 7 Dec,* $10,450 (£7,060)

3
A carved oak sideboard, designed by Charles Rohlfs, 1907, 120cm (47in) high, *NY 7 Dec,* $6,050 (£4,087)

4
An L & J G Stickley stained-oak hall bench, early 20th century, 140cm (55in) wide, *NY 23 Feb,* $2,860 (£2,673)

5
A Mission oak library table, in the manner of Charles Rohlfs, c.1910, 72.5cm (28½in) high, *NY 23 Feb,* $1,320 (£1,234)

6
A Stickley Bros. stained oak coat-rack and umbrella stand, c.1915, 224cm (7ft 4in), *NY 7 Dec,* $3,630 (£2,452)

7
A Gustav Stickley oak cabinet, c.1910, 159cm (5ft 2¾in) high, *NY 23 Feb,* $825 (£771)

8
A Gustav Stickley oak library table, c.1910, 77cm (30¾in) high, *NY 7 Dec,* $1,870 (£1,263)

9
A Roycroft oak rocker, c.1910, *NY 18 May,* $935 (£742)

10
A Gustav Stickley oak Morris chair, c.1910, no. 369, sold with a Gustav Stickley oak footstool, *NY 18 May,* $3,300 (£2,619)

11
A Limbert oak oval centre table, c.1910, no. 146, 73.5cm (29in) high, *NY 18 May,* $770 (£611)

1

2

6

3

4

7

5

8

9

10

11

1
A Waring & Gillow oak wardrobe, c.1910, 191cm (6ft 3in) high, L 17 Oct, £165 ($244)

2
A Heals Ltd 1930s bedroom suite, comprising dressing chest, chest/cabinet, small wardrobe and single bed, dressing chest 141cm (55½in) high, L 17 Oct, £715 ($1,001)

3
A walnut bedside cupboard, designed by Ernest Gimson, 1930s, 84cm (33in) high, L 2 May, £330 ($425)

4
A Heal's oak dresser, 1905, 163cm (5ft 4in) high, L 4 Dec, £825 ($1,155)

5
A sycamore writing desk, designed by Sir Edwin Lutyens, 1930s, inset leather top, 77cm (30¼in) high, L 2 May, £1,760 ($2,270)

6
A William Birch armchair, designed by William Punnett, 1901, the back with a design in stained fruitwoods, 85.5cm (33½in) high, L 5 July, £550 ($759)

7
An oak 'domino' table, after a design by Charles Rennie Mackintosh for the Argyle Street tea rooms of 1897, 80cm (31½in) high, L 17 Oct, £770 ($1,140)

8
A 'Mouseman' oak dining suite, by Robert Thompson of Kilburn, 1930s, comprising table, six side chairs and two armchairs, sideboard and carving table, sideboard 94.5cm (37¼in) high, table 183cm (6ft) long, L 4 Dec, £3,520 ($4,928)

9
A Peter Waals walnut desk, 1920s, 78cm (30¾in) high, L 2 May, £2,090 ($2,696)

10
A pair of 'Mouseman' oak armchairs, by Robert Thompson of Kilburn, 1930s, 78cm (30¾in), L 4 Dec, £440 ($616)

11
A macassar ebony table, designed by Sir Edward Maufe, c.1928, 53cm (21in) high, L 2 May, £275 ($354)

12
A pair of macassar ebony tables, designed by Sir Edward Maufe, c.1928, 54cm (21¼in) high, L 2 May, £506 ($652)

1

2

3

4

5

6

7

8

9

10

11

12

1
A Betty Joel black-painted dining room suite, 1930s, comprising table and six armchairs, *L 5 July,* £1,870 ($2,580)

2
A 1930s sycamore dressing table with bedside cabinet ensuite, *L 5 July,* £990 ($1,366)

3
A 'pop-up' bar table, 1930s, 76cm (30in) diam, *L 17 Oct,* £308 ($456)

4
A burr wood dining room suite, 1930s comprising table, six chairs and sideboard, *L 15 Feb,* £880 ($1,021)

5
A Hille burr maple bedroom suite, *c.*1930, probably designed by Ray Hille, comprising dressing table, two wardrobes, and a bed-head with fitted bedside cabinets, *L 2 May,* £880 ($1,135)

6
An Eavestaff 'Minipiano' pianette and stool, 92.5cm (36½in) high, *L 15 Feb,* £935 ($1,085)

7
A Modernist rug, 1930s, 116 x 244cm *L 5 July,* £242 ($334)

8
A large tufted rug, 1930s, 342 x 255cm *L 17 Oct,* £495 ($733)

9
A carpet, 1930s, 365 x 262cm *L 2 May,* £902 ($1,163)

10
A Modernist carpet, *c.*1930, 182 x 90cm *M 6 Oct,* FF 2,200 (£191; $283)

11
A Walt Disney character rug, 1960s, 113 x 164cm *L 15 Feb,* £638 ($740)

12
A Walt Disney cotton rug, 1950s, 114 x 147cm *L 4 Dec,* £165 ($231)

1

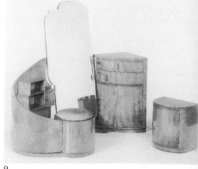

2

3

4

5

6

7

8

9

10

11

12

1
A pair of French mahogany armchairs, *c.*1935, *NY 18 May,* **$1,980 (£1,571)**

2
A pair of 1930s armchairs, faced in macassar, 77cm (30¼in) high, *L 15 Feb,* **£572 ($664)**

3
A pair of vellum armchairs, *c.*1935, in the style of Jean Michel Franck, 57cm (22½in), *M 6 Oct,* **FF 24,975 (£2,172; $3,215)**

4
A gold-leaf commode, designed by André Arbus, *c.*1930, 83in (32¾in) high, *NY 18 May,* **$2,750 (£2,183)**

5
A lacquered nest of tables, *c.*1925, largest 50.5cm (19¾in) high, *M 17 Mar,* **FF 12,210 (£1,090; $1,340)**

6
A Dominique macassar and stained-wood games table, designed by André Domin and Marcel Genevrière, *c.*1930, drawer, 75cm (29½in) high, *NY 18 May,* **$1,320 (£1,048)** *NY 18 May,* **$1,320 (£1,048)**

7
A French dining room suite, 1930s, comprising extending table, eight chairs and sideboard, table 259cm (8ft 6in) extended length, *L 2 May,* **£1,210 ($1,560)**

8
A mahogany and silver-bronze desk, designed by Alfred Porteneuve, *c.*1936, 76.5cm (29¾in), *NY 18 May,* **$7,150 (£5,675)**

9
A French bedroom suite, 1930s, comprising dressing table, small chair, side unit and double bed end, the unit 250cm (8ft 2¾in) wide, *L 2 May,* **£1,430 ($1,844)**

10
A Modernist dressing table, *c.*1935, 156cm (61½in) high, *M 6 Oct,* **FF 39,960 (£3,475; $5,143)**

1

2

3

4

5

6

7

8

9

10

1
A Modernist chromed
metal and mirror glass
side table, 1930s, 55cm
(21½in) high, *L 5 July*,
£143 ($197)

2
A chrome, leather and
mahogany chaise longue,
designed by Ludwig
Mies van der Rohe,
retailed by Knoll
Associates, Inc., uphol-
stered in tan leather,
198cm (6ft 6in) long,
NY 6 Dec,
$2,420 (£1,635)

3
A tubular chrome and
leather armchair,
designed by Le Cor-
busier, Pierre Jeanneret
and Charlotte Pierrand,
*c.*1928, and executed
by Cassina, *c.*1967,
NY 23 Feb
$1,650 (£1,542)

4
A wood and chrome pool-
side trolley, designed by
Gilbert Rohde for the
Troy Sunshade Com-
pany, *c.*1929, with
lime-green cork-lined
tray, 84cm (33in) high,
NY 23 Feb,
$1,100 (£1,028)

5
A pair of chrome and
leather 'Barcelona' side-
chairs, designed by
Ludwig Mies van der
Rohe for the Barcelona
Exhibition of 1929,
retailed by Knoll
Associates Inc., uphol-
stered in tan leather,
NY 6 Dec,
$3,410 (£2,304)

6
A chromed tubular steel
desk and chair with
matching side table,
1930s, desk 78cm (31in)
high, *L 2 May*,
£605 ($780)

7
A chromed metal, glass
and black glass dressing
table, 1930s, attributed
to Desny, mirror marked
'Miroir Blot Paris',
120cm (47¼in) high,
L 2 May,
£638 ($823)

8
A tubular chrome and
green leather stool,
designed by Charlotte
Perriand and Le Cor-
busier, *c.*1929, 53cm
(20¾in) high, *M 6 Oct*,
FF12,765(£1,110;$1,643)

9
A mahogany and chrome
dining table, in the
manner of Donald
Deskey, *c.*1935, the top
hinged and opening to
form a dining surface,
137cm (54in) long,
NY 23 Feb,
$990 (£925)

10
A cheval glass in nickled
tubular metal, by Louis
Sognot, *c.*1925, 180cm
(5ft 11in), *M 6 Oct*,
FF 11,100 (£965; $1,429)

11
A glass and chrome table,
designed by Ludwig
Mies van der Rohe,
1930, for the Tugendhat
House Brno, Czechos-
lovakia, 102cm (40in)
wide, *NY 6 Dec*,
$880 (£595)

1
A black-painted circular table, 1930s, 77cm (30¼in) high, *L 5 July,* £374 ($517)

2
A Marcel Baugniet oak armchair, *c.*1930, 88cm (34½in), *M 6 Oct,* FF 9,435 (£821; $1,215)

3
A pair of Djo Bourgeois armchairs, *c.*1930, 82cm (32¼in), *M 17 Mar,* FF 17,760 (£1,585; $1,949)

4
A Pierre Chareau sycamore stool, *c.*1925, 38cm (15in) high, *M 17 Mar,* FF 23,310 (£2,081; $2,559)

5
A nest of three Isokon plywood tables, designed by Marcel Breuer, 1936, *L 2 May,* £825 ($1,064)

6
A pair of Hermès leather armchairs, designed by Jacques Adnet, *c.*1935, 75cm (29½in), *M 6 Oct,* FF 6,660 (£579; $857)

7
A Gerrit Rietveld 'zig-zag' armchair, *c.*1935, 81cm (31¾in), *M 17 Mar,* FF 55,500 (£4,955; $6,094)

8
A moulded plywood chaise longue, designed by Marcel Breuer, *c.*1935, manufactured probably *c.*1960, 134cm (53in) long, *NY 18 May,* $1,100 (£873) See also p.347 fig.1

9
A Finmar child's table and four chairs, designed by Alvar Aalto, 1930s, table 100cm (39¼in) diam, *L 2 May,* £440 ($567)

10
Two Finmar Ltd. plywood tables, designed by Alvar Aalto, 1930s, 99.5cm (39¼in) wide, and 63cm (24¾in) diam, *L 15 Feb,* £418 ($485)

11
A Piermag inflatable armchair and two pouffes, *c.*1970, 100cm (39¼in) wide, *M 17 Mar,* FF 6,660 (£595; $732)

1

2

3

4

5

6

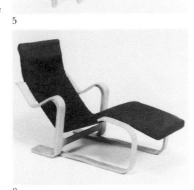

7

8

9

10

11

Post-war Decorative Arts

The last twenty years have witnessed an acceleration in the rate at which historic styles come back into favour. We have witnessed the revival of interest in all things nineteenth-century, a tremendous vogue for Art Nouveau, followed by an even greater enthusiasm for Art Deco and the styles of the late 1920s and 1930s. It seemed inevitable, therefore, that sooner rather than later the interest of researchers, collectors, dealers and curators should focus on the decorative styles and artifacts of the 1940s and 1950s. Older generations may prefer to forget the styles which they associate with the relative austerity of the post-war years and with a period when mass-production methods were ringing the death-knell of traditional craftsmanship in so many areas of domestic goods.

A younger generation, however, is now discovering with fascination the relics of this period, already sufficiently distant to be viewed objectively as a historically definable phase in the history of style. Collectors are hunting, dealers selling and auction houses offering in their catalogues the characteristic products of the post-war era. Publishers are issuing books on this period, which followed Art Deco and Modernism.

—1—
A Fornasetti trompe l'oeil cupboard, *c.*1950, 179cm (5ft 10½in), *M 17 Mar,* **FF 55,500 (£4,955; $6,094)**

—2—
A Johannes Hansen dumb-valet chair, *c.*1953, designed by Hans Wegner in 1951, 94.5cm (37¼in), *M 6 Oct,* **FF 8,325 (£724; $1,071)**

—3—
An H Morris & Co Ltd coffee table, *c.*1949, designed by Neil Morris, 46cm (18in), *L 2 May,* **£484 ($624)**

—4—
A blond wood and green simulated leather occasional table, designed by Gilbert Rohde for Herman Miller, *c.*1940, 68.5cm (27in), *NY 18 May,* **$495 (£393)**

—1—

—2—

—3—

—4—

Whilst generalizations are, by their very nature, incomplete and potentially misleading, it would nonetheless seem reasonable to suggest certain broad principles as a basis for understanding the nature of post-war styles. The war had provided a natural hiatus in the evolution of the decorative arts. The combination of post-war optimism, the need to rebuild manufacturing industries, the progress toward a boom period in growth economies built on a broad-based pattern of consumerism, engendered new decorative styles. The most influential sources of new ideas were Italy, the United States and the Scandinavian countries. France failed to recapture its former supremacy in the decorative arts, with the singular exception of its couture industry. Britain enjoyed a flurry of creativity, stimulated by the Festival of Britain, which provided, in 1951, an opportunity for indulgence in decorative whimsy.

Italian designers and artisans were the most exuberant in their inventive development of novel motifs and forms, in many cases reflecting very clearly the influence of currently fashionable abstract styles in the fine arts. American designers evolved radical new styles for furniture, with an emphasis on curvilinear asymmetrical shapes, a style that has been dubbed Organic Modernism. Scandinavian design tended to be less extreme, although certain designers experimented with the fashionable free-form sculptural style. Through the 1950s, Scandinavian glass, metalwork and furnishings found considerable international success and came to be regarded as a new measure of good taste.

—5—
A Herman Miller wood and glass table, designed by Isamu Noguchi, c.1945, 127.5cm (50¼in) long, M 17 Mar, FF 14,430 (£1,288; $1,584)

—6—
A set of nine Carlo Mollino oak and plywood chairs, c.1950, 89.5cm (35¼in), M 17 Mar, FF 122,100 (£10,901; $13,408)

—7—
A Carlo Mollino wood and black glass table, 1949, 169.5cm (5ft 6½in) wide, M 6 Oct, FF 66,600 (£5,791; $8,571)

—8—
A pair of Carlo Mollino plywood armchairs, c.1950, 74cm (29in) high, M 17 Mar, FF 172,050 (£15,361; $18,894)

—9—
A Carlo Mollino plywood copper and glass table, c.1950, 120.5cm (47½in) long, M 6 Oct, FF 233,100 (£20,270; $29,999)

—10—
An Ar-Flex armchair, designed by Marco Zanuso in 1951, upholstered in cream vinyl, 99cm (39in) high, L 5 July, £110 ($152)

—5—
—6—
—7—
—8—
—9—
—10—

The relative infancy of this area as a subject of interest to collectors is such that the criteria of quality and merit are still in the process of being established. The subject is full of promise for the investor with sufficient knowledge to appreciate what is or is not a good and typical example, what may or may not be demonstrated to be of lasting significance. Let us take the example of 1950s glass. Five years ago there was little price differential between run-of-the-mill pieces and outstanding examples. In the last couple of years, however, levels of connoisseurship have increased and the differential is now more marked. Master works sell for many thousands of pounds, while the more mundane pieces have hardly moved in price. This trend will doubtless continue, with even higher price records being set for the finest and rarest examples by the leading designers and craftsmen.

Study of the period will give the collector or enthusiast much food for thought about the relative importance of design concept and virtuoso craft. For in this period, more than ever before, good design was to become increasingly associated with industrial design for series production, just as much as with the creation of finely made luxury goods. It would seem logical that the rarity and intrinsic technical qualities of the most finely made objects—be they of glass, ceramic, wood, silver or enamel—should command high prices and prove to be good investments. There are many series-produced objects, however, which can be bought for relatively modest sums and yet which are as perfect examples of the stylistic tendencies of their era as are the more precious and rarefied artifacts. A series-produced plywood table designed by the American Charles Eames is as worthy of our interest as a unique plywood and glass table by the Italian Carlo Mollino; a simple, well-proportioned glass vase designed by the Scandinavians Kaj Franck or Timo Sarpaneva can be as aesthetically satisfying as the most complex tour de force of master glasswork from the most creative studios of Murano.

—11—
A laminated wood and painted metal coffee table, designed by Charles Eames, c.1955, 226cm (7ft 5in) long, *NY 6 Dec,* $1,760 (£1,189)

—12—
An Archimede Seguso glass table, c.1950, 90cm (35½in) wide, *M 17 Mar,* FF 45,510 (£4,063; $4,997)

—11—

—12—

—13—
An Archimede Seguso glass vase, *c.*1950, in colourless glass with a white glass serpent, 20cm (8in), *M 17 Mar,*
FF 24,420
(£2,180; $2,681)

—14—
A Seguso Vetri d'Arte 'Siderale' vase, designed by Flavio Poli, *c.*1950, decorated on one side with layers of blue-green and smoked glass, *M 17 Mar,*
FF 38,850 (£3,468; $4,265)

—15—
A Kosta internally decorated glass vase, designed by Vicke Lindstrand, 1950s, smoky pale blue base, 33.5cm (13¼in), *L 5 July,*
£143 ($197)

—16—
Two Iittala glass vases, designed by Tapio Wirkkala, 1950s 13.5 and 5.5cm (5¼ and 2¼in), *L 17 Oct,*
£110 ($163)

—17—
An Iittala 'Lily' vase, designed by Tapio Wirkkala, *c.*1946, 21cm (8¼in), *L 17 Oct,*
£440 ($651)

—18—
A Barovier & Toso 'Saturneo' vase, designed by Ercole Barovier, 1951, 16cm (6¼in), *M 17 Mar,*
FF 14,430 (£1,288; $1,584)

—19—
Two Nuutajarvi-Notsjo glass vases, designed by Gunnel Nyman, *c.*1945, the inner layers tinted amber and deep mauve, 12 and 10.5cm (4¾ and 4¼in), *L 2 May,*
£286 ($368)

—20—
An Iittala glass dish, designed by Tapio Wirkkala, *c.*1950, 7.5cm (3in), *L 17 Oct,*
£82 ($121)

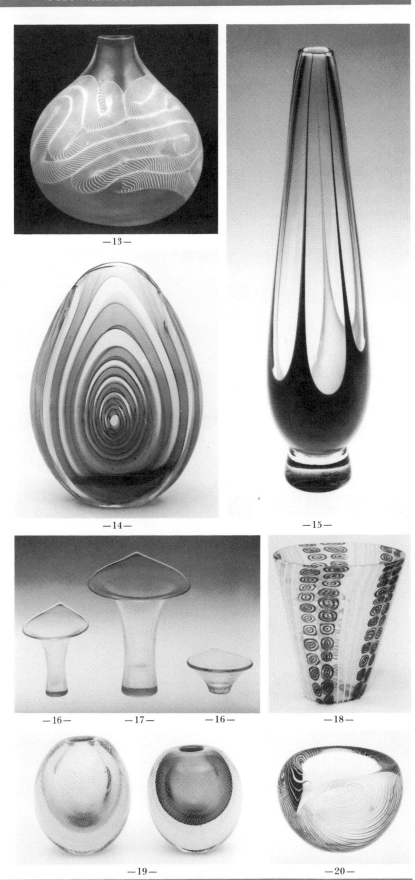

—13—

—14—

—15—

—16—

—17—

—16—

—18—

—19—

—20—

The market-place will surely put an ever rising premium on the combination of rarity and fine craftsmanship. Collectors, however, would be well advised to investigate and consider the full range of objects which survive from the 1940s and 1950s with an eye for purity of concept, for typicalness as well as rarity (which, in itself, has no great virtue), or for complexity of execution.

The market in post-war works has an international following, as befits the international character of the subject. There are specialist dealers in the United States and in Europe, notably in New York, London, Paris, Munich, Milan and Turin. Auction houses are including increasing numbers of post-war pieces in sales of twentieth-century decorative arts, though the market is by no means as extensive as that for the works of the first decades of the century.

The period is particularly interesting for its glass and this medium has already proved very attractive to collectors. Most highly prized are the best works of the foremost Venetian glassworkers and designers, notably Paolo Venini (figs.22, 23, 24), Flavio Poli (fig.14), Archimede Seguso (fig.13), Fulvio Bianconi and Alfredo Barbini, and of the top designers for the leading Scandinavian glassworks, including Tapio Wirkkala (figs.16, 17, 20), Kaj Franck, Gunnel Nyman (fig.19) and Sven Palmquist (fig.21).

Less widely known, but worthy of interest, are the ceramics, which range from elegant designs for series production from such factories as Gustavsberg in Sweden, and Carter, Stabler and Adams in England, to elaborate sculptured or highly decorative works by the Italians Guido Gambone (fig.29), Fausto Melotti or Franco Fantoni.

—21—
An Orrefors 'Ravenna' glass vase, designed by Sven Palmquist, *c.*1955, in blue and purple glass, 14.5cm (5¾in), *L 2 May,* £220 ($283)

—22—
A Venini glass jug, 1950s, the green glass banded in milky blue, 24.5cm (9½in), *L 15 Feb,* £176 ($204)

—23—
A Venini blue glass handkerchief vase, 1950s, with royal blue exterior, 23cm (9in), *L 4 Dec,* £352 ($493)

—24—
A Venini glass vase, in smoked grey glass with red lines, 31cm (12¼in), *M 17 Mar,* FF 6,660 (£594; $731)

—21—

—23—

—22—

—24—

Exciting designs in silver are rare, but, at their best, in work by such designers as Henning Koppel (for Georg Jensen) (see pp.306-311) or Lino Sabattini (for Christofle) (fig.28), can be elegant and inventive. In furniture, Italian, American and Scandinavian designers produced the most interesting work. The Turin-based architect/designer Carlo Mollino (figs.6-9) is highly regarded for his eccentric experiments in sculpting plywood; Charles Eames (fig.11) designed for mass-production, but his early prototypes of the 1940s are keenly collected.

There is still much to be explored, and there are priorities yet to be established, which will give this field great potential for research and discovery. The question begs itself as to whether interest in the 1940s and 1950s will be followed by a revival of interest in the 1960s. The answer is that such is the rate at which the wheel of reappraisal turns full circle that the 1960s are already attracting the interest of collectors.

● PHILIPPE GARNER ●

Further reading:

Mary Banham & Bevis Hillier (ed). *A Tonic to the Nation*, The Festival of Britain, 1951
Philadelphia Museum of Art, *Design since 1945*, 1883
Philippe Garner, *The Contemporary Decorative Arts (from 1940 to the present day)*, 1980
Roberto Aloi, *Esempi di Decorazione Moderna di tutto il mondo*, 1955

—25—
A Lucie Rie porcelain bowl, 1950s, the exterior glazed deep-brown, the interior cream, 12cm (4¾in) diam, L 3 May, £242 ($309)

—26—
A Lucie Rie and Hans Coper stoneware coffee set, 1950s, comprising two cups and saucers and a coffee pot, each glazed in deep brown, light damage, coffee pot 13cm (5in), L 3 May, £286 ($366)

—27—
An American Thermos Bottle Co aluminium thermos and tray, designed by Henry Dreyfus, c.1945, 18.5cm (7¼in), M 6 Oct, FF 8,325 (£724; $1,071)

—28—
A Christofle silver vase, 1960, designed by Lino Sabattini, 17cm (6¾in), M 17 Mar, FF 9,990 (£892; $1,097)

—29—
A decorated earthenware pitcher, Guido Gambone, 1950s, 30cm (11⅞in) high, L 16 Feb, 1984, £693 ($972)

—30—
A Christofle silvered metal tea service, comprising five pieces, teapot 25.5cm (10in) wide, M 17 Mar, FF 13,320 (£1,189; $1,462)

—25—

—26—

—27—

—28—

—29—

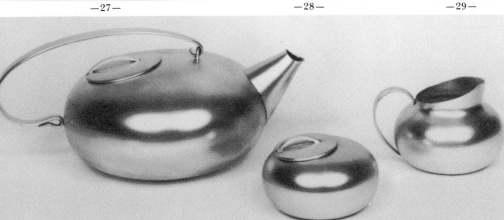

—30—

1
A Philippe bronze and ivory figure of a dancing girl, *c.*1920, marked, 41cm (16in), *L 2 May,* £1,540 ($1,986)

2
A Paul Philippe bronze and ivory figure of a female violin player, *c.*1930, marked, variegated gold/brown patination, two fingers detached, 30cm (11¾in), *S 15 Oct,* £858 ($1,270)

3
A pair of Fath bronze and ivory figures of 'The Young Man of the World' and 'Going Out in the Rain', early 20th century, chocolate-brown and silvered patination, 20cm (8in), *S 16 Apr,* £946 ($1,230)

4
A Mirval gilt-bronze and ivory figure of an exotic dancer, *c.*1930, marked, 64cm (25¼in), *M 17 Mar,* FF 49,950 (£4,459; $5,484)

5
A Blanchot bronze figure of a woman with a boa, *c.*1900, marked, 32.5cm (12¾in), *M 6 Oct,* FF 4,440 (£387; $573)

6
A Bruno Zach bronze figure of a woman smoking, *c.*1925, marked, reddish-brown patina heightened with gilding, cigarette broken, 40cm (15¾in), *NY 18 May,* $1,320 (£1,048)

7
A Bruno Zach bronze and ivory figure of a young woman, *c.*1930, marked, wearing smoking jacket and trousers, 74cm (29in), *L 2 May,* £9,240 ($11,919)

8
A Santiago-Rodriguez Bonome bronze figure of a woman, *c.*1930, marked, light brown patina, 66cm (26in), *NY 18 May,* $1,100 (£873)

9
A patinated spelter figure, *c.*1920, with pink glass globe, 51cm (20in), *C 16 May,* £143 ($190)

10
An Otto Poertzel polychromed-figure of a dancer, *c.*1930, marked, green, copper and gold patinas, total height 37.5cm (14¾in), *NY 18 May,* $990 (£786)

11
A Paul Piel figure of a snake dancer, *c.*1924, marked, total height 27cm (10½in), *NY 18 May,* $1,320 (£1,048)

12
A Bruno Zach bronze and ivory figure of a woman, 'Jockey Girl', *c.*1930, marked, cigarette missing, 60cm (23¾in), *NY 7 Dec,* $6,600 (£4,459)

13
Two Roland Paris polished bronze figures of a Pierrot and Pierrette, 1930s, marked Ernest Graas, Bildgiesserei Berlin SD26, 30.5cm (12in), *L 17 Oct,* £440 ($651)

14
A Bouraine bronze and ivory figure of Pierrette, *c.*1925, marked 25.5cm (10in), *M 6 Oct,* FF 8,880 (£773; $1,144)

1

2

3

4

5

6

7

8

9

10

11

12

13

14

1
A Preiss cold-painted bronze and ivory figure, 'Flame Leaper', c.1930, marked, some wear, 30cm (11¾in), *NY 18 May*, $3,850 (£3,056)

2
A Preiss bronze and ivory figure, 'The Bat Girl', 1930s, marked green/gold cold-painted costume, 24cm (9½in), *L 5 July*, £2,200 ($3,036)

3
A Preiss bronze and ivory figure of a schoolboy, 1930s, marked, wearing gold shorts and silver/gold shirt 21cm (8¼in), *L 4 Dec*, £935 ($1,309)

4
A Preiss bronze and ivory figure of a young girl, c.1930, marked, 21cm (8¼in), *L 2 May*, £1,320 ($1,702)

5
A Preiss carved ivory figure of a young girl with a casket, c.1930s, marked 15cm (6in), *S 15 Oct*, £319 ($472)

6
A Chiparus bronze and ivory figure of a young girl, c.1930, marked 37.5cm (14¾in), *L 5 July*, £1,210 ($1,669)

7
A Preiss cold-painted bronze and ivory figure, 'Moth Girl', c.1930, marked, one antenna lacking and age cracks, 44cm (17¼in), *NY 18 May*, $2,860 (£2,270)

8
A Preiss bronze and ivory figure, 'Con Brio', 1930s, marked, in silver, turquoise and gold cold-painted bikini costume, 39cm (15¼in), *L 4 Dec*, £3,520 ($4,928)

9
A Chiparus polychromed gilt-bronze and ivory figure of a dancer, c.1925, marked 54.5cm (21½in), *NY 7 Dec*, $9,075 (£6,131)

10
A Chiparus parcel-silvered and gilt-bronze figure of a dancer, 'Tanara' c.1925, marked, depatinated, 65cm (25½in), *NY 7 Dec*, $9,350 (£6,317)

11
A Chiparus patinated metal figure of an archer stretching his bow, 1930s, marked, 54cm (21¼in), *L 5 July*, £528 ($729)

1

2

3

4

5

6

7

8

9

10

11

1
A Josef Csaky bronze figure of a pigeon, c.1925, marked, 27.5cm (10¾in), M 17 Mar, FF55,500(£4,955;$6,094)

2
A Decoux bronze figure of a Greek archer, c.1925, signed, 29.5cm (11½in), M 6 Oct, FF 4,662 (£406; $601)

3
A Hagenauer carved wood study of a young negress, 1930s, marked, 26.5cm (10½in), L 2 May, £1,320 ($1,702)

4
A Bouraine bronze group of Diana with fawns, c.1925, marked Etling Paris, partially depatinated, 70cm (27½in), NY 23 Feb, $3,850 (£3,598)

5
A Privat figure of a young woman with a doe, c.1925, in Sèvres biscuit porcelain, marked, 35cm (13¾in), M 6 Oct, FF 5,550 (£483; $715)

6
A Maurice Guiraud-Rivière bronze and marble figure of a dancer, 'Stella', c.1925, marked, depatinated, 66cm (26in), NY 23 Feb, $3,520 (£3,290)

7
A Maurice Guiraud-Rivière parcel-gilt and silvered-bronze figure of a woman, 'The Comet', c.1930, marked Etling Paris, gilding and silvering worn, 60cm (23½in), NY 18 May, $6,600 (£5,238)

8
A pair of Emory P Seidel bronze figural three-light candelabra, c.1925, marked Roman Bronze Works NY, green patina, 29cm (11½in), NY 18 May, $1,760 (£1,397)

9
A Guiraud-Rivière silvered bronze nude study, c.1930, marked, 18cm (7in), L 17 Oct, £462 ($684)

10
A Guy Debe bronze figure of a panther, marked, 77cm (30¼in), A 25 Feb, Dfl 3,944 (£967; $1,083)

11
A Vago Weiss carved wood panther, 1920s, marked, 53cm (20¾in), L 17 Oct, £374 ($554)

12
A Grandcheff patinated bronze group of two fish, 1930s, marked, brown patinated with black and gilt details, 42cm (16½in), L 4 Dec, £528 ($739)

13
A pair of Le Verrier patinated metal bookends, c.1930, marked, 15cm (6in), L 15 Feb, £176 ($204)

14
A Silvestre 'cire perdue' bronze study of Diana, c.1930, marked, 152.5cm (5ft), L 2 May, £7,150 ($9,223)

1

2

3

4

5

7

8

6

9

10

11

12

13

14

 rare John Bird
 ahogany quadrant,
 nglish, *c.*1775, signed,
 djustment to the
 orizon glass signed
 ollond, London,
 cking some pieces,
 cm (20in) radius,
 23 Oct,
 ,050 ($9,075)

 J B Dancer brass
 inocular microscope,
 nglish, *c.*1870, signed,
 cm (20in) high, with
 arious accessories,
 11 June,
 ,870 ($2,431)

 brass universal
 quinoctial ring dial,
 nglish, mid-18th
 entury, unsigned,
 cm (9in) diam,
 11 June,
 ,640 ($3,432)

 Charles Bloud ivory
 ptych dial, Dieppe,
 1660, pin missing and
 rack, 6.5 x 5.5cm (2½ x
 ¼in) closed, *L 11 June,*
 ,320 ($1,716)

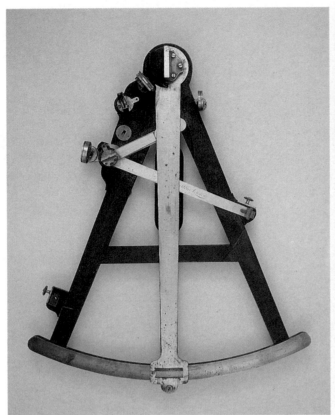

1

3

2

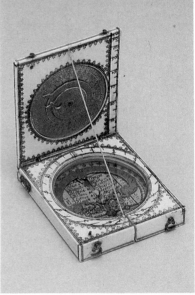

4

1
A Louis XV gilt-bronze
cartel clock, mid-18th
century, the dial signed
Bunon à Paris, 110cm
(3ft 7½in) high, *L 5 July,*
£3,520 ($4,505)

2
A late Louis XVI bronze,
gilt-bronze and marble
calendar mantel clock,
*c.*1790, the dial signed
Robin Aux Galeries du
Louvre and also Dub-
uisson, the movement
signed Robin à Paris,
the case flanked by a
young man and maiden
symbolising Learning,
43cm (17in), *L 5 July,*
£14,300 ($19,734)

3
A white marble and
ormolu lyre clock garni-
ture, *c.*1880, the dial
signed Kinable à Paris,
56.5cm (22¼in); with a
pair of four-light can-
delabra, 47cm (18½in),
L 21 June,
£2,860 ($3,832)

4
A Louis XVI gilt-bronze
and marble mantel clock,
*c.*1785, the dial flanked
by figures of Venus and
Cupid, 34cm (13½in),
L 5 July,
£2,420 ($3,340)

5
A gilt-bronze, porcelain
and champlevé enamel
mantel clock, *c.*1880, with
Japy Frères movement,
the porcelain panels
signed Lefranc, 47cm
(18½in) high, *L 21 June,*
£1,980 ($2,653)

1

2

3

4

5

1 A Chippendale carved mahogany tall-case clock, Philip Garrett, Philadelphia, c.1775, the dial surmounted by a painted panel with a sporting scene, 256cm (8ft 4in), *NY 26 Oct,* $14,300 (£10,070)

2 A Federal mahogany and eglomisé banjo clock, J Billings, Acton, Massachusetts, dated 1829, with a panel depicting a view of Mount Vernon, 86cm (34in), *NY 26 Oct,* $2,750 (£1,936)

3 A Federal carved mahogany, giltwood and eglomisé banjo clock, possibly by Simon Willard, Massachusetts, c.1825, 108cm (42½in), *NY 26 Oct,* $3,300 (£2,323)

4 A silver-mounted ebony bracket timepiece, c.1730, the dial and backplate signed Geo: Graham London, the backplate No. 674 and engraved with leaf scrolls and birds, 34cm (13½in), *L 6 June,* £19,800 ($26,334)

5 A George III ebonised brass inlaid bracket clock, the dial signed Barraud's Cornhill London, 51cm (20in), *HS 16 July,* £1,155 ($1,675)

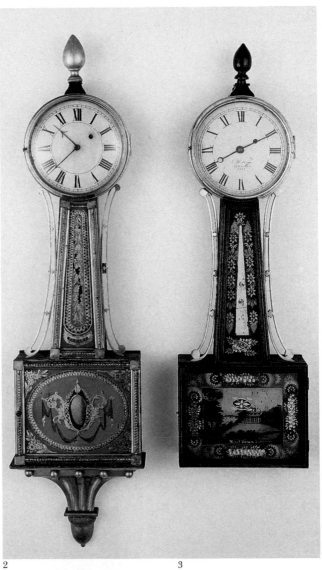

1

2

3

4

5

1
A French violin by Jean Baptiste Vuillaume, Paris, 1867, *L 14 Nov,* £28,600 ($40,000)

2
An Italian violin by Tommaso Balestrieri, Mantua, 1761, 36cm (14¼in) long, *L 14 Nov,* £30,800 ($43,120)

3
An English silver-mounted violin bow, by James Tubbs, London, 61 grams, *L 3 Apr,* £2,200 ($2,838)

4
A gold and tortoiseshell-mounted violin bow by W E Hill & Sons, London, 60 grams, *L 4 July,* £2,640 ($3,643)

5
A French violin by Nicolas Lupot, Paris, first half 19th century, *NY 19 June,* $38,500 (£30,315)

6
A French violoncello by J. B. Vuillaume, Paris, 75cm (29½in), *NY 19 June,* $40,700 (£32,047)

7
A silver-mounted violin bow by Francois Nicolas Voirin, Paris, 56 grams, *L 14 Nov,* £1,650 ($2,310)

8
A gold and tortoiseshell-mounted violin bow by Franz Albert Nürnberger, unused, 59 grams, *L 14 Nov,* £2,750 ($3,850)

1   2   3   4

5   6   7   8

1
A rare Portuguese single manual harpsichord, by Joachim José Antunes, 1785, 249.5 x 99.5cm (8ft 2¼in x 3ft 3in), *L 12 Dec,* £33,000 ($46,200)

2
An English spinet by Thomas Hitchcock the Younger, London, *c.*1715, 186.5cm (6ft 1½in) long, *L 12 Dec,* £11,000 ($15,400)

3
A French boxwood treble (alto) recorder by Rippert, Paris, last quarter 17th century, ivory mounts and beak, *L 12 Dec,* £11,000 ($15,400)

4
A stained pearwood tenor recorder by Jean-Hyacinth-Joseph Rottenburgh, Brussels, first quarter 18th century, *L 12 Dec,* £13,000 ($18,200)

1

2

3

4

1
A New England upright-bouquet weight, 9.4cm (3¾in), *L 1 July,* £11,000 ($15,180)

2
A Clichy faceted concentric millefiori mushroom weight, (slight surface wear), 7cm (2¾in), *NY 15 June,* $3,080 (£2,406)

3
A Baccarat sulphide weight, (tiny chips and minor imperfections), 9.2cm (3⅝in), *NY 15 June,* $1,760 (£1,375)

4
A Baccarat salmon-pink pom-pom and garland weight, 6.5cm (2½in), *L 1 July,* £1,045 ($1,442)

5
A St Louis pink carpet-ground weight, 7.2cm (2¾in), *L 1 July,* £1,870 ($2,581)

6
A Baccarat double clematis weight, 6.4cm (2½in), *L 1 July,* £825 ($1,139)

7
A St Louis miniature white pom-pom weight, on pink spiralling ground, 5cm (2in), *L 1 July,* £715 ($987)

8
A St. Louis miniature crown weight, 4.5cm (1¾in), *NY 15 June,* $825 (£645)

9
A St. Louis miniature fruit weight, 5.1cm (2in), *NY 15 June,* $880 (£688)

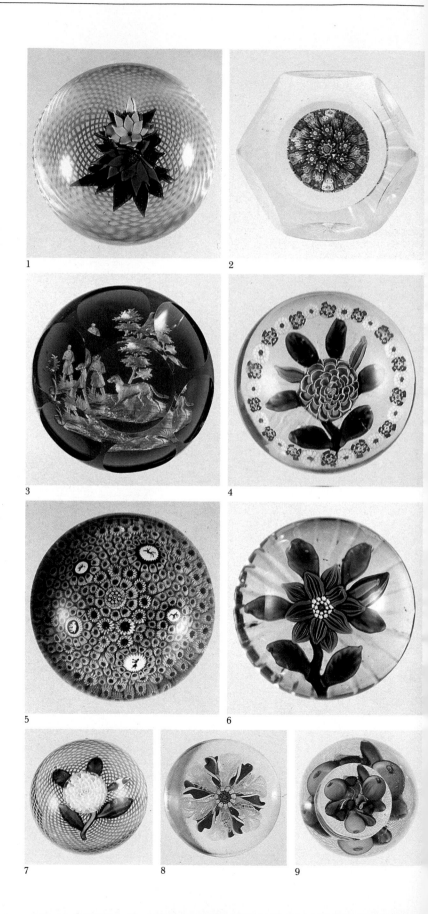

1 Beilby enamelled wine glass, c.1770, 13cm (5in), L 2 July, £880 ($1,214)

2 Beilby decanter and stopper, c.1770, the body decorated in opaque white enamel with a label inscribed 'W,WINE', 28.5cm (11¼in), L 2 July, £2,750 ($3,547)

3 Beilby-enamelled colour-twist cordial, the stem enclosing a central royal-blue corkscrew entwined within opaque-white threads, 17cm (6¾in), L 1 July, £2,090 ($2,884)

4 Beilby-enamelled wine glass, c.1770, the bowl painted with a vignette of an obelisk, 14.5cm (5¾in), L 1 July, £2,090 ($2,884)

5 French turquoise opaline basket, c.1825, decorated in blue and gold, the handle and base in gilded bronze, 9cm (3½in), M 25 June, FF 10,545 (£879; $1,186)

6 French bottle and stopper in turquoise opaline, c.1825, decorated in gold, blue and red, 11cm (4¼in) high, M 25 June, FF 10,545 (£879; $1,186)

7 Baccarat millefiori vase, 15.5cm (6in), NY 15 June, $1,100 (£859)

8 Baccarat millefiori and parcel-gilt goblet, 6cm (2½in), NY 15 June, $1,650 (£1,289)

1   2   3   4

5

6

7   8

1
A Sèvres porcelain jardinière, 1924, decorated with four nude figures, decorated in white, gold, pale blue, green, and black on a light blue ground, 58cm (22¾in), *M 17 Mar,* **FF 122,100 (£10,901; $13,408)**

2
A French gold, enamel, ruby and diamond pendant/brooch, *c.*1900, some losses to enamel, *NY 15 Oct,* **$2,970 (£2,106)**

3
A Guild of Handicraft Ltd. silver, enamel and amethyst buckle/cloak clasp, designed by C R Ashbee, *c.*1902, 14cm (5½in) wide, *L 2 May,* **£7,150 ($9,223)**

4
A Preiss bronze and ivory figure of a flute player, 1930s, marked in metallic cold painted costume, 43.5cm (17in), *L 2 May,* **£2,860 ($3,689)**

5
A De Morgan vase, decorated by Joe Juster, 1880s, painted in turquoise, green and red, some chips, 31cm (12¼in), *L 3 May,* **£1,650 ($2,112)**

1

2

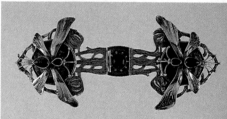

3

4

5

1
A Gallé landscape vase,
c.1900, cameo mark,
in red and grey glass,
lined with brown,
68cm (26¾in), *M 17 Mar,*
FF 39,405
(£3,518; $4,327)

2
A Gallé 'marqueterie-
sur-verre' vase, with
applied and internal
decoration, c.1900,
signed in intaglio, the
grey glass decorated
with violet and ochre
crocus blossoms, the foot
applied in polished
ochre, 44.5cm (17½in),
NY 17 May,
$24,200 (£19,206)

3
A Gallé cameo glass blow
out vase, c.1900, cameo
mark, in bright yellow
glass overlaid in
pink and cherry red,
23.5cm (9¼in) high,
L 4 Dec,
£4,950 ($6,930)

4
A Bernard Leach stone-
ware vase, c.1960,
impressed BL and St
Ives seals, decorated in
ashen-white against a
mottled pale-olive and
brown ground, 26cm
(10¼in), *L 3 May,*
£770 ($985)

1
A Daum Nancy cameo glass and wrought-iron lamp, *c.*1900, signed in cameo Daum Nancy with Croix de Lorraine, in pale raspberry glass overlaid in magenta and mulberry, 78.5cm (31in) high, *NY 7 Dec,* **$21,450 (£14,493)**

2
A Bugatti side chair, *c.*1900, the back, sides and legs covered in vellum and painted with green, red and gold poppies, the vellum-covered seat edged with strips of beaten copper, 93cm (36½in) high, *L 2 May,* **£4,400 ($5,676)**

3
A Gustave Serrurier-Bovy iron and copper coat-stand, 1906, 204cm (6ft 8½in), *M 6 Oct,* **FF 77,700 (£6,757; $10,000)**

4
A Neatby & Evans inlaid mahogany writing bureau, designed by W J Neatby, *c.*1903, 129.5cm (51in) high, *L 2 May,* **£2,860 ($3,689)**

1

2

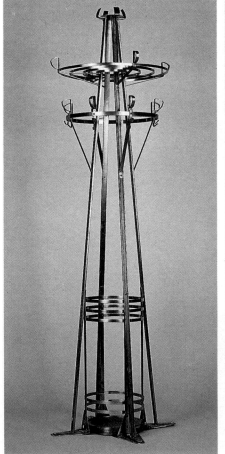

3

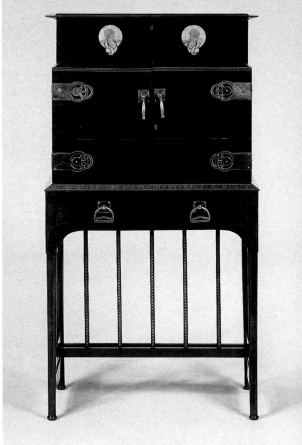

4

**1 An Isokon laminated
plywood chaise longue,**
designed by Marcel
Breuer, 1935/6, 79.5cm
(31¼in) high, *L 4 Dec,*
£5,500 ($7,700)
(See also p.327 fig. 8)

**2 A James Dixon & Sons
electroplated three-piece
tea set,** designed by
Christopher Dresser,
1880, teapot 13.5cm
(5¼in) high, *L 5 July,*
£11,000 ($15,180)

**3 A Robert Oerley wooden
suite,** *c.*1905, comprising
sofa and two armchairs,
sofa 104cm (41in) wide,
M 17 Mar,
**F 66,600
(£5,946; $7,313)**

1

2

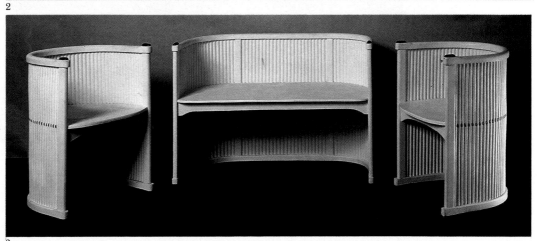

3

1
**A pair of Vieux Paris
vases,** Nast factory,
*c.*1820, each with an
Italianate view, on
claret ground with rich
gilding, 71cm (28in),
NY 4 May,
$26,400 (£22,000)

2
**A pair of Sèvres vases
Hollandaise,** 1757,
painted with Cupid and
trophies within green and
gilt ribbons, some wear
and chips, blue enamel
interlaced Ls, date letter
E, 19cm (7½in), *L 5 Mar,*
£2,750 ($3,080)

1

2

A **Meissen Augsburg-decorated assembled part tea and chocolate service,** 1730-45, comprising 30 pieces, each painted in underglaze blue in the 'Fels-und Vogel' pattern, gilded ground, crossed swords in underglaze blue, coffee pot 20cm (8in) high, fitted travelling case, *NY 4 May,* $18,700 (£15,583)

An early Meissen coffee pot and cover, *c.*1727, painted in colours in the manner of J G Höroldt with two chinoiserie scenes, painted number 2, 20cm (8in), *L 26 Nov,* £13,200 ($18,480)

A **Meissen yellow-ground dish,** *c.*1730, with chinoiserie scenes, hair crack and minor restoration, crossed swords in underglaze blue, 42.5cm (16½in), *L 26 Nov,* £5,500 ($7,700)

Six **Meissen ornithological plates,** mid to late 18th century, crossed swords in underglaze blue, impressed numerals 36 on three and 14 on three, 24cm (9in), *NY 10 Oct,* $2,310 (£1,638)

A **set of twelve Meissen ornithological plates,** 1760, crossed swords in underglaze blue, impressed numerals 22, 25cm (10in), *NY 10 Oct,* $4,675 (£3,316)

An early Meissen teapot and cover, *c.*1723, painted with two chinoiserie scenes, crossed swords in blue enamel, KPM in underglaze blue, 58 in gilding, 12cm (5in), *5 Mar,* £14,300 ($16,016)

1

2

3

4

5

6

1
A Copenhagen group of a shepherd and shepherdess, *c.*1783, modelled as a kneeling youth holding a wreath (partially missing), triple wave mark in underglaze blue, 19.4cm (7⅝in), *NY 21 May,* $660 (£528)

2
A Copenhagen group of pastoral lovers, *c.*1783, modelled as a shepherd-ess and her admirer, triple wave mark in underglaze blue, 18.4cm (7¼in), *NY 21 May,* $660 (£528)

3
A pair of Bow figures of the Four Seasons, *c.*1765, minor chips, red anchor and dagger mark, 23.5cm (9¼in), *L 22 Oct,* £2,860 ($4,290)

4
A Longton Hall straw-berry plate, *c.*1755 painted by the 'Trembly Rose' painter, 27.5cm (10¾in), hair crack; sold with another by the same hand, repaired, 25cm (10¾in), *NY 10 Oct,* $1,100 (£780)

5
A Chelsea 'Hans Sloane' plate, late red/early gold anchor period, *c.*1758, painted with a spray of yellow and red apples, 23cm (9in), *NY 10 Oct,* $7,700 (£5,461)

1

2

3

3

4

5

1 A Worcester claret-ground dish, c.1775, from the Hope-Edwardes Service, painted possibly in the atelier of James Giles, 26cm (10¼in), *L 22 Oct,* £2,200 ($3,300)

2 A Worcester mask jug, c.1770, brightly enamelled on a blue scale ground, 30cm (11¾in), *L 22 Oct,* £4,620 ($6,930)

3 A pair of Worcester Barr, Flight & Barr vases, c.1810, each painted with colourful feathers reserved on a salmon-pink ground, painted mark, 16cm (6¼in), *L 22 Oct,* £7,480 ($11,220)

1

2

3

1
A Spode 'Stone China' dinner service, c.1830, comprising 88 pieces, some chips and cracks, printed mark in under-glaze blue, largest serving dish 52cm (20in), *L 22 Oct,* £4,400 ($6,600)

2
A majolica pedestal, c.1880, probably Brown-Westhead, Moore & Co., 76cm (30in), *L 21 May,* £7,150 ($9,581)

3
A Minton majolica tower jug, dated 1870, impressed Minton mark and date cypher, model number 1231, 33cm (13in) high, *NY 30 Nov,* $880 (£591)

4
A Minton majolica stilton cheese stand, dated 1862, 33.2cm (13¼in), *NY 30 Nov,* $2,750 (£1,846)

1

2

3

4

Silver

Article ● Electroplate *pp* 396-401 *See also* ● Colour illustrations *pp* 491-493
● Decorative arts from 1880 *pp* 301-311 ● Objects of vertu *p* 416 ● Russian works of art *pp* 432-433
● Judaica *pp* 441-446 ● Islamic works of art *p* 621 ● Japanese works of art *p* 682
● Chinese works of art *p* 689

**A German silver-gilt
tankard**, Nicolaus Weiss,
Nuremberg, *c.*1620,
20cm (8in) high, 20oz
(628gr), *G 14 May,*
F 28,600
(£8,363; $11,123)

A parcel-gilt tankard,
probably Baltic, *c.*1690,
engraved with three
scenes of the parable of
the Prodigal Son,
19.5cm (7¾in), 41oz
(1263gr), *G 12 Nov,*
F 24,200
(£7,908; $11,071)

**A South German silver-
gilt tankard**, maker's
mark only SG con-
joined, *c.*1620, the body
with cartouches enclos-
ing David, Perseus and
Hercules, 12cm (4¾in),
oz 6dwt (283gr),
11 Feb,
2,530 ($2,909)

**An Estonian parcel-gilt
tankard**, Joachim
Thomsen, Reval, late
17th century, the cover
applied with an embos-
sed plaque of Jacob
wrestling with the angel,
19cm (7½in) high, 43oz
dwt (1350gr), *L 11 Feb,*
2,530 ($2,909)

**A Danish silver-gilt peg
tankard**, Niels Enevol-
sen, (Copenhagen),
1650, 23.5cm (9¼in),
1oz (1583gr), *G 12 Nov,*
F 15,400 (£5,032; $7,044)

A Swedish tankard,
apparently Bent Olofs-
on, Stockholm, *c.*1640,
1cm (8¼in), 24oz 10dwt
770gr), *G 12 Nov,*
F 30,800
(£10,065; $14,092)

**7
A German parcel-gilt
tankard**, Peter Rohde II,
Danzig, *c.*1670, embos-
sed with Orpheus and
various animals, 22.5cm
(8¾in), 40oz 10dwt
(1260gr), *NY 9 Oct,*
$4,400 (£3,120)

**8
A German parcel-gilt
tankard**, Johann Rein-
hard Raiser I, Augs-
burg, *c.*1680, embossed
with putti emblematic
of Morning, Noon,
Evening and Night,
16.5cm (6½in), 17oz
(528gr), *NY 19 Feb,*
$3,300 (£3,028)

1

2

3

4

5

6

7

8

1
A Swedish parcel-gilt tankard, Abraham Wirgman, Gothenburg, 1715, inset with a medal of Charles XI and Ulrica Eleonora, 20cm (8in), 44oz (1383gr), *G 12 Nov*, SF 14,300 (£4,673; $6,542)

2
A German parcel-gilt tankard, Philipp Stenglin, Augsburg, 1732-33, engraved with bands of Régence strapwork, 16.5cm (6½in), 17oz (525gr), *G 12 Nov*, SF 13,200 (£4,313; $6,038)

3
An American tankard, John Coburn, Boston, c.1760, 23cm (9in), 28oz 10dwt (886gr), *NY 27 June*, $6,050 (£4,654)

4
A William III tankard, William Keatt, London, 1700, 18.5cm (7¼in), 26oz (808gr), *NY 14 Feb*, $2,200 (£1,897)

5
A Queen Anne tankard, Samuel Dell, London, 1703, 25oz 9dwt (791gr), *L 21 Feb*, £3,630 ($4,175)

6
A Queen Anne tankard, Timothy Ley, London, 1705, 19cm (7½in), 31oz (933gr), *L 24 Oct*, £2,530 ($3,795)

7
A George I tankard, William Fawdery, London, 1726, 18.5cm (7¼in), 26oz 10dwt (824gr), *S 17 Apr*, £1,100 ($1,430)

8
A George II tankard, Edward Vincent, London, 1740, 21.5cm (8½in), 38oz 10dwt (1197gr), *NY 26 Apr*, $3,850 (£3,156)

9
A George III small tankard, Sebastian & James Crespell, London, 1775, 12cm (4¾in), 13oz 7dwt (415gr), *L 4 Apr*, £748 ($950)

10
A George III tankard, James Stamp, London, 1777, 19cm (7½in), 23oz (715gr), *S 16 Oct*, £902 ($1,335)

11
A Dutch tankard, Johannes Schiotling, Amsterdam, 1770, 21.5cm (8½in), 50oz (1527gr), *A 1 Apr*, Dfl 53,360 (£12,352; $15,687)

12
A George III tankard, Charles Price, London, 1815, 18cm (7in), 26oz 10dwt (824gr), *S 16 Oct*, £660 ($977)

13
A George III tankard, Joseph Lock, London, 1775, 21.5cm (8½in), 29oz 10dwt (914gr), *L 21 Nov*, £1,100 ($1,584)

14
A George IV tankard, Craddock & Reid, London, 1821, the body with a chased tartan ground and a Highlander, *Glen 26 Aug*, £3,520 ($5,174)

15
A continental tankard, late 19th century, 52cm (20½in), 65oz (2021gr), *NY 14 Feb*, $2,640 (£2,276)

16
A German tankard, Posen, late 19th century, chased with a stag and boar hunt, 49.5cm (19½in), 90oz (2799gr), *NY 14 Feb*, $3,850 ($3,319)

A Queen Anne mug, Thomas Parr, London, apparently 1708, later crested, 11cm (4¼in), 12oz 10dwt (299gr), 17 Oct, £385 ($570)

A pair of George III baluster mugs, perhaps John Schofield, London, 1774, 9cm (3½in), 12oz dwt (373gr), C 9 July, £880 ($1,223)

A George I mug, William Darker, London, 1726, 12.5cm (5in), 10oz 10dwt (326gr), L 4 Apr, £605 ($768)

A George I mug, William Fleming, London, 1721, 9.5cm (3¾in), 9oz 10dwt (292gr), L 24 Oct, £495 ($743)

An American mug, John Brevoort, New York, c.1760, 13.5cm (5¼in), 13oz (404gr), NY 31 Jan, $2,750 (£2,331)

An American mug, Jacob Jacobse Lansing, Albany, c.1740, 11.5cm (4½in), 9oz (280gr), NY 31 Jan, $6,600 (£5,593)

An American mug, Joseph Richardson Jr., Philadelphia, c.1785, cm (3½in), 7oz 10dwt (233gr), NY 31 Jan, $1,430 (£1,212)

An American mug and cover, Robert Evans, Boston, c.1810, 14cm (5½in), 8oz (249gr), NY 14 Feb, $935 (£806)

A George III mug, Edward Fernell, London, 1782, 16.5cm (6½in), 27oz (847gr), 24 Oct, £770 ($1,155)

10
A Chinese export mug, Canton? c.1820, base marked WE/WE/WC and pseudo hallmarks, 9.5cm (3¾in), 11oz (342gr), NY 31 Jan, **$1,430 (£1,212)**

11
An American silver child's mug, J Rafel, New Orleans, c.1857, 8.5cm (3¼in), NY 25 Nov, **$1,320 (£964)**

12
A French mug, maker's mark L R, Paris, c.1825, 15.5cm (6in), 10oz (320gr), F 29 May, **L 900,000 (£350; $462)**

13
A South American mug, stamped Leiba, probably Argentinian, 19th century, 11cm (4¼in) high, 12oz 2dwt (378gr), L 11 Feb, **£330 ($380)**

14
A Charles II flagon, maker's mark D R, London, 1670, engraved with contemporary armorials and Latin inscription, 28cm (11in), 44oz (1368gr), NY 12 Dec, **$9,900 (£7,021)**

1   2

3   4   5

6   7   8

9   10   11

12   13   14

1
A German silver-gilt cup, Johann Jacob Wolrab, Nuremberg, c.1670, detachable head, 16.5cm (6½in) high, 9oz 10dwt (298gr), *G 14 May,* **SF 71,500** (£20,906; $27,805)

2
A German silver-gilt standing cup and cover, Melchior Bair, Augsburg, c.1600, 30cm (11¾in), 10oz 10dwt (332gr), *G 12 Nov,* **SF 49,500** (£16,176; $22,646)

3
A German silver-gilt standing cup and cover, Hans Zeiger, Nuremberg, c.1590, 41cm (16in), 21oz (666gr), *G 12 Nov,* **SF 44,000** (£14,379; $20,130)

4
A German silver-gilt standing cup, Melchior Bair, Augsburg, 1590-95, 21cm (8¼in), 8oz 9dwt (264gr), *L 11 July,* £2,310 ($3,396)

5
A German parcel-gilt standing cup and cover, Nuremberg, c.1640, 31cm (12¼in), 11oz 1dwt (348gr), *L 11 Feb,* £3,520 ($4,048)

6
An Austrian parcel-gilt standing cup, maker's mark H K, Vienna, c.1640, 14.5cm (5¾in), 5oz (166gr), *G 12 Nov,* **SF 6,600** (£2,156; $3,018)

7
A German silver-gilt standing cup, Abraham Kessbair I, Augsburg, c.1670, 17cm (6¾in), 5oz (169gr), *G 12 Nov,* **SF 4,950** (£1,617; $2,263)

8
A German silver-gilt standing cup and cover, Christian Mundt, Hamburg, c.1650, 40.5cm (16in), 14oz (435gr), *NY 9 Oct,* $4,675 (£3,315)

9
A German parcel gilt standing cup and cover, maker's mark S B F, a member of the Ferrn family, Nuremberg, c.1675, 40.5cm (16in), 20oz 10dwt (635gr), *G 14 May,* **SF 30,800** (£9,006; $11,978)

10
A continental standing cup and cover, late 19th century, in 16th century style, 44cm (17¼in), 40oz (1244gr), *NY 14 Feb,* $852 (£734)

11
A German standing cup and cover, late 19th century, in early 17th century style, 45.5cm, (18in), 32oz (995gr), *NY 7 June,* $715 (£567)

12
A German standing cup and cover, c.1880, 44.5cm (17¼in) high, 36oz (1119gr), *L 21 Mar,* £715 ($865)

13
A German beaker-shaped cup and cover, late 19th century, embossed with three allegorical figures, pseudo-hallmarked, 50cm (19¾in) high, 58oz 4dwt (1813gr), *L 21 Mar,* £990 ($1,198)

14
A Charles II silver-gilt caudle cup and cover, Francis Leake, London, 1669, 17cm (6¾in), 31oz 4dwt (964gr), *NY 12 Dec,* $12,100 (£8,582)

15
A Charles II porringer and cover, I W, London, 1669, with armorials, crest and inscription, 19cm (7½in), 28oz 18dwt (898gr), *L 23 May,* £14,300 ($18,876)

16
A Charles II porringer, maker's mark SN, London, 1665, 3oz 15dwt (116gr), *L 23 May,* £1,100 ($1,452)

1
A Charles II caudle cup, maker's mark R S, mullet above and below, London, 1669, embossed with a hound pursuing a lion, 10.5cm (4¼in), 14oz 6dwt (435gr), NY 12 Dec, $3,575 (£2,535)

2
A Queen Anne racing trophy, Seth Lofthouse, London, 1709, 11cm 4¼in), 9oz 16dwt (304gr), L 4 Apr, £660 ($838)

3
A George III two-handled porringer, London, 1764, 7.5cm (3in), 2oz 10dwt (78gr), C 16 Oct, £143 ($212)

4
A George II cup and cover, Francis Nelme, London, 1727, 25.5cm 10in), 50oz (1558gr), L 23 May, £2,145 ($2,831)

5
A George II two-handled cup and cover, Thomas Farren, London, 1733, 22.5cm (9¼in), 40oz 1244gr), NY 26 Apr, $4,400 (£3,607)

6
A George III two-handled cup, Robert Gray & Son, Edinburgh, 1805, 23.5cm 9¼in) high, 22oz 15dwt 707gr), Glen 26 Aug, £418 ($614)

7
A George II two-handled cup and cover, Paul de Lamerie, London, 1744, 32cm (12½in), 66oz 2052gr), NY 12 Dec, $33,000 (£23,404)

8
A silver-gilt cup and cover, A H Benson, London 1894, base engraved Hunt & Roskell, late Storr & Mortimer, 39.5cm (15½in), 102oz 8dwt (3172gr), C 9 July, £6,050 ($8,409)

9
An American two-handled baseball trophy, Whiting Mfg. Co, New York, 1888, acid etched with a view of a baseball game in progress, 21cm (8¼in), 27oz (840gr), NY 27 June, $770 (£592)

10
A German silver-gilt two-handled cup, probably Georg Roth & Co, Hanau, c.1902, importer's mark William Moering for Barr, Moering & Co, London, 1902, 35.5cm (14in) high, 106oz (3297gr), L 21 Mar, £1,980 ($2,396)

11
An American two-handled cup, S Kirk & Son Co, Baltimore, c.1910, chased with a coach and four, 28.5cm (11¼in), 72oz (2239gr), NY 27 June, $1,980 (£1,523)

12
A pair of continental silver-gilt wager cups, c.1892, in 17th century style, 26cm (10¼in), 27oz (840gr), NY 14 Feb, $2,200 (£1,897)

13
A German silver-gilt footed cup, Eustachius Hohman, Nuremberg, late 16th century, engraved with biblical scenes, 10cm (4in), NY 26 June, $22,000 (£17,054)

14
A Transylvanian parcel-gilt beaker, Paulus Brölfft I, (Nagyszeben), c.1590, maker's mark only, 20cm (8in) high, 11oz 18dwt (370gr), L 11 July, £3,300 ($4,851)

15
A German beaker, Cologne, c.1620, gilt interior, 8cm (3¼in), 2oz 10dwt (78gr), NY 9 Oct, $2,420 (£1,716)

1 2 3
4 5 6
7 8
9 10 11
12 13 14 15

1
A Friesian beaker, Wieger Jansen van Isens, Sneek, 1647, with Faith, Hope and Charity within cartouches, 11.5cm (4½in) high, 5oz 10dwt (169gr), *A 1 Apr,*
Dfl 15,660
(£3,625; $4,604)

2
A German parcel-gilt rummer-shaped beaker, Reinhold Riel, Nuremberg, 1660, 12cm (4¾in), 3oz 17dwt (120gr), *L 11 July,*
£1,870 ($2,799)

3
A German parcel-gilt covered beaker, maker's mark G R above a flower Nuremberg, *c.*1680, embossed with three architectural views, 13.5cm (5½in), 4oz 7dwt (138gr), *L 11 July,*
£880 ($1,294)

4
A Charles II goblet, Thomas Mangy, York, 1670, 8cm (3¼in), 3oz (87gr), *L 24 Oct,*
£1,155 ($1,733)

5
A German silver-gilt beaker, maker's mark a housemark, Nuremberg, *c.*1680, 9.5cm (3¾in), 4oz (135gr), *G 12 Nov,*
SF 3,850 (£1,258; $1,761)

6
A Charles II beaker, maker's mark E G mullet above and below, London, 1682, 8.5cm (3¼in), 3oz 8dwt (109gr), *NY 10 Oct,*
$495 (£351)

7
A James II beaker, maker's mark a goose in a dotted circle, London, 1686, 9.5cm (3¾in), 3oz 13dwt (113gr), *L 24 Oct,*
£682 ($1,023)

8
A Danish parcel-gilt covered beaker, Jacob Sørensen, Copenhagen, 1688, 12cm (4¾in), 10oz (313gr), *G 12 Nov,*
SF 13,200 (£4,314; $6,039)

9
A Swedish parcel-gilt beaker, Rudolf Wittkopf, Stockholm, 1700, 16cm (6¼in), 10oz (311gr), *G 12 Nov,*
SF 14,300 (£4,673; $6,542)

10
A German silver-gilt beaker, Johann Sigmund Abrell, Augsburg, *c.*1697, engraved to commemorate the Treaty of Ryswick, 15.5cm (6in) high, 11oz (350gr), *G 14 May,*
SF 66,000
(£19,298; $25,666)

11
A William III tumbler cup, maker's mark VN, London, 1700, 6cm (2¼in), 5oz 16dwt (180gr), *L 24 Oct,*
£660 ($990)

12
A Queen Anne tumbler cup, Eli Bilton, Newcastle, 1793, 5cm (2in), 3oz 2dwt (96gr), *L 21 Feb,*
£495 ($569)

13
A William III two-handled cup, Joseph Walker, Dublin, 1701, 8cm (3in), 5oz 10dwt (171gr), *L 17 Oct,*
£638 ($944)

14
A German silver-gilt beaker, maker's mark, I K, Nuremberg, *c.*1700, 10.5cm (4in), 4oz 10dwt (140gr), *NY 19 Feb,*
$1,320 (£1,211)

1
A German beaker, Gottfried Ihme, Breslau, c.1710, 9.5cm (3¾in), 3oz (95gr), *M 25 June,* SF 6,660 (£555; $708)

2
A Swedish parcel-gilt beaker, Gottfried Dubois, Stockholm, apparently 1737, 17.5cm (7in), 12oz (377gr), *G 12 Nov,* SF 4,950 (£1,617; $2,263)

3
A Louis XV silver-gilt beaker, Joachim-Frederic Kirstein, Strasbourg, c.1760, gilding rubbed, 10cm (4in), 5oz (155gr), *NY 9 Oct,* $1,870 (£1,326)

4
A pair of French beakers, Joseph Moillet, Paris, 1725, 5.5cm (2¼in) high, 6oz 1dwt (188gr), *L 11 Feb,* £935 ($1,075)

5
A German parcel-gilt beaker, Christoph Müller, Breslau, c.1710, the body engraved with three scenes within inscribed borders, 12cm (5in), 5oz 5dwt (165gr), *L 11 Feb,* £1,540 ($1,771)

6
A German beaker, Augsburg, 1739-41, later inscription, 14cm (5½in), 6oz (186gr), *NY 7 June,* $990 (£786)

7
An American beaker, John Adam, Alexandria, VA, c.1820, 8.5cm (3¼in), 4oz (124gr), *NY 31 Jan,* $825 (£699)

8
A thistle cup, David Manson of Dundee, c.1830, initialled, 4.5cm (1¾in), 1oz 5dwt (62gr), *HH 30 Apr,* £605 ($793)

9
A pair of George III goblets, Fogelbert & Gilbert, London, 1780, 14cm (5½in) high, 12oz 1dwt (389gr), *C 9 July,* £880 ($1,223)

10
A pair of George III silver-gilt beakers, William Holmes, London, 1801, 9cm (3½in), 11oz 11dwt (359gr), *L 21 Feb,* £880 ($1,012)

11
A Victorian stirrup cup, Robert Hennell, London, 1875, cast and chased as a hound's head, 16cm (6¼in), 10oz (311gr), *NY 26 Apr,* $2,970 (£2,434)

1   2   3
4
5   6
7
8
9
10   11

1
A Queen Anne chocolate pot, William Denny, London, 1706, 24cm (9½in), 23oz 10dwt (731gr), *NY 10 Oct,*
$7,700 (£5,460)

2
A Queen Anne coffee pot, Benjamin Pyne, London, 1707, 25cm (9¾in), 22oz (688gr), *L 24 Oct,*
£4,620 ($6,930)

3
A Belgian coffee jug, maker's mark MH conjoined below a crown, Mons, *c.*1730, 15cm (6in), 9oz 15dwt (305gr), *L 11 Feb,*
£3,520 ($4,048)

4
A George II coffee pot, Humphrey Payne, London, 1731, 18.5cm (7¼in), 15oz (469gr), *L 24 Oct,*
£1,100 ($1,650)

5
A George II coffee pot, Ayme Videau, London, 1740, 25.5cm (8½in), 24oz 8dwt (758gr), *L 23 May,*
£4,840 ($6,389)

6
A small George II coffee pot, Ayme Videau, London, 1738, 17cm (6¾in) high, 12oz 16dwt (398gr), *L 21 Feb,*
£825 ($949)

7
A George III coffee pot, Thomas Heming, London, 1753, later initialled, 20.5cm (8in), 24oz (749gr), *L 21 Nov,*
£1,100 ($1,584)

8
A George III coffee pot, J Marsh or Moore, London, 1762, 27cm (10½in), 29oz (914gr), *L 21 Nov,*
£1,815 ($2,614)

9
A George II coffee pot, Gurney & Cooke, London, 1753, 24cm (9½in), 24oz (754gr), *L 21 Nov,*
£1,650 ($2,376)

10
A George II coffee pot, William Williams I, London, 1743, 24cm (9½in) high, 24oz 14dwt (768gr), *L 4 Apr,*
£935 ($1,187)

11
A George II coffee pot, Ayme Videau, London, 1754, 23cm (9in) high, 24oz (746gr), *S 12 June,*
£2,200 ($2,926)

12
A George II coffee pot, Thomas Whipham, London, 1757, 25.5cm (10in), 33oz (1026gr), *L 23 May,*
£2,530 ($3,340)

13
An early George III coffee pot, William Grundy, London, 1760, 31.5cm (12½in), 43oz 4dwt (1343gr), *L 23 May,*
£4,400 ($5,808)

14
A George III coffee pot, John Kentember, London, 1770, 27.5cm (10¾in), *L 4 Apr,*
£1,430 ($1,816)

15
A German silver-gilt chocolate pot and coffee pot, Johann Christian Girschner, Augsburg, 1745-47, 27.5cm (10¾in) and 21.5cm (8½in) high, 44oz (1362gr), *G 14 May,*
SF 26,400
(£7,719; $10,266)

16
A German baluster chocolate pot, Jakob Wilhelm Kolb, Augsburg, 1767-69, 26cm (10¼in) high, 10oz 10dwt (578gr), *L 11 Feb,*
£2,200 ($2,530)

1
An Italian coffee pot, maker's mark only I M, c.1760, 24cm (9½in), 18oz (564gr), *G 12 Nov,* SF 8,250 (£2,696; $3,774)

2
An Italian coffee pot, Trento, late 18th century, 19cm (7½in), 8oz 10dwt (264gr), *F 29 May,* L 1,700,000 (£661; $873)

3
A Louis XVI coffee pot, Louis Ducoing, Bordeaux, 1781, 21cm (8¼in), 19oz (591gr), *NY 19 Feb,* $1,870 (£1,716)

4
A French coffee pot, apparently Joseph Rogé, Bordeaux, c.1785, 21cm (8¼in), 15oz (470gr), *G 12 Nov,* SF 3,300 (£1,078; $1,509)

5
A Dutch coffee urn, apparently Berend Strom, Leeuwarden, 1752, and a stand, 19th century, 34cm (13¼in), 42oz 10dwt (1320gr), *G 12 Nov,* SF 8,800 (£2,875; $4,025)

6
A French coffee pot, a member of the Wausraud family, Valenciennes, c.1750, 19cm (11½in) high, 20oz (620gr), *G 14 May,* SF 30,800 (£9,006; $11,978)

7
A Swiss coffee pot, Hans Heinrich Locher I, Zurich, c.1765, 17cm (6¾in) high, 10oz (315gr), *G 14 May,* SF 9,350 (£2,734; $3,636)

8
A Swiss coffee pot, Johann Jakob Dulliker, Bern c.1775, 25cm (9¾in) high, 21oz (644gr), *G 14 May,* SF 6,600 (£1,930; $2,567)

9
A George III hot water jug, ? David Whyte, London, 1768, 28cm (11in), 20oz (622gr), *NY 1 Feb,* 550 (£466)

10
An Italian coffee pot, probably Venice, c.1775, 28.5cm (11¼in) high, 28oz (883gr), *G 14 May,* SF 10,450 (£3,055; $4,063)

11
A George III coffee pot, Henry Chawner, London, 1786, 30cm (11¾in), 23oz 12dwt (733gr), *L 4 Apr,* £1,760 ($2,235)

12
A Maltese coffee pot, apparently Francesco Arnaud, c.1780, 28cm (11in) high, 31oz (955gr), *L 11 Feb,* £2,640 ($3,036)

13
A George III coffee pot, Francis Butty & Nicholas Dumee, London, 1771, 30.5cm (12½in), 30oz 10dwt (948gr), *L 24 Oct,* £3,520 ($5,280)

1   2   3

4   5   6

7

8   9

10

11   12   13

1

A George III hot water jug, Charles Wright, London, 1776, 34cm (13½in), 29oz (902gr), *NY 19 Feb,* $935 (£858)

2

An American coffee pot, Christian Wiltberger, Philadelphia, c.1795, 38.5cm (15in), 42oz (1306gr), *NY 27 June,* $4,400 (£3,385)

3

A coffee jug on stand with burner, John Robins, London, 1779, 46cm (18in), 48oz 12dwt (1508gr), *C 9 July,* £7,150 ($9,939)

4

A George III ewer, Edward Fernell, London, 1784, 29.5cm (11½in), 21oz 5dwt (660gr), *L 12 July,* £1,760 ($2,534)

5

A French silver-gilt coffee pot, Jean-Baptiste-Claude Odiot, Paris, c.1800, 27cm (10½in) high, 26oz (810gr), *G 14 May,* **SF 10,450** (£3,056; $4,064)

6

A French silver-gilt coffee pot, Jean-Baptiste-Claude Odiot, Paris, c.1800, 30cm (11¾in) high, 44oz (1366gr), *G 14 May,* **SF 8,800** (£2,573; $3,422)

7

A German coffee pot, Gustav Friedrich Gerich, Augsburg, 1805, 26.5cm (10½in), 22oz (685gr), *L 11 Feb,* £748 ($860)

8

An Italian coffee pot, maker's mark FC, Genoa, c.1825, 38cm (15in), 47oz 10dwt (1476gr), *F 29 May,* **L 4,600,000** (£1,790; $2,363)

9

A George III coffee pot, Paul Storr, London, 1797, 29.5cm (11½in), 40oz (1244gr), *NY 9 Oct,* $5,225 (£3,705)

10

A George III hot water jug and matching lamp-stand, Rundell, Bridge & Rundell, maker's mark Paul Storr, London, 1813/11, 29.5cm (11½in), 51oz 10dwt (1602gr), *NY 26 Apr,* $4,950 (£4,057)

11

A George IV hot water jug on lampstand, Rundell, Bridge & Rundell, maker's mark, John Bridge, London, 1829, 32cm (13½in), 49oz 10dwt (1539gr), *NY 26 Apr,* $4,125 (£3,381)

12

A French coffee pot, Moutot, Paris, 3rd quarter 19th century, 35.5cm (14in), 67oz (2084gr), *NY 26 Apr,* $1,430 (£1,172)

13

A William IV coffee pot, William Hattersley, London, 1834, 23cm (9in), 28oz 4dwt (870gr), *C 4 Sept,* £462 ($679)

14

A Victorian coffee pot, maker's mark FBT, London, 1875, 23cm (9in), 29oz (915gr), *JHB 31 July,* **R 1,300** (£483; $720)

15

A Victorian coffee pot, Richard Sibley, London, 1844, 25cm (9¾in), 28oz (870gr), *S 17 Apr,* £825 ($1,073)

16

A William IV hot water jug, Edward Barnard & Sons, London, 1833, 30.5cm (12in), 33oz (1026gr), *L 21 Nov,* £935 ($1,346)

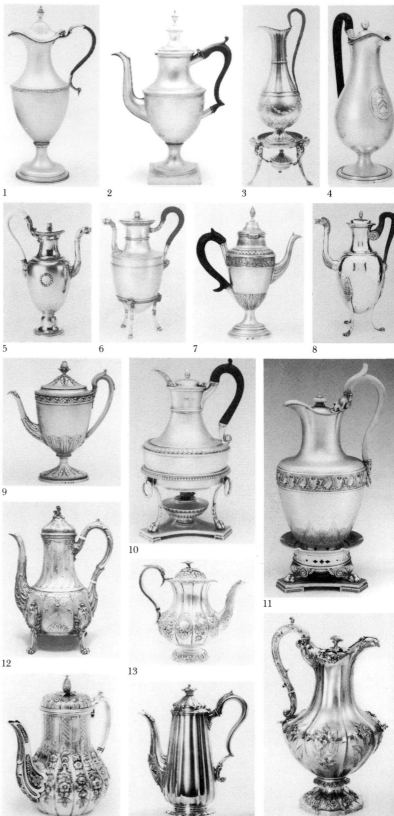

1 2 3 4
5 6 7 8
9
10
11
12 13
14 15 16

1

A George I kettle on lampstand, Seth Lofthouse, London, 1718, 37cm (14½in) high, 81oz (2519gr), *NY 10 Oct,* **$10,175 (£7,216)**

2

A George II silver-gilt tea kettle on lampstand, Samuel Courtauld, London, 1749, 40.5cm (16in) high, 91oz 10dwt (2846gr), *NY 26 Apr,* **$3,850 (£3,156)**

3

A Victorian kettle, stand and burner, J S Hunt, London, 1854, 43cm (17in), 87oz 12dwt (2721gr), *C 15 Jan,* **£1,925 ($2,310)**

4

An early George III tea urn, Thomas Whipham & Charles Wright, London, 1763, 54cm (21¼in) high, 97oz 14dwt (3038gr), *L 21 Feb,* **£2,640 ($3,036)**

5

A George III tea urn, Andrew Folgelberg, London, 1773, 55.5cm (21¾in), 121oz 10dwt (3779gr), *NY 7 June,* **$5,775 (£4,583)**

6

A silver-gilt tea urn, Benjamin Smith III, London, 1840, 47cm (18½in) high, 168oz (5,224gr), *S 12 June,* **£4,070 ($5,413)**

7

A French tea kettle on lampstand, Puiforcat, 43cm (17in) high, 96oz 10dwt (3000gr), *M 25 June,* **FF 9,990 (£833; $1,068)**

8

A Victorian tea kettle, stand, C F Hancock, London, 1866, 40cm (15¾in) high, 64oz (2000gr), *JB 13 Nov,* **R 5,200 (£1,405; $1,968)**

9

A Victorian tea kettle on stand, London, 1884, 31cm (12¼in), 49oz (1524gr), *C 27 Mar,* **£616 ($782)**

10

A Dutch kettle on stand, Bonebakker, Amsterdam, 1892, 40cm (15¾in), 56oz (1740gr), *A 5 Feb,* **Dfl 2,146 (£526; $615)**

1

2

3

4

5

6

7

8

9

10

1
A Swiss teapot, Jean Daniel Barde, Geneva, c.1740, 13cm (5¼in) high, 17oz (530gr), *G 14 May,*
SF 6,600 (£1,930; $2,567)

2
A Belgian teapot, maker's mark I L crowned, Mons, probably 1705, 28.5cm (11¼in), 55oz (1700gr), *G 12 Nov,*
SF 88,000 (£28,758; $40,261)

3
A George I teapot, William Gamble, London, 1715, 17cm (6¾in), *L 24 Oct,*
£4,180 ($6,270)

4
A small Dutch silver-gilt teapot, Adam Loofs, The Hague, 1701, initialled 'A', probably for Augustus, Duke of Clarence, third son of George III, 7.5cm (3in) high, 5oz 6dwt (166gr), *L 11 Feb,*
£4,190 ($4,807)

5
A George I bullet teapot, John East or Joseph Clare, London, 1722, 11cm (4¼in), 12oz 8dwt (385gr), *L 23 May,*
£3,080 ($4,067)

6
A Dutch melon-shaped teapot, Leendert Bouwer, The Hague, 1770, 13.5cm (5¼in), 13oz (404gr), *A 1 Apr,*
Dfl 14,500 (£3,356; $4,263)

7
A George III teapot, stand and tea caddy, Hester Bateman, London, 1788, 32oz 12dwt (1013gr), *L 24 Oct,*
£5,280 ($7,920)

8
A George III teapot and stand, maker's mark W S, London, 1790, 26.5cm (10½in) wide, 19oz 10dwt (606gr), *NY 26 Apr,*
$2,090 (£1,713)

9
An American teapot, John David, Philadelphia, c.1785, 16cm (6¼in), 18oz 10dwt (575gr), *NY 31 Jan,*
$9,350 (£7,924)

10
An American teapot, William Thompson, New York, c.1810, 18.5cm (7½in), 17oz (529gr), *NY 31 Jan,*
$825 (£699)

11
A George III teapot, John Robins, London, 1792, 14.5cm (5¾in), 15oz 10dwt (482gr), *L 23 May,*
£880 ($1,162)

12
A Dutch teapot, Barend van Mecklenburg, Amsterdam, 1791, 13cm (5in), 12oz (373gr), *A 2 Dec,*
Dfl 3,450 (£819; $1,146)

13
A George IV teapot, Rundell, Bridge & Rundell, maker's mark Phillip Rundell, London, 1821, 18.5cm (7¼in), 30oz (933gr), *C 15 Jan,*
£990 ($1,188)

14
A George IV teapot, Robert Garrard, London, 1823, 14cm (5½in), 37oz 10dwt (1166gr), *NY 7 June,*
$770 (£611)

15
A George IV teapot, Paul Storr, London, 1821, 18.5cm (7¼in), 23oz 15dwt (746gr), *C 9 July,*
£1,540 ($2,141)

1   2   3

4   5   6

7   8

9

10

11

13

12

14   15

1
A George III four-piece tea and coffee set, Peter & William Bateman, London, 1810-11, coffee pot 26cm (10¼in), 63oz (1959gr), *NY 7 June*, $3,850 (£3,056)

2
An American three-piece tea set, Christian Wiltberger, Philadelphia, *c.*1795, teapot 28cm (11in), 42oz 8dwt (1322gr), *NY 31 Jan*, $6,600 (£5,593)

3
A George III three-piece tea set, J McKay, Edinburgh, 1818, 45oz 10dwt (1415gr), *C 16 Oct*, £594 ($879)

4
A George III three-piece tea set, maker's mark W S, London, 1816, 57oz (1773gr), *NY 7 June*, $1,430 (£1,135)

5
A George IV three-piece tea set, Leonard Urquhart, Edinburgh, 1827, 75oz 2dwt (2335gr), *Glen 26 Aug*, £902 ($1,326)

6
An American three-piece tea set, Thomas Richards, New York, *c.*1820, 65oz (2021gr), *NY 19 Feb*, $770 (£706)

7
A George IV four-piece tea and coffee set, Paul Storr, London, 1827, coffee pot 23.5cm (9¼in), 84oz (2612gr), *NY 12 Dec*, $6,600 (£4,681)

8
A Victorian four-piece tea set, George Angell, London, 1850, 76oz 3dwt (2363gr), *C 9 July*, £1,485 ($2,064)

9
A Victorian four-piece tea and coffee set, Edward Barnard & Sons, London, 1865/67/68, 68oz 8dwt (2127gr), *L 21 Nov*, £1,980 ($2,851)

10
A Victorian four-piece tea set, William Hattersley, London, 1851, 73oz 15dwt (2301gr), *C 27 Mar*, £1,210 ($1,537)

1

2

3

4

5

6

7

8

9

10

1
A Victorian four-piece tea and coffee set, Reily & Storer, London, 1851, 79oz 4dwt (2463gr), *L 21 Feb*, £2,200 ($2,530)

2
A Victorian four-piece tea and coffee set, Edward Barnard & Sons, London, 1875, 58oz 4dwt (1810gr), *L 21 Feb*, £2,475 ($2,846)

3
A Victorian four-piece tea set, Stephen Smith, London, 1877, 91oz 7dwt (2830gr), *C 9 July*, £2,200 ($3,058)

4
A French tea and coffee service, Odiot, Paris, c.1840, 230oz (7170gr), *G 12 Nov*, **SF 12,100** (£4,033; $5,242)

5
A Victorian four-piece tea and coffee set and tray, The Goldsmiths Alliance Limited, London, maker's mark Samuel Smily, 1868-70 and a plated tea kettle on lampstand, *L 4 Apr*, £4,180 ($5,309)

6
A Victorian parcel-gilt four-piece tea and coffee set, Edward Barnard & Sons, London, 1875/77, 62oz (1928gr), *L 23 May*, £4,400 ($5,808)

7
A French five-piece tea and coffee set, mid-19th century, 230oz (7153gr), *NY 7 June*, $4,950 (£3,929)

8
A French five-piece tea and coffee set, Odiot, Paris, mid-19th century, 254oz (7899gr), *NY 7 June*, $4,125 (£3,274)

9
An American four-piece tea set, Eoff & Shepherd for W Carrington, Charleston, c.1850, 80oz (2488gr); with plated tea tray, *NY 27 June*, $1,430 (£1,100)

10
An American four-piece tea and coffee set, Tiffany & Co, New York, c.1860, 79oz 10dwt (2472gr); & plated tray, *NY 31 Jan*, $2,090 (£1,771))

1

2

3

4

5

6

7

8

9

10

1

An American five-piece
tea and coffee service,
Tiffany & Co. 1891-1907.
93oz (2892gr), *NY 8 Oct,*
$2,860 (£1,932)

2

An American five-piece
tea and coffee set with
tray, Gorham Mfg. Co,
20th century, tray
70.5cm (27¾in), 308oz
10dwt (9594gr),
NY 7 June,
$4,950 (£3,929)

3

A French four-piece
bachelors tea set and tray,
Lavallee, late 19th cen-
tury, 39oz 18dwt (1244gr),
C 15 Jan,
£990 ($1,188)

4

A French four-piece tea
and coffee set with tray,
*c.*1900, in Empire style,
tray 62cm (24½in), 158oz
(4914gr), *NY 19 Feb,*
$2,750 (£2,523)

5

A French four-piece tea
set with matching tea
tray, maker's mark T F,
*c.*1900, tray 72.5cm
(28½in), 319oz (9921gr),
NY 12 Dec,
$6,050 (£4,291)

6

A four-piece tea set,
Goldsmiths & Silver-
smiths Co Ltd, London,
1931/2, 16oz 5dwt
(3614gr), *L 30 May,*
£1,595 ($2,137)

7

A Dutch six-piece tea set,
J M van Kempen & Zn.
Voorschoten, 1906, 96oz
(3000gr), *A 1 Apr,*
Dfl 5,800 (£1,343; $1,705)

8

A Dutch six-piece tea and
coffee set, 1912-13, 119oz
(3701gr), *NY 14 Feb,*
$2,475 (£2,134)

9

A Dutch three-piece tea
set, Gerritsen & Van
Kempen, Zeist, 1944,
63oz (1961gr), with tray,
A 25 Oct,
Dfl 2,760 (£657; $979)

10

A four-piece tea set, Birmingham, 1913, match-
ing plated tea-kettle on
stand, 57oz 10dwt
(1788gr), *C 30 Jan,*
£704 ($831)

1

2

3

4

5

6

7

8

9

10

1

An early George I tea caddy, Thomas Ash, London, 1714, detachable shoulder plate and bun cover, 13cm (5in), 8oz 10dwt (272gr), *L 24 Oct,* **£1,760 ($2,640)**

2

A tea caddy, probably Danish or North German, early 18th century, engraved with scenes from the Old Testament, 12.5cm (5in), 6oz (189gr), *G 12 Nov,* **SF 20,900 (£6,830; $9,562)**

3

A Dutch tea caddy, maker's mark a tulip, Haarlem, 1720, 11cm (4¼in), 3oz (97gr), *A 2 Dec,* **Dfl 3,450 (£819; $1,146)**

4

A George II tea caddy, Christian Hillan, London, 1739, 14.5cm (5¾in), 8oz 17dwt (275gr), *L 31 Jan,* **£605 ($714)**

5

A pair of George II tea caddies and a mixing bowl, Samuel Taylor, London, 1749, 13.5 and 14.5cm (5¼ and 5¾in), 30oz (933gr), *NY 26 Apr,* **$2,530 (£2,074)**

6

A pair of George II tea caddies and a sugar box, John Newton, London, 1741, 14 and 13cm (5½ and 5in), 37oz (1150gr), *L 24 Oct,* **£2,640 ($3,960)**

7

An early George II tea caddy, Smith & Sharp, London, 1760, 13.5cm (5¼in) high, *S 12 June,* **£484 ($644)**

8

A set of three George III tea caddies, Daniel Smith & Robert Sharp, London, 1763, 14cm (5½in), 27oz 2dwt (842gr),' *L 21 Feb,* **£1,925 ($2,214)**

9

A Cape tea caddy, Johan Hendrik Vos, *c.*1770, 7.5cm (3in) wide, 5oz 10dwt (170gr), *JHB 13 Mar,* **R 3,500 (£1,577; $1,798)**

10

A George III tea caddy, maker's mark S A , London, 1795, 10cm (4in), 7oz (218gr), *NY 19 Feb,* **$825 (£757)**

11

A pair of German tea caddies, Johann Diedrich (? David) Laue Jr, Hamburg, 1816-26, 10cm (4in), 21oz (653gr), *NY 7 June,* **$1,320 (£1,048)**

12

A George III tea caddy, Augustin Le Sage, London, 1766, engraved with pseudo Chinese characters, 13.5cm (5¼in), *L 24 Oct,* **£3,080 ($4,620)**

13

A Swiss tea caddy, Charles Louis Rappillard, (Lausanne), *c.*1780, 12cm (4¾in) high, 6oz 10dwt (203gr), *G 14 May,* **SF 6,600 (£1,930)**

14

A George III tea caddy, Daniel Smith & Robert Sharp, London, 1782, 11.5cm (4½in), 13oz (401gr), *L 17 Oct,* **£1,078 ($1,595)**

15

A George III tea caddy, Peter & William Bateman, London, 1814, 9.5cm (3¾in), 5oz 11dwt (172gr), *L 21 Feb,* **£792 ($911)**

16

An Austrian tea caddy, Stephan Mayerhofer, Vienna, 1856, applied with the arms of Hapsburg and Wittelsbach below an Imperial crown, 12.5cm (5in), 38oz 10dwt (1203gr), *G 12 Nov,* **SF 4,620 (£1,509; $2,112)**

17

A pair of George III chinoiserie tea caddies, William Eaton, London, 1815, 14.5cm (5¾in), 49oz 10dwt (1539gr), *NY 26 Apr,* **$5,225 (£4,283)**

1 A George II creamboat, Christian Hillan, London, 1739, the body chased with grotesque masks, 12.5cm (5in) long, 5oz 12dwt (174gr), *L 30 May,* £682 ($914)

2 A George II cream jug, Charles Woodward, London, 1748, 10.5cm (4¼in), 4oz 16dwt (149gr), *L 4 Apr,* £462 ($587)

3 A Swiss cream jug, Jean-Daniel Magnin, Geneva, *c.*1775, 13cm (5in) high, 4oz (138gr), *G 14 May,* SF 2,860 (£836; $1,112)

4 A Dutch hot milk jug, Phillipus Prié, Middelburg 1764, 15cm (6in), 12oz (367gr), *A 2 Dec,* Dfl 11,500 (£2,731; $3,823)

5 An American milk jug, Jonathan Otis, Newport, RI, *c.*1760, 11.5cm (4½in), 4oz (124gr), *NY 31 Jan,* $935 (£792)

6 A George III milk jug, Robert & Samuel Hennell, London, 1903, 13.5cm (5¼in), 12oz 9dwt (387gr), *L 23 May,* £528 ($697)

7 A George III milk jug, Hester Bateman, London, 1788, 13.5cm (5¼in), 2oz 10dwt (83gr), *L 24 Oct,* £275 ($413)

8 A Victorian milk jug, Robert Harper, London, 1865, 14cm (5½in), 6oz (190gr), *JHB 31 July,* R 400 (£149; $222)

9 A cow creamer, maker's mark M F, London, 1903, 17cm (6¾in) long, 7oz 8dwt (217gr), *C 13 Feb,* £341 ($392)

10 A George II cow creamer on later base, the cow John Schuppe, 1758, the base Charles and George Fox, 1842, both London, 15cm (6in) long, 6oz (186gr), *C 15 Jan,* £2,970 ($3,564)

11 A George III cruet set, John Delmester, London, 1765, 28.5cm (11¼in), 51oz 10dwt (1602gr), *NY 7 June,* $2,750 (£2,183)

12 An Italian cruet frame, maker's mark SC, Genoa *c.*1830, complete with two bottles, 32cm (12½in), 23oz (710gr), *F 29 May,* L 1,800,000 (£700; $925)

13 A William IV eight-bottle cruet frame, J H & C Lias, London, 1834, stamped 323, complete with eight cut-glass bottles, 28cm (11in) high, 44oz (1373gr), *L 21 Nov,* £1,320 ($1,901)

14 A George III cruet set, Paul Storr, for Rundell, Bridge & Rundell, London, 1815, fitted with eight silver-mounted cut-glass bottles, four with later bases, 26.5cm (10½in), 42oz 10dwt (1322gr), *NY 12 Dec,* $2,310 (£1,638)

1
A Dutch sugar caster,
probably Cornelis van
Dijk, Delft 1706, 12cm
(4¾in), 3oz (101gr),
A 2 Dec,
Dfl 9,430 (£2,239; $3,134)

2
A Queen Anne caster,
Isaac Liger, London,
1705, engraved with two
later crests, 14.5cm
(5¾in), 9oz (279gr),
L 24 Oct,
£1,155 ($1,733)

3
A Queen Anne caster,
Thomas Farren,
London, 1709, later
crest, 21cm (8¼in), 9oz
(276gr), *L 24 Oct,*
£935 ($1,403)

4
A Dutch sugar caster,
Gregorius van der
Toorn, The Hague,
1743, 13cm (5in), 4oz
(124gr), *A 2 Dec,*
Dfl 7,360 (£1,748; $2,447)

5
A pair of George I cas-
ters. probably Jacob or
Samuel Margas of Lon-
don, *c.*1720, 15.5cm (6in).
10oz 2dwt (562gr),
L 4 Apr,
£1,320 ($1,676)

6
A George I kitchen pep-
per, Thomas Bamford I.
London, 1725, 9cm
(3½in), 3oz 17dwt
(119gr), *L 12 July,*
£1,155 ($1,663)

7
A George I caster, Samuel Welder, London,
1722, 13cm (5in), 4oz
(124gr), *NY 10 Oct,*
$880 (£624)

8
Three George II casters,
Edward Aldridge, Lon-
don 1737/8, engraved
with crest and marquess'
coronet, 18.5cm (7¼in)
and 15cm (6in) high,
25oz 16dwt (802gr),
L 23 May,
£2,750 ($3,630)

9
A set of three George II
casters, Samuel Wood,
London, 1758, 18.5 and
16cm (7¼ and 6¼in),
NY 14 Feb,
$1,100 (£948)

10
A Dutch sugar caster,
Gorinchem, mid-18th
century, 14cm (5½in).
3oz 10dwt (111gr),
A 1 Apr,
Dfl 12,320 (£537; $682)

11
A Belgian mustard pot
and matching sugar cas-
ter, Mechelen, 1758,
19cm (7½in), 19oz (593gr),
A 1 Apr,
**Dfl 18,560
(£4,296; $5,456)**

12
A pair of Dutch sugar
casters, Franciscus Herlé,
Den Bosch, 1775, 18cm
(7in) high, 15oz 10dwt
(486gr), *G 14 May,*
**SF 10,450
(£3,056; $4,064)**

13
A George III caster, Hester Bateman, London,
1788, 14cm (5½in), 2oz
10dwt (82gr), *L 24 Oct,*
£352 ($528)

14
A German sugar caster,
Johan Ernst Holtz-
hausen, Verden, *c.*1745,
16cm (6¼in), 5oz (150gr),
G 12 Nov,
SF 2,530 (£826; $1,156)

15
An American caster, John
Roe, Kingston, NY,
*c.*1770, 14cm (5½in), 4oz
(124gr), *NY 14 Feb,*
$1,980 (£1,707)

16
An American pepper box,
Miles Beach, Litchfield
and Hartford, Conn.,
*c.*1780, 7.5cm (3in), 20oz
(622gr), *NY 27 June,*
$1,210 (£931)

17
A caster and a pair of
pepper shakers,
R Comyns, London,
1961/62, in the form of
penguins, caster 12.5cm
(5in), 12oz (360gr),
CT 4 Nov,
R 750 (£203; $284)

18
A mouse-form salt and
pepper, R. Comyns.
London, 1967, 6cm
(2½in), 3oz (100gr).
CT 4 Nov,
R 300 (£81; $114)

1   2   3   4   5

6   7   8

9   10   11

12   13   14   15   16

17

18

1
A pair of Queen Anne trencher salt cellars, William Pearson, London, 1710, 6.5cm (2½in), and a pair of mid 18th century salt spoons, 4oz 14dwt (146gr), *L 4 Apr,* £687 ($872)

2
A pair of William and Mary trencher salt cellars, London, 1690, 7cm (2¾in) diam, and a pair of mid 18th century spoons, 7oz (217gr), *L 4 Apr,* £715 ($908)

3
A set of four George II salt cellars, original maker's mark overstruck by Jones & Scofield, 1742, 9cm (3½in) diam, 31oz (960gr), *L 17 Oct,* £1,320 ($1,954)

4
A pair of George II salt cellars, David Tanqueray, *c.*1735, 8.5cm (3½in), 12oz 10dwt (389gr), *L 17 Oct,* £385 ($570)

5
A pair of American salt cellars, John Heath, New York, *c.*1765, 9.5cm (3¾in), 5oz 10dwt (171gr), *NY 31 Jan,* £8,800 (£7,458)

6
A pair of early George III salt cellars and spoons, Sebastian & James Crespell, London, 1763, 9.5cm (3¾in) wide, 10oz 2dwt (314gr), *L 23 May,* £1,595 ($2,105)

7
A pair of George III salt cellars, Hester Bateman, London, 1777, 7cm (2¾in) diam, 4oz 10dwt (146gr), *L 24 Oct,* £330 ($495)

8
Four George III salt cellars and spoons, Aldridge & Green, London, 1777, 12cm (4¾in) wide, 27oz 18dwt (870gr), *C 9 July,* £2,090 ($2,905)

9
A George III mustard pot and spoon, Aldridge & Green, London, 1777, 13.5cm (5¼in), 9oz 6dwt (280gr), *C 9 July,* £1,210 ($1,682)

10
Four George III salt cellars, Peter & Ann Bateman, London, 1794, 10.5cm (4¼in) wide, 10oz 11dwt (326gr), *C 15 Jan,* £616 ($739)

11
A set of four George III salt cellars, John Emes, London, 1805, 8.5cm (3¼in) wide, 13oz 16dwt (429gr), *L 30 May,* £660 ($884)

12
A pair of George III salt cellars, Rundell, Bridge & Rundell, maker's mark Paul Storr, London, 1806, 11cm (4½in), 12oz (373gr), *NY 7 June,* $1,210 (£960)

13
A set of six George III silver-gilt salt stands, John Emes, London, 1801, glass liners, 14.5cm (5¾in) wide, and six silver-gilt salt spoons, mid 18th century, 27oz 10dwt (855gr), *L 23 May,* £1,980 ($2,614)

14
A set of six George III salt cellars, William Elliott, London, 1818-19, and six salt spoons, Newcastle, 1832, 9.5cm (3¾in), 34oz (1057gr), *NY 19 Feb,* $1,375 (£1,261)

15
A pair of French silver-gilt double salts, Jacques-Louis-Auguste Leguay, Paris, *c.*1820, 10cm (4in) wide, 15oz (465gr), *G 14 May* SF 6,050 (£1,769; $2,353)

16
A pair of Victorian salt cellars, Hunt & Roskell, London, 1855, maker's mark John Samuel Hunt, 11.5cm (4½in), 37oz (1146gr), *L 24 Oct,* £4,950 ($7,425)

17
A pair of Victorian figural salts, Robert Garrard, London, 1855, 15cm (6in), 29oz 10dwt (917gr), *NY 7 June,* $7,150 (£5,675)

18
A pair of Victorian salt cellars, Martin Hall & Co, London, 1874, 10cm (4in) wide, 4oz 18dwt (155gr), *C 19 June,* £187 ($252)

1
A French cup and saucer, maker's mark Q B, Paris, *c.*1825, 11.5cm (4½in), 12oz (385gr), *M 25 June,* **FF 7,215 (£601; $768)**

2
A French brazier, Lille, probably 1751, 19.5cm (7¾in) diam, 26oz 10dwt (830gr), *M 25 June,* **FF 15,540 (£1,295; $1,653)**

3
A French silver-gilt egg service, Paris, *c.*1800, including six egg-cups, Jean-Baptiste-Lazare Clérin, six egg spoons and six salt spoons, Pierre Desfontaine, cups 7cm (2¾in) high, 20oz (620gr), *M 25 June,* **FF 44,400 (£3,700; $4,723)**

4
An American porringer, Samuel Gray, Boston, *c.*1740, 13.5cm (5¼in), 8oz (249gr), *NY 31 Jan,* **$1,650 (£1,398)**

5
An American porringer, Benjamin Burt, Boston, *c.*1760, 14cm (5½in), 8oz 10dwt (264gr), *NY 27 June,* **$1,210 (£931)**

6
A pair of George III spit roast posts, Thomas Heming, London, 1770, 20.5cm (8in), 11oz (342gr), *NY 14 Feb,* **$1,760 (£1,517)**

7
A Dutch brazier, Gerrit Boverhof, Amsterdam, 1764, 18cm (7in), 13oz (411gr), *A 1 Apr,* **Dfl 10,440 (£2,417; $3,069)**

8
A George I lemon strainer, John Albright, London, 1723, 17.5cm (7in), 2oz (10dwt) (78gr), *NY 10 Oct,* **$825 (£585)**

9
A Queen Anne saucepan, David King, Dublin, 1706-08, later armorials, 28.5cm (11¼in) over handle, 21oz (650gr), *L 17 Oct,* **£2,420 ($3,582)**

10
A brandy warmer, Calcutta, late 18th century, 12.5cm (5in) diam, 14oz (435gr), *C 30 Oct,* **£616 ($917)**

11
A pair of Queen Anne snuffers and stand, Francis Turner, London, 1712, 19.5cm (7½in), 11oz 10dwt (357gr), *L 24 Oct,* **£6,380 ($9,570)**

12
A George III snuffer's tray and pair of snuffers, London, the tray Robert Hennell, 1788, the snuffers William Bennett, 1799, tray 23cm (9in), 6oz 10dwt (202gr), *NY 14 Feb,* **$1,210 (£1,043)**

13
A Swiss chamber candlestick, François Barbier, Geneva, *c.*1765, 20cm (8in) wide, 6oz 10dwt (208gr), *G 14 May,* **SF 7,700 (£2,251; $2,994)**

14
A George III snuffer's tray, John Carter, London, 1770, 18cm (7in) wide, *S 12 June,* **£275 ($366)**

15
A pair of George III chamber candlesticks, Ebenezer Coker, London, 1770, 13.5cm (5¼in) diam, 18oz 15dwt (583gr), *L 30 May,* **£1,870 ($2,506)**

pair of Swiss chamber
candlesticks, Johann
Jakob Dulliker, Bern,
1790, 19.5cm (7¾in)
high, 22oz 10dwt (700gr),
14 May,
F 12,100
(£3,538; $12,100)

George III argyle,
Hester Bateman,
London, 1776, 17cm
(6¾in), 9oz (280gr),
9 July,
1,320 ($1,835)

George III argyle,
Aaron Lestourgen,
London, 1771, 11.5cm
(4½in), 10oz (311gr),
16 Oct,
1,265 ($1,872)

A George II Irish dish
ring, William Townsend,
Dublin, c.1755, 20cm
(8in), 20oz (617gr),
24 Oct,
2,750 ($4,125)

An Irish dish ring, West &
Sons, Dublin, 1918, 18cm
(7in) diam, 10oz 4dwt
(311gr), *C 27 Feb,*
308 ($345)

A George II Irish dish
cross, Robert Calder-
wood, Dublin, c.1735,
with pivoting arms,
24.5cm (9¾in), 19oz
10dwt (606gr), *L 17 Oct,*
2,200 ($3,256)

A George III dish cross,
William Plummer,
London, 1789, detach-
able reeded burner and
cover, 27cm (10¾in)
wide, 14oz 4dwt (435gr),
C 15 Jan,
902 ($1,082)

A George III skep honey
pot, Richard Morton &
Co, Sheffield, 1798,
12.5cm (5in), 13oz
(401gr), and a stand,
Thomas Harper I,
London, 1800, 13cm
(5¼in) diam, *L 24 Oct,*
1,430 ($2,145)

9
**A George III skep honey
pot,** Paul Storr, London,
1793, detachable cover,
11.5cm (4½in), 6oz 10dwt
(202gr), *NY 9 Oct,*
$9,900 (£7,021)

10
**A circular two-handled
biscuit barrel,** Hukin &
Heath, Birmingham,
1936, 15cm (6in) diam,
19oz 8dwt (606gr),
C 13 Nov,
£352 ($493)

11
**A set of three George III
butter shells,** William
Abdy, London, 1784,
each on two whelk sup-
ports, 16cm (6¼in), 14oz
5dwt (443gr), *L 30 May,*
£1,485 ($1,990)

12
A William IV toast rack,
Storr & Mortimer,
London, 1834, 15cm
(5¾in) wide, 9oz 16dwt
(304gr), *L 31 Jan,*
£792 ($934)

13
**A George III preserve
dish,** William Rudkins,
London, 1805, the cut-
glass body with mounts
showing traces of
gilding, 24cm (9½in)
wide, *L 24 Oct,*
£1,265 ($1,897)

14
A Victorian butter dish,
Martin Hall & Co, Shef-
field, 1872, 22.5cm (9in)
wide, 19oz 2dwt (591gr),
C 9 July,
£550 ($765)

1
A George I Irish sugar bowl and cover, David King, Dublin, 1715, 11.5cm (4½in) diam, 7oz 10dwt (233gr), *NY 10 Oct* $4,675 (£3,315)

2
A Hungarian sugar box, maker's mark I G, Nagybánya, *c.*1760, 12.5cm (5in), 6oz 10dwt (211gr), *G 12 Nov,* SF 3,740 (£1,222; $1,710)

3
A George II sugar bowl, Edinburgh, 1739, struck with two maker's marks, that of David Mitchell and of Edward Lothian, 15cm (6in), 6oz 11dwt (202gr), *HH 30 Apr,* £418 ($548)

4
A mid-18th century sugar bowl, Joseph Johns of Limerick, *c.*1755, with lion mask headed fret, 6oz 10dwt (207gr), 12.5cm (5in) diam, *L 17 Oct,* £1,100 ($1,628)

5
A Jamaican sugar bowl and cover, Anthony Danvers, Kingston, *c.*1765, chased with rococo decoration, 15cm (6in), 27oz 10dwt (855gr), *NY 9 Oct,* $1,870 (£1,326)

6
An Italian sugar bowl with cover, Piedmontese, *c.*1770, 12.5cm (5in), 7oz (226gr), *F 29 May,* L 4,000,000 (£1,556; $2,054)

7
A George III sugar basket, Robert Hennell, London, 1781, 14cm (5½in), 7oz 4dwt (223gr), *L 30 May,* £770 ($1,032)

8
A George III sugar basket, Charles Chesterman, London, 1787, 18cm (7in), 8oz (249gr), *NY 9 Oct,* $770 (£546)

9
A George III sweetmeat basket, Hester Bateman, London, 1788, 17.5cm (7in), 7oz 10dwt (233gr), *L 24 Oct,* £1,100 ($1,650)

10
An Italian sugar box and cover, Turin, *c.*1790, 8oz 10dwt (270gr), *L 11 Feb,* £2,200 ($2,530)

11
An American sugar urn and cover, Samuel Richards Jr. & Samuel Williamson, Philadelphia, *c.*1800, 25.5cm (10in), *NY 31 Jan,* $3,520 (£2,983)

12
An Italian sugar bowl and cover, maker's mark C.I.A., Catania, 1811, 16cm (6¼in), 9oz 10dwt (295gr), *NY 19 Feb,* $330 (£303)

13
An Italian sugar bowl with cover, Emmanuel Caber, Milan, *c.*1830, 13.5cm (5¼in) high, 14oz 10dwt (450gr), *F 29 May,* L 2,200,000 (£856; $1,130)

14
An American two-handled sugar bowl and cover, S Kirk, Baltimore, 1828, 22cm (8¾in), 33oz (1026gr), *NY 31 Jan,* $825 (£699)

1   2   3

4   5   6

7   8   9

10   11   12

13   14

1
A German silver-gilt bowl
and cover, Johann Peter
Müller, Augsburg,
1755-57, armorial eng-
raved, 22.5cm (8¾in)
wide overall, 16oz
(500gr), *G 14 May,*
SF 12,100 (£3,538; $4,706)

2
An Italian ecuelle and
cover, Turin, *c.*1780,
assay master Giuseppe
Vernoni, 27cm (10½in),
20oz 12dwt (640gr),
L 11 Feb,
£6,380 ($7,337)

3
A Swiss bowl and cover,
Samuel Siegfried the
Elder or Younger, Zof-
ingen, *c.*1760, 12.5cm
(5in) diam, 10oz 10dwt
(327gr), *G 14 May,*
SF 10,450 (£306; $407)

4
A Swiss bowl, probably
Jean Veyrassat,
Lausanne, *c.*1760, 21.5cm
(8½in) diam, 15oz 10dwt
(485gr), *G 14 May,*
SF 7,150 (£2,091; $2,781)

5
An American silver bowl,
Christian Wiltberger,
Philadelphia, *c.*1795,
16cm (6¼in) diam, 12oz
(373gr), *NY 27 June,*
$1,430 (£1,100)

6
A French Empire silver-
gilt covered bowl and
stand, maker's mark L R
Paris, *c.*1810, 16cm
(6¼in), 28oz 10dwt
(887gr), *G 12 Nov,*
SF 5,500 (£1,797; $2,515)

7
A French silver-gilt cov-
ered cup and stand, Paris,
*c.*1825, 14.5cm (5¾in),
20oz (635gr), *G 14 May,*
SF 3,300 (£965; $1,283)

8
A German parcel-gilt
bowl, Frankfurt a.M,
*c.*1664, a pricked
inscription in the base,
17cm (6¾in) wide over-
all, 5oz (167gr),
G 14 May,
SF 22,000 (£6,433; $8,556)

9
A German silver-gilt
bowl, Johann Gelb,
Augsburg, *c.*1730,
11.5cm (4½in) wide, 3oz
(93gr), *G 14 May,*
SF 6,600 (£1,930; $2,567)

10
A German silver-gilt stand,
Johann Engelbrecht,
Augsburg, *c.*1730, flat-
chased with Régence
ornament, 22cm (8¾in),
11oz 10dwt (362gr),
G 14 May,
SF 9,900 (£2,895; $3,850)

11
A Dutch bowl and cover,
Arnoldus Coolhaas,
Utrecht, 1731, 22.5cm
(9in) wide overall, 20oz
(619gr), *G 14 May,*
SF 20,900 (£6,111; $8,128)

12
A German parcel-gilt
sweetmeat dish, Balthasar
Haydt, Augsburg,
*c.*1675, 18.5cm (7¼in),
5oz 10dwt (171gr),
NY 26 Apr,
$2,090 (£1,713)

1

2

3

4

5

6

7

8

9

10

11

12

1
A James II chinoiserie
monteith bowl, George
Garthorne, London,
1685, the eight panels
flat-chased with various
chinoiserie scenes,
28.5cm (11¼in) diam,
31oz 10dwt (980gr),
NY 9 Oct,
$52,800 (£37,446)

2
A Flemish dish, maker's
mark the sun in splen-
dour, Tournai, *c.*1685,
35cm (13¾in), 15oz
(480gr), *G 12 Nov,*
SF 19,800 (£6,471; $9,059)

3
A Dutch brandy bowl,
Hindrik Muntinck,
Groningen, 1670-71,
11cm (4¼in), 7oz (221gr),
A 2 Dec,
Dfl 4,600 (£1,092; $1,528)

4
A German silver-gilt
basin, Johann Conrad
Treffler, Augsburg,
1682-85, 39cm (15½in),
23oz 10dwt (731gr),
NY 9 Oct,
$9,350 (£6,631)

5
A Friesian brandy bowl,
Pieter Jansen Poelgeest,
Bolsward, 1671, engraved
with figures of the Five
Senses, Hope and Char-
ity, 8.5cm (3¼in) high,
9oz (285gr), *A 1 Apr,*
Dfl 19,720 (£4,565; $5,793)

6
A Friesian brandy bowl,
Rembartus Gerbrandi
de Visscher, Leeuwar-
den, 1698, engraved with
initials and date, 23cm
(9in), 9oz (275gr),
A 1 Apr,
Dfl 13,920 (£3,222; $4,092)

7
An ecuelle and cover, probably Dutch, *c.*1690,
25.5cm (10in) wide, 13oz
(415gr), *A 2 Dec,*
Dfl 20,700
(£4,916; $6,882)

8
A German ecuelle and
cover, Matthäus Baur II,
Augsburg, 1708-10,
23.5cm (9¼in) wide
overall, 13oz 10dwt
(429gr), *G 14 May,*
SF 8,800 (£2,573; $3,422)

9
A French silver-gilt
ecuelle, cover and stand,
Jean-Louis Imlin III,
Strasbourg, *c.*1750, 30cm
(11¾in) wide overall,
49oz (1520gr), *G 14 May,*
SF 68,200
(£19,942; $26,522)

10
A German silver-gilt
ecuelle and cover, Jo-
hann Erhard Heuglin II,
Augsburg, 1729-30, flat-
chased in Régence style,
20.5cm (8in) wide, 13oz
10dwt (420gr), *NY 9 Oct,*
$3,410 (£2,418)

11
An ecuelle and cover,
possibly French Provin-
cial, *c.*1740, 29.5cm
(11½in) wide overall,
27oz (839gr), *G 14 May,*
SF 9,350 (£2,734; $3,636)

1

2

3

4

5

6

7

8

9

10

11

1
A George I bowl, Henry Daniell, Dublin, 1715, 10cm (4in) diam, 6oz (181gr), L 24 Oct, £1,870 ($2,805)

2
An early George II strawberry dish, Robert Calderwood, Dublin, 1728, 21cm (8¼in), 9oz (274gr), L 17 Oct, £1,210 ($1,791)

3
A George II fluted dish, Paul de Lamerie, maker's mark only, (London), c.1730-32, on three feet, 18cm (7in), 11oz 10dwt (358gr), NY 18 Oct, $12,100 (£8,581)

4
A George II bowl, Isaac Cookson, Newcastle, 1746, engraved with crest and motto, 14cm (5½in) diam, 10oz (310gr), L 24 Oct, £1,265 ($1,898)

5
A George II dish, possibly John Carnaby, Newcastle, c.1735, with later crest, 16cm (6¼in), 8oz (244gr), L 4 Apr, £770 ($978)

6
Two dessert dishes, Robert Gainsford, Sheffield, 1828-33, with four foliate supports, 32.5cm (12¾in), 47oz 10dwt (1477gr), L 12 July, £3,630 ($5,227)

7
A Victorian bowl, Frederick Elkington, Birmingham, 1877, the rim applied with a cast classical frieze, gilt interior, 12.5cm (5in), 20oz 10dwt (638gr), NY 7 June, $550 (£437)

8
A German silver two-handled dish, late 19th century, decorated in 17th century style, 14cm (5½in) diam, NY 26 June, $385 (£298)

9
Two matching George III serving dishes, William Hall, London, 1768 and William Fountain, London, 1800, 39.5 and 53cm (15½ and 20¾in), NY 10 Oct, $2,310 (£1,638)

10
A set of twenty-four Queen Anne dinner plates, Philip Rollos, London, 1706, engraved with slightly later armorials, 24cm (9½in), 429oz (13342gr), NY 10 Oct, $187,000 (£132,624)

11
Five matching George II serving dishes, three by William Cripps, two by Lewis Herne & Francis Butty, London, 1758/9, 54.5 to 33.5cm (21½ to 13¼in), 169oz 10dwt (5271gr), NY 10 Oct, $12,100 (£8,581)

12
A set of four George IV graduated serving dishes, Storr & Mortimer, maker's mark Paul Storr, London, 1828, 51.5 to 39cm (20¼ to 15¼in), NY 9 Oct, $15,950 (£11,312)

13
A set of four George III serving dishes, from the Catherine the Great service, George Heming & William Chawner, London, 1776, the borders engraved with the Russian Imperial arms, 33cm (13in), 131oz (4074gr), NY 10 Oct, $12,100 (£8,581)

14
A set of twelve Victorian dinner plates, John Mortimer & John S Hunt, London, 1841, 25.5cm (10in), 242oz (7526gr), NY 26 Apr, $9,900 (£8,115)

15
A set of twenty-four American service plates, Tiffany & Co, New York, c.1930, 28cm (11in), 437oz 10dwt (13606gr), NY 19 Feb, $12,100 (£11,101)

1
A set of twelve Victorian silver-gilt dinner plates, Messrs. Barnard, London, 1872, 25cm (10in), 246oz (7651gr), *NY 19 Feb,* $6,875 (£6,307)

2
A set of fourteen American dinner plates, Tiffany & Co, New York, 20th century, 25cm (9¾in), 273oz (8490gr), *NY 14 Feb,* $4,400 (£3,793)

3
A pair of English cloisonné enamel vases, and gilt-metal stands, Elkington & Co of Birmingham, one dated 1874, 26 cm (10¼in) high, *L 21 Mar,* £660 ($799)

4
An Italian table service, modern, comprising fifty six pieces, and one hundred and fifty four pieces of table silver, 741oz (23045gr), *NY 19 Feb,* $8,800 (£8,073)

5
An American silver-mounted cut-glass punch bowl on stand, and a ladle of different pattern, Dorflinger, *c.*1890-1900, chips, 46cm (18in) diam, *NY 30 Nov,* $5,225 (£3,506)

6
A pair of Continental two-handled vases, 58.5cm (23in), 279oz 10dwt (8568gr), *NY 26 Apr,* $11,000 (£9,016)

7
A reproduction of the Warwick vase, Elkington & Co, London, 1904, 32.5cm (13¾in) wide, 72oz 7dwt (2239gr), *C 9 July,* £1,320 ($1,835)

8
A German jardinière, C A Beumers, Dusseldorf, *c.*1900, detachable gilt-metal liner, 55cm (21¾in) over handles, 94oz (2923gr), *S 16 Oct,* £1,925 ($2,849)

9
A circular rose bowl, William Hutton & Sons Ltd, Sheffield, 1897, 26cm (10¼in) diam, 43oz (1337gr), *C 27 Nov,* £616 ($862)

10
A pair of American silver-gilt vases, Gorham Mfg. Co, 20th century, 65.5cm (25¾in), 213oz (6624gr), *NY 19 Feb,* $3,300 (£3,038)

11
An American centrepiece bowl with a matching pair of tazze, Black, Starr & Frost, New York, *c.*1915, 35.5 and 30cm (14 and 9in), 67oz (2084gr), *NY 12 Dec,* $1,760 (£1,248)

12
A two-handled cup, The Barnards, London, 1910, 26.5cm (10½in), 83oz (2581gr), *NY 7 June,* $2,200 (£1,746)

13
A two-handled bowl, James Ramsay, London, 1934, 35.5cm (14in) diam, 166oz 14dwt (5184gr), *HH 30 Apr,* £1,980 ($2,594)

14
An American art nouveau centrepiece bowl, Gorham Mfg. Co, Providence, RI, Martelé, *c.*1914, retailed by Spalding & Co, Chicago, the deep bell-shaped bowl with wavy everted rim and foot, 29.9cm (11¾in) diam, 17.2cm (6¾in) high, 54oz 12dwt (1,698gr), *NY 7 Dec,* $2,530 (£1,721)

15
An English silver-gilt covered vase, D & J Welby, London, 1928, 44.5cm (17½in) high, 147oz 10dwt (4587gr), *NY 9 Oct,* $1,980 (£1,404)

1
A pair of George III wine coolers, Andrew Fogelberg & Stephen Gilbert, London, 1788, detachable rims by Thomas Ellerton & Richard Sibley I, c.1805, plated liners, 22cm (8¾in), 96oz (2985gr), NY 10 Oct, $17,050 (£12,092)

A Austrian wine cooler, maker's mark G H, Vienna, 1795, with later applied armorials, 32cm (12½in) high, 120oz (3730gr), L 11 Feb, £2,970 ($3,416)

A pair of French wine coolers, Charles-Nicolas Odiot, Paris, c.1840, 25cm (9¾in) high, 138oz 10dwt (4310gr), G 14 May, FF 24,200 (£7,076; $9,411)

A George III silver-gilt wine cooler, Rundell, Bridge & Rundell, London, 1814, maker's mark of Paul Storr for Storr & Co, 136oz (4230gr), L 23 May, £21,450 ($28,314)

A pair of Victorian wine coolers, D & C Houle, London, 1854, 29cm (11in), 277oz 10dwt (8638gr), L 21 Nov, £9,900 ($14,256)

A set of four George III wine coasters, R & D Hennell, London, 1771, 12cm (4¾in), L 24 Oct, £4,950 ($7,425)

A pair of George III wine coasters, Robert Hennell, London, 1776, wood bases, 12.5cm (5in) diam, L 30 May, £2,310 ($3,095)

A pair of George III wine coasters, Emick Romer of London, c.1775, maker's mark and lion passant only, 12.8cm (5in) diam, L 30 May, £1,045 ($1,400)

9
A pair of George IV wine coasters, Emes & Barnard, London, 1820, 16.5cm (6½in), L 17 Oct, £1,155 ($1,709)

10
A set of four George III silver-gilt wine coasters, Robert & Samuel Hennell, London, 1806, 14.5cm (5½in) diam, L 23 May, £6,820 ($9,002)

11
A pair of George IV wine coasters, Samuel Dutton, London, 1824, 14cm (5½in), NY 10 Oct, $2,530 (£1,794)

12
A George III wine funnel, William Burwash, London, 1819, 16cm (6¼in) long, 7oz (218gr), C 16 Oct, £462 ($684)

1

2 3

4 5

6 7 8 9

10 11 12

1

A Portuguese ewer, *c.*1580, the body engraved with the arms of Fonseca, unmarked, 23cm (9in) high, 10oz 2dwt (564gr), *L 11 Feb,* £3,520 ($4,048)

2

A German ewer and basin, maker's mark W H Nuremberg, *c.*1725, chased in Régence style, 22cm (8¾in) high, 59oz (1850gr), *G 12 Nov,* SF 41,800 (£13,660; $19,124)

3

An Italian ewer and basin, Como, *c.*1740, chased with Régence ornament, basin 38cm (14¾in) wide, ewer 22.5cm (8¾in) high, 45oz 16dwt (1430gr), *L 11 Feb,* £6,600 ($7,590)

4

A French silver-gilt ewer, Puiforcat, Paris, early 20th century, in Régence style, 25.5cm (10in), 48oz (1493gr), *NY 9 Oct,* $2,310 (£1,638)

5

A George III beer jug, John Parker & Edward Wakelin, London, 1765, with later chasing, 27cm (10½in), 38oz (1180gr), *JHB 31 July,* R 3,400 (£1,264; $1,883)

6

An Irish baluster beer jug, Dublin, mid 18th century, 21.5cm (8½in), 30oz (933gr), *C 15 Jan,* £1,485 ($1,782)

7

A George III beer jug, Peter & Ann Bateman, London, 1800, 23.5cm (9¼in), 28oz (871gr), *NY 12 Dec,* $2,860 (£2,028)

8

A French ewer and basin, Gabriel-Jacques-André Bompart, Paris, *c.*1810, ewer 36cm (14in) high, 57oz (1770gr), *M 25 June,* FF 44,400 (£3,700; $4,723)

9

A William IV hot-milk or water jug, Storr & Mortimer, London, 1836, in the form of a Pompeian 'acsos', 22.5cm (8¾in), 34oz 11dwt (1074gr), *L 23 May,* £5,280 ($6,970)

10

An American water pitcher, Ball, Black & Co, New York, *c.*1872, 28cm (11in), 38oz (1182gr), *NY 14 Feb,* $990 (£853)

11

A Victorian Armada jug, J Smyth, Dublin, 1864, with later presentation inscription, 37cm (14½in), 38oz (118gr), *C 15 Jan,* £1,485 ($1,782)

1
A Victorian 'Cellini' pattern ewer, Charles Boyton, London, 1884, 29.5cm (11½in), 32oz 2dwt (99gr), *L 21 Feb, 1990* ($1,139)

2
A late 19th century French claret jug, 33cm (13in), *C 16 Oct,* £770 ($1,140)

3
A Victorian silver-gilt wine jug, Charles Reily & George Storer, London, 1839, 31cm (12¼in), 24oz (754gr), *L 24 Oct,* £1,210 ($1,815)

4
A William IV wine jug, William Eley II, London, 1833, in the form of an Italo-Greco *oinochoe,* 30cm (11¾in), 32oz (995gr), *NY 9 Oct,* $1,320 (£936)

5
An American punch set, P L Krider, Philadelphia, *c.*1880, comprising a jug and twelve goblets, goblets gilt inside, jug 44.5cm (17½in), 152oz (4727gr), *NY 27 June,* $3,850 (£2,962)

6
A Victorian ewer, Charles Reily & George Storer, London, 1850, with applied plaques depicting the four seasons and presentation inscription, *L 12 July,* £1,430 ($2,059)

7
A Victorian claret jug, Frederick Elkington, London 1871, 31cm (12¼in), 18oz (560gr), *S 17 Apr,* £440 ($572)

8
A parcel-gilt ewer, German or possibly Italian, third quarter 19th century, in Renaissance taste, 43cm (17in), 61oz (1897gr), *NY 7 June,* $1,650 (£1,310)

9
A pair of silver-gilt ewers, Goldsmiths & Silversmiths Co Ltd, London, 1910, after the designs of John Flaxman for Wedgwood, 44cm (17¼in) high, 253oz (7870gr), *M 25 June,* FF 244,200 (£20,350; $25,979)

10
A Victorian silver mounted glass claret jug, London, 1873, 26.5cm (10½in), *C 15 Jan,* £858 ($1,030)

11
A pair of silver-gilt mounted glass claret jugs, maker's mark C E London, 1887, 33.5cm (13¼in), *C 9 July,* £4,400 ($6,116)

12
A Victorian silver-mounted claret jug, William Hutton & Sons Ltd, London, 1894, the cover in the form of a head of a 'Louis Wain' cat, 20cm (8in), *L 23 May,* £880 ($1,162)

13
A Victorian silver-mounted glass claret jug, George Fox, London, 1869, 27.5cm (10¾in), *C 9 July,* £825 ($1,147)

14
A pair of cut glass and silver-mounted decanters, Birmingham, 1895, 18.5cm (11¼in), *C 27 Mar,* £462 ($587)

15
A Victorian silver-mounted amber glass claret jug in the form of a monkey, London, 1892, 30cm (11¾in), *NY 7 June,* $2,420 (£1,921)

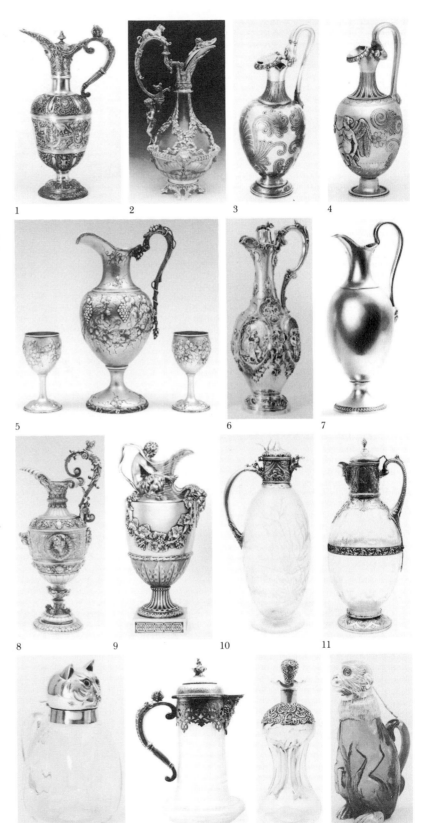

1
A pair of Dutch table candlesticks, Dirk ten Brink Amsterdam, 1693, 19cm (7½in), 16oz 10dwt (520gr), *A 2 Dec,*
Dfl 37,950
(£9,014; $12,619)

2
A pair of Queen Anne table candlesticks, Joseph Bird, London, 1702, 17cm (6¾in), 26oz 10dwt (830gr), *L 24 Oct,*
£9,020 ($13,530)

3
A set of four George I table candlesticks, David Willaume, London, 1715, 21cm (8¼in), 92oz (2861gr), *NY 10 Oct,*
$69,300 (£49,148)

4
A pair of Queen Anne table candlesticks, John Fawdery, London, 1709, 18cm (7in), 32oz (1001gr), *L 24 Oct,*
£7,480 ($11,220)

5
A set of four George I table candlesticks, Dublin, 1717, with four nozzles, *c.*1717, with four nozzles, *c.*1740, 16.5cm (6½in) high, 55oz 2dwt (1713gr), *L 23 May,*
£16,500 ($21,780)

6
Two German table candlesticks, Jacob Schenck the Younger, Hamburg, *c.*1725-30, almost matching, 19.5cm (7¾in), 19oz (601gr), *G 12 Nov,*
SF 10,450 (£3,415; $4,781)

7
A pair of George I table candlesticks, Samuel Margas, London, 1724, 15cm (6in), 24oz 19dwt (775gr), *L 12 July,*
£5,500 ($7,920)

8
An early George II taperstick, London, 1727, maker's mark IH, 11.5cm (4½in), 3oz 17dwt (119gr), *L 23 May,*
£825 ($1,089)

9
An early George II taperstick, Isaac Cookson, Newcastle, 1728, 11cm (4¼in), 4oz 5dwt (132gr), *L 23 May,*
£990 ($1,307)

10
A pair of George II table candlesticks, James Gould, London, 1739, 19cm (7½in), 31oz (964gr), *NY 1 Feb,*
$2,860 (£2,424)

11
A pair of George II table candlesticks, William Cafe, London, 1759, 18.5cm (7¼in), *L 24 Oct,*
£2,310 ($3,465)

12
A pair of Dutch table candlesticks, Jan Pereboom, Leeuwarden, 1774, 20cm (8in), 24oz (760gr), *A 1 Apr,*
Dfl 15,660
(£3,625; $4,604)

13
A pair of George II candlesticks, Lewis Pantin, London, 1734, 29cm (11½in), 80oz 10dwt (2500gr), *L 23 May,*
£39,600 ($52,272)

14
A pair of Dutch table candlesticks, Hendrik van Beest, Rotterdam, 1734, 18.5cm (7¼in), 30oz (948gr), *G 14 May,*
SF 15,400
(£4,503; $5,989)

15
A pair of German table candlesticks, maker's mark JD Jacques Demarolle, Kassel, *c.*1765, 20.5cm (8in), 13oz 10dwt (492gr), *G 12 Nov,*
SF 7,150 (£2,336; $3,270)

1 2 3

4 5 6 7

8 9 10 11 12

13

14

15

1
A pair of Swiss table candlesticks, Charles-Louis Rapillard, Lausanne, c.1760, 21cm (8¼in) high, 19oz (590gr), G 14 May,
SF 12,100
(£3,538; $4,706)

2
A pair of Belgian table candlesticks, Nicolaas Wodon, Namur, 1764, detachable nozzles, 27cm (10½in), 20oz (622gr), A 2 Dec,
Dfl 14,950
(£3,551; $4,971)

3
A pair of French table candlesticks, maker's mark J A D, Lille, 1762 and circa, 27.5cm (10¾in) high, 43oz (1346gr), G 14 May,
SF 9,900 (£2,895; $3,850)

4
A pair of Italian table candlesticks, Giacomo Morrone, Naples, c.1770, 20.5cm (8in) high, 33oz (1042gr), L 11 July,
£2,750 ($4,043)

5
A pair of French table candlesticks, Claude-Pierre Deville, Paris, 1773, 25.5cm (10in), 49oz 10dwt (1548gr), M 25 June,
FF 88,800
(£7,400; $9,447)

6
A pair of Swedish table candlesticks, Jakob Lampa, Stockholm, 1772, detachable nozzles, 24.5cm (9½in), 29oz 10dwt (918gr), G 12 Nov,
SF 30,800
(£10,065; $14,091)

7
A pair of Belgian table candlesticks, maker's mark API, Namur, 1772, 25cm (9¾in), 23oz (714gr), A 1 Apr,
Dfl 16,240
(£3,759; $4,774)

8
A pair of French table candlesticks, Charles-François Legast, Paris, 1769, 28cm (11in) high, 42oz 10dwt (1327gr), G 14 May,
SF 9,900 (£2,895; $3,850)

9
A pair of George II table candlesticks, John Cafe, London, 1750, 21.5cm (8½in), 35oz 6dwt (1088gr), S 17 Apr,
£1,760 ($2,288)

10
A pair of George II table candlesticks, John Cafe, London, 1755, 25.5cm (10in), 41oz 12dwt (1293gr), L 24 Oct,
£1,925 ($2,888)

11
A set of four George II table candlesticks, John Cafe, London, 1754, 23.5cm (9¼in), 82oz 10dwt (2566gr), NY 12 Dec,
$12,100 (£8,582)

12
A pair of George II table candlesticks, William Cafe, London, 1758, 25.5cm (10in), 41oz 10dwt (1290gr), L 31 Jan,
£3,410 ($4,024)

13
A set of four George III table candlesticks, Ebenezer Coker, London, 1762, 27cm (10½in), 91oz (2830gr), L 21 Nov,
£6,380 ($9,187)

14
A set of four early George III table candlesticks, John Carter, London, 1768, (loaded), 32cm (12½in) high, S 12 June,
£2,420 ($3,219)

15
A set of four George III Irish table candlesticks, Dublin, 1782, 27.5cm (10¾in), 103oz (3203gr), NY 7 June,
$6,050 (£4,802)

1
A Maltese oil lamp, Giovani Lebrun, c.1760, 61cm (24in), 59oz 11dwt (1852gr), *L 11 Feb,* £5,060 ($5,819)

2
A George III candelabrum, William Cripps, London, 1754, 37.5cm (14¾in), 59oz 3dwt (1839gr), *L 23 May,* £3,520 ($4,646)

3
A set of ten George III table candlesticks, Green, Roberts, Mosley & Co, Sheffield, 1799, and six plated branches, c.1800, 45.5cm (18in), *L 24 Oct,* £11,550 ($17,325)

4
A pair of German two-light candelabra, maker's mark IGB, Breslau, c.1800, 44.5cm (17½in), 63oz (1959gr), *NY 14 Feb,* $2,310 (£1,991)

5
A pair of Austrian six-light candelabra, late 19th century, 56cm (22in), 130oz 10dwt (4059gr), *NY 7 June,* $2,200 (£1,746)

6
A pair of French five-light candelabra, Paris, c.1900, 51.5cm (20¼in), 239oz 10dwt (7448gr), *NY 9 Oct,* $5,772 (£4,093)

7
A pair of German sixteen-light candelabra, Elimeyer, Dresden, c.1880, 94.5cm (37¼in), 1279oz 10dwt (39792gr), *NY 26 Apr,* $27,500 (£22,541)

8
A pair of American three-light candelabra and a pair of matching table candlesticks, Tiffany & Co, New York, 1891-1907, 40.5cm (16in), 144oz (4478gr), *NY 9 Oct,* $3,850 (£2,730)

9
A pair of five-light candelabra, Collingwood & Co, London, 1969, 48.5cm (19in), 167oz (5194gr), *NY 19 Feb,* $3,080 (£2,826)

10
A pair of three-light candelabra, c.1840, plated, 51cm (20in), *C 27 Mar,* £286 ($363)

1

2

3

4

5

6

7

8

9

10

pair of French table
andlesticks, Odiot,
aris, 1809-19, 27.5cm
10¾in), 29oz (902gr),
Y 26 Apr,
2,750 (£2,254)

pair of Swedish table
andlesticks, Johan Wil-
elm Zimmerman,
tockholm, 1795, 27cm
10½in), 33oz 10dwt
1045gr), G 12 Nov,
F 9,350 (£3,055; $4,277)

pair of table candles-
cks, maker's mark C M,
robably Italian, c.1810,
5.5cm (10in), 23oz
715gr), NY 14 Feb,
770 (£664)

pair of French silver-
ilt dressing table candle-
icks, maker's mark L R,
aris, c.1825, 16.5cm
5½in) high, 12oz 10dwt
390gr), G 14 May,
F 5,500 (£1,608; $2,139)

pair of Italian table
andlesticks, maker's
nark I L, Turin, c.1825,
7cm (10½in), 19oz
0dwt (612gr), F 29 May,
1,900,000 (£739; $976)

pair of French table
andlesticks, maker's
nark F J B, Paris, c.1820,
9cm (11½in) high, 29oz
900gr), M 25 June,
F 17,205 (£1,434; $1,830)

set of four George III
able candlesticks, Nath-
niel Smith & Co, Shef-
eld, 1791-2, loaded,
9cm (11½in), NY 9 Oct,
2,860 (£2,028)

pair of George III table
andlesticks, John Rob-
rts & Co, Sheffield,
oaded, 1809, 18cm (7in),
1 May,
539 ($706)

our George IV table
andlesticks, Smith, Tate,
loult & Tate, Sheffield,
825, loaded, 30.5cm
2in), C 15 Jan,
1,925 ($2,310)

10
A pair of table candle-
sticks, Goldsmiths &
Silversmiths Co Ltd,
London, 1917, 18.5cm
(7¼in), C 13 Nov,
£374 ($524)

11
A set of four table candle-
sticks, Thos. Bradbury &
Sons, London, 1927,
loaded, 19.5cm (7¾in),
NY 8 Oct,
$1,540 (£1,041)

12
A pair of table candle-
sticks, Sheffield, 1899,
maker's mark WL and S,
25.5cm (10in), C 27 Nov,
£506 ($708)

13
A pair of Corinthian col-
umn table candlesticks,
Birmingham 1962,
30.5cm (12in), C 18 Sept,
£374 ($527)

14
A pair of table candle-
sticks, London, 1905,
19cm (11½in), C 27 Mar,
£506 ($643)

1   2   3   4

5   6   7   8

9   10   11

12   13   14

1
A William and Mary salver-on-foot, maker's mark IC crowned, London, 1691, 21cm (8¼in), 9oz 12dwt (298gr), *L 24 Oct,* £935 ($1,403)

2
A George I salver, William Darker, London, 1718, four bracket feet, 28.5cm (11¼in), 25oz (777gr), *NY 10 Oct,* $5,225 (£3,705)

3
A George I Irish salver on foot, Matthew Walker, Dublin, c.1725, central spreading foot, 29.5cm (11½in), 33oz (1026gr), *NY 26 Apr,* $2,200 (£1,803)

4
A pair of George I waiters, Augustine Courtauld, London, 1725, 16cm (6¼in) square, 21oz 13dwt (673gr), *L 24 Oct,* £4,400 ($6,600)

5
An early George II salver, John Tuite, London, 1727, volute supports, 31cm (12¼in), 38oz 15dwt (1205gr), *L 24 Oct,* £3,300 ($4,950)

6
A George II salver, Francis Pages, London, 1730, 22cm (8½in), 20oz 5dwt (629gr), *L 21 Feb,* £2,420 ($2,783)

7
An Austrian salver, maker's mark OG, Vienna, 1717, flat-chased with Régence ornament, 22.5cm (8¾in), 7oz (221gr), *G 12 Nov,* SF 4,180 (£1,366; $1,912)

8
A George II waiter, John Tuite, London, 1733, 16cm (6¼in), square, 9oz (279gr), *L 24 Oct,* £682 ($1,023)

9
A Dutch salver, maker's mark a swan, Gorinchem, 1736 (?), 25.5cm (10in), 17oz (528gr), *A 2 Dec,* Dfl 8,970 (£2,130; $2,982)

10
A Spanish tazza, Madrid, 1747, engraved with armorials, 35cm (13¾in) diam, 50oz 10dwt (1570gr), *L 11 Feb,* £1,650 ($1,898)

11
A George II salver, Coline Allan, Aberdeen, c.1750, with three volute supports, 20cm (8in) diam, 10oz 16dwt (335gr), *Glen 26 Aug,* £715 ($1,051)

12
A George II salver, Dorothy Sarbit, London, 1754, three scroll supports, 32.5cm (12¾in), 30oz (933gr), *NY 14 Feb,* $1,320 (£1,138)

13
An early George III salver, R Rew or Rugg, London, 1760, three hoof feet, 28cm (11in), 22oz 10dwt (699gr), *L 24 Oct,* £935 ($1,403)

14
A George III salver, David Bell, London, 1760, on four volute supports, 40.5cm (16in), 53oz 19dwt (1677gr), *L 24 Oct,* £2,200 ($3,300)

15
A George III salver, London, 1763, 25cm (9¾in) diam, 18oz 15dwt (590gr), *C 4 Sept,* £363 ($534)

16
A Swiss salver, Abraham Moll, Biel, c.1760, 29.5cm (11½in) diam, 16oz 10dwt (520gr), *G 14 May,* SF 9,900 (£2,895; $3,850)

17
A Dutch salver, François Markus Simons, The Hague, 1784, 30cm (11¾in), 34oz (1057gr), *A 17 May,* Dfl 3,712 (£861; $1,145)

18
A George III salver, Crouch & Hannam, London, 1791, four panel supports, 43cm (17in), 73oz 14dwt (2292gr), *L 24 Oct,* £3,520 ($5,280)

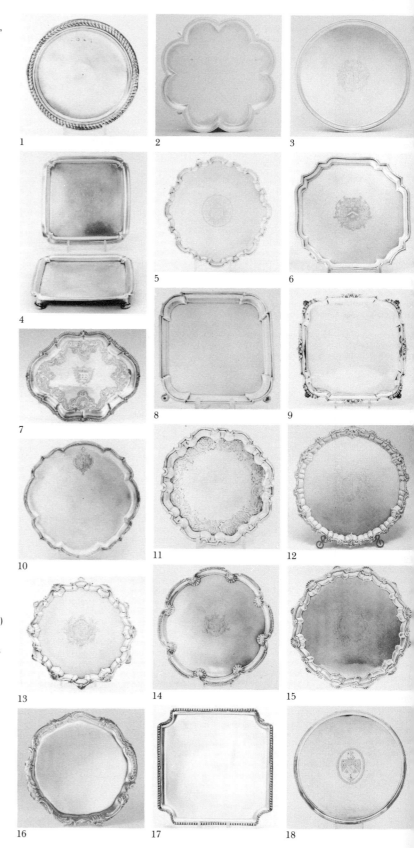

pair of George III
alvers, Ebenezer Coker,
ondon, 1772, 39.5cm
5½in) diam, 99oz
6dwt (3103gr),
23 May,
13,750 ($18,150)

pair of George III
aiters, Robert Salmon,
ondon, 1803, 18cm
in), 17oz (529gr),
Y 14 Feb,
825 (£711)

George IV salver,
William Brown,
ondon, 1823, 23cm
in), 19oz 5dwt (591gr),
16 Oct,
286 ($423)

William IV salver,
Robert W Smith,
Dublin, 1836, with later
rmorials, on four lion
mask and paw supports,
2cm (24½in), 163oz
0dwt (5090gr),
21 Nov,
2,640 ($3,802)

Victorian salver,
maker's mark I W,
London, 1837, 52cm
20½in) diam, 96oz 6dwt
2994gr), *L 21 Feb,*
1,540 ($1,771)

Victorian salver,
Martin Hall & Co,
heffield, 1863, three
law and ball feet, 32cm
12½in), 25oz 13dwt
793gr), *C 30 Oct,*
297 ($442)

Victorian salver,
rederick Elkington,
London, 1879, with fros-
ed surface, 21cm (8¼in),
4oz (435gr), *NY 7 Dec,*
1,045 (£706)

An American oval tray,
iffany & Co, New York,
1900, the rim with a
elief of lions amongst
ines, on six paw feet,
2.5cm (28½in), 245oz
7619gr), *NY 27 June*
4,125 (£3,173)

9
A George III tea tray,
Crouch & Hannam,
London, 1785, 51cm
(20in) wide, 59oz 16dwt
(1859gr), *L 30 May,*
£2,640 ($3,538)

10
**An American "Japanese
style" two-handled tray,**
Gorham Mfg. Co. Pro-
vidence, R I, 1881,
66.8cm (26¼in), 152oz
(4309gr), *NY 7 Dec,*
$8,250 (£5,612)

11
A George III tea tray,
John Mewburn, London,
1804, 70cm (27½in),
141oz 13dwt (4405gr),
L 31 Jan,
£5,500 ($6,490)

12
**A Victorian two-handled
tea tray,** maker's mark B
F, London, 1876, flat-
chased with rococo
decoration, 96cm
(37¾in), 293oz (9112gr),
NY 12 Dec,
$13,200 (£9,362)

13
A tea tray, London, 1931,
56.5cm (22¼in), 65oz
6dwt, (2021gr),
C 15 May,
£616 ($819)

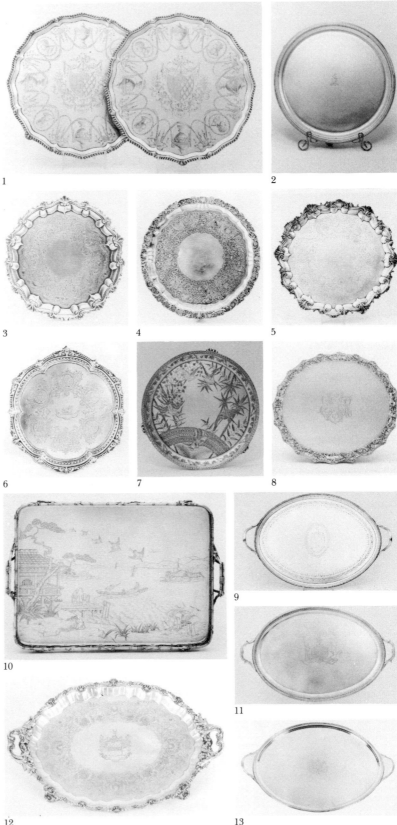

1   2

3   4   5

6   7   8

9

10

11

12   13

1
A George II cake basket,
Peter Archambo, Lon-
don, 1736, 32cm (12½in),
68oz 10dwt (2130gr), *NY
26 Apr*,
$6,325 (£5,184)

2
A George II bread basket,
Paul de Lamerie, Lon-
don, 1742, 35cm (13¾in),
62oz (1933gr), *L 24 Oct*,
£94,600 ($141,900)

3
A George II cake basket,
John Jacob, London,
1747, 34cm (13½in) wide,
69oz 10dwt (2161gr),
L 24 Oct,
£7,150 ($10,725)

4
A George III cake basket,
S Herbert & Co, Lon-
don, 1762, 37cm (14½in),
39oz 10dwt (1228gr),
NY 7 June,
$1,760 (£1,397)

5
A George III cake basket,
Simon Harris, London,
1805, 35cm (13¾in), 31oz
10dwt (980gr), *NY 9 Oct*,
$1,650 (£1,170)

6
A Swedish parcel-gilt bowl
(**Kallskal**), Nicolas
Wraneck, Karlstad,
1765, 41.5cm (16¼in),
42oz (1306gr), *NY 26 Apr*,
$12,650 (£10,368)

7
A Dutch cake basket,
Hendrik Nieuwenhuis,
Amsterdam, 1771, 26cm
(10¼in) long, 16oz 10dwt
(514gr), *A 1 Apr*,
Dfl 32,480
(£7,519; $9,549)

8
A large French bowl,
Puiforcat, in Louis XVI
style, 50cm (19¾in)
wide, 78oz (2420gr), *M
25 June*,
FF 22,200 (£1,850; $2,362)

1

2

3

4

5

6

7

8

A **George II chinoiserie cake basket**, S Herbert & Co, London, 1757, 38cm (15in), 47oz (1462gr), *NY 6 Apr,*
3,630 (£2,975)

A **George III cake basket**, Burrage Davenport, London, 1774, 40.5cm (16in) high, 49oz 12dwt (1539gr), *C 15 Jan,*
3,740 ($4,488)

A **George III oval cake basket**, Young, Greaves and Holland, Sheffield, 1785, 35cm (13¾in), 24oz (746gr), *C 16 Oct,*
605 ($895)

A **George III cake basket**, E Terrey & Co, London, 1819, in 18th century taste, 87oz 12dwt (2725gr), 39cm (15¼in), *24 Oct,*
7,480 ($11,220)

A **George III cake basket**, Solomon Hougham, London, 1807, 32cm (12½in), 33oz (18dwt), *16 Oct,*
594 ($879)

A **George III cake basket**, Peter, Ann & William Bateman, London, 1880, 8cm (15in), 34oz (1057gr), *NY 9 Oct,*
1,760 (£1,248)

A **George III bread basket**, Michael Plummer, London, 1794, 34.5cm (13½in), 59oz (1898gr), *21 Nov,*
4,070 ($5,861)

A **Dutch cake basket**, .N.S. van Voorst, Utrecht, 1839, 31.5cm (12½in) long, 30oz 10dwt (950gr), *A 1 Apr,*
Dfl 4,640 (£1,074; $1,364)

A **French two-handled oval basin**, Jean-Baptiste-Claude Odiot, Paris, 1798-1809, 46.5cm (18¼in) wide, 63oz 10dwt (1975gr), *NY 26 Apr,*
3,300 (£2,705)

10
A **William IV silver-gilt dessert basket**, Edward Barnard & Sons, London, 1833, 20.5cm (8in) wide, 7oz 10dwt (230gr), *L 24 Oct,*
£1,760 ($2,640)

11
A **Victorian silver-gilt cake basket**, D & J Wellby, London, 1888, in Dutch taste, 22.5cm (8¾in), 17oz 16dwt (553gr), *L 21 Nov,*
£825 ($1,188)

12
A **pair of Victorian dessert baskets** maker's mark JC, London, 1894, 21.5cm (8½in) wide, 38oz (1181gr), *L 21 Feb,*
£1,705 ($1,961)

13
A **pair of oval bonbon dishes**, C S Harris, London, 1893, 18.5cm (7¼in), 17oz (528gr), *C 18 Sep,*
£352 ($493)

14
A **Dutch bread basket**, 1901, 34.5cm (13½in), 22oz (658gr), *A 10 Dec,*
Dfl 1,552 (£378; $529)

15
A **two-handled cake stand**, Viners, Sheffield, 1938, 42cm (16½in) wide, 34oz 13dwt (1073gr), *C 27 Feb,*
£550 ($616)

16
A **silver-gilt dessert basket**, The Goldsmiths & Silversmiths Co Ltd, London, 1905, 26cm (11¼in) wide, 45oz 12dwt (1399gr), *S 12 June,*
£2,310 ($3,072)

1 2 3
4 5 6
7 8
9 10
11 12 13
14
15 16

1
**A pair of George III
entrée dishes and covers,**
John Scofield, London,
1795, 38.5cm (15in), 68oz
(2115gr), *NY 9 Oct,*
$1,980 (£1,404)

2
**A pair of George III
vegetable dishes, covers,
and hot water bases,**
Thomas Ellerton &
Richard Sibley I, Lon-
don, 1803, 115oz
(3576gr); with a later
pair of silver-plated
lampstands, 22cm
(8¾in), *NY 12 Dec,*
$5,500 (£3,901)

3
**A pair of George III Irish
entrée dishes and covers,**
James Scott, Dublin,
1807, detachable crest
finials, 29cm (11½in),
106oz (3297gr),
NY 26 Apr,
$3,300 (£2,705)

4
**A pair of George III
entrée dishes, covers and
hot water bases,** Ben-
jamin Smith II, Lon-
don, 1807, the bases cast
with the Manners crest,
32cm (12½in), 260oz
10dwt (8102gr),
NY 12 Dec,
$20,900 (£14,823)

5
**A set of four George III
entrée dishes and covers,**
Paul Storr, London,
1800, 29.5cm (11½in),
224oz (6966gr), *L 24 Oct,*
£10,450 ($15,675)

6
**A set of four George III
entrée dishes and covers,**
Benjamin Smith II and
III, London, 1816, with
screw-on handles, 26cm
(10¼in), 192oz (5971gr),
L 31 Jan,
£3,520 ($4,154)

7
**A pair of George III
entrée dishes and covers,**
Rundell, Bridge &
Rundell, London, 1804,
maker's mark of Paul
Storr for Storr & Co,
29cm (11½in) wide,
117oz (3638gr), *L 23 May,*
£7,920 ($10,454)

8
**A pair of George III
circular dishes and covers,**
Rundell, Bridge &
Rundell, London,
1807/10, maker's mark
Paul Storr for Storr &
Co, 25cm (9¾in), 101oz
10dwt (3160gr),
L 23 May,
£7,150 ($9,438)

9
**A Victorian dish and
cover,** Hunt & Roskell,
London, 1867, 27cm
(10½in) diam, 39oz
10dwt (1235gr),
JHB 13 Mar,
R 1,850 (£833; $950)

10
**A set of four George III
entrée dishes and covers,**
William Elliott,
London, 1813, the cov-
ers with detachable
handles, 30.5cm (12in)
wide, 251oz 10dwt
(7827gr), *L 24 Oct,*
£6,050 ($9,075)

11
**A pair of Victorian entrée
dishes and covers,** Hawks-
worth, Eyre & Co,
Sheffield, 1845, with
detachable handles,
33cm (13in) wide, 88oz
(2736gr), *L 31 Jan,*
£1,815 ($2,142)

12
**A pair of George III
entrée dishes and covers,**
Rundell, Bridge &
Rundell, maker's mark
Paul Storr, London,
1809, with Sheffield
plated warming stands,
27cm (10½in), 145oz
(4509gr), *NY 26 Apr,*
$13,750 (£11,270)

13
**A pair of octagonal entrée
dishes and covers,** Lon-
don, 1909, with detach-
able handles, 26cm
(10¼in) wide, 84oz
(2612gr), *C 16 Oct,*
£880 ($1,302)

14
**An American vegetable
dish, cover and liner,** S
Kirk & Sons, Baltimore,
1861-68, 32.5cm (13in),
59oz (1835gr), *NY 31 Jan,*
$1,870 (£1,585)

1

2

3

4

5

6

7

8

9

10

11

12

13

14

Belgian double-lipped
uce boat, maker's
ark ? C N, Brussels,
727-30, 21.5cm (8½in)
ng, 11oz (342gr),
Y 9 Oct,
,950 (£3,510)

pair of George II sauce
oats, Ayme Videau,
ondon, 1738/9, 19.5cm
¾in), 30oz (933gr),
Y 10 Oct,
,675 (£3,315)

pair of George II sauce
oats, John Pollock,
ondon, 1748, 20.5cm
in) wide, 29oz (903gr),
21 Nov,
,860 (£4,118)

pair of George II sauce
oats, John Jones I,
ondon, 1753, 18.5cm
¼in) long, 20oz 3dwt
26gr), L 31 Jan,
,265 (£1,493)

George II Scottish sauce
oat, Lothian & Robert-
n, Edinburgh, 1751,
cm (7½in), 8oz 10dwt
64gr), NY 19 Feb,
05 (£555)

pair of George II sauce
oats, Pezé Pilleau,
ondon, 1758, 21.5cm
½in), 38oz 5dwt
189gr), the undersides
ith scratch weights,
23 May,
,620 (£6,098)

pair of George II sauce
oats, Paul Crespin,
ondon, 1740, 20.5cm
in), 41oz (1275gr),
Y 12 Dec,
4,300 (£10,142)

pair of George II sauce
oats, John Le Sage,
ondon, 1738, 21cm
¼in), 33oz (1023gr),
24 Oct,
,960 (£5,940)

George II shell-shaped
uce boat, Elizabeth
odfrey, London, 1753,
).5cm (8in), 15oz
66gr), NY 26 Apr,
,980 (£1,623)

10
A George II oval sauce
boat, possibly John
Moore of Dublin, c.1745,
14cm (5½in), 5oz 10dwt
(168gr), L 17 Oct,
£330 ($488)

11
A pair of George III Irish
sauce boats, Matthew
West, Dublin, 1775,
22cm (8¾in), 23oz 17dwt
(741gr), L 4 Apr,
£1,430 ($1,816)

12
A pair of Victorian sauce
boats, Hunt & Roskell,
maker's mark J S Hunt,
London, 1849, 18.5cm
(7¼in), 30oz 7dwt
(943gr), L 21 Nov,
£1,430 ($2,059)

13
A pair of French sauce
boats with liners and fixed
stands, Odiot, Paris,
c.1850, 27cm (10½in)
wide, 79oz (2460gr),
G 12 Nov,
SF 4,400 (£1,437; $2,011)

14
A pair of sauce boats,
Edward Barnard & Son,
London, 1934, in mid-
18th century style,
19.5cm (7¾in), 24oz 6dwt
(746gr), C 4 Sept,
£594 ($873)

15
A pair of sauce boats, in
mid-18th century style,
Birmingham, 1916,
16cm (6¼in), 13oz 10dwt
(420gr), C 27 Nov,
£264 ($370)

16
A pair of sauce boats on
stands, Birmingham,
1936/7, 20cm (8in), 33oz
18dwt, (1057gr),
C 18 Sept,
£330 ($462)

17
A German dolphin-form
sauce boat, with plated
liner and ruby glass
eyes, 26.5cm (10½in),
14oz (435gr), NY 14 Feb,
$1,320 (£1,138)

18
A pair of American sauce
boats, S Kirk & Son,
Baltimore, c.1850,
embossed with a gothic
church and a cottage,
21.5cm (8½in), 33oz
(1026gr), NY 27 June,
$1,540 (£1,185)

1

2

3

4

5

6

7

8

9

10

11

12

13

14

15

16

17

18

1
A pair of George III sauce tureens and covers, Cornelius Bland, London, 1790, 25cm (9¾in), 33oz (1026gr), *L 21 Nov,* £1,485 ($2,138)

2
A set of four George III sauce tureens and covers, John Robins, London, 1786, 24cm (9½in) wide, 83oz 14dwt (2603gr), *L 23 May,* £7,150 ($9,438)

3
A pair of George III sauce tureens and covers, Carter, Smith & Sharp, London, 1780, of oval boat form, 21.5cm (8½in) wide, 44oz (1368gr), *NY 26 Apr,* $4,675 (£3,832)

4
A pair of George III sauce tureens and covers, Richard Cooke, London, 1811, engraved with a ducal crest, 22.5cm (9in) wide, 60oz 18dwt (1893gr), *L 31 Jan,* £2,640 ($3,115)

5
Two pairs of matching George III sauce tureens and covers, William Stroud, London, 1808-16, 23cm (9in) wide, 117oz (3639gr), *NY 9 Oct,* $5,775 (£4,095)

6
A pair of George III sauce tureens and covers, William Frisbee, London, 1807, 21cm (8¼in) wide, 50oz (1555gr), *NY 26 Apr,* $1,980 (£1,623)

7
A pair of George III sauce tureens and covers, Robert Sharp, London, 1802, 24.8cm (9¾in) wide, 54oz 13dwt (1699gr), *L 4 Apr,* £2,145 ($2,724)

8
A William IV shaped oval sauce tureen and cover, Benjamin Smith, London, 1835, detachable handle, 23cm (9in) wide, 34oz (1057gr), *C 16 Oct,* £748 ($1,107)

9
A pair of American sauce tureens and covers, in Empire style, Anthony Rasch & Co, Philadelphia, *c.*1820, 23.5cm (9¼in) wide, 80oz (2488gr), *NY 27 June,* $8,525 (£6,558)

1

2

3

4

5

6

7

8

9

 French soup tureen,
 ver and liner, Jean
annier, Paris, 1774,
morial engraved,
cm (15¼in) wide over-
l, 122oz 10dwt (3820gr),
14 May,
 28,600
8,363; $11,123)

 George III oval soup
reen and cover, Run-
ll, Bridge & Rundell,
aker's mark Paul Storr,
ondon, 1816, 44.5cm
7½in) wide, 162oz
dwt (5050gr), L 21 Nov,
2,320 ($17,741)

1

2

 George IV oval soup
reen and cover, Rebecca
mes & Edward Bar-
rd, London, 1828,
cm (17¾in) wide, 164oz
00gr), NY 26 Apr,
2,100 (£9,918)

 William IV oval pre-
ntation soup tureen and
ver, Elder & Co,
linburgh, 1832, 45cm
7¾in) wide, 127oz
dwt (3968gr), L 21 Nov,
,740 ($5,386)

3

4

 French soup tureen and
over, Odiot, Paris,
1840-50, 29.5cm (11½in)
gh, 77oz (2395gr),
Y 19 Feb,
,650 (£1,514)

 n American oval soup
reen and cover, Tiffany
Co, New York, c.1870,
.5cm (16¼in) wide,
2oz (2239gr), NY 31 Jan,
,320 (£1,119)

5

6

 n American oval
overed tureen, Tiffany
Co, New York, c.1890,
hrysanthemum pat-
rn, 33.5cm (13¼in)
ide, 68oz 10dwt
2130gr), NY 12 Dec,
,700 (£5,461)

 n American oval soup
reen and cover, Tiffany
Co, New York, 1891-
902, decorated in the
Vave' pattern, 30.5cm
2in) wide, 64oz
990gr), NY 12 Dec,
,190 (£2,262)

7

8

1
A pair of Sheffield-plated wine coolers, *c.*1815, detachable rims and liners, 23cm (9in), *NY 12 Dec,* $2,200 (£1,571)

2
A pair of Sheffield-plate tea trays, *c.*1825, 74cm (29in), *L 24 Oct,* £3,080 ($4,620)

3
A pair of Sheffield-plated wine coolers, *c.*1800, detachable rims and liners, 21cm (8½in), *NY 19 Feb,* $2,310 (£2,119)

4
A pair of Sheffield-plated salvers, *c.*1825, flat-chased with rococo decoration, 41cm (16in), *NY 9 Oct,* $880 (£624)

5
A Sheffield-plate venison dish, cover and heater base, *c.*1810, 62cm (24½in) wide, *L 12 July,* £3,190 ($4,594)

6
A set of four Sheffield-plated table candlesticks, *c.*1765, detachable nozzles, 28cm (11in), *NY 14 Feb,* $935 (£606)

7
A Sheffield-plated soup tureen, cover, liner and stand, *c.*1834, 47cm (18½in), *NY 12 Dec,* $4,675 (£3,316)

8
A Sheffield-plate soup tureen, cover and stand, Thomas Law & Co, Sheffield, 1777, dolphin supports and fish finial, tureen 44cm (17¼in) over handles, *L 24 Oct,* £6,380 ($9,570)

1

3

2

4

5

7

6

8

1
A Sheffield-plated
cucumber slicer, *c.*1800,
1cm (8¼in) high,
NY 14 Feb,
990 (£853)

2
A Sheffield plate 'skep'
honey pot, unmarked,
1800, 12.5cm (5in) high,
4 Apr,
495 ($629)

3
A Sheffield-plate coffee
pot, *c.*1770, 29.5cm
11½in), L 17 Oct,
418 ($619)

4
A Sheffield plate dish
cross, *c.*1775, with sli-
ing shell supports, L 21
eb,
242 ($278)

5
A pair of Sheffield plate
chamber candlesticks,
1810, with detachable
ozzles, 16.5cm (6½in),
21 Feb,
407 ($468)

6
A Sheffield plate venison
dish and cover, *c.*1815, a
ection on the border
inged at one end,
3.5cm (25in) wide,
30 May,
1,320 ($1,769)

7
A Sheffield-plated soup
tureen and cover, T & J
Creswick, *c.*1820, 41cm
16in) over handles,
NY 9 Oct,
2,530 (£1,794)

8
A pair of Sheffield-plated
wine coolers, *c.*1800, lack-
ng liners and rims,
4cm (9½in), NY 7 June,
1,045 (£829)

9
A pair of Sheffield plate
wine coolers, *c.*1810,
detachable rims and
iners, 21cm (8¼in) high,
30 May,
2,750 ($3,685)

10
A soup tureen and cover,
1830, replated, 38.5cm
15¼in) overall, C 27 Feb,
506 ($567)

11
A pair of wine coolers,
*c.*1815, detachable col-
lars and liners, 23cm
(9in), S 16 Oct,
£1,265 ($1,872)

12
A pair of Sheffield plate
wine coolers, *c.*1825,
L 31 Jan,
£1,595 ($1,882)

13
A pair of Sheffield plate
tea trays, attributed to
Gainsford & Nicholson
of Sheffield, *c.*1820, 73cm
(28¾in) wide, L 21 Feb,
£2,420 ($2,783)

14
A Sheffield plate tea urn,
*c.*1840, case with label
for I & I Waterhouse,
Sheffield, 44.5cm
17½in), L 31 Jan,
£990 ($1,168)

1

2

3

4

5

6

7

8

9

10

11

12

13

14

Electroplate

By a curious coincidence, patents for two marvels of the Victorian age, photography and electroplating, were granted within a few years of each other between 1836 and 1840. Resulting from many years' experiment, both inventions caused revolutions; photography, for instance, quickly undermined the place which miniature portrait painters and silhouette artists had held for generations. The technique of electroplating, which transformed the silver trade and speedily curtailed the manufacture of Sheffield Plate, depended initially upon Alessandro Volta's invention in 1800 of the electric battery. As early as 1805 Brugnatelli had gilded, albeit imperfectly, medals by means of electrolysis, and it was the work of Michael Faraday, himself the son-in-law of Edward Barnard the manu-

facturing silversmith, in 1821 which prepared the way for later experiments.

The commercial success of electroplating was due almost entirely to the acumen of George Richards Elkington (1801-65) and his cousin, Henry Elkington (1812-52), founders of Elkington and Company Ltd of Birmingham. Through their uncles, Josiah and George Richards, they were connected with the local toy and button trades, businesses in which G. R. Elkington had already been employed for some time. The cousins' subsequent experiment in gilding base metals led to three patents, granted in 1836 and 1837. In 1837 a subsidiary partnership, which lasted until the autumn of 1843, was formed with the proprietors of two Birmingham firms of button makers

—1—
A parcel-gilt decorated electroplated copper electrotype basin, ewer and stand, Elkington & Co, of Birmingham, 1883 and circa, the basin after the original by Leonard Morel-Ladeuil, diam 53.5cm (21in), 40cm (15¾in) high, *L 21 Mar,* **£3,080 ($3,727)**

—2—
A French silver-plated centrepiece, *c.*1880, in the form of a carriage drawn by a swan, Victory prow, detachable liner, 60.5cm (23¾in) long, *NY 9 Oct,* **$2,200 (£1,560)**

—1—

—2—

o exploit these patents. Meanwhile the Elkington cousins, together with a group of assistants, among them the brilliant Alexander Parkes (1813-90), a prolific inventor (Parkesine, a compound of pyroxyline, now more familiarly called Zylonite or Celluloid, was his brainchild), were able to bring the technique of electroplating to perfection early in 1840. This they were only able to do with the reluctant help of John Wright, a Birmingham doctor, whose success in contriving an electrolyte containing potassium cyanide was the deciding factor.

In the late 1830s, convinced of the eventual success of their enterprise, G. R. Elkington began building a large silver and electroplate factory at Newhall Street, Birmingham. Another, for the manufacture of electroplated articles of the plain and useful kind, such as spoons and forks, was built between 1848

—3—
A galleried tea-tray, late 19th century, 71cm (28in), *C 30 Jan*, £132 ($156)

—4—
A Victorian four-piece teaset, *c.*1890, *C 13 Feb*, £330 ($380)

—5—
A three-piece compressed circular teaset, Elkington & Co, struck with 1858/9 date letter, *C 13 Feb*, £170 ($196)

—6—
A tea kettle on stand, *c.*1900, 34.5cm (13½in), *C 30 Oct*, £132 ($196)

—7—
A tea tray, English, *c.*1850, the feet with pattern number 1669, otherwise unmarked, 90.5cm (35½in) wide, *L 12 July*, £3,960 ($5,702)

—8—
A tea kettle, stand and burner, Elkington & Co, 1861, 40.5cm (16in), *C 13 Nov*, £198 ($277)

—3—

—4—

—5—

—6—

—7—

—8—

—9—
A large table centrepiece,
Elkington & Co, struck
with 1883 date letter,
81cm (32in), *C 1 May,*
£1,980 ($2,594)

—10—
A large centrepiece,
Elkington & Co, *c.*1855,
75cm (29½in), *C 15 Jan,*
£1,100 ($1,320)

—11—
**A table centrepiece and
mirror plateau,** Elkington
& Co., struck with 1864
date letter, lacking cut-
glass bowl, 71cm (28in),
C 19 June,
£495 ($668)

—12—
A Victorian centrepiece,
*c.*1860, *C 30 Jan,*
£187 ($221)

—13—
**A centrepiece and mirror
plateau,** *c.*1870, plateau
38cm (15in) diam,
L 4 Apr,
£660 ($883)

—9—

—11—

—12—

—10—

—13—

and 1851 at nearby Brearly Street. Money to finance such an ambitious programme was provided by the introduction in 1842 of a third partner, Josiah Mason (1795-1881), a wealthy pen-nib manufacturer, whereupon the firm's name was changed for the duration of the partnership (which lasted until 1861) to Elkington, Mason and Company. Meanwhile, in 1840 G. R. Elkington had come to an agreement with his brother-in-law, the London working silversmith Benjamin Smith, to open electroplating workshops in the City, and a retail outlet in Regent Street. Although Smith had helped materially not least in procuring suitable designs, the connection ended badly for him when Elkington took control of both premises in 1849, forcing Smith into bankruptcy.

Elkington's patents met with initial resistance in the trade, especially among Sheffield platers, but the company was soon able to gain effective control of the entire plating industry. For within a matter of months the process won enthusiastic general acceptance, and the partners were able to benefit from the licences which they granted to a number of other manufacturing concerns who wished to use the process. Among the earliest firms to be granted licences were Christofle & Cie in France, and, in England, Edward Barnard & Sons of London, Thomas Prime & Son of Birmingham and William Carr Hutton, founder of William Hutton & Sons Ltd, in Sheffield.

Refinements in electroplating techniques were fostered at Elkington's: in 1841, for instance, Parkes patented on their

—14—
A cut-glass claret jug with plated mounts, late 19th century, 30.5cm (12in), *C 19 June,* **£121 ($163)**

—15—
A cut-glass butter dish, with plated mounts, late 19th century, 15cm (6in) diam, *C 27 Feb,* **£61 ($68)**

—16—
A seven bottle cruet frame, three glass bottles with plated mounts, 28.5cm (11¼in), *C 13 Nov,* **£308 ($431)**

—17—
A pair of five-light Corinthian column candelabra, Elkington & Co, struck with their date letter for 1905, 52cm (20½in), *C 4 Sept,* **£880 ($1,294)**

—18—
An inkstand, Edward Barnard & Sons of London, 1840-1846, 35cm (12¾in) long, *L 12 July,* **£1,100 ($1,584)**

—14—

—15—

—16—

—17—

—18—

behalf the technique of making electrotypes for which moulds of unvulcanized rubber were used. By lining these moulds with a conductive wax material, objects, or parts of objects, could be mass-produced in silver or copper (figs.1, & 20). Even old items, including antique silver pieces, could be exactly copied in the finest detail. Much later, in the 1870s, Elkington's were thus able to make electrogilt copper blanks for a range of beautiful *cloisonné* enamels, most of which were designed by A. A. Willms, head of their art department (fig.22). Unfortunately, similar wares from Japan and China, with which they were intended to compete, were more reasonably priced and the firm ceased producing them after eight or nine years.

By the time G. R. Elkington died in 1865, leaving a vast personal fortune, electroplated goods had become universal. In an already expanding market the public's taste for silver and, in

the lower price range, its imitations was insatiable, as even the most hasty look at old trade and exhibition catalogues will prove. Whereas the usual metal preferred for electroplate was nickel, soon the Britannia metal smiths, among them James Dixon & Sons and Atkin Brothers of Sheffield, began producing plated teapots and other domestic articles in this less costly alloy, which persons of even the most moderate means could afford.

The polite deception which Elkington's patents had encouraged was made complete by the patentees themselves in their use of maker's marks; at first glance these bear a remarkable resemblance to silver hallmarks. Other producers followed suit. Barnard's electroplate marks, for example, each of which was struck in a different punch, comprised their current makers' mark for silver entered at Goldsmiths' Hall, a

—19—
A parcel-gilt mustard pot and spoon, four salt cellars and spoons, decorated with electro-type panels, Elkington & Co, *c.*1875, *Belg 11 Dec 1980,* £270 ($483)

—20—
A parcel-gilt copper electrotype jewel casket, Elkington, Mason & Co, *c.*1855, decorated in Renaissance style, 17cm (6¾in), *Belg 3 Sept 1981,* £270 ($483)

—21—
A tureen and cover, in the form of a broody hen, G R Collis & Co, 1850s, 22cm (8¾in), *Belg 17 Dec 1981,* £374 ($669)

—22—
A champlevé enamel electrogilt copper electrotype dish, *c.*1873-80, applied with the label 'Published by Elkington & Co 1405', 15.7cm (6¼in) square, *Belg 17 Dec 1981,* £418 ($748)

—23—
A table lighter, early 20th century, designed as Mr Toad, 11.5cm (4½in), *C 30 Jan,* £176 ($208)

—24—
A spoon warmer, English, PODR mark for 4 December 1872, 19cm (7½in) long, *L 31 Jan,* £209 ($247)

—19—

—20—

—21—

—22—   —23—   —24—

date' letter and the crest and coat-of-arms of the City of London
a reference to the location of their workshops). A minefield for
he collector of electroplate, the study of such marks has been
argely ignored and offers great scope to any courageous
researcher and his publisher alike, (see below).

As a substitute for silver, electroplate of course has its more
prosaic uses. But as a subject for collectors the range is limitless,
rom oak tree and stag pattern centrepieces of the 1850s (fig.10) to
eapots, toast racks and the like of the 1870s and 1880s, whose
advanced forms are instantly recognizable as those created by
Christopher Dresser. Depending on condition and rarity, prices
or pieces designed by Dresser can be exceptionally high (fig.26)
see also pp302 & 347). Yet the generally more modest cost of
most other Victorian electroplate should not be taken as a
disparaging comment on its quality; it is just that much of it is
till very inexpensive.

● JOHN CULME ●

Further reading

John Culme *Nineteenth Century Silver*, 1977

Shirley Bury *Victorian Electroplate*, 1971

Patricia Wardle *Victorian Silver and Silver-Plate*, 1963

H. Bouilhet *Christofle 1830-1980*, 1981

D. Rainwater *American Silver Manufacturers*, 1966

D. & H. I. Rainwater *American Silverplate*, 1968

—25—
A **tea caddy**, Elkington,
Mason & Co, 1852, 17cm
(6¾in), *L 31 Jan*,
£462 ($545)

—26—
A **James Dixon & Sons
coast rack**, designed by
Christopher Dresser,
1880s, 13.5cm (5¼in),
L 4 Dec,
£3,800 ($5,662)

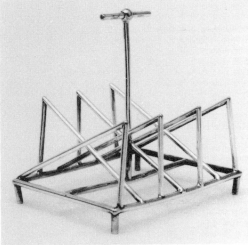

—25—

—26—

Elkington & Co, Birmingham
(manufacturer's label usually
found on electrotypes)

Horace Woodward & Co,
of Atlas Works,
Birmingham *c.*1880

Walker & Hall, Sheffield, *c.*1900
(the device at the top is a trade
mark)

'A1' denotes first quality electroplate

Deykin & Harrison Ltd.,
Birmingham, *c.*1900

Reed & Barton, Taunton,
Mass., *c.*1860 (the device
at the top is a trade mark)

A French manufacturer's mark
on electroplate (the punch is
squared, whereas on silver it is
lozenge-shaped)

Roberts & Belk, Sheffield

1

A set of four George III silver-gilt and cut-glass sweetmeat dishes, William Hall, London, 1793, 19cm (7½in), 40oz 10dwt (1260gr), *NY 12 Dec,* $1,980 (£1,404)

2

Two George III silver-gilt and cut-glass centrepieces, London, 1799-1800, one Pitts & Preedy, no maker's mark, 32.5 and 30.5cm (12¾ and 12in), 82oz 10dwt (2566gr), *NY 12 Dec,* $2,420 (£1,716)

3

A George II silver-gilt epergne, William Robertson, London, 1756, gilding later, 35cm (13¾in), 124oz (3856gr), *NY 26 Apr,* $16,500 (£13,524)

4

A George III epergne, James Young, London, 1788, the central basket surrounded by six detachable reeded arms supporting four circular and two oval baskets, 63cm (24¾in), 76oz 10dwt (2379gr), *NY 19 Feb,* $4,950 (£4,541)

5

A George III centrepiece, Benjamin Smith, London, 1813, three detachable two-light branches and detachable nozzles, 38cm (15in), 163oz (5070gr), and a Sheffield Plate circular mirror plateau, 47cm (18½in) diam., *L 23 May,* £4,400 ($5,808)

6

A George III silver-gilt and cut-glass epergne, Matthew Boulton Co, Birmingham, 1813, 38cm (15in), 149oz (4634gr), *NY 7 June,* $4,400 (£3,492)

7

A George III epergne, Paul Storr, London, 1819, the central column with a capital in the form of the Prince of Wales badge, 54.5cm (21¼in), 192oz 10dwt (5987gr), *NY 9 Oct,* $18,700 (£13,262)

8

A George III epergne, Emick Romer, London, 1777, 37.5cm (14.5in), 119oz 16dwt (3725gr), *L 23 May,* £14,300 ($18,876)

9

A Victorian presentation centrepiece, Edward Barnard & Sons, 1860, with detachable cut-glass bowl, 71.5cm (28in), 188oz (5850gr), *L 23 May,* £3,190 ($4,211)

10

A pair of Victorian parcel-gilt and cut-glass compotes, Frederick Elkington, Birmingham, 1879, in the 'Egyptian' pattern, 22.5cm (8¾in), 55oz 10dwt (1726gr), *NY 9 Oct,* $2,090 (£1,482)

11

A German centrepiece on silver-mounted mirror plateau, late 19th century, in the form of a basket with dolphin handles, plateau 62.5cm (24½in), basket 43oz 10dwt (1353gr), *NY 12 Dec,* $4,675 (£3,316)

12

A table centrepiece, Sheffield, 1911, 17cm (10½in), 40oz (1244gr), *C 30 Jan,* £440 ($519)

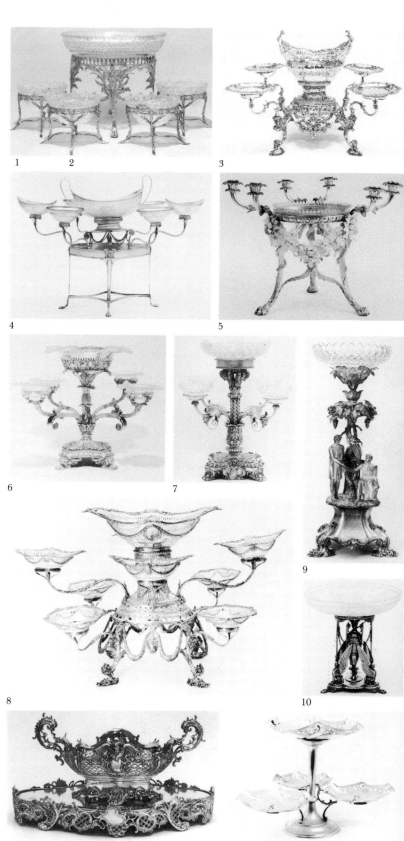

1
A pair of German decorative figures, c.1927, carved ivory faces, 24.5 and 23cm (9½ and 9in), 36oz (1125gr), L 7 Nov, £1,210 ($1,815)

2
A pair of Continental parcel-gilt and gem-set knights on horseback and stands, 20th century, 31cm (12¼in), 114oz (3,545gr), NY 14 Feb, $4,675 (£4,030)

3
A silver-gilt model of a fighting cock, probably Ludwig Neresheimer & Co, Hanau, c.1900, 44cm (17½in), 83oz (2586gr), L 20 June, £2,200 ($2,970)

4
A German model of a strutting cock, Ludwig Neresheimer & Co, Hanau, c.1910, 23.5cm (9¼in), 23oz 10dwt (730gr), L 20 June, £396 ($535)

5
A statue of an officer in the Life Guards, Carrington & Co, London, 1921, 41.5cm (16¼in), NY 14 Feb, $1,650 (£1,422)

6
A model of a rhinoceros, Asprey & Co., Ltd., London, 1971, 15oz (480gr), CT 4 Nov, R 550 (£149; $208)

7
A Continental pheasant, with hinged wings and detachable head, 30cm (11¾in), 10oz (310gr), sold with two silver-plated geese, NY 14 Feb, $797 (£687)

8
A Dutch miniature bureau bookcase, imported London 1897, 7.5cm (3in) high, C 1 May, £88 ($115)

9
A Dutch miniature grand piano, imported London 1897, 6.5cm (6½in) long, C 1 May, £88 ($115)

10
A Dutch miniature chalet, late 19th century, with hinged roof, 6.5cm (2½in) high, C 1 May, £82 ($107)

11
A model of the Statue of Liberty, Elkington & Co, Birmingham, 1918, 34.5cm (13½in), 44oz (1368gr), NY 14 Feb, $1,980 (£1,707)

12
A German nef, Ludwig Neresheimer & Co, Hanau, c.1909, in the form of a Viking war ship, 28.5cm (11¼in), 20oz 10dwt (640gr), L 20 June, £528 ($713)

13
A German nef, Ludwig Neresheimer & Co, Hanau, c.1924, 32cm (12¼in), 28oz (872gr), L 20 June, £880 ($1,188)

14
A Continental nef, late 19th century, 79cm (31in), 170oz (5287gr), NY 14 Feb, $8,525 (£7,349)

15
A Continental model of a coach and pair, late 19th century, the coach with detachable top, 41cm (16in) long, 52oz 10dwt (1633gr), NY 7 June, $2,750 (£2,183)

1   2

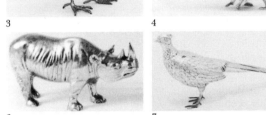

3   4   5

6   7

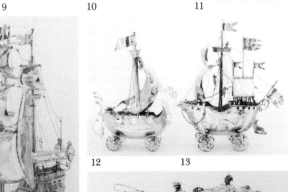

8   9   10   11

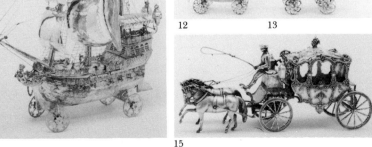

12   13

14   15

1
A Dutch table bell, Middelburg, 1727, 11cm (4¼in), 8oz 10dwt (272gr), *A 1 Apr,*
Dfl 6,960 (£1,611; $2,046)

2
A Dutch table bell, H J Schmidt, Amsterdam, 1875, 17cm (6¾in), *A 5 Feb,*
Dfl 858 (£210; $246)

3
A Dutch table bell, J M van Kempen, Utrecht/ Voorschoten, 1858, 16.5cm (6½in), *A 25 Oct,*
Dfl 603 (£144; $214)

4
A George II inkstand, Benjamin Godfrey, London, 1740, 27.5cm (10¾in) wide, 29oz (901gr), *L 23 May,*
£4,400 ($5,808)

5
A German inkstand, maker's mark only, mid 18th century, 28cm (11in), 32oz (995gr), *NY 9 Oct,*
$1,760 (£1,248)

6
A Victorian inkstand, Robert Hennell, London, 1861, 17cm (6¾in), *NY 14 Feb,*
$825 (£711)

7
A Victorian inkstand, The Soho Plate Co, maker's mark Robinson, Edkins & Aston, Birmingham, 1838, 33.5cm (13¼in) long, 34oz 15dwt (1062gr), *L 21 Nov,*
£1,540 ($2,218)

8
A large inkstand, maker's mark WG over JL, London, 1897, detachable taperstick with chain-hung extinguisher, 37.5cm (14½in), 55oz 18dwt (1741gr), *C 15 Jan,*
£1,870 ($2,244)

9
A French inkstand, Maison Odiot Prevost Cie., Paris, third quarter 19th century, in the manner of Thomas Germain, 26cm (10¼in) wide, 64oz 10dwt (2006gr), *NY 12 Dec,*
$5,225 (£3,706)

10
A Victorian inkstand, E Barnard & Sons, London, 1895, complete with silver-mounted cut glass wells, 36cm (14in) wide, 57oz (1772gr) excluding wells, *L 12 July,*
£1,650 ($2,376)

11
A Victorian inkstand, Charles Reily & George Storer, London, 1843, 32cm (12½in) wide, 32oz 6dwt (1004gr), *L 21 Feb,*
£1,815 ($2,087)

12
A Scottish silver and hard-stone inkwell, maker's mark JR, Edinburgh, 1889, inlaid with multi-coloured agates, gilt interior, 12.5cm (5in), *L 21 Oct,*
£2,200 ($3,300)

13
A silver-mounted horse's hoof inkwell, London, 1905, 13.5cm (5¼in) wide, *C 19 June,*
£132 ($178)

14
A silver-gilt inkstand, commemorating the Wembley Exhibition of 1924, Goldsmiths and Silversmiths Company, London, 1923, *C 30 Jan,*
£363 ($428)

1 2 3

4 5

6 7

8 9

10 11

12 13 14

1
A German parcel-gilt canister, Marx Schaller II, Augsburg, 1670-74, 23oz (710gr), 19cm (7½in) high, *G 12 Nov,*
SF 27,500
(£8,986; $12,580)

2
A Dutch pierced and engraved book cover, 17th century, depicting the Visitation and the Adoration of the Shepherds, 7cm (2¾in) long, *A 1 Apr,*
Dfl8,816 (£2,041; $2,592)

3
A six sectioned pomander-form spice container, probably Dutch, mid 17th century, 4cm (1½in), *NY 26 June,*
$1,870 (£1,450)

4
A German box, maker's mark A B or H V in monogram, Regensberg, *c.*1700, 7cm (2¾in), 2oz (62gr), *NY 26 Apr,*
$440 (£361)

5
A Dutch tobacco jar and cover, Hermanus Heuvel, Amsterdam, 1777, 16cm (6¼in) high, 16oz 10dwt (516gr), *A 2 Dec,*
Dfl 20,125 (£4,780; $6,692)

6
A Dutch tobacco jar and cover, Wijnand Warneke, Amsterdam, 1773, 14cm (5½in) high, 19oz (590gr), *A 1 Apr,*
Dfl 14,500 (£3,356; $4,263)

7
A German oval toilet box, Hans Jakob Schech, Augsburg, *c.*1690, 11.5cm (4½in) long, 4oz (124gr), *NY 26 Apr,*
$1,100 (£902)

8
A Dutch tobacco box, Jacobus de Koning, Amsterdam, 1764, 15.5cm (6in) long, 7oz (217gr), *NY 26 Apr,*
$1,980 (£1,623)

9
A German snuff box, apparently Johann Jakob Bruglocher II, Augsburg, 1741-43, 6.5cm (2½in) wide, *L 11 July,*
£682 ($1,003)

10
Two Danish spice boxes, *c.*1820, one Wolfgang Petersen of Haderslev, the other Reimer Diderich Dethlefsen, Sonderborg, 12 and 13cm (4¾ and 5in), 5oz (155gr), *NY 9 Oct,*
$1,100 (£780)

11
A French silver-gilt snuff box, probably Étienne Septier de la Sellière, Paris, 1752, the cover with a country scene in the manner of Nicholas Lancret, 8cm (3¼in) wide, *L 11 Feb,*
£1,540 ($1,771)

12
A silver-gilt double-lid toilet box, probably German, *c.*1750, unmarked, the cover fitted with a watercolour, 8cm (3in) wide, *L 11 Feb,*
£880 ($1,012)

13
A Dutch fish form spice container, late 19th century, garnet eyes, 9.5cm (3¾in), *NY 26 June,*
$495 (£384)

14
A silver-gilt covered box, probably Augsburg, maker's mark only of Edward Wakelin (London), presumably as retailer, *c.*1750, 7.5cm (3in) high, 6oz (187gr), *NY 10 Oct,*
$1,760 (£1,248)

15
A Russian oval toilet box, Moscow, 1766, with traces of gilding, 23.5cm (9½in), 42oz (1335gr), *L 11 Feb,*
£4,180 ($4,807)

16
A Swiss soap box, Johann Jakob Dulliker (Bern), *c.*1770, 9cm (3½in) high, 6oz (200gr), *G 14 May,*
SF 7,700 (£2,251; $2,994)

17
A silver-gilt sponge box, unmarked, *c.*1725, 11.5cm (4½in) high, 10oz 10dwt (332gr), *L 24 Oct,*
£1,595 ($2,393)

1
A Queen Anne counter box, c.1705, 6.5cm (2½in) high, containing 43 English coins, the majority silver shillings of Edward VI, *L 23 May*, £3,190 ($4,211)

2
An early 18th century tobacco box, c.1700, maker's mark only, apparently of Anthony Stanley of Dublin, 9.5cm (3¾in) wide, *L 21 Nov*, £880 ($1,267)

3
A mid 18th century oval snuff box, maker's mark J W possibly for John Warren of Dublin, 11cm (4¼in), 4oz (124gr), *L 17 Oct*, £715 ($1,058)

4
A set of sixteen Georgian buttons, probably Basil Denn of London, c.1760, 2.5cm (1in) diam, *L 23 May*, £2,090 ($2,759)

5
A vesta case, James Fenton, Birmingham, 1906, 4cm (1½in) diam, *L 11 Mar*, £308 ($351)

6
A George III wine label, Thomas Watson, Newcastle, 1819, 7cm (2¾in) high, *L 11 Mar*, £572 ($652)

7
A set of three George III wine labels, c.1780, for white wine, Madeira and Port; sold with another label and a caddy spoon, all Hester Bateman, London, *L 24 Oct*, £462 ($693)

8
A set of five George III crescent-shaped wine labels, maker's mark I R, script, London, c.1788, 5.5cm (2¼in) long, *NY 7 June*, $550 (£437)

9
A Victorian seal box, Joseph & John Angel, London, 1847, 18cm (7in) diam, 19oz (591gr), *NY 12 Dec*, $2,970 (£2,106)

10
A George III vinaigrette, Matthew Linwood, Birmingham, 1805, with a portrait of Nelson, 4cm (1½in) wide, *L 24 Oct*, £1,650 ($2,475)

11
A George III nutmeg grater, Phipps & Robinson, London, 1796, 5cm (2in) long, *NY 14 Feb*, $385 (£332)

12
A George III nutmeg grater, Thomas & James Phipps, London, 1816, 7cm (2¾in), *NY 14 Feb*, $385 (£332)

13
Two George III nutmeg graters, Samuel Massey, London, 1770, 5cm (2in), *NY 12 Dec*, $770 (£546)

14
A George III silver-gilt vinaigrette, Joseph Willmore, Birmingham, 1813, 4.5cm (1¾in) wide, *L 23 May*, £825 ($1,089)

15
Two American snuff boxes, c.1830, 9 and 8cm (3½ and 3in) long, 6oz (187gr), *NY 27 June*, $825 (£635)

16
A William IV silver-gilt presentation snuff box, Joseph Willmore, Birmingham, 1833, *S 17 Apr*, £616 ($801)

17
A George III silver-gilt vinaigrette, Walter Williams, London, 1819, 4cm (1½in) wide, *L 11 Mar*, £308 ($351)

18
A George IV snuff box, William Simpson, Birmingham, 1829, 8.5cm (3¼in) long, *L 24 Oct*, £638 ($957)

19
A Victorian vinaigrette, Nathaniel Mills, Birmingham 1838, Abbotsford, 4.5cm (1¾in) wide, *L 11 Mar*, £715 ($815)

1
A George III silver-gilt vinaigrette, Nathaniel Mills, Birmingham, 1830, 4.5cm (1¾in), *L 23 May,* £440 ($581)

2
A Victorian vinaigrette, Thomas Lawrence, Birmingham, 1837, the lid with a dye-stamped view of Windsor Castle, 3.5cm (1½in) wide, *L 21 Nov,* £308 ($444)

3
A George III silver-mounted baby tortoise shell snuff box, Joseph Ash, London, 1811, gilt interior, 7.5cm (3in), *L 21 Nov,* £935 ($1,346)

4
A Victorian novelty writing necessaire in the form of a railway lamp, Walter Thornhill & Co, London, 1877, 12.5cm (4¾in), *L 23 May,* £1,265 ($1,670)

5
A Victorian silver-mounted horn snuff mull, unmarked, *c.*1870, 10cm (4in) long, *Glen 26 Aug,* £330 ($485)

6
A Victorian travelling case, Thomas Johnson, London, 1862, complete with 12 engraved jars and bottles, mirror and jewellery drawer below, *L 4 Apr,* £528 ($671)

7
An electro-gilt mounted ram's head snuff mull, Scottish, mid 19th century, 39cm (15¼in) wide, *S 17 Apr,* £770 ($1,001)

8
A silver mounted mirror, Henry Matthews, Birmingham, 1907, 75cm (29½in), *C 30 Oct,* £506 ($753)

9
A pair of silver-plated 'Naughty Nellie' nut crackers, 21.5cm (8½in), *NY 14 Feb,* $357 (£308)

10
A writing set, Goldsmiths & Silversmiths Co Ltd, London, 1904, comprising inkstand, leather blotter and leather stationery box, all silver mounted, blotter 29cm (11½in), 12oz (373gr), *C 16 Oct,* £1,760 ($2,605)

11
A two-compartment silver mounted photograph frame, Chester, 1900, 30cm (11¾in) wide, *C 15 May,* £550 ($732)

12
An ivory pepper grinder, *c.*1900, in the form of a weight, 9cm (3½in), *C 13 Nov,* £50 ($70)

13
A silver and tortoiseshell oval trinket box, Goldsmiths & Silversmiths Co Ltd, London, 1910, 11.5cm (4½in), *C 13 Nov,* £242 ($339)

14
A tortoiseshell and silver mounted mantel clock, William Comyns, London, 1907, 17cm (6¾in) high, *C 19 June,* £572 ($772)

15
A pair of George IV silver-gilt grape scissors, Charles Rawlings, London, 1825, 18cm (7in), 5oz 10dwt (171gr), *NY 10 Oct,* $550 (£390)

1 2 3
4 5 6
7
8
9 10 11
12 13
14 15

1
A pair of early 17th century seal top spoons, probably Robert Matthew of Barnstaple, *c.*1623, with traces of gilding, one engraved 'Feare God', the other 'Praise God', 17.5 and 18.5cm (7 and 7¼in), *L 24 Oct,*
£1,870 ($2,805)

2
A late 17th century Apostle spoon, Thomas Dare junior, Taunton, *c.*1667, St. John, 18.5cm (7¼in), *L 24 Oct,*
£935 ($1,403)

3
An Elizabeth I seal top spoon, maker's mark a bird's claw (?), London, 1565, with traces of gilding, 17cm (6¾in), *L 24 Oct,*
£462 ($693)

4
A 17th century Apostle spoon, Exeter, *c.*1640, St Matthew, *L 21 Feb,*
£495 ($569)

5
A Commonwealth puritan spoon, Stephen Venables, London, *c.*1655, date letter worn, initialled, 10oz 10dwt (46gr), *L 21 Feb,*
£495 ($569)

6
A Dutch spoon, Boele Rijnhout, Amsterdam, *c.*1657, with pineapple finial, *A 2 Dec,*
Dfl 3,105 (£737; $1,031)

7
A Dutch Apostle spoon, Jan Melekers Oostervelt, Leeuwarden, *c.*1630, *A 2 Dec,*
Dfl 2,185 (£519; $726)

8
A Norwegian spoon, Jonas Andersen, (Bergen), *c.*1640, maker's mark only, *L 11 Feb,*
£550 ($633)

9
A Norwegian parcel-gilt spoon, Jost Alberszenn, (Bergen), *c.*1620, maker's mark only, *L 11 Feb,*
£550 ($633)

10
A Norwegian spoon, Bergen, early 17th century, 14cm (5½in), *NY 19 Feb,*
$412 (£378)

11
Twelve Queen Anne tablespoons, William Petley, 1711, Hanoverian pattern, 16oz 14dwt (519gr), *L 23 May,*
£1,045 ($1,379)

12
Twelve George I three prong table forks, Paul Hanet, London, 1716/26, Hanoverian pattern, 25oz 9dwt (791gr), *L 23 May,*
£2,090 ($2,759)

13
A Dutch fish server, Jan Diederik Pont, Amsterdam, 1757, 38cm (15in) long, 8oz 13dwt (269gr), *L 11 Feb,*
£1,760 ($2,024)

14
A George II punch ladle, Francis Spilsbury, London, 1742, 35.5cm (14in), *NY 14 Feb,*
$330 (£284)

15
A pair of Victorian fish servers, Francis Higgins, London, 1865, one handle modelled as a fisherboy holding a net, the other as a fishwife, slice 35cm (13¾in), 15oz (466gr), *NY 26 Apr,*
$2,090 (£1,713)

1
An American tablespoon, Paul Revere Jr., Boston, *c.*1780, 2oz (62gr), *NY 31 Jan,* **$2,200 (£1,864)**

2
An American dessert spoon, Myer Myers, New York or Philadelphia, *c.*1780, *NY 26 June,* **$1,210 (£938)**

3
A pair of American tablespoons, Henricus Boelen, New York, *c.*1750, 3oz 10dwt (109gr), *NY 31 Jan,* **$330 (£280)**

4
An American tablespoon, Jacob Boelen, New York, *c.*1720, 2oz (62gr), *NY 31 Jan,* **$357 (£303)**

5
An American soup ladle, Bernard Dupuy, Raleigh, NC, *c.*1830, Fiddle pattern, 32cm (12½in), 6oz 10dwt (202gr), *NY 31 Jan,* **$770 (£653)**

6
An American soup ladle, Hyde & Goodrich, New Orleans, *c.*1840, Fiddle pattern, 31.5cm (12½in), 5oz (155gr), *NY 31 Jan,* **$357 (£303)**

7
Victorian table silver, London, 1857-85, Rose pattern comprising one hundred and forty three pieces, the majority H & H Lias, twenty-eight pieces Wakely & Wheeler, 327oz 10dwt (10185gr), *L 24 Oct,* **£7,700 ($11,550)**

8
American table silver, Tiffany & Co, New York, *c.*1900, King's pattern, comprising two hundred and seventy five pieces, 326oz (10139gr), *NY 7 June,* **$10,175 (£8,075)**

9
American table silver, Tiffany & Co, New York, *c.*1930, Windham pattern, comprising four hundred and four pieces, 480oz (14928gr), *NY 12 Dec,* **$29,700 (£21,064)**

10
Russian table silver, Karl Magnus Stahle, St Petersburg, 1848, comprising fifty-two pieces, 121oz (3760gr), *M 25 June,* **FF 17,760 (£1,480; $1,889)**

11
A French silver-gilt dessert service, the majority Odiot, Paris, *c.*1860, in the style of Nicolas-Martin Langlois, comprising 73 pieces, 87oz (2700gr), *G 14 May,* **SF 16,500 (£4,824; $6,415)**

12
French table silver, silver and silver-gilt, Puiforcat, Paris, 20th century comprising two hundred and three pieces, 384oz 10dwt (11957gr), *NY 26 Apr,* **$9,350 (£7,664)**

13
A Dutch fish server, 1834, *A 5 Feb,* **Dfl 348 (£85; $100)**

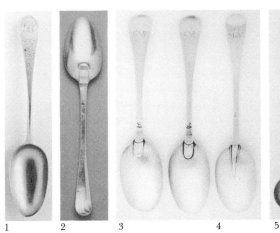

Objects of Vertu

See also
● Colour illustrations *p* 488 ● Silver *pp* 406-407 ● European works of art *pp* 447-468

1
A Swiss gold and champ-levé enamel musical fob seal, early 19th century, enamelled with colourful flowering foliage, 4cm (1½in) high, *NY 11 Dec,* $1,760 (£1,248)

2
A gold and sapphire-set musical fob seal, *c.*1830, 4cm (1½in) high, *NY 17 June,* $1,650 (£1,299)

3
An English gold fob seal, *c.*1830, with watch key and gilt-metal chain, 19th century, *L 8 July,* £330 ($459)

4
A Swiss gold musical fob seal, *c.*1800, the base enclosing a movement which plays 'God Save the King', some repair, 3.5cm (1½in) high, *L 28 Oct,* £880 ($1,311)

5
A gold and citrine quartz desk seal, late 19th century, in the form of the head of the Capitoline Brutus, 7.5cm (3in) high, *NY 21 May,* $1,980 (£1,584)

6
An enamelled gold and lapis lazuli desk seal, with the monogram of Czar Nicholas I, second quarter 19th century, possibly French, in the form of Atlas, the base decorated in Renaissance taste, 12cm (4¾in), *NY 21 May,* $6,325 (£5,060)

7
A gem-set gilt-metal desk seal, English, mid-19th century, 8cm (3¼in) long, *L 21 Oct,* £110 ($165)

8
A gold fob, *c.*1840, comprising four gold chains, gold sliding thimble and amethyst swivel seal, *G 12 Nov,* **SF 1,780 (£575; $805)**

9
A musical necessaire, French, *c.*1840, in the form of a miniature grand piano, with various silver sewing accessories, lacking original legs, 28.5cm (11½in) long, *C 26 June,* £330 ($445)

10
A Continental gold and enamel-mounted desk seal, contained in original fitted case of retailer, *c.*1830, 10.6cm (4⅛in), *NY 10 June,* $1,650 (£1,310)

11
A Swiss gold and enamel vinaigrette, *c.*1830, covered basket form, pendent from a circular handle by a chain, some damage, 3.5cm (1⅜in), *NY 10 June,* $2,200 (£1,746)

12
A Palais Royal ring holder, Vienna,*c.*1820-30 of gilt-metal and painted mother of pearl, painted with views of Austria, 14.7cm (5¾in), *NY 21 May,* $660 (£528)

1   2   3   4

5   6   7   8

9

10   11   12

1
A gold and mother-of-pearl
pen knife, probably
French, mid-18th cen-
tury, the mother-of-pearl
panels applied in burgau
and gold piqué with ivory
leaves, 11cm (4¼in),
G 16 May,
SF 3,040 (£901; $1,198)

2
A silver-gilt mounted
enamel Lady's Companion,
H. W. & L. Dee, London,
1871, painted in pastel
shades, fitted with com-
partments for scent,
smelling salts and
vinaigrette, 13cm (5in),
L 21 Oct,
£748 ($1,122)

3
A Swiss gold, enamel and
pearl-set folding knife,
early 19th century, the
sides enamelled in trans-
lucent blue, 8cm (3¼in),
G 14 Nov,
SF 16,500 (£5,392; $7,548)

4
A French two-colour gold
étui à cire, Paris, 1798-
1809, 7.5cm (3in),
G 16 May,
SF 990 (£289; $385)

5
An English gold and glass
scent bottle, c.1765, the
glass overlaid with
scrolling gold cagework,
gold bird stopper, 5.5cm
(2¼in), G 16 May,
SF 7,700 (£2,251; $2,994)

6
An English gilt-metal
chatelaine, c.1745, hung
with three small boxes,
needle and scissors case,
17.5cm (7in), L 9 July,
£352 ($489)

7
An English gilt-metal
chatelaine, mid-18th
century, the central étui
chased with Diana and
Apollo, fitted with
various accessories
(incomplete), 20.5cm
(8in), L 9 July,
£550 ($765)

8
A silver-gilt mounted
painted porcelain double
scent flask, S. Mordan &
Co, London, c.1880, in
the form of a pair of
opera glasses, mount a
little distressed, 6.5cm
(2½in), L 9 July,
£220 ($306)

9
A two-colour gold-mounted
meerschaum pipe, French,
c.1885, the bowl carved
as the head of a maha-
raja, amber mouthpiece
with later gold repair,
slight repair to bowl,
25cm (9¾in), L 21 Oct,
£682 ($1,023)

10
An English-gilt-metal and
hardstone étui, mid-18th
century, the interior
with gilt-metal, steel and
ivory implements, one
lacking, lid cracked, 9cm
(3½in) high, L 9 July,
£198 ($275)

11
A Palais Royal gilt-metal
spy glass, early 19th
century, mounted with
four panels each painted
with a coquette, gilt-
metal mounts, 9.5cm
(3¾in), L 21 Oct,
£440 ($660)

12
A two-colour gold thimble,
late 19th century, 2cm
(¾in), L 9 July,
£198 ($275)

13
A German carved agate
and gold combination
double scent flask and
bonbonnière, third
quarter 18th century, in
the form of an agate
peasant girl holding one
basket, another on her
back, 12.5cm (5in),
NY 11 Dec,
$24,200 (£17,163)

14
A malacca walking cane,
with ivory top, the band
inscribed W.C. 1698,
84cm (33in), S 14 May,
£220 ($293)

15
An English gold-mounted
glass scent bottle, c.1760,
the body and stopper of
blue glass, the gold cap
with gilt inscription,
6cm (2½in), L 21 Oct,
£902 ($1,353)

16
A Scandinavian gold spice
box, 18th century,
unmarked, possibly
Danish, with later grille
inside, 5cm (2in) high,
G 14 Nov,
SF 6,050 (£1,977; $2,767)

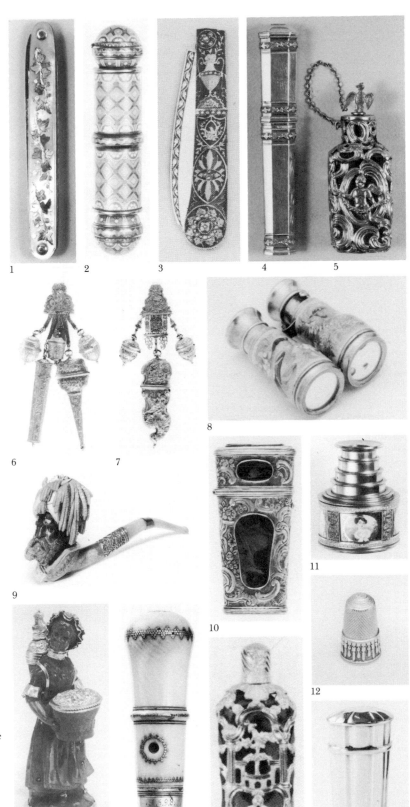

1
An oval tortoiseshell snuff box, dated 1724, 9.5cm (3¾in), *C 11 July,* £374 ($520)

2
An ivory snuff box, probably German, *c.*1730, the lid carved with a scene of a lascivious monk and a young woman, later reeded gilt-metal mounts, 8cm (3in), *L 11 May,* £330 ($376)

3
A German lacquered papier-mâché snuff box, Stockmann, early 19th century, painted with a scene possibly taken from Tasso, worn, 9.5cm (3¾in), *L 21 Oct,* £242 ($363)

4
A German lacquered papier-mâché snuff box, early 19th century, painted with two snuff-takers, chipped, 10cm (4in), *L 9 July,* £242 ($336)

5
A French gilt metal boîte à pomponne, *c.*1775, lined with tortoiseshell, 7cm (2¾in), *L 9 July,* £528 ($734)

6
A French poudre d'écaille snuff box, *c.*1780, the lid impressed with a portrait of Louis XVI against a slate blue ground, tortoiseshell-lined, 8cm (3in), *L 9 July,* £440 ($612)

7
A lacquered snuff box, probably German *c.*1840, scratched, *C 17 Jan,* £154 ($185)

8
A horn snuff box, late 18th century, the lid with a polychrome decoration of one of the first balloon trials, 7cm (2¾in), *A 3 June,* **Df 16,032 (£1,365; $1,842)**

9
An English pressed horn snuff box, John Obrisset, 1712, the lid decorated with the arms of Sir Francis Drake, 10cm (4in), *L 11 Mar,* £286 ($326)

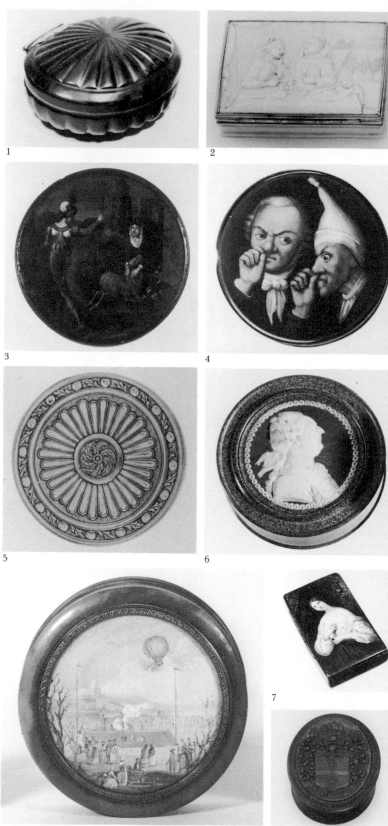

1
An Italian lapis lazuli and mosaic snuff box, Luigi Mascelli, Rome, 1804-25, with silver-gilt mounts, 9.5cm (3¾in), G 14 Nov, SF 9,350 (£3,055; $4,277)

2
A Roman micromosaic plaque, early 19th century, showing a view of the Ponte Lucano, set into a gold-mounted composition snuff box, 9cm (3½in), G 14 Nov, SF 8,800 (£2,875; $4,025)

3
A tortoiseshell and mosaic snuff box, c.1830, inset with a Roman micromosaic plaque of a swan, chased gold frame, some damage, 8.5cm (3¼in), L 8 July, £418 ($581)

4
An English gold snuff box inset with a Roman mosaic, A. J. Strachan, London, 1816, 7.5cm (3in), L 8 July, £4,840 ($6,728)

5
An English hardstone and gold snuff box, mid-18th century, the brown agate lid, body and base with gold mounts, unmarked, 6cm (2½in), G 14 Nov, SF 9,900 (£3,235; $4,529)

6
A gold and hardstone snuff box, English, mid-18th century, the front with a gold mask within scrolls, plain gold mounts, unmarked, 8cm (3in), G 14 Nov, SF 3,080 (£1,006; $1,408)

7
An English silver and aventurine glass snuff box, c.1740, maker's mark L.M., 7cm (2¾in), L 9 July, £198 ($275)

8
An English gilt-metal and hardstone snuff box, Birmingham, c.1750, the lid set with a brown agate panel, 6.5cm (2½in), L 11 Mar, £176 ($201)

9
A double-opening hardstone snuff box, German, c.1770, with agate panels, the sides decorated in the manner of Heinrici with architectural ruins, gilt-metal mounts, base panel replaced and cracked, 10.5cm (4¼in), L 21 Oct, £308 ($462)

10
An English gilt-metal and agate snuff box, Birmingham, c.1750, 6cm (2¼in), L 11 Mar, £110 ($125)

11
A Neapolitan tortoiseshell piqué snuff box, c.1760, 8cm (3in), F 29 May, L 1,600,000 (£623; $822)

12
A tortoiseshell piqué snuff box, probably English, c.1730, the lid inlaid in gold piqué posé et point with the reconciliation of Mercury with Apollo, gold hinges and foliate mounts (one missing), some chips, 8cm (3in), L 11 Mar, £396 ($451)

13
A gold and enamel snuff box, early 19th century, decorated overall with a translucent blue and red enamel trellis, 7cm (2¾in), G 14 Nov, SF 3,850 (£1,258; $1,761)

14
A gilt-metal and mother-of-pearl snuff box, probably German, c.1740, the lid inlaid with tortoiseshell and gold, 7cm (2¾in), L 11 Mar, £418 ($477)

1
A French gold snuff box, Paris, 1732-8, maker's mark probably that of Claude-Auguste Prévost, the lid chased with Syrinx leaning on an urn, 7.5cm (3in), *G 16 May*, **SF 22,000 (£6,433; $8,556)**

2
A French four-colour gold snuff box, Dominique-François Poitreau, Paris, 1759, 8cm (3in), *G 16 May*, **SF 26,400 (£7,719; $10,267)**

3
A French three-colour gold oval snuff box, Jean-Louis Bouillerot, Paris, 1767, 9cm (3½in) long, *NY 10 June*, **$5,225 (£4,146)**

4
A French three-colour gold snuff box, Jean Formey, Paris, 1763, 8cm (3in), *L 28 Oct*, **£8,580 ($12,784)**

5
A French gold snuff box, René-Antoine Bailleul, Paris, 1770-71, 6.5cm (2½in), *G 14 Nov*, **SF 4,400 (£1,437; $2,011)**

6
A French two-colour gold and tortoiseshell snuff box, Louis-Antoine Martigny, Paris, 1773, 8.5cm (3¼in), *G 14 Nov*, **SF 7,150 (£2,336; $3,270)**

7
A French gold and enamel snuff box, Charles le Bastier, Paris, 1778, enamel restored, 8cm (3in), *L 28 Oct*, **£8,250 ($12,293)**

8
A Swiss four-colour gold snuff box, *c.*1775, the lid chased with a panel of articles of amorous significance, 7cm (2¾in), *G 16 May*, **SF 8,800 (£2,573; $3,422)**

9
A French two-colour gold and poudre d'écaille powder box, late 18th century, apparently unmarked, the navy blue ground dotted with gold discs, tortoiseshell lining, 6cm (2½in), *G 16 May*, **SF 3,520 (£1,029; $1,369)**

10
A French two-colour gold and lacquer powder box, *c.*1780, striped in red-gold on green lacquer, cable-twist mounts, tortoise-shell lining, 8cm (3in), *L 11 Mar*, **£385 ($439)**

11
A French two-colour gold pill box, Jean-Bernard Cherrier, Paris, 1781, 4cm (1½in), *L 28 Oct*, **£1,980 ($2,950)**

12
A French three-colour gold snuff box, Paris, 1786, maker's mark rubbed, 8cm (3in), *L 28 Oct*, **£2,860 ($4,261)**

13
A French two-colour gold box, Paris 1789-92, 5.5cm (2¼in), *G 16 May*, **SF 4,180 (£1,222; $1,626)**

14
A Swiss four-colour gold snuff box, late 18th century, 6.5cm (2½in), *G 16 May*, **SF 6,050 (£1,769; $2,353)**

15
A Swiss two colour gold and enamel snuff box, early 19th century, makers mark J.O., 9.2cm (3½in), *G. 14 Nov*, **SF 12,100, (£3,954; $5,536)**

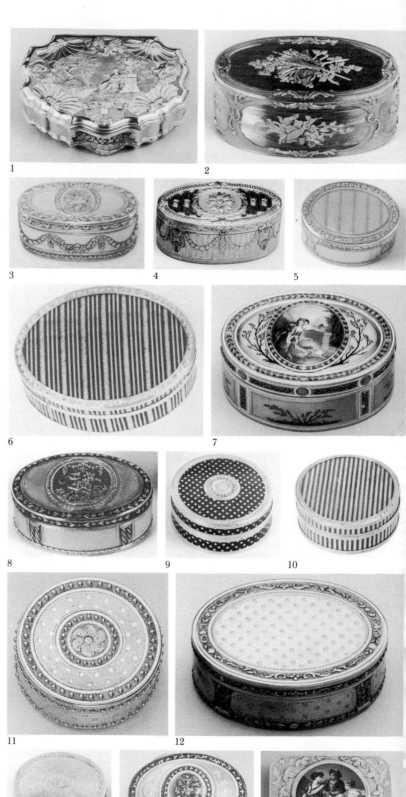

1
2
3
4
5
6
7
8
9
10
11
12
13
14
15

Swiss gold and enamel
snuff box, 19th century,
the base and sides
enamelled translucent
royal blue, 7cm (2¾in),
NY 10 June,
3,300 (£2,619)

A French tortoiseshell,
gold and enamel snuff box,
Adrien-Jean-Maximilien
Vachette, Paris, 1810,
inset with a gold medal
commemorating the
marriage of Napoleon I
and Marie-Louise of
Austria, 9cm (3½in) wide,
G 14 Nov,
SF 22,000 (£7,189; $10,064)

A George III gold box,
A. J. Strachan, London,
1809, 5cm (2in),
NY 10 June,
1,320 (£1,047)

A Swiss gold snuff box,
maker's mark R.P.C.,
c.1810, 9.5cm (3¾in),
NY 10 June,
1,430 (£1,134)

An English gold snuff box,
A. J. Strachan, London,
1823, 9.5cm (3¾ in),
L 28 Oct,
£1,430 ($2,145)

An English four-colour
gold jewelled toothpick
case, A. J. Strachan,
London, 1817, 7cm
(2¾in), L 28 Oct,
£3,520 ($5,245)

An 18ct. gold presentation
snuff box, Charles
Rawlings, London, 1825,
8.5cm (3¼in), L 28 Oct,
£2,640 ($3,934)

A Swiss gold and enamel
snuff box, c.1820, 9.5cm
(3½in), NY 11 Dec,
4,950 (£3,510)

An 18ct. gold vinaigrette,
Edward Edwards,
London, 1830, in Bir-
mingham taste, 2.5cm
(1in), L 28 Oct,
£440 ($656)

10
An English gold vin-
aigrette, Joseph Willmore,
Birmingham, 1833,
2.5cm (1in), L 28 Oct,
£308 ($459)

11
A Swiss four-colour gold
snuff box, Neuchâtel,
early 19th century, 8cm
(3in), A 1 Apr,
Dfl 6,032 (£1,396; $1,773)

12
A Swiss gold musical box,
c.1830, 8cm (3in),
L 28 Oct,
£3,080 ($4,589)

13
A gold snuff box, maker's
mark Am, Vienna, 1840,
6.5cm (2½in), L 11 Mar,
£440 ($502)

14
A Swiss gold snuff box,
mid-19th century, maker's
mark rubbed, 8cm (3in).
G 14 Nov,
SF 2,090 (£683; $956)

15
A Swiss gold snuff box,
Neuchâtel, 19th century,
8.5cm (3¼in), G 14 Nov,
SF 4,180 (£1,366; $1,912)

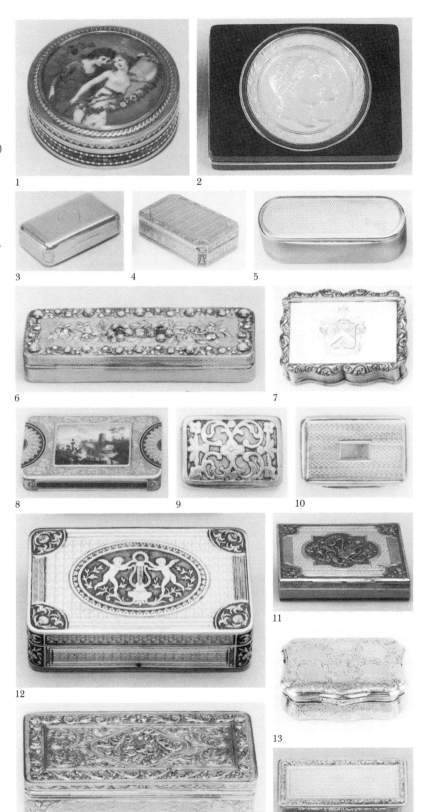

1

2

3

4

5

6

7

8

9

10

11

12

13

14

15

1
**An enamelled silver ciga-
rette case,** *c.*1910, 9cm
(3½in) wide, *S 16 Oct,*
£715 ($1,058)

2
**An enamelled cigarette
case,** early 20th century,
depicting a nude bather,
scratches, 9cm (3½in)
wide, *C 27 Nov,*
£110 ($154)

3
**An enamelled silver vesta
case,** Sampson Mordan &
Co. Ltd., London, 1896,
5cm (2in) high, *L 21 Oct,*
£220 ($330)

4
**An enamelled cigarette
case,** probably German,
*c.*1910, 9cm (3½in),
L 11 Mar,
£1,045 ($1,191)

5
**An enamelled cigarette
case,** German, *c.*1905,
painted with a portrait of
Una Gitana, 9cm (3½in)
high, *L 11 Mar,*
£352 ($401)

6
**A German enamelled
cigarette case,** Louis
Kuppenheim, Pforzheim,
*c.*1910, 10cm (4in) high,
L 8 July,
£682 ($948)

7
A Victorian vesta case,
Sampson Mordan & Co.,
London, 1889, painted
with a cut-out of a royal
flush, 5.7cm (2¼in),
L 11 Mar,
£495 ($564)

8
**A Victorian enamelled
silver vesta case,**
S. Mordan & Co.,
London, 1891, one chip
and some surface
scratches, 5.5cm (2¼in),
L 11 Mar,
£462 ($527)

9
**An enamelled silver vesta
case,** S. Mordan & Co.,
London, 1885, painted
on one side with the King
of Hearts and on the
other with the Ace of
Hearts, gilt interior, one
chip, 4.5cm (1¾in),
L 11 Mar,
£462 ($527)

10
**An enamelled silver
cigarette case,** probably
German, London import
marks 1910, the con-
cealed inner compart-
ment painted with a saucy
underwater scene,
enamel repaired, 9cm
(3½in) high, *L 11 Mar,*
£440 ($502)

11
**A Swiss silver-gilt and
enamel singing bird box,**
mid 19th century, 10.5cm
(4¼in) long, *NY 17 June,*
$4,125 (£3,248)

12
A singing bird box,
probably French, early
20th century, with gilt
brass and royal blue
enamel case, 10cm (4in)
wide, *L 1 Oct,*
£495 ($723)

An Italian tortoiseshell
piqué fan, c.1700, the
vellum leaf painted with a
battle scene and coat-of-
arms, several repairs,
28cm (11½in) long, L 9 July,
£1,430 ($1,988)

An ivory brisé fan, French,
c.1720, re-ribboned, minor
repairs, 21.5cm (8½in)
long, L 9 July,
£418 ($581)

A biblical fan, Italian,
early 18th century, minor
repairs, 27cm (10½in)
long, L 21 Oct,
£308 ($462)

A pierced and carved ivory
fan, probably English,
mid-18th century, 28.5cm
(11¼in), L 21 Oct,
£187 ($281)

A French ivory fan, c.1765,
coiled gilt sticks, the paper
leaf printed with the
departure of a hero, 27cm
(10½in), L 21 Oct,
£165 ($248)

An English printed fan,
1837, commemorating the
accession of Queen
Victoria, leaf torn, 27cm
(10½in) long, L 21 Oct,
£165 ($248)

A mother-of-pearl fan,
possibly Viennese, c.1860,
slight damage, sold with
a case, 28.5cm (11¼in),
L 11 Mar,
£330 ($376)

8
A French mother-of-pearl
fan, c.1880, signed F.
Houghton, 33cm (13in)
long, L 9 July,
£715 ($994)

9
An ivory brisé fan, 1780,
decorated with carved
vignettes and three carved
medallions, slight staining,
25cm (9¾in) long, L 11 Mar,
£330 ($376)

10
A printed dance fan,
English, 1798, the paper
leaf printed 'The New
Caricature Dance Fan for
1794', small repairs, 25cm
(9¾in) long, L 9 July,
£242 ($336)

11
A mother-of-pearl fan,
second half of the 19th
century, the leaf of
Brussels *point de gaze* lace,
29.5cm (11½in) long,
L 9 July,
£495 ($688)

12
An ivory brisé fan, Vienna,
c.1905, with gilt metal
mounts, studded with
jewels and painted with a
crowned portrait. 9.5cm
(7¼in) long. L 11 Mar.
£286 ($326)

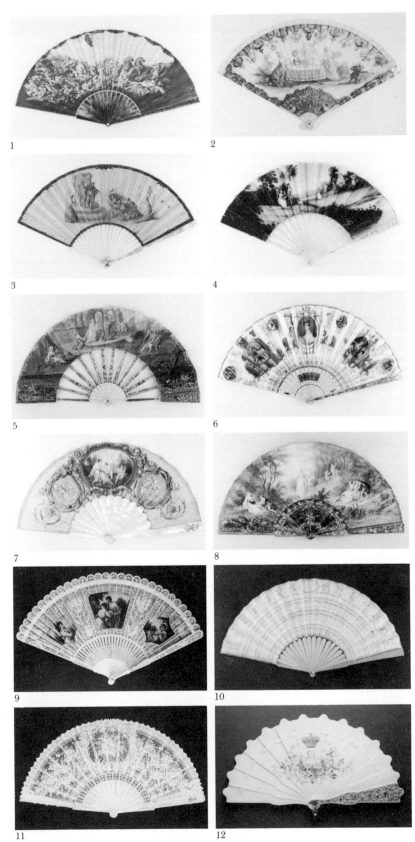

1
An oval Staffordshire patch box, early 19th century, the lid printed with a view of Abbey Church, Bath, some restoration, 5cm (2in), *L 22 Oct*, **£198 ($297)**

2
A South Staffordshire snuff box, *c*.1765, with polychrome colours on green, the yellow ground with blue and gold stars, 5cm (2in), *L 26 Feb*, **£484 ($542)**

3
A 'purple' ground' Staffordshire étui, *c*.1765, the sides and top painted with pastoral vignettes, gilt-metal mounts, the interior with three implements, some chipping and restoration, 9cm (3½in), *L 22 Oct*, **£770 ($1,155)**

4
A Birmingham/Battersea snuff box, *c*.1755, transfer-printed in sepia, gilt-metal mounts, 7cm (2¾in), *L 22 Oct*, **£638 ($957)**

5
A 'purple scroll group' étui, *c*.1760, painted with a polychrome portrait of a young lady and with flowers, gilt-metal mounts, with pen knife and bodkin, top restored, 8cm (3in), *L 22 Oct*, **£770 ($1,155)**

6
An oval snuff box, probably Liverpool, *c*.1770, the lid printed in black, metal mounts, hinge damaged, 8cm (3in), *L 22 Oct*, **£286 ($429)**

7
An early Birmingham snuff box, *c*.1750, the interior painted with a portrait bust of Bonnie Prince Charlie, gilt-metal mounts, 5.5cm (2¼in), *L 22 Oct*, **£495 ($743)**

8
A Birmingham snuff box, *c*.1755-60, metal mounts, damaged, 7.5cm (3in), *L 26 Feb*, **£396 ($444)**

9
A Birmingham snuff box, *c*.1760, painted with Mademoiselle Camargo, after Lancret, gilt mounts, minor cracks, 7.5cm (3in), *L 26 Feb*, **£638 ($715)**

10
A Birmingham enamel and silver-plate patch box, *c*.1750, with original steel mirror, 4cm (1½in), *L 26 Feb*, **£220 ($246)**

11
A Birmingham egg pendant, *c*.1765, gilt-metal mounts and loop, 3.5cm (1½in), *L 22 Oct*, **£286 ($429)**

12
A Wednesbury theatrical pill box, *c*.1805, the dark blue box decorated in raised white with a profile portrait of the boy actor William Betty (1791-1874), 4.5cm (1¾in), *L 22 Oct*, **£715 ($1,073)**

1

2

3

4

5

6

7

8

9

10

11

12

A **Bilston candlestick**,
770, gilt-metal mounts,
ater matching detach-
ble nozzle, some
amage, 27cm (10½in),
22 Oct,
605 ($907)

A **pair of pink-ground
Bilston candlesticks**,
1775, gilt-metal
mounts, one restored,
7cm (10½in), L 22 Oct,
1,045 ($1,568)

A **Bilston chamber candlestick**, c.1765-70, brass
detachable nozzle,
andle restored, 19cm
7½in), L 22 Oct,
1,210 ($1,815)

A **Bilston standish**, c.1765,
vith ink pot and two
ounce pots, painted
vith harbour and
astoral scenes within
ilded scrolls, slight
damage, 23cm (9in)
vide, L 22 Oct,
3,300 ($4,950)

A **Bilston plaque**, c.1765,
ilt-metal mount, one
hip and some restora-
ion, 20cm (8in) wide,
22 Oct,
770 ($1,155)

A **Bilston Queen's Head**,
onbonnière, c.1770, the
id formed as a crown
lecorated with blue
jewels', gilt-metal
nounts, 7.5cm (3in),
22 Oct,
2,860 ($4,290)

A **Bilston pug dog bon-
bonnière**, c.1775, with
vellow fur and black face
narkings, chip to rim,
over rubbed, 5cm (2in),
10 July,
1,375 ($1,911)

A **Bilston bullfinch bonbonnière**, c.1770, with red
reast and blue-grey
ead, restored, 5.5cm
¼in) long, L 26 Feb,
495 ($554)

9
A **Bilston patch box**, late
18th century, the lid
painted with a recum-
bent ewe, dark blue
ground, original steel
mirror, 4cm (1½in),
L 26 Feb,
£286 ($320)

10
A **Bilston patch box**,
c.1800, painted with the
bust of Mary Magdalene,
some damage, 5.5cm
(2¼in), L 26 Feb,
£88 ($99)

11
A **Bilston snuff box**,
c.1765, the lid painted
with a scene of a boatman
ferrying across a river,
shaded blue ground,
gilt-metal mounts, slight
chip, 5cm (2in), L 22 Oct,
£1,650 ($2,475)

12
A **Bilston rainbow scent
bottle**, c.1765, one side
with the 'Finch and
Fruit' design, the reverse
with a shepherd, the gilt-
metal stopper in the
shape of a cherub's head,
7cm (2¾in), L 22 Oct,
£2,090 ($3,135)

13
A **white-ground Staffordshire scent flask**, c.1765,
painted with a couple
after Watteau, gilt-metal
stopper, slight chip, 8cm
(3in), L 22 Oct,
£1,430 ($2,145)

14
A **Staffordshire snuff box**,
c.1770, printed with "Les
Poussins" after a design
by Boucher, powder
blue ground, slight
chipping, 8cm (3in),
L 22 Oct,
£825 ($1,238)

1
A 'purple scroll' group
snuff box, c.1765, with
polychrome medallion
and spandrel with
purple scrolls, some
restoration, 6cm (2¼in),
L 26 Feb,
£242 ($271)

2
An American export
Staffordshire snuff box,
c.1800, with a portrait
of George Washington,
restored, 5cm (2in),
L 22 Oct,
£605 ($908)

3
A Staffordshire patch box,
early 19th century, the
lid painted with a
triumphant huntsman,
5.5cm (2¼in), *L 26 Feb,*
£638 ($715)

4
A Staffordshire motto box,
late 18th century, 'A
Trifle from Chester',
4cm (1½in), *L 26 Feb,*
£198 ($222)

5
A French étui, late 19th
century, with panels of
flowers on a deep blue
ground and gilt-metal
mounts, 9.5cm (3¾in),
L 26 Feb,
£209 ($234)

6
A French étui, late 19th
century, with panels of
flowers on a turquoise
ground, 9.5cm (3¾in),
L 26 Feb,
£231 ($259)

7
A Battersea portrait
plaque, 1753-56,
engraved by Simon-
François Ravenet and
printed with a portrait
of the Duke of Cumber-
land, original gilt-metal
frame, 8.5cm (3¼in)
high, *L 22 Oct,*
£770 ($1,155)

8
A Staffordshire patch box,
c.1796, with a view of
'Iron Bridge, Wear-
mouth, Sunderland'
slight damage, 5cm (2in),
wide, *L 22 Oct,*
£275 ($413)

9
A German snuff box,
c.1757, the lid painted
with a plan of Prague at
the time of its attack by
Frederick the Great's
army, gilt-metal mounts,
sides restored, 8cm
(3¼in), wide, *L 11 Mar,*
£715 ($815)

10
A Birmingham snuff box,
c.1755, the lid printed
in red, gilt-metal mounts,
lid restored, 7.5cm
(3in), *L 26 Feb,*
£242 ($271)

11
A German table snuff box,
c.1762, the lid painted
with a battle scene
between mounted Prus-
sians and Poles, gilt-
metal mounts, some
cracks, 13cm (5in),
L 11 Mar,
£968 ($1,104)

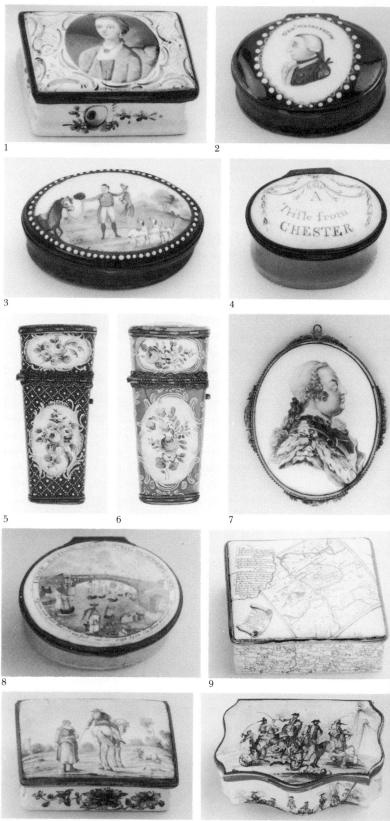

Silhouettes and Portrait Miniatures

Article ● Silhouettes *pp 426-429*
See also ● Colour illustrations *pp 489*

1
A gentleman, by Jean Baptiste Jacques Augustin, signed and dated 1800, 7cm (2¾in), *L 11 Mar,* £4,180 ($4,765)

2
A gentleman, by Vincent Bertrand, signed and dated 1815, 6.8cm (2½in), *G 16 May,* SF 1,650 (£482; $641)

3
Charlotte Palmer, daughter of Sir Henry Palmer Bt, by Henry Pierce Bone, inscribed and dated 1848, enamel, 8.6cm (3⅜in), *L 11 Mar,* £968 ($1,104)

4
Three children, by George Chinnery, *c.*1800, 14cm (5½in) wide, *L 4 Dec,* £902 ($1,335)

5
A gentleman, by John Comerford, *c.*1810, 9cm (3½in), *G 16 May,* SF 1,320 (£385; $512)

6
A Dutch nobleman, by Alexander Cooper, *c.*1630, on vellum, 4.5cm (1¾in), *L 11 Mar,* £13,750 ($15,675)

7
A gentleman, by Samuel Cooper, signed and dated 1651, on vellum, 4.9cm (1⅞in), *L 8 July,* £2,750 ($3,822)

8
A Knight of the Garter, by Peter Cross, *c.*1680, 3.5cm (1½in), *L 4 Dec,* £638 ($994)

9
An officer, by Richard Crosse, *c.*1775, gold frame inset with diamonds, 3.5cm (1½in), *L 4 Dec,* £715 ($1,058)

10
A gentleman, by Richard Crosse, *c.*1780, 6cm (2⅜in), *L 11 Mar,* £462 ($527)

11
A gentleman, stated to be F. A. Sage, by Thomas Seir Cummings, 1838, 6.5cm (2½in), *NY 10 June,* $1,045 (£829)

12
A young lady, by Moritz Michael Daffinger, signed *c.*1820, watercolour on card, 7.4cm (2⅞in), *L 8 July,* £825 ($1,146)

Augustin, Jean Baptiste Jacques, d.Paris 1832

Bertrand, Vincent, b.1770, fl.Paris

Bone, Henry Pierce, 1779-1855, London

Chinnery, George, b.London 1774, d.Macao 1852

Comerford, John, b.Kilkenny *c.*1779, d.Dublin 1832

Cooper, Alexander, b.*c.*1605, d.Stockholm 1660, fl.Holland & England

Cooper, Samuel, 1609-72, England

Cosway, Richard, b.Devon 1743, d.London 1821

Cross, Peter, *c.*1645-1724, England

Crosse, Richard, 1742-1820 Devon

Cummings, Thomas Seir, b.Bath 1804, d.New Jersey 1894

Daffinger, Moritz Michael, 1790-1849, Vienna

1

2

3

4

5

6

7

8

9

10

11

12

1
A young lady, by Arthur Devis, signed and dated 1748, oil on card, 5cm (2in), *L 4 Dec,*
£1,540 ($2,279)

2
A gentleman, bearing signature 'Dumont', 6.5cm (2½in), *G 14 Nov,*
SF 990 (£324; $454)

3
A young lady, in the manner of Dumont, *c.*1795, 5.4cm (2in), *G 16 May,*
SF 990 (£289; $384)

4
Gurney Barclay, Esq., (1786-1820), by John Cox Dillman Engleheart, signed and dated 1820, 8.9cm (3½in), *L 8 July,*
£638 ($886)

5
Mrs William Stevens of Cowley, by John Cox Dillman Engleheart, *c.*1815, 8.6cm (3⅜in), *L 11 Mar,*
£330 ($376)

6
Mrs Ellen Thistlewaite by George Engleheart, *c.*1785, 5.3cm (2¹in), *L 11 Mar,*
£748 ($853)

7
A cavalry officer, by George Engleheart, *c.*1790, 7cm (2¾in), *L 4 Dec,*
£792 ($1,172)

8
A gentleman, by George Engleheart, *c.*1785, 5.5cm (2¼in), *L 4 Dec,*
£550 ($814)

9
A young lady, by Madame Sophie Feytaud, signed and dated 1831, 9.6cm (3¾in), *G 16 May,*
SF 1,870 (£546; $726)

10
Emperor Franz I of Austria, by E. *** Bernhard Chevalier de Guérard, signed *c.*1805, 8.5cm (3¼in), *L 4 Dec,*
£1,705 ($2,523)

11
Mary Brodie, by Charles Hayter, signed and dated 1796, 8.5cm (3⅜in), *L 8 July,*
£418 ($581)

12
Archduke Henry and Archduchess Amalie of Austria, by Josef Heigel, *c.*1800, 6.5cm (2½in) diam., *L 4 Dec,*
£770 ($1,140)

13
A young lady, by Joseph Highmore, signed and dated 1732, oil on copper, 11cm (4¼in), *L 4 Dec,*
£4,840 ($7,163)

14
Sarah Siddons, by Horace Hone, signed and dated 1785, 9cm (3½in), *L 4 Dec,*
£2,420 ($3,582)

15
A gentleman, by Horace Hone, signed and dated 1818, 8.5cm (3½in), *L 4 Dec,*
£352 ($521)

Daniel, Abraham, d.Plymouth 1806, fl.Bath

Daniel, Joseph, b.1760, d.Bath 1803, fl.Bristol, Bath & London

Devis, Arthur, b.Preston 1711, d.London 1787

Dumont, François, b.Luneville 1751, d.Paris 1831

Engleheart, George, 1750/53-1829, London

Engleheart, John Cox Dillman, b.Kew 1782/4, d.Tunbridge Wells 1862 fl.London

Feytaud, Sophie, fl.Bordeaux *c.*1830

Guérard, E. Bernhard Chevalier de, d.Naples 1836, fl.Vienna

Hayter, Charles, 1761-1835, fl.London

Heigel, Joseph, b.Munich 1780, d.Paris 1837

Highmore, Joseph, b.London 1693, d.Canterbury 1780

Hone, Horace, 1754/6-1825, London

1   2   3
4   5   6
7   8   9
10   11   12
13   14   15

1
Captain Martin, by Nathaniel Hone, signed and dated 1757, 3.5cm (1½in), *L 4 Dec*, £462 ($684)

2
A gentleman, by Nathaniel Hone, signed and dated 1764, enamel, 4.5cm (1¾in), *L 11 Mar*, £968 ($1,104)

3
Hortense de Beauharnais, (1783-1837) who married Louis, later King of Holland, in 1802, by Victor Hubert, *c.*1805, 8cm (3in), *G 14 Nov*, SF 1,210 (£395; $553)

4
A young lady, by Ozias Humphry, *c.*1770, 3.9cm (1½in), *L 11 Mar*, £396 ($451)

5
A gentleman, by Philip Jean, *c.*1780, 6cm (2½in), *L 4 Dec*, £550 ($814)

6
A young lady, by James Leakey, *c.*1805, 7.2cm (2⅞in), *L 11 Mar*, £484 ($552)

7
Alexander I, Emperor of Russia, by Jacques-Marie Le Gros, *c.*1818, 6.1cm (2½in), *G 16 May*, SF 1,870 (£546; $726)

8
A gentleman, attributed to Edward G. Malbone, *c.*1800, 8cm (3in), *NY 10 June*, $1,485 (£1,178)

9
A young lady, by Jeremiah Meyer, *c.*1775, 4cm (1½in), *L 4 Dec*, £638 ($944)

10
A gentleman, by Jeremiah Meyer, *c.*1780, 5.5cm (2¼in), *L 4 Dec*, £2,420 ($3,730)

11
Henry Frederick, Prince of Wales, by Isaac Oliver, signed with monogram in gold, *c.*1610, on vellum, 5cm (2in), *L 11 Mar*, £6,380 ($7,273)

12
A young lady, by Charles Antoine Claude Berny d'Ouville, *c.*1815, set within the lid of a gold mounted burr walnut box, 5.7cm (2¼in), *L 11 Mar*, £1,485 ($1,698)

13
A gentleman, by Charles Antoine Claude Berny d'Ouville, *c.*1835, 10.5cm (4in), *G 16 May*, SF 935 (£273; $363)

14
A young man, by Charles Antoine Claude Berny d'Ouville, signed and dated 1836, 11.4cm (4½in), *G 16 May*, SF 1,760 (£514; $683)

15
A young lady, by Peter Paillou, *c.*1810, 6.3cm (2½in), *L 8 July*, £330 ($458)

Hone, Nathaniel, b.Dublin 1718, d.London 1774

Humphry, Ozias, b.Devon 1742, d.London 1810

Jean, Philip, b.Jersey 1755, d.Kent 1802, fl.India & London

Leakey, James, b.Exeter 1775, d.1865

Le Gros, Jacques Marie, b.Haiti, fl.Paris

Malbone, Edward G., b.Newport R.I. 1777, d.Savannah 1807

Meyer, Jeremiah, b.Tübingen 1735, d.Kew 1789

Mosnier, Jean-Laurent, b.1743, fl.Paris, London & St. Petersburg

Oliver, Isaac, b.before 1568, d.1617, fl.England & Italy

d'Ouville, Charles Antoine Claude Berny, b.*c.*1775, d.1842, fl.Paris

Paillou, Peter, b.*c.*1757, d.after 1831, fl.Glasgow & London

1   2   3
4   5   6
7   8   9
10   11   12
13   14   15

1
A gentleman, by Raphael Peale, *c.*1810, 7cm (2¾in), *NY 10 June,* $1,320 (£1,047)

2
A gentleman, by Thomas Peat, *c.*1790, 5.6cm (2¼in), *L 11 Mar,* £374 ($426)

3
A young lady, by Andrew Plimer, *c.*1795, 6.5cm (2½in), *L 4 Dec,* £825 ($1,221)

4
A young lady, by Andrew Plimer, *c.*1795, set within the lid of a gold mounted contemporary tortoiseshell box, 7.5cm (3in), *L 4 Dec,* £902 ($1,335)

5
A young man, by Andrew Plimer, *c.*1800, 7.5cm (3in), *L 4 Dec,* £770 ($1,140)

6
A young lady, by Andrew Plimer, *c.*1800, gold frame inset with pearls, 7.5cm (3in), *L 4 Dec,* £880 ($1,302)

7
An officer of infantry, by Nathaniel Plimer, *c.*1795, 7cm (2¾in), *L 4 Dec,* £1,045 ($1,547)

8
A gentleman, stated to be Mr Vanderoot, by Nathaniel Rogers, *c.*1825, 7cm (2¾in), *NY 10 June,* $935 (£742)

9
A lady, attributed to Nanette Rosenzweig, *c.*1820, 7.5cm (3in), *NY 10 June,* $605 (£408)

10
A young lady, by Sir William Charles Ross, *c.*1840, in ormolu frame, cast by Miers & Co., 20cm (7⅞in), *L 8 July,* £6,380 ($8,868)

11
A Russian officer, by Pietro de Rossi, signed *c.*1815, 6.5cm (2½in), *L 4 Dec,* £1,870 ($2,768)

12
A young lady, by Jean Andre Rouquet, *c.*1750, enamel, 3.5cm (1¼in), *G 14 Nov,* SF 3,520 (£1,150; $1,610)

13
A gentleman, by Pierre Rouvier, signed and dated 1789, 5cm (2in), *G 14 Nov,* SF 2,640 (£863; $1,208)

14
James Simon Adam Fordate, by Karl von Saar, signed and dated 1836, 10.1cm (4in), *L 11 Mar,* £550 ($627)

15
A gentleman, in the manner of Karl von Saar, *c.*1820, 9.5cm (3¾in), *NY 10 June,* $660 (£523)

Peale, Raphael, b.Annapolis 1774, d.Philadelphia 1825

Peat, Thomas, fl. 1791-1831, London & Glasgow

Plimer, Andrew, b.Shropshire 1764, d.Brighton 1837

Plimer, Nathaniel, b.Shropshire 1757, d.Brighton 1822

Rogers, Nathaniel, 1788-1844, Bridge-hampton, Long Island

Rosenzweig, Nanette, fl. 1820s, Austria

Ross, William Charles, 1794/5-1860, London

Rossi, Pietro de, 1761-1831, St. Petersburg

Rouquet, Jean Andre, b.Geneva 1701, d.Charenton 1758, fl. London & Paris

Rouvier, Pierre, fl. Paris after 1742

Saar, Karl von, 1797-1853, Vienna

1
A gentleman, by Henry Spicer, c.1780, enamel, 5.5cm (2¼in), L 4 Dec, £506 ($749)

2
A young lady, by Peter Edward Stroely, c.1800, 7.5cm (3in), G 14 Nov, SF 1,980 (£647; $906)

3
A young lady, by Adalbert Suchy, signed c.1825, 7cm (2¾in), L 4 Dec, £880 ($1,302)

4
Charles Henry, 6th Duke of Richmond and Lennox, (1818-1903) by Robert Thorburn, 13.5cm (5¼in), L 4 Dec, £495 ($733)

5
Catherine the Great, probably by Augustus Toussaint, signed with monogram and dated 1765, enamel, 6cm (2⅜in), L 8 July, £605 ($840)

6
A gentleman, by Jean François Marie Huet-Villiers, signed and dated 1806, 5.4cm (2⅛in), L 11 Mar, £462 ($527)

7
A gentleman, by Christian Friedrich Zincke, c.1730, enamel, gold frame inset with diamonds, 4.5cm (1¾in), L 4 Dec, £1,320 ($1,954)

8
A lady and gentleman, in the manner of Zincke, c.1720, enamel, 5.5cm (2¼in), L 4 Dec, £3,520 ($5,210)

9
A young lady, by Christian Friedrich Zincke, c.1730, enamel, 4.4cm (1¾in), L 11 Mar, £1,100 ($1,254)

10
Thomas Budgen, by Christian Friedrich Zincke, c.1725, enamel, 4.4cm (1¾in), L 11 Mar, £462 ($527)

11
William Savage Esq., by Christian Friedrich Zincke, c.1725, enamel, 4cm (1½in), G 14 Nov, SF 1,870 (£611; $855)

12
A gentleman, French School, c.1750, 6.3cm (2½in), L 8 July, £495 ($688)

13
A musician stated to be Francesco Solo, Italian School, c.1770, 5.5cm (2¼in), NY 10 June, $770 (£611)

14
A French officer of field rank, Italian School, c.1796, pointing at a map of the Italian province of Lodi, where Napoleon defeated the Austrians on 10 May 1796, 6.1cm (2⅜in), L 8 July, £968 ($1,345)

15
Madame Beaumoir, French School, c.1825, 4.5cm (1¾in), L 11 Mar, £374 ($426)

Smart, John, b.1742/3, d.London 1811, fl. India & England

Snelling, Matthew, b.Kings Lynn 1621, d.1678, fl. London

Spicer, Henry, b.Norfolk 1743, d.London 1804

Stroely, Peter Edward, b.Dusseldorf, 1768, d.London after 1826

Suchy, Adalbert, b.Bohemia 1783, d.Vienna 1849

Thorburn, Robert, 1818-1885, fl. Scotland & London

Thouron, Jacques, b.Geneva 1760, d.Paris 1789

Toussaint, Augustus, b.London c.1750, d.c.1800

Zincke, Christian Friedrich, b.Dresden 1683/4, d.London 1767

Silhouettes

A silhouette is an extremely individual form of portraiture and is, in every sense, the most economical method of taking a likeness. Its strength, and its attraction, rests on the total elimination of all unnecessary detail and the fascinating contrast of both light and shade.

The market for silhouettes had not risen dramatically until Sotheby's offered the collection of the late Leonard Morgan-May in February 1985. This collection was the most comprehensive to have appeared on the market for at least ten years and the prices paid for most of the works offered were far above those expected. However, silhouettes may be bought for figures from £70-£500 ($100 to $700) in usual circumstances—which make them amongst the least expensive of 18th and 19th century works of art available today.

Silhouette portraiture was among the earliest to be practised. According to the Roman writer Pliny, it was a young lady from Corinth who outlined the shadow of her lover's profile on a sunlit wall and thus created the first shadow portrait. Although a shadow portrait of William III and Mary is said to have been taken in the 17th century, it was not until about 1780 that a definite school of British silhouette artists emerged.

Beetham, Mrs Isabella, c.1752-1825
Started cutting silhouettes in paper c.1774, went on to paint profiles on card, plaster, ivory and glass. Worked in London.

Buncombe, Charles, fl.1795-1830
Painted profiles on card or paper, mainly of officers. Worked in Newport, Isle of Wight.

Buncombe, John, fl.1820-30
Son of Charles, worked in Newport, Isle of Wight.

Bruce, George, fl.c.1792-1837
Worked on ivory and plaster, in Edinburgh.

Clarke, W, fl.1780-81
Painted on card coated with plaster, in Chester, Harrogate and Durham.

Field, Henry William, 1810-82
Son of John, worked with him at Mier's studio until father and son set up business together c.1830. Worked on card, paper and ivory, in London.

Field, John, 1772-1848
Assistant to John Miers, c.1791; see above entry.

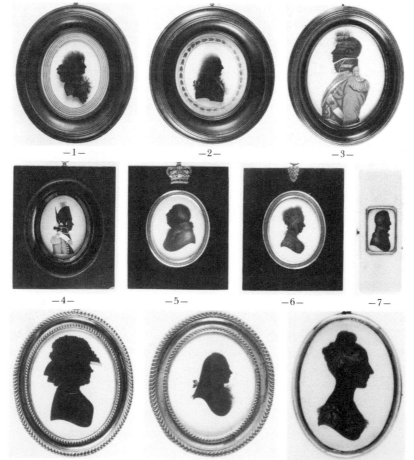

—1—
Mrs Isabella Beetham,
a young lady, c.1790, painted on convex glass against a plaster ground, turned wood frame, 9.6cm (3¾in), L 22 Feb, **£858 ($978)**

—2—
Mrs Isabella Beetham,
a gentleman, c.1785, painted on convex glass against a plaster ground, turned wood frame, 9.6cm (3¾in), L 22 Feb, **£1,078 ($1,229)**

—3—
In the manner of Charles Buncombe, a coloured profile of an officer of the 79th Foot, turned wood frame, 10cm (4in), L 22 Feb, **£440 ($502)**

—4—
Charles Buncombe, a coloured profile of Nunn Davie, an officer in the Life Guards, c.1795, painted on paper, papier-mâché frame, 12cm (4¾in), L 22 Feb, **£902 ($1,028)**

—5—
John Field, King George III, dated 1812, painted on plaster, papier-mâché frame, 7.6cm (3in), L 22 Feb, **£1,485 ($1,693)**

—6—
John Field, a bronzed profile of a lady, c.1820, painted on plaster, papier-mâché frame, 7.6cm (3in), L 22 Feb, **£330 ($376)**

—7—
John Field, a bronzed profile of an officer, signed Miers, c.1805, painted on ivory, set within the lid of a gold-mounted ivory patch box, L 22 Feb, **£440 ($502)**

—8—
W*** Clarke, a lady, c.1780, painted on plaster-coated card, hammered brass frame, 8.6cm (3½in), L 22 Feb, **£374 ($426)**

—9—
George Bruce, a gentleman, c.1795, painted on convex plaster, hammered brass frame, 7.3cm (2⅞in), L 22 Feb, **£396 ($451)**

—10—
John Field, a bronzed profile of a lady, signed Miers, c.1810, painted on ivory, gold pendant frame, 3.5cm (1⅜in), L 22 Feb, **£242 ($277)**

However, the Golden Age of the silhouette artist was, in comparison with that of the miniature painter, a short one, and collectors of silhouettes usually restrict their collecting period from 1770 to 1825. There were over three hundred professional artists practising at this time and on top of that, literally hundreds more who enjoyed amateur status. It is the work of these amateurs that the collector might avoid in many respects because the silhouettes tend to be in poor condition, partly as a result of being unframed: they were gummed into the family scrapbook without documentation.

Frames are an important part of a silhouette and should not be considered separately. Fortunately a large number of artists made their own frames, which included a trade label, rendering authentication fairly simple.

Amongst the earliest artists was Mrs Sarah Harrington, who placed an advertisement in the *Leeds Mercury* in November 1776 announcing that she 'takes likenesses' at 2/6d. She cut from paper, using common scissors and even the eyelashes were made with precise 'snips'. Mrs Harrington was a 'hollow-cut' artist meaning that she cut the portrait out of a sheet of white paper and placed another sheet of black paper behind the portrait. Fig. 14 shows a typical example of her style, mounted in the type of brass frame associated with her work.

Although the labours of the paper cutter silhouette artists were generally less expensive, the best can be acquired today for as little as £100 ($140).

Gibbs, Hinton, fl.late 1790s-c.1822
Worked on glass, in London.

Hamlet, William the elder, fl.1785-1816
Worked on card and glass, in Bath.

Hamlet, William the Younger, fl.1779-1816
Son of the above, used his father's trade label. Worked on card, paper and glass, in Bath.

Harrington, Mrs Sarah, fl.1774-87(?)
In 1775 patented the first recorded machine for taking profiles. Cut profiles in paper and painted on card and silk.

Hervé, Henry I., fl.c.1800-20
Worked on card, glass, plaster and ivory, as well as cutting paper, in London.

Kelfe, Mrs M. Lane, fl.c.1778-94
Painted profiles on card or paper, ivory and glass.

Lea, Arthur, 1768-1828
Painted under the surface of convex glass backed with a slab of plaster. fl.1799-1818.

Lewis, T, fl.c.1808-1830s
Worked on card or paper.

London, T, 1798-c.1810
Worked on paper and ivory, in Kidderminster and Worcester.

Miers, John, c.1758-1810
Painted on card, plaster and ivory. Worked in Leeds, then London.

—11—
A profile of a young lady of the Gosset family, c.1780, painted on paper, wood frame, 29.2cm (11½in), L 22 Feb, £2,145 ($2,445)

—12—
Henry Hervé, a bronzed profile of a young lady, c.1805, painted on plaster, papier-mâché frame, 8.5cm (3⅜in), L 22 Feb, £396 ($451)

—13—
William Hamlet the elder, a profile of William, 1st Marquess of Lansdowne, inscribed on the reverse and dated 1785, painted on flat glass, gilt-gesso frame, 22.3cm (8¾in), L 22 Feb, £990 ($1,129)

—14—
Mrs Sarah Harrington, a hollow-cut profile of a gentleman, c.1785, hammered frame, 10.1cm (4in), L 22 Feb, £396 ($451)

—15—
Attributed to T* Lewis,** a profile of a young girl, c.1835, painted against a wash landscape, gilt-gesso frame, 11.1cm (3⅜in), L 21 Oct, £242 ($363)

—16—
Mrs M* Lane Kelfe,** a lady, signed and dated Bath 1784 on the verso, painted on paper, turned wood frame, 9cm (3½in), L 22 Feb, £308 ($351)

—17—
Arthur Lea, General Pedizler, c.1815, painted on convex glass against a plaster ground, 9cm (3½in), verre églomisé border, turned wood frame, 9cm (3½in), L 22 Feb, £1,595 ($1,818)

—18—
John Miers, a pair of profiles of Rev. and Mrs Wood, c.1783, painted on plaster, terracotta frames, L 22 Feb, £605 ($690)

—19—
John Miers, The Countess of Hardwick, c.1815, painted on plaster, turned wood frame, 8.4cm (3¼in), L 22 Feb, £418 ($477)

—11— —12— —13— —14— —15— —16— —17— —18— —19—

Mrs Isabella Beetham, Mrs Harrington's mother, was both a cutter of paper and a painter on the underside of glass, and was probably the first professional shadow painter of all time. Her husband, formerly an actor, made a handsome fortune by inventing the roller mangle and his ingenuity was also responsible for the wonderfully decorated glasses which in some cases surround her profiles.

Silhouettes on glass were very much a German fashion however, and the precious little glass painted profiles, often conversational in concept, with a gold background, are both rare and expensive, (fig. 30). The rarity is, in part, due to their considerable delicacy, since a broken glass silhouette is irreparable and worthless.

The most sought after silhouettes amongst collectors today are those of the 18th century painted on glass; that is to say the work of Mrs Beetham, Jacob Spornberg, Hinton Gibbs, Charles Rosenberg, and William Hamlet, and also those quite superb German and Viennese examples with a black profile, against a gold ground.

Examples of coloured silhouettes, which in itself is almost a contradiction, were also popular in the 1780s and artists such as William Phelps and John Buncombe, to mention the two most prolific, are highly sought after. Prices for these vary between

Miers, William, 1793-1863
Son of John. Framemaker and engraver of metal and seals, profilist on paper and card. In partnership with John Field 1828-29, in London.

Phelps, W, fl.1784-c.1791
Worked on card, paper, glass and plaster, in London.

Rosenberg, Charles, 1745-1844
Probably Austrian by birth, arrived in England 1761. Profile painter to King George III. Worked on paper and glass, in Bath.

Spornberg, Jacob, 1768-after 1840
Worked on glass, in Bath.

Thomason, J, fl. 1786-c.1800
Painted on plaster, ivory and glass. Worked in the north of England and Dublin, probably also in London and Scotland.

Torond, Francis, c.1743-1812
Of French origin. Worked on paper and card until 1786, in London, Bath and perhaps Exeter.

Wellings, William, fl.1778-96
Worked on card or paper and ivory, in London.

Wheeler, Thomas, fl.c.1783-1810(?)
Painted on plaster, paper and glass, also miniatures.

—20—
John Miers, a young lady, c.1805, signed, painted on ivory, gold pendant frame, 4cm (1½in), *L 22 Feb,* **£220 ($251)**

—21—
John Miers, a gentleman, c.1780, painted on ivory, cracked, gold pendant frame, 5.7cm (2¼in), *L 22 Feb,* **£418 ($477)**

—22—
W* Phelps,** Miss Mary Ann Lovell as a child, 1786, painted on plaster, hammered brass frame, 8.5cm (3⅜in), *L 22 Feb,* **£935 ($1,066)**

—23—
Jacob Spornberg, an Etruscan profile of a lady of the Anstey family, signed and dated Bath 1793, painted on convex glass, with Greek-style border, giltwood frame, 8.6cm (3⅜in), *L 22 Feb,* **£990 ($1,129)**

—24—
Jacob Spornberg, an Etruscan profile of Captain W. Sotheby, signed and dated Bath 1793, painted on convex glass, giltwood frame, 8.9cm (3½in), *L 22 Feb,* **£2,860 ($3,260)**

—25—
J* Thomason,** a profile of Miss Ruth Leslie, c.1790, painted on plaster, hammered brass frame, 8.9cm (3½in), *L 21 Oct,* **£143 ($215)**

—26—
Francis Torond, a profile of a gentleman, c.1785, signed, painted on card, 9.6cm (3¾in), *L 21 Oct,* **£407 ($611)**

—27—
Francis Torond, a conversational profile of a lady and gentleman, c.1780, signed, painted on paper, giltwood and gesso frame, the reverse with Bath frame maker's label, 43cm (17in), *L 22 Feb,* **£6,160 ($7,022)**

—20— —21— —22—
—23— —24— —25—
—26— —27—

£500 ($700) and £1,000 ($1,400). John Buncombe, of Isle of Wight fame, painted the faces in black and coloured the naval uniforms—a pleasing and most striking likeness thus evolved.

No article on silhouettes would be complete without mention of one of the most esteemed painters of profile portraits, John Miers, who was born in Leeds in about 1758. He began work in his native town and after a protracted tour of many of the principal cities of Britain, eventually settled in London in 1788. Miers specialised in painting delicately shaded portraits on specially prepared ovals of white plaster of Paris. His frames of pinchbeck, papier mâché or lustrous wood were in the most perfect taste, and often backed with his highly informative and detailed trade label. The silhouette of the Countess of Hardwick, c.1815, (fig.19) is a good example of his work, but although it realised a high sum (£418; $477), profiles by Miers usually realise as little as £150 ($210).

Works on plaster, although quite common, command high prices. However, the highly successful business of John Miers produced such vast quantities of his work that unless they are of top quality in every respect (including the frame and trade label) they are almost too common to demand competitive prices today.

Miers died in 1821, but his very extensive business was continued by his son, William, in partnership with his famous pupil, John Field—one of the most notable exponents of shading with bronze paint to pronounce the textiles. The bronzed silhouette by John Field of King George III, dated 1812, (fig. 5) is a typical 'bronzed' example of his work.

At its outset, profile taking was a dignified art, but slowly its status became tarnished by various tawdry innovations, until it deteriorated into a kind of side-show, where an adroit 'scissor man' supplied black portraits at great speed from pieces of paper and mounted the result on white card for sixpence a time! By 1830, the fine and detailed paintings on glass and plaster of

Paris, card and glass, were gone: gone too was the superb artistry of master craftsmen. In exchange, patrons had to be content with an uninspired black and white silhouette. By 1840 the photograph, or Daguerreotype, was favoured for its accuracy and the art of the silhouette was rebutted as uncommercial.

● RICHARD ALLEN ●

Further reading

Sue McKechnie, *British Silhouette Artists and their Work, 1760-1860*, 1978

Arthur Mayne, *British Profile Miniaturists*, 1970

—28—

—30—
Continental School, a verre églomisé profile of a gentleman, c.1780, painted on a gold medallion, ebonised frame, 14cm (5½in), *L 22 Feb*, £462 ($527)

—31—
Continental School, a verre églomisé profile of a lady, c.1780, painted on a gold medallion, ebonised frame, 14cm (5½in), *L 22 Feb*, £462 ($527)

—32—
Continental School, a double-sided verre églomisé profile of a lady and gentleman, c.1790, on gold ground, 3.2cm (1¼in), *L 22 Feb*, £242 ($276)

—33—
Thomas Wheeler, a young lady, c.1790, painted on plaster, hammered brass frame, 9.5cm (3¾in), *L 22 Feb*, £220 ($251)

—34—
Continental School, a double-sided verre églomisé profile of a lady and gentleman, c.1780, on gold ground, gold pendant frame, 3.2cm (1¼in), *L 22 Feb*, £330 ($376)

—28—
William Wellings, a profile of William Pitt (1759-1806), signed and dated 1781, painted on paper, giltwood frame, Pitt is holding his speech in support of Fox's motion for peace with the American colonies, which he delivered on 12 June 1781, 26.6cm (10½in), *L 22 Feb*, £2,640 ($3,010)

—29—
William Wellings, a profile of John, Earl of St Vincent, (1735-1823) signed and dated 1783, Loughborough Hall shown in the distance, painted on paper, within verre églomisé border, giltwood frame, 28.3cm (11¼in), *L 22 Feb*, £2,860 ($3,260)

—29—

—30—

—31—

—32—

—33—

—34—

Russian Works of Art

Article ● Russian cloisonńe enamel 1880-1917 *pp 436-439* *See also* ● Colour illustrations *p 490*

1
A glass portrait tumbler,
Imperial or Bakmetyev
Glass Manufactory,
*c.*1820, with a portrait
of Count Platov, 10.5cm
(4¼in), *L 20 Feb,*
£935 ($1,075)

2
**A lacquered papier-mâché
box,** Lukutin, *c.*1830,
painted with dancing
peasants and a balalaika
player, slight chips,
13.5cm (5¼in) wide,
L 20 Feb,
£550 ($633)

3
A lacquer box, *c.*1849,
oval, painted with two
chess players, some
chips, 8.5cm (3¼in),
L 20 Feb,
£440 ($506)

4
**A biscuit figure of a
peasant,** Gardner fac-
tory, late 19th century,
right arm re-glued,
14cm (5½in), *L 12 June,*
£264 ($351)

5
An Imperial wine glass,
Imperial Glass Manu-
factory, *c.*1910, the bowl
engraved and gilt with
the cypher of Emperor
Nicholas II, for use on
the Imperial yacht
Standart, 15.5cm (6in)
high, *L 12 June,*
£605 ($805)

6
Four porcelain figures,
19th century, *c.*1900, a
young woman and a
balalaika player both by
Gardner, a figure in
16th century dress by
Popov, and a group of
Georgians by Kuznetsov,
heights 18.5 to 28cm
(7¼ to 11in), *NY 11 Dec,*
$1,870 (£1,326)

7
**Two Russian porcelain
groups,** Gardner, late
19th century, heights 25
and 20.5cm (9 and
8¼in), *NY 11 June,*
$935 (£742)

8
**A Russian porcelain
group: 'Three Tipsy Men',**
Gardner, late 19th
century, 24.5cm (9½in)
high, *NY 11 June,*
$1,350 (£1,134)

9
**A Russian porcelain group
of a Polish couple,**
Gardner, late 19th
century, 26.5cm (10½in)
high, *NY 11 June,*
$990 (£785)

10
**Five Russian porcelain
figures,** 19th century,
heights 17 to 18.5cm (6¾
to 7¼in), *NY 11 Dec,*
$2,475 (£1,755)

1613-1645	Michael I
1645-1676	Alexis I
1676-1682	Feodor II
1682-1725	Peter I
1725-1727	Catherine I
1727-1730	Peter II
1730-1740	Anna I
1740-1741	Ivan VI
1741-1762	Elizabeth
1762	Peter III
1762-1796	Catherine II
1796-1801	Paul I
1801-1825	Alexander I
1825-1855	Nicholas I
1855-1881	Alexander II
1881-1894	Alexander III
1894-1917	Nicholas II

1
An Imperial porcelain Easter egg, 1900, with the cypher of Empress Alexandra Feodorovna and sprays of pink roses within grey laurel, 8.5cm (3¼in), *L 12 June*, £330 ($439)

2
An Imperial porcelain egg, late 19th century, painted on one side with St. George and the Dragon and on the other with the veil of St Veronica, unmarked, 9cm (3½in), *G 16 May*, SF 935 (£273; $363)

3
An Imperial porcelain cup and saucer, period of Nicholas I, the cup with a portrait of Nicholas I by Lifantiev, signed and dated 1843, *L 20 Feb*, £1,433 ($1,648)

4
A Russian Imperial wine cooler from the cabinet service, period of Catherine the Great, each side with an Italianate scene, 18cm (7in) high, *NY 11 June*, $2,530 (£2,007)

5
A porcelain egg, late 19th century, the white ground painted with violets, unmarked, 10.5cm (4in) high, *G 16 May*, SF 385 (£113; $150)

6
An Imperial porcelain dish, 1910, with later painting, the border inscribed 'We celebrate while working 1. May 1920', marked with the cypher of Nicholas II and overglaze blue mark of the Lomonosov Factory, Petrograd, 1920, 28cm (11in), *L 20 Feb*, £715 ($822)

7
Three Imperial porcelain cups with saucers, period of Alexander III, each one later painted with Soviet propaganda and inscribed '25 October 1917', and marked with the cypher of Alexander III and overglaze blue mark of the Lomonosov Factory, Petrograd, 1922, *L 20 Feb*, £3,300 ($3,795)

8
An Imperial porcelain plate, *c.*1900, the centre later painted with a hammer and sickle amid brightly coloured flowers, marked with the cypher of Nicholas II and overglaze blue mark of the Lomonosov Factory, Petrograd, 1920, 25cm (9¾in) diam., *L 20 Feb*, £825 ($949)

9
Eleven Russian Imperial porcelain dinner plates, period of Nicholas I *NY 11 Dec*, $2,860 (£2,028)

10
Twelve soup plates, the borders with the Imperial arms, each marked with the cypher of Nicholas I, one plate with chipped base, 24.5cm (9½in) diam., *L 20 Feb*, £12,100 ($13,915)

11
An Imperial porcelain plate from the Würtemberg service, *c.*1810, small chip, inner gilded border rubbed, marked with the underglaze blue cypher of Alexander I, 24cm (9½in) diam., *L 12 June*, £220 ($293)

12
A set of twelve Russian Imperial porcelain dinner plates, period of Nicholas I, 25cm (9¾in) diam., *NY 11 June*, $2,310 (£1,833)

13
A set of twelve Russian Imperial porcelain soup plates, period of Nicholas II; sold with a pair of Popov porcelain fruit serving plates, mid-19th century, 25.5cm (10in) diam., *NY 11 June*, $1,320 (£1,047)

1
A silver covered beaker,
Moscow, 175?, 21.5cm
(8½in) high, *NY 14 Feb*,
$825 (£711)

2
**A group of four silver
beakers,** second half of
the 18th century,
G 16 May,
SF 3,300 (£965; $1,283)

3
A silver table cigar box,
Moscow, 1900, engraved
to simulate tax bands,
maker's mark unclear,
17cm (7¾in) wide,
NY 11 Dec,
$2,860 (£2,028)

4
**A silver and parcel-gilt
trompe l'oeil table cigar
box,** Khlebnikov, Mos-
cow, 1908-17, engraved
to simulate woodgrain
and taxbands, 17.5cm
(7in) wide, *G 14 Nov*,
SF 6,050 (£1,977; $2,768)

5
**A silver and enamel
commemorative cigarette
case,** Moscow, late 19th
century, the case applied
with fifteen coats-of-
arms, the base with gold
signatures, 10.5cm
(4¼in) wide, *G 14 Nov*,
SF 4,400 (£1,438; $2,013)

6
A gold cigarette case, St.
Petersburg, late 19th
century, the lid with
white and red enamel
monogram and Imperial
crown, cabochon sapph-
ire thumbpiece, 9.5cm
(4in) wide, *G 14 Nov*,
SF 6,600 (£2,157; $3,020)

7
**A silver-gilt filigree cache-
pot,** C. F. B. Jörkman, St.
Petersburg, 1786, 11.5cm
(4½in), *G 16 May*,
SF 4,400 (£1,287; $1,712)

8
**A silver matching teapot
and hot water jug,**
Moscow, 1829, 17cm
(6¾in) high, *NY 11 June*,
$1,650 (£1,309)

9
**A silver ten-piece tea and
coffee set,** Nicholls and
Plincke, St. Petersburg,
1861/2, each piece with
the monogram 'MM'
below an Imperial
crown, probably for
Grand Duke Michal-
aevich, grandson of
Nicholas I, *NY 11 Dec*,
$8,250 (£5,851)

10
**A silver tea and coffee
service with tray,** Pavel
Fedorovich Sazikov,
Moscow, 1855, *F 29 May*,
L 7,000,000
(£2,724; $3,595)

11
A silver-gilt covered salt,
Moscow, 1859, the lid
surmounted by the
Russian Imperial eagle,
14.5cm (5¾in), *NY 14 Feb*,
$605 (£522)

12
**A pair of parcel-gilt
silver kovshi,** *c.*1900,
11.5cm (4½in) long,
NY 14 Feb,
$605 (£522)

13
A silver mug, Moscow,
1845, 12cm (4¾in) high,
M 25 June,
FF 5,550 (£458; $619)

14
A set of table silver
Grachev, St. Petersburg,
late 19th century,
comprising 87 pieces,
each piece mono-
grammed, *G 16 May*,
SF 17,600
(£5,146; $6,844)

15
A silver cake basket,
Ovchinnikov, Moscow,
1864, 28cm (11in) wide,
NY 11 June
$990 (£785)

1

A pair of silver wine coasters, C. Tengelsten, St. Petersburg, 1843, turned wood bases with initials and crest, 18cm (7in) diam., *G 16 May,* **SF 4,400** (£1,287; $1,712)

2

A silver-mounted cut-glass kovsh, G. Sbitndev, Moscow, *c.*1900, 43.5cm (17¼in) long, *G 14 Nov,* **SF 18,700** (£6,111; $8,556)

3

A pair of silver candelabra, Nicholls & Plincke, St. Petersburg, *c.*1880, 62cm (24½in), *NY 11 Dec,* $11,000 (£7,801)

4

A pair of silver candelabra, Ovchinnikov, Moscow, 1886, 21cm (8½in), *NY 11 June,* $1,760 (£1,396)

5

A silver samovar, Jacob Wiberg, Moscow, 1846, 56.5cm (22¼in), *NY 11 Dec,* $8,250 (£5,851)

6

A three-piece parcel-gilt tea service, G. Klingert, Moscow, 1890, each engraved to simulate raffia work, *L 20 Feb,* £1,320 ($1,518)

7

A silver trompe l'oeil vase, St. Petersburg, 1883, engraved to simulate basketwork, 10cm (4in), *G 16 May,* **SF 1,870** (£547; $728)

8

A silver trompe l'oeil caviar bowl, Nicholls & Plinke, St. Petersburg, 1885, engraved to similate a wickerwork basket, 11.5cm (4½in), *G 16 May,* **SF 4,180** (£1,222; $1,625)

9

A trompe l'oeil silver and glass vodka set, N. Yanichkin, St. Petersburg, *c.*1886, one glass liner replaced, *L 12 June,* £1,430 ($1,902)

10

A trompe l'oeil silver sugar bowl and cover, G. Ivanov, Moscow, 1869, the body engraved to simulate wickerwork and the cover a bound napkin, several dents, 9cm (3½in), *L 12 June,* £352 ($468)

11

A parcel-gilt cake basket, Khlebnikov, Moscow, 1878, chased to simulate basketweave with an overlaid napkin, 37.5cm (14¾in) wide, *NY 11 Dec,* $3,960 (£2,808)

12

A silver-gilt and niello beaker, Moscow, 1833, 8.5cm (3¼in), *G 16 May,* **SF 1,760** (£515; $685)

13

A silver and niello cigarette case, Moscow, 1887, slight dents, 8.5cm (3¼in) wide, *L 20 Feb,* £275 ($316)

14

A silver and niello snuff box, Moscow, 1826, the lid with representation of the monument to Minin and Pojharsky, some dents, 7cm (2¾in), *L 12 June,* £385 ($512)

15

A parcel-gilt and niello coffee pot, O. Kurliukov, Moscow, late 19th century, with medallions enclosing views of St Basil's Cathedral and a monument, 16cm (6¼in),, *G 16 May,* **SF 3,520** (£1,029; $1,369)

1
A Fabergé two-colour gold cigarette case, workmaster M. Perchin, St. Petersburg, late 19th century, 10.5cm (4¼in) wide, *L 28 Oct*, £3,520 ($5,245)

2
A Fabergé gold-mounted rock crystal and enamel box, workmaster M. Perchin, St. Petersburg, late 19th century, chipped, 5cm (2in), *L 28 Oct*, £4,620 ($6,884)

3
A Fabergé silver-gilt and enamel cigarette case, workmaster A. Hollming, St. Petersburg, 1908-17, enamelled in translucent white, chipped, 9cm (3½in), *G 16 May*, SF 5,720 (£1,673; $2,225)

4
A Fabergé two-colour gold and enamel sealing wax case, workmaster M. Perchin, St. Petersburg, late 19th century, enamelled in translucent pink, chipped, 12cm (4¾in) long, *G 16 May*, SF 9,350 (£2,734; $3,636)

5
A Fabergé gold and enamel desk timepiece, workmaster H. Wigström, St. Petersburg, late 19th century, with key, 7cm (2¾in), *G 16 May*, SF 18,700 (£5,468; $7,272)

6
A Fabergé gold-mounted enamel timepiece, workmaster M. Perchin, St. Petersburg, late 19th century, 12cm (4¾in), *G 16 May*, SF 38,500 (£11,257; $14,972)

7
A Fabergé silver-gilt, translucent powder blue enamel and jewelled cigarette case, workmaster August Holmström, St. Petersburg, *c.*1910, 9.5cm (3¾in) long, *NY 11 June*, $10,450 (£8,293)

8
A Fabergé silver-gilt and enamel kovsh, workmaster Anders Nevalainen, St. Petersburg, *c.*1890, 12cm (4¾in) long, *NY 11 Dec*, $7,150 (£5,070)

9
A miniature Easter egg pendant, *c.*1900, unmarked, probably Fabergé, with moonstone base and enamelled peach top, diamond-set borders, 2.5cm (1in) long, *NY 11 June*, $3,300 (£2,619)

10
A gold-mounted white and translucent red enamel miniature Easter egg, *c.*1900, 1.8cm (¾in) high, *G 14 Nov*, SF 6,050 (£1,977; $2,768)

11
A Fabergé jewelled gold-mounted enamel buckle, workmaster M. Perchin, St. Petersburg, late 19th century, presented to Queen Louisa of Denmark by Empress Marie Feodorovna, 7.5cm (3in), *G 16 May*, SF 8,800 (£2,573; $3,422)

12
A Fabergé gold, silver and enamel match case, workmaster Fyodor Afanassiev, St. Petersburg, *c.*1900, enamelled in green, black and white stripes, 4.5cm (1¾in) high, *NY 11 Dec*, $4,400 (£3,120)

13
A Fabergé silver-gilt and translucent enamel miniature cup, workmaster Anders Nevalainen, St. Petersburg, *c.*1900, 4cm (1½in) high, *NY 11 Dec*, $6,600 (£4,680)

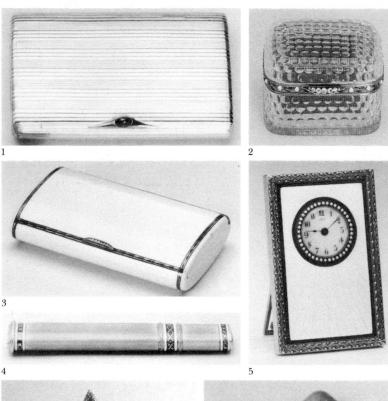

1

2

3

4

5

6

7

8

9

10

11

12

13

1
A Fabergé nephrite, silver and enamel bell push, workmaster Johan Victor Aarne, St. Petersburg, c.1900, 5.5cm (2¼in) wide, *NY 11 Dec,* $4,675 (£3,315)

2
A Fabergé silver-gilt pencil-holder, Moscow, 1899-1908, 4.5cm (1¾in) high, *G 14 Nov,* SF 2,640 (£863; $1,208)

3
A Fabergé silver and nephrite charka, St. Petersburg, c.1897, 9cm (3½in), *NY 11 Dec,* $6,050 (£4,290)

4
A Fabergé jewelled gold and hardstone forget-me-not spray, workmaster H. Wigström, St. Petersburg, late 19th century, 8.5cm (3¼in), *L 20 Feb,* £11,550 ($13,282)

5
Three Fabergé silver-mounted cut-glass toilet jars, workmaster Julius Rappoport, St. Petersburg, c.1900, 16 & 14.5cm (6¼ & 5¾in), *NY 11 Dec,* $4,620 (£3,276)

6
A Fabergé gold and jewelled moustache-comb, workmaster M. Perchin, St. Petersburg, c.1890, 6cm (2½in), *NY 11 Dec,* $3,850 (£2,730)

7
A pair of Fabergé silver-mounted glass claret jugs, Moscow, c.1900, 38cm (15in), *NY 11 June,* $8,525 (£6,765)

8
A pair of Fabergé gold and enamel cufflinks, workmaster Wilhelm Reimer, St. Petersburg, c.1890, *NY 11 Dec,* $2,750 (£1,950)

9
A Fabergé silver sugar basket, Moscow, c.1910, 11cm (4¼in), *NY 11 Dec,* $2,475 (£1,755)

10
A Fabergé gold and nephrite miniature bowl, workmaster M. Perchin, St. Petersburg, late 19th century, 13cm (5in), *G 16 May,* SF 18,700 (£5,468; $7,272)

11
A Fabergé silver-mounted ceramic bowl, workmaster Andrei Gorianov, St. Petersburg, c.1900, 7cm (2¾in) diam., *NY 11 June,* $1,430 (£1,134)

12
A Fabergé silver pin tray, workmaster Stephan Wäkevä, Moscow, 1900, 14.5cm (5¾in), *NY 11 June,* $1,430 (£1,134)

13
A carved rock crystal, gold, silver and jewelled parasol handle, c.1900, unmarked, probably Fabergé, 7cm (2¾in) high, *NY 11 Dec,* $4,400 (£3,120)

14
A Fabergé jewelled hard-stone desk pad, work-master H. Wigström, St. Petersburg, 1908-17, 20.5cm (8in), *L 28 Oct,* £14,300 ($21,307)

15
A Fabergé two-colour gold and hardstone magnifying glass, workmaster M. Perchin, St. Petersburg, late 19th century, 16.5cm (6½in), *L 28 Oct,* £7,700 ($11,473)

16
A Fabergé silver-mounted nephrite tray, workmaster Anders Nevalainen, St. Petersburg, c.1890, 28.5cm (11¼in) long, *NY 11 June,* $7,150 (£5,674)

17
A Fabergé topaz quartz, two-colour gold and enamel desk seal, workmaster Fyodor Afanassiev, St. Petersburg, c.1900, 6cm (2½in), *NY 11 June,* $5,225 (£4,146)

18
An Imperial Fabergé gold, enamel and rock crystal desk seal, workmaster M. Perchin, St. Petersburg, late 19th century, *G 14 Nov,* SF 8,250 (£2,696; $3,775)

19
A Fabergé gold-mounted enamel cigarette case, workmaster H. Wigström, St. Petersburg, late 19th century, 8.5cm (3¼in), *G 16 May,* SF 14,300 (£4,181; $5,561)

Russian Cloisonné Enamel 1880-1917

Cloisonné enamelling was a craft much practised in Russia from the latter part of the 19th century until after the Revolution of 1917. It was the revival of interest within Russia in the country's history, and in traditional Russian designs, that led to the rediscovery of a taste for the colourful art of cloisonné enamel. Many designs on enamelled pieces are similar to the painted designs and carved decoration found on old houses and churches: for example, the painted walls of St. Basil's Cathedral in Moscow's Red Square.

The technique of cloisonné enamelling is based on the building of small cloisons (partitions) to contain the enamel. These are formed by bands of silver, or more commonly fine silver-gilt twisted wire, which are soldered onto the silver surface of an object following a previously drawn design. The cells thus formed are then filled with enamel colours, the chemical components of which are sand, soda, magnesium, lead, potash and metal oxides. Since the enamel shrinks during the firing and cooling, further applications are needed, resulting in numerous layers. Several firings are required in the kiln at between 600° and 800° centigrade. Finally, the surface is polished to give it shine and brilliance. Most enamel colours change their hue during firing; the artist therefore has to be certain of his intended effect in advance, which requires great skill.

—1—
A silver-gilt and shaded cloisonné enamel vase, Maria Semyonova, Moscow, 1908-1917, with multicolour enamel flowers against a green ground, 16.5cm (6½in) high, *G 14 Nov,* **SF 6,600 (£2,157; $3,020)**

—2—
A silver-gilt and multi-coloured enamel liqueur set, Gustav Klingert, Moscow, 1891, tray 24cm (9½in) diam, *NY 11 Dec,* **$3,300 (£2,340)**

—3—
A silver-gilt and enamel Easter egg, Gustav Klingert, Moscow, *c.*1890, with stylised multi-coloured foliage, and reserves of turquoise between silver filigree scrolls, 6cm (2½in) high, *NY 11 Dec,* **$1,980 (£1,404)**

—4—
A set of twelve silver-gilt and enamel demi-tasse spoons, Gustav Klingert, Moscow, *c.*1890, the back of the bowls with multi-coloured stylised foliage and blue bead borders, 14cm (5½in), *NY 11 June,* **$990 (£785)**

See also colour illustrations on p.490

—1—

—2—

—3—

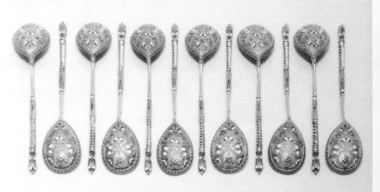

—4—

The best known makers in the late 19th and early 20th centuries were Maria Semyonova (fig.1), Ivan Sazikov, Gustav Klingert (figs.2, 3, 4), Ivan Saltikov (figs.5, 6,), Pavel Ovchinnikov (figs.7, 10) and Feodor Rückert (figs.8, 9, 11, 12, 13). It is pieces by Rückert, one of the greatest of enamellers, which fetch the highest prices in the saleroom today. He had his own workshop; his enamels were retailed by the house of

Fabergé (fig.8) and by Pavel Ovchinnikov (fig.11). Rückert's work is characterized by its muted colours, in which tones of blue, green and grey are used. He often combined cloisonné enamelling with paintings enamelled en plein (on an open field) with scenes from Russian history: a most difficult technique.

Pieces are normally marked with the initials of the maker. Another unusual mark can also be found: a number, followed by

—5—
A pair of silver-gilt and cloisonné enamel travelling egg cups, I Saltikov, Moscow, late 19th century, 6.5cm (2½in), L 20 Feb, £1,210 ($1,391)

—6—
A silver-gilt and shaded cloisonné enamel tea-glass holder, I Saltikov, Moscow, 1899-1908, with multicolour floral scolls, 6.5cm (2½in), G 16 May, SF 1,210 (£3,538; $4,706)

—7—
A silver-gilt and enamel covered cup, Ovchinnikov, Moscow, c.1885, 16cm (6¼in) high, NY 11 June, $1,760 (£1,396)

—8—
A Fabergé shaded cloisonné enamel kovsh, workmaster F Ruckert, Moscow, 1899-1908, 11cm (4¼in), L 12 June, £1,045 ($1,390)

—9—
A silver and shaded enamel kovsh, Fyodor Ruckert, Moscow, c.1900, the front enamelled with the Russian Imperial eagle, 9cm (3½in), NY 11 Dec, $1,980 (£1,404)

—10—
A silver-gilt and plique-à-jour enamel sherbet cup, Ovchinnikov, Moscow, 1890, the base with loisonné enamel lowers, 11cm (4¼in), NY 11 Dec, 2,200 (£1,560)

—11—
A silver-gilt and shaded enamel bowl, Fyodor Ruckert, retailed by Ovchinnikov, Moscow, 1890, 8.5cm (3¼in) diam, NY 11 June, 3,300 (£2,619)

—12—
A silver-gilt and shaded enamel pictorial kovsh, Fyodor Ruckert, Moscow, c.1900, enamelled in blue and green and with a detail of 'The Boyar Wedding' after Constantin Makovsky, 14.5cm (5¾in) long, NY 11 Dec, $6,600 (£4,680)

—13—
A silver-gilt and shaded enamel three-handled cup, Moscow, c.1900, apparently unmarked, almost certainly by Fyodor Ruckert, 11cm (4¼in) high, NY 11 June, $7,700 (£6,111)

—5—

—7—

—10—

—12—

—6—

—8—

—9—

—11—

—13—

Fabergé (St Petersburg)

Fabergé (Moscow)

Gustav Klingert

Pavel Ovchinnikov

the letter A. In the last years of the 19th century artists collaborated to found workshops, called Artels: thirty Moscow Artels are known. The work of the second Artel was retailed by Fabergé; examples of the work of other Artels illustrated here are from the sixth (fig.15), eleventh (fig.14, 17) and twentieth Artel (fig.16) respectively.

A variety of objects were made in cloisonné enamel, the most popular being cigarette cases, small bowls and beakers, tea services and salt cellars. Salt-chairs, typically Russian objects, are relatively expensive today. Collectors are especially interested in large presentation pieces, such as *kovshi*, beakers and caskets; these often bear inscriptions giving information about the occasion of the gift and the people involved.

Although collectors are becoming increasingly interested in these enamel objects, it is still possible to buy many good pieces, of a quality to make them the stars of a collection, for a sum

—14—
A silver-gilt and shaded enamel table cigar box, The Eleventh Artel, Moscow, *c.*1910, 19cm (7½in) long, *NY 11 Dec,* $7,700 (£5,460)

—15—
A silver-gilt and shaded enamel pictorial cigarette case, The Sixth Artel, Moscow, *c.*1910, with colourful foliage on a deep green ground, 11.5cm (4½in) long, *NY 11 Dec,* $3,025 (£2,145)

—16—
A silver-gilt and shaded enamel cigarette case, the Twentieth Artel, Moscow, *c.*1910, 10.5cm (4¼in) long, *NY 11 June,* $2,200 (£1,746)

—17—
A silver-gilt and shaded enamel pictorial table cigarette box, The Eleventh Artel, Moscow, *c.*1910, the cover enamelled *en plein* with a warrior at a tombstone, after Victor Vasnetsov (1846-1926), the border and sides enamelled in the Old Russian style, 12cm (4¾in) long, *NY 11 June,* $8,800 (£6,984)

—18—
A silver-gilt and shaded enamel matching sugar basket, creamer and sugar tongs, Vasili Agafonov Moscow, *c.*1900, 12 to 11cm (4¼ to 4¾in) long, *NY 11 Dec,* $3,080 (£2,184)

—19—
A silver-gilt and shaded enamel bowl, Ja B, *c.*1880, painted with flowers against pale green and grey grounds, 9cm (3½in) diam, *G 16 May,* **SF 1,430 (£418; $556)**

—20—
A silver-gilt and enamel sugar basket, Moscow, 1891, maker's mark unclear, 12cm (4¾in), *NY 11 June,* $825 (£654)

—14—

—15—

—16—

—17—

—18—

—19—

—20—

Feodor Rückert

Ivan Saltikov

Ivan Sazikov

Maria Semyonova

Eleventh Artel

ranging from about £600 ($840). The more 'Russian' the object, in shape and decoration, the more interesting it will be to the collector. Pieces made in the Art Nouveau style are also gaining in popularity. Buyers must be aware that condition is most important: any damage or restoration, even if it is difficult to detect at first sight, will be reflected in the price realized. Sometimes small delicate pieces in mint condition will fetch more at auction than an elaborate but damaged presentation piece. Enamel is a very hard substance, but it can easily be chipped if carelessly handled. Pieces which have been kept in their original case, often with a silk or velvet lining, are therefore sought eagerly.

In recent years many copies have been seen, making the market more difficult. At first sight some of these appear to be of good quality. Some bear fake marks, often with the initials of Feodor Rückert or Pavel Ovchinnikov. Anyone who wishes to start collecting in this field should seek expert advice and guidance. To train his or her eye, the aspiring collector should study the fine enamelling which is to be seen on the very best pieces and compare them with other objects of lesser quality.

● HEINRICH GRAF VON SPRETI ●

Further reading

Les émaux russe XIe-XIXe, Collections des Musees: Musées du Kremlin de Moscow, Musee Historique d'etat L'Ermitage, 1974

Alexander von Solodkoff, *Russian Gold and Silver*, 1981

—21—
A shaded cloisonné enamel casket, maker's mark BMA, Moscow, 1908/1917, 12cm (4¾in) wide, *L 28 Oct,* £2,970 ($4,425)

—22—
A silver-gilt and enamel salt throne, Anton Kuzmichev, Moscow, c.1890, the seat with the Cyrillic inscription 'Without Salt, Without Bread is only Half a Meal', the back in the form of a country cottage surmounted by the Russian Imperial eagle, 14.5cm (5¾in) high, *NY 11 June,* $2,310 (£1,833)

—23—
A silver and enamel table bell, Antip Kuzmichev, Moscow, c.1900, with blue borders, 12cm (4¾in) high, *NY 11 June,* $1,320 (£1,047)

—24—
A set of six silver-gilt and enamel spoons, Antip Kuzmichev, Moscow, c.1890, 14cm (5¾in) long, *NY 11 June,* $715 (£567)

—21—

—22—

—23—

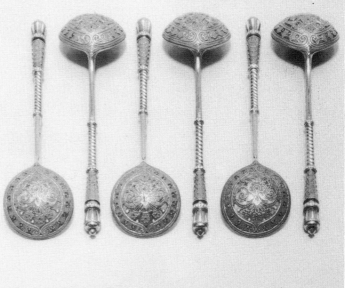

—24—

1
Evgenie Lanceray. A bronze equestrian group of a man smoking a pipe, late 19th century, signed, 47cm (18½in) long, *NY 11 June*, $2,420 (£1,920)

2
Evgenie Lanceray. A bronze equestrian group of a mounted soldier, signed, *NY 11 Dec*, $2,310 (£1,638)

3
A malachite and ormolu mantle clock, late 19th century, 39.5cm (15½in), *NY 11 June*, $5,225 (£4,146)

4
Vasili Gratchev. A bronze equestrian group of a soldier, late 19th century, signed, 36cm (14¼in), *NY 11 June*, $2,860 (£2,269)

5
Gratchev. A bronze group of a mounted cossack and his sweetheart, late 19th century, golden brown rubbed patination, 23.5cm (9¼in), *S 11 June*, £671 ($882)

6
Vasili Gratchev. A bronze equestrian group, late 19th century, signed, 36cm (14in), *NY 11 June*, $1,980 (£1,571)

7
A bronze bust of Emperor Nicholas I, *c.*1850, later mount, base chipped, 16.5cm (6½in), *L 20 Feb*, £220 ($253)

8
Nicholas I. Liberich. A bronze model of a bear, late 19th century, signed, 52cm (20½in) high, *NY 14 Feb*, $3,300 (£2,845)

9
Leonid Vladimirovitch Posen. A bronze group, late 19th century, depicting a rabbi on his way to the Zaddik before the Sabbath, 56cm (22in) wide, *J 18 May*, $9,500 (£7,143)

1

2

3

4

5

6

7

8

9

Judaica

1
A pair of English parcel-gilt silver Torah finials, Joseph Rappaport, London, 1919, 30cm (13½in), *NY 26 June,*
$660 (£512)

2
A pair of German parcel-gilt silver Torah finials, Friedrich Wilhelm Borcke, Berlin, c.1825, later bells, 35.5cm (14in), *NY 25 Nov,*
$4,950 (£3,390)

3
A pair of German parcel-gilt and silver Torah finials, Andreas Mielach, Augsburg, 1805, 31cm (12in) high, *J 18 May,*
$11,000 (£8,271)

4
A pair of Dutch parcel-gilt silver Torah finials, mid-18th century, unmarked, some damage and old repairs, 45.5cm (18in) high, *J 18 May,*
$17,000 (£12,782)

5
A pair of German silver Torah finials, Posen, late 19th century, now lacking bells, 30.5cm (12in), *NY 25 Nov,*
$1,760 (£1,205)

6
A German silver Torah shield, Frankfurt a.M., c.1770, 23cm (9in) high, *J 18 May,*
$7,000 (£5,263)

7
A parcel-gilt and silver Torah shield, probably Austrian, last quarter 18th century, unmarked, 21cm (8¼in) high, *J 18 May,*
$4,500 (£3,383)

8
A German silver-gilt Torah shield, Franz Anton Gutwein, Augsburg, 1802, slight damage, 29cm (11½in), high *NY 25 Nov,*
$5,500 (£3,767)

9
An Austro-Hungarian silver Torah shield, maker's mark JB, Vienna, with inscription dated 1873, suspension chains lacking, 34cm (13½in), *NY 26 June,*
$1,980 (£1,535)

10
An Austrian silver Torah shield, Vienna, 1804, lacks suspension chains, 19cm (7½in), *NY 26 June,*
$2,750 (£2,132)

11
A silver Torah shield, probably Austrian, c.1840, unmarked, 31.8cm (12½in) high, *J 18 May,*
$1,200 (£902)

12
An American silver-gilt Torah shield, Ludwig Wolpert, 1960's, stamped maker's mark and Toby Pascher Workshop, the Jewish Museum, 23cm (9in), *NY 26 June,*
$1,760 (£1,364)

Torah. Hebrew for law. Specifically the five books of Moses written on a parchment scroll that forms the focus of synagogue liturgy and is kept in the Aron Hakodesh.

Ornaments include:

Torah finials and *Rimmonim.*

Torah Shield or Breast Plate (*Tas*), hung on the front of the Torah scroll.

Torah Pointer (*Yad*)

Torah Crown (*Keter*) usually to fit over the Torah when it is not in use.

Aron Hakodesh. Commonly named the *Ark.* The cupboard containing the Torah scrolls in the synagogue.

1

2

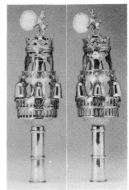

3

4

5

6

7

8

9

10

11

12

1

A Polish silver Torah pointer, 18th century, index finger worn, 27cm (10½in), *NY 26 June*, $825 (£640)

2

An Italian carved coral and bone Torah pointer, mid-19th century, some splits, 14.5cm (5¾in), *NY 26 June*, $1,320 (£1,023)

3

A Torah pointer, probably Austrian, mid-19th century, unmarked, 31cm (12¼in) long, *J 18 May*, $1,100 (£827)

4

An Austro-Hungarian silver cased Esther scroll, Vienna, 1846, some wear, case 27cm (10½in) long overall, *NY 26 June*, $1,650 (£1,279)

5

A rare German travelling Torah with original silver and fabric fittings, unmarked, probably Berlin or Breslau, mid-19th century, *NY 26 June*, $39,600 (£30,698)

6

A Polish silver filigree cased Esther scroll, *c.*1925, length overall 28cm (11in), *NY 26 June*, $825 (£640)

7

An Austrian silver Etrog box, maker's mark P.S., Vienna, 1739, later Hebrew inscription, 20cm (8in) wide, *J 18 May*, $6,000 (£4,511)

8

An Italian silver Torah ark key, 18th century, 10cm (4in), *NY 25 Nov*, $4,125 (£2,825)

9

A Bezalel silver Etrog box, *c.*1920, stamped Bezalel, Jerusalem, 15.2cm (6in) wide, *J 18 May*, $2,100 (£1,579)

10

A Palestinian parcel-gilt filigree Megillah case, Bezalel, early 20th century, containing a parchment scroll of Esther, 22.5cm (8½in), *L 24 Apr*, £990 ($1,297)

11

A Russian silver Purim bowl, Moscow, 1845, the decoration probably Persian, mid-19th century, 15cm (6in), *NY 26 June*, $2,310 (£1,791)

12

A silver and mahogany Purim noisemaker, Joseph and Alexander Reichman, Jerusalem, 1984, 20cm (8in), *NY 25 Nov*, $3,575 (£2,449)

Megillah. Manuscript Book of Esther recited on Purim.

Purim. Festival commemorating the events in the Book of Esther.

Etrog. A citrus fruit used on Sukkoth.

Sukkoth. The autumn festival of the Tabernacles.

1

2

3

4

6

7

8

9

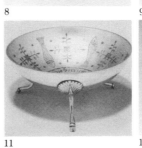

5

10

11

12

1
A Polish silver-gilt Kiddush cup, mid-18th century, 13.5cm (5¼in), NY 25 Nov, $3,850 (£2,637)

2
A Polish silver Passover Kiddush goblet, early 19th century, maker's mark KG, 15cm (6in), NY 26 June, $2,860 (£2,217)

3
A German silver-gilt Festival Kiddush cup, Hieronymus Mittnacht, Augsburg, 1761-3, 12cm (4¾in), NY 25 Nov, $16,500 (£11,301)

4
A Polish silver Kiddush beaker, early 19th century, 7cm (2¾in), NY 26 June, $1,100 (£853)

5
A German silver-gilt Sabbath beaker, probably Johann Friedrich Schutteler, Lippstadt, c.1825, 7.5cm (3in), L 24 Apr, $1,990 ($1,297)

6
A German silver spice tower, late 18th century, 22cm (8½in) high, J 18 May, $17,000 (£12,782)

7
A Bohemian filigree spice box, R. G., Prague, 1815, 13.5cm (5¼in), L 24 Apr, $880 ($1,153)

8
A German silver spice tower, Christian Friedrich Mueller, Berlin, 1780s, replacement door, 25.5cm (10in), NY 25 Nov, $8,800 (£6,027)

9
A Polish silver filigree spice tower, 18th century, 25.5cm (10in), NY 25 Nov, $7,425 (£5,086)

10
A Polish silver fruit-form spice container, maker's mark a stag, probably for Hirsch, early 19th century, 12.5cm (5in), NY 25 Nov, $1,760 (£1,205)

11
A Polish silver book-form spice container, early 19th century, 6.5cm (2½in), NY 25 Nov, $3,575 (£2,449)

12
An Austro-Hungarian filigree spice box, mid-19th century, 20.5cm (8in), L 24 Apr, £418 ($556)

13
A German pewter spice container, dated 1753, some moulding lacking, 9cm (3½in) wide, J 18 May, $3,000 (£2,256)

14
A German silver spice box, possibly Frankfurt a.M., early 19th century, 6.8cm (2½in) wide, J 18 May, $1,600 (£1,203)

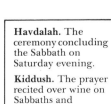

Havdalah. The ceremony concluding the Sabbath on Saturday evening.

Kiddush. The prayer recited over wine on Sabbaths and festivals.

Seder. The ritual meal held at home on Passover eve.

1
An American silver Mezuzah case, Ludwig Wolpert, New York, 1960's, stamped Toby Pascher Workshop, The Jewish Museum, New York, 11.5cm (4½in), *NY 26 June,*
$660 (£512)

2
A German silver travelling Hanukah lamp, Berlin, *c.*1830, 10cm (4in) high, *J 18 May,*
$5,500 (£4,135)

3
An Austro-Hungarian silver Hanukah lamp, maker's mark E.W., late 19th century, 21.1cm (8¼in) high, *J 18 May,*
$1,700 (£1,278)

4
An American silver Mezuzah, Ilya Schor, 1950's, 16.5cm (6½in) high, *NY 25 Nov,*
$15,400 (£10,548)

5
A German silver Hanukah lamp, Posen, late 19th century, 30.5cm (12in), *NY 26 June,*
$5,500 (£4,264)

6
A Ukrainian silver and filigree Hanukah lamp, maker's mark M.L.M., 1881, of 'Baal Shem Tov' type, 15cm (6in) high, *J 18 May,*
$3,750 (£2,820)

7
A German silver Hanukah lamp, maker's mark M incuse, Berlin, 1854-60, 20cm (8in) high, *NY 25 Nov,*
$12,100 (£8,288)

8
A German brass Hanukah lamp, second half 19th century, 62.5cm (24½in), *L 24 Apr,*
£1,210 ($1,585)

9
An Italian cast brass Hanukah lamp, 17th century, 16.5cm (6½in), *NY 26 June,*
$1,100 (£853)

10
A Polish cast brass Hanukah lamp, 18th century, 30.5cm (12in), *NY 25 Nov,*
$3,025 (£2,072)

11
A Polish brass Hanukah lamp, mid-19th century, 18cm (7in), *NY 25 Nov,*
$935 (£640)

12
An Italian bronze Hanukah lamp, early 19th century, later servant light, *NY 26 June,*
$3,575 (£2,771)

13
A Bohemian cast brass Hanukah lamp, Prague, *c.*1800, the sides cast and chased with Moses and Aaron, lacking servant light, 19cm (7½in) high, *J 18 May,*
$3,500 (£2,632)

14
A Dutch sheet brass Hanukah lamp, 18th century, 23cm (9in) high, *NY 26 June,*
$1,100 (£853)

Mezuzah. Small scroll containing a prayer fixed to the right doorpost of each door.

Hanukah. The midwinter (December) festival of lights.

Menorah. Hebrew for candelabrum. Now commonly the eight-branched Hanukah lamp lit on each day of the festival.

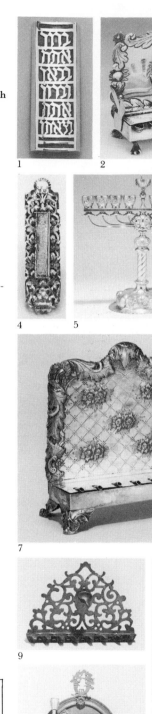

1

A Polish brass two-light Sabbath wall sconce, mid 19th century, 28cm (11in) *J 18 May,* $1,000 (£752)

2

A pair of Italian brass seven-light Sabbath candelabra, late 19th century, detachable drip pans, 43cm (17in), *NY 26 June,* $660 (£512)

3

A pair of Polish four-light cast brass Sabbath candelabra, mid 19th century, 52cm (20in) high, *J 18 May,* $2,300 (£1,729)

4

A pair of American silver two-light Sabbath candelabra, Ilya Schor, New York, dated 1942, 32cm (12½in), *NY 25 Nov,* $33,000 (£22,603)

5

A pair of Polish silver Sabbath candlesticks, I. A. Goldman, Warsaw, 1875, later English drip pans, 30.5cm (12in), *NY 26 June,* $1,210 (£938)

6

A Dutch or Italian brass hanging Sabbath lamp, *c.*1700, 43cm (17in) high overall, *NY 26 June,* $1,870 (£1,450)

7

A pair of Sabbath candlesticks, Aaron Katz, London, 1894, in Polish style, 41cm (16¼in) *L 24 Apr,* £770 ($1,009)

8

A German silver Havdalah candlestick, Johann Samuel Beckensteiner, Nuremberg, *c.*1760, 19.4cm (7½in) high, *J 18 May,* $8,500 (£6,391)

9

A Baltic parcel-gilt beaker, Christopher Mansfeld, Reval *c.*1700, with later inscription, 10.5cm (4in), *L 24 Apr,* £1,925 ($2,522)

10

A Continental pewter festival wine jug, 18th century, 53cm (20in) high, *J 18 May,* $2,200 (£1,654)

11

A Continental pewter Passover dish, 3rd quarter 18th century, 41cm (16in) diam., *J 18 May,* $2,000 (£1,504)

12

A German pewter Passover dish, maker's initials probably D.V.D., *c.*1768, 39cm (15¼in) diam., *L 24 Apr,* £2,860 ($3,747)

13

A Dutch delft festival plate, De Porceleyne Claeuw, late 18th century, some chips, 23cm (9in), *NY 26 June,* $3,190 (£2,473)

14

A Continental ceramic Passover plate, 18th century, damaged, 22.4cm (8¾in), *J 18 May,* $450 (£338)

1

2

3

4

5

6

7

8

9

10

11

12

13

14

1
A brass Burial Society comb, probably Hungarian, dated 1881, 15cm (6in) wide, *NY 25 Nov,* $5,775 (£3,955)

2
An Austro-Hungarian silver Burial Society charity box, late 19th century, 23cm (9in), *NY 26 June,* $6,050 (£4,690)

3
A pair of Dutch nesting silver circumcision beakers, Amsterdam, 1853, 4.9cm (2in) high, *J 18 May,* $5,000 (£3,759)

4
An Austrian parcel gilt silver Burial Society covered goblet, by Johann Elias Gribinger, Vienna, 1697, the inscription dated 1804, 33.5cm (13¼in) high overall, *NY 26 June,* $35,200 (£27,287)

5
A continental circumcision knife, tortoiseshell, silver and steel, late 18th century, 18cm (7in), *NY 25 Nov,* $1,650 (£1,130)

6
An English circumcision cup, Urquart and Hart, London, 1792, 9cm (3½in), *L 24 Apr,* £715 ($937)

7
A German silver-gilt double circumcision cup, Johann Becker, Augsburg, 1755-57, height assembled 12.5cm (5in), *NY 25 Nov,* $13,200 (£9,041)

8
A pair of Bohemian silver circumcision cups, maker's mark PR, Prague, 1846, sold with another goblet, 7.5cm (3in) and and 17cm (6¾in) high, *NY 25 Nov,* $2,970 (£2,034)

9
A German carved and painted wood circumcision ceremony box, late 17th century, 11 x 20cm (4¼ x 8in), *NY 25 Nov,* $33,000 (£22,603)

10
An Italian silver amulet case, Turin, master or assayer's mark GB, mid 18th century, 14cm (5½in) high, *NY 25 Nov,* $5,225 (£3,579)

11
A Bezalel silver inlaid brass urn, c.1910, 16.5cm (6½in), *NY 26 June,* $1,320 (£1,023)

12
An American silver necklace, Ludwig Wolpert, 1960's, unsigned, composed of Hebrew letters spelling out 'If I forget thee, Oh Jerusalem', 43cm (17in) long, *NY 26 June,* $1,760 (£1,364)

13
A continental silver amulet case, probably German, early 19th century, 7.5cm (3in) high overall, *NY 26 June,* $880 (£682)

14
A German silver presentation goblet, c.1850, stamped '13', 10cm (4in), *NY 26 June,* $660 (£512)

15
An Italian gold and enamel marriage and Sabbath ring, probably Venetian, 16th century, 4cm (1½in) high, *NY 26 June,* $25,300 (£19,612)

16
A Continental gun metal cased open-faced pocket watch, early 20th century, 5cm (2in) diam., *J 18 May,* $3,500 (£2,632)

European Works of Art

1

A silver devotional pendant, early 17th century, South German, engraved on one side with the Resurrection, and the other with the Virgin, after Durer, 7.5cm (3in), *L 12 Dec*, £440 ($616)

2

An enamelled gold and Baroque pearl reliquary pendant, late 16th century, South German, some enamelling restored, 3cm (1¼in), *L 12 Dec*, £990 ($1,386)

3

A South Italian gold, enamel and pearl pendant, 17th century, in the form of a nef, enamel chipped, *L 12 Dec*, £2,530 ($3,542)

4

A Franco-Flemish enamelled gold medallion, late 17th century, of the young St. John the Baptist, later gold case, medallion 2cm (¾in), *L 12 Dec*, £660 ($924)

5

An English late Gothic gold posy ring, 15th century, with the inscription 'loialte dort', *L 2 Apr*, £3,080 ($3,911)

6

An English gold and enamel Loyalist pendant, mid-17th century, enclosing two enamel portraits of Charles I and Henrietta Maria, 2.5cm (1in) wide, *L 12 Dec*, £495 ($693)

7

A gold and enamel reliquary cross, late 16th century, probably Northern Europe, 6cm (2½in) high, *L 12 Dec*, £2,200 ($3,080)

8

A South German gold, enamel and diamond dress jewel, early 17th century, later brooch bar with pearls, 3.5cm (1¼in) wide, *L 12 Dec*, £1,320 ($1,848)

9

A Spanish gold and enamelled devotional pendant, 17th century, with a figure of the Virgin Immaculata, later brooch pin, enamel chipped, 4.5cm (1½in), high, *L 2 Apr*, £1,760 ($2,235)

10

A Gothic gold and agate signet ring, first half 14th century, probably North Italian, engraved with Biblical inscriptions, 2cm (¾in) diam., *L 12 Dec*, £8,360 ($11,704)

11

A jewel-set enamelled gold chain, early 17th century, South German or Austrian, the components originally assembled differently, the chains 19th century, 50cm (19¾in), *NY 21 May*, $5,775 (£4,620)

12

An enamelled gold necklace set with jewels, late 16th century, South German, formerly of longer length, 28cm (11in), *NY 21 May*, $17,600 (£14,080)

13

A diamond-set enamelled gold pendant, 16th century and later, some enamel loss, 11.5cm (4½in), *NY 21 May*, $23,100 (£18,480)

Article • Ivories *pp 452-455*
See also • Colour illustrations *pp 482-484*

1   2   3

4   5   6

7   8   9

10

11   12   13 *(front and rear views)*

1
A Tuscan silver and copper-gilt chalice, early 15th century, 20.5cm (8in), *L 12 Dec,* £4,180 ($5,852)

2
A Tuscan gilt copper and silver-gilt chalice, 15th century, 20.5cm (8in), *L 2 Apr,* £1,650 ($2,095)

3
A German copper-gilt coconut cup, possibly Bohemian, late 16th century, later finial, 36.5cm (14¼in), *NY 22 Nov,* $3,850 (£2,637)

4
A Saxon serpentine cup and cover, late 17th century, the lid with later gilt bronze putto, repaired, 34cm (13½in), *NY 10 May,* $1,760 (£1,431)

5
A Limoges painted enamel plaque, mid-16th century, 15cm (6in), *NY 22 Nov,* $1,760 (£1,205)

6
Two Limoges painted enamel biblical plaques, one by Leonard Limousin, second quarter 16th century, depicting Christ at the Pillar, signed with initials, (illustrated), the other depicting the Betrayal, slight restoration, each 17 x 14cm (6¾ x 5½in), *NY 10 May,* $3,520 (£2,862)

7
A Saxon serpentine tankard, early 18th century, mounted in pewter, 18cm (7in), *NY 16 Feb,* $715 (£616)

8
A Limoges polychrome enamel plaque of the Crucifixion, from the Penicaud workshops, 16th century, 23.5 x 27.5cm (9¾ x 10¾in), *L 2 Apr,* £3,960 ($5,029)

9
A Limoges painted enamel mirror plaque, Jean de Court, last quarter of the 16th century, depicting the crowned Jupiter, mounted in silver-gilt mirror case, 11 x 9cm (4½ x 3½in), *NY 21 May,* $9,350 (£7,480)

10
A Limoges pyx, 13th century, 12cm (4¾in), *L 2 Apr,* £2,200 ($2,794)

11
A Limoges champlevé enamel head of a pastoral staff, 13th century, the supporting angel probably of later date, some loss of enamel, 28.5cm (11¼in), *NY 21 May,* $46,750 (£37,400)

12
A Limoges polychrome enamel bowl, 17th century, from the Laudin workshops, with a profile bust of Minerva, some repair, 12.5cm (5in) across, *L 25 Apr,* £220 ($284)

13
A Limoges champlevé enamel and copper pyx, 13th century, 10.5cm (4¼in), *L 12 Dec,* £3,410 ($4,774)

14
A Limoges enamel salt, 16th century, attributed to Pierre Reymond, showing scenes from the life of Hercules, small restorations, 8.5cm (3¼in), *L 12 Dec,* £1,375 ($1,925)

1
A Flemish Gothic oak figure of Mary Magdalene, possibly Antwerp, early 16th century, traces of paint, 87cm (34¼in), *NY 10 May,* $4,950 (£4,024)

2
A French limestone group of the Virgin and Child, probably Burgundy, early 16th century, traces of original paint and gilding, some replacement and restoration, 52.5cm (20¾in), *NY 10 May,* $13,750 (£11,179)

3
A Netherlandish oak group of the Nativity, c.1500, 20cm (11½in), *L 4 July,* £6,820 ($9,412)

4
A North Netherlandish oak group of the Virgin and Child, c.1500, 43.5cm (17in), *NY 10 May,* $5,500 (£4,472)

5
An Austrian wood group of the Virgin and Child, second half 15th century, probably Tyrol, her clothes gilded, some repairs, 147.5cm (58in), *L 12 Dec,* £11,000 ($15,400)

6
A Hispano-Flemish walnut figure of Saint James, first half 16th century, gilt and painted, 103cm (40½in), *NY 10 May,* $4,125 (£3,354)

7
A Netherlandish oak figure of an evangelist, perhaps Utrecht, early 16th century, probably St John, 114cm (44¾in), *NY 22 Nov,* $3,850 (£2,637)

8
A Tuscan painted terracotta figure of the Virgin, probably Florence early 16th century, attributed to the 'Master of the Unruly Children', once forming part of a Nativity, 57cm (22½in), *NY 22 Nov,* $9,075 (£6,216)

9
A Central European lindenwood group of Saint Martin, probably Bavarian, early 16th century, traces of polychrome, 71cm (28in), *NY 10 May,* $10,450 (£8,496)

10
A pair of Swabian polychrome and gilt limewood reliefs of saints, c.1500, 46cm (18½in), *L 4 July,* £7,700 ($10,626)

11
A Malines polychrome wood figure of the Virgin and Child, early 16th century, 34.5cm (13½in), *L 12 Dec,* £3,080 ($4,312)

1   2   3

4   5

6   7   8

9

10

11

1
A pair of Venetian bronze and iron figures, 16th century, in the manner of Roccatagliata, 30.5cm (12in), *L 12 Dec,*
£2,200 ($3,080)

2
A pair of North Italian bronze cherubs, 17th century, 18.5cm (7¼in), *L 2 Apr,*
£605 ($768)

3
A North Italian bronze figure of a rearing horse, Padua, early 16th century, dark brown lacquer over brown bronze, 17.5cm (7in) long, *NY 10 May,*
$2,860 (£2,325)

4
A French bronze figure of the reclining Cleopatra, late 16th century, rich brown patina, 28cm (11in), *L 12 Dec,*
£6,600 ($9,240)

5
A Netherlandish bronze bull, first half 17th century, 44.5cm (17½in), *L 2 Apr,*
£4,180 ($5,308)

6
An Italian bronze figure of Hercules and Cerberus, Lombardy, late 16th century, dark lacquer over brown bronze, 15.5cm (6in), *NY 10 May,*
$2,530 (£2,057)

7
An Italian bronze figure of Antinous Belvedere, *c.*1600, 23cm (9in), *L 12 Dec,*
£3,850 ($5,390)

8
A South German gilt bronze lion rampant, *c.*1600, re-gilt, 20cm (8in), *L 12 Dec,*
£2,530 ($3,542)

9
An Italo-Flemish bronze figure of Venus after the bath, 17th century, after Giambologna, 22.5cm (8¾in), *L 2 Apr,*
£748 ($950)

10
A Florentine bronze rearing horse, from the workshop of Giambologna, early 17th century, olive brown patina, 31cm (12¼in) high, *NY 10 May,*
$14,300 (£11,626)

11
An Italo-Flemish bronze figure of a putto, 17th century, attributed to the workshops of Francois Duquesnoy, 17cm (6¾in), *L 2 Apr,*
£770 ($977)

12
An Italian bronze model of a bull, 17th century, after Giambologna, later lacquer, 25.5cm (10in), *L 12 Dec,*
£3,300 ($4,620)

13
A Flemish bronze bust of the boy Christ, late 17th century, after Duquesnoy, 16.5cm (6½in), *L 12 Dec,*
£990 ($1,386)

14
A French bronze figure of a goddess, cast from a model by Michel Anguier, after 1652, golden lacquer over red gold bronze, 54.5cm (21½in), *NY 10 May,*
$8,800 (£7,154)

15
A Florentine bronze figure of a youth, *c.*1700, from the workshops of Massimiliano Soldani, after the antique, 30.5cm (12in), *L 2 Apr,*
£2,420 ($3,073)

16
An Italian bronze figure of Silenus, 18th century, after the antique, 34cm (13½in), *L 4 July,*
£1,705 ($2,353)

17
A bronze group of Marcus Aurelius, late 18th/early 19th century, 39.5cm (15½in) high, *L 2 Apr,*
£1,210 ($1,536)

1
A South German fruit-wood group of Saint Michael, early 17th century, some pieces replaced, 24cm (9½in), *NY 22 Nov,* $6,050 (£4,144)

2
A North German pear-wood figure of a dancing girl, early 18th century, attributed to Johann Heinrich Meissner, 20.5cm (8in), *L 12 Dec,* £4,620 ($6,468)

3
A pair of Dutch or North German fruitwood busts, of Harlequin and Columbine, c.1700, 21cm (8¼in), *L 12 Dec,* £2,200 ($3,080)

4
A pearwood relief of the Virgin and Child, c.1600, after Dürer, monogrammed AD1517, 12cm (4½in) high, *L 2 Apr,* £5,720 ($7,264)

5
A white marble portrait relief of Louis XIV, c.1690, 18.5cm (7¼in) high, *L 4 July,* £1,045 ($1,442)

6
A pair of Italian marble lions, c.1800, of the Egyptian type, 137cm (54in) long, *L 2 Apr,* £8,250 ($10,477)

7
A marble bust of the Roman empress Livia, 18th century, probably English, 46cm (18in), *L 2 Apr,* £1,760 ($2,235)

8
A life-size plaster bust of the Duke of Wellington, by Peter Turnerelli, 1812, 71cm (28in), *L 2 Apr,* £990 ($1,257)

9
A marble bust of George Washington, after Houdon, c.1800, 50.5cm, (20in), *L 12 Dec,* £3,300 ($4,620)

10
An English marble bust of William Pitt, from the workshop of Joseph Nollekens, signed Nollekens FT 1808, 71cm (28in), *L 12 Dec,* £3,190 ($4,466)

11
An Italian marble bust of Augustus, 19th century, the shoulders of verde antico, 71cm (28in), *L 12 Dec,* £6,050 ($8,470)

12
A French terracotta bust of a young girl, c.1810, in the manner of Chinard, 44.5cm (17½in), *L 12 Dec,* £4,180 ($5,852)

13
A French terracotta bust of a gentleman, late 18th century, attributed to Clement Jayet, 69cm (27¼in), *L 2 Apr,* £2,750 ($3,492)

1   2   3   4   5

6   7

8   9   10

11   12   13

Ivories

Although examples of ivory carving can be found which date from prehistoric times, it was the Egyptians, from the eighth to the fourth millenia, who made the greatest artistic contribution by their work in this highly prized medium. Phoenician ivories found their way into Spain and Italy and influenced both Etruscan and Greek culture, although the predominance of marble carving in the latter lessened the production of ivory carvings. In Roman times, the adaptation of the jewel box to a pyx or container for the Christian Holy Sacrament, and of the consular diptychs to the portable religious diptychs of the Carolingian to 14th century gothic period, formed the basis of the enormous quantity of European ivory carving of the mediaeval, renaissance and baroque eras.

Elephant tusks were the main source of ivory, though walrus or narwhal were also common in Northern Europe, particularly in Romanesque times, since the supply of tusks, so plentiful in antiquity, was considerably depleted by the middle ages, due to the decline in the number of elephants. Historically, ivory has always been regarded as a luxury and as a symbol of purity and of the Virgin—the 'ivory tower'.

The most important gothic centres of ivory carving were those of 14th century Paris, where the carvers were attached to the guilds relating to the objects which they made, such as the guilds of the comb makers, tablet makers, casket makers and so on. In the 16th century, a guild of ivory carvers was established in France, although, strangely enough, the carvers of the renaissance were far less prolific than their successors were to be during the great revival launched during the 18th and 19th centuries by the workshops of Dieppe. In 15th century Italy, the bone carvers of the Embriachi family executed hundreds of small plaques, carved with figures of both secular and religious significance, which were intended to be fitted into caskets, portable altars, mirrors and other articles. In Germany—particularly in the south, in Bavaria and in the Tirol—the baroque carvers, such as Adam Lencke and Ignaz Elhafen, performed extraordinary feats, creating entwined figures and reliefs of galloping classical warriors after designs by Rubens and Lebrun.

—1—
A Flemish ivory crucifix, dated 1656, 56cm (22in) high, *L 4 July,* **£6,600 ($9,108)** Inset: date and monogram

—2—
A French ivory diptych leaf of the Crucifixion, early 14th century, 8.5 x 6.5cm (3¼ x 2½in), *L 2 Apr,* **£2,310 ($2,933)**

—3—
An ivory pax, mid 14th century, French, 18.5cm (7¼in), *L 12 Dec,* **£3,960 ($5,544)**

—2—

—1—

—3—

In the courts of Denmark and Florence, noblemen, even kings, whiled away their time by making cups and towers by concentrically turning ivories, or *tours de force.* In Goa, small figures of the Virgin and of the infants Christ and St. John, rendered with almost Indian features, were executed in large numbers from the 17th to the 19th centuries for the Indo-Portuguese Roman Catholics, and similar figures were made by the Chinese Jesuits. Throughout Europe there was never any lack of demand for Crucifix figures, the largest of which can be three feet high or more.

—4—
A South German ivory relief of the Flagellation, 17th century, 17cm (6¾in), L 2 Apr, £2,750 ($3,492)

—5—
A French ivory spoon, 17th century, the handle with emblematic figures of Justice and Power, 15cm (6in), L 12 Dec, £1,100 ($1,540)

—6—
A South German ivory ewer, in the manner of Michael Maucher, late 17th century, 22cm (8¾in), NY 22 Nov, $3,300 (£2,260)

—7—
A French Gothic ivory panel of the Crucifixion, 14th century, 11cm (4¼in), NY 22 Nov, $1,320 (£904)

—8—
A French ivory figure of an old woman, 18th century, 10cm (4in), L 2 Apr, £1,045 ($1,327)

—9—
A French ivory figure of J J Rousseau, last quarter 18th century, Dieppe, 16.5cm (6½in), L 2 Apr, £1,155 ($1,466)

—10—
A Flemish ivory figure of Leda and the Swan, late 17th century, in the manner of Bossuit, 22.5cm (8¾in), L 12 Dec, £2,970 ($4,158)

—11—
A French ivory figure of Voltaire, last quarter 18th century, Dieppe, 17cm (6¾in), L 2 Apr, £1,155 ($1,466)

—12—
An ivory figure of a beggar boy, early 18th century, perhaps English, 19cm (7½in), L 2 Apr, £1,650 ($2,095)

—4— —5— —6—

—7—

—8—

—9—

—10— —11— —12—

The allure and beauty of ivory combined with its historical interest for collectors, particularly in mediaeval pieces, led to the production of many forgeries in the 19th century. A fairly recent publication (see below by Leeuwenberg) has identified such copyists as 'the master of the pointed noses' and has discussed the possibility that many of the 14th century reliefs, from diptychs with pierced architectural backgrounds, are of later date. Some of the examples named include pieces which had for many years been accepted as totally genuine and had been preserved in some of the world's most prestigious museums and collections. The effect of this controversy has probably been to contribute to the sometimes unnecessary doubts of those uncertain whether to enter this field of collecting and certainly one would be wise to seek advice from a specialist before starting a collection of gothic ivories.

When preserved away from the light, ivory can lose its luminosity and turn brown or yellow. This effect can be produced by staining the ivory with tea, and cracks of age can be simulated by exposure to intense heat. However, once pointed out, these deceptions will not take in the discerning eye a second time.

Some ten years ago international legislation was introduced for the protection of ivory-bearing species, making it necessary to prove import and export of all forms of ivory carving, even in cases of extremely old pieces. This act has now been more clearly defined and papers of origin are no longer required for antique pieces except in the United States of America and Japan.

Probably the best ivory collections for the person who wishes to study the whole period are those at the Victoria & Albert Museum, London, and the Bavarian National Museum,

—13—
A French ivory rappoir, early 18th century, carved with the Rape of Proserpine, 20cm (8in), *L 2 Apr,* £880 ($1,117)

—14—
An ivory-handled knife and fork, early 18th century, South German, with silver ferrules, 15 and 16cm (6 and 6¼in) long, *L 12 Dec,* £1,155 ($1,617)

—15—
A German turned ivory cup and cover, in the manner of Lorenz Spengler, *c.*1750-60, 24cm (9½in), *NY 10 May,* $3,190 (£2,593)

—16—
A German ivory group of the Virgin and Child, early 18th century, the Virgin with silver gilt and enamelled crown, 28cm (11in), *NY 22 Nov,* $2,640 (£1,808)

—17—
An English ivory portrait relief, of Alexander Pope, *c.*1740, attributed to Van der Hagen, 9cm (3½in), *L 12 Dec,* £1,320 ($1,848)

—13—

—14—

—15—

—16—

—17—

Munich. The enthusiasm of the private collector for ivories of all styles and periods, from the most modest Goanese figure to the important ivory portrait busts of the famous English carver, David le Marchand, is undiminished. However, it is still possible to buy a small gothic relief from a 14th century diptych for under £1,000 ($1,400). Perhaps the religious aspect of such a piece is initially less attractive to the modern collector, though it will not distract the real connoisseur from appreciating the wonderful quality, both artistic and spiritual, of these exquisite little carvings.

● ELIZABETH WILSON ●

Further reading:

O. Beigbeder, *Ivory,* 1965

J. Leeuwenberg, *Early 19th century, Gothic Ivories,* Aachener Kunstblätter, vol. 39, 1969

E. von Philippovich, *Eifenbein,* 1982

—18—
A South German fruitwood and ivory figure of an old beggar, first half 18th century, attributed to Simon Troger, 39.5cm (15½in), *L 12 Dec,* £3,300 ($4,620)

—19—
A German ivory cup and cover, c.1750, interior with silver gilt liner stamped with Frankfurt marks of Johanne Peter Beyer, 35.5cm (14in), *L 12 Dec,* £11,000 ($15,400)

—20—
A South German ivory vessel, 18th century, Nuremberg, the inside lined in silver, the base also mounted in silver, marked by Gregory Nicholas Bierfreundt, later handle and stem, 30cm (11¾in), *NY 16 Feb,* $5,500 (£4,741)

—21—
An ivory relief of St Catherine, mid 18th century, South German, in the manner of the monogrammist HE, 12cm (4¾in), *L 12 Dec,* £660 ($924)

—22—
An ivory presentation gavel, English, 1875, carved in the form of a capstan, 15cm (6in), *L 12 Dec,* £1,100 ($1,540)

—23—
A Flemish ivory double cup, first half of the 19th century, 20cm (8in), *NY 22 Nov,* $1,320 (£904)

—18—

—19—

—20—

—21—

—22—

—23—

Nineteenth century ivories are illustrated on p.456

1
A pair of carved ivory figures, representing Love and Youth, French, c.1895, one repaired at the feet, 24cm (3½in) and 25cm (9¾in), *L 21 Mar,* £1,265 ($1,531)

2
A pair of silver-mounted carved ivory figures of a 'Buttenmann' and his wife, probably Austro-Hungarian, c.1895, unmarked, 22cm (8½in) and 21cm (8¼in) high, *L 21 Mar,* £4,400 ($5,324)

3
A jewelled carved ivory figure, French, late 19th/early 20th century, of vierge ouvrante type, 20.5cm (8in) high, *L 21 Mar,* £858 ($1,038)

4
An ivory figure of Marie Antoinette, French, late 19th/early 20th century, cracks, 23cm (9in), *NY 30 Mar,* $880 (£709)

5
A silver-mounted ivory tankard, German, c.1890, the mounts chased in late 16th century taste, unmarked, 45.5cm (18in) high, *L 21 Mar,* £5,720 ($6,921)

6
A German carved ivory tankard, Gebrüder Gutgesell, Hanau, early 20th century, cracked, 34.5cm (13½in) high, *L 20 June,* £2,750 ($3,713)

7
A carved ivory tankard, German, c.1880, with detached finial, some damage, 50.5cm (20in) high, *L 20 June,* £3,080 ($4,158)

8
An ivory tankard, German, late 19th century, 42.5cm (18in) high, *L 20 June,* £3,300 ($4,455)

9
A silver-mounted carved ivory tankard, Hippolyte Verberckt, Antwerp, mid-19th century, 31.5cm (12½in) high, *L 20 June,* £3,740 ($5,049)

10
An ivory tankard, German, 19th century, 26.5cm (10½in), *NY 16 Feb,* $4,675 (£4,030)

11
A carved ivory figure of a mediaeval king, German, mid-late 19th century, 62cm (24½in) high, *L 21 Mar,* £2,200 ($2,662)

12
An ivory group, French, late 19th century, with two couples in 18th century Watteau-style costume and two gipsy fortune tellers, gilt-metal mounted base, 26.5cm (10½in) high, *L 7 Nov,* £16,500 ($24,750)

13
An ivory cup and cover, German, 19th century, 29cm (11½in), *NY 16 Feb,* $880 (£759)

1
A Viennese enamel-mounted ebonised wood musical casket, c.1895, 18.5cm (7¼in), L 20 June, £1,320 ($1,782)

2
A Viennese enamel dish, late 19th century, gilt-metal mounts, small chips, 31cm (12¼in) wide, L 20 June, £2,530 ($3,416)

3
A Viennese enamel tankard, Hermann Böhm, c.1895, silver mounts, 27.5cm (10¾in), L 20 June, £5,500 ($7,425)

4
A Viennese rock crystal and enamel cup and cover, c.1895, 18cm (7in), F 29 May, L 1,800,000 (£700; $925)

5
A Viennese enamel horn and stand, c.1895, with silver mounts, some wear, 39.5cm (15½in), L 20 June, £3,300 ($4,455)

6
A Viennese enamel centrepiece, late 19th century, with gilt-metal mounts, painted with figures after Watteau and Boucher, 22cm (8½in), L 21 Oct, £638 ($957)

7
A pair of Viennese silver and enamel large urns, probably Hermann Böhm, c.1895, 55cm (21½in), NY 10 June, $37,400 (£29,682)

8
A Viennese enamel miniature stein, ewer and compote, late 19th/early 20th century, stein and ewer with silver mounts, height of compote 9.5cm (3¾in), NY 10 June, $1,760 (£1,396)

9
Two Viennese silver and enamel cream jugs, late 19th century, 9 and 10cm (3½ and 4in), NY 11 Dec, $1,100 (£780)

10
A Viennese silver and enamel vase, Hermann Böhm, late 19th century, 22cm (8¾in), NY 11 Dec, $1,870 (£1,326)

11
A Hungarian jewelled silver-gilt and hardstone cup, mid-19th century, cold-painted and set with garnets, carbuncles and turquoises, brown agate bowl, 17cm (6¾in), L 21 Oct, £638 ($957)

12
A Viennese silver-gilt and enamel coronation coach, Ludwig Politzer, late 19th century, 18.5cm (7¼in) long, NY 11 Dec, $3,850 (£2,730)

13
A jewel-set enamelled gold architectural pendant, of Diana and Acteon, attributed to Reinhold Vasters, c.1875, 11.5cm (4½in), NY 21 May, $16,500 (£13,200)

14
A Viennese silver-gilt and enamel cup and cover, Hermann Böhm, late 19th century, 19cm (7½in), NY 10 June, $1,760 (£1,396)

15
A copper gilt and champlevé enamel ciborium, in Limoges 13th century style, probably Paris, 30.5cm (12in), L 31 Oct, £3,080 ($4,620)

16
A silver and silver-gilt reliquary group of the Virgin and Child, in French Gothic style, from the Marcy Workshops, 42cm (16½in), L 31 Oct, £4,620 ($6,930)

17
A boxwood group of the Virgin and Child, late 14th century style, 21cm (8¼in), L 31 Oct, £440 ($660)

1
An Austrian gilt bronze chamberlain's key, 19th century, bearing the initials FI for Franz Joseph of Austria and the Habsburg eagle, stamped with maker's mark PSW, 18.5cm (7¼in), *L 31 Oct,* £242 ($363)

2
A combined steel pistol and key, in 18th century style, 24cm (9½in), *L 31 Oct,* £1,100 ($1,650)

3
An iron double folding key, 17th century, 12cm (4¾in) closed, *L 31 Oct,* £352 ($528)

4
An English steel key, early 18th century, 14.5cm (5¾in), *L 31 Oct,* £715 ($1,073)

5
An English key, 18th century, 8.5cm (3¼in), *L 31 Oct,* £352 ($528)

6
A French steel lock and key, early 18th century, 19 x 15.5cm (7½ x 6in), *L 25 Apr,* £715 ($922)

7
A South German steel lock and key, late 17th/early 18th century, 16.5 x 9cm (6½ x 3½in), *L 25 Apr,* £1,650 ($2,128)

8
A Central European iron cupboard lock, mid-16th century, 24.5cm (9¾in), *NY 11 May,* $935 (£760)

9
A German iron key and chamber, late 17th century, key 15cm (6in), *L 31 Oct,* £352 ($528)

10
A South German steel double-padlock, early 18th century, struck with maker's mark of lion rampant, 17cm (6¾in) high, with two keys, one repaired, *L 4 July,* £2,970 ($4,099)

11
A bronze nest of weights, 17th century, probably Nuremburg, for 32 Marcs, 16cm (6¼in), *L 2 Apr,* £2,860 ($3,632)

12
A large bronze nest of weights, *c.*1681-1715, by Jonas Paulus Schirmer of Nurnberg, for 64lbs, some weights replaced, all converted to English lbs and stamped with Victorian verification marks, 28cm (11in) high without handle, *L 4 July,* £9,900 ($13,662)

13
A Venetian bronze door-knocker, late 16th century, 33cm (13in), *L 25 Apr,* £2,860 ($3,632)

14
A gilt copper and brass Minnekästchen, by Michel Mann, early 17th century, Augsburg, engraved with God and various saints, 5cm (2in) high, *L 12 Dec,* £2,860 ($4,004)

15
A French iron casket, early 16th century, 19cm (7½in) long, *L 12 Dec,* £1,375 ($1,925)

16
A German Baroque iron strong box, 17th century, 91cm (36in) wide, *NY 22 Nov,* $2,750 (£1,884)

17
A 17th century Nuremburg iron bound chest, 56 x 104cm (22 x 41in), *HS 16 July,* £1,980 ($2,871)

1

2   3   4   5

6   7   8   9

10   11   12

13   14   15

16   17

1
A bronze pot, 17th
century, 12.5cm (5in),
A 6 Sept,
Dfl 1,610 (£370; $544)

2
An Italian bronze mortar,
16th century, 13cm
(5¼in), *NY 22 Nov,*
$3,740 (£2,562)

3
A German Gothic mortar,
*c.*1400, some old
damages to rim, 15cm
(6in) high, *L 4 July,*
£1,100 ($1,485)

4
A bronze mortar, *c.*1660,
probably Nuremberg,
25.5cm (10in), *L 31 Oct,*
£825 ($1,238)

5
A German bronze mortar,
dated 1569, dolphin
handles, 14cm (5½in),
L 2 Apr,
£1,870 ($2,374)

6
**A North Italian bronze
mortar,** by Cavadini,
late 16th century, with
reliefs of harpies and
lionesses, golden brown
patina, 37cm (14½in),
NY 11 May,
$4,950 (£4,024)

7
**An Italian Renaissance
bronze mortar,** 16th
century, 14cm (5½in)
high, *NY 16 Feb,*
$935 (£806)

8
A bronze cauldron, 17th
century, 16cm (6¼in),
A 11 Feb,
Dfl 1,624 (£398; $466)

9
An Italian bronze mortar,
probably 17th century,
the sides cast with the
Medici arms, 13cm
(5in), with pestle,
NY 22 Nov,
$495 (£339)

1

A bronze lavabo, 16th century, 12cm (4¾in) high, *A 3 June*, **Dfl 4,872 (£1,102; $1,488)**

2

A pair of South German wrought iron wall lights, early 18th century, enriched with gilding, later wooden mounts, 56cm (22in), *L 4 July*, **£3,960 ($5,465)**

3

A Dutch brass teapot, 18th century, 16.5cm (6½in) high, *A 20 May*, **Dfl 986 (£229; $304)**

4

An English iron rushlight and candleholder, 18th century, 31cm (12¼in), *L 25 Apr*, **£605 ($780)**

5

Two similar rushlight and candleholders, 18th century, the bases in the form of banded wooden tubs, 34cm (13¼in), *L 25 Apr*, **£242 ($546)**

6

An English iron candle-stick, 16th century, 23cm (9in), *L 25 Apr*, **£440 ($567)**

7

A pair of Nuremberg brass snuffers, 17th century, the lid repoussé with Adam and Eve, 17cm (6¾in), *L 31 Oct*, **£550 ($825)**

8

A Dutch brass tobacco box, 18th century, with copper sides, the lid engraved with the story of Abraham and the sacrifice of Isaac, 18cm (7in), *S 17 Sept*, **£121 ($182)**

9

A pair of Italian gilt iron shears, early 17th century, the blades engraved with figures of male saints, 19.5cm (7¾in), *L 31 Oct*, **£440 ($660)**

10

A Dutch brass oval tobacco box, 18th century, 12cm (4¾in), *S 17 Sept*, **£50 ($74)**

11

A South German or Austrian brass and iron flat-iron, early 18th century, handle replaced, 18cm (7in), *L 31 Oct*, **£990 ($1,485)**

12

An Iserlohner brass tobacco box, second half 18th century, the base commemorating the Treaty between Russia, Prussia and Sweden in 1762 and signed IAKM (Iohann Adam Keppelman), 14.5cm (5¾in), *L 25 Apr*, **£242 ($312)**

13

A Dutch brass tobacco box, 18th century, the lid engraved with arms of the United Provinces, the base with anti-clerical medallions and caricatures, 12.5cm (5in) wide, *L 25 Apr*, **£242 ($312)**

14

An English steel rasp and tobacco box, second half 18th century, inscribed 'Tobacco leaves Ive often hid from Beging Knaves beneath this lid', 11cm (4¼in), *L 25 Apr*, **£385 ($496)**

15

An Iserlohner brass tobacco box, second half 18th century, the lid with a portrait of Ferdinand, Duke of Brunswick, copper sides, 16cm (6¼in), *L 25 Apr*, **£462 ($595)**

16

An early 18th century brass footman, 30.5cm (12in) high. *HS 4 June*. **£682 ($921)**

1   2
3   4   5   6
7   8
9   10   11
12   13   14   15   16

1
A maple and brass bed-warmer, late 18th century, 108cm (42½in), *NY 2 Feb,* $660 (£600)

2
An English brass warming pan, early 17th century, later wood handle, 31cm (12in) diam, *L 25 Apr,* £165 ($212)

3
A brass and iron bed-warmer, late 17th century, 115cm (45in), *C 3 Oct,* £418 ($585)

4
An English brass chestnut roaster, early 19th century, 54cm (21¼in), *NY 2 Feb,* $1,210 (£1,100)

5
An English brass caster, *c.*1750, 19cm (7½in), *HS 4 June,* £550 ($743)

6
A brass hanging lamp, 17th century, 29.5cm (11½in), *L 25 Apr,* £275 ($355)

7
A composed set of five copper measures, *c.*1840, gill to half gallon, 9 to 24cm (3½ x 9½in), with copper spirit funnel, *C 17 Jan,* £352 ($423)

8
An English brass wax jack, snuffers and stand, 18th century, *NY 2 Feb,* $1,540 (£1,400)

9
An English brass tankard, 18th century, 20cm (8in), *NY 2 Feb,* $6,050 (£5,127)

10
An English brass tankard, 18th century, 19cm (7½in), *NY 26 Oct,* $2,750 (£1,936)

11
A brass dish, 17th/18th century, with biblical scene in relief, 64cm (25¼in) diam, *A 3 June,* **Dfl 2,668** (£678; $916)

12
A Flemish brass charger, 17th/18th century, the well embossed with Adam and Eve, 68cm (26¾in) diam, *L 31 Oct,* £418 ($627)

13
A brass alms dish, 17th century, 40.5cm (16in) diam, *C 11 July,* £330 ($459)

14
A Venetian brass dish, late 16th century, with Arabic inscription, 48.5cm (19in) diam, *NY 11 May,* $2,200 (£1,789)

1
A Flemish brass candle-stick, last quarter 16th century, one old patch to stem, 20.5cm (8in), *L 25 Apr,* £825 ($1,064)

2
A brass Nuremberg bell-based candlestick, late 16th/early 17th century, by Stephan Schirmer, 21cm (8¼in), *L 25 Apr,* £1,155 ($1,489)

3
A pair of Nuremberg brass candlesticks, 17th century, maker's mark PM, 25.5cm (10in), *L 31 Oct,* £3,080 ($4,620)

4
A pair of Spanish brass candlesticks, 16th century, 7.5cm (3in), *L 31 Oct,* £528 ($792)

5
A Flemish brass candle-stick, c.1500, some wear, 25cm (9¾in), *L 31 Oct,* £935 ($1,403)

6
A pair of bronze pricket candlesticks, Italian, c.1600, 38.5cm (15¼in), *NY 11 May,* $1,760 (£1,431)

7
A pair of Flemish late Gothic dinanderie pricket candlesticks, late 15th/early 16th century, one pricket detached, one stem repaired, 36cm (14¼in), *NY 22 Nov,* $3,025 (£2,072)

8
A pair of Flemish Gothic dinanderie pricket candlesticks, late 15th/early 16th century, one stem repaired, 28cm (11in), *NY 22 Nov,* $2,475 (£1,695)

9
A pair of Spanish brass candlesticks, mid-17th century, 24cm (9½in), *L 31 Oct,* £418 ($627)

10
A set of four brass candlesticks, English, c.1750, 23cm (9¼in), *S 9 July,* £2,035 ($2,727)

11
A pair of brass table candlesticks, English, c.1735, 22cm (8½in), *C 17 Jan,* £528 ($634)

12
A Charles II brass candlestick, second half 17th century, 17.5cm (7in), *L 25 Apr,* £1,320 ($1,703)

13
A pair of brass telescopic ejector candlesticks, English, c.1800, 24cm (9½in) when extended, *S 9 July,* £143 ($192)

14
A pair of brass ejector candlesticks, English, late 18th century, 18cm (7in), *HS 4 June,* £374 ($505)

15
A pair of paktong candle-sticks, second quarter 18th century, 16cm (6¼in), *L 25 Apr,* £1,485 ($1,915)

16
A pair of paktong candle-sticks, 18th century, 24cm (9½in), *NY 2 Feb,* $2,420 (£2,050)

17
A pair of brass chamber candlesticks, English, c.1800, 11cm (4½in), *NY 1 Feb,* $440 (£400)

18
A pair of brass chamber candlesticks, c.1770, 10 x 14cm (4 x 5½in), *C 11 July,* £264 ($367)

19
A brass hanging candle-holder, first quarter 19th century, 25cm (9¾in) wide, *NY 2 Feb,* $880 (£800)

1
An American pewter
basin, Richard Austin,
Boston, *c.*1800, 20cm
(8in) diam, *NY 27 June,*
$330 (£253)

2
An American pewter
basin, Samuel Danforth,
Hartford, Connecticut,
*c.*1800, 17cm (6½in)
diam, *NY 27 June,*
$385 (£296)

3
An American pewter
plate, Frederick Bassett,
last half 18th century,
22cm (8½in) diam,
NY 27 June,
$385 (£296)

4
An American pewter **mug,**
Joseph Danforth,
Middleton, Connecti-
cut, *c.*1785, 15cm (6in),
NY 27 June,
$880 (£676)

5
An American pewter **mug,**
Nathaniel Austin,
Charlestown, Mass.,
late 18th century, 15cm
(6in) high, *NY 27 June,*
$3,960 (£3,046)

6
An American pewter **mug,**
Samuel Hamlin, Provi-
dence, Rhode Island,
late 18th/early 19th
century,15cm (6in),
NY 27 June,
$2,200 (£1,692)

7
An American pewter **mug,**
Nathaniel Austin,
Charlestown, Mass., late
18th century, 15cm
(6in) high, *NY 27 June,*
$1,320 (£1,015)

8
An American pewter
chamberstick, Roswell
Gleason, Dorchester,
Mass., *c.*1835, 7cm (3in)
high, *NY 27 June,*
$495 (£380)

9
An American pewter
flagon, Boardman & Co,
New York, *c.*1825, 28cm
(11in), *NY 27 June,*
$1,430 (£1,100)

10
An American drum-form
teapot, possibly New
York, *c.*1790, 17cm
(6½in) high, *NY 27 June,*
$3,630 (£2,792)

11
An American pewter
porringer, Samuel
Hamlin, Providence,
Rhode Island, late 18th
century, 20cm (8in)
long, *NY 27 June,*
$660 (£507)

12
An American pewter
candlestick, J B Wood-
bury, Philadelphia,
*c.*1840, 19cm (7½in),
NY 27 June,
$275 (£211)

13
A pair of American pewter
candlesticks, Flagg &
Homan, Cincinnati,
Ohio, 19th century,
23cm (9in), *NY 27 June,*
$605 (£465)

14
An American pewter
porringer, Thomas and
Sherman Boardman,
Hartford, Connecticut,
*c.*1820, 19cm (7½in),
NY 27 June,
$440 (£338)

15
A pewter water **jug,**
possibly American, late
18th/early 19th century,
30cm (12in), *NY 27 June,*
$220 (£169)

16
An American pewter
beaker, Timothy Boardman & Co, New York,
*c.*1825, 13cm (5¼in)
high, *NY 27 June,*
$880 (£676)

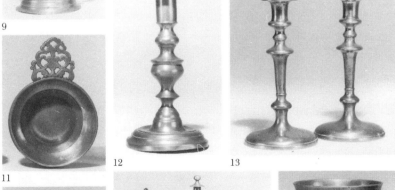

1
A William and Mary 'wriggled-work' pewter portrait beaker, c.1689-94, by John Kenton of London, engraved with portraits of the monarchs, 13cm (5in), *L 25 Apr,* **£2,970 ($3,831)**

2
A pewter ball-knopped candlestick, second half 17th century, maker's mark CB, later sconce, 22cm (8¾in), *L 25 Apr,* **£492 ($634)**

3
A pair of pewter pricket candleholders, early 18th century, perhaps Austrian, faults, 79cm (31in), *L 25 Apr,* **£528 ($681)**

4
A Dutch black-lacquered pewter urn, decorated with gilt birds, 18th/19th century, 44cm (17¼in), *A 11 Feb,* **Dfl 1,015 (£249; $291)**

5
A Stuart pewter candlestick, last quarter 17th century, 18cm (7in), *L 25 Apr,* **£5,060 ($6,527)**

6
A Charles II pewter charger, c.1670, probably by William Wette, 58.5cm (23in), *L 25 Apr,* **£1,100 ($1,419)**

7
A Flemish pewter dish, (**Kardinaalschotel**), c.1700, by CP of Antwerp, probably Cornelis Peeters I, 32.5cm (12¾in), *L 25 Apr,* **£770 ($993)**

8
A pewter 'wriggled-work' plate, English, c.1720, by John Duncombe, 22.5cm (8¾in), *L 25 Apr,* **£506 ($653)**

9
A small garnish of wavy-edged pewter flatware, English, mid 18th century, by Jonas Durand Jr of London, consisting of four dishes, 33cm (13in) diam, and fourteen plates, 24.5cm (9½in) diam, *L 31 Oct,* **£2,200 ($3,300)**

10
A Dutch pewter chamber-pot, The Hague, 19th century, marked 'IM' for Johannis Nicolaas Meeuws, 16cm (6¼in), *A 4 Sept,* **Dfl 862 (£198; $291)**

11
A French pewter ecuelle and cover, 18th century, *A 3 June,* **Dfl 1,160 (£262; $354)**

12
A Regency oval pewter tureen and cover, c.1820, wooden handles, 42cm (16½in) long overall, *L 25 Apr,* **£572 ($738)**

13
A Dutch pewter inkwell, 18th century, 6cm (2½in) high, *A 3 June,* **Dfl 1,798 (£407; $549)**

14
A pewter urn, early 19th century, painted red and stencilled with gold leaves and flowers, some retouching, 38cm (15in), *NY 1 Feb,* **$935 (£850)**

15
Three French pewter culinary moulds, late 19th century, hinged, *C 17 Jan,* **£363 ($436)**

1
A James I pewter flagon, c.1610, some repairs, 38.5cm (15¼in), *L 31 Oct*, £1,430 ($2,145)

2
A pewter tappit-hen flagon, Scottish, 18th century, 27cm (10½in), *A 3 June*, Dfl 2,204 (£499; $673)

3
A French pewter 'cimarre' flagon, 18th century, 25.5cm (10in), *A 3 June*, Dfl 5,104 (£1,155; $1,559)

4
A Swiss pewter schnabel-stitze, c.1783, by Johannes Zimmermann of Zurich, 32.5cm (12¾in), *L 31 Oct*, £330 ($495)

5
A Dutch pewter flagon, Amsterdam 1751, maker's mark MB, 25cm (9¾in), *A 3 June*, Dfl 1,392 (£315; $425)

6
A pewter flagon, probably Bruges, 17th/18th century, 26.5cm (10½in), *A 3 June*, Dfl 3,364 (£761; $1,027)

7
A Dutch pewter flagon, Maastricht 1696, 28cm (11in), *A 3 June*, Dfl 4,640 (£1,050; $1,417)

8
A pewter 'Rembrandt' flagon, last quarter of the 18th century, by Berend Derk Helderman, Deventer, 25.5cm (10in), *A 3 June*, Dfl 7,192 (£1,627; $2,197)

9
A William and Mary pewter 'wriggled-work' portrait tankard, c.1689-94, made by Richard Donne of London, engraved with portraits of the monarchs, 18cm (7in), *L 31 Oct*, £14,300 ($21,450)

10
A French pewter 'cruche à lait', early 19th century, marked Pissavy à Lyon, *A 3 June*, Dfl 3,480 (£787; $1,063)

11
A Swiss pewter bauch-kanne, 18th century, Valais, by Pier Antoin Simaval, 33cm (13in), *L 25 Apr*, £440 ($568)

12
A pewter and wood tankard, German, mid-18th century, 16cm (6¼in), *A 3 June*, Dfl 4,872 (£1,102; $1,488)

13
A Gothic pewter flagon, 14th century, in fine state of preservation, excavated near Tonbridge, Kent, 24cm (9½in) high overall, *L 31 Oct*, £21,450 ($32,175)

14
A Saxon pewter tankard, dated 1767, maker's marks of Johan Andeas Burckhardt of Zwickau, 25cm (9½in), *L 31 Oct*, £308 ($462)

15
A Swiss pewter stegkanne, second half 18th century, by Johann Heinrich Petersohn of Bern, 26.5cm (10½in), *A 3 June*, Dfl 4,640 (£1,050; $1,417)

16
A Swiss pewter prismen-kanne, mid-18th century, by Johannes Weber of Zurich, 40cm (15¾in), *L 25 Apr*, £495 ($624)

1
A Norwegian polychrome and carved wood marriage candelabra, 18th/19th century, perhaps Setesdal, the stem carved with the inscription 'Norsk Fine Eine Hustru', 56.8cm (22¼in), *L 31 Oct*, £2,640 ($3,960)

2
A Norwegian burrwood tankard, dated 1721, the lid carved with a roundel enclosing the Royal Norwegian Lion, 29.5cm (11½in), *L 31 Oct*, £1,430 ($2,145)

3
A Norwegian carved wood tankard, second half 17th century, carved with biblical figures, some restoration to feet, 23.1cm (9¼in), *L 31 Oct*, £11,000 ($16,500)

4
A Norwegian stavework pitcher, 18th century, perhaps Numedal, the sides painted with cartouches enclosing traces of initials, 22.9cm (9in), *L 31 Oct*, £1,870 ($2,805)

5
A Norwegian wood skala, late 18th century, the rim painted with an inscription and the date 179?, 41.2cm (16¼in), *L 31 Oct*, £1,155 ($1,733)

6
A Norwegian wood ale bowl, *c.*1775, the exterior of the rim painted with an inscription and the date 1775, 25.2cm (9¾in), *L 31 Oct*, £1,870 ($2,805)

7
A Norwegian burrwood tankard, 18th century, probably Hedmark, the lid carved with the Royal Norwegian Lion, some worming and damage, 26cm (10¼in), *L 31 Oct*, £440 ($660)

8
A Dutch cheese sellers sign, dated 1766, inscribed 'Kaashande-lary', 140cm (45in), *L 31 Oct*, £1,210 ($1,815)

9
A Norwegian polychrome wood ale bowl, late 18th/early 19th century and a Norwegian painted wood scoop, 19th century, 36.2cm (14¼in), *L 31 Oct*, £935 ($1,403)

10
A Norwegian painted wood Trøys, 18th/19th century, inscribed inside with the date 1847, the paint perhaps later, 35.5cm (14in), *L 31 Oct*, £1,265 ($1,898)

11
A Norwegian carved burrwood tankard, first half 18th century, Telemark, the handle with an old brass repair, three ball feet missing, traces of red paint, 22.8cm (9in), *L 31 Oct*, £3,960 ($5,940)

12
A pair of Norwegian birchwood 'lion' peg tankards, 18th century, 23cm (9in), *S 9 July*, £880 ($1,179)

13
A Norwegian painted and carved wood tankard, late 18th/early 19th century, Gudbrandsdal, painted primarily in red, green and ochre, 17cm (6¾in), *L 31 Oct*, £308 ($462)

14
An Austrian wood and bone casket, 17th century, 28.2cm (11¼in), *L 31 Oct*, £770 ($1,155)

15
An Upper Rhine cedarwood casket, *c.*1500, 38.8cm (15¼in), *L 2 Apr*, £660 ($838)

1
A South German minia-
ture table cabinet,
early 17th century, of
ebonised wood mounted
with gilt copper reliefs
of Faith, Justice,
Judith and the head of
Holofernes, 15.8cm
(6¼in), *L 2 Apr,*
£1,100 ($1,397)

2
A Nuremberg Hafner
Ware stove tile, mid-
16th century, worked
in polychrome relief
with the portrait of the
Countess of Branden-
burg, 29 x 25cm (11½
x 9¾in), *L 12 Dec,*
£1,650 ($2,310)

3
A blackjack, mid-17th
century, with later
silver mounts, 38cm
(15in), *C 31 Jan,*
£374 ($441)

4
A painted leather fire
bucket, Columbia Eagle
Fire Society, branded
J Fenno, Boston, 19th
century, decorated with
American eagle and
shield, 33cm (13in),
NY 2 Feb,
$2,640 (£2,400)

5
A pair of leather and
silver-mounted ewers,
c.1780, lined with metal,
one with handle lack-
ing, 51cm (20in),
C 11 July,
£2,200 ($3,058)

6
A silver roundel, late
17th century, with a
portrait of William III
on horseback, 12cm
(4¾in), *L 12 Dec,*
£495 ($693)

7
An onyx cameo, early
19th century, carved
with the head of Medusa
inspired by the Farnese
cup), chipped, 8cm
(3¼in) diam, *L 12 Dec,*
£1,100 ($1,540)

8
A German mother-of-
pearl portrait relief,
mid-18th century,
attributed to Johann
Ludwig Meil, 10.2cm
(4in), *L 12 Dec,*
£5,720 ($8,008)

9
A German honestone
portrait roundel, early
16th century, dated
1514, 8.6cm (3¼in),
L 2 Apr,
£5,720 ($7,264)

10
A German honestone
roundel, mid-18th
century, 6.5cm (2½in),
L 12 Dec,
£330 ($462)

11
A fruitwood double snuff
box, late 18th century,
carved with a portrait
of Charles III of
Spain and Sicily, 7.5cm
(3in), *L 25 Apr,*
£154 ($198)

12
A horn snuff box, by O
Brisset, signed and
dated 1727, the cover
depicting George II on
horseback, 11cm (4¼in),
C 17 Jan,
£132 ($158)

13
A Dutch East Indies snuff
box, *c.*1800, 10.3cm
(4in), *L 25 Apr,*
£110 ($141)

14
A French fruitwood
flask, late 17th century,
carved with portrait
heads of the Virgin and
St Joseph, 10cm (4in),
L 25 Apr,
£165 ($212)

15
A wooden tobacco box,
carved with biblical
scenes, 18th century,
A 25 Feb,
Dfl 1,972 (£483; $541)

16
A Scottish staghorn snuff
mull, *c.*1714, 8.5cm
(3¼in), *L 25 Apr,*
£330 ($425)

17
A French fruitwood
spectacles case, late 17th
century, 8cm (3¼in),
L 25 Apr,
£165 ($212)

1
A polychrome wax portrait by J Heuberger, 1841, on slate ground inscribed 'J Heuberger 1841', 17cm (5¾in), *L 31 Oct,* £275 ($413)

2
A polychrome wax portrait, possibly by J H Hagbold, *c.* 1800, glass ground painted with clouds on the underside, 7.8cm (3in), *L 31 Oct,* £165 ($248)

3
A wax portrait relief of Robert Burns by John Fillans, 1857, 10cm (4in), *L 31 Oct,* £176 ($264)

4
A wax portrait, of William Roscoe of Liverpool, by Samuel Percy, early 19th century, in a glazed giltwood frame, 33 x 30.5cm (13 x 12in), *L 2 Apr,* £2,640 ($3,352)

5
A wax portrait bust, by G G Parker, possibly Simon Bolivar, mid-19th century, signed, 21.5cm (8½in), *L 31 Oct,* £187 ($281)

6
A pink wax portrait bust, of Princess Charlotte of Wales and Saxe-Coburg, by Samuel Percy, 1814, 17.8cm (7in), *L 12 Dec,* £242 ($339)

7
A pair of wax portrait reliefs, by Giovanni Antonio Santarelli, with trade labels dated 1805 and 1807, mounted in original gilt and gessoed wood frames, 10.6cm (4¼in), *L 4 July,* £1,045 ($1,442)

8
A pair of wax portrait reliefs of Matthew Boulton and James Watt, by Peter Rouw, signed and dated 1803, both cracked, 17cm square (6¾in), *L 31 Oct,* £605 ($908)

9
A wax portrait relief of Queen Charlotte, by Peter Rouw, dark glass ground, inscribed on the back of the wax with the sitter's name and 'Peter Rouw Sculptor, Modeller of Gems & Cameos to His R H the Prince Regent, 22 Carmarthen Street, Fitzroy Square, London 1814', 14cm (5½in), *L 31 Oct,* £605 ($908)

10
A wax relief, of Sir John Thorold Bt, by Peter Rouw, 1809, pink wax on glass ground, signed and dated, later papier-mâché frame, 11cm (4¼in), *L 12 Nov,* £275 ($385)

11
A pair of wax portrait busts, by Samuel Percy, late 18th century, signed 'Percy No. 642, No. 643' in original frames and backing paper with inscription dated 'October 1786', 16.5cm (6½in), *L 31 Oct,* £286 ($429)

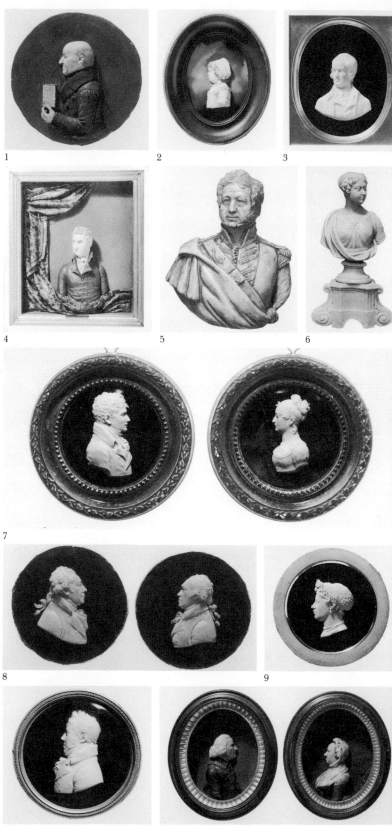

19th and 20th Century Sculpture

Article ● Marble sculpture *pp* 477-480

See also ● Colour illustrations *p* 481 ● Decorative arts from 1880 *pp* 334-336
● Russian works of art *p* 440 ● European works of art *pp* 450-451

1
An alabaster group of young woman and child, *c.*1880, Italian, 48cm (19in), *C 18 Apr,* £330 ($429)

2
An alabaster bust, *c.*1900, 61cm (24in), *C 17 Jan,* £264 ($317)

3
Giovanni Broggi, an alabaster figure of a girl, *c.*1890, signed, 66cm (26in), *L 20 June,* £1,045 ($1,411)

4
P Barranti, an alabaster group of a youth and young maid at a fountain, 1902, signed, repaired, 81cm (32in), *S 11 June,* £792 ($1,041)

5
Anton van Wouw, Bad News, 1907, signed and inscribed 'G Nisini-fuse Roma', rich brown patination, 30cm (11¾in), *JHB 18 Mar,* **R 32,000** (£14,414; $17,441)

6
Edmund Caldwell, a bronze figure of a buffalo, 32.5cm (12¾in), *JHB 18 Mar,* **R4,500** (£2,027; $2,453)

7
Anton van Wouw, Lehman, The Postman, 1901, signed, dark brown patination, 45cm, (17¾in), *JHB 18 Mar,* **R 12,000** (£5,405; $6,540)

8
Anton van Wouw, The Dagga Smoker, signed and inscribed 'S A Joh-Burg' and 'Fonderia G Nisini, Roma', dark patination, *JHB 18 June,* **R 20,000** (£7,813; $10,548)

Edmund Caldwell,
b.1852 Canterbury

Anton van Wouw,
1862-1945

1

2

3

4

5

6

7

8

1
Gilbert Bayes, The Remounts, signed and dated 1915, rich brown patination, 23cm (9in), *L 12 Apr,* £2,640 ($3,379)

2
Sir Joseph Edgar Boehm, a bronze group of a girl on horseback with boy and dog, signed, dated 1865, rich brown patination, 43cm (14in), *L 2 Oct,* £3,300 ($4,851)

3
Thomas Thornycroft, Young Victoria on Horseback, signed and dated 1853, brown patination, 56cm (22in), *L 12 June,* £3,520 ($4,682)

4
Joseph Durham, a bronze model of Albert, Prince Consort, signed and with foundry mark Elkington & Co, rich coppery/black patination, 67cm (26½in), *S 23 July,* £1,650 ($2,442)

5
Bertram MacKennal, Salome, signed, dark brown patination, on a marble plinth, 33cm (13in), *L 2 Oct,* £5,720 ($8,408)

6
Bertram MacKennal, Circe, signed and inscribed, dark brown patination, 60.5cm (23½in), *L 12 June,* £16,500 ($21,945)

7
Gilbert Bayes, A Young Diana, signed and dated 1915, rich brown patination, 28cm (11in), *L 12 Apr,* £1,980 ($2,534)

8
Goscombe John, The Drummer Boy, signed, rich brown patination, 44cm (17¼in), *L 12 June,* £4,180 ($5,560)

9
Albert Toft, a bronze figure of a foundry worker, signed and dated 1914, dark-green patination, 35cm (13¾in), *S 11 June,* £858 ($1,128)

10
Henry Alfred Pegram, a bronze group of Man and Mermaid, signed, bronze patination, 55cm (21¾in), *L 2 Oct,* £3,850 ($5,660)

11
Felix Weiss, a bronze portrait bust of Conrad Veidt, signed and dated 1932, dark-brown patination, 45cm (17½in) high, *S 19 Feb,* £176 ($202)

12
John Henry Foley, a pair of bronze figures of Oliver Goldsmith and Edmund Burke, mid-19th century, inscribed Elkington & Co, brown coppery patination, 51cm (20in), *S 11 June,* £858 ($1,128)

13
Sir George Frampton, a bronze figure of Peter Pan, brown patination, on ebonised wood socle, 18cm (7in), *L 2 Oct,* £3,080 ($4,528)

Gilbert Bayes, 1872-1953, fl.London

Sir Joseph Edgar Boehm, 1834-90, London

Joseph Durham, 1814-77, London

John Henry Foley, RA, 1818-74

Sir George James Frampton, RA, 1860-1928, fl.London

Sir William Goscombe John, 1860-1952, fl.London

Sir Edgar Bertram MacKennal, b.1863 Melbourne, Australia, d.1931, fl.London and Paris

Henry Alfred Pegram, RA, 1862-1937, fl.London

Thomas Thornycroft, 1815-85, fl.London

Albert Toft, 1862-1949, fl.London

Felix Weiss, b.1908 Vienna, fl.Paris and London

1   2   3

4   5   6   7

8   9   10

11   12   13

1
Frédéric-Auguste Bartholdi, a white metal figure of 'Liberty Enlightening the World', *c.*1885, grey/black patina, signed and with Avoiron foundry mark, 99cm (39in), *NY 30 Nov*, $5,500 (£3,691)

2
Louis-Simon Boizot, a bronze group of the Abduction of Persephone, late 19th century, brown patina, 52cm (21½in), *NY 22 June*, $715 (£559)

3
Louis Chalon, a bronze figure of a Valkyrie on horseback, *c.*1910, signed, brown patination, *L 21 Mar*, £1,760 ($2,130)

4
After Coustou, a pair of bronze Marly horses, *c.*1870, each 58cm (22¾in), *C 17 Jan*, £495 ($594)

5
Jean Didier Debut, a bronze figure of an Arabian woman, Fatma, late 19th century, signed, worn golden-brown patina, 81cm (32in), *NY 30 Mar*, $1,320 (£1,064)

6
Edouard Drouot, a bronze figure of a miner, *c.*1880, signed, rich brown patination, 38cm (15in), *L 21 Mar*, £902 ($1,091)

7
Jean-Didier Debut, a bronze figure of an Arabian warrior, *c.*1890, signed and stamped with 'Bronze Garanti au Titre' seal, rich red and brown patination, *L 21 Mar*, £572 ($692)

8
Alfred Dubucand, a bronze group of an Arab boy and a donkey, *c.*1870, signed, light and dark patination, *L 21 Mar*, £1,320 ($1,597)

9
Alfred Dubucand, a bronze group of a hunting horse and two hunting dogs, *c.*1870, signed, light brown patination, 22cm (9in), *L 20 June*, £825 ($1,114)

10
E Drappier, a bronze group of blacksmiths, early 20th century, black patina, 54cm (21¼in) high, *NY 30 Mar*, $1,760 (£1,419)

11
Eugene Delaplanche, a bronze group of mother and child, late 19th century, signed and with F Barbedienne foundry mark, dark brown patina, 54cm (21½in), *NY 30 Mar*, $1,980 (£1,596)

12
Leon-Noel Delagrange, a bronze bust of an Egyptian: Morgiane, late 19th/early 20th century, signed, 49.5cm (19½in), *NY 22 June*, $715 (£559)

Frédéric-Auguste Bartholdi, 1834-1904, fl.Paris

Louis Simon Boizot, 1843-1909,

Louis Chalon, b.1866, fl.Paris

Jean Didier Debut, 1824-93, fl.Paris

Leon Noel Delagrange, 1872-1910, fl.Paris

Eugene Delaplanche, 1836-91, fl.Paris

E Drappier, fl.early 20th century

Edouard Drouot, b.1859, fl.Paris

Alfred Dubucand, b.1828, Paris

1
Isidore Bonheur, a bronze group of a horse and jockey, *c.*1870, signed and inscribed with the Peyrol foundry stamp, rich red/brown patination, 61cm (24in), *L 20 June,* £11,000 ($14,850)

2
Isidore Bonheur, a bronze figure of a racehorse, *c.*1870, signed, brown patination, 34cm (13½in), *L 20 June,* £1,760 ($2,376)

3
Antoine Louis Barye, a bronze figure of the 'Cheval Percheron', *c.*1850, signed, green and black patination, 20cm (8in), *L 7 Nov,* £3,630 ($5,445)

4
Alfred Barye and Emile Guillemin, a spelter group of an Arab on horseback, late 19th century, signed and with the 'Fabrication Francais' seal, 81cm (31in), *L 20 June,* £2,860 ($3,861)

5
Alphonse-Alexandre Arson, a bronze group of a bird protecting her young, *c.*1867, signed, brown patina, 31cm (12¼in), high, *NY 22 June,* $1,210 (£945)

6
Alfred Barye, a spelter group of a jockey on horseback, *c.*1880, signed, black patination, 21cm (8¼in), *L 7 Nov,* £308 ($462)

7
Albert-Ernest Carrier-Belleuse, an ivory, silvered and parcel-gilt bronze figure, Graziella, *c.*1890, signed, 74cm (29¼in), *NY 30 Mar,* $2,750 (£2,217)

8
Jean-Jules Allasseur, a bronze group of Moses rescued from the waters, third quarter 19th century, brown patina, 64cm (25¼in), *NY 30 Nov,* $2,310 (£1,550)

9
Isidore Bonheur, a bronze group of a bull and dog, early 20th century, signed, black patina, 63.5cm (25in), *NY 22 June,* $1,540 (£1,203)

10
Albert-Ernest Carrier-Belleuse, a gilt and silvered-bronze of Rembrandt, *c.*1900, signed, lacquered gold/silver patina, 53cm (21in), *NY 22 June,* $550 (£430)

11
Albert Ernest Carrier-Belleuse, a bronze figure of a soldier, *c.*1870, signed, brown patination, 63cm (24¾in), *L 21 Mar,* £770 ($932)

12
Albert Ernest Carrier-Belleuse, a gilt-bronze figure of a bacchante and cherub, late 19th century, signed, 51cm (20in), *NY 30 Nov,* $2,310 (£1,550)

Jean Jules Allasseur, 1818-1903, fl.Paris

Alphonse-Alexandre Arson, 1822-80, fl.Paris

Alfred Barye, son of Antoin Louis, fl.Paris

Antoine Louis Barye, 1796-1875, fl.Paris

Isidore Jules Bonheur, b.1827, fl.Paris

Albert Ernest Carrier-Belleuse, 1824-87, fl.England and France

Pietro Calvi, 1833-84, Milan

Christophe Fratin, *c.*1800-64

Emmanuel Fremiet, 1824-1910, fl.Paris

Adrien Etienne Gaudez, 1845-1902, fl.Paris

Paul Joseph Raymond Gayrard, 1807-55, fl.Paris

Jean Francois Theodore Gechter, 1796-1844, fl.Paris

Emile Coriolan Hippolyte Guillemin, 1841-1907, Paris

1
Christophe Fratin,
a bronze figure of
'Rainbow', *c*.1840,
signed and inscribed
with the founder's mark
'Quesnel fondr.', rich
brown patination, 31cm
(12¼in), *L 5 July,*
£3,300 ($4,554)

2
Christophe Fratin, a
bronze group of a cow
and a bull, *c*.1850,
signed, one stamped
Fratin, rich brown
patination, 24cm (9½in),
L 21 Mar,
£528 ($639)

3
Emmanuel Fremiet, a
bronze group of a pair
of horses and jockeys,
c.1860, signed, 47cm
(18½in), *L 7 Nov,*
£13,750 ($20,625)

4
Emmanuel Fremiet, a
bronze group of a horse
and jockey, *c*.1880,
signed, dark and red/
brown patination,
45.5cm (18in), *L 5 July,*
£5,500 ($7,590)

5
Joseph Raymond Gayrard,
a bronze group of a
young man and woman,
c.1850, signed, rich
dark brown patination,
49.5cm (19½in), *L 20 June,*
£682 ($921)

6
Adrien Etienne Gaudez,
a bronze figure of a
woman, Mignon, late
19th century, brown
patina, 56.5cm (22¼in),
NY 22 June,
$1,100 (£859)

7
Adrien Etienne Gaudez, a
bronze figure of Saint
Cecile, *c*.1890, signed,
89cm (35in), *L 21 Mar,*
£638 ($772)

8
Guiseppe Grandi, a
bronze figure of a man,
signed, dull green/
brown patination, 66cm
(26in), *L 21 Mar,*
£990 ($1,198)

9
Emile Lambert, a bronze
figure, entitled 'Voltaire,'
c.1890, signed, 45cm
(17¾in), *C 17 Jan,*
£462 ($554)

10
H Keck, a bronze figure
of a blacksmith, early
20th century, black
patina, *NY 30 Mar,*
$880 (£709)

11
**Jean Francois Theodore
Gechter,** a bronze group
of a greyhound with a
hare, *c*.1843, signed,
brown patination, 37cm
(14½in), *L 21 Mar,*
£1,650 ($1,997)

12
**Ievegueni Alexandrovich
Lanceray,** a bronze figure
of a horse, late 19th
century, signed in
cyrillic, dark brown
patination, 15.5cm
(6¼in), *L 21 Mar,*
£572 ($692)

13
Henri Louis Levasseur,
a bronze figure of a
woman perched on a
half-moon, *c*.1900,
signed & inscribed
Tiffany & Co, 78cm
(30¾in), *NY 22 June,*
$2,200 (£1,719)

14
Alfred-Desire Lanson, a
bronze figure of an
oriental woman playing
an instrument, *c*.1890,
green, earth and golden
brown patina, 81cm
(32in), *NY 22 June,*
$1,540 (£1,203)

Guiseppe Grandi,
1843-91, fl.Milan
and Turin

**Emile Placide
Lambert,** 1828-97,
fl.Paris

**Ievegueni Alexandro-
vich Lanceray,** 1848-
86, St Petersburg,
fl.Paris

Alfred-Desire Lanson,
1851-98, fl.Paris

Prosper Lecourtier,
1855-1924, studied
under Fremiet,
fl.Paris

Henri Louis Levasseur,
b.1853, studied under
Delaplanche, fl.Paris

1

2

3

4

5

6

7

8

9

10

11

12

13

14

1
Pierre Jules Mêne, a bronze group of 'l'Accolade', c.1870, with a mare and stallion standing side by side, signed, dark brown patination, 34cm (13¼in), *L 5 July*, £3,520 ($4,858)

2
Pierre Jules Mêne, a cast-iron group of 'l'Accolade', Russian, late 19th/early 20th century, base stamped in cyrillic, black patination, 32cm (12½in) high, *S 19 Feb*, £353 ($405)

3
Pierre Jules Mêne, a bronze group of 'l'Accolade', c.1860, signed, rich brown patination, 20cm (8in), *L 7 Nov*, £1,485 ($2,228)

4
Pierre Jules Mêne, a bronze group of a setter, a pointer and a partridge, c.1880, signed, light and dark patination, 23cm (9in), *L 21 Mar*, £880 ($1,065)

5
Pierre Jules Mêne, a bronze group of 'Vainqueur du Derby', c.1863, signed, rich brown patination, 42.5cm (16¾in), *L 5 July*, £7,480 ($10,322)

6
Pierre Jules Mêne, a bronze figure of 'Cheval Libre', c.1860, signed, dark brown patination, 18.5cm (7½in), *L 20 June*, £858 ($1.158)

7
Pierre Jules Mêne, a bronze figure of a deer, signed, brown patination, *L 21 Mar*, £572 ($692)

8
Pierre Jules Mêne, a bronze figure of a falconner, c.1880, signed, brown patination, 65cm (25½in), *L 7 Nov*, £1,155 ($1,733)

9
Marius Jean Antonin Mercie, a bronze group entitled 'Gloria Victis', c.1880, signed, brown and gilt patination, 89cm (35in), *L 21 Mar*, £2,530 ($3,061)

10
Auguste Moreau, a spelter figure of a young woman, c.1900, signed, 102cm (40in), *L 21 Mar*, £528 ($639)

11
Hippolyte Moreau, a bronze bust of a young woman, c.1890, signed, light red/brown and dark brown patination, 58cm (23in), *L 7 Nov*, £935 ($1,403)

12
Hippolyte Moreau and Prosper Lecourtier, a bronze group entitled 'Piqueur au Relais, Salon des Beaux Arts', c.1870, signed, with foundry seal Societe de Bronze de Paris, light and dark brown patination, 80cm (31½in), *L 7 Nov*, £4,400 ($6,600)

Pierre Jules Mêne, 1810-71, fl.Paris

Marius Jean Antoine Mercie, 1845-1916, fl.Paris

August Moreau, born Dijon, fl.19th/20th century

Hippolyte Moreau, b.1832 Dijon, fl.Paris

1 2

3 4

5 6 7

8 9

10 11 12

1
Jules Moigniez, a bronze group of a turkey and a cockerel, c.1860, signed, brown patination, 21.5cm (8½in), *L 21 Mar,* £682 ($825)

2
René Paris, a bronze group of 'A Two Year Old's Canter', c.1910, signed, dark red brown patination, 20cm (8in), *L 5 July,* £1,540 ($2,125)

3
Benedict Rougelet, A bronze figure of a ballerina, c.1887, signed, rich brown patination, 41cm (16in), *L 7 Nov,* £1,045 ($1,568)

4
R Ripamonti, a bronze group of Napoleon on horseback: Waterloo, 1908, signed, thick dark-brown/green patination, 64cm (25in), *S 16 Apr,* £1,100 ($1,430)

5
Jules Moigniez, a bronze group of 'Mon Etoile', c.1860, signed, yellow/golden brown and brown patination, 32.5cm (12¾in), *L 5 July,* £1,650 ($2,277)

6
Emile-Louis Picault, a bronze figure of a woman at a memorial: Le Souvenir, c.1900, signed, green patina, 63.5cm (25in), *NY 22 June,* $660 (£516)

7
Jules Moigniez, a gilt-bronze figure of a heron, c.1885, 54cm (21¼in), *NY 22 June,* $2,090 (£1,633)

8
Jules Moigniez, a gilt-bronze group of a bird feeding her fledglings, late 19th century, signed, weathered/depatinated, 49cm (19¼in), *NY 22 June,* $990 (£773)

9
Emile Picault, a pair of bronze figures of a falconer with a dog and a young woman, c.1880, signed and stamped Bellman Ivey & Carter, brown patination, 77.5cm (30½in), *L 21 Mar,* £2,860 ($3,461)

10
Henri-Honore Plé, a bronze figure of an Arab, c.1885, signed, dark brown patina, 141cm (55½in), *NY 22 June,* $11,550 (£9,023)

11
Jean Jacques Pradier, a bronze figure of Venus, signed and founder's mark Susse Freres, depatinated, 33cm (13in), *NY 30 Mar,* $770 (£620)

12
Louis Polét, a bronze group of a youth and a lioness, early 20th century, signed and with Exposition gold medal stamp of 1900, mid and dark brown patination, 56cm (22in), *S 19 Feb,* £605 ($696)

13
Emile Pinedo, a bronze group of an Arabian on a camel, late 19th century, signed, with foundry seal 'Syndicate de Fabr de Bronze', light and dark brown, silver and gilt patination, 78cm (30½in), *L 20 June,* £6,160 ($8,316)

Emile Louis Picault, *born c.1840,* fl. Paris

Emile Pinedo, fl.Paris, first exhibited 1870

Henri Honore Plé, 1853-1922, fl.Paris

Jean Jacques Pradier, 1792-1852, fl.Rome and Paris

Riccardo Ripamonti, 1849-1930, Milan

Benedict Rougelet, 1834-94, fl.Paris

1
Alexandre Schoenwerk,
a bronze figure of a
woman, c.1870, signed,
rich brown patination,
33cm (13in), *L 7 Nov,*
£715 ($1,073)

2
V Szczeblewski, a bronze
figure, 'A Whistling
Cabin Boy', 1889, dark
brown patination, 43cm
(17in), *C 18 Apr,*
£1,012 ($1,316)

3
Jean Jules Salmson, a
pair of bronze figures of
an Arabian man and
woman, c.1870, signed,
dark brown patination,
56cm (22in) and 53cm
(21in), *L 21 Mar,*
£2,310 ($2,795)

4
Georges van der Straeten,
A bronze bust of a
young woman, c.1890,
signed and with the
'Societe de bronze de
Paris' seal, gilt/green
and red/brown patina-
tion, 60cm (23½in),
L 20 June,
£770 ($1,040)

5
Thyllmani, a pair of
bronze figures, Italian,
late 19th century, signed,
black/green patination,
91cm (36in), *S 23 July,*
£1,815 ($2,686)

6
Charles Raoul Verlet,
a gilt-bronze group of
Orpheus and Cerberus,
signed and inscribed
F Barbedienne Fondeur,
late 19th/early 20th
century, 100.5cm
(39½in), *NY 30 Mar,*
$5,500 (£4,435)

7
**A cold painted bronze
group of two Arabians,**
c.1900, 16cm (6¼in),
L 7 Nov,
£902 ($1,353)

8
*** Waagen, a bronze
group of 'Kabyle au
Retour de la Chasse',
c.1870, signed, light,
dark and red brown
and cream patination,
91.5cm (36in), *L 7 Nov,*
£8,250 ($12,375)

9
After the Antique, a
bronze figure of Nar-
cissus, late 19th century,
green patination,
63.5cm (25in), *L 20 June,*
£550 ($743)

10
Joseph Uphues, a bronze
figure of a hunter,
late 19th century,
signed, brown pati-
nation, 127cm (50in),
L 21 Mar,
£2,310 ($2,795)

11
After the Antique, a
bronze group of Lao-
coon and the Serpent,
late 19th century, green-
brown patination, 61cm
(24in), *C 18 Apr,*
£682 ($887)

12
After the Antique, a
bronze figure of a faun,
1880, signed Duchemin,
mid-green/brown
patination, 59cm (23in)
high, *S 19 Feb,*
£880 ($1,012)

Jean Jules Salmson,
1832-1902, fl.Paris

Alexandre Schoenwerk,
1820-85, fl.Paris

Georges van der
Straeten, *born* 1856,
fl.Paris and Ghent

Joseph Uphues, 1850-
1911, fl.Berlin

Charles Raoul Verlet,
1857-1923, fl.Paris

1

2　3

4

5　6

7

8　9

10

11　12

19th century Marble Sculpture

Prices realised at auction for an equivalent sculpture in marble or bronze have usually been heavily weighted in favour of the latter. This reflects the buying public's image of the greater value of bronzes and makes few allowances for artistic considerations. However, the prices realised for a few pieces of marble sculpture sold at Sotheby's in 1985, may well indicate a change in taste and increased interest in this field. The Benzoni marble group (fig. 1) illustrates a type of marble sculpture which is now in strong demand. It sold for £30,800 ($46,200), a price which would have been difficult to achieve a few years ago.

It is not always necessary to spend large sums to purchase a fine marble. Fig. 4 is by the 'Symbolist' artist Stephen Sinding. His work in marble is not common and can be very appealing. This good quality piece must represent a sensible investment. However, in any consideration of 19th century marble sculpture, it is important to appreciate the two distinct areas into which the market divides: that of originals and copies of popular models.

—1—
Giovanni Maria Benzoni (1809-73), a marble group of a young man and woman, c.1861, signed and dated, 172cm (67½in), *L 7 Nov*, **£30,800 ($46,200)**

—2—
Edward Onslow Ford, a marble bust of a young woman, late 19th century, signed, 48cm (19in), *S 11 June*, **£1,100 ($1,447)**

—3—
Albert Toft, (1862-1949) a marble figure of a young woman, signed and dated '84, 49cm (19½in), *L 12 Apr*, **£495 ($634)**

—4—
Stephen Sinding, (1846-1922) a marble group of two young lovers, c.1890, signed, 16.5cm (6½in), *L 7 Nov*, **£1,265 ($1,898)**

—5—
William Theed the Younger, (1804-91) a pair of marble figures of Rebecca and Ruth, c.1868, both signed, 99cm (39in) and 102cm (40in), *L 21 Mar*, **£4,950 ($5,990)**

—1—

—2—

—3—

—4—

—5—

In the case of the first, successful and well regarded artists might begin work on a sculpture as a result of receiving a commission. The major drawback to this type of work was that on many occasions it gave the sculptor little artistic freedom. When embarking upon non-commissioned work, the sculptor generally modelled his subject in clay (a relatively cheap material requiring no expensive finishing treatment) and then mounted the piece to show at a public exhibition or competition. The cost of producing the original 'study' was low, so that if the sculptor did not receive acclaim for his work, it could be kept and exhibited at a more opportune time. If it was well received, the artist might either produce the subject in marble, or have an edition cast in bronze. Because of the considerable expense involved in requesting a foundry to make a casting mould, unless the sculptor had specific orders for a piece, he might carve the 'study' in marble. On many occasions exhibiting the subject in marble would bring further praise from the critics, as marble was seen as a more suitable medium for a finished work than clay.

—6—
Odoardo Fantacchiotti, a marble figure of a child with puppy, Florence, mid 19th century, signed, 125cm (4ft 1in), *NY 30 Mar,* $8,360 (£6,741)

—7—
Odoardo Tabacchi, a marble figure of a diver, Turin, second half of the 19th century, signed, 103cm (40½in), *F 26 Mar,* L7,000,000 (£2,806; $3,563)

—8—
Peter Barzanti, a marble figure of Venus, c.1900, signed, 80cm (31½in), *L 21 Mar,* £1,430 ($1,730)

—9—
Guilio Tadolini, (1849-1918) a marble figure entitled 'Before the Bath', c.1875, signed, 116cm (45½in), *L 7 Nov,* £8,800 ($13,200)

—10—
P. Barranti, a marble figure of a classical maiden, late 19th century, signed, 88cm (35in), *S 16 Apr,* £1,595 ($2,074)

—11—
Ernst Seger, a marble and ivory figure of a young woman, c.1890, signed, 24cm (9¼in), *L 20 June,* £715 ($965)

—6—

—7—

—8—

—9—

—10—

—11—

Many artists sculpted marble themselves or at least personally supervised the first example of a work. Not every sculptor, however, had the ability to carve in marble, a discipline very different from modelling a soft material such as clay. Indeed it was not necessary to have these skills, as by the 19th century a substantial group of professional marble carvers had been established, largely in response to the vogue for erecting monuments. The carving was divided into three stages, each executed by an individual craftsman. The first would carve the general form of the piece; the second would then carve this into the limbs; and the third would put in the detail. At this point the artist might add the fine details which create the expression and feeling of the piece.

A marble sculpture is likely to be considerably rarer than its bronze equivalent and when dated, more likely to be of the period. The creation of a bronze edition was very different, for it was usual for the sculptor never to handle or manage the production of a cast of his work. Dating, too, is sometimes difficult as a bronze dated 1860, for example, might have been re-cast much later from an 1860s model.

Secondly there is the range of pieces which were made in large numbers and which were often inspired by, or indeed straight copies of, 18th century or antique models. Although made to a high standard, these pieces should be purchased today as decorative objects, rather than 'sculpture', and their market value assessed accordingly. Examples of this type are illustrated as figs. 8, 15, 16 and 17.

—12—
A marble bust of a young woman, c.1850, her face covered by a veil, 53cm (21in), L 7 Nov,
£1,760 ($2,640)

—13—
A marble figure of a naked young bacchante, c.1880, 53cm (21in), L 21 Mar,
£1,760 ($2,130)

—14—
A white and rouge marble bust of a woman, Beatrice, c.1890, inscribed 'Prof. G Besfil Italy', NY 22 June,
$1,650 (£1,289)

—15—
*** **Marnaghini,** a marble bust of 'La Frileuse', c.1890, inspired by Houdon, signed, 71cm (28in), L 20 June,
£1,705 ($2,302)

—16—
A pair of marble figures of putti, mid 19th century, inspired by Pigalle, 76cm (30in), L 20 June,
£2,530 ($3,416)

—17—
A marble bust of a classical youth, Italian, 19th century, 63cm (25in) high, on a composition and marble pedestal, 104cm (41in) high, S 19 Feb,
£638 ($734)

—12—   —13—   —14—

—15—   —16—   —17—

Although potential purchasers can be recommended to buy 19th century marble sculpture, the condition of a piece must be carefully considered. Pieces in poor condition are expensive to repair and in cases where sections are missing, such as fingers, the restoration is rarely satisfactory. In the first half of this century most things 19th century were viewed with little respect and some superb pieces were placed outside as garden ornaments, despite the fact that they were originally intended for interior display. The condition of these pieces obviously varies, but erosion of detail by the weather cannot be repaired. In some cases the marble may not be worth restoring or indeed moving with a view to sale. The salts within it may have been expanded by moisture which gives the marble a sugary texture and makes it very brittle. Other forms of weathering, such as verdigris and general dirt, can normally be removed, but it is essential to consult a specialist restorer.

Further reading

Christopher Payne, *Animals in Bronze,* 1986

Peter Fusco, *The Romantics to Rodin,* exhibition catalogue, Los Angeles County Museum of Art, 1980

H.W. Janson, *19th Century Sculpture,* 1985

● ROBERT BOWMAN ●

—18—
A pair of marble lions, last quarter 19th century, inspired by Antoine Louis Barye, 137cm (54in), *L 7 Nov,* £13,200 ($19,800)

—19—
A marble figure of a reclining nude, after Canova, late 19th century, 58cm (23in), *NY 30 Mar,* $990 (£798)

—18—

—19—

1
Marius-Jean-Antonin Mercie, a Barbedienne parcel-gilt bronze figure of David, *c.*1875, signed and stamped with the 'Collas Reduction Mechanique' seal, brown and gilt patination, 89.5cm (35¼in), *L 20 June,* **£4,400 ($5,940)** Compare with a bronze in Vol I of Sotheby's Guide p.421 fig. 1, without gilding.

2
Pietro Calvi, a painted white marble and bronze bust of an Arabian, late 19th century, signed, 71cm (28in), *G 25 June,* **SF 35,200 (£10,203; $13,774)**

3
Prosper Lecourtier, a bronze group of 'La Fantasia', late 19th century, signed, light and dark brown patination, 84cm (33in), *L 20 June,* **£5,940 ($8,019)**

4
Pierre Jules Mêne, a bronze group of 'L'Amazone', *c.*1865, signed, brown patination, 45cm (17¾in), *L 5 July,* **£5,280 ($7,286)**

1

2

3

4

1
**A bronze relief of the
'Ecce Homo'**, mid-16th
century, probably a
tabernacle door, rich
brown patina beneath
black lacquer, 35cm
(12¼in) high, *L 12 Dec,*
£107,800 ($150,920)

2
**A Florentine glazed
terracotta Madonna and
Child**, workshop of
Giovanni della Robbia,
*c.*1510-20, blue glazed
background probably
of later date, losses and
repair, 67 x 48cm (26½
x 18¾in), *NY 22 Nov,*
$26,400 (£18,082)

3
**A jewel-set enamelled
gold pendant**, in the form
of a lion rampant, decor-
ated with champlevé
enamel mounted with
diamonds, rubies and
pearls, 7.5cm (3in),
NY 21 May,
$9,075 (£7,260)

1

2

3

1
A French bronze group of Hercules and the Erymanthian boar, mid-17th century, 75cm (29½in), *L 2 Apr,* £33,000 ($41,910)

2
A Venetian marble group of Aeneas and Anchises, by Giovanni Antonio Carra, early 17th century, *L 12 Dec,* £17,600 ($24,640)

3
A rare Trapani holy water stoup, late 17th century, of gilt copper applied with enamel and coral reliefs depicting biblical subjects, the central relief depicting the Holy Family, 52cm (20½in) high, *L 12 Dec,* £30,800 ($43,120)

4
A German gold double portrait medallion, early 17th century, by Daniel Kellerthaler, of Johann Georg I of Saxony and his wife, with three enamelled suspension chains, 10.5cm (4¼in) high overall, *L 2 Apr,* £13,200 ($16,764)

5
A Saxon gold and enamel chain of office, of the household of Christian II of Saxony, reigned 1591-1611, *L 2 Apr,* £66,000 ($83,820)

1

2

3

4 & 5

1
A Netherlandish pear-wood group of the Virgin and Child, *c.*1700, in the manner of Mattens van Beveren, 23cm (9in),
L 4 July,
£10,450 ($14,421)

2
'A Powerful Man', by Franz Xavier Messerschmidt, *c.*1770, a self-portrait bust of the sculptor, in a lead and tin alloy, 42.5cm (16¾in) high, *L 2 Apr,*
£143,000 ($181,610)

3
A rare Italian terracotta male portrait bust, dated 1545, modelled in the tradition of Benedetto Majano, colour probably restored, 39.5cm (15½in) high, *L 12 Dec,*
£24,200 ($33,880)

1

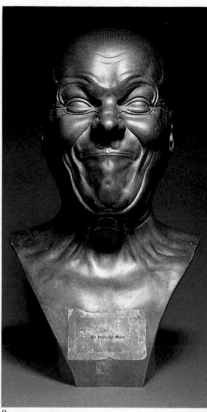

2

3

1
A 1934 Bentley 3½-litre three position 'Sedanca' drophead coupé, coachwork by Gurney Nutting, *L 24 June*, £37,400 ($50,116)

2
A 1932 Alfa Romeo 8C 2300 Cabriolet (super-charged), coachwork by Farina, *L 9 Dec*, £126,500 ($177,100)

3
A 1937 MG 'TA' Midget two-seater Sports, *L 24 June*, £11,000 ($14,740)

1

2

3

1
An early Marklin two-funnelled passenger liner 'London', German, *c.*1922, some rust and some pieces missing, 68cm (26¾in), *L 1 Oct*, £4,180 ($6,103)

2
A Bing limousine, German, *c.*1908, finished in cream and burgundy, *L 1 Oct*, £5,720 ($8,351)

3
A Marklin tinplate battleship 'HMS Gladiator', German, *c.*1902, catalogue no. 1091, with massive clockwork motor and key-wind through funnel above, some pieces missing and some rust, 62cm (23¾in) long, *L 21 May*, £5,720 ($7,665)

4
A Bing gauge III 'Black Prince' spirit-fired 4-4-0 locomotive and tender, German, *c.*1905, with filling accessories, some damage to paintwork, *L 21 May*, £3,080 ($4,127)

1

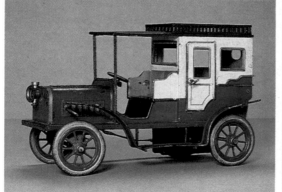

2

3

4

1 A Kammer and Reinhardt bisque character doll, German, c.1910, impressed K star R 107 5, in original Scottish costume, 56cm (22in), L 21 May, £10,450 ($14,003)

2 A Schmitt & Fils bisque doll, French, c.1880, impressed SCH and crossed hammers in a shield 4, 63.5cm (25in), L 1 Oct, £5,940 ($8,672)

3 A carved and painted wood rocking horse, English, c.1870, with remains of leather saddle and one stirrup, on shaped rocker, 203cm (80in), L 17 July, £1,100 ($1,595)

4 A musical automaton lute player, by G. Vichy, French, 1890, one finger missing, 74cm (29in), L 21 May, £7,480 ($10,023)

1

2

3

4

1
A French gold and enamel fan, second half 19th century, painted in the manner of Boucher, the guards bearing the discharge mark of Henri Clavel, the sticks with the inscribed signature: De Lafons A Paris, 27cm (10½in), *L 9 July,* £7,150 ($9,939)

2
A French mother-of-pearl fan, mid-18th century, 29cm (11½in) *L 11 Mar,* £792 ($903)

3
A Swiss four-colour gold and enamel snuff box, early 19th century, 8.5cm (3¼in), *G 14 Nov,* SF 27,500 (£8,986; $12,580)

4
An Italian lapis lazuli and mosaic snuff box, Luigi Mascelli, Rome, 1804-25, with silver-gilt mounts, 9.5cm (3¾in), *G 14 Nov,* SF 9,350 (£3,055; $4,277)

5
A French three-colour gold snuff box, Jean-François Defer, Paris, 1766, 9cm (3½in), *L 28 Oct,* £7,150 ($10,654)

6
A Swiss four-colour gold snuff box, *c.*1830, the lid and base chased with urns of flowers, 9cm (3½in), *L 28 Oct,* £2,860 ($4,261)

7
A gold and citrine vinaigrette, Scottish or English, *c.*1830, 2cm (¾in), *L 28 Oct,* £440 ($656)

8
A German gold and mother-of-pearl snuff box, mid-18th century, the lid with a scene of Vertumnus wooing Pomona, 8.5cm (3¼in), *L 28 Oct,* £23,100 ($34,419)

9
A Staffordshire snuff box, *c.*1765, the lid decorated after a print by Robert Hancock, gilt-metal mounts, 7cm (2¾in), *L 22 Oct,* £1,430 ($2,145)

1

2

3

4

5

6

8

7

9

1
A gentleman, by
Abraham or Joseph
Daniel, *c*.1795,
7cm (2¾in), *L 4 Dec*,
£968 ($1,433)

2
A young lady, attributed
to Madame Hande-
bourg-Lescot, *c*.1835,
7.4cm (3in), *L 11 Mar*,
£902 ($1,028)

3
An elderly lady, by Jean-
Laurent Mosnier, signed
and dated 1776, 3.5cm
(1¼in), *G 14 Nov*,
SF 4,180 (£1,366; $1,912)

4
**Charles III, duc de
Lorraine,** (1543-1608)
school of Clouet, *c*.1585,
on vellum, 5cm (1½in),
L 4 Dec,
£7,920 ($11,722)

5
Lady 'Pamela' Fitzgerald,
by George Engleheart,
signed, *c*.1795. Stephanie
Caroline Anne Syms,
known as 'Pamela', mar-
ried Lord Edward
Fitzgerald (1763-98) in
1792. 7.9cm (3⅛in),
L 8 July,
£3,300 ($4,587)

6
A lady, by Jacques
Thouron, signed *c*.1780,
enamel, gilt-bronze
frame, 4.5cm (1¾in),
G 14 Nov,
SF 19,800 (£6,470; $9,058)

7
Mrs Thomas Staniforth
née Elizabeth Goore
(1737-82), by Richard
Cosway, signed and dated
1796, 8.9cm (3½in),
L 11 Mar,
£3,190 ($3,637)

8
John Bullock Esq., aged
58, by John Smart, signed
and dated 1772, 3.8cm
(3½in), *L 11 Mar*,
£2,310 ($2,633)

9
A young man, by Matthew
Snelling, signed and
dated Feb. 1653, 6.3cm
(2½in), *L 11 Mar*,
£8,800 ($10,032)

1

2

3

4

5

6

7

8

9

1
A Fabergé hardstone
figure of a carpenter,
workmaster H Wig-
ström, St Petersburg,
1908-17, carved from
various semi-precious
hardstones, 12.5cm
(5in), *L 20 Feb,*
£82,500 ($94,875)

2
A Fabergé silver and
translucent enamel desk
clock, workmaster
M Perchin, St Peters-
burg, *c.*1900, 20.5cm
(8in) high, *NY 11 Dec,*
$24,200 (£17,163)

3
A silver-gilt and shaded
enamel beaker, NA, St
Petersburg, late 19th
century, with multi-
coloured flowerheads on
blue ground, with
Russian presentation
inscription, 14.5cm
(5½in), *G 16 May,*
SF 9,900 (£2,895; $3,850)

4
A silver-gilt and shaded
enamel kovsh, BMA,
Moscow, 1908-17,
painted in multicolour
enamel, 33.5cm (13¼in)
long, *G 16 May,*
**SF 26,400
(£7,719; $10,266)**

5
A silver-gilt and shaded
enamel cigarette case,
Agafonov, St Peters-
burg, late 19th century,
8.5cm (3¼in) wide,
G 16 May,
SF 2,640 (£772; $1,027)

6
A Fabergé hardstone
carving of a Pekinese,
*c.*1900, with diamond-
set eyes, 6.5cm (2½in),
G 16 May,
SF 7,700 (£2,251; $2,994)

7
A Fabergé jewelled
enamel pill box, work-
master H Wigström,
St Petersburg, 1899-
1908, the lid set with a
ruby and diamonds,
4.5cm (1¾in), *L 28 Oct,*
£4,400 ($6,556)

8
A Fabergé gold-mounted
and diamond-set white
onyx miniature Easter
egg, *c.*1900, 2.1cm (¾in)
high, *G 14 Nov,*
SF 4,400 (£1,438; $2,013)

1

2

3

4

5

6

7

8

An American pepper box, Myer Myers, New York, 1767, 7.4cm (3in) high, oz (62gr), *NY 31 Jan*, 14,300 (£12,119)

A George III two-handled cup and cover, William Cripps, London, 1762, applied with the arms of the East India Company, 42.5cm (16¾in) high, 117oz 16dwt 3,648gr), *L 24 Oct*, 8,800 ($13,200)

A Commonwealth sweetmeat tazza, London, 862, maker's mark indecipherable, 24.8cm 9¾in) diam, 13oz 8dwt 416gr), *L 24 Oct*, 5,500 ($8,250)

A pair of Victorian parcelgilt pilgrim bottles, Charles & George Fox, London, 1854, 48.3cm 19in) high, 141oz 4,385gr), *NY 7 June*, 13,750 (£10,913)

A set of four George IV silver-gilt table candlesticks, Rundell, Bridge & Rundell, London, 828, maker's mark of John Bridge, engraved with crest and motto of Neeld for Joseph Neeld (1789-1856), great nephew of Philip Rundell, 31cm (12¼in), 30oz (7183gr), *L 24 Oct*, 31,900 ($47,850)

1

2

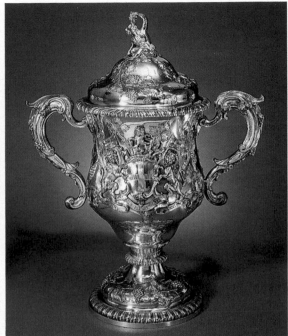

3

4

5

1
A French chocolate pot,
François-Thomas Germain, Paris, 1764,
18.5cm (7¼in), 25oz
(780gr) *L 24 Oct,*
£46,200 ($69,300)

2
A French silver-gilt teapot and stand, Jean-Charles Cahier, Paris,
*c.*1820, with the monogram of the Grand
Duchess Maria Pavlovna
of Russia, 21.5cm (8½in)
high overall, 58oz
(1805gr) *G 14 May,*
SF 20,900
(£6,111; $8,128)

3
**A German silver-gilt toilet
box,** Peter Neuss II,
Augsburg, 1689,
engraved with architectural and marine
views, 10.7cm (4½in)
wide, 6oz 10dwt (204gr),
G 14 May,
SF 46,200
(£13,509; $17,967)

4
**A German silver-gilt
tumbler cup,** Cornelius
Poppe, Augsburg, 1717-
18, 5.1cm (2in) high,
2oz 15dwt (85gr),
NY 9 Oct,
$3,850 (£2,730)

5
**A German silver-gilt
ecuelle and cover,** Peter
Neuss II, Augsburg,
1689, 19cm (7½in) wide
overall, 11oz (340gr),
G 14 May,
SF 55,000
(£16,082; $21,389)

6
**A French ecuelle and
cover,** Thomas Germain,
1735/38, and a stand,
Antoine Plot, *c.*1766, all
Paris, 29.7cm (11½in)
wide, 60oz (1864gr),
G 12 Nov,
SF 286,000
(£93,464; $130,849)

1
A German parcel-gilt nef, maker's mark AP conjoined, Regensburg, c.1610, detachable deck, 46.5cm (18¼in), 42oz (1313gr), *G 12 Nov,* **SF 550,000** (£179,739; $251,634)

2
A German ewer and basin, Johann Gottlob Jaeckel, Breslau, c.1765, presented by Friedrich the Great to General Friedrich Bogislaw von Tauentzien, 26.7cm (10½in) high and 47cm (18½in) wide, 59oz (1835gr), *G 12 Nov,* **SF 38,500** (£12,581; $17,613)

1

2

1
A gold and tinted crystal intaglio pendant, *c.*1870, and a pair of earrings *en suite, L 23 May,* £2,530 ($3,340)

2
A gold and enamel necklace, possibly Melillo, Italian, *c.*1860, decorated in a floral design of oriental taste, *L 23 May,* £6,380 ($8,422)

3
A gold bracelet, Castellani, *c.*1860, *L 23 May,* £4,400 ($5,808)

4
A gold pendant, Italian, *c.*1860, designed as an Etruscan bulla, *L 23 May,* £1,540 ($2,033)

5
A gold brooch, Castellani, *c.*1860, *L 23 May,* £880 ($1,162)

6
A gold and tinted crystal intaglio pendant, *c.*1870, *L 5 Dec,* £715 ($1,051)

7
A gold and hardstone intaglio necklace, probably Italian, *c.*1865, *L 23 May,* £2,750 ($3,630)

1 2 3 4 5 (*From bottom left to top right*)

6

7

1
Carlo Giuliano, a gold, enamel, ruby, turquoise, seed pearl and diamond demi-parure, *c.*1865, in Egyptian style, comprising: a Necklace, a hinged bangle and a pair of earrings, signed C G, cased by C F Hancock & Co, *L 29 Oct,* £28,600 ($42,614)

2
Carlo Giuliano, a gold, enamel and gem-set bracelet, *c.*1870, each rectangular plaque set with blue-green beryls and a zircon within enamel foliate motifs, signed C G, *L 29 Oct,* £13,200 ($19,668)

3
Carlo and Arthur Giuliano, a gold polychrome enamel and seed pearl necklace, *c.*1890, clasp signed C & A G, *L 29 Oct,* £11,000 ($16,390)

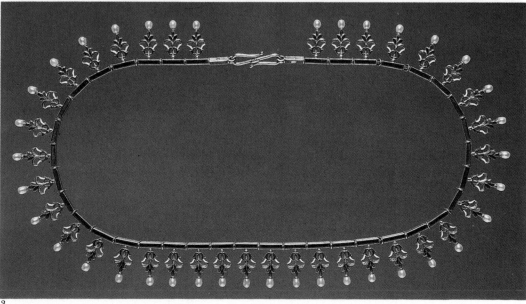

1
A platinum, gold, plique-a-jour enamel and diamond brooch, *c.*1910, some damage, *NY 12 June,* $3,080 (£2,444)

2
A pair of diamond and coloured stone clips, *c.*1930, *NY 23 Apr,* $8,800 (£7,040)

3
A sapphire and diamond double-clip/brooch, J E Caldwell, *c.*1935, mounted in platinum, *NY 15 Oct,* $7,425 (£5,266)

4
A sapphire and diamond brooch, *c.*1910, of stylised wing design, *L 7 Mar,* £3,300 ($3,696)

5
A black opal and diamond brooch, with a pair of earrings en suite, *L 7 Mar,* £2,860 ($3,203)

6
A pair of diamond pendent earrings, second quarter 19th century, lacking fittings, *L 5 Dec,* £8,250 ($12,128)

7
An opal and diamond brooch/pendant, last quarter 19th century, *L 5 Dec,* £1,210 ($1,779)

8
A diamond and pearl pendant, *c.*1900, with platinum chain, 38cm (15in), *NY 22 Apr,* $6,600 (£5,280)

9
A shell and gem-set brooch, last quarter 19th century, the shells applied with a cat's eye and diamond spider and an opal and diamond fly, *L 5 Dec,* £825 ($1,213)

10
A diamond brooch/pendant, last quarter 19th century, *L 3 Oct,* £770 ($1,140)

11
A diamond brooch, by Van Cleef & Arpels, mounted in 18 ct white gold, *G 15 May,* SF 9,900 (£2,895; $3,850)

Jewellery

1
A gold and sapphire ring, 19th century, *L 5 Dec,* £880 ($1,294)

2
A ruby and diamond tie-pin, French, *c.*1910, with platinum mount, *NY 15 Oct,* $550 (£390)

3
A diamond ring, *c.*1900, pavé-set with cushion-shaped stones, *L 5 Dec,* £605 ($889)

4
A diamond ring, the bombé bezel pierced with foliate motifs, *Glen 26 Aug,* £660 ($970)

5
A sapphire and diamond cluster ring, *c.*1820, *L 23 May,* £748 ($987)

6
A diamond ring, early 19th century, *L 29 Oct,* £3,080 ($4,589)

7
A diamond ring, *c.*1820, *L 29 Oct,* £3,080 ($4,589)

8
A gold, enamel and diamond memorial ring, late 18th century, with a rose-diamond urn on a blue Bristol glass background, *L 23 May,* £935 ($1,234)

9
A rubellite and diamond ring, late 19th century, with gold and silver mount, *NY 15 Oct,* $5,060 (£3,589)

10
A diamond ring, last quarter 19th century, *L 23 May,* £2,200 ($2,904)

11
A garnet and diamond ring, Cartier, *c.*1920, with platinum mount, *NY 22 Apr,* $2,200 (£1,760)

12
A sapphire and diamond ring, *c.*1930, with platinum band, *NY 22 Apr,* $3,850 (£3,080)

13
A diamond and ruby ring, *c.*1910, the diamonds set in platinum, *NY 15 Oct,* $1,540 (£1,092)

14
A gold and gem-set ring, *Glen 26 Aug,* £308 ($453)

15
A gold and diamond dress ring, French, *c.*1900, *L 7 Mar,* £7,150 ($8,008)

16
A diamond ring, last quarter 19th century, *L 7 Mar,* £6,380 ($7,146)

17
A black opal and diamond ring, *L 3 Oct,* £1,760 ($2,605)

18
A pearl and diamond crossover ring, on an expanding shank, *L 7 Nov,* £935 ($1,403)

19
A ruby and diamond ring, *c.*1925, with platinum mount, *NY 10 Dec,* $4,675 (£3,315)

20
A platinum, diamond, coloured stone and onyx tiepin, *c.*1925, *NY 15 Oct,* $1,540 (£1,092)

21
A gold, silver and diamond ring, 19th century, designed as a serpent, *NY 10 Dec,* $9,350 (£6,631)

1
A gold and carbuncle bracelet, c.1865, slightly imperfect, L 11 July, £715 ($1,051)

2
A gold, Geneva enamel and gem-set bracelet, c.1830, designed as a row of miniatures depicting girls in Austro-Hungarian costumes, L 23 May, £3,740 ($4,937)

3
A gold, enamel and diamond serpent bracelet, c.1845, the body hinged and sprung and decorated with royal blue guilloché enamel, L 29 Oct, £10,450 ($15,571)

4
A gold and turquoise expanding bracelet, c.1840, designed as a coiled serpent with cabochon ruby eyes, inscribed and dated: J Dismore & Son, 1 Nov 1841, case, L 29 Oct, £3,520 ($5,245)

5
A diamond cluster brooch, first quarter 19th century, contemporary fitted case, L 29 Oct, £4,180 ($6,228)

6
A gold, enamel, half-pearl and diamond hinged bangle, L 7 Nov, £418 ($627)

7
A gold and carbuncle, hinged bracelet, L 11 July, £660 ($970)

8
A pair of gold, diamond and enamel flower brooches, 18th century, NY 12 June, $1,760 (£1,397)

9
A four-coloured gold and gem-set pendant, c.1830 the reverse with a hair compartment, Glen 26 Aug, £286 ($420)

10
A gold, onyx and half-pearl brooch, edged by white cloisonné enamel, L 5 Dec, £440 ($647)

11
A rose diamond brooch, 19th century, L 29 Oct, £3,520 ($5,245)

12
A pair of pendent ear-rings, late 18th century, set throughout with rose diamonds, L 23 May, £1,375 ($1,815)

13
A pair of topaz and diamond pendant earrings, Catalan 19th century, L 23 May, £825 ($1,089)

14
A gold, enamel and diamond chatelaine, early 19th century, applied with blue enamel, slightly damaged, NY 12 June, $880 (£698)

15
A gold, blue enamel, half-pearl and ruby necklace, c.1840, designed as a serpent, the eyes set with cabochon rubies, slightly imperfect, L 23 May, £1,210 ($1,597)

16
A pearl and diamond brooch, last quarter 19th century, L 23 May, £990 ($1,307)

17
A three-coloured gold and gem-set bracelet, c.1825, the clasp set with a pink topaz, step cut emeralds and half-pearls, L 29 Oct, £2,640 ($3,934)

18
A Berlin ironwork bracelet, c.1830, clasp marked 'Geiss a Berlin', decorated in the traditional manner, S 24 July, £440 ($651)

1
A gold, enamel and pearl
longchain, late 19th
century, enamel imper-
fect, L 29 Oct,
£1,650 ($2,459)

2
A gold and enamel watch-
chain, mid-19th century,
with floral motif links,
L 5 Dec,
£1,320 ($1,940)

3
A gold and glass bead
necklace, last quarter
19th century, NY 22 Apr,
$2,090 (£1,672)

4
A gold necklace, French,
last quarter 19th century,
NY 22 Apr,
$1,430 (£1,144)

5
A gold and amethyst long
chain, late 19th century,
142cm (56in), NY 22 Apr,
$2,530 (£2,024)

6
An 18 ct two-coloured
gold chain necklace,
Cartier, 83cm (32¾in),
St M 21 Feb,
FF 4,180 (£1,290; $1,484)

7
A platinum and moon-
stone chain, c.1925,
152.5cm (60in),
NY 22 Apr,
$4,125 (£3,300)

8
A gold, enamel, ruby and
diamond bracelet, L 7 Feb,
£990 ($1,158)

9
A gold and amethyst long-
chain, first quarter 19th
century, set with mixed-
cut stones, L 3 Oct,
£1,650 ($2,442)

10
A platinum, seed pearl
and diamond choker
necklace, separating to
form a pair of bracelets,
c.1910, 32.5cm (12¾in),
NY 15 Oct,
$11,550 (£8,191)

11
A turquoise and diamond
necklace, last quarter
19th century, L 7 Mar,
£1,870 ($2,094)

1
A carved opal brooch/
pendant, Child and
Child, late 19th century,
L 11 July,
£2,200 ($3,234)

2
A gold and Roman mosaic
brooch, *c.*1870, depict-
ing a maenad, *L 5 Dec,*
£418 ($614)

3
A gold, hardstone cameo
and seed pearl pendant,
mid-19th century,
NY 15 Oct,
$1,210 (£858)

4
A gold, sardonyx cameo
and half-pearl brooch/
pendant, *c.*1865, depicting a classical god,
L 5 Dec,
£935 ($1,374)

5
A gold and hardstone
cameo brooch, mid-19th
century, *NY 22 Apr,*
$770 (£616)

6
A gold and shell cameo
brooch, *c.*1865, *L 5 Dec,*
£605 ($889)

7
A gold, half-pearl and
cornelian cameo demi-
parure, mid-19th
century, comprising a
brooch/pendant, signed
Girometti, and a pair of
earrings, *L 5 Dec,*
£1,430 ($2,102)

8
A 9ct gold cameo brooch/
pendant, *JHB 31 July,*
R 220 (£82; $122)

9
A cameo habillé,
*c.*1870, mounted as a
brooch in a gold frame,
carved in shell and
inlaid with malachite,
mother of pearl and
coral, *Glen 26 Aug,*
£1,320 ($1,940)

10
An oval shell cameo
brooch, *c.*1880,
C 9 July,
£286 ($398)

11
A platinum, diamond and
enamelled portrait
pendant, *c.*1915,
NY 15 Oct,
$1,100 (£780)

12
An onyx cameo, gold,
pearl and diamond
brooch, last quarter 19th
century, probably
representing Queen
Elizabeth I, *L 7 Feb,*
£1,100 ($1,287)

13
An onyx cameo, diamond
and seed pearl brooch/
pendant, E Girardet,
early 20th century,
depicting one of the
Dancing Hours,
NY 22 Apr,
$2,200 (£1,760)

14
A hardstone cameo and
diamond pendant,
G 15 May,
SF 6,050 (£1,769; $2,353)

15
A diamond and hardstone
cameo brooch, last
quarter 19th century,
the agate carved with
the head of Hercules,
C 9 July,
£1,540 ($2,141)

16
A gold brooch, *c.*1860, set
with a Wedgwood jasper
plaque, *L 23 May,*
£880 ($1,162)

17
A carved coral and
diamond brooch, the two
corals carved with
heads of goddesses,
St M 21 Feb,
SF 6,600 (£2,037; $2,343)

18
A gold, turquoise and
half-pearl bracelet,
*c.*1830, set with an oval
eye miniature, probably
of King Leopold of the
Belgians, *L 5 Dec,*
£935 ($1,374)

19
A gold and enamelled
miniature pendant, 19th
century, the reverse
with locket compart-
ment, some repair to
frame, *NY 22 Apr,*
$550 (£440)

1

A gold and onyx demi-parure, Italian, c.1860, comprising a necklace and bracelet in classical revival style, approx 38cm (15in), *NY 12 June*, $4,180 (£3,317)

2

A gold and Roman mosaic necklace, Castellani, c.1860, and a pair of earrings *en suite*, imperfect, *L 5 Dec*, £9,350 ($13,745)

3

A pair of gold and malachite earrings, third quarter 19th century, *NY 12 June*, $880 (£698)

4

A garnet and diamond pendant/locket, mid-19th century, the reverse with locket compartment, *NY 15 Oct*, $3,630 (£2,574)

5

A gold, enamel and gem-set cross/pendant, in Holbeinesque taste, Ernesto Rinzi, c.1870, *L 23 May*, £3,960 ($5,227)

6

An enamel, pearl and diamond pendant, last quarter 19th century, decorated with lilac, white and black piqué enamel, fitted case by R & S Garrard, *L 23 May*, £4,180 ($5,518)

7

A gold, ruby, diamond and polychrome enamel Holbeinesque pendant, c.1870, later fitting, *L 23 May*, £2,750 ($3,630)

8

A gold, enamel, half-pearl and carbuncle Holbeinesque pendant, c.1870, crimson, blue and green champlevé enamel slightly imperfect, *L 23 May*, £1,210 ($1,597)

9

A gold and micro-mosaic brooch, Castellani, c.1870, the design formed of blue and green tessarae, *NY 12 June*, $3,410 (£2,706)

10

A gold, enamel, emerald and diamond cameo brooch/pendant, last quarter 19th century, with an onyx cameo of Medusa, decorated with black and white enamel, *L 23 May*, £1,980 ($2,614)

11

A gold and onyx cameo brooch, Italian, mid-19th century, two cameos signed Luigi Rosi, Roma, *NY 15 Oct*, $1,870 (£1,326)

12

A gold, enamel and hardstone intaglio brooch, c.1860, centred by an agate carved with a warrior, and decorated in white, black, red and green enamel, some wear, *NY 15 Oct*, $1,045 (£741)

13

A gold, enamel and gem-set pendant, Phillips of Cockspur Street, c.1875, the centre with a step cut peridot within a border of scarlet and white enamel, and pearl and diamond trefoils, signed with the Prince of Wales feathers, case, *L 29 Oct*, £3,520 ($5,245)

14

A gold and enamelled brooch/pendant, Giacinto Melillo, c.1860, in original fitted case, *S 16 Oct*, £1,870 ($2,768)

The Giuliano Family

Seldom has so great an opportunity presented itself of studying the work of the celebrated family of jewellers, Giuliano, as that afforded in October 1985 by the sale of the John Sheldon collection. Over thirty jewels, many of them small masterpieces, had been chosen for his personal collection by a man who had devoted his life to jewellery and had spent over fifty years as a prominent member of the trade in London. The result was a dazzling and formidable display of the jeweller's art—in the context of the 19th century, the most important ever to be offered at auction, establishing many auction record prices for the maker.

By the mid-19th century the vogue for jewels of classical inspiration was already firmly established, largely through the extraordinary expertise of Alessandro Castellani but also fuelled by the archaeological discoveries at Herculaneum and Pompeii. The exact connection between Castellani and Carlo Giuliano is uncertain, but it is thought that when Giuliano came to London in the early 1860s, it was with the idea of running an outlet of Castellani's in Frith Street, Soho, as a workshop rather than as retail premises. Whatever else Giuliano owes to Castellani, he certainly drew great inspiration from him for the archaeological jewels he made during his early years in London. By 1863 he had entered his own mark at Goldsmith's Hall—the simple initials CG—and by 1874 his work was in sufficient demand for him to open his own retail shop at 115 Piccadilly. The business flourished and Giuliano gained an enviable reputation as the leading art jeweller in London. Carlo's two sons, Carlo Joseph and Arthur Alphonse, both of whom had learnt their skills from their father, took over the family business on his death in 1895, changing their mark to C & AG and eventually moving the premises in 1912 to 48 Knightsbridge. The business was closed in 1914 on Arthur's death.

—1—
Carlo Giuliano, a gold, seed pearl and enamel necklace, c.1880, supporting a gold, black and white piqué enamel and diamond locket, enamel slightly imperfect, *L 29 Oct,* £4,400 ($6,556)

—2—
Carlo Giuliano, a gold, enamel and pearl pendant, c.1880, black and white piqué enamel with a button pearl at the centre and edged with seed pearls, enamel slightly imperfect, signed C G, *L 29 Oct,* £1,210 ($1,803)

—3—
Carlo and Arthur Giuliano, a gold, enamel and sapphire pendant cross, c.1900, decorated with red guilloché and white enamel, with a star sapphire set on the terminal, signed C & A G, *L 23 May,* £660 ($871)

—4—
Carlo Giuliano, a gold, enamel and gemstone necklace and pendant, c.1890, decorated with black and white piqué enamel, on a necklace of seven rows of seed pearls, slightly imperfect, *L 23 May,* £5,720 ($7,550)

For colour illustrations of Giuliano jewellery see p. 495 and Vol.I p.291

—1—   —2—

—3—   —4—

By far the most important inspiration for Giuliano during the years between 1870 and his death in 1895 was derived from the jewels of the 15th and 16th centuries — the Renaissance in Europe — notably the designs of Hans Holbein, the court painter to Henry VIII. He also profited from the great discoveries and interest in Egyptology; an interesting early example of this is fig.1 p.495, retailed not by Giuliano himself but by Hancock's and datable to c.1865. The motifs in this parure are essentially a pastiche of Egyptian designs, and in its use of Calibré-cut turquoises in channelled settings the piece is also reminiscent of French jewels of the period. All the elements of the Giuliano style are present, however: the subtle chromatic sense (using stones for their colour rather than

for their value); the fine black and white piqué enamel; the attention to detail, for example the delicately wrought flowerheads supporting the fringe of the necklace, and most importantly, the sense of the jewellery having been conceived as a whole by a designer of outstanding taste.

Fig.5 is absolutely typical of the 'renaissance' jewels — lozenge-shaped, delicately enamelled, elaborately pierced. Great attention has been paid to the colours; here, a monochrome palette of black enamel flecked with white, and with a single pearl. The use of diamonds, though necessary in this context, is unusual in Giuliano's jewellery in this size; normally these stones are used as highlights rather than as the focus of the jewel.

—5—
Carlo Giuliano, a gold, enamel, pearl and diamond pendant, c.1870, on a necklace decorated with blue and black enamel and alternating with seed pearls, both signed C G, *L 29 Oct,* £13,750 ($20,488)

—6—
Carlo Giuliano, a gold, enamel and gem-set demiparure, c.1870, comprising a pendant, a necklace, and a pair of earrings, signed C G, *L 5 Dec,* £7,700 ($11,319)

—7—
Carlo Giuliano, a gold, enamel and gem-set pendant, c.1870, decorated with blue enamel flecked with white, set with a brown zircon and two rose-diamonds, and with single pearl drop, on a seed pearl necklace, signed C G, *L 29 Oct,* £14,300 ($21,307)

—8—
Carlo Giuliano, a gold, enamel and gem-set Holbeinesque pendant, c.1870, decorated with black, blue and white piqué enamel and set with cabochon rubies and seed pearls, signed C G, *L 29 Oct,* £3,520 ($5,245)

—9—
Carlo Giuliano, a gold, black and white enamel, pearl and diamond pendant, c.1880, designed as a Greek cross, with diamond centre, signed C G, *L 29 Oct,* £4,180 ($6,228)

—10—
Carlo and Arthur Giuliano, a gold, enamel and gem-set pendant, c.1890, set with central garnet and with cabochon emerald drop, with black and white piqué enamel, signed C & A G, *L 29 Oct,* £6,380 ($9,506)

—6—

—5—

—7—

—8—

—9—

—10—

After Giuliano's death, his sons concentrated on lighter, less substantial jewels. The quality of the enamelling was retained, and—typically—the monochrome palette, but this was now used in a way more reminiscent of French 17th century jewels. Skeins of seed pearls and enamelled gold chains became common (fig.16). Delicate quatrefoil and cruciform pendants (figs.10 and 17) were favoured, as were small bar brooches.

As in all fields, once the market is sufficiently well established, the temptation for the unscrupulous to pass off fakes grows greater. With Giuliano, however, we are fortunate in that the quality of the workmanship is extremely difficult, if

not financially unviable, to reproduce. Most fakes, therefore, are jewels contemporary with the genuine Giuliano work, but by lesser craftsmen, and spurious marks have been added subsequently. This can happen in two ways. The first is where a bona fide Giuliano mark, perhaps on a pendant loop or the hinge of a brooch pin, is taken from a damaged or insubstantial Giuliano jewel and added to an impressive fake. In such cases, care must obviously be taken to establish whether the loop or pin is in keeping with the jewel itself; traces of soft (lead) solder will offer a strong clue, and the quality of the enamel under a lens may well appear finer than that on the body of the

—11—
Carlo Giuliano, a gold, enamel and gem-stone bracelet, c.1870, the border decorated with black piqué enamel and the sides and backs with similar motifs and decorations, signed C G, maker's fitted case, *L 29 Oct,* £7,150 ($10,654)

—12—
Carlo Giuliano, a gold and enamel pendant, c.1880, with hair compartment within a border of blue and white piqué enamel and a row of half-pearls, signed C G, *L 29 Oct,* £1,320 ($1,967)

—13—
Carlo Giuliano, a gold, enamel and gem-set hinged bangle, c.1865, decorated with black and white piqué and blue enamel, with two carbuncles and a cabochon yellow zircon at the front, signed C G, *L 29 Oct,* £7,700 ($11,473)

—14—
Carlo and Arthur Giuliano, a gold, enamel and gem-set necklace, c.1900, front designs decorated in green, blue, cream and brick-red enamel supporting a deep graduated fringe with forms of pearls and cushion-shaped rubies, on a chain of wave-scroll links decorated with green and blue guilloché enamel, *L 29 Oct,* £8,250 ($12,293)

—15—
Carlo and Arthur Giuliano, a gold, enamel and gem-set necklace, c.1900, the detachable pendant and chain both decorated with black and white piqué enamel and white enamel, the pendant set with an oval opal and diamonds, and with single pearl drop, slightly imperfect, signed C & A G, *L 29 Oct,* £7,700 ($11,473)

—11—

—12—

—13—

—14—

—15—

jewel itself. The second method of faking marks is where a spurious mark is struck onto the fake jewel itself or where a cast mark is added. Familiarity with Giuliano marks (many of which, it must be admitted, are badly struck), can make one suspicious of spurious examples, particularly when they are uncharacteristically clear. Cast marks are particularly easy to spot, since the surface shows a particular granular appearance under magnification. Nevertheless, fakes are rare and their existence should not deter the collectors; after all, any form of imitation is merely flattery.

● DAVID BENNETT ●

Further reading

Geoffrey C. Munn, *Castellani and Giuliano*, 1984.

—16—
Carlo and Arthur Giuliano, a gold, enamel, pearl and diamond necklace, *c.*1900, all decorated with white enamel flecked with black, the front set with diamonds and pearls, signed C & A G, *L 29 Oct*, £10,450 ($15,571)

—17—
Carlo and Arthur Giuliano, a gold, enamel, pearl and diamond pendant, *c.*1890, set with a central diamond, and with three baroque pearl drops, signed C & A G, *L 29 Oct*, £2,640 ($3,934)

—18—
Carlo and Arthur Giuliano, a gold, enamel and gem-set necklace, *c.*1900, the pendant decorated with black and white flecked enamel, with a cluster of star ruby and sapphire and a diamond at the centre, and large pearl drop, signed C & A G, *L 29 Oct*, £14,850 ($22,127)

—19—
Carlo and Arthur Giuliano, a gold, enamel, pearl and diamond pendant, *c.*1890, with fresh water pearl drop, signed C & A G, *L 29 Oct*, £2,420 ($3,606)

—16—

—17—

—18—

—19—

A Carlo Giuliano mark on a pendant

A fake Carlo Giuliano mark on a brooch

A Carlo and Arthur Giuliano mark on a pendant loop

1
An emerald and diamond brooch/pendant, last quarter 19th century, *L 5 Dec,* £3,530 ($5,189)

2
A diamond brooch, last quarter 19th century, designed as an open-work lozenge of leaf and bud motifs, *L 5 Dec,* £1,540 ($2,264)

3
A gold, enamel and diamond Prince-of-Wales-feathers brooch, 19th century, applied with deep green enamel, slightly damaged, *NY 22 Apr,* $1,210 (£968)

4
A diamond, emerald and ruby coronet brooch, *c.*1900, mounted in gold and platinum, one diamond missing, *NY 15 Oct,* $1,650 (£1,170)

5
A half-pearl and diamond pendant, last quarter 19th century, *L 5 Dec,* £2,420 ($3,557)

6
An enamel and diamond brooch, *c.*1900, with shaded mauve enamels and small brilliants, *G 15 May,* SF 6,050 (£1,769; $2,353)

7
A pearl, enamel and diamond circular brooch/pendant, last quarter 19th century, with central blue guilloché enamel plaque, *L 3 Oct,* £770 ($1,140)

8
A turquoise and diamond brooch, late 19th century, *L 7 Nov,* £572 ($858)

9
A diamond crescent brooch, *c.*1880, *L 3 Oct,* £605 ($895)

10
An enamel and diamond pendant, mid-19th century, *L 5 Dec,* £1,100 ($1,617)

11
A rose diamond and pearl brooch, 19th century, *G 15 May,* SF 3,080 (£901; $1,198)

12
A diamond brooch, *c.*1900, *L 25 Apr,* £495 ($639)

13
A peridot and diamond pendant/brooch, Shreve, Crump & Low & Co, *c.*1900, gold and platinum mount, *NY 22 Apr,* $1,980 (£1,584)

14
A sapphire and diamond hinged bangle, *c.*1900, *L 29 Oct,* £3,520 ($5,245)

15
A diamond and pearl hinged bangle, last quarter 19th century, *JHB 13 Nov,* R 4,200 (£1,135; $1,589)

16
A gold, diamond and jasper necklace, *c.*1900, 41cm (16in) long, *NY 10 Dec,* $1,320 (£936)

1
A pair of cultured baroque pearl and diamond pendent earrings, *G 15 May,* SF 4,640 (£1,357; $1,804)

2
A pair of amethyst and diamond pendent earrings, *L 11 July,* £880 ($1,294)

3
A pair of platinum, gold and diamond pendent earrings, *c.1910, NY 15 Oct,* $2,090 (£1,482)

4
A pair of natural pearl and diamond pendent earclips, Cartier, *c.1920, NY 15 Oct,* $5,500 (£3,901)

5
A pair of emerald and diamond earclips, *NY 10 Dec,* $935 (£663)

6
A demantoid garnet and diamond brooch/pendant, *C 1 Oct,* £484 ($707)

7
A giardinetto brooch, set with rubies, emeralds and sapphires, *L 20 June,* £440 ($594)

8
A set of gold, enamel and opal buttons, *c.1900, NY 12 June,* $935 (£742)

9
A sapphire and diamond brooch, *L 7 Nov,* £550 ($825)

10
A platinum and diamond brooch/pendant, Black, Starr & Frost, *c.1910, NY 12 June,* $2,200 (£1,746)

11
An emerald, diamond and pearl brooch, *G 15 May,* SF 6,600 (£1,930; $2,567)

12
A seed pearl and diamond brooch, *c.1900, L 25 Apr,* £495 ($638)

13
A platinum, diamond and pearl brooch/pendant, *c.1910, NY 12 June,* $1,650 (£1,310)

14
A diamond bar brooch, *Glen 26 Aug,* £660 ($970)

15
A 15 ct. gold gem-set brooch/pendant, *C 1 Oct,* £572 ($835)

16
A diamond oval pendant, *c.1910,* the wreath with white and piqué enamel borders, enamel slightly imperfect, *L 20 June,* £715 ($965)

17
A seed pearl and diamond sautoir, *c.1910, G 15 May,* SF 2,860 (£836; $1,112)

1
A diamond, sapphire and ruby brooch, *c.*1930, designed as a terrier, *NY 15 Oct,* $660 (£468)

2
A diamond and sapphire butterfly brooch, 19th century, *NY 22 Apr,* $3,850 (£3,080)

3
A diamond donkey brooch, 19th century, cabochon ruby eyes, bearing a gold and coral basket, *G 15 May,* SF 8,250 (£2,412; $3,208)

4
An enamel and diamond brooch, Boucheron, London, the snail's shell decorated in green and white enamel, *L 3 Oct,* £1,155 ($1,709)

5
An 18 ct gold and gem skiing bird brooch, highlighted by five small single cut diamonds and a small seed pearl, emerald eyes, *St M 21 Feb,* SF 1,320 (£407; $469)

6
An opal and diamond dragonfly brooch, *c.*1890, mounted en tremblant, *G 15 May,* SF 9,900 (£2,895; $3,850)

7
A diamond, ruby and demantoid garnet brooch, designed as a donkey, *L 23 May,* £572 ($755)

8
A mauve and pale-blue pliqué à jour enamel silver butterfly brooch, *S 17 Apr,* £121 ($157)

9
A ruby, sapphire and diamond brooch, Van Cleef & Arpels, New York, *c.*1940, the four birds with cabochon ruby bodies, mounted in 14 ct. gold, *NY 15 Oct,* $5,500 (£3,901)

10
A diamond, ruby and sapphire brooch, *c.*1930, designed as a bird within a circle, *NY 12 June,* $1,650 (£1,310)

11
A gold, enamel, tiger's-eye and diamond brooch, French, last quarter 19th century, maker's mark CD, *L 23 May,* £935 ($1,234)

12
A gold, diamond and coloured stone brooch, 19th century, the cockerel with a baroque pearl body, *NY 15 Oct,* $2,640 (£1,872)

13
A demantoid garnet and diamond brooch, *c.*1900, one stone deficient, *L 25 Apr,* £550 ($709)

14
A pearl and diamond brooch, *c.*1910, designed as a cockerel, mounted in gold and platinum, the tail feathers formed of a baroque pearl, *NY 12 June,* $1,320 (£1,048)

15
A gold and pearl brooch, designed as a dragon, *G 15 May,* SF 935 (£273; $364)

16
A pearl and diamond brooch, designed as a bird on its nest, *L 23 May,* £682 ($900)

17
A demantoid garnet and diamond brooch, designed as a lizard, last quarter 19th century, *L 5 Dec,* £825 ($1,213)

18
A three-coloured gold and diamond bar brooch, designed as a fishing rod with rose diamond fish, *Glen 26 Aug,* £462 ($679)

19
A gold and polychrome enamel brooch, designed as a pheasant, enamel slightly imperfect, *Glen 26 Aug,* £264 ($388)

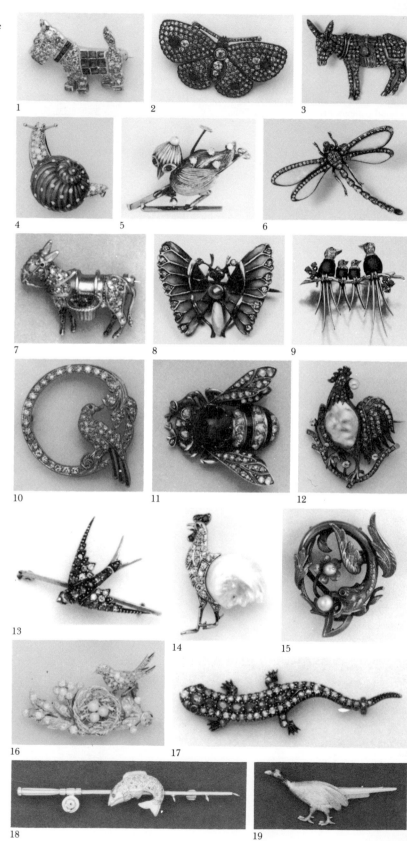

1

A diamond bracelet,
G 15 May,
SF 8,800 (£2,573; $3,422)

2

A lady's diamond watch
bracelet, *L 3 Oct,*
£3,520 ($5,210)

3

A diamond bracelet,
L 3 Oct,
£2,420 ($3,582)

4

An emerald and diamond
brooch, *L 3 Oct,*
£5,060 ($7,489)

5

A moonstone and
diamond brooch, *c.1910,*
mounted in gold and
platinum, *NY 22 Apr,*
$2,530 (£2,024)

6

A pair of sapphire and
diamond clips, Cartier,
c.1930, NY 15 Oct,
$5,225 (£3,706)

7

A diamond plaque
brooch, French, *c.1925,*
L 23 May,
£3,080 ($4,066)

8

A sapphire and diamond
brooch, *c.1925,*
NY 22 Apr,
$10,450 (£8,360)

9

A diamond double-clip,
mounted in platinum,
G 15 May,
SF 6,050 (£1,769; $2,353)

10

A diamond brooch,
Glen 26 Aug,
£660 ($970)

11

A diamond plaque
brooch, mounted in
platinum, *G 15 May,*
SF 8,800 (£2,573; $3,422)

12

A sapphire and diamond
brooch, *L 7 Nov,*
£792 ($1,188)

13

A ruby and diamond
brooch, *c.1925,* signed
Bert H Satz, *NY 10 Dec,*
$3,575 (£2,535)

14

A diamond plaque
brooch, *c.1930,* in a
stylised buckle design,
L 5 Dec,
£2,640 ($3,881)

15

A lady's diamond wrist-
watch, *L 5 Dec,*
£748 ($1,100)

16

A lady's platinum, gold,
seed pearl and diamond
wristwatch, Cartier,
c.1920, NY 10 Dec,
$9,900 (£7,021)

17

A diamond and sapphire
brooch, Cartier, *c.1935,*
designed as a speedboat,
NY 12 June,
$4,125 (£3,274)

18

A lady's platinum and
diamond bracelet watch,
c.1930, L 5 Dec,
£4,290 ($6,306)

1
A gold, turquoise and seed
pearl watch and chain,
Ch Oudin, Palais-
Royal, 19th century, one
stone missing, *NY 15 Oct,*
$1,540 (£1,092)

2
A gold, lapis lazuli,
diamond and pearl fob
and watch chain, 19th
century, *NY 15 Oct,*
$2,860 (£2,028)

3
A gold and enamel watch
with chain, by Golay Fils
& Stahl, Geneva, *c.*1910,
St M 21 Feb,
SF 4,180 (£1,290; $1,484)

4
A lady's platinum and
diamond wristwatch,
Marcus & Co., *c.*1920,
movement by C H
Meylan, *NY 22 Apr,*
$1,980 (£1,584)

5
A gold, ruby bead,
sapphire and diamond
hatpin, in the form of a
parasol, *NY 23 Apr,*
$605 (£484)

6
A platinum, diamond and
tortoiseshell hair comb,
*c.*1900, *NY 22 Apr,*
$2,200 (£1,760)

7
A gold, platinum, ruby
and diamond clutch
purse, Ostertag, Paris,
*c.*1930, 17cm (6¾in),
NY 23 Apr,
$3,300 (£2,640)

8
A platinum, diamond
and sapphire lorgnette,
*c.*1915, *NY 12 June,*
$2,420 (£1,921)

9
A diamond and onyx
lorgnette, *c.*1930,
St M, 21 Feb,
SF 3,850 (£1,188; $1,355)

10
An 18 ct gold, enamel
and diamond cigarette
case, *c.*1925, *NY 12 June,*
$1,210 (£960)

11
An 18 ct gold, platinum,
diamond and black
enamel compact, Cartier,
NY 12 June,
$1,210 (£1,525)

12
A black silk and diamond
evening bag, Ostertag,
Paris, with platinum
frame, damaged,
NY 23 Apr,
$8,250 (£6,600)

13
A 14 ct gold, enamel,
carved jade and diamond
compact and lipstick
case, *c.*1915, slight
wear, *NY 12 June,*
$605 (£480)

1
A platinum, sapphire
and diamond lapel watch,
c.1925, crystal and one
hand missing, *NY 15 Oct,*
$5,775 (£4,096)

2
A two-colour 18 ct. gold
lapel watch, French,
c.1930, *NY 12 June,*
$825 (£655)

3
An onyx and diamond
dress set, comprising a
pair of cufflinks, four
buttons and two studs,
one link imperfect,
L 3 Oct,
£3,520 ($5,210)

4
A pair of sapphire and
diamond earclips, Van
Cleef & Arpels, New
York, *NY 15 Oct,*
$7,425 (£5,266)

5
A pair of jade and
diamond pendent ear-
rings, c.1920, later
fittings, *L 23 May,*
£825 ($1,089)

6
A pair of onyx and
diamond pendent ear-
rings, c.1925, *L 3 Oct,*
£1,210 ($1,791)

7
A yellow and white gold
and enamel lapel-watch,
French, c.1925, the dial
concealed by an opening
ribbed motif, *NY 10 Dec,*
$4,125 (£2,925)

8
A gold, diamond and
citrine quartz brooch,
Paul Flato, c.1940, some
stones missing,
NY 23 Apr,
$3,850 (£3,080)

9
A pair of onyx and
diamond cufflinks,
St M 23 Feb,
SF 6,050 (£1,867; $2,129)

10
A jade, pearl and diamond
sureté-pin, c.1925,
Glen 26 Aug,
£880 ($1,294)

11
A black onyx and diamond
brooch, French, c.1930,
NY 15 Oct,
$2,310 (£1,638)

12
A pair of moonstone,
sapphire and diamond
cufflinks, c.1930,
NY 15 Oct,
$2,860 (£2,028)

13
An 18 ct. gold, platinum,
diamond and enamel
necklace, David Webb,
with alternating blue
and reddish brown
enamelled links,
NY 10 Dec,
$7,425 (£5,265)

14
A gold and diamond
bracelet, by Van Cleef &
Arpels, *L 5 Dec,*
£7,590 ($11,157)

15
An 18 ct. pink gold
bracelet, c.1940,
NY 10 Dec,
$2,090 (£1,482)

16
A gold link bracelet,
c.1940, *NY 15 Oct,*
$1,650 (£1,170)

Orders, Medals and Decorations

1
Germany, Saxon Duchies, Order of Ernestine, Grand Cross sash badge, unmarked, in gold and enamels, 105mm (4in) overall, *L 27 June,*
£660 ($898)

2
Germany, Brunswick, Order of Henry the Lion, *c.*1860, Commander's neck badge, in gold and enamels, 82mm (3¼in), *L 27 June,*
£550 ($748)

3
The Most Eminent Order of the Indian Empire (C.I.E.), Companion's breast badge, type 1, in gold and enamels, *L 27 June,*
£935 ($1,272)

4
Lloyd's medal for Meritorious Services, 1906, silver, *L 6 Nov,*
£660 ($990)

5
Royal Naval Long Service and Good Conduct medal, William IV, 'anchor type' (George Radford, Blacksmith, HMS *Vindictive,* 22 years), *L 6 Nov,*
£374 ($561)

6
Davison's medal for the Battle of Trafalgar, 1805, in pewter, *L 6 Nov,*
£935 ($1,403)

7
Arctic discoveries medal, 1815-55, (Wm. Lee, HMS *Pioneer), L 27 June,*
£198 ($269)

8
Upper Canada Preserved, silver medal, 1812, *L 27 June,*
£176 ($239)

9
Liverpool Shipwreck and Humane Society, marine silver medal, 1839, unnamed, *L 28 Feb,*
£77 ($89)

10
A Lifesaving pair, comprising a Royal National Lifeboat Institution, gold medal; A French Ministère de la Marine et des Colonies, gold medal, 37mm (1½in), *L 6 Nov,*
£2,530 ($3,795)

11
A Royal Red Cross pair for the Quetta earthquake, 1935, (Staff Nurse G. Lincoln), *L 6 Nov,*
£506 ($759)

12
A Royal Red Cross and bar group of three (Miss A. M. MacDonnell), *L 6 Nov,*
£1,430 ($2,145)

1
Army of India medal,
1799, 1 clasp, Ava (Lieut.
T. S. Kirby, Arty.),
L 28 Feb,
£462 ($536)

2
Army of India, 1799, 1
clasp, Kirkee and Poona,
(Joshua Foxwell, Eur.
Regt.), *L 7 Nov,*
£990 ($1,485)

3
Army of India, 1799, 4
clasps, Battle of Deig,
Capture of Deig, Nepaul,
Ava, (Lt. Col. T.P. Smith,
49th N.I.), *L 7 Nov,*
£3,740 ($5,610)

4
Army of India, 1799,
1 clasp, Nagpore, (P.
Kelly, 1st Foot), *L 7 Nov,*
£605 ($908)

5
**A pair of medals com-
prising:** Army of India,
1799, 1 clasp Bhurtpoor,
and Candahar, Ghuznee
and Cabul 1842, both
awarded to Col. W. An-
derson, Bengal Artillery,
L 28 Feb,
£770 ($893)

6
Sutlej Campaign medal,
1845, rev. Ferozeshuhur,
1 clasp, Sobraon (David
Elsworth, 29th Regt.),
L 28 Feb,
£187 ($217)

7
Punjab Campaign medal,
1848, 2 clasps, Goojerat,
Chilianwala (1st Lieut.
W. M. Gowan, H. Arty.),
L 28 Feb,
£198 ($230)

8
Indian Mutiny medal,
1857, 2 clasps, Lucknow,
Defence of Lucknow (W.
Ford, 78th Highlanders)
L 27 June,
£308 ($419)

9
Abyssinia medal, 1867
(H. Cooper, Chf. Engr.,
H.M.S. *Daphne*) *L 7 Nov,*
£143 ($215)

10
Ashantee medal, 1873,
1 clasp, Coomassie (Pte.
C. Smith, 2nd Bn. 23rd
R. W. Fus.), *L 7 Nov,*
£121 ($182)

11
First China medal, 1842
(Richard Murchy, 49th
Regiment Foot), *L 28 Feb,*
£132 ($153)

12
Third China medal, 1900,
1 clasp, Relief of Pekin
(A. Young, Pte., R.M.,
H.M.S. *Aurora*), *L 28 Feb,*
£132 ($153)

13
Carib War silver medal,
1773, *L 27 June,*
£770 ($1,047)

14
Empress of India medal,
1877 (unnamed as issued),
L 7 Nov,
£209 ($314)

15
A miniature medal,
Queen's South Africa,
1899, 24 clasps,
L 27 June,
£93 ($126)

1
A pair awarded to Lieut. Edward Scones, 52nd Foot, comprising: Military General Service medal, 1793, 1 clasp, Toulouse, Waterloo medal, 1815, *S 3 Apr,* £825 ($1,064)

2
Transport medal, 1899, 2 clasps, S. Africa, 1899-1902, China 1900 (H. Coutts, 2nd Engineer, H.M.T. *Glegyle*), *L 7 Nov,* £418 ($627)

3
A First World War Distinguished Conduct medal, awarded to Cpl. J. Peach, 5th Dragoon Guards, *L 7 Nov,* £209 ($413)

4
A First World War Military Cross group, awarded to Lieut. C. E. Hughes-Davies, Royal Field Artillery, *L 7 Nov,* £121 ($182)

5
A Battle of Britain A.F.C., D.F.M. group awarded to Sq. Ldr. R. V. Ellis, *L 7 Nov,* £5,720 ($8,580)

6
A Second World War George medal, awarded to A. R. P. Warden William Purchase, for bravery in rescuing seven people who were buried in debris during an air raid, *L 7 Nov,* £440 ($660)

7
A posthumous George Cross for bomb disposal in 1941, awarded to O. S. Bennett Southwell, 23rd January 1941, *L 27 June,* £5,500 ($7,480)

8
Naval General Service medal, 1793, 1 clasp, 1 Nov. Boat Service, 1809 (J. Brutton, Lieut., R.M.), *L 7 Nov,* £605 ($908)

9
Naval General Service medal, 1793, 1 clasp, Stately, 22 March 1808, awarded to Webb Hall, Ordinary Seaman, *L 27 June,* £770 ($1,047)

10
Naval General Service medal, 1793, 3 clasps, Trafalgar, St. Domingo and 24 May Boat Service 1814 (Thomas Robinson), *L 7 Nov,* £880 ($1,320)

11
Naval General Service medal, 1793, 1 clasp, Syria (Geo., Bedwell, Boy, H.M.S. *Ganger*), *L 28 Feb,* £165 ($191)

12
Naval General Service medal, 1793, 2 clasps 1798 Lion and Trafalgar, awarded to George Decoeurdoux, *L 27 June,* £3,300 ($4,488)

13
Royal Naval Long Service and Good Conduct medal, William IV, 'anchor type', awarded to William Wittern, HMS *Benbow, L 27 June,* £396 ($539)

14
Naval Long Service and Good Conduct medal, Victoria, 1½in. type (Ge. Keys, Chf. Boatsns. Mte. H.M.S. *Pantaloon*, 22 yrs), *L 28 Feb,* £165 ($191)

15
A First World War Distinguished Service Order group, awarded to Commander H. G. Higgins, Royal Navy, for bravery in action against enemy submarines, *L 27 June,* £638 ($868)

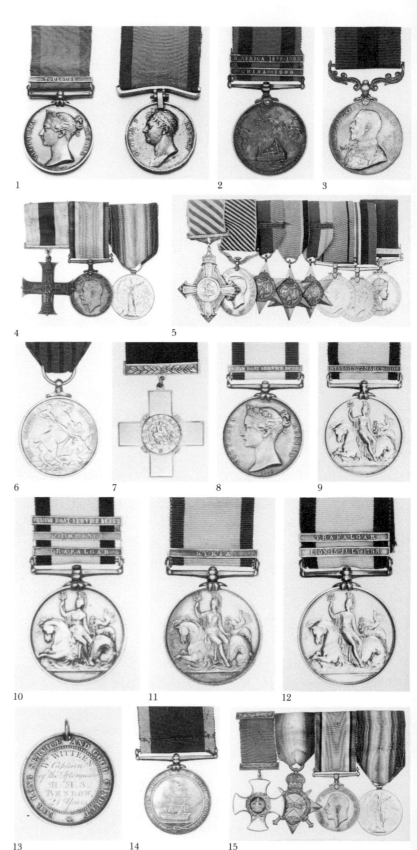

1

2

3

4

5

6

7

8

9

10

11

12

13

14

15

Arms and Armour

Article ● A warning to owners *pp* 521-523

See also ● Sporting guns *pp* 538-539 ● Islamic works of art *pp* 622-623
● Japanese works of art *p* 681

1
A Victorian Trooper's helmet, 19th century, of the Royal Life Guards, *C 31 Jan,* £880 ($1,038)

2
An Austrian Lancer's Tschapka, *c.*1900, *L 6 Nov,* £462 ($693)

3
An Austrian Dragoon helmet, late 19th century, some flaking to black paint, *L 6 Nov,* £495 ($742)

4
An officer's helmet of the 3rd (Prince of Wales's) Dragoon Guards, Pattern 1871, slight wear, *L 6 Nov,* £935 ($1,402)

5
A helmet of Duke of Lancaster's Own Yeomanry, *c.*1870, *L 6 Nov* £385 ($577)

6
A helmet of West Yorkshire Yeomanry, 19th century, *L 6 Nov,* £682 ($1,023)

7
A helmet of Royal Artillery Militia, *c.*1910, *L 6 Nov,* £187 ($280)

8
A Victorian Scottish Highlanders Light Infantry officer's dirk, with cairngorm pommel, in matching sheath with companion knife and fork, dirk blade 28.5cm (11¼in), *S 26 June,* £693 ($935)

9
A Scottish dirk and matching skean dhu, 19th century, stamped Forsyth, Glasgow, with nickel-plated mounts, and companion knife and fork, dirk 38cm (15in), *C 31 Jan,* £352 ($415)

10
A Scottish regimental dirk, late 19th/early 20th century, in original japanned tin case with skean dhu, sporran, a dress sporran and other items (ten altogether), *L 6 Nov,* £935 ($1,402)

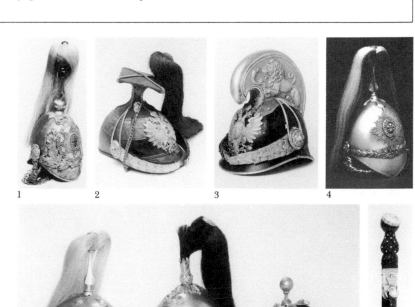

1 2 3 4

5 6 7 8

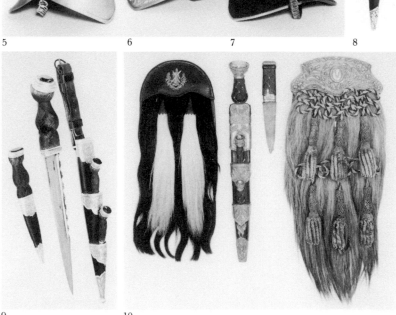

9 10

1
An Italian morion, late 16th century, of two pieces, some damage and wear, 32.5cm (12½in), *L 6 Nov,* £682 ($1,023)

2
A cuirassier's helmet, 17th century, rear lame partly detached, *L 23 Apr,* £1,100 ($1,474)

3
A morion, 17th century, two small holes, *L 5 Feb,* £880 ($1,038)

4
A pig-faced bascinet, in late 14th century style, marked with a Gothic letter Y, sold with a leg defence, 29.5cm (11¾in) high, *NY 11 May,* $3,960 (£3,220)

5
A pair of pauldrons and rerebraces, late 16th/17th century, etched with allegorical figures, regilt, 44.5cm (17½in), *NY 22 Nov,* $2,090 (£1,432)

6
A German black and white three quarter armour, late 16th century and later, the etched decoration 19th century, *NY 11 May,* $2,310 (£1,878)

7
A composite full length armour, second quarter 16th century and later, *NY 11 May,* $4,400 (£3,577)

8
A cuirassier's three quarter armour, *c.*1640, retaining original buckles, *L 23 Apr,* £5,500 ($7,370)

9
A composite browned cavalry munition armour, late 16th century and later, some repairs, *NY 11 May,* $3,850 (£3,130)

10
A composite three quarter cavalry armour, third quarter 16th century and later, *NY 11 May,* $5,500 (£4,472)

11
A composite pikeman's half armour, early 17th century, *NY 11 May,* $1,760 (£1,431)

12
A three quarter munition armour, early 17th century and later, 137cm (54in) high, *NY 22 Nov,* $5,775 (£3,955)

13
A South German full length armour, late 19th century, some finger lames and spurs lacking, *NY 11 May,* $9,900 (£8,049)

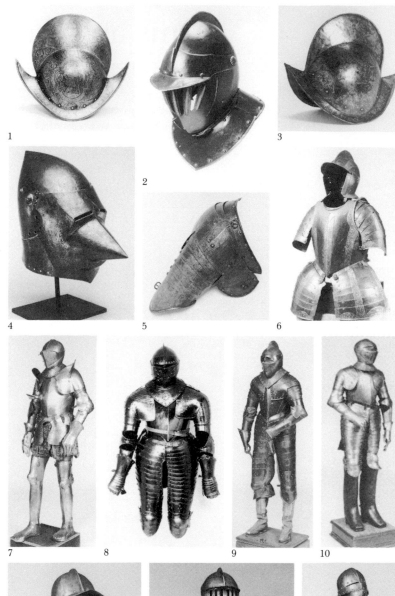

1
A bois durci powder flask,
19th century, 13cm
(5¼in), L 23 Apr,
£143 ($192)

2
A powder flask, mid-19th
century, embossed with
scenes from Aesop's
Fables, 12cm (4¾in),
L 23 Apr,
£60 ($80)

3
An ivory inlaid powder-
horn probably Swiss,
dated 1621, 30cm (12½in),
NY 11 May,
$3,850 (£3,130)

4
A powder horn, 17th
century, 28.5cm (11in),
L 23 Apr,
£1,100 ($1,474)

5
A central European bone
veneered powder flask,
17th century, gilt-brass
mounts, 17.5cm (7in),
NY 15 Feb,
$990 (£853)

6
An ivory powder flask,
South German, late 16th
century, iron mounts,
21cm (8¼in), NY 22 Nov,
$1,650 (£1,130)

7
A model parapet gun,
18th century, mounted on
wood carriage, 33.5cm
(13¼in), NY 15 Feb,
$2,420 (£2,086)

8
A Venetian bronze
mortar, by Giovanni
Mazzaroli, c.1700, lacking
wheels, 25.5cm (10in),
NY 15 Feb,
$3,520 (£3,034)

9
An English model horse
artillery cannon, 19th
century, mounted with
wrought iron, length
of cannon 47cm (18½in),
NY 15 Feb,
$1,650 (£1,422)

10
Two silver models of
English field cannon, 1898
and 1901, 25.5 and 22cm
(10 and 8½in), NY 15 Feb,
$1,320 (£1,138)

11
A North German target
crossbow, Ian Sander,
Hanover, 18th century,
inlaid with bone and
mother-of-pearl, 68.5cm
(27in), NY 15 Feb,
$2,970 (£2,560)

12
A German crossbow, pos-
sibly Saxon, dated 1636,
some restoration, 62cm
(24½in) long, NY 11 May,
$2,530 (£2,057)

13
A North Italian pierced
steel halberd, dated 164?,
sold with another hal-
berd, heights of blades 52
and 56cm (20½ and 22in),
NY 22 Nov,
$1,320 (£904)

14
A South German etched
halberd, dated 1589,
height of blade including
socket 63cm (24¾in),
NY 22 Nov,
$17,600 (£12,055)

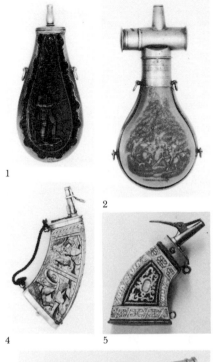
1

2

3

6

4

5

8

7

9

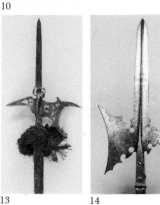
10

11

12

13   14

1
A German wheel lock carbine, early 17th century, 113cm (44¼in), *L 23 Apr,* £3,850 ($5,159)

2
A brass barrelled flintlock blunderbuss, *c.*1700, signed 'R. Silk', 81cm (32in), *L 5 Feb,* £770 ($909)

3
A Warner .50 rimfire carbine, *c.*1864, stamped Greene Rifle Works, Worcester, Mass. Pat D 1864, 95cm (37½in), *L 6 Nov,* £418 ($627)

4
A Colt percussion revolving carbine, *c.*1860, iron butt plate, barrel 53cm (21in), *L 6 Nov,* £1,375 ($2,062)

5
A German percussion hunting rifle, J. Adam Kuchenreuter in Regensburg, mid-19th century, 71.5cm (28in), *NY 15 Feb,* $3,630 (£3,129)

6
A pair of Irish silver-mounted double-barrelled percussion pistols, mid-19th century, the locks inscribed Trulock & Son, *L 6 Nov,* £825 ($1,237)

7
A cased Tranter percussion single-trigger revolver, *c.*1864, retailed by J. W. Edge, Manchester, *L 6 Nov,* £770 ($1,155)

8
A pair of French gold-embellished flintlock rifled sporting pistols, *c.*1817, inscribed Boutet et fils à Versailles, metal corroded, stocks damaged, *L 6 Nov,* £4,840 ($7,260)

9
A pair of Swiss percussion target pistols, third quarter 19th century, inlaid 'T. Wagner in Bern', case 39.5cm (15½in), *NY 15 Feb,* $3,850 (£3,319)

10
A cased pair of breech loading percussion pistols, Bertonnet a Paris, *c.*1849, 38.5cm (15¼in), *NY 22 Nov,* $2,860 (£1,959)

11
A pair of French percussion pocket pistols, Gastinne Renette, mid-19th century, 21cm (8¼in), *NY 15 Feb,* $1,650 (£1,422)

12
A double-barrelled flintlock coaching carbine, early 19th century, signed Wogdon & Barton, minor damage, 79cm (31in), *L 6 Nov,* £935 ($1,403)

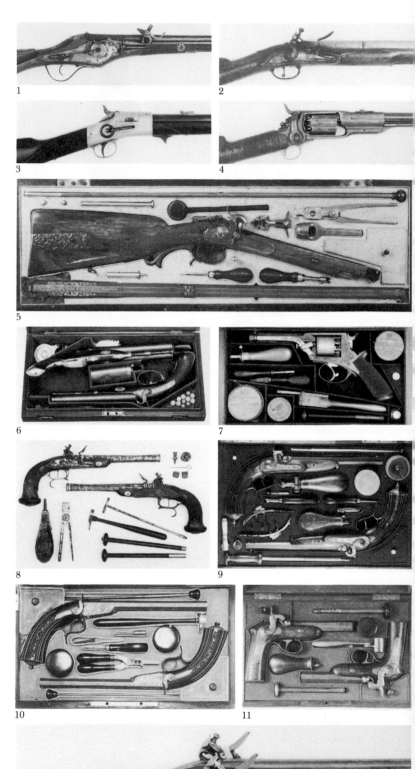

1

A Savage percussion revolver, c.1860-61, length of barrel 18cm (7in), NY 15 Feb, $660 (£569)

2

A Webley longspur percussion revolver, mid-19th century, barrel pitted, 30.5cm (12in), L 23 Apr, £385 ($516)

3

A Remington Model 1871 Army rolling block pistol, c.1872-88, length of barrel 20.5cm (8in), NY 15 Feb, $825 (£711)

4

An Adams patent five shot percussion revolver, c.1860, barrel stamped 'Manufactured by Mass Arms Co., Chicopee Falls', 32cm (12½in), C 31 Jan, £187 ($220)

5

A Volcanic lever action Number One pocket pistol, c.1857-60, action faulty, length of barrel 9cm (3½in), NY 15 Feb, $935 (£806)

6

A miquelet lock ripoll pistol, early 18th century, ramrod lacking, action defective, 23cm (9in), L 23 Apr, £1,265 ($1,695)

7

A pair of flintlock double-barrelled tap-action silver-mounted pistols, c.1810, slight damage, the barrels cleaned and patinated, L 6 Nov, £748 ($1,122)

8

An officer's silver mounted flintlock pistol, c.1780, the lock signed 'T. Richards', some wear, 37cm (14½in), L 23 Apr, £528 ($708)

9

A French flintlock holster pistol, mid-18th century, made for the Middle Eastern market, 47cm (18½in), L 23 Apr, £605 ($811)

10

A North Italian Snaphaunce, pistol, probably Brescian, early 18th century, repaired and polished, 36cm (14¼in), NY 15 Feb, $3,300 (£2,845)

11

A Wilkinson breech loading blunderbuss pistol, c.1831, retaining some original colour, L 6 Nov, £2,750 ($4,125)

12

A flintlock tinder lighter, late 18th century, mechanism defective, 17cm (6¾in), L 23 Apr, £407 ($545)

13

A flintlock eprouvette, late 18th century, some wear, 14.6cm (5¾in), L 5 Feb, £220 ($250)

14

A pair of French four barrel flintlock pistols, Lambert Dit Biron, last quarter 18th century, walnut grips, 32.5cm (12¾in), NY 15 Feb, $3,080 (£2,655)

15

A double-barrelled tap action boxlock pocket pistol, c.1800, signed D. Egg, London, small notch on both barrels, L 6 Nov, £660 ($990)

16

A percussion six shot pepperbox revolver, c.1860, with 3in rotating fluted barrels, 20cm (8in), C 2 May, £198 ($259)

17

A matchlock eprouvette, 17th century, 11cm (4¼in), L 23 Apr, £308 ($413)

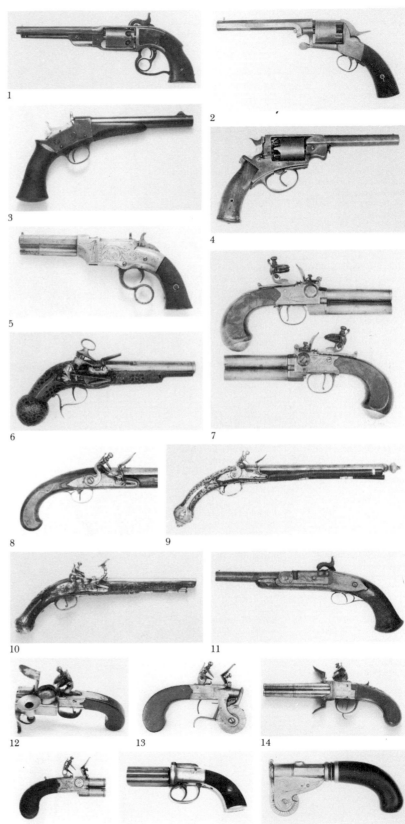

1
An officer's backsword,
18th century, blade
pitted, 102cm (40in),
L 23 Apr,
£462 ($619)

2
A schiavona, 18th century, with Solingen wolf
mark and orb and cross,
minor rusting, 108cm
(42½in), *L 23 Apr,*
£495 ($663)

3
**A South German hunting
sword,** early 17th century,
blade later, 73cm (28¾in),
L 23 Apr,
£2,640 ($3,538)

4
A hand and half sword,
late 16th century, blade
engraved 'Ioannes*
Wands* Me* Fecit*
Solingen', 107cm (42in),
L 5 Feb,
£1,540 ($1,817)

5
A broadsword, possibly
Northern European,
early 17th century, grip
replaced, 117cm (46in),
L 23 Apr,
£550 ($737)

6
A basket hilted sword,
mid-18th century, the
blade punched 'GR *
Harvey 1755', grip re-
stored, 117cm (46in),
L 23 Apr,
£528 ($708)

7
A rapier, North Euro-
pean, *c.*1630, Solingen
running wolf mark,
superficial rust and
minor pitting, *L 6 Nov,*
£1,430 ($2,145)

8
A hunting knife, probably
French, *c.*1870, hilt
decorated in gold with
scrolling foliage, 51cm
(20¼in), *L 23 Apr,*
£495 ($663)

9
**A French (?) cavalry
officer's sword,** late 18th
century, one plaque
lacking from hilt, 98cm
(38½in), *L 23 Apr,*
£1,430 ($1,916)

10
An Italian stiletto, late
16th century, 33cm (13in),
NY 11 May,
$2,860 (£2,325)

11
A smallsword, mid-18th
century, top mount
engraved 'Jeffery, Cutler
to His Majesty, Strand',
81cm (32in), *S 9 Jan,*
£572 ($686)

12
**A Scottish basket hilted
officer's backsword,**
probably by Jeffery,
London, *c.*1770,
blade 86.3cm (34in),
S 26 June,
£660 ($891)

13
**A Household Cavalry
trooper's sword,** *c.*1805, the
blade signed 'Bate'(?),
104cm (41in), *L 23 Apr,*
£462 ($619)

14
A naval officer's sword,
late 18th/early 19th cen-
tury, hilt slightly loose,
92cm (36¼in), *L 23 Apr,*
£495 ($663)

15
**A Georgian Light
Dragoon officer's sword,**
early 19th century, the
blade inscribed 'Tho.
Bate', point reshaped,
87cm (34¼in), *L 23 Apr,*
£495 ($663)

16
**A Light Dragoon officer's
sword,** early 19th cen-
tury, the blade inscribed
'Woolley Deakin & Co',
minor damage to scab-
bard and hilt, 92cm
(36½in), *L 23 Apr,*
£440 ($590)

17
**A combination flintlock
sword-pistol,** late 18th
century, some repair,
79cm (31in), *L 23 Apr,*
£440 ($590)

18
**A silver mounted small-
sword,** *c.*1740, restoration
to scabbard, 100cm
(39¼in), *L 23 Apr,*
£462 ($619)

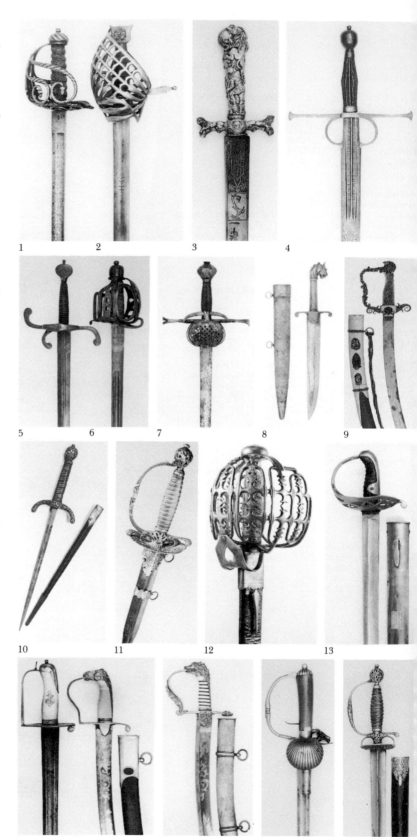

A Warning to Owners

The possessors of antique arms and armour, or indeed of almost any other artefact, may in simple terms be divided into three groups: collectors, investors and those who acquire their possessions by inheritance or some other happy accident. It is to the third group that the following observations are, in the main, directed. Dealers have not been included in this classification because, by the very nature of their profession, they must be considered to be in but temporary possession of their stock-in-trade. With the auction houses, they form an important link, serving and supplying the two first groups in particular and offering, one must hope, a means of profitable and convenient disposal to the third. My main object in addressing 'accidental' owners is to help them to ensure that the disposal of their unwanted arms or armour is indeed profitable and not inhibited, eroded or ruined by ignorance, poor advice or preconceived notions.

In general, the items in question are those in which the owner has little interest except possibly as familiar ornaments, and of which he or she has little or no technological or historical understanding—apart perhaps from the acceptance of frequently apocryphal family tradition or legend. Therefore, when the time for disposal arrives, the actual state of the piece is seen in a fresh light, which may cause the owner some concern. It is at this moment that great and irrevocable harm may be done and hundreds of pounds subtracted from the unsuspected potential value of the item. A fine patina composed of old oil, dust and many years of handling—indicating to a possible buyer that the weapon is a much sought-after 'sleeper'—may

—1—
A four-barrelled rimfire pistol, 19th century, with Birmingham proof, main spring lacking, 18.5cm (7¼in), *L 6 Nov,* £286 ($429)

—2—
A cased Tranter .32 rimfire revolver, c.1865, inscribed Coggswell & Harrison, 223 & 224, Strand, London, some wear to original blued finish, 21.5cm (8½in), *L 6 Nov,* £462 ($693)

—3—
An Imperial German Garde du Corps helmet, late 19th/early 20th century, back of guard stamped 'GKR 2E 2', minor wear, *L 23 Apr,* £1,540 ($2,064)

—4—
A North African Snaphance Kabyle gun, 19th century, slight damage to decoration, *L 6 Nov,* £682 ($1,023)

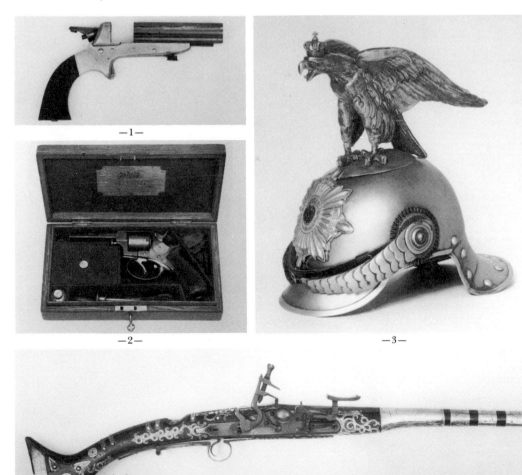

—1—

—2—

—3—

—4—

suddenly be seen as 'dirt' and removed by one of the many harsh household methods to hand. Or perhaps a thin coating of stable rust, concealing the valuable original colour of the metal, will be seen by a widowed housewife as damaging to her reputation or pride and removed by an obliging friend with an electric wire brush or emery cloth.

These common processes can, in seconds, render the piece totally unattractive to a discerning buyer. If the item originally was of great potential interest or value such treatment may result in large sums being spent on restoration which, however skilful, renders it permanently second-rate. Prospective vendors should reflect that such sums will be subtracted automatically at the time of sale by a knowledgeable buyer. Therefore it may be seen that pride in presenting a bright and shiny object for appraisal and valuation may indeed suffer a fall. Some examples which illustrate these points can be seen in the accompanying photographs of items sold by Sotheby's in England, on the Continent of Europe and in the United States. For instance fig. 10 although sold, failed to reach the figure hoped for because, in spite of being a genuine and normally

attractive piece, it had been cleaned with a commercial rust-remover which, typically, left the surface with a dead, pitted and unreal appearance. Such chemicals, whilst ideal for de-rusting industrial ironwork and the chassis of vintage cars, should never be used on any item of which the original surface is of interest or value. Figs.6, 7, 8 and 9 were amongst a group of eight pistols which had been in the ownership of the same family since the 18th and early 19th centuries. They had suffered the usual neglect and misuse when their working life was over. They were originally of good quality, intended for use rather than display, and typified the arms commissioned or simply purchased by gentlemen of the period. Had any amateur attempt been made to 'tidy them up' before sale their potential would have been ruined and they would have been reduced to shiny junk with ineptly glued stocks. They all sold well, several exceeding the upper estimates, and will repay restoration in the proper skilled hands. Fig.5 sold in New York for $1,650 (£1,341). It is unlikely that it would have reached this figure had the previous owner not resisted the temptation to burnish out the pitting and patination. Even the finest armour,

—5—
A German fluted helmet, in 16th century Maximilian style, some pitting, 28cm (11in), *NY 11 May,* $1,650 (£1,341)

—6—
A percussion double-barrelled over-and-under single trigger travelling pistol, *c.*1825, inscribed J. Egg, London, butt-cap damaged, barrels rust-stained, *L 6 Nov,* £1,100 ($1,650)

—7—
A flintlock duelling pistol, *c.*1770, inscribed East Smithfield, London, 34.5cm (16½in), *L 6 Nov,* £385 ($578)

—8—
A pair of silver-mounted flintlock travelling pistols, late 18th century, re-barrelled and later fore-ends, inscribed H Nock London and Higginbotham, one butt cracked, metal stained overall, 32.5cm (13in), *L 6 Nov,* £792 ($1,188)

—9—
A pair of steel-mounted flintlock belt pistols, early 18th century, lockplates inscribed I Drew, some damage, lightly rusted overall, *L 6 Nov,* £715 ($1,072)

—10—
A left-hand dagger, Italian, early 17th century, the blade of diamond section, 59cm (23¼in), *L 6 Nov,* £1,650 ($2,475)

—5—

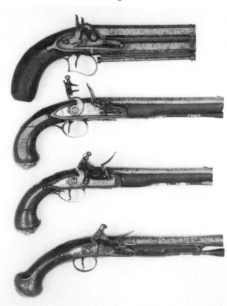

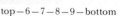
top—6—7—8—9—bottom

—10—

maintained in a private or public collection virtually since its manufacture in the 15th or 16th century, is unlikely to be found without some evidence of oxidization, and a mirror-like surface will undoubtedly raise suspicions of restoration or replacement of elements in the mind of a discriminating buyer.

A large quantity of armour was made in Europe during the 19th century for the mansions and castles of the nouveaux riches. When it became unfashionable in the early 20th century much of it was relegated to attics, cellars and stables, where it acquired a patina of rust and dirt. The shortage of genuine armour, and the revival of interest in armour as a decorative item, have recently caused this hitherto scorned class to command increasingly impressive prices in the salerooms. Fig. 11, sold in London for £4,400 ($5,896) is a good example. Although the amateur cleaning of such armour is unlikely to offend the purist, it is still better left to the buyer to have the work carried out professionally.

Figs. 13, 15, and 16 represent a much-abused class of weapon. Good swords are becoming increasingly rare and many genuine and collectable examples have been ruined for ever by dismantling and burnishing. It is sad that collectors have been by no means guiltless in this respect.

The cleaning, or rather overcleaning, of brass, bronze, silver and gilt metal has long been either a domestic temptation or an imposed duty, and weapons have suffered from the houseproud owner as much as utensils and ornaments. The evidence lies in worn hallmarks, inscriptions and decoration and in unsightly accretions of dried polish. Fig.12 is a good example of such vulnerable objects which have escaped unscathed, and also illustrates the increasing interest in good 18th and 19th century model cannon.

The message to the prospective vendor is clear. Those who have to dispose of hitherto neglected arms should never, whatever their state, attempt to improve them before sale, and the expert valuer or potential buyer should be afforded the opportunity to judge the piece 'as is'. Conservation and, if necessary, restoration should be left to those with the necessary skill and experience.

● MICHAEL BALDWIN ●

Further reading

C. Blair and L. Tarassuk (editors), *The Complete Encyclopaedia of Arms and Weapons*, 1982

D. Harding (editor), *Weapons 5000 BC to 2000 AD*, 1980

—11—
A Victorian armour, in 16th century style, minor damage, and rust, 170cm (67in) high, *L 23 Apr,* £4,400 ($5,896)

—12—
A model cannon, 18th century, bronze barrel, mounted on wooden field carriage, elevating crank missing, barrel 22.5cm (8¾in), *L 6 Nov,* £528 ($792)

—13—
A schiovona, 18th century, leather bound grip, 101cm (39¾in), *L 5 Feb,* £935 ($1,103)

—14—
An officer's hanger, late 18th century, the blade inscribed 'Sandwich le 12m Avril 1782' and 'La Ville de Paris le 12me Avril 1782', 76.5cm (30in), *L 23 Apr,* £352 ($472)

—15—
A general officer's Mameluke sword pattern 1831, mid 19th century, maker Manton & Co, England, 99cm (39in), *L 23 Apr,* £330 ($442)

—16—
A Scottish regimental broadsword, mid 19th century, the double-edged blade with V.R. cypher, 96.5cm (38in), *C 2 May,* £264 ($346)

—11— —12— —13— —14— —15— —16—

Sports and Pastimes

Including • Advertising material • Automobilia • Cameras • Corkscrews • Fishing tackle • Games • Golf and cricket • Musical boxes and mechanical musical instruments • Rock 'n roll • Sporting guns
See also • Colour illustrations p 485

1
A carved ivory chess set, probably English, mid-to late 19th century, 32 pieces, 7.5cm (3in) to 4cm (1½in), *NY 10 June,* $770 (£611)

2
A Continental carved amber chess set, probably German, mid-19th century, 32 pieces, 8.5cm (3¼in) to 3cm (1¼in), *NY 10 June,* $660 (£523)

3
An Indian carved ivory chess set, probably Bengal, early 19th century, Hindus vs British, 32 pieces, 9.5cm (3¾in) to 5.5cm (2¼in), *NY 10 June,* $4,840 (£3,841)

4
An Anglo-Indian carved ivory chess set, 19th century, 32 pieces, 11cm (4¼in) to 5cm (2in), *NY 10 June,* $935 (£742)

5
A German carved ivory chess set, late 18th/early 19th century, 32 pieces, 13.5cm (5¼in) to 6.5cm (2½in), *NY 10 June,* $1,320 (£1,047)

6
A French 'Naive' chess set, c.1800, in carved and turned bone, some damage, the king 6cm (2¼in), *L 23 Jan,* £308 ($365)

7
A fruitwood and mahogany chess set, probably French, mid-19th century, the king 7.5cm (3in), *L 23 Jan,* £770 ($912)

8
A Victorian coromandel and brass-bound games compendium, c.1870, the hinged cover revealing a folded gaming board, and various accessories, 36cm (14in), *S 11 June,* £792 ($1,041)

9
A Victorian burr walnut 'Royal Cabinet of Games', by Asprey & Sons, c.1860, containing various games and accessories, 32cm (12½in) wide, *S 16 Apr,* £517 ($672)

10
A musical game by Ann Young, Edinburgh, early 19th century, mahogany case, with various accessories, 44cm (17½in), long, *L 3 Apr,* £858 ($1,107)

11
Parker Bros. 'The Game of Merry Christmas,' American, c.1898, 56.5cm (22¼in), *L 1 Oct,* £330 ($412)

1
A 'Hidden-Drum-and-Bells' cylinder musical box, Swiss, c.1860, probably by Bremond, 56cm (22in) wide, *L 1 Oct,* £682 ($996)

2
A 'Bells-in-Sight' cylinder musical box, Swiss, late 19th century, 52cm (20½in) wide, *L 23 Jan,* £748 ($886)

3
A 'Bells, Castanets and Drums-in-Sight' musical box, late 19th century, 67cm (26½in) wide, *S 17 Oct,* £1,760 ($2,605)

4
A lever-wound 'sublime harmony' cylinder musical box, playing six airs, 65.5cm (25½in) wide, *A 25 Nov,* Dfl 5,290 (£1,251; $1,751)

5
A Samuel Troll cylinder musical box, Swiss, third quarter 19th century, no.2192, 56cm (22in) wide, *L 23 Jan,* £495 ($587)

6
A Nicole Frères Mandoline two-per-turn cylinder musical box, Swiss, c.1880, no.44740, playing twelve operatic airs, comb with replaced teeth, 56cm (22in) wide, *L 23 Jan,* £1,430 ($1,695)

7
A Mojon Manger and Co interchangeable cylinder musical box, Swiss, c.1880, the movement restored, 92cm (36in) wide, *L 23 Jan,* £2,640 ($3,128)

8
A Raymond Nicole overture cylinder musical box, Swiss, mid-19th century, 38cm (15in) wide, *L 23 Jan,* £4,620 ($5,475)

9
An 11-inch Polyphon disc musical box, German, c.1900, with twelve discs, 39cm (15½in) wide, *C 20 Mar,* £462 ($568)

10
An 11-inch Polyphon disc musical box, German, c.1910, 24cm (13¼in) wide, with eighteen metal discs, 24cm (13¼in) wide, *L 1 Oct,* £357 ($514)

11
A 19½-inch Polyphon disc muscial box, German, c.1900, 69cm (27in), with twenty-four metal discs, *L 1 Oct,* £2,310 ($3,373)

12
An 11¾in Symphonion disc muscial box, German, c.1900, with 13 discs, *C 26 June,* £1,452 ($1,960)

13
A perifery-driven disc musical box, Regina, New Jersey, U.S.A., no.33696, c.1900, with handle and original tune sheet, 56.5cm (22¼in) wide, *A 25 Nov,* Dfl 5,060 (£1,196; $1,675)

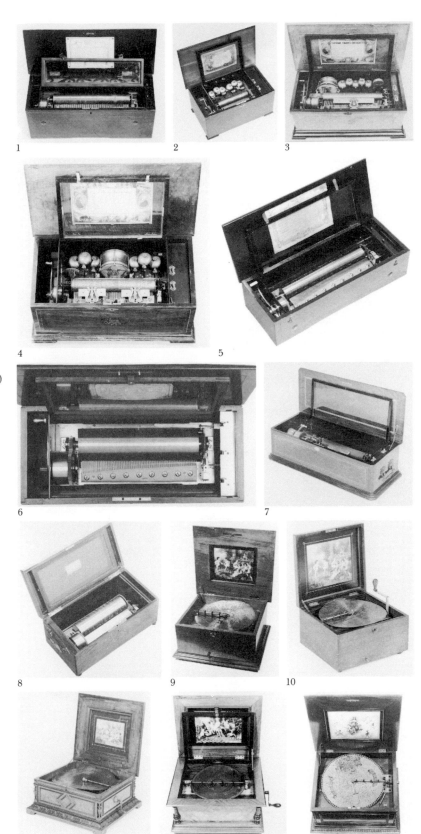

1

A cylinder organ, *c.*1880, playing nine airs, in walnut case, *A 25 Nov,* **Dfl 1,840** (£435; $609)

2

A Putteman's café barrel piano, Belgian, late 19th century, playing ten tunes, movement worn, 161cm (63½in) high, *C 29 Nov,* £495 ($693)

3

A Frati 26-note barrel-organ, late 19th century, in oak case, playing ten tunes, movement restored, 64cm (25in) wide, *L 23 Jan,* £2,530 ($2,999)

4

A Chordephone mechanical zither, German, *c.*1900, the ebonised sound box on ash base, 81cm (32in) wide, with twenty-two metal discs, *L 1 Oct,* £4,400 ($6,424)

5

A Regina 15½ in style 35 automatic changer disc musical box, American, *c.*1902, 173cm (68in) high, *NY 29 June,* $8,250 (£6,346)

6

A Columbia gramophone, American, *c.*1900, with 'Dulcetto' reproducer, with various accessories, *L 1 Oct,* £220 ($321)

7

A Gramophone and Typewriter Co. double spring Monarch gramophone, English, *c.*1905, tone arm and support rubbed, turntable 25.5cm (10in), *C 26 June,* £396 ($534)

8

A Gramophone and Typewriter Co. Gramophone, English, *c.*1905, with red painted morning glory horn, turntable, 25.5cm (10in), *C 26 June,* £352 ($475)

9

A horn gramophone, German, *c.*1905, the mahogany base with gilt brass decoration, complete with brass 'morning glory' horn, *L 1 Oct,* £825 ($1,205)

10

An E M Ginn Mark XB gramophone, English, *c.*1933, with papier mâché horn, 73cm (29in) diam, at mouth, on original stand, *C 22 Oct,* £638 ($957)

1   3   5

2

4

6   7   8

9   10

1
A 15½-inch **Polyphon disc musical box**, German, *c.*1900, in stained wood wall-mounting case with coin chute to either side, 85cm (33½in) high, together with four metal discs, *C 22 Oct*,
£1,320 ($1,980)

2
A **Nicole Frères, lever-wound interchangeable 'sublime harmony' Piccolo cylinder musical box**, Geneva, no.47423, *c.*1880, playing six airs, the table with cylinder storage drawers, 160cm (63in) wide, *A 25 Nov*,
Dfl 33,925 (£8,082; $11,228)

3
A 19⅝-inch **Polyphon autochange disc musical box**, German, *c.*1905, contained in stained-wood case on reproduction disc storage bin, 229cm (90in) high, *L 1 Oct*,
£8,250 ($12,045)

4
A **Gem roller organ**, American, late 19th century, manufactured by the Autophone Company, 30.5cm (12in) wide, *L 23 Jan*,
£528 ($626)

5
An **Ehrlich reed organ**, Leipzig, type Mignon, no.48881, *c.*1910, 49cm (19¼in) wide, *A 25 Nov*,
Dfl 1,840 (£435; $609)

6
An **Atlas Organette** reed organ, *c.*1900, with four polychrome wood musicians, 58.5cm (23in) wide, *A 25 Nov*,
Dfl 977 (£231; $323)

7
A **cylinder organ**. Ch. Anciaume à Paris, *c.*1880, playing eight airs, in palisander wood case, 73cm (28¾in) high, *A 25 Nov*,
Dfl 20,700 (£4,894; $6,851)

1

2

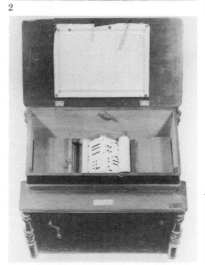

3

4

5

6

7

1
A J Lancaster & Son folding stereo camera, English, c.1890, mahogany and brass, with twin Lancaster lenses, 8.5 x 17cm (3¼ x 6¾in), *C 20 Mar,* £264 ($325)

2
A Gandolfi field camera, English, c.1970, with Kodak Ektar 12in f/4.5 in Universal Synchro shutter no. 5, 20.5 x 25.5cm (8 x 10in), *L 20 Feb,* £495 ($569)

3
A Dallmeyer studio camera, 25.5 x 30.5cm (10 x 12in), with f/7/7 lens, *L 13 June,* £220 ($293)

4
An R & J Beck Ltd., mahogany and brass biunial lantern, English, late 19th century, with electric illuminants, 62cm (24½in) high, *L 23 Oct,* £462 ($693)

5
A J Solomon magnesium lamp, French, late 19th century, no. 4828, 30.5cm (12in) long, *L 23 Oct,* £396 ($594)

6
A Kodak studio camera, with Taylor, Taylor & Hobson lens, leather bellow and mahogany body, with various accessories, 24 x 24cm (9½ x 9½in), *L 13 June,* £250 ($333)

7
A tailboard portrait camera, English, late 19th century, 12 x 10cm (4¾ x 4in), with 14½in Cooke f/3.4 portrait lens, *C 26 June,* £275 ($371)

8
A mahogany zograscope, English, early 19th century, 65cm (25½in), *L 23 Oct,* £198 ($297)

9
A mahogany panorama pantoptique, probably English, early 19th century, 46cm (18in) long, together with twenty tissue slides, *L 23 Oct,* £880 ($1,320)

10
A Brewster-type stereoscopic viewer, English, c.1870, the case veneered in tortoiseshell with ivory mounts, 17cm (6¾in) long, *L 11 June,* £462 ($600)

11
A Beinhauer Brothers 'Magic Disc' phenakistiscope, German, c.1825, with various accessories, *L 11 June,* £550 ($715)

12
A Kendal & Son phenakistiscope or 'Living Picture', English c.1825, with fifteen hand tinted cardboard discs, 20cm (8in) long, *C 20 Mar,* £660 ($812)

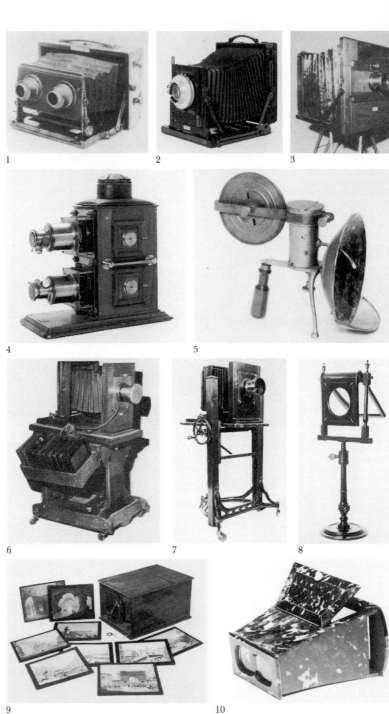

1   2   3

4   5

6   7   8

9   10

11   12

1
A Leica I Interchange-
able, *c.*1930, no. 37394,
with Elmar 50mm f/3.5
lens, *L 23 Oct,*
£550 ($825)

2
A Leica IIIG, *c.*1957,
no. 904508, with Sum-
marit 5cm f/1.5 lens,
no. 1471734, *L 23 Oct,*
£198 ($297)

3
A wood and copper plate
camera, L. Gaumont &
Cie, Paris, *A 2 Apr,*
Dfl 551 (£128; $165)

4
A sliding-box wet-plate
camera, mid-19th cen-
tury, with Petzval-type
lens signed Lerebours
et Secretan no. 8186, 16 x
11.5cm (6¼ x 4½in),
L 20 Feb,
£572 ($658)

5
A Leica III, *c.*1953,
no. 110612, with Sum-
mar 5cm f/2 lens
no. 256634, *L 11 June,*
£165 ($214)

6
A Horne & Thornthwaite
folding wet-plate camera,
English, *c.*1855, with
portrait lens, with
various accessories,
32 x 23 x 20cm (12½ x 9
x 8in), *L 23 Oct,*
£2,420 ($3,630)

7
A Schneider & Munzke
55MM cine camera, Ger-
man, 1930's, the hand-
cranked mechanism
with Astra 52mm f/2.7
lens, with various
accessories, *L 11 June,*
£308 ($400)

8
A Leica IIIA, *c.*1937,
no. 248124, with Elmar
5cm f/3.5 lens, together
with three other lenses
and screw mounts,
L 11 June,
£330 ($429)

9
A Black Leica IIIG,
no. 987976, *c.*1960,
together with 200mm
Telyt and 35mm Sume-
ron lenses, *L 23 Oct,*
£1,980 ($2,970)

10
A Lehmann cane-handle
camera, German, *c.*1903,
35mm f/9 meniscus lens,
79cm (31¼in), *L 23 Oct,*
£3,520 ($5,280)

1

2

3

4

5

6

7

8

9

10

1
A Telefunken radio, 1928,
type 4, 20cm (8in) high,
A 7 Oct,
Dfl 1,178 (£278; $411)

2
A Telefunken radio, 1928,
type 3W, *A 7 Oct,*
Dfl 1,667 (£394; $583)

3
An Erres radio, 1945, type
KY 457, 39cm (15¼in)
high, *A 7 Oct,*
Dfl 126 (£29; $42)

4
A Phillips radio, 1947,
type 760 x 62cm (24½in)
high, *A 7 Oct,*
Dfl 218 (£51; $75)

5
A Phillips radio 1937/38,
type 890 A, 40cm (15¾in)
high, *A 7 Oct,*
Dfl 195 (£46; $68)

6
A Phillips radio, 1933/34,
type 634 A, 49cm (19¼in)
high, *A 7 Oct,*
Dfl 391 (£92; $136)

7
A Phillips radio, 1933/34,
type 834 A, 44cm (17¼in)
high, *A 7 Oct,*
Dfl 460 (£108; $159)

8
A Phillips loudspeaker,
1927, type 2007,
A 7 Oct,
Dfl 414 (£97; $143)

9
A Waldorp radio,
1946, type 46 A, 80cm
(31½in) high, *A 7 Oct,*
Dfl 977 (£230; $340)

10
**A Phillips type 6028T
projection television,**
*c.*1951, comprising
projector in maple-
veneered casing and
screen in suite unit with
loudspeaker, screen unit
74 x 137cm (29 x 54in),
L 11 June,
£286 ($372)

11
**An Ahrens 'Test Your
Strength' amusement
machine,** *c.*1922, lacking
back plate, 203cm (80in),
C 29 Nov,
£880 ($1,232)

12
**A Wurlitzer Model 800
jukebox,** 1940s, with
twenty-four selections,
156cm (5ft 1½in) high,
NY 29 June,
$5,500 (£4,231)

13
**A Wurlitzer Model 1015
jukebox,** *c.*1946, with
twenty-four selections,
case restored, 152.5cm
(5ft) high, *NY 29 June,*
$7,920 (£6,092)

1
Taddy & Co.'s 'Orders of Chivalry' cigarette cards, 1911 (25); together with Ogden's 'Orders of Chivalry', 1907 (50), *S 6 Mar,*
£143 ($160)

2
F & J Smith's 'Cricketers' cigarette cards (1-50), 1912, *S 6 Mar,*
£154 ($172)

3
Wills' 'Builders of the Empire', 1898 (50); together with Franklyn Davey 'Historic Events' 1924 (50), *S 6 Mar,*
£52 ($59)

4
Original artwork for an advertising poster, 'Guinness for Strength' 1934, in watercolour and pastels, 56 x 46cm (22 x 18in), *C 22 Oct,*
£1,320 ($1,980)

5
Original artwork for Guinness advertising poster, 1955, entitled 'Lovely day for a Guinness', in coloured pastels and pencil, 45 x 31cm (17½ x 12in), *C 22 Oct,*
£924 ($1,386)

6
A collection of advertising inserts, *c.*1890-1905, comprising 166 examples, not stuck down, very good condition, *C 26 June,*
£506 ($683)

7
Players 'Digger' tobaccos showcard *c.*1928, 145cm (57in), *C 20 Mar,*
£330 ($406)

8
'Players Please' standing showcard, 1937, 102cm (40in), *C 20 Mar,*
£308 ($379)

9
A pair of composition figurative advertising signs, *c.*1935, for Facchino Cone Ice Cream, painted, 56cm (22in) high, *L 21 Feb,*
£374 ($430)

10
A Players Navy Cut pressed tin lifebelt display sign, early 1920's, slight abrasions, 39cm (15½in) diam, *C 20 Mar,*
£187 ($230)

1

2

3

4

5

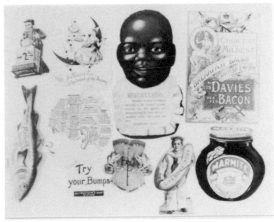

6

7

8

9

10

1
A set of seven Beatles Suffolk Downs concert tickets, 1966, in seven different colours, *NY 29 June*, $825 (£635)

2
A Beatles French 45 RPM records display, 38 x 37cm (15 x 14½in), sold with a selection of Beatles 45s, *NY 29 June*, $495 (£381)

3
An Apple paperweight and wall plaque, both of brass, plaque 20cm (8in) high, *NY 29 June*, $440 (£338)

4
An early Beatles poster, July 27th 1962, signed by Paul McCartney, 76 x 52cm (30 x 20½in), *L 29 Aug*, £2,530 ($3,719)

5
John Lennon original Bag One 1969, each numbered 74/300, signed by John Lennon, the sheets 51 x 76cm (20 x 30in), *NY 29 June*, $14,300 (£11,000)

6
A signed photograph of The Beatles, *c*.1962, with Mike Millward of the Fourmost, 35.5 x 28.5cm (14 x 11½in), *L 29 Aug*, £297 ($437)

7
A Beatles concert poster for their 1965 Shea Stadium performance, 56 x 39.5cm (22 x 15½in), *NY 29 June*, $1,760 (£1,354)

8
A signed Beatles concert programme, 1963, Gaumont Theatre, Southampton, 26.5cm (10½in) high, sold with another, unsigned, *L 29 Aug*, £660 ($772)

9
A Beatles autographed souvenir programme cover, Royal Hall Harrogate, March 8, 1963, 35.5 x 28cm (14 x 11in), *NY 29 June*, $990 (£762)

10
Two English Buddy Holly posters, 1958, relating to his only English tour, 76 x 101cm (30 x 40in), *L 29 Aug*, £660 ($970)

11
A celluloid from 'Yellow Submarine', 28 x 41cm (11 x 16in), *NY 29 June*, $1,210 (£931)

12
Cliff Richard's first acetate recording, *c*.1958, *L 29 Aug*, £3,080 ($4,528)

13
A presentation 'Silver' disc for 'Led Zeppelin II' framed, *L 29 Aug*, £1,155 ($1,698)

14
A presentation 'Gold' disc for The Who 'Live at Leeds', *c*.1973, framed, *L 29 Aug*, £715 ($1,051)

1

2

3

4

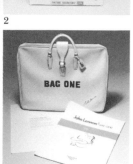

5

6

7

8

9

10

11

12

13

14

1
eter Townsend's double
eck electric guitar, a
ibson 6-12 semi-acoustic
uitar, 1957, *NY 29 June*,
,050 (£4,654)

2
inger Baker's 'Ludwig'
rum kit, *c.*1975, the
rum shells constructed
om orange and lemon
oloured perspex, the
arger bass drum 56cm
22in) diam., *L 29 Aug*,
,960 ($5,821)

3
at Stevens' ARP 'Omni'
ynthesizer, 99cm (39in)
ide, *L 29 Aug*,
506 ($744)

4
imi Hendrix's Gibson SG
ype 2 custom guitar,
1969, serial no. 899617,
ome wear, *L 29 Aug*,
7,700 ($11,319)

5
liff Richard's Ibanez
Concord electric acoustic
uitar, model no. 698M,
earing his signature,
10.5cm (43½in) long,
. 29 Aug,
2,200 ($3,234)

6
Beatles promotional dis-
lay poster for 'Meet the
eatles', 37 x 51.5cm
14½ x 20½in), *NY 29 June*,
935 (£719)

7
An album cover slick for
he Beatles butcher cover
Yesterday and Today',
he proof cover of the un-
cceptable version of the
lbum, 30.5 x 30.5cm (12 x
2in), *NY 29 June*,
880 (£677)

8
A Billy Fury stage suit,
.1963, *L 29 Aug*,
605 ($889)

9
Elvis Presley's black suede
acket, American, *c.*1969,
orn by him in concert in
1969, *L 29 Aug*,
4,950 ($7,277)

10
George Harrison's stage
uit, *c.*1964, *L 29 Aug*,
3,520 ($5,174)

1
An A.A. brass member's badge, 17cm (6¾in) high, *L 9 Dec*, £220 ($308)

2
A brass commercial A.A. member's badge, 13.5cm (5¾in) high, *L 9 Dec*, £60 ($84)

3
A brass R.A.C. associate badge for 1915, 13.5cm (5½in) high, *L 9 Dec*, £462 ($647)

4
A Bentley 'B' radiator mascot, on cap suitable for a 3½-litre Bentley, 9.5cm (3¾in) high, *L 9 Dec*, £88 ($123)

5
A Gordon Crosby Jaguar SS mascot, 20.5cm (8in) long, *L 9 Dec*, £374 ($524)

6
A Watson & Sons Ltd. dashboard aneroid barometer, 10cm (4in) diam., *L 9 Dec*, £440 ($616)

7
An eight-day dashboard timepiece, 10cm (4in) diam., *L 9 Dec*, £77 ($108)

8
A rare Lucas PLG40 tribar centre spotlight, suitable for a Rolls-Royce Phantom, restored, 15cm (6in), *L 9 Dec*, £495 ($693)

9
A pair of Powell & Hanmer brass headlamps, English, *c.*1912, lens 14cm (5½in) diam., *NP 30 Mar*, £187 ($237)

10
A pair of Carl Zeiss 8-inch headlamps, restored, *L 9 Dec*, £770 ($1,078)

11
A brass rear lamp, probably from a 1928 Mercedes 770, 21cm (8¼in), *L 9 Dec*, £330 ($462)

12
A Rolls-Royce Phantom radiator grille, 84cm (33in) high, *L 24 June*, £1,705 ($2,285)

13
A nickle-plated boa-constrictor motor horn, 1920s, 183cm (72in) long, *L 24 June*, £176 ($236)

14
A 'Shell' glass petrol pump globe, English, 1930s, 40.5cm (16in) high, *L 9 Dec*, £308 ($431)

15
A pair of motorist's 'indicating' gauntlets, English, 1920s, the right hand glove mounted with two small electric light bulbs, *NP 30 Mar*, £94 ($119)

16
A Coracle travelling picnic set, *c.*1930, with all accessories, 52cm (20½in) wide, *L 24 June*, £550 ($737)

1   2   3   4   5

6   7   8

9   10

11   13   14

12

15   16

Michaux velocipede,
ench, *c.*1870, *L 24 June,*
,265 ($1,695)

56-inch ordinary or
ennyfarthing' bicycle,
nglish, *c.*1880,
9 Dec,
,925 ($2,695)

Quadrant tricycle,
nglish, *c.*1882,
9 Dec,
,950 ($6,930)

Bantam Krypto bicycle,
nglish, *c.*1896, *L 24 June,*
,001 ($1,341)

Centaur cross frame
entleman's bicycle,
nglish, *c.*1900,
9 Dec,
462 ($647)

wooden pedal bicycle,
rly 20th century,
dially spoked 61cm
4in) diam, wheels,
30 Apr,
550 ($710)

James Model 8 2¼hp
lo motorcycle, *c.*1915,
24 June,
,155 ($1,548)

1932 Ariel model MB32
50cc solo motorcycle,
A 6 Oct,
836 ($1,237)

1936 Scott Squirrel
00cc solo motorcycle,
9 Dec,
,045 ($1,463)

1952 Moto Guzzi
alcone 498cc solo motor-
ycle, *MA 6 Oct,*
,650 ($2,442)

1970 Harley Davidson
lectra Glide 1200cc solo
otorcycle with trailer,
stomised in 'Mardi
ras' style, *MA 6 Oct,*
,915 ($4,314)

1982 Hesketh V1000
lo motorcycle, un-
egistered, *L 9 Dec,*
,575 ($5,005)

1
A Riley 9hp two seater
Special, *c.*1934, *L 9 Dec,*
£2,530 ($3,442)

2
A 1934 Hispano-Suiza
type K6 30/120 two-door
close coupled saloon,
coachwork by Freestone
& Webb, in need of over-
haul and repainting,
L 9 Dec,
£45,100 ($63,140)

3
A 1934 Hillman Minx
10/30hp saloon, *L 24 June,*
£1,595 ($2,137)

4
A 1936 Daimler New
Fifteen four-door saloon,
L 24 June,
£1,320 ($1,769)

5
A 1937 Citroen Fifteen
sports roadster two seater
with dickey, *L 24 June,*
£8,250 ($11,055)

6
A 1937 Morris Eight Series
I two-seater tourer,
NP 30 Mar,
£2,420 ($3,073)

7
A 1947 MG TC two seater
sports tourer, *L 9 Dec,*
£9,350 ($13,090)

8
A 1953 Bentley R Type
standard steel saloon,
L 24 June,
£7,480 ($10,023)

9
A 1960 Jaguar XK 150
fixed head coupe,
L 9 Dec,
£5,610 ($7,854)

10
A 1964 Ferrari 330 GT
Mk 1 Coupe 2+2, *L 9 Dec,*
£11,000 ($15,400)

1

2

3

4

5

6

7

8

9

10

governess cart, English,
te 19th century,
P 30 Mar,
352 ($447)

1904 Phoenix Trimo,
½hp with replica basket
orecar, *L 24 June,*
6,050 ($7,370)

1905 De Dion Bouton
hp two seater, *L 9 Dec,*
12,650 ($17,710)

1912 Fiat 15hp
mousine landaulette,
P 30 Mar,
12,650 ($16,066)

1927 Hispano-Suiza
16B 37.2hp two-seater
oadster, coachwork by
Dietrich, *L 9 Dec,*
39,600 ($55,440)

1926 Chrysler E80
mperial roadster, *L 9 Dec,*
28,600 ($40,040)

1931 Daimler V-30
ouble six coupe de ville,
oachwork by Thrupp
nd Maberley, *NP 30 Mar,*
8,800 ($11,176)

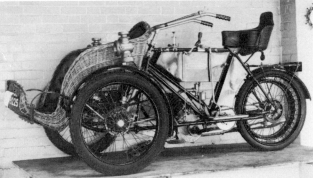

1   2

3   4

5

6   7

1
J. Blanch & Son. A pair of 12-bore single-trigger backlock ejector guns, 25in sleeved barrels, 6lb 8oz and 6lb 9oz, figured stocks 37cm (14½in), nitro proof, no. 2 restocked, *Glen 26 Aug,*
£3,300 ($4,851)

2
Boss & Co. A lightweight 12-bore single-trigger assisted-opening over-and-under sidelock ejector gun, 26in barrels, 6lb 4oz, well-figured stock 37cm (14½in), nitro proof, brushed and reblacked, re-stocked, *Glen 26 Aug,*
£9,900 ($14,553)

3
John Dickson & Son. A 12-bore assisted-opening 'round-action' ejector gun, 28in barrels, 6lb 4oz, stock 37cm (14½in), nitro proof, *Glen 26 Aug,*
£2,640 ($3,881)

4
A Dickson & Murray patent three-barrelled 16-bore bar-in-wood trigger plate action non-ejector gun, by John Dickson & Son, 28in barrels, 7lb 9oz, stock 37.5cm (14¾in), proof exemption bores oversized, *S 24 Apr,*
£8,580 ($11,240)

5
William Evans. A 12-bore sidelock ejector gun, 28in barrels, 6lb 8oz, stock 39cm (15¼in), nitro proof, *Glen 26 Aug,*
£2,310 ($3,396)

6
Holland & Holland. A pair of 12-bore 'Royal' detachable sidelock ejector guns, 30in barrels, 6lb 12oz and 6lb 11oz, stocks 38.5cm (15¼in), nitro proof, fore-ends chipped, no. 2 bores marked, *S 24 Apr,*
£9,020 ($11,816)

7
Holland & Holland. A 12-bore 'Royal' sidelock ejector gun, 30in barrels, 6lb 14oz, stock 35.5cm (14in), *L 26 Nov,*
£3,850 ($5,390)

8
Holland & Holland. A pair of left-handed light-weight 12-bore 'Royal Brevis' self-opening side-lock ejector guns, 28in chopper lump barrels, 6lb 5oz, stocks 37.5cm (14¾in), *L 26 Nov,*
£13,200 ($18,480)

9
Holland & Holland. A 12-bore 'Model de Luxe' self-opening sidelock ejector pigeon gun, built 1948, 28¾in chopper lump barrels, 7lb 6oz, figured stock 37cm (14½in), nitro proof, *L 26 Nov,*
£9,460 ($13,244)

10
Thos. Horsley. An 1863-patent top-lever, snap-action, bar-in-wood, 12-bore pinfire gun, 30in damascus barrels, 6lb 14oz, stock 37cm (14½in), bores marked and marginal, *S 24 Apr,*
£770 ($1,009)

11
H. J. Hussey Ltd. A pair of 'Imperial Ejector' 12-bore sidelock ejector guns, 27in barrels, 6lb 11oz and 6lb 12oz, figured stocks 38.5cm (15in), nitro proof, *Glen 26 Aug,*
£6,600 ($9,702)

12
W. J. Jeffery. A 16-bore sidelock ejector gun, built 1911, 28in barrels, locks and top lever with engraving of pheasants in landscape, retaining much colour, 6lb 1oz, stock 36cm (14¼in), nitro proof, bores worn, *S 24 Apr,*
£2,420 ($3,170)

13
A. Lancaster. A matched pair of D.B. 20-bore bar-in-wood hammer non-ejector sporting guns, 29¾in barrels, figured walnut stocks 36cm (14¼in), no. 1 nitro re-proof, no. 2 original black powder proof, *L 23 Jan,*
£2,640 ($3,115)

14
Joseph Lang & Son. A 20-bore sidelock ejector gun, 28in chopper lump barrels, 5lb 8oz, figured stock 35cm (13¾in), nitro proof, bores marked and dented, *Glen 26 Aug,*
£3,190 ($4,689)

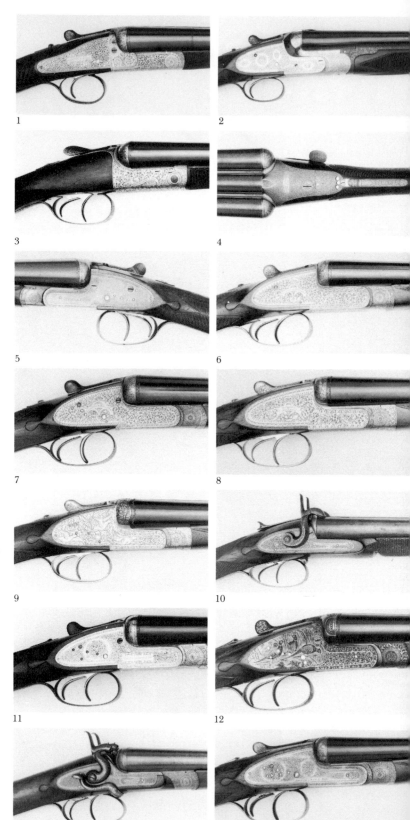

1   2
3   4
5   6
7   8
9   10
11   12
13   14

Charles Lancaster. A .303 patent smooth-oval bore self-opening backlock ejector rifle, 28in barrels, 7lb, figured stock 36cm (14¼in), nitro proof, *S 26 Nov,*
£2,310 ($3,234)

Charles Lancaster. A Spencer-Roper patent 12-bore pump-action repeating gun, 27in barrel, walnut stock 37cm (14¼in), London black powder proof, *L 23 Jan,*
£1,540 ($1,817)

Theophilus Murcott. A patent snap-action lever-cocking hammerless side-lock non-ejector gun, 30in barrels, 7lb 9oz, stock 36cm (14¼in), original black powder proof, *S 24 Apr,*
£715 ($937)

J. Purdey & Sons. A Grade 'C' 38-bore (.500 3in) hammer non-ejector rifle, 28in barrels, stock 37cm (14½in), *S 24 Apr,*
£1,430 ($1,873)

J. Purdey & Sons. A pair of 12-bore self-opening sidelock ejector guns, 29½in chopped lump *Whitworth* steel barrels, 6lb 11oz, stocks 37cm (14½in), *L 26 Nov,*
£13,200 ($18,480)

Purdey. An 8-bore hammer non-ejector wild-fowling gun, 32½in barrels, 10lb 15oz, stock 36cm (14¼in), recent nitro proof, in its brass-bound oak case with many accessories, *Glen 26 Aug,*
£3,520 ($5,174)

J. Purdey & Sons. A light-weight pair of 12-bore self-opening sidelock ejector guns, 28in chopper lump barrels, 6lb 5oz, stocks 37cm (14½in), nitro proof, no. 1 restocked by the makers, *Glen 26 Aug,*
£14,300 ($21,021)

8
J. Woodward & Sons. A 12-bore sidelock ejector pigeon gun, built in 1938, 30in chopper lump barrels, 7lb 10oz, highly-figured stock 37cm (14½in), nitro proof, in oak and leather case with many accessories, *Glen 26 Aug,*
£8,250 ($12,128)

9
Karl Hauptmann. An Austrian 12-bore boxlock ejector sporting gun, 27in barrels, 6lb 5oz, stock 36cm (14¼in), Austrian nitro proof, bores with some pits and dents, *L 23 Jan,*
£1,100 ($1,298)

10
Wilhelm Brenneke, Leipzig, A 'System Brenneke' 7 x 65Rmm under-and-over boxlock non-ejector sporting rifle, with 25¼in *Boehler* steel barrels, and two telescopic sights, 7lb 10oz, stock 35.5cm (14in), German nitro proof, *L 23 Jan,*
£1,595 ($1,882)

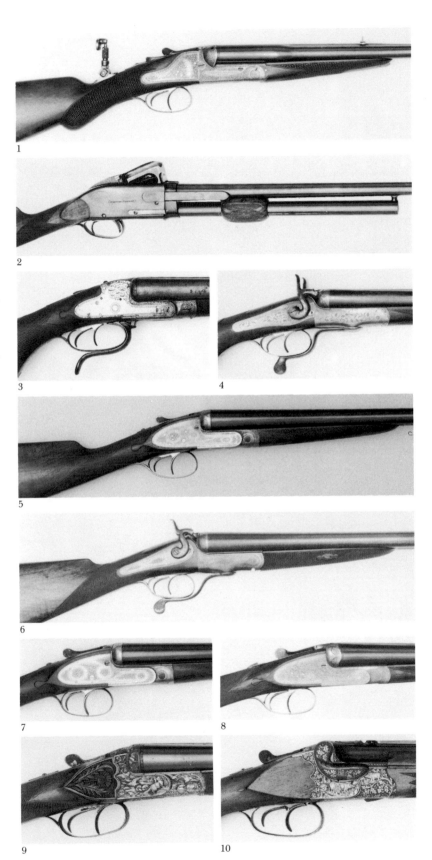

1

2

3   4

5

6

7   8

9   10

1
A registered design reel by Bowness & Bowness, PODR mark for 1876, *S 24 Apr,*
£110 ($144)

2
A crank-handled salmon reel, *c.*1840, 10cm (4in), *L 23 Jan,*
£105 ($124)

3
A trolling wynch by Farlows *c.*1850, retaining much bronzing, 9cm (3½in) diam., *L 23 Jan,*
£748 ($883)

4
A walnut Nottingham-style 'Silex no. 2' reel by Hardy's, 11.5cm (4½in), *S 6 Nov,*
£132 ($198)

5
A 'Triumph' coarse fishing reel by Hardy's, 8cm (3¼in), *S 6 Nov,*
£110 ($165)

6
A Scottish 'Pirn' or trolling wynch, 18th century, one pillar lacking, 11.5cm (4½in), *S 6 Nov,*
£330 ($495)

7
A 'turntable' casting reel by C. Farlow & Co. Ltd., drum 4.5cm (1¾in) diam, *S 6 Nov,*
£220 ($330)

8
A 3¼-inch 'Bouglé' light-weight fly reel by Hardy's, finish worn, *S 24 Apr,*
£638 ($836)

9
A multiplying reel by J. B. Crook & Co., New York, of nickel silver, 6.5cm (2½in), *L 23 Jan,*
£286 ($337)

10
A 2¾inch 'Silex Multi-plyer' by Hardy's, *L 23 Jan,*
£231 ($273)

11
A 2⅝-inch transitional pattern brass and nickel silver 'Perfect' reel by Hardy's, retaining much bronzing, *L 23 Jan,*
£3,300 ($3,894)

12
A 3½-inch 1891 model 'Perfect' fly reel by Hardy's, check defective, retaining much bronzing, *L 23 Jan,*
£2,750 ($3,245)

13
A transitional 1896-pattern 3½-inch 'Perfect' salmon reel by Hardy's, some wear, *S 6 Nov,*
£440 ($660)

14
A brown trout *c.*1912, in bow-fronted case, with inscription, 73cm (29in) long, *C 26 June,*
£242 ($326)

15
A stuffed perch by J. Cooper & Sons, the fish 12½in, 1lb 3oz and caught 1928, case 47cm (18½in) wide, *S 6 Nov,*
£176 ($264)

16
A stuffed roach by J. Cooper & Sons, in bow-fronted case with inscription, the 2lb fish caught 1946, 48cm (19in) wide, *S 24 Apr,*
£187 ($245)

17
A stuffed barbel, the fish 28in, 9lb and caught 1921, case slightly chipped, 94.5cm (37¼in) wide, *L 23 Jan,*
£275 ($325)

1

2

3

4

5

6

7

8

9

10

11

12

13

14

15

16

17

1
A feathery golf ball, Scottish, *c.*1840s, worn, 4.5cm (1¾in) diam, *L 24 July,*
£825 ($1,221)

2
A feathery golf ball, *c.*1840, probably Gourlay, 4cm (1½in) diam., *L 24 July,*
£1,760 ($2,604)

3
A 9ct gold golf medal, *c.*1920, inscribed 'St. Nicholas Golf Club Prestwick', 4cm (1½in), *L 24 July,*
£660 ($976)

4
A Peter McEwan long-nosed driver, *c.*1885, with hickory shaft, some damage, *L 24 July,*
£770 ($1,139)

5
An early long-nosed grassed driver, *c.*1835, with hickory shaft, *L 24 July,*
£1,155 ($1,709)

6
An R. Forgan & Son long-nosed driving putter, St. Andrews, *c.*1890, with original hickory shaft, *L 24 July,*
£242 ($358)

7
A Hugh Philp long-nosed putter, St. Andrews, *c.*1835, *L 24 July,*
£2,420 ($3,581)

8
An R. Ramsbottom left-handed mashie, Manchester, *c.*1900, *L 24 July,*
£715 ($1,058)

9
A rut iron, *c.*1845, hickory shafted, *L 24 July,*
£418 ($618)

10
A G. Alexander 'patent' wood, *c.*1895, *L 24 July,*
£418 ($618)

11
A golfing bronze, *c.*1910, signed W. Inick, 30.5cm (12in), *L 24 July,*
£715 ($1,058)

12
W. & F. Faulkner 'Golf Terms', 1901, eleven cards from a set of twelve, *L 24 July,*
£242 ($358)

13
A pair of Royal Doulton 'Uncle Toby Series' ceramic candlesticks, *c.*1920, small chip and hairline crack, 16.5cm (6in), *L 24 July,*
£495 ($732)

14
A brass golf-ball mould, Scottish, *c.*1920s, maker's plaque 'John White & Coy', 8cm (3¼in) diam., *L 24 July,*
£363 ($537)

15
A Royal Doulton 'Ivory Ware' ceramic jardinière, the ochre ground printed in black with golfing figures, restored, 36cm (14¼in), *L 24 July,*
£825 ($1,221)

16
A Doulton Lambeth cricketing subject mug, 13.5cm (5¼in), *C 12 Mar,*
£66 ($75)

17
A moulded biscuit figure of Dr. W. G. Grace, Continental, *c.*1890, 24cm (9½in), *L 24 July,*
£385 ($569)

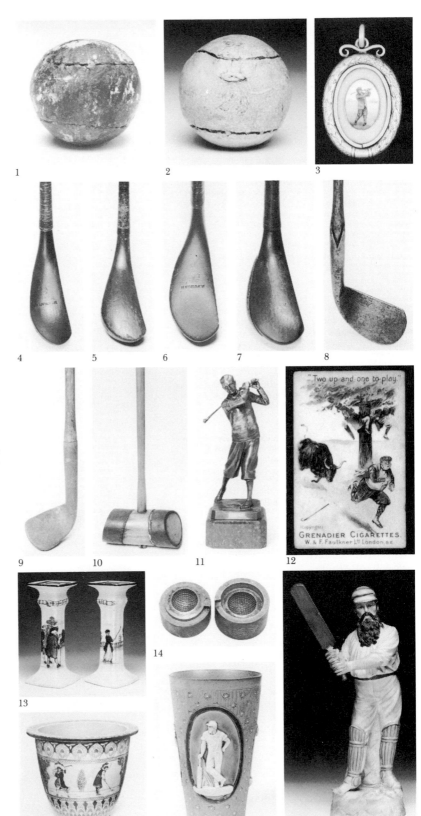

1
An 1868 Twigg patent steel corkscrew, marked faintly TWIGG'S PATENT AMERICA JAN 21 1868, *L 29 May*, £380 ($502)

2
An 1868 Twigg patent steel corkscrew, marked G. TWIGG'S PATENT U.S. AMERICA JAN 21 1868, *L 20 Mar*, £420 ($517)

3
An English corkscrew with brass barrel inscribed ROBERT JONES & SON BIRMINGHAM REGISTERED NO. 423 8TH OCTR 1840, brush and ring missing, damaged, *L 25 Sept*, £510 ($765)

4
An English 1894 Murray & Stalker patent corkscrew, one arm marked PATENT NO. 234, very rare, *L 29 May*, £1,700 ($2,244)

5
An English-style bronze corkscrew, mid-19th century, *L 29 May*, £4,200 ($5,544)

6
A Dutch silver pocket corkscrew, mid-18th century, sheath decorated with flowers and fruit, *L 25 Sept*, £190 ($285)

7
A 'Goliath' steel double-lever corkscrew, marked GEHA and PATENTAMTL. GESCH. PATENTED-BREVETE, design patented by George Haussmann of Cassel in England in 1903, *L 20 Mar*, £300 ($369)

8
A German pocket cork-screw, *L 20 Mar*, £170 ($209)

9
An American steel cork-screw, 19th century, *L 25 Sept*, £105 ($158)

10
An English miniature bow corkscrew, early 18th century, silver-plated one finger bow, *L 29 May*, £280 ($370)

11
A Charles Hull's 1864 patent Royal Club cork-screw, all-metal construction, *L 25 Sept*, £600 ($900)

12
An 18th century com-bination five-tool bow corkscrew, *L 11 Dec*, £132 ($185)

13
An American steel bar corkscrew, late 19th century, body marked ENTERPRISE MFC. CO. PHILA. PA U.S.A. NO. 113, *L 20 Mar*, £220 ($271)

14
A King's corkscrew, *L 29 May*, £230 ($305)

15
A French complex all-metal lever corkscrew, marked on lever LE DÉSIRÉ BTE S.G.D.G., *L 29 May*, £400 ($528)

16
A silver-plated decanting cradle, *L 20 Mar*, £550 ($677)

17
An electroplated decan-ting cradle, *L 29 May*, £400 ($528)

18
A wooden decanting cradle, *L 11 Dec*, £715 ($1,001)

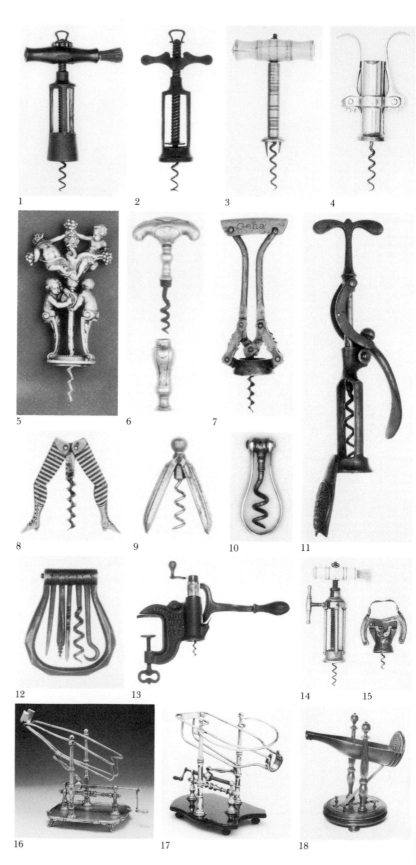

1   2   3   4

5   6   7

8   9   10   11

12   13   14   15

16   17   18

Dolls and Toys

Article ● Toy cars *pp 552-555*
See also ● Colour illustrations *pp 486-487*

1

A dappled blue-grey rocking horse, English, late 19th century, some flaking, 106.5cm (42in) long, *L 21 May,* £440 ($590)

2

A rocking horse, English, late 19th century, 127cm (50in) long, *L 1 Oct,* £715 ($1,044)

3

A Triang painted wooden rocking horse, English, *c.*1920, 124.5cm (49in) high, *C 26 June,* £440 ($594)

4

A dog cart, early 20th century, repainted, 136cm (53½in), *C 26 June,* £121 ($163)

5

A team of four carved wood galloping horses, English, *c.*1885, mounted on iron framework, some wear and missing pieces, 90cm (35in) long, *S 4 Nov,* £605 ($908)

6

A Noah's Ark and large quantity of carved and painted wooden animals, German, mid-19th century, some damage, 236 pieces, *L 21 May,* £2,200 ($2,948)

7

A Noah's Ark, German, late 19th century, containing approx 147 figures mounted on later wooden bases, *L 1 Oct,* £990 ($1,445)

8

A Schoenhut circus, American, *c.*1900, with various accessories, *L 1 Oct,* £495 ($723)

9

A felt and bisque candy container, German, early 20th century, Santa sitting on a log, 23cm (9in) high, *NY 13 Apr,* $495 (£396)

10

A candy container, George Washington on horse, German, *c.*1910, the horse concealing the candy, 25cm (10in), *NY 13 Apr,* £880 ($704)

11

A rooster and hen candy container, probably German, early 20th century, the hen's nest concealing the candy, *NY 13 Apr,* $330 (£264)

1

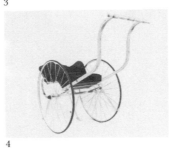

6

2

7

3

8

4

5

9   10   11

1

A Steiff blonde long plush teddy bear, German, c.1905, Steiff metal disc removed, 51cm (20in), *L 21 May,* £2,090 ($2,801)

2

A gold plush teddy bear, English, c.1910, 48cm (19in), *L 21 May,* £220 ($295)

3

A Steiff silver plush teddy bear, German, c.1905, with Steiff disc in ear, some wear, 76cm (30in), *L 1 Oct,* £3,740 ($5,460)

4

An early Steiff teddy bear, German, c.1905, pads worn, growl inoperative, *C 26 June,* £748 ($1,009)

5

A Steiff blonde plush teddy bear, German, c.1903, with Steiff metal disc in ear, growler missing, some wear, 62cm (24½in), *L 1 Oct,* £1,430 ($2,088)

6

A Steiff teddy bear, German, c.1905, 24cm (9½in), *L 21 May,* £352 ($472)

7

A pink-blonde long plush teddy bear, German, c.1908, worn, growler inoperative, 39cm (15¼in), *L 9 May,* £418 ($539)

8

A Steiff blonde plush teddy bear, German, c.1905, with Steiff metal disc in ear, pads renewed, 41cm (16in), *L 23 Jan,* £792 ($935)

9

A Steiff cinnamon long plush teddy bear, German, c.1905, Steiff disc removed from ear, once with growler, 53cm (21in), *L 1 Oct,* £1,430 ($2,088)

10

A Steiff dual plush dog on wheels, German, c.1930, with Steiff metal disc in ear, with voice-box (inoperative), 35.5cm (14in), *L 23 Jan,* £286 ($337)

11

A Steiff beige plush teddy bear, German, c.1910, metal disc in ear, growler inoperative, 66cm (26in), *L 1 Oct,* £2,310 ($3,373)

12

A fabric fur teddy bear, English, c.1910, growler inoperative and replacement pads, 43cm (17in) high, *S 7 Aug,* £121 ($180)

13

A fabric fur bear on wheels, possibly by Steiff, German, c.1920, sound-box inoperative, worn, 29cm (11½in), *S 7 Aug,* £231 ($344)

14

A fabric fur teddy bear, c.1909, growler, inoperative, 62cm (24½in), *S 7 Aug,* £209 ($311)

15

A fabric fur teddy bear, possibly by Steiff, 28cm (11in) high, with a fabric fur bear, 21.5cm (8½in) high, *S 7 Aug,* £209 ($311)

16

A Steiff fabric fur bear on wheels, German, c.1920, Steiff button in ear, some moth, 38cm (13in), *S 7 Aug,* £330 ($492)

17

A fabric fur teddy bear, probably by Steiff, German, with growler, 33cm (13in) high, *S 7 Aug,* £286 ($426)

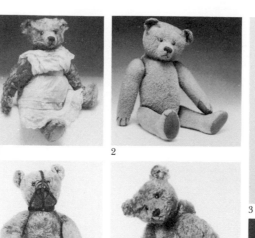

1   2

4

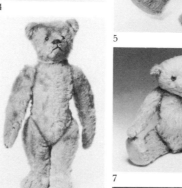

5

3

6   7   8

9   10   11

12   13   14   15   16   17

1
A perambulator, 61cm (24in) high, *A 8 Oct,* **DFl 977** (£230; $340)

2
A metal and wood push-chair, 65cm (25½in) high, *A 8 Oct,* **Dfl 1,488** (£115; $170)

3
A dolls' three-wheeled pram, English, *c.*1880, upholstered in red velvet, 61cm (24in) high, *L 23 Jan,* **£352** ($415)

4
A painted wood dolls' double pram, English, late 19th century, 84cm (33in) high, *L 23 Jan,* **£770** ($909)

5
A wooden and iron perambulator, 60cm (23½in) high, *A 8 Oct,* **Dfl 948** (£224; $331)

6
A carved and painted model of a butcher's shop, English, mid-19th century, 51 x 71cm (20 x 28in), *L 17 July,* **£2,640** ($3,828)

7
A wooden dolls' house, English, late 19th century, with eleven pieces of furniture, 88cm (34¾in) high, *L 21 May,* **£660** ($884)

8
A toy oven, end 19th century, with accessories, *A 8 Oct,* **Dfl 1,495** (£353; $522)

9
A late Victorian dolls' house, some repainting, 79cm (31in) high, *C 26 June,* **£132** ($178)

10
An American lithographed paper-on-wood firehouse with pumper, by Bliss, early 1900s, 43cm (17in) high, *NY 13 Apr,* **$1,430** (£1,144)

11
An American lithographed paper-on-wood butcher shop, possibly by Bliss, late 19th century, 38cm (15in) high, *NY 13 Apr,* **$1,210** (£928)

12
An American lithographed paper-on-wood dollhouse by Bliss, late 19th century, the hinged front façade opening to reveal two rooms, 41cm (16in) high, *NY 13 Apr,* **$1,210** (£928)

1

2

3

4

5

6

7   8   9

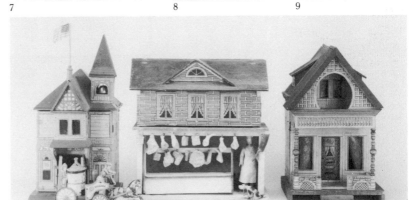

10   11   12

1
A rare wax portrait doll by
Mrs. Lucy Peck, of the
the young Queen
Victoria, English, *c.*1850,
one leg broken, 71cm
(28in), *C 22 Oct,*
£495 ($743)

2
A Jules Steiner 'Walking/
Talking' bisque shoulder
headed doll, French,
*c.*1860, the cardboard
body containing the Key-
wind mechanism with
three wheels, mechanism
faulty (38cm, 15in),
S 4 Nov,
£660 ($990)

3
A shoulder-papier-mâché
doll, *c.*1835, in original
white muslin dress, 24cm
(9½in), *L 21 May,*
£495 ($663)

4
A Grodnertal wooden doll,
German, *c.*1810, in
original hooped silk
dress, some wear, dress
slightly torn, 38cm
(15in), *L 21 May,*
£1,430 ($1,916)

5
A Grodnertal wooden doll,
German, *c.*1830, com-
plete with a quantity of
contemporary and later
clothing, 26cm (10in),
C 26 June,
£660 ($891)

6
A pine lay figure, mid-19th
century, some wear and
chips, 67cm (26½in),
L 21 May,
£880 ($1,179)

7
A George II wooden doll,
English, *c.*1740, in
original green saque
dress, underskirt and
corset, some damage and
wear, one thigh replaced,
61cm (24in), *L 21 May,*
£15,400 ($20,636)

8
A shoulder-papier-mâché
doll, German, *c.*1840,
nose rubbed and small
chips, 43cm (17in),
L 23 Jan,
£528 ($623)

9
A wooden doll, German,
*c.*1805, in original dress,
slight damage, 44cm
(17¼in), *L 1 Oct,*
£880 ($1,285)

10
A shoulder-papier-mâché
doll, German, *c.*1840, in
original clothes, one
thumb broken, 41cm
(16in), *L 1 Oct,*
£1,430 ($2,088)

1

A Jules Steiner bisque-head Bébé, French, incised J. Steiner/Bte SGDG/ Paris/F1 re A 9, 41cm (16in), *NY 29 June,* $1,760 (£1,354)

2

A Bru bisque swivel-head Bébé, French, incised circle dot, Bte SGDG, in original dress, 41cm (16in), *NY 29 June,* $6,050 (£4,654)

3

A swivel-neck bisque fashion doll, probably by Simonne, French, *c.*1875, some chips, legs restored, 24cm (9½in), *L 9 May,* £396 ($511)

4

A shoulder-bisque doll, French, probably by Bru, French, *c.*1875, impressed C, unclothed, 30.5cm (12in), *L 21 May,* £1,045 ($1,400)

5

A Rabery & Delphieu bisque-head Bébé, French, incised R2D, 53.5cm (21in), *NY 29 June,* $2,475 (£1,904)

6

A Bru Jeune bisque doll, French, *c.*1875, impressed BRU Jne, 6, three fingers missing, chips, 46cm (18in), *L 23 Jan,* £7,150 ($8,437)

7

A Schoenau and Hoffmeister 'Princess Elizabeth' bisque doll, German, *c.*1930, impressed Porzellanfabrik Burggrub Princess Elizabeth 6½ DRGM, in original pink frilled cotton dress, 58.5cm (23in), *L 23 Jan,* £1,870 ($2,027)

8

A Danel Et Cie Paris bisque Bébé, French, *c.*1890, impressed PARIS BEBE TETE DEP*ee*, 10, stringing loose, chip, 66cm (26in), *L 21 May,* £1,760 ($2,358)

9

A shoulder-Parian bisque doll, mid-19th century, short firing line from right eye, 38cm (15in), *L 23 Jan,* £330 ($389)

10

A Kestner bisque-head googly-eyed doll, German, *c.*1910, incised G Made in H/Germany/JDK/221, Ges gesch, 33cm (13in), *NY 29 June,* $3,850 (£2,961)

11

A Schoenau & Hoffmeister 'Princess Elizabeth' bisque doll, German, *c.*1940, impressed Porzellanfabrik, Burggrub, Princess Elizabeth 5 DRGM, kiln spot below mouth, 52cm (20½in), *L 21 May,* £1,100 ($1,474)

12

A J. D. Kestner bisque doll, German, *c.*1890, impressed K½ 214 14½, six fingers missing, 71cm (28in), *L 23 Jan,* £220 ($260)

1
A Kammer & Reinhardt 'Mein Liebling' bisque doll, German, *c*.1900, head impressed K*R 117 Simon & Halbig 55, 53cm (21in), *C 20 Mar,*
£3,190 ($3,924)

2
A Kammer and Reinhardt bisque-headed 'Kaiser' baby doll, German *c*.1909, impressed 100 50, one hand broken, 50cm (19¾in), *S 7 Aug,*
£429 ($639)

3
A Kammer & Reinhardt bisque character doll of 'Max', German, *c*.1910, unmarked, firing spot on left eyebrow, 41cm (16in), *L 21 May,*
£5,720 ($7,665)

4
A Jumeau bisque doll, French, *c*.1880, in original clothes and box, 58cm (22¾in), *A 8 Oct,*
Dfl 11,040 (£2,609; $3,861)

5
A Jumeau bisque swivel-head fashion doll, French, *c*.1870, impressed 1, in original satin dress, 38cm (15in), *L 23 Jan,*
£1,760 ($2,077)

6
An F. G. bisque swivel-head fashion doll, French, *c*.1880, impressed FG on one shoulderplate, 6 on the other and 6 on the head, 57cm (22½in), *L 23 Jan,*
£2,310 ($2,726)

7
A swivel-head shoulder-bisque fashion doll, French, *c*.1880, impressed L Depose 1 D, in original silk dress, one finger repaired, 37cm (14½in), *L 23 Jan,*
£1,100 ($1,298)

8
An Emile Jumeau bisque doll, French, *c*.1880, impressed DEPOSE E 8 J and with red H check mark, fingers cracked, the body stamped JUMEAU Medaille d'Or Paris, 48cm (19in), *L 1 Oct,*
£2,860 ($4,176)

9
An SFBJ Jumeau bisque doll, French, *c*.1907, impressed 1907 16, unclothed and unstrung, 89cm (35in), *L 23 Jan,*
£1,870 ($2,207)

10
A Jules Steiner bisque doll, French, *c*.1885, impressed J STEINER Bte, SGDG Paris Fre A 5, in original courtier's outfit, 33cm (13in), *L 1 Oct,*
£1,540 ($2,248)

11
An Armand Marseille bisque doll, German, *c*.1910, impressed 971 0, small chip, 35cm (13¼in), *L 21 Feb,*
£264 ($304)

12
An Armand Marseille black bisque My Dream Baby doll, German, *c*.1925, impressed 341/4K, 38cm (15in), *L 21 May,*
£385 ($516)

13
An SFBJ bisque doll, French, *c*.1915, impressed 60 6, with Jumeau-look face, stringing perished, chip, 43cm (17in), *L 21 Feb,*
£242 ($278)

14
An SFBJ bisque boy doll, French, *c*.1910, impressed 237 Paris 4, unclothed and unstrung, hairline crack, 36cm (14in), *L 23 Jan,*
£462 ($545)

15
A Jules Steiner bisque Bébé, French, *c*.1880, the head impressed 'Steiner Paris FRE A.7', chip to right ear, 36cm (14in), *C 20 Mar,*
£880 ($1,082)

1
A Gebruder Heubach bisque-headed character doll, German, c.1912, impressed 69 69 5, body associated, 38cm (15in), *S 7 Aug*, £396 ($590)

2
A Gebruder Heubach bisque piano baby, German, c.1900, leg impressed 3100, firing flaws to arms, 22.5cm (8¾in), *S 7 Aug*, £99 ($148)

3
A Gebruder Heubach/ Einco bisque googley-eyed doll, German, c.1910, impressed Einco 3, 28cm (11in), *L 23 Jan*, £1,540 ($1,817)

4
A Gebruder Heubach bisque piano baby, German, c.1910, one finger broken, 24cm (9½in), *S 7 Aug*, £143 ($213)

5
A Heubach Koppelsdorf painted black bisque doll, German, c.1900, impressed 399.2/0 DRGM, unclothed, 38.5cm (15¼in), *L 21 May*, £352 ($472)

6
A Demalcol bisque character doll, German, c.1910, impressed 5/0, 24cm (9½in), *L 21 May*, £286 ($383)

7
A Grace S. Putnam Bye-Lo bisque baby, German, c.1923, impressed Copr, by Grace S Putnam MADE IN GERMANY, stamped BYE-LO-BABY Pat.-applied-for copy by Grace Storey Putnam, 25.5cm (10in), *L 21 May*, £286 ($383)

8
A shoulder-Parian bisque doll, German, c.1870, with painted features and original red dress, 58.5cm (23in), *L 1 Oct*, £660 ($964)

9
A Simon & Halbig bisque oriental doll, German, c.1900, impressed S H 1099 DEP 5½in, in original silk dress, 35.5cm (14in), *L 21 May*, £880 ($1,179)

10
A 'scarf-head' Parian bisque doll, German, c.1870, with curly blonde hair held by a blue draped scarf, thumb missing, leg cracked, 46cm (18in), *L 1 Oct*, £2,090 ($3,051)

11
A Kammer & Reinhardt/ Simon & Halbig bisque doll, German, c.1900, impressed HALBIG/ KstarR 58, two teeth and one finger missing, 57cm (22½in), *L 23 Jan*, £330 ($389)

12
A Simon & Halbig shoulder-bisque character doll, German, c.1889, impressed S & H 1250 DEP 4½, with original silk dress, 42cm (16½in), *L 1 Oct*, £572 ($835)

13
A Simon & Halbig bisque lady doll, German, c.1910, impressed 1159 Halbig 8 S & H, in cream silk dress applied with pearls, stringing loose, flaking on neck, 57cm (22½in), *L 23 Jan*, £1,155 ($1,363)

1
A shoulder-china doll's head, German, *c.*1870, 11.5cm (4½in), *L 21 May,* £495 ($663)

2
A shoulder-china head, French, *c.*1860, unmarked, 10cm (4in), *L 1 Oct,* £825 ($1,205)

3
A shoulder porcelain doll, German, *c.*1860, one leg restored, 61cm (24in), *C 25 July,* £440 ($647)

4
A rare Dressel and Kister china half-doll, German, early 20th century, 15cm (6in), *S 4 Nov,* £352 ($524)

5
A William Goebels china half doll, German, early 20th century, impressed faintly 333, with green mask and red bobbed hair, 11cm (4¼in), *L 1 Oct,* £462 ($677)

6
A Dressel and Kister china 'Pierrette' half doll, early 20th century, with highly painted face and black skull cap, *L 1 Oct,* £220 ($321)

7
Two shoulder-china heads, German, *c.*1850, 7.5cm (3in), *L 21 Feb,* £286 ($329)

8
A composition Shirley Temple doll, American, *c.*1935, embossed SHIRLEY TEMPLE 60, in original clothes and with original extra clothes and trunk, 38cm (15in), *L 21 May,* £352 ($472)

9
A Lenci 'Butterfly' doll, Italian, 42cm (16½in), *A 8 Oct,* Dfl 2,530 (£598; $885)

10
A Lenci-type boy golfer doll, *c.*1930, replacement golf club, 49cm (19¼in), *S 6 Feb,* £638 ($753)

11
A Kathe Kruse cloth doll, German, *c.*1930 in original clothes, 43cm (17in), *A 2 Apr,* Dfl 2,204 (£510; $658)

12
An early Steiff felt sailor doll, German, *c.*1910, 38cm (15in), *L 1 Oct,* £286 ($418)

13
A Lenci felt doll, Italian, *c.*1925, 29cm (11½in), *C 22 Oct,* £352 ($528)

14
A Lenci cloth doll, Italian, 1930, in original clothes and hat applied with a white cat, 23cm (9in), *L 21 May,* £198 ($265)

15
A Chad Valley 'Bambina' Princess Elizabeth cloth doll, English, *c.*1930, in original yellow net dress, 44.5cm (17½in), *L 23 Jan,* £242 ($286)

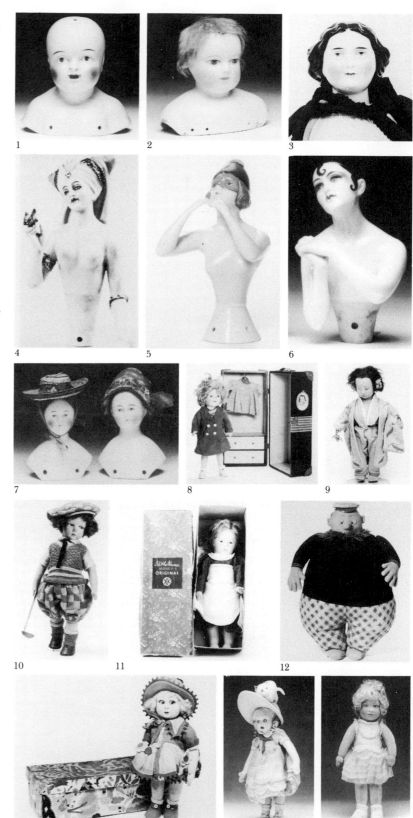

1
A bisque-headed Marotte, French, c.1880, 28.5cm (11¼in), A 8 Oct, **Dfl 1,437 (£339; $501)**

2
An Armand Marseille shoulder-bisque Marotte doll, German, c.1900, impressed 3200 A 10/ox DEP, 30.5cm (12in), L 23 Jan, **£165 ($195)**

3
A bisque-headed Pierrot, French, c.1925, marked MVR, 50.5cm (19¾in), A 8 Oct, **Dfl 3,105 (£734; $1,086)**

4
A musical automaton of a drinking Chinaman, mechanism inoperative, 35cm (13¾in) high, L 21 May, **£825 ($1,106)**

5
A French musical automaton by Lambert, c.1880, impressed 1300 DEP SH, replacement wig and blouse, some damage, 55cm (21½in) high, S 1 May, **£770 ($993)**

6
A bisque-headed doll, German, c.1895, 37cm (14½in), A 8 Oct, **Dfl 3,565 (£842; $1,246)**

7
A musical automaton flower seller, by Leopold Lambert, French, c.1880, the Jumeau head stamped DEPOSE TETE JUMEAU Bte. SGDG 4, two fingers broken, 50cm (19¾in), L 21 May, **£1,980 ($2,653)**

8
A 'Spinning Jenny' bone automaton, English, early 19th century, 18cm (7in) high, L 17 July, **£4,180 ($6,061)**

9
A singing bird automaton, French, c.1860, 50cm (19¾in) high, A 25 Nov, **Dfl 5,290 (£1,251; $1,751)**

10
A singing bird automaton, c.1880, 56cm (22in) high, A 25 Nov, **Dfl 4,600 (£1,087; $1,522)**

11
A singing bird automaton, French, early 20th century, 51cm (20in), L 1 Oct, **£528 ($771)**

12
A seated drinking musical automaton, French, c.1880, probably by Decamps, some damage, 48cm (19in), C 26 June, **£1,045 ($1,410)**

13
A mechanical walking automaton, the 'Heathen Chinee', American, late 19th century, impressed Patd. Sept. 21.75, chips on face, key missing, 24cm (9½in), S 1 May, **£319 ($412)**

14
A Puss-In-Boots automaton, probably by Decamps, French, c.1915, 41cm (16in), L 1 Oct, **£638 ($375)**

15
A Decamps musical automaton of a knitting woman, French, c.1880, the Jumeau head stamped in red DEPOSE TETE JUMEAU Bte. SGDG 5, 43cm (17in), L 1 Oct, **£4,620 ($6,745)**

16
A musical automaton, with porcelain Jumeau head, 29cm (11½in), A 8 Oct, **Dfl 5,980 (£1,413; $2,091)**

17
A 'barking' bulldog, French, c.1910, inset wheels to the paws, 47cm (18½in) long, C 26 June, **£286 ($386)**

18
A clockwork mechanical bear, American, Ives, 35cm (14in), NY 29 June, **$550 (£423)**

19
A clockwork mechanical bear, American, Ives, 24cm (9½in), NY 29 June, **$412 (£316)**

1 2 3

4 5 6 7

8 9 10 11

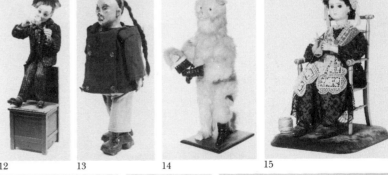

12 13 14 15

16 17 18 19

Toy Cars

So many people collect toys today, whether Dinky die-cast vehicles, Hornby railway stock of both large and small gauge, or the scarcer and more expensive toys made before the Second World War, that the press has come to regard this hobby as unremarkable. Matters were very different, however, ten years ago, when toys first began to be taken seriously by the auction rooms; the amazement of the saleroom correspondents spilled over onto front page news as toys fetched first hundreds and then thousands of pounds.

At first sight, it may indeed seem eccentric for an adult to collect toy cars avidly. In fact, peoples' reasons for collecting are varied. Some may be interested in full-size motor cars and collect representative models of their own particular favourites.

Others may be drawn to collect toys which illustrate the historical and technical development of the motor car. Others again, may appreciate the design of a toy, finding an aesthetic satisfaction in its sculptural quality. Some buy, of course, solely for investment.

The manufacturers of tinplate toys in the early part of this century were centred in Germany, mainly around the Nuremburg area in Bavaria. There, large factories, including Bing, Märklin, Carette and Gunthermann produced a diverse assortment of tinplate toys: cars, boats, trains and aeroplanes. Most company's wares can be identified by their individual trademarks and a selection of the most common of these is reproduced.

—1—
A Bing clockwork tin-plate limousine, German, *c.*1910, lithographed in white, some repainting, *C 22 Oct,*
£1,210 ($1,815)

—2—
A Carette hand painted landaulette, German, *c.*1910, no. 3358/41 in Carette catalogue, retouched, some chips, 24cm (9½in) long, *L 23 Jan,*
£1,870 ($2,216)

—3—
A tinplate and clockwork limousine, probably by Carette, *c.*1912, distressed condition, 35cm (13⅞in) long, *S 6 Feb,*
£374 ($441)

—4—
A Carette lithographed tinplate limousine, German, *c.*1911, finished in red lined cream and gold, lacking one side lamp, some wear, *L 23 Jan,*
£1,540 ($1,825)

—5—
A J Distler tinplate limousine, German, *c.*1928, lithographed dark blue, one wheel detached, 36cm (14in) long, *L 1 Oct,*
£990 ($1,445)

—6—
A Distler tinplate saloon car, German, *c.*1925, lithographed dark blue and black, the driver in two-tone orange jacket and hood, 31cm (12in) long, *L 23 Jan,*
£880 ($1,043)

—7—
A G & K tinplate clock-work 'Cyclon' motorcycle and passenger, German, *c.*1920, 16cm (6¼in) long, *L 1 Oct,*
£1,760 ($2,570)

—8—
A G & K tinplate clock-work 'Cyclon' motorcycle and side car, *c.*1920, 16cm (6¼in) long, *L 1 Oct,*
£627 ($915)

—1—

—2—

—3—

—4—

—5—

—6—

—7—

—8—

Gebrüder Bing, German, early 1880s until 1924 (when the mark changed to 'BW' and production continued through the 1960s)

Carette, German, 1886 to 1917

These German factories produced vehicles which, although loosely modelled on full-size production line cars, can seldom be accurately identified as any particular model. Later, in the 1920s, many of the toy designs faithfully copied contemporary vehicles on the road. In the case of the French car manufacturer, Citroën, for example, tinplate toys of their own full-size cars were produced by an offshoot of the main car plant called 'Jouets Citroën'. Hoping to encourage future generations of loyal car buyers by producing toy cars, Andre Citroën wished the first words of a child to be 'Papa, Mama and… Citroën': a successful marketing ploy by this car producer which continued to sell these toys over a period of some twenty years.

Hand-painted tin cars from the period prior to the First World War by European manufacturers have attracted particular interest from collectors and have commanded high auction prices for many years due to their rarity and aesthetic appeal. Recent times, however, have seen a rapid growth in the demand for toy cars made from the 1930s up to the early 1960s. These later vehicles tend not to be finished in the hard, baked, enamel-like paint of the earlier models, but are normally found to be decorated by a lithographic process, by which details and colours were printed onto flat tin sheets before these were cut, pressed and moulded into their finished shapes. These later vehicles were made not only by European companies (including Tipp, Lehmann, Shuco, Paya, Jep, Ingap and Rossignol), but also, particularly after the Second World War, by Japanese manufacturers, whose profile in the market place now increased.

Some of the vehicles produced in Japan in the 1950s displayed impressive details, faithfully copying the exaggerated chrome fins, bumpers and radiator grilles which glittered so ostentatiously on full-size Cadillacs, Buicks and Fords. These toys, normally friction- or battery-powered, are eagerly sought by today's collectors of the full-size American cars; they can still be found at relatively modest prices, at general antique fairs, where their modern styling is often not fully appreciated. In a similar way, the small mechanical toy cars produced by the German factory, Shuco, in the 1930s, 1950s and 1960s, each scarcely larger than a die-cast Dinky toy, can still be bought at jumble sales, where uninitiated sellers link their small dimensions to lack of appeal.

—9—
A Jouets Citroen tinplate open tourer, French, c.1930, some damage, 37cm (14½in) long, C 20 Mar, £935 ($1,150)

—10—
A C I J tinplate P2 Alfa Romeo racing car, French, c.1935, 52.5cm (20¾in), L 23 Jan, £660 ($782)

—11—
A J Ph Meier racing car tinplate penny toy, German, c.1914, 9.5cm (3¾in) long, L 21 May, £176 ($236)

—12—
A horseless carriage tinplate penny toy, German, c.1902, lead weighted, 7.5cm (3in) long, L 21 May, £187 ($251)

—13—
A Lehmann tinplate clockwork autobus, German, c.1905, with driver, 20cm (8in) long, NY 29 June $1,650 (£1,269)

—14—
A Lehmann tinplate clockwork, 'Berolina' convertible automobile, German, c.1914, 18cm (7in), NY 29 June, $2,750 (£2,115)

—15—
A Lehmann tinplate car, German, c.1910, A 28 June, Dfl 1,276 (£289; $390)

—9—

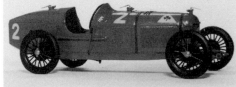
—10—

—11— —12—

—13—

—14—

—15—

Andre Citroën, France, 1923 to 1950

Kingsbury, America, 1895 until Second World War

Doll et Cie, German, 1898 to late 1930's

Marklin, German, 1859 to present day

The Meccano company of Liverpool introduced the first die-cast vehicles in 1934 to accompany, and act as accessories for, their popular Hornby model railways. These small toys (1/43 in scale) were an instant success and very soon the company was producing a wide variety of different vehicles. These models, produced prior to the outbreak of the Second World War, have been highly prized for many years, but only within the last eighteen months has the demand for Dinky toys from the 1950s and 1960s increased significantly. Today a Dinky Supertoy, dating from the 1960s, in mint condition and in its original box, could be priced at £400 or £500 ($560 or $700) in a specialized dealer's shop. Other companies imitated Dinky toys both before and after the war, hoping to share the success of this important new market. The trade names of these include Corgi, Matchbox, Taylor and Barrett, and Spot-On in Britain, Manoil in the United States of America, and Märklin, Solido and Palitoy in the European continent.

In the United States, toy manufacturers tended to produce much more robust vehicles than their European counterparts, made from thicker gauge steel sheets and even from cast-iron. Originally, the American toy-making industry was centred in Connecticut, where the early workshops fitted their toy trains and carriages in the 1870s and 1880s with the mechanisms from the clock-making factories close by. These 'clockwork' toys very quickly became popular; later toy makers refined the movements and reduced their size to fit them into smaller vehicles. During the 1920s and 1930s American toys became more refined, and the products of some companies, such as Kingsbury, Arcade and Buddy L, are comparable in style, quality and decoration to some toys produced in Europe at that time.

When assessing the importance and value of a toy the following points should be noted. Care should be taken to ensure that a toy is in good condition and relatively rust-free;

—16—
A collection of Dinky and Corgi toys, 1950s and 60s, approx seventy pieces, 6 illustrated, *L 1 Oct,* £2,090 ($3,051)

—17—
A collection of Dinky promotional vans, English, *c.*1955, comprising seven pieces (three illustrated), *L 1 Oct,* £1,265 ($1,847)

—18—
Two 23A Dinky racing sports cars, English, 1934, representing George Eyston's 'Humbug', *L 21 May,* £242 ($324)

—19—
An Arcade painted cast-iron 'General' steam shovel, American, *c.*1932, finished in red and green, tyres warped, 25.5cm (10in) long, *NY 29 June,* $220 (£196)

—20—
A Brimtoy limousine, English, *c.*1925, lithographed scarlet and black-lined gold, mint and boxed, 27cm (10½in) long, *L 1 Oct,* £605 ($883)

—21—
A Dinky 28G 'Kodak Film' delivery van, English, *c.*1934, finished in yellow, slight wear, *L 23 Jan,* £462 ($547)

—16—

—17—

—18—

—19—   —20—   —21—

this is particularly important in toys decorated by lithography rather than hand-painted. Whereas a craftsman competent in toy restoration could restore most hand-painted vehicles affected by a limited amount of rust, a lithographic finish is almost impossible to reproduce accurately to cover a damaged area. Restoration, if executed poorly, will adversely affect the desirability and value of a toy, as will missing pieces and damaged details. The date of the toy and the name of the company which produced it are equally important; these can be ascertained in most cases by consulting the relevant textbook. Finally, aesthetic appeal is a very important factor for the potential purchaser; no-one, after all, would want to own an object that they personally found unattractive, no matter how rare or desirable it might be in the eyes of the rest of the collecting world.

● HILARY KAY ●

Further reading

David Pressland, *The Art of the Tin Toy,* 1976

Allen Levy, *A Century of Model Trains,* 1974

Cecil Gibson, *The History of British Dinky Toys 1934-1964,* 1966

Peter Randall, *The Products of Binns Road,* 1977

Gwen White, *Toys, Dolls, Automata, Marks and Labels,* 1975

—22—
A Lehmann tinplate clockwork 'Tut Tut' car, German, 1904-1926, 18cm (7in) high, *NY 29 June,* $522 (£402)

—23—
A tinplate and clockwork horseless carriage, possibly by Gunthermann, c.1900, the vehicle finished in grey with lilac and yellow, ochre interior, damaged, *S 6 Feb,* £682 ($805)

—24—
A Lehmann tinplate clockwork 'Naughty Nephew' automobile, EPL no. 495, German, c.1910, 13cm (5in) long, *L 1 Oct,* £385 ($562)

—25—
A Schuco Texi 5735, German, c.1950, the red tinplate sports car with seated blonde female driver, 24cm (9½in) long, *L 21 May,* £209 ($280)

—26—
A Gunthermann tinplate Golden Arrow record car, German, c.1935, 53cm (21in) long, *L 21 May,* £330 ($442)

—27—
A Tipp & Co tinplate fire engine, German, c.1935, lithographed scarlet, with four firemen, 25.5cm (10in) long, *L 1 Oct,* £330 ($482)

—28—
A Tipco tinplate convertible Führer car, navy blue, with composition figure of Hitler in the back, 23cm (9in) long, *NY 29 June,* $825 (£635)

—29—
A Tipp & Co tinplate and clockwork drop-head coupé, finished in orange and grey, with tinplate driver, some wear, 46cm (18in) long, *S 4 Nov,* £858 ($1,287)

—30—
A Tipp tinplate charabanc, German, c.1932, finished in scarlet and yellow, some rust, 43cm (17in) long, *L 1 Oct,* £462 ($675)

—22—

—23—

—24—

—25—

—26—

—27—

—28—

—29—

—30—

Photographs of marks Courtesy New Cavendish Books, from 'The Art of the Tin Toy, by David Pressland

Paya, Spain, early 1900's to present day

Schuco, German, 1912 to present day

Günthermann, German 1887 to 1965

1
A Hornby '0' gauge 4-4-2
electric locomotive
'Lord Nelson', c.1900,
with tender, L 21 May,
£165 ($221)

2
A Hornby '0' gauge 4-4-0
electric 'Eton' locomotive
and tender, c.1930,
L 21 May,
£396 ($579)

3
A Hornby '0' gauge
Riviera 'Blue' train set,
English, c.1927, com-
prising 4-4-2 Nord
engine and matching
tender no. 31801,
L 21 May,
£286 ($383)

4
A Bing gauge '1' clock-
work train set, German,
c.1905, comprising 0-4-0
clockwork loco and
tender, two coaches and a
goods wagon, with a
quantity of track,
L 23 Jan,
£1,100 ($1,304)

5
A Hornby gauge '0' elec-
tric 4-4-2 locomotive
'Flying Scotsman'
no. 4472, with matching
tender, L 23 Jan,
£110 ($130)

6
A Hornby electric 4-4-0
locomotive 'County of
Bedford' no. 3821, in
green lined black and
gold, with matching
tender, L 23 Jan,
£440 ($521)

7
A Hornby 'O' gauge 4-6-2
electric 'Princess
Elizabeth' locomotive and
tender, c.1952, no. 6201,
finished in maroon livery,
lacking bogie wheels and
with some metal fatigue,
L 21 May,
£715 ($958)

8
A Rock & Garner tinplate
central station, German,
c.1880, 42cm (16½in)
wide, L 21 May,
£2,310 ($3,095)

9
A Bing gauge '1' spirit
fired 4-4-4 locomotive and
tender, German, c.1906,
finished in black, front
bogie detached, lacking
two headlamps, L 1 Oct,
£1,540 ($2,248)

10
A Bing spirit-fired gauge
'1' 4-4-0 locomotive,
German, c.1905, with
matching tender, some
damage, 48cm (19in),
C 26 June,
£1,045 ($1,410)

11
A Bassett-Lowke gauge '0'
clockwork 4-6-0 loco-
motive no. 1108, with
matching tender, L 23 Jan,
£264 ($313)

12
A Bassett-Lowke gauge '0'
electric 4-6-2 locomotive
'Flying Scotsman'
no. 60103, with matching
tender, L 23 Jan,
£418 ($495)

13
A gauge '0' clockwork
4-6-4 Stephenson Baltic
tank locomotive no. 329,
Marklin, c.1923,
finished in Southern
green livery (Ex
LBSCR), S 1 May,
£638 ($823)

14
A Marklin gauge '1' tin-
plate bogie cattle
truck, German, c.1902,
some wear, 24.5cm
(9¾in) long, C 26 June,
£110 ($148)

15
A Marklin gauge one
CIWR bogie restaurant
car, German, c.1919,
no. 1932, 40cm (15¾in),
C 22 Oct,
£396 ($594)

16
A Marklin gauge '1'
tinplate electric 0-4-0
steeplecab locomotive,
German, lacking one
mounting step, 26cm
(10in), C 22 Oct,
£308 ($462)

17
A Marklin tinplate gauge
'1' double decker carriage,
German, c.1907, 24cm
(9½in) long, NY 13 Apr,
$3,960 (£3,168)

18
An early tinplate toy,
carpet train, French,
c.1880, possibly by
Faivre, two wheels miss-
ing and some damage,
44cm (17½in), C 22 Oct,
£605 ($908)

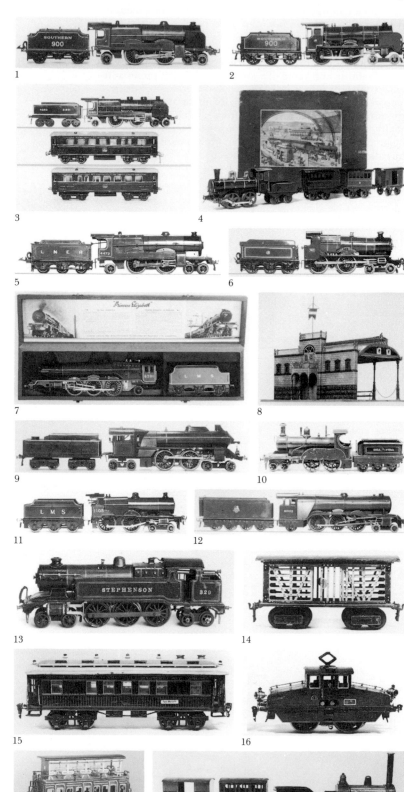

1
A Tipp & Co tinplate petrol pump group, German, c.1935, 24cm (9½in) wide, *L 1 Oct*, £286 ($418)

2
A model of a steam-fired Burrell traction engine, 'Winston Churchill', English, modern, inscribed Michael Holden Engineers, Banbury, England, no. 453, 88cm (34½in) long, *L 1 Oct*, £1,045 ($1,526)

3
A brass fire pumper, by Stevens Model Dockyard, English, c.1880s, finished in faded scarlet paint, 33cm (13in) long, *L 1 Oct*, £770 ($1,124)

4
A brass and copper engineered model of a single cylinder agricultural traction engine, 20th century, 37cm (14½in), *C 22 Oct*, £264 ($396)

5
A Lehmann tinplate clockwork 'Ikarus' aeroplane, no. 653, German, with paper wings, wingspan 38cm (15in), *NY 29 June*, £4,620 ($3,554)

6
A JEP seaplane, type F260, French, *A 8 Oct*, Dfl 1,610 (£380; $562)

7
An Orobr tinplate clockwork Terradactyl monoplane, German, c.1914, with pilot, 27cm (10½in) long, *L 1 Oct*, £825 ($1,205)

8
A Tipp & Co tinplate bomber, lithographed with swastikas, with four cast alloy bombs, 36.5cm (14¼in) wing span, *L 21 May*, £495 ($663)

9
A Marklin painted tin clockwork battleship 'New York', German, c.1905, replaced turret and lifeboats, lacking mechanism, 91cm (36in) long, *NY 13 Apr*, $9,900 (£7,920)

10
A German painted tin clockwork riverboat, Uebelacker, early 1900s, the plaque numbered DRP 66476, lacking flag and ship's wheel, 51cm (20in) long, *NY 13 Apr*, $3,520 (£2,816)

11
A Marklin tinplate Graf zeppelin, German, c.1910, no. 5402 in Marklin catalogue, handpainted cram lined silver and black, some wear, 32cm (12½in) long, *L 23 Jan*, £2,310 ($2,737)

12
A Tipp & Co Graf zeppelin, German, c.1928, 44cm (17¼in), *A 8 Oct*, Dfl 2,127 (£502; $742)

13
A Marklin painted tin clockwork battleship 'Missouri', German, c.1933, stamped in red with the maker's insignia, two anchors lacking, 71cm (28in) long, *NY 13 Apr*, $9,350 (£7,480)

14
A Marklin painted tin gunboat 'New York', German, c.1904, with four-wheel carriage (lacking anchor and mechanism), 56cm (22in) long, *NY 13 Apr*, $9,350 (£7,480)

15
A Bing tinplate clockwork torpedo boat, German, c.1900, some chips, lacks mast, 57cm (22½in) long, *L 1 Oct*, £550 ($803)

16
A Bing tinplate three-funnelled transatlantic liner, German, c.1918, Bing catalogue no. 10/321/5, some pieces missing, some repainting, 64cm (25¼in) long, *L 21 May*, £935 ($1,253)

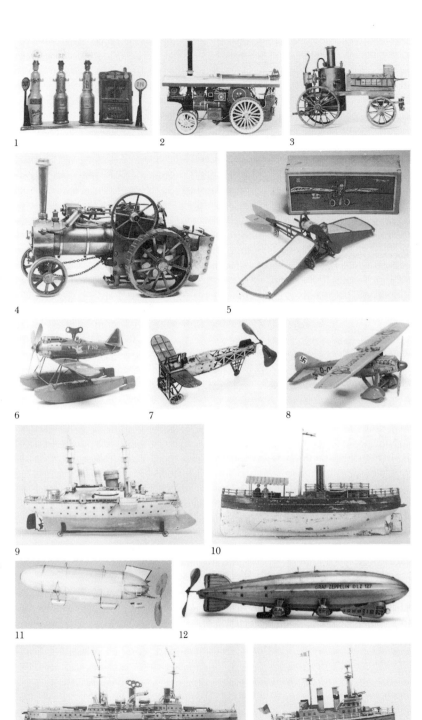

1   2   3

4   5

6   7   8

9   10

11   12

13   14

15   16

1
A knife-grinder tinplate
steam accessory toy,
German, c.1910, driven
either by steam or clock-
work, 14cm (5½in),
C 26 June,
£88 ($118)

2
A Lehmann Man-Da-
Rin, EPL no. 565, Ger-
man, c.1905, with red
and blue lithographed
sedan chair, 18cm (7in)
long, *L 21 May,*
£880 ($1,179)

3
A tinplate bagatelle
player, German, c.1912,
with articulated right
arm, 19cm (7½in) long,
L 21 May,
£330 ($442)

4
A Shimer cast-iron
horse-drawn pony cart,
American, c.1890, with
female driver, 25.5cm
(10in) long, *NY 29 June,*
$330 (£254)

5
An American cast-iron
horse-drawn English trap
pull toy, probably Ken-
ton, late 19th century,
38cm (15in) long,
NY 13 Apr,
$1,650 (£1,320)

6
A trotter toy, French,
c.1900, the bisque-
headed figure dressed
in satin suit above a
strong clockwork mech-
anism, 34cm (13½in)
long, *L 21 May,*
£1,265 ($1,695)

7
A French tinplate clock-
work tricyclist, late 19th
century, the bisque-
headed figure in
original blue and beige
silk costume, 21.5cm
(8½in) high, *NY 29 June,*
$2,750 (£2,115)

8
A Lehmann tinplate and
clockwork 'Anxious Bride'
novelty toy, c.1910, 23cm
(9in) long, *S 6 Feb,*
£638 ($753)

9
An F Martin 'Le Gai
Violiniste', French,
c.1905, no. 160, with
hand-painted face and
original clothes, 21cm
(8¼in), *L 21 May,*
£440 ($560)

10
A Muller & Kadedar
tinplate Ferris wheel,
German, c.1905, hand-
painted, with five gon-
dolas, 33cm (13in) high,
L 21 May,
£440 ($590)

11
A German tinplate dou-
ble ferris wheel, c.1910,
with fly wheel driven
mechanism, each wheel
with four gondolas and
four passengers, 82cm
(32in) high, *NY 13 Apr,*
$9,350 (£7,480)

12
A collection of Heyde
Roman figures, French,
dating from c.1890, some
figures distressed,
L 21 May,
£385 ($516)

13
A Britain's no. 3/117 best
soldier assortment retail
display, including Her
Majesty the Queen
mounted taking salute,
Horse Guards,
Dragoons, Guards,
Bandsmen, etc, 33 fig-
ures, *S 6 Feb,*
£1,100 ($1,298)

14
A painted wooden toy
stable, with two horses
and a wagon, c.1910,
67.5cm (26in) high,
S 1 May,
£638 ($823)

15
A Hubley painted cast-
iron horse-drawn Royal
Circus giraffe cage,
American, 1919-1926,
including a driver and a
giraffe with her baby,
40cm (16in) long,
NY 13 Apr,
$3,740 (£2,192)

16
A Hubley painted cast-
iron horse-drawn Royal
Circus farmer's van,
American, c.1919-1926,
with a driver and bob-
bing farmer's head,
38cm (15in), *NY 13 Apr,*
$3,630 (£2,904)

1
A cast spelter alarm clock, in the form of Paul Kruger, French, c.1900, the alarm activating the figure's right arm with pistol match-holder, ash tray to hat, lacking match-strike from base, 24cm (9½in), *L 17 July*, £220 ($319)

2
A cast iron automaton timepiece, American, c.1860, internal mechanism causing the negress to flutter her eyes, skirt repainted, 43cm (17in) high, *C 22 Oct*, £418 ($627)

3
A Bradley & Hubbard cast iron mantle clock, c.1860, depicting King Cole sitting astride a beer barrel, *L 17 July*, £1,430 ($2,074)

4
A cast iron 'Giant in the Tower' mechanical bank, English, late 19th century, 23.5cm (9¼in), *L 23 Jan*, £1,760 ($2,086)

5
A tinplate 'Chocolate Club' dispenser bank, German, c.1935, some wear, 13cm (5in), *L 23 Jan*, £71 ($84)

6
A cast iron 'Dinah' mechanical bank, English, c.1910, paint worn, 17cm (6¾in), *L 23 Jan*, £88 ($104)

7
An 'Organ Grinder and Performing Bear' cast-iron mechanical bank, Griffith no.195, mechanism broken, 17.5cm (7in) long, *NY 15 Feb*, $1,540 (£1,328)

8
A 'Boy Scout Camp' cast-iron mechanical bank, Griffith no.24, 25.5cm (10in) long, *NY 15 Feb*, $4,400 (£3,793)

9
A 'Boy Robbing Bird's Nest' cast-iron mechanical bank, Griffith no.23, 20cm (8in) high, *NY 15 Feb*, $3,300 (£2,845)

10
A 'Darktown Battery' cast-iron mechanical bank, Griffith no.68, some rust, 25.5cm (10in) long, *NY 15 Feb*, $715 (£616)

11
A 'Mason' cast-iron mechanical bank, Griffith no.163, 19cm (7½in) long, *NY 15 Feb*, $1,650 (£1,422)

12
A 'Panorama' cast-iron mechanical bank, Griffith no.200, crack and chip, 16.5cm (6½in), *NY 15 Feb*, $4,675 (£4,030)

13
A cast-iron two frogs mechanical bank, American late 19th century, some damage, 21cm (8½in) long, *L 21 May*, £286 ($383)

14
A 'Clown on Globe' cast-iron mechanical bank, Griffith no.59, 23cm (9in), *NY 15 Feb*, $605 (£522)

15
A General Butler cast-iron still bank, 17.5cm (7in) high, *NY 15 Feb*, $1,760 (£1,517)

1   2   3   4

5   6   7

8   9

10   11   12

13   14   15

1
**A Distler tinplate Mickey
Mouse organ grinder,**
German, *c.*1930,
lithographed with
Minnie dancing above
the wheeled instrument,
15cm (6in) long,
L 21 May,
£440 ($560)

2
**A Lionel Donald Duck
rail car,** American, *c.*1935,
tinplate and composi-
tion, in original card-
board box, 29cm
(11½in) wide, *L 23 Jan,*
£242 ($287)

3
**A Marx walking Popeye
tinplate clockwork toy,**
American, 1930s,
inoperative, 21.5cm
(8½in) high, *NY 29 June,*
$247 (£190)

4
**A Minnie Mouse carousel
figure,** French, *c.*1935,
carved and painted
wood, 96.5cm (38in)
long, *L 23 Jan,*
£1,760 ($2,086)

5
**An American clockwork
celluloid Mickey Mouse**
on rocking horse, 19cm
(7½in) high, *NY 29 June,*
$715 (£550)

6
**A Walt Disney 'Pinnochio'
celluloid,** numbered
5/275, bearing certified
seal, image 19 x 24.5cm
(7½ x 9¾in), *L 23 Jan,*
£187 ($222)

7
**A Walt Disney celluloid
from 'Fantasia',** 1940,
depicting Mickey
Mouse as the sorceror,
signed in pencil by
Walt Disney, 20cm (8in)
square, *NY 29 June,*
$3,630 (£2,792)

8
**A Walt Disney celluloid
from 'Snow White',** 1937,
depicting Dopey within
a bubble, 21.5cm (8½in)
square, *NY 29 June,*
$1,430 (£1,100)

9
**A Walt Disney celluloid
from 'Snow White',** 1937,
27.5 x 35cm (10¾ x
13¾in), *NY 29 June,*
$2,640 (£2,031)

10
**A Walt Disney celluloid
from 'Pinocchio',** 1939,
depicting Jiminy
Cricket, 18 x 22cm
(7¼ x 8¾in),
NY 29 June,
$1,430 (£1,100)

11
**A Walt Disney celluloid
from 'Dumbo',** 1941,
depicting Dumbo with
his mother, 21.5 x
26.5cm (8½ x 10½in),
NY 29 June,
$880 (£677)

12
**A Walt Disney celluloid,
from 'Fantasia',** 1940,
19 x 22cm (7½ x 9in),
L 21 May,
£550 ($737)

See also
p.324, figs 11 & 12

**1 A Yokuts coiled poly-
chrome gambling tray,**
woven on a saw grass
ground in black bracken
fern root and redbud,
68cm (26¾in),
NY 21 June,
$24,200 (£18,906)

**2 A Four Mile polychrome
picture bowl,** *c.*1350-
1400 AD, painted on a
deep orange slip in
black and cream detail,
22cm (8¾in), *NY 21 June,*
$19,800 (£15,469)

**3 A classic Navajo wearing
blanket,** woven on a
deep red cochineal
ravelled and commer-
cial yarn ground in
natural ivory and indigo
blue, 178.5 x 121.5cm
(70¼ x 48in), *NY 21 June,*
$24,200 (£18,906)

1

2

3

1
A Mayan polychrome plate, Uaxactun Late Classic, *c.*550-950 AD, with a warrior in the tondo, possibly one of the Hero Twins, the three glyphs on the left hand side denoting the date of the event, 39.5cm (15½in), *NY 26 Nov,* **$9,350 (£6,404)**

2
A Mayan carved vessel, Northern Peten region, Late Classic, *c.*550-950 AD, the sides carved with the aged God L, 16cm (6¼in), *NY 26 Nov,* **$9,350 (£6,404)**

3
An Olmec seated baby, possibly from Zumpango del Rio, Guerrero, Middle Preclassic, *c.*1150-550 BC, *NY 26 Nov,* **$51,700 (£35,410)**

4
A Costa Rican portrait head, probably Atlantic Watershed region *c.*800-1500 AD, 19.5cm (7¾in), *NY 31 May,* **$14,300 (£11,172)**

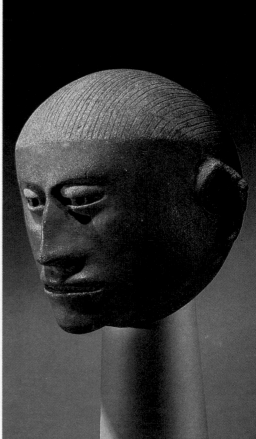

1
An Akan/Kwahu terra-cotta portrait head, representing a person of royal lineage, sculpted by a female artist, black pigment with traces of red clay, 38cm (15in), *NY 15 Nov,* $4,675 (£3,292)

2
A Chokwe wood face mask, Cihongo, Lubalo region, Sukamuna chiefdom, of typical form, fine reddish patina, 20cm (8in), *L 2 Dec,* £3,850 ($5,698)

3
A Yombe wood figure, the coiffure arranged in the typical tall transversal crescent, fine patina, 80cm (31½in), *L 2 Dec,* £10,450 ($15,466)

4
A Kuba wood cup, carved in the form of a human head, 21cm (8¼in), *L 2 Dec,* £9,350 ($13,838)

1

2

3

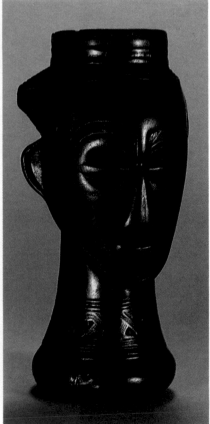

4

1
A Kazakh Bordjalou rug,
274 x 104cm (9ft x 3ft
5in), *L 16 Oct,*
£1,320 ($1,954)

2
A Caucasian gelim, 310 x
133cm (10ft 2in x 4ft
4in), *G 25 June,*
SF 9,900 (£2,870; $3,874)

3
An Uzbek rug, with a
Susani design, 180 x
103cm (5ft 11in x 3ft
4in), *L 16 Oct,*
£4,180 ($6,186)

1

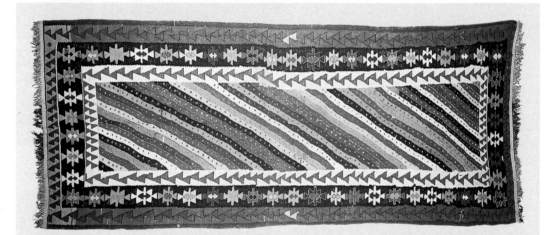

2

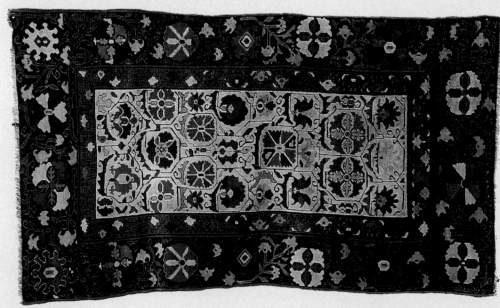

3

1
A Ziegler carpet, 764 x
423cm (25ft 1in x 13ft
10½in), *G 14 May,*
SF 44,000
(£12,865; $17,111)

2
A Bakshaish rug, last
quarter 19th century,
246 x 193cm (8ft 1in x
6ft 4in), *NY 18 May,*
$9,900 (£7,857)

1

2

1
A Persian slip-painted pottery bowl, 11th century, 23.4cm (9¼in) diam, *L 16 Apr,* £385 ($501)

2
A Persian Minai pottery bowl, *c.*1200, Kashan, a band of *kufic* inscription below the rim, 20.3cm (8in) diam, *L 16 Apr,* £4,510 ($5,863)

3
A small Persian slip-painted pottery bowl, 9th/10th century, Nishapur, with a pseudo *kufic* inscription, 13.2cm (5¼in) diam, *G 25 June,* SF 3,300 (£957; $1,291)

4
An Isnik pottery jug, *c.*1530-50, decorated in the 'Damascus' palette of cobalt-blue, turquoise and black, 20cm (7⅞in) high, *L 15 Oct,* £8,250 ($12,210)

5
A Persian lustre pottery jug, last quarter 12th century, Kashan, in brownish lustre on a blue ground in the 'Rayy' style, 12.5cm (5in) high, *G 25 June,* SF 9,900 (£2,870; $3,874)

6
A Persian underglaze-painted pottery cup-bowl, 14th century, 14cm (5½in) diam, *L 15 Oct,* £8,250 ($12,210)

1

2

3

4

5

6

1
An Isnik pottery dish,
second half 16th century,
30.5cm (12in) diam,
L 15 Oct,
£14,300 ($21,164)

2
**An early Ottoman brass
candlestick,** early 16th
century, inscribed [in
translation]: 'To its owner,
Happiness, Well-being,
and Long life as long as
the dove coos. Perpetual
Glory and Prosperity...'
23.4cm (9¼in) high,
L 16 Apr,
£14,300 ($18,590)

3
**An early 16th century
Ottoman cast silver-gilt
jug,** stamped below the
rim with a *tughra*,
probably of Sultan Selim,
I, 1512-1520, 10.1cm (4in)
high, *L 16 Apr,*
£77,000 ($100,000)

4
**A gold and silver inlaid
cast bronze inkwell,** *c.*1275,
al-Jazira or Western
Persia, with an inscrip-
tion round the shoulder,
5.9cm (2¾in) high,
L 16 Apr,
£39,600 ($51,480)

1

2

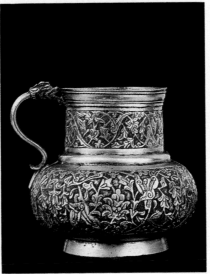

3

4

1
A Satsuma earthenware vase and cover, early Meiji period, of lotus form, painted in enamels and gilt, 41.2cm (16¼in), *L 12 Nov,* £6,600 ($9,306)

2
Masanao: a fine ivory study of a rat, 18th century, the details finely rendered in slightly worn and well toned ivory which bears old cracks, the eyes inlaid, signed, 4.8cm (1⅞in), *L 13 Nov,* £19,000 ($26,790)

3
Sokoku: a very good boxwood figure of a Sarumawashi, Meiji period, the details delicately rendered in the pale wood, signed, 3.5cm (1⅜in), *L 13 Nov,* £1,600 ($2,256)

4
Chokusai: a study of a reclining cat, 19th century, turning back to look at a bird, broken winged, on its back, a loose feather in the cat's forepaw, the bird's eyes inlaid, signed, 4cm (1½in), *L 14 June,* £3,520 ($4,682)

1

2

3

4

1
**A gold lacquer box and
cover,** Meiji period,
decorated in gold *taka-
makie, hiramakie, togi-
dashi* and *kirigane,* rims
mounted in silver, the
interior with nine fitted
jars of *manju* form, 11.5
x 3.5cm (4½ x 1¼in),
L 6 Mar,
£3,630 ($4,066)

2
**Minamoto Seisho: a two-
case inro,** 19th century,
decorated with a tiger
drinking at a stream, all
in gold *takamakie, hiramakie* and *e-nashiji,* signed
with *kakihan,* 6cm
(2½in), *L 6 Mar,*
£1,540 ($1,725)

3
A gold lacquer cabinet,
19th century, bearing a
nashiji ground decorated
with a panoramic land-
scape illustrating the
53 stations of the Tokaido
Road, the two doors open
to reveal four drawers,
silver mounts, slight re-
pairs, 27.5 x 19.6 x 26cm
(10⅞ x 7¾ x 10¼in),
L 12 Nov,
£9,500 ($13,395)

4
A large lacquer vase,
Meiji period, in the
form of a rope bag, the
neck hung with silver
tassels, details in gold,
silver, black *takamakie*
and foil, silver mounts,
slight chips and cracks,
45.5cm (18in), *L 12 Nov,*
£4,400 ($6,204)

1 (*above*)   2   3

4

1
A Kakiemon figure of a bijin, late 17th century, her kimono decorated in enamels, the skirt damaged toward the front, the base missing, 39.2cm (15½in), *L 12 Nov,* **£7,000 ($9,870)**

2
An Imari jar and cover, late 17th century, decorated with *kiku* in shades of green, yellow and grey enamels, iron-red and touches of gilding within underglaze-blue cartouches, 21.5cm (8½in), *L 6 Mar,* **£2,860 ($3,203)**

3
Hayashi Kodenji: a cloisonné vase, Meiji period, worked with butterflies against a midnight-blue ground, silver rim and base, signed *Aichi, Hayashi ko,* 31cm (12¼in), *L 13 June,* **£9,900 ($13,167)**

4
Chin Jukan: a large Satsuma earthenware jar and cover, Meiji period, enamelled and gilt with panels of *ho-o* and chrysanthemum, small chip, signed, with enamelled *mon,* 77cm (30¼in), *L 13 June,* **£12,650 ($16,825)**

1

2

3

4

1 Hiroshige: Oban: A sudden shower over Ohashi Bridge and Atake, from the series 'The Hundred Famous Views of Edo' date-seal, Year of Snake (Ansei 4, 1857), and publisher's mark, Shitaya Uoei, *L 22 May,* £17,600 ($23,408)

2 Harunobu: Chuban: Two young women in a room open to a balcony, a poem by Jakuren Hoshi in a tablet at the top right, fine impression and good colour, *L 22 May,* £2,200 ($2,926)

3 Kiyomine: Oban: The head and shoulders of a geisha applying rouge on her lips, from the set 'Comparison of Brocade Beauties of the Eastern Capital', publisher's mark, Eijudo, fine impression, good colour, *L 22 May,* £7,040 ($9,363)

4 Hiroshige II: Oban tate-e album, mounted with 77 prints (two illustrated) from the series Shokoku Meisho Kyakkei, publisher's mark Shitaya Uoei, dated 1859, '60, '61 and '64, good impressions and colour, mostly from early editions; also six prints from the series 'The Souvenirs of Edo', dated 1861, publisher's mark Uoei, good impressions and colour, *NY 7 Nov,* $57,750 (£40,384)

1

2

3

4

1
A pair of gilt-bronze figures of guardians, Ming dynasty, traces of gilding and red lacquer, 62.5cm (24½in), *NY 17 Apr,* $11,000 (£8,593)

2
A blue and white bottle vase, Qianlong mark and period, 30.5cm (12in), *HK 21 May,* HK$60,500 (£6,263; $8,392)

3
A pair of blue and white bottle vases, Kangxi, each decorated with a mythical beast galloping beneath a phoenix, *NY 4 Dec,* $18,700 (£12,635)

4
An archaic bronze wine vessel (gu), late Shang dynasty, decorated in relief with elongated masks, the silver-green patina with extensive malachite encrustation around the rim, 32cm (12½in), *L 10 Dec,* £55,000 ($77,000)

1
A large tileworks figure of Guandi, Ming dynasty, 95cm (37½in), *NY 5 June*, $9,900 (£7,795)

2
A pair of figures of dogs of Fo, Kangxi, with hair markings incised beneath the overall egg and spinach glazes, 30cm (12in), *M 23 June*, FF 199,800 (£16,100; $21,574)

3
A pair of figures of cocks, Qianlong, enamelled in white with black details, 35cm (13¾in), *M 23 June*, FF 83,250 (£6,708; $8,989)

4
A figure of a harnessed Fereghan horse, Tang dynasty, 53.5cm (21in) long, *L 10 Dec*, £67,100 ($93,940)

5
Two 'famille-rose' figures of pheasants, Qianlong, 36cm (14in) and 35cm (13¾in), *M 23 June*, FF 61,050 (£4,919; $6,592)

1

2

3

4

5

1
A pair of coral-ground bowls, Daoguang seal marks and period, 12.7cm (5in), *HK 22 May,* **HK$55,000** (£5,694; $7,629)

2
A pair of jardinières, Yongzheng, 46.8cm (18⅜in) high, *L 16 July,* £19,800 ($28,710)

3
A Jianyao tea-bowl, Song dynasty, 12.5cm (5in), *L 10 Dec,* £1,595 ($2,233)

4
A flambé-glazed vase, Qianlong seal mark and period, of hexagonal lobed section, 19cm (7½in), *NY 4 June,* $8,800 (£6,929)

5
A green dragon jar and cover, seal mark and period of Jiaqing, 22cm (8½in), *L 18 June,* £5,500 ($7,425)

6
A rhinoceros horn libation cup, carved with figures in a boat, the handle formed from a pine tree, 15.7cm (6⅛in), *HK 22 May,* **HK$30,800** (£3,188; $4,272)

7
A spinach jade censer and cover, 18th century, the underside carved as an open chrysanthemum flower, 19cm (7½in) wide, *HK 22 May,* **HK$44,000** (£4,555; $6,104)

1

2

3

4

5

6

7

1
**A Thai gilt-bronze
Buddha head**, Chien
Sen style, *c*.15th century,
with worn gilding over
a dark jade-green
patina, 12.5cm (5in),
L 10 June,
£880 ($1,170)

2
**A Lucknow polychrome-
enamelled silver-gilt
Pan-box** (*Pan-dan*), mid-
19th century, 12.1cm
(4¾in) diam, *NY 21 Sept*,
$1,045 (£786)

3
**A Gandhara grey schist
figure of Buddha**, 3rd/4th
century, 66cm (26in),
NY 20 Sept,
$11,000 (£8,271)

4
**A Tibetan copper-gilt
figure of Aksobhya
Buddha**, 15th/16th
century, 39.4cm (15½in),
NY 20 Sept,
$6,325 (£4,756)

1

2

3

4

1
An Etruscan terracotta antefix in the form of the head of a boar, 5th century BC, 25.5cm (10in), *L 9 Dec*, £4,400 ($6,160)

2
A Roman marble portrait head of a man, period of Emperor Maximinus I of Thrace, 235-8 AD, height 30.5cm (12in), *NY 21 Nov*, $22,000 (£15,385)

3
An Attic black-figure neck amphora, in the manner of the Antimenes painter, belonging to the Group of Toronto 305, *c.*510-500 BC, 43cm (17in), *L 17 July*, £9,900 ($13,860)

4
A large Roman bronze lamp, late 1st century BC/2nd century AD, the handle terminating in a theatrical mask, 30cm (12in) long, *L 17 July*, £2,200 ($3,080)

1

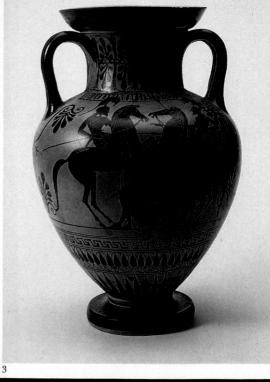

2

3

4

Antiquities

1
An Egyptian turquoise faience necklace, New Kingdom, 1554-1080 BC, 56cm (22in) long, *NY 21 Nov,* $715 (£500)

2
A group of rock crystal and glass face beads, *c.* 1st century BC, strung as a necklace, 36cm (14¼in) long, *NY 21 Nov,* $2,750 (£1,923)

3
An opaque dark blue sand-core trefoil glass oinochoe, 6th-4th century BC, with yellow and white spiral trailing, 11cm (4¼in), *L 9 Dec,* £1,650 ($2,310)

4
A dark blue mould-blown glass amphoriskos, *c.* 1st century AD, some weathering, 10cm (4in), *L 9 Dec,* £1,650 ($2,310)

5
An opaque white sandcore glass amphoriskos, 4th-3rd century BC, part of rim restored, 11.5cm (4½in), *L 20 May,* £418 ($564)

6
A cobalt blue bottle, 1st century AD, decorated with white trailing, 10cm (4in), *NY 22 Nov,* $2,310 (£1,615)

7
A dark blue sandcore glass alabastron, 6th-4th century BC, decorated with yellow and white trailing, 10cm (4in), *L 17 July,* £1,100 ($1,540)

8
A bluish-green mould-blown glass 'lotus-bud' beaker, with human mask decoration, 1st century AD, base restored, 12.5cm (5in), *L 9 Dec,* £660 ($924)

9
An olive-green mould-blown glass grape flask, *c.* 2nd century AD, 13.5cm (5¼in), *L 20 May,* £715 ($965)

10
An iridescent pale green glass twin-handled flask, Eastern Mediterranean, *c.* 4th century AD, with multi-coloured iridescence, 17cm (6¾in), *L 9 Dec,* £1,100 ($1,540)

11
A pale greenish-brown glass jug, *c.* 4th century AD, some iridescence and encrustation, 15cm (6in), *L 20 May,* £462 ($623)

12
A blue-green ribbed bowl, 1st century AD, some cracking, 13cm (5in) diam., *NY 22 Nov,* $770 (£538)

13
Sassanian yellowish-green facet-cut bowl, *c.* 6th century AD, 7.5cm (3in) high, *L 9 Dec,* £3,520 ($4,928)

See also
● Colour illustrations *p 576*

1

2

3

4

5

6

7

8

9

10

11

12

13

1
A limestone votive stela,
19th Dynasty, 1305-1196
BC, carved in sunk relief
in two registers, height as
framed 31.5cm (12½in),
NY 22 Nov,
$2,090 (£1,462)

2
**A sandstone relief frag-
ment,** Ptolemaic period,
305-30 BC, carved with
the king, Ptolemy III or
IV, 28.5 x 47.5cm (11¼ x
18¾in), *NY 21 Nov,*
$2,310 (£1,615)

3
**A plaster funerary mask of
a girl,** 2nd century AD,
painted in flesh tones,
black, red, white, and
green, 26cm (10¼in),
NY 9 Feb,
$2,310 (£2,081)

4
**A plaster mummy portrait
of a man,** 2nd century
AD, 23cm (9in) high,
NY 21 Nov,
$4,400 (£3,077)

5
**An Egyptian mummy of a
child,** Roman period,
c. 1st century AD,
wrapped in linen and
polychrome-painted
cantonnage, 37cm
(14½in), *L 9 Dec,*
£2,090 ($2,926)

6
**An Egyptian bronze figure
of a cat,** Saite period,
*c.*664-525 BC, 15cm (6in),
L 20 May,
£3,740 ($5,049)

7
An Egyptian bronze figure
of the God Thoth, 26th
Dynasty, *c.*664-525 BC,
13.5cm (5¼in), *L 20 May,*
£1,210 ($1,633)

8
**An 'Egyptian Blue' figure
of a baboon,** 26th Dynasty,
664-525 BC, or earlier,
sacred to the god Thoth,
inserted moon-disk
missing, 6cm (2½in) high,
NY 8 Feb,
$2,200 (£1,982)

9
**A magnesite marble bust
of Isis,** Ptolemaic period,
305-30 BC, or earlier,
from a figure of the
goddess nursing Horus,
missing headdress
inserted, 8cm (3in) high,
NY 21 Nov,
$2,860 (£2,000)

10
**An Egyptian bronze figure
of Harpocrates,** 26th
Dynasty, *c.*664-525 BC,
wearing the *hem-hem*
crown, 22cm (8¾in), sold
with another Egyptian
bronze figure of Harpo-
crates, 12.5cm (5in),
L 9 Dec,
£2,090 ($2,926)

11
A bronze figure of Sekhmet,
26th Dynasty, 664-525
BC, 12.5cm (5in) high,
NY 8 Feb,
$2,640 (£2,378)

12
**A miniature bronze falcon
sarcophagus,** 26th/30th
Dynasty, 664-525 BC,
surmounted by a figure of
the Horus falcon,
restored, 16cm (6½in)
long, *NY 8 Feb,*
$2,200 (£1,982)

1
A bronze figure of Maat,
22nd/26th Dynasty,
946-525 BC, plume
missing, 6cm (2½in) high,
NY 22 Nov,
$935 (£654)

2
**An Egyptian pale
turquoise-glazed com-
position Ushabti figure,**
from Saqqara, 26th
Dynasty, reign of Amasis,
*c.*550 BC, of the overseer
of the royal fleet, Heka-
em-saf, 18.5cm (7¼in),
L 9 Dec,
£1,210 ($1,694)

3
**An Egyptian pale turquoise
glazed composition
Ushabti figure,** from
Saqqara, 26th Dynasty,
*c.*550 BC, of the royal
scribe Hor-maa-Kheru,
15.5cm (6in), *L 9 Dec,*
£770 ($1,078)

4
**An Egyptian bronze figure
of Osiris,** 26th Dynasty,
664-525 BC, wearing the
atef crown, 27.5cm
(10¾in), *L 9 Dec,*
£2,640 ($3,696)

5
**An Egyptian bronze figure
of Imhotep,** 26th Dynasty,
664-525 BC, 14.5cm
(5¾in), *L 17 July,*
£6,600 ($9,240)

6
**An Egyptian limestone
male bust,** Ptolemaic
period, *c.*305-30 BC,
38cm (15in), *L 9 Dec,*
£4,180 ($5,852)

7
**A basalt head of a man or
god,** 12th Dynasty, reign
of Sesostris II, 1897-1878
BC, from a seated figure,
24.5cm (9½in), *NY 8 Feb,*
$5,500 (£4,955)

8
**A turquoise-blue faience
sistrum,** 26th Dynasty,
664-525 BC, in the form
of a janus head of the
goddess Hathor, the
hawks re-attached and
with crowns missing,
26.5cm (10½in), *NY 8 Feb,*
$6,875 (£6,194)

9
**A Diorite bust of
Wennufer,** late 27th/early
30th Dynasty, *c.*425-375
BC, black pillar with two
fragmentary columns of
inscription: "Wen-nufer,
son of Pedy-hor..." 13cm
(5in), *NY 8 Feb,*
$26,400 (£23,784)

10
**A bronze figure of the
Horus falcon,** 22nd/26th
Dynasty, 946-525 BC,
dark green, brown and
black patina, 25cm (9¾in)
high, *NY 21 Nov,*
$30,800 (£21,538)

11
A wood figure of a man,
6th Dynasty, 2290-2155
BC, figure 30cm (11½in),
NY 8 Feb,
$3,850 (£3,468)

12
A wood figure of Isis,
Ptolemaic period, 305-30
BC, wearing a red skirt
and with black details,
34cm (13½in), *NY 9 Feb,*
$3,300 (£2,973)

13
**An Egyptian cartonnage
mummy mask,** New King-
dom, *c.*1300-1200 BC,
polychrome painted,
49cm (19¼in), *L 20 May,*
£1,320 ($1,782)

1 2 3 4 5

6 7

8

9 10

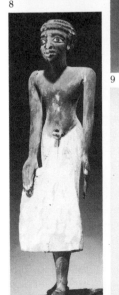

11 12 13

1
A bronze figure of Hermes-Thoth, *c.* 1st century AD, after a Polykleitan work of the 5th century BC, missing separately carved left arm and cloak, 12.5cm (5in), *NY 22 Nov,* $1,430 (£1,000)

2
A Greek bronze helmet, Magna Graecia, 6th century, BC, of Corinthian type, 30cm (12in), *NY 21 Nov,* $18,700 (£13,077)

3
A Roman bronze protome spout, 2nd century AD, in the form of a Dionysiac feline head, 10cm (4in) high, *NY 8 Feb,* $1,980 (£1,784)

4
A Roman bronze figure of a goat, *c.* 3rd century AD, 12cm (4¾in), *L 17 July,* £7,150 ($10,010)

5
A Greek bronze figure of a prancing horse, 5th century BC, 8cm (3in), *L 17 July,* £1,430 ($2,002)

6
A Roman bronze figure of Aphrodite, *c.* 1st century BC/1st century AD, 21.5cm (8½in), *L 17 July,* £8,250 ($11,550)

7
A bronze figure of the Apis bull, Greco-Egyptian *c.* 1st century AD, 9.5cm (3¾in) high, *NY 21 Nov,* $4,675 (£3,269)

8
A Roman bronze recumbent kid, *c.* 2nd century AD, 9cm (3½in) long, *NY 8 Feb,* $2,860 (£2,577)

9
A bronze figure of a divinity, *c.* 1st/2nd century AD, 11.5cm (4½in) high, *NY 21 Nov,* $4,950 (£3,462)

10
A Roman bronze figure of a Lar, 2nd century AD, eyes once inlaid, 10cm (4in), *NY 21 Nov,* $1,980 (£1,385)

11
An Etruscan bronze balsamarium, *c.* 3rd century BC, in the form of a head of a goddess, 11cm (4¼in), *L 17 July,* £2,420 ($3,388)

12
A Roman bronze figure of Jupiter, *c.* early 2nd century AD, after a work of the 4th century BC, perhaps by Bryaxis, scepter missing, his left hand once grasping a thunderbolt, some corrosion and encrustation, 12cm (4¾in), *NY 8 Feb,* $12,650 (£11,396)

13
An Etruscan bronze mirror, *c.* 4th/3rd century BC, engraved with four female and one male figure, 28.5cm (11¼in), *L 9 Dec,* £1,320 ($1,848)

14
A large Roman bronze handle, *c.* 3rd century AD, the foot in the form of the bust of Herakles, 34.5cm (13½in), *L 9 Dec,* £1,980 ($2,772)

1

2

3

4

5

6

7

8

9

10

11

12

13

14

1
A Sicilian terracotta female
figure, early 5th century
BC, 24cm (9½in), *L 9 Dec,*
£1,980 ($2,772)

2
An Etruscan terracotta
head of a young woman,
4th century BC, 29cm
(11½in), *L 18 July*
£605 ($847)

3
An Etruscan polychrome-
painted terracotta antefix,
second half 6th
century BC, 18.5cm
(7¼in), *L 17 July,*
£3,850 ($5,390)

4
A large Etruscan
polychrome-painted
terracotta antefix, second
half 6th century BC,
23cm (9in), *L 20 May,*
£2,200 ($2,970)

5
An Etruscan pottery ribbed
stamnos, central Italy,
*c.*700-675 BC, 44.5cm
(17½in), *L 20 May,*
£1,155 ($1,559)

6
A Sicilian terracotta figure
of Artemis, late 3rd cen-
tury BC, carrying a torch
and with a doe at her feet,
23cm (9in), *L 20 May,*
£770 ($1,039)

7
An Etruscan terracotta
antefix, 6th century BC,
in the form of a male
mask, *L 20 May,*
£1,430 ($1,930)

8
An Italo-Corinthian terracotta balsamarium, *c.*600-
575 BC, in the form of a
couchant ram, 10cm (4in)
long, *NY 21 Nov,*
$550 (£385)

9
A Geometric Greek pottery
jar, 8th century BC,
decorated in dark-brown
slip, 37.5cm (14¾in),
L 20 May,
£1,760 ($2,376)

10
A Cypriot pottery amphora,
*c.*700-650 BC, painted in
brown over a buff slip,
57cm (22½in), *NY 22 Nov,*
$1,870 (£1,308)

11
A South Italian Greek
bronze trefoil oinochoe,
5th century BC, 26cm
(10¼in), *L 17 July,*
£528 ($739)

12
A bronze piriform flagon,
3rd/1st century BC,
42cm (16½in), *L 9 Dec,*
£1,100 ($1,540)

13
A late Hellenistic or early
Roman silver bowl, *c.*
1st century BC/1st cen-
tury AD, 11cm (4¼in)
diam., *L 9 Dec,*
£990 ($1,386)

14
An Etruscan terracotta
mask, *c.* 4th/3rd cen-
tury BC, from an antefix
in the form of the head
of a satyr, 20cm (8in),
L 9 Dec,
£1,100 ($1,540)

1

2

3

4

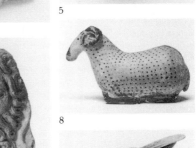
5

6

7

8

9

10

11

12

13

14

1
A Roman marble relief fragment, *c.* 2nd century AD, carved with Hermes holding the kerykeion and leading two horses, 49.5cm (19½in), *NY 21 Nov,* $12,650 (£8,846)

2
A Roman marble sarcophagus fragment, Antonine, *c.*160-180 AD, carved with Orestes weeping over the sacrifice of Iphigenia, 49.5cm (19½in), *NY 8 Feb,* $9,075 (£8,176)

3
A Roman marble draped figure of Athena, *c.* 2nd century AD, 73.5cm (29in), *L 9 Dec,* £7,700 ($10,780)

4
A Roman marble sarcophagus fragment, 2nd century AD, 28cm (11in), *NY 8 Feb,* $1,540 (£1,387)

5
A Roman marble torso of a young man, *c.* 1st-2nd century AD, holding a bird in his left hand, 58.5cm (23in), *L 9 Dec,* £7,700 ($10,780)

6
A Roman marble cinerary urn, *c.* 2nd century AD, 21 x 38cm (8¼ x 15in), *L 18 July,* £1,430 ($2,002)

7
A Roman marble headless male cuirassed torso, 2nd century AD, an architectural fragment probably part of a pilaster, *L 9 Dec,* £6,050 ($8,470)

8
A Roman marble cinerary urn, first half 3rd century AD, 23cm (9in), *L 9 Dec,* £1,210 ($1,694)

9
A Roman marble Hecateion, Eastern Mediterranean, *c.* 3rd century AD, a solar disk headdress surmounting the triple-bodied goddess, 36cm (14¼in), *L 17 July,* £1,980 ($2,772)

10
The front from a Roman marble pilaster-capital, second quarter 2nd century, AD, *L 9 Dec,* £3,300 ($4,620)

11
A Roman marble pilaster-capital, second quarter 2nd century AD, 51 x 53.5cm (20 x 21in), *L 9 Dec,* £4,180 ($5,852)

1
An Hellenistic marble head of a prince, Alexandrian, late 4th/3rd century BC, perhaps a portrait of Ptolemy II Philadelphos, 14cm (5½in) high, *NY 21 Nov*, $7,979 (£5,577)

2
A marble head of the Apollino, *c.* 1st century BC/1st century AD, 15cm (6in), *NY 22 Nov*, $2,475 (£1,731)

3
An Hellenistic marble head of a maenad, 2nd/1st century BC, 19cm (7½in), *NY 21 Nov*, $16,500 (£11,538)

4
A fragmentary Roman marble head of a young woman, *c.* 3rd century AD, 15cm (6in), *L 9 Dec*, £1,430 ($2,002)

5
A Roman marble head of a woman, *c.* 1st century AD, 37cm (14½in), *L 9 Dec*, £2,640 ($3,696)

6
A Roman marble head of a young woman, *c.* 2nd century AD, 33cm (13in), *L 9 Dec*, £2,860 ($4,004)

7
A Roman marble head of a maenad, *c.* 2nd century AD, 30cm (11¾in), *L 17 July*, £3,520 ($4,928)

8
A fragmentary Roman marble head of a satyr, *c.* 2nd century AD, 14.5cm (5¾in), *L 17 July*, £1,540 ($2,156)

9
A Roman marble head of a young woman, *c.* 2nd century AD, 34.5cm (13½in), *L 9 Dec*, £7,700 ($10,780)

10
A Roman marble head, *c.* 1st century AD, 33cm (13in), *L 17 July* £3,740 ($5,236)

11
A Roman marble head of Eros, *c.* 1st century AD, 18cm (7in), *L 20 May*, £2,090 ($2,821)

12
A marble head of a Bacchante, 2nd century AD, after a work of the 4th century BC, unfinished, 19.5cm (7¾in), *NY 8 Feb*, $2,750 (£2,477)

13
A Roman marble portrait head of a man, late Republican, 1st century BC, 30.5cm (12in) high, *NY 21 Nov*, $6,600 (£4,615)

14
A Roman marble portrait head of a man, Augustan, *c.*25-15 BC, 24.5cm (9¾in), *NY 8 Feb*, $12,650 (£11,396)

1

2

3

4

5

6

7

8

9

10

11

12

13

14

1
An Apulian red-figure
Kylix, 4th century BC,
40.5cm (16in) diam.,
L 18 July,
£1,210 ($1,694)

2
An Attic red-figure Kylix,
5th century BC, the
interior depicting a
figure of Apollo, 29cm
(11½in), *L 20 May,*
£880 ($1,188)

3
A pair of South Italian
Greek pottery column
Kraters, 4th century BC,
by the Patera Painter,
47.5cm (18¾in), *L 9 Dec,*
£7,700 ($10,780)

4
An Attic red-figure bell-
Krater, by the Retorted
Painter, *c.*380-360 BC,
40.5cm (16in), *L 20 May,*
£2,420 ($3,267)

5
An Apulian teano-ware
Kalathos, *c.* early 3rd
century BC, decorated in
cream slip over the
brownish-black glaze,
25cm (10in) diam.,
NY 8 Feb,
$825 (£743)

6
An Attic black figure 'Eye'
cup, type A, end of 6th
century BC, decoration
with added red and white
details, 30.5cm (12in)
diam., *L 9 Dec,*
£1,210 ($1,694)

7
An Attic black-glaze
Lekanis, second half 5th
century BC, cover 19.5cm
(7¾in) diam., *NY 22 Nov,*
$1,760 (£1,231)

8
Two Attic Sesille
Kantharoi, Saint-Valentin
class, *c.* late 5th
century BC, both painted
in added black and white,
12cm (4¾in) high,
NY 22 Nov,
$1,760 (£1,231)

9
A South Italian Greek
pottery **Rhyton**, 4th
century BC, in the form
of the head of a ram,
yellow and white painted
details, 20.5cm (8in),
L 18 July,
£2,860 ($4,004)

10
An Euboean black-figure
basin-shaped **vase**, late 6th
century BC, 12cm (9¾in)
diam., *L 17 July,*
£550 ($770)

11
A pair of South Italian
Greek pottery **Oinochoai**,
3rd century BC, 38cm
(15in), *L 20 May,*
£1,760 ($2,376)

12
An Attic pottery trefoil
Oinochoe, *c.*480-470 BC,
19.5cm (7¾in), *L 9 Dec,*
£1,430 ($2,002)

13
An Attic black-figure
Kyathos, *c.* late 6th
century BC, the exterior
painted with a Dionysiac
revel, details in purple
and white, 10.5cm (4in)
diam., *NY 8 Feb,*
$3,575 (£3,221)

1
An Attic black-figure trefoil oinochoe, 6th century BC, the decoration enriched with white and red paint, 26.5cm (10½in), *L 9 Dec*, £1,870 ($2,618)

2
A Paestan pottery amphora, 4th century BC, 45.5cm (18in), *L 9 Dec*, £1,320 ($1,848)

3
An Attic white-ground neck amphora, early 5th century BC, painted on each side with Apollo, *NY 9 Feb*, $1,540 (£1,387)

4
A South Italian Greek pottery pelike, 4th century BC, 24cm (9½in), *L 20 May*, £1,045 ($1,410)

5
An Attic black-figure pelike, *c.* late 6th/ early 5th century BC, attributed to the Theseus Painter, painted on both sides with a man playing the double-flute for a departing warrior, 33.5cm (13¼in), *NY 8 Feb*, $12,100 (£10,901)

6
An Attic black-figure amphora, 6th century BC, decorated in white and purple slip, 39cm (15¼in), *L 20 May*, £1,760 ($2,376)

7
An Attic black-figure-horse-head amphora, 6th century BC, *L 9 Dec*, £7,150 ($10,010)

8
An Attic red-figure pelike, *c.*450 BC, 31cm (12¼in), *NY 21 Nov*, $4,070 (£2,846)

9
An Attic black-figure amphora, 6th century BC, 24cm (9½in), *L 18 July*, £2,970 ($4,158)

10
A 'Gnathia Ware' pottery volute krater, last quarter 4th century BC, decorated in white and yellow, 84cm (33in), *L 9 Dec*, £4,400 ($6,160)

11
An Attic black-figure neck amphora, *c.*510-500 BC, with red and white details, 41.5cm (16¼in), *L 17 July*, £8,800 ($12,320)

12
An Hellenistic black-glazed pottery trefoil Oinochoe, *c.* 3rd century BC, 35cm (13¾in), *L 20 May*, £1,155 ($1,559)

1

2

4

5

6

7

8

3

9

10

11

12

1
**An Hellenistic terracotta
figure of a young woman,**
c. late 4th century BC,
22cm (8¾in), *L 20 May,*
£330 ($445)

2
**An Hellenistic terracotta
figure of Eros,** *c.* 3rd
century BC, seated on a
goose, 13cm (5in), *L 9 Dec,*
£770 ($1,078)

3
**An Hellenistic terracotta
figure of a young woman,**
c. 3rd/2nd century
BC, 22cm (8¾in), *L 9 Dec,*
£880 ($1,232)

4
**An Hellenistic terracotta
figure of a young woman,**
c. 3rd/2nd century
BC, with traces of poly-
chrome decoration, 47cm
(18½in), *L 17 July,*
£3,080 ($4,312)

5
**An Hellenistic terracotta
figure of a goddess,** Asia
Minor, *c.* 2nd century
BC, perhaps Demeter,
remains of pigment and
gilding, *NY 8 Feb,*
$17,050 (£15,360)

6
**A Greek terracotta figure
of a goddess,** *c.*470-460 BC,
23cm (9in), *NY 8 Feb,*
$1,650 (£1,486)

7
**A Greek terracotta
aryballos,** 6th/4th century
BC, in the form of an alabastron in a sandal, 10cm
(4in) long, *NY 8 Feb,*
$440 (£396)

8
**An Hellenistic terracotta
theatre mask,** Sicily,
4th/3rd century BC,
14cm (5½in), *NY 22 Nov,*
$1,320 (£923)

9
**An Hellenistic terracotta
head of a woman,** Italy or
Asia Minor, 3rd/2nd
century BC, 12cm (4¾in),
NY 22 Nov,
$1,320 (£923)

Pre-Columbian Art

See also ● Colour illustrations *p* 562

1
A Costa Rican jade pendant, Guanacaste/Nicoya area, *c.*300-700 AD, 12cm (4¾in) high, *NY 26 Nov*, $1,650 (£1,130)

2
A Quimbaya seated figure, Cauca Region, *c.*500-1000 AD, faint remains of black facial decoration, 30.5cm (12in), *NY 26 Nov* $935 (£640)

3
A Costa Rican male figure, Atlantic Watershed region, *c.*700-1000 AD, in volcanic stone, 31.5cm (12½in), *NY 31 May*, $2,750 (£2,148)

4
A pair of Tairona gold ear ornaments, *c.*1000-1500 AD, 6cm (2¼in), *NY 26 Nov*, $2,310 (£1,582)

5
A Tairona gold nose ornament, Santa Marta region *c.*1000-1500 AD, ornamented with bands of braiding, 7cm (2¾in), *NY 31 May*, $3,520 (£2,750)

6
A Costa Rican stone metate, 800-1200 AD, 47.5cm (18¾in), *NY 26 Nov*, $550 (£376)

7
A Costa Rican stone metate, Las Mercedes region, 800-1500 AD, 34cm (13½in), *NY 31 May*, $440 (£344)

8
A Costa Rican male figure, Atlantic Watershed region, 700-1000 AD, in light brown volcanic stone, 24.5cm (9¾in), *NY 26 Nov*, $660 (£452)

9
A Guangala female figural whistle, Bahia phase, 500 BC-500 AD, painted in ochre, red and black, 34cm (13½in), *NY 26 Nov*, $880 (£602)

10
A Manabi head fragment, Jama Coaque, 500 BC-500 AD, 23cm (9in), *NY 31 May*, $1,100 (£859)

11
A large Costa Rican warrior, Atlantic Watershed region, *c.*700-1000 AD, 73cm (28¾in), *NY 31 May*, $4,125 (£3,222)

12
An Ecuadorian vessel, possibly Chorrera, *c.*1200-500 BC, covered overall in a brown mottled slip, 16.5cm (6½in), *NY 31 May*, $1,210 (£945)

13
A Manabi standing figure, Jama Coaque, *c.*500 BC-500 AD, wearing elaborate jewellery and helmet with curved fish finials, details in bright green pigment, 32cm (12½in), *NY 26 Nov*, $1,760 (£1,205)

1

2

3

4

5

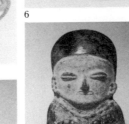
6

7

8

9

10

11

12

13

1
A Mayan blackware bowl,
Late Classic, c.550-950
AD, carved with three
rhomboids, each en-
closing a centipede-
bodied warrior, 15cm
(6in), *NY 31 May,*
$990 (£773)

2
**A Proto-Mayan grayware
bowl,** possible Izapan,
Late Preclassic, c.300-100
BC, carved with an
Olmecoid 'Jaguar paw'
on each side, 17.5cm
(6¾in), *NY 31 May,*
$2,090 (£1,633)

3
**A Mayan polychrome
vessel,** Soyapango, El
Salvador, Late Classic,
c.550-950 AD, painted
with a frieze including a
monster-headed priest
holding ritual imple-
ments, 21.5cm (8½in),
NY 26 Nov,
$1,650 (£1,130)

4
**A Mayan carved tripod
vase,** Northern Peten
region, Early Classic,
c.250-550 AD, in
Teotihuacan style, 15cm
(6in), *NY 26 Nov,*
$8,800 (£6,027)

5
**A Mayan painted tripod
plate,** Late Classic,
55)-950 AD., painted in
bl ick and shades of
orange. 34cm (13¼in),
NY 31 May,
$660 (£516)

6
A Mayan head Hacha,
Pacific Slope region, Late
Classic, c.550-950 AD,
possibly a depiction of a
death deity, in greyish-
black stone, 19cm (7¼in),
NY 31 May,
$2,090 (£1,633)

7
A Mayan warrior, Jaina,
Late Classic, c.350-950
AD, with remains of
bright Maya blue, ochre
and red pigment along
the face, 24cm (9½in),
NY 26 Nov,
$7,425 (£5,085)

8
A Mayan seated lord, Jaina,
Late Classic, c.550-950
AD, with his face
elaborately tattooed,
with remains of white and
blue pigment, 15.5cm
(6in), *NY 26 Nov,*
$2,310 (£1,582)

9
A Colima dog, Protoclassic,
c.100 BC-250 AD, and
painted overall in
reddish-brown, 27.5cm
(10¾in), *NY 31 May,*
$1,430 (£1,117)

10
A Colima water carrier,
Protoclassic, c.100 BC-
250 AD, painted overall
in reddish-brown, 46cm
(18¼in), *NY 31 May,*
$4,950 (£3,867)

11
A Colima water carrier,
Protoclassic, 100 BC-
250 AD, painted overall
in red, 19.5cm (7¾in),
NY 31 May,
$770 (£602)

12
**A pair of Colima Shaman
figures,** Protoclassic, c.100
BC-250 AD, painted
overall in reddish brown,
29 and 30.5cm (11¼ and
12in), *NY 31 May,*
$1,320 (£1,031)

13
A Colima standing dog,
Protoclassic, c.100 BC-
250 AD, painted overall
in light brown, 44.5cm
(17½in), *NY 31 May,*
$2,640 (£2,063)

14
A Colima vessel, Protoclassic, 100 BC-250 AD,
33.5cm (13¼in),
NY 26 Nov,
$990 (£678)

1
A Colima warrior, Proto-classic, 100 BC-250 AD, painted overall in reddish-brown with areas of buff, 30cm (11¾in), *NY 31 May,* $1,430 (£1,117)

2
A Mixtec tripod bowl, Postclassic, 1200-1400 AD, the geometric motifs repeated on the interior 26cm (10¼in), *NY 31 May,* $660 (£516)

3
A Jalisco crouching dwarf, Protoclassic, c.100 BC-250 AD, painted in reddish-brown and buff with details in black, 17cm (6¾in), *NY 31 May,* $660 (£516)

4
A Veracruz dignitary, Classic c.250-550 AD, mouth and eyes ritually painted in black bitumen, 61cm (24in), *NY 31 May,* $4,125 (£3,223)

5
A Colima effigy urn, Postclassic, 900-1400 AD, 31.5cm (12½in), *NY 26 Nov,* $715 (£489)

6
A Veracruz priest, Late Classic, c.550-950 AD, 50cm (19½in), *NY 26 Nov,* $3,850 (£2,636)

7
A Nopiloa mould-made female figure, Late Classic, c.550-950 AD, 22.5cm (9in), *NY 31 May,* $2,970 (£2,320)

8
A Veracruz standing warrior, Late Classic, c.550-950 AD, the face and torso ritually covered in black bitumen, 48cm (19in), *NY 31 May,* $3,300 (£2,578)

9
A Veracruz basalt head hacha, Late Classic, c.550-950 AD, 19cm (7½in), *NY 31 May,* $1,100 (£859)

10
A Veracruz warrior, Classic, c.250-550 AD, 59.5cm (23½in), *NY 31 May,* $3,850 (£3,008)

11
A Veracruz dancer, possibly Nopiloa, Late Classic, c.550-950 AD, covered overall in a pale ochre slip, 34cm (13¼in), *NY 26 Nov,* $2,640 (£1,808)

12
A Diquis gold fishhook, c.700-1500 AD, 4.5cm (1¾in), *NY 26 Nov,* $990 (£678)

1
A Chancay wood mask, c.1300-1500 AD, 28cm (11in), *NY 26 Nov*, $1,540 (£1,054)

2
A Chancay figure, c.1100-1400 AD, painted overall in cream, 60cm (23¾in), *NY 26 Nov*, $1,430 (£979)

3
A Middle Chimu gilt copper Tumi, c.1000-1250 AD, the double-sided finial surmounted by addorsed hummingbirds, 23.5cm (9¼in), *NY 26 Nov*, $990 (£678)

4
A Middle Chimu gold beaker, c.1000-1250 AD, four ridged bivalves around the rim, 15cm (5¾in), *NY 31 May*, $5,500 (£4,297)

5
An early Mochica vessel, c. 400-100 BC, painted overall in plum with decoration in cream, 21 cm (8¼in), *NY 31 May*, $1,540 (£1,203)

6
An Early/Middle Mochica blackware head vessel, c.100-500 AD, the open mouth and eyes inlaid with white shell 19.5cm (7¾in), *NY 26 Nov*, $2,200 (£1,506)

7
A Middle Mochica figural vessel, 100-500 AD, painted overall in cream and reddish-brown, 23.5cm (9¼in), *NY 31 May*, $247 (£193)

8
A Middle Mochica portrait head, c.200-500 AD, painted in cream, tan and reddish brown, 30.5cm (12in), *NY 31 May*, $2,750 (£2,148)

9
A Middle Mochica portrait head, 100-500 AD, wearing a close-fitting turban with chin strap, 15cm (6in), *NY 26 Nov*, $440 (£301)

10
A late Mochica copper effigy vessel, c.400-700 AD, the carinated neck filled as a rattle, wearing a removable headband, 13.5cm (5¼in), *NY 26 Nov*, $1,870 (£1,280)

11
A Middle Mochica captive vessel, c.100-500 AD, with wrists bound at the back, with a long rope around his neck, 29cm (11in), *NY 26 Nov*, $1,100 (£753)

12
A Middle Mochica portrait head, 100-500 AD, painted in buff and reddish-brown, 20cm (7¾in), *NY 31 May*, $550 (£430)

13
A Nazca polychrome jar, 200-500 AD, painted in black, white and red on a beige ground, 17cm (6¾in), *NY 31 May*, $660 (£516)

14
A Mochica jaguar head vessel, c.200-500 AD, polychrome decoration, 15cm (6in), *L 27 Mar*, £242 ($307)

15
An Early Nazca polychrome vessel, 100-500 AD, painted in red, grey, black and tan with a large demon figure wearing a serpent belt, 20cm (8in), *NY 26 Nov*, $550 (£376)

16
A Nazca figural vessel, 200-500 AD, 17cm (6¾in), *NY 31 May*, $385 (£301)

1

2

3

4

5

6

7

8

9

10

11

12

13

14

15

16

American Indian Art

See also ● Colour illustrations p 561

1
A transitional Navajo wedge weave blanket, 184 x 143.5cm (72½ x 56½in), *NY 21 June*, **$4,675 (£3,652)**

2
A Navajo regional rug, Sunrise, Klagetoh, 1955, 294.5 x 180cm (116 x 71in), *NY 22 June*, **$2,750 (£2,148)**

3
A late classic Navajo serape, with red ground overlaid in white, mustard and indigo blue and green, 173 x 130cm (68 x 51in), *NY 16 Nov*, **$4,400 (£3,098)**

4
A Navajo Germantown blanket, woven on a bright red ground in black and white, 209.5 x 133cm (82½ x 52½in), *NY 21 June*, **$1,980 (£1,547)**

5
A classic Navajo chief's blanket, woven with a Third Phase pattern in shaded cochineal red and deep indigo blue, 168.5 x 133cm (66½ x 52½in), *NY 21 June*, **$14,300 (£11,172)**

6
A Navajo fringed Germantown blanket, with 'eyedazzler' pattern in white, black, yellow, pale blue and green, red, maroon and pink, 140 x 93cm (55 x 36½in), *NY 16 Nov*, **$2,200 (£1,549)**

7
A transitional Navajo chief's blanket, woven in a Third Phase pattern in red, green, ivory, brown and indigo blue, 180.5 x 150.5cm (71 x 59¼in), *NY 16 Nov*, **$5,775 (£4,066)**

8
A classic Navajo child's blanket, 132 x 84cm (52 x 33in), *NY 16 Nov*, **$14,300 (£10,070)**

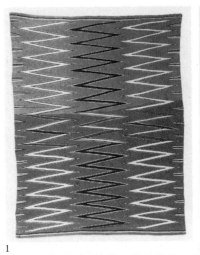

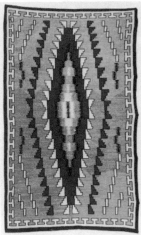

1   2   3

4   5

6   7   8

1
A classic Saltillo serape, slit at the centre, 236 x 163cm (93¼ x 64½in), *NY 21 June,* $7,975 (£6,230)

2
A classic Saltillo serape, in black and shades of brown and rust on a mustard ground, 248 x 132cm (98 x 52in), *NY 16 Nov,* $6,875 (£4,841)

3
A classic Saltillo serape, woven in two vertical panels, 232 x 132cm (91½ x 52in), *NY 21 June,* $9,625 (£7,520)

4
An Eastern Plains red catlinite pipe, dated 1893, 71.5cm (28in), *NY 16 Nov,* $4,950 (£3,485)

5
An Eastern Plains red catlinite pipe, 54cm (21¼in), NY 21 June, $880 (£688)

6
A Micmac birchbark box, with wood lining, decorated overall with dyed porcupine quills, 22cm (8¾in), *NY 22 June,* $550 (£430)

7
An Eastern Woodlands birchbark fish creel, 40cm (15¾in), *NY 22 June,* $550 (£430)

8
A Haida model canoe, painted in black and red, with figures of a native, an oriental and a white man, 57cm (22½in), *NY 16 Nov,* $2,750 (£1,936)

9
A Hopi Hemis Kachina dance mask, 59.5cm (23¼in), *NY 21 June,* $7,975 (£6,230)

10
A Hopi Kachina doll, Sai-astasana, the Zuni Rain Priest of the North, 37.5cm (14¾in), *NY 21 June,* $2,200 (£1,719)

11
A Hopi Kachina doll, Nuvak-china, 40cm (14½in), *NY 21 June,* $1,210 (£945)

12
A Hopi Kachina doll, Malo, 34.5cm (13¾in), *NY 21 June,* $1,210 (£945)

13
A Hopi Hemis Kachina doll, 41cm (16in), *NY 21 June,* $1,650 (£1,289)

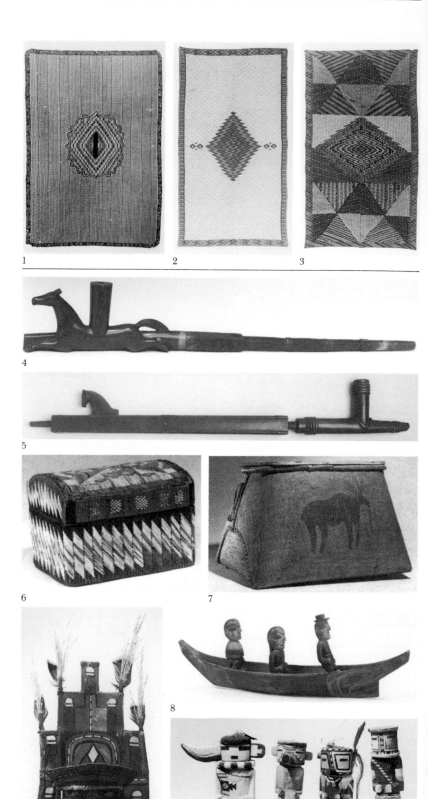

1
A Haida portrait mask, naturalistically carved, with Europeanised coiffure, red and black tattoos and traces of original pigment, 23.5cm (9¼in), *NY 16 Nov*, $8,800 (£6,197)

2
A Seneca Shaman's rattle, carved in the form of a human hand, the sunken nail areas painted red, 30cm (11¾in), *NY 21 June*, $2,750 (£2,148)

3
A Great Lakes beaded cloth bandoleer, trimmed with glass beads and blue wool tassels, 97.5cm (38½in), *NY 21 June*, $1,430 (£1,117)

4
A Northwest Coast twined spruce root hat, probably Haida, 44cm (17¼in) diam, *NY 16 Nov*, $8,800 (£6,197)

5
A Great Lakes beaded cloth bandoleer, stitched in white, black, green and blue glass beads on a red ground, 104cm (41in), *NY 16 Nov*, $2,750 (£1,936)

6
A Northern Plains club, the head formed by two pointed horns joined by a beaded hide strip, the handle with hair, 62cm (24½in), *L 2 Dec*, £605 ($895)

7
A Plains Indian club, Iwatajinga, 78cm (30¾in), *L 2 Dec*, £605 ($895)

8
A pair of Cheyenne beaded hide girl's boot moccasins, with mustard dye, each beaded round the cuff and foot, 52cm (20½in), *NY 21 June*, $3,850 (£3,008)

9
A Plains painted buffalo robe, decorated in black and red pigment, 2641cm (8ft 8in), *NY 16 Nov*, $4,675 (£3,292)

10
A Northern Plains beaded cloth shirt, 75.5cm (29¾in), *NY 21 June*, $4,950 (£3,867)

11
A pair of Northern Plains beaded hide cuffs, 17.5cm (7in), *NY 22 June*, $385 (£301)

12
A Sioux man's dance breastplate, composed of two long columns of tubular bone 'hair-pipes', 47cm (18½in), *NY 21 June*, $2,310 (£1,805)

1
A Plains beaded hide man's vest, lined with cotton, 47cm (18½in), *NY 16 Nov,* $1,100 (£774)

2
A pair of Sioux beaded hide moccasins, 27.9cm (11in), *NY 21 June,* $605 (£473)

3
A pair of Eastern Woodlands beaded hide child's moccasins, 12.5cm (4¾in), *NY 21 June,* $1,320 (£1,031)

4
A Tlingit ceremonial dance blanket, Chilkat, finger woven in mountain goat's wool and plaited cedar bark, 162.5cm (64in), *NY 21 June,* $9,350 (£7,305)

5
A Great Lakes beaded hide pad saddle, decorated with white beaded panels with coloured foliate motifs, 49.5cm (19½in), *NY 16 Nov,* $2,530 (£1,781)

6
A Navajo silver and turquoise squash blossom necklace, 36.5cm (14¼in), *NY 21 June,* $1,210 (£945)

7
A Pueblo shell and stone necklace, composed of clam shell beads alternating with shell and turquoise stone pendants, 39.5cm (15½in), *NY 21 June,* $1,210 (£945)

8
A Navajo silver tobacco canteen, 18cm (7in) high, *NY 16 Nov,* $880 (£619)

9
Six Navajo silver and turquoise bracelets, 6 to 6.5cm (2¼ to 2½in) wide, *NY 16 Nov,* $475 (£339)

10
Seven Southwest silver bracelets, comprising six expanding turquoise-set bands and an openwork sandcast bracelet, *NY 16 Nov,* $475 (£339)

11
An Eskimo ceremonial mask, St Michael's area, with black, red and white pigment, remains of feather decoration, 29cm (11½in) high, *NY 16 Nov,* $4,125 (£2,904)

12
An Eskimo coiled whale baleen basket, carved with a polar bear watching over a seal pup, 9.5cm (3¾in), *NY 16 Nov,* $2,530 (£1,781)

13
An Eskimo ivory tusk, Nunivak Island, details in baleen and black and red pigment, 85cm (33½in), *NY 16 Nov,* $6,600 (£4,647)

14
An Eskimo model kyak, the light wood frame covered with stretched sealskin, with a number of implements including a sealskin float, two wood and bone harpoons and a wood and bone paddle, 75cm (29½in), *L 27 Mar,* £242 ($307)

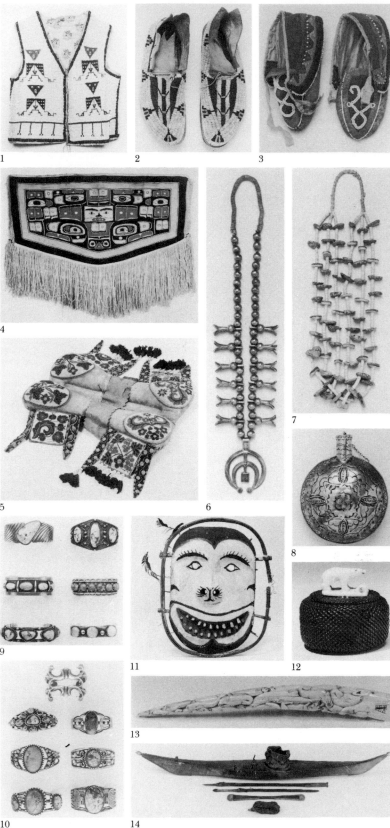

1
A Four Mile polychrome geometric bowl, *c.*1350-1400 AD, 30cm (11¾in), *NY 21 June*, $2,200 (£1,719)

2
A Tularosa black-on-white Olla, *c.*1100-1250 AD, 29cm (11½in), *NY 21 June*, $3,575 (£2,793)

3
A classic Chaco Canyon black-on-white mug, *c.*1100 AD, 16cm (6¼in), *NY 21 June*, $3,300 (£2,578)

4
A Mimbres black-on-white geometric bowl, *c.*950-1150 AD, the tapering end probably used as a spout, 38cm (15in), *NY 21 June*, $3,300 (£2,578)

5
An Acoma polychrome jar, 24cm (10½in), *NY 21 June*, $990 (£773)

6
A Hopi polychrome jar, painted on the shoulder against a deep cream slip in black and red, 27.5cm (11in), *NY 21 June*, $880 (£688)

7
A Hopi seed jar, painted over an orange slip in black and red with a stylised eagle pattern, signed 'Fannie Nampeyo', 33.5cm (13¼in) diam, *NY 16 Nov*, $2,640 (£1,859)

8
A Hopi seed jar, painted over an orange slip in black and orange, signed 'Fannie Nampeyo', 21.5cm (8½in), *NY 16 Nov*, $1,210 (£852)

9
A Mohave effigy jar, in the form of a female figure, painted in red on a buff ground, 24cm (9½in) high, *NY 16 Nov*, $1,100 (£774)

10
A San Ildefonso blackware vase, inscribed on the base, 'Blue Corn San Ildefonso Pueblo', 22.5cm (8¾in), *NY 21 June*, $1,210 (£945)

11
A Jeddito black-on-cream picture bowl, *c.*1100-1300 AD, 23cm (9in), *NY 21 June*, $2,750 (£2,148)

12
A San Ildefonso redware platter, inscribed on the base, 'Maria/Popovi', 35.5cm (14in), *NY 21 June*, $6,050 (£4,727)

13
A San Ildefonso blackware jar, inscribed Maria/Popovi, 17.2cm (6¾in) diam, *NY 21 June*, $1,210 (£945)

14
A Casas Grandes polychrome Olla, *c.*1350-1400 AD, 29.5cm (11¾in), *NY 21 June*, $2,640 (£2,063)

15
A Zia polychrome jar, painted over a pinkish cream slip in black and deep orange, 30.5cm (12in), *NY 21 June*, $2,090 (£1,632)

16
A Zuni polychrome jar, with thin solid walls and tall rounded sides, 34cm (13½in), *NY 21 June*, $3,410 (£2,664)

17
A Pueblo polychrome storage jar, Cochiti or San Ildefonso, painted over a burnished cream slip in black and red, 56cm (22in), *NY 21 June*, $14,300 (£11,172)

1

3

2

5

4

6

10

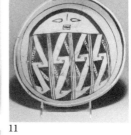

11

12

13

14

1
A Hupa twined poly-chrome fancy basket, woven in bear grass and maidenhair fern over hazelshoot warps, 15cm (6in), *NY 21 June,* $495 (£387)

2
A Pomo coiled gift basket, tightly woven on a single rod willow foundation in sedge and dyed bulrush root, with clam shell disks at the rim, traces of feathers, 13.5cm (5¼in), *NY 21 June,* $990 (£773)

3
A Yokuts coiled poly-chrome treasure basket, remains of feathers, 20.5cm (8in), *NY 21 June,* $1,760 (£1,375)

4
A Panamint coiled poly-chrome storage bowl, 45.5cm (18in), *NY 21 June,* $3,575 (£2,793)

5
A Panamint coiled bowl, woven on a willow ground in dyed bulrush root, 23cm (9in), *NY 21 June,* $1,540 (£1,203)

6
A Washoe coiled poly-chrome basket, *degikup,* tightly woven in willow, bracken fern root and redbud, 21.5cm (8½in), *NY 21 June,* $1,980 (£1,547)

7
An Apache coiled storage jar, woven in willow and devil's claw, 31.5cm (12¼in), *NY 21 June,* $990 (£773)

8
An Attu twined basket, tightly woven in rye grass, embroidered in red, maroon, bright green, pale blue and shades of pink silk thread, 10cm (4in), *NY 21 June,* $1,045 (£816)

9
A Western Apache coiled polychrome jar, woven in willow, devil's claw and reddish yucca root, 57cm (22½in), *NY 21 June,* $8,525 (£6,660)

10
A Western Apache coiled storage jar, with meander pattern woven in willow, black devil's claw and red yucca root, 61cm (24in) high, *NY 16 Nov,* $2,420 (£1,704)

11
Two Achomawi twined baskets, 23 and 36cm (9 and 14in) diam, *NY 16 Nov,* $450 (£321)

12
An Apache coiled bowl, woven with a spoked wheel and diamond pattern, 33.5cm (13in) diam, *NY 16 Nov,* $660 (£464)

13
A Tlingit twined spruce root basket, embroidered in green and brown dyed grass with totemic faces and geometric motifs, 28cm (11in) diam, *NY 16 Nov,* $990 (£697)

Tribal Art

1
**A Naga seated male
figure,** 49cm (19¼in),
L 26 June,
£198 ($267)

2
A male ancestor figure,
probably Naga, wearing
strands of red and
blue and white glass
beadwork, 36.5cm
(14½in), *NY 16 May,*
$495 (£392)

3
**A Nias wood male ancestor
figure,** wearing the
ceremonial gold coif-
fure, dark patina,
53.5cm (21in), *L 24 June,*
£7,700 ($10,318)

4
**A Trobriand Islands wood
stool,** with incised and
limed embellishments,
38cm (15in), *L 26 June,*
£264 ($356)

5
**A New Guinea wood
trophy head,** *chumbuli,*
conus shell incised
eyes, 21cm (8in),
L 27 Mar,
£495 ($629)

6
**An Indonesian wood
figure,** Tau-tau, prob-
ably Dyak, the arms
missing, traces of black
paint, 133cm (52½in),
L 26 June,
£1,980 ($2,673)

7
**A New Guinea over-
modelled skull,** the facial
contours recreated by
deep red clay, set with
cowrie shells, the back
of the head with
attached human hair,
20cm (8in), *L 26 June,*
£572 ($772)

8
**A Trobriand Islands
shield,** Massim area,
Milne Bay Province,
83cm (32¾in), *NY 15 Nov,*
$6,050 (£4,260)

9
A New Guinea shield,
with a rattan handle
attached behind, the
mid-section covered
with wickerwork fibre
panel, 81cm (32in),
NY 16 May,
$660 (£523)

10
**A Trobriand Islands wood
pig,** with deeply carved
and lime-filled deco-
rations, 40cm (15¾in),
L 2 Dec,
£550 ($814)

11
A New Guinea dance staff,
Maprik, carved with
male and female figure,
remains of red, black
and white clay pigment,
127cm (50in), *NY 15 Nov,*
$1,320 (£929)

12
A New Guinea stool, in
the form of a turtle,
89cm (35in) long,
NY 16 Nov,
$1,600 (£1,142)

Article ● African furniture *pp* 608-609
See also ● Colour illustrations *p* 563

1
A New Ireland memorial carving, *malanggan,* the figure painted with red, black and white details, holding a shaft and a pipe, 161cm (63½in), *NY 15 Nov,* $8,800 (£6,197)

2
A Solomon Islands ceremonial paddle, Buka Island or Buka Passage, one side of the blade with an incised *kokorra* head, red and black pigment, 137cm (54in), *L 2 Dec,* £715 ($1,058)

3
A Solomon Islands club, Malaita, plaited *coir* binding on the grip, reddish-brown patina, 67cm (26¼in), *NY 16 May,* $220 (£174)

4
A Solomon Islands wood bowl, a half dolphin figure at either end, decorated with mother-of-pearl inlays, 33.5cm (13¼in), *L 27 Mar,* £1,100 ($1,397)

5
A Solomon Islands wood cup or drum, both supporting figures with shell inset eyes, 33cm (13in), *L 27 Mar,* £1,760 ($2,235)

6
An Abelam mask, with matching beard and coiffure, traces of pigment, 43cm (17in), *L 26 June,* £418 ($564)

7
A Washkuk wood head, painted red, white and black, 126cm (49½in), *L 26 June,* £242 ($327)

8
A Sepik wood figure, wearing a fibre loin cloth, 238cm (94in), *L 26 June,* £825 ($1,114)

9
A Fijian Gunstock club, *cali,* old patina, 107cm (42in), *L 26 June,* £308 ($416)

10
A Murik Lakes wood mask, old dark patina, 35.5cm (14in), *L 27 Mar,* £3,520 ($4,470)

11
An Austral Islands paddle, the blade of leaf form, the handle with a ring of stylised figures, 99cm (39in), *L 26 June,* £198 ($267)

12
A Santa Cruz dance club, strong with fibres, 99cm (39in), *L 26 June,* £110 ($148)

13
A Fijian wood bowl, tanoa, for the Yaqona ceremony, old patina, 52.5cm (20¾in), *L 26 June,* £286 ($386)

14
A Tongan headrest, 47.5cm (18¾in), *L 2 Dec,* £550 ($814)

1
A Maori whalebone hand-club, *wahaika*, a stylised *tiki* figure on the haft, yellow patina, 36.5cm (14¼in), *NY 15 Nov,* $1,430 (£1,007)

2
A Maori wood handclub, *wahaika*, a finely carved *tiki* figure above the handle, deep brown patina, 40cm (15¾in), *L 26 June,* £1,870 ($2,525)

3
A Maori treasure box, *waka huia*, the handles carved as *tiki* figures, painted with brown varnish, 53.5cm (21in), *L 2 Dec,* £2,420 ($3,582)

4
A Maori housepost figure, *poutokoma Nawa*, the face with elaborate *moko* tattooing, 42.5cm (16¾in), *L 24 June,* £3,960 ($5,304)

5
A Maori greenstone pendant, *Hei tiki*, of typical form, 6.5cm (2¾in), *L 2 Dec,* £605 ($895)

6
An Easter Island wood pipe, the bowl carved as a human head, brown patina, 20cm (8in), *L 2 Dec,* £660 ($977)

7
A Maori ceremonial club (?), the head above the handle with *moko* tattooing and shell inset eyes, old dark patina, 137cm (54in), *L 2 Dec,* £1,210 ($1,791)

8
A Cook Islands chief's seat, *no'oanga*, carved from a single piece of *tamanu* wood, honey brown patina, 44cm (17½in) long, *NY 15 Nov,* $1,870 (£1,316)

9
An Easter Island wood figure, two cracks with old gum repairs, 44cm (17½in), *L 27 Mar,* £1,430 ($1,816)

10
A large Hawaiian Islands meat bowl, *'umeke ipu kai'* of highly polished *koa* wood, rich brown patina, crack to interior, 53.5cm (21in), *NY 16 May,* $2,860 (£2,269)

11
A Hawaiian Islands ivory wristlet, *kupe'e palaoa*, honey-yellow patina, *NY 15 Nov,* $935 (£658)

12
A Marquesas Islands ivory man's ear ornament, *ha'akai*, the spur with carved male *tiki* figure, 8.5cm (3¼in) long, *NY 15 Nov,* $1,760 (£1,239)

13
Two Marquesas Islands wood stilt steps, *vaeake*, with dark glossy patina, 41 and 35.5cm (16 and 14in), *L 27 Mar,* £4,180 ($5,309)

14
A South-East Australian wood shield, probably from the Murray River area, of densely grained wood, 85cm (33½in), *L 26 June,* £1,650 ($2,228)

1   2   3   4
5   6
7   8   9
10
11   12   13   14

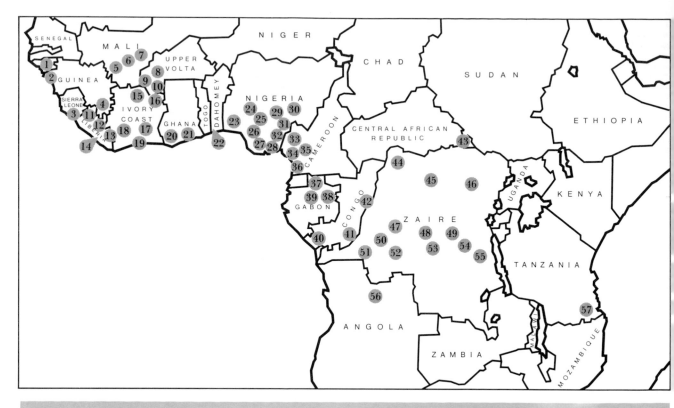

21 AKAN	48 BENA KANIOKA	32 EKOI	13 KRAN	11 MBETE	4 TOMA
20 ASHANTI	23 BENIN	37 FANG	49 KUBA	3 MENDE	40 VILI
43 AZANDE	1 BIJOGO	22 FON	33 KUYU	8 MOSSI	50 YAKA
2 BAGA	26 BINI	12 GREBO	39 KWELE	24 NGBAKA	18 YAURE
38 BAKOTA	9 BOBO	17 GURO	10 LOBI	24 NUPE	42 YOMBE
6 BAMANA	30 CHAMBA	54 HEMBA	53 LUBA	31 OYO	25 YORUBA
36 BAMILEKE	56 CHOKWE	28 IBIBIO	45 LULUWA	51 PENDE	55 ZANDE
35 BANGWA	14 DAN	27 IBO	57 MAKONDE	15 SENUFO	
19 BAULE	7 DOGON	29 IDOMA	5 MALINKE	52 SONGE	
41 BEMBE	34 DUALA	16 KOULANGO	46 MANGBETU	47 TEKE	

1
A Bambara wood mask,
fine dark patina, 42.5cm
(16¾in), *L 27 Mar,*
£770 ($978)

2
**A Bambara wood antelope
head-dress,** Tchi-wara,
of typical form, the tall
horns decorated with
flattened metal sheets,
77cm (30¼in), *L 26 June,*
£528 ($713)

3
**A Bambara antelope
head-dress,** Tchi-wara,
of typical form, 110.5cm
(43½in), *L 26 June,*
£264 ($356)

1   2   3

1
A Senufo equestrian group, Boundiali Village, *bandéguélé,* used in divination as a manifestation of the diviner's spirit, brown patina, 25.5cm (10in), *NY 15 Nov,* $1,980 (£1,394)

2
A Yaure wood mask, pierced coffee-bean eyes, holes for attachment at the back, fine black patina, 20.5cm (8in), *L 26 June,* £1,210 ($1,634)

3
A Yaure face mask, a metal plaque attached by two brass tacks to the forehead area, areas of encrustation, 39cm (15½in), *NY 16 May,* $2,750 (£2,182)

4
Three Dan chairs, 30.5 to 35.5cm (12 to 14in), *NY 16 Nov,* $850 (£607)

5
A Senufo male figure, 40cm (15¾in), *NY 16 Nov,* $1,200 (£857)

6
A Senufo heddle pulley, incised scarification markings on chin, cheeks and temples, rich black patina, a highly worn area at the back, 20cm (8in), *NY 16 May,* $605 (£480)

7
A Senufo chair, a bird's head projecting out at each side, a bird at the back (head broken away), brown patina, 66cm (26in), *NY 16 May,* $1,430 (£1,134)

8
A Guro wood mask, with human and antelope features, the ears painted black, 35cm (13¾in), *L 24 June,* £5,500 ($7,370)

9
A Guro Zamle mask, 35cm (13¾in), *L 26 June,* £440 ($594)

10
A Senufo helmet mask, two holes pierced for vision between the eyes and the nostrils, the whole covered in white kaolin, 63cm (24¾in), *L 27 Mar,* £495 ($629)

11
An Ashante stool, 63.5cm (25in) long, *NY 16 Nov,* $1,000 (£714)

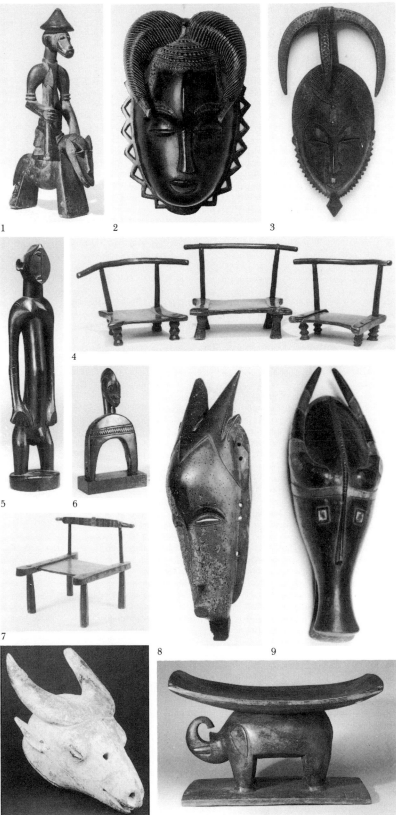

1
An Ashanti linguist's staff, *okyeame poma*, carved with a hen and rooster depicting the proverb (*ebe*), 'the hen knows when dawn will break but leaves it to the cock to make all the noise', sheathed overall in gold leaf, 181.5cm (71½in), *NY 16 May*, $1,430 (£1,134)

2
A Senufo washstand table, 62cm (24½in) long, *NY 16 Nov*, $550 (£392)

3
A Senufo washstand, solidly carved from a single piece of wood, aged brown patina, 67cm (26½in), *NY 16 May*, $1,760 (£1,396)

4
An Ashanti stool, with pedestal carved in the form of a powder keg, the platform decorated with a rifle and shot pouch belt in relief, 57.5cm (22½in), *NY 16 Nov*, $475 (£339)

5
An Ashanti stool, supported by a pair of opposed male figures, 68cm (27in) long, *NY 16 Nov*, $700 (£500)

6
An Ashanti stool, concave rectangular seat, shiny brown patina, 50.5cm (20in), *NY 16 May*, $770 (£611)

7
A Nafana Bedu masquerade mask, painted in black and white, 114cm (44¾in), *NY 16 Nov*, £750 ($535)

8
An Ashanti male figure, seated on an *asipim* chair, scarification marking on chest, cheeks and forehead, rich brown patination, light brown on chair, 36cm (14¼in), *NY 16 May*, $2,090 (£1,658)

9
An Ashanti stool, golden brown patina, 38cm (15in), *L 26 June*, £990 ($1,337)

10
An Ashanti hide head-dress, *Krobonkye*, worn by a sword bearer, senior chief or official, composed of antelope hide painted with black pigment, decorated with gold sheathed attachments, 27cm (10¾in), *NY 16 May*, $935 (£742)

11
A Benin ivory bracelet, depicting four figures, honeyed patina, 14cm (5½in), *L 2 Dec*, £3,300 ($4,884)

12
A pair of Ashanti stools, 24 x 30cm (9½ x 11¾in), *L 27 Mar*, £110 ($140)

13
An Ashanti bronze Kuduo, the sides with intricate raised motifs, the lid with a figure of a crocodile, 12cm (5in), *L 27 Mar*, £440 ($559)

14
An Ashanti stool, the curved rectangular seat with 'rainbow' supports, minor damages, 43cm (17in), *L 27 Mar*, £352 ($447)

15
An Ashanti linguist's staff, *okyeame poma*, covered entirely in gold leaf, 156cm (61½in), *NY 16 May*, $3,575 (£2,837)

16
A Voodoo fetish staff, probably Fon, encrusted sacrificial patina, 40.5cm (16in), *NY 15 Nov*, $990 (£697)

17
An Owo/Yoruba ivory finial, probably 17th/18th century, the shaft surmounted by a male figure in European attire, 18cm (7in), *NY 15 Nov*, $2,530 (£1,781)

18
An early Benin bronze memorial head of an Oba, thinly cast, the almond shaped eyes with iron inset pupils, dark patina, 22cm (8½in), *L 24 June*, £352,000 ($471,680)

1

A Bambara wood figure, encrusted patina, 55cm (21½in), *L 24 June,* £20,900 ($28,006)

2

A Dan wood portrait figure, metal inset teeth, incised scarification marks at the back, fine black patina, 48.5cm (19in), *L 26 June,* £880 ($1,188)

3

A Grebo wood mask, the four protruding eyes with inset mirrors, black crusty patina, used during ceremonies of the Poro Society, 57cm (22½in), *L 24 June,* £12,100 ($16,214)

4

A Baga wood shrine object, *elek,* the skull decorated with brass studs, old dark patina, 60cm (23½in), *L 2 Dec,* £2,420 ($3,582)

5

A Kran ceremonial ladle, Kaobli (Doube River) area, East Liberia, the handle in the form of a female figure, used on the appointment of tribal chiefs or the higher members of the Poro Society, which ended with a ritual distribution of rice, 76cm (30in), *L 24 June,* £14,300 ($19,162)

6

A Mbete wood mask, of classical form, fine black patina, 42cm (16½in), *L 2 Dec,* £1,870 ($2,768)

7

A Baule wood face mask, painted red, white and black, fine patina, some wear, 53cm (21in), *L 24 June,* £3,080 ($4,127)

8

A Toma wood mask, Nyangbay, black crusty patina, used in the ceremonies of the Poro Society, 56cm (22in), *L 24 June,* £4,950 ($6,633)

9

A Baule pith helmet, covered overall with gold leaf, 33cm (13in), *NY 16 May,* $1,430 (£1,134)

1

2

3

4

5

6

7

8

9

1
An Oyo equestrian group, the rider in full armour, crusty patina 22cm (8¾in), *L 24 June,* £11,000 ($14,740)

2
A pair of bronze Ogboni-Edan, the cylindrical bodies with a small bird attached, the heads linked by a bronze chain, 21cm (8¼in), *L 26 June,* £308 ($416)

3
Two Yoruba twin figures, *ibeji,* each wearing a beadwork cloak, the female has one pupil remaining, 29cm (11½in), *NY 16 May,* $2,200 (£1,746)

4
A Koulango bronze male figure, greenish patina, 8cm (3¼in), *L 24 June,* £1,320 ($1,769)

5
A Yoruba bronze ring, 18th century or earlier, cast with twenty six elements with various motifs including a crowned figure and four sacrificial human victims, greenish-brown patina, 26.5cm (10½in) diam, *NY 15 Nov,* $8,800 (£6,197)

6
A Yoruba stool, with thick circular seat and base both with incised geometric designs, the whole with limed and painted decoration, 40cm (16in), *L 26 June,* £440 ($594)

7
A Yoruba wood Ifa divination bowl, the whole with traces of paint, 28cm (11in), *L 27 Mar,* £418 ($531)

8
A Yoruba Gelede mask, with pierced eyes and nostrils, painted red, black and blue, 31.5cm (12½in), *L 2 Dec,* £286 ($423)

9
A Yoruba divination cup, *agere Ifa,* heavily encrusted, 26.5cm (10½in), *NY 16 May,* $3,300 (£2,619)

10
A Yoruba wood dance wand, with female figure, some worm damage to handle, old black patina, 34cm (13½in), *L 2 Dec,* £286 ($423)

11
A Yoruba equestrian group, the rider armed with flintlock gun and sword, 33cm (13in), *L 2 Dec,* £825 ($1,221)

12
A Yoruba wood equestrian figure, the diminutive horse mounted by a rider holding ceremonial objects, 81cm (32in), *L 2 Dec,* £1,650 ($2,442)

13
A Yoruba wood mirror, with a sliding panel and a male and female figure, 41cm (16in), *L 2 Dec,* £6,600 ($9,768)

14
A pair of Yoruba wood twin figures, Ere Ibeji, both wearing brass bracelets, very worn facial features, 29cm (11½in), *L 26 June,* £528 ($713)

15
A Bini wood deformation mask, the face with bulging coffee-bean eyes, fine black patina, 27cm (10½in), *L 26 June,* £3,740 ($5,049)

1

An Ibo title stool, the base with incised design and with four standing birds, 28cm (11in), *L 27 Mar,* **£748 ($950)**

2

An Ibo wood mask, *Mwo* the face painted white, 59cm (23¼in), *L 2 Dec,* **£440 ($651)**

3

A Kuyu wood head, the blackened coiffure decorated with cowrie shells and an insect-like creature covered in skin, 50cm (19¾in), *L 2 Dec,* **£1,045 ($1,547)**

4

An Ekoi head, Cross River, the large open mouth with painted wood teeth, on a circular basketwork base, 24cm (9½in), *L 26 June,* **£286 ($386)**

5

A Nupe stool, of unusual form, old patina, 30cm (12in), *L 26 June,* **£88 ($119)**

6

A Bali elephant mask, encrusted dark brown patina, 89cm (35in), *NY 16 May,* **$3,025 (£2,400)**

7

A Cameroons stool/table, 61cm (24in), *L 27 Mar,* **£770 ($978)**

8

Two Cameroon stools, each with a concave oval seat, the details incised, aged brown patina, 33 and 27cm (13 and 11in), *NY 16 May,* **$330 (£261)**

9

A Bamileke male figure, the left foot fragmentary, encrusted brown patina, 19cm (7¾in), *NY 16 May,* **$880 (£698)**

10

An Idoma wood head, black crusty patina, 46cm (18in), *L 27 Mar,* **£715 ($908)**

11

A Cameroon stool, the openwork mid-section carved with animals' heads, 40cm (17in), *NY 16 Nov,* **$450 (£321)**

12

A Bakota wood reliquary figure, overlaid with copper and brass sheeting, the body partly missing, 30cm (11¾in), *L 2 Dec,* **£3,300 ($4,884)**

13

A Kota wood and brass reliquary figure, of abstract form, with applied bone disk eyes, dark brown patina, 44cm (17½in), *NY 15 Nov,* **$19,800 (£13,943)**

14

A Bamileke chief's throne, supported by rows of leopards, the seat slightly damaged, 122cm (48in), *L 24 June,* **£4,950 ($6,633)**

15

A Fang wood helmet mask, Komo River area, southern Fang territory, zig-zag decoration painted white with kaolin, holes pierced around the base for attachment, worn on top of the head, 29cm (11½in), *L 27 Mar,* **£1,760 ($2,235)**

16

A Kwele face mask, the back pierced twice for attachment, fine dark brown patina with heavy encrustation and traces of pigment on the mouth and eyes, 38cm (15in), *NY 16 May,* **$1,980 (£1,571)**

1
A Pende chief's lance,
mikumbu, the shaft
carved with human
figures, 180cm (71in),
NY 16 May,
$935 (£742)

2
A Kuba wood cup, of
typical form, 17.5cm
(7in), *L 27 Mar,*
£330 ($419)

3
**A Bembe male fetish
figure,** drilled on the
underside for placement
of fetish material, dark
brown patina on the
legs, chest and head,
light brown on the
torso, 24.5cm (9½in),
NY 16 May,
$605 (£480)

4
A Luluwa pipe, in the
form of a hand, a
crouching figure form-
ing the shaft, brown
patina, 24.5cm (9½in)
long, *NY 15 Nov,*
$2,200 (£1,549)

5
**A Pende ivory whistle
pendant,** in the form of a
human figure, pale
yellow and brown
patina, 8.5cm (3¼in),
NY 15 Nov,
$4,950 (£3,485)

6
A Pende cup, carved
with human faces
wearing a solemn
expression, blackish-
brown patina, 9.5cm
(3¾in) high, *NY 15 Nov,*
$1,870 (£1,316)

7
A Xosa pipe, the figures
with metal inlay and
bead inset eyes, height
of bowl 7cm (2¼in),
L 27 Mar,
£825 ($1,048)

8
A Mangbetu container,
made in three sections
as a male figure, the
head of light wood, the
central section of bark,
the whole with dark
patina, 51.5cm (20¼in),
L 2 Dec,
£12,100 ($17,908)

9
A Yaka Colonial figure,
of a standing sailor, with
polychrome decoration,
46cm (18in), *L 27 Mar,*
£440 ($559)

10
A Xosa pipe, with metal
inlay decoration, 10cm
(4in), *L 27 Mar,*
£1,980 ($2,515)

11
A Xosa pipe, 16cm
(6¼in), *L 27 Mar,*
£1,760 ($2,235)

12
**A Ngoni-Tonga wood
mask,** the prominent
pierced mouth open to
reveal the carved
teeth, brown and black
patina, 27cm (10½in),
L 27 Mar,
£4,950 ($6,287)

13
A Yaka whistle, sur-
mounted by a human
head, black patina,
17.5cm (7in), *NY 15 Nov,*
$1,650 (£1,161)

14
A Kongo staff, with iron
point, the finial carved
in the form of a clenched
hand, rich light brown
patina, 159cm (62¾in),
NY 16 May,
$2,090 (£1,658)

15
A Zande adze, the finely
shaped iron blade
emerging from the
mouth of the human
head terminal, the head
with inset copper wire
embellishments, 43cm
(17in), *L 26 June,*
£495 ($668)

16
A Makonde wood mask,
the semicircular lug ears
pierced (the left one
partly missing),
encrusted resin indi-
cating the eyebrows,
17.5cm (7in), *L 26 June,*
£1,100 ($1,485)

1 2 3 4 5 6 7 8 9 10 11 12 13 14 15 16

1
A Chokwe face mask,
wearing a fragmentary
fibre and cloth head-
covering, remains of
kaolin, encrusted black
patina, 21cm (8¼in),
NY 16 May,
$880 (£698)

2
**A Luba/Hemba female
figure**, *mboko*, carved
of light wood and
painted black, the toes
and fingernails with
reddish pigment, 22cm
(8¾in), *NY 16 May*,
$1,650 (£1,309)

3
A Chokwe sceptre, 55cm
(21¾in), *L 26 June*,
£4,180 ($5,643)

4
**A Hemba wood caryatid
stool**, with massive
coiffure teminating in a
diamond motif at the
back, dark patina, 38cm
(15in), *L 24 June*,
£15,400 ($20,636)

5
A Hemba male figure, in
the classical Nyembo
style, wearing a fibre
skirt, black patina with
areas of encrustation,
61cm (24in), *NY 16 May*,
$19,800 (£15,714)

6
A Vili wood fetish figure,
used to exorcise sick-
ness, with inset
circular mirror on the
abdomen, glass inset
eyes, crusty patina,
26.5cm (10½in),
L 24 June,
£4,620 ($6,191)

7
A Teke wood male figure,
the right foot partly
missing, 71cm (28in),
L 26 June,
£880 ($1,188)

8
**A Luba wood Kifwebe
panel mask**, *Kalengula*,
brown patina with
lighter incisions, 80cm
(31½in), *L 24 June*,
£3,300 ($4,422)

9
A Luba wood stool,
the circular top partly
missing at the back,
black patina, 50cm
(19¾in), *L 27 Mar*,
£418 ($531)

10
**A Songe wood fetish
figure**, with metal studs,
the abdomen and head
with holes for fetish
material, brown patina,
18.5cm (7¼in), *L 2 Dec*,
£660 ($977)

11
A Kuba pipe, in two
sections, the head in the
form of an abstract
human figure, back
section of shaft probably
a replacement, total
length 43cm (17in),
NY 16 Nov,
$500 (£357)

12
**A Yombe wood female
figure**, scarification
marks on the back and
abdomen, the coiffure
darkened, 23cm (9in),
L 27 Mar,
£1,320 ($1,676)

13
**Two Songe ceremonial
axes**, each with copper
sheeting on the shaft,
29 and 50.5cm (15¼
and 19¾in), *NY 16 May*,
$550 (£436)

14
A Kuba wood cup, the
handle with a flattened
human head, inlaid
with ivory pieces,
18.5cm (7¼in), *L 2 Dec*,
£1,650 ($2,442)

15
A Kuba wood cup, 14cm
(5½in), *L 2 Dec*,
£1,100 ($1,628)

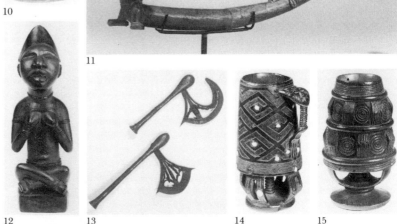

African Furniture

African art has in recent years found its place in the art market. It has been discovered by many museums, collectors and dealers, who have focused their attention on masks and figures; so, too, have the astonishing numbers of books and publications which have followed this trend. In 1980 the distinguished scholar Roy Sieber published the catalogue to the exhibition 'African Furniture and Household Objects' which travelled to several cities in the United States. This helped everyone to the realization that a piece of furniture can be as good as a sculpture, an ancestor figure or a mask. Despite increased popularity, however, until two or three years ago stools and furniture were relegated to the lower end of the art market. It was purely incidental that the record for the most expensive work of African art sold at auction between 1979 and 1985 was held by a stool (fig.1).

The fast and unexpected escalation of prices which climaxed in the £264,000 ($541,200) paid for the Master of Buli stool, left many collectors behind; they could no longer afford the objects they loved and had to seek less obvious works of art to placate their collecting appetite. New collectors approaching this field were also being discouraged by the need to spend large sums of money to be able to purchase items of good quality.

—1—
A Luba wood 'Master of Buli' wood stool,
L 21 June, 1979,
£264,000 ($541,200)

—2—
An Ashanti wood stool,
L 26 June, 1984,
£935 ($1,328)

—3—
A Senufo wood seat,
L 26 June, 1984,
£605 ($859)

—4—
A Senufo wood bed,
L 26 June, 1984,
£1,430 ($2,031)

—1—

—2—

—3—

Further examples of African furniture are illustrated on the preceeding pages.

—4—

Sotheby's sale of African furniture in June 1984 (the first of its kind) was obviously perfectly timed to focus attention on a new area for collectors of African art. The prices achieved were in most cases quite unexpected (figs. 2, 3, 4,). Old and new collectors could, for the first time, choose from a wide selection of first class material. The magic word 'furniture' also attracted completely new categories of buyers: interior decorators looking for new ideas and, more simply, people looking for unusual but perfectly adequate furniture.

The house is often the centre of an African's world and within it furniture is very scarce, particularly by comparison with the West. A Shona warrior possesses one neckrest and often very little else. His status and wealth is reflected in that object in the same way that a car or country house reflects the wealth of a European (fig.5). The same concept applies to stools, bowls and other household objects. One must not forget that, unlike European furniture, the African production was very limited. Many African tribes were composed of only a few hundred individuals.

Sculptures very seldom survive more than fifty or sixty years. Most are made of wood which, in the African climate, deteriorates with alarming speed. The humidity, termites and continuous use, often add a patina and a special feeling which enhances their extraordinary sculptural qualities. Despite this, however, these works of art have often reached us in impeccable condition.

All these factors contribute to the fascination of African art for collectors. They also help us to understand why the prices for furniture have continued to rise so steadily. But if we look at the prices fetched by these objects over the last two or three years, it is not difficult to realize that, although prices have certainly gone up, they have not reached the level of figures or masks. A top quality stool from Zaire can still be purchased for one-fifth of the price of a mediocre figure from the same area. More books and exhibition catalogues are being published and the demand from unconventional collectors and those who buy at irregular intervals is steadily growing. The chance of being able to acquire an ancient work of art of fine quality for a few hundred pounds or dollars, might not last for very much longer.

● ROBERTO FAINELLO ●

Further reading

Roy Sieber, *African Furniture and Household Objects*, 1980

Elsy Leuzinger, *The Art of Black Africa*, 1972

W. Fagg, *Tribes and Forms in African Art*, 1965

—5—
A Shona neckrest, old dark patina, 11.5cm (4½in), *L 26 June,* £1,430 ($1,931)

—6—
A Mashona neckrest, rich reddish-brown patina, 19cm (7½in), *NY 15 Nov,* $2,860 (£2,014)

—7—
A Zulu headrest, with openwork support carved in the form of two wheels flanking a reclining human figure, 44.5cm (17½in), *NY 16 Nov,* $900 (£642)

—8—
A Bena-Kanioka wood neckrest, fine dark patina, 18cm (7in), *L 2 Dec,* £6,600 ($9,768)

—9—
A Zairian headrest, with remains of brass tack and nail decoration, 21.5cm (8½in), *NY 16 Nov,* $650 (£464)

—5—

—6—

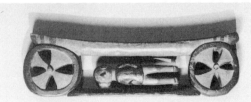

—7—

—8—

—9—

Islamic Works of Art

Article ● Persian metalwork *pp 615-619*   *See also* ● Colour illustrations *pp 567-568*

Major Islamic Dynasties

	A.H.*	A.D.		A.H.*	A.D.		A.H.*	A.D.
Umayyads	41-132	661- 750	Seljuqs	429-590	1038-1194	Ottomans	680-1342	1281-1924
Abassids	132-656	749-1258	Selijuqs of Rum	470-707	1077-1307	Muzzaffarids	713- 795	1314-1393
Samanids	204-395	819-1005	Ayyubids	567-648	1171-1250	Timurids	771- 912	1370-1506
Fatimids	297-567	909-1171	Delhi Sultanate	602-962	1206-1555	Safavids	907-1145	1501-1732
Buyids	320-454	932-1062	Mamluks	648-922	1250-1517	Mughals	932-1274	1526-1858
Ghaznavids	366-582	971-1186	Il-Khanids	654-754	1256-1353	Qajars	1193-1342	1779-1924

*The Islamic era began in 622 A.D. which corresponds to A.H.1. (anno hijra = year of the flight of Muhammed to Medina) and is calculated in lunar years. Unless otherwise stated, dates in this book and Sotheby Islamic catalogues are in Christian years (A.D.).

1
A millefiori glass bowl probably 9th century Mesopotamian 6.7cm (2⅝in) high, *G 25 June,* **SF 22,000** **£6,377; $8,609)**

2
A pale blue free-blown glass jug, 9th-10th century, probably Persian, broken and restored, 14.5cm (5½in) high, *L 17 Apr,* £154 ($200)

3
A Syrian greenish colourless free-blown glass beaker, late 13th century, perhaps Aleppo, slight surface weathering, 11.6cm (4½in) high, *G 25 June,* **SF 4,400 (£1,275; $1,722)**

4
A Persian free-blown glass flask, almost colourless, 9th-10th century, repaired, 17.5cm (6¾in) high, *L 17 Apr,* £825 ($1,073)

5
A Persian emerald-green mould-blown glass flask, with applied decoration, 9th-10th century, 15.5cm (6⅛in) high, *L 15 Oct,* £1,045 ($1,546)

6
A small pale green mould-blown glass bowl, 11th-12th century, Persian or perhaps Egyptian, 12cm (4¾in) diam, *L 15 Oct,* £605 ($895)

7
A brown mould-blown glass jug, 11th-12th century, probably Persian, 15.2cm (6in) high, *L 15 Oct,* £440 ($651)

8
A Persian manganese-purple mould-blown glass bottle, with applied decoration, 11th-12th century, cracked, *L 15 Oct,* £825 ($1,221)

9
An aubergine vase, 9th-12th century, decorated with white festoons, 12.7cm (5in) high, *NY 21 Nov,* $5,060 (£3,538)

1

2

3   4   5   6

7   8   9

1
A Persian slip-painted
pottery bowl, 10th-12th
century, Nishapur,
18.8cm (7⅜in) diam,
L 6 Feb,
£209 ($236)

2
A Persian slip-painted
pottery bowl, 9th-10th
century, Nishapur with
four *kufic* inscriptions
27.5cm (12in) diam,
L 17 Apr,
£935 ($1,216)

3
A small Persian slip-
painted pottery bowl, 9th-
10th century, Nishapur,
in manganese-brown and
tomato red on a white
ground, 13cm (5in) diam,
G 25 June,
SF 4,400 (£1,275; $1,722)

4
An Ilkhanid turquoise-
glazed bowl, Sultanabad,
late 13th century 20.3cm
(8in) diam, *NY 21 Nov,*
$715 (£500)

5
A Persian slip-painted
pottery plate, 9th-10th
century, Nishapur,
26.6cm (10½in) diam,
L 16 Apr,
£528 ($686)

6
A Persian slip-painted
pottery bowl, 10th century, Nishapur, 33cm
(13in) diam, *L 15 Oct,*
£385 ($569)

7
A Persian slip-painted
pottery bowl, 9th-10th
century, Nishapur,
22.1cm (8¾in) diam,
L 16 Apr,
£605 ($787)

8
A Persian slip-painted
pottery bowl, 9th-10th
century, Nishapur, deco-
rated in manganese-
brown on a cream
ground, 24.1cm (9½in)
diam, *L 15 Oct,*
£1,430 ($2,116)

9
A Persian buff-ware pottery
bowl, 9th-10th century,
Nishapur, with a central
kufic inscription, 22cm
(8⅝in) diam, *L 16 Apr,*
£572 ($744)

10
A Seljuk champlevé bowl,
Garrus district, 12th
century, 17.8cm (7in)
diam., *NY 21 Nov,*
$2,310 (£1,165)

11
A Persian splashed-ware
pottery bowl, 9th-10th
century, Nishapur, with
a pseudo inscription on
one side, 19cm (7½in)
diam, *L 15 Oct,*
£352 ($520)

12
A Persian underglaze-
painted pottery bowl, late
13th century, 20.3cm
(8in) diam, *L 16 Apr,*
£1,650 ($2,145)

13
A Persian slip-painted
pottery bowl, 10th-11th
century, decorated in
manganese-brown and
yellow on a cream
ground, 19.1cm (7½in)
diam, *L 16 Apr,*
£440 ($572)

14
A Persian slip-painted
pottery bowl, 11th century,
in manganese-brown and
yellow staining black on
a cream ground, 17.5cm
(6⅞in) diam, *G 25 June,*
SF 6,050 (£1,754; $2,367)

15
A Persian 'Amol ware'
pottery bowl, 11th-12th
century, North Persia,
decorated in green and
sgraffiato, 20cm (8in) diam,
L 16 Apr,
£550 ($715)

16
A Persian underglaze-
painted pottery bowl, 13th
century, 19.2cm (8in)
diam, *L 6 Feb,*
£660 ($745)

17
A Persian lustre pottery
bowl, second half 13th
century, in brownish-
gold lustre and cobalt-
blue on a white ground,
Kashan, 19.8cm (7⅞in)
diam., *G 25 June,*
SF 3,300 (£957; $1,291)

18
A Persian underglaze-
painted pottery bowl, late
13th-14th century,
decorated in cobalt-blue
on a white ground, 22cm
(8¾in) diam., *L 15 Oct,*
£660 ($976)

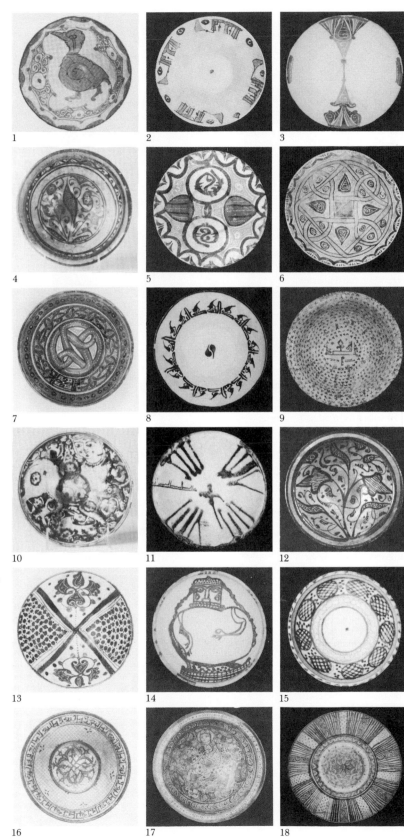

1
2
3
4
5
6
7
8
9
10
11
12
13
14
15
16
17
18

1
An Isnik pottery plate,
second half 16th century,
36.1cm (14¼in) diam,
L 15 Oct,
£1,750 ($2,590)

2
An Isnik pottery tile,
last quarter 16th
century, 24.7cm (9¾in)
square, *G 25 June,*
SF 2,200 (£638; $861)

3
An Isnik pottery jug,
17th century, decorated
in cobalt-blue, green,
black, and raised
sealing-wax red, 24.4cm
(9⅝in) high, *L 17 Apr,*
£660 ($858)

4
**An Isnik blue and white
pottery jug,** third quarter
16th century, 23.8cm
(9⅜in) high, *L 16 Apr,*
£13,200 ($17,160)

5
**An Isnik pottery bowl and
cover,** 17th century,
decorated in cobalt-
blue, black, green, tur-
quoise and raised
sealing-wax red, 31.7cm
(12½in) high, *G 25 June,*
SF 18,700 (£5,420; $7,317)

6
**A Mesopotamian tin-
glazed pottery bowl,** 9th-
10th century, decorated
in cobalt-blue on a buff
ground, 20.5cm (8in)
diam, *G 25 June,*
SF 2,750 (£797; $1,076)

7
**A Syrian monochrome
pottery sweatmeat dish,**
12th-13th century,
Raqqa, with an iridised
turquoise glaze, 26.4cm
(10⅜in) diam, *L 15 Oct,*
£990 ($1,465)

8
**A Mesopotamian tin-
glazed pottery bowl,** 9th
century, the exterior
with four purple slashes,
20.4cm (8in) diam,
L 16 Apr,
£1,100 ($1,430)

9
**A Syrian monochrome
pottery bowl,** 12th-13th
century, decorated in
cream under an iridised
glaze, 15.6cm (6⅛in)
diam, *L 15 Oct,*
£605 ($895)

10
An Isnik pottery tankard,
*c.*1580, restored, 22.5cm
(8⅞in) high, *L 16 Apr,*
£11,000 ($14,300)

11
Two Syrian pottery vases,
12th-13th century,
Rakka, decorated with a
turquoise glaze, each
18.5cm (7¼in) high,
L 16 Apr,
£3,080 ($4,004)

1
A Persian underglaze-painted pottery jug, 1200-1220, *Kashan*, the neck with a cursive inscription of Arabic verse, 18.1cm (7⅛in) high, *L 16 Apr*, £990 ($1,287)

2
A Persian monochrome moulded pottery albarello, 12th-13th century, 16cm (6⅜in) high, *L 6 Feb*, £605 ($683)

3
A Persian lustre pottery jug, last quarter 17th century, *Kashan*, in brownish-gold lustre in the 'Rayy' style on a cream ground, 18cm (7in) high, *G 25 June*, SF 3,300 (£957; $1,291)

4
A Persian lustre pottery jug, 1200-1220, *Kashan*, in the 'Rayy miniature' style, with cursive inscription of Persian verse round the body and neck, 16.5cm (6½in) high, *L 16 Apr*, £1,100 ($1,430)

5
A Persian lustre pottery bowl, 13th century, 17.7cm (7in) diam, *L 6 Feb*, £330 ($372)

6
Two Persian lustre star tiles, late 13th century, the border with reserved cursive inscription, 20.2cm (8in) diam, *L 15 Oct*, £1,045 ($1,546)

7
A Persian lustre pottery bottle, 13th century, 19cm (7½in) high, *L 6 Feb*, £275 ($310)

8
A Persian underglaze-painted pottery jar, late 13th-14th century, 24.5cm (9⅝in) high, *L 15 Oct*, £385 ($569)

9
A Persian lustre pottery frieze tile, 13th century, 32.2 x 31.5cm (13 x 12½in), *L 16 Apr*, £990 ($1,287)

10
Two Seljuk lustre-painted star tiles, Sultanabad, 13th century, 20.7cm (8in) diam, *NY 21 Nov*, $1,540 (£1,077)

11
A Persian lustre pottery jug, 13th century, 19cm (7½in) high, *L 6 Feb*, £220 ($248)

12
A Persian monochrome-painted pottery cock's head ewer, 12th-13th century, *Kashan*, with a turquoise glaze, 18.5cm (7¼in) high, *G 25 June*, SF 11,000 (£3,188; $4,304)

13
A Persian 'white-ware' moulded pottery jug, 12th century, with touches of cobalt-blue, 14.5cm (5¾in) high, *G 25 June*, SF 1,980 (£574; $775)

1

4

7

11

2

5

8

12

3

6

9

10

13

1
A Mamluk slip-painted pottery bowl, 14th-15th century, Syria or Egypt, decorated in green on a brown ground, 18.4cm (7⅛in) diam, *L 17 Apr,* £5,280 ($6,864)

2
A Safavid blue-and-white dish, early 17th century, *Kirman,* the interior painted in the Chinese manner, 26.3cm (10½in), *NY 8 Feb,* $3,520 (£3,171)

3
A Mamluk blue-and-white hexagonal tile, 15th century, Syria, 17cm (6¾in) diam, *L 15 Oct,* £495 ($732)

4
A large Qajar pottery tile, 18th-19th century, decorated in shades of blue, green, yellow, purple and manganese brown with a *mehrab*-shaped panel 58.5 x 38.7cm (23 x 15¼in), *L 17 Apr,* £1,045 ($1,359)

5
A Seljuk turquoise-glazed ewer, 13th century, *Kashan,* 26.3cm (10½in) high, *NY 8 Feb,* $1,760 (£1,586)

6
A Safavid blue-and-white tile, 17th century, 18cm (7in) square, *L 15 Oct,* £385 ($569)

7
A Kutahya pottery dish, 18th century, in green, yellow, manganese-purple and raised sealing-wax red and outlined in black, 19.2cm (7½in) diam, *L 17 Apr,* £1,320 ($1,716)

8
A Qajar pottery jar, 19th century, decorated with courtly figures and animals, 30.5cm (12in) high, *L 17 Apr,* £935 ($1,216)

9
An Ayyubid lustre-painted jar, 12th century, Rakka, the body painted over a white ground in brown lustre and cobalt-blue, 28.2cm (11⅛in) high, *NY 8 Feb,* $7,975 (£7,185)

10
A Kutahya pottery dish, 18th century, decorated in cobalt-blue, green, beige and sealing-wax red, 22.7cm (9in) diam, *L 17 Apr,* £440 ($572)

11
A Safavid 'Gombroon' pottery bowl, 17th century, with colourless glaze over a white hard-paste body carved with a pierced design, 19.7cm (7¾in) diam, *L 17 Apr,* £1,760 ($2,288)

12
A large Cantigalli pottery bowl, in the Isnik 'Rosette and Saz leaf' style, *c.*1880, Cantigalli factory, Florence, 40.5cm (16in) diam, *L 17 Apr,* £1,320 ($1,716)

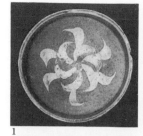

1

2

3

6

4

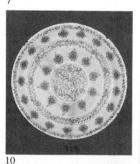

5

8

9

7

10

11

12

Persian Metalwork

For many, Islamic art is unexplored territory. The field covers an enormous geographical and historical span, further complicated by unfamiliar names, endlessly shifting political boundaries and a chronology based on a lunar calendar beginning 600 years after Christ. The purpose of this article is to draw a rough framework tracing the output of one identifiable area: the metalwork production of Persia.

Persia was a leader in metalwork production in the Islamic world from the outset. Khorassan province in the north-east had a strong tradition of high-quality craftsmanship from pre-Islamic times and the advantage of rich gold and silver deposits; while copper is abundant all over the Middle East and Kerman had zinc mines. For the first few centuries after the Muslim conquest of Persia the continuation of Sassanian styles and techniques predominate. Typical pieces which have survived until the present are small silver bowls decorated with confronting animals (fig.1) or fantastic beasts within roundels, royal figures or hunting scenes. Alongside these rich court pieces we find heavy cast bronze objects in relatively large quantities, for example ewers (figs.2 & 4), buckets, cauldrons, pestle and mortars (fig.3) and rosewater sprinklers. These utilitarian pieces are often unadorned or roughly incised with a *kufic* inscription.

—1—
A Persian silver bowl, 6th/7th century, decorated with four birds and scroll in repoussé, 17.5cm (7in) wide, *G 25 June,* **SF 8,000 (£2,319; $3,130)**

—2—
A Persian cast-bronze ewer, 9th-10th century, with a *kufic* inscription below the rim, Eastern Persia, 35.5cm (14in) high, *L 16 Apr,* **£4,180 ($5,434)**

—3—
A small Persian bronze mortar and pestle, 10th-12th century, with a pseudo-*kufic* inscription, 12cm (4¾in) diam, *L 15 Oct,* **£836 ($1,237)**

—4—
A Persian bronze ewer, 9th-10th century, Khorassan, 30cm (11¾in) high, *L 15 Oct,* **£6,600 ($9,768)**

—1—

—3—

—2—

—4—

The first major changes occurred in the 12th—13th centuries during the so-called 'Seljuk' period, apparently precipitated by an acute shortage of silver around 1100. The silversmiths turned their mastery of sheet-metalworking to baser metals, especially brass, and an extremely brittle alloy known as high-tin bronze or bell metal which has a silvery appearance but is so friable that it shatters when hit and is therefore difficult to work. Their patrons were mainly rich merchants (Khorassan straddled the silk routes as well as the gold mines) who demanded opulant and showy pieces. The craftsmen unable to provide the traditional silver pieces (which had often been gilded and inlaid with niello to provide a three-coloured effect) turned instead to larger, more impressive objects in base metal heavily inlaid with gold, silver and copper. The new shapes

include candlesticks, lampstands (fig.8), large ribbed ewers, (see Sotheby's sale in London, 16 April, 1986, lot 127), scalloped basins (fig.5) and inkwells (fig.10) (a symbol of educated status). Lesser pieces and cast vessels were also still produced, notably a wide variety of pierced incense burners either of cylindrical form on three feet (fig.6) or in the form of animals: birds (figs.7 & 9) and cats being very popular.

The decorative motifs in this period are highly symbolic and largely preoccupied with the triumph of light over darkness: good over evil. Hence the lion (light) is frequently shown vanquishing other animals. The rosette (sun) is a predominant motif often on a star-trellis representing the cosmos (fig.5) and zodiacal symbols in conjunction with their solar houses appear time and again. Arabic inscription was another form of

—5—
A Persian copper-inlaid brass basin (Lagan), 12th century, with a *kufic* inscription, 49cm (19¼in) diam, *G 25 June*, **SF 14,300 (£4,145; $5,596)**

—6—
A Persian bronze incense burner (ud-suz), 10th-12th century, Khorassan, 15.8cm (6¼in) high, *L 15 Oct*, **£198 ($293)**

—7—
A Persian bronze incense burner, in the form of a bird, 12th century, 23.5cm (9¼in), *G 25 June*, **SF 22,000 (£6,376; $8,607)**

—8—
A Persian bronze lamp-stand, 12th-13th century, the parts possibly not belonging, 35cm (13¾in) high, *L 15 Oct*, **£1,045 ($1,463)**

—9—
A Persian cast-bronze chick, 12th century, 6cm (2½in), *L 16 Apr*, **£374 ($486)**

—10—
A Persian silver and copper-inlaid cast-bronze inkwell (Davat), Khorassan, late 12th century, with inscriptions, 9.8cm (3⅞in) high, *L 16 Apr*, **£1,045 ($1,359)**

Brass
Copper and zinc (20%)

Bronze
Copper 70%, lead 25%, zinc 4%, tin 1%, approx. (quaternary alloy)

High-tin bronze
Copper and tin (20%)

Niello
A black compound used as inlay on silver.

Steel
Iron and carbon.

Tinned copper
Copper decorated with a coating of tinning. Predominantly used in Iran from 15th century onwards.

Tombak
Copper decorated with a coating of gilding. Unique to the Ottoman court.

—5—

—6—

—7—

—8—

—9—

—10—

decoration popular in the 13th century usually bestowing a seemingly endless flow of blessings on the owner. Figs. 12 and 14 show inscriptions of this type as the primary embellishment with slim, elegant silver cursive script (*naskhi*) on a spiralling ground. Meanwhile in another school of metalwork beginning in western Iran, new and highly decorative forms of script develop as an integral part of intricate and complex decorative schemes. These usually appear on expensive, high quality pieces richly inlaid with gold and silver such as the casket in fig. 11. As well as the human-headed script such as on this piece, foliated and animated epigraphy developed to such an extent that at its extreme a line of Arabic appears as a procession of figures and is illegible to all but the most skilled eye. (See Sotheby's sale in London, 16 April 1986, lot 68).

In the 14th century emphasis shifts from Khorassan to Fars in south-western Iran where the Muzaffarid rulers encouraged a flourishing of the arts. The most common pieces found in the salerooms are squat, deep sided bowls (*tas*) (fig.15 & 16) on which monumental script is combined with panels of elongated courtly figures closely resembling the drawing of contemporary miniatures. The inscriptions still include Arabic benedictions and also, for the first time, Persian verse. Astrological themes continue alongside Mongol symbols such as phoenixes, dragons and fish whorls.

In comparison few pieces from the short but innovative Timurid period survive but their influence on the Safavid style is undeniable. New shapes include long-necked bottles and ewers and, most familiar of all, squat, bulbous jugs (fig.17). These jugs were not only copied by later Persian and Ottoman Turkish metalworkers but also by Chinese potters. Distinctive changes in techniques and designs in surface decoration also herald a new era. The silver and gold inlay becomes thin foil and fine wires confined to an intricate tracery of foliate arabesques and lobed cartouches of *nastaliq* inscription. At the same time there is an increase of tinned-copper vessels with engraved decoration offset against a hatched ground filled with

—11—
A Persian gold and silver-inlaid cast brass casket (Dorj), Western Persia, early 14th century, 12.7cm (5in) high, *L 16 Apr,* £42,900 ($55,770)

—12—
A Persian silver-inlaid bronze jug (mashrabe), 12th-13th century, Eastern Persia, handle missing, 21cm (8¼in) high, *L 15 Oct,* £1,650 ($2,442)

—13—
A Persian cast-bronze ewer, 12th-13th century, 20.5cm (8in) high, *L 16 Apr,* £550 ($715)

—14—
A Persian silver-inlaid bronze jug (mashrabe), Eastern Persia, 12th-13th century, 20.5cm (8⅛in) high, *L 17 Apr,* £935 ($1,216)

—15—
A Fars silver-inlaid brass bowl (tas), 14th century, 17.5cm (7in) diam, *L 17 Oct, 1984,* £7,480 ($9,350)

—16—
A Fars silver-inlaid brass bowl (Tas), 14th century, with a *thuluth* inscription, 24cm (9½in) diam. *G 25 June,* **SF 14,850 (£4,304; $5,811)**

—17—
A Timurid brass jug, signed by Ruhalla Shah'ali, dated AH896/1490 AD, 12.5cm (5in), *L 16 Apr,* £3,850 ($5,005)

—11— —12— —13— —14— —15— —16— —17—

black composition.

There is no stylistic break between the Timurid and the Safavid periods, rather a continuation of these trends until silver inlay disappears and tinned-copper or brass predominate. Human and animal representations are largely replaced by vigorous scrolling arabesques bearing a profusion of split-palmettes, trefoils, lotus blossoms and cloud bands (fig.19). Some new forms include large basins, footed bowls and 'pillar' torch stands. The supreme achievement is open-work steel. Pierced plaques (fig.18), battle standards and decorative panels were formed out of sheets of steel and the designs cut away

to a hair's breadth. These usually took the form of religious phrases against a typical scrolling ground.

After this pinnacle there was no major development in skill or artistry. During the Qajar period enamelling in bright polychrome on gold became popular but the expense restricted it to a court vogue. Favourite subjects are European (fig.20) or Qajar courtly ladies against floral sprays which are perhaps gaudy to modern taste. Steel too was brightly embellished with gold and silver damascening, often used as naturalistic detailing on an assortment of creatures: from hawks and cockerels to stags and elephants (figs. 21, 22 & 23). Other

—18—
A Safavid open-work steel plaque, mid 16th century, 38cm (15in) long.
L 15 Oct,
£36,300 ($53,724)

—19—
A Safavid copper bowl, 17th century, with inscription cartouches, 16.4cm (6½in) diam,
L 17 Apr,
£550 ($715)

—20—
A Qajar enamelled copper Ghalian cup, *c.*1860, 5.7cm (2⅜in) high,
L 17 Apr,
£880 ($1,144)

—21—
A small Qajar steel bird, 19th century, decorated in gold and silver damascening, 10cm (4in),
L 17 Apr,
£615 ($799)

—22—
A Qajar steel stag, decorated in gold and silver damascening, 31.5cm (12½in), *L 17 Apr,*
£550 ($715)

—23—
A Qajar steel cockerel, 19th century, decorated in silver and gold damascening, 35cm (13¾in).
G 25 June,
SF 7,700 (£2,231; $3,011)

—18—

—19—

—20—

—21—

—22—

—23—

common Qajar vessels are large ewers and basins (fig.24) and circular swing mirrors on stands (fig.25).

The Islamic Art market is currently experiencing some uncertainties for political and economic reasons but that is not greatly affecting Persian metalwork other than to emphasize the importance of high quality workmanship and good condition. An inlaid piece finely worked and with a large proportion of the silver remaining will command a high price (fig. 15) whereas a piece which has been cleaned so vigorously that the silver and perhaps the sharpness of the engraving have been rubbed away (fig. 16) will not be as valuable despite its age or shining appearance! Early bronze vessels ideally should have a sound provenance and one should examine them carefully in case they have been made up of several unrelated pieces. Of the later periods large, Safavid brass pieces remain popular but tinned-copper vessels (fig.26), unless in exceptional condition or with particularly interesting inscriptions, go relatively unremarked. The highlights of two important Islamic Works of

Art sales in the last year have been, unsurprisingly, Safavid steel plaques.

● CAROLINE RUSSETT ●

Further reading

Baer (Eva), *Metalwork in Medieval Islamic Art,* New York 1983.

Melikian-Chirvani (Assadullah Souren), *Islamic Metalwork from the Iranian World,* Victoria and Albert Museum Catalogue, London, 1978.

—24—
A Qajar steel ewer, 19th century, with incised decoration and gold damascening, 34.5cm (13½in), *L 17 Oct, 1984*
£1,100 ($1,375)

—25—
A Qajar steel mirror case and stand, second half 19th century, decorated in gold damascening with a *nastaliq* inscription, 59.5cm (23½in), *L 13 Nov, 1984*
£704 ($860)

—26—
A Safavid tinned-copper basin, *c.*1600, with inscription cartouches, 17.1cm (6¾in) diam, *L 15 Oct,*
£440 ($651)

—24—

—25—

—26—

1
An Egyptian cast-bronze ewer, 9th/10th century, Nishapur, 20.6cm (8⅛in) high, *L 16 Apr*, £2,640 ($3,432)

2
A Fatimid cast-bronze bucket, 11th century, Egypt, with *kufic* inscription below the rim, 11.6cm (4½in) diam., *L 16 Apr*, £6,050 ($7,865)

3
An Anatolian silver-inlaid brass candlestick, late 13th century, 20cm (7⅞in) high, *G 25 June*, SF 9,900 (£2,870; $3,874)

4
A Mamluk brass tray, *c.*1293-1341, bordered inside and outside with inscription bands and roundels, 46cm (18in) diam, *L 16 Apr*, £3,630 ($4,719)

5
A Mamluk silver-inlaid brass candlestick base, 14th century, the body with a bold *thuluth* inscription, 20cm (8in) high, *L 16 Apr*, £7,700 ($10,010)

6
A Mamluk style silver-inlaid candlestick, 14th century, with a *thuluth* inscription, 27cm (10½in) high, *G 25 June*, SF 5,500 (£1,594; $2,152)

7
A Mamluk brass bowl, 14th century, Syria or Egypt, with a Hebrew inscription, 18.2cm (7in) diam., *L 15 Oct*, £1,430 ($2,116)

8
A Mamluk bronze lunch-box, 15th century, Syria or Egypt, with traces of tinning, 24.8cm (9¾in) wide, *L 17 Apr*, £1,980 ($2,574)

9
An Ottoman tinned-copper tankard, 16th century, 24.5cm (9½in) high, *L 15 Oct*, £3,520 ($5,209)

10
A Veneto-Saracenic silver-inlaid brass ewer, last quarter 15th century, 26.8cm (10½in) high, *L 16 Apr*, £5,280 ($6,864)

11
A Mamluk tinned-copper pouring vessel, *c.*1500, 26.7cm (10½in) diam., *G 25 June*, SF 1,320 (£383; $517)

12
An Ottoman gilt-copper (Tombak) basin, *c.*1800, 35cm (13¾in) diam, *G 25 June*, SF 9,900 (£2,870; $3,874)

13
An Ottoman gilt-copper (Tombak) beaker and cover, *c.*1800, 11.8cm (4¾in) high, *L 17 Apr*, £792 ($1,030)

14
A Veneto-Saracenic brass bowl and cover, *c.*1500, Egypt with pseudo-*kufic* inscriptions, 12.6cm (5in) diam, *L 15 Oct*, £2,750 ($4,070)

15
An Ottoman silver box and cover, 18th century, 7.8cm (3¼in) high, *L 17 Apr*, £440 ($572)

16
An Ottoman brass candlestick, with the *waqf* date A.H.1255/1839 AD, 38cm (15in) high, *G 25 June*, SF 1,650 (£478; $646)

1 2 3

4 5 6

7

8 9

10

11

12 13

14 15 16

1
**An Ottoman gilt-copper
(Tombak) dish and cover,**
*c.*1800, 13.7cm (5½in)
high, *L 16 Oct,*
£2,640 ($3,907)

2
An Ottoman silver box,
19th century, chased
with *mehrab*-shaped
panels, 25½cm (10in)
high, *L 17 Apr,*
£2,420 ($3,146)

3
**A set of four Ottoman
silver cups,** late 19th
century, 13cm (5¼in)
high, *L 16 Oct,*
£1,210 ($1,790)

4
**A silver and copper-inlaid
brass bowl,** dated 1907
AD, Syria or Egypt,
16.6cm (6½in) diam.,
L 16 Oct,
£550 ($814)

5
An Ottoman silver box,
late 19th/early 20th
century, marked with a
tughra, 27cm (10½in)
high, *L 16 Oct,*
£2,640 ($3,907)

6
**An Ottoman silver travel-
ling scribe set,** 18th-19th
century, 21cm (8¼in),
L 16 Oct,
£935 ($1,383)

7
**A brass travelling scribe
set,** 19th century, Egypt
or Syria, with inscrip-
tion cartouches, 33.5cm
(13⅜in), *G 25 June,*
SF 2,200 (£638; $861)

8
**A large silver inlaid copper
tray,** with wooden stand,
dated AH 1350/1931
AD, Egypt, decorated in
the Mamluk style, 70cm
(27⅝in) diam., *L 17 Apr,*
£1,210 ($1,573)

9
**An Ottoman silver ewer,
stand and basin,** 19th
century, 24.5cm (9⅝in)
high, *G 25 June,*
SF 9,900 (£2,870; $3,874)

10
**A silver and copper inlaid
brass vase,** *c.*1900, Syria
or Egypt, 38cm (15in)
high, *L 17 Apr,*
£1,540 ($2,002)

11
An Ottoman silver mirror,
19th century, marked
with a *tughra,* 30.5cm
(12in), *L 16 Oct,*
£1,760 ($2,604)

12
**A silver-inlaid brass
casket,** *c.*1900, Syria or
Egypt, in the Mamluk
style, the sides with
inscriptions, marquetry
wood interior, 19.6cm
(7¾in) square, *L 16 Oct,*
£2,420 ($3,581)

13
An Ottoman silver box,
19th century, with
mehrab-shaped panels,
9.5cm (3¾in) diam.,
G 25 June,
SF 1,320 (£383; $517)

1
An Indian steel mace,
19th century, 76cm
(30in), *L 17 Apr,*
£220 ($286)

2
A Qajar steel mace,
19th century, 77.5cm
(30½in), *L 17 Apr,*
£308 ($400)

3
A Qajar steel axe, 82cm
(32in), *L 17 Apr,*
£242 ($315)

4
**A Persian cast-bronze
mace-head,** 13th-14th
century, 7.5cm (3in),
L 17 Apr,
£418 ($543)

5
A set of Egyptian armour,
*c.*1870, consisting of
helmet, breastplate and
back plate, 39cm
(15¼in) and 40cm
(15½in), *L 17 Apr,*
£2,640 ($3,432)

6
An Indian axe, late 18th
century, the head of
Persian form, with
panels of gold *koftgari,*
the hammer signed and
dated, 57cm (22½in),
L 16 Oct,
£1,760 ($2,605)

7
A Qajar steel helmet,
decorated with
arabesques and car-
touches containing
figures and inscriptions,
L 16 Oct,
£880 ($1,302)

8
**A Persian silver and gold
inlaid steel helmet (Kulah
Khud), and armguard
(Bazuband),** 18th
century, *G 25 June,*
SF 28,600
(£8,290; $11,191)

9
**A Persian armguard
(Bazuband),** 18th cen-
tury, 34cm (13½in),
L 17 Apr,
£550 ($715)

10
A Persian steel shield,
18th-19th century, 47cm
(18½in), *L 16 Oct,*
£660 ($976)

11
**A set of Qajar steel
armour,** early 19th cen-
tury, comprising
helmet, shield and
associated armguard,
L 16 Oct,
£990 ($1,465)

1
A Persian dagger (Kard), the hilt of ivory with gold damascend grip strap, with green leather, sheath, 38cm (15in), *L 17 Apr,* £418 ($543)

2
A Persian dagger (Khanjar), the hilt inlaid with a red stone, in green velvet scabbard, 35cm (13¾in), *L 17 Apr,* £605 ($787)

3
A Turkish dagger (Jambiya), 18th-19th century, the hilt and scabbard mounts of brass, 56cm (22in), *L 16 Oct,* £418 ($619)

4
An Indian dagger (Katar), with damascend hilt and grip bars, 44cm (17½in), *L 16 Oct,* £352 ($521)

5
A Yemeni dagger (Khanjar), 19th century, the hilt of rhinoceros horn, the sheath of leather with small dagger in separate compartment, 31cm (12in), *L 16 Oct,* £935 ($1,384)

6
A Turkish sword (Yataghan), the hilt with ivory grip and brass mounts, the steel blade with maker's stamp, 71cm (28in), *L 16 Oct,* £330 ($488)

7
A Balkan Miquelet gun from Roumelia, 18th-19th century, 177cm (69½in), *L 16 Oct,* £1,760 ($2,605)

8
An Ottoman Miquelet fullstocked gun, *c.*1800, maker's mark and dated AH 1237/1821 AD, 100cm (39½in), *L 16 Oct,* £2,200 ($3,080)

9
An Ottoman Balkan rifle, 19th century, 140cm (55in), *L 16 Oct,* £1,650 ($2,442)

10
An Ottoman Miquelet rampart gun, 17th century, with brass inset maker's mark, 160cm (63in), *L 16 Oct,* £3,300 ($4,884)

11
A Moroccan snaphaunce gun, mid-19th century, lock with maker's stamp, 171cm (67in), *L 16 Oct,* £495 ($733)

12
A pair of Balkan Miquelet pistols, 46.5cm (18¼in), *L 16 Oct,* £1,540 ($2,279)

13
A Persian percussion pistol, 19th century, the barrel with maker's marks, inscribed (in translation) 'The Work of Haji Mustafa', 44.5cm (17½in), *L 17 Apr,* £143 ($186)

14
An Ottoman Balkan pistol, *c.*1700, 53cm (21in), *L 17 Apr,* £715 ($930)

15
An Ottoman flintlock blunderbuss, *c.*1800, the barrel bearing pseudo maker's marks, 48.3cm (19in), *G 25 June,* SF 9,350 (£2,701; $3,659)

16
A Cossack Miquelet rifle, early 19th century, with mounts of nielloed silver, the lock with maker's stamp, and ten cartridges, 133cm (51½in), *L 16 Oct,* £5,500 ($8,140)

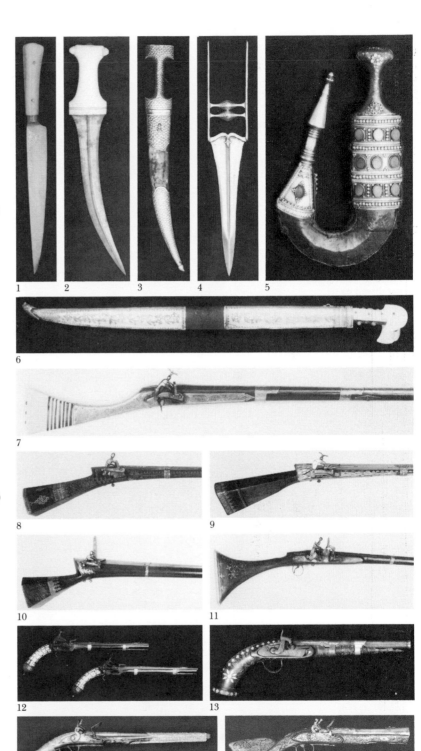

1
An Ottoman silk and metal thread brocade panel, 17th century, mounted, 181 x 68cm (71 x 27in), *L 15 Oct,* **£2,200 ($3,256)**

2
A Safavid velvet panel, early 17th century, 71 x 68cm (2ft 4in x 2ft 3in), *L 15 Oct,* **£880 ($1,302)**

3
A Safavid silk and metal thread brocade coat, 17th-18th century, 91cm (36in), *L 16 Oct,* **£880 ($1,302)**

4
An Ottoman velvet and metal thread panel, Turkey, 17th century, parts of the border now missing, 91 x 37cm (36 x 14in), *L 16 Apr,* **£4,840 ($6,292)**

5
A Bokhara Susani, 239 x 150cm (94 x 59in), *L 16 Apr,* **£1,540 ($2,279)**

6
A Bokhara Susani, 225 x 168cm (88½ x 66in), *L 17 Apr,* **£3,300 ($4,290)**

7
An Indo-Portuguese coverlet border fragment, Goa, 18th century, with Mughal influence, mounted, 148 x 71cm (58 x 28in), *L 17 Apr,* **£1,430 ($1,859)**

8
An 18th century Ottoman embroidery, mounted, 221 x 150cm (87 x 59in), *L 17 Apr,* **£2,420 ($3,146)**

9
An Ottoman silk and velvet panel, 18th century, 145 x 66cm (57 x 26in), *NY 22 Nov,* **$1,100 (£753)**

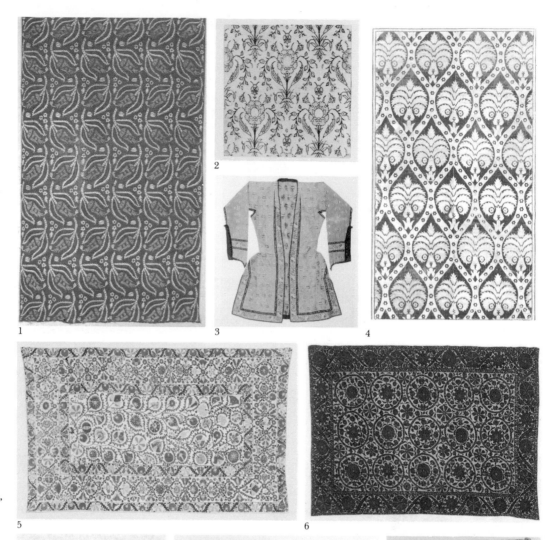

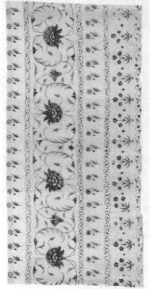

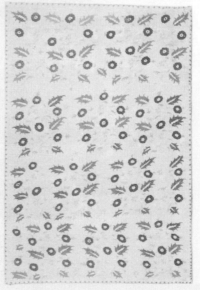

Oriental Rugs and Carpets

See also
● Colour illustrations *pp* 564-565 ● European carpets *pp* 132-134

1
A Persian Tekke part silk carpet, with madder field, 347 x 236cm (11ft 5in x 7ft 9in), *L 31 July*, £2,420 ($3,606)

2
A Tekke carpet, with madder field, 268 x 227cm (8ft 9½in x 7ft 5in), *G 14 May*, **SF 3,300** (£965; $1,283)

3
A Yomut carpet, with walnut field and ivory border, 361 x 220cm (11ft 10in x 7ft 3n), *G 12 Nov*, **SF 4,620** (£1,509; $2,112)

4
A Yomut 'dyrnak gul' carpet, with madder field, 317 x 180cm (10ft 5in x 5ft 11in), *S 19 Nov*, £440 ($616)

5
A Beluch rug, with indigo field and madder border, 175 x 91cm (5ft 9in x 3ft), *S 26 Mar*, £352 ($447)

6
A Beluch prayer rug, the camel *mehrab* with Tree of Life with madder and indigo flowers, walnut border, 140 x 90cm (4ft 7in x 2ft 11½in), *S 19 Nov*, £440 ($616)

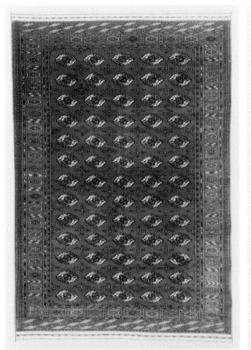

1

2

3

4

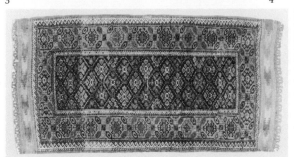

5

6

1
A Kazakh Lambalo rug, the madder field with green and ivory medallions, 196 x 126cm (6ft 5in x 4ft 2in), *G 13 May,* **SF 6,050** (£1,769; $2,353)

2
A Kazakh Gendje rug, with madder field, 193 x 160cm (6ft 4in x 5ft 3in), *L 17 Apr,* **£4,370** ($5,681)

3
A Kazakh prayer rug, the ivory mehrab with blue polygon, blue and red border, 150 x 99cm (4ft 11in x 3ft 3in), *NY 18 May,* **$3,300** (£2,619)

4
A Kazakh Loripambak rug, the madder field with ivory medallion, 231 x 167cm (7ft 7in x 5ft 5½in), *L 17 Apr,* **£4,950** ($6,435)

5
A Kazakh Frachlo rug, the green field with saffron and ivory medallions, 211 x 150cm (6ft 11in x 4ft 11in), *L 17 Apr,* **£5,500** ($7,150)

6
A Kazakh Karatchoph rug, the green field with ivory medallion, saffron border, 242 x 172cm (7ft 11in x 5ft 8in), *L 17 Apr,* **£15,400** ($20,482)

7
A Kazakh Sewan rug, the madder field with bird medallion and Trees of Life, 220 x 168cm (7ft 3in x 5ft 6in), *L 17 Apr,* **£4,400** ($5,720)

8
A Kazakh rug, the indigo field with madder, walnut and indigo medallions, polychrome border, 213 x 137cm (7ft x 4ft 6in), *L 16 Oct,* **£1,540** ($2,279)

1

2

3

4

5

6

7

8

1
A Garabagh runner, the plum field with indigo medallions, 549 x 107cm (18ft 11in x 3ft 6in), *C 18 Apr,* £495 ($644)

2
A Daghestan rug, 193 x 138cm (6ft 4in x 4ft 6in), *L 16 Oct,* £2,420 ($3,582)

3
A Chichi rug, the indigo field with red, ivory, saffron and pale blue design, 142 x 107cm (4ft 8in x 3ft 6in), *M 25 June,* FF 7,770 (£648; $874)

4
A Shirvan kilim, the field woven with ivory, red and blue hexagons, 226 x 165cm (7ft 5in x 5ft 5in), *NY 8 May,* $770 (£611)

5
A Daghestan prayer rug, with ivory *mehrab,* 133 x 115cm (4ft 4in x 3ft 9in), *L 31 July,* £1,705 ($2,540)

6
A South Caucasian carpet, dated AH 1240/ 1824 AD, the saffron field with design in madder, aubergine and walnut, 414 x 188cm (13ft 7in x 6ft 2in), *L 17 Apr,* £1,870 ($2,431)

7
A Garabagh carpet, the madder field with indigo medallions, 280 x 120cm (9ft 2in x 3ft 11in), *G 14 May,* SF 5,500 (£1,608; $2,138)

8
A Kuba rug, with indigo field and ivory border, 259 x 115cm (8ft 6in x 3ft 9in), *L 6 Feb,* £1,650 ($1,865)

9
A Shirvan rug, with indigo field and ivory border, 180 x 96cm (5ft 11in x 2ft 2in), *L 16 Oct,* £1,650 ($2,442)

1

3

2

5

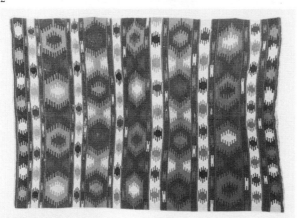

4

6

7

8

9

1
A Shirvan prayer rug,
the ivory *mehrab*
enclosing stylised
plants, 136 x 110cm (4ft
5in x 3ft 7in), *L 6 Feb*,
£1,925 ($2,175)

2
A Shirvan rug, with
madder field, 283 x
143cm (9ft 3in x 4ft 8in),
L 17 Apr,
£2,640 ($2,432)

3
A Shirvan carpet, the
indigo field with
madder medallions, 331
x 181cm (10ft 10in x 5ft
11in), *S 24 Sept*,
£2,860 ($4,290)

4
A Shirvan rug, with
indigo field and ivory
love bird border, 295
x 145cm (9ft 8in x 4ft
9in), *C 12 July*,
£440 ($612)

5
A Shirvan carpet, the
madder field with
indigo bar motifs,
indigo and madder
borders, 290 x 152cm (9ft
6in x 5ft), *S 26 Mar*,
£1,265 ($1,607)

6
A Soumakh rug, 310 x
193cm (10ft 2in x 6ft
4in), *L 6 Feb*,
£385 ($435)

7
A Soumakh rug, with
madder field and ivory
border, 220 x 126cm (7ft
3in x 4ft 2in), *L 17 Apr*,
£935 ($1,216)

8
A Bergama runner, the
madder field with ivory
medallions, 480 x 110cm
(15ft 9in x 3ft 7in),
L 16 Oct,
£1,100 ($1,628)

1

2

3

4

5

6

7

8

1
A Pirbedil rug, with indigo field and walnut border, 174 x 120cm (5ft 8in x 3ft 11in), *L 31 July,* **£2,090 ($3,114)**

2
A Gonakghend rug, with indigo field, 168 x 120cm (5ft 6in x 3ft 11in), *L 31 July,* **£1,210 ($1,803)**

3
A Gonakghend rug, with ivory field and black flowerhead border, 155 x 113cm (5ft 1in x 3ft 8½in), *L 16 Oct,* **£1,760 ($2,605)**

4
A Verne rug, the field with madder and indigo panels, 218 x 155cm (7ft 2in x 5ft 1in), *G 25 June,* **SF 35,200 (£10,203; $13,774)**

5
A Khila carpet, with indigo field and madder border, 284 x 160cm (9ft 4in x 5ft 3in), *L 16 Oct,* **£990 ($1,465)**

6
A Lenkoran runner, the dark-camel field with madder and ivory dragon motifs, 315 x 107cm (10ft 4in x 3ft 6in), *S 29 Jan,* **£825 ($978)**

7
A Talysh runner, with cornflower blue field, and ivory and brick red borders, 249 x 117cm (8ft 2in x 3ft 10in), *NY 26 Oct,* **$2,750 (£1,937)**

8
A Talysh runner, with madder field and ivory border, 280 x 106cm (9ft 2in x 3ft 6in), *L 16 Oct,* **£2,090 ($3,093)**

9
An Akstafa runner, with dark indigo field and ivory border, 330 x 112cm (10ft 10in x 3ft 8in), *S 29 Jan,* **£1,210 ($1,434)**

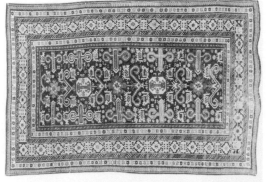
1

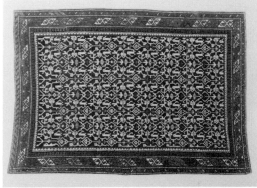
2

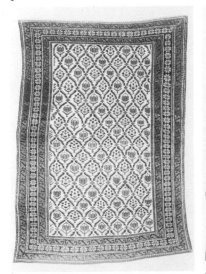
3

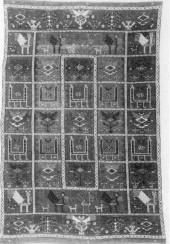
4

5

6

7

8

9

1
A Gabeh rug, the indigo field with madder medallions, ivory border, 206 x 160cm (6ft 9in x 5ft 3in), *L 6 Feb,* **£748 ($845)**

2
A Ghashghai rug, the dark indigo field with ivory medallion, camel and indigo borders, 198 x 222cm (6ft 5in x 4ft), *S 24 Sept,* **£858 ($1,287)**

3
An Afshar rug, 99 x 53cm (3ft 3in x 1ft 9in), *NY 23 Nov,* **$3,300 (£2,260)**

4
A Ghashghai gelim, with madder field, 282 x 167cm (9ft 3in x 5ft 5½in), *L 31 July,* **£275 ($410)**

5
An Afshar mat, with polychrome *gul* panels, 58.5 x 56cm (1ft 11in x 1ft 10in), *C 17 Jan,* **£187 ($224)**

6
A Ghashghai carpet, the indigo field with red medallions, ivory border, 255 x 145cm (8ft 5in x 4ft 9in), *M 25 June,* **FF 7,215 (£601; $812)**

7
An Afshar rug, the indigo field with madder medallion, 127 x 112cm (4ft 2in x 3ft 8in), *L 31 July,* **£418 ($623)**

8
A Ghashghai carpet, the indigo field with madder and ivory medallions, walnut border, 260 x 182cm (8ft 6in x 6ft), *L 16 Oct* **£1,375 ($2,028)**

1

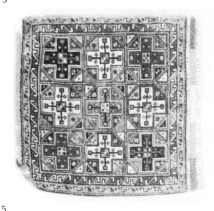

3

5

7

2

4

6

8

1
A **Bidjar rug,** the red ground with blue *herati* pattern, cream border, 218 x 145cm (7ft 2in x 4ft 9in), *NY 23 Nov,* $11,000 (£7,534)

2
A **Bidjar carpet,** the indigo field with madder medallion, 269 x 175cm (8ft 10in x 5ft 9in), *L 17 Apr,* £3,300 ($4,290)

3
A **Bakhtiari rug,** with madder border, single guard stripes, 224 x 137cm (7ft 4in x 4ft 6in), *L 17 Apr,* £935 ($1,216)

4
A **Bakhtiari rug,** the madder field with indigo pole medallion, 218 x 142cm (7ft 2in x 4ft 8in), *S 26 Mar,* £616 ($782)

5
A **Bakhtiari carpet,** with ivory field and indigo border, 350 x 261cm (11ft 6in x 8ft 7in), *L 16 Oct,* £5,720 ($8,466)

6
A **Mahal carpet,** with madder field and walnut border, 333 x 233cm (10ft 11in x 7ft 8in), *L 31 July,* £660 ($983)

7
A **Heriz carpet,** the madder field with indigo medallion, indigo border, 476 x 294cm (15ft 7in x 9ft 8in), *L 31 July,* £2,090 ($3,114)

8
A **Heriz carpet,** 620 x 445cm (20ft 4in x 14ft 7in), *NY 23 Nov,* $16,500 (£11,301)

1

2

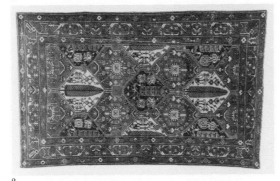
3

4

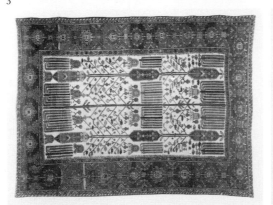
5

6

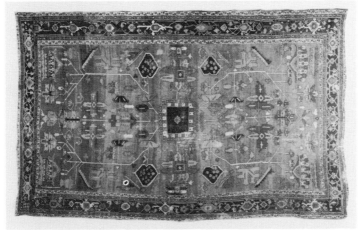
7

8

1
A Heriz carpet, the madder field with indigo medallion, madder border, 407 x 333cm (13ft 4in x 10ft 11in), *L 16 Oct,* **£2,750 ($4,070)**

2
A Heriz carpet, with wine red field and midnight blue border, 338 x 297cm (11ft 1in x 9ft 9in), *NY 2 Feb,* **$9,350 (£7,923)**

3
A Serapi carpet, 325 x 277cm (10ft 8in x 9ft 1in), *NY 18 May,* **$18,700 (£17,841)**

4
A Veramin carpet, with madder field and indigo border, 337 x 252cm (11ft 1in x 8ft 3in), *L 17 Apr,* **£5,500 ($7,150)**

5
A Sultanabad carpet, 516 x 371cm (16ft 11in x 12ft 2in), *NY 8 Oct,* **$7,700 (£5,203)**

6
A North Persian rug, with indigo field and madder border, 188 x 132cm (6ft 2in x 4ft 4in), *L 31 July,* **£935 ($1,393)**

7
A Northwest Persian runner, the brick field with palmettes in blue, mocha, rose and ivory, 505 x 99cm (16ft 7in x 3ft 3in), *NY 23 Nov,* **$2,530 (£1,733)**

8
A Northwest Persian prayer rug, the ivory *mehrab* with red medallion, deep blue border, 213 x 170cm (7ft x 5ft 7in), *NY 23 Nov,* **$17,600 (£12,055)**

1

2

3

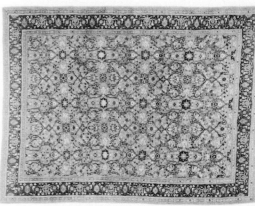

4

5

6

7

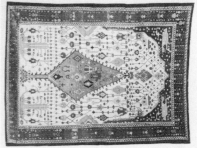

8

1
A Faraghan rug, 193 x 130cm (6ft 4in x 4ft 3in), *NY 23 Nov*, **$27,500 (£18,836)**

2
A Sarough Faraghan rug, with ivory field and indigo border, 194 x 136cm (6ft 4in x 4ft 5in), *L 17 Apr*, **£17,050 ($22,165)**

3
A Sarough carpet, 635 x 409cm (20ft 10in x 13ft 5in), *NY 2 Feb*, **$22,000 (£18,644)**

4
A Faraghan rug, the indigo field with ivory medallions, madder border, *G 25 June*, **SF 16,500 (£4,783; $6,457)**

5
A Sarough rug, the madder field with indigo medallion, 195 x 132cm (6ft 5in x 4ft 4in), *L 6 Feb*, **£1,100 ($1,243)**

6
A Sarough rug, the indigo field with ivory columns, walnut and indigo border, 200 x 129cm (6ft 7in x 4ft 3in), *G 14 May*, **SF 12,650 (£3,699; $4,919)**

7
A Sarough Faraghan prayer rug, the cream *mehrab* with brick red palmette tree, dark blue border, 196 x 137cm (6ft 5in x 4ft 6in), *NY 18 May*, **$9,900 (£7,857)**

8
A Senneh rug, the shaped ivory field with indigo medallion, madder border, 197 x 137cm (6ft 5½in x 4ft 6in), *S 16 July*, **£704 ($943)**

9
A Senneh rug, with indigo field and madder border, 192 x 132cm (6ft 4in x 4ft 4in), *G 14 May*, **SF 22,000 (£6,433; $8,566)**

1

2

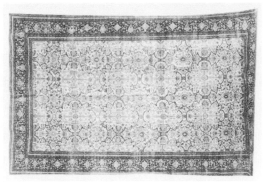

3

4

5

6

7

8

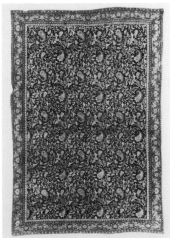

9

1
A Kazvin Tree of Life rug, with indigo field and madder border, 182 x 129cm (6ft x 4ft 3in), *L 16 Oct,*
£1,540 ($2,279)

2
A Tabriz Tree of Life rug, with ivory field and madder border, 198 x 145cm (6ft 6in x 4ft 9in), *L 6 Feb,*
£660 ($746)

3
A Tabriz silk rug, the madder field with ivory medallion and spandrels, *L 17 Apr,*
£5,500 ($7,150)

4
A Malayer rug, the ivory field with madder medallion and walnut spandrels, madder border, 190 x 126cm (6ft 3in x 4ft 2in), *S 16 July,*
£792 ($1,101)

5
A Tabriz carpet, 648 x 331cm (21ft 3in x 13ft 10in), *NY 18 May,*
$44,000 (£34,920)

6
A Tabriz carpet, with pale indigo field and beige border, 395 x 277cm (12ft 11in x 9ft 1in), *L 6 Feb,*
£1,265 ($1,429)

7
A Tabriz rug, the madder field with pale green medallion, 175 x 123cm (5ft 9in x 4ft), *L 6 Feb,*
£605 ($684)

8
A Tabriz carpet, with saffron field and indigo border, 324 x 285cm (10ft 7½in x 9ft 4in), *L 17 Apr,*
£1,980 ($2,574)

9
A Nain part silk carpet, with indigo field and beige border, 282 x 165cm (9ft 3in x 5ft 1in), *G 12 Nov,*
SF 7,700 (£2,516; $3,522)

1   2   3

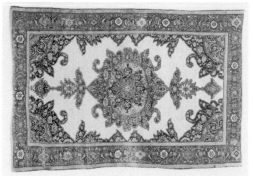

4   5

6   7

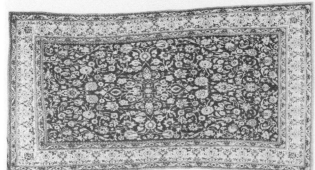

8   9

1

A **Tehran rug**, with ivory field, 204 x 140cm (6ft 8in x 4ft 7in), *S 24 Sept,* £495 ($743)

2

A **Mashhad carpet**, the indigo field with central madder and green medallion, madder border, 351 x 239cm (11ft 6in x 7ft 10in), *L 17 Apr,* £9,350 ($12,155)

3

A **Mashhad rug**, the madder field with ivory medallion, madder border, *L 6 Feb,* £495 ($559)

4

A **Kashan raised silk prayer rug**, with pale indigo *mehrab* and indigo border, 206 x 129cm (6ft 9in x 4ft 3in), *G 14 May,* **SF 11,000 (£3,216; $4,278)**

5

A **Kashan rug**, the madder field with indigo medallion, indigo border, 202 x 135cm (6ft 7in x 4ft 5in), *L 6 Feb,* £715 ($808)

6

A **Kurk Kashan pictorial rug**, depicting the story of Babak, dark indigo border, 198 x 130cm (6ft 6in x 4ft 3in), *S 21 May,* £2,970 ($3,980)

7

A **Kashan carpet**, the ivory *mehrab* surrounded by foliage and birds in red, ivory and blue, red border, 204 x 134cm (6ft 8½in x 4ft 4¾in), *M 25 June,* **FF 37,185 (£3,099; $4,183)**

8

A **Kashan Natanz rug**, with ivory field and indigo border, 199 x 129cm (6ft 6in x 4ft 3in), *L 31 July,* £1,980 ($2,950)

9

A **pair of Kashan silk rugs**, each with beige field and madder border, 202 x 133cm (6ft 7in x 4ft 4in), *C 18 Apr,* £2,200 ($2,860)

1

2

3

4

5

6

7

8

9

1
A Kashan carpet, with ivory field and beige border, 326 x 226cm (10ft 8in x 7ft 5in), *L 31 July,*
£1,430 ($2,131)

2
A Kashan rug, with madder field and indigo border, 203 x 135cm (6ft 8in x 4ft 5in), *L 31 July,*
£1,540 ($2,295)

3
A Ghom rug, with ivory field and border, 213 x 138cm (7ft x 4ft 6½in), *S 26 Mar,*
£638 ($810)

4
A Ghom silk rug, the field with ivory bands, green border, 165 x 107cm (5ft 5in x 3ft 6in), *C 4 Oct,*
£902 ($1,263)

5
A Ghom silk carpet, the ivory field with madder medallion, ivory border, 306 x 195cm (10ft ½in x 6ft 5in), *L 17 Apr,*
£6,050 ($7,865)

6
A Tabriz Benlian carpet, the ivory field with madder medallion, indigo border, 447 x 362cm (15ft 8in x 11ft 10½in), *L 17 Apr,*
£8,800 ($11,440)

7
A Tabriz carpet, 455 x 340cm (14ft 11in x 11ft 2in), *NY 18 May,*
$15,400 (£12,222)

8
An Esfahan rug, with madder field and indigo border, 232 x 150cm (7ft 7in x 4ft 11in), *L 31 July,*
£2,970 ($4,425)

1

2

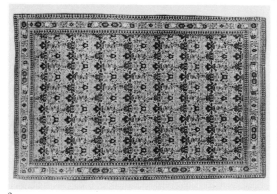
3

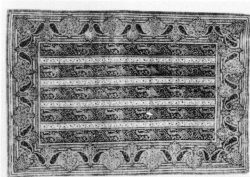
4

5

6

7

8

1
A Ghom silk rug, with camel field and madder border, 212 x 138cm (6ft 11in x 4ft 6in), *G 14 May*, **SF 6,050** (£1,769; $2,353)

2
A Ghom silk prayer rug, with pale indigo *mehrab* and walnut border, 172 x 110cm (5ft 8in x 3ft 7in), *G 12 Nov*, **SF 9,900** (£3,235; $4,529)

3
An Esfahan carpet, with ivory field and border, 302 x 205cm (9ft 11in x 6ft 9in), *G 12 Nov*, **SF 38,500** (£12,581; $17,613)

4
An Esfahan rug, with ivory field and indigo border, 218 x 133cm (7ft 2in x 4ft 4in), *S 24 Sept*, £902 ($1,353)

5
An Esfahan prayer rug, with ivory *mehrab* and madder border, 216 x 144cm (7ft 1in x 4ft 9in), *L 17 Apr*, £1,430 ($1,859)

6
A pair of Esfahan rugs, with madder field and indigo border, 223 x 140cm (7ft 4in x 4ft 7in), *S 16 July*, £1,870 ($2,599)

7
A Kerman prayer rug, with ivory field and indigo border, 236 x 147cm (7ft 9in x 4ft 10in), *L 31 July*, £2,640 ($3,934)

8
A Kerman pictorial rug, with a medallion depicting Nur Ali Shah, madder border of portrait roundels, 207 x 135cm (6ft 9½in x 4ft 5in), *G 14 May*, **SF 5,500** (£1,608; $2,139)

9
A Kerman pictorial rug, depicting the Garden of Eden, indigo border, 216 x 142cm (7ft 1in x 4ft 8in), *L 17 Apr*, £2,200 ($2,860)

1

2

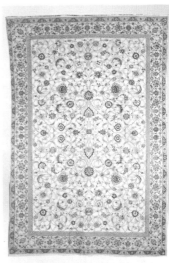
3

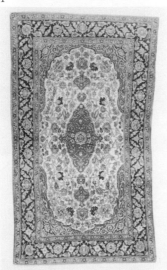
4

5

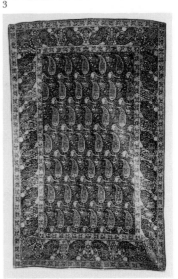
6

7

8

9

1
A Konya prayer rug,
the brick field with
sky blue medallions,
224 x 102cm (7ft 4in x
3ft 4in), *NY 23 Nov,*
$3,575 (£2,449)

2
A Konya prayer rug,
163 x 114cm (5ft 4in x
3ft 9in), *NY 18 May,*
$15,400 (£12,222)

3
A West Anatolian rug,
with a Transylvanian
design within a white
and cornflower blue
border, 246 x 191cm
(8ft 1in x 6ft 3in),
NY 18 May,
$6,050 (£4,801)

4
A Ladik prayer rug,
with madder *mehrab*
within a saffron border,
164 x 108cm (5ft 5in x 3ft
7in), *L 17 Apr,*
£10,450 ($13,585)

5
An Ushak rug, 137 x
107cm (4ft 6in x 3ft 6in),
NY 18 May,
$22,000 (£17,460)

6
A Melas rug, the madder
field with a Tree of
Life, surrounded by
seven borders, 171 x
113cm (5ft 7in x 3ft 8in),
L 17 Apr,
£12,100 ($15,730)

7
A Melas prayer rug, with
madder *mehrab* and
saffron floral border,
168 x 107cm (5ft 6in x
3ft 6in), *L 17 Apr,*
£2,750 ($3,575)

8
A Melas prayer rug, with
madder *mehrab* and
saffron gul border, 159
x 107cm (5ft 3in x 3ft
6in), *S 24 Sept,*
£495 ($743)

1

2

3

4

5

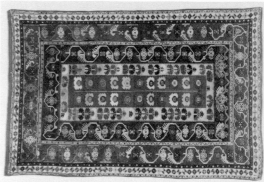

6

7

8

1
A Malatya kilim, 386 x
188cm (12ft 8in x 6ft
2in), *NY 18 May*,
$3,740 (£2,968)

2
A Rashwan kilim, 374 x
152cm (12ft 3in x 5ft),
NY 18 May,
$1,760 (£1,396)

3
**A Kum Kapour prayer
rug**, signed Zare,
(1903-6), 122 x 184cm
(4ft x 2ft 9in),
NY 18 May,
$60,500 (£48,015)

4
A Borlu carpet, with
madder field and camel
border, 395 x 285cm
(12ft 11in x 9ft 4in),
L 6 Feb,
£1,320 ($1,492)

5
**A Sharkoy gelim prayer
carpet**, with madder
field, 367 x 334cm (12ft x
10ft 11in), *L 17 Apr*,
£2,090 ($2,717)

6
**A Turkish silk and metal
thread prayer rug**, with
madder *mehrab*, beige
cartouche and roundel
border, 190 x 142cm
(6ft 3in x 4ft 8in),
G 14 May,
SF 9,900 (£2,895; $3,850)

7
**A Keyseri silk prayer
carpet**, with madder
mehrab and ivory
border, 256 x 181cm (8ft
5in x 5ft 11in), *G 14 May*,
SF 8,250 (£2,412; $3,208)

8
A Hereke silk prayer rug,
the ivory *mehrab* with
ochre spandrels, 147 x
103cm (4ft 10in x 3ft 4in),
S 24 Sept,
£1,595 ($2,393)

1   2   3

4   5

6   7   8

1
A Peking carpet, with indigo field and ivory border, 411 x 392cm (13ft 6in x 12ft 10in), *L 17 Apr,* £8,250 ($10,725)

2
A Chinese carpet, with indigo field and beige and indigo border, 305 x 223.5cm (10ft x 7ft 4in), *C 12 July,* £484 ($673)

3
A Chinese rug, with indigo field and indigo lattice border, 184 x 95cm (6ft ½in x 3ft 1in), *S 24 Sept,* £286 ($429)

4
A Chinese carpet, *c.*1800, with saffron field and border, 453 x 305cm (14ft 10in x 6ft 10in), *L 17 Apr,* £12,100 ($15,730)

5
A Pao Tou carpet, Guangxu, in shades of brown, peach and honey, 200 x 129cm (6ft 7in x 4ft 2¾in), *L 1 Nov,* £440 ($669)

6
A Peking silk rug, Guangxu, the blue and iron red ground with a medallion of a Buddhist lion, 249 x 155cm (8ft 2in x 5ft 1in), *L 1 Nov,* £2,970 ($4,455)

7
A rare Chinese rug, 19th century, the ochre ground with a chocolate brown and white tiger, 239 x 140cm (8ft 2in x 4ft 7in), *L 1 Nov,* £7,700 ($11,550)

8
An Agra carpet, *c.*1900, the ivory field woven in magenta, puce and fawn design, 488 x 366cm (16ft x 12ft), *NY 2 Nov,* $6,050 (£4,201)

9
An Agra carpet, with indigo palmette border, 268 x 174cm (8ft 9½in x 5ft 9in), *C 4 Oct,* £715 ($1,001)

10
An Indo-Persian carpet, 749 x 588cm (24ft 8in x 19ft 5in), *L 16 Oct,* £3,850 ($5,698)

1

2

3

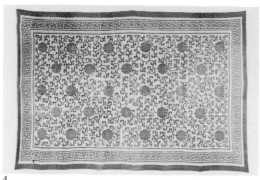
4

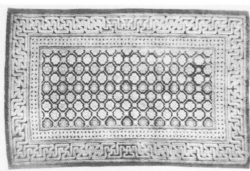
5

6

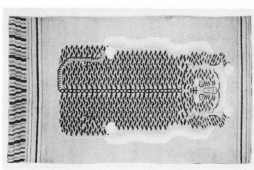
7

8

9

10

Asian Works of Art

Article ● Tibetan bronzes *pp* 648-652   *See also* ● Colour illustrations *p* 575

1
A Thai ivory figure of Buddha, 17th/18th century, with brownish patina, 25cm (9⅞in), *L 10 June*, £1,650 ($2,195)

2
A South Indian ivory figure of Krishna, 19th century, with burnished patina, 20.3cm (8in), *L 10 June*, £1,045 ($1,390)

3
A Mughal ivory panel, probably from a casket, Deccan, 17th/18th century, 23.5 x 7.5cm (9¼ x 3in), *L 10 June*, £902 ($1,200)

4
A pair of Indian ivory figures, 18th/19th century, with traces of vermilion, 14cm (5½in), 13.5cm (5¼in), *L 10 June*, £1,430 ($1,902)

5
A Pair of Indian ivory sandals, *c.*18th century 25cm (9⅞in), *L 11 June*, £462 ($614)

6
An Indian ivory figure of Ganesha, 18th/19th century, with brownish patina, 9cm (3½in), *L 10 June*, £1,265 ($1,682)

7
A pair of Indian ivory sandals, 18th/19th century, 25cm (9¾in), *NY 21 Sept*, $1,430 (£1,075)

8
A Tibetan copper-gilt figure of a cow (?), 15th/16th century, 13.3cm (5¼in) wide, *NY 20 Sept*, $935 (£703)

9
A Sukhothai roof finial, 14th century, the scales incised and picked out in brown on a creamy slip beneath a transparent glaze, 51.3cm (20in), *L 10 June*, £132 ($176)

10
A Sawankhalok roof finial, 14th century, the details all incised and picked out in brown over a greenish-white glaze, 48.7cm (19in), *L 10 June*, £308 ($410)

1   2   3

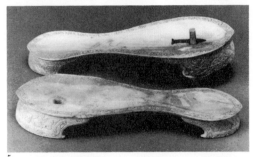

4

5

6   7

9

8   10

1
An Indian white marble fragment depicting elephants, 18th/19th century, 67.5cm (26½in), *L 10 June,* £605 ($805)

2
An Agra pietra dura-work marble panel, probably a railing section, 18th/19th century, 45 x 25.5cm (17½ x 10in), *NY 21 Sept,* $3,575 (£2,688)

3
A pair of decorative Indian white marble lions, 61cm (24in), *NY 21 Sept,* $6,050 (£4,549)

4
An Indian parcel-gilt polychrome-painted wood elephant, 19th century, 154cm (60½in), *L 10 June,* £1,650 ($2,195)

5
A Mughal buff sandstone Jali screen, *c.*18th century, 76cm (30in), *NY 21 Sept,* $935 (£703)

6
An Indian white marble chair, 87.5cm (34½in), *NY 21 Sept,* $5,500 (£4,135)

7
An Indian marble bench, 172cm (67¾in) wide, *L 10 June,* £2,200 ($2,926)

8
A pair of Indian buff sandstone elephants, probably Uttar Pradesh, 17th century, 76cm (30in), *NY 21 Sept,* $16,500 (£12,406)

9
A Mughal white marble panel, 17th/18th century, 47 x 70cm (18½ x 27½in), *NY 21 Sept,* $550 (£414)

10
An Indian wood brass-inlaid four-fold screen, *c.*1900, 185cm (72¾in), *L 10 June,* £550 ($732)

11
An Indian polychrome-painted wood figure of a horse, 19th century, 34cm (13⅜in), *NY 21 Sept,* $1,540 (£1,158)

1

2

3

4

5

6

7

8

9

10

11

1
A Central Indian buff
sandstone stele depicting
Vishnu, c.12th century,
87cm (34in), *NY 20 Sept*,
$2,860 (£2,150)

2
A Nepalese polychrome
painted wood figure of
the Dharmapala Haya-
griva, c.18th century,
72.5cm (28½in),
NY 20 Sept,
$4,125 (£3,102)

3
A North-West Indian buff
sandstone caryatid, prob-
ably early 19th century,
173cm (69in), *NY 21 Sept*,
$7,700 (£5,789)

4
A Jain pink sandstone
head, c.10th century, the
whole with traces of
paint, 38cm (15in),
NY 20 Sept,
$12,650 (£9,511)

5
A Kashmir grey stone
head of Vishnu, c.9th century, 10.8cm (4⅛in),
NY 20 Sept,
$770 (£579)

6
A Central Indian buff
sandstone stele depicting
Siva and Parvati, 11th/
12th century, 92.8cm
(36½in), *NY 20 Sept*,
$19,800 (£14,887)

7
A Central Indian buff
sandstone stele depicting
Durga slaying the buffalo
demon, c.12th century,
61cm (24in), *L 10 June*,
£1,595 ($2,121)

8
A Central Indian buff
sandstone stele depicting
the dancing Ganesha,
c.11th century, 63.5cm
(25in), *NY 20 Sept*,
$4,400 (£3,308)

9
An Eastern Indian black
stone miniature stupa,
c.11th century, 33cm
(13in), *L 10 June*,
£1,870 ($2,487)

10
A Central Indian red
sandstone fragment
depicting the river-
goddess Ganga, 4th/5th
century, 38cm (15in),
NY 20 Sept,
$7,150 (£5,376)

11
A Central Indian buff
sandstone figure of the
goddess Sarasvati, c.12th
century, 47cm (18½in),
NY 20 Sept,
$3,575 (£2,688)

12
A South Indian granite
standing figure of
Parvati(?), late Chola,
12th/13th century,
86.5cm (34in),
NY 20 Sept,
$7,700 (£5,789)

13
A Central Indian Jain
pinkish-buff sandstone
figure of a Tirthankara,
7th/8th century, 70cm
(27½in), *NY 20 Sept*,
$9,900 (£7,444)

14
A Central Indian buff
sandstone female head,
8th/10th century,
59.6cm (23½in),
NY 20 Sept,
$14,850 (£11,165)

1
A Thai buff sandstone head of Buddha, Haripunjay style, 12th/13th century, the whole with slight traces of polychrome, 19cm (7½in), *L 10 June,* £3,300 ($4,389)

2
A Thai bronze figure of Buddha, 12th/13th century, the whole with dark green patina, 28.5cm (11¼in), *L 10 June,* £9,900 ($13,167)

3
A Thai bronze bust of Buddha, Sukothai style, *c.*14th century, 70cm (27½in), *L 10 June,* £8,250 ($10,973)

4
A Thai bronze head of Buddha, Chien Sen style, *c.*15th century, 34.5cm (13½in), *L 10 June,* £3,300 ($4,389)

5
A Thai bronze bust of Buddha, late Sukothai style, *c.*15th century, the whole with turquoise-coloured patina, 26.5cm (10⅜in), *L 10 June,* £2,420 ($3,219)

6
A Thai bronze figure of Buddha, Ayuthia style, 16th/17th century, the whole with traces of red lacquer and gilding, 61cm (24in), *L 10 June,* £1,430 ($1,902)

7
A Thai gilt-bronze figure of Buddha, 19th century, with traces of red lacquer, 101.5cm (40in), *L 10 June,* £572 ($761)

8
A Thai gilt-bronze reclining figure of Buddha, 18th/19th century, 171cm (67¼in), *L 10 June,* £5,500 ($7,315)

9
A Thai gilt-bronze figure of a kneeling devotee, 19th century, 58cm (22¾in), *L 10 June,* £462 ($614)

10
A Thai gilt-bronze figure of Buddha, *c.*18th century, 108cm (42½in), *L 10 June,* £825 ($1,097)

11
A Khmer grey sandstone male head, Kulen style, 9th century, 21cm (8¼in), *NY 20 Sept,* $7,700 (£5,789)

12
A Khmer grey sandstone female figure, Baphuon style, probably 11th century, 75cm (29½in), *L 10 June,* £9,680 ($12,874)

1

2

3

4

5

6

7

8

9

10

11

12

1
A Khmer grey sandstone
female head, Baphuon
style, 11th century,
19.5cm (7½in), L 10 June,
£3,960 ($5,267)

2
A Khmer grey sandstone
female head, possibly of
Uma, Baphuon style,
11th century, 15.5cm
(6⅛in), L 10 June,
£4,620 ($6,145)

3
A Khmer pink sandstone
lion, c.12th century, with
traces of polychrome,
75cm (29½in), L 10 June,
£4,950 ($6,584)

4
A Khmer grey sandstone
female head, Baphuon
style, 11th century,
14.5cm (5¾in), L 10 June,
£1,045 ($1,390)

5
A Khmer buff sandstone
head of Avalokitesvara,
Bayon style, 12th/13th
century, 21.5cm (8½in),
NY 20 Sept,
$5,500 (£4,135)

6
A Khmer grey sandstone
male head, Angkor Wat
style, c.12th century,
15cm (6in), L 10 June,
£1,320 ($1,756)

7
A Khmer bronze figure of
Vishnu on Garuda, 12th/
13th century, the whole
with green patina, 19cm
(7½in), L 10 June,
£1,210 ($1,609)

8
A Gandhara grey schist
Bodhisattva head,
Swat Valley style,
2nd/3rd century, 36.8cm
(14½in), NY 20 Sept,
$6,325 (£4,756)

9
A Gandhara grey schist
head of Maitreya Buddha,
Swat Valley style, 3rd/
4th century, 20.5cm
(8in), NY 20 Sept,
$1,100 (£827)

10
A Gandhara grey schist
Buddha head, 3rd/4th
century, 16.5cm (6½in),
NY 20 Sept,
$1,320 (£992)

11
A Gandhara grey schist
frieze, 3rd/4th century,
63.5cm (25in), L 10 June,
£2,860 ($3,804)

12
A Gandhara grey schist
figure of Buddha, 3rd/
4th century, 38.7cm
(15¼in), NY 20 Sept,
$3,410 (£2,564)

13
A Gandhara grey schist
figure of Buddha, 3rd/
4th century, 81.5cm
(32in), NY 20 Sept,
$15,400 (£11,579)

14
A Gandhara grey schist
bust of a Bodhisattva,
3rd/4th century, 52.7cm
(20¾in), NY 20 Sept,
$7,700 (£5,789)

15
A Gandhara stucco
Bodhisattva head, 4th/
5th century, 21cm
(8½in), L 10 June,
£2,640 ($3,511)

1   2   3

4   5   6

7   8   9

10   11

12   13   14   15

1
An Indian parcel-gilt
ewer, 19th century,
14.5cm (5¾in), *L 11 June*,
£330 ($439)

2
A Tibetan silver butter-
lamp (*Cho-kung*), 23cm
(9½in), *L 10 June*,
£550 ($732)

3
An Indian pierced silver
fruit bowl, 19th century,
21.5cm (11½in),
NY 21 Sept,
$660 (£496)

4
A Thai silver-gilt bowl,
with nielloed border,
19th century, 22.3cm
(8¾in) diam, *L 11 June*,
£462 ($614)

5
A Kashmiri silver jug
and basin, 19th century,
40cm (15¾in) diam,
NY 21 Sept,
$990 (£744)

6
An Indian silver pan-box,
19th century, 11.2cm
(4⅜in) diam, *L 11 June*,
£550 ($732)

7
A Khmer bronze bell,
12th century, 21cm
(8¼in), *L 10 June*,
£880 ($1,170)

8
An Indian parcel-gilt
silver pan-box, with fitted
compartments, 18th/
19th century, 23.2cm
(9⅛in), *NY 21 Sept*,
$880 (£662)

9
An Indian parcel-gilt
silver rosewater-sprinkler,
*c.*18th century, 29.2cm
(11½in), *NY 21 Sept*,
$1,870 (£1,406)

10
An Indian silver-gilt
ewer, *c.*18th century,
33.5cm (13¼in),
NY 21 Sept,
$7,150 (£5,376)

11
An Indian 'Bidri' bowl
inscribed with Koranic
verse, 19th century,
12.3cm (5in) diam,
L 11 June,
£528 ($702)

12
A South Indian bronze
bowl, 98cm (38½in)
diam, *NY 21 Sept*,
$7,150 (£5,376)

13
An Indian silver-gilt pan-
box, probably Lucknow,
late 18th/early 19th
century, 22cm (8⅝in),
NY 21 Sept,
$1,320 (£992)

14
An Indian parcel-gilt
silver Huqqa, late 18th/
early 19th century,
71cm (28in), *NY 21 Sept*,
$880 (£662)

15
An Indian octagonal
silver casket, 19th century,
16.3cm (6⅜in), *L 11 June*,
£495 ($658)

1
A Mongolian silver coral and turquoise-inset sword and scabbard, 19th century, 106cm (41¾in), *L 10 June,* £1,320 ($1,756)

2
A Gangetic Valley copper harpoon, Uttar Pradesh, *c.*1500-1200 BC, with dark green patina, blade repaired, 38.1cm (15in), *NY 20 Sept,* $825 (£620)

3
A Mughal jade-hilted ram's head dagger, *c.*18th century, 29cm (11½in), *NY 21 Sept,* $3,575 (£2,688)

4
A Mughal jade-hilted dagger set with rubies, *c.*18th century, 35.5cm (14in), *NY 21 Sept,* $6,325 (£4,756)

5
A Tibetan rock-crystal ritual dagger (*Phur-bu*), probably 17th/18th century, 25.5cm (10in), *NY 20 Sept,* $2,750 (£2,068)

6
A Balinese dagger (*kris*), 19th century, the ebony grip mounted with gold panels set with diamonds and rubies, 64cm (25¼in), *NY 15 Feb,* $2,420 (£2,086)

7
An Indian enamelled gold and white sapphire-inset sarpesh, 19th century, 11cm (4¼in), *L 10 June,* £1,760 ($2,341)

8
A Mughal jade gold-inset dagger hilt, 18th/19th century, 12.5cm (4⅞in), *NY 21 Sept,* $1,320 (£992)

9
A pair of Kharanphool enamelled gold earrings, 19th century, 5.5cm (2⅛in), *NY 21 Sept,* $2,860 (£2,150)

10
An Indian gold bazu-band, set with emeralds, rose-diamonds and a ruby, 18th/19th century, 12.2cm (4¾in), *NY 21 Sept,* $9,350 (£7,030)

11
A South Indian gold bracelet, Toda, 8.3cm (3¼in) diam., *NY 21 Sept,* $2,200 (£1,654)

12
A Nepalese gold earring, from an image, inset with foiled rubies and other stones, 19th century, 8cm (3⅛in), *NY 21 Sept,* $7,700 (£5,789)

13
A Jaipur enamelled gold sarpest plume, set with diamonds, emeralds and rubies, 19th century, 5.5cm (2⅛in), *NY 21 Sept,* $1,760 (£1,323)

14
A Ladakh woman's head-dress, (*Perak*), 104cm (41in), *L 10 June,* £1,210 ($1,609)

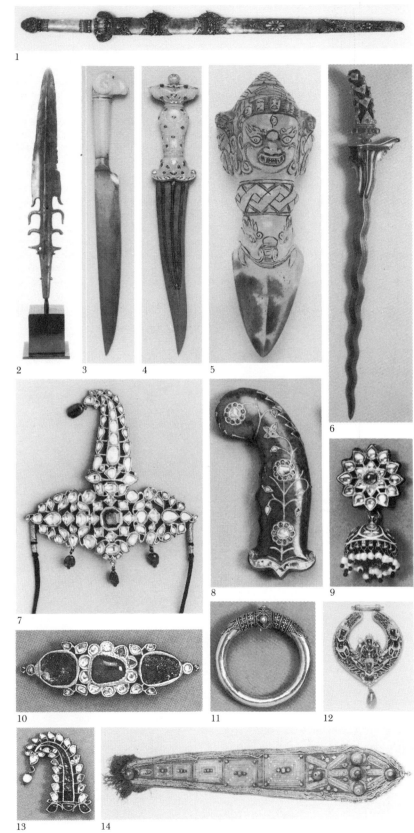

1
2 3 4 5
6
7
8 9
10 11 12
13 14

Tibetan Bronze Images

The market for Tibetan art provides infinite opportunities for the collector, particularly the 'uninitiated' or those with limited means. Being a highly specialised subject, there are comparatively few collectors world-wide, resulting in a less competitive, and in consequence less expensive, market. It would be possible to make a collection today of Tibetan Buddhist bronzes, spanning most periods and styles from the 12th to the 20th century, without any one item costing more than £1,000 ($1,500) and many costing less than £500 ($750).

There are excellent study collections representative of Tibetan art in many European museums and some of the finest objects to have left Tibet as a result of the Chinese Communist takeover in 1959 have found their way to museums in India, America and elsewhere. The first known Europeans to enter Tibet were two intrepid Portuguese Jesuit missionaries, Father Antonio d'Andrade and Father Marques, in 1624. However,

Tibet remained a closed country until the late 19th century and it was not until after the British military expedition led by Colonel Younghusband in 1904, that the country became accessible to travellers. Consequently Tibetan art has only been collected outside Tibet for the last eighty years.

The iconology of Tibetan Buddhism (or Lamaism) is a vast and complex subject, the study of which is far from complete in the West. Based on the original Indian Buddhist pantheon, its often terrifying and seemingly incomprehensible deities evolved largely through a melange of regional superstitions and the shamanistic beliefs of pre-Buddhist Tibet. In addition, the early religious kings, Indian teacher-scholars, yogins and mystics, historical figures such as Gesar of gLing and Kuan-Te, and later reformers, abbots, Grand-, Dalai- and Panchen-Lamas, all added to the pantheon, each with his own iconographical recipe as laid down by sacred texts.

—1—
A Tibetan copper figure of Gautama Buddha (*Sakya-muni*), 12th century, 19.3cm (7⅝in), *NY 20 Sept*, $8,250 (£6,203)

—2—
A Western Tibetan brass figure of the Saviouress Sitatara, the Green Tara (*sGrol-dkar*) *c.*12th century, 14.7cm (5¾in), *NY 20 Sept*, $1,925 (£1,447)

—3—
A Nepalese copper-gilt figure of the Saviouress Syamatara, *c.*12th century, 16cm (6¼in), *NY 20 Sept*, $4,400 (£3,308)

—4—
A Western Tibetan bronze figure of the crowned Amitabha Buddha, *c.*14th century, 14cm (5½in), *NY 20 Sept*, $1,540 (£1,158)

—5—
A Tibetan bronze figure of the Saviouress Syamatara, probably *c.*14th century, 16.5cm (6½in), *L 10 June*, £880 ($1,170)

—6—
A Western Tibetan bronze figure of Aksobhya Buddha, 14th/15th century, 24.5cm (9⅝in), *L 11 June*, £385 ($512)

—1—

—2—

—3—

—4—

—5—

—6—

Bronze images were by far the most common, although wood, terracotta, silver and gold were also used. They were usually executed by the *cire perdu* or 'lost wax' method, the image once cast being gilded, chased, applied with polychrome details or set with semi-precious stones. Sacred talismans were inserted into the hollow figure which was then sealed with a metal plate. Images were seen most frequently in monasteries, displayed *en masse* on altars, but in secular life they were also kept in houses, tents or private chapels. Merit was accumulated both by worshipping and commissioning images. On inscribed bronzes occasionally the name of the commissioner (but rarely of the artist) is given, amidst invocations. The styles of Tibetan images, a few cases excepted, cannot easily be located geographically, despite obvious influences from the immediately surrounding areas of India, (frequently providing the prototype), China, Nepal, Ladakh, Kashmir, Central Asia and Mongolia.

Some of the most popular deities are listed below and the sample illustrations broadly reflect the styles and influences which these countries had on Tibetan art. The history and teachings of Buddhism are comparatively little known in the West: readers of this introduction to Tibetan bronzes may find a very brief outline history of Buddhism in Tibet of interest.

According to historical tradition, Prince Siddharta Gautama (the Buddha or 'enlightened one' as he subsequently became known) was born in the 6th century B.C. By the time of his death *c.*483 B.C. the seeds of Buddhism had been sewn with the establishment of his disciples in monasteries throughout north-eastern India. After the adoption of Buddhism by the great Emperor Ashoka (273-232 B.C.) the new religion spread throughout his vast empire. The Muslim invasion in the 12th and 13th centuries effectively quoshed Buddhism in India, through which the whole basis of Tibetan Buddhism had been absorbed.

—7—
A Tibetan coppery-bronze figure of the Mahasiddha Virupa 14th/15th century, 15cm (6in), *NY 20 Sept,* $5,775 (£4,342)

—8—
A Tibetan copper gilt figure of the Buddha Bhaisajyaguru (*sMan-la*), 16th/17th century, 27.5cm (10¾in), *NY 20 Sept,* $2,750 (£2,067)

—9—
A Tibetan copper figure of Jalendra, 15th/16th century, 24.5cm (10in), *NY 20 Sept,* $18,700 (£14,060)

—10—
A Nepalese copper-gilt figure of the Bodhisattva Manjusri, 15th/16th century, 16.5cm (6½in), *NY 20 Sept,* $6,930 (£5,210)

—11—
A Tibetan copper figure of the Dakini Vajravarahi, *c.*16th century, 24cm (9½in), *NY 20 Sept,* $2,640 (£1,985)

—12—
A Tibetan gilt-copper figure of Padmasambhava, *c.*17th century, 17.5cm (7in), *L 11 June,* £792 ($1,053)

—13—
A Tibetan gilt-copper figure of Gautama Buddha, *c.*16th century, 16.5cm (6½in), *L 10 June,* £440 ($585)

—14—
A Tibetan gilt-copper figure of Vajradhara, 16th/17th century, 21.5cm (8½in), *L 10 June,* £660 ($878)

—7—

—8—

—11—

—9—   —10—

—12—   —13—

—14—

Tibet was ruled by *Srong-brtsan-sgam-po* from *c*.609-649. He is thought to have been responsible for the introduction of Buddhism through his marriage with two Buddhist princesses, one Chinese, the other Nepalese. It was not until *c*.779, however, that the first Tibetan monastery was founded and Tibetans were trained as monks for the first time. This came about largely though the influence of two Indian *gurus* (religious teachers), *Santarakshita* and *Padmasambhava*, who came to Tibet, possibly by royal invitation. The latter became famous as a learned yogin and mystic who performed magic feats, his name meaning 'born from the lotus flower'. He was later adopted by the *rNying-ma-pa* (or 'Red Cap' sect) as their founder, and images of him proliferated.

With the embracing of *Mahayana* Buddhism in about 972, the foundation stone of Tibetan Buddhism was laid, from which its own pantheon of disparate gods gradually emerged. The Indian *Mahayana* ('Greater Vehicle') school believed in the gradual progression towards buddhahood through the ideal of a *bodhisattva*, one who through the accumulation of great

knowledge and merit over a lengthy period, has reached the stage of being able to attain buddhahood, but does not, in order to help others along the same path. This became one of the central themes of *Mahayana* Buddhism.

Between the 9th and 12th centuries, numerous sects were founded by scholar/teachers or were based on their teachings. They included *Atista* (982-1054) and his austere disciple *Brom-ston* and *Mar-pa* (1012-1096). The latter's disciple, *Mi-la ras-pa* (1040-1123) is known primarily as Tibet's most famous writer of religious songs, but also for his austerity: he meditated for months in snow-bound caves clad only in a cotton loin-cloth. One of the most powerful sects, the *Sa-skya-pa*, was founded through the teachings of the translator, *Brog-mi* (992-1072), ultimately providing viceroys of Tibet under Genghiz Khan in the mid-13th century. In the 14th century political and religous power was divided by a series of secular rulers, but the founding of the *dGe-lugs-pa* (or 'Yellow Cap' sect) by the great reformer *Tsong-kha-pa* (1357-1419) eventually led to the religious and political re-unification of Tibet under the Dalai

—15—
A Tibetan copper-gilt figure of a Dakini, 17th century, 24cm (9½in), *NY 20 Sept*, $3,850 (£2,894)

—16—
A Tibetan bronze figure of Candavajrapani, *c*.17th century, 12cm (4¾in), *L 11 June*, £440 ($585)

—17—
A Tibetan gilt-copper figure of a monk, *c*.17th century, *L 11 June*, £495 ($658)

—18—
A Tibetan bronze figure of Avalokitesvara, (*Thugsrje-chen-po bcu-gcig-zhal*), 17th/18th century, 9.5cm (3¾in), *L 11 June*, £220 ($292)

—19—
A Tibetan gilt-copper figure of Maitreya, (*Byamspa*) *c*.18th century, 17.8cm (7in), *L 10 June*, £660 ($878)

—20—
A Sino-Tibetan gilt-bronze figure of the Dharmapala Mahakala, (*mGon-dkar*), 18th century, *L 10 June*, £638 ($849)

—15—

—16—

—17—

—18—

—19—

—20—

Lamas. The successive reincarnated grand lamas of the *dGe-lugs-pa* were granted the title of *Dalai* (from *Ta-le* meaning 'ocean' implying 'Ocean of Wisdom') when in 1578 the reigning Grand Lama met with the Mongol leader. The great fifth Dalai Lama was installed as ruler of Tibet in 1642, and the country prospered until his death in 1682. The palace of the Dalai Lamas at Lhasa, the *Potala*, was begun in 1645. Most importantly, the country was united under a strong political and spiritual leader, with the support of the 'Yellow' church, which was soon to be predominant. The present Dalai Lama (the fourteenth) was born in 1935.

● BRENDAN LYNCH ●

Further reading

A. Gordon, *The Iconography of Tibetan Lamaism*, 1967

D. Snellgrove & H. E. Richardson, *A Cultural History of Tibet*, 1971

A. Waddell, *The Buddhism of Tibet or Lamaism*, 1895

—21—
A Chinese parcel-gilt bronze figure of the Dharmapala Hayagira, Qianlong, 18th century, 37.5cm (14¾in), *NY 20 Sept,* $14,300 (£10,752)

—22—
A Sino-Tibetan bronze figure of the Bodhisattva Manjusri, seated on the back of a ferocious lion, *c.*18th century, 53.5cm (21in), *NY 20 Sept,* $9,625 (£7,237)

—23—
A Sino-Tibetan gilt-bronze figure of the Dharmapala Yama (*Chos-rgyal phi-sgrub*), 18th century, 18cm (7in), *L 11 June,* £1,155 ($1,536)

—24—
A Tibetan gilt-copper figure of a Lama, probably Tsong-Kha-Pa (1357-1419), *c.*18th century, 18.5cm (7¼in), *L 10 June,* £605 ($805)

—25—
A Sino-Tibetan gilt-bronze figure of the Dharma-pala Vajrabhairava in Yab-Yum with his Sakti, 18th century, 20cm (8in), *L 11 June,* £1,100 ($1,463)

—21—

—22—

—23—

—24—

—25—

Name of deity in Sanskrit and Tibetan	Category	Rôle	Aspect/Attributes
Sakyamuni *Sa-kya thub-pa*	Buddha (male)	Buddha of present world cycle.	Meditating. Various *mudras*.
Maitreya *Byams-pa*	Buddha (male)	Buddha of the future.	Preaching. May hold water-bottle.
Vajradhara *rDo-rje chang*	Adibuddha (male)	Primordial Buddha of the 'Yellow Cap' sect.	As Buddha supreme & eternal; holds *vajra* & *ghanta*.
Aksobhya *Mi-bskyod-pa*	Tagatha or Dhyanibuddha (male)	Buddha of Meditation.	Earth-touching *mudra* & *vajra*.
Avalokitesvara *sPyan-ras-gzigs*	Bodhisattva (male)	God of Mercy & Patron Saint of Tibet, from whom the Dalai Lamas claim descent.	Numerous aspects; Original is as a benevolent bodhisattva.
Padmapani *Phynag-na Pad-ma*	Bodhisattva & form of Avalokitesvara (male)	The lotus bearer.	Standing holding flowering lotus.
Manjusri *Jam-dpal*	Bodhisattva & form of Avalokitesvara (male)	God of Wisdom.	Sword (to destroy ignorance) & book (of wisdom).
Sitatara *sGrol-dkar* (White Tara)	Bodhisattva & form of Avalokitesvara (female)	Saviouress of mankind.	Benevolent goddess; holds two flowering lotuses.
Syamatara *sGrol-ljan* (Green Tara)	Bodhisattva & form of Avalokitesvara (female)	Saviouress of mankind.	Benevolent goddess; holds single lotus.
Vasudhara *Nor-rgyun-ma*	Bodhisattva (female)	Goddess of Wealth & Plenty.	Holds vase of jewels & spike of grain in two of her six hands.
Vajravarahi *rDo-rje phag-mo* ('Diamond Sow')	Dakini (feminine deities of lesser rank, usually) ferocious.)	Granter of superhuman power.	Has boar's head above right ear; holds ritual chopper, skull-bowl & staff with skeletal finial.
Hevajra *Kye-rdo-rje*	Yi-dam (tutelary deity chosen by person or sect) (male)	Protector	In sexual union (*yab-yum*) with his consort (*sakti*); has 8 heads, 16 arms—each holding a *kapala*—& 4 legs.
Kubera *rNam-thos-sras*	Dharmapala (defenders of Buddhism)	God of Wealth	Holds a lemon & a mongoose vomiting jewels; has ferocious expression.
Vajrabhairava *rDo-rje hjigs-byed*	Dharmapala (male)	Tutelary form of Manjusri, who overcomes Yama, Lord of Death. Guardian deity of the 'Yellow Cap' sect.	Has ferocious bull's head & 8 human heads, 34 arms & 16 legs with which he tramples Hindu gods & animals.
Four Lokapala *Jig-rten skyuong*	Lokapala (male)	Guardians of the four cardinal points who guard entrance to the Buddhist paradise (*Sukhavati*).	All 4 wear Mongolian dress: boots & chain-mail armour & have ferocious expression; each has his own attributes.
Tsong-Kha-Pa (1357-1419)	Religious Reformer (male)	Founded the *dGe-lugs-pa* or 'Yellow Cap' sect.	Wears peaked cap; monastic robes; holds 2 lotuses which support a sword & book. Benevolent aspect.
Padmasambhava *Pad-ma byung-gnas*	Indian teacher-scholar (male)	Came to Tibet in the 7th cent. Was later adopted as founder of the *rNying-ma-pa* or 'Red hat' sect.	Wears plumed cap & monastic robes; face has tantric meditative expression.
Dam-can	Demon King (male)	Indigenous country-rulers/gods of Tibet. Said to have been subdued by Padmasambhava.	Wear wide brimmed hats & ride animals.

—26—
A Sino-Tibetan gilt-bronze figure of the Dharmapala Sri-Devi, 18th century, 28cm (11in), *NY 20 Sept,* $9,350 (£7,030)

—27—
A Sino-Tibetan gilt-bronze figure of the goddess Usnisavijaya, 18th century, 16.8cm (6⅝in), *L 10 June,* £715 ($951)

—28—
A Sino-Tibetan gilt-bronze figure of the Dharmapala Yama, 18th century, 17cm (6⅝in), *L 10 June,* £990 ($1,317)

—26—　　　　—27—　　　　—28—

Japanese Works of Art

Article ● Japanese prints *pp 663-669*   *See also* ● Colour illustrations *pp 568-571*

Early Muromachi	1331-93	Momoyama 1573-1615	Early Edo	1615-1688	Meiji	1868-1912
Middle Muromachi	1393-1467		Middle Edo	1688-1803	Taisho	1912-1926
Late Muromachi	1467-1573		Late Edo	1803-1868	Showa	1926-

1

A pliqué-à-jour box and cover, Meiji/Taisho period, decorated with various flowers on a celadon green ground, silver mounts, cover cracked, 12.5cm (5in), *L 24 July,* £770 ($1,140)

2

An ovoid cloisonné vase, Taisho period, enamelled in shades of green and grey, on a mauve pink ground, chrome mounts, unsigned, 25.5cm (10in), *NY 3 Oct,* $1,760 (£1,257)

3

Namikawa Yasuyuki: A cloisonné vase and cover, Meiji period, depicting three *ho-o* in flight, crack, signed *Kyoto Namikawa,* 9cm (3½in), *L 6 Mar,* £1,980 ($2,218)

4

Namikawa Yasuyuki: A cloisonné vase, Taisho period, decorated with stems of red campion on a pale green body, silver rim and base, slight firing fault, signed *Kyoto, Namikawa,* 8.5cm (33¼in), *L 6 Mar,* £1,650 ($1,848)

5

A cloisonné enamel baluster vase, Meiji period, in shades of pink, rose, white, yellow and bright and olive green, on a midnight blue ground, 146cm (57½in), *NY 11 Apr,* $2,860 (£2,288)

6

Ota: A cloisonné enamel vase, Meiji period, in shades of pale brown, blue, pink and green on a dark robin's-egg blue ground, stamped with the artist's seal, 17.8cm (7in), *NY 11 Apr,* $825 (£660)

7

Shibata: A cloisonné vase, Meiji period, decorated with flowers on the black ground, rim and foot in gilt, slight scratches, 12.5cm (5in), *L 24 July,* £2,200 ($3,256)

8

A pair of cloisonné vases, Meiji period, of quadrangular ovoid form, all with pale grey grounds, silver mounts, unsigned, 24cm (9½in), *NY 3 Oct,* $4,125 (£2,946)

9

A pair of Hayashi type cloisonné vases, Meiji period, enamelled in shades of orange, green, grey and blue with hawks perched in maple trees, on a midnight blue ground, unsigned, 30cm (11¾in), *NY 3 Oct,* $2,750 (£1,964)

Hiragana } **Katakana** } forms of phoenetic script

Kakihan stylised script signature (written seal)

Kanemono horizontal scroll

Kiku chrysanthemum, adopted as badge of Emperor

Mon badge or crest

Sagemono hanging scroll

Saya Gata Testatire inscription on box

Sosho (characters) 'grass writing'

Tsukuru } **Sei** } character **Saku** } mean 'made' (appears after signature)

Yaki character meaning 'fired', used on pottery after signature

---

1

2

3

4

5

6

7

8

9

1
A pair of cloisonné vases,
Meiji period, each with
wisteria on a dark blue
ground, silver rim and
base, stamped KMS,
15.5cm (6in), *L 24 July,*
£660 ($977)

2
**Hayashi Kodenji: A clois-
onné enamel vase,** Meiji
period, decorated on
the celadon green
ground with three Man-
churian cranes, signed
Nagoya, Hayashi saku,
15cm (6in), *L 13 June,*
£1,430 ($1,902)

3
**Tadashi: A pair of clois-
onné vases,** *c.*1900, each
midnight-blue ground
inlaid with a bird of
prey in a wisteria tree,
signed, minor scratches,
15cm (6in), *S 25 Mar,*
£275 ($349)

4
**Namikawa Yasuyuki: A
cloisonné vase and cover,**
Meiji period, decorated
with birds and flowers
on a black ground,
signed *Kyoto Namikawa,*
9cm (3½in), *L 13 June,*
£2,255 ($2,999)

5
**Namikawa Yasuyuki: A
cloisonné koro and cover,**
Meiji period, decorated
with cockerel, hen and
chicks, cover chipped,
signed *Kyoto Namikawa,*
12cm (4¾in), *L 6 Mar,*
£8,360 ($9,363)

6
A pair of cloisonné vases,
*c.*1900, in the style of
Namikawa, with flowers
and insects on a yellow
ground, one slightly
damaged, 16.5cm
(6½in), *S 25 Mar,*
£484 ($615)

7
**Gonda Hirosuke: A pair
of cloisonné vases,** early
1900's, each decorated
with pink, purple and
blue water-iris, impres-
sed marks, 15cm (6in),
S 25 Mar,
£242 ($307)

8
A pair of cloisonné vases,
Meiji period, in the
style of *Hayashi Kodenji,*
applied with silvered
rim and foot, unsigned,
12.2cm (4¾in), *L 12 Nov,*
£1,100 ($1,410)

9
**Shibata: A pair of clois-
onné vases,** Meiji period,
each with a *ho-o* in
flight, silver rim and
foot, signed *Kyoto Shi-
bata,* 18.8cm (7⅜in),
L 12 Nov,
£4,000 ($5,640)

10
A cloisonné charger,
*c.*1900, with multi-
coloured foliage border,
60cm (22¾in), *S 10 July,*
£715 ($958)

11
**Ando (attributed to): A pair
of good cloisonné vases,**
Meiji period, decorated
with black and golden
carp in rippling water,
one with minor dam-
age, unsigned, 30.8cm
(12⅛in), *L 12 Nov,*
£3,200 ($4,512)

12
**A cloisonné sake kettle
and cover,** Meiji period,
decorated with flowers
and a stylised stream on
a black ground, 14cm
(5½in), *L 6 Mar,*
£1,540 ($1,725)

13
**A cloisonné tea pot and
cover,** Meiji period,
16.5cm (6½in), *L 24 July,*
£528 ($781)

1   2   3

4

5

6   7   8   9

10   11

12   13

1
A set of twelve fish knives and forks, Meiji period, the handles formed from *kozuka*, many of Goto School, some pieces signed, with fitted leather box, *L 12 Nov*, £2,800 ($3,948)

2
Gonda Hirosuke: A pair of Musen enamel vases, Meiji period, each decorated with purple, blue and white irises, slight crack to one base, engraved mark, 14.5cm (5¾in), *L 13 June*, £1,760 ($2,341)

3
A cloisonné bottle and cover, early Meiji period, decorated with panels of landscapes, *rakkan* and legendary figures, 19.5cm (7¾in), *L 13 June*, £352 ($468)

4
Ikai Snajiro: A pliqué-à-jour vase, Meiji period, with pink roses and foliage on a royal-blue ground, silver rim and foot, signed *Katakana Ikai*, *L 13 June*, £1,980 ($2,633)

5
Gonda Hirosuke: A pair of Musen enamel vases, Meiji period, each delicately worked with leafy stems of red and white roses on a pale grey ground, stamped mark, 18cm (7⅛in), *L 12 Nov*, £600 ($846)

6
An enamelled shibuichi vesta case, Meiji period, decorated in *Hirata* style, the *shibuichi* body inlaid in gold and silver *honzogan*, 5.3cm (2¼in), *L 12 Nov*, £850 ($1,198)

7
A pliqué-à-jour vase, Meiji period, decorated with stems of red berries and green leaves on a pale celadon ground, silver rim and foot, stamped mark, 9cm (3½in), *L 24 July*, £770 ($1,140)

8
A pliqué-à-jour bowl, Meiji period, the pale blue/green body decorated with chrysanthemum, silver rims, some cracks, 14cm (5½in), *L 13 June*, £990 ($1,317)

9
Kumeno Teitaro: A pair of pliqué-à-jour vases, Meiji period, each decorated with orange and purple *kiku* on a celadon green ground, silver rim and foot, the silver stamped *jun-gin*, and mark, *L 13 June*, £1,210 ($1,609)

10
A pliqué-à-jour vase, Meiji period, decorated with roses, wild poppies and chrysanthemum, stamped *jun-gin*, 20cm (8in), *L 13 June*, £6,380 ($8,485)

11
Namikawa Sosuke: A cloisonné tray, Meiji period, after a painting by *Watanabe Shotei*, signed *Shotei* with *kakihan*, and inlaid seal, 27.6cm (10¾in), *L 13 June*, £9,020 ($11,997)

Iroe-takazogan relief inlay of coloured metals.

Nanako lit. "Fish-skin". Punching technique, giving a pebbled appearance to metal.

Shakudo alloy of silver and copper, black in colour.

Shibuichi metal alloy of gold, silver and copper, dull grey in appearance.

Sentoku metal alloy, brassy in appearance

1
Gyoshun: A Shibayama kodansu, Meiji period, each side inset with a gold lacquer panel, the interior with three graduated drawers decorated in gold *hiramakie*, signed, 14cm (5½in) wide, *L 13 June,*
£4,620 ($6,145)

2
A pair of Shibayama vases, Meiji period, applied with tall lacquered ivory handles, one finial missing, small chips, 13.3cm (5¼in), *L 6 Mar,*
£1,430 ($1,602)

3
A pair of Shibayama vases, Meiji period, each with a gold lacquer body worked in gold and coloured *hiramakie* and *togidashi,* inset with ivory panels, some inlay missing, feet chipped, 30cm (11¾in), *L 13 June,*
£3,740 ($4,974)

4
Masayasu: A Shibayama vase and cover, Meiji period, applied with birds on prunus branches, some inlay missing, 32.5cm (12¾in), *L 6 Mar,*
£770 ($862)

5
Masayuki: A Shibayama vase, Meiji period, the silver body enamelled and inset with four gold lacquer panels, signed, 24cm (9½in), *L 13 June,*
£935 ($1,244)

6
Masatami: A Shibayama card vase, Meiji period, engraved signature, 11cm (4¼in), sold with a bezique counter, *C 17 Apr,*
£572 ($744)

7
A pair of Shibayama and metalwork vases, Meiji period, inlaid with hardstones and mother-of-pearl, some inlay missing, signed, 33cm (13in), *C 2 Oct,*
£1,100 ($1,606)

8
A pair of Shibayama koro and covers, *c.*1900, some inlay missing, one handle missing, one glued, 23cm (9in), *S 10 July,*
£1,375 ($1,843)

9
A pair of gold ground lacquer and Shibayama vases, Meiji period, inlaid in a variety of hardstones and mother-of-pearl, slight chips, signed, 23.2cm (9⅛in), *C 2 Oct*
£3,300 ($4,818)

10
A Shibayama tsuba, Meiji period, inlaid with enamel roundels and with cranes, 9.9cm (3⅞in), *L 12 Nov,*
£950 ($1,339)

11
A Shibayama miniature cabinet, Meiji period, 13cm (5¼in), *S 10 July,*
£770 ($1,032)

12
A composed Shibayama garniture, Meiji period, with details in ivory, silver and enamel, vases signed *Nobukazu,* 15cm (5¾in), *L 13 June,*
£2,090 ($2,780)

13
A silver and Shibayama vase and cover, Meiji period, inlaid with a variety of hardstones, mother-of-pearl and stained ivory, signed, repairs and faults, 18.4cm (7¼in), *C 2 Oct,*
£1,045 ($1,525)

14
A silver and Shibayama vase and cover, Meiji period, signed, foot damaged, finial missing, *C 10 July,*
£385 ($535)

15
Masayuki: A lacquer and ivory two panel table screen, Meiji period, inlaid with mother-of-pearl and wood, the ground decorated in gold *togidashi* and *hiramakie,* the reverse lacquered in *togidashi,* signed, 21.6cm (8½in) high, *NY 3 Oct,*
$1,980 (£1,414)

1

2

3

4

5

6

7

8

9

10

11

12

13

14

15

1
A Matsugatani-style dish,
late 17th/early 18th century, decorated in underglaze-blue and covered with a pale celadon glaze, small chips, 16cm (6¼in),
L 24 July,
£440 ($651)

2
Two figures of a standing man and a lady, Ko-Imari, Genroku period, 13.5cm (5¼in) and 14cm (5½in), *A 4 June,*
Dfl 2,204 (£499; $673)

3
A figure of an actor,
Ko-Imari, Genroku period, 17cm (6¾in),
A 4 June,
Dfl 812 (£184; $248)

4
An Arita apothecary's bottle, late 17th century, decorated in underglaze-blue, 30cm (9¾in),
L 13 June,
£2,860 ($3,804)

5
An Arita apothecary bottle, third quarter 17th century, decorated with a pair of *shishi,* 53cm (21in), *A 4 June,*
Dfl 41,760
(£9,448; $12,755)

6
An early Arita Kendi, late 17th century, decorated in Kakiemon style enamels, *A 4 June,*
Dfl 15,080 (£3,412; $4,606)

7
An Arita group of two wrestlers, late 17th century, the details in iron-red and black enamel, one chip, some firing faults, 28cm (11in),
L 13 June,
£4,950 ($6,584)

8
An Arita blue and white garniture, late 17th century, comprising five pieces each decorated with *shishi* beneath *ho-o* in flight, some restoration, jars 48cm (19in),
L 6 Mar,
£9,350 ($10,472)

9
An Arita blue and white vase and cover, late 17th century, the octagonal body painted with peony, *kiku* prunus and foliage, cover restored,
L 13 June,
£2,860 ($3,804)

10
An Arita dish, late 17th century, decorated in underglaze-blue, 46.4cm (18¼in), *L 12 Nov,*
£750 ($1,057)

11
A large Arita blue and white beaker vase, late 17th century, painted in underglaze-blue, 57.8cm (22¾in), *L 12 Nov,*
£800 ($1,128)

12
An Arita model of a cat, late 17th century, decorated with patches of iron-red, brown enamel and gilding, one ear damaged, 26cm (10¼in),
L 12 Nov,
£3,800 ($5,358)

13
Three Arita blue and white vases, *c.*1700, covers missing, one with chipped foot, 22.8cm (9in), *C 2 Oct,*
£825 ($1,204)

1
An Imari figure of a courtier, late 17th century, his *kimono* decorated in underglaze-blue, coloured enamels, iron-red and gilt, 32.5cm (12¾in), *L 13 June,* £638 ($849)

2
An Imari figure of a man, late 17th century, his *kimono* painted in underglaze-blue, coloured enamels and gilding, 38cm (15in), *L 13 June,* £1,320 ($1,756)

3
An Imari porcelain figure of bijin, late 17th century, her *kimono* decorated in underglaze-blue, iron-red enamel and gilding, glaze crackled, 54.5cm (21½in), *L 13 June,* £3,080 ($4,096)

4
An Imari saucer dish, late 17th century, 33cm (13in), *L 12 Nov,* £420 ($592)

5
A set of three Imari dishes, late 17th/early 18th century, decorated in underglaze-blue, iron-red green enamel and gilding, one with cracks, 23.8cm (9⅜in), *L 12 Nov,* £1,100 ($1,551)

6
An Imari charger, late 17th century, decorated in underglaze-blue, iron-red, black enamel and gilding, 54.5cm (21.5in), *L 12 Nov,* £1,600 ($2,256)

7
A pair of Imari dishes, late 17th/early 18th century, each decorated in underglaze-blue, green, aubergine and black enamels, iron-red and gilt with a central pomegranate, chip and some flaking, 34cm (13½in), *L 13 June,* £550 ($732)

8
An Imari dish, late 17th century, slight rubbing to the gilding, 33cm (13in), *C 16 Jan,* £253 ($304)

9
A pair of Imari jars and covers, late 17th/early 18th century, decorated in underglaze-blue, iron-red enamels and gilding, one small firing crack, 27cm (10⅝in), *L 12 Nov,* £6,000 ($8,460)

10
An Imari jar and cover, late 17th century, decorated in underglaze-blue, iron-red, black and aubergine enamels and gilt with panels of *ho-o,* the cover with a *shishi* finial, 63cm (24¾in), *L 24 July,* £1,980 ($2,930)

11
An Imari garniture, late 17th/early 18th century, comprising five pieces, each decorated in underglaze-blue, iron-red, coloured enamels and gilt, the jar covers with *shishi* finials, some restoration, jars 60cm (23½in), *L 6 Mar,* £3,520 ($3,942)

12
An Imari ribbed jar, 18th century, with twelve panels of decoration painted in typical palette, the interior painted with flowering plum, 26cm (10¼in), *NY 11 Apr,* $1,100 (£880)

13
An Imari garniture, late 17th century, comprising a jar and cover surmounted by a *bijin* and a pair of beaker vases, decorated in underglaze-blue, iron-red, green enamels and gilt, chips, one beaker damaged, 66cm (26in), *L 13 June,* £2,640 ($3,511)

14
An Imari shaving basin, 18th century, cracks, 26.5cm (10½in), *A 4 Sept,* **Dfl 2,530 (£582; $855)**

1 2 3 4
5 6 7
8 9 10
11 12
13 14

1
An Imari tokuri, late 17th century, decorated in iron-red, enamels, gilding and underglaze-blue wash, 15.3cm (6in), *L 12 Nov,* £700 ($987)

2
An Imari bowl and cover, 18th century, painted in underglaze-blue, iron red, yellow and green, cover chipped, 33.2cm (13⅛in), 29.2cm (11½in) diam, *NY 11 Apr,* $1,760 (£1,408)

3
An Imari saucer dish, 18th century, painted in underglaze blue, iron red and gilding, 56cm (22in), *L 6 Mar,* £1,540 ($2,310)

4
An Imari fish bowl, Meiji period, painted in underglaze-blue, copper red, creamy yellow and gold, 54.5cm (21½in) high, *NY 25 June,* $1,870 (£1,450)

5
A very large Imari jardiniere, Meiji period, decorated in typical palette and painted in underglaze-blue, 40.6cm (16in) high, 43.2cm (17in) diam, *NY 3 Oct,* $2,200 (£1,571)

6
A pair of Imari dishes, Meiji period, 45.5cm (18in), *C 16 Jan,* £484 ($581)

7
A pair of Imari vases, Meiji period, 64cm (25¼in), *C 16 Jan,* £1,980 ($2,376)

8
An Imari figure of a bijin, Meiji period, her *kimono* decorated in underglaze-blue, iron-red, coloured enamels and gilt, 49cm (19¼in), *L 13 June,* £682 ($907)

9
A pair of Imari vases, Meiji period, painted in underglaze-blue, iron-red and gilt, 47cm (18½in), *L 12 Nov,* £1,600 ($2,256)

10
Watano: A pair of Kutani vases, Meiji period, each painted in iron-red, coloured enamels and gilt, signed, 56cm (22in), *L 13 June,* £1,650 ($2,195)

11
An Imari bowl, mid 19th century, painted and gilded, with reserves containing *samurai* and *bijin,* 61cm (24in), *NY 3 Oct,* $3,850 (£2,750)

12
An Imari charger, late 19th century, 63cm (24¾in), *S 10 July,* £880 ($1,179)

13
A pair of Imari plates, 19th century, decorated in underglaze-blue, overglaze coloured enamels, iron-red and gilding with panels of Dutch ships and conversing Dutchmen, painted mark *Fuki Choshun,* 23.6cm (9¼in), *L 13 June,* £550 ($732)

14
A large Imari jar, 19th century, painted in underglaze-blue, coloured enamels and gilding, 51.5cm (20¼in), *L 6 Mar,* £1,320 ($1,478)

15
A large Kutani jardiniere, Meiji period, painted with figures in a mountainous setting, repair in base, painted *Fuki* mark, 33cm (13in), *L 12 Nov,* £550 ($775)

16
A pair of Kutani porcelain jars, late 19th century, 20.5cm (8in), *S 3 Apr,* £374 ($482)

1
Kisen: A Satsuma earthenware Koro and cover, 19th century, in coloured enamels and gilding, signed *Kisen* with apocryphal date Genroku 4, 15.8cm (6¼in), *L 12 Nov,*
£1,200 ($1,692)

2
Shozan: A Satsuma earthenware koro and cover, Meiji period, signed, 21.5cm (8⅛in), *L 12 Nov,*
£800 ($1,128)

3
A Satsuma earthenware koro and cover, Meiji period, painted and gilt with panels of *rakkan,* the cover with a *shishi* finial, tail chipped, 30cm (11¾in), *L 24 July,*
£935 ($1,384)

4
A Satsuma earthenware well bucket, Meiji period, of shallow form, painted in enamels and gilding with *shishi* amid *Kusudama* and flowering cherry, slightly rubbed, 13.5cm (5¼in), *L 24 July,*
£605 ($895)

5
A Satsuma earthenware caddy and cover, Meiji period, signed, 15cm (6in), *S 25 Mar,*
£990 ($1,257)

6
A Satsuma earthenware bowl, 19th century, the exterior bearing a gilt *rinzu* ground, the interior with a central *kiku* panel and lappet border, signed *Nihon Meisho,* 12.8cm (5in), *L 12 Nov,*
£1,000 ($1,410)

7
Juko: A Satsuma earthenware beaker vase, 19th century, painted over the heavily crackled glaze with a *ho-o* flying over peonies and rocks, in coloured enamels and glazes, signed *Juko ga,* 21cm (8¼in), *L 12 Nov,*
£400 ($564)

8
Shurakudo Yoshiyuki: A pair of Satsuma earthenware vases, mid 19th century, signed, 12cm (4⅞in), *L 12 Nov,*
£560 ($789)

9
A pair of Satsuma vases, Meiji period, boldly enamelled with stems of iris, signed *Satsuma Masasara Yaki,* 30.5cm (12in), *L 12 Nov,*
£680 ($958)

10
A Satsuma vase, mid 19th century, decorated in green enamel and gilding with *kiri-mon* on a ground of foliate scrolls, 31.6cm (12½in), *L 12 Nov,*
£400 ($564)

11
Hozan: A Satsuma jar and cover, Meiji period, painted in green enamel and gilding, the neck with an *asa-no-ha* design in iron red and gilding, signed *Hozan sei,* 33cm (13in), *L 12 Nov,*
£1,400 ($1,974)

12
A Satsuma earthenware vase and cover, painted and gilt with *Rakan,* figure finial, chipped neck, 37cm (14½in), *C 26 Nov,*
£253 ($367)

13
Matsumoto Hozan: A Satsuma earthenware vase, Meiji period, decorated in delicate coloured enamels and gilding, signed, 18.5cm (7¼in), *L 6 Mar,*
£2,090 ($2,341)

14
Gosuido Shozan: A Satsuma earthenware vase, Meiji period, enamelled and gilt with seven sages and thirteen *rakan,* signed with *kakihan* and *mon,* 25.5cm (10in), *L 13 June,*
£605 ($805)

15
Ryuun Fuzan: A Satsuma earthenware study of a shishi, Meiji period, a patterned sash around her body, signed, 29cm (11½in), *L 13 June,*
£1,045 ($1,390)

16
Imamura Minetaro: A blue and white Hirado jar and cover, Meiji period, painted with a tiger behind bamboo stems, signed, 21.5cm (8½in), *L 12 Nov,*
£1,300 ($1,833)

1
Kinkozan: An earthen-
ware Koro and cover,
Meiji period, the body
with panels of courtiers
in a garden, the blue
ground gilt with scrolls
and *mon*, impressed
Kinkozan tsukuru, 11cm
(4¼in), *L 6 Mar,*
£396 ($444)

2
Kinkozan: An earthen-
ware vase and cover,
Meiji period, in the
form of a small shrine,
gilt *Kinkozan tsukuru*,
16cm (6¼in), *L 24 July,*
£770 ($1,140)

3
Kinkozan: A pair of ear-
thenware cups, Meiji
period, painted and
gilded with chrysanthe-
mum, blossoms, incised
signature, 8.2cm (3¼in),
NY 10 Apr,
$660 (£545)

4
Kinkozan: An earthenware
vase, Meiji period,
pierced with diaper and
painted with swallows
and wisteria, impressed
Kinkozan tsukuru, gilt
Sozan ga, 18.4cm (7¼in),
L 12 Nov,
£2,900 ($4,089)

5
Kinkozan: An earthenware
vase, Meiji period, pain-
ted with panels of fig-
ures, the blue ground
gilt with scrolls and
flowers, panels signed
Yuzan, gilt and impres-
sed *Kinkozan tsukuru*,
26.5cm (10⅜in),
L 12 Nov,
£780 ($1,099)

6
Kinkozan: An earthenware
dish, Meiji period, pain-
ted and gilt with man-
darin ducks on a stream,
signed, 22cm (8¾in),
L 6 Mar,
£506 ($567)

7
A Kyoto-ware bottle, 18th
century, decorated in
blue and green enamel
and gilding, the neck
with *saya-gata* diaper,
24.2cm (9½in), *L 12 Nov,*
£950 ($1,339)

8
An earthenware model of
a tiger, 19th century,
covered with a crackled
cream glaze, details in
iron-red and gilding,
25.5cm (10in), *L 12 Nov,*
£500 ($705)

9
A pair of earthenware
vases, painted and gilt
with *Rakan*, chip to one,
19.5cm (7¾in), *C 26 Nov,*
£319 ($463)

10
A pair of earthenware
vases, Meiji period, each
with a slightly waisted
body painted with pan-
els of figures on a lake-
shore, signed, 10cm
(3⅞in), *L 12 Nov,*
£480 ($676)

11
An earthenware ovoid
vase, Edo period, delic-
ately enamelled and
gilded with *ho-o* birds,
chip, 42.5cm (16¾in),
NY 25 June,
$825 (£640)

12
A pair of earthenware
vases, painted and heavi-
ly gilded, 61cm (24in),
C 26 Nov,
£330 ($479)

13
A vase, Meiji period,
moulded in relief with
lilies and partly painted
pink, painted mark
Seieiken Hanju, 31.5cm
(12½in), *L 6 Mar,*
£418 ($468)

14
Kushiyama: An earthen-
ware koro and cover,
painted with panels of
women and children in
a garden with a cock and
hens, cover repaired,
signed, 16.5cm, *L 12 Nov,*
£520 ($733)

1
Kinkozan: An earthenware vase, late Meiji period, impressed *Kinkozan tsukuru*, 27cm (10⅝in), *L 12 Nov,* £1,800 ($2,538)

2
A blue and white porcelain figure of Daruma, holding a whisk, 17in (43cm), *C 26 Nov,* £231 ($355)

3
A blue and white porcelain charger, mid 19th century, painted with a scene of a fishing village, travellers crossing a bridge in the foreground, 56cm (22in), *NY 3 Oct,* $1,760 (£1,257)

4
A pair of Fukagawa vases, Meiji period, each decorated in underglaze-blue, iron-red, coloured enamels and gilt, painted leaf mark, 25.5cm (10in), *L 13 June,* £770 ($1,024)

5
A pair of Fukugawa vases, with two panels of fish and iris, on a blue and gilt ground, 21.5cm (8½in), *C 26 Nov,* £198 ($287)

6
A pair of Fukagawa blue and white vases, Meiji/Taisho period, each painted with *shishi*, signed *Nihizan, Fukagawa sei*, 76cm (30in), *L 24 July,* £1,155 ($1,709)

7
A Fukagawa fish bowl, Meiji period, signed, 23.5cm (9¼in), *C 17 Apr,* £660 ($858)

8
Hankinzan: An earthenware bowl, Meiji period, painted and gilt with panels of figures and landscapes signed *Hankinzan go*, 13cm (5⅛in), *L 12 Nov,* £2,800 ($3,948)

9
Kizan: An earthenware cup and saucer, Meiji period, the interior painted with butterflies and the sides with flowers, 9.5cm (3¾in), *L 6 Mar,* £308 ($345)

10
Keitokuen Watano: A Kutani vase, enamelled in purple, yellow, green, black and blue, signed, 46.5cm (18¼in), *L 6 Mar,* £880 ($986)

11
Yabu Meizan: An unguent bottle and cover, Meiji period, painted in subtle enamels highlighted with gilt, stopper chipped, signed 14cm (5½in), *NY 11 Apr,* $3,300 (£2,640)

12
An Hichozan Shunga vase and cover, late 19th century, painted in iron-red and enamels, the domed cover surmounted by a *kiku*-form knop, 52cm (32½in), *L 12 Nov,* £1,200 ($1,692)

13
Ryozan: An earthenware vase, Meiji period, delicately enamelled and gilded, signed *Kyoto Ryozan*, 30.5cm (12in), *NY 10 Apr,* $1,650 (£1,091)

14
School of Makuzu Kozan: A tapered bottle vase, painted with carp swimming behind a fish net, minor rubbing, signed *Kozan*, 20.4cm (8in) high, *NY 25 June,* $880 (£682)

15
Yabu Meizan: An earthenware vase, Meiji period, painted and gilt with a stem of clematis, signed, 23.5cm (9¼in), *L 13 June,* £825 ($1,097)

16
A Takeitsu earthenware vase, signed *Satsuma mon*, 24.5cm (9¾in), *C 17 Apr,* £715 ($930)

Japanese Prints

In about 1600, at the end of the Civil Wars, Japan closed itself to the rest of the world and began adapting its war-orientated society to peacetime conditions. The resulting urbanization and commercialization of the country brought about a rapid change in its feudal structure. The middle class now acceded to a position of wealth and power by controlling the goods and services that society required. The merchants became patrons of art, music and theatre, and style-setters, and artists, writers and craftsmen responded with new designs and themes derived from the customs which their patrons observed and the leisure activities which they pursued. The paintings, screens and prints that document this life are called *ukiyo-e,* 'pictures of the floating world'.

—1—
Hiroshige: *Oban tate-e:* Komagata Temple, Azuma Bridge, from *Edo Meisho,* very good impression, good colour, *NY 6 Nov,* $2,475 (£1,731)

—2—
Hiroshige: *Oban yoko-e,* Yokkaichi, from the Hoeido *Tokaido* set, good impression and colour, *NY 6 Nov,* $1,650 (£1,153)

—3—
Hiroshige: *Aiban yoko-e: Hara,* from the *Gyosho Tokaido* set, very good impression, good clolour, *NY 6 Nov,* $935 (£653)

—4—
Hiroshige: *Oban tate-e,* Kiba Lumber Yard, from *Edo Meisho,* Fukagawa, good impression, moderate colour, *NY 6 Nov,* $1,320 (£923)

—5—
Hiroshige: *Aiban yoko-e: Mariko,* from the *Gyosho Tokaido* set, very good impression, good colour, *NY 6 Nov,* $412 (£288)

—1—

—2—

—3—

—4—

—5—

See also
colour illustrations
on p.571

Paintings and screens were commissioned works and were expensive by the very nature of the materials needed to produce them. Woodblock prints were introduced as an inexpensive means of capitalizing on the rage for the new styles. Prints were designed for the ordinary person and were intended to evoke the pleasures and events surrounding him: picnics under the cherry trees, parties on river-boats, evenings with courtesans and actors. The artists who created them were of the same class and lived with or around the people and places idealized in their prints. For them, print-making was a way of making a living as painting commissions were rarer and time-consuming. What is remarkable in this field is the consistently high level of artistry and production achieved by print-designers and publishers.

—6—
Hiroshige: *Oban yoko-e, Nagakubo,* from the *Kisokaido* set, good impression, moderately good colour, *NY 6 Nov,* $2,090 (£1,461)

—7—
Hiroshige: *Oban yoko-e: Oi,* from the *Kisokaido* set, good impression, moderately good colour, *NY 6 Nov,* $5,775 (£4,038)

—8—
Hiroshige: *Oban tate-e:* a woman holding a bamboo vase and a branch of plum, from the set 'Five Festivals of the Year', published by Shorindo, good impression and colour, *NY 6 Nov,* $467 (£326)

—9—
Hiroshige: from *Edo Meisho, Oban tate-e:* Sudden Shower at Ohashi Bridge, Snake 9, 1857, good impression, moderately good colour, *NY 6 Nov,* $8,800 (£6,153) See also p.571 fig.1

—10—
Hiroshige: *Oban tate-e album,* the complete set of the 'Upright Tokaido' set, publisher's mark Tsutaya Kichizo, date seal Snake 7 (1855), good and moderately good impressions, good colour, *NY 25 June,* $6,600 (£5,116)

—11—
Hiroshige: *Oban tate-e triptych:* Beauties watching fireworks on a summer night in Ryogoku, publisher's seal Yamadaya, *c.*1850, very good impression and colour, *NY 6 Nov,* $1,980 (£1,384)

—6—

—7—

—8—

—9—

—10—

—11—

At the beginning of the 17th century, prints appeared as black and white illustrations in books of poetry, popular novels and guides to the pleasure quarters of the cities. By the close of the century, publishing houses were releasing single black and white sheets, and subsequently introduced designs commissioned from contemporary artists; generally black and white prints enhanced with hand-applied colour and lacquer and metallic dusts. In the mid-18th century Harunobo (fig.13 and p.571 fig.2) created the first multiple-colour image, which replaced the black and white prints except in illustrated books and albums.

Although prints are known by the artist who designed and signed them, it was the publisher, whose seal appears on the print, who commissioned the design and orchestrated the production and distribution. To create a print, the artist's original drawing was mounted on a block of cherry or pear wood and the lines cut by a team of engravers. Once the artist had specified the colours, separate blocks were made for each colour to be used. The printer prepared inks—black (*sumi*) for the line image, made from soot and glue, and colours made from rice paste and mineral pigments—and transferred the image by rubbing the *hosho* paper by hand with a circular bamboo *baren*.

Once the original edition was completed, the blocks might be recut and the colour changed, or sold to another publisher. Generally, publishers left no records of numbers and quantities of editions, block changes, or designs commissioned. Scholars have been able to document many of these changes, but even today, not all of the hundreds of woodblock prints are recorded. Kunisada's output, for example, was so enormous that his images rarely reappear from sale to sale.

—12—
Hiroshige: *Oban yoko-e:* Toka Festival at Ebisu Shrine, Imamiya, from the set *Naniwa Meisho dzu-e*, published by Eisendo, *c.*1834, very good impression and colour, *NY 6 Nov*, $550 (£384)

—13—
Harunobu: *Chuban:* A girl hopping on to the bow of a pleasure-boat moored by a bank, fairly good impression, faded, *L 22 May*, £1,650 ($2,195)

—14—
Hiroshige: *Oban yoko-e:* Musicians and figures under large parasols walking down a wide street behind a boy blowing bubbles, from *Toto Meisho*, publisher's seal Kikakudo, good impression and colour, *NY 25 June*, $385 (£298)

—15—
Hiroshige: *Oban yoko-e, Kakegawa,* from the Hoeido *Tokaido* set, moderately good impression, good colour, *NY 25 June*, $990 (£767)

—16—
Hiroshige II: *Oban:* The Kiso Gorge in Snow, Shinshu Province, from the series 'The Famous Places of Edo', date-seal, Year of Goat, 1859, very good impression and colour, *L 22 May*, £1,870 ($2,487) Compare with fig.4 p.571

—12—

—14—

—15—

—13—

—16—

The greatest theme of *ukiyo-e* is the beautiful woman, or *bijin*. The designs of Utamaro, Kiyonaga and Eishi, to name only three, bring to life the dazzling costumes and accoutrements of the new styles as well as the expressions of a new age. This is probably best demonstrated in prints portraying the courtesan: Kiyomine's *geisha* painting her lips (p.571 fig.3), Utamaro's courtesan on her way to work (fig.18) and Eisui's Mutsu holding a cup (fig.17). While these are not portraits in the western sense, the artist usually knew the sitter and included her name and often her place of employment on the print itself. Although the prints may seem to concentrate on the elegant hairstyles or dresses of the young women depicted, they do not ignore character; this is seen in many prints, particularly those by Utamaro, where the pathos of a young woman unhappily in love or a young mother caring for her child is handled with directness and sympathy.

Actor prints depicted real performers in recorded *kabuki* roles. The success of these designs depended both on the popularity of the actor and on the graphic ingenuity of the print itself. The costume of the actor allowed wonderful combinations of pattern and colour that were never repeated in the hundreds of images released. Although *ukiyo-e* prints have the consistency of subject-matter and treatment that we associate with a style, the details are handled differently from print to print. In the two *surimono* (that is, privately commissioned single-sheet prints) by Kunisada of the actor Danjuro VII in virtually the same role, the artist varies the pose of the figure and the pattern of his clothing to distinguish the two prints (figs.20 and 21).

The landscape, exemplified by Hokusai and Hiroshige, was the great 19th-century contribution to woodblock printing. Unlike most figure prints, which were issued singly or in small

—17—
Eisui: *Oban:* The head and shoulders of the courtesan Mutsu of Tsuru-ya holding a sake cup, publisher's seal *Maruya Bun'emon*, good impression, colour slightly faded, *L 22 May*, £2,200 ($2,926)

—18—
Utamaro: *Naga-ban:* A geisha on her way to a night assignment, from the set 'The Three Beauties of the Present Day', publisher's mark, Murataya Jirobei, good impression, faded, *L 22 May*, £1,760 ($2,341)

—19—
Shunsho: *Hosoban:* an actor in a female role standing with a scroll of a samurai, very good impression and colour, *NY 25 June*, $1,320 (£1,023)

—20—
Kunisada: square *surimono*, Ichikawa Danjuro VII as a samurai from a Kakekiyo play, good impression and colour, *NY 7 Nov*, $1,430 (£1,000)

—21—
Kunisada: *Kakuban surimono:* Ichikawa Danjuro VII as a villain in a Kabuki play, good impression and colour, *NY 7 Nov*, $1,100 (£769)

—17—

—18—

—19—

—20—

—21—

sets, landscapes were distributed in large series, generally in album form. The complete set of Hokusai's 'Thirty-six Views of Mount Fuji' contains 46 sheets, Hiroshige's 'Fifty-three Stations of the Tokaido', 55. So popular were these series that the sets were broken up and the prints were sold individually; also repeated editions were printed, giving rise to vast differences in quality and value between early well-printed and de luxe editions and later editions produced from worn or altered blocks. The de luxe edition of Hiroshige II's 'One Hundred Famous Views of the Provinces' sold in New York (p.571, fig.4) for $57,750 (40,384) while in the same sale half the number of prints from a later edition of the same series sold for $8,800 (£5,594).

—22—
Ichiyusai Kuniyoshi
'Ceramics of Owari Province': *Tanto tsuritai*, 'Want to fish a lot', no. 28 from 'The Propitious Products of Mountains and Seas'. Publisher: Sanoki. *L 22 May*, £253 ($336)

—23—
Ichiyusai Kuniyoshi
'Giant Octopuses in Namekawa, Etchu Province', Oo itai, 'Ouch!...', no. 7 from 'The Propitious Products of Mountains and Seas'. Publisher, Tsutakichi, *L 22 May*, £462 ($614)

—24—
Eisho: *Oban:* An *Okubi-e* of the courtesan Shinateru of Okamoto-ya, from the series 'The Contest of Beauties of the Pleasure Quarter', publisher's mark, Yamaguchiya Chesuke, good impression, much faded, *L 22 May*, £1,430 ($1,902)

—25—
Shunei: *Hosoban:* The actor Morita Kanya in the role of a samurai, publisher's mark Kawaguchi Uenoya, good impression and colour, *NY 25 June*, $935 (£725)

—26—
Kampo: *Oban:* The head and shoulders of an actor, dated Taisho 12 (1923), with publisher's mark, Sato Shotaro, fine impression, *L 22 May*, £220 ($293)

—27—
Attributed to Harunobu: *Chuban yoko-e:* a woman and a young boy on a veranda near a flowering garden and stream, unsigned, very good impression, good colour, *NY 25 June*, $2,420 (£1,876)

Captions to figs 28-30 on p.668

—22—   —23—   —24—

—25—   —26—   —27—

—28—   —29—   —30—

Hiroshige and Hokusai also produced the best known prints of birds and flowers, animals and water life (fig.31). Other artists picked up themes of heroes and legends from the early printed books. After the arrival of Commodore Perry in 1853 and the opening of Japan to the west, prints of foreigners became popular, and print makers such as Yoshitoshi began to experiment with western pictorial technique. In the majority of 20th-century designs, the artist combines these techniques with the subjects and conventions of traditional *ukiyo-e*. (See Shinsui, figs.32 and 33).

In the current market, prints of actors and landscapes from the first quarter and middle of the 19th-century are the most available. Of the landscapes the majority are by Hiroshige. At auction, prints are sold singly or in small groups, depending on the popularity of the design, the condition of the print and the rarity of its appearance in sales. Rarity influences the value of the print but seldom compensates for poor condition. Only in the case of recognized great prints such as Hokusai's 'Great Wave off Kanagawa' or a Sharaku actor portrait, are collectors willing to accept unsatisfactory condition or a poor impression because of the importance of the design. This is not to say that condition fails to affect the price of the print: a 'Great Wave' in poor condition has sold for $9,900 (£7,070) (fig.38) whereas one in better condition has sold for $24,200 (£10,521) (fig.37). Although collectors will opt for a poorer impression of a major design over a group of mediocre designs in excellent condition,

—28—
Kiyonaga: *Oban tate-e:* a woman seated in a palanquin conversing with another woman and two men, good impression, moderate colour, *NY 25 June,*
$1,210 (£945)

—29—
Kiyonaga: *Oban:* The left-hand sheet from a diptych from the set 'Tosei Yuri Bijin Awase', 'A Contest of Fashionable Beauties of the Gay Quarters', depicting a party on the verandah of a brothel at Nakasu, good impression, faded, *L 22 May,*
£2,750 ($3,657)

—30—
Shinsui: *Oban:* The portrait of a young married woman with the coiffure called maru-mage, date Taisho 13 (1924), shichigatsu (July): publisher's mark, Watanabe Shozaburo, fine impression and colour, *L 22 May,*
£1,870 ($2,487)

—31—
Hiroshige: *Uchiwa-e Kacho-e,* small brown bird on flowering cherry, good impression and colour, *NY 6 Nov,*
$1,430 (£1,000)

—32—
Hiroshige, *Omi Hakkei: Oban yoko-e:* Ishiyama no Shugetsu (Autumn Moon at Ishiyama), good impression and colour, *NY 6 Nov,*
$2,310 (£1,615)

—33—
Hasui: *Aiban yoko-e,* Kazusa Beach, Hizen Province, from the set 'Nihon Fukei Senshu', dated Taisho II (1922), good impression and colour, *NY 7 Nov,*
$825 (£576)

—31—

—32—

—33—

—34—

—35—

—36—

they will generally restrict their collections to good but affordable prints in good condition. Fortunately, this can still be accomplished as demonstrated by the examples illustrated.

● JANE OLIVER ●

Further Reading

Laurence Binyon & J.J. O'Brien Sexton, *Japanese Colour Prints*, 1923

J. Hillier, *The Japanese Print: A New Approach*, 1960

Richard D. Lane, *Masters of the Japanese Print*, 1962

—34—
Hasui: *Aiban tate-e:* Kinya Street at Nagasaki, from the set 'Nihon Fukei Senshu', dated Taisho 12 (1923), very good impression and colour, *NY 7 Nov,* **$1,045 (£730)**

—35—
Hasui: *Oban yoko-e,* Snow Dawn at Ogi Port, Sado, from the set 'Tabi Miyage Dai Ni Shu', Taisho 10 (1921), very good impression and colour, *NY 25 June,* **$1,320 (£1,023)**

—36—
Kiyochika: *Oban yoko-e,* blue and pale pink morning glories, dated Meiji 12 (1879), good impression, moderately good colour, *NY 25 June,* **$1,650 (£1,279)**

—37—
Hokusai: *Oban yoko-e,* Under the wave off Kanagawa (the 'Great Wave'), from the series 'The Thirty-Six Views of Mt Fuji', *NY 3 July 1980,* **$24,200 (£10,521)**

—38—
Hokusai: *Oban yoko-e,* Under the wave off Kanagawa (the 'Great Wave'), from the series 'The Thirty Six Views of Mt Fuji', *NY 14 May 1983,* **$9,900 (£7,070)**

—37—

—38—

1

A lacquer basin, Meiji period, decorated in gold and silver, *hiramakie* with pine, persimmon and bamboo, crack, 60cm (23½in), *L 13 June,* £825 ($1,097)

2

A lacquer model of a sack, Meiji period, decorated in gold *hiramakie, kirigane* and *nashiji* with panels of *shi-shi,* cover missing, 28.5cm (11¼in), *L 6 Mar,* £3,520 ($3,942)

3

A silver mounted lacquer kodansu, Meiji period, decorated overall in *nashiji,* the interior of black lacquer, 39.4cm (15½in) wide; sold with a lacquer tray, 27.3cm (10¾in) square, *NY 11 Apr,* $880 (£704)

4

A pair of inlaid lacquer kodansu, Meiji period, each with a single door inlaid in ivory and mother-of-pearl, enclosing four smaller drawers, decorated on the *roiro* ground with cranes, slight chips and cracks, 25.5cm (10in), *L 12 Nov,* £800 ($1,128)

5

A black and gold lacquer bunko, Meiji period, decorated on the cover and sides with large gold *mon* on a black lacquer ground, the interior *nashiji,* 40.7cm (16in) wide, *NY 11 Apr,* $3,300 (£2,640)

6

A tabako-bon, 19th century, decorated with butterflies in gold *hiramakie,* the sides with a river among *kiku,* some foil flaking, 22.5cm (9in) wide, *L 12 Nov,* £1,300 ($1,833)

7

Sanyo: a lacquer kobako, 20th century, decorated in eggshell, black, gold and coloured *takamakie* with peony blossoms, the interior with *mura-nashiji* on a *roiro* ground, signed, 36.5cm (14½in) wide, *NY 11 Apr,* $1,760 (£1,408)

8

An inlaid lacquer kodansu, Meiji period, decorated on the *kinji* ground in gold and coloured *takamakie* and inlaid in mother-of-pearl, 13cm (5⅛in), *L 12 Nov,* £800 ($1,128)

9

A lacquer kobako, Meiji period, decorated on all sides in gold *hiramakie, nashiji* ground, minor wear, 17.2cm (6¾in) wide, *NY 25 June,* $770 (£600)

10

A Sake bowl, Meiji period, decorated with Shoki dressed in flowing robes, chips, surface scratches, 54.5cm (21½in), *L 6 Mar,* £3,300 ($3,696)

1

2

4

3

6

5

7

8

9

10

Bunko document box.

Hibachi portable brazier.

Jukobako tiered incense box.

Karabitsu large lacquered container.

Kendi ewer of Persian inspiration.

Kizeruzutsu pipe case.

Kobako incense box.

Kodansu perfume cabinet.

Kogo small incense box.

Koro incense burner on three legs.

Mizuire water dropper.

Natsume tea caddy.

Suzuribako writing box.

Suzuri inkstone.

Tabako-bon tobacco box.

See p.677 for glossary of types of decoration

1
An inlaid lacquer chest,
Showa period, decorated
on the *kinji* ground in
gold *takamakie* with an
aoi mon and inlaid in
aogai with petal motifs,
silver lock plate, 34cm
(13⅜in), *L 12 Nov,*
£1,700 ($2,397)

2
**An inlaid lacquer small
chest,** Momoyama per-
iod, decorated in gold
lacquer and mother-of-
pearl on a *roiro* ground,
some losses and chips,
bronze mounts, 24.5cm
(9¾in) wide, *NY 11 Apr,*
$880 (£704)

3
**A lacquer Namban cof-
fer,** Momoyama period,
decorated on the black
ground in gold *hiram-
akie* and *raden*, lock-
plate replaced, 22cm
(8¾in) wide, *L 13 June,*
£1,320 ($1,756)

4
A lacquer takigaraire
(ash-holder for The
Perfume Game), 18th
century, *fundame*
interior, 6.7cm (3⅝in),
L 12 Nov,
£400 ($564)

5
**A lacquer box, cover and
interior tray,** late 18th/
early 19th century,
decorated in gold and
takamakie with a flowering plum tree, slight
crack and chips, 18cm
(7in) wide, *L 13 June,*
£616 ($819)

6
A lacquer karabitsu, late
18th/early 19th century,
decorated with peonies
in shades of gold *hiram-
akie* and *e-nashiji* reserved on scrolling peonies
in green, red and yellow
lacquer, gilt copper
mounts, slight chips,
59cm (23¼in) wide,
L 6 Mar,
£3,080 ($3,450)

7
**A black lacquer writing
box,** 19th century,
decorated in gold lac-
quer, cracks, 45.5cm
(18in) wide, *A 4 June,*
Dfl 5,452 (£1,233; $1,665)

8
A gold lacquer box, 19th
century, in the form of
two overlapping boxes,
the top decorated on the
kinji ground in gold,
takamakie, togidashi and
kirigane the sides with
irises among staves on a
nashiji ground 21.3cm
(8½in) wide, *L 12 Nov,*
£1,450 ($2,044)

9
**A lacquer sake bottle
(Tokuri),** 18th century,
decorated with the sun
setting, the reverse
showing the crescent
moon, all in gold and
coloured *takamakie, hir-
amakie* and *e-nashiji,*
slight damage, 18cm
(7in), *L 13 June,*
£1,320 ($1,756)

10
A lacquer kogo, Meiji
peirod, in the form of a
deep brown aubergine
with *kimpun* dusted
brown stem supporting
a silvery brown rat,
5.7cm (2¼in), *NY 11 Apr,*
$990 (£792)

11
A lacquer kobako, Meiji
period, decorated in
gold *hiramakie* and *takamakie* with *aogai* highlights with, Jurojin and
his crane, 10.7cm (4¼in),
NY 11 Apr,
$302 (£242)

12
**Jokasai: A two-tiered lac-
quer Jukobako,** 19th century, decorated in gold
and coloured *takamakie*
with large insects, details
in *aogai*, signed, saku,
5.4cm (2¼in) wide,
L 13 June,
£1,650 ($2,195)

13
A gold lacquer box, Meiji
period in the form of a
seated crane, details in
gold *hiramakie* and red,
12cm (5in), *L 13 June,*
£1,100 ($1,463)

14
**A lacquer bunko with
interior tray,** 19th century, decorated with two
work boats, slight cracks
and chips, 38 x 30.5cm
(15 x 12in), *L 13 June,*
£1,430 ($1,902)

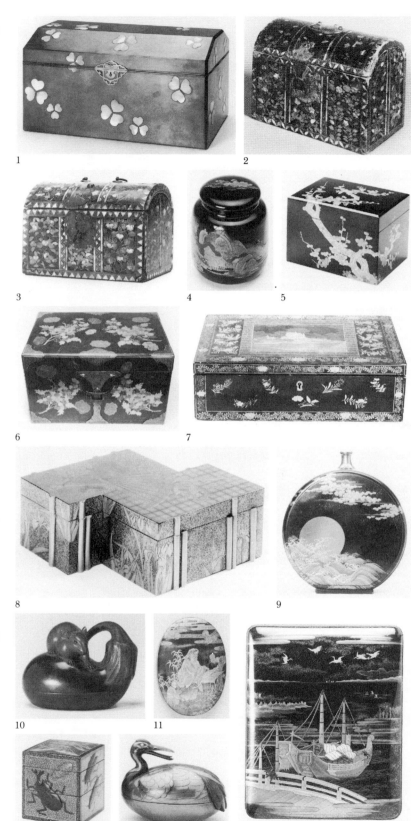

1
Kajikawa Family: A gold lacquer four-case inro, 19th century, decorated with Narihira riding past Fujiyama, the reverse showing an attendant, all in gold and coloured *takamakie*, slight fading, signed *Kajikawa*, 9cm (3½in), *L 14 June*, £660 ($878)

2
Shiomi Masanari: A four-case lacquer inro, 19th century, decorated with the seven scholars in the bamboo grove, some losses, signed with seal, the manju lacquered with Yin/Yang symbol, 8cm (3⅛in), *NY 11 Apr*, $5,225 (£4,180)

3
Tokosai Masashige: A dated two-case inro, 1833, the oval form decorated with five fan-shaped panels of *nashiji* and *kinji*, showing flowers, slight chips, signed, 7cm (2¾in), *L 14 June*, £495 ($658)

4
Shoshusai Rosho: A four-case inro, Meiji period, decorated with a youth comforting a *bijin*, signed, 10.5cm (4in), with *guri* lacquer Ojime and ivory netsuke depicting a hare, signed *Koyo, L 14 June*, £3,520 ($4,682)

5
Shokasai: An inro, late 19th century, in the form of a suit of armour, slight chips, signed, 15.5cm (5¾in), *L 6 Mar*, £2,310 ($2,587)

6
A metal inlaid lacquer four-case inro, mid 19th century, inlaid in gold, silver and *shakudo* with a Narihira on horseback, slight chips, and wear, signed *Mitsutoshi* with seal, 8.3cm (3¼in) high, *NY 25 June*, $1,100 (£853)

7
A two-case inro, 19th century, in the form of Hotei seated in his sack, unsigned, 8.5cm (3¼in), with small plain gold lacquered ojime, and an ivory netsuke of Daikoku standing on a rice bale, signed *Ikko* (Kazutora), *L 14 June*, £1,210 ($1,609)

8
A three-case inro, late 19th century, decorated with boys illustrating the legend of Shiba Onko, unsigned, 9cm (3½in), with ivory two-part manju, *L 6 Mar*, £1,320 ($1,478)

9
A gold lacquer and shibayama six-case inro, late 19th century, unsigned, 8.5cm (3¼in), with ivory ball-straped netsuke, signed *Chounsai, L 6 Mar*, £1,540 ($1,725)

10
A five-case inro, 19th century, bearing a *kinji* ground, decorated with Jurojin and his deer, slight wear, unsigned, slightly worn, unsigned, 9.9cm (3⅞in), *L 13 Nov*, £1,200 ($1,692)

11
Eisai Kimitatsu: A gold lacquer five-case inro, 19th century, decorated on the *kinji* ground in gold *takamakie* with figures of Jo and Uba with emblems of longevity, details in Shibayama style, signed, 9cm (3½in), *L 6 Mar*, £715 ($801)

12
A gold lacquer four-case inro, 19th century, decorated with Kikujido seated on a river bank, the background of gold *takamakie* with *okibirame* and *e-nashiji* details, slight fading, unsigned, 8.5cm (3¼in), with a gold lacquered manju, signed *Nobusada, L 14 June*, £1,430 ($1,902)

13
A walrus ivory three-case inro, Meiji period, unsigned, 7.5cm (2¾in), *L 14 June*, £682 ($907)

1   3

4   5   6

7   8   9   10

11   12   13

1
**Yoshimitsu: A bronze
ojime of a Chinese sage,**
19th century, signed,
2.3cm (⅞in), *NY 3 Oct,*
$770 (£550)

2
**A silver ojime of crab and
lotus,** 19th century, unsigned, 1.6cm (⅝in),
NY 3 Oct,
$715 (£510)

3
A gold ojime, late 19th
century, signed in seal,
2.3cm (⅞in), *L 13 Nov,*
£1,200 ($1,692)

4
A gold ojime, late 19th
century, unsigned,
2.1cm (⅞in), *L 13 Nov,*
£2,600 ($3,666)

5
Norinaga: A gold ojime,
late 19th century,
signed, 1.2cm (½in),
L 13 Nov,
£550 ($775)

6
A lacquer five-case inro,
*c.*1800, unsigned, 9.5cm
(3¾in), *Hu 28 Jan,*
$605 (£545)

7
A four-case inro, 18th
century, unsigned, 7cm
(2¾in), *L 24 July,*
£220 ($326)

8
**Koma Ankyo (Yasutada):
A four-case gold lacquer
inro,** 19th century, signed
*Koma Ankyo (Yasutada)
saku,* 9.2cm (4½in),
L 13 Nov,
£750 ($1,057)

9
**Kajikawa Fusataka:
A four-case inro,** 19th
century, decorated after
a painting by Hogen
Eisen, signed, 8cm (3¼in),
and a soft metal Ojime,
L 6 Mar,
£715 ($801)

10
**Kajikawa Family: A gold
lacquer four-case inro,**
19th century, decorated
with Kanyu on horse-
back, signed *Kajikawa* with
red pot seal, 8cm (3in),
with a brass and copper
Ojime, unsigned,
L 14 June,
£638 ($849)

11
**Koma Kyuhaku: A two-
case inro of wide form,**
19th century, decorated
with Raiden and Futen
creating a storm, signed,
6.5cm (2½in), with a
copper Ojime and a wood
netsuke unsigned,
L 14 June,
£1,540 ($2,048)

12
Jokasai: A five-case inro,
19th century, signed *Jo-o*
with *kakihan,* 9cm (3½in),
and a *shibuichi* ojime,
signed *Shumin* with
kakihan, L 6 Mar,
£1,100 ($1,232)

13
Kakosai: A four-case inro,
19th century, signed, 8cm
(3⅛in), *L 13 Nov,*
£1,600 ($2,256)

14
**Yamada Joka: A large
inro,** 19th century,
decorated with the Seven
Gods of Good Fortune,
signed, 13.1cm (5⅛in),
L 13 Nov, £1,600 ($2,256)

15
**Kajikawa Family: A gold
lacquer four-case inro,**
19th century, signed *kajikawa saku* with red pot
seal, 9cm (3½in), *L 24 July,*
£440 ($651)

16
**Kajikawa Juei: A four-
case inro,** 19th century,
signed with *kakihan,*
8.5cm (3¼in), *L 14 June,*
£935 ($1,244)

17
**Kajikawa Family: A gold
lacquer four-case inro,**
19th century, decorated
with the story of the
Capture of the Oil Thief,
signed *Kajikawa,* 8cm
(3in), *L 14 June,*
£572 ($761)

18
**Kajikawa Family: A gold
lacquer four-case inro,**
19th century, decorated
with Narihira on horse-
back viewing Fujiyama,
signed *Kajikawa saku,*
8.6cm (3⅜in), with an
ivory netsuke, unsigned,
L 13 Nov, £880 ($1,128)

19
**Kajikawa Family: A four-
case inro,** 19th century,
signed *Kajikawa saku* with
red pot seal, with a metal
ojime, 7.3cm (2⅞in),
L 13 Nov,
£2,200 ($3,102)

1 2 3 4 5

6 7 8 9

10 11 12

13 14 15 16

17 18 19

1
Kokei: A wood study of a goat, 18th century, the eyes inlaid in green glass, signed, 5cm (2in), *L 14 June*, £2,090 ($2,780)

2
Masanao: A wood study of a scribe, late 19th century, the wood well stained and slightly worn, signed, 5cm (2in), *NY 11 Apr*, $275 (£220)

3
A wood double mask netsuke, late 19th century, one side depicting Okame, the other a Kyogen mask, unsigned, 5cm (2in), *NY 3 Oct*, $550 (£393)

4
A figure of Ashinaga, early 19th century, toe restored, unsigned, 4.5cm (1¾in), *L 13 Nov*, £340 ($479)

5
Ichiun: A wood figure of a monkey, 19th century, the eyes inlaid, signed, 3.5cm (1¼in), *L 14 June*, £990 ($1,317)

6
Deme Uman: A wood mask of a smiling man, probably late 18th century, signed, 4.5cm (1¾in), *Hu 28 Jan*, $440 (£396)

7
Tametaka: A wood model of a snake, late 18th/early 19th century, signed, 4.5cm (1¾in), *Hu 28 Jan*, $4,620 (£4,162)

8
Tomokazu (after): A boxwood study of a monkey, 19th century, the eyes of pale translucent horn, inscribed Tomokazu, 3.5cm (1⅜in), *L 13 Nov*, £320 ($451)

9
Kaigyokudo Masateru: A wood group of two rats, late 19th century, clambering on top of a gourd, the eyes inlaid, signed, 3.8cm (1½in), *L 13 Nov*, £850 ($1,198)

10
Style of Sukenaga: A formalised figure of Daruma, 19th century, seated, enveloped in his voluminous robe, yawning after his nine-year meditation, unsigned, 4cm (1½in), *L 6 Mar*, £594 ($665)

11
Matsuda Sukenaga: A boxwood study of Daruma, 19th century, signed, 3.8cm (1½in), *L 13 Nov*, £800 ($1,128)

12
A figure of Daruma, 19th century, the back of his robe engraved with a grotesque face, unsigned, 4.5cm (1¾in), *L 14 June*, £748 ($995)

13
Ipposai: A two-part manju, carved on the face in *shishiaibori* with an *ushidoji* seated on the back of an ox, signed, 5cm (2in), *L 24 July*, £220 ($326)

14
Renkyo: A metal and stag antler manju, late 19th century, signed, 4cm (1½in), *NY 3 Oct*, $825 (£589)

15
Koju: A two-part ivory manju, carved in *shishiaibori* with a woman kneeling beside the recumbent Jurojin, their robes engraved with *karakusa* and medallions, signed with *kakihan*, 4cm (1½in), *L 14 June*, £385 ($512)

Inro small set of infitting boxes, for medicines usually of lacquer, hung at waist.

Netsuke toggle used to suspend pipe, inro etc. from waistband (obi).

Ojime small bead holding inro cords.

Manju netsuke of flattened bun form.

Kagamibuta netsuke with ivory bowl and infitting metal disc.

Okimono standing ornaments, figures, etc.

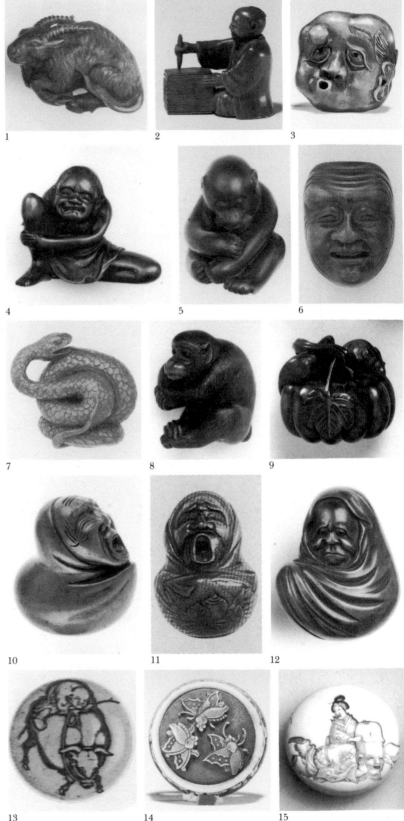

1 2 3

4 5 6

7 8 9

10 11 12

13 14 15

1

An ivory study of a Manzai dancer, *c.*1800, the details rendered in well patinated and worn ivory, unsigned, 6.4cm (2½in), *NY 11 Apr,* $605 (£484)

2

Ikkosai: An ivory group of a monkey and octopus, the monkey struggling to free itself from the octopus's tentacles, the eye pupils inlaid in horn, signed, 3cm (1¼in), *Hu 28 Jan,* $2,860 (£2,577)

3

Kangyoku: An ivory study of a hare, 20th century, lightly stained, the eyes inlaid with pink coral, signed, 4.2cm (1⅝in), *NY 11 Apr,* $1,760 (£1,408)

4

Asakusa School: An ivory study of a cartwheel, the details boldly rendered in well stained and slightly worn ivory, cracks, unsigned, 4.2cm (1¾in), *NY 11 Apr,* $495 (£396)

5

Masatsugu: An ivory group of Hotei and Karako, late 18th/early 19th century, well rendered in patinated and well worn ivory, signed, 4.5cm (1¾in), *NY 3 Oct,* $1,540 (£1,100)

6

Okatomo (School): A study of a cockerel, early 19th century, seated with a chick, inscribed *Okatomo, aged 81,* 4cm (1½in), *L 14 June,* £1,430 ($1,902)

7

An ivory study of Hotei, 18th century, cracks, unsigned, 5cm (2in), *L 6 Mar,* £242 ($271)

8

An ivory study of a grazing horse, late 18th century, rendered in well patinated and worn ivory, unsigned; sold with a Kyoto School study of a hawk, late 19th century, inscribed Tomotada, 5cm (2in), *NY 3 Oct,* $1,100 (£786)

9

Tomotoshi: A figure of Daruma, late 19th century, stretching after his nine-year meditation, his body partly covered by his tattered voluminous robes, signed, 7cm (2¾in), *L 6 Mar,* £330 ($370)

10

An ivory figure of Sennin, late 18th century, wearing his traditional leafy cloak, unsigned, 6.5cm (2½in), *Hu 28 Jan,* $495 (£446)

11

Kaigyokusai Masatsugu: A study of a seated monkey, 19th century, the eyes inlaid in horn, 4cm (1½in), *L 6 Mar,* £2,420 ($2,710)

12

A study of a cat on a rice bale, 19th century, the animal crouching on a sliding panel which opens to reveal a rat, some wear, unsigned, 5cm (2in), *L 6 Mar,* £484 ($542)

13

A figure of a Dutchman, 18th century, holding a puppy in his arms, 12cm (4¾in), *L 6 Mar,* £1,760 ($1,971)

14

Karaku of Osaka: An ivory model of a foxwoman, mid 19th century, dancing on one foot, signed, 4cm (1½in), *L 6 Mar,* £770 ($862)

15

Ichiro: An ivory figure of a Samurai, holding a drawn dagger in a cloth before him, an inro slung at his back, his robe with inlaid *raden* medallions, signed, 5.5cm (2¼in), *L 6 Mar,* £330 ($370)

16

Shukosai Anraku: An ivory study of a Daruma doll, 19th century, a *hossu* beside him, signed, 5cm (2in), *Hu 28 Jan,* $2,640 (£2,378)

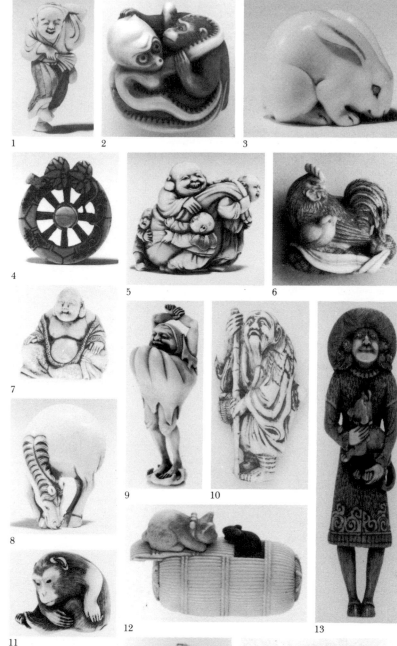

1
A figure of a musician, 19th century, the details expressively rendered in slightly worn and well toned ivory, unsigned, 3.8cm (2½in), *L 13 Nov,* £350 ($493)

2
A figure of a Karako, 19th century, his coat engraved with scrolling *kiku-mon,* and his hair tufts inlaid with dark horn, unsigned, 3.8cm (1½in), *L 13 Nov,* £260 ($366)

3
Yasuyuki: A figure of a baby boy, late 19th century, the ivory partly stained brown and with variously inlaid details, signed on a green stained tablet, 3.5cm (1⅜in), *L 13 Nov,* £2,500 ($3,525)

4
Ransen: A small figure of Jurojin, 19th century, the ivory slightly worn, signed, 4.2cm (1⅝in), *L 13 Nov,* £250 ($352)

5
Ikkyu: A study of an octopus, 19th century, the details well rendered, the eyes inlaid with dark horn, signed, 3.8cm (1½in), *L 13 Nov,* £660 ($930)

6
A study of a cat, late 18th century, the details well rendered in slightly worn ivory which bears a good patina, unsigned, 4.8cm (1⅞in), *L 13 Nov,* £620 ($874)

7
Style of Garaku: A study of a dog, late 18th/early 19th century, the details slightly worn in well toned ivory, eyes inlaid, unsigned, 4.4cm (1¾in), *L 13 Nov,* £820 ($1,156)

8
Suketada: A wood study of two puppies, 19th century rendered in slightly stained boxwood, signed, 4.2cm (1⅝in), *NY 3 Oct,* $825 (£589)

9
An ivory study of a Dutch monkey trainer, 18th century, one toe restored, 8.3cm (3¼in), *L 13 Nov,* £1,950 ($2,749)

10
Ogasawara Issai (style of): A fine wood figure of a Ronin, probably 18th century, unsigned, 6.4cm (2½in), *L 13 Nov,* £2,700 ($3,807)

11
Sosui: A wood model of a crow, 20th century, inlaid eye pupils, signed, 6.5cm (2½in), *Hu 28 Jan,* $935 (£842)

12
A wood study of a Sarum-awashi, 18th century, boldly rendered in well patinated and worn ivory, the leggings inlaid with dark horn buttons, unsigned, 6.4cm (2½in), *NY 3 Oct,* $467 (£334)

13
Tomochika: A group of two puppies, 19th century, the pupils inlaid, cracks, signed, 3.5cm (1¼in), *L 6 Mar,* £330 ($370)

14
Meikeisai Hojitsu: A wood study of a Shojo, 19th century, holding a ladle over one shoulder and standing before a large basket, signed, 4cm (1½in), *L 14 June,* £682 ($907)

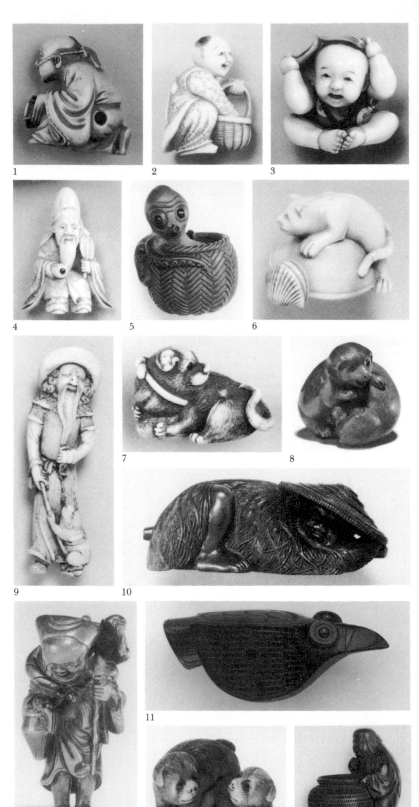

Types of Decoration

Aogai. Blue/green mother-of-pearl shell inlay.

Cloisonne. Enamelware in which the design is delineated by wires.

E-nashiji. Nashiji forming design rather than background.

Fundame. Dull or matt gold or silver lacquer.

Hiramakie. Flat lacquer decoration.

Hirame. Small metal flakes.

Ishime. Roughened surface technique.

Kinji. Bright gold lacquer.

Kirigane. Minute squares of gold foil applied to lacquer.

Mura-nashiji. Clouds of nashiji.

Nashiji. (lit: pearskin) powdered metals, usually gold under a transparent lacquer forming a dense ground.

Okibirame. Setting of dull gold flakes larger than fundame in lacquer.

Plique-a-jour. Enamelware in which the metal body is removed.

Raden. White shell used for inlay.

Roiro. Polished black lacquer.

Shakudo. Alloy of gold, silver and copper, black in colour.

Shibayama. Technique of inlaying minute pieces of various materials into ivory and lacquer; name of family that developed technique.

Shibuichi. Metal alloy of gold, silver and copper, dull grey in appearance.

Shippo. Enamels used in cloisonne work.

Takamakie. Relief design in lacquer.

Togidashi. Burnished lacquer design flush with surface.

1
An ivory okimono of a farmer and ox, Meiji period, unsigned, 34.5cm (13½in), L 14 June, £1,430 ($1,902)

2
An ivory okimono of a vegetable farmer, Meiji period, signature panel missing, 21cm (8¼in), L 24 July, £880 ($1,302)

3
A carved ivory okimono of a bijin, signed, 21cm (8¼in), C 2 Oct, £253 ($369)

4
A Japanese carved ivory okimono, Meiji period, signed on red lacquer tablet, 18.4cm (7¼in), C 2 Oct, £385 ($562)

5
Meiji (Akitsugu): An ivory figure of a fisherman with two boys, Meiji period, signed, 17.5cm (7in), L 24 July, £935 ($1,384)

6
An ivory okimono of two peasants, Meiji period, base cracked, signature plaque missing, 15cm (6in), L 24 July, £660 ($977)

7
Shinho and Kazumine: A lacquered wood and ivory figure of a bijin, Meiji period, playing a *samisen*, cracked and slightly worn, 40.6cm (16in), NY 11 Apr, $1,430 (£1,144)

8
An ivory okimono of a fisherman, Meiji period, signed, slight chips, 17cm (6¾in), C 10 July, £165 ($229)

9
A bronze and ivory figure depicting a man seated, smoking a pipe and holding a *kizeruzutsu*, Meiji period, cast signature probably Seiya, 33cm (13in), C 10 July, £1,210 ($1,682)

1

2

3

4

5

6

7

8   9

1
Gyokushin: A large ivory figure of a bijin, Meiji period, signed, 49.5cm (19½in), *L 12 Nov*, £2,800 ($3,948)

2
Rinyu: An ivory figure of Kannon, Meiji period, holding a basket of lotus, signed, 68.7cm (27in), *L 12 Nov*, £1,600 ($2,256)

3
Sesso: An ivory figure of Jurojin, Meiji period, the ivory stained for effect, signed, 46cm (18⅛in), *L 12 Nov*, £800 ($1,128)

4
Shumei: ivory figure of a bijin, Meiji period, signed, 23.5cm (9¼in), *NY 3 Oct*, $880 (£628)

5
Yosei: An ivory Okimono of a cafe proprietor, Meiji/Taisho period, the figure holding a tray in his right hand and a lantern in his left, signed, 17.5cm (6¾in), *L 14 June*, £528 ($702)

6
Hozan: An ivory figure of a man in ceremonial costume, Meiji period, small cracks, signed, 29.5cm (11½in), *L 14 June*, £1,760 ($2,341)

7
An ivory carving, Meiji period, signed *Tamayuki*, base glued, 20cm (8in), *S 25 Mar*, £286 ($363)

8
An ivory carving of a drummer, Meiji period, signed, 8cm (3¼in), *S 10 July*, £297 ($398)

9
Tokyo School: An ivory group of a man and a boy, late 19th century, chip and slight cracks, signed *Komin with seal*, 25.5cm (10in), *NY 3 Oct*, $1,430 (£1,021)

10
Keiji: A Tokyo School ivory figure of a fisherman and his son, Meiji period, slightly chipped, signed, 26.5cm (10½in), *L 12 Nov*, £1,400 ($1,974)

11
Ishin: An ivory group of a man and his son, Meiji period, signed, 28.5cm (11¼in), *L 12 Nov*, £520 ($733)

12
Gyokusui: An ivory figure of a young boy, Meiji period, playing a large *biwa*, his robe engraved with *sosho* characters, signed, 10cm (4in), *L 14 June*, £935 ($1,244)

Bijin beautiful girl

Eboshi court hat

ho-o phoenix

Hossu fly-switch

Oni demon

Oshirorie Chinese or mandarin ducks

Minogame 'hairy tailed' turtle, symbol of long life

Sarumawashi monkey trainer

Shi-shi lion dog

Takarabune treasure ship of the Seven Gods of Good Fortune

1

2

3

4

5

6

7

8

9

10

11

12

1
An ivory okimono, Meiji period, signed *Toshiaki*, 12.1cm (4¾in), *NY 11 Apr*, $1,430 (£1,144)

2
An ivory okimono of a toymaker, late 19th century, the ivory finely carved and lightly stained, signed *Horaku*, 9cm (3½in), *NY 3 Oct*, $1,210 (£864)

3
A wood and ivory okimono of a wheelwright, Meiji period, unsigned base, 24.2cm (9½in), *L 12 Nov*, £820 ($1,156)

4
An ivory two fold miniature screen, Meiji period, well carved on the interior with a scene of Immortals, the exterior carved with egrets and lotus, 14cm (5½in), *NY 10 Apr*, $2,200 (£1,818)

5
A carved ivory okimono depicting Fukurokoju, Meiji period, engraved signature, 19cm (7½in), *C 16 Jan*, £792 ($950)

6
A pair of ivory tusk vases, and covers, Meiji period, carved with monkeys applied signature seal, slight damage, 32cm (16½in), *C 16 Jan*, £1,815 ($2,178)

7
Shigemitsu: A carved ivory brushpot, Meiji period, carved with hunters resting beneath a tree, stained and well patinated, slightly worn, crack and chip, signed, 30.5cm (12in), *NY 25 June*, $770 (£600)

8
Seiya: A bronze and ivory figure of a bijin, Meiji period, signed, 21cm (8¼in), *C 17 Apr*, £1,100 ($1,430)

9
A pair of ivory vases, Meiji period, each carved in relief with a procession of children, unsigned, 14.5cm (5¾in), *L 14 June*, £1,210 ($1,609)

10
A carved teak takarabune, Meiji period, the boat fitted with figures of the Seven Lucky Gods, minor losses and repairs, 29.8cm (11¾in) high, *NY 25 June*, $825 (£640)

11
An ivory tanto, Meiji period, the whole carved as a dragon, the *tsuba* decorated with branches of pine, 55.5cm (22in), *L 14 June*, £880 ($1,170)

1   2

3   4

5   6   7

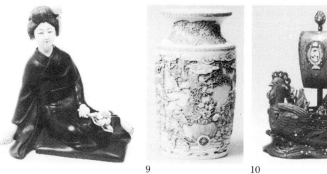

8   9   10

11

1
An iron tsuba, 18th century, applied in coloured enamels, 7cm (2¾in), *L 13 June,* £550 ($732)

2
An iron tsuba, 19th century, fashioned with two seated elephants, 8.5cm (3¼in), *L 13 June,* £484 ($644)

3
Furukawa Yoshinaga: A shakudo tsuba, 18th century, pierced with two *shishi* beneath peony, signed *Goto Takanori Monjin Furukawa Yoshinaga* with *kakihan,* 7cm (2¾in), *L 13 Nov,* £620 ($874)

4
Choshu School: A shakudo tsuba, 19th century, pierced with a flowering cherry tree, 7.8cm (3⅛in) with wood box, *L 13 Nov,* £420 ($592)

5
Haruaki Hogen: A copper tsuba, 19th century, depicting Daikoku seated upon two rice bales, signed *Mosetsushu zu Haruaki Hogen sei,* 9.5cm (3¾in), *L 13 June,* £1,485 ($1,975)

6
Kazuchika: A tsuba, 19th century, applied in relief with Wasobioye seated upon the hand of the giant Dr Kochi, signed *Kazuchika tsukuru,* 9.5cm (3¾in), *L 13 June,* £1,210 ($1,609)

7
Fujiwara Kiyonaga: A tsuba, 19th century, applied with an old woman carrying a basket with an emerging snake, signed with *kakihan,* 9.5cm (3¾in), *L 13 June,* £1,540 ($2,048)

8
Seiryoken Hagitani Katsuhira (ascribed to): A shibuichi tsuba, mid 19th century, applied with Daikoku playing with rats, signed, *L 6 Mar,* £880 ($1,320)

9
Tsuchiya Masachika (ascribed to): A copper tsuba, 19th century, applied with a sage opening a box out of which appears an oni, details in gilt, signed *Ansei 5th year (1858),* with *kakihan, L 13 June,* £308 ($410)

10
Nomura Masahide: An oval shakudo tsuba, applied with three crayfish, signed with *kakihan, L 13 June,* £1,100 ($1,463)

11
Ishiguro Masayoshi: A silver tsuba, 19th century, carved and incised with flowering *kiku* and peony, signed *Jugakusai Ishiguro Masayoshi* with *kakihan,* 8.2cm (3¼in), *L 13 Nov,* £1,700 ($2,397)

12
Shimamura Mitsuyoshi: A white metal tsuba, 19th century, decorated with Murasaki kneeling before a *suzuribako,* signed, 7.9cm (3⅛in) with fitted leather box, *L 13 Nov,* £950 ($1,339)

13
Hamano Naoyuki: A shibuichi tsuba, 19th century, applied with Yoshitsune and Benkei, signed *Gaiundo Hamano Naoyuki* with *kakihan, L 13 June,* £825 ($1,097)

14
Ittosai Riuo: A copper tsuba, mid 19th century, applied with the hag of the 'Lonely House of Adachigahara', 8.5cm (3¼in), *L 6 Mar,* £748 ($1,122)

15
A shibuichi and copper tsuba, 19th century, 7cm (2¾in), *L 13 June,* £264 ($351)

See glossary on p.677

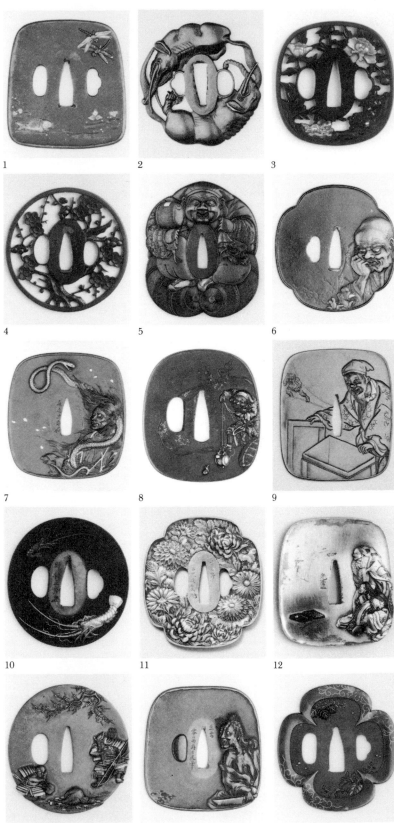

1

2

3

4

5

6

7

8

9

10

11

12

13

14

15

1
A shibuichi o-kozuka, 19th century, applied with Yasusuke, details in silver, copper, *shakudo* and gilt, *L 13 Nov*, £620 ($874)

2
A gilt kozuka, 19th century, carved and applied in coloured enamels on a *nanako* ground, *L 13 Nov*, £220 ($310)

3
Umetada School: A shakudo kozuka, 19th century, applied with butterflies and a grasshopper, *L 13 Nov*, £440 ($620)

4
Motoharu: A shibuichi kozuka, 19th century, applied with a *bijin*, signed with *kakihan*, *L 3 June*, £220 ($293)

5
Kikuoka Mitsuaki: A Shakudo Nanako set, late Edo/early Meiji period, applied in relief with bound reeds, *kiri*, fan and incense burner, signed with *Kakihan*, *L 6 Mar*, £209 ($314)

6
Jochiku: A shakudo set, mid-Edo period, applied in relief with two dragonflies, signed, *L 6 Mar*, £968 ($1,452)

7
Furukawa Jochin: A shakudo nanako set, late 18th century, applied in *iroe-takazogan* with the three Sake Tasters, details in copper, gold and silver, signed, *L 13 Nov*, £400 ($564)

8
Iwamoto Riokan: A shakudo set, late 18th century, applied with fish, details in gilt, *shibuichi* and *shakudo*, signed with *kakihan*, *L 13 Nov*, £460 ($648)

9
A shakudo set, 19th century, applied on a fine *nanako* ground in gold and *shakudo*, unsigned, *L 13 Nov*, £300 ($423)

10
Omori Hidenaga: An associated shakudo nanako set, 19th century, applied with a peony and butterflies, signed with *kakihan*, *L 13 Nov*, £300 ($423)

11
A mounted Koto Wakizashi blade, 40.8cm (16in), *L 13 Nov*, £2,500 ($3,525)

12
Sukesada (ascribed to): A Shinto Tachi, silvered metal fittings, blade 66.5cm (26¼in), *L 13 June*, £1,815 ($2,414)

13
Kanesada: A mounted Wakizashi, blade 44.5cm (17½in), *L 13 June*, £660 ($878)

14
An Aikuchi in carved wood mounts, blade 29.5cm (11½in), boxwood saya and tsuba, details in mother-of-pearl and horn, *L 13 June*, £495 ($658)

Aikuchi dagger.

Daisho pair of long and short swords.

Fuchi-kashira hilt end and band on sword handle.

Handachi long sword in court mount.

Katana sword blade mounted to hang edge upwards.

Koto old swords (14th to early 16th century)

Kozuka hilt of small knife accompanying sword in scabbard.

Kozuka hilt of small knife accompanying sword in scabbard.

Shinto new swords (mid 16th to 18th century).

Tachi sword blade mounted to hang edge downwards, court mount.

Tanto dagger with tsuba.

Tsuba sword guard.

Wakizashi short sword.

1 2
3 4 5
6
7 8
9 10
11
12
13
14

1
A pair of inlaid bronze vases, Meiji period, worked in relief with birds and flowers, one leaf missing, 45cm (17¾in), *L 6 Mar,* £990 ($1,109)

2
An inlaid bronze saucer dish, Meiji period, signed *Horyushi Juto (?)* with seal, *L 6 Mar,* £935 ($1,047)

3
A silver inlaid bronze vase, Meiji period, inlaid in silver, with bamboo, scratched, signed with artist's seal, 36.3cm (14¼in), *NY 25 June,* $2,090(£1,620)

4
Yoshikane: An inlaid bronze vase, Meiji period, applied and inlaid in gold, silver, and bronze, silver foot, signed, 36.2cm (14¼in), *NY 11 Apr,* $2,860 (£2,288)

5
A bronze Koro and cover, Meiji period, with six pierced panels each applied with a *kirin,* some areas repatinated, 55.5cm (21¾in), *L 6 Mar,* £1,265 ($1,417)

6
A bronze jardiniere, 19th century, 60cm (23¾in) diam, *L 13 June,* £990 ($1,317)

7
Isshin: A bronze vase, Meiji/Taisho period, decorated with silver upon a green patinated ground, signed, 21.3cm (8⅜in), *L 12 Nov,* £260 ($366)

8
A bronze ovoid vase, Meiji period, fitted with a band of garden flowers, inlaid gilt seal, scratches, 21.6cm (8½in), *NY 10 Apr,* $550 (£455)

9
Komai (attributed to): An inlaid iron vase and cover, Meiji period, with a panel of shrines in a lakeside setting, 19cm (7½in), *L 24 July,* £902 ($1,335)

10
A pair of inlaid bronze vases, Meiji period, inlaid in silver, *shakudo* and *sentoku,* signed *Hamada yaki gido zo,* 17.8cm (7in), *NY 11 Apr,* $1,320 (£1,056)

11
Komai: An inlaid iron cabinet, Meiji period, the two doors decorated with landscape views, incised mark, 11cm (4¼in), *L 24 July,* £1,430 ($2,116)

12
Komai: An inlaid iron jar and cover, Meiji period, decorated with iris and *ho-o,* interior gilt and engraved, inlaid seal, 8cm (3in), *L 24 July,* £660 ($977)

13
An inlaid iron box, Meiji period, in the form of a travelling storage box, inlaid in gold and silver, signed *Yoshiyama,* 12.1cm (4¾in) wide, *NY 25 June,* $990 (£767)

14
An inlaid and enamelled silver bowl, Meiji period with eight silvered copper panels of various birds, stamped, *ju-gin,* 24cm (9½in), *L 13 June,* £1,045 ($1,390)

15
A Koshosai silver and enamel vase and cover. Meiji period, decorated with *kiku* in coloured enamels, engraved signature, 12cm (4¾in), *C 17 Apr,* £825 ($1,073)

16
A silver tea kettle, late 19th century, 15cm (6in) high, *C 17 Apr,* £330 ($429)

1

2

3

4

5

6

7

8

9

10

11

12

13

14

15

16

1
A Komai Koro, cover and stand, Meiji period, signed, 10. 5cm (4¼in), *C 16 Jan,* £682 ($818)

2
Komai: A pair of brush pots, Meiji period, inlaid mark *Kyoto ju Komai sei,* 8.5cm (3¼in), *L 6 Mar,* £462 ($517)

3
Yoshiteru: An enamelled silver vase, Meiji period, chased with cranes, *kiku* and flowering cherry, signed on a gilt tablet, 26.7cm (10½in), *L 12 Nov,* £550 ($775)

4
A large copper study of a mythological creature, 19th century, tongue missing, 180cm (71in), *L 12 Nov,* £900 ($1,269)

5
Takami: A bronze figure of a young woman, early 20th century, signed, 33cm (13in), *L 12 Nov,* £480 ($676)

6
A Miyao bronze of a peasant, Meiji period, engraved signature, piece missing, 33cm (13in), *C 17 Apr,* £1,705 ($2,217)

7
A bronze figure of a samurai, *c.*1900, signed, blemish to leg, 27.5cm (10¾in), *S 25 Mar,* £638 ($810)

8
Genryusai Seiya: A bronze figure of a tiger, well modelled with dark brown patina, signed, 45.6cm (18in), *NY 3 Oct,* $1,210 (£864)

9
A bronze group of an elephant and two tigers, Meiji period, ivory tusks, signed with a seal mark *Shokoku saku,* 25.5cm (10in), *NY 3 Oct,* $1,540 (£1,100)

10
A bronze figure of Hotei, Meiji period, staff missing, 31.8cm (12½in), *NY 25 June,* $605 (£469)

11
Gyoko: A bronze figure of an archer, Meiji period, signed, 37cm (14½in), *L 13 June,* £2,420 ($3,219)

12
A bronze model of an eagle, *c.*1900, 40.5cm (16½in), *S 14 Nov,* £1,045 ($1,463)

1

2

3

4

5

6

7

8

9

10

11

12

1

A carved wood figure of an Arhat, Meiji period, 99cm (39in), *NY 25 June,* $1,760 (£1,364)

2

A gilt wood figure of Shaka Nyorai, Edo period, 123.5cm (48¾in), *L 12 Nov,* £1,950 ($2,749)

3

A pair of painted wood figures of Koma Inu, late 17th/early 18th century, 46cm (18in), *NY 3 Oct,* $2,860 (£2,042)

4

A pair of wood figures of Koma Inu, 17th century, 54cm (21¼in), *M 24 June,* FF 61,050 (£5,088; $6,868)

5

An inlaid lacquer Tsuitate, Meiji period, 129 x 93cm, 130 x 116cm (51 x 45¾in), *L 6 Mar,* £1,430 ($1,602)

6

A hardwood display cabinet, Meiji period, 181.5cm (71½in), *NY 11 Apr,* $2,090 (£1,672)

7

A gold lacquer shodana, 19th century, with drawers decorated in gold *takamakie, hiramakie, kirigane,* gold and silver foil and gold insets, silver metal mounts, 91 x 93cm (35¾ x 36¼in), *L 6 Mar,* £3,080 ($3,450)

8

A red lacquered cabinet-on-stand, late 19th century, gilt within a *wan* diaper, fitted with drawers, 112cm x 60cm (44 x 23½in), *S 10 July,* £528 ($708)

9

A carved hardwood and lacquer cabinet on stand, with carved ivory, mother-of-pearl and gold and black lacquer, 218 x 155cm (86in x 61in), *L 6 Mar,* £1,430 ($1,602)

10

An inlaid lacquer display cabinet, Meiji period, inset with lacquer panels, 230cm (90½in), *L 12 Nov,* £2,000 ($2,820)

1

2

3

4

5

6

7

8

9

10

Chinese Works of Art

Article ● Ming Blue and White Porcelain *pp* 706-710 *See also* ● Colour illustrations *pp* 572-574

Chinese Dynasties and Reign Titles

		MING				QING			
Shangyin	c.1600-c.1027 BC	Liao	916-1125	Hongwu	1368-1398	Jiajing	1522-1566	Shunzhi	1644-1661	Xianfeng	1851-1861
Zhou	1027-475	Song	560-1279	Yongle	1403-1424	Longqing	1567-1572	Kangxi	1662-1722	Tongzhi	1862-1873
Qin	221-206	Jin	1115-1234	Xuande	1426-1435	Wanli	1573-1619	Yongzheng	1723-1735	Guangxu	1874-1907
Han	206-220 AD	Yuan	1279-1368	Chenghua	1465-1487	Tianqi	1621-1627	Qianlong	1736-1795	Xuantong	1908-1912
Sui	581-618			Hongzhi	1488-1505	Chongzheng	1628-1643	Jiaqing	1796-1820	Hongxian	1916
Tang	618-907			Zhengde	1506-1521			Daoguang	1821-1850		

1
A pair of stone figures of camels, Ming dynasty, 127cm (50in) long, *NY 17 Apr*, $71,500 (£55,859)

2
A cast-iron head of Guanyin, early Ming dynasty, partially covered with gesso, 21.5cm (8½in), *L 1 Nov*, £1,870 ($2,805)

3
A stone head of Guanyin, Ming dynasty, wearing a diadem with the figure of Amitabha, 35cm (13¾in) high, *L 18 June*, £2,750 ($3,713)

4
A carved wood figure of a priest, Ming dynasty, 51cm (20⅛in) high, *L 2 May*, £1,320 ($1,703)

5
A pair of plaster figures, early 19th century, of a mandarin and his lady in court dress, the heads detachable and nodding, 27.6cm (10⅞in) high, *M 23 June*, FF 26,640 (£2,147; $2,877)

6
A stone figure of the goddess Guanyin, 142cm (56in), *NY 16 Feb*, $1,650 (£1,422)

7
A polychrome wood figure of Guandi, the god of war, Jiaqing, 104.5cm (41⅛in) high, *L 2 May*, £5,060 ($6,527)

1

2

3

4

5

6

7

1
An inlaid bronze figure of Guanyin, Kangxi, signed *Shi Sou*, 12.5cm (5in), *L 1 Nov,* £935 ($1,403)

2
A gilt-bronze figure of a Buddhist sage, Ming dynasty, seated in *dhyanasana*, traces of blue, green and red pigmentation, 18.2cm (7in), *L 1 Nov,* £440 ($660)

3
A bronze figure of Guanyin, Song dynasty, seated *rajalalitasana* on a lotus pedestal, 24cm (9½in), *NY 4 Dec,* $2,200 (£1,486)

4
A gilt-bronze figure of Wenshu, 18th century, the deity seated on a *fu*-lion, 22cm (8¾in), *NY 5 June,* $3,850 (£3,031)

5
A pair of bronze figures of acolytes, Ming dynasty, 31cm (12¼in), *L 2 May,* £935 ($1,206)

6
A gilt-bronze figure of Buddha as the Supreme Physician, Ming dynasty, 49.5cm (19½in), *L 2 May,* £3,630 ($4,683)

7
A silver-wire inlaid bronze figure of Guanyin, 18th century, 58cm (22¾in), *NY 17 Apr,* $2,420 (£1,890)

8
A gilt-bronze seated Buddha, Ming dynasty, 61cm (24in), *NY 5 June,* $8,250 (£6,496)

9
A gilt-bronze figure of Buddha, Ming dynasty, seated in *dhyanasana,* 28cm (11in), *L 1 Nov,* £858 ($1,287)

10
A gilt-bronze figure of a monk, 18th century, seated in *dhyanasana,* 24.5cm (9½in), *NY 5 June,* $990 (£779)

11
An inscribed gilt-bronze figure of a dignitary, mark and period of Yongzheng, inscribed at the front *Zhu Ba, Yong Zheng Nian Zao,* 'Casting no. 8, made in the Yongzheng reign', 44.5cm (17½in), *L 1 Nov,* £726 ($1,089)

12
A bronze figure of Guanyin, Ming dynasty, with hands in *dhyana mudra,* 32cm (12½in), *NY 5 June,* $880 (£692)

13
A gilt-bronze figure of Amitayus, Qianlong mark and period, seated in *dhyanasana,* incised nine-character mark of Qianlong corresponding to the year 1761, 25.5cm (10in), *NY 5 June,* $605 (£476)

14
A gilt-bronze figure of a dignitary, Ming dynasty, 37cm (14½in), *L 2 May,* £297 ($383)

1 2 3 4 5 6

7 8 9 10

11 12 13 14

1
A ritual bronze food
vessel (*gui*), 11th/10th
century BC, cast on each
side with a large *taotie*
mask, 24cm (9½in),
L 18 June,
£5,500 ($7,425)

2
An archaic bronze food
vessel and cover (*ding*),
Warring States, olive
brown patina with pat-
ches of green and rust
encrustation, 23cm (9in)
wide, *NY 4 June*,
$3,960 (£3,118)

3
A bronze covered vessel
(*liding*) Warring States,
the dark surface with
greenish encrustations,
21cm (8¼in), *L 10 Dec*,
£1,430 ($2,002)

4
An archaic bronze wine
vessel (*zun*), Western Zhou
dynasty, the central bulb
cast with two *taotie* masks,
mottled silver green
patina, 24.5cm (9½in),
NY 4 June,
$13,200 (£10,393)

5
A bronze vessel and cover
(*hu*), Han dynasty, cast
with *taotie*, 18.5cm (7¼in),
NY 5 June,
$627 (£493)

6
An archaic bronze food
vessel (*gui*), pale greyish
patina 23.5cm (9½in),
NY 4 June,
$8,800 (£6,929)

7
A bronze shoudai mirror,
1st century BC/1st cen-
tury AD, the outer field
with phoenix, dragon,
tiger and tortoise in
thread relief, 17.5cm
(7in), *L 10 Dec*,
£330 ($462)

8
An archaic bronze
libation vessel, Shang
dynasty, of *jue* form,
23.5cm (9¼in), *L 18 June*,
£4,400 ($5,940)

9
An archaic bronze 'TLV'
mirror, 1st century BC/
1st century AD, of Wang
Meng type, silver patina
with some bright green
encrustation, 19cm
(7½in), *NY 4 Dec*,
$1,760 (£1,189)

10
An archaic bronze vessel,
Zhou dynasty, mottled
green patina with earth
encrustation, 19.5cm
(7¾in), *NY 4 Dec*,
$1,100 (£743)

11
An archaic bronze
cauldron (*li*), late Shang
dynasty, the sides cast
with three *taotie* masks,
14.5cm (5¾in), *L 10 Dec*,
£11,000 ($15,400)

12
An archaic bronze food
vessel (*ding*), Shang
dynasty, decorated with a
band of *kui* dragons,
encrusted dark green
patina, 15cm (6in),
NY 5 June,
$2,310 (£1,818)

1
A bronze censer, 19th century, six character mark of Xuande, 54cm (21¼in), *L 2 May,* £880 ($1,135)

2
A bronze censer, 19th century, the sides cast with a band of masks, lion mask handles, 33cm (13in) over handles, *NY 17 Apr,* $1,045 (£816)

3
A bronze tripod censer, Ming dynasty, with three elephant-head feet, 18cm (7in) over handles, *NY 17 Apr,* $660 (£515)

4
A pair of bronze figures of geese, rich dark patina 73 and 59cm (28¾ and 23¼in), *L 1 Nov,* £3,740 ($5,610)

5
A bronze censer, in the form of a goose, late 17th century, 41.5cm (16½in), *S 25 Mar,* £595 ($754)

6
A pair of bronze rabbits, 17th century, silver inlay representing the markings, 12cm (4¾in), *L 1 Nov,* £1,375 ($2,063)

7
A bronze figure of a *fu lion,* Ming dynasty, 7.5cm (3in) long, *NY 17 Apr,* $825 (£644)

8
A bronze arrow vase, Ming dynasty, cast in relief with dragons, waves, and lotus, 42cm (16½in), *L 1 Nov,* £418 ($627)

9
A pair of bronze gold-splash vases, 19th century, cast Xuande mark, 27.5cm (10¾in), *C 10 July,* £858 ($1,193)

10
A bronze censer, late Ming dynasty, signed Hu Wenming, cast with a frieze of fish, crab and dragons, 14.5cm (5¾in), *L 10 Dec,* £440 ($616)

11
A gold-splash bronze censer, 17th/18th century, seal mark of Xuande, 17.5cm (7in), *L 1 Nov,* £715 ($1,073)

12
A gold-splash bronze censer, 17th/18th century, six character mark of Xuande, 11cm (4¼in), *L 2 May,* £990 ($1,277)

13
A gold-splash bronze wine vessel, 17th/18th century, mark of Xuande on base, 27cm (10½in), *HK 22 May,* HK$22,000 (£2,277; $3,052)

14
A gold-splash bronze vase, 17th/18th century, four seal-character hallmark, 46.5cm (18¼in), *L 2 May,* £1,595 ($2,058)

1 2 3 4 5 6 7 8 9 10 11 12 13 14

1
A silver teapot and cover,
19th century, etched with
bamboo sprays, 16.5cm
(6½in), *L 1 Nov,*
£605 ($908)

2
**A Chinese export silver
coffee pot,** Khecheong,
Canton, *c.*1835, base
marked KHC and pseudo
marks, 27cm (10½in), 42oz
(1306gr), *NY 30 Jan,*
$4,620 (£4,088)

3
**A silver compressed cir-
cular fruit bowl,** late 19th
century, 21cm (8½in)
diam, 21oz 12dwt (671gr),
C 16 Jan,
£341 ($409)

4
**A silver three-piece tea
set,** Woshing, Shanghai,
late 19th century, teapot
13.5cm (5¼in) high, 41oz
6dwt (1285gr), *L 11 Feb,*
£660 ($1,155)

5
**A silver three-piece tea
set,** late 19th century,
48oz 18dwt (1520gr),
C 16 Jan,
£660 ($792)

6
**A Chinese export silver
teapot,** Khecheong, Can-
ton, *c.*1840, in George IV
style, 17cm (6½in), 50oz
(1,555gr), *NY 31 Jan,*
$19,800 (£16,780)

7
A silver brushpot, decor-
ated in relief with the
'Hundred Boys' at play,
13cm (5in) high,
NY 17 Apr,
$8,250 (£6,445)

8
**A silver three-piece tea
set,** late 19th century,
each piece chased with a
dragon, 29oz (902gr),
C 2 Oct,
£308 ($449)

9
A silver tea tray, late 19th
century, engraved with
exotic birds amongst
prunus branches, 54.5cm
(21½in) 64oz 10dwt
(2006gr), *C 2 Oct,*
£660 ($963)

10
**A Chinese export tea
kettle on lampstand,**
Wang Hing, late 19th
century, 30cm (11¾in),
30oz (933gr), *NY 27 June,*
$412 (£317)

11
A silver bowl, *c.*1900,
decorated with a dragon
relief, marked from Wang
Hing & Co, Hong Kong,
19cm (7½in), *L 2 May,*
£616 ($795)

12
A silver mug, 19th century, decorated with a
spray of chrysanthemum,
11.5cm (4½in), *L 2 May,*
£572 ($738)

13
A silver bowl, *c.*1900, with
bamboo canes and cir-
cular reserve in repoussé,
marked on the base 'Tuck
Chang' and with two
characters, made by Tuck
Chang & Co, Shanghai,
17cm (6¾in), *L 2 May,*
£242 ($312)

 8 *(tea set)* 9 *(tray)*

1
A pair of cloisonné
enamel vases, Jiaqing,
36cm (14in), *L 2 May*,
£660 ($851)

2
A cloisonné enamel
covered censer (*fangding*),
Qianlong mark, in
archaic bronze style,
brightly decorated on a
turquoise ground, later
fu-lion finial, 52cm
(20½in) high, *NY 2 Oct*,
$3,575 (£2,554)

3
A pair of cloisonné
enamel *gu* form vases,
Qianlong, decorated with
Indian lotus blossoms on
a turquoise ground, 63cm
(24½in), *NY 17 Apr*,
$5,500 (£4,296)

4
A cloisonné enamel jar-
diniere, Qianlong, later
mounted by Barbedienne
of Paris, 87.8cm (34½in)
high, *L 2 May*,
£9,900 ($12,771)

5
A pair of cloisonné bowls,
Qianlong, each decorated
with lotus, 16.5cm (6½in)
wide, *NY 5 June*,
$1,045 (£822)

6
A cloisonné enamel cen-
ser, Qianlong mark and
period, brightly decor-
ated on a turquoise
ground, the *nianhao*
incised on the base with
the additional character
Qiang, 14cm (5½in),
HK 22 May,
HK$13,200
(£1,366; $1,831)

7
A pair of cloisonné
enamel wall vases, 18th
century, decorated with
coloured flowers on a
turquoise ground,
L 2 May,
£825 ($1,064)

8
A late Ming cloisonné
enamel box and cover,
17th century, decorated
with red and green
motifs on a lapis-blue
ground, 10.5cm (4in),
L 2 May,
£440 ($568)

9
A cloisonné censer, 17th
century, with colourful
lotus meanders on a tur-
quoise body, 12.5cm
(5in), *L 2 May*,
£308 ($397)

10
A cloisonné enamel vase,
16th century, of archaic
gu form, 26cm (10¼in),
HK 22 May,
HK$19,800
(£2,050; $2,747)

1   2   3

4   5   6

7   8   9   10

1
A pair of cloisonné vases,
Guangxu, 31cm (12¼in),
C 10 July,
£616 ($856)

2
A cloisonné goose censer,
20th century, 38cm
(15in), *C 17 Apr,*
£440 ($572)

3
**A pair of cloisonné
enamel jars and covers,**
Daoguang, 24cm (9½in),
L 1 Nov,
£902 ($1,353)

4
**A pair of cloisonné
enamel vases,** Jiaqing,
decorated in imitation of
the 'Hundred Deer' pat-
tern, 50cm (19¾in),
L 2 May,
£3,630 ($4,983)

5
**A pair of cloisonné
enamel figures of quail,**
Jiaqing, for use as incense
burners, the wings form-
ing removable covers,
13.5cm (5¼in), *L 2 May,*
£2,530 ($3,264)

6
**A pair of cloisonné
enamel vases,** Jiaqing,
enamelled with butter-
flies and flowers on a
turquoise ground, 24cm
(9½in), *L 2 May,*
£385 ($497)

7
A Changfu, *c.*1900, with
dark blue satin ground,
edged with metallic trim,
gilded buttons, *C 3 May,*
£605 ($774)

8
**A blue ground dragon
robe,** late 18th century,
embroidered with gold
dragons and peonies in
blue, yellow, peach and
white, 142cm (56in) long,
NY 17 Apr,
$1,980 (£1,546)

9
**An orange brocade
chuba,** 18th century, with
brocade metallic gold
dragons clutching pearls,
152cm (5ft) long,
NY 17 Apr,
$1,100 (£859)

10
**An Imperial theatre cos-
tume,** Kangxi, the jacket
with black silk ground,
the leg panels with
yellow silk ground, all
decorated with gold
dragons, jacket 81cm
(32in) long, *NY 17 Apr,*
$5,225 (£4,082)

11
An export fan, Chinese
school, *c.*1860, in watercolour, cut silk and painted ivory on paper, with
three views showing
Macao, the Hongs at
Canton and Hong Kong,
sticks 22cm (8¾in),
NY 17 Apr,
$1,870 (£1,460)

12
**An Imperial theatre cos-
tume,** 18th century, the
red silk ground with gold
imitating chain mail,
122cm (48in) long,
NY 17 Apr,
$2,310 (£1,804)

13
**A Chinese export ivory
and painted silk fan,**
*c.*1785, the paper-backed
silk painted in various
colours with European
ladies and gentlemen,
length outstretched 54cm
(21¼in), *NY 30 Jan,*
$550 (£487)

1

2

3

4

5

6

7

8

9

10

11

12

13

1
A huang huali seal chest,
(*guanpixiang*), 16th/17th
century, the top lifting to
reveal a demountable
tray, 39cm (15¼in) high,
NY 4 Dec,
$9,900 (£6,689)

2
**A Ming rosewood
armchair,** early 17th century, *L 2 May,*
£6,820 ($8,798)

3
**An elmwood side cab-
inet,** 17th/18th century,
with brass handles,
hinges and lockplates,
216cm (7ft 1in) wide,
L 1 Nov,
£1,540 ($2,310)

4
A nanmu cupboard, 18th
century, 171cm (67¼in)
high, *L 2 May,*
£2,860 ($3,689)

5
A tilimn table, late 18th
century, 106cm (41¾in)
wide, *L 2 May,*
£3,190 ($4,115)

6
A huang huali low table,
18th century, reduced in
height, 92.5cm (36½in)
wide, *NY 17 Apr,*
$2,310 (£1,804)

7
**A pair of hongmu coin
chests,** 18th/19th century,
49.5cm (19½in) high,
NY 17 Apr,
$5,225 (£4,082)

8
**A pair of marble-top
hongmu brocade stools,**
18th/19th century, 52cm
(20½in) high, *NY 17 Apr,*
$2,860 (£2,234)

9
A carved hongmu table,
18th/19th century,
reduced in size, replace-
ment plaques on frieze,
94.5cm (37¼in) wide,
NY 2 Oct,
$1,980 (£1,414)

10
**A pair of huang huali
side chairs,** late 18th
century, 102cm (40in),
C 17 Jan,
£550 ($660)

11
**A zitan polished wood
writing box,** 17th cen-
tury, with *ruyi* shaped
brass appliques and clasp,
32cm (12½in) wide,
HK 24 May,
HK$11,550
(£1,196; $1,603)

12
**A huang huali polished
wood writing box,** 17th
century, with *ruyi* shaped
brass mounts, and pulls,
38cm (15in) wide,
HK 24 May,
HK$15,400
(£1,594; $2,136)

1

2

3

4

5

6

7

8

9

11

10

12

1
A pair of rosewood stools, 19th century, 52cm (20½in) high, *C 18 Apr,* £418 ($534)

2
A pair of stools, 19th century, each with cane seat, 51cm (20in) high, *L 2 May,* £2,090 ($2,696)

3
A nan mu chest, 19th century, the top with two removable panels, 93.5cm (37in) wide, *L 1 Nov,* £1,100 ($1,650)

4
A pair of hong mu side tables, 19th century, 94cm (37in) high, *L 1 Nov,* £1,705 ($2,558)

5
A set of six rosewood dining chairs, mid 19th century, *L 2 May,* £1,210 ($1,561)

6
A hong mu display cabinet, 19th century, 101.5cm (40in) high, *NY 17 Apr,* $2,420 (£1,890)

7
A pair of Ming style faded hong mu side cabinets, late 19th century, 142cm (56in) high, *NY 2 Oct,* $2,750 (£1,964)

8
A pair of hong mu armchairs, 19th century, 95cm (37½in), *NY 17 Apr,* $3,080 (£2,406)

9
A nest of four huali tables, *c.*1900, 48cm (19in) wide, *S 25 Mar,* £484 ($615)

10
A hong mu spindleback bench, 19th century, 90cm (35in) high, *NY 17 April,* $4,400 (£3,437)

11
A rosewood torchère, *c.*1900, the top with inset marble slab, 91cm (36in), *C 11 July,* £115 ($160)

12
A rosewood urn stand, *c.*1900, with rouge marble top, 81cm (32in) high, *C 18 Apr,* £440 ($572)

13
A rosewood display cabinet, 1900, 212cm (83½in) high, *C 17 Jan,* £935 ($1,122)

1
A Pekin glass vase, 19th century, the white metal decorated in *café-au-lait* overlay, 18.4cm (7¼in) high, *L 2 May,*
£418 ($539)

2
A pair of imperial yellow Peking glass ovoid vases, carved with floral and bird reserves, 21.5cm (8½in), *NY 2 Oct,*
$1,650 (£1,179)

3
A pair of glass overlay meiping vases, Guangxu, decorated on the milk-white metal in high relief in red with two truncated heart-shaped panels, 17.5cm (6⅞in), *L 2 May,*
£330 ($426)

4
A Pekin glass vase, of purplish-blue translucent tone, incised Qianlong mark on the base, 26.5cm (10½in), *HK 24 May,*
HK$5,720 (£592; $793)

5
A faceted Peking glass vase, Qianlong mark and period, imitating realgar, suffused with orange swirls tinged with red, 15cm (6in), *HK 22 May,*
HK$17,600
(£1,822; $2,441)

6
A Pekin glass jar, decorated on the translucent white ground in bright lime green, 13cm (5⅛in) high, *L 2 May,*
£308 ($397)

7
An Imperial yellow Peking glass vase, 18th century, 20.5cm (8in), *L 1 Nov,*
£1,870 ($2,805)

8
A Pekin glass vase, mark and period of Qianlong, the metal of vivid ruby tone, 9cm (3½in), *L 1 Nov,*
£572 ($858)

9
A glass overlay jar and cover, Qianlong mark and period, the bubble-suffused ground carved and overlaid in ruby-red, 18cm (7¼in), *HK 22 May,*
HK$60,500
(£6,263; $8,392)

10
A jade snuff bottle, 1800/1880, the yellowish-green stone suffused with ochre inclusions, carved with archaic bronze cash, *NY 1 July,*
$880 (£676)

11
A yellow jade snuff bottle, 1780/1850, carved with a wickerwork pattern, *NY 2 Dec,*
$2,640 (£1,772)

12
A lavender jadeite snuff bottle, 1800/1880, *NY 1 July,*
$3,850 (£2,961)

13
A jade snuff bottle, 1750/1820, carved as a melon, the stone stained black, *NY 1 July,*
$247 (£190)

1
A jadeite snuff botte, the mottled green stone suffused with emerald-green dappling, *NY 2 Dec*, $880 (£591)

2
An amber snuff bottle, 1750/1850, suffused on one side with ribbon-like darker markings and a fine crackle, *L 2 May*, £2,420 ($3,121)

3
An amber snuff bottle, 1750/1820, carved with a wickerwork pattern, *NY 1 July*, $6,600 (£5,076)

4
An embellished amber snuff bottle, decorated with soapstone of various shades and lacquer, *NY 2 Dec*, $2,640 (£1,772)

5
A chalcedony snuff bottle, 1800/1880, the mushroom-coloured stone with a dark inclusion depicting an eagle attacking a cat, *NY 2 Dec*, $2,090 (£1,403)

6
A coral snuff bottle, carved in relief with a sage and attendant crossing a bridge, *NY 2 Dec*, $1,430 (£960)

7
A chalcedony snuff bottle, carved using dark inclusions in the stone with Liu Hai and the toad, *NY 2 Dec*, $1,430 (£960)

8
A lacquer burgauté snuff bottle, decorated with purple, silver and green mother-of-pearl depicting an egret beside lotus, *NY 16 Apr*, $605 (£476)

9
A soapstone snuff bottle, carved with clusters of lotus and magnolia, *NY 16 Apr*, $302 (£237)

10
A turquoise snuff bottle, 1820/1880, carved with archaic bronze-form cash, *NY 1 July*, $1,320 (£1,015)

11
A turquoise matrix snuff bottle, 1820/1880, the stone suffused with a metallic black matrix, *L 2 May*, £1,155 ($1,489)

12
A turquoise snuff bottle, incised with an inscription, a Qianlong seal mark on the base, *NY 16 Apr*, $1,430 (£1,125)

13
A cinnabar lacquer snuff bottle, decorated in relief with an attendant leading a horse and maiden, *NY 16 Apr*, $357 (£281)

14
An Imperial-style ivory snuff bottle, four character Qianlong mark, carved in relief with a group of boys pulling at an elephant carrying a lady on its back, *L 2 May*, £6,600 ($8,514)

15
An ivory snuff bottle, 1750/1850, carved with a wickerwork pattern, *NY 1 July*, $2,970 (£2,284)

16
An ivory snuff bottle, 1800/1880, in the form of a curled lotus leaf, *NY 2 Dec*, $4,125 (£2,768)

17
A cloisonné enamel snuff bottle, 19th century, *NY 1 July*, $1,650 (£1,269)

18
An embellished brass snuff bottle, decorated with chips of soapstone, coral, malachite and mother-of-pearl, *NY 1 July*, $1,870 (£1,438)

19
An agate snuff bottle, 1800/1880, encircled by bands of white and caramel brown, *L 2 May*, £418 ($539)

20
A 'peanut' agate snuff bottle, 1800/1860, carved using ochre inclusions with three peanuts on top of a cluster of Chinese dates, *NY 1 July*, $715 (£550)

1   2   3   4
5   6   7   8
9   10   11   12
13   14   15   16
17   18   19   20

1
A glass inside-painted
snuff bottle, modern
school, possibly Gweilin,
NY 16 Apr,
$192 (£151)

2
A rock crystal inside-
painted snuff bottle, by
Ye Zhongsan, signed and
dated 1919, painted with
a continuous scene
depicting the Eight
Immortals, *NY 16 Apr,*
$1,430 (£1,125)

3
A glass inside-painted
snuff bottle, by Ma
Shaoxuan, signed,
NY 16 Apr,
$2,860 (£2,251)

4
An inside-painted glass
snuff bottle, by Ye
Zhongsan the Younger,
signed and dated 1929,
depicting Huang Chen-
yen riding on a donkey,
NY 1 July,
$302 (£232)

5
An inside-painted glass
snuff bottle, by Yen
Yutian, signed, *NY 2 Dec,*
$220 (£148)

6
A glass inside-painted
snuff bottle, by Ma
Shaoxuan, signed and
dated 1913, *NY 16 Apr,*
$660 (£519)

7
A glass inside-painted
snuff bottle, by Shi
Chuan, signed, painted
with a Manchu warrior,
L 2 May,
£330 ($425)

8
A glass overlay snuff
bottle, 1800/80, the green
ground overlaid in
cinnabar red with a fish,
NY 1 July,
$3,190 (£2,453)

9
A glass overlay snuff
bottle, the white ground
carved in translucent
blue on each side,
NY 2 Dec,
$3,850 (£2,584)

10
A glass overlay snuff
bottle, 1800/60, the
bubble-suffused ground
decorated in green,
NY 16 Apr,
$3,850 (£3,031)

11
A glass overlay snuff
bottle, 1800/60, the coffee
ground overlaid in green,
NY 1 July,
$1,100 (£846)

12
A glass overlay snuff
bottle, 1750/1850, the
clear ground decorated
with two fan-tailed fish,
NY 16 Apr,
$1,320 (£1,039)

13
A glass overlay snuff
bottle, 1780/1850, the
bubble-suffused ground
decorated in purplish
blue, *NY 16 Apr,*
$2,200 (£1,732)

14
A seal-type glass overlay
snuff bottle, Yangzhou
School, the clear ground
overlaid in black with
birds and butterflies,
NY 1 July,
$1,320 (£1,015)

15
A glass overlay snuff
bottle, 1750/1850, the
opaque ground overlaid
in blue with *mon*-like
medallions, *NY 2 Dec,*
$2,750 (£1,846)

16
A seal-type glass overlay
snuff bottle, Yangzhou
School, the white ground
decorated in dark brown,
NY 16 Apr,
$880 (£692)

17
A glass overlay snuff
bottle, 1820/1880, the
white ground decorated
in black with a pair of
dragons, *NY 16 Apr,*
$880 (£692)

18
A glass overlay snuff
bottle, 1780/1850, the
'snowflake' ground
decorated in red with a
fan-tailed carp, *NY 1 July,*
$412 (£316)

19
A glass overlay snuff
bottle, 1750/1850, the
opaque ground overlaid
in green with a design of
flowering lotus, *NY 2 Dec,*
$1,320 (£886)

20
A double overlay glass
snuff bottle, decorated
with blooms and buds in
red and green, *NY 2 Dec,*
$935 (£628)

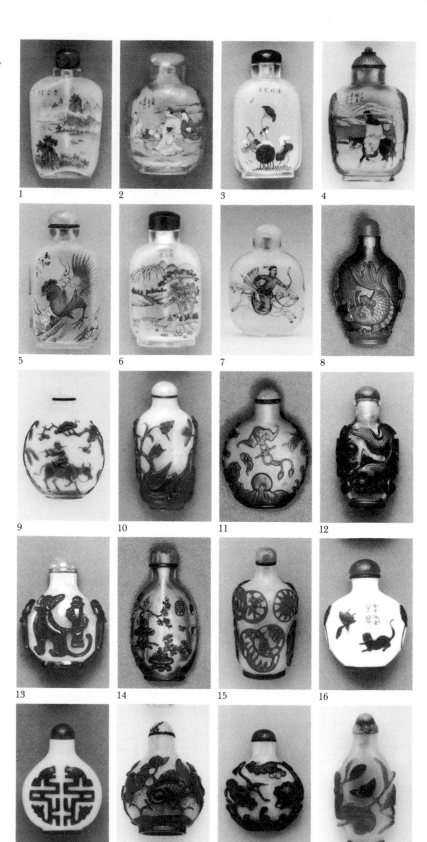

1
**A glass overlay snuff
bottle,** 1800/1850, the
bubble-suffused ground
decorated in green with
fruiting pods, *L 2 May,*
£121 ($156)

2
**A chalcedony snuff
bottle,** carved in relief
with white doves,
L 2 May,
£506 ($652)

3
**A glass overlay snuff
bottle,** 1800/1860, the
'snowflake' ground
decorated in green with
fruiting pods, *NY 2 Dec,*
$880 (£590)

4
**A hair crystal snuff
bottle,** 18th century, the
stone suffused through-
out with black tourma-
line needles, *NY 1 July,*
$5,775 (£4,442)

5
**A hair crystal snuff
bottle,** 1780/1880, the
stone suffused with black
tourmaline needles,
NY 2 Dec,
$550 (£369)

6
**A rock crystal coin snuff
bottle,** *c.*1800, after a
Spanish Eight Reales
piece, the obverse carved
with an effigy of Charles
V, *NY 1 July,*
$1,430 (£1,100)

7
**A Peking glass snuff
bottle,** 1780/1880, the
ruby metal of rich tone,
NY 2 Dec,
$880 (£591)

8
**A Peking glass snuff
bottle,** 18th century, the
metal of whitish-green
tone imitating jade, *NY
16 Apr,*
$660 (£519)

9
**A Peking glass snuff
bottle,** Qianlong mark
and period, carved with
six panels enclosing
flowering sprays,
mottled green, *NY 1 July,*
$7,150 (£5,500)

10
**An imperial yellow glass
snuff bottle,** 1760/1860,
NY 16 Apr,
$4,125 (£3,248)

11
**A slip-decorated Yixing
snuff bottle,** Daoguang,
the shoulders enamelled
in blue, a recessed panel
decorated in ochre slip,
NY 1 July,
$2,200 (£1,692)

12
**A 'soft paste' porcelain
snuff bottle,** Jiaqing,
NY 2 Dec,
$3,410 (£2,289)

13
A porcelain snuff bottle,
Daoguang seal mark and
period, enamelled with
dragons, *NY 16 Apr,*
$935 (£736)

14
**A 'famille-rose' porcelain
snuff bottle,** Daoguang
seal mark and period,
NY 1 July,
$880 (£676)

15
A moulded snuff bottle,
1840/1880, in the form of
a curled lotus leaf,
enamelled in green,
yellow, white and
aubergine, *NY 16 Apr,*
$467 (£367)

16
**A 'famille-rose' porcelain
snuff bottle,** Daoguang
seal mark and period,
NY 16 Apr,
$880 (£692)

17
An agate snuff bottle,
1780/1850, the stone of
richly coloured caramel
and white, *L 2 May,*
£1,320 ($1,702)

18
An agate snuff bottle,
1800/1880, the stone
banded in white and
caramel brown, *NY 1 July,*
$660 (£507)

19
An agate snuff bottle,
1820/1880, the metallic
stone encircled by a band
of white and shades of
grey and brown,
NY 16 Apr,
$880 (£692)

20
**A Suzhou agate snuff
bottle,** 1750/1850, carved
on the front using a dark
inclusion to depict Liu
Hai mounting a rocky
promontory, *NY 2 Dec,*
$7,150 (£4,799)

1
A jade figure of a quail,
Ming dynasty, 7.5cm
(3in), *L 10 Dec,*
£1,210 ($1,694)

2
**A spinach jade triple vase
group,** Qianlong, carved
as two hawthorn trunks
and a *lingzhi*-form vase,
19cm (7½in), *NY 2 Oct,*
$1,540 (£1,100)

3
A white jade *bidong,*
Qianlong, carved with a
continuous landscape
scene, 11.5cm (4½in),
NY 17 Apr,
$4,400 (£3,437)

4
**A pair of spinach jade
vases,** Jiaqing, each carved with three phoenix
heads, 10cm (4in),
L 1 Nov,
£4,400 ($6,600)

5
**A pair of white jade
bowls,** Qianlong, the
stone of faint greenish
tint, 13.5cm (5¼in) diam,
NY 17 Apr,
$4,675 (£3,652)

6
A white jade beaker, 18th
century, 9cm (3½in) high,
NY 17 Apr,
$990 (£773)

7
**A white jade vase and
cover,** Jiaqing, with a
frieze of dragon motifs,
27.9cm (11in), *L 2 May,*
£9,020 ($11,636)

8
**A pale green jade bird
vase,** Jiaqing, the pear-
shaped vessel supported
on the back of a phoenix,
17cm (6¾in), *NY 17 Apr,*
$2,530 (£1,976)

9
A pale green jade vase,
Qianlong, decorated with
a frieze of *taotie* masks,
16.8cm (6⅝in) high,
L 2 May,
£1,078 ($1,391)

10
**A miniature white jade
Leys Jar** (zhadou), 18th
century, 7.5cm (3in),
NY 5 June,
$605 (£476)

11
**A greenish-white jade
ewer,** 18th century, of
archaistic bronze form,
the central section car-
ved with a *taotie* band,
17cm (6¾in), *HK 22 May,*
HK $19,800
(£2,050; $2,747)

12
A Moghul jade vessel,
18th century, the stone of
faint greenish tint, car-
ved in the form of a
chrysanthemum flower,
8.5cm (3¼in), *L 1 Nov,*
£440 ($660)

13
**A pale green lotus-form
coupe,** 18th century,
14.5cm (5¾in), *NY 5 June,*
$605 (£476)

14
A spinach jade buffalo,
with pale green
suffusions, 26.5cm
(10½in), *NY 5 June,*
$2,200 (£1,732)

1
A jadeite figure of a lady, a ruyi sceptre in the right hand, a fruit in the left, the stone of mottled apple-green with splashes of lavender and russet, 30.5cm (12in), *HK 22 May,*
HK $35,200
(£3,644; $4,883)

2
A jade hanging vase and cover, the body carved with descending dragons, 33.5cm (13¼in), *L 1 Nov,*
£902 ($1,353)

3
A white jade bowl and cover, the cover carved with a frieze of chrysanthemums, 11.5cm (4½in), *L 1 Nov,*
£440 ($660)

4
A carved jade peach-form coupe, the stone of celadon and brown colour, 10cm (4in) long, *NY 17 Apr,*
$1,320 (£1,031)

5
A celadon jade group, early 19th century, carved with a boy seated on an elephant, the stone softly polished with some areas of cloudy beige, 11cm (4½in), *NY 17 Apr,*
$2,310 (£1,804)

6
A pair of green jade vases and covers, each with central section carved with *taotie* masks, 18.5cm (8½in), *NY 17 Apr,*
$1,320 (£1,031)

7
A yellowish-green jadeite tripod censer and cover, the cover with three *lingzhi* handles, 18cm (7in), *NY 17 Apr,*
$2,420 (£1,890)

8
A green jade figure of a Maiden Immortal, 19th century, 30cm (11¾in), *L 1 Nov,*
£605 ($908)

9
A jadeite group, 19th century, carved as two lotus flowers and two buds with stalks tied with sprays of millet, 20.3cm (8in), *L 2 May,*
£1,870 ($2,412)

10
A pair of greyish-white jade libation cups, 12cm (4¾in) long, *NY 17 Apr,*
$467 (£364)

11
A spinach jade butterfly-handled bowl, 19th century, the sides carved with the *Bajixiang,* 28.5cm (11¼in) wide, *NY 17 Apr,*
$6,050 (£4,726)

12
A green jadeite bronze-form vessel, 19th century, of archaistic form, carved with a band of *taotie* masks, the stone of whitish tone with areas of deep green, 13.5cm (5¼in), *NY 5 June,*
$3,630 (£2,858)

1
An early Ming cinnabar lacquer box and contemporary cover, early 15th century, 21.5cm (8½in), *HK 22 May,*
HK $60,500
(£6,263; $8,392)

2
A bamboo carving of an official on horseback, late 18th century, 20.5cm (8in), *HK 24 May,*
HK $4,400 (£455; $609)

3
A cinnabar lacquer box and cover, 18th century, carved in the centre with a cluster of a peach, pomegranate and persimmon, 16.5cm (6½in), *L 2 May,*
£352 ($454)

4
A pair of cinnabar lacquer vases, 19th century, 27.5cm (11in), *L 1 Nov,*
£396 ($594)

5
A bamboo brushpot, 17th century, carved with a scholar looking up at a bat in flight, 15cm (6in), *HK 22 May,*
HK $13,200
(£1,366; $1,831)

6
A huang huali pail and cover, 18th/19th century, with *ruyi* shaped detachable handles, brass mounts, 22.5cm, (8¾in), *NY 17 Apr,*
$660 (£515)

7
A huang huali brushpot, 18th century, the wood with deep honey-coloured patina, 19.6cm (7¾in) high, *L 2 May,*
£902 ($1,164)

8
A bamboo group, 19th century, of a water-buffalo and its young, 19cm (7½in), *L 1 Nov,*
£286 ($429)

9
A rhinoceros horn libation cup, 16th/17th century, of pale honey brown colour, carved as two pine branches growing up a segment of pine trunk, 11cm (4½in) long, *NY 17 Apr,*
$3,300 (£2,578)

10
A rhinoceros horn libation cup, 17th century, carved in the form of a large lotus leaf with veined interior, 15.2cm (6in) high, *L 2 May,*
£902 ($1,164)

11
A rhinoceros horn libation cup, late 17th century, carved in relief with prunus sprays, a branch forming the handle, 13cm (5in), *L 1 Nov,*
£1,650 ($2,475)

12
A rhinoceros horn libation cup, 17th/18th century, carved in the form of an open lotus blossom, 13.5cm (5¼in) high, *L 2 May,*
£880 ($1,135)

13
A rhinoceros horn libation cup, 18th century, the base with the seal of 'Zhisheng', 13.5cm (5¼in), *NY 17 Apr,*
$3,740 (£2,921)

14
A rhinoceros horn libation cup, 18th century, carved in relief with *taotie* bands, 18.5cm (7¼in), *NY 17 Apr,*
$3,300 (£2,578)

15
A large rhinoceros horn libation cup, 19th century, carved with a long cluster of lotus blossoms, 82cm (32¼in), *NY 5 June,*
$2,530 (£1,992)

1
An ivory figure of Shoulao, Ming dynasty, following the line of the original tusk, wood stand, 27cm (10⅝in) high, *L 2 May*, £682 ($880)

2
An ivory figure of a sage, Ming dynasty, 26.7cm (10⅝in) high, *L 2 May*, £748 ($965)

3
An ivory figure of a scholar, Ming dynasty, the ivory of rich honey tone, 10cm (4¼in), *NY 17 Apr*, $4,070 (£3,179)

4
An ivory oviform jar and cover, 18th/19th century, of archaistic form and motif, 23cm (17in), *NY 16 Feb*, $935 (£806)

5
An ivory figure of an Immortal, Ming dynasty, in long scholar's robe and holding a fly whisk, the ivory of rich honey tone, 23cm (9in), *NY 5 June*, $2,090 (£1,645)

6
A pair of Chinese ivory figures of warriors, Guangxu, the details picked out in black, 31.5cm (12½in), *C 2 Oct*, £682 ($995)

7
A pair of ivory figures, Guangxu, one holding an inhaler to a nostril, the other an instrument to his ear, 23.5cm (9¾in) high, *L 2 May*, £572 ($738)

8
An ivory figure of a maiden, 18th century, holding a basket containing a fish, 26.5cm (10½in), *L 1 Nov*, £385 ($578)

9
An ivory figure of a maiden with a baby, 19th century, traces of blue pigmentation, 29cm (11½in), *L 1 Nov*, £495 ($743)

10
An ivory vase and cover, 19th century, carved with phoenix and exotic birds amid foliage, later *fu*-lion finial, 32.5cm (12¾in), *NY 5 June*, $1,540 (£1,212)

11
An ivory brushpot, 19th century, etched and stained black with two figures on a raft, 12.5cm (5in), *L 1 Nov*, £275 ($413)

12
A pierced ivory tusk vase, c.1900, 18.4cm (7in), *C 10 July*, £165 ($229)

13
A woven ivory oval casket and cover, 28.8cm (11⅜in) wide, *L 2 May*, £2,420 ($3,122)

14
An ivory carving of a deity, 46cm (18⅛in) high, *L 2 May*, £1,210 ($1,561)

15
A pair of ivory figures of celestial guardians, with inlaid wood stands, 35.5cm (14in) high, *L 2 May*, £616 ($794)

16
A pair of ivory figures of an emperor and empress, the former holding a sceptre and the latter a seal chop wrapped in cloth, 30.5cm (12in), *NY 16 Feb*, $1,760 (£1,517)

17
A pair of ivory figures of immortal maidens, one holding a flowering stem and a fan, the other holding a peacock-form headdress and rearranging her hair, 47cm (18½in), *NY 16 Feb*, $1,925 (£1,659)

1 2 3 4 5

6 7 8 9 10

11 12 13

14 15 16 17

1
A Neolithic jar, 3rd/2nd millenium BC, decorated in red and black, 38cm (15in), *L 10 Dec,* £4,950 ($6,930)

2
A green-glazed jar (hu), Han dynasty, the central double rib divided on each side by a moulded *taotie* mask, 39cm (15¼in), *HK 21 May,* HK $24,750 (£2,562; $3,433)

3
A green-glazed jar (hu), Han dynasty, 30cm (12in), *L 10 Dec,* £550 ($770)

4
A sancai glazed pottery cup, Tang dynasty, splashed in green, cream and amber glazes, 5cm (2in) high, *NY 4 June,* $1,980 (£1,559)

5
A sancai glazed pottery tazza, Tang dynasty, the cream glaze splashed with brown and green, 12.5cm (5in) wide, *NY 4 June,* $2,640 (£2,078)

6
A blue-glazed buff pottery cup, Tang dynasty, the interior with slightly degraded straw glaze, 8cm (3in) wide, *NY 4 June,* $2,750 (£2,165)

7
A sancai glazed pottery stembowl, Tang dynasty, with splashed glazes of dark green, brown and cream on pinkish buff ware, 14.5cm (15¾in), *L 18 June,* £2,200 ($2,970)

8
A sancai glazed pottery offering set, Tang dynasty, comprising tray, seven wine cups and a jar, all splashed in brown, cream and green glazes, the interior of the tray unglazed, tray 22.5cm (8¾in), *NY 4 June,* $6,875 (£5,413)

9
An amber-glazed pottery flask, Liao dynasty, 28.3cm (11in), *NY 4 Dec,* $7,975 (£5,388)

10
A Junyao bowl, Song dynasty, applied with finely speckled lavender-blue/mushroom glaze, 12cm (4¾in), *L 10 Dec,* £1,320 ($1,848)

11
A Yueyao cake mould, Song dynasty, impressed with a *shou* character, beneath a transparent pale olive-green glaze, *HK 24 May,* HK $6,050 (£626; $838)

12
A phosphatic splashed stoneware jar, Tang dynasty, of Huangdao-type, the dark brown glaze with lavender splashes, lip unglazed, 17.2cm (6¾in), *NY 4 Dec,* $5,225 (£3,530)

13
A Henan black-glazed jar, Song dynasty, 20cm (8in), *NY 4 Dec,* $3,300 (£2,229)

14
A Henan globular jar, Song dynasty, applied inside and out with black glaze, the exterior decorated with russet splashes, 11.5cm (4½in), *L 10 Dec,* £7,700 ($10,780)

1
A Jizhou bowl, Song dynasty, covered in brown glaze, covered with two long-tailed phoenix in ochre tones, 12cm (4¾in), *HK 21 May,* **HK $13,200** (£1,366; $1,831)

2
A Henan black-glazed vase, Song dynasty, of truncated *meiping*-form, the dark-brown glaze draining to white along the extremities, 21.5cm (8½in), *NY 4 June,* **$57,750** (£45,472)

3
A ribbed Henan vase, Song dynasty, applied with black glaze and lines of white slip, 15cm (6in), *L 18 June,* **£7,480** ($10,098)

4
A splashed Henan bowl, Song dynasty, applied with a dark glaze decorated with five russet splashes, 17.5cm (7in), *L 18 June,* **£2,970** ($4,010)

5
A Junyao lotus-bud waterpot and cover, Song dynasty, the interior and exterior with a faintly crackled milky lavender-blue glaze draining to mushroom at the lip, 9.5cm (3¾in), *HK 21 May,* **HK $68,750** (£7,116; $9,535)

6
A carved Cizhou pillow, Song dynasty, carved through the cream-coloured slip to the chocolate ground, 20.5cm (8½in), *L 18 June,* **£990** ($1,337)

7
A Jianyao teabowl, Song dynasty, applied with russet glaze, the base and footrim unglazed, 12.5cm (5in), *L 18 June,* **£440** ($594)

8
A soft Junyao waterpot, Yuan dynasty, with pale blue opaque glaze, 5cm (2in), *HK 21 May,* **HK $8,250** (£854; $1,144)

9
A Cizhou pillow, Jin dynasty, in the form of a recumbent tiger, 35.5cm (14in), *L 18 June,* **£2,860** ($3,861)

10
A carved Cizhou-type jar, Yuan dynasty, carved through the white slip, and applied with transparent glaze, 25.5cm (10in), *L 10 Dec,* **£902** ($1,263)

11
A painted Cizhou pillow, Jin dynasty, painted with a poem in white slip on a chocolate brown ground, beneath a clear glaze, 44cm (17¼in), *NY 4 Dec,* **$7,975** (£5,388)

12
A painted Cizhou vase, Song/Yuan dynasty, decorated in ferruginous brown on a cream slip, and with translucent milky glaze, 35cm (13¾in), *L 10 Dec,* **£462** ($647)

13
A Henan black-glazed vase, Song/Yuan dynasty, 21.5cm (8½in), *L 18 June,* **£550** ($743)

14
A Henan iron-splashed jar, Song/Yuan dynasty, the body painted in iridescent iron brown on black ground, 20cm (8in), *NY 4 June,* **$6,600** (£5,196)

15
A Jianyao bowl, Song dynasty, covered in a lustrous black glaze suffused with russet flecks, 12cm (4¾in), *HK 24 May,* **HK $2,200** (£227; $304)

16
A painted Cizhou jar, Yuan dynasty, painted with a songbird among bamboo in dark brown over the white slip beneath a finely cracked ivory glaze, 32.5cm (12¾in), *NY 4 June,* **$15,400** (£12,125)

17
A painted Cizhou bowl, Jin dynasty, painted in orange-red and green on white slip beneath a clear glaze, the foot with five spur marks, 17.5cm (7in), *NY 4 June,* **$6,600** (£5,196)

1
A glazed pottery figure, of a horse, Tang dynasty, covered in straw-coloured glaze with brown splashes, 31.5cm (12½in), *L 18 June*, £2,530 ($3,416)

2
A painted pottery figure of a prancing horse, Tang dynasty, 42.5cm (16¾in), *NY 4 Dec*, $27,500 (£18,581)

3
A painted pottery figure of an attendant, Tang dynasty, wearing an orange coat and green shoes, holding a blue vase, 27cm (10½in), *NY 4 Dec*, $11,000 (£7,432)

4
A sancai pottery figure of a lady, Tang dynasty, 25.5cm (10in), *HK 21 May*, **HK $28,600** (£2,961; $3,967)

5
A painted red pottery figure of a lady, Tang dynasty, 14cm (5½in), *NY 4 Dec*, $1,320 (£891)

6
A painted pottery figure of a guardian, Tang dynasty, the pinkish pottery with traces of red, green and black pigment, 51.5cm (23¼in), *NY 4 June*, $3,630 (£2,858)

7
A pair of straw-glazed figures of attendants, Tang dynasty, 26.5cm (10½in), *L 10 Dec*, £462 ($647)

8
A pair of straw-glazed figures of attendants, Tang dynasty, 25.5cm (10in), *L 10 Dec*, £462 ($647)

9
A glazed pottery figure of a groom, Tang dynasty, of foreign type, 43.5cm (17¼in), *L 10 Dec*, £2,970 ($4,158)

10
A sancai figure of a dignitary, Tang dynasty, glazed in chestnut and cream, 77cm (30¼in), *L 18 June*, £6,050 ($8,168)

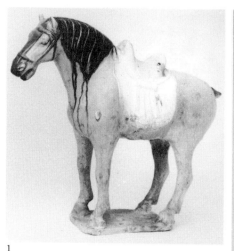

1

4

2

3

5

6

7

8

9

10

1
A painted pottery figure of a soldier, Northern Wei dynasty, 34.5cm (13½in), *NY 4 Dec,* $4,620 (£3,121)

2
A grey pottery figure of a court lady, Wei dynasty, 32cm (12½in), *L 10 Dec,* £1,100 ($1,540)

3
A grey pottery figure of a lady, Han dynasty, the robe outlined in red pigment, 32cm (12½in), *L 18 June,* £1,650 ($2,228)

4
A grey pottery horse's head, Han dynasty, with traces of red pigmentation, 14cm (5½in), *L 18 June,* £1,815 ($2,450)

5
A pottery horse's head, Han dynasty, traces of trappings in white pigment, 16cm (6¼in), *L 10 Dec,* £352 ($493)

6
A grey pottery figure of an animal, Han dynasty of rhinoceros-like appearance, unglazed with traces of red pigment, 29.5cm (11½in), *L 18 June,* £2,200 ($2,970)

7
A painted grey pottery figure of a horse, Han dynasty, traces of white pigment, 27cm (10½in), *NY 4 Dec,* $3,520 (£2,378)

8
A straw-glazed pottery figure of a camel, Sui dynasty, 36cm (14¼in), *NY 4 Dec,* $3,520 (£2,378)

9
A red pottery figure of a maiden, Sui dynasty, 27cm (10½in), *L 18 June,* £770 ($1,040)

10
A straw-glazed figure of an earth spirit, early Tang dynasty, traces of red polychrome, glaze degraded and iridescent in areas, 33.5cm (13¼in), *NY 4 Dec,* $1,540 (£1,040)

11
A glazed equestrian figure, Tang dynasty, the horse partly glazed in chestnut and the figure wearing a green robe, 42cm (16½in), *L 18 June,* £10,450 ($14,108)

12
A sancai-glazed pottery figure of an equestrienne, Tang dynasty, the lady splashed in chestnut and green, and with unglazed head, 41.5cm (16¾in), *NY 4 June,* $29,700 (£23,385)

13
A painted pottery figure of a camel, Tang dynasty, traces of red, tan and black pigment, earth encrustation, 42cm (16½in), *NY 4 June,* $3,850 (£3,031)

14
A glazed pottery figure of a Bactrian camel, Tang dynasty, splashed in chestnut and green, 41.5cm (16¼in), *L 18 June,* £8,250 ($11,138)

15
A glazed pottery figure of a Bactrian camel, Tang dynasty, of small size, 34.5cm (13½in) long, *L 10 Dec,* £1,320 ($1,848)

16
A straw-glazed figure of a braying camel, Tang dynasty, traces of red and brown details, *NY 5 June,* $15,950 (£12,559)

17
A red pottery figure of a horse, Tang dynasty, traces of pigment and burial dirt, 29.5cm (11½in), *NY 4 Dec,* $3,190 (£2,155)

1 2 3 4

5 6 7

8 9 10 11

12 13 14

15 16 17

Ming Blue and White Porcelain

When the 14th century potters, under the Yuan dynasty of the Mongols, developed the technique of painting in cobalt blue under the glaze of high-fired white wares, they struck an artistic vein of surpassing richness. Six centuries later we are still mining it, though it is all but exhausted; but the first and greatest beneficiaries were the Ming potters in Jingdezhen. From the end of the 14th century to the middle of the 17th century, through the vagaries of Imperial taste and patronage and the uncertainty over supply of raw materials from abroad, they continued the development of this new ware. Though their names are for the most part lost, the potters of the Ming have left us a tremendous legacy of confident forms and bold decorative designs which have not been equalled since.

Naturally enough it is the classic wares produced during the reign of the early Ming emperors Yongle (1403-24) and Xuande (1426-35) which generally command the highest prices today.

Though the shapes employed were often derived from Near Eastern models—as, for instance, the Yongle ewer (fig.1) and the Xuande tankard (fig.2)—the vigour and control of the painting and the intelligent and characteristically Chinese use of the white areas to set off the whole, eloquently express the new-found cultural strength of the Chinese after their defeat of the Mongols. The market for such pieces goes from strength to strength and is dominated by powerful buyers from Japan and the Far East, who place a large premium on condition. Generally speaking, a hair crack may reduce the value of a fine Imperial piece by as much as two-thirds and more serious damage may remove nine-tenths or more. This seems severe, but in the eyes of many collectors, and especially Far Eastern ones, a significant part of the aesthetic appeal of fine ceramics lies in a sense of permanence and integrity.

The last classical reign of the 15th century was that of the

—1—
An early Ming blue and white ewer, Yongle, 30cm (12in), L 18 June, £68,200 ($92,070)

—2—
An early Ming blue and white tankard, Xuande mark and period, after a Near Eastern shape, 13cm (5in), NY 4 June, $66,000 (£51,969)

—3—
A Ming blue and white fruit bowl, Xuande mark and period, 29cm (11½in), HK 21 May, HK$726,000 (£75,155; $100,708)

—4—
A pair of blue and white bowls, 16th century, six character marks of Xuande on the base, 12cm (4¾in), HK 21 May, HK $16,500 £1,708; ($2,289)

—5—
A blue and white bowl, second half of the 16th century, painted with a roundel enclosing a flying crane, four character mark fu gui jia qi meaning 'a rich, noble and beautiful piece', 29.5cm (11½in), L 18 June, £418 ($564)

—1—

—2—

—3—

—4—

—5—

Chenghua emperor (1465-87). Porcelain of this period is extemely rare and has an entirely different character from that of earlier reigns. Pieces tend to be smaller and more delicately potted; the painting is executed in a softer, purer cobalt blue and the whole is applied with a smoother, thinner glaze, the better to bring out the decoration. The overall effect is of warmth and cultural refinement. These wares are deeply admired by collectors, who are prepared to pay prices comparable to those for the earlier wares.

The move towards more delicate construction, greater use of white areas and less reliance on strongly defined borders of petal panels, keyfret bands and stiff leaves, is continued through the reigns of Hongzhi (1488-1505) and Zhengde (1506-21) into the sixteenth century. Though pieces from these periods are less sought after than those from the Chenghua era, they can still command high prices—as for instance the very fine saucer dish painted with clouds and dragons from the Zhengde period

(fig.7). There is a very marked stylistic shift between the blue and white wares discussed above and those of the next three reign periods: Jiajing (1522-66), Longqing (1567-72) and Wanli (1573-1619). A new kind of cobalt blue, the famous 'Mohammedan blue', was imported during the Jiajing reign; it is unmistakable and at best produces a rich purplish colour of remarkable vibrancy. Equally important was the reorganization of the official kilns in 1530 to streamline and increase production. The subsequent ease of manufacture led not only to a huge increase in the number of wares, but also made possible larger and more complex shapes, like the octagonal facetted bowl and cover, painted with phoenix and cranes (fig.10), the massive jar painted with Shou Lao and acolytes (fig.6), and the imposing jar and cover painted with numerous boys at work and play (fig.9).

The situation remained more or less unchanged through the Longqing reign and the first half of the Wanli reign, as shown by

—6—
A blue and white jar, mark and period of Jiajing, showing the God of Longevity and various figures including the Eight Immortals with their attributes, 50cm (19¾in), *L 18 June,* **£9,350 ($12,623)**

—7—
A Ming blue and white saucer dish, Zhengde mark and period, 22.5cm (8¾in), *NY 4 June,* **$49,500 (£38,976)**

—8—
A blue and white box cover, mark and period of Jiajing, 19.5cm (7¾in), *L 18 June,* **£1,045 ($1,411)**

—9—
A Ming blue and white wine jar and cover, Jiajing mark and period, 45.5cm (18in), *NY 4 June,* **$170,500 (£134,252)**

—10—
A blue and white covered bowl, Jiajing, 14.5cm (5¾in), *L 18 June,* **£748 ($1,010)**

—11—
A pair of blue and white dishes, Jiajing marks and period, 11.5cm (4½in), *HK 24 May,* **HK$3,740 (£387; $518)**

—6—

—7—

—9—

—8—

—10—

—11—

the charming eight-lobed jar painted with tree shrews amid scrolling fruiting melons (fig.13) and the large *meiping* painted with dragons and lotus (fig.12), though there is a tendency toward a greater density of decoration, well illustrated by the massive dragon and phoenix vase (fig.18). For all their grandeur and imaginative construction, the wares discussed above have an undeniable roughness, best seen in the unfinished footrims and the quick angularity of some of the

painting, which does not compare with the supple and painstaking craftsmanship of the fifteenth century wares. In recognition of this, prices for pieces of comparable size are considerably lower, sometimes by as much as a factor of ten, which brings many well within reach of less ambitious collectors.

During the first half of the 17th century the official kilns, increasingly beleaguered by lack of court funding, went into a steep decline, culminating in their virtual closure on the

—12—
A late Ming blue and white Meiping, mark and period of Wanli, 52cm (20½in), *L 10 Dec*, £4,950 ($6,930)

—13—
A blue and white jar, Wanli, of eight-lobed form, 18cm (7in), *L 18 June*, £1,540 ($2,079)

—14—
A blue and white double-duck waterdropper and cover, *c.*1500, modelled as a pair of conjoined mandarin ducks, 12.5cm (5in), *NY 4 June*, $1,980 (£1,559)

—15—
A blue and white dish, mark and period of Jia-jing, 31cm (12¼in), *L 10 Dec*, £715 ($1,001)

—16—
A pair of blue and white jars, 16th century, 11.5cm (4½in), *L 10 Dec*, £495 ($693)

—17—
A blue and white jar, *c.*1600, 19.5cm (7¾in), *S 14 Nov*, £308 ($431)

—18—
A blue and white dragon and phoenix vase, Wanli mark and period, 57cm (22½in), *NY 4 June*, $42,900 (£33,779)

—19—
A blue and white jar, 16th century, 17.5cm (6¾in), *L 18 June*, £495 ($668)

—20—
A blue and white bottle, 17th century, 26.5cm (10½in), *C 2 Oct*, £385 ($562)

—12—

—13—

—14—

—15—

—16—

—17—

—18—

—19—

—20—

death of the Wanli emperor. Having perhaps forseen this earlier in the century, many of the Jingdezhen potters now turned their attention to the newly developing export markets, in Holland and Japan especially. Pieces for the insatiable Dutch market, generally called Kraak ware, were exported in their millions during this period, stacked on board the East Indiamen of the Dutch East India Company (VOC). Characteristically thin-walled and painted with flower-like designs of radiating panels, they have, at best, a crispness to the touch and a pleasing clarity in their silver-blue, freely painted motifs. The large dish (fig.21) unusually painted with a central writhing dragon, is in the upper price range for a Kraak piece, from which it can be judged that smaller items may be

purchased for very reasonable sums.

Wares made for the Japanese market—variously called Tenkei blue and white, after the Japanese rendition of Tianqi (1621-7), during whose reign they were first produed, or *ko sumetsuke* ('old blue and white)—are generally of small size and have coarse, thick-walled bodies, typically painted with simple, sketchy landscapes and diminutive human figures. They are much appreciated in Japan for their evident lack of affectation and for the untrammelled painterliness of their decoration, but are unfortunately rather rare in the West.

Both Kraak wares and Tenkei blue and white wares may be classified among Transitional wares (that is, wares which are transitional in style between the Ming and Qing dynasties), but

—21—
A Ming blue and white dish, Wanli period, 50cm (19¾in) diam, *NY 17 Apr,* $1,265 (£988)

—22—
A 'Kraak' vase, Wanli, painted in underglaze blue, 31.5cm (12½in), *C 2 Oct,* £1,650 ($2,409)

—23—
A blue and white Kendi, Wanli, 17cm (6¾in), *L 18 June,* £385 ($520)

—24—
A jar, Wanli, 12cm (4¾in), *A 26 June,* **Dfl 6,612** (£1,466; $1,979)

—25—
An inscribed polychrome Swatow dish, 17th century, decorated in turquoise, green and iron-red, *HK 21 May,* **HK$39,600** (£4,099; $5,493)

—26—
A late Ming blue and white censer, Wanli, 33cm (13in) diam, *NY 17 Apr,* $1,320 (£1,031)

—27—
A good Kraak dish, Wanli, painted in blue, 49cm (19¼in), *C 10 July,* £1,265 ($1,758)

—28—
A pair of dishes, Wanli, each painted in underglaze blue with a frog, 14.5cm (5¾in), *L 10 Dec,* £462 ($647)

—21—

—25—

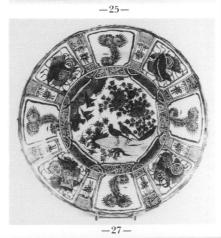

—27—

—23—

—22—　　—24—

—26—

—28—

those which spring most readily to mind in this context are the domestic wares of the last Ming reign: that of Chongzhen (1628-43). Characteristically they have clean, simplified shapes, like the sleeve vase (fig.29) and the cylindrical brushpot (fig. 30), and are painted in a pure tone of underglaze blue which has aptly been described as 'violets in milk', beneath a softening, bubbled glaze. The execution of the painting is vigorous and very expressive of movement, as can be well seen in the jardinière painted with flowers and birds in flight (fig.31). In spirit this group suggests a return to the earlier Ming preference for simple, strong potting and bold, uncluttered decoration. It is interesting to speculate about what course Chinese ceramics would have taken if the Ming had succeeded in beating off the Manchu invaders; but it was not to be, and the Transitional style was destined instead to act as one of the inspirations for the sophisticated and technically refined wares of the Kangxi reign, the first great artistic period of the Qing dynasty.

● DAVID PRIESTLEY ●

Further reading

Sir Harry Garner, *Oriental Blue and White*, 1954

S.T. Yeo & J. Martin, *Chinese Blue and White Ceramics*, 1978

D. Lion-Goldschmidt, *Ming Porcelain*, 1978

R.S. Kilburn (The Oriental Ceramic Society of Hong Kong), *Transitional Wares and their Forerunners*, 1981

—29—
A blue and white sleeve vase, Transitional, painted with the legend of the scholar borne on clouds before a vision of the Lady of the Moon, 47.5cm (18¾in), *NY 17 Apr,* $3,300 (£2,578)

—30—
A Chinese blue and white brushpot, Transitional, 18.5cm (7¼in), *C 17 April,* £1,760 ($2,288)

—31—
A blue and white jardinière, Transitional, painted with a pair of birds flitting among peonies, prunus and bamboo, 21.4cm (8⅜in) high, *L 16 July,* £682 ($989)

—32—
A pair of late Ming bottles, Wanli, 27.5cm (10¾in), *L 18 June,* £1,320 ($1,782)

—33—
A Ming blue and white dish, mark and period of Wanli, 16cm (6¼in), *L 10 Dec,* £660 ($924)

—34—
A Ming blue and white bowl, Wanli mark and period, decorated with Sanscrit characters, 18.5cm (7¼in), *NY 4 June,* $1,870 (£1,472)

—29—

—30—

—31—

—32—

—33—

—34—

Ming Dynasty

Hongwu 1368-98

Jianwen 1399-1402

Yongle 1403-24

Hongxi 1425

Xuande 1426-35

Zhengtong 1436-49

Jingtai 1450-56

Tianshun 1457-64

Chenghua 1465-87

Hongzhi 1488-1505

Zhengde 1506-21

Jiajing 1522-66

Longqing 1567-72

Wanli 1573-1619

Taichang 1620

Tianqi 1621-27

Chongzhen 1628-43

1
A tileworks figure, Ming dynasty, of a Demon lunging to one side, glazed in green with details in ochre and brown, 34cm (13½in), *L 1 Nov,* **£1,320 ($1,980)**

2
A glazed pottery equestrian figure, Ming dynasty, the rider wearing a green-glazed tunic, and red-painted hat, left hand and head detachable, 54.5cm (21½in), *L 18 June,* **£1,980 ($2,673)**

3
A ridgetile figure of a deity, Ming dynasty, glazed in turquoise and yellow, 42cm (16½in), *L 18 June,* **£1,650 ($2,228)**

4
A tileworks figure, Ming dynasty, of a dignitary on horseback, decorated in cream, green and brown enamels, 43cm (17in) high, *M 24 June,* **FF 31,080 (£2,590; $3,497)**

5
A lead glazed pottery figural rooftile, Ming dynasty, with a demon riding a *fu*-lion, with green glaze and details picked out in yellow and cream, 56.5cm (22¼in) high, *NY 17 Apr,* **$2,750 (£2,148)**

6
A pair of glazed pottery figures of male and female attendants, Ming dynasty, in green-glazed outer robes over ochre inner robes, 38 and 33cm (15 and 13in), *NY 5 June,* **$1,650 (£1,299)**

7
A pair of polychrome dishes, Ming dynasty, each decorated with lotus picked out in green, yellow and turquoise enamels on a *rouge-de-fer* ground, 17cm (6¾in), *L 18 June,* **£528 ($713)**

8
A blue and white dish, Transitional, decorated with a snarling kylin, 35.5cm (14in), *HK 24 May,* **HK $8,250 (£854; $1,144)**

9
A blue and white double-gourd vase, Transitional, 33cm (13in), *L 19 Nov,* **£968 ($1,375)**

10
A blue and white ewer, Transitional, 37.5cm (14¾in), *L 19 Nov,* **£1,760 ($2,499)**

11
A polychrome jar and cover, Transitional, painted in underglaze blue, iron-red, green and yellow, 41cm (16⅛in), *L 16 July,* **£770 ($1,117)**

12
A polychrome jar, Transitional, painted in green, yellow, iron-red and aubergine enamels, 20.5cm (8in), *L 10 Dec,* **£1,320 ($1,848)**

13
A blue and white jar, Transitional, 16cm (6¼in), *NY 17 Apr,* **$1,210 (£945)**

14
A polychrome ovoid jar, Transitional, decorated in iron-red, green and yellow, 18.5cm (7¼in), *L 10 Dec,* **£715 ($1,001)**

15
A blue and white sleeve vase, Transitional, 44.4cm (17½in) high, *L 16 July,* **£3,300 ($4,785)**

16
A blue and white jardinière, Transitional, painted with the five symbolic animals, the dragon, the phoenix, the kylin, the tiger and the tortoise, 43cm (17in) high, *L 16 July,* **£1,430 ($2,074)**

1
A blue and white jar, Transitional, 24cm (9½in), *S 10 July*, £385 ($516)

2
A pair of blue and white shallow bowls, 17th century, six character marks of Jiajing, 12cm (4¾in), *L 18 June*, £1,320 ($1,782)

3
A Ming style blue and white stemcup, seal mark and period of Qianlong, painted with a frieze of *lança* characters, 14.5cm (5¾in), *L 10 Dec*, £1,045 ($1,463)

4
A blue and white Zhadou, seal mark and period of Daoguang, painted in 15th century style, 8.5cm (3¼in), *L 10 Dec*, £1,430 ($2,002)

5
A Ming style blue and white meiping, 18th century, 17.5cm (7in), *L 10 Dec*, £792 ($1,109)

6
A Ming style blue and white flask, Qianlong seal mark and period, 46cm (18in), *HK 24 May*, HK $23,100 (£2,391; $3,204)

7
A Ming style blue and white meiping, Yongzheng, 33.5cm (13¼in), *HK 21 May*, HK $44,000 (£4,555; $6,104)

8
A blue and white basin, Yongzheng, the interior decorated in Ming style with a frieze of Buddhist emblems, 26.5cm (10½in), *L 10 Dec*, £990 ($1,386)

9
A Ming style moon flask, Qianlong, of characteristic form, painted in 15th century style, 29cm (11½in), *L 10 Dec*, £1,045 ($1,463)

10
A blue and white bottle vase, Qianlong seal mark and period, 36cm (14in), *HK 21 May*, HK $30,800 (£3,188; $4,272)

11
A blue and white dragon vase, Kangxi mark and period, 24.5cm (9¾in), *NY 4 June*, $22,000 (£17,323)

12
A blue and white ovoid jar, Yongzheng mark and period, painted with two archaistic dragons, 14cm (5½in), *NY 4 June*, $11,550 (£9,094)

13
A pair of blue and white bowls, Daoguang seal marks and period, each with exterior painted with the Eight Immortals, 15cm (5in), *HK 21 May*, HK $16,500 (£1,708; $2,289)

14
A blue and white 'palace' bowl, mark and period of Kangxi, 16cm (6¼in), *L 18 June*, £1,100 ($1,485)

15
A blue and white double-ogee bowl, Qianlong seal mark and period, painted in Ming style, 17cm (6¾in), *HK 21 May*, HK $26,400 (£2,733; $3,662)

1
A pair of blue and white
jars, Kangxi, each pain-
ted with three Buddhist
lions, 33.5cm (13in),
L 19 Nov,
£638 ($906)

2
A pair of candlesticks,
Qianlong, 19cm (7½in),
A 4 June,
Dfl 4,408 (£997; $1,346)

3
A blue and white Ming
style jardinière, 18th century, 37cm (14½in),
L 18 June,
£1,430 ($1,931)

4
A blue and white ginger
jar, Kangxi, 21.5cm
(8½in), *L 16 July,*
£330 ($479)

5
A blue and white garni-
ture, Kangxi, aiye marks,
22.5cm (8¾in) and 23cm
(9in), *M 23 June,*
FF 24,420
(£1,968; $2,637)

6
A blue and white vase,
Kangxi, painted with a
continuous scene of
mounted warriors, 18.5cm
(7¼in), *HK 21 May,*
HK $15,400
(£1,594; $2,136)

7
A blue and white
jardinière, *c.*1800, 15cm
(6in), *C 17 Sept,*
£209 ($293)

8
A set of four large dishes,
Kangxi, painted in
underglaze blue, aiye
marks, 37.6cm (14⅞in)
diam, *L 16 July,*
£1,265 ($1,834)

9
A pair of dishes, Kangxi,
31.5cm (12½in), *A 4 June,*
Dfl 4,756 (£1,076; $1,453)

10
A blue and white dish,
Qianlong, 43.5cm
(17¼in), *C 16 Jan,*
£286 ($343)

11
A blue and white dish,
Qianlong, 38cm (15in),
S 10 July,
£242 ($324)

12
A set of three blue and
white dishes, Qianlong,
55.2cm (21¾in) diam,
L 16 July,
£2,200 ($3,190)

13
A blue and white meat
plate, Qianlong, 33cm
(13in), *C 17 Sept,*
£121 ($169)

14
A blue and white covered
vase, 19th century, 64cm
(25¼in), *M 24 June,*
FF 22,200
(£1,850; $2,498)

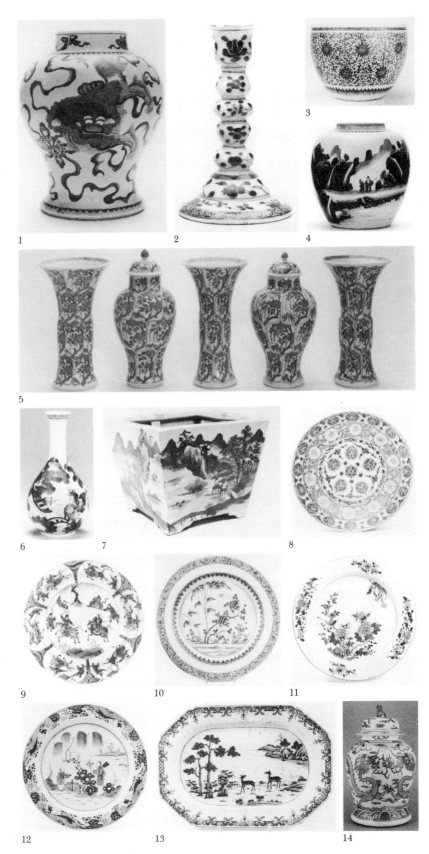

1
A blue and white rouleau
vase, Kangxi, painted
with two figures on a
mountainous landscape,
22.5cm (8¾in),
HK 24 May,
HK $3,520 (£364; $488)

2
A blue and white rouleau
vase, Kangxi, 46.5cm
(18¼in), *HK 21 May,*
HK $31,900
(£3,302; $4,425)

3
A blue and white vase,
Kangxi, of *rouleau* form,
44.5cm (17½in), *L 16 July,*
£1,870 ($2,712)

4
A blue and white jar and
cover, 17th century, 47cm
(18½in), *L 16 July,*
£1,265 ($1,834)

5
A blue and white covered
jar, Kangxi, painted with
Precious Objects, 23cm
(9in), *L 19 Nov,*
£682 ($968)

6
A blue and white censer,
Kangxi, painted with a
continuous scene of a
sage in a landscape,
22.5cm (8¾in) wide,
HK 24 May,
HK $5,280 (£547; $733)

7
A blue and white brush-
pot, Kangxi, decorated
with a group of digni-
taries in front of an altar,
15cm (6in), *HK 21 May,*
HK $9,350
(£968; $1,297)

8
A blue and white brush-
pot (*bidong*), Kangxi,
painted with a con-
tinuous mountainous
landscape, 15cm (6in),
NY 4 June,
$2,640 (£2,079)

9
A blue and white jar-
diniere, Kangxi, painted
with four different fish
amongst aquatic weeds,
four character mark of
Chenghua, 21.5cm
(8¾in), *L 19 Nov,*
£968 ($1,375)

10
A pair of blue and white
covered pots, Kangxi,
painted with a scene of
three horsemen against a
landscape of willows and
rocks, *yu* mark, 14.6cm
(5¾in) high, *L 16 July,*
£528 ($766)

11
A blue and white
hexagonal spittoon,
Kangxi, 15cm (6in) diam,
C 26 Nov,
£220 ($319)

12
A blue and white box and
cover, Kangxi, painted
with a lotus meander,
four character mark of
Chenghua, 10.5cm (4¼in)
wide, *HK 24 May,*
HK $6,600 (£683; $915)

13
A blue and white bowl,
Kangxi, painted with a
frieze of foliate-tailed
dragons above a band of
ruyi heads, six character
mark of Chenghua,
20.4cm (8in), *L 16 July,*
£528 ($766)

14
A blue and white beaker
vase, Kangxi, painted
with figures on a terrace,
27.5cm (10¾in),
HK 24 May,
HK $5,500 (£569; $762)

15
A blue and white yen-yen
vase, Kangxi, painted
with deer in a river
landscape, 47cm (18½in),
HK 21 May,
HK $20,900
(£2,164; $2,899)

16
A blue and white yen-yen
vase, Kangxi, 44.5cm
(17½in), *S 25 Mar,*
£605 ($768)

1
A biscuit figure of the
Hare in the Moon, 18th
century, applied with a
crackled turquoise glaze,
27.5cm (10¾in),
M 23 June,
FF 44,400
(£3,578; $4,794)

2
A turquoise-glazed vase,
Kangxi, 15cm (6in),
M 23 June,
FF 6,105 (£492; $659)

3
A turquoise-glazed
jardiniere, 18th century,
18cm (7in), *M 23 June,*
FF 17,760
(£1,431; $1,918)

4
A turquoise-glazed vase,
Kangxi, 16.5cm (6½in),
M 23 June,
FF 7,770 (£626; $839)

5
A turquoise-glazed moon
flask, Kangxi, 24.5cm
(9½in), *M 23 June,*
FF 57,720
(£4,651; $6,232)

6
A turquoise-glazed
brushrest, Kangxi,
modelled in the form of
the Five Sacred Moun-
tains, 14cm (5½in),
M 23 June,
FF 10,545 (£850; $1,139)

7
A pair of turquoise-
glazed waterdroppers,
Kangxi, in the form of a
monkey with a double-
gourd clasped between
his knees, 8.5cm (3¼in),
M 23 June,
FF 19,980
(£1,610; $2,157)

8
A Longquan celadon
yen-yen vase, Yuan
dynasty, 68.5cm (27in),
L 18 June,
£27,500 ($37,125)

9
A celadon bowl, Ming,
interior and exterior with
a band of lotus meander,
olive-green glaze, 37.5cm
(14¾in), *NY 5 June,*
$3,300 (£2,598)

10
A Longquan celadon
censer, Song dynasty,
with pale green glaze,
14.5cm (5¾in),
HK 21 May,
HK $55,000
(£5,694; $7,629)

11
A celadon barrel-form
garden seat, Ming
dynasty, the top carved
with floral motifs, 43cm
(17in), *NY 2 Oct,*
$2,090 (£1,493)

12
A celadon jardiniere with
gilt lacquer stand, Ming
dynasty, sea-green glaze,
the stand gilt painted
with bats amidst clouds,
height overall 66.5cm
(26¼in), *NY 2 Oct,*
$6,600 (£4,714)

13
A Longquan celadon
figure of Budai, Ming
dynasty, transparent sea-
green glaze, 27.5cm
(10¾in), *HK 21 May,*
HK $26,400
(£2,733; $3,662)

14
A celadon dish, Ming
dynasty, 24cm (9½in),
C 17 Apr,
£297 ($386)

15
A Longquan celadon
ewer, late 14th century,
incised with floral scroll
between lotus petals, sea-
green glaze, 12cm (4¾in),
HK 21 May,
HK $18,700
(£1,936; $2,594)

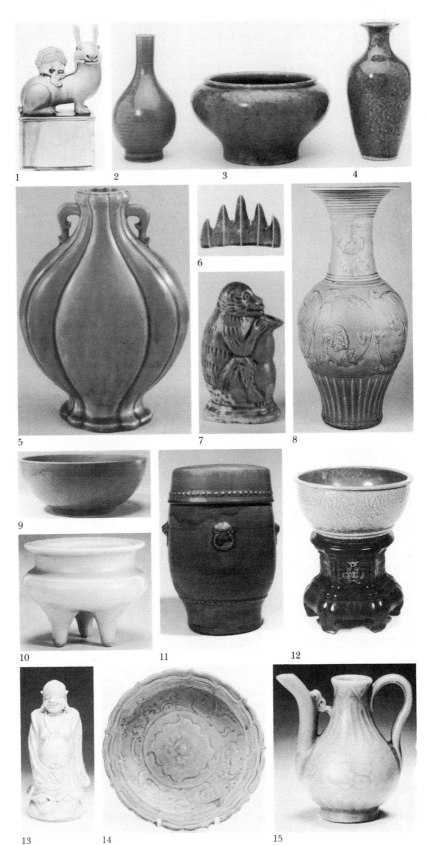

1
A **waterdropper** in the form of a Buddhist lion, Kangxi, glazed in green, 8.5cm (3¼in), *M 23 June*, **FF 6,660 (£537; $719)**

2
A **figure of a Fabulous Animal**, Kangxi, glazed in green, 11.5cm (4½in), *M 23 June*, **FF 13,320 (£1,073; $1,438)**

3
A **waterdropper** in the form of a parrot, Kangxi, with overall green glaze, 11.5cm (4½in), *M 23 June*, **FF 11,100 (£894; $1,199)**

4
A **pair of 'tea-dust' stembowls**, first half 19th century, with minutely speckled dark yellowish green glaze, three character marks, *Zhiben Tang*, 17.5cm (7in), *L 10 Dec*, **£1,155 ($1,617)**

5
A **teadust vase**, Qianlong mark and period, with fine yellowish-green glaze with traces of gold flecks, incised seal mark in gilt, *HK 22 May*, **HK $37,400 (£3,872; $5,188)**

6
A **vase**, 18th century, with thick brown glaze freely dusted with greenish gold, possibly in imitation of an 'oil spot' glaze, 23cm (9in), *L 10 Dec*, **£572 ($800)**

7
A **'robin's egg' glazed Yixing teapot and cover**, 18th century, with feathered lavender-blue and turquoise glaze on the purplish-brown ware, partly legible seal mark, reading *??Jin Zhi*, 19cm (7½in), *L 10 Dec*, **£1,760 ($2,464)**

8
A **'robin's egg' vase**, 18th century, with characteristic glaze of turquoise streaked in blue, 18cm (7in), *L 10 Dec*, **£528 ($739)**

9
A **copper-red waterpot**, Qianlong seal mark and period, the exterior with raspberry-coloured glaze, 5.5cm (2¼in), *HK 24 May*, **HK $6,050 (£626; $839)**

10
A **mazarin blue vase**, seal mark and period of Qianlong, the interior white, 40cm (15¾in), *L 18 June*, **£770 ($1,040)**

11
A **sang-de-boeuf vase**, seal mark and period of Qianlong, of *meiping* form, 28cm (11in), *M 23 June*, **FF 23,310 (£1,878; $2,517)**

12
A **sang-de-boeuf vase**, 18th/19th century, 42cm (18½in), *S 3 Apr*, **£462 ($596)**

13
A **copper-red vase**, Qianlong seal mark and period, with raspberry-coloured glaze, 28cm (11in), *HK 22 May*, **HK $13,200 (£1,366; $1,831)**

14
A **Guan-type vase**, Qianlong seal mark and period, of faceted *hu*-form, with crackled glaze of pale ash tone in imitation of Song guanyao, 24cm (9½in), *NY 4 Dec*, **$7,700 (£5,202)**

15
A **pair of blue-glazed bowls**, Qianlong seal marks and period, covered in deep blue glaze thinning to white on the rim, 18cm (7in), *HK 22 May*, **HK $15,400 (£1,594; $2,136)**

16
A **liver-red bowl**, seal mark and period of Qianlong, the interior plain white, 15cm (6in), *L 10 Dec*, **£495 ($693)**

17
A **yellow-glazed saucer dish**, Yongzheng mark and period, 14cm (5½in), *HK 22 May*, **HK $37,400 (£3,872; $5,188)**

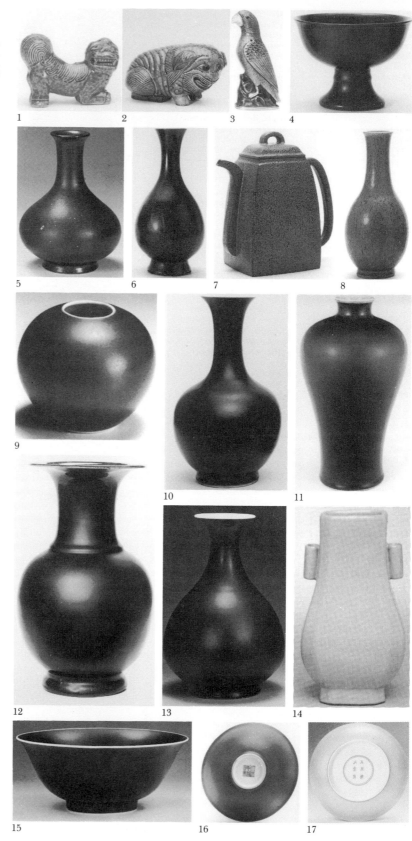

1

A flambé meiping, Qianlong, with purple glaze suffused with cascades of lavender, 20.5cm (8in), *HK 22 May,* **HK $15,400** (£1,594; $2,136)

2

A white-glazed beehive waterpot, mark and period of Kangxi, the sides carved in relief with cloud scrolls, 7.5cm (3in), *L 10 Dec,* £1,485 ($2,079)

3

A 'clair-de-lune' stem-bowl, seal and period of Yongzheng, 22cm (8¾in), *L 18 June,* £2,750 ($3,713)

4

A Guan-type quadruple vase, Yongzheng mark and period, with faintly crackled ash-grey glaze, 10cm (4in), *HK 24 May,* **HK $7,480** (£744; $997)

5

A carved celadon bottle vase, 19th century, 54cm (21¼in), *S 3 May,* £935 ($1,197)

6

A Longquan celadon vase, early Ming dynasty, of archaic *gu* form, with bubble-suffused sea-green glaze, 23.5cm (9¼in), *HK 21 May,* **HK $29,700** (£3,075; $4,120)

7

A celadon-glazed meiping, 18th century, 43cm (17in), *HK 24 May,* **HK $10,450** (£7,799; $10,451)

8

A carved celadon vase, seal mark and period of Qianlong, carved with a design of tiered petals, 33cm (13in), *L 10 Dec,* £990 ($1,386)

9

A 'blanc-de-chine' figure of Guanyin, Kangxi, 13.5cm (5¼in), *M 23 June,* **FF 3,330** (£268; $360)

10

A 'blanc-de-chine' figure of Guanyin, Jiaqing, impressed double-gourd mark, 35cm (13¾in), *M 23 June,* **FF 4,440** (£358; $479)

11

A 'blanc-de-chine' figure of Guanyin enthroned, late 17th/early 18th century, 38cm (15in), *NY 30 Jan,* $2,640 (£2,336)

12

A 'blanc-de-chine' vase, 18th century, of archaic beaker form following a bronze original, *M 23 June,* **FF 4,662** (£376; $503)

13

A 'blanc-de-chine' group of three Europeans, late 17th/early 18th century, 14cm (5½in), *NY 30 Jan,* $1,870 (£1,655)

14

A 'blanc-de-chine' figure of a hound, 18th century, for use as a taper holder, 24cm (9⅜in), *L 16 July,* £352 ($510)

15

A 'blanc-de-chine' libation cup, 18th century, of rhinoceros horn form, 14cm (5½in), *L 16 July,* £308 ($447)

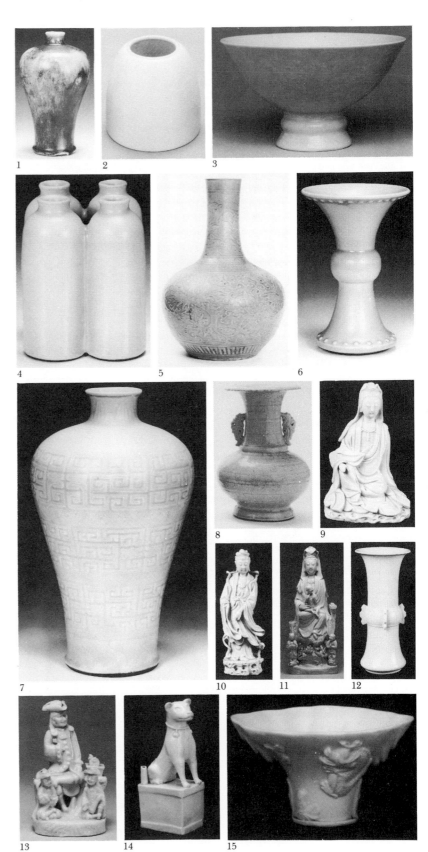

1
A pair of ruby-ground 'famille-rose' vases, Qianlong seal marks and period, each of square section and archaic *hu* form, 18.5cm (7¼in),
HK 22 May,
HK $39,600
(£4,037; $5,410)

2
A pair of pink-ground 'famille-rose' jars and covers, Qianlong seal mark and period, the shoulders moulded with a beribboned lime-green sash, 23.5cm (9¼in),
NY 4 June,
$57,200 (£45,039)

3
A wucai dragon and phoenix bowl, seal mark and period of Daoguang, painted with green and red dragons between two descending phoenix, 16cm (6½in), *L 18 June,*
£880 ($1,188)

4
A pair of yellow-ground bowls, seal marks and periods of Daoguang, each with four landscape medallions, 15cm (6in),
L 10 Dec,
£2,420 ($3,388)

5
A pair of 'famille-rose' dishes, Jiaqing seal marks and period, each on four short feet, 15cm (6in),
HK 24 May,
HK $27,500
(£2,846; $3,813)

6
A grisaille-decorated brushpot, Jiaqing, the exterior painted in Chinese taste, with a landscape, 14cm (5½in),
L 10 Dec,
£880 ($1,232)

7
A 'famille-rose' vase, Daoguang seal mark and period, decorated overall with flowering lotus scrolls, 17.5cm (7in),
HK 24 May,
HK $11,550
(£1,196; $1,603)

8
A pair of green dragon dishes, Daoguang seal marks and period, 17.5cm (7in), *HK 22 May,*
HK $28,600
(£2,961; $3,967)

9
A pair of famille-rose dishes, seal marks and period of Daoguang, painted with scenes after Jiao Bingzhen's 1696 edition of Geng Zhi Tu Shu (Book of Ploughing and Weaving), 14cm (5½in), *L 18 June,*
£660 ($891)

10
A pair of enamelled jars and covers, Daoguang seal marks and period, 15.5cm (6in), *HK 24 May,*
HK $9,350
(£968; $1,297)

11
A pair of iron-red decorated wine cups, Tongzhi marks and period, 6cm (2½in) diam, *HK 24 May,*
HK $11,000
(£1,139; $1,526)

12
A 'famille-rose' winecup, four character mark and period of Hongxian, painted with two pomegranates in red and yellow, 7.5cm (3in),
L 18 June,
£935 ($1,262)

13
A 'famille-rose' bowl, mark and period of Guangxu, decorated with four stylised phoenix, gilded borders, 30cm (8¼in), *L 18 June,*
£440 ($594)

14
A 'famille-rose' butterfly vase, Guangxu seal mark and period, 40cm (15¾in), *NY 2 Oct,*
$1,430 (£1,021)

1   2   3   4   5   6   7   8   9   10   11   12   13   14

1
A doucai ovoid vase,
Kangxi, six character
mark of Chenghua, 19cm
(7½in), *L 18 June,*
£1,100 ($1,485)

2
**A copper-red decorated
bottle,** Kangxi, the sides
painted with three
bushy-tailed fabulous
animals, 17.5cm (7in),
L 10 Dec,
£935 ($1,309)

3
**A 'famille-verte'
moulded meiping,**
Kangxi, decorated with a
dragon in pursuit of a
'flaming pearl', 38.5cm
(15¼in), *NY 4 Dec,*
$23,100 (£15,608)

4
A 'famille-rose' vase,
Yongzheng, painted with
a group of three ladies
carrying baskets of
flowers, 23cm (9in),
HK 24 May,
HK $3,080 (£318; $426)

5
**A 'famille-verte' month
cup,** Kangxi mark and
period, painted with a
narcissus emblematic of
the twelfth month, 5cm
(2in) high, *HK 22 May,*
HK $16,500
(£1,708; $2,289)

6
**A pair of 'famille-rose'
saucer dishes,** marks and
period of Yongzheng,
11cm (4in), *L 18 June,*
£572 ($772)

7
**A pair of doucai saucer
dishes,** marks and period
of Yongzheng, each
decorated with a central
pomegranate spray,
19.5cm (7¾in), *L 10 Dec,*
£2,200 ($3,080)

8
A 'rose-verte' vase, Yong-
zheng, 37cm (14½in),
M 23 June,
FF 42,180
(£3,399; $4,554)

9
A plate, Yongzheng,
20.5cm (8in), *A 4 Sept,*
Dfl 488 (£112; $165)

10
A Chinese taste dish,
Yongzheng, enamelled
in 'famille-rose' palette,
20cm (8in), *L 16 July,*
£308 ($447)

11
A doucai jar and cover,
seal mark and period of
Qianlong, 12cm (4¾in),
L 18 June,
£2,200 ($2,970)

12
A yellow-ground vase,
seal mark and period of
Qianlong, of *meiping*
form, decorated in
underglaze blue in 15th
century style, 21.5cm
(8½in), *L 10 Dec,*
£3,520 ($4,928)

13
**A green dragon jar and
cover,** Qianlong seal
mark and period, 21.5cm
(8½in), *NY 4 Dec,*
$12,100 (£8,175)

14
**A pair of 'famille-rose'
chicken dishes,** Qianlong
seal marks and period,
each decorated with a
chicken boy dancing in
front of two chickens,
19.5cm (7¾in),
HK 24 May,
HK $14,850
(£1,537; $2,198)

15
A 'famille-rose' bowl,
Qianlong mark and
period, decorated with
three goats on a mossy
bank, the six character
nianhao incised on the
base, 20.5cm (8in),
HK 22 May,
HK $38,500
(£3,986; $5,341)

16
**A celadon-ground
'famille rose' ovoid jar,**
Qianlong seal mark and
period, decorated with
narcissus, berry and
lingzhi, 50cm (19¾in),
HK 24 May,
HK $6,600 (£683; $915)

1
A 'famille-verte' dish,
Kangxi, the broad well
with sprays of peony and
chrysanthemum, 38.5cm
(15in), *L 19 Nov*,
£286 ($406)

2
A 'famille-verte' plate,
Kangxi, painted with
three figures and an
Immortal, 26.9cm
(11⅜in), *L 16 July*,
£330 ($479)

3
A 'famille-verte' saucer
dish, Kangxi, seal mark
in underglaze blue, 27cm
(10½in), *S 25 Mar*,
£231 ($293)

4
A pair of 'famille-verte'
chargers, Kangxi period,
each decorated with a
xiechai and phoenix
above, 38.5cm (15¼in),
NY 5 June,
$2,750 (£2,165)

5
A pair of 'famille-verte'
vases, Daoguang, fitted
as lamps, 49cm (19¼in),
C 10 July,
£1,650 ($2,294)

6
A 'famille-verte' figure of
a Hehe twin, Kangxi,
27.5cm (10¾in), *NY 5 June*,
$1,100 (£866)

7
A 'famille-verte' biscuit
figure of Zhong Liquan,
Kangxi, wearing a robe
with green, black and
yellow checks, 15.5cm
(6in), *NY 4 June*,
$3,520 (£2,771)

8
An enamelled biscuit
figure of a scholar, 19th
century, 22.5cm (6¾in),
S 10 July,
£374 ($501)

9
A biscuit figure of Kwei-
Sing, Kangxi, 33cm
(13in), *C 16 Jan*,
£220 ($264)

10
A 'famille-noire' vase,
Guangxu, six character
mark of Kangxi, 53.5cm
(21in), *L 19 Nov*,
£946 ($1,343)

11
A pair of 'famille-noire'
vases and covers, each
decorated in 'famille-
verte' palette on a black
ground, 63cm, (24¾in),
M 23 June,
FF 46,620
(£3,757; $5,034)

12
A pair of 'famille-noire'
fishbowls, 52cm (21¼in)
diam, *NY 2 Oct*,
$3,300 (£2,357)

1   2   3

4   5   6

7   8   9

10   11   12

1
A pair of mugs, Kangxi, painted in iron-red, 16cm (6¼in), *C 2 Oct*, £605 ($883)

2
A Chinese Imari coffee pot and cover, Qianlong, 23.5cm (9¼in), *C 17 Apr*, £1,155 ($1,502)

3
A Chinese Imari cruet set, Qianlong, 13.5cm (5¼in), *A 4 Sept*, Dfl 2,415 (£555; $816)

4
A pair of Chinese Imari canisters and covers, Kangxi, painted in underglaze blue and iron-red heightened with gilding, 25.5cm (10in), *L 16 July*, £1,870 ($2,712)

5
A Chinese Imari bowl, 17th century, 31.5cm (12⅜in), *L 16 July*, £462 ($670)

6
A set of three Chinese Imari dishes, Kangxi, each enamelled in characteristic palette of underglaze blue, iron-red and gilding, 34.5 to 41.5cm (13½ to 16½in), *L 19 Nov*, £1,100 ($1,562)

7
A Chinese Imari tureen and cover, Kangxi, painted with a continuous scene of fishing boats on a river, 24cm (9½in), *L 19 Nov*, £1,650 ($2,343)

8
A Chinese Imari fish bowl, Qianlong, 63.5cm (25in), *C 16 Jan*, £1,870 ($2,244)

9
A blue and white bidet, Qianlong period, *c.*1770, 60.5cm (23¾in) long, *NY 31 Jan*, $1,430 (£1,212)

10
A part dinner service, Daoguang period, *c.*1820 or later, comprising sixty pieces, each painted in blue enamel heightened in gilding, cracks, *NY 31 Jan*, $11,000 (£9,322)

11
A pair of 'faux bois' vases and covers, Guangxu, 87.6cm (34½in), *L 16 July*, £3,300 ($4,785)

12
A garniture-de-cheminee, Kangxi, comprising a pair of beaker vases and three baluster vases and covers, each painted in iron-red and gilding, 22.5 and 27cm (8¾ and 10½in), *L 19 Nov*, £2,640 ($3,749)

13
A pair of crackle glaze vases, late 19th century, 50cm (22in), *S 31 May*, £880 ($1,162)

1
A pair of Canton 'famille-rose' garden seats, 44.5cm (17½in), *C 17 Apr*, £660 ($858)

2
A 'famille-rose' garden seat, Jiaqing, the top pierced with a cash medallion in the centre, 47cm (18½in), *L 16 July*, £1,155 ($1,675)

3
A pair of 'famille-rose' garden seats, 44.5cm (17½in), *L 16 July*, £7,040 ($10,208)

4
A tureen and cover, Qianlong, decorated with panels painted in 'famille-rose' enamels, 23.5cm (9¼in), *L 16 July*, £792 ($1,148)

5
A pair of 'famille-rose' teapots and covers, Qianlong, *A 4 June*, Dfl 3,712 (£840; $1,134)

6
A 'famille-rose' tureen and cover, Qianlong, 29cm (11½in), *L 19 Nov*, £1,650 ($2,343)

7
A 'famille-rose' teapot, cover and stand, Qianlong, painted with alternating panels in pink and yellow infilled with stylised lotus, 15.5cm (6⅛in), *L 16 July*, £330 ($479)

8
A soup tureen and cover, Qianlong, 35cm (14in) wide, *NY 31 Jan*, $2,090 (£1,771)

9
A 'famille-rose' teapot and cover, Qianlong, 23cm (9in), *L 19 Nov*, £990 ($1,406)

10
A 'famille-rose' export tea cup and saucer, Qianlong, 11.5cm (4½in), *HK 24 May*, HK $6,600 (£683; $915)

11
A 'famille-rose' bell mug, Qianlong, painted in Mandarin-style, 15cm (6in), *S 10 July*, £385 ($516)

12
A 'famille-rose' writing stand, of triple form, Qianlong, 16cm (6¼in), *A 4 June*, Dfl 9,280 (£2,100; $2,834)

13
A 'famille-rose' fishbowl, first half 19th century, 47cm (18½in), *L 16 July*, £1,210 ($1,755)

14
A 'famille-rose' brushpot, 1770-90, painted with a lady looking at a small boy, the reverse with a poem, 12cm (4¾in), *NY 30 Jan*, $330 (£292)

15
A Canton 'famille-rose' jardinière and stand, 19th century, 16cm (6¼in), *M 23 June*, FF 4,662 (£376; $503)

16
A 'Compagnie-des-Indes' ice pail, Qianlong, with lion mask handles, *M 23 June*, FF 11,100 (£894; $1,199)

17
A 'famille-rose' ice pail, Qianlong, painted with roundels of floral sprays and sprigs, below a broad underglaze blue border, 26cm (10¼in), *L 16 July*, £935 ($1,356)

1
An export ruby-ground soup plate, 1730-40, 23cm (9in), *NY 30 Jan*, $715 (£633)

2
A set of fourteen 'Compagnie-des-Indes' plates, Qianlong, decorated in pink enamel, 23cm (9in) diam, *A 4 June*, **Dfl 7,192 (£1,627; $2,197)**

3
A set of eighteen Canton 'famille-rose' dishes, Jiaqing, painted with a court scene of a lady giving audience to an official, 19.5cm (7⅝in), *L 16 July*, £1,320 ($1,914)

4
A set of three 'famille-rose' plates, Qianlong, 23cm (9in), *S 3 Apr*, £297 ($383)

5
A pair of 'famille-rose' plates, Yongzheng/Qianlong, 22.5cm (8¾in), *S 10 July*, £82 ($111)

6
A 'famille-rose' dish, Qianlong, 44cm (17¼in), *M 23 June*, **FF 16,095 (£1,297; $1,738)**

7
A 'famille-rose' dish, Qianlong, 38.7cm (15¼in), *L 16 July*, £418 ($606)

8
A pair of 'famille-rose' plates, early Qianlong, painted with a cock standing on rockwork, 23.1cm (9⅛in), *L 16 July*, £825 ($1,196)

9
A pair of 'famille-rose' dishes, Qianlong, 38cm (15in), *L 19 Nov*, £1,045 ($1,484)

10
A pair of 'famille-rose' dishes, Qianlong, 36cm (14in), *L 19 Nov*, £440 ($625)

11
A pair of 'famille-rose' dishes, Qianlong, 31cm (12¼in), *L 19 Nov*, £1,980 ($2,812)

12
An export 'famille-rose' barber's bowl, Qianlong, 26.5cm (10½in), *NY 31 Jan*, $605 (£513)

13
A 'famille-rose' plate, Qianlong, 22.5cm (8¾in), *S 14 Nov*, £154 ($215)

14
A set of three 'famille-rose' plates, Qianlong, 23cm (9in), *S 14 Nov*, £187 ($262)

15
A pair of 'famille-rose' dishes, Yongzheng, 38.5cm (15¼in), *NY 4 June*, $3,300 (£2,598)

16
A 'famille-rose' plate, Yongzheng, painted with the Immortal Maiden He Xiangu, 22.5cm (8¾in), *M 23 June*, **FF 6,105 (£492; $659)**

17
A 'tobacco leaf' meat dish, Qianlong, decorated in underglaze blue and 'famille-rose' enamels, 31cm (12¼in), *M 23 June*, **FF 16,650 (£1,342; $1,798)**

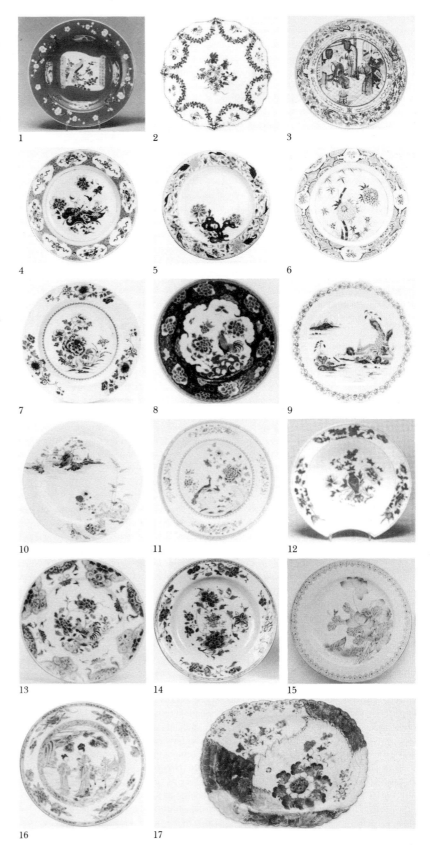

1
An export lotus punch bowl, Qianlong, painted in 'famille-rose' enamels, 54cm (21¼in) diam, *NY 10 Oct*, $10,450 (£7,411)

2
A 'Mandarin palette' punch bowl, Qianlong, 26.5cm (10½in), *S 25 Mar*, £660 ($838)

3
An export lotus bowl, Qianlong, painted with iron-red-edged petals shading from rose to pale pink, beneath gilt sprays, 20.5cm (8in) diam, *NY 31 Jan*, $495 (£419)

4
A baluster vase and cover, Qianlong, decorated in 'famille-rose' enamels, 45cm (17¾in), *L 19 Nov*, £1,155 ($1,640)

5
A pair of Canton 'famille-rose' covered jars, 19th century, decorated with panels of dignitaries, ladies and attendants in summer houses, 63cm (24¾in), *L 16 July*, £5,720 ($8,294)

6
A bowl and saucer dish en suite, Guangxu, for the near eastern market, 39.7cm (5⅝in) diam, *L 16 July*, £4,180 ($6,061)

7
A 'famille-rose' bowl and stand, Qianlong, stand 15.5cm (9in), *S 10 July*, £209 ($280)

8
A Canton 'famille-rose' flower vase and cover, 19th century, 24cm (9½in), *M 23 June*, FF 5,328 (£429; $575)

9
A Canton 'famille-rose' spittoon, 19th century, 28cm (11in), *S 14 Aug*, £550 ($820)

10
A pair of 'famille-rose' vases, 19th century, painted with figures of dignitaries and maidens divided by inscriptions, 62cm (24½in), *L 19 Nov*, £550 ($781)

11
A Canton 'famille-rose' vase, Guangxu, decorated with panels enclosing figure scenes and butterflies, 90cm (35½in), *L 19 Nov*, £2,970 ($4,217)

12
A pair of Cantonese 'famille-rose' vases, 45cm (17¾in), *C 12 Feb*, £748 ($1,309)

13
A 'famille-rose' guglet, Qianlong, painted with a scene of combatants, 23.5cm (9¼in), *S 14 Nov*, £176 ($246)

14
A beaker vase, Qianlong, decorated in 'famille-rose' palette, 45cm (17½in), *L 19 Nov* £825 ($1,172)

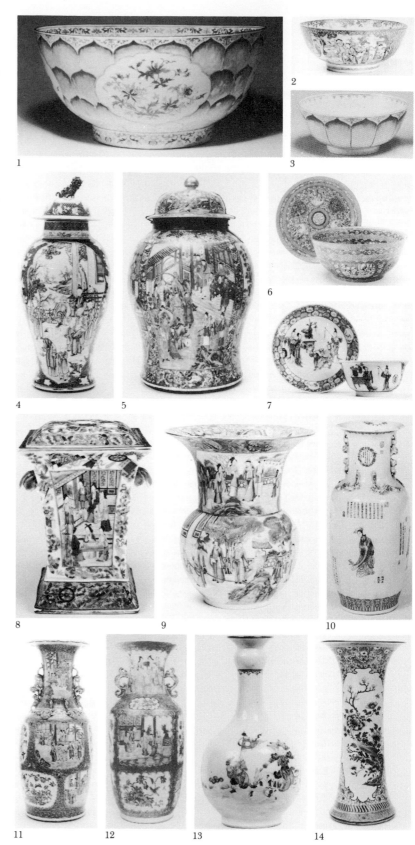

1
A pair of figures of
cranes, Qianlong, each
enamelled in white,
M 23 June,
FF 310,800
(£25,044; $33,560)

2
A pair of figures of
fabulous animals, Qianlong, in *rouge-de-fer* and
green enamel with
gilding, 18cm (7in),
M 23 June,
FF 53,280
(£4,293; $5,753)

3
A 'Compagnie-des-Indes'
cock tureen and cover,
Qianlong, the plumage
in *rouge-de-fer* heightened
in gilding, *M 23 June,*
FF 199,800
(£16,100; $21,574)

4
A **joss-stick holder,**
Jiaqing, in the form of a
puppy, decorated in
sepia, gilding, bright
green and iron-red,
16.5cm (6½in), *L 19 Nov,*
£792 ($1,125)

5
A pair of exportware
figures of chimeras,
Qianlong, each decorated
in iron-red, turquoise,
green and blue, 18cm
(7in), *L 19 Nov,*
£2,310 ($3,280)

6
An exportware **goose
tureen and cover,** Qian-
long, decorated in iron-
red, sepia, aubergine,
blue and green, 35cm
(13¾in), *L 19 Nov,*
£12,980 ($18,432)

7
A 'famille-rose' **wall vase
figure,** Qianlong, 21cm
(8¼in), *S 25 Mar,*
£231 ($293)

8
A pair of figures of **white
cocks,** Qianlong, each
white-glazed with brown-
glazed beak and comb
and wattles left in the
biscuit, 38cm (15in),
L 19 Nov,
£1,650 ($2,343)

9
A 'famille-rose' **group of
the Hehe Erxian,** Qian-
long, showing the twins
with a toad in front, 20cm
(8in), *M 23 June,*
FF 8,325 (£671; $899)

10
A pair of 'famille-rose'
peacocks, 19th century,
58cm (22¾in), *NY 17 Apr,*
$2,640 (£2,062)

11
A Canton 'famille-rose'
joss-stick holder, 19th
century, 14cm (5½in),
S 14 Aug,
£352 ($524)

12
A 'famille-rose' **dish,**
Qianlong, encircled by a
raised gilded fillet,
43.2cm (17in), *L 16 July,*
£418 ($606)

13
A pair of 'famille-rose'
dishes, Qianlong, 42cm
(16½in), *L 16 July,*
£792 ($1,148)

14
A pair of **export dishes,**
Qianlong, each painted
in a 'Mandarin' palette,
30.5cm (12½in) long,
NY 31 Jan,
$1,210 (£1,025)

1

A pair of 'famille-verte' shell-shaped dishes, Kangxi, 19cm (7½in), *A 26 June*, **Dfl 4,408** (£977; $1,319)

2

A 'famille-verte' baluster jar and cover, Kangxi, 49.5cm (19½in), *NY 4 Dec*, **$5,500** (£3,716)

3

A 'famille-verte' cistern, Kangxi, 41.5cm (16⅛in), *L 16 July*, **£2,750** ($3,988)

4

A powder-blue ground 'famille-verte' triple-gourd vase, Kangxi, reserved with panels enclosing kylins and birds, 27.5cm (10¾in), *L 16 July*, **£440** ($638)

5

A 'famille-jaune' vase, Kangxi, 43cm (17in), *NY 4 June*, **$8,525** (£6,712)

6

A 'famille-verte' bottle vase, Kangxi, with three panels each enclosing a different scene of a scholar and attendant, 44cm (17¼in), *NY 4 June*, **$17,050** (£13,425)

7

A 'famille-verte' jar and cover, Kangxi, decorated with groups of Precious Objects and flowering sprays, 17.8cm (7in), *L 16 July*, **£660** ($957)

8

A pair of 'famille-verte' candlesticks, Kangxi, of European silver shape, 17cm (6¾in), *M 23 June*, **FF 39,960** (£3,220; $4,315)

9

A 'famille-verte' beaker vase, Kangxi, of *gu* form, the central bulb studded with four *shou* characters, 19.2cm (7½in), *L 16 July*, **£440** ($638)

10

A 'famille-verte' kendi and cover, Kangxi, 23.5cm (9¼in), *L 19 Nov*, **£1,485** ($2,109)

11

A 'famille-verte' bowl, Kangxi, 33.5cm (13¼in), *F 28 May*, **L 800,000** (£311; $410)

12

A potiche, mark and period of Kangxi, decorated in underglaze blue with peonies, 20.5cm (8in), *L 19 Nov*, **£858** ($1,218)

13

A 'famille-verte' brush-pot, Kangxi, decorated with a scholar and attendants, 12cm (4¾in), *HK 22 May*, **HK $19,800** (£2,050; $2,747)

14

A 'famille-verte' bowl, Kangxi, 18.8cm (7⅜in), *L 16 July*, **£704** ($1,021)

15

A pair of 'famille-verte' Qilin-form censers, Kangxi, the heads forming covers, one with green face and one with white, 23cm (9in), *NY 4 June*, **$6,325** (£4,980)

16

A pair of 'famille-verte' salt-cellars, Kangxi, 5.5cm (2¼in), *A 4 June*, **Dfl 2,320** (£525; $709)

1
A part tea service, comprising eleven pieces, Qianlong, painted *en grisaille* with 'The Crucifixion', plates 12.5cm (5in) and 15.5cm (6in), *A 4 June,* **Dfl 13,080** (£2,959; $3,995)

2
A Masonic mug, Qianlong, painted with Masonic symbols between borders of blue and gilt, 12.5cm (4⅞in), *L 16 July,* £1,760 ($2,552)

3
A Masonic bowl, *c.*1800, the exterior painted in brown, rose, iron-red, black, puce, salmon and gold with Masonic devices, 29.5cm (11½in) diam, *NY 30 Jan,* $1,650 (£1,460)

4
A Masonic large mug, *c.*1795, with 'The Pillars at the Entrance to King Solomon's Temple', 14cm (5½in) high, *NY 30 Jan,* $990 (£876)

5
A tureen, cover and stand, Qianlong, decorated in 'famille-rose' enamels with the arms of La Bouvais of Brittany, 34.5cm (13½in), *M 23 June,* **FF 1,050** (£4,919; $6,592)

6
A child's teapot and cover, *c.*1795, painted after a mezzotint by Francesco Bartolozzi from a painting by William Hamilton of 'Playing at Marbles', 9.5cm (3¾in) high, *NY 30 Jan,* $825 (£730)

7
A blue-ground milk jug and cover, *c.*1805, with roundel painted in iron-red, rose, blue, yellow, brown and grey, 16cm (6¼in) high, *NY 30 Jan,* $440 (£389)

8
A yellow-ground caudle cup and cover, *c.*1815, 15cm (6in), *NY 30 Jan,* £935 ($827)

9
A tea caddy, *c.*1800, with American eagle decoration, traces of gilding, 12.5cm (5in) high, *NY 31 Jan,* $495 (£419)

10
A plate, *c*1795, with American eagle decoration, salmon and gilt border, 24.5cm (9½in) diam, *NY 31 Jan,* $495 (£419)

11
A teapot and cover and a pair of teabowls and saucers, *c.*1810, for the American market, each piece painted in brown heightened in gilding with an eagle, 9 and 14cm (3½ and 5½in) diam, *NY 31 Jan,* $1,210 (£1,025)

12
A teapot and cover, *c.*1795, with a figure of 'Hope' on either side, painted in blue, rose, black and gilt, 13.5cm (5¼in) high, *NY 30 Jan,* $880 (£779)

13
An American eagle tureen, cover and stand, 19th century, 40.5cm (16in), *L 16 July,* £4,400 ($6,380)

14
A lighthouse coffee pot and cover, 1800-10, painted on either side with a gilt-heightened brown eagle, 24cm (9½in), *NY 30 Jan,* $1,650 (£1,460)

15
An armorial tea service, *c.*1780, comprising thirty-five pieces, each painted in blue, iron-red, gold and grey, gilt-edged rims, tea and coffee pots 14 and 23cm (5½ and 9in) high, *NY 31 Jan,* $3,410 (£2,890)

1
A Dutch-decorated
saucer dish, *c.*1730,
painted with a ship flying
iron-red, white and blue
Dutch flags above a sea
shading from turquoise
to mauve, 21cm (8¼in),
NY 30 Jan,
$3,025 (£2,677)

2
A pair of armorial plates,
*c.*1725, each painted in
blue, iron-red, gold,
white, black and brown,
28cm (11in), *NY 31 Jan,*
$990 (£839)

3
An armorial charger,
dated 1733, painted in
brown, pink, blue, white,
green and gold against a
yellow roundel with a
Dutch coat-of-arms, 39cm
(15½in), *NY 30 Jan,*
$5,500 (£4,867)

4
A pair of armorial saucer
dishes, 1750-70, each
painted in underglaze
blue with the arms of
Mareschal of Forez, 25
and 24.5cm (9¾ and
9½in), *NY 31 Jan,*
$550 (£466)

5
A pair of armorial dishes,
Kangxi, each decorated
in underglaze blue,
rouge-de-fer and gilding
and with the arms of
Ataide, 43cm (17in),
M 23 June,
FF 77,700
(£6,261; $8,370)

6
An armorial dish, Qian-
long, the centre decor-
ated in 'famille-rose'
enamels with the arms of
Forbes, 36cm (14in),
M 23 June,
FF 18,870
(£1,521; $2,038)

7
An armorial saucer dish,
18th century, decorated
in *rouge-de-fer* and
gilding with a coat-of-
arms, 37cm (14½in),
M 23 June,
FF 13,320
(£1,073; $1,438)

8
A 'famille-verte' armorial
dish, Kangxi, decorated
with the arms of Holland
in gilding and iron-red,
27.5cm (10⅜in), *L 16 July,*
£1,155 ($1,675)

9
A pair of armorial plates,
Yongzheng, painted in
'famille-rose' enamels
with the arms of God-
frey, 21.5cm (8½in),
L 16 July,
£880 ($1,276)

10
A pair of armorial soup
plates, *c.*1760, painted in
black, gold, iron-red and
blue, the rim in 'famille
rose' enamels, 22 and
21.5cm (8¾ and 8½in),
NY 31 Jan,
$3,080 (£2,610)

11
An 'Italian Comedy'
plate, 1720-25, painted in
brown, blue, iron-red,
gilt and black, with a
figure of Harlequin,
21.5cm (8½in), *NY 31 Jan,*
$2,475 (£2,097)

12
A pair of 'famille-rose'
European subject plates,
early Qianlong, depict-
ing a European merch-
ant and servant, 23cm
(9¼in), *M 23 June,*
FF 16,650
(£1,342; $1,798)

13
A plate, Qianlong,
decorated in *rouge-de-fer,*
orange and gold with
'The Baptism of Christ',
27.5cm (10¾in), *A 4 June,*
Dfl 2,204 (£499; $673)

14
A plate, painted with
'The Judgement of Paris',
Qianlong, 23cm (9in),
A 4 June,
Dfl 1,740 (£394; $532)

15
A blue and white
'Deshima Island' plate,
18th century, 19.5cm
(7¾in), *NY 30 Jan,*
$660 (£584)

16
An armorial meat dish,
Qianlong, for the Con-
tinental market, decor-
ated in enamels and
gilding, 35.6cm (14in);
sold with a smaller dish
en suite, 23.5cm (9¼in),
L 16 July,
£1,375 ($1,994)

17
A 'Blue Fitzhugh' platter,
*c.*1800, 34cm (13½in),
NY 30 Jan,
$715 (£633)

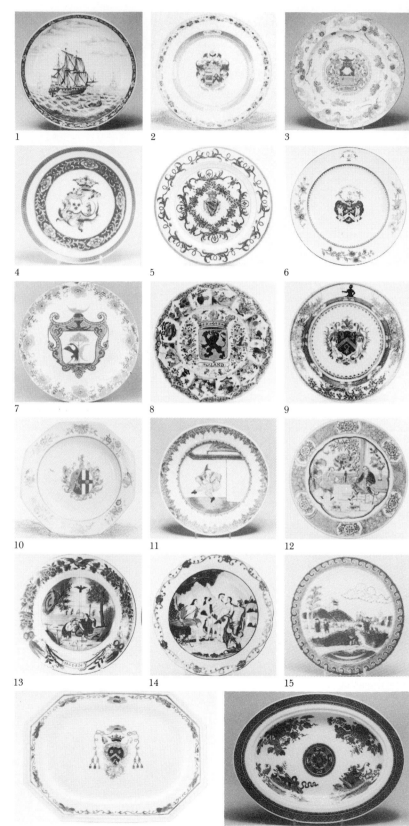

1
A crested platter, *c.*1760, painted in shades of underglaze blue with a water buffalo scene, the rim with a border of English flowers, 42cm (16½in), *NY 31 Jan,* $412 (£349)

2
An armorial platter, *c.*1745, the centre painted with a view of the church at Fort St George in Madras, in green, brown, grisaille, blue, yellow and white, 43cm (17in) long, *NY 30 Jan,* $1,540 (£1,363)

3
A 'Compagnie des Indes' armorial plate, Qianlong, painted in 'famille-rose' colours, 41cm (16in), *F 28 May,* L 1,800,000 (£699; $923)

4
A blue and white baluster jar and cover, Kangxi, with four roundels depicting fashionable French ladies, after prints by Henri, Robert and Nicolas Bonnart of *c.*1685-1700, artemisia leaf mark within a double circle in underglaze blue, 39cm (15½in) high, *NY 30 Jan,* $5,225 (£4,624)

5
A European subject coffee pot and cover, Qianlong, painted in Meissen style in 'famille-rose' enamels, 25.5cm (10in), *FF 16,095* (£1,297; $1,738)

6
An armorial punch bowl, 1795-1805, painted in iron-red, blue, gold, green and gilt, 32.5cm (13in), *NY 10 Oct,* $1,540 (£1,092)

7
An armorial punch bowl, *c.*1790, painted in iron-red, grisaille, brown and yellow with the arms of Trinity House, 36.5cm (14½in), *NY 30 Jan,* $2,860 (£2,531)

8
A 'foxhunting' punch bowl, Qianlong, richly enamelled in Mandarin palette, the exterior with scenes of a European fox hunt, 29.5cm (11½in), *L 19 Nov,* £3,190 ($4,530)

9
A blue and white bowl, 1790-1810, 23cm (9in) diam, *NY 30 Jan,* $660 (£584)

10
A Chinese export European subject punch bowl, Qianlong, 30cm (11¾in), *C 16 Jan,* £858 ($1,030)

11
An armorial large mug, *c.*1775, painted on the front in iron-red, blue, grisaille, gold, rose, white and green, the sides with 'Mandarin palette' sprays, 15.5cm (6¼in), *NY 10 Oct,* $1,430 (£1,014)

12
A 'famille-rose' jug, Qianlong, with a 'G.R.' monogram, 19cm (7½in), *S 10 July,* £352 ($472)

13
A 'famille-rose' butter tub, cover and stand, Qianlong, painted with a goddess and three putti on a cloud, within a scalloped purple border, 12.6cm (5in) diam, *L 16 July,* £396 ($574)

14
A 'famille-rose' tureen and cover, Qianlong, decorated in Meissen style around the sides with panels of European merchants supervising the loading of cargo on a quayside, 23cm (9in) wide, *L 16 July* £528 ($766)

15
An armorial soup tureen, cover and deep platter, *c.*1790, painted in gold, blue, iron-red, pink, green and brown, 30 and 40cm (13 and 15½in), *NY 31 Jan,* $4,950 (£4,195)

Index

continued